Oxford School French Dictionary

Editorial Manager: Valerie Grundy
New Edition: Nicholas Rollin
with the assistance of Natalie Pomier

OXFORD
UNIVERSITY PRESS

OXFORD
UNIVERSITY PRESS

Great Clarendon Street, Oxford OX2 6DP

Oxford University Press is a department of the University of Oxford.
It furthers the University's objective of excellence in research,
scholarship, and education by publishing worldwide in

Oxford NewYork

Auckland Bangkok Buenos Aires Cape Town Chennai
Dar es Salaam Delhi Hong Kong Istanbul Karachi Kolkata
Kuala Lumpur Madrid Melbourne Mexico City Mumbai Nairobi
São Paulo Shanghai Taipei Tokyo Toronto

Oxford is a registered trade mark of Oxford University Press
in the UK and in certain other countries

© Oxford University Press 1997

First published in 1997
Revised edition 2002
New edition 2004

Database right Oxford University Press (maker)

British Library cataloguing in Publication Data available

ISBN 0-19-910927-3

10 9 8 7 6 5 4 3

Printed in Italy by G.

INTRODUCTION

This dictionary has been specially written for students who are in their first years of learning French all the way through to preparing for exams. We have paid particular attention to making the dictionary user-friendly. With the help of colour headwords, alphabet tabs, easy-to-follow signposts and examples, the right translation can quickly be found. French verbs on both sides of the dictionary are numbered to direct the student to the appropriate verb table in the centre pages.

Throughout the writing of this dictionary we have worked in close consultation with students, teachers, inspectors, and examining boards. We gratefully acknowledge the examining boards AQA (formerly NEAB and SEG), OCR, and EDEXCEL, who have read and commented on the dictionary text.

Since the first edition of this dictionary there have been many changes in French life. Not least has been the introduction of the euro. This new edition takes full account of these changes and many new words and examples have been included in order to provide the best possible learner's dictionary of French at this level.

HOW A BILINGUAL DICTIONARY WORKS

A bilingual dictionary contains two languages. When you look up a word in one of the languages, it gives the translation for that word in the other language. This dictionary is divided into two halves separated by a section of blue-edged pages. In the first half you look up French words, which are in alphabetical order, to find out what they mean in English and in the second half you look up English words, also in alphabetical order, to find out how to say them in French. The blue-edged pages are verb tables and you can see how to use them further on in this section.

At each entry you will find not only **translations** but other information that will help you get the right translation and use the word correctly. Here is a guide to the different things you will find in an entry:

headword	a word you look up in the dictionary
translation	translations are the only things that are in 'ordinary' type in the dictionary. They are always typed like this, and something which is typed in a different way can never be a translation
noun	word class (part of speech): tells you whether the word you are looking up is a noun, a verb, an adjective, or some other part of speech. A headword can be more than one part of speech. For instance, **book** can be a noun (she was reading a book) or a verb (I've booked the seats)

(*signpost*)	helpful information: to guide you to the right translation, to show you how to use the translation, or to give you extra information
example	a phrase or sentence using the word you have looked up. You should read through them carefully to see if they are close to what you want to understand or say
Masc.	gender: after a French noun, to tell you that it is masculine
Fem.	gender: after a French noun, to tell you that it is feminine. *Fem.* also shows the feminine form of some adjectives
●	indicates a phrasal verb such as to carry on
★	shows an idiomatic expression such as over the moon
[27]	verb number – tells you which verb pattern to look at in the blue-edged centre pages of the dictionary

USING THE DICTIONARY

To find out what a French word means

Suppose you want to find out what the French word **bouton** means. You need to use the first half of the dictionary to find the French words that you are looking for. To help you do this, the guide words at the top of each page show the alphabetical range of words on the pages you have open. Notice that hyphens and spaces between words in French words make no difference to the alphabetical order.

When you find the entry for **bouton** you will find the translation. But you will also see that **bouton** is a noun and because all nouns are either masculine or feminine in French, you are given the gender *Masc.* (*Masc.* = masculine, *Fem.* = feminine).

However, it often happens that a French word has more than one English translation so you will see that the translation for **bouton** is divided into sections numbered **1** and **2**.

bouton *noun Masc.* **1** button;
 2 spot, pimple.

The first translation is **button** and the second is **spot** or **pimple**. You will need to look at both translations to work out which one fits the French sentence you are trying to understand. So:

il y a quatre boutons sur ma veste *means* there are four buttons on my jacket

BUT

j'ai un bouton sur le nez *means* I've got a spot on my nose

The plurals of most French nouns are formed by adding an -s, as in **boutons** in the first sentence. Exceptional plural forms can be found after the headword:

animal *noun* animal *Masc.* (*plural* **animaux**).

French like English has certain words that you would use when chatting with friends but not in more formal situations. French words like this are marked *informal* in the dictionary, like **bouquin** here:

bouquin *noun Masc.* (*informal*) book.

Note that the usual word for **book** is **livre**.

To find an English word and how to say it in French

You can see that it is quite easy, once you know how the dictionary works, to look up a French word and find out what it means. Students usually find it harder to use the dictionary to find out how to say something in French. This dictionary is written specially to help you do this and to make it easy to find the right way of saying things in French.

Suppose you want to know how to say **garden** in French. Look up the word in the second part of the dictionary. If you follow the same method of going through the alphabetical order of the headwords as you did when you were looking up a French word, you will find **garden** on page 435.

garden *noun* jardin *Masc.*

Now you can see that the French word for **garden** is **jardin**. But if you want to make a sentence using a noun like **jardin** you need to know whether it is masculine or feminine. The *Masc.* after **jardin** tells you that it is masculine so *in the garden* is **dans le jardin**. It is not always as easy as this to know which French word you need. Sometimes there will be more than one French word for the English word you are looking up. When the dictionary entry gives you more than just one translation, it is very important to take the time to read through the whole entry. If you look up **plug** the entry looks like this:

plug *noun* **1** (*electrical*) prise *Fem.*; **2** (*in a bath or sink*) bonde *Fem.*; **to pull out the plug** retirer la bonde.

You can see that **1** tells you that the French word for an electrical plug is **prise** and **2** tells you that the word for a bath plug or a sink plug is **bonde**.

Remember that information which is either in brackets or italics, or both, is there to help you, but it *will never be* the translation itself. Wherever there is more than one translation, depending on what meaning of the English word you are looking for, the dictionary will always help you to choose the right one. Often it is not enough to find the translation of one word. In the case of more common words the dictionary also gives you a selection of common phrases you will often want to use. In the entry for **hair** below you can find out how to use the translation in different expressions:

hair *noun* **1** cheveux *Masc. plural*; **to have short hair** avoir les cheveux courts; **to brush your hair** se brosser les cheveux; **to wash your hair** se laver les cheveux; **to have your hair cut** se faire couper les cheveux; **she's had her hair cut** elle s'est fait couper les cheveux; **2 a hair** (*from the head*) un cheveu; (*from the body*) un poil.

HOW TO USE THE VERB TABLES

On the French side of the dictionary all the headwords which are verbs look like this: **faire** *verb* [10]. On the English side of the dictionary all the verbs given as translations of English verbs look like this: **frighten** *verb* effrayer [59].

If you look at the pages edged in blue in the centre of the dictionary, you will find tables showing you how to use the different types of French verbs.

The verb **faire** above has the number 10. If you look at number 10 in the verb tables, you will see that because **faire** is a very common and very irregular verb it has a whole page to itself giving you all the tenses you will need. The verb **effrayer** has number 59 after it. When you look up verb table number 59, you will see the verb **payer**. This means that the verb endings given for **payer** will also be the endings for **effrayer**. So **payer** is there to show you the pattern that other verbs like it, such as **effrayer**, will follow.

With practice you will soon be able to find your way easily around the dictionary and identify what you are looking for in an entry. Some entries may seem long and complicated at first glance. Reading carefully through the signposts and examples will lead you to the translation you need.

Aa

a *verb* SEE **avoir**.

à *preposition* (*note that 'à + le' becomes 'au' and 'à + les' becomes 'aux'*) **1** at; **à la maison** at home; **à l'école** at school; **au bureau** at the office; **à deux heures** at two o'clock; **2** in; **à Londres** in London; **à la campagne** in the country; **au printemps** in the spring; **3** to; **aller à Londres** to go to London; **donner quelque chose à quelqu'un** to give something to somebody; **4** by; **à la main** by hand; **à vélo** by (*or* on a) bicycle; **5** with; **une petite fille aux yeux bleus** a little girl with blue eyes; **6** à **trois kilomètres d'ici** three kilometres from here; **7** **ce bracelet est à Natalie** this bracelet is Natalie's.

abandonner *verb* [1] **1** to give up; **elle a abandonné les maths** she has given up maths; **j'abandonne** I give up; **2** to abandon; **un enfant abandonné** an abandoned child.

abat-jour *noun* Masc. lampshade.

abats *plural noun* Masc. **les abats** offal (*liver, kidneys, heart, etc*).

abattoir *noun* Masc. slaughterhouse.

abattre *verb* [21] **1** to shoot down; **deux policiers ont été abattus par des gangsters hier** two policemen were shot down by gangsters yesterday; **2** to slaughter (*an animal*); **3** to demolish (*a building*).

abbaye *noun* Fem. abbey; **l'abbaye de Cluny** Cluny Abbey.

abbé *noun* Masc. priest.

abcès *noun* Masc. abscess.

abeille *noun* Fem. bee; **une piqûre d'abeille** a bee sting.

abîmer *verb* [1] **1** to damage; **la pluie avait abîmé la porte** the rain had damaged the door; **tu vas t'abîmer les yeux** you'll ruin your eyesight; **des fruits abîmés** fruit which is going bad; **2** **s'abîmer** to get damaged; **les pommes vont s'abîmer** the apples are going to go bad; **la viande s'abîme vite** meat goes off quickly.

aboiement *noun* Masc. barking; **on entendait des aboiements** we could hear dogs barking.

abolir *verb* [2] to abolish.

abominable *adjective* abominable.

abondance *noun* Fem. **une abondance de** plenty of, lots of; **il y a des fruits en abondance** there's plenty of fruit.

abonné, abonnée *noun* Masc., Fem. **1** season ticket holder; **2** subscriber (*to a magazine, journal, etc*).
abonné *adjective* **être abonné** to have a subscription (*to a magazine, journal, etc*); to have a season ticket (*for the bus, train, theatre, etc*).

abonnement *noun* Masc. **1** subscription; **2** season ticket.

abonner *verb* [1] **s'abonner à** to subscribe to; **je me suis abonné pour un an** I have a year's subscription.

abord *noun* Masc. **1** **d'abord** first; **tout d'abord** first of all; **je vais**

1

a
d'abord faire du thé I'll make some tea first; **2 d'abord** at first; **j'ai d'abord cru qu'il était français** I thought at first that he was French; **3 les abords** the surroundings.

abordable *adjective* **1 des prix abordables** affordable prices; **2 une personne abordable** an approachable person.

aborder *verb* [1] **1** to tackle (*a problem, a piece of work, a subject, etc*); **2** to approach.

aboutir *verb* [2] **1 aboutir à** to lead to; **la rue aboutit à une petite place** the street leads to a little square; **2 aboutir à** to end up in; **nous avons abouti à Paris** we ended up in Paris; **3** to succeed, to be successful (*of discussions or negotiations*).

aboyer *verb* [39] to bark.

abrégé *noun Masc.* summary. **abrégé** *adjective* **la version abrégée** the abridged version.

abréger *verb* [15] to shorten.

abréviation *noun Fem.* abbreviation.

abri *noun Masc.* **1** shelter; **trouver un abri** to take shelter; **les sans-abri** the homeless; **2** shed; **3 à l'abri de** sheltered from; **à l'abri du vent** sheltered from the wind, out of the wind; **à l'abri de la lumière** in a dark place.

abricot *noun Masc.* apricot; **de la confiture d'abricots** apricot jam; **une tarte aux abricots** an apricot tart.

abricotier *noun Masc.* apricot tree.

abriter *verb* [1] **1** to shelter; **2 s'abriter** to take shelter.

abrupt *adjective* **1** steep; **une pente abrupte** a steep slope; **2** abrupt.

abrutir *verb* [2] **1** to deafen; **2** to stupefy.

absence *noun Fem.* **1** absence; **pendant mon absence** while I was out, while I was away; **2 l'absence de** the lack of.

absent *adjective* **1 être absent** to be out, to be away; **je serai absent pendant une heure** I'll be out for an hour; **elle a été absente tout le mois de mai** she was away for the whole of May; **2** absent; **3** absent-minded.

absenter *verb* [1] **s'absenter** to go out, to go away; **je m'absente quelques minutes** I'm just popping out for a few minutes.

absolu *adjective* absolute.

absolument *adverb* absolutely.

absorbant *adjective* **1** absorbing; **un livre absorbant** an absorbing book; **2** absorbent (*material*).

absorber *verb* [1] **1** to absorb; **2** to take (*food or drink*).

abstenir *verb* [81] **s'abstenir de** to refrain from.

abstrait *adjective* abstract.

absurde *adjective* absurd.

absurdité *noun Fem.* absurdity; **dire des absurdités** to talk nonsense.

abus *noun Masc.* abuse; **l'abus d'alcool** alcohol abuse.

buser verb [1] **1 abuser de** to misuse; **abuser de l'alcool** to drink too much (regularly); **2 abuser de** to take advantage of, to exploit; **elle abuse de ta gentillesse** she's taking advantage of your kindness.

busif (Fem. **abusive**) adjective **1** excessive; **2** unfair.

cajou noun Masc. mahogany; **une table en acajou** a mahogany table.

ccablant adjective overwhelming.

ccabler verb [1] to overwhelm.

ccéder verb [24] **1 accéder à** to reach, to get to ; **pour accéder à la salle de bains, il faut passer par la chambre** to get to the bathroom you have to go through the bedroom; **2 accéder au pouvoir** to come to power.

ccélérateur noun Masc. accelerator; **appuyer sur l'accélérateur** to accelerate.

ccélération noun Fem. acceleration.

ccélérer verb [24] **1** to speed up (the rhythm, process, etc); **2** to accelerate (in a car).

ccent noun Masc. **1** accent; **un accent étranger** a foreign accent; **parler français sans accent** to speak French without an accent; **2** accent (on a letter in written French) **un accent aigu** an acute accent; **un accent grave** a grave accent; **un accent circonflexe** a circumflex; **3 mettre l'accent sur quelque chose** to put the emphasis on something.

accentuer verb [1] to emphasize.

acceptation noun Fem. acceptance.

accepter verb [1] **1** to accept; **accepter une invitation** to accept an invitation; **2 accepter de faire** to agree to do; **elle a accepté de m'aider** she agreed to help me.

accès noun Masc. **1** access; **accès interdit** no entry; **2 un accès de colère** a fit of anger.

accessible adjective **1** accessible; **un livre accessible** a book which is easy to read; **2 des prix accessibles** affordable prices.

accessoire noun Masc. accessory; **les accessoires** accessories (gloves, handbags, etc).
accessoire adjective incidental.

accident noun Masc. **1** accident; **avoir un accident** to have an accident; **un accident de la route** a road accident; **2** hitch; **il y a eu un petit accident** there's been a slight hitch.

accidenté adjective **1** injured; **2** damaged; **3 'chaussée accidentée'** 'uneven road surface'.

acclamations plural noun Fem. cheering.

accommodant adjective easy-going.

accompagnateur, **accompagnatrice** noun Masc., Fem. **1** tourist guide; **2** courier (for a group on a package holiday); **3** accompanying adult (with a child); **4** accompanist (for example, a pianist accompanying a singer).

a
b
c
d
e
f
g
h
i
j
k
l
m
n
o
p
q
r
s
t
u
v
w
x
y
z

a
b
c
d
e
f
g
h
i
j
k
l
m
n
o
p
q
r
s
t
u
v
w
x
y
z

accompagner *verb* [1] **1** to accompany; **je t'accompagne** I'll go with you, I'll come with you; **je t'accompagne jusqu'à chez toi** I'll see you home; **2 accompagné de** accompanied by; **elle est partie accompagnée de son frère** she left accompanied by her brother; **3** to accompany (*on the piano, for example*).

accomplir *verb* [2] to carry out (*a task, project, mission, etc*).

accord *noun* Masc. **1** agreement; **2 d'accord** all right, OK; **je suis d'accord** I agree; **je suis d'accord avec Rosie** I agree with Rosie; **Paul est d'accord pour venir avec nous** Paul's agreed to come with us; **se mettre d'accord** to come to an agreement; **ils se sont mis d'accord sur le prix** they came to an agreement over the price; **3** chord (*in music*).

accordéon *noun* Masc. accordeon; **jouer de l'accordéon** to play the accordeon.

accorder *verb* [1] **1** to grant (*a favour, permission, etc*); **2** to tune (*a musical instrument*); **3 s'accorder** to agree.

accotement *noun* Masc. verge (*on the edge of the road*); hard shoulder (*on the motorway*); **'accotements non stabilisés'** 'soft verges' (*as road sign*).

accouchement *noun* Masc. childbirth, delivery.

accoucher *verb* [1] to give birth.

accoutumé *adjective* **1** usual; **2 accoutumé à** used to, accustomed to.

accoutumer *verb* [1] **s'accoutumer à** to become accustomed to.

accro *noun* Masc. (*informal*) addict; **accro** *adjective* (*informal*) **être accro de quelque chose** to be hooked on something.

accroc *noun* Masc. **1** tear; **tu as un accroc à ta jupe** you've got a tear in your skirt; **2** hitch; **sans accroc(s)** without a hitch.

accrocher *verb* [1] **1** to hang; **accrocher un tableau au mur** to hang a picture on the wall; **accroché au mur** hanging on the wall; **2** to catch, to snag (*something on a nail or thorn, for example*).

accroupir *verb* [2] **s'accroupir** to crouch (down), to squat.

accueil *noun* Masc. **1** welcome; **un accueil chaleureux** a warm welcome; **ma famille d'accueil est très sympathique** my host family very nice; **2** reception desk; **Madame Jones est priée de se présenter à l'accueil** would Ms Jones please go to the reception desk.

accueillant *adjective* **1** (*of a person*) hospitable, welcoming; **2** (*of a place*) inviting, friendly.

accueillir *verb* [35] **1** to welcome; **2** to receive, to greet.

accumuler *verb* [1] **1** to collect; **2 s'accumuler** to pile up.

accusation *noun* Fem. accusation

accusé de réception *noun Masc.* **envoyer une lettre avec accusé de réception** to send a letter recorded delivery.

accuser *verb* [1] to accuse; **il m'a accusé d'avoir volé son stylo** he accused me of stealing his pen.

acharner *verb* [1] **s'acharner à faire** to persist in doing.

achat *noun Masc.* purchase; **je te montre mes achats** I'll show you what I've bought.

acheter *verb* [16] **1** to buy; **je vais acheter du pain** I'm going to buy some bread; **2 acheter quelque chose à quelqu'un** to buy somebody something; **je t'achète un sandwich?** shall I buy you a sandwich?; **je lui ai acheté un cadeau** I bought him (*or* her) a present; **3 acheter quelque chose à quelqu'un** to buy something from somebody; **j'ai vendu ma voiture – c'est Lisa qui me l'a achetée** I've sold my car – Lisa bought it from me.

acheteur, acheteuse *noun Masc., Fem.* buyer.

achever *verb* [50] **1** to finish (*a piece of work*); **2** to finish off (*meaning 'kill'*).

acide *noun Masc.* acid.
acide *adjective* sharp, sour.

acier *noun Masc.* steel.

acné *noun Fem.* acne.

acoustique *noun Fem.* acoustics.

acquérir *verb* [17] to acquire.

âcre *adjective* pungent.

acrobate *noun Masc. & Fem.* acrobat.

acrobatie *noun Fem.* acrobatics.

acte *noun Masc.* act.

acte de naissance *noun Masc.* birth certificate.

acteur, actrice *noun Masc., Fem.* actor, actress.

actif (*Fem.* **active**) *adjective* active; **la vie active** working life.

action *noun Fem.* action, act; **une bonne action** a good deed.

activement *adverb* actively.

activer *verb* [1] **1** to speed up; **2 s'activer** to hurry up.

activité *noun Fem.* activity.

activité professionnelle *noun Fem.* occupation.

actualité *noun Fem.* **1** current affairs; **2 les actualités** the news.

actuel (*Fem.* **actuelle**) *adjective* present, current; **la situation actuelle** the present situation.

actuellement *adverb* at the moment; **elle est actuellement à Rome** she's in Rome at the moment.

adapté *adjective* **1** suitable; **adapté à** suitable for, suited to; **2** adapted.

adapter *verb* [1] **1** to adapt; **2 s'adapter à** to adapt to, to get used to.

additif *noun Masc.* additive.

addition *noun Fem.* **1** addition; **2** bill (*in a restaurant*) **l'addition, s'il vous plaît** can I have the bill please.

additionner *verb* [1] to add up.

a

adhésif (Fem. **adhésive**) *adjective* adhesive; **ruban adhésif** sticky tape.

b

adieu (*plural* **adieux**) *noun Masc.* goodbye, farewell (*the usual expression is 'au revoir' since 'adieu' is properly used to mean 'goodbye for ever'*).

c

d

e

adjectif *noun Masc.* adjective.

f

adjoint, adjointe *noun Masc., Fem.* **1** assistant; **2** deputy.

g

admettre *verb* [11] **1** to admit; **j'admets qu'elle a raison** I admit that she's right; **2 admettre dans** to admit to (*a restaurant, a club, etc*).

h

i

j

administratif (Fem. **administrative**) *adjective* administrative.

k

l

administration *noun Fem.* administration.

m

admiratif (Fem. **admirative**) *adjective* admiring; **des regards admiratifs** admiring glances.

n

o

admiration *noun Fem.* admiration.

p

admirer *verb* [1] to admire.

q

adolescence *noun Fem.* adolescence.

r

adolescent, adolescente *noun Masc., Fem.* teenager, adolescent.
adolescent *adjective* teenage, adolescent.

s

t

u

adopter *verb* [1] to adopt.

v

adoptif (Fem. **adoptive**) *adjective* **un enfant adoptif** an adopted child.

w

x

adoption *noun Fem.* adoption.

adorable *adjective* adorable.

y

adorer *verb* [1] to adore, to love.

z

adresse *noun Fem.* **1** address; **quelle est ton adresse?** what's your address?; **se tromper d'adresse** to get (*or* go to) the wrong address; **2** skill; **elle l'a fait avec beaucoup d'adresse** she did it very skilfully; **3** speech, address.

adresser *verb* [1] **1 adresser une lettre à quelqu'un** to send somebody a letter; **2 adresser la parole à quelqu'un** to speak to somebody; **3 s'adresser à** to enquire at; **adressez-vous à la réception** enquire at reception; **4 s'adresser à** to be aimed at; **le film s'adresse aux adolescents** the film is aimed at teenagers.

adroit *adjective* skilful.

adulte *noun Masc. & Fem., adjective* adult.

adverbe *noun Masc.* adverb.

adversaire *noun Masc. & Fem.* opponent.

adverse *adjective* opposing.

aération *noun Fem.* ventilation.

aérer *verb* [24] to air.

aérobic *noun Masc.* aerobics.

aéro-club *noun Masc.* flying club.

aérogare *noun Fem.* (flight) terminal (*in an airport*).

aéronautique *noun Fem.* aeronautics.

aéroport *noun Masc.* airport; **à l'aéroport** at (*or* to) the airport.

aérosol *noun Masc.* aerosol.

affaire *noun Fem.* **1** matter, business; **c'est une drôle d'affaire** it's a funny business;

c'est une autre affaire that's another matter; **2** affair, political crisis.

affaires *plural noun Fem.* **1 les affaires** business; **un homme d'affaires** a businessman; **une femme d'affaires** a businesswoman; **un voyage d'affaires** a business trip; **2** business; **occupe-toi de tes affaires!** mind your own business!; **3** belongings, things; **tu peux laisser tes affaires dans la chambre** you can leave your things in the bedroom.

affamé *adjective* starving.

affamer *verb* [1] to starve.

affecter *verb* [1] **1** to affect; **2 affecter de faire** to pretend to do.

affection *noun Fem.* affection; **j'ai beaucoup d'affection pour lui** I'm very fond of him.

affectueusement *adverb* affectionately.

affectueux (*Fem.* **affectueuse**) *adjective* affectionate.

affiche *noun Fem.* **1** poster; **2** notice.

afficher *verb* [1] to put up (*a poster or a notice*).

affliger *verb* [52] **1** to distress, to grieve; **2 affliger de** to afflict with.

affluence *noun Fem.* crowds; **aux heures d'affluence** at peak times.

affolant *adjective* (*informal*) frightening.

affoler *verb* [1] **1 affoler quelqu'un** to throw somebody into a panic;

2 s'affoler to panic; **ne t'affole pas** don't panic.

affreux (*Fem.* **affreuse**) *adjective* **1** awful, dreadful; **2** hideous.

afin *preposition* **1 afin de faire** in order to do; **2 afin que** in order that.

africain *adjective* African.

Africain, Africaine *noun Masc., Fem.* African.

Afrique *noun Fem.* Africa; **en Afrique** in (*or* to) Africa.

agaçant *adjective* annoying.

agacer *verb* [61] to annoy.

âge *noun Masc.* age; **quel âge as-tu?** how old are you?; **à l'âge de cinq ans** at the age of five; **je ne sais pas son âge** I don't know how old he (*or* she) is; **il a l'âge de mon père** he's the same age as my father.

âgé *adjective* **1** old; **les personnes âgées** old people; **2 âgé de** aged; **une femme âgée de trente ans** a woman aged thirty.

agence *noun Fem.* **1** agency; **2** branch (*of a bank*).

agence de voyages *noun Fem.* travel agent's.

agence immobilière *noun Fem.* estate agent's.

agenda *noun Masc.* diary.

agenouiller *verb* [1] **s'agenouiller** to kneel down.

agent *noun Masc.* **1** official; **2** agent.

agent commercial *noun Masc.* sales representative.

a
b
c
d
e
f
g
h
i
j
k
l
m
n
o
p
q
r
s
t
u
v
w
x
y
z

a

agent de police noun Masc.
police officer; **une femme agent de
police** a woman police officer.

b

c

aggraver verb [1] **1** to make worse;
aggraver la situation to make
things worse; **2 s'aggraver** to get
worse; **la situation s'aggrave**
the situation is deteriorating, things are
getting worse.

d

e

f

agir verb [2] **1** to act; **2** to behave; **3 il
s'agit de** it is about; **il s'agit de ton
frère** it's about your brother; **de
quoi s'agit-il?** what's it about?

g

h

i

agitation noun Fem. **1** hustle and
bustle; **2** unrest; **3** restlessness.

j

k

agité adjective **1** restless, agitated;
2 rough (sea); **3** bustling (street);
4 mener une vie agitée to lead a
hectic life.

l

m

agiter verb [1] to shake; **agiter la
main** to wave your hand.

n

agneau (plural **agneaux**) noun
Masc. lamb; **un gigot d'agneau** a leg
of lamb.

o

p

agrafe noun Fem. **1** staple; **2** hook
(on a garment).

q

r

agrafer verb [1] **1** to staple; **2** to
fasten.

s

agrafeuse noun Fem. stapler.

t

agrandir verb [2] to enlarge.

agrandissement noun Masc.
enlargement (of a photo).

u

agréable adjective pleasant, nice.

v

agréé adjective **1** registered;
2 authorized.

w

x

agréer verb [32] **1** to agree to;
**2 veuillez agréer l'expression de
mes sentiments distingués** Yours
faithfully, Yours sincerely (this is

y

z

one of a number of fixed expressions
used to end any formal or business
letter).

agresser verb [1] **1** to attack; **2** to
mug.

agresseur noun Masc. attacker.

agressif (Fem. **agressive**)
adjective aggressive.

agression noun Fem. **1** attack;
2 mugging.

agressivité noun Fem.
aggressiveness.

agricole adjective agricultural.

agriculteur, agricultrice
noun Masc., Fem. farmer.

ahuri adjective amazed, stunned.

ai verb SEE **avoir**.

aide¹ noun Fem. **1** help; **avec l'aide
de Claire** with Claire's help; **venir à
l'aide de quelqu'un** to help
somebody; **2** aid (financial aid given
to a person or a country).

aide² noun Masc. & Fem. **1** assistant;
2 helper.

aider verb [1] **1** to help; **il m'a aidé à
mettre la table** he helped me set the
table; **est-ce que je peux t'aider?**
would you like some help?; **2** to give
aid to (financial aid to a person,
group, or country).

aigle noun Masc. & Fem. eagle.

aiglefin noun Masc. haddock.

aigre adjective **1** sour; **2** sharp.

aigu (Fem. **aiguë**) adjective **1** high-
pitched; **2** acute.

aiguille noun Fem. **1** needle; **une
aiguille à coudre** a sewing needle;
une aiguille à tricoter a knitting

needle; **2** hand (*of a clock or watch*); **dans le sens des aiguilles d'une montre** clockwise; **ça tourne dans le sens des aiguilles d'une montre** it turns clockwise.

aiguilleur du ciel *noun Masc.* air traffic controller.

aiguiser *verb* [1] to sharpen.

ail *noun Masc.* garlic.

aile *noun Fem.* wing; ★ **voler de ses propres ailes** to stand on your own two feet (*literally: to fly with your own wings*).

ailleurs *adverb* **1** elsewhere, somewhere else; **2 d'ailleurs** besides, moreover; **3 par ailleurs** also, in addition.

aimable *adjective* kind, nice; **vous êtes très aimable** that's very kind of you.

aimant *noun Masc.* magnet.

aimer *verb* [1] **1** to like; **est-ce que tu aimes les fraises?** do you like strawberries?; **aimer faire quelque chose** to like doing something; **elle aime aller au cinéma** she likes going to the cinema; **elle aimerait aller au cinéma** she'd like to go to the cinema; **2 aimer mieux** to prefer; **j'aime mieux les fraises que les framboises** I prefer strawberries to raspberries, I like strawberries better than raspberries; **j'aimerais mieux aller au cinéma** I'd prefer to go to the cinema, I'd rather go to the cinema; **3** to love; **je t'aime** I love you; **4 s'aimer** to like each other, to love each other.

aîné, aînée *noun Masc., Fem.* **l'aîné(e)** the eldest, the oldest (*child*).
aîné *adjective* elder, older (*of two*) eldest, oldest (*of more than two*); **leur fille aînée** their elder (or eldest) daughter.

ainsi *adverb* **1** thus; **2** in this way; **3 ainsi que** as well as, along with.

aïoli *noun Masc.* garlic mayonnaise.

air *noun Masc.* **1** air; **aller prendre l'air** to go out and get some fresh air; **2 un courant d'air** a draught; **3 avoir l'air (...)** to look (...); **avoir l'air bon** to look good; **avoir l'air fatigué** to look tired; **4 avoir l'air de** to look like; **il a l'air d'un policier** he looks like a policeman; **5 avoir l'air d'être** to look as if you are; **elle a l'air d'être perdue** she looks as if she's lost; **6 avoir l'air de faire** to look as if you are doing; **il a l'air de comprendre** he looks as if he understands; **7 sourire d'un air heureux** to smile happily; **8** tune.

air bag™ *noun Masc.* airbag (*in a car*).

aire de jeu *noun Fem.* playground.

aire de pique-nique *noun Fem.* picnic area.

aire de services *noun Fem.* motorway service station.

aise *noun Fem.* **être à l'aise** to be comfortable, to feel at ease; **être mal à l'aise** to feel uncomfortable.

aisselle *noun Fem.* armpit.

ajout *noun Masc.* addition.

ajouter *verb* [1] to add; **ajoutez un œuf** add an egg.

a b c d e f g h i j k l m n o p q r s t u v w x y z

a

alarme *noun Fem.* alarm; **sonner l'alarme** to sound the alarm.

album *noun Masc.* album.

album de bandes dessinées *noun Masc.* comic book.

album de photos *noun Masc.* photograph album.

album de timbres *noun Masc.* stamp album.

alcool *noun Masc.* alcohol.

alcoolique *noun Masc. & Fem., adjective* alcoholic.

alcoolisé *adjective* **une boisson alcoolisée** an alcoholic drink; **une boisson non alcoolisée** a non-alcoholic drink.

alcootest *noun Masc.* Breathalyzer™.

alcôve *noun Fem.* alcove.

alentours *plural noun Masc.* **1** surroundings; **2 aux alentours de** in the vicinity (*or* neighbourhood) of.

algèbre *noun Fem.* algebra.

Algérie *noun Fem.* Algeria.

algérien (*Fem.* **algérienne**) *adjective* Algerian.

algues *plural noun Fem.* seaweed.

alibi *noun Masc.* alibi.

aliment *noun Masc.* food.

alimentaire *adjective* **des produits alimentaires** food products; **l'industrie alimentaire** the food industry.

alimentation *noun Fem.* **1** groceries; **2** diet.

allée *noun Fem.* path, drive.

alléger *verb* [15] **1** to lighten; **2** to reduce.

Allemagne *noun Fem.* Germany.

allemand *noun Masc.* German (*language*).
allemand *adjective* German.

Allemand, Allemande *noun Masc., Fem.* German (*person*).

aller¹ *verb* [7] **1** to go; **aller à Paris** to go to Paris; **je vais à Paris** I'm going to Paris, I go to Paris; **2** (*used with another verb in much the same way as 'going to' is used in English*) **je vais écrire à ma mère ce soir** I'm going to write to my mother this evening; **3** (**comment**) **ça va?** how are you?; **ça va bien** I'm fine; **comment va ta mère?** how's your mother?; **elle va bien** she's fine; **4** to suit; **cette robe te va bien** that dress really suits you; **est-ce que jeudi te va?** does Thursday suit you?; **5 s'en aller** to leave; **je m'en vais!** I'm off!

aller² *noun Masc.* **1 faire des allers et retours** to go to and fro; **2 un aller simple** a single ticket; **un aller-retour** a return ticket; **Avignon aller simple, s'il vous plaît** a single to Avignon please.

allergie *noun Fem.* allergy.

allergique *adjective* **être allergique à** to be allergic to; **elle est allergique aux chats** she's allergic to cats.

alliance *noun Fem.* **1** wedding ring; **2** alliance.

allié, alliée *noun Masc., Fem.* ally.

alligator *noun Masc.* alligator.

allô *exclamation* hello (*only used on the telephone*).

allocation *noun Fem.* benefit, allowance.

allocation chômage *noun Fem.* unemployment benefit.

allocations familiales *plural noun Fem.* family allowance.

allonger *verb* [52] **1** to lengthen; **2** to extend; **3 s'allonger** to lie down.

allumer *verb* [1] **1** to light; **allumer le feu** to light the fire; **2** to switch on; **allumer la lampe** to switch on the lamp; **3** to switch on the lights.

allumette *noun Fem.* match; **une boîte d'allumettes** a box of matches.

allure *noun Fem.* **1** speed; **à toute allure** at top speed; **2** appearance (*of a person*).

alors *adverb* **1** then, at that time; **elle travaillait alors à Paris** she was working in Paris then; **2** so; **alors, comment ça va?** so how are you?; **3 alors que** while; **alors qu'elle faisait ses devoirs** while she was doing her homework.

alouette *noun Fem.* skylark.

Alpes *noun Fem.* **les Alpes** the Alps.

alphabet *noun Masc.* alphabet.

alphabétique *adjective* alphabetical; **dans l'ordre alphabétique, par ordre alphabétique** in alphabetical order.

alpin *adjective* alpine.

alpinisme *noun Masc.* mountaineering.

alsacien (*Fem.* **alsacienne**) *adjective* from Alsace, Alsatian.

Alsacien, Alsacienne *noun Masc., Fem.* Alsatian.

alternatif (*Fem.* **alternative**) *adjective* alternative.

altitude *noun Fem.* altitude.

alu *noun Masc.* (*informal*) aluminium; **du papier alu** kitchen foil.

aluminium *noun Masc.* aluminium.

amalgame *noun Masc.* mixture.

amande *noun Fem.* **1** almond; **2** kernel (*of a fruit stone*).

amant *noun Masc.* lover.

amateur *noun Masc.* enthusiast; **un amateur de musique** a music lover. **amateur** *adjective* amateur; **un photographe amateur** an amateur photographer.

ambassade *noun Fem.* embassy; **l'ambassade de France** the French Embassy.

ambassadeur *noun Masc.* ambassador.

ambiance *noun Fem.* atmosphere; **une bonne ambiance** a good atmosphere.

ambigu (*Fem.* **ambiguë**) *adjective* ambiguous.

ambitieux (*Fem.* **ambitieuse**) *adjective* ambitious.

ambition *noun Fem.* ambition.

ambulance *noun Fem.* ambulance.

a
b
c
d
e
f
g
h
i
j
k
l
m
n
o
p
q
r
s
t
u
v
w
x
y
z

ambulancier, **ambulancière**
noun Masc., Fem. ambulance driver.

âme *noun Fem.* soul.

amélioration *noun Fem.*
improvement.

améliorer, **s'améliorer** *verb*
[1] to improve.

aménagé *adjective* **1** equipped;
une cuisine aménagée an
equipped kitchen; **2** converted.

aménager *verb* [52] **1** to convert,
to do up (*a building, a room, etc*); **2** to
develop (*an area*); **3** to construct, to
improve (*a road or road system*).

amende *noun Fem.* fine; **une
amende de 500 euros** a 500-euro
fine.

amener *verb* [50] **1** to bring; **elle a
amené son cousin** she brought her
cousin (with her); **2** to take; **amener
un enfant à l'école** to take a child to
school.

amer (*Fem.* **amère**) *adjective* bitter.

américain *adjective* American.

Américain, **Américaine** *noun*
Masc., Fem. American.

Amérique *noun Fem.* America.

ami, **amie** *noun Masc., Fem.* friend;
un ami à moi a friend of mine; **un
ami à Lisa** a friend of Lisa's.
ami *adjective* friendly.

amiante *noun Masc.* asbestos.

amical (*Masc. plural* **amicaux**)
adjective friendly.

amicale *noun Fem.* association.

amicalement *adverb* **1** in a
friendly way; **2** Best wishes (*at the
end of a letter*).

amitié *noun Fem.* **1** friendship; **faire
quelque chose par amitié** to do
something out of friendship;
2 amitiés love (*at the end of a letter*).

amortisseur *noun Masc.* shock
absorber.

amour *noun Masc.* love.

amoureux (*Fem.* **amoureuse**)
adjective in love; **être amoureux de**
to be in love with.

amour-propre *noun Masc.* self-
esteem.

amovible *adjective* detachable.

amphi *noun Masc.* (*informal*) lecture
theatre (*in a university*).

amphithéâtre *noun Masc.*
1 amphitheatre; **2** lecture theatre.

ample *adjective* **1** loose-fitting
(*jacket, dress, etc*); **2** ample
(*quantity*).

ampleur *noun Fem.* size, scope.

ampli *noun Masc.* (*informal*)
amplifier.

amplificateur *noun Masc.*
amplifier.

ampoule *noun Fem.* **1** light bulb;
2 blister.

amusant *adjective* **1** funny; **une
histoire amusante** a funny story;
2 entertaining.

amuse-gueule *noun Masc.* **des
amuse-gueule** nibbles (*crisps, nuts
etc*).

amuser *verb* [1] **1** to amuse; **2** to
entertain; **3 s'amuser** to play;
4 s'amuser to enjoy oneself, to have
a good time; **on s'est bien amusé**
we really enjoyed ourselves, we had
a really good time.

an *noun Masc.* year; **elle a dix ans** she's ten (years old); **le nouvel an, le jour de l'an** New Year's Day; **il va en Normandie tous les ans** he goes to Normandie every year; ★ **bon an, mal an** year in, year out (*literally: good year, bad year*).

analgésique *noun Masc.* analgesic, painkiller.

analphabète *adjective* illiterate.

analyse *noun Fem.* **1** analysis; **2 une analyse de sang** a blood test.

analyser *verb* [1] to analyse.

ananas *noun Masc.* pineapple.

anatomie *noun Fem.* anatomy.

ancêtre *noun Masc. & Fem.* ancestor.

anchois *noun Masc.* anchovy.

ancien (Fem. **ancienne**) *adjective* **1** (*coming before a noun*) former; **l'ancien président** the former president, the ex-president; **mon ancienne école** my old school; **un ancien élève** a former pupil; **2** (*coming after a noun*) old; **une maison ancienne** an old house; **une table ancienne** an antique table.

ancien combattant *noun Masc.* war veteran.

ancre *noun Fem.* anchor.

ane *noun Masc.* donkey.

anémone *noun Fem.* anemone.

anesthésie *noun Fem.* anaesthesia; **une anesthésie** an anaesthetic.

anesthésiste *noun Masc. & Fem.* anaesthetist.

ange *noun Masc.* angel; ★ **être aux anges** to be over the moon, to be

absolutely delighted (*literally: to be at the level of the angels*).

angine *noun Fem.* throat infection; **avoir une angine** to have a throat infection.

anglais *noun Masc.* English (*language*); **parler l'anglais** to speak English.
anglais *adjective* English.

Anglais, Anglaise *noun Masc., Fem.* Englishman, Englishwoman; **les Anglais** the English; **il y a une Anglaise dans notre classe** there's an English girl in our class.

angle *noun Masc.* **1** angle; **un angle droit** a right angle; **2** corner; **à l'angle de la rue** at the corner of the street; **le magasin qui fait l'angle** the shop on the corner.

Angleterre *noun Fem.* England; **en Angleterre** in (*or* to) England; **aller en Angleterre** to go to England.

Anglo-Normande *adjective* **les îles Anglo-Normandes** the Channel Islands.

anglophone *noun Masc. & Fem.* English speaker.
anglophone *adjective* English-speaking.

angoisse *noun Fem.* anxiety.

angoissé *adjective* anxious.

anguille *noun Fem.* eel.

anguleux (Fem. **anguleuse**) *adjective* bony.

animal (*plural* **animaux**) *noun Masc.* animal.

a

animateur, animatrice noun Masc., Fem. **1** group leader; **2** organizer; **3** presenter.

animation noun Fem. **1** liveliness, life; **il y a beaucoup d'animation dans le quartier le soir** there's a lot going on in the area at night; **2** organization (of a group, a programme, etc).

animé adjective **1** lively (person or discussion); **2** busy (place).

animer verb [1] **1** to run (a course); **2** to lead (a group); **3** to present (a programme or a show); **4** to liven up (an occasion); **5** s'animer to liven up.

anis noun Masc. aniseed.

anneau (plural anneaux) noun Masc. ring.

année noun Fem. year; **l'année prochaine** next year; **l'année dernière** last year; **les années 70** the seventies; **Bonne année** Happy New Year.

annexe noun Fem. **1** appendix (of book); **2** annexe (of building).

anniversaire noun Masc. **1** birthday; **fêter son anniversaire** to celebrate one's birthday; **Bon anniversaire, Joyeux anniversaire** Happy Birthday; **2** anniversary.

annonce noun Fem. **1** advertisement; **les petites annonces** the small ads (in a newspaper); **2** announcement; **3** sign.

annoncer verb [61] **1** to announce; **2** to forecast; **ils annoncent de la neige pour demain** snow is forecast for tomorrow.

annuaire noun Masc. directory; **l'annuaire téléphonique** the telephone directory.

annuel (Fem. annuelle) adjective annual, yearly; **un événement annuel** a yearly event.

annuler verb [1] to cancel; **le vol a été annulé** the flight has been cancelled.

anonyme adjective anonymous.

anorak noun Masc. anorak.

anorexie noun Fem. anorexia.

anormal (Masc. plural anormaux) adjective abnormal.

anse noun Fem. handle (of a basket, cup, jug, or teapot).

Antarctique noun Masc. **l'Antarctique** the Antarctic.

antenne noun Fem. **1** aerial (for a radio or television); **2** antenna (of a insect, a radio mast, or a spacecraft).

anthropologie noun Fem. anthropology.

antibiotique noun Masc. antibiotic; **prendre des antibiotiques** to be on antibiotics.

antichoc adjective shockproof; **u casque antichoc** a crash helmet.

anticiper verb [1] to foresee, to anticipate.

antidérapant adjective nonslip, nonskid.

antidote noun Masc. antidote.

antigel noun Masc. antifreeze.

antillais adjective West Indian.

Antillais, Antillaise noun Masc., Fem. West Indian.

ntilles *plural noun Fem.* **les Antilles** the West Indies.

ntilope *noun Fem.* antelope.

ntipathique *adjective* unpleasant.

ntiquaire *noun Masc. & Fem.* antique dealer.

ntiquité *noun Fem.* antique.

ntiseptique *noun Masc.,* *adjective* antiseptic.

ntitabac *adjective* antismoking.

ntiterroriste *adjective* antiterrorist.

ntivol *noun Masc.* anti-theft device.

nxieux (Fem. **anxieuse**) *adjective* anxious.

oût *noun Masc.* August; **en août, au mois d'août** in August.

percevoir *verb* [66] **1** to catch sight of; **2 s'apercevoir de** to notice; **s'apercevoir que** to notice that.

perçu *noun Masc.* **1** insight; **2** glimpse.

péritif *noun Masc.* drink (*usually alcoholic, before a meal*).

phte *noun Masc.* mouth ulcer.

platir *verb* [2] **1** to flatten; **2** to smooth out.

postrophe *noun Fem.* apostrophe.

pparaître *verb* [57] **1** to appear; **2** to seem; **il apparaît que** it seems that.

appareil *noun Masc.* **1** device, appliance, piece of equipment; **2** telephone; **c'est Paul à l'appareil** it's Paul speaking; **3 un appareil (dentaire)** a brace (*for teeth*).

appareil photo *noun Masc.* camera.

apparemment *adverb* apparently.

apparence *noun Fem.* appearance.

apparent *adjective* **1** visible, obvious; **2** apparent.

apparition *noun Fem.* appearance.

appartement *noun Masc.* flat; **'appartement à louer'** 'flat to let'.

appartenir *verb* [81] **appartenir à** to belong to; **est-ce que ce stylo t'appartient?** does this pen belong to you?, is this pen yours?; **à qui appartiennent ces chaussures?** who do these shoes belong to?

appel *noun Masc.* **1** call, appeal; **un appel d'aide** a call for help; **2 un appel (téléphonique)** a telephone call; **3 faire appel à** to appeal to; **4 faire l'appel** to take the register (*at school*).

appeler *verb* [18] **1** to call; **ils l'ont appelé Roger** they called him Roger; **2 s'appeler** to be called; **il s'appelle Frank** he's called Frank, his name is Frank; **je m'appelle Anne** my name is Anne; **comment t'appelles-tu?, tu t'appelles comment?** what's your name?; **3** to phone; **4** to call; **appeler un taxi** to call a taxi.

appendice *noun Masc.* appendix (*organ*).

a b c d e f g h i j k l m n o p q r s t u v w x y z

appendicite *noun Fem.* appendicitis.

appétissant *adjective* appetizing.

appétit *noun Masc.* appetite; **'bon appétit'** 'enjoy your meal'.

applaudir *verb* [2] to applaud.

applaudissements *plural noun Masc.* applause.

application *noun Fem.* 1 care; 2 application.

appliquer *verb* [1] 1 to apply; 2 **s'appliquer** to take care; 3 **s'appliquer à** to apply to; **cela ne s'applique pas à vous** that doesn't apply to you.

apporter *verb* [1] to bring.

apprécier *verb* [1] to appreciate.

appréhender *verb* [1] 1 to arrest; 2 to dread.

apprenant, apprenante *noun Masc., Fem.* learner.

apprendre *verb* [64] 1 to learn; **apprendre à lire** to learn to read; 2 to hear; **j'ai appris que tu vas partir** I hear you're leaving; 3 to teach; **apprendre quelque chose à quelqu'un** to teach somebody something; **elle leur apprend le français** she's teaching them French; **elle leur apprend à parler français** she's teaching them to speak French.

approche *noun Fem.* approach.

approcher *verb* [1] 1 to move (something) closer; **approche ta chaise** move your chair closer; **approche ta chaise de la table** move your chair closer to the table; 2 **approcher quelqu'un** to go up to

somebody; 3 **s'approcher de quelque chose** to go (*or* come) near to something.

approprié *adjective* appropriate.

approuver *verb* [1] 1 to approve of 2 to approve (*a document, project, budget, etc*).

approximatif (Fem. approximative) *adjective* approximate, rough.

approximativement *adverb* approximately, roughly.

appui *noun Masc.* support.

appuyer *verb* [41] 1 **appuyer sur quelque chose** to press something **appuie sur le bouton** press the button; 2 to lean; **appuyer quelqu chose contre le mur** to lean something against the wall.

après *adverb* afterwards, later; **un heure après** an hour later; **peu après** shortly afterwards; **longtemps après** a long time later.
après *preposition* 1 after; **après dix heures** after ten o'clock; **aprè l'école** after school; 2 **après avoi fait** after doing; 3 **après que** after

après-demain *adverb* the day after tomorrow.

après-midi *noun Masc. OR Fem.* afternoon; **cet après-midi** this afternoon; **demain après-midi** tomorrow afternoon; **hier après-midi** yesterday afternoon; **tous le après-midi** every afternoon.

après-rasage *noun Masc.* aftershave.

aptitude *noun Fem.* aptitude; **son aptitude pour le dessin** his aptitude for drawing.

aquarelle *noun Fem.* watercolours; **une aquarelle** a watercolour (painting).

aquarium *noun Masc.* **1** fish tank; **2** aquarium.

arabe *noun Masc.* Arabic.
arabe *adjective* **1** Arab; **2** Arabic.

Arabe *noun Masc. & Fem.* Arab.

araignée *noun Fem.* spider; **une toile d'araignée** a spider's web.

arbitraire *adjective* arbitrary.

arbitre *noun Masc.* referee, umpire.

arbre *noun Masc.* tree.

arbre généalogique *noun Masc.* family tree.

arc *noun Masc.* **1** bow (*as in 'bow and arrow'*); **2** arch.

arc-en-ciel *noun Masc.* rainbow.

archéologie *noun Fem.* archeology.

archéologue *noun Masc. & Fem.* archeologist.

archet *noun Masc.* bow (*for a musical instrument such as a violin.*).

archevêque *noun Masc.* archbishop.

architecte *noun Masc. & Fem.* architect.

architecture *noun Fem.* architecture.

Arctique *noun Masc.* **l'Arctique** the Arctic.

ardoise *noun Fem.* slate.

arène *noun Fem.* **1** arena; **2** bullring.

arête *noun Fem.* fishbone; **ce poisson est plein d'arêtes** this fish is full of bones.

argent *noun Masc.* **1** money; **dépenser de l'argent** to spend money; **2** silver; **une cuillère en argent** a silver spoon.

argent de poche *noun Masc.* pocket money.

argile *noun Fem.* clay.

argot *noun Masc.* slang.

aristocrate *noun Masc. & Fem.* aristocrat.

aristocratie *noun Fem.* aristocracy.

arithmétique *noun Fem.* arithmetic.

arme *noun Fem.* weapon.

armé *adjective* **1** armed; **2 armé de** armed with, equipped with.

arme à feu *noun Fem.* firearm.

armée *noun Fem.* army.

armée de l'air *noun Fem.* Air Force.

armée de terre *noun Fem.* Army.

armoire *noun Fem.* **1** cupboard; **2** wardrobe.

arobase *noun Masc.* at, @ (*in email addresses*); **jean-point-dupont-arobase-mondecom-point-com** jean-dot-dupont-at-mondecom-dot-com.

aromates *plural noun Masc.* herbs and spices.

aromathérapie noun Fem. aromatherapy.

aromatisé adjective flavoured.

arôme noun Masc. **1** flavouring; **2** aroma.

arracher verb [1] **1 arracher quelque chose à quelqu'un** to snatch something from somebody; **2** to rip out, to rip off (a page or pages); **3** to pull up (weeds or vegetables).

arrangement noun Masc. arrangement.

arranger verb [52] **1** to arrange; **arranger une réunion** to arrange a meeting; **2** to arrange (flowers, books, etc); **3** to sort out; **4** to fix; **5 s'arranger** to get better; **ça va s'arranger** it will sort itself out; **6 s'arranger avec quelqu'un** to sort it out with somebody; **tu t'arranges avec Paul** sort it out with Paul.

arrestation noun Fem. arrest.

arrêt noun Masc. **1** stop; **un arrêt de bus** a bus stop; **2 sans arrêt** non-stop.

arrêter verb [1] **1** to stop; **arrêter la voiture** to stop the car; **2** to switch off (an engine, a machine, etc); **3 arrêter de faire** to stop doing; **il a arrêté de fumer** he's stopped smoking; **elle n'arrête pas de travailler** she never stops working; **4 s'arrêter** to stop; **on va s'arrêter à la boulangerie** we'll stop at the baker's.

arrhes plural noun Fem. deposit; **verser des arrhes** to pay a deposit.

arrière noun Masc. back; **à l'arrière** in the back (of a car); **regarder en arrière** to look back.
arrière adjective back (door, pocket, etc).

arrière-goût noun Masc. aftertaste.

arrière-grand-mère noun Fem. great-grandmother.

arrière-grand-père noun Masc. great-grandfather.

arrière-grands-parents plural noun Masc. great-grandparents.

arrière-petits-enfants plural noun Masc. great-grandchildren.

arrivage noun Masc. **1** delivery (of goods); **2** batch (of students).

arrivée noun Fem. arrival.

arriver verb [1] **1** to arrive; **arriver à Londres** to arrive in London, to get to London; **je suis arrivé à cinq heures** I arrived at five o'clock, I got there (or here) at five o'clock; **j'arrive!** just coming!; **2** to happen; **un accident est arrivé** an accident has happened; **tu sais ce qui m'est arrivé?** do you know what happened to me?; **3 arriver à faire** to manage to do; **je n'arrive pas à tourner la clef** I can't manage to turn the key.

arrogant adjective arrogant.

arrondi adjective rounded.

arrondissement noun Masc. arrondissement; **elle habite à Paris dans le neuvième arrondissement** she lives in Paris in the ninth arrondissement (large French cities are divided into numbered *administrative areas called 'arrondissements').*

arroser *verb* [1] to water; **arroser les plantes** to water the plants; **on va arroser l'anniversaire de mon frère** we're going to have a few drinks to celebrate my brother's birthday.

arrosoir *noun Masc.* watering can.

art *noun Masc.* art; **une galerie d'art** an art gallery; **l'art de faire** the art of doing.

art dramatique *noun Masc.* drama.

artère *noun Fem.* **1** artery; **2** arterial road; **3** main road.

arthrite *noun Fem.* arthritis.

artichaut *noun Masc.* artichoke.

article *noun Masc.* **1** article (*in a newspaper, magazine, etc*); **2** item (*for sale*); **articles de sport** sports equipment; **articles de toilette** toiletries; **3** article (*in grammar*); **l'article défini** the definite article; **l'article indéfini** the indefinite article.

articulation *noun Fem.* joint; **articulation du coude/de la hanche** elbow/hip joint.

artificiel (*Fem.* **artificielle**) *adjective* artificial.

artisan *noun Masc.* craftsman.

artisanal (*Masc. plural* **artisanaux**) *adjective* **1** traditional; **2** hand-crafted.

artisanat *noun Masc.* arts and crafts.

artiste *noun Masc. & Fem.* **1** artist; **2** performer.

as[1] *verb* SEE **avoir**.

as[2] *noun Masc.* ace.

ascenseur *noun Masc.* lift; **prendre l'ascenseur** to take the lift.

asiatique *adjective* Asian.

Asie *noun Fem.* Asia.

asile *noun Masc.* **1** refuge; **2 le droit d'asile** political asylum.

aspect *noun Masc.* **1** aspect; **2** appearance; **d'un aspect bizarre** strange-looking; **3** side; **l'aspect positif** the positive side.

asperger *verb* [52] to sprinkle.

asperges *plural noun Fem.* asparagus.

asphyxier, s'asphyxier *verb* [1] to suffocate.

aspirateur *noun Masc.* vacuum cleaner.

aspirine *noun Fem.* aspirin.

assaisonnement *noun Masc.* **1** seasoning; **2** dressing.

assaisonner *verb* [1] **1** to season; **2** to put the dressing on (*a salad*).

assassin, assassine *noun Masc., Fem.* murderer.

assassinat *noun Masc.* murder.

assassiner *verb* [1] to murder.

assemblée *noun Fem.* meeting.

assembler *verb* [1] **1** to put together, to assemble (*a kit, a machine, etc*); **2** to gather together; **3 s'assembler** to gather (*of a group, crowd, demonstration, etc*); ★ **qui se ressemble s'assemble** birds of a feather flock together (*literally: those who are similar gather together*).

a
b
c
d
e
f
g
h
i
j
k
l
m
n
o
p
q
r
s
t
u
v
w
x
y
z

asseoir verb [20] **s'asseoir** to sit down; **s'asseoir sur une chaise** to sit down on a chair; **assieds-toi** take a seat; **asseyez-vous** do sit down SEE ALSO **assis**.

assez adverb **1 assez de** enough; **assez de pain** enough bread; **2** enough; **elle ne mange pas assez** she doesn't eat enough; **3** enough; **est-ce que l'eau est assez chaude?** is the water hot enough?; **4** quite; **leur maison est assez grande** their house is quite big; **assez souvent** quite often; **assez joli** quite pretty; **5 j'en ai assez (de)** (informal) I'm fed up (with).

assiette noun Fem. plate; **une assiette plate** a dinner plate; **une assiette creuse, une assiette à soupe** a soup plate; ★ **je ne suis pas dans mon assiette aujourd'hui** I'm not my usual self today.

assis adjective **être assis** to be sitting; **elle était assise dans un fauteuil** she was sitting in an armchair; **rester assis** to remain seated.

assistance noun Fem. **1** audience; **dans l'assistance** in the audience; **2** assistance.

assistant, assistante noun Masc., Fem. assistant.

assister verb [1] **1** to assist; **2** to aid (a country, the poor, etc); **3 assister à** to be present at, to be at; **j'ai assisté à leur mariage** I was at their wedding.

association noun Fem. association.

associé, associée noun Masc., Fem. associate, partner.

associer verb [1] **1 associer quelqu'un à quelque chose** to include somebody in something; **2 s'associer à un groupe** to join a group; **3 s'associer pour faire** to get together to do.

assommer verb [1] **1 assommer quelqu'un** to knock somebody senseless; **2 assommer quelqu'un** (informal) to bore somebody stiff; **3 être assommé par une nouvelle** to be stunned by a piece of news.

assorti adjective matching; **rideaux et coussins assortis** matching curtains and cushions; **une veste assortie à sa robe** a jacket to match her dress.

assortiment noun Masc. assortment, selection.

assortir verb [2] **1** to match; **2 s'assortir à** to match.

assouplissant noun Masc. fabric softener.

assourdir verb [2] **1** to deafen; **2** to muffle.

assourdissant adjective deafening.

assumer verb [1] **assumer la responsabilité de quelque chose** to take responsibility for something; **assumer une fonction** to hold a position.

assurance noun Fem. **1** confidence; **avec assurance** confidently; **2** insurance.

assurance automobile *noun Fem.* car insurance.

assurance maladie *noun Fem.* health insurance; **est-ce que vous avez une assurance maladie?** do you have health insurance?

assurance voyage *noun Fem.* travel insurance.

assuré *adjective* **1** confident; **2** insured.

assurer *verb* [1] **1** to assure; **je vous assure que c'est vrai** I assure you it's true; **2** to insure; **assurer sa voiture** to insure one's car; **3** to provide (*a service*); **4** to carry out (*a task or a responsibility*); **5 s'assurer** to make sure.

astérisque *noun Masc.* asterisk.

asthmatique *adjective* asthmatic.

asthme *noun Masc.* asthma.

asticot *noun Masc.* maggot.

astiquer *verb* [1] to polish.

astrologie *noun Fem.* astrology.

astrologue *noun Masc. & Fem.* astrologer.

astronome *noun Masc. & Fem.* astronomer.

astronomie *noun Fem.* astronomy.

astronomique *adjective* astronomical.

astuce *noun Fem.* **1** cleverness; **2 une astuce** a trick (*for managing to do something*); **il doit y avoir une astuce** there must be a trick to it.

astucieux (*Fem.* **astucieuse**) *adjective* clever; **c'était très**

astucieux de sa part de faire ça it was very crafty of her to do that.

atelier *noun Masc.* **1** workshop; **2** studio (*of an artist, a sculptor, etc*); **3** work group.

athée *noun Masc. & Fem.* atheist.

Athènes *noun* Athens.

athlète *noun Masc. & Fem.* athlete.

athlétique *adjective* athletic.

athlétisme *noun Masc.* athletics.

Atlantique *noun Masc.* **l'Atlantique** the Atlantic.

atlas *noun Masc.* atlas.

atmosphère *noun Fem.* atmosphere.

atome *noun Masc.* atom.

atomique *adjective* atomic.

atomiseur *noun Masc.* spray, atomizer.

atout *noun Masc.* **1** trump card; **c'est atout pique** spades are trumps; **2** asset, advantage.

atroce *adjective* dreadful, terrible.

atrocité *noun Fem.* **1** atrocity; **2** monstrosity.

attachant *adjective* lovable.

attache *noun Fem.* **1** tie, string, strap; **2 attaches familiales** family ties.

attacher *verb* [1] **1 attacher ses cheveux** to tie (*or* fix) your hair back; **2 s'attacher** to stick (*to the pan*).

attaque *noun Fem.* attack.

attaquer *verb* [1] **1** to attack; **2** to tackle (*a job*).

attarder *verb* [1] **s'attarder** to linger.

atteindre *verb* [60] **1** to reach; **2** to achieve.

atteint *adjective* **être atteint d'une maladie** to be suffering from an illness.

attendant *in phrase* **en attendant** meanwhile, in the meantime.

attendre *verb* [3] **1** to wait; **tu peux attendre deux minutes?** can you wait two minutes?; **2** to wait for; **j'attends le bus** I'm waiting for the bus; **je t'attends dehors** I'll wait for you outside; **3** **s'attendre à** to expect.

attendrissant *adjective* touching.

attentat *noun Masc.* **1** **un attentat (à la bombe)** a bomb attack, a bombing; **2** assassination attempt.

attente *noun Fem.* wait; **une attente de vingt minutes** a twenty-minute wait.

attentif (*Fem.* **attentive**) *adjective* **1** attentive; **2** careful.

attention *noun Fem.* **1** attention; **2** **faire attention à** to be careful of; **faites attention aux pickpockets!** look out for pickpockets!; **3** **attention!** watch out!; **attention au chien!** beware of the dog!

atterrir *verb* [2] to land.

atterrissage *noun Masc.* landing.

attirant *adjective* attractive.

attirer *verb* [1] to attract; **attirer l'attention de quelqu'un sur quelque chose** to attract (*or* draw) somebody's attention to something.

attitude *noun Fem.* attitude.

attraction *noun Fem.* attraction.

attraper *verb* [1] **1** to catch; **2** **attraper un rhume** to catch a cold; **3** to catch hold of.

attrayant *adjective* attractive.

attrister *verb* [1] to sadden.

au SEE **à**.

aubaine *noun Fem.* godsend.

aube *noun Fem.* dawn; **à l'aube** at dawn.

aubépine *noun Fem.* hawthorn.

auberge *noun Fem.* inn; ★ **on n'est pas sorti de l'auberge** our problems are not over yet (*literally: we're not out of the inn*).

auberge de jeunesse *noun Fem.* youth hostel.

aubergine *noun Fem.* aubergine.

aucun *adjective* no; **en aucun cas** under no circumstances; **sans aucun doute** without any doubt. **aucun** *pronoun* none; **aucun des deux** neither of them; **aucun d'entre eux** none of them.

aucunement *adverb* in no way.

audace *noun Fem.* daring.

audacieux (*Fem.* **audacieuse**) *adjective* daring.

au-delà de *preposition* beyond.

au-dessous *adverb* **1** underneath; **2** below; **3** **au-dessous de** underneath; **au-dessous de la table** underneath the table; **4** **au-dessous de** below; **au-dessous de la limite** below the limit.

u-dessus *adverb* **1** above; **2 au-dessus de** above.

udience *noun Fem.* audience.

udiovisuel (*Fem.* **audiovisuelle**) *adjective* audiovisual.

uditeur, auditrice *noun Masc., Fem.* listener.

udition *noun Fem.* audition.

ugmentation *noun Fem.* increase; **l'augmentation des prix** the increase in prices; **une augmentation de salaire** a pay rise.

ugmenter *verb* [1] **1** to raise, to increase; **augmenter les prix** to raise prices; **2** to rise, to go up; **le prix a augmenté** the price has gone up.

ujourd'hui *adverb* today; **nous sommes lundi aujourd'hui** today is Monday.

uparavant *adverb* before, beforehand.

uprès de *preposition* beside, next to.

uquel *pronoun* **le garçon auquel je parle** the boy I'm talking to.

ura, aurai, auras, aurez, aurons, auront *verb* SEE **avoir**.

u revoir *exclamation* goodbye.

ussi *adverb* **1** also, too; **moi aussi** me too; **j'ai aussi invité ton frère** I also invited your brother, I invited your brother as well; **2 aussi ...que** as ...as; **mon panier est aussi lourd que le tien** my basket is as heavy as yours; **3 aussi bien que** as well as; **les enfants aussi bien que les**

adultes children as well as adults.

aussi *conjunction* so, therefore.

aussitôt *adverb* immediately.

Australie *noun Fem.* Australia.

australien (*Fem.* **australienne**) *adjective* Australian.

Australien, Australienne *noun Masc., Fem.* Australian.

autant *adverb* **1** as much, so much; **je n'ai jamais mangé autant** I've never eaten so much; **2 autant que** as much as, as many as; **tu en as autant que moi** you have as much (or as many) as me; **3 autant de ...que** as much ...as, as many ...as; **tu as autant de problèmes que moi** you have as many problems as I do.

autel *noun Masc.* altar.

auteur *noun Masc.* author.

authentique *adjective* genuine.

auto *noun Fem.* car.

autobiographie *noun Fem.* autobiography.

autobus *noun Masc.* bus.

autocar *noun Masc.* coach.

autocollant *noun Masc.* sticker. **autocollant** *adjective* self-adhesive.

autodéfense *noun Fem.* self-defence.

auto-école *noun Fem.* driving school.

automate *noun Masc.* robot.

automatique *adjective* automatic.

automatiquement *adverb* automatically.

a
b
c
d
e
f
g
h
i
j
k
l
m
n
o
p
q
r
s
t
u
v
w
x
y
z

23

automne *noun Masc.* autumn; **en automne** in autumn.

automobile *noun Fem.* car. **automobile** *adjective* **l'industrie automobile** the car industry.

automobiliste *noun Masc. & Fem.* motorist.

autoradio *noun Masc.* car radio.

autorisation *noun Fem.* **1** permission; **2** permit.

autoriser *verb* [1] **1** to allow, to authorize; **2 autoriser quelqu'un à faire** to allow somebody to do.

autoritaire *adjective* authoritarian, strict.

autorité *noun Fem.* authority.

autoroute *noun Fem.* motorway; **l'autoroute de l'information** the information super-highway.

auto-stop *noun Masc.* hitchhiking; **faire de l'auto-stop** to hitchhike.

auto-stoppeur, auto-stoppeuse *noun Masc., Fem.* hitchhiker.

autour *adverb* **1** around; **2 autour de** round, around; **autour de la table** round the table.

autre *adjective* **1** other; **l'autre couteau** the other knife; **l'autre jour** the other day; **2 un/une autre** another; **tu peux me passer un autre verre?** can you pass me another glass?; **3 quelqu'un d'autre** somebody else; **personne d'autre** nobody else.

autre *pronoun* **1 un/une autre** another one; **donne-moi un autre** give me another one; **2 les autres** the others; **où sont les autres?** where are the others?

autrefois *adverb* in the past, in the old days.

autrement *adverb* **1** differently; **autrement dit** in other words; **2** otherwise.

autre part *adverb* somewhere else.

Autriche *noun Fem.* Austria.

autrichien (*Fem.* **autrichienne**) *adjective* Austrian.

Autrichien, Autrichienne *noun Masc., Fem.* Austrian.

autruche *noun Fem.* ostrich.

aux SEE **à**.

auxiliaire *noun Masc. & Fem.*, *adjective* auxiliary.

auxquelles *pronoun* **les filles auxquelles je parlais** the girls I was talking to.

auxquels *pronoun* **les garçons auxquels je parlais** the boys I was talking to.

avalanche *noun Fem.* avalanche.

avaler *verb* [1] **1** to swallow; **2** to inhale.

avance *noun Fem.* **1** advance, progress; **2 je suis arrivé dix minutes en avance** I arrived ten minutes early; **avoir dix minutes d'avance** to be ten minutes early; **3 être en avance** to be early; **4 à l'avance** in advance.

avancer *verb* [61] **1** to move forward, to advance; **2 avancer quelque chose** to move something forward; **3 ma montre avance de cinq minutes** my watch is five minutes fast.

avant *adverb* **1** before; **longtemps avant** a long time before; **2** forward; **plus avant** further forward.

avant *preposition* **1** before; **avant Noël** before Christmas; **avant six heures** before six o'clock; **elle est arrivée avant moi** she arrived before me; **2 avant de faire** before doing; **avant de partir je vais téléphoner à ma mère** before leaving (*or* before I leave) I'll phone my mother; **3 avant que** before.

avant *noun Masc.* front.

avant *adjective* front; **la roue avant** the front wheel.

avantage *noun Masc.* advantage.

avantageux (*Fem.* **avantageuse**) *adjective* **1 des prix avantageux** attractive prices; **2 des conditions avantageuses** favourable conditions.

avant-bras *noun Masc.* forearm.

avant-dernier, avant-dernière *noun Masc., Fem.* **l'avant-dernier** the last but one.

avant-dernière *adjective* second last, last but one.

avant-hier *adverb* the day before yesterday.

avare *noun Masc. & Fem.* miser.

avare *adjective* mean, miserly.

avec *preposition* with; **avec Marie** with Marie; **avec un couteau** with a knife; **avec ça?** anything else? (*in a shop*).

avenir *noun Masc.* future; **l'avenir** the future; **à l'avenir** in the future.

aventure *noun Fem.* adventure.

avenue *noun Fem.* avenue.

averse *noun Fem.* shower.

avertir *verb* [2] **1** to inform; **2** to warn.

avertissement *noun Masc.* warning.

aveuglant *adjective* blinding.

aveugle *adjective* blind.

aveuglément *adverb* blindly.

aveugler *verb* [1] to blind.

avez *verb* SEE **avoir**.

aviation *noun Fem.* **1** aviation; **2** aircraft industry; **3** flying; **4** air force.

avion *noun Masc.* aeroplane, plane; **aller à Paris en avion** to go to Paris by plane, to fly to Paris; **par avion** by airmail.

aviron *noun Masc.* **1** rowing; **faire de l'aviron** to row; **2** oar.

avis *noun Masc.* **1** opinion; **à mon avis** in my opinion; **2 changer d'avis** to change one's mind; **3** notice.

avocat[1]**, avocate** *noun Masc., Fem.* **1** solicitor; **2** barrister.

avocat[2] *noun Masc.* avocado (pear).

avoine *noun Fem.* oats; **des flocons d'avoine** porridge oats.

avoir *verb* [5] **1** to have (got); **elle a trois frères** she has (*or* she's got) three brothers; **tu as beaucoup de livres** you have (*or* you've got) a lot of books; **2** (*talking about age*) **avoir dix ans** to be ten; **Claudie a dix ans** Claudie's ten; **quel âge a-t-il?** how old is he?; **3 avoir chaud** to be hot; **j'ai chaud** I'm hot; **j'ai froid** I'm cold; **4** (*used with another verb, like 'have' in English, to form past tenses*) **j'ai perdu mon stylo** I have lost my

a
b
c
d
e
f
g
h
i
j
k
l
m
n
o
p
q
r
s
t
u
v
w
x
y
z

pen; **j'ai vu ta mère hier** I saw your mother yesterday; **5 j'en ai pour dix minutes** it'll take me ten minutes; **6 il y a** there is, there are; **il y a un livre sur la table** there's a book on the table; **il y a trois livres sur la table** there are three books on the table; **7 il y a** ago; **il y a trois ans** three years ago; **8 qu'est-ce qu'il y a?** what's the matter?

avons *verb* SEE **avoir**.

avortement *noun Masc.* abortion.

avouer *verb* [1] to confess, to admit.

avril *noun Masc.* April; **en avril, au mois d'avril** in April.

azalée *noun Fem.* azalea.

azote *noun Masc.* nitrogen.

Bb

babouin *noun Masc.* baboon.

baby-foot *noun Masc.* table football; **jouer au baby-foot** to play table football; **on va faire une partie de baby-foot** we're going to have a game of table football.

bac *noun Masc.* **1** (*informal*) SHORT FOR **baccalauréat**; **2** tub.

bac à glace *noun Masc.* ice tray.

bac à sable *noun Masc.* sandpit.

baccalauréat *noun Masc.* baccalaureate (*school-leaving certificate sat at the age of 17-18 and giving access to higher education*); **passer le baccalauréat** to sit the baccalaureate; **réussir au**

baccalauréat to pass the baccalaureate.

bâche *noun Fem.* tarpaulin.

badaud, **badaude** *noun Masc., Fem.* passerby, onlooker.

baffe *noun Fem.* (*informal*) slap.

baffle *noun Masc.* speaker (*on a music system*).

bagage *noun Masc.* **un bagage** a piece of luggage; **des bagages** luggage; **où sont tes bagages?** where is your luggage?; **j'ai fait me bagages** I've packed.

bagarre *noun Fem.* fight.

bagarrer *verb* [1] **se bagarrer** to fight.

bagnole *noun Fem.* (*informal*) car

bague *noun Fem.* ring.

baguette *noun Fem.* **1** baguette, French bread stick; **2** stick; **3** drumstick; **4** chopstick.

baguette magique *noun Fem.* magic wand.

Bahamas *noun Fem. plural* **les îles Bahamas** the Bahamas.

baie *noun* **1** bay (*on the sea*); **2** berry; **3 une baie vitrée** a pictur window.

baignade *noun Fem.* swimming; **'baignade interdite'** 'no swimming'.

baigner *verb* [1] **se baigner** to go swimming.

baignoire *noun Fem.* bath.

bail (*plural* **baux**) *noun Masc.* lease **un bail de trois ans** a three-year lease.

bâiller *verb* [1] to yawn.

ain noun Masc. bath; **prendre un bain** to have a bath.

aiser noun Masc. kiss; **bons baisers** love and kisses (at the end of a letter).

aisse noun Fem. drop, fall; **être en baisse** to be falling; **la température est en baisse** the temperature is falling.

aisser verb [1] **1** to lower; **baisser le store** to lower (or pull down) the blind; **baisser le volume** to turn down the volume; **baisser la lumière** to turn down the lights; **baisser les prix** to cut prices; **2 se baisser** to bend down.

al noun Masc. dance; **un bal populaire** a village dance (or disco).

alade noun Fem. walk, drive; **faire une balade (à pied)** to go for a walk; **faire une balade (en voiture)** to go for a drive; **faire une balade à la campagne** to go for a walk (or drive) in the country.

alader verb [1] **1 se balader** to go for a walk (or drive); **se balader en Écosse** to tour around Scotland; **2 balader quelque chose** to carry something around.

aladeur noun Masc. Walkman™, personal stereo.

alai noun Masc. broom, (long-handled) brush; **passer le balai** to sweep the floor.

Balance noun Fem. Libra (sign of the Zodiac).

alance noun Fem. scales; **une balance de cuisine** kitchen scales.

balancer verb [61] **1** to sway; **2** to swing; **3** (informal) to throw, to chuck; **balance-moi les clés!** chuck me the keys!; **4** (informal) to chuck out; **je vais balancer tous ces vieux bouquins** I'm going to chuck out all these old books.

balançoire noun Fem. **1** swing; **2** seesaw.

balayer verb [59] **1** to sweep; **balayer la cuisine** to sweep the kitchen floor; **2** to sweep up; **balayer les miettes** to sweep up the crumbs.

balayeur, balayeuse noun Masc., Fem. roadsweeper.

balbutier verb [1] to mumble.

balcon noun Masc. balcony.

baleine noun Fem. whale.

baliser verb [1] **1** to signpost; **2** to mark out.

balle noun Fem. **1** ball; **2** bullet.

ballerine noun Fem. **1** ballerina; **2** ballerina shoe; **3** ballet shoe.

ballet noun Masc. ballet.

ballon noun Masc. **1** ball; **2** balloon; **3** (informal) Breathalyzer™; ★ **souffler dans le ballon** to be breathalyzed.

ball-trap noun Masc. clay pigeon shooting.

balnéaire adjective seaside; **une station balnéaire** a seaside resort.

bambou noun Masc. bamboo.

banal adjective ordinary; **peu banal** unusual.

banane noun Fem. **1** banana; **2** bumbag.

a
b
c
d
e
f
g
h
i
j
k
l
m
n
o
p
q
r
s
t
u
v
w
x
y
z

banc *noun* Masc. bench; **assis sur un banc** sitting on a bench.

bancaire *adjective* **1** banking; **2 une carte bancaire** a bank card.

bancal *adjective* **1** rickety; **2** wobbly.

bande *noun* Fem. **1** group; **une bande de jeunes** a group of young people; **2** gang; **une bande de criminels** a criminal gang; **3** strip (*of fabric or paper*); **4** tape (*for recording*); **5** bandage.

bande-annonce *noun* Fem. trailer (*for a film*).

bandeau (*plural* **bandeaux**) *noun* Masc. **1** headband; **2** blindfold.

bande d'arrêt d'urgence *noun* Fem. hard shoulder (*on motorway*).

bande de fréquence *noun* Fem. wavelength (*on radio*).

bande dessinée *noun* Fem. **1** comic strip; **2** comic book.

bande publique *noun* Fem. Citizen's Band, CB radio.

bande rugueuse *noun* Fem. rumble strip (*on motorway*).

bande sonore *noun* Fem. **1** soundtrack (*of film*); **2** rumble strip (*on motorway*).

bandit *noun* Masc. bandit.

banditisme *noun* Masc. crime.

banlieue *noun* Fem. **la banlieue** the suburbs; **une banlieue** a suburb; **une maison de banlieue** a house in the suburbs; **un train de banlieue** a commuter train.

banque *noun* Fem. **1** bank; **aller à la banque** to go to the bank; **2** banking; **travailler dans la banque** to work in banking.

banquet *noun* Masc. banquet.

banquette *noun* Fem. **1** wall seat (*in a cafe or restaurant*); **2** seat (*in a car, bus, or train*).

banquier *noun* Masc. banker.

baptême *noun* Masc. christening.

baptiser *verb* [1] **1** to christen; **2** to name; **3** to nickname.

baquet *noun* Masc. tub.

bar *noun* Masc. bar.

baraque *noun* Fem. (*informal*) house.

Barbade *noun* Fem. **la Barbade** Barbados.

barbadien (Fem. **barbadienne**) *adjective* Barbadian.

Barbadien, Barbadienne *noun* Masc.,Fem. Barbadian.

barbant *adjective* (*informal*) boring.

barbe *noun* Fem. beard; ★ **c'est la barbe!** what a drag!; ★ **faire quelque chose à la barbe de quelqu'un** to do something behind somebody's back (*literally: to do something in somebody's beard*).

barbe à papa *noun* Fem. candyfloss.

barbecue *noun* Masc. barbecue.

barbelé *noun* Masc. barbed wire.

barbouiller *verb* [1] **1** to smear; **tu es tout barbouillé de confiture** you've got jam all over your face;

to daub; **barbouillé de slogans** daubed with slogans.

barbu *noun Masc.* **un barbu** a man with a beard.

barbu *adjective* bearded.

barème *noun Masc.* scale.

barmaid *noun Fem.* barmaid.

barman *noun Masc.* barman.

baromètre *noun Masc.* barometer.

barque *noun Fem.* rowing boat.

barquette *noun Fem.* tub, container; **une barquette de fraises** a punnet of strawberries.

barrage *noun Masc.* **1** dam; **2** roadblock.

barre *noun Fem.* bar; **une barre de fer** an iron bar; **une barre de chocolat** a chocolate bar.

barreau (*plural* **barreaux**) *noun Masc.* bar; **derrière les barreaux** behind bars (*in prison*).

barrer *verb* [1] **1** to block; **'route barrée'** 'road closed'; **2** to cross out; **barrer trois mots** to cross out three words; **3 se barrer** (*informal*) to clear off, to leave; **je me barre!** I'm off!; ★ **on est mal barré** (*informal*) we're in trouble.

barrette *noun Fem.* hairslide.

barrière *noun Fem.* **1** fence; **2** gate.

bar-tabac *noun Masc.* cafe (*selling cigarettes, tobacco, and stamps as well as drinks and snacks*).

bas *noun Masc.* **1** bottom, lower part; **en bas de la page** at the bottom of the page; **2** stocking.

bas *adjective* (*Fem.* **basse**) low.

bas *adverb* **1** low; **plus bas** further down; **parler plus bas** to lower one's voice; **2 en bas** at the bottom, down below, downstairs; **les voisins d'en bas** the neighbours in the flat below.

bas-côté *noun Masc.* verge (*on the roadside*).

basculant *adjective* **un camion à benne basculante** a dump truck.

bascule *noun Fem.* **1** rocker; **un fauteuil à bascule** a rocking chair; **un cheval à bascule** a rocking horse; **2** seesaw.

basculer *verb* [1] to topple over.

base *noun Fem.* **1** basis; **être à la base de quelque chose** to be at the root of something; **2** base; **à base de chocolat** chocolate-based; **3 de base** basic; **les ingrédients de base** the basic ingredients.

base-ball *noun Masc.* baseball.

base de données *noun Fem.* database.

baser *verb* [1] to base; **basé sur** based on.

basilic *noun Masc.* basil; **une sauce au basilic** a basil sauce.

basket *noun Masc.* **1** basketball; **2** sports shoe, trainer; ★ **lâche-moi les baskets!** (*informal*) get off my back!

basketteur, basketteuse *noun Masc., Fem.* basketball player.

basque *noun Masc.* Basque (*language*).
basque *adjective* Basque.

Basque *noun Masc. & Fem.* Basque (*person*).

a
b
c
d
e
f
g
h
i
j
k
l
m
n
o
p
q
r
s
t
u
v
w
x
y
z

basse *noun Fem.* bass (*in music.*).
basse *adjective* SEE **bas.**.

bassin *noun Masc.* **1** pond; **2** pelvis.

bassine *noun Fem.* bowl.

bassiste *noun Masc. & Fem.* bassist.

bataille *noun Fem.* **1** battle; **la bataille de Trafalgar** the Battle of Trafalgar; **la bataille du pouvoir** the battle for power; **une bataille de boules de neige** a snowball fight; **2** a card game (*similar to beggar-my-neighbour*); ★ **avoir les sourcils en bataille** to have bushy eyebrows; ★ **elle avait les cheveux en bataille** her hair was all over the place.

bateau (*plural* **bateaux**) *noun Masc.* boat, ship; **faire du bateau** to go boating (*or* sailing).

bateau à moteur *noun Masc.* motorboat.

bateau de plaisance *noun Masc.* pleasure boat.

bateau-mouche *noun Masc.* pleasure boat (*a large river boat for sightseeing trips*).

bateau pneumatique *noun Masc.* rubber dinghy.

bâti *adjective* built; **bien bâti** well-built.

bâtiment *noun Masc.* **1** building; **les bâtiments de l'école** the school buildings; **2 le bâtiment** the building trade; **travailler dans le bâtiment** to work in the building trade; **3** ship.

bâtir *verb* [2] to build.

bâtisse *noun Fem.* building.

bâton *noun Masc.* stick.

bâton de ski *noun Masc.* ski stic

bâtonnet *noun Masc.* stick.

bâtonnet de poisson *noun Masc.* fish finger.

bâtonnet ouaté *noun Masc.* cotton bud.

batte *noun Fem.* bat (*for cricket, baseball, etc*).

batterie *noun Fem.* **1** battery; **2** drum kit, drums.

batterie de cuisine *noun Fer* pots and pans.

batteur *noun Masc.* **1** drummer; **2** whisk.

batteur électrique *noun Mas* (electric) mixer.

battre *verb* [21] **1** to beat (*in a gam* **Nicole m'a battu au tennis** Nico. beat me at tennis; **2** to beat, to batter; **battre un chien** to beat a dog; **3** to beat (*a mixture*); **battre le œufs** to whisk the eggs; **battre la crème** to whip the cream; **4 se battre** to fight; **5 battre des main** to clap your hands; **6 le cœur bat** the heart beats; **7 la porte bat** the door bangs.

bavard *adjective* talkative.

bavarder *verb* [1] to chat, to chatter.

baver *verb* [1] to dribble.

bavure *noun Fem.* **1** smudge; **2** blunder.

bazar *noun Masc.* **1** general store; **2** (*informal*) mess.

BCBG SHORT FOR **bon chic bon gen** chic and stylish (*in appearance*).

B.D. *noun Fem.* comic strip SHORT FOR **bande dessinée**.

eau, bel (*before a vowel or silent 'h'*) (*Fem.* **belle**) (*Masc. plural* **beaux**) *adjective* **1** beautiful, lovely; **une belle maison** a beautiful house; **un bel homme** a handsome man; **fais de beaux rêves!** sweet dreams!; **2 il fait beau** it's a nice day; ★ **faire le beau** to sit up and beg (*of a dog*).

eaucoup *adverb* **1** a lot; **tu m'en as donné beaucoup** you've given me a lot; **tu ne m'en as pas donné beaucoup** you haven't given me much; **cinquante euros c'est beaucoup** fifty euros is a lot; **2** a lot; **il lit beaucoup** he reads a lot; **il ne lit pas beaucoup** he doesn't read much; **3** very much; **j'aime beaucoup ta robe** I like your dress very much, I really like your dress; **j'aime beaucoup aller au cinéma** I really like going to the cinema; **4 beaucoup de** a lot of; **beaucoup d'argent** a lot of money; **elle a beaucoup d'argent** she has a lot of money; **elle n'a pas beaucoup d'argent** she doesn't have much money; **il a beaucoup d'amis** he has a lot of friends; **il n'a pas beaucoup d'amis** he doesn't have many friends; **5 beaucoup plus** much more; **beaucoup moins** much less; **beaucoup trop** far too much; **beaucoup trop court** far too short.

eau-fils (*plural* **beaux-fils**) *noun Masc.* **1** son-in-law; **2** stepson.

eau-frère (*plural* **beaux-frères**) *noun Masc.* brother-in-law.

beau-père (*plural* **beau-pères**) *noun Masc.* **1** father-in-law; **2** stepfather.

beauté *noun Fem.* beauty.

beaux-arts *plural noun Masc.* fine arts; **école des beaux-arts** art school.

beaux-parents *plural noun Masc.* parents-in-law, in-laws.

bébé *noun Masc.* baby.

bec *noun Masc.* beak.

bêche *noun Fem.* spade.

bégayer *verb* [59] to stammer.

beige *adjective* beige.

beignet *noun Masc.* **1** fritter; **2** doughnut.

bel *adjective* SEE **beau**.

belette *noun Fem.* weasel.

belge *adjective* Belgian.

Belge *noun Masc. & Fem.* Belgian.

Belgique *noun Fem.* Belgium.

bélier *noun Masc.* ram.

Bélier *noun Masc.* Aries (*sign of the Zodiac*).

belle *noun Fem.* **1 ma belle** darling; **2 la Belle au bois dormant** Sleeping Beauty.
belle *adjective* SEE **beau**.

belle-famille *noun Fem.* in-laws.

belle-fille (*plural* **belles-filles**) *noun Fem.* **1** daughter-in-law; **2** stepdaughter.

belle-mère (*plural* **belles-mères**) *noun Fem.* **1** mother-in-law; **2** stepmother.

belle-sœur (*plural* **belles-sœurs**) *noun Fem.* sister-in-law.

31

a
b
c
d
e
f
g
h
i
j
k
l
m
n
o
p
q
r
s
t
u
v
w
x
y
z

a

b

c

d

e

f

g

h

i

j

k

l

m

n

o

p

q

r

s

t

u

v

w

x

y

z

bénédiction *noun Fem.* blessing.

bénéfice *noun Masc.* profit; **faire un bénéfice de dix mille euros** to make a profit of ten thousand euros.

bénéfique *adjective* beneficial.

bénévole *noun Masc. & Fem.* voluntary worker.
bénévole *adjective* voluntary, unpaid.

bénir *verb* [2] to bless.

benne *noun Fem.* skip (*for rubbish*).

béquille *noun Fem.* crutch.

berceau (*plural* **berceaux**) *noun Masc.* cradle.

bercer *verb* [61] to rock (*a baby*).

berceuse *noun Fem.* **1** lullaby;
2 rocking chair.

béret *noun Masc.* beret.

berge *noun Fem.* bank (*of a river or canal*).

berger, bergère *noun Masc., Fem.* shepherd, shepherdess.

berger allemand *noun Masc.* Alsatian (dog).

besoin *noun Masc.* need; **avoir besoin de quelque chose** to need something; **j'ai besoin d'un marteau** I need a hammer; **avoir besoin de faire** to need to do; **j'ai vraiment besoin de me reposer** I really need to take a rest.

bestiole *noun Fem.* (*informal*) creepy-crawly.

bétail *noun Masc.* **1** livestock;
2 cattle.

bête *noun Fem.* animal.
bête *adjective* stupid.

bêtise *noun Fem.* stupidity; **faire une bêtise** to do something stupi

béton *noun Masc.* concrete.

bétonnière *noun Fem.* cement mixer.

betterave (rouge) *noun Fem.* beetroot.

beurre *noun Masc.* butter; ★ **un œ au beurre noir** a black eye (*literall an eye with black butter*).

beurrer *verb* [1] to butter.

bibelot *noun Masc.* ornament.

biberon *noun Masc.* (feeding) bott

bible *noun Fem.* bible; **la Bible** the Bible.

bibliothécaire *noun Masc. & Fer* librarian.

bibliothèque *noun Fem.* **1** librar
2 bookcase.

bic™ *noun Masc.* **un stylo bic**™ a Biro™.

biche *noun Fem.* doe.

bicyclette *noun Fem.* bicycle; **fair de la bicyclette** to cycle.

bidet *noun Masc.* bidet.

bidon *noun Masc.* can.
bidon *adjective* (*informal*) phoney

bidonville *noun Masc.* shanty tow

bidule *noun Masc.* (*informal*) whatsit, thingamajig.

bien *noun Masc.* **1** good; **le bien et l mal** good and evil; **ça te fera du bien** that'll do you good;
2 possession; **tous leurs biens** all their possessions.
bien *adjective* **1** good, nice; **des gens bien** nice people; **ce sera bie de le revoir** it will be nice to see hi

again; **2** well; **je ne me sens pas bien** I don't feel well; **3** happy, comfortable; **on est bien ici** it's nice here; **on est très bien dans ce fauteuil** this chair's really comfortable.

bien *adverb* **1** well; **elle chante bien** she sings well; **bien joué!** well done!; **tu vas bien?** are you well?; **2** well; **bien habillé** well dressed; **cette couleur te va bien** that colour suits you; **3** very, really; **bien triste** really sad; **bien chaud** really hot; **4** very much; **j'aime bien ta robe** I like your dress very much, I really like your dress; **j'aimerais bien savoir** I'd really like to know; **j'aimerais bien aller au cinéma** I'd really like to go to the cinema; **'veux-tu du thé?' – 'oui, je veux bien'** 'would you like some tea?' – 'yes, I'd love some'; **'tu aimes le poisson?' – 'oui, je l'aime bien'** 'do you like fish?' – 'yes, I do'; **je veux bien le faire** I'm quite happy to do it; **5** much; **bien mieux** much better; **bien plus chaud** much hotter; **6 bien de** many, a number of; **bien des gens** many people; ★ **c'est bien fait pour elle!** serves her right!

bien entendu *adverb* of course.

bien-être *noun Masc.* well-being.

bien que *conjunction* although.

bien sûr *adverb* of course.

bientôt *adverb* soon; **à bientôt** see you soon.

bienvenu, bienvenue[1] *noun Masc., Fem., adjective* welcome; **soyez le bienvenu (or la bienvenue)!** welcome!

bienvenue[2] *noun Fem.* welcome; **bienvenue!** welcome!; **bienvenue en France!** welcome to France!; **souhaiter la bienvenue à quelqu'un** to welcome somebody.

bière *noun Fem.* beer; **boire de la bière** to drink beer; **trois bières, s'il vous plaît** three beers, please.

bière blonde *noun Fem.* lager.

bière brune *noun Fem.* brown ale.

bifteck *noun Masc.* steak.

bifurcation *noun Fem.* fork (*in the road*).

bigoudi *noun Masc.* hair curler.

bijou (*plural* **bijoux**) *noun Masc.* jewel, piece of jewellery.

bijouterie *noun Fem.* jeweller's (shop).

bijoutier, bijoutière *noun Masc., Fem.* jeweller.

bilan *noun Masc.* balance sheet; ★ **faire le bilan de quelque chose** to assess something.

bilingue *adjective* bilingual.

billard *noun Masc.* **1** billiards; **jouer au billard** to play billiards; **2** billiard table.

billard américain *noun Masc.* pool.

billard anglais *noun Masc.* snooker.

billard électrique *noun Masc.* pinball machine.

bille *noun Fem.* **1** marble; **jouer aux billes** to play marbles; **2** billiard ball.

billet *noun Masc.* **1** note, banknote; **un billet de cent euros** a

a
b
c
d
e
f
g
h
i
j
k
l
m
n
o
p
q
r
s
t
u
v
w
x
y
z

hundred-euro note; **2** ticket; **un billet de train** a train ticket.

billion *noun Masc.* billion.

biochimie *noun Fem.* biochemistry.

biographie *noun Fem.* biography.

biologie *noun Fem.* biology.

biologique *adjective* **1** biological; **2** organically grown.

biologiste *noun Masc. & Fem.* biologist.

bip *noun Masc.* beep; **'après le bip sonore'** 'after the tone' (*on an answering machine*).

biscotte *noun Fem.* continental toast.

biscuit *noun Masc.* biscuit.

bise *noun Fem.* (*informal*) kiss; **faire la bise à quelqu'un** to kiss somebody on the cheek; **grosses bises** lots of love.

bissextile *adjective* **une année bissextile** a leap year.

bistro, **bistrot** *noun Masc.* bistro, cafe.

bizarre *adjective* odd, strange.

blague *noun Fem.* (*informal*) **1** joke; **sans blague!** no kidding!; **2** trick; **faire une blague à quelqu'un** to play a trick on somebody.

blaguer *verb* [1] (*informal*) to joke.

blaireau (*plural* **blaireaux**) *noun Masc.* **1** badger; **2** shaving brush.

blâmer *verb* [1] **1** to criticize; **2** to blame.

blanc *noun Masc.* **1** white; **peint en blanc** painted white; **2** white meat, breast; **3** white wine; **4** blank;

laisser un blanc to leave a blank.
blanc *adjective* (*Fem.* **blanche**) **1** white; **2** blank; **une feuille blanche** a blank sheet of paper.

Blanc, **Blanche** *noun Masc., Fem.* white man, white woman.

blanche *adjective* SEE **blanc**.

blanchir *verb* [2] to whiten.

blanchisserie *noun Fem.* laundry

blé *noun Masc.* wheat.

blessé, **blessée** *noun Masc., Fem.* injured person, casualty.
blessé *adjective* injured.

blesser *verb* [1] **1** to hurt, to injure **2 se blesser** to hurt oneself; **tu t'es blessé?** did you hurt yourself?

blessure *noun Fem.* **1** injury; **2** wound.

bleu[1] *noun Masc.*, *adjective* blue; **peint en bleu** painted blue; **bleu marine** navy blue.

bleu[2] *noun Masc.* bruise.

bleuet *noun Masc.* cornflower.

bloc *noun Masc.* **1** block; **un bloc de ciment** a block of cement; **2 un bloc de papier à lettres** a writing pad.

bloc-notes *noun Masc.* notepad.

blond *adjective* blonde, fair-haired.

bloqué *adjective* **1** blocked; **2** jammed; **3** stuck.

bloquer *verb* [1] **1** to block; **2** to jam.

blouse *noun Fem.* overall.

blouson *noun Masc.* jacket.

blue-jean noun Masc. jeans; **j'ai acheté un blue-jean** I bought a pair of jeans.

bobine noun Fem. reel.

bocal (plural **bocaux**) noun Masc. jar.

bœuf noun Masc. **1** bullock; **2** beef; **est-ce que tu aimes le bœuf?** do you like beef?

bof exclamation (informal) **'c'était bien hier soir?' – 'bof!'** 'did you have a good time last night?' – 'nothing special'.

bohémien, bohémienne noun Masc., Fem. gipsy.

boire verb [22] to drink; **qu'est-ce que tu veux boire?** what would you like to drink?; **il n'y a rien à boire** there's nothing to drink.

bois noun Masc. wood; **une table en bois** a wooden table; ★ **avoir la gueule de bois** (informal) to have a hangover (literally: to have a mouth made of wood).

boisson noun Fem. drink; **une boisson fraîche** a cold drink.

boîte noun Fem. **1** tin; **une boîte de sardines** a tin of sardines; **2** box; **une boîte d'allumettes** a box of matches; **3** (informal) **une boîte de nuit** a nightclub; **aller dans une boîte** to go to a club; **4** (informal) firm, company.

boîte aux lettres noun Fem. post box.

boiter verb [1] to limp.

bol noun Masc. **1** bowl; **un bol de riz** a bowl of rice; **2** (informal) luck; **un coup de bol** a stroke of luck; ★ **en avoir ras le bol** (informal) to be fed

up (literally: to have a bowlful); **j'en ai ras le bol d'attendre** I'm fed up with waiting.

bombarder verb [1] **1** to bombard; **2** to bomb, to shell.

bombe noun Fem. **1** bomb; **2** spray can (containing hairspray, fly spray, etc).

bôme noun Fem. boom (of a sail).

bon (Fem. **bonne**) adjective **1** good; **un bon repas** a good meal; **bon en français** good at French; **2 un bon kilomètre**, at least a kilometre; **3** right; **le bon numéro** the right number; **la bonne adresse** the right address; **c'est bon** it's OK, it's fine.
bon noun **1** voucher; **2 cela a du bon** that has its good points; **pour de bon** for good.
bon adverb **sentir bon** to smell good (or nice); **il fait bon aujourd'hui** it's a nice day today; **il fait bon dans mon appartement** it's lovely and warm in my flat.

bon anniversaire greeting happy birthday.

bon appétit exclamation enjoy your meal.

bonbon noun Masc. sweet.

bonbonne noun Fem. **1 une bonbonne à gaz** a gas cylinder; **2** demijohn.

bond noun Masc. leap; **se lever d'un bond** to leap to your feet.

bondé adjective crowded, packed; **bondé d'étudiants** packed with students.

bondir verb [2] to leap; **bondir de joie** to jump for joy.

bonheur *noun Masc.* **1** happiness; **2** pleasure; **avoir le bonheur de faire** to have the pleasure of doing.

bonhomme (*plural* **bonshommes**) *noun Masc.* fellow, man.

bonhomme de neige *noun Masc.* snowman.

bonjour *greeting* hello, good morning, good afternoon; ★ **être simple comme bonjour** to be really easy, to be as easy as pie (*literally: to be as simple as hello*).

bon marché *adjective* cheap.

bonne *noun Fem.* maid.
bonne *adjective* SEE **bon**.

bonne année *greeting* happy New Year.

bonne chance *exclamation* good luck.

bonne heure *in phrase* **de bonne heure** early.

bonne nuit *greeting* goodnight.

bonnet *noun Masc.* hat, bonnet.

bon retour *exclamation* safe journey back.

bon sens *noun Masc.* common sense.

bonsoir *greeting* good evening.

bonté *noun Fem.* kindness.

bon voyage *exclamation* have a good trip.

boom *noun Masc.* boom (*time of prosperity*).

bord *noun Masc.* **1** edge (*of a table, cliff, etc*); **2** rim (*of a glass, cup, vase, etc*); **3** side, edge (*of a road, path, etc*); **au bord de la route** on the edge of

the road; **4** bank (*of a stream or lake*); **5 au bord de la mer** at the seaside.

bordeaux *adjective* maroon.

border *verb* [1] **1** to line; **bordé d'arbres** tree-lined; **2** to edge, to trim.

bordure *noun Fem.* **1** border; **2** edge; **3 en bordure de** on the edge of.

borne *noun Fem.* **1** kilometre marker (*the equivalent of a milestone*); **2** bollard.

Bosnie *noun Fem.* Bosnia.

bosse *noun Fem.* bump.

bosser *verb* [1] (*informal*) to work

botanique *noun Fem.* botany.
botanique *adjective* **les jardins botaniques** the botanic gardens.

botte *noun Fem.* **1** boot; **des bottes de cuir** leather boots; **des bottes de caoutchouc** wellington boots; **2 une botte de foin** a bale of hay.

bottine *noun Fem.* ankle boot.

bouc *noun Masc.* billy goat.

boucan *noun Masc.* (*informal*) din, racket.

bouc émissaire *noun Masc.* scapegoat.

bouche *noun Fem.* mouth.

bouche-à-bouche *noun Masc.* mouth-to-mouth resuscitation.

bouche d'égout *noun Fem.* manhole.

bouchée *noun Fem.* mouthful.

boucher[1] *verb* [1] **1** to cork (*a bottle*); **2** to block up, to fill (*a hole, gap, or crack*); **3 se boucher** to get

bouleverser

blocked up; **4 se boucher le nez** to hold one's nose.

boucher[2] *noun Masc.*, *Fem.* butcher.

boucherie *noun Fem.* butcher's (shop).

bouchon *noun Masc.* **1** cork; **2** screw-cap; **3** traffic jam.

boucle *noun Fem.* **1** buckle; **2** curl.

bouclé *adjective* curly.

boucle d'oreille *noun Fem.* earring.

Bouddha *noun Masc.* Buddha.

bouddhisme *noun Masc.* Buddhism.

bouder *verb* [1] **1** to sulk; **2 bouder quelque chose** to stay away from something.

boudin *noun Masc.* black pudding.

boudin blanc *noun Masc.* white pudding.

boue *noun Fem.* mud.

bouée *noun Fem.* **1** rubber ring; **2** buoy.

bouée de sauvetage *noun Fem.* lifebelt.

boueux (*Fem.* **boueuse**) *adjective* muddy.

bouffe *noun Fem.* (*informal*) food.

bouffée *noun Fem.* **une bouffée d'air frais** a breath of fresh air.

bouffer *verb* [1] (*informal*) to eat.

bougeoir *noun Masc.* candlestick.

bouger *verb* [52] to move.

bougie *noun Fem.* **1** candle; **2** spark plug.

bouillabaisse *noun Fem.* Mediterranean fish soup (*made with several varieties of fish and vegetables*).

bouillant *adjective* boiling; **faire cuire à l'eau bouillante** cook in boiling water.

bouillir *verb* [23] to boil; **faire bouillir le lait** to boil the milk; **le lait bout** the milk is boiling.

bouilloire *noun Fem.* kettle.

bouillon *noun Masc.* stock (*made with meat, fish, or vegetables*).

bouillon-cube *noun Masc.* stock cube.

bouillotte *noun Fem.* hot-water bottle.

boulanger, boulangère *noun Masc.*, *Fem.* baker.

boulangerie *noun Fem.* bakery, baker's.

boule *noun Fem.* **1** bowl; **jouer aux boules** to play bowls; **2** scoop (*of ice-cream*); **vous voulez combien de boules?** how many scoops would you like?

bouleau (*plural* **bouleaux**) *noun Masc.* birch tree.

boule de neige *noun Fem.* snowball.

boulette *noun Fem.* pellet.

boulette de viande *noun Fem.* meatball.

boulevard *noun Masc.* boulevard.

boulevard périphérique *noun Masc.* ring road.

bouleverser *verb* [1] **1** to overwhelm, to shatter; **être bouleversé** to be overwhelmed (*or* shattered); **2** to disrupt (*a schedule, plans, etc*); **3** to turn upside down.

a
b
c
d
e
f
g
h
i
j
k
l
m
n
o
p
q
r
s
t
u
v
w
x
y
z

boulot noun Masc. (*informal*)
1 work; **j'ai trop de boulot** I've got too much work to do; **c'est un boulot immense** it's a huge amount of work; **2** job; **elle cherche du boulot** she's looking for a job.

boum noun Fem. (*informal*) party.

bouquet noun Masc. bunch, bouquet (*of flowers or herbs*).

bouquin noun Masc. (*informal*) book.

bouquiner verb [1] (*informal*) to read.

bouquiniste noun Masc. & Fem. secondhand bookseller.

bourdon noun Masc. bumblebee.

bourg noun Masc. market town.

bourgeois, bourgeoise noun Masc., Fem. middle-class person.
bourgeois adjective middle-class.

bourgeon noun Masc. bud.

Bourgogne noun Fem. Burgundy.

bourratif (Fem. **bourrative**) adjective very filling.

bourré adjective **1 bourré de** crammed with, stuffed with; **2** drunk.

bourrer verb [1] to cram.

bourse noun Fem. grant.

Bourse noun Fem. stock exchange.

bousculer verb [1] to push, to jostle.

boussole noun Fem. compass.

bout noun Masc. **1** end; **au bout de** at the end of; **2** tip (*of nose or finger*); **3 un bout de papier** a scrap of paper; **un petit bout de fromage** a little bit of cheese; **4 au bout de**
after; **au bout d'une demi-heure** after half an hour.

bouteille noun Fem. bottle.

boutique noun Fem. shop.

bouton noun Masc. **1** button; **2** spot, pimple.

bouton d'or noun Masc. buttercup.

boxe noun Fem. boxing.

boxeur noun Masc. boxer.

bracelet noun Masc. **1** bracelet; **2** bangle.

bracelet-montre noun Masc. wristwatch.

braise noun Fem. embers (*of a fire*).

brancard noun Masc. stretcher.

branche noun Fem. branch.

branché adjective (*informal*) trendy.

brancher verb [1] **1** to plug in (*an iron, a television, etc*); **2** to connect (*electricity, gas, water, telephone*).

bras noun Masc. sleeve; **en bras de chemise** in one's shirtsleeves.

bras de fer noun Masc. arm wrestling.

brasse noun Fem. breaststroke.

brasserie noun Fem. **1** brasserie, cafe-restaurant; **2** brewery.

brave adjective nice (*person*).

break noun Masc. estate car.

brebis noun Fem. ewe.

bref (Fem. **brève**) adjective short, brief.

Brésil noun Masc. Brazil.

brésilien noun Masc. Brazilian Portuguese (*language*).

brésilien, **brésilienne** *adjective*
Brazilian.

Brésilien, **Brésilienne** *noun*
Masc., Fem. Brazilian.

Bretagne *noun Fem.* Brittany.

bretelle *noun Fem.* **1** strap; **2** slip
road; **3 des bretelles** braces.

breton *noun Masc.* Breton
(*language*).

Breton, **Bretonne** *noun Masc.*,
Fem. Breton.

breton (*Fem.* **bretonne**) *adjective*
Breton.

brevet *noun Masc.* certificate.

bribes *plural noun Fem.* bits,
fragments.

bricolage *noun Masc.* DIY, do-it-
yourself.

bricoler *verb* [1] to do DIY.

bricoleur, **bricoleuse** *noun*
Masc., Fem. DIY enthusiast.

brièvement *adverb* briefly.

brillamment *adverb* brilliantly.

brillant *adjective* **1** shiny;
2 brilliant.

briller *verb* [1] to shine.

brin *noun Masc.* sprig (*of herb or
plant*); **un brin d'herbe** a blade of
grass.

brindille *noun Fem.* twig.

brioche *noun Fem.* brioche, bun.

brique *noun Fem.* **1** brick; **2** carton
(*of fruit-juice, milk, etc*).

briquet *noun Masc.* lighter.

brise *noun Fem.* breeze.

briser *verb* [1] to break.

britannique *adjective* British.

Britannique *noun Masc. & Fem.*
British person; **les Britanniques**
the British.

brocante *noun Fem.* **1** junk shop;
2 second-hand goods.

broche *noun Fem.* **1** brooch; **2** spit
(*for roasting*).

brochet *noun Masc.* pike.

brochette *noun Fem.* **1** skewer;
2 kebab; **une brochette de viande**
a meat kebab.

brochure *noun Fem.* **1** booklet;
2 brochure.

brocolis *plural noun Masc.*
broccoli.

broder *verb* [1] to embroider.

broderie *noun Fem.* embroidery;
des broderies embroidery.

bronchite *noun Fem.* bronchitis;
avoir une bronchite to have
bronchitis.

bronzage *noun Masc.* suntan.

bronzer *verb* [1] to tan.

brosse *noun Fem.* brush.

brosse à cheveux *noun Fem.*
hairbrush.

brosse à dents *noun Fem.*
toothbrush.

brosser *verb* [1] **1** to brush; **2 se
brosser les dents** to brush your
teeth.

brouette *noun Fem.* wheelbarrow.

brouillard *noun Masc.* fog.

brouillon *noun Masc.* rough draft.

bru *noun Fem.* daughter-in-law.

brugnon *noun Masc.* nectarine.

bruit *noun Masc.* **1** noise; **entendre
un bruit** to hear a noise; **entendre le**

bruit d'une voiture to hear the sound of a car; **2** rumour.

brûlant *adjective* **1** boiling hot; **2** burning hot.

brûlé *noun Masc.* **un goût de brûlé** a burnt taste; **ça sent le brûlé** there's a smell of burning.

brûler *verb* [1] **1** to burn; **2 se brûler** to burn yourself.

brûlure *noun Fem.* burn.

brume *noun Fem.* mist.

brun *adjective* **1** brown; **2** dark-haired.

brushing *noun Masc.* blow-dry; **se faire faire un brushing** to have a blow-dry.

brut *adjective* **1** raw (*material*); **2** crude (*oil*); **3** gross (*income*); **4** dry (*champagne*).

brutal (*Masc. plural* **brutaux**) *adjective* **1** violent, brutal; **2** sudden.

brutalement *adverb* **1** suddenly; **2** violently.

Bruxelles *noun* Brussels.

bruyant *adjective* noisy, loud.

bruyère *noun Fem.* heather.

bu *verb* SEE **boire**.

bûche *noun Fem.* log.

budget *noun Masc.* budget.

buffet *noun Masc.* **1** sideboard; **2** buffet.

buisson *noun Masc.* bush.

buissonnière *adjective* **faire l'école buissonnière** to play truant.

Bulgarie *noun Fem.* Bulgaria.

bulle *noun Fem.* bubble.

bulletin *noun Masc.* report, bulletin.

bulletin de salaire *noun Masc.* payslip.

bulletin scolaire *noun Masc.* school report.

bureau (*plural* **bureaux**) *noun Masc.* **1** desk; **elle est à son bureau** she is at her desk; **2** office; **au bureau** at (*or* to) the office.

bureaucratie *noun Fem.* bureaucracy.

bureau de poste *noun Masc.* post office.

bureau de tabac *noun Masc.* tobacconist's.

bureau de tourisme *noun Masc.* tourist information office.

burin *noun Masc.* chisel.

bus *noun Masc.* bus.

buse *noun Fem.* buzzard.

buste *noun Masc.* bust.

but *noun Masc.* **1** goal, aim, purpose; **2** goal (*in football, hockey*); **marquer un but** to score a goal; **3** target.

buté *adjective* stubborn.

buvable *adjective* drinkable.

buvard *noun Masc.* blotter; **du papier buvard** blotting paper.

buvette *noun Fem.* bar (*at a dance, village fair, etc*).

buvez, buvons *verb* SEE **boire**.

Cc

ça *pronoun* **1** that, this; **donne-moi ça** give me that; **ça c'est un**

...moineau that's a sparrow;
2 comment ça va?,ça va? how are
you?; **ça va bien merci** I'm fine
thanks; **3 c'est ça** that's right; **ça
ne fait rien** it doesn't matter.

...à *adverb* **çà et là** here and there.

...abane *noun Fem.* hut, shed.

...abas *noun Masc.* shopping bag.

...abillaud *noun Masc.* cod.

...abine *noun Fem.* **1** cubicle; **cabine
de douche** shower cubicle; **cabine
d'essayage** fitting room (*in a
clothes shop*); **2** cabin (*on a ship*);
3 cab (*on a lorry*).

...abinet *noun Masc.* **1** office (*of a
solicitor*); **2** surgery (*of a doctor or
dentist*); **3 cabinet de médecins**
medical practice.

...abine téléphonique *noun
Fem.* phone box.

...abinets *plural noun Masc.* toilet.

...âble *noun Masc.* **1** cable; **2** rope.

...âblé *adjective* **être câblé** to have
cable television.

...abosser *verb* [1] to dent.

...acahuète *noun Fem.* peanut; **des
cacahuètes grillées** roasted
peanuts.

...acao *noun Masc.* cocoa.

...ache *noun Fem.* hiding place.

...aché *adjective* hidden.

...ache-cache *noun Masc.* **jouer à
cache-cache** to play hide and seek.

...achemire *noun Masc.*
1 cashmere; **2 motif cachemire**
paisley pattern.

cache-nez *noun Masc.* (thick)
scarf.

cache-pot *noun Masc.* flowerpot
holder.

cacher *verb* [1] **1** to hide; **cacher
quelque chose** to hide something;
**elle a caché son portefeuille dans
un tiroir** she's hidden her wallet in a
drawer; **2 se cacher** to hide; **il s'est
caché derrrière la porte** he hid
behind the door.

cachet *noun Masc.* **1** tablet; **un
cachet d'aspirine** an aspirin;
2 official stamp (*made with a rubber
stamp*); **3 le cachet de la poste** the
postmark.

cachette *noun Fem.* **1** hiding
place; **2 en cachette** secretly, on
the sly.

cachot *noun Masc.* dungeon.

cactus *noun Masc.* cactus.

cadavre *noun Masc.* corpse, body.

caddie *noun Masc.* trolley (*in the
supermarket*).

cadeau (*plural* **cadeaux**) *noun
Masc.* present; **faire un cadeau à
quelqu'un** to give somebody a
present; **du papier cadeau**
wrapping-paper; **je vous fais un
paquet-cadeau?** shall I gift-wrap it
for you?

cadenas *noun Masc.* padlock.

cadence *noun Fem.* rhythm.

cadet, cadette *noun Masc., Fem.*
younger child, youngest child.
cadet (*Fem.* **cadette**) *adjective*
younger, youngest.

cadran *noun Masc.* **1** face (*of a
watch or clock*); **2** dial (*on an*

a
b
c
d
e
f
g
h
i
j
k
l
m
n
o
p
q
r
s
t
u
v
w
x
y
z

41

a
b
c
d
e
f
g
h
i
j
k
l
m
n
o
p
q
r
s
t
u
v
w
x
y
z

instrument such as the speedometer in a car).

cadran solaire *noun Masc.* sundial.

cadre *noun Masc.* **1** frame (*of a picture, mirror, or window*); **2** surroundings, setting; **3** executive (*a person with a management job in a company*); **4** frame (*of a bicycle*).

cafard *noun Masc.* **1** cockroach; **2** depression; **avoir le cafard** to be down in the dumps.

café *noun Masc.* **1** coffee; **café instantané, café soluble** instant coffee; **café moulu** ground coffee; **café en grains** coffee beans; **café au lait** coffee with milk; **prendre un café** to have a coffee; **2** cafe.

café-crème *noun Masc.* white coffee.

caféine *noun Fem.* caffeine.

cafétéria *noun Fem.* cafeteria.

cafetière *noun Fem.* **1** coffee pot; **2** coffee maker.

cage *noun Fem.* cage.

cageot *noun Masc.* crate.

cagibi *noun Masc.* store cupboard.

cagnotte *noun Fem.* **1** kitty (*of money*); **2** jackpot.

cagoule *noun Fem.* hood.

cahier *noun Masc.* **1** exercise book; **2** notebook.

caille *noun Fem.* quail.

cailler *verb* [1] to curdle.

caillou (*plural* **cailloux**) *noun Masc.* pebble, stone.

caisse *noun Fem.* **1** till, cash register; **2** cash desk; **3** checkout (*i a supermarket*); **4** box, crate.

caisse à outils *noun Fem.* toolbox.

caisse d'épargne *noun Fem.* savings bank.

caissier, caissière *noun Masc. Fem.* **1** checkout assistant; **2** cashie

cajou *noun* **une noix de cajou** a cashew nut.

cake *noun Masc.* fruit cake.

calamité *noun Fem.* disaster, calamity.

calcaire *noun Masc.* **1** limestone; **2** furring (*the sediment which clogs up kettles, steam irons, etc*). **calcaire** *adjective* **eau calcaire** hard water; **l'eau ici est très calcaire** the water here is very hard.

calcium *noun Masc.* calcium.

calcul *noun Masc.* **1** calculation; **2** arithmetic.

calculatrice *noun Fem.* pocket calculator.

calculer *verb* [1] to calculate, to work out.

calculette *noun Fem.* pocket calculator.

caleçon *noun Masc.* **1** boxer short **2** leggings.

calembour *noun Masc.* pun, play on words.

calendrier *noun Masc.* **1** calenda **2** schedule.

calepin *noun Masc.* notebook.

aler *verb* [1] **1** to wedge; **2** to prop up; **3 ma voiture a calé** my car stalled.

alibre *noun Masc.* **1** size, grade (*of eggs, fruit, or vegetables*); **2** calibre, bore (*of a gun*).

âlin *noun Masc.* cuddle; **fais-moi un câlin** give me a cuddle (*usually said to a child*); **fais un calin à ta grand-mère** give your gran a cuddle. **câlin** *adjective* affectionate.

âliner *verb* [1] to cuddle.

almant *noun Masc.* sedative. **calmant** *adjective* soothing.

almar *noun Masc.* squid.

alme *noun Masc.* peace and quiet. **calme** *adjective* **1** calm; **2** quiet.

almement *adverb* calmly.

almer *verb* [1] **1 calmer quelqu'un** to calm somebody down; **2 se calmer** to calm down; **calme-toi** calm down; **3** to soothe; **l'aspirine a calmé la douleur** the aspirin soothed the pain.

alorie *noun Fem.* calorie.

alque *noun Masc.* **un calque** a tracing; **papier-calque** tracing paper.

alvados *noun Masc.* calvados (*apple brandy made in Normandy*).

amarade *noun Masc. & Fem.* friend; **camarade de classe** classmate.

ambriolage *noun Masc.* burglary.

ambrioler *verb* [1] **cambrioler une maison** to burgle a house; **ils ont été cambriolés** they were burgled.

cambrioleur, cambrioleuse *noun Masc., Fem.* burglar.

caméra *noun Fem.* cine-camera.

caméscope *noun Masc.* camcorder.

camion *noun Masc.* truck, lorry.

camion-citerne *noun Masc.* tanker lorry.

camionnette *noun Fem.* van.

camionneur *noun Masc.* lorry driver, truck driver.

camp *noun Masc.* camp.

campagnard, campagnarde *noun Masc., Fem.* country person. **campagnard** *adjective* country; **la vie campagnarde** country life.

campagne *noun Fem.* **1** country, countryside; **à la campagne** in the country, in the countryside; **aller se promener à la campagne** to go for a country walk; **2** campaign.

camper *verb* [1] to camp.

campeur, campeuse *noun Masc., Fem.* camper.

camping *noun Masc.* **1** camping; **faire du camping** to go camping; **2 un camping, un terrain de camping** a campsite.

camping-car *noun Masc.* camper van.

camping-gaz™ *noun Masc.* camping stove.

Canada *noun Masc.* Canada; **au Canada** in (*or* to) Canada.

canadien (*Fem.* **canadienne**) *adjective* Canadian.

Canadien, Canadienne noun
Masc., Fem. Canadian.

canal (plural **canaux**) noun Masc.
canal.

canapé noun Masc. sofa.

canapé-lit noun Masc. sofa bed.

canard noun Masc. duck.

canari noun Masc. canary.

cancer noun Masc. cancer; **avoir un
cancer** to have cancer.

Cancer noun Masc. Cancer (sign of
the Zodiac).

candidat, candidate noun
Masc., Fem. **1** candidate; **2** applicant.

candidature noun Fem. **poser sa
candidature à un poste** to apply for
a job.

cane noun Fem. female duck.

caneton noun Masc. duckling.

canette noun Fem. **une canette de
bière** a small bottle of beer.

canevas noun Masc. canvas.

caniche noun Masc. poodle.

canicule noun Fem. **1** scorching
heat; **2** heat wave.

canif noun Masc. penknife.

caniveau (plural **caniveaux**)
noun Masc. gutter.

canne noun Fem. walking stick.

canne à pêche noun Fem. fishing
rod.

canne à sucre noun Fem. sugar
cane.

cannelle noun Fem. cinnamon.

canoë noun Masc. **1** canoe; **2 faire
du canoë** to go canoeing.

canon noun Masc. **1** gun; **2** barrel
(of a gun); **3** cannon.

canot noun Masc. small boat,
dinghy; **un canot pneumatique** a
rubber (or inflatable) dinghy.

canot de sauvetage noun
Masc. lifeboat.

cantatrice noun Fem. opera
singer.

cantine noun Fem. canteen;
manger à la cantine to have school
lunch.

caoutchouc noun Masc. **1** rubber
des bottes en caoutchouc
wellington boots; **2** rubber band.

cap noun Masc. **1** cape, headland;
2 course (of a ship).

capable adjective capable; **être
capable de faire** to be capable of
doing.

capacité noun Fem. **1** ability;
2 capacity.

cape noun Fem. cape, cloak.

capitaine noun Masc. captain; **le
capitaine des pompiers** the chief
fire officer.

capital (plural **capitaux**) noun
Masc. capital (financial).
capital adjective **1 d'une
importance capitale** of major
importance; **2 une question
capitale** a key question; **3 la peine
capitale** capital punishment.

capitale noun Fem. capital city; **la
capitale française** the French
capital.

capot noun Masc. bonnet (of a car).

câpre noun Fem. caper.

aprice *noun Masc.* **1** whim; **2** tantrum; **faire un caprice** to throw a tantrum.

apricorne *noun Masc.* Capricorn (sign of the Zodiac).

apsule *noun Fem.* **1** cap, top (*of a bottle*); **2** capsule.

apter *verb* [1] **1 capter une chaîne (de télévision)** to get a (television) channel; **2 capter l'attention de quelqu'un** to catch somebody's attention.

aptif, captive *noun Masc., Fem.* captive.

aptivant *adjective* **1** fascinating; **2** gripping, riveting.

aptivité *noun Fem.* captivity; **être gardé en captivité** to be kept in captivity.

apturer *verb* [1] to capture.

apuche *noun Fem.* hood.

apuchon *noun Masc.* **1** hood; **2** top, cap (*of a pen*).

apucine *noun Fem.* nasturtium.

ar[1] *conjunction* because.

ar[2] *noun Masc.* coach, bus; **voyager en car** to travel by coach; **un voyage en car** a coach journey.

arabine *noun Fem.* rifle.

aractère *noun Masc.* **1** character, nature; **avoir mauvais caractère** to be bad-tempered; **2** character; **leur maison a beaucoup de caractère** their house has a lot of character; **3** character, letter; **en gros caractères** in large print.

aractéristique *noun Fem., adjective* characteristic.

carafe *noun Fem.* carafe, jug (*for wine or water*).

Caraïbes *noun plural Fem.* **les îles Caraïbes** the Caribbean Islands; **aller aux Caraïbes** to go to the Caribbean.

caramel *noun Masc.* **1** caramel; **2** toffee.

caravane *noun Fem.* caravan.

carbone *noun Masc.* **1** carbon; **2** carbon paper.

carbonisé *adjective* burnt to a cinder.

carburant *noun Masc.* fuel.

carburateur *noun Masc.* carburettor.

carcasse *noun Fem.* carcass.

cardiaque *adjective* **une crise cardiaque** a heart attack.

cardinal (*plural* **cardinaux**) *noun Masc.* **1** cardinal; **2** cardinal number.

carême *noun Masc.* Lent.

caresser *verb* [1] to stroke, to caress.

cargaison *noun Fem.* cargo.

caricature *noun Fem.* caricature.

caricaturiste *noun Masc. & Fem.* caricaturist, cartoonist.

carie *noun Fem.* **la carie dentaire** tooth decay; **avoir une carie** to have a hole in your tooth.

carillon *noun Masc.* **1** church bells; **2** wind chimes.

caritatif (*Fem.* **caritative**) *adjective* charitable; **une association caritative** a charity.

carnaval *noun Masc.* carnival.

a
b
c
d
e
f
g
h
i
j
k
l
m
n
o
p
q
r
s
t
u
v
w
x
y
z

carnet noun Masc. **1** notebook; **2** book (of tickets or stamps).

carnet de chèques noun Masc. chequebook.

carotte noun Fem. carrot.

carpe noun Fem. carp.

carpette noun Fem. rug.

carré noun Masc., adjective square; **un mètre carré** a square metre.

carreau (plural **carreaux**) noun Masc. **1** floor tile; **2** wall tile; **3** windowpane; **4 du tissu à carreaux** checked fabric; **5 du papier à carreaux** squared paper; **6** diamonds (suit of playing cards); **le roi de carreau** the king of diamonds.

carrefour noun Masc. crossroads, junction.

carrelage noun Masc. **1** tiled floor; **2** tiling, tiles.

carrelet noun Masc. plaice.

carrément adverb downright, completely; **c'est carrément malhonnête** it's downright dishonest.

carrière noun Fem. **1** career; **2** quarry.

carrosserie noun Fem. **1** bodywork (of car, etc); **2** bodywork repairs.

cartable noun Masc. **1** satchel, schoolbag; **2** briefcase.

carte noun Fem. **1** card; **2** playing card; **jouer aux cartes** to play cards; **un jeu de cartes** a pack of cards, a card game; **3** map; **4** menu.

carte à jouer noun Fem. playing card.

carte à mémoire noun Fem. smart card.

carte à microprocesseur noun Fem. smart card.

carte à puce noun Fem. smart card.

carte bancaire noun Fem. bank card.

carte d'abonnement noun Fem. season ticket.

carte d'anniversaire noun Fem. birthday card.

carte de crédit noun Fem. credit card.

carte d'embarquement noun Fem. boarding card.

carte de fidelité noun Fem. loyalty card.

carte d'identité noun Fem. identity card.

carte de séjour noun Fem. resident's permit.

carte des vins noun Fem. wine list.

carte de téléphone noun Fem. telephone card.

carte de visite noun Fem. business card.

carte de vœux noun Fem. greetings card.

carte postale noun Fem. postcard.

carte routière noun Fem. road map.

carte SIM noun Fem. SIM card.

carte téléphonique noun Fem. phonecard.

carton noun Masc. **1** cardboard; **une chemise en carton** a cardboard folder; **carton ondulé** corrugated cardboard; **2** cardboard box.

cartouche noun Fem. cartridge.

cas noun Masc. **1** case; **au cas où tu oublierais** in case you forget; **en aucun cas** on no account; **en tout cas** in any case, at any rate; **2** case; **trois cas de rougeole** three cases of measles.

cascade noun Fem. **1** waterfall; **2** stunt.

cascadeur, cascadeuse noun Masc., Fem. stuntman, stuntwoman.

case noun Fem. **1** square (on a board game); **2** box (on a form); **3** hut.

casher adjective kosher.

casier noun Masc. **1** pigeonhole; **2** locker; **3** rack.

casino noun Masc. casino.

casque noun Masc. **1** crash helmet; **2** safety helmet, hard hat; **3** headphones, headset.

casquette noun Fem. cap; **une casquette de base-ball** a baseball cap.

casse-croûte noun Masc. snack.

casse-noisettes noun Masc. nutcrackers.

casse-pieds adjective (informal) **elle est casse-pieds!** she's a pain in the neck!

casser verb [1] **1** to break; **casser un verre** to break a glass; **2 se casser** to break; **le verre s'est cassé** the glass broke; **3 se casser la jambe** to break your leg; ★ **se**

casser la tête to go to a lot of trouble (literally: to break your head); **ne te casse pas la tête!** don't go to a lot of trouble!

casserole noun Fem. saucepan.

casse-tête noun Masc. **1** puzzle; **2** problem.

cassette noun Fem. cassette, tape.

cassis noun Masc. blackcurrant; **sirop de cassis** blackcurrant cordial.

cassoulet noun Masc. oven-baked beans (with meat and sausage).

castor noun Masc. beaver.

catalogue noun Masc. catalogue.

catastrophe noun Fem. disaster, catastrophe.

catch noun Masc. wrestling.

catcheur, catcheuse noun Masc., Fem. wrestler.

catégorie noun Fem. category.

cathédrale noun Fem. cathedral.

catholicisme noun Masc. (Roman) Catholicism.

catholique noun Masc. & Fem., adjective (Roman) Catholic.

cauchemar noun Masc. nightmare; **faire un cauchemar** to have a nightmare.

cause noun Fem. **1** cause; **la cause du problème** the cause of the problem; **2 à cause de** because of; **3 la cause de quelque chose** the reason for something; **fermé pour cause de maladie** closed for reasons of illness; **4** cause; **une bonne cause** a good cause.

a
b
c
d
e
f
g
h
i
j
k
l
m
n
o
p
q
r
s
t
u
v
w
x
y
z

causer *verb* [1] **1** to cause; **2** to talk, to chat; **causer de quelque chose** to talk (*or* chat) about something; **causer avec quelqu'un** to talk (*or* chat) to somebody.

caution *noun Fem.* **1** deposit (*when renting a flat or house*); **2** bail.

cavalier, cavalière *noun Masc., Fem.* rider.

cave *noun Fem.* cellar.

caveau (*plural* **caveaux**) *noun Masc.* vault.

caverne *noun Fem.* cave.

ce[1], **cet** (*before a vowel or mute 'h'*) (*Fem.* **cette**) *adjective* **1** this, that; **ce stylo ne marche pas** this pen doesn't work; **cette semaine** this week; **ce couteau-ci** this knife; **2** that; **passe-moi cette assiette** pass me that plate; **cette chaise-là** that chair; **3** **cette nuit** last night, tonight.

ce[2], **c'** (*before an 'e'*) *pronoun* **1** this, that, it; **qui est-ce?** who is it?; **c'est moi** it's me; **qu'est-ce que c'est?** what is it?; **c'est la première maison à gauche** it's the first house on the left; **2** he, she, they; **c'est un médecin** he's a doctor; **ce sont les enfants de Paul** they're Paul's children; **3** **ce qui** what; **mange ce qui reste** eat what's left; **4** **ce que** what; **prends ce que tu veux** take what you want; **5** **c'est tout ce qui reste** that's all that's left; **prends tout ce que tu veux** take everything you want.

ceci *pronoun* this; **ceci n'est pas à moi** this is not mine.

cécité *noun Fem.* blindness.

céder *verb* [24] **1** to give in; **2** **'cédez le passage'** 'give way' (*at a road junction*); **3** **céder sa place** to give up your seat; **4** **céder à quelque chose** to give in to something.

cédille *noun Fem.* cedilla.

cèdre *noun Masc.* cedar.

ceinture *noun Fem.* **1** belt; **2** waistband; **3** waist.

ceinture de sauvetage *noun Fem.* lifebelt.

ceinture de sécurité *noun Fem.* seatbelt.

cela *pronoun* this, that, it (*'cela' is used in the same way as 'ça' but is more formal*); **cela ne me concerne pas** that does not concern me; **cela ne fait rien** that doesn't matter.

célébration *noun Fem.* celebration.

célèbre *adjective* famous.

célébrer *verb* [24] to celebrate.

céleri *noun Masc.* celery.

célibataire *noun Masc. & Fem.* **1** bachelor; **2** single woman. **célibataire** *adjective* single; **elle est célibataire** she's single.

celle *pronoun* SEE **celui**.

celle-ci *pronoun* SEE **celui-ci**.

celle-là *pronoun* SEE **celui-là**.

celles *pronoun* SEE **ceux**.

celles-ci *pronoun* SEE **ceux-ci**.

celles-là *pronoun* SEE **ceux-là**.

cellule *noun Fem.* **1** (prison) cell; **2** cell (*in biology and medicine*); **3** unit.

celui, celle *pronoun* the one; **'quel livre?'** – **'celui qui est sur la table'** 'which book?' – 'the one on the table'; **'quelle casserole?'** – **'celle qui est sur la cuisinière'** 'which saucepan?' – 'the one on the cooker'.

celui-ci, celle-ci *pronoun* this one.

celui-là, celle-là *pronoun* that one.

cendre *noun Fem.* ash; **les cendres** the ashes.

cendrier *noun Masc.* ashtray.

Cendrillon *noun* Cinderella.

censé *adjective* supposed; **être censé faire/être** to be supposed to do/be; **je suis censé être là à dix heures** I'm supposed to be there at ten o'clock.

cent[1] *number* a hundred, one hundred; **trois cents personnes** three hundred people; **deux cent cinquante personnes** two hundred and fifty people (*note that there is no 's' on 'cent' when it is followed by another number*).

cent[2] *noun Masc.* cent (*one hundredth of a euro or dollar*).

centaine *noun Fem.* **une centaine de personnes** a hundred people, a hundred or so people; **plusieurs centaines de personnes** several hundred people; **des centaines de lettres** hundreds of letters.

centenaire *noun Masc.* centenary.

centième *number* hundredth.

centime *noun Masc.* **1** cent (*one hundredth of a euro*); **2** centime (*one hundredth of former French currency: the franc*).

centimètre *noun Masc.* **1** centimetre; **un centimètre carré** a square centimetre; **un centimètre cube** a cubic centimetre; **2** tape measure.

central *noun Masc.* **un central téléphonique** a telephone exchange.
central *adjective* (*Masc. plural* centraux) **1** central; **2** main.

centrale *noun Fem.* power station; **une centrale nucléaire** a nuclear power station.

centraliser *verb* [1] to centralize.

centre *noun Masc.* centre; **au centre de** in the centre of.

centre commercial *noun Masc.* shopping centre, mall.

centre de loisirs *noun Masc.* leisure centre.

centre sportif *noun Masc.* sports centre.

centre-ville *noun Masc.* town centre, city centre.

cependant *adverb* however.

cercle *noun Masc.* circle; **en cercle** in a circle.

cercueil *noun Masc.* coffin.

céréale *noun Fem.* cereal, grain.

cérémonie *noun Fem.* ceremony.

cerf *noun Masc.* stag.

cerf-volant *noun Masc.* kite.

cerise *noun Fem.* cherry.

a
b
c
d
e
f
g
h
i
j
k
l
m
n
o
p
q
r
s
t
u
v
w
x
y
z

cerisier *noun Masc.* cherry tree.

certain *adjective* **1** certain, sure; **être certain de** to be certain (*or* sure) of; **2** certain; **un certain nombre de** a certain number of; **3** some; **certaines personnes** some people.

certains *pronoun* some; **certains de mes amis** some of my friends.

certainement *adverb* **1** most probably; **2** certainly; **3** of course.

certes *adverb* admittedly.

certificat *noun Masc.* certificate.

certifier *verb* [1] to certify.

cerveau (*plural* **cerveaux**) *noun Masc.* **1** brain; **2** mind.

ces *adjective* **1** these; **c'est Sara qui m'a acheté ces fleurs** it was Sara who bought me these flowers; **2** those; **ces livres que je t'ai prêtés** those books I lent you; **ces arbres-là** those trees.

CES *noun Masc.* (*Collège d'enseignement secondaire*) secondary school (*from 11 to 15, when students can go on to a 'lycée' for a further 3 years*).

cesse *noun Fem.* **sans cesse** constantly.

cesser *verb* [1] to stop; **cesser de faire** to stop doing.

cessez-le-feu *noun Masc.* ceasefire.

c'est-à-dire *phrase* that is, that's to say.

cet, **cette** *adjective* SEE **ce**.

ceux, **celles** *pronoun* the ones; **'quels livres?'** – **'ceux qui sont sur la table'** 'which books?' – 'the ones

on the table'; **'quelles chaussettes?'** – **'celles que tu m'as prêtées hier'** 'which socks?' – 'the ones you lent me yesterday' SEE **celui**.

ceux-ci, **celles-ci** *pronoun* these ones.

ceux-là, **celles-là** *pronoun* those ones.

chacal *noun Masc.* jackal.

chacun, **chacune** *pronoun* **1** each; **ils ont chacun un billet** they each have a ticket; **2** everyone; **comme chacun sait** as everyone knows.

chagrin *noun Masc.* grief.

chaîne *noun Fem.* **1** chain; **2** channel (*on* TV).

chaîne hi-fi *noun Fem.* hi-fi system.

chaîne laser *noun Fem.* CD player.

chaîne stéréo *noun Fem.* stereo system.

chair *noun Fem.* **1** flesh; **2** meat; **la chair à saucisse** sausage meat; ★ **avoir la chair de poule** to have goose pimples (*literally: to have hen's flesh*).

chaise *noun Fem.* chair.

châle *noun Masc.* shawl.

chalet *noun Masc.* chalet.

chaleur *noun Fem.* heat, warmth.

chaleureux (*Fem.* **chaleureuse**) *adjective* warm.

chambre *noun Fem.* **1** bedroom; **dans ma chambre** in my bedroom; **2** (hotel) room; **une chambre pour une personne** a single room; **une**

chambre pour deux personnes a double room; **3 la musique de chambre** chamber music.

chambre d'amis *noun Fem.* spare bedroom.

chambre de commerce *noun Fem.* chamber of commerce.

chambres d'hôte *plural noun Fem.* bed and breakfast.

chameau (*plural* **chameaux**) *noun Masc.* camel.

champ *noun Masc.* field.

champagne *noun Masc.* champagne.

champ de bataille *noun Masc.* battlefield.

champ de courses *noun Masc.* racetrack.

champignon *noun Masc.* **1** mushroom; **des champignons de Paris** button mushrooms; **2** fungus.

champion, championne *noun Masc., Fem.* champion.

championnat *noun Masc.* championship.

chance *noun Fem.* **1** luck; **un coup de chance** a stroke of luck; **Bonne chance!** Good luck!; **j'ai eu la chance de pouvoir passer un an en France** I was lucky enough to be able to spend a year in France; **avoir de la chance** to be lucky; **tu as de la chance d'avoir une sœur pareille!** you're lucky to have a sister like that!; **2** chance.

chancelier *noun Masc.* chancellor.

chandail *noun Masc.* jumper.

chandelier *noun Masc.* **1** candlestick; **2** candelabra.

change *noun Masc.* exchange rate; **bureau de change** bureau de change (*for changing money*).

changeant *adjective* changeable.

changement *noun Masc.* change.

changer *verb* [52] **1** to change; **tu n'as pas changé** you haven't changed; **2 changer quelque chose** to change something; **changer les draps** to change the sheets; **changer une prise** to change a plug; **3 changer quelque chose)** to exchange something (*in a shop*); **4 changer de** to change; **changer de train** to change trains; **changer d'avis** to change your mind; **j'ai changé d'avis** I've changed my mind; **5 se changer** to get changed, to change your clothes.

chanson *noun Fem.* song.

chant *noun Masc.* **1** singing; **2** song.

chantage *noun Masc.* blackmail.

chanter *verb* [1] to sing.

chanteur, chanteuse *noun Masc., Fem.* singer.

chantier *noun Masc.* **1** building site; **2** roadworks.

chantonner *verb* [1] to hum.

chaos *noun Masc.* chaos.

chaotique *adjective* chaotic.

chapeau (*plural* **chapeaux**) *noun Masc.* **1** hat; **2 chapeau!** well done!

chapeau melon *noun Masc.* bowler hat.

chapelle *noun Fem.* chapel.

a b c d e f g h i j k l m n o p q r s t u v w x y z

a

chapelure noun Fem. breadcrumbs.

b

chapiteau (plural **chapiteaux**) noun Masc. **1** marquee; **2** big top (circus tent).

c

d

chapitre noun Masc. chapter.

e

chaque adjective each, every.

f

char noun Masc. **1** (military) tank; **2** carnival float.

g

charabia noun Masc. (informal) gobbledygook, rubbish.

h

charade noun Fem. riddle.

i

charbon noun Masc. coal.

j

charbon de bois noun Masc. charcoal.

k

l

charcuterie noun Fem. **1** pork butcher's (selling salads and ready-prepared dishes as well as pork, bacon, ham, sausages, etc); **2** pork products (ham, salami, pâté, etc).

m

n

charcutier, charcutière noun Masc., Fem. pork butcher.

o

p

chardon noun Masc. thistle.

charge noun Fem. **1** load; **2** responsibility; **avoir la charge de** to be responsible for; **3 charges** costs, charges.

q

r

s

charger verb [52] **1** to load; **2** to charge (a battery).

t

chariot noun Masc. **1** trolley (in a supermarket); **1** waggon.

u

charité noun Fem. charity.

v

charmant adjective charming.

w

charme noun Masc. **1** charm; **2** spell.

x

charmer verb [1] to charm.

y

z

charnière noun Fem. hinge.

charpentier noun Masc. carpenter.

charrette noun Fem. cart.

charrue noun Fem. plough.

charte noun Fem. charter.

charter adjective **un vol charter** charter flight.

chasse noun Fem. hunting, shooting.

chasse d'eau noun Fem. (toilet) flush; **tirer la chasse d'eau** to flush the toilet.

chasse-neige noun Masc. snowplough.

chasser verb [1] to chase off.

chasseur noun Masc. hunter.

chat noun Masc. cat.

châtaigne noun Fem. sweet chestnut.

châtaignier noun Masc. sweet chestnut tree.

châtain adjective **les cheveux châtains** brown hair.

château (plural **châteaux**) noun Masc. **1** castle; **2** large country house.

château d'eau noun Masc. water tower.

chatouiller verb [1] to tickle.

chatroom noun Masc. chatroom.

chatte noun Fem. (female) cat.

chaud adjective hot, warm; **du lait chaud** hot milk; **un pull chaud** a warm jumper; **j'ai chaud** I'm hot; **il fait chaud ici** it's hot here.

chaudière noun Fem. boiler; **une chaudière à gaz** a gas boiler.

chauffage noun Masc. heating.

chauffage central *noun Masc.* central heating.

chauffe-eau *noun Masc.* water heater.

chauffer *verb* [1] **1** to heat, to heat up; **2** to warm.

chauffeur *noun Masc.* **1** driver; **un chauffeur de taxi** a taxi driver; **2** chauffeur.

chaumière *noun Fem.* thatched cottage.

chaussée *noun Fem.* roadway.

chaussette *noun Fem.* sock.

chausson *noun Masc.* **1** slipper; **2** ballet shoe.

chaussure *noun Fem.* shoe.

chauve *adjective* bald.

chauve-souris *noun Fem.* bat.

chavirer *verb* [1] to capsize.

chef *noun Masc.* **1** leader; **2** head; **3** boss; **4** chef de cuisine chef.

chef-d'œuvre *noun Masc.* masterpiece.

chemin *noun Masc.* **1** country road; **2** track, path; **3** way; **perdre son chemin** to lose your way; **en chemin** on the way.

chemin de fer *noun Masc.* railway.

cheminée *noun Fem.* **1** chimney; **2** fireplace; **3** mantelpiece.

cheminot *noun Masc.* railway worker.

chemise *noun Fem.* shirt.

chemise de nuit *noun Fem.* nightdress.

chemisier *noun Masc.* blouse.

chêne *noun Masc.* **1** oak tree; **2** oak; **une table en chêne** an oak table.

chenil *noun Masc.* **1** dog kennel; **2** kennels.

chenille *noun Fem.* caterpillar.

chèque *noun Masc.* cheque; **un carnet de chèques** a cheque book.

chèque de voyage *noun Masc.* traveller's cheque.

chéquier *noun Masc.* cheque book.

cher (Fem. **chère**) *adjective* **1** dear; **Chère Anne** Dear Anne; **2** expensive, dear; **pas trop cher** reasonably priced.
cher *adverb* **coûter cher** to be expensive.

chercher *verb* [1] **1** to look for; **qu'est-ce que tu cherches?** what are you looking for?; **je cherche mes lunettes** I'm looking for my glasses; **je cherche un emploi** I'm looking for a job; **2 chercher quelque chose** to look something up (*in a dictionary, for example*); **3 aller chercher** to go and get (*or* fetch) (*somebody or something*); **je vais chercher des verres** I'll go and get some glasses; **4** to pick up; **je viendrai te chercher à l'école** I'll come and pick you up from school; **5 chercher à faire** to try to do.

chercheur, chercheuse *noun Masc., Fem.* scientist.

chéri, chérie *noun Masc., Fem.* darling.

chérir *verb* [2] to cherish.

cheval (*plural* **chevaux**) *noun Masc.* **1** horse; **à cheval** on horseback; **monter à cheval** to ride

a
b
c
d
e
f
g
h
i
j
k
l
m
n
o
p
q
r
s
t
u
v
w
x
y
z

a
a horse; **2 faire du cheval** to go horseriding.

b

c
cheval à bascule *noun Masc.* rocking horse.

d
chevalet *noun Masc.* easel.

chevet *noun Masc.* **1** bedhead; **au chevet de quelqu'un** at somebody's bedside; **un livre de chevet** a bedside book; **une lampe de chevet** a bedside lamp; **2** bedside table.

e

f

g

h
cheveu (*plural* **cheveux**) *noun Masc.* **1 un cheveu** a hair; **2 les cheveux** hair; **il a les cheveux blonds** he has blond hair; ★ **avoir un cheveu sur la langue** to have a lisp (*literally: to have a hair on one's tongue*); ★ **couper les cheveux en quatre** to split hairs (*literally: to cut hairs in four*).

i

j

k

l

m

n
cheville *noun Fem.* ankle.

o
chèvre[1] *noun Fem.* goat, nanny-goat.

p
chèvre[2] *noun Masc.* goat's cheese.

chèvrefeuille *noun Masc.* honeysuckle.

q

r
chevreuil *noun Masc.* **1** roe deer; **2** venison.

s
chez *preposition* **1 chez quelqu'un** at (*or* to) somebody's house; **je vais chez Paul ce soir** I'm going to Paul's this evening; **elle est chez les Brown** she's at the Browns'; **viens chez moi** come round to my place; **il est chez lui** he's at home; **je rentre chez moi maintenant** I'm going home now; **fais comme chez toi** make yourself at home; **2 chez le boucher** at (*or* to) the butcher's; **je l'ai rencontrée chez le coiffeur**

t

u

v

w

x

y

z

hier I met her at the hairdresser's yesterday; **je vais chez le coiffeur demain** I'm going to the hairdresser's tomorrow.

chic *adjective* **1** chic, well-dressed; **2** nice; **c'était vachement chic de ta part** it was really nice of you; **3 Chic!** (*informal*) Cool!

chicorée *noun Fem.* **1** endive; **2** chicory powder (*for adding to coffee*).

chien *noun Masc.* dog; **'chien méchant'** 'beware of the dog'.

chien d'aveugle *noun Masc.* guide dog.

chien de berger *noun Masc.* sheepdog.

chien de garde *noun Masc.* guard dog.

chienne *noun Fem.* (female) dog, bitch.

chiffon *noun Masc.* **1** rag; **2** duster.

chiffre *noun Masc.* figure; **un numéro à cinq chiffres** a five-figure number.

chignon *noun Masc.* bun, chignon.

chimie *noun Fem.* chemistry.

chimique *adjective* chemical.

chimpanzé *noun Masc.* chimpanzee.

Chine *noun Fem.* China.

chinois *noun Masc.* Chinese (*language*).
chinois *adjective* Chinese.

Chinois, Chinoise *noun Masc., Fem.* Chinese man, Chinese woman; **les Chinois** the Chinese.

chiot *noun Masc.* puppy.

chips *noun Fem.* crisp; **un paquet de chips** a packet of crisps.

chirurgical (*Masc. plural* **chirurgicaux**) *adjective* surgical; **une intervention chirurgicale** an operation.

chirurgie *noun Fem.* surgery.

chirurgie au laser *noun Fem.* laser surgery.

chirurgien *noun Masc.* surgeon.

chirurgien-dentiste *noun Masc.* dental surgeon.

choc *noun Masc.* **1** shock; **ça m'a fait un choc** it gave me a shock; **2** crash.

chocolat *noun Masc.* chocolate; **chocolat au lait** milk chocolate; **chocolat blanc** white chocolate; **chocolat en poudre** drinking chocolate; **un gâteau au chocolat** a chocolate cake; **un chocolat chaud** a hot chocolate.

chœur *noun Masc.* **1** choir (*professional*); **2** chorus.

choisir *verb* [2] to choose.

choix *noun Masc.* **1** choice; **un bon choix** a good choice; **2 un grand choix** a wide choice (*or* variety).

chômage *noun Masc.* unemployment; **être au chômage** to be unemployed.

chômeur, chômeuse *noun Masc., Fem.* unemployed person.

chope *noun Fem.* beer mug.

choquer *verb* [1] to shock.

chorale *noun Fem.* choir (*amateur*).

choriste *noun Masc. & Fem.* **1** member of a choir; **2** member of a chorus; **3** backing singer.

chose *noun Fem.* thing; **les choses qui m'intéressent** the things that interest me; **j'ai plusieurs choses à te dire** I have several things to tell you; **je prends la même chose** I'll have the same.

chou (*plural* **choux**) *noun Masc.* cabbage.

chouchou[1], **chouchoute** *noun Masc., Fem.* teacher's pet.

chouchou[2] *noun Masc.* scrunchy (*for holding back your hair*).

choucroute *noun Fem.* sauerkraut (*pickled cabbage with different types of sausage, ham, and bacon*).

chou de Bruxelles *noun Masc.* Brussels sprout.

chouette *noun Fem.* owl. **chouette** *adjective* (*informal*) great; **c'est chouette!** that's great!; **leur maison est très chouette** their house is really lovely.

chou-fleur (*plural* **choux-fleurs**) *noun Masc.* cauliflower.

chrétien, chrétienne *noun Masc., Fem., adjective* Christian.

christianisme *noun Masc.* Christianity.

chrome *noun Masc.* chromium.

chronique *noun Fem.* **1** column, page (*devoted to a particular journalist in a newspaper*); **2** (radio) programme. **chronique** *adjective* chronic.

chronomètre *noun* Masc. stopwatch.

chrysanthème *noun* Masc. chrysanthemum.

chuchoter *verb* [1] to whisper.

chut *exclamation* shh!

chute *noun* Fem. **1** fall; **faire une chute de 5 mètres** to fall 5 metres; **2 chutes de neige** snowfall; **chutes de pluie** rainfall; **3** fall, drop (*in price, value, temperature*).

chuter *verb* [1] to fall, to drop.

Chypre *noun* Fem. Cyprus.

ci *adverb* **ce mois-ci** this month; **ces timbres-ci** these stamps; **ces jours-ci** these last few days.

cible *noun* Fem. target.

ciboulette *noun* Fem. **de la ciboulette** chives.

cicatrice *noun* Fem. scar.

ci-contre *adverb* opposite.

ci-dessous *adverb* below.

ci-dessus *adverb* above.

cidre *noun* Masc. cider.

ciel (*plural* **cieux**) *noun* Masc. **1** sky; **au ciel** in the sky; **2** heaven.

cigale *noun* Fem. cicada.

cigare *noun* Masc. cigar.

cigarette *noun* Fem. cigarette.

cigogne *noun* Fem. stork.

ci-inclus *adjective* enclosed; **la copie ci-incluse** the enclosed copy. **ci-inclus** *adverb* enclosed.

ci-joint *adverb* **veuillez trouver ci-joint** please find enclosed (*in a letter*).

cil *noun* Masc. eyelash.

ciment *noun* Masc. cement.

cimetière *noun* Masc. **1** cemetery; **2** graveyard.

cinéaste *noun* Masc. & Fem. film director.

ciné-club *noun* Masc. film club.

cinéma *noun* Masc. **1** cinema; **aller au cinéma** to go to the cinema; **2** (*informal*) play-acting; **arrête ton cinéma!** stop that nonsense!

cinéphile *noun* Masc. & Fem. keen cinema-goer.

cinglé *adjective* (*informal*) crazy.

cinq *number* five; **Lucie a cinq ans** Lucie's five; **à cinq heures** at five o'clock; **le cinq avril** the fifth of April.

cinquantaine *noun* Fem. **une cinquantaine (de)** about fifty; **une cinquantaine de personnes** about fifty people; **avoir la cinquantaine** to be about fifty.

cinquante *number* fifty.

cinquantième *number* fiftieth.

cinquième *noun* Fem. (*in a French school*) the equivalent of Year 8. **cinquième** *noun* Masc. **au cinquième** on the fifth floor. **cinquième** *adjective* fifth.

cintre *noun* Masc. clothes hanger.

cirage *noun* Masc. shoe polish.

circonférence *noun* Fem. circumference.

circonflexe *noun* Masc. **un accent circonflexe** a circumflex.

circonstance *noun* Fem. circumstance.

rcuit noun Masc. **1** circuit (*in an athletics stadium*); **2** tour; **3** (electrical) circuit.

rculaire noun Fem., adjective ircular.

rculation noun Fem. **1** traffic; **il y a beaucoup de circulation ce soir** there's a lot of traffic this evening; **2** circulation.

rculer verb [1] **1** to run (*of a bus or train*); **ce train ne circule pas le dimanche** that train doesn't run on Sundays; **2** to circulate.

re noun Fem. wax.

rer verb [1] to polish.

rque noun Masc. circus; **au cirque** t (*or* to) the circus.

seaux plural noun Masc. scissors; **une paire de ciseaux** a pair of cissors.

tadin, citadine noun Masc., em. city dweller.

tation noun Fem. quotation.

té noun Fem. **1** city, town; **2** housing estate; **3 une cité universitaire** university halls of esidence.

ter verb [1] to quote.

terne noun Fem. tank.

toyen, citoyenne noun Masc., em. citizen.

tron noun Masc. lemon; **une tarte au citron** a lemon tart.

tronnade noun Fem. still emonade.

tronnier noun Masc. lemon tree.

tron vert noun Masc. lime.

trouille noun Fem. pumpkin.

civet noun Masc. stew.

civil noun Masc. **1** civilian; **2 un policier en civil** a plain-clothes policeman.
civil adjective **1** civilian; **2 un mariage civil** a civil wedding (*as opposed to a church wedding*).

civilisation noun Fem. civilization.

civique adjective civic.

clair adjective **1** light; **bleu clair** light blue; **2 la chambre est très claire** the bedroom is very light; **3** clear.
clair adverb clearly; **voir clair** to see clearly.

clair de lune noun Masc. moonlight.

clairement adverb clearly.

clapier noun Masc. rabbit hutch.

claque noun Fem. slap.

claqué adjective (*informal*) exhausted, wiped out.

claquer verb [1] **claquer la porte** to slam the door.

clarifier verb [1] to clarify.

clarinette noun Fem. clarinet; **jouer de la clarinette** to play the clarinet.

clarté noun Fem. **1** light; **2** clarity.

classe noun Fem. **1** class; **elle est dans ma classe à l'école** she's in my class (or year) at school; **en classe** in class; **2** classroom; **3 première/deuxième classe** first/second class; **4** (social) class.

classement noun Masc. **1** classification; **2** placing; **3** grading; **4** filing.

57

classer verb [1] **1** to classify; **2** to grade; **3** to file.

classeur noun Masc. **1** ring binder, file; **2** filing cabinet.

classique adjective **1** classical; **2** classic; **3** usual; **c'est classique!** that's typical!

clavier noun Masc. keyboard.

clé noun Fem. **1** key; **fermer quelque chose à clé** to lock something; **2** spanner.

clef = CLÉ.

clémentine noun Fem. clementine.

clic noun Masc. click (with mouse); **un clic sur le bouton droit de la souris** a right-click; **un clic sur le bouton gauche de la souris** a left-click.

client, cliente noun Masc., Fem. **1** customer; **2** client.

clientèle noun Fem. customers.

cligner verb [1] **cligner des yeux** to blink.

clignotant noun Masc. indicator (on a motor vehicle).

clignoter verb [1] to flash.

climat noun Masc. climate.

climatisation noun Fem. air-conditioning.

climatisé adjective air-conditioned.

clin d'œil noun Masc. wink; **faire un clin d'œil à quelqu'un** to wink at somebody; ★ **en un clin d'œil** in a flash.

clinique noun Fem. clinic, private hospital.

clip noun Masc. **1** video clip; **2** clip brooch; **3** clip-on earring.

cliquer verb [1] **cliquer sur quelque chose** to click on something (using a computer mouse); **cliquer en appuyant sur ▌ bouton gauche de la souris** to le click; **cliquer deux fois sur l'icôn** to double-click the icon.

cliqueter verb [48] **1** to jingle; **2 ▌** rattle.

clochard, clocharde noun Masc., Fem. tramp, down-and-out.

cloche noun Fem. bell.

clocher noun Masc. **1** steeple; **2** be tower.

cloison noun Fem. **1** partition; **2** partition wall; **3** screen.

cloître noun Masc. cloister.

clos adjective closed.

clôture noun Fem. **1** fence; **2** close **3** closing.

clou noun Masc. **1** nail; **2** stud.

clou de girofle noun Masc. clov ▌

clouer verb [1] **clouer quelque chose** to nail something down.

clown noun Masc. clown.

club noun Masc. club; **un club de foot** a football club.

cobaye noun Masc. guinea pig.

Coca™ noun Masc. Coke™.

cocaïne noun Fem. cocaine.

coccinelle noun Fem. ladybird.

cocher verb [1] to tick.

cochon noun Masc. pig.
cochon adjective (Fem. **cochonne**) (informal) dirty (joke, story).

ochon d'Inde *noun Masc.* guinea pig.

ocktail *noun Masc.* **1** cocktail; **2** cocktail party.

oco *noun Masc.* **une noix de coco** a coconut.

ocorico *noun Masc.* cock-a-doodle-do.

ocotte *noun Fem.* **1** casserole; **2** hen (*in baby talk*); **3** chocolate hen (*traditionally sold at Easter*).

ocotte-minute™ *noun Fem.* pressure cooker.

ode *noun Masc.* **1** code; **le code de la route** the highway code; **2** codes dipped headlights.

ode postal *noun Masc.* postcode.

œur *noun Masc.* **1** heart; **2** hearts (*suit of playing cards*); **le roi de cœur** the king of hearts; **3 par cœur** by heart; **apprendre quelque chose par cœur** to learn something by heart; ★ **avoir mal au cœur** to feel sick.

offre *noun Masc.* **1** chest; **2** safe; **3** boot (*of a car*).

offre-fort *noun Masc.* safe.

ogner *verb* [1] to bump, to bang; **se cogner la tête** to bang your head.

oiffer *verb* [1] **se coiffer** to brush (*or* comb) your hair.

oiffeur, coiffeuse¹ *noun Masc., Fem.* hairdresser.

oiffeuse² *noun Fem.* dressing table.

oiffure *noun* **1** hairdressing; **2** hairstyle; **tu as changé de coiffure** you've changed your hairstyle.

coin *noun Masc.* **1** corner; **au coin** in the corner; **au coin de** in the corner of; **2 le café du coin** the local cafe; **les gens du coin** the local people; ★ **au coin du feu** by the fireside (*literally: in the corner of the fire*).

coincé *adjective* stuck, jammed.

coincer *verb* [61] to jam.

coïncidence *noun Fem.* coincidence.

col *noun Masc.* **1** collar; **2** neck; **3** (mountain) pass.

colère *noun Fem.* anger; **être en colère** to be angry.

colin *noun Masc.* hake.

colique *noun Fem.* diarrhoea.

colis *noun Masc.* parcel.

collant *noun Masc.* **un collant** (a pair of) tights.
collant *adjective* sticky.

colle *noun Fem.* **1** glue; **2** detention; **une heure de colle** an hour's detention.

collecte *noun Fem.* collection (*of money*).

collection *noun Fem.* collection.

collectionner *verb* [1] to collect.

collectionneur, collectionneuse *noun Masc., Fem.* collector.

collège *noun Masc.* secondary school (*from 11 to 15, when students can either leave school altogether or go on to a 'lycée' for a further 3 years*).

a
b
c
d
e
f
g
h
i
j
k
l
m
n
o
p
q
r
s
t
u
v
w
x
y
z

collégien, collégienne noun
Masc., Fem. schoolboy, schoolgirl.

collègue noun Masc. & Fem.
colleague.

coller verb [1] **1** to stick; **2** to stick
down; **3** to glue; **4** to press.

collier noun Masc. **1** necklace;
2 collar (for a dog, cat, etc).

colline noun Fem. hill.

collision noun Fem. collision.

colombe noun Fem. dove.

colonel noun Masc. colonel.

colonie noun Fem. colony.

colonie de vacances noun
Fem. holiday camp (for children).

colonne noun Fem. column.

colonne vertébrale noun Fem.
spine.

colorant noun Masc. colouring.

coloré adjective **1** coloured;
2 colourful.

colorer verb [1] to colour.

colorier verb [1] to colour in.

coloris noun Masc. colour; **existe
en plusieurs coloris** several
colours available.

combat noun Masc. **1** fighting; **2** un
combat de boxe a boxing match.

combattant noun Masc. **un
ancien combattant** a war veteran.

combattre verb [21] to fight.

combien adverb **1** how much; **tu
en veux combien?** how much do
you want?; **c'est combien?** how
much is it?; **ça coûte combien?**
how much does it cost?; **je vous dois
combien?** how much do I owe you?,
how much is that?; **2** how many; **tu**

en veux combien? how many do
you want?; **3 combien de** how
much; **combien d'argent?** how
much money?; **4 combien de** how
many; **combien de tasses?** how
many cups?; ★ **nous sommes le
combien aujourd'hui?** what's the
date today? (literally: we are the how
many today?).

combinaison noun Fem.
1 combination; **2** jumpsuit;
3 overalls; **4** slip, petticoat.

combiné noun Masc. receiver (of a
telephone).

comble noun Masc. **1 le comble
de** the height of; **le comble du
luxe** the height of luxury; **2 ça
c'est le comble!** that's the last
straw!

comédie noun Fem. comedy.

comédien, comédienne noun
Masc., Fem. actor, actress.

comestible adjective edible.

comique noun Masc. comic,
comedian.
comique adjective funny.

comité noun Masc. committee.

commandant noun Masc.
1 major; **2** squadron leader;
3 commandant-en-chef
commander in chief.

commande noun Fem. order; **sur
commande** to order.

commander verb [1] **1** to order;
avez-vous commandé? have you
ordered?; **2** to be in charge.

comme preposition **1** like; **une
montre comme la tienne** a watch
like yours; **2** like; **comme ça** like
this; **3** as a; **travailler comme**

serveur dans un café to work as a waiter in a cafe; **4 qu'est-ce que tu veux comme glace?** what kind of ice cream would you like?

comme *conjunction* **1** as; **comme tu veux** as you like; **2** as, since; **comme je suis malade** as (*or* since) I'm ill; **3** as; **comme je fermais la porte** as I was closing the door; **4 comme si** as if.

comme *adverb* **comme il est gentil!** he's so nice!; **comme c'est bon!** it's so good!; **comme il fait chaud!** it's so hot!; ★ **blanc comme la neige** as white as snow; ★ **fort comme un bœuf** as strong as an ox.

ommencement *noun Masc.* beginning, start.

ommencer *verb* [61] **1** to begin, to start; **le film a commencé** the film has started; **2 commencer à faire, commencer de faire** to start (*or* begin) to do; **elle a commencé à faire ses devoirs** she's started to do her homework; **je commence à comprendre** I'm beginning to understand; **il commence à pleuvoir** it's starting to rain.

omment *adverb* **1** how; **comment as-tu fait ce gâteau?** how did you make this cake?; **je ne sais pas comment le faire** I don't know how to do it; **2 comment vas-tu?** how are you?; **comment ça va?** how are you?; **comment va ta mère?** how's your mother?; **3 comment t'appelles-tu?** what's your name?; **il s'appelle comment, ton frère?** what's your brother's name?; **4 pardon?**; **5 comment est leur maison?, elle est comment,**

leur maison? what's their house like?

commentaire *noun Masc.* **1** comment; **2** commentary.

commenter *verb* [1] **commenter quelque chose** to comment on something.

commerçant, commerçante *noun Masc., Fem.* shopkeeper.

commerce *noun Masc.* **1** shop; **2 le commerce** business; **je fais des études de commerce** I'm doing business studies; **3 le commerce** trade.

commercial (*Masc. plural* **commerciaux**) *adjective* **1** commercial; **2 un centre commercial** a shopping centre.

commettre *verb* [11] **1 commettre une erreur** to make a mistake; **2 commettre un crime** to commit a crime.

commissariat *noun Masc.* police station.

commission *noun Fem.* **1** committee; **2** commission; **3** message; **4** errand; **5 faire les commissions** to do the shopping.

commode *noun Fem.* chest of drawers.
commode *adjective* **1** convenient, handy; **2** easy.

commun *adjective* **1** common; **2** shared; **3** joint; **4 en commun** in common; **ils n'ont rien en commun** they have nothing in common; **5 en commun** jointly, together; **6 les transports en commun** public transport.

a
b
c
d
e
f
g
h
i
j
k
l
m
n
o
p
q
r
s
t
u
v
w
x
y
z

communauté noun Fem. community.

communication noun Fem.
1 une communication téléphonique a telephone call;
2 communication; se mettre en communication avec quelqu'un to get in touch with someone.

communion noun Fem. communion.

communiquer verb [1] 1 to communicate; 2 communiquer quelque chose to pass something on.

communisme noun Masc. communism.

communiste noun Masc. & Fem., adjective communist.

compact adjective 1 dense;
2 compact; 3 un disque compact a compact disc, a CD.

compagnie noun Fem. 1 company, firm; 2 company; elle m'a tenu compagnie she kept me company.

compagnie aérienne noun Fem. airline.

compagnon noun Masc. companion.

comparable adjective comparable.

comparaison noun Fem. comparison; en comparaison de in comparison with.

comparatif (Fem. comparative) adjective comparative.

comparé adjective comparé à compared to (or with).

comparer verb [1] to compare.

compartiment noun Masc. compartment.

compas noun Masc. compass.

compatir verb [2] to sympathize.

compensation noun Fem. compensation.

compenser verb [1] compenser quelque chose to compensate for something.

compétence noun Fem. 1 ability 2 skill; 3 competence.

compétent adjective competent.

compétitif (Fem. compétitive) adjective competitive.

compétition noun Fem. competition.

complémentaire adjective further, supplementary.

complet noun Masc. suit.
complet adjective (Fem. complète) 1 complete; 2 total; 3 full (speaking of a hotel or a train); 4 le pain complet wholemeal bread.

complètement adverb completely.

compléter verb [24] 1 to complete 2 to fill in (a form).

complexe noun Masc., adjective complex.

complication noun Fem. complication.

complice noun Masc. & Fem. accomplice.

compliment noun Masc. compliment; faire des compliments à quelqu'un to compliment somebody.

compliqué *adjective* complicated.

compliquer *verb* [1] to complicate.

complot *noun Masc.* plot.

comportement *noun Masc.* behaviour.

comporter *verb* [1] **1** to include; **2** to consist of; **3** se comporter to behave.

composé *adjective* **1** composé de made up of; **2** une salade composée a mixed salad.

composer *verb* [1] **1** to make up; **2** to put together; **3** to compose (*music*); **4** composer un numéro (de téléphone) to dial a (telephone) number; composez le 00 44 pour le Royaume Uni dial 00 44 for the United Kingdom.

compositeur, compositrice *noun Masc., Fem.* composer.

composition *noun Fem.* composition.

composter *verb* [1] to punch (*a ticket*); 'n'oubliez pas de composter votre billet' remember to punch your ticket (*in France it is an offence not to punch your ticket on trains and buses at the start of your journey in one of the machines provided for this*).

compote *noun Fem.* stewed fruit; la compote de pommes apple puree.

compréhensible *adjective* understandable.

compréhensif (*Fem.* compréhensive) *adjective* understanding.

compréhension *noun Fem.* comprehension; un test de compréhension a comprehension test.

comprendre *verb* [64] **1** to understand; je comprends I understand; j'ai compris I understood; j'ai mal compris I misunderstood; **2** to include; **3** se comprendre to understand each other; **4** ça se comprend that's understandable.

comprimé *noun Masc.* tablet.

compris *adjective* **1** included; service compris service included; non compris not included; **2** y compris including; tout le monde y compris les enfants everybody including the children.

compromis *noun Masc.* compromise.

comptabilité *noun Fem.* accounting, accountancy.

comptable *noun Masc. & Fem.* accountant.

compte *noun Masc.* **1** account; un compte bancaire a bank account; un compte d'épargne a savings account; j'ai cent livres sur mon compte I have a hundred pounds in my account; **2** le compte est bon the amount is correct; **3** se rendre compte de quelque chose to realize something; se rendre compte que to realize that; je me suis rendu compte que j'avais oublié mes clés I realized I had forgotten my keys; **4** tenir compte de quelque chose to take something into account; **5** en fin de compte all things considered.

a
b
c
d
e
f
g
h
i
j
k
l
m
n
o
p
q
r
s
t
u
v
w
x
y
z

compter *verb* [1] **1** to count; **compter les visiteurs** to count the visitors; **2 compter sur quelqu'un** to count on somebody; **3** to count (*to be valid*); **ça ne compte pas** that doesn't count.

compte rendu *noun Masc.* report.

compteur *noun Masc.* meter.

compteur de vitesse *noun Masc.* speedometer.

comptine *noun Fem.* nursery rhyme.

comptoir *noun Masc.* **1** counter; **2** bar.

concentré *adjective* concentrated.

concentré de tomate *noun Masc.* tomato puree.

concentrer *verb* [1] **se concentrer (sur)** to concentrate (on).

conception *noun Fem.* design.

concernant *preposition* concerning.

concerner *verb* [1] to concern; **en ce qui me concerne** as far as I'm concerned.

concert *noun Masc.* concert; **un concert de rock** a rock concert.

concessionnaire *noun Masc. & Fem.* dealer, agent.

concierge *noun Masc. & Fem.* caretaker.

conclure *verb* [25] to conclude.

conclusion *noun Fem.* conclusion.

concombre *noun Masc.* cucumber.

concours *noun Masc.* competition.

concret (*Fem.* **concrète**) *adjectiv.* **1** concrete; **2** practical.

concurrence *noun Fem.* competition; **il y a beaucoup de concurrence** there's a lot of competition.

concurrent, concurrente *noun Masc., Fem.* competitor.

condamner *verb* [1] to sentence (*criminal*).

condition *noun Fem.* **1** condition; **en bonne condition** in good condition; **2 à condition de/que** provided that; **tu peux emprunter mon vélo à condition de me le rendre ce soir** you can borrow my bike provided you let me have it back this evening; **3 dans ces conditions** in that case.

conditionnel *noun Masc.* conditional tense.

conditionner *verb* [1] to packag.

conducteur, conductrice *noun Masc., Fem.* driver.

conduire *verb* [26] **1** to drive; **apprendre à conduire** to learn to drive; **un permis de conduire** a driving licence; **je te conduis à la gare** I'll drive you to the station; **2 t** take; **je vous conduis à votre chambre** I'll take you to your room **3 se conduire** to behave.

conduite *noun Fem.* behaviour; **mauvaise conduite** bad behaviour.

conférence *noun Fem.* **1** lecture; **2** conference.

onfesser *verb* [1] **se confesser** to go to confession.

onfiance *noun Fem.* **1** trust; **avoir confiance en quelqu'un, faire confiance à quelqu'un** to trust somebody; **je te fais confiance** I'll leave it to you; **2** confidence.

onfiant *adjective* confident.

onfidence *noun Fem.* secret.

onfier *verb* [1] **1 confier quelque chose à quelqu'un** to entrust something to somebody; **2 se confier à quelqu'un** to confide in somebody.

onfirmation *noun Fem.* confirmation.

onfirmer *verb* [1] to confirm.

onfiserie *noun Fem.* **1** sweet shop; **1** confectionery.

onfisquer *verb* [1] to confiscate.

onfit *adjective* **les fruits confits** crystallized fruits.

onfiture *noun Fem.* jam; **la confiture d'abricots** apricot jam.

onflit *noun Masc.* conflict.

onfondre *verb* [69] to confuse, to mix up.

onfort *noun Masc.* comfort; **tout confort** with all mod cons.

onfortable *adjective* comfortable.

onfrontation *noun Fem.* **1** confrontation; **2** clash.

onfus *adjective* **1** confused; **2** embarrassed.

confusion *noun Fem.* **1** confusion; **2** embarrassment.

congé *noun Masc.* **1** holiday (*from work*); **Robert est en congé aujourd'hui** Robert's on holiday today; **quel est ton jour de congé?** when's your day off?; **je pars en congé le dix** I'm on holiday from the tenth; **prendre une semaine de congé** to take a week's holiday; **2** leave; **Sylvie est en congé de maladie** Sylvie is on sick leave.

congélateur *noun Masc.* freezer.

congeler *verb* [45] to freeze.

congère *noun Fem.* snowdrift.

congestion *noun Fem.* congestion.

congrès *noun Masc.* conference.

conifère *noun Masc.* conifer.

conjoint, conjointe *noun Masc., Fem.* spouse (*husband or wife*).

conjonctivite *noun Fem.* conjunctivitis.

conjugaison *noun Fem.* conjugation.

connaissance *noun Fem.* **1** knowledge; **tes connaissances en français** your knowledge of French; **2** acquaintance; **3** consciousness; **perdre connaissance** to lose consciousness.

connaître *verb* [27] **1** to know; **est-ce que tu connais Gaby?** do you know Gaby?; **je ne connais pas Londres** I don't know London; **je la connais depuis trois ans** I've known her for three years; **2 se connaître** to know each other; **on se connaît** we know each other; **3 s'y**

connaître en quelque chose to know about something; **je ne m'y connais pas du tout en informatique** I know absolutely nothing about computers.

connecter verb [1] to connect.

connexion noun Fem. connection.

connu adjective well-known; **elle est très connue en France** she's very well-known in France.

consacrer verb [1] to devote.

consciemment adverb consciously.

conscience noun Fem. conscience; **avoir mauvaise conscience** to have a guilty conscience.

consciencieux (Fem. **consciencieuse**) adjective conscientious.

conscient adjective **1** aware; **être conscient de quelque chose** to be aware of something; **2** conscious.

conseil noun Masc. **1** advice; **un conseil** a piece of advice; **donner un conseil à quelqu'un** to give someone a piece of advice; **des conseils** advice; **suivre les conseils de quelqu'un** to follow someone's advice; **2** council.

conseiller[1], **conseillère** noun Masc., Fem. adviser.

conseiller[2] verb [1] **1** to advise; **conseiller à quelqu'un de faire** to advise somebody to do; **je te conseille de voir un médecin** I advise you to see a doctor; **2** to recommend; **pouvez-vous me conseiller un dentiste?** Can you recommend me a dentist?

consentement noun Masc. consent.

consentir verb [58] **consentir à quelque chose** to agree to something.

conséquence noun Fem. **1** consequence; **2 en conséquence** consequently.

conséquent adjective **par conséquent** consequently.

conservateur, **conservatrice** noun Masc., Fem. **1** conservative; **2** (museum) curator.

conservation noun Fem. **1** conservation; **2 lait longue conservation** long-life milk.

conserve noun Fem. **1 les conserves** canned food; **2 en conserve** canned; **des légumes e conserve** canned vegetables.

conserver verb [1] **1** to keep; **je t'ai conservé une place** I've kept you a seat; **'à conserver au frais'** 'keep in a cool place'; **2 se conserver** to keep; **ce fromage se conserve bien** this cheese keeps well.

considérable adjective considerable; **un pourcentage considérable des étudiants** a considerable percentage of the students.

considérablement adverb considerably.

considération noun Fem. consideration.

considérer verb [24] to consider.

consigne noun Fem. **1** left luggage office; **2** deposit (*on a returnable* *bottle*); **3** instructions; **consignes à suivre en cas d'incendie** fire regulations.

consistant *adjective* substantial; **un repas consistant** a substantial meal.

consister *verb* [1] **consister en** to consist of, to consist in.

consommateur, **consommatrice** *noun Masc., Fem.* **1** consumer; **2** customer (*in a cafe*).

consommation *noun Fem.* **1** consumption (*of fuel, electricity, gas*); **2** drink.

consommer *verb* [1] **1** to use (*fuel*); **2** to have a drink (*in a cafe*).

consonne *noun Fem.* consonant.

conspiration *noun Fem.* conspiracy.

conspirer *verb* [1] to conspire, to plot.

constamment *adverb* constantly.

constant *adjective* constant.

constater *verb* [1] to notice.

constipé *adjective* constipated.

construction *noun Fem.* construction, building.

construire *verb* [26] to build; **construire une maison** to build a house; **faire construire une maison** to have a house built.

consul *noun Masc.* consul.

consulat *noun Masc.* consulate.

consultation *noun Fem.* **1** consultation; **2** (doctor's) surgery hours.

consulter *verb* [1] **1** to consult; **2** to hold surgery.

contact *noun Masc.* contact; **prendre contact avec quelqu'un** to contact somebody.

contacter *verb* [1] to contact.

contagieux (*Fem.* **contagieuse**) *adjective* infectious.

contamination *noun Fem.* contamination.

contaminer *verb* [1] to contaminate.

conte *noun Masc.* tale, story; **un conte de fées** a fairy tale.

contempler *verb* [1] to look at, to contemplate.

contemporain, **contemporaine** *noun Masc., Fem., adjective* contemporary.

contenant *noun Masc.* container.

conteneur *noun Masc.* container.

contenir *verb* [77] to contain; **'ne contient pas de sucre'** 'does not contain sugar'.

content *adjective* pleased, glad, happy; **être content de quelque chose** to be pleased with something; **elle est très contente de son nouveau travail** she's very pleased with her new job; **je suis content de te voir** I'm pleased to see you.

contenter *verb* [1] **1** to satisfy; **2 se contenter de faire** to content oneself with doing.

contenu *noun Masc.* contents.

contesté *adjective* controversial.

contester *verb* [1] to dispute, to challenge, to question.

a
b
c
d
e
f
g
h
i
j
k
l
m
n
o
p
q
r
s
t
u
v
w
x
y
z

a **contexte** noun Masc. context.

b **continent** noun Masc. continent.

c **continu** adjective continuous.

continuation noun Fem. continuation.

d

e **continuer** verb [1] to continue, to go on (with); **continue!** go on!; **elle a continué son histoire** she went on with her story; **continuer à faire, continuer de faire** to go on doing; **elle a continué à parler** she went on talking.

f

g

h

i **contour** noun Masc. outline, contour.

j **contourner** verb [1] to go round.

k **contraceptif** noun Masc. contraceptive.

l **contraception** noun Fem. contraception.

m

n **contractuel, contractuelle** noun Masc., Fem. traffic warden.

o **contradiction** noun Fem. contradiction.

p

q **contradictoire** adjective contradictory.

contraindre verb [31] to force.

r

s **contraire** noun Masc. **1 le contraire** the opposite; **c'est le contraire de ce que je pensais** it's the opposite of what I thought; **2 au contraire** on the contrary. **contraire** adjective opposite.

t

u

v

w **contrairement** adverb **contrairement à** contrary to, unlike; **contrairement à ce qu'il nous a dit** contrary to what he told us.

x

y

z **contrariant** adjective annoying.

contrarier verb [1] **1** to upset; **2** annoy.

contraste noun Masc. contrast.

contraster verb [1] to contrast.

contrat noun Masc. contract.

contravention noun Fem. **1** parking ticket; **2** speeding ticket

contre preposition **1** against; **contre le mur** against the wall; **2 être contre quelque chose** to b against something; **je suis plutôt contre** on the whole, I'm against it **3 jouer contre quelqu'un** to play against somebody; **4** versus; **5 échanger quelque chose contr** to exchange something for (something else); **6 par contre** on th other hand; ★ **le pour et le contre** the pros and cons.

contrebande noun Fem. **1** smuggling; **2** smuggled goods.

contrebasse noun Fem. double bass.

contredire verb [47] to contradic

contrefaçon noun Fem. **1** forgery **méfiez-vous des contrefaçons** beware of forgeries; **2** forged signature; **3** counterfeit banknote.

contremaître noun Masc. forema

contremaîtresse noun Fem. supervisor.

contreplaqué noun Masc. plywood.

contribuable noun Masc. & Fem. taxpayer.

contribuer verb [1] **contribuer à** to contribute to.

contribution *noun Fem.* contribution.

contrôle *noun Masc.* **1** control; **2** class test (*at school*); **j'ai un contrôle de français cet après-midi** I've got a French test this afternoon; **3 contrôle de police** police check; **4 contrôle des passeports** passport control; **contrôle des billets** ticket inspection.

contrôle continu *noun Masc.* continuous assessment.

contrôle des naissances *noun Masc.* birth control.

contrôler *verb* [1] **1** to check; **2** to control.

contrôleur, contrôleuse *noun Masc., Fem.* ticket inspector.

contrôleur aérien, contrôleuse aérienne *noun Masc., Fem.* air traffic controller.

controversé *adjective* controversial; **une décision controversée** a controversial decision.

convaincant *adjective* convincing.

convaincre *verb* [79] **1** to convince; **je ne suis pas convaincu** I'm not convinced; **2** to persuade; **je l'ai convaincu d'acheter un ordinateur** I persuaded him to buy a computer.

convenable *adjective* **1** suitable; **2** decent.

convenir *verb* [81] **1 convenir à** to suit, to be suitable for; **est-ce que dix heures te convient?** does ten

o'clock suit you?; **2 convenir de faire** to agree to do.

convention *noun Fem.* **1** agreement; **2** convention.

conversation *noun Fem.* conversation.

convertir *verb* [2] to convert.

conviction *noun Fem.* conviction.

convive *noun Masc. & Fem.* guest.

convivial (*Masc. plural* conviviaux) *adjective* **1** friendly; **une atmosphère conviviale** a friendly atmosphere; **2** user-friendly.

convoi *noun Masc.* **1** convoy; **2 'convoi exceptionnel'** 'dangerous load'.

convoquer *verb* [1] **1** to invite (*to a meeting*); **2** to summon.

coopératif (*Fem.* coopérative) *adjective* cooperative.

coopération *noun Fem.* cooperation.

coopérative *noun Fem.* cooperative.

coopérer *verb* [24] to cooperate.

coordonnées *plural noun Fem.* address and telephone number.

coordonner *verb* [1] to coordinate.

copain *noun Masc.* **1** friend, mate (*male*); **je sors avec les copains** I'm going out with my mates; **2** boyfriend; **elle est partie en vacances avec son copain** she's gone on holiday with her boyfriend.

copie *noun Fem.* **1** copy; **2** paper (*on which an exam or class exercise has been written*); **j'ai un tas de copies**

à corriger ce soir I've got a pile of marking to do this evening.

copier *verb* [1] to copy.

copier-coller *verb* [1] to cut and, paste; **copiez-collez le tableau** cut and paste the table.

copieux (*Fem.* **copieuse**) *adjective* hearty; **un petit déjeuner copieux** a hearty breakfast.

copine *noun Fem.* **1** friend, mate (*female*); **je sors avec les copines** I'm going out with my mates; **2** girlfriend; **il est parti en vacances avec sa copine** he's gone on holiday with his girlfriend.

coq *noun Masc.* cockerel.

coque *noun Fem.* **1** hull (*of a boat*); **2** shell (*of a nut*); **3 un œuf à la coque** a soft-boiled egg.

coquelicot *noun Masc.* poppy.

coqueluche *noun Fem.* whooping-cough.

coquet (*Fem.* **coquette**) *adjective* **1** flirtatious; **2** pretty.

coquetier *noun Masc.* eggcup.

coquillage *noun Masc.* **1** shellfish; **2** seashell.

coquille *noun Fem.* **1** shell; **2** misprint.

coquille Saint-Jacques *noun Fem.* scallop.

coquin *adjective* cheeky, naughty.

cor *noun Masc.* horn (*musical instrument*).

corail (*plural* **coraux**) *noun Masc.* coral.

Coran *noun Masc.* **le Coran** the Koran.

corbeau *noun Masc.* crow.

corbeille *noun Fem.* basket; **une corbeille à papier** a wastepaper basket; **une corbeille à linge** a linen basket.

corbillard *noun Masc.* hearse.

corde *noun Fem.* **1** rope; **2** string (*o a racket, a bow, or an instrument such as a guitar or violin*);
★ **pleuvoir des cordes** to be pouring down (*literally: to be raining ropes*).

corde à linge *noun Fem.* clothes line.

corde à sauter *noun Fem.* skipping rope.

corde d'attache *noun Fem.* guy rope.

cordial (*Masc. plural* **cordiaux**) *adjective* warm, cordial.

cordialement *adverb* **1** warmly **2 cordialement à vous** Yours sincerely.

cordonnerie *noun Fem.* shoe repairer's.

cordonnier *noun Masc.* shoe repairer.

corne *noun Fem.* horn.

cornemuse *noun Fem.* bagpipes; **jouer de la cornemuse** to play the bagpipes.

cornet *noun Masc.* **1 un cornet de glace** an ice cream cone; **2 un cornet de frites** a bag of chips (*in fact sold in a cardboard cornet*).

corniche *noun Fem.* **1** ledge; **2** cornice; **3 (route de) corniche** coastal road.

cornichon *noun Masc.* gherkin.

70

ornouailles *noun Fem.* Cornwall.

orps *noun Masc.* body.

orrect *adjective* **1** correct; **2** reasonable, fine; **à un prix correct** at a reasonable price; **le repas était tout à fait correct** the meal was absolutely fine.

orrectement *adverb* **1** correctly; **est-ce que vous avez rempli le formulaire correctement?** have you filled in the form correctly?; **2** properly; **3** reasonably well.

orrecteur orthographique *noun Masc.* spell checker.

orrection *noun Fem.* correction.

orrespondance *noun Fem.* **1** letters, correspondence; **2 acheter quelque chose par correspondance** to buy something by mail order; **3** connection (*a train or flight*); **j'ai raté ma correspondance** I missed my connection; **un vol en correspondance** a connecting flight.

orrespondant, correspondante *noun Masc., Fem.* pen friend.

orrespondre *verb* [3] to correspond.

orrida *noun Fem.* bullfight.

orriger *verb* [52] **1** to correct; **2** to mark; **elle est en train de corriger ses copies** she's doing her marking.

orsage *noun Masc.* **1** blouse; **2** bodice.

corse *adjective* Corsican.

Corse[1] *noun Fem.* Corsica.

Corse[2] *noun Masc. & Fem.* Corsican (*person*).

corsé *adjective* full-bodied, strong.

corvée *noun Fem.* chore.

cosmétiques *plural noun Masc.* cosmetics.

costaud *adjective* strong, sturdy.

costume *noun Masc.* **1** suit; **2** costume.

côte *noun Fem.* **1** coast; **2** hill; **3** rib; **4** chop; **une côte d'agneau** a lamb chop.

côté *noun Masc.* **1** side; **de l'autre côté (de)** on the other side (of); **de l'autre côté de la rue** on the other side of the street; **2 d'un autre côté** on the other hand; **3 à côté** nearby; **mon frère habite à côté** my brother lives nearby; **4 à côté de** next to, beside; **elle était assise à côté de moi** she was sitting next to me.

Côte d'Azur *noun Fem.* French Riviera.

côtelette *noun Fem.* chop; **une côtelette de porc** a pork chop.

cotisation *noun Fem.* **1** subscription; **2** contribution.

coton *noun Masc.* **1** cotton; **un pull en coton** a cotton jumper; **2** sewing cotton; **3** cotton wool.

cou *noun Masc.* neck.

couchage *noun Masc.* **un sac de couchage** a sleeping bag.

couchant *adjective* **le soleil couchant** the setting sun; **au soleil couchant** at sunset.

a
b
c
d
e
f
g
h
i
j
k
l
m
n
o
p
q
r
s
t
u
v
w
x
y
z

a
b
c
d
e
f
g
h
i
j
k
l
m
n
o
p
q
r
s
t
u
v
w
x
y
z

couche noun Fem. **1** layer; **2** coat (of paint); **3** nappy.

couche d'ozone noun Fem. ozone layer.

coucher verb [1] **1** to sleep; **tu peux coucher chez Sophie** you can sleep at Sophie's house; **2 se coucher** to go to bed; **elle se couche à dix heures** she goes to bed at ten o'clock; **se coucher avec quelqu'un** to sleep with someone; **3 coucher un enfant** to put a child to bed.

coucher de soleil noun Masc. sunset; **un coucher de soleil magnifique** a magnificent sunset.

coucou noun Masc. **1** cuckoo; **2** cowslip.

coude noun Masc. elbow.

coudre verb [28] to sew; **coudre un bouton** to sew on a button.

couette noun Fem. duvet, continental quilt.

couler verb [1] **1** to flow; **2 avoir le nez qui coule** to have a runny nose; **3 faire couler un bain** to run a bath; **4** to sink.

couleur noun Fem. colour; **de quelle couleur est ta voiture?** what colour is your car?

couleuvre noun Fem. grass snake.

coulisses plural noun Fem. wings (in a theatre).

couloir noun Masc. corridor.

couloir d'autobus noun Masc. bus lane.

coup noun Masc. blow; **il a reçu un coup à l'estomac** he was hit in the stomach; ★ **boire un coup** (informal) to have a drink; ★ **donner un coup de balai** to sweep the floor; ★ **un coup de peinture** a lick of paint; ★ **sur le coup** at first; ★ **tenir le coup** to last out; ★ **tout d'un coup** all of a sudden.

coupable noun Masc. & Fem. culprit; **coupable** adjective guilty.

coup d'œil noun Masc. glance; **jeter un coup d'œil à quelque chose** to have a quick look at something.

coup de chance noun Masc. stroke of luck.

coup de feu noun Masc. (gun)shot.

coup de main noun Masc. **donner un coup de main à quelqu'un** to give somebody a hand.

coup de pied noun Masc. kick.

coup de poing noun Masc. punch.

coup de soleil noun Masc. **attraper un coup de soleil** to get sunburnt.

coup de téléphone noun Masc. phone call.

coup de tonnerre noun Masc. clap of thunder.

coup de vent noun Masc. gust of wind.

coupe noun Fem. **1** cup (for sports); **la Coupe du Monde** the World Cup; **2** haircut; **3** fruit dish.

couper verb [1] **1** to cut; **se faire couper les cheveux** to have your hair cut; **2 se couper** to cut yourself; **se couper le doigt** to cut your finger; **3** to cut off, to turn off (gas, electricity); **4 excuse-moi, je**

t'ai coupé la parole sorry, I interrupted you.

coup franc *noun Masc.* free kick.

couple *noun Masc.* couple.

couplet *noun Masc.* **1** verse (*of song*); **2** couplet.

coupon *noun Masc.* **1** remnant (*of fabric*); **2** coupon.

coupure *noun Fem.* cut; **une coupure de courant** a power cut.

cour *noun Fem.* **1** school playground; **2** inner courtyard (*in an apartment block or hotel*); **3** court (*of a king or queen*); **4** law court.

courage *noun Masc.* **1** courage, bravery; **2** energy; **avoir le courage de faire** to have the energy to do; **3 bon courage!** good luck!

courageux (*Fem.* **courageuse**) *adjective* brave.

couramment *adverb* fluently.

courant *noun Masc.* **1 être au courant de quelque chose** to know about something; **est-ce que ta sœur est au courant?** does your sister know?; **je te tiens au courant** I'll let you know what happens; **2** current; **3** electricity; **couper le courant** to cut off (*or* turn off) the electricity; **une panne de courant** a power cut.
courant *adjective* **1** common; **2** usual; **3** current.

courant d'air *noun Masc.* draught.

courbe *noun Fem.* curve.

courber *verb* [1] to bend.

coureur, coureuse *noun Masc., Fem.* runner.

courge *noun Fem.* (vegetable) marrow.

courgette *noun Fem.* courgette.

courir *verb* [29] **1** to run; **traverser la rue en courant** to run across the street; **2 courir un risque** to run a risk.

couronne *noun Fem.* crown.

courrier *noun Masc.* mail, post.

courrier électronique *noun Masc.* electronic mail, email.

cours *noun Masc.* **1** class, lesson; **le cours de français** the French lesson; **suivre des cours d'espagnol** to go to Spanish classes; **2** course (*of events*); **au cours de** in the course of.

course *noun Fem.* **1** race; **2** running; **3 les courses** shopping; **faire des courses** to do some shopping; **je fais mes courses à midi** I do my shopping at lunchtime.

courses hippiques *plural noun Fem.* horse racing.

court *adjective* short.

court-circuit *noun Masc.* short-circuit.

court de tennis *noun Masc.* tennis court.

couru *verb* SEE **courir**.

cousin, cousine *noun Masc., Fem.* cousin; **mon cousin germain** my first cousin.

coussin *noun Masc.* cushion.

coût *noun Masc.* cost; **le coût de la vie** the cost of living.

a
b
c
d
e
f
g
h
i
j
k
l
m
n
o
p
q
r
s
t
u
v
w
x
y
z

73

couteau (*plural* **couteaux**) *noun* Masc. knife; **un couteau à pain** a bread knife.

coûter *verb* [1] to cost; **ça coûte combien?** how much is it?; **ça coûte dix euros** it's ten euros; **coûter cher** to be expensive; **est-ce que ça t'a coûté cher?** was it expensive?

coutume *noun* Fem. custom.

couture *noun* Fem. **1** sewing, dressmaking; **faire de la couture** to sew; **2** seam.

couturier *noun* Masc. fashion designer.

couturière *noun* Fem. dressmaker.

couvent *noun* Masc. convent.

couvercle *noun* Masc. **1** lid; **2** screwtop.

couvert *noun* Masc. place setting; **les couverts** the cutlery; **mettre les couverts** to set the table.
couvert *adjective* **1** covered; **un marché couvert** a covered market; **2 couvert de** covered with; **3** overcast, cloudy.

couverture *noun* Fem. **1** blanket; **2** cover (*of a book*).

couvre-lit *noun* Masc. bedspread.

couvrir *verb* [30] **1** to cover; **2 se couvrir** to cloud over; **ça s'est couvert dans l'après-midi** it clouded over in the afternoon.

crabe *noun* Masc. crab.

cracher *verb* [1] to spit.

crachin *noun* Masc. drizzle.

craie *noun* Fem. chalk.

craindre *verb* [31] to be afraid of.

crainte *noun* Fem. fear.

crampe *noun* Fem. cramp.

crâne *noun* Masc. skull; **avoir mal au crâne** (*informal*) to have a headache.

crâner *verb* [1] (*informal*) to show off.

crapaud *noun* Masc. toad.

craquement *noun* Masc. creak.

craquer *verb* [1] **1** to split; **2** to creak; **3** (*informal*) to crack up; ★ **j'ai craqué** I couldn't resist it!

crasse *noun* Fem. filth.

cravate *noun* Fem. tie.

crawl *noun* Masc. crawl (*in swimming*); **nager le crawl** to swim crawl.

crayon *noun* Masc. pencil.

créatif (Fem. **créative**) *adjective* creative.

création *noun* Fem. creation.

créativité *noun* Fem. creativity.

crèche *noun* Fem. **1** crèche, day nursery; **2** nativity scene (*as a Christmas decoration*).

crédit *noun* Masc. **1** credit; **2** funding.

crédit immobilier *noun* Masc. mortgage.

créer *verb* [32] to create.

crémaillère *noun* Fem. chimney hook (*used in olden times to hang a pot for cooking over the fire*); ★ **pendre la crémaillère** to have a house-warming party (*literally: to hang the chimney hook*).

crème *noun* Fem., *adjective* cream.

crème anglaise noun Fem. custard.

crème Chantilly noun Fem. whipped cream.

crémerie noun Fem. cheese shop.

crémeux (Fem. **crémeuse**) adjective creamy.

crêpe noun Fem. pancake.

crépon noun Masc. crepe paper.

crépuscule noun Masc. twilight.

cresson noun Masc. watercress.

creuser verb [1] **1** to dig; **2** to hollow out; ★ **se creuser la cervelle** (informal) to rack your brains.

creux noun Masc. hollow.

creux adjective (Fem. **creuse**) **1** hollow; **2 une assiette creuse** a soup plate.

crevaison noun Fem. puncture.

crevé adjective **1** burst; **2** (informal) knackered.

crever verb [50] **1** to burst; **un pneu crevé** a burst tyre, a puncture; **2** (informal) to die; **je crève de faim!** I'm starving!

crevette noun Fem. prawn.

cri noun Masc. cry, shout.

criard adjective garish.

cric noun Masc. (car) jack.

cricket noun Masc. cricket; **jouer au cricket** to play cricket.

crier verb [1] **1** to shout; **2** to scream.

crime noun Masc. crime.

criminel, criminelle noun Masc., Fem., adjective criminal.

crinière noun Fem. mane.

criquet noun Masc. grasshopper.

crise noun Fem. **1** crisis; **2** attack (of an illness).

crise cardiaque noun Fem. heart attack.

cristal (plural **cristaux**) noun Masc. crystal.

critère noun Masc. criterion.

critique[1] noun Masc. critic.

critique[2] noun Fem. **1** criticism; **les critiques** criticism; **2** review (of a film, book, etc).

critique[3] adjective critical.

critiquer verb [1] to criticize.

Croatie noun Fem. Croatia.

croche-pied noun Masc. **faire un croche-pied à quelqu'un** (informal) to trip somebody up.

crochet noun Masc. **1** hook; **2** detour; **3** crochet.

crocodile noun Masc. crocodile.

croire verb [33] **1 croire que** to think that; **je crois qu'il est parti** I think he's left; **tu crois que c'est trop tard?** do you think it's too late?; **je ne crois pas** I don't think so; **2** to believe; **je n'arrive pas à le croire** I can't believe it; **3 croire à** to believe in; **4 je n'en croyais pas mes yeux!** I couldn't believe my eyes!

croiser verb [1] **1** to cross; **croiser les jambes** to cross your legs; **croiser les bras** to fold your arms; **2 croiser quelqu'un** to bump into somebody (meet by chance); **j'ai croisé Odile devant la banque** I bumped into Odile outside the bank.

croisière noun Fem. cruise.

croissance noun Fem. growth.

croissant noun Masc. croissant.

a
b
c
d
e
f
g
h
i
j
k
l
m
n
o
p
q
r
s
t
u
v
w
x
y
z

croître *verb* [34] to grow.

croix *noun Fem.* cross.

Croix-Rouge *noun Fem.* Red Cross.

croquant *adjective* crunchy.

croque-monsieur *noun Masc.* toasted ham sandwich with cheese sauce on top.

croque-mort *noun* (*informal*) *Masc.* undertaker.

croquer *verb* [1] to munch.

croquis *noun Masc.* sketch.

crottes *plural noun Fem.* droppings; **des crottes de chien** dog dirt.

croustillant *adjective* crispy.

croûte *noun Fem.* **1** crust; **2** rind (*of cheese*); **3** scab.

croûton *noun Masc.* crouton.

croyance *noun Fem.* belief.

cru[1] *verb* SEE **croire**.

cru[2] *adjective* raw, uncooked.

cruauté *noun Fem.* cruelty; **ils ont été traités avec beaucoup de cruauté** they were treated with great cruelty.

cruche *noun Fem.* (large) jug.

crudités *plural noun Fem.* raw vegetables (*served with dips as a starter*).

cruel (Fem. **cruelle**) *adjective* cruel.

crustacé *noun Masc.* shellfish.

crypte *noun Fem.* crypt.

Cuba *noun Fem.* Cuba.

cubain *adjective Fem.* Cuban.

Cubain, **Cubaine** *noun Masc., Fem.* Cuban.

cube *noun Masc.* cube.
cube *adjective* cubic; **un mètre cube** a cubic metre.

cueillir *verb* [35] to pick (*fruit or flowers*).

cuiller *noun Fem.* **1** spoon; **2** spoonful.

cuillère *noun Fem.* = **cuiller**.

cuillerée *noun Fem.* spoonful.

cuir *noun Masc.* leather; **des chaussures en cuir** leather shoes

cuir chevelu *noun Masc.* scalp.

cuire *verb* [36] to cook.

cuisine *noun Fem.* **1** kitchen; **2** cooking; **faire la cuisine** to cook to do the cooking.

cuisiner *verb* [1] to cook.

cuisinier, **cuisinière**[1] *noun Masc., Fem.* cook.

cuisinière[2] *noun Fem.* cooker; **une cuisinière à gaz** a gas cooker; **une cuisinière à électrique** an electri cooker.

cuisse *noun Fem.* thigh.

cuisse de poulet *noun Fem.* chicken leg, chicken thigh.

cuit *adjective* cooked; **bien cuit** we done (*meat*).

cuivre *noun Masc.* copper.

cuivre jaune *noun Masc.* brass; **u chandelier en cuivre jaune** a bras candlestick.

culot *noun Masc.* (*informal*) cheek; **quel culot!** what a cheek!, what a nerve!; **elle a du culot!** she's got a nerve!

culotte *noun Fem.* **une (petite) culotte** knickers, panties.

ulpabilité *noun Fem.* guilt.

ultivateur, **cultivatrice** *noun Masc., Fem.* farmer.

ultiver *verb* [1] **1** to grow; **2** to cultivate.

ulture *noun Fem.* **1** farming; **2** growing; **de culture biologique** organically produced; **3** crop; **4** culture.

ulturel (*Fem.* **culturelle**) *adjective* cultural.

ulturisme *noun Masc.* body-building.

ure *noun Fem.* course of treatment.

uré *noun Masc.* parish priest.

ure-dents *noun Masc.* toothpick.

urer *verb* [1] **se curer les ongles** to clean your nails; **se curer les dents** to pick your teeth.

urieux (*Fem.* **curieuse**) *adjective* **1** strange, odd; **2** curious, inquisitive.

uriosité *noun Fem.* curiosity.

urseur *noun Masc.* cursor (*on a computer screen*).

uve *noun Fem.* vat, tank.

uvette *noun Fem.* bowl; **la cuvette des wc** the lavatory bowl.

ybercafé *noun Masc.* Internet café; **où est-ce qu'il y a un cybercafé?** where is there an Internet café?

ybernaute *noun Masc. & Fem.* web surfer, cybernaut.

yclable *adjective* **une piste cyclable** a cycle track.

ycle *noun Masc.* cycle.

yclisme *noun Masc.* cycling.

cycliste *noun Masc. & Fem.* cyclist.

cyclone *noun Masc.* hurricane.

cygne *noun Masc.* swan.

cylindre *noun Masc.* **1** cylinder; **2** roller.

cynique *adjective* cynical.

cyprès *noun Masc.* cypress (tree).

Dd

d' *preposition* SEE **de**.

dactylo *noun Masc. & Fem.* typist.

dactylographie *noun Fem.* typing.

daigner *verb* [1] to deign.

daim *noun Masc.* **1** suede; **des chaussures en daim** suede shoes; **2** fallow deer.

dalle *noun Fem.* paving slab.

daltonien (*Fem.* **daltonienne**) *adjective* colour-blind.

dame *noun Fem.* **1** lady; **2** queen (*in cards or chess*).

dames *plural noun Fem.* draughts; **jouer aux dames** to play draughts.

dancing *noun Masc.* dance hall.

Danemark *noun Masc.* Denmark; **au Danemark** to (*or* in) Denmark.

danger *noun Masc.* danger.

dangereux (*Fem.* **dangereuse**) *adjective* dangerous.

danois *noun Masc.* Danish (*language*).
danois *adjective* Danish.

Danois, , **Danoise** *noun Masc., Fem.* Danish.

a
b
c
d
e
f
g
h
i
j
k
l
m
n
o
p
q
r
s
t
u
v
w
x
y
z

dans *preposition* **1** in; **elle est dans la cuisine** she's in the kitchen; **2** into; **va dans la cuisine** go into the kitchen; **3 dans trois mois** in three months' time; **4 boire dans un verre** to drink out of a glass.

danse *noun Fem.* **1** dance; **2** dancing; **faire de la danse** to go to dancing classes.

danse classique *noun Fem.* ballet.

danser *verb* [1] to dance.

danseur, **danseuse** *noun Masc., Fem.* dancer.

d'après *preposition* **1** according to; **d'après le ministre** according to the minister; **2** based on; **un film d'après le roman de** a film based on the novel by; **3** in the style of; **un tableau d'après Degas** a painting in the style of Degas.

date *noun Fem.* date.

date de naissance *noun Fem.* date of birth.

date limite *noun Fem.* closing date.

date limite de vente *noun Fem.* sell-by date.

datte *noun Fem.* date (*fruit*).

dauphin *noun Masc.* dolphin.

davantage *adverb* **1** more; **2** longer.

de, **d'** (*before a vowel or a silent 'h'*) (*note that 'de + le' becomes 'du' and 'de + les' becomes 'des'*).
de *preposition* **1** of; **une boîte d'allumettes** a box of matches; **le pied de la table** the leg of the table, the table leg; **2 le père de Marie** Marie's father; **la maison de tes parents** your parents' house; **3** from; **elle vient de Paris** she comes from Paris; **elle rentre du bureau à six heures** she comes home from the office at six o'clock; **4** made from; **une table de bois** a wooden table; **5** by; **le prix a augmenté de vingt euros** the price has gone up (by) twenty euros.
de *determiner* **du café** (some) coffee; **veux-tu du café?** would you like (some) coffee?; **je n'ai pas de café** I don't have any coffee; **nous avons des pommes et des oranges** we have apples and oranges; **veux-tu de l'eau?** would you like some water?

dé *noun Masc.* **1** dice; **2 un dé à coudre** a thimble.

dealer *noun Masc.* drug pusher.

déballer *verb* [1] to unpack.

débardeur *noun Masc.* camisole top, vest-style top.

débarquer *verb* [1] **1** to disembark; **2** to land; **3** (*informal*) to turn up; **elle a débarqué chez moi** she turned up at my place.

débarras *noun Masc.* junk room; ★ **bon débarras!** good riddance!

débarrasser *verb* [1] **1** to clear out (*a room*); **débarrasser la table** to clear the table; **2 se débarrasser de quelque chose** to get rid of something; **je me suis débarrassé de tous ces vieux bouquins** I got rid of all those old books.

débat *noun Masc.* debate.

débattre verb [21] to discuss, to negotiate; **'prix à débattre'** 'price negotiable'.

débile adjective (informal) stupid, crazy; **tu es débile ou quoi?** are you stupid or something?; **c'est complètement débile!** that's completely crazy!

déblayer verb [59] to clear.

débordé adjective **être débordé** to be up to your eyes in work.

débordement noun Masc. **1** overflowing; **2** flood.

déborder verb [1] to overflow.

débouché noun Masc. job prospect; **il y a peu de/beaucoup de débouchés pour les jeunes diplômés** there are few/many openings for recent graduates.

déboucher verb [1] **1** to uncork (a bottle); **2** to unblock (a drain or pipe); **3 déboucher sur** to lead into.

déboussoler verb [1] (informal) to confuse.

debout adverb **1** standing; **rester debout** to remain standing; **je suis resté debout toute la journée** I've been on my feet all day; **se mettre debout** to stand up; **tout le monde s'est mis debout** everybody stood up; **2** upright; **mettre quelque chose debout** to stand something upright; **3** up (out of bed); **je suis debout à six heures tous les jours** I'm up at six every day; ★ **ça ne tient pas debout** it doesn't make any sense (literally: it doesn't stand upright).

déboutonner verb [1] to unbutton.

débrancher verb [1] **1** to unplug (an iron, a television set, etc); **2** to disconnect (the electricity, gas, water, telephone).

débris noun Masc. **1** fragment; **2** piece of wreckage.

débrouiller verb [1] **se débrouiller** to manage; **je peux me débrouiller tout seul** I can manage by myself; **débrouille-toi!** get on with it!

début noun Masc. beginning, start; **le début de** the beginning of; **au début** at the beginning, to start with; **on commencera début mars** we'll start at the beginning of March; **en début d'après-midi** in the early afternoon.

débutant, **débutante** noun Masc., Fem. beginner.

débuter verb [1] to begin, to start.

décaféiné adjective decaffeinated.

décalage noun Masc. **1** gap; **2** discrepancy.

décalage horaire noun Masc. time difference (between time zones); **il y a une heure de décalage horaire entre la France et la Grande-Bretagne** there's an hour's time difference between France and Britain.

décaler verb [1] to move (forward or back).

décapiter verb [1] to behead.

décapotable adjective **une voiture décapotable** a convertible (car).

a
b
c
d
e
f
g
h
i
j
k
l
m
n
o
p
q
r
s
t
u
v
w
x
y
z

décapsuleur noun Masc. (bottle) opener.

décéder verb [24] to die; **elle est décédée au mois de novembre** she died in November.

décembre noun Masc. December; **en décembre, au mois de décembre** in December.

décemment adverb decently.

décennie noun Fem. decade.

décent adjective decent.

déception noun Fem. disappointment.

décès noun Masc. death.

décevant adjective disappointing.

décevoir verb [66] to disappoint.

décharge noun Fem. (public) rubbish tip.

décharger verb [52] to unload.

déchets plural noun Masc. **1** waste; **les déchets nucléaires** nuclear waste; **2** rubbish.

déchiffrer verb [1] to decipher.

déchirant adjective heart-rending.

déchirer verb [1] **1** to tear; **j'ai déchiré mon pantalon** I've torn my trousers; **2** to tear up; **déchirer une enveloppe** to tear up an envelope; **3** to tear off; **déchirer une feuille** to tear off a sheet of paper; **4** to tear out; **déchirer une page** to tear out a page; **5 se déchirer** to tear, to rip.

décidé adjective determined.

décidément adverb really.

décider verb [1] **1** to decide; **décider de faire** to decide to do; **j'ai décidé de vendre mon vélo** I've

decided to sell my bike; **2 se décider** to make up your mind; **il faut qu'on se décide une fois pou toutes** we must make up our mind once and for all; **3 se décider à faire** to decide to do.

décimal (Masc. plural décimaux) adjective decimal.

décimale noun Fem. decimal.

décision noun Fem. decision.

déclaration noun Fem. **1** statement; **2** declaration.

déclarer verb [1] to declare.

déclencher verb [1] **1** to cause; **2** to set off; **déclencher l'alarme t** set off the alarm.

déclic noun Masc. click.

décliner verb [1] to decline.

décollage noun Masc. takeoff (of plane).

décollé adjective ★ **avoir les oreilles décollées** to have stickin out ears (literally: to have ears whic have come unstuck).

décoller verb [1] **1** to take off (of plane); **2 décoller quelque chose** to peel something off; **3 se décolle** to come unstuck, to peel off; **le papier peint est en train de se décoller** the wallpaper's peeling o

décolleté adjective low-cut.

décolorer verb [1] **se décolorer t** fade; **se faire décolorer les cheveux** to have your hair lightened.

décombres plural noun Masc. rubble.

décongeler verb [45] to defrost.

déconseillé *adjective* not recommended; **'déconseillé pour les enfants'** 'not recommended for children'.

déconseiller *verb* [1] **déconseiller à quelqu'un de faire** to advise somebody not to do; **nous lui avons déconseillé de voyager toute seule** we advised her not to travel alone.

décontracté *adjective* relaxed, laid-back; **mon patron est très décontracté** my boss is very laid-back.

décontracter *verb* [1] **se décontracter** to relax.

décor *noun Masc.* **1** decor; **2** setting.

décorateur, décoratrice *noun Masc., Fem.* interior designer.

décoratif (*Fem.* **décorative**) *adjective* **1** ornamental; **2** decorative.

décoration *noun Fem.* **1** decorating; **2** interior design.

décorer *verb* [1] to decorate.

découper *verb* [1] **1** to cut out; **découper un article dans un journal** to cut an article out of a newspaper; **2** to carve (*meat*); **c'est Marie-Laure qui va découper le poulet** Marie-Laure's going to carve the chicken.

décourageant *adjective* discouraging.

décourager *verb* [52] to discourage.

découvert *noun Masc.* overdraft.

découverte *noun Fem.* discovery.

découvrir *verb* [30] to discover.

décrire *verb* [38] to describe.

décrocher *verb* [1] **1** to lift the receiver (*of a telephone*); **'décrochez'** 'lift the receiver'; **il faut décrocher avant de composer le numéro** you have to lift the receiver before dialling; **2** to take down (*a picture, curtains, etc*).

déçu *adjective* disappointed; **nous sommes tous très déçus** we're all very disappointed.

dedans *adverb* inside **1** elle a ouvert la boîte mais il n'y avait rien dedans she opened the box but there was nothing in it; **2** là-dedans in there.

dédommager *verb* [52] to compensate.

déduction *noun Fem.* deduction.

déduire *verb* [26] **1** to deduce; **2** to deduct.

déesse *noun Fem.* goddess.

défaire *verb* [10] **1** to undo, to untie; **2** se défaire to come undone; **3** se défaire de to get rid of.

défaite *noun Fem.* defeat.

défaut *noun Masc.* **1** flaw, defect; **2** à défaut de for want of.

défavorisé *adjective* underprivileged; **les défavorisés** the underprivileged.

défectueux (*Fem.* **défectueuse**) *adjective* faulty; **une prise défectueuse** a faulty plug.

défendre *verb* [3] **1** to forbid; **2** to defend.

défendu *adjective* forbidden.

défense *noun* **1** défense de fumer no smoking; **2** defence;

a
b
c
d
e
f
g
h
i
j
k
l
m
n
o
p
q
r
s
t
u
v
w
x
y
z

3 protection; **la défense de l'environnement** the protection of the environment; **4** tusk (*of an elephant*).

défi *noun Masc.* challenge.

déficit *noun Masc.* deficit.

défigurer *verb* [1] to disfigure.

défilé *noun Masc.* **1** parade; **2** procession; **3** march.

défiler *verb* [1] **1** to parade; **2** to march; **3** to come and go.

définir *verb* [2] to define.

définitif (Fem. **définitive**) *adjective* final, definitive.

définition *noun Fem.* definition.

définitivement *adverb* **1** for good; **2** definitely.

défoncer *verb* [61] to smash in (*a door*).

déformer *verb* [1] **1** to bend out of shape; **2** to distort; **3** to stretch (*a garment or shoes*).

défouler *verb* [1] **1** se défouler to let off steam; **2** to unwind.

défunt *noun Masc.* **le défunt** the deceased.

dégagé *adjective* **1** clear; **2** casual.

dégager *verb* [52] **1** to clear; **2** to free (*a trapped person*).

dégâts *plural noun Masc.* damage.

dégel *noun Masc.* thaw.

dégeler *verb* [45] to thaw.

dégénérer *verb* [24] **1** to degenerate; **2** to go from bad to worse.

dégivrer *verb* [1] **1** to defrost; **2** to de-ice.

dégonfler *verb* [1] to let down (*a tyre, an airbed, etc*).

dégouliner *verb* [1] to trickle.

dégourdi *adjective* smart, bright; **un gamin dégourdi** a bright kid.

dégoût *noun Masc.* disgust.

dégoûtant *adjective* **1** filthy; **tes mains sont dégoûtantes** your hands are filthy; **2** disgusting.

dégoûté *adjective* disgusted.

dégoûter *verb* [1] **1** to disgust; **2** dégoûter quelqu'un de quelque chose to put somebody off something; **ça m'a dégoûté du poisson** that put me off fish.

dégrader *verb* [1] **1** to damage; **2** se dégrader to deteriorate.

dégraisser *verb* [1] to dryclean.

degré *noun Masc.* degree.

dégringoler *verb* [1] (*informal*) to tumble down.

déguisé *adjective* **1** in fancy dress, in disguise; **2** une soirée déguisée a fancy-dress party; **3** disguised.

déguiser *verb* [1] **1** to disguise; **2** se déguiser to dress up in fancy dress.

dégustation *noun Fem.* tasting; **'dégustation de glaces'** 'a fine selection of ice creams'.

déguster *verb* [1] **1** to savour, to enjoy; **2** to taste (*wine, cheese, etc*).

dehors *adverb* **1** outside; **je t'attends dehors** I'll wait for you outside; **j'ai passé toute la journée dehors** I've been outside all day; **2** en dehors de apart from; **en dehors de la salade, tout est prê**

everything's ready apart from the salad.

déjà *adverb* **1** already; **tu pars déjà?** are you leaving already?; **je t'ai déjà dit de ne pas faire ça!** I told you not to do that!; **2** before; **tu es déjà venu ici?** have you been here before?

déjeuner *noun Masc.* lunch; **petit déjeuner** breakfast.

déjeuner *verb* [1] **1** to have lunch; **nous déjeunons à une heure** we have lunch at one o'clock; **2** to have breakfast.

délabré *adjective* dilapidated.

délacer *verb* [61] to unlace.

délai *noun Masc.* period of time, waiting period.

délavé *adjective* **1** faded; **2** washed-out.

délecter *verb* [1] **se délecter à faire** to delight in doing.

délégué, déléguée *noun Masc., Fem.* **1** delegate; **2** representative.

délibéré *adjective* deliberate.

délibérer *verb* [24] to discuss.

délicat *adjective* **1** delicate; **2** tactful.

délice *noun Masc.* delight; **c'est un vrai délice!** it's absolutely delicious!

délicieux (*Fem.* **délicieuse**) *adjective* delicious.

délinquance *noun Fem.* **1** crime; **2** delinquency.

délinquant, délinquante *noun Masc., Fem.* offender.

délirant *adjective* (*informal*) crazy; **c'est complètement délirant!** it's completely crazy!

délire *noun Masc.* **1** (*informal*) madness; **2** frenzy.

délirer *verb* [1] (*informal*) to be crazy; **il délire!** he's crazy!

délit *noun Masc.* criminal offence.

délivrer *verb* [1] to free, to liberate.

déloyal (*Masc. plural* **déloyaux**) *adjective* disloyal.

deltaplane *noun Masc.* **1** hang-glider; **2 faire du deltaplane** to go hang-gliding.

déluge *noun Masc.* **1** downpour; **2 le Déluge** the Flood (*in the Bible*).

demain *adverb* tomorrow; **à demain!** see you tomorrow!; **après-demain** the day after tomorrow.

demande *noun Fem.* **1** request; **2** demand; **3** application; **faire une demande d'emploi** to apply for a job; **'demandes d'emplois'** 'situations wanted'; **4** claim; **faire une demande de remboursement auprès d'une compagnie d'assurance** to make a claim on insurance.

demandé *adjective* **très demandé** very much in demand, very popular.

demander *verb* [1] **1 demander quelque chose** to ask for something; **2 demander quelque chose à quelqu'un** to ask somebody (for) something; **demande à ton père!** ask your father!; **il m'a demandé ton adresse** he asked me for your address; **3 demander à quelqu'un de faire** to ask somebody to do; **elle m'a demandé de**

a
b
c
d
e
f
g
h
i
j
k
l
m
n
o
p
q
r
s
t
u
v
w
x
y
z

téléphoner she asked me to phone; **4 se demander** to wonder; **je me demande ce qu'elle est en train de faire** I wonder what she's doing.

demandeur d'emploi noun Masc. job-seeker.

démangeaison noun Fem. itch.

démanger verb [52] **ça me démange** it itches.

démanteler verb [45] to dismantle.

démaquillant noun Masc. make-up remover.

démaquiller verb [1] se **démaquiller** to remove your make-up.

démarche noun Fem. **1** walk; **2** step.

démarrer verb [1] **1** to start (of engine or car); **la voiture ne veut pas démarrer** the car won't start; **2** to drive off; **3** to start up, to start off; **le projet va démarrer en juin** the project will start up in June.

démarreur noun Masc. starter (in a car).

démêler verb [1] to untangle.

déménagement noun Masc. (house) move, removal.

déménager verb [52] **1** to move (house); **2** to move out; **nous déménageons la semaine prochaine** we're moving out next week; **3 déménager quelque chose** to move something.

déménageur noun Masc. removal man.

dément adjective crazy.

démentir verb [53] **1** to deny; **2** to refute.

démesuré adjective excessive.

demeure noun Fem. residence, mansion.

demeurer verb [1] to reside, to liv

demi[1] adjective **1** half; **trois et dem** three and a half; **elle a trois ans e demi** she's three and a half; **une heure et demie** an hour and a hal **2 une demi-pomme** half an apple; **une demi-bouteille** half a bottle; **3 à deux heures et demie** at half past two; **à trois heures et demie a** half past three.

demi[2] noun Masc. half (of beer).

demi-cercle noun Masc. semicircle.

demi-douzaine noun Fem. half dozen.

demie noun Fem. half-hour; **à la demie** on the half-hour.

demi-écrémé adjective semi-skimmed.

demi-finale noun Fem. semifinal

demi-frère noun Masc. half brother.

demi-heure noun Fem. **une dem heure** half an hour; **toutes les demi-heures** every half hour.

demi-journée noun Fem. half a day.

demi-litre noun Masc. half a litre.

demi-pension noun Fem. half board.

demi-sel adjective slightly salted

demi-sœur noun Fem. half sister

démission *noun Fem.* resignation; **donner sa démission** to resign.

démissionner *verb* [1] to resign.

demi-tarif *adjective* half-price.

demi-tour *noun Masc.* **faire demi-tour** to turn back.

démocrate *noun Masc. & Fem.* democrat.

démocrate *adjective* democratic.

démocratie *noun Fem.* democracy.

démocratique *adjective* democratic.

démodé *adjective* old-fashioned.

demoiselle *noun Fem.* young lady.

demoiselle d'honneur *noun Fem.* bridesmaid.

démolir *verb* [2] to demolish, to wreck.

démolition *noun Fem.* demolition.

démon *noun Masc.* demon.

démonstrateur, **démonstratrice** *noun Masc., Fem.* demonstrator (*for products*).

démonstratif (*Fem.* **démonstrative**) *adjective* demonstrative.

démonstration *noun Fem.* **1** demonstration (*of a product, appliance, etc*); **2** display.

démonter *verb* [1] to dismantle, to take apart.

démontrer *verb* [1] to demonstrate, to prove.

démoraliser *verb* [1] to demoralize.

démouler *verb* [1] to turn out (*a cake, mousse, etc, from a tin or mould*).

démuni *adjective* **1** poverty stricken; **2** penniless.

dénoncer *verb* [61] to denounce.

dénouer *verb* [1] to undo.

denrée *noun Fem.* foodstuff.

dense *adjective* dense.

densité *noun Fem.* density.

dent *noun Fem.* tooth; **avoir mal aux dents** to have toothache.

dentaire *adjective* dental.

dent de sagesse *noun Fem.* wisdom tooth.

dentelé *adjective* **1** jagged; **2** serrated; **3** perforated.

dentelle *noun Fem.* lace.

dentier *noun Masc.* denture, false teeth.

dentifrice *noun Masc.* toothpaste.

dentiste *noun Masc. & Fem.* dentist.

déodorant *noun Masc.* deodorant.

dépannage *noun Masc.* repair; **'dépannages'** 'emergency repairs'; **le service de dépannage** the breakdown service; **un véhicule de dépannage** a breakdown vehicle.

dépanner *verb* [1] **1** to fix, to repair; **2 dépanner quelqu'un** (*informal*) to help somebody out.

dépanneuse *noun Fem.* breakdown truck.

départ *noun Masc.* **1** departure; **je t'appellerai avant mon départ** I'll phone you before I leave; **elle m'a appelé avant son départ** she

a
b
c
d
e
f
g
h
i
j
k
l
m
n
o
p
q
r
s
t
u
v
w
x
y
z

a

phoned me before she left; **2 au départ** at first, to start with.

b

c

d

département noun Masc. department (As well as other sorts of department, this is a French numbered administrative area, rather like a county in Britain. The two numbers on the end of vehicle registrations in France show the number of the department where the car is registered).

e

f

g

dépassé adjective outdated, old-fashioned.

h

dépasser verb [1] **1** to overtake; **2** to exceed; **3 ça me dépasse!** it's beyond me!

i

j

k

dépêcher verb [50] **se dépêcher** to hurry up; **dépêche-toi!** hurry up!

l

m

dépendance noun Fem. outbuilding.

n

o

dépendre verb [3] **1 dépendre de** to depend on; **ça dépend de l'heure** it depends on the time; **ça dépend** it depends; **2** to be dependent on.

p

q

dépenser verb [1] to spend.

r

dépenses plural noun Fem. **1** expenses; **2** spending.

s

t

dépensier (Fem. **dépensière**) adjective extravagant.

u

v

dépilatoire adjective **une crème dépilatoire** a hair-removing cream.

w

dépistage noun Masc. screening.

x

dépit noun Masc. **en dépit de** in spite of.

y

z

déplacé adjective out of place.

déplacement noun Masc. trip; **le frais de déplacement** travel expenses.

déplacer verb [61] **1** to move; **2 se déplacer** to travel.

déplaire verb [62] **déplaire à quelqu'un** to be displeasing to somebody; **cela me déplaît** I don't like that.

déplaisant adjective unpleasant.

dépliant noun Masc. leaflet.

déplier verb [1] to unfold.

déporter verb [1] to deport.

déposer verb [1] **1** to put down; **2** to drop off; **il m'a déposé à la gare** he dropped me off at the station; **3 déposer un chèque** to pay in a cheque.

dépôt noun Masc. **1** warehouse; **2** depot; **3** deposit.

dépôt d'ordures noun Masc. rubbish tip.

dépoussiérer verb [24] to dust.

dépressif (Fem. **dépressive**) adjective depressive.

dépression noun Fem. depression; **une dépression nerveuse** a nervous breakdown.

déprimant adjective depressing.

déprimer verb [1] **1** to depress; **2** get depressed; **elle déprime en ce moment** she's depressed at the moment.

depuis preposition **1** since; **depuis vendredi** since Friday; **je suis à Paris depuis mardi** I've been in Paris since Tuesday; **j'habite à Londres depuis avril** I've been living in London since April; **2** for

elle habite à Londres depuis cinq ans she's lived in London for five years; **je le connais depuis longtemps** I've known him for a long time; **3 tu es là depuis combien de temps?** how long have you been here?; **tu le sais depuis combien de temps?** how long have you known?; **depuis quand es-tu à Paris?** how long have you been in Paris?; **4 depuis que** since; **depuis que ton frère est à Londres** since your brother's been in London.

depuis *adverb* since; **je ne l'ai pas revu depuis** I haven't seen him since.

député *noun Masc.* deputy (*the French equivalent of a member of Parliament*).

déraciner *verb* [1] to uproot.

déranger *verb* [52] to disturb; **'ne pas déranger'** 'do not disturb'; **excusez-moi de vous déranger** sorry to bother you ; **est-ce que cela vous dérange si j'ouvre la fenêtre?** do you mind if I open the window?; **cela ne me dérange pas du tout** I don't mind at all; **ça vous dérange de venir me chercher?** do you mind coming to pick me up?

déraper *verb* [1] **1** to skid; **2** to get out of control.

dérisoire *adjective* pathetic, trivial; **je l'ai acheté pour une somme dérisoire** I bought it for next to nothing.

dériveur *noun Masc.* sailing dinghy.

dermatologue *noun Masc. & Fem.* dermatologist.

dernier (*Fem.* **dernière**) *adjective* **1** last; **le dernier train part à minuit** the last train leaves at midnight; **jeudi dernier** last Thursday; **la semaine dernière** last week; **l'année dernière** last year; **2** latest; **leur dernier album** their latest album; **3 en dernier** last; **il est arrivé en dernier** he arrived last.

dernier cri *noun Masc.* latest fashion; **le dernier cri en matière d'équipement hifi** the latest in audio equipment.

dernièrement *adverb* recently.

dérouler *verb* [1] **1** to unroll, to unwind; **2 se dérouler** to take place; **ça s'est très bien déroulé** it went very well.

déroutant *adjective* puzzling.

derrière *noun Masc.* **1** back (*of an object or a house*); **2** bottom, backside.
derrière *preposition* behind; **derrière la porte** behind the door.
derrière *adverb* behind; **être derrière** to be in the back (*of the car*).

des *article* some, any SEE **de, un**.

dès *preposition* **1** from; **dès l'âge de cinq ans** from the age of five; **2 dès que** as soon as.

désagréable *adjective* unpleasant.

désarroi *noun Masc.* confusion.

désastre *noun Masc.* disaster.

désavantage *noun Masc.* disadvantage.

désavouer *verb* [1] **1** to deny; **2** to disown.

a
b
c
d
e
f
g
h
i
j
k
l
m
n
o
p
q
r
s
t
u
v
w
x
y
z

descendre *verb* [3] **1** to go down;
descendre les escaliers to go
down the stairs; **2** to come down; **je
descends dans trois secondes!**
I'll be down in a second!; **3** to get off
(*a train or bus*); **je descends à
Dijon** I'm getting off at Dijon; **4** to
get down; **pouvez-vous descendre
ma valise, s'il vous plaît?** could
you get my case down for me,
please?; **5** to take (*or* bring)
downstairs; **je vais descendre mes
bagages** I'm going to take my
luggage downstairs; **est-ce que tu
peux descendre une chaise de là-
haut?** could you bring a chair down
from upstairs?

descente *noun Fem.* descent.

descriptif (Fem. **descriptive**)
adjective descriptive.

description *noun Fem.*
description.

déséquilibrer *verb* [1]
déséquilibrer quelqu'un to throw
somebody off balance.

désert *noun Masc.* desert.
désert *adjective* deserted.

déserter *verb* [1] to desert.

désespéré *adjective* **1** desperate;
2 in despair; **3 une situation
désespérée** a hopeless situation.

désespérer *verb* [24] to despair,
to give up hope.

désespoir *noun Masc.* despair.

déshabiller *verb* [1] **1 se
déshabiller** to undress, to get
undressed; **2 déshabiller
quelqu'un** to undress somebody.

désherbant *noun Masc.*
weedkiller.

désherber *verb* [1] to weed.

déshérité *noun Masc.* **les
déshérités** the underprivileged.

déshériter *verb* [1] to disinherit.

déshydraté *adjective* dehydrate

désigner *verb* [1] **1** to point out;
2 to denote.

désinfectant *noun Masc.*
disinfectant.

désinfecter *verb* [1] to disinfect

désir *noun Masc.* **1** wish; **2** desire.

désirer *verb* [1] to want; **que
désirez-vous?** what would you lik

désobéir *verb* [2] **1** to be
disobedient; **2 désobéir à
quelqu'un** to disobey somebody.

désobéissant *adjective*
disobedient.

désobligeant *adjective*
unpleasant.

désodorisant *noun Masc.* air
freshener.

désolé *adjective* **être désolé** to b
sorry; **je suis désolé** I'm sorry;
désolé de te déranger sorry to
disturb you.

désopilant *adjective* hilarious.

désordonné *adjective* untidy.

désordre *noun Masc.* **1** untidines
mess; **être en désordre** to be in a
mess; **2** disorder.

désorganisé *adjective*
disorganized.

désorienté *adjective*
disorientated, confused.

désormais *adverb* **1** from now o
2 from then on.

esquels, desquelles
pronoun (= *de lesquels, de lesquelles*)
of which, of whom.

essécher *verb* [24] **1** to dry out;
2 se dessécher to dry out.

esserrer *verb* [1] to loosen.

essert *noun* Masc. dessert,
pudding.

esservir *verb* [58] **le train
dessert Vienne et Valence** the
train calls at Vienne and Valence.

essin *noun* Masc. **1** drawing; **un
cours de dessin** a drawing class;
2 un dessin a drawing; **3** design.

essin animé *noun* Masc.
(animated) cartoon.

essiner *verb* [1] to draw.

essin humoristique *noun*
Masc. cartoon.

essous *noun* Masc. **1** underside;
le dessous du pied the sole of the
foot; **2 les voisins du dessous** the
neighbours below; **3 les dessous**
underwear; **4 en dessous**
underneath; **5 en dessous de**
below.

essous *adverb* underneath.

essous-de-plat *noun* Masc.
table mat (*for dish*).

essus *noun* Masc. **1** top; **le dessus
du carton** the top of the box; **un
pantalon gris et un dessus rose**
grey trousers and a pink top; **2 les
voisins du dessus** the neighbours
above; **3 en dessus** above; **4 au
dessus de** above.

essus *adverb* on top; **quelqu'un a
écrit dessus** somebody's written on
it.

dessus-de-lit *noun* Masc.
bedspread.

destin *noun* Masc. **1** fate; **2** destiny.

destinataire *noun* Masc. & Fem.
addressee.

destination *noun* Fem.
destination; **le train à destination
de Nice** the train for Nice; **les
passagers à destination de Rome**
passengers travelling to Rome.

destiner *verb* [1] **1 destiner
quelque chose à** to design
something for; **2 être destiné à** to
be intended for; **3 être destiné à
faire** to be intended to do.

détachable *adjective* detachable.

détachant *noun* Masc. stain
remover.

détacher *verb* [1] **1** to untie; **2** to
undo; **3** to tear off; **4** to remove; **5** to
remove the stains from; **6 se
détacher** to come off, to come
undone.

détail *noun* Masc. **1** detail; **en détail**
in detail; **2 regarder quelque
chose dans le détail** to look closely
at something; **3** retail.

détailler *verb* [1] to detail, to
itemize; **une facture détaillée** an
itemized bill.

détecter *verb* [1] to detect.

détective *noun* Masc. detective.

déteindre *verb* [60] **1** to fade; **2** to
run (*in the wash*).

détendre *verb* [3] **1** to be relaxing;
2 to relax; **3 se détendre** to relax.

détendu *adjective* relaxed.

a
b
c
d
e
f
g
h
i
j
k
l
m
n
o
p
q
r
s
t
u
v
w
x
y
z

détenir verb [81] **1** to detain; **2** to keep.

détente noun Fem. relaxation.

détenu, détenue noun Masc., Fem. prisoner, detainee.

détergent noun Masc. detergent.

détériorer verb [1] **se détériorer** to deteriorate.

détermination noun Fem. determination.

déterminer verb [1] to fix.

détestable adjective appalling, revolting.

détester verb [1] to hate.

détour noun Masc. detour; ★ **ça vaut le détour** it's well worth seeing (literally: it's worth the detour).

détournement noun Masc. **un détournement d'avion** a highjacking.

détourner verb [1] **1** to divert; **2 détourner un avion** to highjack a plane; **3 détourner les yeux** to look away.

détritus plural noun Masc. rubbish, refuse.

détruire verb [26] to destroy.

dette noun Fem. debt.

deuil noun Masc. **1** bereavement; **2** mourning.

deux number **1** two; **deux enfants** two children; **elle a deux ans** she's two; **il est deux heures** it's two o'clock; **2 deux fois** twice; **3** second (in dates); **le deux juin** the second of June; **4** both; **les deux frères** both brothers; **tous les deux, toutes les deux** both; **ils sont malades tous les deux, tous les deux sont**

malades they're both ill, both of them are ill.

deuxième noun **au deuxième o**ˉ the second floor.
deuxième adjective **pour la deuxième fois** for the second tim

deuxièmement adverb secondly.

deux-points noun Masc. colon.

dévaliser verb [1] to rob.

dévaluer verb [1] to devalue.

devant noun Masc. front.
devant preposition **1** in front of; **elle était devant moi dans la queue** she was in front of me in th queue; **il l'a dit devant ses parent** he said it in front of his parents; **2** outside; **devant la boulangerie** outside the baker's.

développement noun Masc. development; **les pays en voie de développement** developing countries.

développer verb [1] **1** to develo **2** to expand; **3 se développer** to expand; **la ville se développe** the town is expanding.

devenir verb [81] to become; **elle est devenue médecin/infirmière** she went into medicine/nursing.

déverser verb [1] **1** to pour out; **2** to tip out.

déviation noun Fem. diversion.

deviner verb [1] **1** to guess; **2** to foresee.

devinette noun Fem. riddle.

devis noun Masc. quote, estimate.

evises *plural noun Fem.* (foreign) currency.

evisser *verb* [1] to unscrew.

evoir *noun Masc.* **1** exercise, test; **2 devoirs** homework; **faire ses devoirs** to do your homework; **3** duty.

devoir *verb* [8] **1** to owe; **elle me doit vingt euros** she owes me twenty euros; **je vous dois combien?** how much do I owe you?; **2** to have to; **je dois partir à dix heures** I have to (*or* I must) leave at ten o'clock; **3 tu dois être fatigué** you must be tired; **elle doit avoir quarante ans** she must be forty; **il a dû oublier** he must have forgotten; **4 tu devrais partir** you ought to leave; **tu aurais dû partir** you should have left; **5 elle doit arriver à cinq heures** she's supposed to arrive at five o'clock.

évorer *verb* [1] to devour.

évoué *adjective* devoted.

évouement *noun Masc.* devotion.

évouer *verb* [1] **se dévouer à** to devote oneself to.

iabète *noun Masc.* diabetes.

iabétique *noun Masc. & Fem.*, *adjective* diabetic.

iable *noun Masc.* devil.

iabolo *noun Masc.* fruit cordial and lemonade; **un diabolo menthe** a mint cordial and lemonade.

iagnostic *noun Masc.* diagnosis.

iagnostique *adjective* diagnostic.

diagnostiquer *verb* [1] to diagnose.

diagonal (*Masc. plural* **diagonaux** *adjective* diagonal.

diagonale *noun Fem.* diagonal; **en diagonale** diagonally.

diagramme *noun Masc.* graph.

dialecte *noun Masc.* dialect.

dialogue *noun Masc.* dialogue.

dialyse *noun Fem.* dialysis.

diamant *noun Masc.* diamond.

diamètre *noun Masc.* diameter.

diapo *noun Fem.* (*informal*) slide SHORT FOR **diapositive**.

diapositive *noun Fem.* slide.

diarrhée *noun Fem.* diarrhoea.

dico *noun Masc.* (*informal*) dictionary SHORT FOR **dictionnaire**.

dictateur *noun Masc.* dictator.

dictature *noun Fem.* dictatorship.

dictée *noun Fem.* dictation.

dicter *verb* [1] to dictate.

dictionnaire *noun Masc.* dictionary.

dicton *noun Masc.* saying.

diesel *noun Masc.* diesel.

diététique *noun Fem.* **un magasin de diététique** a health-food shop. **diététique** *adjective* dietary.

dieu (*plural* **dieux**) *noun Masc.* god.

Dieu *noun Masc.* God; **mon Dieu!** good heavens!

différemment *adverb* differently.

différence *noun Fem.* **1** difference; **quelle est la différence (entre)?**

a
b
c
d
e
f
g
h
i
j
k
l
m
n
o
p
q
r
s
t
u
v
w
x
y
z

91

what's the difference (between)?; **2 à la différence de** unlike.

différend noun Masc. disagreement.

différent adjective **1** different; **différent de** different from; **2** various, different; **différentes personnes** various people, different people.

difficile adjective **1** difficult, hard; **difficile à faire** difficult to do; **leur maison est difficile à trouver** their house is difficult to find; **c'est difficile à imaginer** it's hard to imagine; **2** hard to please, fussy.

difficilement adverb with difficulty.

difficulté noun Fem. difficulty; **avoir de la difficulté à faire** to have difficulty in doing; **j'ai eu de la difficulté à vous joindre** I had difficulty getting in touch with you.

difforme adjective deformed, misshapen.

difformité noun Fem. deformity.

diffuser verb [1] **1** to broadcast; **2** to distribute; **3** to spread.

digérer verb [24] to digest.

digestif noun Masc. (after-dinner) liqueur.

digestion noun Fem. digestion.

digital (Masc. plural **digitaux**) adjective digital.

digne adjective **1** worthy; **digne de** worthy of; **digne de foi** trustworthy; **2** dignified.

dignité noun Fem. dignity.

digue noun Fem. **1** sea wall; **2** dyke.

dilemme noun Masc. dilemma.

diligent adjective diligent.

diluant noun Masc. thinner.

diluer verb [1] **1** to dilute; **2** to thin (paint).

dimanche noun Masc. **1** Sunday; **nous sommes dimanche aujourd'hui** it's Sunday today; **dimanche dernier** last Sunday; **dimanche prochain** next Sunday; **2** on Sunday; **je t'appellerai dimanche soir** I'll ring you on Sunday evening; **3 le dimanche** on Sundays; **fermé le dimanche** closed on Sundays; **4 tous les dimanche** every Sunday.

dimension noun Fem. size.

diminuer verb [1] **1** to reduce; **2** t come (or go) down; **3** to decrease; **4** to die down.

dinde noun Fem. turkey (as meat).

dindon noun Masc. turkey (when alive).

dîner noun Masc. dinner, supper; **inviter quelqu'un à dîner** to invit somebody to dinner.
dîner verb [1] to have dinner; **vien dîner chez nous ce soir** come to dinner with us this evening.

dingue adjective (informal) crazy.

dinosaure noun Masc. dinosaur.

diplomate noun Masc. & Fem. diplomat.
diplomate adjective diplomatic.

diplomatie noun Fem. diplomacy

diplomatique adjective diplomatic.

diplôme noun Masc. **1** diploma, certificate; **2** (university) degree.

diplômé adjective qualified.

ire verb [9] **1** to say; **elle dit qu'elle est malade** she says she's ill; **2** to tell; **dire quelque chose à quelqu'un** to tell somebody something; **j'ai dit à Anne que tu l'appellerais** I told Anne you'd ring her; **dire à quelqu'un de faire** to tell somebody to do; **je leur ai dit de venir à cinq heures** I told them to come at five o'clock; **on dirait qu'il va pleuvoir** it looks like rain; **dire la vérité** to tell the truth; **dire l'heure** to tell the time; **dire des mensonges** to tell lies.

irect adjective **1** direct; **un vol direct** a direct flight; **2** (in broadcasting) **en direct de** live from.

irectement adverb **1** directly; **2 aller directement à** to go straight to.

irecteur, directrice noun Masc., Fem. **1** director; **2** manager; **3** head (of a school).

irecteur général, directrice générale noun Masc., Fem. managing director.

irection noun Fem. **1** direction; **en direction de** towards, in the direction of; **2** management; **3** steering (of a vehicle).

irigeant, dirigeante noun Masc., Fem. leader.

iriger verb [52] **1** to direct; **2** to manage; **3** to conduct (an orchestra); **4 se diriger vers** to make for; **elle s'est dirigée vers la porte** she made for the door.

iscerner verb [1] **1** to make out; **2** to detect.

discipline noun Fem. **1** discipline; **2** subject (of study).

discipliner verb [1] **1** to discipline; **2** to control.

disco noun Masc. **1** disco; **2** disco music.

discothèque noun Fem. **1** disco, discotheque; **2** music library.

discours noun Masc. speech.

discret (Fem. **discrète**) adjective **1** discreet; **2** quiet; **3** subtle.

discrétion noun Fem. discretion.

discrimination noun Fem. discrimination.

discussion noun Fem. discussion.

discutable adjective questionable; **une décision discutable** a questionable decision.

discuter verb [1] **1** to talk; **on peut discuter tranquillement chez moi** we can talk in peace at my house; **2** to argue; **ça se discute** it's arguable; **3 discuter de quelque chose** to discuss something; **on va en discuter demain** we'll discuss it tomorrow.

disparaître verb [27] **1** to disappear; **2 faire disparaître quelque chose** to get rid of something; **3** to die; **4** to die out (traditions, customs).

disparition noun Fem. **1** disappearance; **2 une espèce en voie de disparition** an endangered species; **3** death.

disparu, disparue noun Masc., Fem. **1** missing person; **2 les disparus** the dead.

a
b
c
d
e
f
g
h
i
j
k
l
m
n
o
p
q
r
s
t
u
v
w
x
y
z

disparu *adjective* **1** missing; **2** lost; **3** dead; **4** extinct.

dispenser *verb* [1] **1** to hand out; **2** to give; **3 dispenser quelqu'un de** to exempt somebody from.

disperser *verb* [1] **1** to break up (*a crowd or demonstration*); **2 se disperser** to break up; **la foule s'est dispersée** the crowd broke up.

disponibilité *noun Fem.* availability.

disponible *adjective* available.

disposé *adjective* **1** arranged, laid out; **2 être disposé à faire** to be willing to do.

disposer *verb* [1] **1** to arrange, to lay out; **2 disposer de quelque chose** to have something (at your disposal).

dispositif *noun Masc.* **1** device; **2** system.

disposition *noun Fem.* **1** arrangement, layout; **2 à ta disposition** at your disposal; **3** measure.

dispute *noun Fem.* argument.

disputé *adjective* **1** contested; **2** controversial.

disputer *verb* [1] **1 se disputer** to argue; **ils se sont disputés** they had an argument; **2 se disputer quelque chose** to fight over something; **3 se faire disputer** (*informal*) to get told off; **je me suis fait disputer par mon patron** I got told off by my boss.

disqualifier *verb* [1] to disqualify.

disque *noun Masc.* **1** record; **passe un disque** to play a record (or CD); **2** disc; **3** (computer) disk.

disque compact *noun Masc.* compact disc, CD.

disque dur *noun Masc.* hard disk (*of a computer*).

disquette *noun Fem.* (computer) diskette.

disséquer *verb* [24] to dissect.

dissertation *noun Fem.* essay.

dissident, dissidente *noun Masc., Fem.* dissident.

dissimuler *verb* [1] to conceal.

dissocier *verb* [1] to separate.

dissolvant *noun Masc.* **1** nail polish remover; **2** solvent.

dissoudre *verb* [67] **1 dissoudre quelque chose** to dissolve something; **2 se dissoudre** to dissolve.

dissuader *verb* [1] **1 dissuader quelqu'un de faire** to persuade somebody not to do, to put somebody off doing; **il m'a dissuadé d'y aller** he persuaded me not to go; **2** to deter; **pour dissuader les voleurs** in order to deter thieves.

distance *noun Fem.* **1** distance; **une distance de cinq kilomètres** a distance of five kilometres; **c'est à quelle distance d'ici?** how far is it from here?; **à distance** from a distance; **l'enseignement à distance** distance learning; **2 ga**

distant *adjective* distant; **distant de** far away from; **un village distant**

de trois kilomètres a village three kilometres away.

istiller *verb* [1] to distil.

istillerie *noun Fem.* distillery.

istinct *adjective* distinct.

istinctif (*Fem.* **distinctive**) *adjective* distinctive.

istinction *noun Fem.* distinction.

istingué *adjective* distinguished.

istinguer *verb* [1] **1** to make out; **j'ai distingué un bateau à l'horizon** I made out a boat on the horizon; **2 distinguer entre** to distinguish between.

istraction *noun Fem.*
1 entertainment; **on a besoin d'un peu de distraction** we need a bit of entertainment; **2** leisure; **3** leisure activity, form of entertainment; **4** absent-mindedness.

istraire *verb* [78] **1** to amuse, to entertain; **ça m'a distrait un peu** that cheered me up a bit; **2** to distract; **3 se distraire** to amuse yourself, to enjoy yourself.

istrait *adjective* absent-minded.

istribuer *verb* [1] **1** to hand out, to distribute; **2 distribuer les cartes** to deal (*in a card game*); **3 distribuer le courrier** to deliver the mail.

istributeur *noun Masc.*
1 distributor; **2 un distributeur automatique** a vending machine; **3 un distributeur de tickets** a ticket machine; **4 un distributeur de billets** a cash dispenser.

istribution *noun Fem.*
1 distribution; **2** handing out;

3 delivery (*of mail*); **4** cast (*of a play*).

diverger *verb* [52] to diverge.

divers *adjective* various; **dans divers pays** in various countries.

divertir *verb* [2] **1** to amuse, to entertain; **2 se divertir** to amuse oneself.

divertissant *adjective* amusing, entertaining.

divin *adjective* divine.

diviser *verb* [1] to divide.

division *noun Fem.* division.

divorce *noun Masc.* divorce.

divorcé *adjective* divorced; **mes parents sont divorcés** my parents are divorced.

divorcer *verb* [61] to get divorced; **ils ont divorcé après dix ans de mariage** they got divorced after being married for ten years.

dix *number* ten; **elle a dix ans** she's ten; **il est dix heures** it's ten o'clock; **le dix juillet** the tenth of July.

dix-huit *number* eighteen; **il a dix-huit ans** he's eighteen; **à dix-huit heures** at six p.m.

dixième *noun Masc.* **au dixième** on the tenth floor.
dixième *adjective* tenth.

dix-neuf *number* nineteen; **elle a dix-neuf ans** she's nineteen; **à dix-neuf heures** at seven p.m.

dix-sept *number* seventeen; **elle a dix-sept ans** she's seventeen; **à dix-sept heures** at five p.m.

a
b
c
d
e
f
g
h
i
j
k
l
m
n
o
p
q
r
s
t
u
v
w
x
y
z

dizaine *noun Fem.* **1** ten; **2 une dizaine de personnes** about ten people.

docteur *noun Masc.* doctor.

document *noun Masc.* document.

documentaire *noun Masc.*, *adjective* documentary.

documentaliste *noun Masc. & Fem.* librarian.

documentation *noun Fem.* **1** documentation; **2** material; **3** research.

documenter *verb* [1] **se documenter sur quelque chose** to gather information on something.

dodo *noun Masc.* **faire dodo** (*baby talk*) to sleep; **on va faire dodo** time to tuck up in bed.

dogmatique *adjective* dogmatic.

doigt *noun Masc.* finger; **se couper le doigt** to cut your finger; **avoir mal au doigt** to have a sore finger; ★ **être à deux doigts de** to be within an inch of (*literally: to be two fingers away from*).

doigt de pied *noun Masc.* toe.

domaine *noun Masc.* **1** estate; **2** field, domain.

dôme *noun Masc.* dome.

domestique *noun Masc. & Fem.* servant.
domestique *adjective* domestic.

domicile *noun Masc.* **1** place of residence; **2 à domicile** at home; **travailler à domicile** to work at home.

dominant *adjective* **1** dominant; **2** main.

dominer *verb* [1] **1** to dominate; **2** to control.

Dominicain, Dominicaine *noun Masc.,Fem.* Dominican.

dominicain *adjective* Dominican; **la République dominicaine** the Dominican Republic.

domino *noun Masc.* domino; **jouer aux dominos** to play dominoes.

dommage *noun Masc.* **1 c'est dommage** it's a pity; **c'est dommage qu'elle n'y soit pas allée** it's a pity she didn't go; **2 les dommages** damage.

dompter *verb* [1] to tame.

DOM-TOM SHORT FOR **département et territoires d'outre-mer** (*French overseas departments and territories*).

don *noun Masc.* **1** gift; **faire don de** give; **2** donation; **dons en argent** cash donations; **3** gift, talent; **elle** un don pour les langues** she has gift for languages; **avoir le don de faire quelque chose** to have the gi of doing something.

donc *conjunction* so, therefore.

donne *noun Fem.* deal (*in card games*).

donné *adjective* given; **étant donn que** given that.

donnée *noun Fem.* **1** fact; **2 données** data.

donner *verb* [1] **1** to give; **donner quelque chose à quelqu'un** to giv somebody something; **elle m'a donné dix euros** she gave me ten euros; **donne-moi ton adresse** giv me your address; **2** to give away; **il donné tous ses livres** he gave awa

96

all his books; **3 ma fenêtre donne sur la rue** my window looks onto the street; **4 se donner à quelque chose** to devote yourself to something.

ont *relative pronoun* whose, of which; **une personne dont j'ai oublié le nom** a person whose name I've forgotten; **la maison dont je parle** the house I'm talking about; **six verres dont l'un est cassé** six glasses, one of which is broken.

oré *adjective* **1** gold; **2** gilt; **3** golden.

orénavant *adverb* from now on; **dorénavant je serai là tous les jours** from now on I'll be here every day.

orer *verb* [1] **1** to gild; **2 faire dorer** to brown (*meat or vegetables*).

ormir *verb* [37] to sleep; **tu as bien dormi?** did you sleep well?; **elle va dormir chez moi** she's going to spend the night at my house; **il dort** he's asleep.

ortoir *noun Masc.* dormitory.

os *noun Masc.* back; **avoir mal au dos** to have backache; **faire quelque chose dans le dos de quelqu'un** to do something behind somebody's back; **elle me tournait le dos** she had her back to me; **il m'a tourné le dos** he turned his back on me.

osage *noun Masc.* **1** amount; **2** mixture.

ose *noun Fem.* **1** dose; **2** measure.

dossier *noun Masc.* **1** file; **2** application form; **remplir un dossier** to fill in an application form; **3 dossier médical** medical records; **4 le dossier d'une chaise** the back of a chair.

douane *noun Fem.* **la douane** customs; **passer la douane** to go through customs.

douanier *noun Masc.* customs officer.

double *noun Masc.* **1 le double (de)** twice as much, twice as many; **2** copy, duplicate; **3** double. **double** *adjective* double.

doublé *adjective* **1** lined; **2** dubbed (*film*).

doublement *adverb* doubly.

doubler *verb* [1] **1** to double; **2** to overtake; **il m'a doublé dans un virage** he overtook me on a bend; **3** to line (*a garment*); **4** to dub (*a film*).

doublure *noun Fem.* lining.

douce *adjective* SEE **doux**.

doucement *adverb* **1** gently; **2** slowly; **3** softly.

douceur *noun Fem.* **1** softness; **2** gentleness; **3** mildness (*of weather*).

douche *noun Fem.* shower; **prendre une douche** to take a shower.

doucher *verb* [1] **se doucher** to have a shower.

doué *adjective* gifted; **être doué pour quelque chose** to have a gift for something.

a

b

douillet (*Fem.* douillette) *adjective* cosy.

c

douleur *noun Fem.* **1** pain; **2** grief.

d

douloureux (*Fem.* douloureuse) *adjective* painful.

e

doute *noun Masc.* **1** doubt; **2 sans doute** probably.

f

douter *verb* [1] **1** to doubt; **douter de** to have doubts about; **2 se douter de** to suspect; **je m'en doutais** I thought as much.

g

h

i

douteux (*Fem.* douteuse) *adjective* **1** doubtful; **2** dubious.

j

Douvres *noun* Dover.

k

doux (*Fem.* douce) *adjective* **1** soft; **2** gentle; **3** mild; **4** sweet.

l

douzaine *noun Fem.* **1** dozen; **2 une douzaine (de)** a dozen or so.

m

n

douze *number* twelve; **elle a douze ans** she's twelve; **le douze juillet** the twelfth of July.

o

p

douzième *noun Masc.* **au douzième** on the twelfth floor. **douzième** *adjective* twelfth.

q

r

dragée *noun Fem.* sugared almond.

s

draguer *verb* [1] (*informal*) **draguer quelqu'un** to chat somebody up; **il est toujours en train de draguer les nanas** he's always chatting up the girls; **se faire draguer** to get chatted up; **Carole s'est fait draguer par ton copain** Carole got chatted up by your mate.

t

u

v

w

x

y

dramatique *adjective* **1** tragic; **2** dramatic; **l'art dramatique** drama.

z

drame *noun Masc.* **1** tragedy; **2** drama; **il en a fait tout un drame** he made a big scene about it.

drap *noun Masc.* sheet.

drapeau (*plural* drapeaux) *noun Masc.* flag.

drap-housse *noun Masc.* fitted sheet.

dresser *verb* [1] **1** to train (*an animal*); **2** to put up (*a tent*); **3** to draw up (*a list*); **4 se dresser** to stand up.

drogue *noun Fem.* drug; **la drogue** drugs; **les drogues douces** soft drugs; **les drogues dures** hard drugs.

droguer *verb* [1] **1** to drug, to give drugs to; **2 se droguer** to take drugs.

droguerie *noun Fem.* hardware shop.

droit *noun Masc.* **1** right; **les droits de l'homme** human rights; **2 avoir le droit de faire** to be allowed to do; **je n'ai pas le droit de sortir ce soir** I'm not allowed to go out tonight; **3 avoir le droit de faire** to have the right to do; **tu n'as pas le droit de me critiquer** you have no right to criticize me; **4 le droit** law; **un étudiant en droit** a law student; **5** fee; **les droits d'inscription** enrolment fees.

droit *adjective* **1** straight; **une ligne droite** a straight line; **cette ligne n'est pas droite** this line is crooked; **2** right; **ma main droite** my right hand; **3 un angle droit** a right angle.

droit *adverb* straight; **continuez tout droit** go straight ahead.

droite *noun Fem.* **1** right; **à droite** on the right; **tourner à droite** to turn right; **à ta droite** on your right; **2 la droite** the right (*in politics*).

droitier (*Fem.* **droitière**) *adjective* right-handed.

drôle *adjective* **1** funny; **une histoire drôle** a funny story; **un film très drôle** a really funny film; **2** odd; **un drôle de film** an odd film.

drôlement *adverb* **1** (*informal*) really; **c'était drôlement bon!** it was really good!; **2** oddly, peculiarly.

dû, due, dus *verb* SEE **devoir**.

du *article* some, any SEE **de**.

duc *noun Masc.* duke.

duchesse *noun Fem.* duchess.

dune *noun Fem.* dune.

duo *noun Masc.* duet.

duplex *noun Masc.* maisonette.

duquel *pronoun* (= de lequel).

dur *adjective* **1** hard; **2** tough (*meat*); **3** difficult, hard.
dur *adverb* **travailler dur** to work hard.

durant *preposition* **1** for; **des années durant** for years; **2** during.

durcir *verb* [2] **1** to harden; **2 se durcir** to harden.

durée *noun Fem.* length.

durement *adverb* harshly.

durer *verb* [1] **1** to last; **2 durer pendant trois mois** to go on for three months.

dureté *noun Fem.* **1** hardness; **2** toughness; **3** difficulty.

duvet *noun Masc.* sleeping bag.

DVD *noun Masc.* DVD.

dynamique *adjective* dynamic, lively.

dyslexique *noun Masc. & Fem.* dyslexic.

Ee

eau *noun Fem.* water; **est-ce que tu veux de l'eau?** would you like some water?; **un verre d'eau** a glass of water; **eau gazeuse** sparkling mineral water; **eau plate** still mineral water; **'eau potable'** 'drinking water'; **'eau non potable'** 'not drinking water'; ★ **tomber à l'eau** to fall through (*literally: to fall into the water*); **nos projets sont tombés à l'eau** our plans have fallen through; ★ **mettre l'eau à la bouche de quelqu'un** to make somebody's mouth water; **ta sauce sent tellement bon que ça me met l'eau à la bouche** your sauce smells so good it's making my mouth water.

eau de Javel *noun Fem.* bleach.

eau de toilette *noun Fem.* toilet water.

eau minérale *noun Fem.* mineral water.

a
b
c
d
e
f
g
h
i
j
k
l
m
n
o
p
q
r
s
t
u
v
w
x
y
z

ébaucher verb [1] **1** to sketch; **2** to outline.

ébéniste noun Masc. & Fem. cabinet maker.

éblouir verb [2] to dazzle.

éblouissant adjective dazzling.

éboueur noun Masc. refuse collector.

ébouillanter verb [1] to scald.

ébranler verb [1] to shake.

ébullition noun Fem. boiling point; **porter à ébullition** to bring to the boil.

écaille noun Fem. **1** scale (of a fish or reptile); **2** tortoiseshell.

écailler verb [1] **s'écailler** to flake; **la peinture s'écaille** the paint's flaking.

écart noun Masc. **1** gap, distance; **faire un écart** to swerve; **la voiture a fait un écart pour éviter le chien** the car swerved to avoid the dog; **2** difference; **3 à l'écart de** away from.

écarté adjective **1 un village écarté** a remote village; **2 les jambes écartées** with legs apart; **3 les bras écartés** with arms outstretched.

écarter verb [1] **1** to move apart; **écarter les rideaux** to open the curtains; **2** to move back.

échafaudage noun Masc. scaffolding.

échalote noun Fem. shallot.

échange noun Masc. exchange; **en échange (de)** in exchange (for), in return (for).

échanger verb [52] to exchange, t swap; **nous avons échangé nos adresses** we exchanged addresses

échangeur noun Masc. (motorway interchange.

échantillon noun Masc. sample.

échapper verb [1] **1 échapper à** escape, to escape from, to get away from; **le week-end nous échappons à la ville** at weekends we get away from the town; **2 s'échapper** to escape.

écharde noun Fem. splinter.

écharpe noun Fem. scarf.

échasse noun Fem. stilt.

échec noun Masc. failure.

échecs plural noun Masc. chess; **jouer aux échecs** to play chess.

échelle noun Fem. **1** ladder; **2** scal

échelon noun Masc. **1** rung; **2** grade.

échiquier noun Masc. chessboard.

écho noun Masc. **1** echo; **2 des échos** rumours.

échographie noun Fem. (medical scan; **passer une échographie** to have a scan.

échouer verb [1] to fail; **échouer** **un examen** to fail an exam.

éclabousser verb [1] to splash.

éclair noun Masc. **1** flash of lightning; **2 un éclair au chocola** a chocolate eclair.

éclairage noun Masc. lighting.

éclairagiste noun Masc. & Fem. lighting engineer.

éclaircie noun Fem. sunny interval.

éclairer *verb* [1] to light (up).

éclat *noun Masc.* **1** splinter, fragment; **2** brightness; **3** splendour; **4** un éclat de rire a roar of laughter.

éclatant *adjective* brilliant; **des murs d'une blancheur éclatante** brilliant white walls.

éclater *verb* [1] **1** to burst; **un pneu a éclaté** a tyre has burst; **2** to shatter; **l'ampoule a éclaté** the bulb shattered; **3** to break out (*war or fighting*); **4 éclater de rire** to burst out laughing; **éclater en sanglots** to burst into tears.

éclipse *noun Fem.* eclipse.

écluse *noun Fem.* lock (*on a canal or river*).

écœurant *adjective* sickly.

écœurer *verb* [1] to make (somebody) feel sick.

école *noun Fem.* school; **aller à l'école** to go to school.

école de conduite *noun Fem.* driving school.

école de langue *noun Fem.* language, school.

école maternelle *noun Fem.* (state) nursery school (*age 2 – 6*).

école primaire *noun Fem.* primary school (*age 6 –11*).

écolier, écolière *noun Masc., Fem.* schoolchild.

écologie *noun Fem.* ecology.

écologique *adjective* **1** ecological; **2** environmentally friendly.

écologiste *noun Masc. & Fem.* ecologist.

économe *noun Masc.* potato peeler.
économe *adjective* economical.

économie *noun Fem.* **1** economy; **2** economics; **3** les économies savings; **faire des économies** to save up.

économique *adjective* **1** economical; **2** economic.

économiser *verb* [1] to save.

économiste *noun Masc. & Fem.* economist.

écorce *noun Fem.* **1** bark (*of a tree*); **2** peel (*of an orange or a lemon*).

écorcher *verb* [1] **s'écorcher le genou** to graze your knee.

écorchure *noun Fem.* graze.

écossais *noun Masc.* tartan (cloth).
écossais *adjective* **1** Scottish; **2** tartan; **une jupe écossaise** a tartan skirt.

Écossais, Écossaise *noun Masc., Fem.* Scotsman, Scotswoman, Scot; **les Écossais** the Scots.

Écosse *noun Fem.* Scotland; **elle habite en Écosse** she lives in Scotland.

écourter *verb* [1] to shorten.

écouter *verb* [1] to listen to; **j'écoute beaucoup la radio** I listen to the radio a lot; **écoute-moi** listen to me.

écouteur *noun Masc.* **1** receiver (*on a telephone*); **2** headphones.

écran *noun Masc.* **1** screen; **à l'écran** on the screen; **le petit écran** television; **2 la crème écran total** sun block.

a b c d **e** f g h i j k l m n o p q r s t u v w x y z

écrasant *adjective* crushing, overwhelming; **une victoire/ défaite écrasante** a crushing victory/defeat.

écraser *verb* [1] **1** to crush; **écrasez les noix** crush the walnuts; **2** to squash; **tu vas écraser les pêches!** you'll squash the peaches!; **3 écraser une cigarette** to stub out a cigarette; **4 se faire écraser** to get run over; **Attention! Tu vas te faire écraser!** Watch out! You'll get run over!; **5 s'écraser** to crash; **leur voiture s'est écrasée contre un mur** their car crashed into a wall.

écrémé *adjective* **le lait écrémé** skimmed milk; **le lait demi-écrémé** semi-skimmed milk.

écrevisse *noun Fem.* crayfish.

écrire *verb* [38] **1** to write; **elle m'a écrit une lettre** she wrote me a letter; **2 s'écrire** to write to each other; **ils s'écrivent tous les jours** they write to each other every day; **3 s'écrire** to be spelled; **comment ça s'écrit?** how do you spell it?

écrit *noun Masc.* **1** (piece of) writing; **2** written paper (*of an exam*); **il a réussi à l'oral mais il a raté l'écrit** he passed the oral but failed the written paper; **3 à l'écrit** in writing. **écrit** *adjective* written.

écriture *noun Fem.* handwriting.

écrivain *noun Masc.* writer.

écrou *noun Masc.* nut (*screwed onto a bolt*).

écrouler *verb* [1] **s'écrouler** to collapse.

écume *noun Fem.* **1** foam, froth; **2** scum.

écureuil *noun Masc.* squirrel.

écurie *noun Fem.* stable.

eczéma *noun Masc.* eczema.

EDF SHORT FOR **Électricité de France** French electricity company.

Édimbourg *noun* Edinburgh.

éditer *verb* [1] to publish.

éditeur *noun Masc.* publisher.

édition *noun Fem.* **1** publishing; **elle travaille dans l'édition** she works in publishing; **2** edition; **une édition de poche** a paperback edition.

édredon *noun Masc.* eiderdown.

éducateur, **éducatrice** *noun Masc., Fem.* special needs teacher.

éducatif (*Fem.* **éducative**) *adjective* educational.

éducation *noun Fem.* education; **elle a reçu une bonne éducation** she had a good education.

éducation physique *noun Fem.* physical education, PE.

éduquer *verb* [1] to educate.

effacer *verb* [61] to rub out.

effaceur *noun Masc.* correction pen.

effarant *adjective* amazing.

effarer *verb* [1] to alarm.

effectivement *adverb* indeed (*used to show agreement with what someone has just said*); **il est effectivement extrêmement gentil** he is indeed extremely nice; **oui, elle m'a effectivement téléphoné hier** yes, that's right, sh did phone me yesterday; **'Tu as oublié tes clés' – 'Ah oui, effectivement!'** 'You've left your keys behind' – 'Oh yes, so I have!'; **'Il est maintenant trop tard pour y aller' – 'Oui, effectivement'** 'It's too late to go now' – 'Yes, so it is.'

ffectuer verb [1] to make, to carry out.

ffet noun Masc. **1** effect; **2 en effet** indeed (used to show agreement with what someone has just said); **elle avait en effet raison** she was indeed right; **'il fait très froid' – 'Oui, en effet'** 'It's very cold' – 'Yes, it is, isn't it?'; **'Tu as laissé la porte ouverte' – 'Oui, en effet'** 'You've left the door open' – 'Yes, so I have'.

fficace adjective **1** efficient; **elle est très efficace** she's very efficient; **2** effective; **c'est un remède très efficace** it's a very effective remedy.

fficacité noun Fem. **1** efficiency; **il est connu pour son efficacité** he's known for his efficiency; **2** effectiveness.

ffondrer verb [1] **s'effondrer** to collapse.

fforcer verb [61] **s'efforcer de faire** to try hard to do; **elle s'efforce de rester calme** she tries hard to remain calm.

ffort noun Masc. effort; **faire un effort** to make an effort; **il n'a même pas fait l'effort de m'appeler** he couldn't even be bothered to phone me.

ffrayant adjective frightening.

effrayer verb [59] to frighten.

effroi noun Masc. terror.

effronté adjective cheeky.

effroyable adjective dreadful.

égal, **égale** (Masc. plural **égaux**) noun Masc., Fem. equal.
égal adjective **1** equal; **une distance égale** an equal distance; **des quantités égales** equal quantities; **être égal à** to be equal to; **2 ça m'est égal** I don't mind; **'Tu veux aller au cinéma ou rester à la maison?' – 'Ça m'est égal'** 'Do you want to go to the cinema or stay at home?'– 'I don't mind'.

également adverb also; **elle est également prof d'allemand** she's also a German teacher.

égaler verb [1] to equal; **trois plus cinq égale huit** three plus five equals eight.

égaliser verb [1] to equalize; **ils ont égalisé dans la dernière minute** they equalized in the last minute.

égalité noun Fem. **1** equality; **2 les deux joueurs sont à égalité** the two players are level.

égard noun Masc. **1 à l'égard de** towards; **à mon égard** towards me; **2 à cet égard** in this respect.

égaré adjective stray; **un chien égaré** a stray dog.

égarer verb [1] **1** to mislay; **j'ai égaré mes lunettes** I've mislaid my glasses; **2 s'égarer** to get lost; **nous sommes égarés dans les petites rues** we got lost in the back streets.

103

a
b
c
d
e
f
g
h
i
j
k
l
m
n
o
p
q
r
s
t
u
v
w
x
y
z

égayer *verb* [59] **1** to brighten up; **j'ai acheté quelques fleurs pour égayer la pièce** I've bought some flowers to brighten up the room; **2** to cheer up; **un peu de musique va nous égayer un peu** a bit of music will cheer us up a bit.

églantine *noun Fem.* wild rose.

églefin *noun Masc.* haddock.

église *noun Fem.* church; **aller à l'église** to go to church.

égoïsme *noun Masc.* selfishness.

égoïste *adjective* selfish.

égout *noun Masc.* sewer.

égoutter *verb* [1] **1** to drain (*vegetables*); **2** to strain (*pasta*); **3** to drip.

égratignure *noun Fem.* scratch.

Égypte *noun Fem.* Egypt.

eh bien *exclamation* well; **eh bien, ça me fait plaisir de te revoir** well, it's nice to see you again.

élancer *verb* [61] **s'élancer** to dash.

élargir *verb* [2] to widen.

élastique *noun Masc.* **1** rubber band; **2** elastic.
élastique *adjective* **1** elastic; **2** elasticated.

électeur, électrice *noun Masc., Fem.* voter.

élection *noun Fem.* election; **une élection présidentielle** a presidential election; **se présenter aux élections** to be a candidate in the elections.

électricien, électricienne *noun Masc., Fem.* electrician.

électricité *noun Fem.* electricity.

électrique *adjective* **1** electric; **2** electrical.

électronique *noun Fem.* electronics.
électronique *adjective* electronic

élégant *adjective* elegant.

élément *noun Masc.* **1** element; **2** part.

élémentaire *adjective* basic, elementary.

éléphant *noun Masc.* elephant.

élevage *noun Masc.* **1** farming (*of livestock*); **2** farm; **un élevage de porcs** a pig farm.

élevé *adjective* high; **une note élevée** a high mark.

élève *noun Masc. & Fem.* student, pupil.

élever *verb* [50] **1 élever un enfant** to bring up a child; **elle a été élevée en Écosse** she was brought up in Scotand; **2** to breed (*animals*); **3 élever la voix** to raise one's voice; **4 s'élever** to rise; **5 s'élever à** to amount to; **la facture s'élève à cinq cents euros** the bill amounts to five hundred euros.

éleveur, éleveuse *noun Masc., Fem.* breeder.

éliminer *verb* [1] **1** to eliminate; **2** to rule out; **nous ne pouvons pas éliminer cette possibilité** we cannot rule out that possibility.

élire *verb* [51] to elect.

elle *pronoun* **1** she; **où est Sylvie? — elle est dans la cuisine** where's Sylvie? — she's in the kitchen; **2** her; **Paul est avec elle** Paul's with her; **3** it (*when referring to an object which is feminine in French*); **où est ma tasse? — elle est sur la table** where's my cup? — it's on the table.

elle-même *pronoun* **1** herself; **elle me l'a dit elle-même** she told me herself; **2** itself (*referring to an object which is feminine in French*); **la pièce elle-même est jolie mais les meubles sont hideux** the room itself is pretty but the furniture is hideous.

elles *pronoun* they, them **1** they (*referring to female people or feminine objects*); **elles sont arrivées** they've arrived; **2** them; **avec elles** with them.

éloigné *adjective* distant; **la colline la plus éloignée** the most distant hill.

éloigner *verb* [1] **s'éloigner (de)** to move away (from).

Élysée *noun Masc.* the Élysée Palace (*the official residence of the French President*).

email *noun Masc.* enamel.

emballage *noun Masc.* wrapping.

emballer *verb* [1] **1** to wrap, to pack; **2** (*informal*) to get enthusiastic; **elle s'est vraiment emballée pour son nouveau boulot** she's got really enthusiastic about her new job; **ça ne m'emballe pas vraiment** I'm not that keen.

embarquement *noun Masc.* boarding; **une carte d'embarquement** a boarding card.

embarquer *verb* [1] **1** (*informal*) to go off with; **elle a embarqué toutes mes chaises** she's gone off with all my chairs; **2 s'embarquer** to board.

embarras *noun Masc.* **1** embarrassment; **2** dilemma.

embarrassé *adjective* **1** embarrassed; **2** cluttered.

embarrasser *verb* [1] **1** to embarrass; **2** to clutter up.

embaucher *verb* [1] to take on (*an employee*); **ils embauchent en ce moment** they're taking people on at the moment.

embêtant *adjective* annoying; **c'est vraiment embêtant!** it's really annoying!

embêter *verb* [1] **1** to annoy; **arrête de m'embêter!** stop annoying me!; **2 s'embêter** to be bored; **on ne s'embête pas ici** there's plenty going on here; **on ne s'embête pas!** we're having a great time!

embouteillage *noun Masc.* traffic jam.

embrasser *verb* [1] to kiss; **je t'embrasse** lots of love (*at the end of a letter or said on the phone to a friend*).

embrayage *noun Masc.* clutch (*in a vehicle*).

émeraude *noun Fem.* emerald.

a
b
c
d
e
f
g
h
i
j
k
l
m
n
o
p
q
r
s
t
u
v
w
x
y
z

a

émerger *verb* [52] to emerge.

b

émeute *noun Fem.* riot.

c

émission *noun Fem.* programme (*on television or radio*).

d

emménager *verb* [52] to move in (*to a flat or house*); **nous avons emménagé la semaine dernière** we moved in last week.

e

f

emmener *verb* [50] to take; **c'est sa sœur qui l'emmène à l'école** it's his sister who takes him to school; **tu veux que je t'emmène?** would you like a lift?

g

h

i

émotif (Fem. **émotive**) *adjective* emotional.

j

k

émotion *noun Fem.* emotion.

l

émouvant *adjective* moving.

emparer *verb* [1] **s'emparer de** to seize.

m

empêcher *verb* [1] **1** to prevent, to stop; **rien ne t'empêche d'essayer** there's nothing to stop you trying; **2 elle n'a pas pu s'empêcher de rire** she couldn't help laughing.

n

o

p

empereur *noun Masc.* emperor.

q

empiler *verb* [1] to pile up.

r

empirer *verb* [1] to get worse.

s

emplacement *noun Masc.* site.

t

emploi *noun Masc.* **1** job; **2** use; **le mode d'emploi** instructions for use.

u

v

emploi du temps *noun Masc.* timetable (*at school*).

w

employé, **employée** *noun Masc., Fem.* employee.

x

y

employer *verb* [39] **1** to employ; **2** to use.

z

employeur, **employeuse** *noun Masc., Fem.* employer.

empoisonné *adjective* poisoned.

empoisonner *verb* [1] to poison.

emporter *verb* [1] to take (away); **'plats à emporter'** 'takeaway meals'.

empreinte *noun Fem.* footprint.

empreinte digitale *noun Fem.* fingerprint.

emprisonner *verb* [1] to imprison.

emprunt *noun Masc.* loan.

emprunter *verb* [1] to borrow.

emprunt-logement *noun Masc.* mortgage.

EMT *noun* (= *éducation manuelle et technique*) technology (*at school*).

ému *adjective* moved.

en *preposition* **1** in; **elle habite en Écosse** she lives in Scotland; **en été** in summer; **en avril** in April; **un livre en anglais** a book in English; **habillé en noir** dressed in black; **j'étais en pyjama** I was in my pyjamas; **2** into; **aller en ville** to go into town; **traduire en anglais** to translate into English; **3** to; **aller en Italie** to go to Italy; **4** by; **en avion** by plane; **5** made of; **une table en bois** a table made of wood, a wooden table; **6 en vacances** on holiday; **7 en ami** as a friend; **8 en rentrant à la maison j'ai rencontré Tom** as I was coming home I met Tom; **je me suis brûlé en repassant ma chemise** I burned myself (while) ironing my shirt.

en *pronoun* **1 j'en ai** I've got some; **je n'en veux pas** I don't want any;

tu en as combien? how many (of them) do you have?, how much (of it) do you have?; **elle en a quatre** she's got four; **'qui a un stylo?' — 'j'en ai un'** 'who's got a pen?' — 'I've got one' (notice that in this sort of expression 'en' is often not translated at all); **2 elle m'en a parlé** she told me about it; **3 j'ai emprunté ton fer à repasser — est-ce que tu en as besoin?** I borrowed your iron — do you need it?

encadrement noun Masc. 1 frame; 2 framing; 3 door frame.

encadrer verb [1] to frame.

enceinte noun Fem. 1 surrounding wall; 2 enclosed space; 3 loudspeaker.

enceinte adjective pregnant.

encens noun Masc. incense.

encercler verb [1] to surround, to circle.

enchanté adjective 1 delighted; 2 (when meeting someone) **enchanté/enchantée** pleased to meet you.

enchère noun Fem. bid; **une vente aux enchères** an auction sale.

encombrant adjective bulky.

encombrer verb [1] 1 to clutter; 2 to obstruct.

encore adverb 1 still; **elle est encore au bureau** she's still at the office; **il reste encore de la viande** there's still some meat left; **2 pas encore** not yet; **il n'est pas encore rentré** he hasn't come home yet, he's not home yet; **3 again**; **je l'ai encore oublié** I've forgotten it again; **4 more**; **encore un peu** a little

more; **encore une fois** one more time; **attendre encore une semaine** to wait for another week; **5 even**; **encore mieux** even better.

encourageant adjective encouraging.

encouragement noun Masc. encouragement.

encourager verb [52] 1 to encourage; **elle m'a encouragé à suivre des cours de dessin** she encouraged me to go to drawing classes; 2 to cheer on (a team).

encre noun Fem. ink.

encyclopédie noun Fem. encyclopedia.

endive noun Fem. chicory.

endommager verb [52] to damage.

endormi adjective asleep.

endormir verb [37] 1 **endormir quelqu'un** to send somebody to sleep; 2 **s'endormir** to fall asleep, to go to sleep.

endroit noun Masc. 1 place; **un bon endroit pour** a good place for; 2 the right side (of a garment); 3 **à l'endroit** the right way up.

énergie noun Fem. energy.

énergique adjective energetic.

énervé adjective irritated, annoyed.

énerver verb [1] 1 to irritate, to annoy; **ça m'énerve!** this is getting on my nerves!; 2 **s'énerver** to get annoyed.

enfance noun Fem. childhood.

a

b

c

d

e

f

g

h

i

j

k

l

m

n

o

p

q

r

s

t

u

v

w

x

y

z

enfant noun Masc. & Fem. child; **un enfant unique** an only child.

enfantin adjective **1** easy; **2** childish.

enfer noun Masc. hell.

enfermer verb [1] **1** to shut up; **2 s'enfermer** to shut yourself up; **elle s'est enfermée dans sa chambre** she shut herself up in her room.

enfiler verb [1] **1** to put on; **je vais juste enfiler mon pull** I'll just put my jumper on; **2 enfiler une aiguille** to thread a needle.

enfin adverb **1** at last; **je l'ai enfin fini** I've finished it at last; **2** finally; **elle a enfin réussi** she finally succeeded.

enflé adjective swollen; **il a le genou enflé** his knee is swollen.

enflure noun Fem. swelling.

enfoncer verb [61] **1** to push in; **2 s'enfoncer dans** to sink into.

enfreindre verb [2] to disobey; **elle a enfreint les règles** she disobeyed the rules.

engagement noun Masc. commitment.

engager verb [52] **1** to take on (an employee); **2** to commit; **3 s'engager à faire** to promise to do; **je me suis engagé à organiser le repas** I promised to organize the meal.

engelure noun Fem. chilblain.

engin noun Masc. device.

engourdi adjective numb; **j'ai les doigts engourdis par le froid** my fingers are numb with cold.

engourdir verb [2] **s'engourdir** to go numb.

engrais noun Masc. fertilizer.

engueuler verb [1] (informal) to tell off; **elle m'a engueulé** she gave me a telling off; **se faire engueuler** to get a telling off.

énième adjective umpteenth; **pour la énième fois** for the umpteenth time.

énigme noun Fem. riddle.

enivrer verb [1] **1 enivrer quelqu'un** to make somebody drunk; **2 s'enivrer** to get drunk.

enjeu (plural **enjeux**) noun Masc. **1** stake (in a gambling game); **2** what is at stake.

enlèvement noun Masc. kidnapping.

enlever verb [50] **1** to take off (garment); **il a enlevé sa veste** he took off his jacket; **2** to remove; **enlever une tache** to remove a stain; **tu peux enlever les assiettes** you can clear the plates; **3** to kidnap.

enneigé adjective **1** snowy; **2** snow-covered.

ennemi, ennemie noun Masc., Fem. enemy.

ennui noun Masc. **1** boredom; **2** problem; **avoir des ennuis** to have problems.

ennuyé adjective **1** bored; **2** embarrassed.

ennuyer verb [41] **1** to bore; **son discours m'a ennuyé** I found his speech boring; **2** to bother; **je t'ennuie?** am I bothering you?;

3 s'ennuyer to be (*or* get) bored; **j'ai fini par m'ennuyer** I got bored in the end; **on s'ennuie ici** it's boring here.

ennuyeux (*Fem.* ennuyeuse) *adjective* **1** boring; **2** annoying; **ça c'est vraiment ennuyeux** that's really annoying.

énorme *adjective* huge.

énormément *adverb* **1** tremendously; **2 énormément de masses** of; **j'ai énormément de choses à faire avant de partir** I've got masses of things to do before I leave.

enquête *noun Fem.* **1** investigation; **2** inquiry; **3** survey.

enregistrement *noun Masc.* **1** recording; **2** check-in (*at airport*).

enregistrer *verb* [1] **1** to record; **2** to register; **3** to check in (*at airport*).

enrhumer *verb* [1] **s'enrhumer** to catch a cold; **être enrhumé** to have a cold.

enrichir *verb* [2] **1** to make rich; **2** to enrich.

enrichissant *adjective* rewarding.

enrouler *verb* [1] to wind.

enseignant, enseignante *noun Masc., Fem.* teacher.

enseigne *noun Fem.* sign; **enseigne lumineuse** neon sign.

enseignement *noun Masc.* **1** teaching; **2** education.

enseigner *verb* [1] to teach.

ensemble *noun Masc.* **1** outfit; **j'ai acheté un joli ensemble pour le mariage** I've bought a lovely outfit for the wedding; **2 l'ensemble de** the whole of; **3 dans l'ensemble** on the whole.

ensemble *adverb* together; **on va y aller ensemble** we'll go together; **ils sont ensemble depuis trois ans** they've been together for three years.

ensoleillé *adjective* sunny.

ensommeillé *adjective* sleepy.

ensuite *adverb* then; **on va aller à la banque et ensuite chez Marianne** we'll go to the bank and then to Marianne's.

entamer *verb* [1] to start; **ce paquet n'a pas encore été entamé** this packet hasn't been started yet.

entasser *verb* [1] to pile up.

entendre *verb* [3] **1** to hear; **est-ce que tu l'entends?** can you hear it?; **se faire entendre** to make yourself heard; **2 j'ai entendu dire que ...** I've heard that ...; **3** to mean; **qu'est-ce que tu entends par là?** what do you mean by that?; **4 s'entendre bien** to get on well.

entendu *exclamation* **1** okay, fine; **2 bien entendu** of course.

entente *noun Fem.* **1** understanding; **2** agreement.

enterrement *noun Masc.* funeral, burial.

enterrer *verb* [1] to bury.

entêté *adjective* stubborn.

entêter *verb* [1] **s'entêter à faire** to persist in doing.

a
b
c
d
e
f
g
h
i
j
k
l
m
n
o
p
q
r
s
t
u
v
w
x
y
z

a
b
c
d
e
f
g
h
i
j
k
l
m
n
o
p
q
r
s
t
u
v
w
x
y
z

enthousiasme *noun Masc.* enthusiasm.

enthousiasmer *verb* [1] **s'enthousiasmer** to get enthusiastic.

enthousiaste *adjective* enthusiastic.

entier (*Fem.* entière) *adjective* **1** whole; **une pomme entière** a whole apple; **le monde entier** the whole world; **2 je n'ai pas lu sa lettre en entier** I haven't read his letter right through; **3 le lait entier** full-fat milk.

entièrement *adverb* completely, entirely.

entorse *noun Fem.* sprain; **se faire une entorse à la cheville** to sprain your ankle.

entouré *adjective* **entouré de** surrounded by; **elle est entourée d'amis** she's surrounded by friends.

entourer *verb* [1] to surround; **entourer de** to surround with.

entracte *noun Masc.* interval (*at the theatre*).

entraînement *noun Masc.* **1** training; **2** practice.

entraîner *verb* [1] **1** to lead to; **entraîner des problèmes** to lead to problems; **2** to take; **il m'a entraîné chez sa copine** he took me off to his girlfriend's; **3 entraîner une équipe** to train a team; **4** to drag; **5 s'entraîner** to train; **elle s'entraîne tous les matins** she trains every morning.

entre *preposition* **1** between; **entre la porte et la fenêtre** between the door and the window; **on va le**

partager entre nous we'll share it between us; **2** among; **entre eux** among themselves; **3 l'un d'entre eux** one of them.

entrée *noun Fem.* **1** entrance; **à l'entrée de** at the entrance to; **billets à l'entrée** tickets at the door; **2** hall(way); **3** admission; **4** starter, first course.

entremets *noun Masc.* dessert.

entrepôt *noun Masc.* warehouse.

entreprendre *verb* [64] **1** to undertake; **2** to start.

entreprise *noun Fem.* firm, business.

entrer *verb* [1] **1** to go in; **entrer dans un magasin** to go into a shop; **entrer à l'hôpital** to go into hospital; **2** to come in; **entrer dans** to come into; **Entrez!** Come in!

entre-temps *adverb* meanwhile.

entretenir *verb* [81] **1** to maintain (*a building, a road, etc*); **2** to support.

entretien *noun Masc.* **1** interview; **elle a été convoquée à un entretien** she's been invited for interview; **2** discussion; **j'ai eu un entretien avec mon patron** I had a discussion with my boss; **3** upkeep; **l'entretien de la maison** the upkeep of the house.

entrevue *noun Fem.* interview.

entrouvert *adjective* ajar, half-open.

envahir *verb* [2] to invade.

enveloppe *noun Fem.* envelope; **une enveloppe matelassée** a padded envelope.

envelopper *verb* [1] to wrap up.

envers noun Masc. **1** wrong side; **2 à l'envers** upside down, inside out, back to front.
envers preposition towards, to.

envie noun Fem. **1** urge; **avoir envie de faire** to want to do, to feel like doing; **j'ai envie de te voir** I want to see you; **j'ai envie d'aller au cinéma** I feel like going to the cinema; **2 avoir envie de quelque chose** to feel like something; **j'ai envie d'une glace** I feel like an ice cream; **3 ces frites me font envie** I fancy some of those chips.

envier verb [1] to envy.

envieux (Fem. **envieuse**) adjective envious.

environ adverb about; **environ trente personnes** about thirty people.

environnement noun Masc. environment.

environs plural noun Masc. surroundings; **aux environs de** near.

envisager verb [52] **envisager de faire** to plan to do; **qu'est-ce que vous envisagez de faire?** what are you planning to do?

envoi noun Masc. **1** dispatch; **faire un envoi de** to send; **2** consignment.

envoler verb [1] **s'envoler** to fly away.

envoyer verb [40] to send; **envoyer quelque chose à quelqu'un** to send somebody something; **elle m'a envoyé une carte** she sent me a card; **elle m'a envoyé chercher les verres** she sent me to get the glasses.

épais (Fem. **épaisse**) adjective thick; **une tranche épaisse** a thick slice.

épaisseur noun Fem. thickness.

épargne noun Fem. savings; **une banque d'épargne** a savings bank; **un compte d'épargne** a savings account.

épatant adjective (informal) fantastic, great.

épaule noun Fem. shoulder.

épaulette noun Fem. **1** shoulder strap; **2** shoulder pad.

épave noun Fem. wreck.

épée noun Fem. sword.

épeler verb [18] to spell.

éphémère adjective fleeting.

épi noun Masc. ear (of corn); **un épi de maïs** a corn cob.

épice noun Fem. spice.

épicé adjective spicy, hot; **je n'aime pas les choses épicées** I don't like spicy food.

épicerie noun Fem. grocer's (shop); **à l'épicerie** at the grocer's.

épicier, épicière noun Masc., Fem. grocer.

épidémie noun Fem. epidemic.

épilepsie noun Fem. epilepsy.

épiler verb [1] **s'épiler les sourcils** to pluck your eyebrows; **une pince à épiler** eyebrow tweezers; **s'épiler les jambes** to shave your legs (or use wax or cream to remove hair).

a
b
c
d
e
f
g
h
i
j
k
l
m
n
o
p
q
r
s
t
u
v
w
x
y
z

épinards *plural noun* Masc. spinach; **est-ce que tu aimes les épinards?** do you like spinach?

épine *noun* Fem. thorn.

épineux (Fem. **épineuse**) *adjective* prickly.

épingle *noun* Fem. pin; **une épingle de sûreté** a safety pin.

épingler *verb* [1] to pin.

éplucher *verb* [1] to peel.

épluchures *plural noun* Fem. peelings.

éponge *noun* Fem. **1** sponge; **2** towelling.

éponger *verb* [52] **1** to mop up; **2** to sponge.

époque *noun* Fem. time; **à cette époque-là** at that time.

épouse *noun* Fem. wife.

épouser *verb* [1] to marry.

épouvantable *adjective* dreadful.

épouvantail *noun* Masc. scarecrow.

épouvante *noun* Fem. terror; **un film d'épouvante** a horror film.

épouvanter *verb* [1] to terrify.

époux *noun* Masc. husband.

épreuve *noun* Fem. **1** test; **2** exam; **l'épreuve de français** the French exam; **3** event (*sports*); **4** ordeal.

éprouver *verb* [1] to feel, to experience.

éprouvette *noun* Fem. test tube.

EPS *noun* (*éducation physique et sportive*) PE.

épuisant *adjective* exhausting; **c'est un travail épuisant** it's exhausting work.

épuisé *adjective* **1** exhausted, worn out; **je suis épuisé** I'm worn out; **2** out of stock; **3** out of print.

épuiser *verb* [1] to wear out; **cette discussion m'a épuisé** that discussion's worn me out.

équateur *noun* Masc. equator.

équestre *adjective* **un centre équestre** a riding school.

équilibré *adjective* balanced.

équilibre *noun* Masc. balance.

équipage *noun* Masc. crew.

équipe *noun* Fem. team.

équipé *adjective* **1** equipped; **2 une cuisine équipée** a fitted kitchen.

équipement *noun* Masc. equipment.

équipements *plural noun* Masc. **les équipements sportifs** sports facilities.

équitation *noun* Fem. riding.

équivalent *adjective* equivalent.

érable *noun* Masc. maple tree; **le sirop d'érable** maple syrup.

errer *verb* [1] to wander.

erreur *noun* Fem. mistake; **par erreur** by mistake.

es *verb* SEE **être**[2].

escabeau *noun* Masc. stepladder.

escalade *noun* Fem. rock-climbing.

escalier *noun* Masc. **1** stairs; **dans l'escalier** on the stairs; **2** staircase; **3 un escalier mécanique, un escalier roulant** an escalator.

scargot noun Masc. snail.

scarpin noun Masc. court shoe.

sclavage noun Masc. slavery.

sclave noun Masc. & Fem. slave.

scompte noun Masc. discount; **un escompte de 10%** a 10% discount.

scorter verb [1] to escort.

scrime noun Fem. fencing (the sport).

scroc noun Masc. crook, swindler.

scroquer verb [1] to swindle.

scroquerie noun Fem. swindle; **quelle escroquerie!** what a swindle!

space noun Masc. space.

spacer verb [61] to space out.

spadon noun Masc. swordfish.

spadrille noun Fem. espadrille.

spagne noun Fem. Spain.

spagnol noun Masc. Spanish (language).

espagnol adjective Spanish.

spagnol, Espagnole noun Masc., Fem. Spaniard; **les Espagnols** the Spanish.

spèce noun Fem. **1** sort; **une espèce de** a sort of; **on a mangé du poisson avec une espèce de sauce épicée** we had fish with a sort of spicy sauce; **2** species; **3 espèce d'idiot!** you idiot!; **4 en espèces** in cash.

spérer verb [24] to hope; **ils espèrent pouvoir venir** they're hoping to be able to come; **j'espère qu'elle n'a pas oublié** I hope she hasn't forgotten; **j'espère bien!** I certainly hope so.

espiègle adjective mischievous.

espion, espionne noun Masc., Fem. spy.

espionnage noun Masc. spying, espionage.

espionner verb [1] to spy on.

espoir noun Masc. hope.

esprit noun Masc. **1** mind; **ça ne m'est pas venu à l'esprit** it didn't cross my mind; **2** wit; **avoir de l'esprit** to be witty.

esquimau™ (plural esquimaux) noun Masc. ice lolly.

esquisse noun Fem. sketch.

esquisser verb [1] to sketch.

essai noun Masc. **1** trial; **2** test; **3** attempt, try.

essaim noun Masc. swarm.

essayer verb [59] **1** to try; **essayer de faire** to try to do; **j'ai essayé de t'appeler** I tried to phone you; **2** to try on; **essayer une robe** to try on a dress; **voulez-vous l'essayer?** would you like to try it on?; **3** to test.

essence noun Fem. **1** petrol; **essence sans plomb** unleaded petrol; **2** essential oil.

essentiel (Fem. **essentielle**) adjective essential; **c'est l'essentiel** that's the main thing.

essentiellement adverb **1** mainly; **2** essentially.

essorage noun Masc. spin-dry.

essorer verb [1] to spin-dry.

essoufflé adjective out of breath.

essuie-glace noun Masc. windscreen wiper.

a
b
c
d
e
f
g
h
i
j
k
l
m
n
o
p
q
r
s
t
u
v
w
x
y
z

a

essuie-tout noun Masc. (paper) kitchen towel.

b

c **essuyer** verb [41] to wipe; **essuyer la vaisselle** to do the drying-up; **s'essuyer les mains** to dry your hands.

d

e **est**¹ verb SEE **être**².

f **est**² noun Masc. east; **l'est de Paris** the east of Paris; **dans l'est de la France** in the east of France; **l'Europe de l'Est** Eastern Europe.

g

h **est** adjective **1** east; **2** eastern.

i **est-ce que** (used for asking questions) **est-ce qu'il pleut?** is it raining?; **est-ce que Julie est partie?** has Julie left?; **où est-ce qu'il habite?** where does he live?

j

k

l **esthéticienne** noun Fem. beautician.

m **estime** noun Fem. respect.

n **estimer** verb [1] **1** to esteem; **2** to value; **3 j'estime que** ... I think that ....

o

p **estival** (Masc. plural **estivaux**) adjective summer.

q

estivant, estivante noun Masc., Fem. summer visitor.

r

s **estomac** noun Masc. stomach; **avoir mal à l'estomac** to have stomachache.

t

u **Estonie** noun Fem. Estonia.

v **estrade** noun Fem. platform.

w **estragon** noun Masc. tarragon; **une sauce à l'estragon** a tarragon sauce.

x

y **et** conjunction and.

établir verb [2] **1** to establish; **2 établir une liste** to draw up a list;

z

3 s'établir à son compte to set up in business.

établissement noun Masc. **1** institution; **établissement scolaire** school; **2** organization.

étage noun Masc. floor; **au premier étage** on the first floor; **au dernier étage** on the top floor; **à l'étage** upstairs.

étagère noun Fem. **1** shelf; **2** set of shelves.

étain noun Masc. **1** tin; **2** pewter.

étalage noun Masc. window display.

étaler verb [1] **1** to spread; **2** to spread out; **3** to roll out (pastry).

étanche adjective **1** watertight; **2** waterproof.

étang noun Masc. pond.

étape noun Fem. **1** stage; **2** stopping place.

état noun Masc. state, condition; **en mauvais état** in a bad state; **en bon état** in good condition; **en état de marche** in working order; **être dans tous ses états** to be in a state.

État noun Masc. state, State.

États-Unis plural noun Masc. **les États-Unis** the United States; **aux États-Unis** in (or to) the United States.

été¹ verb SEE **être**².

été² noun Masc. summer; **en été** in summer; **l'été dernier** last summer; **des vêtements d'été** summer clothes.

éteindre verb [60] **1** to turn off, to switch off; **éteindre la lumière** to turn out the lights; **2** to put out (*a fire or cigarette*); **3 s'éteindre** to go out.

teint *adjective* extinct (*volcano*).

tendre *verb* [3] **1** to spread out; **2** to stretch out (*your arms or legs*); **3 étendre le linge** to hang out the washing; **4 s'étendre** to stretch; **5 s'étendre** to spread.

ternel (*Fem.* **éternelle**) *adjective* eternal.

ternité *noun Fem.* eternity.

ternuement *noun Masc.* sneeze.

ternuer *verb* [1] to sneeze.

tes *verb* SEE **être**².

thnie *noun Fem.* ethnic group.

thnique *adjective* ethnic.

tinceler *verb* [18] to sparkle, to twinkle.

tincelle *noun Fem.* spark.

tiquette *noun Fem.* **1** label; **2** etiquette.

tirer *verb* [1] to stretch.

toffe *noun Fem.* fabric.

toile *noun Fem.* star; **une étoile filante** a shooting star.

tonnant *adjective* **1** surprising; **2** astonishing.

tonnement *noun Masc.* **1** surprise; **2** astonishment.

tonner *verb* [1] **1** to surprise; **ça m'a beaucoup étonné** that really surprised me; **ça ne m'étonne pas du tout** that doesn't surprise me at all; **2 s'étonner** to be surprised; **s'étonner de quelque chose** to be surprised at something.

touffant *adjective* stifling.

étouffer *verb* [1] **1** to stifle; **2** to suffocate; **3 s'étouffer** to choke.

étourderie *noun Fem.* **1** absent-mindedness; **2 une étourderie** a careless mistake.

étourdi, **étourdie** *noun Masc., Fem.* scatterbrain.
étourdi *adjective* scatterbrained.

étourdir *verb* [2] to daze, to stun.

étourneau *noun Masc.* starling.

étrange *adjective* strange.

étranger¹, **étrangère** *noun Masc., Fem.* **1** foreigner; **2** stranger.
étranger, **étrangère** *adjective* foreign; **un pays étranger** a foreign country.

étranger² *noun Masc.* **à l'étranger** abroad.

étrangler *verb* [1] **1** to strangle; **2** to choke.

être¹ *noun Masc.* being; **un être humain** a human being.

être² *verb* [6] **1** to be; **nous sommes dans la cuisine** we're in the kitchen; **elle est malade** she's ill; **c'est moi** it's me; **2 elle est infirmière** she's a nurse; **3 être à quelqu'un** to belong to somebody, to be somebody's; **ce livre est à Paul** this book is Paul's; **ce livre est à moi** this book is mine; **4 il est 6 heures** it's 6 o'clock; **5 nous sommes le 7 mars** it's the 7th of March (today); **6** (*used with certain verbs to form past tenses: for a list of these, see the centre pages*) **je suis allé à Paris** I went to Paris; **nous sommes rentrés à 7 heures** we got home at 7 o'clock; **7** (*used to form the passive of verbs*) **ses robes sont**

a
b
c
d
e
f
g
h
i
j
k
l
m
n
o
p
q
r
s
t
u
v
w
x
y
z

faites par sa mère her dresses are made by her mother.

étroit *adjective* **1** narrow; **2** close.

étroitement *adverb* closely.

étude *noun Fem.* **1** study; **2** **études** studies; **faire des études de médecine** to study medicine.

étudiant, étudiante *noun Masc., Fem.* student.

étudier *verb* [1] to study.

étui *noun Masc.* case.

eu *verb* SEE **avoir**.

euro *noun Masc.* euro; **l'euro est divisé en cents/centimes** the euro is divided into cents.

Europe *noun Fem.* Europe; **en Europe** in (*or* to) Europe.

européen (*Fem.* **européenne**) *adjective* European.

euthanasie *noun Fem.* euthanasia.

eux *pronoun* **1** them; **avec eux** with them; **des amis à eux** friends of theirs; **2** they.

eux-mêmes *pronoun* themselves.

évacuer *verb* [1] to evacuate; **la police a fait évacuer l'immeuble** the police evacuated the building.

évader *verb* [1] **s'évader** to escape.

évaluer *verb* [1] to assess.

évanouir *verb* [2] **s'évanouir** to faint.

évaporer *verb* [1] **s'évaporer** to evaporate.

évasion *noun Fem.* escape.

éveillé *adjective* awake.

éveiller *verb* [1] **1** to arouse; **2** to awaken.

événement *noun Masc.* event.

éventail *noun Masc.* fan.

éventualité *noun Fem.* possibilit

éventuel (*Fem.* **éventuelle**) *adjective* possible.

éventuellement *adverb* **1** possibly; **2** if necessary.

évêque *noun Masc.* bishop.

évidemment *adverb* of course.

évidence *noun Fem.* **être en évidence** to be clearly visible; **de toute évidence** clearly; **de toute évidence il a oublié de venir** he' clearly forgotten to come; **mettre quelque chose en évidence** to reveal something.

évident *adjective* obvious.

évier *noun Masc.* sink.

éviter *verb* [1] to avoid; **éviter de faire** to avoid doing; **ça t'évitera d sortir** that'll save you having to g out.

évolué *adjective* advanced.

évoluer *verb* [1] **1** to develop; **nou ne savons pas comment la situation va évoluer** we do not know how the situation will develo **2** to progress; **l'informatique a beaucoup évolué ces dernières années** computer science has progressed a great deal in recent years; **3** to change; **les choses or évolué depuis** things have chang since.

évolution *noun Fem.* **1** development; **2** progress; **3** evolution.

a b c d e f g h i j k l m n o p q r s t u v w x y z

exact *adjective* **1** correct; **c'est exact** that's absolutely right; **2** exact, precise.

exactement *adverb* exactly.

exagéré *adjective* **1** exaggerated; **2** excessive.

exagérer *verb* [24] **1** to exaggerate; **2** to go too far.

examen *noun Masc.* **1** exam; **passer un examen** to sit an exam; **réussir à un examen** to pass an exam; **un examen blanc** a mock exam; **2 un examen médical** a medical examination.

examinateur, examinatrice *noun Masc., Fem.* examiner.

examiner *verb* [1] to examine.

exaspérant *adjective* exasperating.

exaspérer *verb* [24] to exasperate.

excellence *noun Fem.* excellence.

excellent *adjective* excellent.

excentrique *noun Masc. & Fem.*, *adjective* eccentric.

excepté *preposition* except.

exception *noun Fem.* exception; **à l'exception de** with the exception of.

exceptionnel (*Fem.* **exceptionnelle**) *adjective* **1** exceptional; **2** special.

exceptionnellement *adverb* exceptionally.

excès *noun Masc.* excess.

excès de vitesse *noun Masc.* speeding.

excessif (*Fem.* **excessive**) *adjective* excessive.

excessivement *adverb* excessively; **il est excessivement timide** he's incredibly shy.

excitant *noun Masc.* stimulant. **excitant** *adjective* exciting.

excitation *noun Fem.* excitement.

excité *adjective* **1** frenzied; **2** over-excited; **3** thrilled.

exciter *verb* [1] **s'exciter** to get excited.

exclamation *noun Fem.* exclamation.

exclamer *verb* [1] **s'exclamer** to exclaim.

exclu *adjective* **il n'est pas exclu que** ... it's not impossible that ....

exclusif (*Fem.* **exclusive**) *adjective* exclusive.

excursion *noun Fem.* excursion, trip.

excuse *noun* **1** apology; **présenter ses excuses** to apologize; **2** excuse.

excuser *verb* [1] **1** to forgive; **excusez-moi!** sorry!; **excusez-moi de vous déranger** sorry to disturb you; **2 s'excuser** to apologize; **je m'excuse** I'm sorry; **je m'excuse d'être en retard** sorry I'm late.

exécuter *verb* [1] **1** to execute; **2** to carry out.

exemplaire *noun Masc.* copy; **six exemplaires du dictionnaire** six copies of the dictionary.

exemple *noun Masc.* example; **par exemple** for example; **donner l'exemple** to set an example.

a
b
c
d
e
f
g
h
i
j
k
l
m
n
o
p
q
r
s
t
u
v
w
x
y
z

exercer *verb* [61] **1** to exercise (*a right*); **2** to practise (*an art or a profession*); **3** to exert (*authority*); **4 s'exercer** to practise.

exercice *noun Masc.* exercise; **exercices de mise en forme** fitness exercises.

exhiber *verb* [1] **1** to show off; **2** to display.

exhibitionniste *noun Masc.* flasher.

exigeant *adjective* hard to please.

exiger *verb* [52] **1** to demand; **2** to require.

exil *noun Masc.* exile.

exilé, exilée *noun Masc., Fem.* exile.

existence *noun Fem.* existence.

exister *verb* [1] to exist.

exotique *adjective* exotic.

expansion *noun Fem.* **1** expansion; **2** growth.

expédier *verb* [1] to send (off); **expédier un paquet** to send off a package.

expéditeur, expéditrice *noun Masc., Fem.* sender.

expédition *noun Fem.* expedition.

expérience *noun Fem.* **1** experience; **avoir de l'expérience** to be experienced; **2** experiment; **faire une expérience** to carry out an experiment.

expérimenté *adjective* experienced.

expert *noun Masc.* expert.

explication *noun Fem.* explanation.

explicite *adjective* explicit.

expliquer *verb* [1] to explain.

exploit *noun Masc.* **1** achievemen **2** feat.

exploiter *verb* [1] **1** to exploit; **2** use, to make use of.

explorer *verb* [1] to explore.

exploser *verb* [1] to explode, to blow up.

explosif (Fem. **explosive**) *adjecti* explosive.

explosion *noun Fem.* **1** explosio **2** boom.

export *noun Masc.* export.

exportateur, exportatrice *noun Masc., Fem.* exporter.

exportation *noun Fem.* export.

exporter *verb* [1] to export; **la Russie exporte beaucoup de pétrole** Russia exports a lot of oil.

exposé *noun Masc.* talk; **Gaby a fa un exposé sur le Japon** Gaby ga a talk about Japan. **exposé** *adjective* **1** exposed; **2** o display.

exposer *verb* [1] **1** to exhibit; **2** t expose; **3** to explain.

exposition *noun Fem.* **1** exhibition; **une exposition d'a africain** an exhibition of African art; **2** exposure.

exprès *adjective* express. **exprès** *adverb* **1** deliberately; **tu l'as fait exprès** you did it deliberately, you did it on purpose **a fait exprès de le casser** he bro it on purpose; **c'est fait exprès** it meant to be like that; **2** specially; **je suis venu exprès pour te voir** I've come specially to see you.

xpress *noun Masc.* **1** fast train; **2** espresso coffee.

xpression *noun Fem.* expression.

xprimer *verb* [1] **1** to express; **2 s'exprimer** to express yourself; **je n'exprime mal** I'm expressing myself badly.

xpulser *verb* [1] **1** to evict; **2** to xpel.

xquis *adjective* exquisite, delightful.

xtase *noun Fem.* ecstasy.

xtensif (*Fem.* **extensive**) *adjective* xtensive.

xtension *noun Fem.* extension.

xtérieur *noun Masc.* **1** outside; **à 'extérieur** outside; **2** exterior.

xtérieur *adjective* **1** outside; **2** outer.

xternat *noun Masc.* day school.

xterne *noun Masc. & Fem.* day upil.

xtincteur *noun Masc.* fire xtinguisher.

xtinction *noun Fem.* extinction; **ne espèce en voie d'extinction** n endangered species.

xtra *adjective* (*informal*) great, antastic; **ta sauce est vraiment xtra!** your sauce is really fantastic!

xtraction *noun Fem.* **1** extraction; **2** mining.

xtraire *verb* [78] **1** to extract; **2** to nine.

xtrait *noun Masc.* extract.

extraordinaire *adjective* extraordinary, amazing.

extra-terrestre *noun Masc. & Fem.* extra-terrestrial, alien (*from outer space*).

extravagant *adjective* **1** eccentric; **des vêtements extravagants** eccentric clothes; **2** extravagant.

extrême *noun Masc., adjective* extreme.

extrêmement *adverb* extremely.

Extrême-Orient *noun Masc.* the Far East.

extrémité *noun Fem.* **1** end; **2** tip; **3** edge; **4** extreme.

Ff

F SHORT FOR **francs**; **30 F** 30 francs.

fabricant *noun Masc.* manufacturer.

fabrication *noun Fem.* manufacture.

fabriquer *verb* [1] to make; **fabriqué en France** made in France; **qu'est-ce que tu fabriques?** (*informal*) what are you up to?

fabuleux (*Fem.* **fabuleuse**) *adjective* fabulous.

fac *noun Fem.* (*informal*) university; **être en fac d'anglais** to be doing a degree in English.

face *noun Fem.* **1** face; **face à face** face to face; **2 en face** opposite; **en face de l'école** opposite the school;

a
b
c
d
e
f
g
h
i
j
k
l
m
n
o
p
q
r
s
t
u
v
w
x
y
z

a
b
c
d
e
f
g
h
i
j
k
l
m
n
o
p
q
r
s
t
u
v
w
x
y
z

la maison d'en face the house opposite; **le magasin en face de chez nous** the shop opposite our house; **3 faire face à quelque chose** to face up to something; **4 face à** facing; **face au mur** facing the wall; **5 pile ou face?** heads or tails?

fâché *adjective* **1** angry; **elle est fâchée contre moi** she's angry with me; **2 il est fâché avec son frère** he's fallen out with his brother.

fâcher *verb* [1] **1 se fâcher** to get angry; **se fâcher contre quelqu'un** to get angry with somebody; **elle s'est fâchée contre moi** she got angry with me; **2 se fâcher avec quelqu'un** to fall out with somebody.

facile *adjective* easy; **c'est facile** it's easy; **c'est facile à comprendre** it's easy to understand.

facilement *adverb* easily.

facilité *noun Fem.* easiness.

faciliter *verb* [1] to make (something) easier; **ça devrait nous faciliter les choses** that should make things easier for us.

façon *noun Fem.* **1** way; **il y a plusieurs façons de le faire** there are several ways of doing it; **d'une façon extraordinaire** in an extraordinary way; **de quelle façon?** in what way?; **2 de toute façon** anyway.

façonner *verb* [1] **1** to make; **2** to shape.

facteur[1] *noun Masc.* factor.

facteur[2] *noun Masc.* postman; **est-ce que le facteur est passé?** has the postman been?

factrice *noun Fem.* postwoman.

facture *noun Fem.* bill; **la facture d'électricité** the electricity bill.

facultatif (*Fem.* **facultative**) *adjective* optional.

faculté *noun Fem.* faculty.

fade *adjective* tasteless; **la sauce est un peu fade** the sauce is a bit tasteless.

faible *noun Masc.* **avoir un faible pour** to have a soft spot for.
faible *adjective* **1** weak; **elle est encore très faible** she's still very weak; **2 elle est faible en chimie** she's not very good at chemistry; **3 un faible bruit** a faint noise.

faiblesse *noun Fem.* weakness.

faiblir *verb* [2] **1** to weaken; **2 le vent a faibli** the wind's died down a bit.

faïence *noun Fem.* earthenware; **des assiettes en faïence** earthenware plates.

faillir *verb* [42] **faillir faire** to nearly do; **j'ai failli tomber** I nearly fell; **j'ai failli rater le train** I nearly missed the train.

faillite *noun Fem.* bankruptcy; **faire faillite** to go bankrupt.

faim *noun Fem.* hunger; **avoir faim** to be hungry; **j'ai très faim** I'm really hungry; **je meurs de faim!** I'm starving!; **je n'ai plus faim** I've had enough to eat; **ces gâteaux me donnent faim** those cakes make me feel hungry.

fainéant adjective lazy.

faire verb [10] **1** to make; **faire un gâteau** to make a cake; **je vais me faire un café** I'm going to make myself a coffee; **faire du bruit** to make a noise; **2** to do; **qu'est-ce que tu fais?** what are you doing?; **il est en train de faire ses devoirs** he's doing his homework; **faire du français** to do French; **fais comme tu veux** do as you like; **3 qu'as-tu fait du couteau?** what have you done with the knife?; **4 il fait froid** it's cold; **il fait chaud** it's hot; **5 quel temps fait-il?** what's the weather like?; **il fait beau** it's a nice day; **il fait beau en été ici** the weather's nice here in summer; **6 ça ne fait rien** it doesn't matter; **7 faire faire quelque chose** to have (or get) something done; **elle a fait réparer son vélo** she got her bike repaired; **il s'est fait couper les cheveux** he's had his hair cut; **8 faire chauffer de l'eau** to heat some water; **faire cuire quelque chose** to cook something; **9 ne t'en fais pas** don't worry.

faire-part noun Masc. announcement (of birth, marriage, or death).

fais verb SEE **faire**.

faisan noun Masc. pheasant.

faisons verb SEE **faire**.

fait[1] verb SEE **faire**.

fait[2] noun Masc. **1** fact; **en fait** actually; **en fait je l'ai vu hier** in fact I saw him yesterday; **2 au fait** by the way; **au fait, est-ce que tu as fermé la porte?** by the way, did you shut the door?

fait d'actualité noun Masc. news item.

faites verb SEE **faire**.

falaise noun Fem. cliff.

fallait verb SEE **falloir**.

falloir impersonal verb [43] **1 il faut le faire** it has to be done, you must do it; **il ne faut pas faire ça** you mustn't do that; **il ne fallait pas faire ça** you shouldn't have done that; **il faudra partir à six heures** we'll have to leave at six o'clock; **2 il me faut un stylo** I need a pen; **il leur faut une voiture** they need a car; **qu'est-ce qu'il te faut?** what do you need?; **3 il faut que tu le fasses** (subjunctive) you must do it; **il faut que tu prennes tes clés** you must take your keys; **4 comme il faut** properly; **tu ne l'as pas fait comme il faut** you haven't done it properly; **marche comme il faut!** walk properly.

famé adjective **un quartier mal famé** a rough area.

fameux (Fem. **fameuse**) adjective first-rate; **le repas n'était pas fameux** the meal wasn't great.

familial (Masc. plural **familiaux**) adjective family; **la vie familiale** family life; **les allocations familiales** child benefit.

familiariser verb [1] **se familiariser avec** to become familiar with.

familiarité noun Fem. familiarity.

a
b
c
d
e
f
g
h
i
j
k
l
m
n
o
p
q
r
s
t
u
v
w
x
y
z

121

familier (*Fem.* **familière**) *adjective* familiar; **un endroit familier** a familiar place.

famille *noun Fem.* **1** family; **un déjeuner en famille** a family lunch; **une famille nombreuse** a big family; **2** relatives; **j'ai de la famille à Londres** I have relatives in London.

famille monoparentale *noun Fem.* single-parent family.

fanatique *noun Masc. & Fem.* fanatic.

faneé *adjective* withered; **les fleurs sont fanées** the flowers are withered.

fanfare *noun Fem.* brass band.

fantaisie *noun Fem.* **1** imagination; **2** **des bijoux de fantaisie** costume jewellery.

fantaisiste *adjective* **1** unreliable; **il est un peu fantaisiste** he's rather unreliable; **2** **une idée fantaisiste** a wild idea.

fantastique *adjective* fantastic.

fantôme *noun Masc.* ghost.

farce *noun Fem.* **1** practical joke; **un magasin de farces et attrapes** a joke shop; **2** stuffing (*for a chicken, for example*).

farci *adjective* stuffed; **des tomates farcies** stuffed tomatoes.

farcir *verb* [2] to stuff (*a chicken, for example*).

fard à paupières *noun Masc.* eye shadow.

fardeau (*plural* **fardeaux**) *noun Masc.* burden.

farfelu *adjective* bizarre; **c'est un type farfelu** he's a bizarre bloke; **elle a toujours des idées farfelue** she always has crazy ideas.

farine *noun Fem.* **1** flour; **2** baby cereal.

fascinant *adjective* fascinating; **son histoire était absolument fascinante** his story was absolute**l** fascinating.

fascination *noun Fem.* fascination.

fasciner *verb* [1] to fascinate; **ça me fascine** I find that fascinating

fascisme *noun Masc.* fascism.

fast-food *noun Fem.* fast food.

fastidieux (*Fem.* **fastidieuse**) *adjective* tedious; **c'est un travail fastidieux** it's tedious work.

fatal *adjective* **1** inevitable; **c'était fatal** it was bound to happen; **2** fata**l**

fatalité *noun Fem.* fate.

fatidique *adjective* fateful.

fatigant *adjective* tiring.

fatigue *noun Fem.* tiredness.

fatigué *adjective* tired; **je suis fatigué** I'm tired; **tu as l'air fatigu**é you look tired.

fatiguer *verb* [1] **1** to tire (somebody) out; **la promenade m'** **fatigué** the walk tired me out; **2 s**é **fatiguer** to get tired.

faubourg *noun Masc.* suburb.

fauché *adjective* (*informal*) broke **je suis fauché cette semaine** I'm broke this week.

femelle

aucher *verb* [1] **1** to mow, to scythe; **2** (*informal*) to nick; **quelqu'un m'a fauché mon vélo** somebody's nicked my bike.

aucon *noun Masc.* falcon, hawk.

audra, faudrait *verb* SEE **falloir**.

aufiler *verb* [1] **se faufiler à travers la foule** to thread your way through the crowd.

aune *noun Fem.* wildlife.

ausse *adjective* SEE **faux**[1].

aussement *adverb* wrongly.

ausser *verb* [1] **1** to distort; **2** to bend.

aut *verb* SEE **falloir**.

aute *noun Fem.* **1** mistake, error; **faire une faute** to make a mistake; **une faute d'orthographe** a spelling mistake; **2** fault; **c'est (de) ma faute** it's my fault; **c'est là faute de Sophie** it's Sophie's fault; **3** **faute de** for lack of; **faute de temps** for lack of time; **faute de mieux** for want of anything better; **4** **sans faute** without fail.

auteuil *noun Masc.* armchair.

auteuil roulant *noun Masc.* wheelchair.

autif (*Fem.* **fautive**) *adjective* faulty.

auve *noun Masc.* wild animal. **fauve** *adjective* tawny.

aux[1] (*Fem.* **fausse**) *adjective* **1** wrong; **c'est faux** it's wrong; **2** untrue; **c'est totalement faux** it's totally untrue; **3** false; **une fausse barbe** a false beard; **4** imitation; **une table en faux marbre** an imitation marble table; **5** **chanter faux** to sing out of tune.

faux[2] *noun Masc.* fake, forgery; **cette pièce est un faux** this coin's a forgery.

faux[3] *noun Fem.* scythe.

faux ami *noun Masc.* false friend (*a word in a foreign language which looks very like a word in your own language but does not mean the same thing at all*).

faux-filet *noun Masc.* sirloin.

faveur *noun Fem.* favour; **en faveur de** in favour of.

favorable *adjective* favourable.

favorablement *adverb* favourably.

favori (*Fem.* **favorite**) *adjective* favourite.

favoriser *verb* [1] to favour.

fax *noun Masc.* **1** fax; **envoyer un fax** to send a fax; **2** fax machine.

fédéral (**fédéraux**) **fédéral** *adjective* federal.

fédération *noun Fem.* federation.

fée *noun Fem.* fairy; ★ **avoir des doigts de fée** to have nimble fingers (*literally: to have the fingers of a fairy*).

féerique *adjective* magical.

feignant *adjective* (*informal*) lazy.

fêler *verb* [1] **se fêler** to crack.

félicitations *plural noun Fem.* congratulations.

féliciter *verb* [1] to congratulate.

fêlure *noun Fem.* crack.

femelle *noun Fem.*, *adjective* female (*animal*).

féminin noun Masc. **le féminin** the feminine (*in French and other grammars*); **au féminin** in the feminine.

féminin adjective **1** female; **le sexe féminin** the female sex; **2** feminine; **elle est très féminine** she's very feminine; **3** women's; **les vêtements féminins** women's clothing; **la presse féminine** women's magazines; **les questions féminines** women's issues.

féministe noun Masc. & Fem. feminist.

femme noun Fem. **1** woman; **c'est une femme très intéressante** she's a very interesting woman; **2** wife; **la femme de David** David's wife.

femme au foyer noun Fem. housewife.

femme d'affaires noun Fem. businesswoman.

femme de ménage noun Fem. cleaning lady.

fendre verb [3] **1** to split; **2** to crack.

fenêtre noun Fem. window; **regarder par la fenêtre** to look out the window; ★ **jeter l'argent par les fenêtres** to throw your money away (*literally: to throw money out of the windows*).

fenouil noun Masc. fennel.

fente noun Fem. **1** slit; **2** slot; **3** crack.

fer noun Masc. iron.

fer à cheval noun Masc. horseshoe.

fer à repasser noun Masc. iron (*for ironing things with*).

fer forgé noun Masc. wrought iron.

férié adjective **un jour férié** a public holiday.

ferme[1] noun Fem. **1** farm; **2** farmhouse.

ferme[2] adjective firm.

fermé adjective closed; **'fermé le dimanche'** closed on Sundays.

ferme d'éoliennes noun Fem. wind farm.

fermenter verb [1] to ferment.

fermer verb [1] **1** to close, to shut; **peux-tu fermer la porte, s'il te plaît** shut the door please; **il a fermé les yeux** he closed his eyes; **2** to turn off (*the lights, the tap, the water, etc*); **n'oublie pas de fermer les robinets** don't forget to turn off the taps; **3 se fermer** to close, to shut.

fermeture noun Fem. **1** closing; **heures de fermeture** closing times; **2** fastening (*on a garment*).

fermeture annuelle noun Fem. annual closure.

fermeture éclair noun Fem. zip.

fermier, fermière noun Masc., Fem. **1** farmer; **2 la fermière** the farmer's wife.
fermière adjective farm; **produits fermiers** farm produce; **un poulet fermier** a free-range chicken.

fermoir noun Masc. clasp.

féroce adjective **1** fierce; **2** ferocious.

ferraille noun Fem. scrap metal.

rroviaire *adjective* rail; **le réseau ferroviaire** the rail network.

rtile *adjective* fertile.

rtilité *noun Fem.* fertility.

esse *noun Fem.* buttock; **fesses** bottom.

stin *noun Masc.* feast.

stival *noun Masc.* festival.

ête *noun Fem.* **1** public holiday; **2** party; **faire la fête** to celebrate; **3 les fêtes de fin d'année** the festive season; **4** fête, fair; **5** saint's name day (*in France each day of the year is associated with the name of a saint and many people still celebrate the day of the saint they are named after*).

ête des Mères *noun Fem.* Mother's Day (*in France on the last Sunday in May*).

ête des Pères *noun Fem.* Father's Day.

ête foraine *noun Fem.* funfair.

ête Nationale *noun Fem.* Bastille Day.

ter *verb* [1] to celebrate.

eu *noun Masc.* **1** fire; **faire du feu** to light a fire; **prendre feu** to catch fire; **2** light; **as-tu du feu?** have you got a light?; **3 les feux de signalisation** the traffic lights; **un feu rouge** a red light; **4 faire cuire à feu doux** cook on a gentle heat; ★ **il n'y a pas le feu** there's no hurry (*literally: there isn't a fire*).

eu d'artifice *noun Masc.* **1** firework; **2** firework display.

euillage *noun Masc.* leaves.

feuille *noun Fem.* **1** leaf; **2 une feuille de papier** a sheet of paper.

feuilleté *noun Masc.* savoury pasty. **feuilleté** *adjective* **de la pâte feuilletée** puff pastry.

feuilleter *verb* [48] **feuilleter un livre** to leaf through a book.

feuilleton *noun Masc.* serial, soap (*on television*).

feutre *noun Masc.* **1** felt; **2 un feutre** a felt-tip pen.

fève *noun Fem.* broad bean.

février *noun Masc.* February; **en février, au mois de février** in February.

fiable *adjective* reliable.

fiançailles *plural noun Fem.* engagement (*to be married*).

fiancé, **fiancée** *noun Masc., Fem.* fiancé, fiancée. **fiancé** *adjective* **être fiancé à quelqu'un** to be engaged to somebody.

fiancer *verb* [61] **se fiancer** to get engaged.

fibre *noun Fem.* fibre.

ficeler *verb* [18] to tie up.

ficelle *noun Fem.* **1** string; **2** thin baguette (*of French bread*).

fiche *noun Fem.* **1** form; **remplir une fiche** to fill in a form; **2** index card; **3** plug.

fiche d'inscription *noun Fem.* registration form.

ficher *verb* (*informal*) [1] **1** to do; **qu'est-ce que tu fiches?** what do you think you're doing?; **2 je m'en fiche!** I don't care!; **3 fiche-moi la paix!** leave me alone!

a b c d e f g h i j k l m n o p q r s t u v w x y z

125

fichier *noun Masc.* file.

fichu *adjective* (*informal*) done for; **ma voiture est fichue** my car's had it.

fiction *noun Fem.* fiction.

fidèle *adjective* **1** faithful; **2** loyal.

fier[1] (*Fem.* **fière**) *adjective* proud.

fier[2] *verb* [1] **se fier à** to trust.

fierté *noun Fem.* pride.

fièvre *noun Fem.* fever; **avoir de la fièvre** to have a temperature.

figer *verb* [52] **1 se figer** to congeal; **2** to freeze to the spot.

figue *noun Fem.* fig.

figuier *noun Masc.* fig tree.

figure *noun Fem.* **1** face; **2** figure.

figurer *verb* [1] **1** to appear; **2 se figurer** to imagine.

fil *noun Masc.* **1** thread; **du fil à coudre** sewing thread; **2** wire, flex (*of a telephone or electrical appliance*); **3 un coup de fil** (*informal*) a phone call; **passer un coup de fil** to make a phone call; **passe-moi un coup de fil** give me a ring.

fil de fer *noun Masc.* wire; **fil de fer barbelé** barbed wire.

file *noun Fem.* **1 une file d'attente** a queue; **2** lane (*on a road*).

filer *verb* [1] **1** to speed along; **2** (*informal*) to give; **elle m'a filé deux CD** she gave me two CDs (*which she didn't want any more*).

filet *noun Masc.* **1** net; **2** fillet; **un filet de poisson** a fish fillet.

fille *noun Fem.* **1** girl; **une petite fille** a little girl; **une jeune fille** a young woman; **2** daughter.

fillette *noun Fem.* little girl.

filleul, filleule *noun Masc., Fem.* godson, goddaughter.

film *noun Masc.* film.

film comique *noun Masc.* comedy (*film*).

film d'épouvante *noun Masc.* horror film.

filmer *verb* [1] to film.

film policier *noun Masc.* thriller

fils *noun Masc.* son.

filtre *noun Masc.* filter.

filtrer *verb* [1] to filter.

fin[1] *noun Fem.* end; **à la fin** in the end; **à la fin du film** at the end of the film; **sans fin** endless.

fin[2] *adjective* **1** fine; **2** slender.

final (*Masc. plural* **finaux**) *adjective* final.

finale *noun Fem.* final, cup final.

finalement *adverb* **1** in the end, finally; **2** after all.

finance *noun Fem.* finance.

financer *verb* [61] to finance.

fines herbes *plural noun Fem.* mixed herbs.

finir *verb* [2] **1** to finish, to end; **le film finit à dix heures** the film finishes at ten o'clock; **2 finir de faire** to finish doing; **j'ai fini de faire la vaisselle** I've finished doing the washing-up; **3 finir quelque chose** to finish something; **as-tu**

fluide

fini tes devoirs? have you finished your homework?; **j'ai fini le sucre** I've finished the sugar, I've used up all the sugar; **4 finir par faire** to end up doing; **il a fini par accepter** he accepted in the end.

finlandais noun Masc. Finnish (language).

finlandais adjective Finnish.

Finlande noun Fem. Finland.

firme noun Fem. firm.

fisc noun Masc. tax office.

fissure noun Fem. crack.

fixe adjective **1** fixed; **2 un emploi fixe** a steady job; **3 aux heures fixes** at set times.

fixer verb [1] **1** to fix (to attach); **2** to set (a date, a price); **fixer les élections legislatives** to set the date for the general elections.

flacon noun Masc. (small) bottle.

flamand noun Masc. Flemish (language).

flamand adjective Flemish.

Flamand, Flamande noun Masc., Fem. Fleming (Dutch-speaking Belgian).

flamant noun Masc. flamingo.

flamber verb [1] to blaze.

flamme noun Fem. flame.

flan noun Masc. custard tart.

flanc noun Masc. side.

flâner verb [1] to stroll.

flaque noun Fem. **une flaque d'eau** a puddle.

flash noun Masc. **1** flash (on a camera); **2** newsflash.

flatter verb [1] to flatter.

flatteur (Fem. **flatteuse**) adjective flattering.

flèche noun Fem. **1** arrow; **2** spire.

fléchette noun Fem. dart; **jouer aux fléchettes** to play darts.

fléchir verb [2] **1** to bend; **2** to weaken.

fleur noun Fem. flower; **un tissu à fleurs** a flower-patterned fabric; **être en fleurs** to be in flower.

fleuri adjective **1** flowery; **du tissu fleuri** flowery material; **2 ton jardin est très fleuri** you've got lots of flowers in your garden.

fleurir verb [2] **1** to flower, to blossom; **2** to flourish.

fleuriste noun Masc. & Fem. florist.

fleuve noun Masc. river.

flexible adjective flexible.

flic noun Masc. (informal) policeman, cop.

flipper noun Masc. pinball machine.

flirter verb [1] to flirt.

flocon noun Masc. flake; **un flocon de neige** a snowflake.

flocons d'avoine plural noun Masc. porridge oats.

floral (Masc. plural **floraux**) adjective floral.

flotte noun Fem. fleet (of ships).

flotter verb [1] to float.

flou adjective **1** blurred; **une image floue** a blurred image; **2** vague; **ses projets sont un peu flous** her plans are a bit vague.

fluide noun Masc., adjective fluid.

a
b
c
d
e
f
g
h
i
j
k
l
m
n
o
p
q
r
s
t
u
v
w
x
y
z

fluo *adjective* (*informal*) fluorescent; **vert fluo** fluorescent green.

fluor *noun Masc.* fluorine.

fluorescent *adjective* fluorescent.

flûte *noun Fem.* flute; **jouer de la flûte** to play the flute.

flûte à bec *noun Fem.* recorder.

focaliser *verb* [1] to focus.

foi *noun Fem.* faith.

foie *noun Masc.* liver; **une crise de foie** an upset stomach.

foin *noun Masc.* hay.

foire *noun Fem.* fair.

fois *noun Fem.* **1** time; **une fois** once; **deux fois** twice; **trois fois** three times; **trois fois dix** three times ten; **plusieurs fois** several times; **la première fois** the first time; **trois fois plus grand** three times as big; **2 à la fois** at the same time; **trois à la fois** three at a time; **3 une fois que** once; **une fois que j'aurai pris une douche** once I've had a shower; **4 j'ai vu une fois** ... I once saw ...; **il était une fois** ... once upon a time ...; **5 à chaque fois** whenever, each time; **à chaque fois que nous sortons, nous verrouillons la porte** whenever we go out, we lock the door.

folie *noun Fem.* madness; **c'est de la folie!** it's crazy!

folk *noun Masc.* folk music.

folle *noun Fem.*, *adjective* SEE **fou**.

foncer *verb* [61] (*informal*) to rush; **tout le monde a foncé vers la porte** everybody rushed for the door.

fonction *noun Fem.* **1** job; **une voiture de fonction** a company ca **2** function.

fonctionnaire *noun Masc. & Fem* civil servant.

fonctionnel (*Fem.* **fonctionnelle** *adjective* functional.

fonctionnement *noun Masc.* working; **comprendre le fonctionnement de quelque chose** to understand how something works.

fonctionner *verb* [1] to work.

fonction publique *noun Fem.* civil service.

fond *noun Masc.* **1** bottom; **au fond du lac** at the bottom of the lake; **a fond de la bouteille** in the bottor of the bottle; **2** back; **au fond du tiroir** at the back of the drawer; **au fond de la salle** at the back of the room; **3** end; **au fond du couloir** the end of the corridor; **4** background; **5 au fond** basicall

fondamental (*Masc. plural* **fondamentaux**) *adjective* basic, fundamental.

fondateur, **fondatrice** *noun Masc., Fem.* founder.

fondation *noun Fem.* foundation.

fond de teint *noun Masc.* make-up, foundation.

fonder *verb* [1] **1** to found; **2** to bas

fondre *verb* [3] to melt.

fondu *adjective* melted.

font *verb* SEE **faire**.

fontaine *noun Fem.* **1** fountain; **2** drinking fountain.

onte *noun Fem.* **1** cast iron; **une poêle en fonte** a cast iron frying pan; **2** melting (*of metal*); **3** thawing (*of ice*).

oot *noun* (*informal*) **un match de foot** a football match; **jouer au foot** to play football.

ootball *noun Masc.* football.

ootballeur *noun Masc.* footballer.

ooting *noun Masc.* jogging; **faire du footing** to go jogging.

orain *noun Masc.* fairground worker.

forain *adjective* **une fête foraine** a funfair.

orce *noun Fem.* **1** strength; **2** force; **de force** by force; **3** force; **force de vente** sales force; **4** à **force de** by; **à force de travailler toute la nuit, elle a fini sa dissertation** she finished her essay by working all night.

orcément *adverb* **1** inevitably; **il y a forcément une solution** there has to be a solution; **2 pas forcément** not necessarily.

orcer *verb* [61] **1** to force; **2 se forcer** to force yourself.

orêt *noun Fem.* forest.

orfait *noun Masc.* fixed price.

orgeron *noun Masc.* blacksmith.

ormalité *noun Fem.* formality.

ormat *noun Masc.* format, size.

ormation *noun Fem.* training; **elle a une formation d'infirmière** she's a trained nurse.

ormation continue *noun Fem.* continuing education.

forme *noun Fem.* **1** shape, form; **2 être en forme** to be on form; **se mettre en forme** to get fit; **tu as l'air en forme** you're looking well.

formel (*Fem.* **formelle**) *adjective* **1** positive, categorical; **2** formal.

formellement *adverb* strictly; **formellement interdit** strictly forbidden.

former *verb* [1] **1** to form; **2** to train, to educate.

formidable *adjective* (*informal*) great, fantastic; **le film était formidable** the film was fantastic.

formulaire *noun Masc.* form; **remplir un formulaire** to fill in a form.

formule *noun Fem.* **1** formula; **Formule Un** Formula One (*car racing*); **2** form; **3** format.

fort *adjective* **1** strong; **il est très fort** he's very strong; **le café est très fort** the coffee's very strong; **2 être fort en quelque chose** to be good at something; **elle est très forte en maths** she's very good at maths; **3** stout.
fort *adverb* **1** extremely; **c'était fort bon** it was extremely good; **2** hard; **frapper fort** to knock (*or* hit) hard; **3** loudly; **chanter fort** to sing loudly; **parle plus fort** speak louder.

forteresse *noun Fem.* fortress.

fortifiant *noun Masc.* tonic.

fortifier *verb* [1] **1** to strengthen; **2** to fortify.

fortuit *adjective* accidental.

fortune *noun Fem.* **1** fortune; **faire fortune** to make a fortune; **2 de**

a
b
c
d
e
f
g
h
i
j
k
l
m
n
o
p
q
r
s
t
u
v
w
x
y
z

fortune makeshift; **un lit de fortune** a makeshift bed.

fossé noun Masc. ditch.

fossette noun Fem. dimple.

fou, folle noun Masc., Fem. madman, madwoman; **un fou m'a doublé dans un virage** a madman overtook me on a bend.

fou (Fem. **folle**) adjective **1** mad; **devenir fou** to go mad; **2** crazy, amazing; **on a passé une soirée folle** we had an amazing evening; **il y avait un monde fou** there were masses of people; **3 être fou de** to be mad about; ★ **attraper un fou rire** to get the giggles.

foudre noun Fem. lightning; **être frappé par la foudre** to be struck by lightning.

fouet noun Masc. **1** whip; **2** whisk (for eggs, cream, etc).

fouetter verb [1] **1** to whip; **2** to whisk (eggs, cream, etc); ★ **avoir d'autres chats à fouetter** to have other fish to fry (literally: to have other cats to whip).

fougère noun Fem. **1** fern; **2** bracken.

fouille noun Fem. search.

fouiller verb [1] **1** to search; **fouiller quelqu'un** to search somebody; **la police a fouillé la chambre/la maison** the police searched the room/house; **2 fouiller dans quelque chose** to rummage through something.

fouillis noun Masc. mess.

foulard noun Masc. scarf.

foule noun Fem. **1** crowd; **2 une foule de** masses of.

four noun Masc. oven; **cuit au four** roasted, baked.

four à micro-ondes noun Masc. microwave oven.

fourche noun Fem. garden fork, pitchfork.

fourchette noun Fem. fork.

fourgon noun Masc. van.

fourgonnette noun Fem. (small) van.

fourmi noun Fem. ant; ★ **avoir des fourmis dans les jambes** to have pins and needles in your legs (literally: to have ants in your legs)

fourmiller verb [1] **fourmiller de** to be swarming with.

fourneau (plural **fourneaux**) noun Masc. stove.

fournée noun Fem. batch (of cakes, bread).

fournir verb [2] to supply.

fournisseur noun Masc. supplier.

fournitures plural noun Fem. stationery; **les fournitures de bureau** office stationery; **les fournitures scolaires** school equipment (stationery, school bags etc).

fourré adjective **1** filled; **fourré au chocolat** with a chocolate filling; **2** fur-lined.

fourrure noun Fem. **1** fur; **2** fur coat.

foyer noun Masc. **1** home; **rester au foyer** to stay at home (rather than going out to work); **une femme au foyer** a housewife; **2** hearth; **3** household; **4** hostel.

fracas noun Masc. crash.

acasser verb [1] to smash.

action noun Fem. fraction.

acture noun Fem. fracture.

acturer verb [1] **1** to break open; **2** to fracture.

agile adjective **1** fragile; **2** frail.

agment noun Masc. fragment.

aîche adjective SEE **frais** 2.

aîcheur noun Fem. **1** coolness; **2** freshness.

ais 1 plural noun Masc. **1** expenses; **les frais de déplacement** travel expenses; **2** costs.

ais 2 (Fem. fraîche) adjective **1** cool, cold; **il fait frais ce matin** it's a chilly morning; **2** cool; **'boissons fraîches'** 'cool drinks'; **servir frais** serve chilled; **conserver au frais** keep in a cool place; **3** fresh; **des légumes frais** fresh vegetables; **'peinture fraîche'** 'wet paint'.

aise noun Fem. strawberry; **une glace à la fraise** a strawberry ice cream.

amboise noun Fem. raspberry; **un yaourt à la framboise** a raspberry yoghurt.

anc 1 noun Masc. franc (the currency of Switzerland; name of the currencies used in France, Belgium and Luxembourg until replaced by the euro; 100 French francs = 15.24 euros).

anc 2 (Fem. franche) adjective frank.

ançais noun Masc. French; **j'apprends le français** I'm learning French; **Laura parle français** Laura speaks French.

français adjective French; **un film français** a French film.

Français, Française noun Masc., Fem. Frenchman, Frenchwoman; **les Français** the French.

France noun Fem. France; **aller en France** to go to France; **habiter en France** to live in France.

franche adjective SEE **franc** 2.

franchement adverb **1** frankly; **franchement, je ne le crois pas** frankly, I don't believe him; **2** really; **le film était franchement nul** the film was really awful.

franchir verb [2] to cross.

franchise noun Fem. **1** frankness, honesty; **2** franchise.

francophone adjective French-speaking.

frange noun Fem. fringe.

frangin noun Masc. (informal) brother.

frangine noun Fem. (informal) sister.

frangipane noun Fem. almond cream.

franglais noun Masc. Franglais (a mixture of French and English).

frapper verb [1] **1** to hit; **2** frapper à la porte to knock on the door; **3** to strike; **être frappé par** to be struck by; **ça m'a beaucoup frappé** that made a big impression on me; **4** frappé par le chômage** hit by unemployment.

fraude noun Fem. **1** fraud; **2** cheating.

a
b
c
d
e
f
g
h
i
j
k
l
m
n
o
p
q
r
s
t
u
v
w
x
y
z

131

fredonner *verb* [1] to hum.

freezer *noun Masc.* freezer compartment (*in a fridge*).

frein *noun Masc.* brake; **les freins** the brakes; **le frein à main** the handbrake.

freiner *verb* [1] **1** to brake; **2** to slow down.

frêle *adjective* frail.

frelon *noun Masc.* hornet.

frémir *verb* [2] **1** to shudder; **2** to tremble.

frêne *noun Masc.* ash tree.

fréquemment *adverb* frequently.

fréquence *noun Fem.* frequency.

fréquenté *adjective* **1** busy; **un restaurant très fréquenté** a very busy restaurant; **2 un quartier mal fréquenté** a rough area.

fréquenter *verb* [1] **1** to go around with (*people*); **2** to go often to (*a place*).

frère *noun Masc.* brother.

fric *noun Masc.* (*informal*) money.

frictionner *verb* [1] to rub.

frigidaire™ *noun Masc.* fridge.

frigo *noun Masc.* (*informal*) fridge; **au frigo** in the fridge.

frileux (*Fem.* frileuse) *adjective* **être frileux** to feel the cold; **je ne suis pas frileuse** I don't feel the cold.

frime *noun Fem.* (*informal*) **c'est de la frime!** it's all show!

fringues *plural noun Fem.* (*informal*) clothes.

fripé *adjective* crumpled.

frire *verb* [74] **faire frire quelque chose** to fry something.

frisé *adjective* **1** curly; **2** curly-haired.

frisée *noun Fem.* curly endive, frisé (*a sort of lettuce*).

friser *verb* [1] to curl.

frisson *noun Masc.* shiver.

frissonner *verb* [1] **1** to shiver; **2** to shudder.

frit *adjective* fried.

frite *noun Fem.* chip, French fry; **steak frites** steak and chips.

friture *noun Fem.* **friture de poissons** fried fish.

froid *noun Masc.* **1 le froid** the col‹ **2 avoir froid** to be cold; **j'ai froid** I' cold; **3 il fait froid aujourd'hui** it’ cold today; **4 prendre froid** to catc‹ a chill.
froid *adjective* cold; **tes mains so‹ froides** your hands are cold.

froidement *adverb* coldly.

froideur *noun Fem.* coldness.

froisser *verb* [1] **1** to crease; **2 se froisser** to crease; **la soie se froiss‹ facilement** silk crushes easily; **3 s‹ froisser** to take offence; **4 se froisser** to strain (*a muscle*).

frôler *verb* [1] to brush against.

fromage *noun Masc.* cheese.

fromagerie *noun Fem.* cheese shop.

froment *noun Masc.* wheat.

froncer *verb* [61] **froncer les sourcils** to frown.

front *noun Masc.* **1** forehead; **2 faire front à** to face up to.

frontière *noun Fem.* border; **nous avons passé la frontière à Bâle** we crossed the border at Basle.

frotter *verb* [1] to rub; **se frotter les yeux** to rub your eyes.

fruit *noun Masc.* **les fruits** fruit; **acheter des fruits** to buy some fruit; **un fruit** a piece of fruit; **veux-tu un fruit?** would you like some fruit?

fruité *adjective* fruity.

fruits de mer *plural noun Masc.* seafood; **une omelette aux fruits de mer** a seafood omelette.

frustrant *adjective* frustrating.

frustrer *verb* [1] **1** to thwart; **2** to frustrate.

fugue *noun Fem.* **1 faire une fugue** to run away; **2** fugue.

fuir *verb* [44] **1** to run away, to flee; **2 fuir quelque chose** to run away from something; **3** to leak; **la bouilloire fuit** the kettle's leaking.

fuite *noun Fem.* **1** flight; **2 prendre la fuite** to flee; **3** leak.

fulgurant *adjective* dazzling.

fumé *adjective* smoked; **du saumon fumé** smoked salmon.

fumée *noun Fem.* smoke; ★ **il n'y a pas de fumée sans feu** there's no smoke without fire.

fumer *verb* [1] **1** to smoke; **2 fumer une cigarette** to smoke a cigarette; **il fume la pipe** he smokes a pipe; ★ **fumer comme un pompier** to smoke like a chimney (*literally: to smoke like a fireman*).

fumeur, fumeuse *noun Masc., Fem.* smoker; **zone non-fumeur** no-smoking area.

fumier *noun Masc.* manure.

funambule *noun Masc. & Fem.* tightrope walker.

funèbre *adjective* **1** funeral; **pompes funèbres** undertaker's; **2** gloomy.

funérailles *plural noun Fem.* funeral.

funiculaire *noun Masc.* funicular.

fur *noun Masc.* **1 au fur et à mesure** as you go along; **je corrige les erreurs au fur et à mesure** I correct the mistakes as I go along; **2 au fur et à mesure que** as.

furet *noun Masc.* ferret.

fureur *noun Fem.* **1** rage, fury; **2** frenzy; ★ **faire fureur** to be all the rage; **ces boucles d'oreilles font fureur en ce moment** these earrings are all the rage at the moment.

furibond *adjective* furious.

furieusement *adverb* furiously.

furieux (*Fem.* **furieuse**) *adjective* furious; **elle est furieuse contre son copain** she's furious with her boyfriend.

furoncle *noun Masc.* boil.

fusain *noun Masc.* charcoal (*for drawing*).

fuseau *noun Masc.* ski pants.

fusée *noun Fem.* rocket.

fusible *noun Masc.* fuse.

fusil *noun Masc.* gun.

fusiller *verb* [1] to shoot.

a
b
c
d
e
f
g
h
i
j
k
l
m
n
o
p
q
r
s
t
u
v
w
x
y
z

fusionner *verb* [1] to merge.

fût *noun Masc.* cask, barrel.

futé *adjective* **1** crafty; **2** bright, clever.

futur *noun Masc.* future (*tense*).
futur *adjective* future; **son futur mari** her husband-to-be.

Gg

gâcher *verb* [1] **1** to waste; **gâcher la nourriture** to waste food; **2** to spoil; **ça m'a gâché la journée!** that's spoiled my day!

gâchis *noun Masc.* waste.

gadget *noun Masc.* gadget.

gaffe *noun Fem.* (*informal*) blunder; **j'ai fait une gaffe** I've done something stupid; ★ **fais gaffe!** watch out!

gage *noun Masc.* forfeit (*in a game*).

gagnant, gagnante *noun Masc., Fem.* winner.
gagnant *adjective* winning.

gagner *verb* [1] **1** to win; **il a gagné** he's won; **gagner le match** to win the match; **2** to earn (*money*); **elle gagne bien sa vie** she makes a good living; **3 gagner du temps** to save time.

gai *adjective* cheerful.

gaieté *noun Fem.* cheerfulness.

gain *noun Masc.* **1** earnings; **2 c'est un gain de temps** it saves time.

galaxie *noun Fem.* galaxy.

galerie *noun Fem.* gallery.

galerie marchande *noun Fem.* shopping arcade.

galet *noun Masc.* pebble.

galette *noun Fem.* **1** biscuit; **2** round flat cake or loaf.

galette des Rois *noun Fem.* Twelfth Night cake (*a cake eaten on Twelfth Night; it contains a 'fève', literally a bean, but usually a small ceramic figure; the person who gets this is the king or queen and is given a cardboard crown to wear*).

galipette *noun Fem.* somersault (*child's*).

Galles *noun* **le pays de Galles** Wales.

Gallois, Galloise *noun Masc., Fem.* Welshman, Welshwoman; **les Gallois** the Welsh.

gallois *noun Masc.* Welsh (*language*).
gallois *adjective* Welsh.

galoper *verb* [1] to galop.

gamba *noun Fem.* king prawn.

gamin, gamine *noun Masc., Fem.* (*informal*) kid; **elle a trois gamins** she has three kids.

gamme *noun Fem.* **1** range; **la nouvelle gamme de produits de beauté** the new range of beauty products; **2** scale (*in music*).

gammé *adjective* **la croix gammée** the swastika.

gangster *noun Masc.* gangster.

gant *noun Masc.* glove.

gant de boxe *noun Masc.* boxing glove.

gant de ménage *noun Masc.* rubber glove.

gant de toilette *noun Masc.* facecloth.

garage noun Masc. garage.

garagiste noun Masc. & Fem.
1 garage owner; **2** motor mechanic.

garantie noun Fem. guarantee.

garantir verb [2] to guarantee.

garçon noun Masc. **1** boy; **2** young
man; **un brave garçon** a nice chap;
3 waiter; **4 un vieux garçon** a
bachelor.

garçon de café noun Masc.
waiter (in a cafe).

garde noun Masc. & Fem. **1** guard;
2 nurse; **3 être de garde** to be on
duty; **la pharmacie de garde** the
duty chemist's; **mettre quelqu'un
en garde** to warn somebody;
★ **prends garde!** watch out, be
careful!

garder verb [1] **1** to keep; **est-ce
que tu peux garder mon sac?** can
you keep my bag for me?; **je t'ai
gardé du gâteau** I've kept you some
cake; **je t'ai gardé une place** I've
kept you a seat; **2** to keep on; **elle a
gardé son manteau** she kept her
coat on; **3** to look after; **je garde
mon petit-fils ce soir** I'm looking
after my grandson this evening;
4 garder la maison to guard the
house.

garderie noun Fem. day nursery.

garde-robe noun Fem. wardrobe.

gardien, gardienne noun Masc.,
Fem. **1** security guard; **2** caretaker;
3 attendant (in a car park or
museum).

gardien de but noun Masc.
goalkeeper.

gardien de la paix noun Masc.
policeman.

gare noun Fem. (railway) station.

garer verb [1] **1 garer une voiture**
to park a car; **2 se garer** to park.

gare routière noun Fem. coach
station.

garni adjective **bien garni** full, well-
stocked.

garnir verb [2] **1** to decorate; **2** to
stock (shelves, fridge).

garniture noun Fem. **1** side-dish;
2 filling (for sandwich); **3** topping
(for pizza); **4** trimming, decoration.

gars noun Masc. (informal) guy.

Gascogne noun Fem. Gascony.

gasoil noun Masc. diesel (oil).

gaspiller verb [1] to waste.

gastronome noun Masc. & Fem.
gourmet.

gastronomie noun Fem.
gastronomy.

gâteau (plural **gâteaux**) noun
Masc. cake; **un gâteau au chocolat** a
chocolate cake.

gâter verb [1] **1** to spoil; **2 se gâter**
to go bad; **la viande se gâte** the
meat is going bad; **le temps se gâte**
the weather's breaking.

gauche noun Fem. **1** left; **à gauche**
on the left; **les Anglais conduisent
à gauche** the English drive on the
left; **tournez à gauche** turn left; **à
ma gauche** on my left; **2 la gauche**
the Left (in politics); **des idées de
gauche** left-wing ideas.
gauche adjective left, left-hand; **sa
main gauche** his left hand.

gaucher (Fem. **gauchère**) adjective
left-handed.

a
b
c
d
e
f
g
h
i
j
k
l
m
n
o
p
q
r
s
t
u
v
w
x
y
z

gaufre *noun Fem.* waffle.

gaufrette *noun Fem.* wafer.

gaz *noun Masc.* gas; **le chauffage à gaz** gas central heating; **nous nous chauffons au gaz** we have gas heating.

gazeux (*Fem.* **gazeuse**) *adjective* fizzy; **eau gazeuse** fizzy mineral water.

gazole *noun Masc.* diesel (oil).

gazon *noun Masc.* grass, lawn.

géant, géante *noun Masc., Fem.* giant.
géant *adjective* huge.

gel *noun Masc.* **1** frost; **2 le gel des prix** the price freeze; **3** gel.

gelé *adjective* frozen.

gelée *noun Fem.* **1** jelly; **œuf en gelée** egg in aspic; **2** frost.

geler *verb* [45] to freeze; **il gèle dehors** it's freezing outside.

gélule *noun Fem.* capsule.

Gémeaux *plural noun Masc.* Gemini (*sign of the Zodiac*).

gémir *verb* [2] to moan.

gênant *adjective* **1** annoying; **ce bruit est très gênant** that noise is very annoying; **2** awkward; **c'est une situation gênante** it's an awkward situation.

gencive *noun Fem.* gum (*part of your mouth*).

gendarme *noun Masc.* policeman.

gendarmerie *noun Fem.* police station.

gendarmerie nationale *noun Fem.* (French) national police force.

gendre *noun Masc.* son-in-law.

gêne *noun Fem.* **1** embarrassment; **2** inconvenience; **3** discomfort.

gêné *adjective* embarrassed.

gêner *verb* [1] **1** to bother; **est-ce que mon sac vous gêne?** is my bag in your way?; **2** to embarrass; **3** to block (*traffic*); **ta voiture gêne** your car's in the way.

général (*plural* **généraux**) *noun Masc.* general; **le général Dubois** General Dubois.
général (*Masc. plural* **gènéraux**) *adjective* general; **en général** in general, generally; **de façon générale** generally.

généralement *adverb* generally.

génération *noun Fem.* generation.

généreux (*Fem.* **généreuse**) *adjective* generous.

générique *noun Masc.* (film) credits.

générosité *noun Fem.* generosity.

genêt *noun Masc.* broom (*the bush*).

génétique *noun Fem.* genetics.

Genève *noun* Geneva.

génial (*Masc. plural* **géniaux**) *adjective* **1** brilliant; **une idée géniale** a brilliant idea; **2** (*informal*) great; **c'était génial!** it was great!

génie *noun Masc.* **1** genius; **2** engineering.

genou (*plural* **genoux**) *noun Masc.* knee; **avoir mal au genou** to have a sore knee; **être à genoux** to be kneeling; **se mettre à genoux** to kneel down; **sur mes genoux** on my lap.

genre *noun Masc.* kind; **un genre de sauce épicée** a kind of spicy sauce; **un peu dans le genre de ton pull** a bit like your sweater.

gens *plural noun Masc.* people; **beaucoup de gens** lots of people; **les gens disent que** ... people say that ....

gentil (*Fem.* **gentille**) *adjective* **1** kind, nice; **elle est très gentille** she's really nice; **2** kind; **c'est très gentil de ta part** it's very kind of you; **3** good; **sois gentil et mange ta viande** be a good boy and eat up your meat.

gentillesse *noun Fem.* kindness.

gentiment *adverb* **1** nicely; **demande gentiment** ask nicely; **2** kindly.

géographie *noun Fem.* geography.

géologie *noun Fem.* geology.

géométrie *noun Fem.* geometry.

gérant, **gérante** *noun Masc., Fem.* manager, manageress.

gérer *verb* (24) to manage, to run.

germain *adjective* **un cousin germain** a first cousin.

gésier *noun Masc.* gizzard.

geste *noun Masc.* gesture.

gestion *noun Fem.* management; **gestion de fichiers** file management (*on a computer*).

gibier *noun Masc.* game (*for example, venison, pheasant*).

gifle *noun Fem.* slap (*in the face*).

gifler *verb* [1] to slap (*in the face*).

gigantesque *adjective* huge, gigantic; **un repas gigantesque** a huge meal.

gigaoctet *noun Masc.* gigabyte; **un disque dur de 20 gigaoctets** a twenty gigabyte hard disk.

gigot *noun Masc.* leg of lamb.

gilet *noun Masc.* **1** cardigan; **2** waistcoat.

gilet de sauvetage *noun Masc.* life-jacket.

gingembre *noun Masc.* ginger.

girafe *noun Fem.* giraffe.

gitan, **gitane** *noun Masc., Fem.* gipsy.

gîte (rural) *noun Masc.* holiday house.

glaçage *noun Masc.* **1** glazing; **2** icing.

glace *noun Fem.* **1** ice cream; **une glace au chocolat** a chocolate ice cream; **2** ice; **3** mirror; **se regarder dans la glace** to look at yourself in the mirror; **4** window (*in a car*).

glacé *adjective* **1** icy cold; **j'ai les mains glacées** my hands are freezing; **2 un thé glacé** an iced tea.

glacier *noun Masc.* glacier.

glacière *noun Fem.* cool-box.

glaçon *noun Masc.* ice cube.

glissant *adjective* slippery.

glisser *verb* [1] to slip, to slide; **attention, ça glisse!** be careful, it's slippery!

global (*Masc. plural* **globaux**) *adjective* total.

a

globalisation noun Fem. globalization.

gloire noun Fem. fame, glory.

glorieux (Fem. **glorieuse**) adjective glorious.

glossaire noun Masc. glossary.

gobelet noun Masc. cup, tumbler; **un gobelet en carton** a paper cup.

godasse noun Fem. (informal) shoe.

gogo (informal) **à gogo** as much as you like; **pizza à gogo** as much pizza as you can eat.

golden noun Fem. Golden Delicious (apple).

golf noun Masc. **1** golf; **jouer au golf** to play golf; **2** golf course.

golfe noun Masc. gulf.

golfeur, golfeuse noun Masc., Fem. golfer.

gomme noun Fem. rubber.

gommer verb [1] to rub out.

gonfler verb [1] **1** to pump up (tyres); **2** to blow up (a balloon).

gorge noun Fem. **1** throat; **j'ai mal à la gorge** I've got a sore throat; **j'avais la gorge serrée** I had a lump in my throat; **il chantait à pleine gorge** he was singing at the top of his voice; **2** gorge.

gorgée noun Fem. sip; **une gorgée de thé** a sip of tea.

gorille noun Masc. gorilla.

gosse noun Masc. & Fem. kid.

goudron noun Masc. tar.

gourde noun Fem. water bottle.

gourmand adjective greedy.

gourmandise noun Fem. **1** greed; **2 elle aime les gourmandises** she likes sweet things.

gousse noun Fem. **une gousse d'ail** a clove of garlic.

goût noun Masc. taste; **ça a un goût bizarre** it has a strange taste; **de bon goût** in good taste; ★ **chacun ses goûts** it takes all sorts to make a world.

goûter noun Masc. **1** teatime snack; **2** children's party.
goûter verb [1] **1** to taste, to try; **est-ce que tu as goûté le gâteau?** have you tried the cake?; **2** to have a teatime snack.

goutte noun Fem. drop; **une goutte de** a drop of; **goutte à goutte** drop by drop.

gouvernement noun Masc. government.

gouverner verb [1] to govern, to rule.

grâce noun Fem. **grâce à** thanks to; **la soirée a été un grand succès grâce à toi** the evening was a great success thanks to you.

gracieux (Fem. **gracieuse**) adjective graceful.

grade noun Masc. rank; **monter en grade** to be promoted.

gradins plural noun Masc. terraces (in a stadium).

graduel (Fem. **graduelle**) adjective gradual.

graffiti plural noun Masc. graffiti.

grain noun Masc. **1** grain; **un grain de sable** a grain of sand; **2 du poivre en grains** peppercorns; **3 du**

café en grains coffee beans; **4 un grain de beauté** a beauty spot; **5 un grain de raisin** a grape.

raine *noun Fem.* seed.

raisse *noun Fem.* fat, grease.

rammaire *noun Fem.* grammar.

ramme *noun Masc.* gramme.

rand *adjective* **1** big; **une grande maison** a big house; **c'est ma grande sœur** she's my big sister; **2** tall; **un grand arbre** a tall tree; **ton frère est très grand** your brother's very tall; **elle est plus grande que moi** she's taller than me; **3** great; **un grand artiste** a great artist; **un grand ami** a great friend; **4** main; **les grandes lignes** main (railway) lines.

grand *adverb* wide; **la porte était grande ouverte** the door was wide open.

rand bassin *noun Masc.* main pool *(for experienced swimmers)*.

rand-chose *pronoun* much; **pas grand-chose** not much; **il ne reste pas grand-chose** there's not much left.

Grande-Bretagne *noun Fem.* Great Britain.

rande personne *noun Fem.* grown-up.

rande surface *noun Fem.* hypermarket.

randes vacances *plural noun Fem.* summer holidays.

randeur *noun Fem.* size; **grandeur nature** life-size.

randir *verb* [2] to grow, to grow up.

rand magasin *noun Masc.* department store.

grand-mère *(plural* **grands-mères)** *noun Fem.* grandmother.

grand-père *(plural* **grands-pères)** *noun Masc.* grandfather.

grands espaces *plural noun Masc.* open spaces.

grands-parents *plural noun Masc.* grandparents.

grange *noun Fem.* barn.

graphiste *noun Masc. & Fem.* graphic designer.

grappe *noun Fem.* **une grappe de raisin** a bunch of grapes.

gras *(Fem.* **grasse)** *adjective* **1** fatty, greasy; **40% matière grasse** 40% fat *(on cheese or yoghurt label)*; **2 une peau grasse** oily skin; ★ **faire la grasse matinée** to have a lie-in.

gratitude *noun Fem.* gratitude.

gratte-ciel *noun Masc.* skyscraper.

gratter *verb* [1] **1 gratter quelque chose** to scratch something; **2 se gratter** to scratch (yourself); **3** to itch; **ça gratte** it itches.

gratuit *adjective* free; **le concert est gratuit** the concert's free; **'entrée gratuite'** 'admission free'.

grave *adjective* **1** serious; **un grave accident** a serious accident; **2 ce n'est pas grave** it doesn't matter; **3** serious; **une expression grave** a serious expression; **4** deep; **une voix grave** a deep voice.

gravement *adverb* seriously; **elle est gravement malade** she's seriously ill.

gravure *noun Fem.* engraving, print.

a
b
c
d
e
f
g
h
i
j
k
l
m
n
o
p
q
r
s
t
u
v
w
x
y
z

a · b · c · d · e · f · **g** · h · i · j · k · l · m · n · o · p · q · r · s · t · u · v · w · x · y · z

gré *noun Masc.* **contre son gré** against his will.

grec *noun Masc.* Greek (*language*).
grec (*Fem.* **grecque**) *adjective* Greek.

Grec, **Grecque** *noun Masc., Fem.* Greek (person).

Grèce *noun Fem.* Greece.

grêle *noun Fem.* hail.

grelotter *verb* [1] to shiver.

grenade *noun Fem.* **1** grenade; **2** pomegranate.

grenadine *noun Fem.* grenadine (*pomegranate cordial*).

grenier *noun Masc.* attic, loft; **au grenier** in the attic.

grenouille *noun Fem.* frog; **les cuisses de grenouille** frogs' legs.

grève *noun Fem.* strike; **une grève des trains** a train strike; **le métro est en grève** the underground's on strike; **faire grève** to go (*or* be) on strike.

gréviste *noun Masc. & Fem.* striker.

grièvement *adverb* seriously; **grièvement blessé** seriously injured.

griffe *noun Fem.* claw.

griffonner *verb* [1] to scribble.

grillade *noun Fem.* grilled meat, meat for grilling; **une grillade de porc** a pork steak.

grillage *noun Masc.* wire netting.

grille *noun Fem.* **1** metal gate; **2** railings; **3** wire fence.

grillé *adjective* **1** grilled; **2** toasted; **du pain grillé** toast.

grille-pain *noun Masc.* toaster.

griller *verb* [1] **1** to grill; **2** to toast

grillon *noun Masc.* cricket (*the creature not the game*).

grimace *noun Fem.* **faire des grimaces** to make faces.

grimper *verb* [1] to climb; **grimper dans un arbre** to climb a tree.

grincer *verb* [61] to creak, to squeak.

grincheux (*Fem.* **grincheuse**) *adjective* grumpy.

grippe *noun Fem.* flu; **avoir la grippe** to have flu; **une grippe intestinale** gastric flu.

gris *adjective* grey.

grisaille *noun Fem.* dull overcast weather.

grogner *verb* [1] **1** to growl; **2** to grumble.

gronder *verb* [1] **1** **gronder quelqu'un** to tell somebody off; **se faire gronder** to get a telling-off; **2** to rumble (*thunder, for example*).

gros (*Fem.* **grosse**) *adjective* **1** big; **un gros morceau** a big piece; **un gros problème** a big problem; **2** fat **un gros monsieur** a fat man; **3** un **gros rhume** a bad cold; **4** un **gros fumeur** a heavy smoker; **5** un **gros mot** a swear word; **6** en gros roughly.

groseille *noun Fem.* redcurrant.

groseille à maquereau *noun Fem.* gooseberry.

grosse *adjective* SEE **gros**.

grossesse *noun Fem.* pregnancy

rosseur noun Fem. **1** lump; **2** size.

rossier (Fem. **grossière**) adjective **1** rude; **2** crude; **une idée grossière de** a rough idea of; **une erreur grossière** a bad mistake.

rossir verb [2] to put on weight; **il a beaucoup grossi** he's put on a lot of weight.

rosso modo adverb roughly.

rotesque adjective ridiculous.

rotte noun Fem. cave.

roupe noun Masc. group; **travailler/voyager en groupe** to work/travel in a group.

rouper verb [1] **1** to group; **2 se grouper** to gather, to form a group.

roupe sanguin noun Masc. blood group.

rue noun Fem. crane.

uépard noun Masc. cheetah.

uêpe noun Fem. wasp.

uère adverb **ne ...guère** hardly; **je ne l'ai guère vu depuis Noël** I've hardly seen him since Christmas.

uérir verb [2] **1** to cure; **le médecin l'a guéri** the doctor cured him; **2** to get better; **j'ai été malade mais je suis maintenant guéri** I've been ill but I'm better now.

uérison noun Fem. recovery (from an illness or injury).

uerre noun Fem. war; **le pays est actuellement en guerre** the country is at war at the moment; **la Seconde Guerre mondiale** World War II.

uetter verb [1] to watch out for.

gueule noun Fem. mouth (of an animal; considered rude if used of a person); **(ferme) ta gueule!** (rude) shut up!

gueule de bois noun Fem. (informal) **avoir la gueule de bois** to have a hangover.

gueuler verb [1] (informal) to yell.

gui noun Masc. mistletoe.

guichet noun Masc. **1** ticket office (in a station or museum); **2** box office (in a theatre or cinema); **3** counter, window (in a bank or post office).

guichet automatique noun Masc. cashpoint.

guide noun Masc. guide.

guider verb [1] to guide.

guidon noun Masc. handlebars.

guillemets plural noun Masc. inverted commas; **entre guillemets** in inverted commas.

guirlande noun Fem. **des guirlandes** tinsel; **des guirlandes en papier** paper chains.

guirlande électrique noun Fem. fairy lights, Christmas-tree lights.

guitare noun Fem. guitar; **jouer de la guitare** to play the guitar.

guitariste noun Masc. & Fem. guitarist.

gym noun Fem. (informal) PE, gymnastics.

gymnase noun Masc. gym; **je te verrai au gymnase** I'll see you in the gym.

gymnastique noun Fem. gymnastics, exercises.

a
b
c
d
e
f
g
h
i
j
k
l
m
n
o
p
q
r
s
t
u
v
w
x
y
z

Hh

a
b
c
d
e
f
g
h
i
j
k
l
m
n
o
p
q
r
s
t
u
v
w
x
y
z

habile *adjective* clever; **elle est habile de ses mains** she's clever with her hands; **de manière habile** cleverly.

habillé *adjective* **1** dressed; **je ne suis pas encore habillé** I'm not dressed yet; **2** smart (*for example, a dress or suit*).

habiller *verb* [1] **1** habiller quelqu'un to dress somebody; **2** s'habiller to get dressed; **habille-toi vite!** get dressed quick!; **3** s'habiller to dress up; **s'habiller en clown** to dress up as a clown.

habitant, habitante *noun Masc., Fem.* inhabitant.

habitation *noun Fem.* house.

habiter *verb* [1] to live; **ils habitent à Paris** they live in Paris.

habitude *noun Fem.* **1** habit; **c'est une mauvaise habitude** it's a bad habit; **2** d'habitude usually; **d'habitude il arrive à midi** he usually arrives at twelve; **3** comme d'habitude as usual; **j'ai pris le bus comme d'habitude** I took the bus as usual; **4** avoir l'habitude de faire to be used to doing; **j'ai l'habitude de travailler le soir** I'm used to working in the evening.

habitué, habituée *noun Masc., Fem.* regular (*in a cafe, shop, etc*).

habitué *adjective* être habitué à quelque chose to be accustomed to something.

habituel (*Fem.* habituelle) *adjective* usual.

habituer *verb* [1] **s'habituer à quelque chose** to get used to something; **je m'y suis habituée** I've got used to it.

hache *noun Fem.* axe.

haché *adjective* chopped; **du bœuf haché** mince.

hacher *verb* [1] **1** to chop (*vegetables*); **2** to mince (*meat*).

hachis Parmentier *noun Masc.* shepherd's pie.

haddock *noun Masc.* smoked haddock.

haie *noun Fem.* **1** hedge; **2** les haies hurdles (*sport*).

haine *noun Fem.* hatred.

haïr *verb* [46] to hate.

Haïti *noun Masc.* Haiti.

haïtien *Fem.* haïtienne *adjective* Haitian.

Haïtien, Haïtienne *noun Masc., Fem.* Haitian.

haleine *noun Fem.* breath; **être hors d'haleine** to be out of breath.

hall *noun Masc.* **1** (entrance) hall; **2** concourse (*in a station*).

halles *plural noun Fem.* covered market.

halogène *adjective* halogen; **une lampe halogène** a halogen lamp.

halte *noun Fem.* stop; **halte!** stop!; **faire une halte** to stop somewhere.

halte-garderie *noun Fem.* playgroup.

haltérophilie *noun Fem.* weightlifting.

hamac *noun Masc.* hammock.

ameau (*plural* **hameaux**) *noun*
Masc. group of houses.

ameçon *noun Masc.* fish hook.

amster *noun Masc.* hamster.

anche *noun Fem.* hip.

andball *noun Masc.* handball;
jouer au handball to play handball.

andicap *noun Masc.* handicap.

andicapé, handicapée *noun*
Masc., Fem. handicapped person.
handicapé *adjective* handicapped,
disabled.

anté *adjective* haunted.

arceler *verb* [45] **1** to pester; **2** to
harass.

areng *noun Masc.* herring.

aricot *noun Masc.* bean; **haricot
vert** French bean; **haricot blanc**
haricot bean.

armonica *noun Masc.* mouth
organ; **jouer de l'harmonica** to play
the mouth organ.

armonie *noun Fem.* harmony.

armoniser *verb* [1] to
coordinate, to harmonize.

arnais *noun Masc.* harness.

arpe *noun Fem.* harp.

asard *noun Masc.* **1** chance; **par
hasard** by chance; **je l'ai rencontré
par hasard** I met him by chance;
2 au hasard at random; **elle a
choisi un livre au hasard** she chose
a book at random; **3 à tout hasard**
just in case; **prends un manteau à
tout hasard** take a coat just in case;
4 à tout hasard on the off chance.

asardeux (*Fem.* **hasardeuse**)
adjective risky.

hâte *noun Fem.* **à la hâte** hurriedly;
elle est partie à la hâte she left in
a rush.

hausse *noun Fem.* increase, rise;
une hausse des prix a rise in
prices; **les prix sont en hausse**
prices are rising.

hausser *verb* [1] **1** to raise;
2 hausser les épaules to shrug
your shoulders.

haut *noun Masc.* **1** top; **le haut de
l'échelle** the top of the ladder;
**regarder quelqu'un de haut en
bas** to look somebody up and down;
2 l'arbre fait 10 mètres de haut
the tree is 10 metres high; **3 en haut**
upstairs; **elle est en haut** she's
upstairs; **4 en haut de** at the top of;
en haut de l'escalier at the top of
the stairs.

haut *adjective* **1** high; **la branche
la plus haute** the highest branch;
2 à haute voix aloud; **lire à haute
voix** to read aloud.

haut *adverb* high; **plus haut dans
l'arbre** higher up the tree; **'voir plus
haut'** 'see above' (*in a book*); **haut
les mains!** hands up!

hautbois *noun Masc.* oboe.

hauteur *noun Fem.* height; **la
hauteur de la pièce** the height of
the room; **dans le sens de la
hauteur** upright; **l'avion prend de
la hauteur** the plane's gaining
height; **il n'est pas à la hauteur de
son travail** he's not up to his job.

haut-parleur *noun Masc.* loudspeaker.

Haye *noun* **La Haye** The Hague.

a
b
c
d
e
f
g
h
i
j
k
l
m
n
o
p
q
r
s
t
u
v
w
x
y
z

hebdomadaire *noun* Masc. weekly magazine.

héberger *verb* [52] to put up; **Jess va nous héberger** Jess'll put us up.

hein *exclamation* (*informal*) what?, eh?

hélas *exclamation* unfortunately; **elle est déjà partie, hélas** she's already left, unfortunately; **hélas non** I'm afraid not.

hélicoptère *noun* Masc. helicopter.

hémorragie *noun* Fem. haemorrhage.

hennir *verb* [2] to neigh.

herbe *noun* Fem. **1 l'herbe** grass; **2** herb; **les fines herbes** mixed herbs; **les herbes de Provence** mixed herbs; **3 une mauvaise herbe** a weed.

hérisson *noun* Masc. hedgehog.

héritage *noun* Masc. inheritance.

hériter *verb* [1] to inherit.

hermétique *adjective* airtight.

héroïne *noun* Fem. **1** heroine; **2** heroin.

héros *noun* Masc. hero.

hésitation *noun* Fem. hesitation.

hésiter *verb* [1] to hesitate; **à ta place, je n'hésiterais pas!** if I were you, I wouldn't hesitate!; **j'ai beaucoup hésité avant d'accepter** I thought about it for a long time before I agreed; **j'hésite entre le poulet et le poisson** I can't decide whether to have the chicken or the fish.

hêtre *noun* Masc. **1** beech tree; **2** beech wood.

heure *noun* Fem. **1** hour; **une heure plus tard** an hour later; **deux heures de train** two hours in the train; **une demi-heure** half an hour; **une heure et demie** an hour and a half; **Londres est à une heure d'avion de Paris** London is an hour from Paris by air; **toutes les quatre heures** every four hours; **toutes les heures: il y a des trains toutes les heures** there are trains every hour; **payé à l'heure** paid by the hour; **cent kilomètres à l'heure** a hundred kilometres an hour; **2** time; **quelle heure est-il?** what time is it?; **il est sept heures** it's seven o'clock; **à huit heures du matin** at eight o'clock in the morning; **tu te lèves à quelle heure demain?** what time are you getting up tomorrow?; **à neuf heures** at nine o'clock; **à six heures et demie** at half past six; **3 être à l'heure** to be on time; **4 à l'heure du déjeuner** at lunchtime; ★ **de bonne heure** early; **je me lève de bonne heure demain** I'm getting up early tomorrow.

heures d'affluence *plural noun* Fem. peak time, rush hour.

heureusement *adverb* fortunately.

heureux (Fem. **heureuse**) *adjective* **1** happy; **elle est heureuse d'être ici** she's happy to be here; **2** lucky, fortunate.

heurter *verb* [1] to hit, to bump into; **la voiture a heurté un camion** the car collided with a lorry.

eurtoir noun Masc. (door) knocker.

exagone noun Masc. **1** hexagon; **2** l'Hexagone France (*French journalists often refer to France as l'Hexagone as it has a six-sided shape on the map*).

ibou (*plural* **hiboux**) noun Masc. owl.

ideux (Fem. **hideuse**) adjective hideous.

ier adverb yesterday; **je l'ai vue hier** I saw her yesterday; **hier matin** yesterday morning; **avant-hier** the day before yesterday.

i-fi noun Fem. hi-fi; **une chaîne hi-fi** a stereo system.

ippique adjective equestrian; **un concours hippique** a horse show; **un club hippique** a riding school.

ippodrome noun Masc. racecourse.

ippopotame noun Masc. hippopotamus.

irondelle noun Fem. swallow.

istoire noun Fem. **1** history; **l'histoire française** French history; **2** story; **l'histoire de ma vie** the story of my life; **3** matter; **c'est une histoire d'argent** it's a matter of money; ★ **faire des histoires** to kick up a fuss.

istorique adjective **1** historic; **un monument historique** a historic monument; **2** historical.

it-parade noun Masc. **le hit-parade** the charts (*pop music*).

iver noun Masc. winter; **en hiver** in winter.

HLM noun Masc. OR Fem. (= *habitation à loyer modéré*) council flat; **nous habitons dans un HLM à Valence** we live in a council flat in Valence; **les HLM** council housing.

hocher verb [1] **hocher la tête** to shake your head, to nod.

hockey noun Masc. hockey; **jouer au hockey** to play hockey; **le hockey sur glace** ice hockey.

hollandais noun Masc. Dutch (*language*).
hollandais adjective Dutch.

Hollandais, Hollandaise noun Masc., Fem. Dutchman, Dutchwoman; **les Hollandais** the Dutch.

Hollande noun Fem. Holland; **en Hollande** in (*or* to) Holland.

homard noun Masc. lobster.

homéopathique adjective homeopathic.

hommage noun Masc. tribute, homage; **rendre hommage à quelqu'un/quelque chose** to pay tribute to someone/something.

homme noun Masc. man; **l'homme de la rue** the man in the street; **l'homme moderne est plus grand que ses ancêtres** modern man is taller than his ancestors.

homme d'affaires noun Masc. businessman.

homme d'État noun Masc. statesman.

homogénéisé adjective homogenized.

a
b
c
d
e
f
g
h
i
j
k
l
m
n
o
p
q
r
s
t
u
v
w
x
y
z

a

b

c

d

e

f

g

h

i

j

k

l

m

n

o

p

q

r

s

t

u

v

w

x

y

z

homosexuel, homosexuelle
noun, Masc., Fem.
homosexuelle *adjective*
homosexual.

Hongrie *noun Fem.* Hungary.

hongrois *noun Masc.* Hungarian
(*language*).
hongrois *adjective* Hungarian.

honnête *adjective* honest,
respectable.

honnêtement *adverb* honestly,
frankly; **honnêtement je ne sais
pas ce que tu veux dire** I honestly
don't know what you mean.

honnêteté *noun Fem.* honesty; **en
toute honnêteté** in all honesty.

honneur *noun Masc.* honour.

honorer *verb* [1] to honour.

honte *noun Fem.* shame; **avoir
honte de quelque chose** to be
ashamed of something; **j'ai
vraiment honte** I'm really ashamed
of myself; **tu n'as pas honte!** what a
thing to say (*or* do)!

honteux (*Fem.* **honteuse**) *adjective*
disgraceful.

hôpital *noun Masc.* hospital; **être à
l'hôpital** to be in hospital.

hoquet *noun Masc.* hiccup; **avoir le
hoquet** to have hiccups.

horaire *noun Masc.* timetable,
schedule; **les horaires de train** the
train timetable.

horizon *noun Masc.* horizon; **à
l'horizon** on the horizon.

horizontal (*Masc. plural*
horizontaux) *adjective* horizontal.

horloge *noun Fem.* clock.

horodateur *noun Masc.* parking
ticket machine.

horoscope *noun Masc.* horoscope

horreur *noun Fem.* **1** horror; **quel
horreur!** how awful!; **2 avoir
horreur de quelque chose** to hate
something; **j'ai horreur d'être en
retard** I hate being late.**j'ai horreur
des escargots!** I can't stand snails

horrible *adjective* horrible.

horrifier *verb* [1] to horrify.

hors *preposition* **1 hors de** outside
hors de France outside France;
2 être hors jeu to be offside; **3 les
boutiques hors taxe** the duty-free
shops; ★ **être hors de soi** to be
beside yourself; **j'étais hors de moi**
I was beside myself.

hors-d'œuvre *noun Masc.* starter
(*to a meal*).

hortensia *noun Masc.* hydrangea.

hospitalier *adjective* **un centre
hospitalier** a hospital.

hospitaliser *verb* [1] **elle a été
hospitalisée** she's been taken into
hospital.

hospitalité *noun Fem.* hospitality

hostilité *noun Fem.* hostility.

hôte[1] *noun Masc.* host.

hôte[2] *noun Masc., Fem.* **1** guest; **hôte
payant** paying guest; **2** host.

hôtel *noun Masc.* hotel; **un hôtel de
luxe** a luxury hotel; **passer deux
nuits à l'hôtel** to spend two nights
in a hotel.

hôtel de ville *noun Masc.* town
hall.

ôtesse *noun Fem.* **1** hostess; **2** receptionist.

ôtesse d'accueil *noun Fem.* receptionist.

ôtesse de l'air *noun Fem.* flight attendant.

ousse *noun Fem.* cover (*for a chair or a machine*); **une housse de couette** a duvet cover.

oux *noun Masc.* holly.

ublot *noun Masc.* **1** window (*in a plane*); **2** porthole (*in a boat*).

uer *verb* [1] to boo; **la foule a hué l'arbitre** the crowd booed the referee.

uile *noun Fem.* oil; **huile de tournesol** sunflower oil; **huile d'olive** olive oil; **huile solaire** suntan oil.

uit *number* **1** eight; **Paul a huit ans** Paul's eight; **le huit juillet** the eighth of July; **2 huit jours** a week; **il y a huit jours** a week ago.

uitième *noun Masc.* **au huitième** on the eighth floor.

huitième *adjective* eighth.

uître *noun Fem.* oyster.

umain *adjective* human.

umanitaire *adjective* humanitarian.

umeur *noun Fem.* mood; **il est de bonne humeur** he's in a good mood; **elle est de mauvaise humeur** she's in a bad mood; **je ne suis pas d'humeur à faire ça** I'm not in the mood to do that.

umide *adjective* damp.

umidité *noun Fem.* damp.

humoristique *adjective* humorous; **un dessin humoristique** a cartoon.

humour *noun Masc.* humour; **avoir de l'humour** to have a sense of humour.

hurler *verb* [1] to yell, to howl.

hutte *noun Fem.* hut.

hydratant *adjective* moisturizing.

hygiène *noun Fem.* hygiene.

hygiénique *adjective* **1** hygienic; **2 une serviette hygiénique** a sanitary towel; **3 du papier hygiénique** toilet paper.

hymne *noun Masc.* hymn; **l'hymne national** the national anthem.

hypermarché *noun Masc.* hypermarket.

hypermétrope *adjective* long-sighted.

hypertension *noun Fem.* high blood pressure.

hypnotiser *verb* [1] to hypnotize.

hypocondriaque *noun Masc. & Fem., adjective* hypochondriac.

hypocrite *noun Masc. & Fem.* hypocrite.

hypothèse *noun Fem.* hypothesis.

hystérie *noun Fem.* hysteria.

Ii

iceberg *noun Masc.* iceberg.

ici *adverb* **1** here; **il y a trop de monde ici** there are too many people here; **les gens d'ici** the local

a
b
c
d
e
f
g
h
i
j
k
l
m
n
o
p
q
r
s
t
u
v
w
x
y
z

a people; **2 jusqu'ici** this far; **les bus ne viennent pas jusqu'ici** the buses don't come this far; **3 jusqu'ici** so far; **jusqu'ici il a fait beau** so far the weather's been good.

b

c

d **icône** noun Fem. icon.

e **idéal** (plural **idéaux**) noun Masc., adjective ideal; **l'idéal serait de louer une voiture** the ideal thing would be to hire a car.

f

g **idée** noun Fem. idea; **quelle bonne idée!** what a good idea!; **je n'ai aucune idée** I've no idea; **se faire des idées** to imagine things.

h

i

j **identifier** verb [1] to identify.

k **identique** adjective identical.

l **identité** noun Fem. identity; **une carte d'identité** an identity card.

m **idiot, idiote** noun Masc., Fem. idiot; **ne fais pas l'idiot!** don't fool around!
idiot adjective stupid; **c'est vraiment idiot!** it's really stupid!

n

o

p **ignorance** noun Fem. ignorance.

ignorant adjective ignorant.

q **ignorer** verb [1] **1** not to know; **j'ignore leur adresse** I don't know their address; **j'ignore les détails** I don't know the details; **2** to ignore; **ils l'ont ignoré** they ignored him.

r

s

t **il** pronoun **1** he; **il parle français** he speaks French; **2** it; **'où est mon sac?' – 'il est sur la chaise'** 'where's my bag?' – 'it's on the chair; **il pleut** it's raining.

u

v

w

x **île** noun Fem. island.

illégal (Masc. plural **illégaux**) adjective illegal.

y

z **illimité** adjective unlimited.

illisible adjective illegible.

illumination noun Fem. floodlighting; **les illuminations de Noël** the Christmas lights.

illuminer verb [1] to floodlight.

illusion noun Fem. illusion; **elle se fait des illusions** she's fooling herself.

illustration noun Fem. illustration.

illustré noun Masc. comic.
illustré adjective illustrated.

illustrer verb [1] to illustrate.

ils pronoun they; **ils sont en vacances** they're on holiday.

il y a SEE avoir.

image noun Fem. picture; **il y a de belles images dans ton livre** there are some lovely pictures in your book.

imaginaire adjective imaginary.

imagination noun Fem. imagination.

imaginer verb [1] to imagine; **je n'arrive pas à l'imaginer** I can't imagine it; **elle va appeler, j'imagine** I suppose she'll phone.

imbattable adjective unbeatable.

imbécile noun Masc. & Fem. fool; **faire l'imbécile** to fool around.
imbécile adjective idiotic.

imitation noun Fem. imitation.

imiter verb [1] to imitate.

immangeable adjective inedible.

immanquablement adverb inevitably.

immatriculation *noun Fem.* registration (*of a car*); **une plaque d'immatriculation** a numberplate.

immédiat *adjective* immediate; **dans l'immédiat** for the time being; **je n'ai pas de projets dans l'immédiat** I don't have any plans for the time being.

immédiatement *adverb* immediately.

immense *adjective* huge.

immeuble *noun Masc.* **1** block of flats; **2** building; **un immeuble de six étages** a six-storey building; **3 un immeuble de bureaux** an office block.

immigration *noun Fem.* immigration.

immigré, immigrée *noun Masc., Fem.* immigrant.

immobile *adjective* motionless.

immobilier (*Fem.* **immobilière**) **une agence immobilière** an estate agent's.

immobiliser *verb* [1] to immobilize.

immodéré *adjective* excessive.

immoral (*Masc. plural* **immoraux**) *adjective* immoral.

immuniser *verb* [1] to immunize.

impact *noun Masc.* impact.

impair *adjective* odd; **un nombre impair** an odd number.

impardonnable *adjective* unforgivable.

imparfait *noun Masc.* imperfect (tense); **à l'imparfait** in the imperfect.

imparfait *adjective* imperfect.

impasse *noun Fem.* dead end.

impatience *noun Fem.* impatience.

impatient *adjective* impatient.

impeccable *adjective* **1** perfect; **un accent français impeccable** a perfect French accent; **2** spotless; **l'appartement est impeccable** the flat's spotless; **3** (*informal*) great; **'je viendrai te chercher chez toi à midi' – 'impeccable!'** 'I'll come and pick you up at your place at twelve' – 'great!'

impensable *adjective* unthinkable.

imper *noun Masc.* (*informal*) SHORT FOR **imperméable** raincoat.

impératif *noun Masc.* imperative; **à l'impératif** in the imperative.

impératrice *noun Fem.* empress.

imperfection *noun Fem.* imperfection.

imperméable *noun Masc.* raincoat.

impertinent *adjective* cheeky.

impitoyable *adjective* merciless.

impliquer *verb* [1] **1** to mean; **cela implique que nous n'aurons pas assez d'argent** this means that we won't have enough money; **2 être impliqué dans quelque chose** to be involved in something.

impoli *adjective* rude.

importance *noun Fem.* importance; **ça n'a pas d'importance** it doesn't matter.

important *adjective* **1** important; **il est important de savoir que …** it's important to know that …;

2 considerable; **une réduction importante** a considerable reduction; **il y aura des retards importants** there will be considerable delays.

importations *plural noun Fem.* imports.

importer *verb* [1] **1** to import (*goods*); **2** to matter; **'lequel veux-tu?' – 'n'importe!'** 'which one do you want?' – 'it doesn't matter!'; **n'importe où** anywhere; **viens n'importe quand** come any time; **n'importe qui sait faire ça** anyone can do that; **il dit n'importe quoi** he's talking nonsense; **elle le fait n'importe comment** she does it any old how.

imposant *adjective* imposing.

imposer *verb* [1] **1** to impose; **imposer à quelqu'un de faire quelque chose** to make somebody do something; **la maman de Katy lui a imposé de rester à la maison** Katy's mum made her stay at home; **2 s'imposer** to establish oneself.

impossibilité *noun Fem.* impossibility.

impossible *adjective* impossible. **impossible** *noun* **faire l'impossible** to do your utmost; **nous ferons l'impossible pour les contacter** we'll do our utmost to contact them.

impôt *noun Masc.* tax.

imprécis *adjective* vague.

impression *noun Fem.* impression; **sa première impression** his first impression; **elle a fait très bonne impression** she made a very good impression; **j'ai l'impression qu'il n'est pas heureux** I have a feeling he's not happy.

impressionnant *adjective* impressive.

impressionner *verb* [1] to impress.

imprévisible *adjective* unpredictable.

imprévu *adjective* unexpected.

imprimante *noun Fem.* printer (*fo a computer*).

imprimante laser *noun Fem.* laser printer.

imprimé *noun Masc.* form (*to fill ir* **imprimé** *adjective* printed.

imprimer *verb* [1] to print.

improviser *verb* [1] to improvise

improviste *noun* **à l'improviste** unexpectedly; **mon oncle est arriv à l'improviste** my uncle arrived unexpectedly.

imprudent *adjective* **1** careless; **2** rash.

impuissant *adjective* helpless.

impulsif (*Fem.* **impulsive**) *adjectiv* impulsive.

inabordable *adjective* **1** inaccessible; **2 des prix inabordables** prohibitive prices.

inacceptable *adjective* unacceptable.

inaccessible *adjective* inaccessible.

inachevé *adjective* unfinished.

inadapté *adjective* unsuitable.

admissible *adjective* intolerable.

aperçu *adjective* **passer inaperçu** to go unnoticed; **son départ est passé inaperçu** her departure went unnoticed.

attendu *adjective* unexpected; **une visite inattendue** an unexpected visit.

attention *noun Fem.* lack of attention; **une faute d'inattention** a careless mistake.

audible *adjective* inaudible.

auguration *noun Fem.* inauguration, opening.

augurer *verb* [1] **1** to open (*an exhibition, a new building*); **2** to unveil (*a monument*).

capable *adjective* **1** incapable; **je suis incapable de bouger!** I'm incapable of moving!; **2** incompetent; **il est complètement incapable** he's completely incompetent.

cassable *adjective* unbreakable.

cendiaire *noun Masc. & Fem.* arsonist.

ncendiaire *adjective* **une bombe incendiaire** an incendiary bomb.

cendie *noun Masc.* fire; **l'incendie a détruit l'église** the fire destroyed the church.

certain *adjective* **1** uncertain; **le résultat est toujours incertain** the result is still uncertain; **2** unsettled (*weather*).

certitude *noun Fem.* uncertainty.

incident *noun Masc.* incident; **en cas d'incident** if anything should happen.

inciter *verb* [1] to encourage; **le père d'André l'a incité à apprendre la guitare** André's father encouraged him to learn to play the guitar.

inclure *verb* [25] **1** to include; **2** to enclose.

inclus *adjective* including; **il y aura trente invités, enfants inclus** there will be thirty guests, including children; **jusqu'à samedi inclus** up to and including Saturday.

incollable *adjective* **le riz incollable** easy-cook rice.

incolore *adjective* colourless.

incommode *adjective* **1** awkward; **2** uncomfortable.

incomparable *adjective* incomparable.

incompétent *adjective* incompetent.

incompréhensible *adjective* incomprehensible.

inconditionnel, inconditionnelle *noun Masc., Fem.* devotee; **c'est un inconditionnel du jazz** he's a real jazz fan.
inconditionnel (*Fem.* **inconditionnelle**) *adjective* unconditional.

inconfortable *adjective* uncomfortable.

inconnu, inconnue *noun Masc., Fem.* stranger.
inconnu *adjective* unknown; **elle m'est inconnue** I don't know her.

a
b
c
d
e
f
g
h
i
j
k
l
m
n
o
p
q
r
s
t
u
v
w
x
y
z

inconsciemment *adverb*
unconsciously.

inconscient *adjective*
1 unthinking; **2** unconscious (*in a faint*).

incontestable *adjective*
unquestionable.

incontournable *adjective*
unavoidable; **c'est un fait incontournable** it's an undeniable fact.

inconvénient *noun Masc.*
1 drawback; **il y a plusieurs inconvénients** there are several drawbacks; **2 l'inconvénient, c'est que …** the difficulty is that …; **3 si vous n'y voyez pas d'inconvénient** if you have no objection.

incorporer *verb* [1] to blend in (*ingredients in cooking*); **incorporez l'huile une goutte à la fois** blend in the oil drop by drop.

incorrect *adjective* **1** incorrect; **2** rude.

incrédule *adjective* incredulous.

incroyable *adjective* incredible; **elle a des connaissances incroyables** her knowledge is incredible.

inculper *verb* [1] **inculper quelqu'un de** to charge somebody with (*a crime*); **elle a été inculpée de vol** she was charged with theft.

Inde *noun Fem.* India; **en Inde** in (*or* to) India.

indécis *adjective* **1** undecided; **elle est toujours indécise** she hasn't decided yet; **2** indecisive.

indemne *adjective* unharmed.

indemnisation *noun Fem.*
compensation; **une demande d'indemnisation** a claim for compensation.

indemniser *verb* [1] to compensate; **demander à être indemnisé** to demand compensation.

indéniable *adjective* undeniable

indépendamment *adverb*
independently.

indépendance *noun Fem.*
independence.

indépendant *adjective*
1 independent; **2 cuisine indépendante** separate kitchen; **3 une maison indépendante** a detached house.

index *noun Masc.* **1** index; **2** forefinger.

indicateur *noun Masc.* **1** timetab (*in a rail or coach station*); **l'indicateur des départs** the departures board; **2** street directory; **3** gauge (*for example, fo oil levels*); **4 un panneau indicate** a road sign.

indicateur de pression *nou Masc.* pressure gauge.

indicatif *noun Masc.* **1** dialling code; **l'indicatif pour l'Espagne e 34** the dialling code for Spain is 3 **2** theme tune; **3** indicative (*of a verb*).

indications *plural noun Fem.*
directions.

indice *noun Masc.* clue.

indien (*Fem.* **indienne**) *adjective*
Indian.

différent *adjective* indifferent.

digène *adjective* native; **les ndigènes** the locals.

digeste *adjective* indigestible.

digestion *noun Fem.* ndigestion; **avoir une indigestion** o have indigestion.

dignation *noun Fem.* ndignation.

digne *adjective* **1** unworthy; disgraceful.

digner *verb* [1] **s'indigner** to get ndignant.

diqué *adjective* recommended; **ce 'est pas très indiqué** it's not a ery good idea.

diquer *verb* [1] to point out, to how; **pouvez-vous m'indiquer la are?** can you show me the way to he station?; **le nom est indiqué sur n grand panneau** the name is on a ig sign; **cela indique que ...** this hows that ....

direct *adjective* indirect.

discipliné *adjective* unruly.

discret (*Fem.* **indiscrète**) *djective* **1** indiscreet; **ne le lui dis as, elle est très indiscrète** don't ell her, she can't keep a secret; **2 si e n'est pas indiscret** if it's not eing nosy.

discutable *adjective* nquestionable.

dispensable *adjective* ssential; **les vêtements ndispensables** essential clothing; **est indispensable** it's essential.

disposé *adjective* unwell.

individu *noun Masc.* individual; **c'est un drôle d'individu** he's a funny bloke.

individuel (*Fem.* **individuelle**) *adjective* **1** individual; **2** separate; **une chambre individuelle** a single room; **une maison individuelle** a detached house.

indolore *adjective* painless.

indulgent *adjective* indulgent; **notre prof de maths est trop indulgent avec nous** our maths teacher isn't strict enough with us.

industrialisé *adjective* **les pays industrialisés** the industrialized countries.

industrie *noun Fem.* industry.

industriel (*Fem.* **industrielle**) *adjective* industrial; **une ville industrielle** an industrial city.

inédit *adjective* **1** unpublished; **2** new.

inefficace *adjective* **1** inefficient; **en tant que patron il est très inefficace** as a boss he's very inefficient; **2** ineffective; **un remède inefficace** an ineffective remedy.

inégal (*Masc. plural* **inégaux**) *adjective* **1** uneven; **2** unequal.

inespéré *adjective* unhoped-for; **un succès inespéré** an unhoped-for success.

inévitable *adjective* **1** inevitable; **c'était inévitable** it was bound to happen; **2** unavoidable; **des problèmes inévitables** unavoidable problems.

inexact *adjective* **1** incorrect; **2** inaccurate.

a
b
c
d
e
f
g
h
i
j
k
l
m
n
o
p
q
r
s
t
u
v
w
x
y
z

inexpérimenté *adjective* inexperienced.

infarctus *noun Masc.* heart attack.

infect *adjective* foul; **le repas était infect!** the meal was foul!

infecter *verb* [1] **1** to infect; **2 s'infecter** to go septic.

infection *noun Fem.* infection.

inférieur *adjective* **1** lower; **sur une marche inférieure** on a lower step; **des prix inférieurs à la moyenne** lower than average prices; **2** smaller; **la taille inférieure** the smaller size; **3** inferior, worse; **de qualité inférieure** of a lower quality.

infernal (*Masc. plural* **infernaux**) *adjective* frightful, dreadful.

infini *adjective* infinite.

infinitif *noun Masc.* infinitive (*in grammar*); **à l'infinitif** in the infinitive.

infirme *noun* **les infirmes** the disabled.
infirme *adjective* disabled; **est-il infirme?** does he have a disability?

infirmerie *noun Fem.* medical room.

infirmier, infirmière *noun Masc., Fem.* nurse.

infirmité *noun Fem.* disability.

inflammable *adjective* flammable.

inflation *noun Fem.* inflation.

influence *noun Fem.* influence; **il a une bonne influence sur son frère** he's a good influence on his brother.

influencer *verb* [61] to influence.

informaticien, informaticienne *noun Masc. Fem.* computer scientist.

information *noun Fem.* **1** information; **une information très utile** a very useful piece of information; **2 les informations** the news (*on TV or radio*); **les informations sont à vingt heure** the news is at eight o'clock.

informatique *noun Fem.* computer science, IT.
informatique *adjective* comput**un système informatique** a computer system.

informatiser *verb* [1] to computerize.

informer *verb* [1] **1** to inform; **2 s'informer** to find out; **je peux m'informer si tu veux** I can find o if you like.

infrarouge *adjective* infra-red.

infusion *noun Fem.* herbal tea.

ingénierie *noun Fem.* engineeri

ingénieur *noun Masc.* engineer; **faire des études d'ingénieur** to study engineering.

ingénieux (*Fem.* **ingénieuse**) *adjective* ingenious; **c'était très ingénieux de sa part** that was ve ingenious of her.

ingrat *adjective* **1** ungrateful; **2** **travail ingrat** unrewarding work

ingrédient *noun Masc.* ingredie

inhabité *adjective* uninhabited.

inhabituel (*Fem.* **inhabituelle**) *adjective* unusual.

inhalateur *noun Masc.* inhaler.

inhumain *adjective* inhuman.

imaginable *adjective* unimaginable, unthinkable.

interrompu *adjective* uninterrupted; **2** continuous.

tial (*Masc. plural* **initiaux**) *adjective* initial.

tiale *noun Fem.* initial; **mes initiales sont là-dessus** my initials re on it.

tiation *noun Fem.* introduction (*to a new place or skill*); **une journée d'initiation** an introductory day (*to a course, for example*); **une initiation à l'anglais** an introduction to English.

tiative *noun Fem.* initiative.

tier *verb* [1] **1 initier quelqu'un à** introduce somebody to (*a skill*); to initiate (*an idea or plan*); **s'initier à quelque chose** to learn about something; **elle s'initie à la photo** she's starting to learn photography.

ecter *verb* [1] to inject.

ection *noun Fem.* injection.

ure *noun Fem.* insult.

urier *verb* [1] to insult; **il m'a injurié** he swore at me.

uste *adjective* unfair.

ocent *adjective* innocent.

ombrable *adjective* countless.

ovation *noun Fem.* innovation.

over *verb* [1] to break new ground.

occupé *adjective* empty.

ondation *noun Fem.* flood; **des inondations** flooding.

onder *verb* [1] to flood.

inoubliable *adjective* unforgettable.

inouï *adjective* incredible.

inox *noun Masc.* stainless steel; **une casserole en inox** a stainless steel pan.

inoxydable *adjective* **un évier en acier inoxydable** a stainless steel sink.

inquiet (*Fem.* **inquiète**) *adjective* anxious, worried.

inquiétant *adjective* worrying.

inquiéter *verb* [24] **1** to worry; **je ne veux pas t'inquiéter** I don't want to worry you; **ça m'inquiète un peu** I find that a bit worrying; **ce qui m'inquiète, c'est qu'elle n'a pas téléphoné** what I find worrying is the fact that she hasn't phoned; **2 s'inquiéter** to worry, to be worried; **elle va s'inquiéter si nous sommes en retard** she'll worry if we're late; **ne t'inquiète pas!** don't worry!

inquiétude *noun Fem.* anxiety.

insatisfait *adjective* dissatisfied.

inscription *noun Fem.* **1** enrolment (*for a course or in a school*); **2** registration.

inscrire *verb* [38] **1** to enrol, to register (*someone for a course or school*); **elle m'a inscrit pour l'examen** she's entered me for the exam; **2 s'inscrire** to enrol; **s'inscrire au club de foot** to join the football club.

insecte *noun Masc.* insect.

insérer *verb* [24] to, insert.

a
b
c
d
e
f
g
h
i
j
k
l
m
n
o
p
q
r
s
t
u
v
w
x
y
z

a b c d e f g h i j k l m n o p q r s t u v w x y z

insertion *noun Fem.* **1** insertion (*of an advertisement in a paper, for example*); **2** integration (*when somebody joins a new community*); **l'insertion des jeunes dans la société** the integration of young people into society.

insignifiant *adjective* insignificant.

insister *verb* [1] to insist; **il faut insister** keep on trying; **la clé est un peu tordue, il faut insister un peu** the key's a bit bent, you have to push it really hard.

insolation *noun Fem.* sunstroke; **attraper une insolation** to get sunstroke.

insolent *adjective* insolent.

insoutenable *adjective* unbearable.

inspecter *verb* [1] to inspect.

inspecteur, inspectrice *noun Masc., Fem.* inspector.

inspection *noun Fem.* **1** inspection; **2** inspectorate (*an official department*).

inspiration *noun Fem.* inspiration.

inspirer *verb* [1] **1** to inspire; **ça ne m'inspire pas** that doesn't appeal to me; **2** to breathe in; **inspire fort!** breathe in deep!; **3 s'inspirer** to be inspired by; **il s'est inspiré de Picasso** he was inspired by Picasso.

instable *adjective* unstable; **il fait un temps instable** the weather's unsettled.

installation *noun Fem.* **1** installation, putting in; **2** move (*to a house or town*); **avant son installation à Paris** before he

moved to Paris; **3 des installatio sportives** sports facilities.

installer *verb* [1] **1** to install, to in (*central heating or a dishwash for example*); **2** to connect (*gas, electricity, a phone*); **3 s'installer** settle, to settle in; **installez-vous** sit down; **je me suis installée à mon bureau** I settled down at m desk.

instant *noun Masc.* moment; **pou l'instant** for the moment; **à tout instant** all the time.

instantané *adjective* instant; **d café instantané** instant coffee.

instinct *noun Masc.* instinct.

institut *noun Masc.* institute; **un institut de beauté** a beautician'.

instituteur, institutrice *no Masc., Fem.* primary school teache

institution *noun Fem.* **1** institution; **2** private school.

institutrice *noun Fem.* SEE **instituteur**.

instructeur, instructrice *noun Masc., Fem.* instructor.

instruction *noun Fem.* **1** education; **instruction civique** civics; **2 instructions** instruction **instructions de lavage** washing instructions.

instruire *verb* [26] **1** to teach, to train; **2 s'instruire** to learn.

instruit *adjective* educated.

instrument *noun Masc.* **1** instrument; **un instrument de mesure** a measuring instrument **les instruments de bord** the controls; **2 un instrument de**

nusique a musical instrument; **un nstrument à cordes** a string nstrument.

su noun **à mon insu** without my knowing.

suffisance noun Fem. shortage.

suffisant adjective
1 insufficient; **2** inadequate; **c'est nsuffisant** it's not good enough.

sultant adjective insulting.

sulte noun Fem. insult.

sulter verb [1] to insult.

supportable adjective
unbearable; **je la trouve nsupportable** I can't stand her.

tact adjective intact.

tégral (Masc. plural **intégraux**) adjective complete.

tégrale noun Fem. complete works (usually music); **l'intégrale des Beatles** the complete Beatles collection.

tellectuel, intellectuelle noun Masc., Fem., adjective ntellectual.

telligence noun Fem. ntelligence.

telligent adjective clever, ntelligent.

tendance noun Fem. administration (in a school).

tense adjective intense.

tensif (Fem. **intensive**) adjective ntensive.

tention noun Fem. intention; **avoir l'intention de faire** to mean to do; **j'avais l'intention d'y aller**

mais je n'ai pas pu I meant to go but I wasn't able to.

interdiction noun Fem. ban; 'interdiction de fumer' 'no smoking'.

interdire verb [47] to forbid; **je t'interdis de le faire** I forbid you to do it.

interdit adjective forbidden; 'entrée interdite' 'no entry'; **il est interdit de fumer dans la salle** smoking is forbidden in the theatre.

intéressant adjective
1 interesting; **c'est un film très intéressant** it's a very interesting film; **2 à un prix intéressant** at a good price.

intéressé[1] adjective interested; **être intéressé par quelque chose** to be interested in something.

intéressé[2]**, intéressée** noun Masc., Fem. person concerned.

intéresser verb [1] **1** to interest; **ça ne m'intéresse pas** that doesn't interest me; **2 s'intéresser à** to be interested in; **elle s'intéresse beaucoup à l'informatique** she's very interested in computing.

intérêt noun Masc. **1** interest; **ce livre est sans intérêt** this book is really boring; **2 tu as intérêt à faire** you'd better do; **tu as intérêt à le finir avant ce soir!** you'd better get it finished by this evening!

intérieur noun Masc. inside, interior; **l'intérieur du placard** the inside of the cupboard; **où est-elle? – à l'intérieur** where is she? – inside (in the house).

a
b
c
d
e
f
g
h
i
j
k
l
m
n
o
p
q
r
s
t
u
v
w
x
y
z

a **intérieur** *adjective* inside, internal;
le côté intérieur the inside.

b **intermédiaire** *noun Masc. & Fem.*
c go-between.
intermédiaire *adjective*
d intermediate; **avez-vous la taille**
e **intermédiaire?** do you have the size
in between?

f **internat** *noun Masc.* boarding
g school.

international (*Masc. plural*
h **internationaux**) *adjective*
international.

i **interne** *noun Masc. & Fem.* boarder
j (*in a school.*).
interne *adjective* internal.

k **Internet** *noun Masc.* Internet; **sur**
l **Internet** on the Internet.

interpeller *verb* [1] **1** to call out to;
m **2 la police l'a interpellé** the police
n have taken him in for questioning.

interphone™ *noun Masc.* entry
o phone.

p **interprète** *noun Masc. & Fem.* **1** (*in*
the theatre) actor; (*in music*)
q performer, soloist; **2** interpreter.

r **interpréter** *verb* [24] **1** to perform,
s to play (*a role in the theatre or a piece*
of music), to sing (*a song*); **2** to
t interpret (*a language or a remark*).

u **interrogatif** *noun Masc.*
interrogative.

v **interrogation** *noun Fem.* **1** test (*at*
w *school*); **2** questioning.

interroger *verb* [52] **1** to question,
x to ask; **il m'a interrogé sur mon**
y **séjour en France** he asked me
about my stay in France; **2** to test (*at*
z *school*).

interrompre *verb* [69] to
interrupt; **interrompre quelqu'un**
to interrupt somebody; **il a**
interrompu son travail he broke o
his work.

interrupteur *noun Masc.* switch

interruption *noun Fem.*
1 interruption; **2 sans interruptio**
without stopping.

intervalle *noun Masc.* **1** interval;
2 dans l'intervalle in the
meantime.

intervenir *verb* [81] to intervene

intervention *noun Fem.*
intervention.

interview *noun Fem.* interview (*c*
TV, radio, for a magazine).

intestin *noun Masc.* intestine.

intime *adjective* intimate; **un**
journal intime a diary (*kept by*
somebody).

intimider *verb* [1] to intimidate.

intimité *noun Fem.* intimacy; **dan**
l'intimité in private.

intolérable *adjective* intolerable

intolérant *adjective* intolerant.

intoxication *noun Fem.*
poisoning.

intoxiquer *verb* [1] to poison.

intrigue *noun Fem.* plot (*of a nove*
play, etc).

introduction *noun Fem.*
introduction.

introduire *verb* [26] **1** to introdu(
(*an idea, a measure, a new product*
2 s'introduire to get into; **un**
cambrioleur s'est introduit dans

l'appartement a burglar got into the flat.

trus, **intruse** noun Masc., Fem. intruder.

tuitif (Fem. **intuitive**) adjective intuitive.

tuition noun Fem. intuition.

usable adjective hard-wearing.

utile adjective pointless; **il est inutile de l'appeler** there's no point telephoning him; **inutile de dire que** ... needless to say ....

utilement adverb pointlessly; **je l'ai cherché inutilement** I looked for it in vain.

utilisable adjective unusable.

valide noun Masc. & Fem. disabled person.

vasion noun Fem. invasion.

venter verb [1] to invent.

vention noun Fem. invention.

verse noun Masc. **l'inverse** the opposite; **l'inverse est vrai** the opposite is true.

inverse adjective opposite; **en sens inverse** in the opposite direction; **dans l'ordre inverse** in reverse order.

vestigation noun Fem. investigation.

vestissement noun Masc. investment.

visible adjective invisible.

vitation noun Fem. invitation.

vité, **invitée** noun Masc., Fem. guest; **nous avons des invités ce soir** we have people coming round this evening.

inviter verb [1] to invite; **ils m'ont invité à dîner** they invited me to dinner.

involontaire adjective unintentional.

invraisemblable adjective **1** unlikely; **une explication invraisemblable** an unlikely explanation; **2** (informal) amazing.

ira, **irai**, **iraient**, **irais**, **irait**, **iras** verb SEE **aller**.

iris noun Masc. iris.

irlandais noun Masc., **irlandais** adjective Irish.

Irlandais, **Irlandaise** noun Masc., Fem. Irishman, Irishwoman; **les Irlandais** the Irish.

Irlande noun Fem. Ireland; **la République d'Irlande** the Republic of Ireland.

Irlande du Nord noun Fem. Northern Ireland.

ironie noun Fem. irony.

ironique adjective ironic.

irons, **iront** verb SEE **aller**[1].

irradier verb [1] to irradiate.

irréel, **irréelle** adjective unreal.

irréfléchi adjective thoughtless.

irrégularité noun Fem. irregularity.

irrégulier (Fem. **irrégulière**) adjective irregular.

irrésistible adjective irresistible.

irresponsable adjective irresponsible.

irritable adjective irritable.

irritation noun Fem. irritation.

a
b
c
d
e
f
g
h
i
j
k
l
m
n
o
p
q
r
s
t
u
v
w
x
y
z

irriter verb [1] **1** to irritate; **cela m'irrite** that makes me cross; **2 s'irriter** to get irritated.

islamique adjective Islamic.

isolation noun Fem. insulation; **isolation acoustique** soundproofing.

isolé adjective **1** remote; **2** lonely.

isoler verb [1] **1** to insulate (a room or building); **2** to isolate (a sick person or a prisoner).

Israël noun Masc. Israel.

israélien (Fem. **israélienne**) adjective Israeli.

issue noun Fem. exit; **issue de secours** emergency exit; **une rue sans issue** a dead end.

Italie noun Fem. Italy; **en Italie** in (or to) Italy.

italien noun Masc. Italian (language).
italien adjective Italian.

Italien, Italienne noun Masc., Fem. Italian (person).

itinéraire noun Masc. route.

itinérant adjective travelling.

ivoire noun Masc., adjective ivory.

ivre adjective drunk.

ivresse noun Fem. drunkenness.

ivrogne noun Masc. & Fem. drunkard.

Jj

j' pronoun SEE **je**.

J.-C. noun Masc. short for Jésus-Christ; **200 avant J.-C.** 200 BC; **400 après J.-C.** 400 AD.

jacinthe noun Fem. hyacinth.

jalousie noun Fem. **1** jealousy; **2** slatted blind.

jaloux (Fem. **jalouse**) adjective jealous; **elle est jalouse de mes résultats d'examen** she's jealous of my exam results.

jamaïquain adjective Jamaican.

Jamaïquain, Jamaïquaine noun Masc., Fem. Jamaican.

Jamaïque noun Fem. Jamaica.

jamais adverb **1** never; **elle ne fume jamais** she never smokes; **on ne sait jamais** you never know; **jamais plus!** never again!; **2** ever; **plus grand que jamais** bigger than ever; **si jamais il pleut** if by any chance it rains; **à jamais** forever.

jambe noun Fem. leg; **se casser la jambe** to break your leg.

jambon noun Masc. ham; **jambon blanc** cooked ham; **jambon de pays** cured raw ham.

janvier noun Masc. January; **en janvier, au mois de janvier** in January.

Japon noun Masc. Japan; **au Japon** in (or to) Japan.

japonais noun Masc. Japanese (language).
japonais adjective Japanese.

Japonais, Japonaise noun Masc., Fem. Japanese (person).

jardin noun Masc. garden; **Patrick est au jardin** Patrick's in the garden; **une chaise de jardin** a garden chair.

jardinage noun Masc. gardening.

a b c d e f g h i j k l m n o p q r s t u v w x y z

ardinier, **jardinière**¹ *noun Masc.*, *Fem.* gardener.

ardinière² *noun Fem.* (large) plant pot.

ardin public *noun Masc.* park (*in a town*).

aune *noun Masc.* **1** yellow; **2 un jaune d'œuf** an egg-yolk.
jaune *adjective* yellow; **une robe jaune** a yellow dress.

aunisse *noun Fem.* jaundice.

avel *noun* **eau de Javel** bleach.

azz *noun Masc.* jazz; **j'aime le jazz** I like jazz.

e, **j'** (*before a vowel or silent 'h'*) *pronoun* I; **je sais où il habite** I know where he lives; **j'habite à Lyon** I live in Lyons.

ean *noun Masc.* **1** (pair of) jeans; **j'ai acheté un jean** I've bought some jeans; **2** denim; **une jupe en jean** a denim skirt.

et *noun Masc.* **1** jet (*of water or steam*); **les jets d'eau de Versailles** the fountains at Versailles; **2** jet (plane).

etée *noun Fem.* jetty.

eter *verb* [48] **1** to throw; **jette-moi le ballon** throw me the ball; **2** to throw away; **j'ai jeté ces vieilles chaussures** I've thrown away those old shoes; **3 jeter un coup d'œil** to have a look; **est-ce que tu peux jeter un coup d'œil aux pommes de terre?** can you have a look at the potatoes?

eton *noun Masc.* **1** counter (*for a board game*); **2** token (*for a machine*).

jeu (*plural* **jeux**) *noun Masc.* **1** game; **faire un jeu** to play a game; **gagner par trois jeux à deux** to win by three games to two; **2** gambling; **3** acting; ★ **ce n'est pas du jeu!** (*informal*) that's not fair!

jeu-concours *noun Masc.* competition.

jeu de cartes *noun Masc.* **1** pack of cards; **2** game of cards.

jeu de hasard *noun Masc.* game of chance.

jeu de mots *noun Masc.* pun.

jeu de société *noun Masc.* board game.

jeudi *noun Masc.* **1** Thursday; **nous sommes jeudi aujourd'hui** it's Thursday today; **jeudi prochain** next Thursday; **jeudi dernier** last Thursday; **2** on Thursday; **je l'ai vu jeudi soir** I saw him on Thursday evening; **3 le jeudi** on Thursdays; **fermé le jeudi** closed on Thursdays; **4 tous les jeudis** every Thursday.

jeune *noun Masc. & Fem.* young person; **une émission destinée aux jeunes** a programme aimed at young people.
jeune *adjective* young; **un jeune homme** a young man; **une jeune femme** a young woman; **une jeune fille** a girl.

jeunesse *noun Fem.* **1** young people; **la jeunesse d'aujourd'hui** young people today; **2** youth; **dans ma jeunesse** in my youth.

jeu-vidéo *noun Masc.* video game.

a
b
c
d
e
f
g
h
i
j
k
l
m
n
o
p
q
r
s
t
u
v
w
x
y
z

jogging noun Masc. **1 faire du jogging** to go jogging; **2 un jogging** a track-suit.

joie noun Fem. joy.

joindre verb [49] **1** to get hold of (*often by telephone*); **je n'ai pas pu la joindre** I wasn't able to get hold of her; **2** to enclose (*in a letter or parcel*); **3** to put together; **les pieds joints** feet together; ★ **joindre les deux bouts** to make ends meet (*financially*).

joli adjective pretty.

jongler verb [1] to juggle.

jongleur, jongleuse noun Masc., Fem. juggler.

jonquille noun Fem. daffodil.

joue noun Fem. cheek.

jouer verb [1] **1** to play; **elle joue avec le chien** she's playing with the dog; **à toi de jouer!** your go!; **bien joué!** well done!; **2 jouer à** to play (*a sport*); **on va jouer au foot** we're going to play football; **3 jouer de** to play (*an instrument*); **Robert joue de la guitare** Robert plays the guitar; **4** to act; **il joue bien dans ce film** he's really good in this film.

jouet noun Masc. toy.

joueur, joueuse noun Masc., Fem. player.

jour noun Masc. **1** day; **les jours de la semaine** the days of the week; **trois jours plus tard** three days later; **le jour où** the day when; **un de ces jours** one of these days; **2 de nos jours** nowadays; **de nos jours, ils sont assez fréquents** nowadays they are quite common; **3 mettre quelque chose à jour** to bring

something up to date; **4** daylight, light; **il fait jour** it's daylight; **en plein jour** in broad daylight; **jour ◂ nuit** night and day.

jour de l'an noun Masc. New Year Day.

jour férié noun Masc. public holiday.

journal (*plural* journaux) noun Masc. **1** newspaper, magazine; **le journal du soir** the evening paper **du papier journal** newspaper (*for wrapping*); **2** news (*on TV or radic* **le journal de vingt-deux heures** the ten o'clock news; **3 un journa◂ intime** a diary.

journalisme noun Masc. journalism.

journaliste noun Masc. & Fem. journalist.

journée noun Fem. day; **toute la journée** all day, the whole day; **il e payé à la journée** he's paid by the day.

jour ouvrable noun Masc. working day.

joyeux (Fem. joyeuse) adjective happy; **Joyeux Anniversaire** Happ Birthday; **Joyeux Noël** Merry Christmas.

judaïsme noun Masc. Judaism.

judicieux (Fem. judicieuse) adjective sensible; **un choix judicieux** a wise choice.

judo noun Masc. judo.

juge noun Masc. judge.

ge d'instruction *noun Masc.* examining magistrate.

ge de ligne *noun Masc.* line judge (*in tennis*).

ge de touche *noun Masc.* linesman (*in football, rugby*).

gement *noun Masc.* judgement.

ger *verb* [52] to judge.

if, juive *noun Masc., Fem.* Jew.
juif, juive *adjective* Jewish.

illet *noun Masc.* July; **en juillet, au mois de juillet** in July; **le quatorze juillet** Bastille Day (*July 14, a national holiday to celebrate the taking of the Bastille prison in Paris by the people at the beginning of the French Revolution in 1789*).

in *noun Masc.* June; **en juin, au mois de juin** in June.

ive *noun Fem., adjective* SEE **juif.**

meau (*plural* **jumeaux**)
jumelle *noun Masc., Fem.* twin; **des vrais jumeaux** identical twins.

meler *verb* [18] to twin (*towns*);
Oxford est jumelé avec Grenoble Oxford is twinned with Grenoble.

melles *plural noun Fem.*
1 binoculars; **2** SEE **jumeau.**

ment *noun Fem.* mare.

ngle *noun Fem.* jungle.

pe *noun Fem.* skirt.

pon *noun Masc.* petticoat.

rer *verb* [1] to swear.

ridique *adjective* legal; **le système juridique** the legal system.

ry *noun Masc.* **1** jury; **2** board of examiners.

jus *noun Masc.* **1** juice; **un jus d'orange** an orange juice; **2** gravy.

jus de fruits *noun Masc.* fruit juice.

jusqu'à *preposition* **1** as far as (*a place*); **ce train va jusqu'à Paris** this train goes as far as Paris; **nous avons marché jusqu'à la mer** we walked as far as the sea; **il m'a accompagné jusqu'à chez moi** he took me all the way home; **2** until; **elle reste jusqu'à mardi** she's staying until Tuesday; **jusqu'à quand reste-t-il?** how long is he staying for?; **jusqu'à présent, jusqu'à maintenant** up to now; **3 jusqu'à ce que** until.

juste *adjective* **1** right, correct; **le mot juste** the right word; **ce que tu dis est juste** what you say is right; **2** fair; **ce n'est pas juste!** it's not fair!; **3** in tune; **elle chante juste** she sings in tune; **4** c'est un peu **juste** it's a bit tight; **une heure est un peu juste** an hour's a bit tight.
juste *adverb* just; **juste à temps** just in time; **il vient tout juste d'arriver** he's only just arrived.

justement *adverb* **1** precisely;
2 just; **je parlais justement de toi** I was just talking about you;
3 correctly; **comme elle a dit très justement** as she so rightly said.

justesse *noun Fem.* **1** correctness;
2 de justesse only just; **il a eu son avion, mais de justesse** he caught his plane, but only just.

justice *noun Fem.* justice.

a
b
c
d
e
f
g
h
i
j
k
l
m
n
o
p
q
r
s
t
u
v
w
x
y
z

justifier verb [1] to justify.

juteux (Fem. **juteuse**) adjective juicy.

juvénile adjective youthful.

Kk

K.O. adjective **1 mettre quelqu'un K.O.** to knock somebody out (in boxing); **2 je suis complètement K.O.** (informal) I'm completely knackered.

kaki noun Masc. persimmon.
kaki adjective khaki.

kangourou noun Masc. kangaroo.

karaté noun Masc. karate.

karting noun Masc. go-karting.

kascher adjective kosher.

kermesse noun Fem. (school) fête.

ketchup noun Masc. ketchup.

kidnapper verb [1] to kidnap.

kidnappeur, **kidnappeuse** noun Masc., Fem. kidnapper.

kilo noun Masc. kilo; **deux kilos de pommes** two kilos of apples; **j'ai pris trois kilos** I've put on three kilos.

kilogramme noun Masc. kilogramme.

kilométrage noun Masc. mileage.

kilomètre noun Masc. kilometre; **à dix kilomètres d'ici** ten kilometres from here; **Paris est à combien de kilomètres de Dijon?** how many kilometres is it from Paris to Dijon?; **elle a combien de kilomètres**

votre voiture? what's the mileage on your car?

kinésithérapeute noun Masc. Fem. physiotherapist.

kinésithérapie noun Fem. physiotherapy.

kiosque noun Masc. kiosk.

kiwi noun Masc. kiwi (the bird and the fruit).

klaxon™ noun Masc. horn (on a car).

klaxonner verb [1] to sound the horn (in a car).

km SHORT FOR **kilomètre; km/h** kph (kilometres per hour).

koala noun Masc. koala bear.

kraft noun Masc. **le papier kraft** brown paper.

K-way™ noun Masc. cagoule.

Ll

la, **l'** (before a vowel or silent 'h') definite article, pronoun SEE **le**.

là adverb **1** there; **est-ce que Paul est là?** is Paul there?; **c'est là qu'habite mon frère** that's where my brother lives; **2** here; **viens là** come here; **Danielle n'est pas là e ce moment** Danielle's not here at the moment; **3** then; **c'est là que j'ai pensé à toi** that's when I thought of you.

-là adverb **cette maison-là** that house; **ces gens-là** those people; **à ce moment-là** at that moment.

à-bas *adverb* **1** there; **qu'est-ce que vous avez fait là-bas?** what did you do there?; **2** over there; **notre maison est là-bas** our house is over there.

abo *noun Masc.* (*informal*) lab.

aboratoire *noun Masc.* laboratory.

aboratoire de langues *noun Masc.* language laboratory.

abourer *verb* [1] to plough.

abyrinthe *noun Masc.* maze, labyrinth.

ac *noun Masc.* lake; **le lac d'Annecy** Lake Annecy.

acer *verb* [61] **lacer ses chaussures** to tie your shoelaces.

acet *noun Masc.* lace (*for shoes*); **des chaussures à lacets** lace-up shoes.

âche *adjective* **1** cowardly; **2** loose (*a belt or rope, for example*).

âcher *verb* [1] **1** to drop (*an object*), to let go of (*a rope or branch*); **lâche-moi!** let go of me!; **ne lâche pas la corde!** don't let go of the rope!; **2** to drop; **elle a lâché son sac** she dropped her bag; **3** to give way; **la corde a lâché** the rope gave way.

âcheté *noun Fem.* cowardice.

acrymogène *adjective* **le gaz lacrymogène** teargas.

à-dedans *adverb* in there; **il y a un oiseau là-dedans** there's a bird in there; **il n'y a rien là-dedans** there's nothing inside.

à-dessous *adverb* under there; **les verres sont là-dessous** the glasses are under there.

là-dessus *adverb* **1** on there; **tu peux mettre les assiettes là-dessus** you can put the plates on there; **2** about it; **ils sont d'accord là-dessus** they agree about it; **a-t-il dit quelque chose là-dessus?** did he say anything about it?; **3** with that; **là-dessus il est sorti** with that, he went out.

là-haut *adverb* **1** up here, up there; **il est là-haut dans l'arbre** he's up there in the tree; **2** upstairs; **maman est là-haut** Mum's upstairs.

laid *adjective* ugly.

laideur *noun Fem.* ugliness.

laine *noun Fem.* wool; **un pull en laine** a woollen jumper.

laine vierge *noun Fem.* pure new wool.

laïque *adjective* **une école laïque** a state school.

laisse *noun Fem.* lead (*for a dog*).

laisser *verb* [1] **1** to leave; **j'ai laissé mes clés chez toi** I've left my keys at your house; **bon, je vous laisse** right, I must be off now; **2 laisser quelqu'un faire** to let somebody do; **laisse-le parler!** let him speak!; **laissez-la faire, elle reviendra** leave her alone, she'll come back; **3 il se laisse insulter** he puts up with being insulted; **elle s'est laissée aller** she's let herself go.

laisser-aller *noun Masc.* carelessness.

lait *noun Masc.* milk; **un thé au lait** a cup of tea with milk; **un café au lait** a white coffee.

lait demi-écrémé noun Masc. semi-skimmed milk.

lait écrémé noun Masc. skimmed milk.

laitier (Fem. **laitière**) adjective **les produits laitiers** milk products (such as yoghurt).

laiton noun Masc. brass.

laitue noun Fem. lettuce.

lame noun Fem. blade.

lamelle noun Fem. thin strip.

lamentable adjective awful.

lampadaire noun Masc. **1** standard lamp; **2** street lamp.

lampe noun Fem. lamp, light; **allumer la lampe** to turn on the lamp.

lampe de poche noun Fem. torch.

lampe électrique noun Fem. torch.

lance noun Fem. spear.

lancement noun Masc. launch.

lancer verb [61] **1** to throw; **il m'a lancé le ballon** he threw the ball to me; **2** to launch (a product, a spacecraft); **ils vont lancer leur nouveau produit en juin** they're going to launch their new product in June; **3 se lancer dans quelque chose** to embark on something.

landau noun Masc. pram.

lande noun Fem. moor.

langage noun Masc. language, type of language; **le langage administratif** official jargon.

langouste noun Fem. crayfish.

langue noun Fem. **1** tongue; **tirer la langue** to stick your tongue out; **2** language; **une langue étrangère** a foreign language; **ma langue maternelle** my mother tongue; ★ **je l'ai sur le bout de la langue** it's on the tip of my tongue.

lanière noun Fem. strap.

lapin noun Masc. rabbit; ★ **il m'a posé un lapin** (informal) he stood me up.

laque noun Fem. **1** hairspray; **2** lacquer, gloss paint.

laquelle pronoun SEE **lequel**.

lard noun Masc. streaky bacon.

lardons plural noun Masc. diced bacon; **salade aux lardons fumés** green salad with diced smoked bacon.

large noun Masc. open sea; **au large** offshore.
large adjective wide; **un large sourire** a broad smile; **être large de deux mètres** to be two metres wide.

largement adverb **c'est largement suffisant** that's more than enough; **j'ai largement le temps** I've got plenty of time.

largeur noun Fem. width.

larme noun Fem. tear; **en larmes** in tears; **rire aux larmes** to laugh till you cry.

laryngite noun Fem. laryngitis.

lasagnes plural noun Fem. lasagna; **manger des lasagnes** to eat lasagna.

laser noun Masc. laser; **une platine laser** a compact disc player.

asser verb [1] **se lasser** to get tired.

assitude noun Fem. weariness.

atin noun Masc., adjective Latin.

auréat, lauréate noun Masc., Fem. winner; **un lauréat du prix Nobel** a Nobel Prize winner.

aurier noun Masc. laurel; **un laurier commun** a bay tree; **une feuille de laurier** a bay leaf.

aurier-rose noun Masc. oleander.

avable adjective washable; **lavable en machine** machine-washable.

avabo noun Masc. washbasin.

avage noun Masc. **1** washing; **2** wash (on a washing-machine programme); **3** car wash.

avande noun Fem. lavender.

ave-linge noun Masc. washing machine.

aver verb [1] **1** to wash; **2 se laver** to wash; **se laver les mains** to wash your hands; **se laver les dents** to brush your teeth.

averie noun Fem. launderette.

ave-vaisselle noun Masc. dish washer.

e, la, l', les definite article **1** the; **le chat** the cat; **la maison** the house; **les enfants** the children; **'quelle chemise?' – 'la verte'** 'which shirt?' – 'the green one'; **2** ('les' is often not translated) **je n'aime pas les chiens** I don't like dogs; **elle se lave les cheveux** she's washing her hair; **3 le père de mon ami** my friend's father; **4** a, an; **cinq euros le kilo** five euros a kilo.

le, la, l', les pronoun him, her, it, them; **je la vois tous les soirs** I see her every evening; **je le vois tous les soirs** I see him every evening; **où est-ce que tu les as mis?** where did you put them?; **il l'a acheté chez Meyer** he bought it at Meyer's.

lécher verb [24] to lick.

lèche-vitrines noun Masc. **faire du lèche-vitrines** to go window-shopping.

leçon noun Fem. lesson; **une leçon de géographie** a geography lesson.

lecteur, lectrice noun Masc., Fem. **1** reader (of a book); **2** foreign language assistant (in a university).

lecteur de cassettes noun Masc. cassette player.

lecteur de disquettes noun Masc. floppy disk drive.

lecteur laser noun Masc. CD player.

lecture noun Fem. reading; **j'aime la lecture** I like reading; **le soir il fait de la lecture** he reads in the evenings.

légal (Masc. plural **légaux**) adjective legal.

légende noun Fem. **1** caption (to a picture); **2** key (to a map); **3** legend.

léger (Fem. **légère**) adjective **1** light; **une veste légère** a light jacket; **un repas léger** a light meal; **2** slight; **un léger retard** a slight delay; **3** weak; **un café léger** a weak coffee; ★ **faire quelque chose à la légère** to do something without thinking.

a
b
c
d
e
f
g
h
i
j
k
l
m
n
o
p
q
r
s
t
u
v
w
x
y
z

a

légèrement *adverb* **1** lightly;
légèrement parfumé lightly
perfumed; **2** slightly; **il est
légèrement blessé** he's slightly
hurt; **elle est légèrement plus
grande que moi** she's slightly taller
than me.

légèreté *noun Fem.* lightness.

législatif (Fem. **législative**)
adjective legislative; **les élections
législatives** the general election.

légume *noun Masc.* vegetable; **des
légumes verts** green vegetables.

lendemain *noun Masc.* **le
lendemain** the next day; **Marc est
arrivé le lendemain** Marc arrived
the next day; **le lendemain matin**
the next morning; **le lendemain de
l'accident** the day after the
accident.

lent *adjective* slow.

lentement *adverb* slowly.

lenteur *noun Fem.* slowness; **avec
lenteur** slowly.

lentille *noun Fem.* **1** lentil; **soupe
aux lentilles** lentil soup; **2** lens;
lentilles de contact contact lenses;
elle met ses lentilles she's putting
in her contact lenses.

léopard *noun Masc.* leopard.

lequel, **laquelle**, **lesquels**,
lesquelles *pronoun* **1** which
one?, which?; **'passe-moi les
verres' – 'lesquels?'** 'pass me the
glasses' – 'which ones?'; **2** which,
who; **la voiture dans laquelle ils
roulaient** the car they were driving
in, the car in which they were
driving; **le monsieur avec lequel je
discutais** the man to whom I was

talking (*often not translated*), the
man I was talking to.

les *definite article,*, *pronoun* SEE **le**.

lesquelles, **lesquelles** SEE
lequel.

lessive *noun Fem.* **1** washing; **faire
la lessive** to do the washing;
2 washing powder, washing liquid

lettre *noun Fem.* **1** letter; **écrire une
lettre** to write a letter; **2** letter (*of the
alphabet*); **une lettre minuscule** a
small letter; **une lettre majuscule** a
capital letter; ★ **il prend tout ce
qu'on lui dit à la lettre** he takes
everything you say literally.

lettres *plural noun Fem.* arts (*at
university*).

leur *pronoun* them (*meaning 'to
them'*); **je leur donne de l'argent** I
give them money.
leur *adjective* (*plural* **leurs**) their;
leur voiture their car; **leurs
enfants** their children.
leur *pronoun* **le leur, la leur, les
leurs** theirs; **ça, c'est notre
maison, et ça, c'est la leur** that's
our house and that's theirs; **nous
avons appelé nos parents et ils
ont appelé les leurs** we phoned our
parents and they phoned theirs.

levant *adjective* **le soleil levant** the
rising sun.

lever¹ *verb* [50] **1** to lift, to raise;
levons nos verres! let's raise our
glasses!; **levez la main!** put your
hand up!; **il a levé les yeux** he
looked up; **2 se lever** to get up (*out of
bed or from a chair*); **je me lève à
sept heures** I get up at seven
o'clock; **nous nous sommes levés**

tôt we got up early; **quand le soleil se lève** when the sun rises.

ever[2] *noun Masc.* **au lever du soleil** at sunrise.

ève-tard *noun Masc.* late riser.

ève-tôt *noun Masc.* early riser.

evier *noun Masc.* lever.

èvre *noun Fem.* lip.

évrier *noun Masc.* greyhound.

evure *noun Fem.* yeast.

exique *noun Masc.* word list.

ézard *noun Masc.* lizard.

aison *noun Fem.* **1** link, connection; **une liaison routière** a road link; **une liaison radio** radio contact; **une liaison satellite** a satellite link; **2** (love) affair.

asse *noun Fem.* wad, bundle (*of papers or banknotes*).

ibellule *noun Fem.* dragonfly.

ibération *noun Fem.* release, liberation; **la libération des femmes** women's liberation; **la Libération (de 1944)** the Liberation (of 1944) (*the end of the German occupation of France*).

ibérer *verb* [24] **1** to free, to release (*a prisoner or hostage*); **2** to vacate (*a hotel room or flat*).

iberté *noun Fem.* freedom.

ibraire *noun Masc. & Fem.* bookseller.

ibrairie *noun Fem.* bookshop.

ibrairie-papeterie *noun Fem.* bookseller's and stationer's.

ibre *adjective* **1** free; **vous êtes libre de partir** you are free to go; **2** free (*of a seat or telephone*); **est-ce**

que cette place est libre? is this seat free?

librement *adverb* freely.

libre-service *noun Masc.* self service, self-service shop or restaurant; **un libre-service bancaire** a cash dispenser.

licence *noun Fem.* degree (*at university*); **elle a une licence de chimie** she has a chemistry degree.

licencier *verb* [1] **licencier quelqu'un** to make somebody redundant.

lien *noun Masc.* link; **mes liens avec la famille** my links with my family; **un lien d'amitié** a bond of friendship.

lierre *noun Masc.* ivy.

lieu (*plural* **lieux**) *noun Masc.* **1** place; **un lieu public** a public place; **date et lieu de naissance** date and place of birth; **lieu de travail** place of work; **2 en premier lieu** in the first place; **3 avoir lieu** to take place; **le mariage aura lieu en juin** the marriage will take place in June; **4 au lieu de** instead of; **au lieu de prendre le bus, il est parti à pied** instead of taking the bus, he went off on foot; **5 les lieux** the premises; **peut-on visiter les lieux?** can one visit the premises?; **la police est arrivée sur les lieux** the police are now at the scene.

lieutenant *noun Masc.* lieutenant.

lièvre *noun Masc.* hare.

lifting *noun Masc.* face-lift.

a
b
c
d
e
f
g
h
i
j
k
l
m
n
o
p
q
r
s
t
u
v
w
x
y
z

a
b
c
d
e
f
g
h
i
j
k
l
m
n
o
p
q
r
s
t
u
v
w
x
y
z

ligne noun Fem. **1** line; **une ligne droite** a straight line; **une ligne blanche** a white line (*on the road*); **à la ligne!** new paragraph! (*in a dictation*); **2** line (*of a bus or train*); **la ligne Paris-Dijon** the Paris-Dijon line; **une ligne de chemin de fer** a railway line; **les grandes lignes** the main lines (*sign at a railway station*); **3** cable; **ligne électrique** electric cable; **4** (telephone) line; **la ligne est mauvaise** it's a bad line; **restez en ligne, monsieur** hold the line, sir; **5** figure; **pour garder la ligne** to keep your figure, to stay slim; **6** fishing line.

ligne d'arrivée noun Fem. finishing line.

ligne de touche noun Fem. touch line.

lilas noun Masc. lilac.

limace noun Fem. slug.

lime noun Fem. file; **une lime à ongles** a nail file.

limite noun Fem. **1** limit; **une limite d'âge** an age limit; **2 la date limite** the closing date; **3 sans limites** endless; **une patience sans limites** endless patience; **4 à la limite** if it comes to it, at a pinch; **à la limite, je peux te prêter l'argent** if it comes to it, I can lend you the money; **5 dans la limite de** within the limits of; **dans la limite des places disponibles** subject to available seating space; **dans la limite du possible** as far as possible; **6** boundary; **les limites du village** the village boundaries; **7** maximum, last; **vitesse limite** maximum speed; **âge limite**

maximum age; **date limite de vente** sell-by date.

limiter verb [1] **1** to limit; **2 se limiter** to limit oneself; **je me limite à deux cafés par jour** I limit myself to two coffees a day.

limonade noun Fem. lemonade.

lin noun Masc. linen; **une jupe en lin** a linen skirt.

linge noun Masc. **1** linen (*sheets, towels, etc*); **linge de maison** household linen; **du linge sale** dirty linen; **2** washing; **as-tu du linge pour la machine?** have you any washing for the machine?; **une corde à linge** a washing line; ★ **elle était blanche comme un linge** she was white as a sheet.

lingerie noun Fem. lingerie.

Lion noun Masc. Leo (*sign of the Zodiac*).

lion noun Masc. lion.

liqueur noun Fem. liqueur.

liquidation noun Fem. clearance sale, closing-down sale; **'liquidation totale!'** 'everything must go!'

liquide noun Masc. **1** liquid; **2** cash; **payer quelque chose en liquide** to pay cash for something. **liquide** adjective liquid.

lire verb [51] to read; **lire un roman** to read a novel; **elle sait lire maintenant** she can read now; **elle m'a lu une histoire** she read me a story; **un auteur qui est très lu** a popular author; **lire à haute voix** to read aloud; ★ **lire entre les lignes** to read between the lines.

s *verb* SEE **lire**.

sible *adjective* legible.

sse *adjective* smooth.

ste *noun Fem.* list; **faire une liste** to make a list; **faire la liste de** to make a list of.

ste d'attente *noun Fem.* waiting list.

t[1] *verb* SEE **lire**.

t[2] *noun Masc.* bed; **aller au lit** to go to bed; **faire son lit** to make one's bed; **un lit à une place** a single bed; **un lit à deux places** a double bed; **une chambre à deux lits** a twin-bedded room; **au lit!** bedtime!

terie *noun Fem.* bedding.

tière *noun Fem.* litter (*for an animal's bed*); **la litière pour chat** cat litter.

tre *noun Masc.* litre; **un litre d'eau** a litre of water.

ttéralement *adverb* literally.

ttérature *noun Fem.* literature; **la littérature française** French literature.

vraison *noun Fem.* delivery; **'livraisons à toute heure'** we deliver any time'; **'livraisons à domicile'** 'we deliver'.

vre[1] *noun Masc.* book; **un livre pour enfants** a children's book; **un livre de poche** a paperback.

vre[2] *noun Fem.* **1** pound (*in money*); **une livre sterling** a pound sterling; **2** pound (*in France = 500 grammes*); **une livre de tomates** a pound of tomatoes.

vrer *verb* [1] **1** to deliver; **2** to hand over; **3 se livrer** to surrender.

livret *noun Masc.* booklet.

livret de famille *Masc.*, **livret de famille** *noun* family record book (*with details of births, marriages, and deaths*).

livret scolaire *noun Masc.* school report book.

local (*plural* **locaux**) *noun Masc.* place (*usually a building*); **locaux commerciaux** business premises; **dans les locaux du lycée** on school premises.
local (*Masc. plural* **locaux**) *adjective* local; **un journal local** a local paper; **dix heures heure locale** ten a.m. local time.

localement *adverb* locally.

locataire *noun Masc. & Fem.* tenant.

location *noun Fem.* **1** renting; **un appartement de location** a rented flat; **'locations'** 'to rent'; **2** hire, rental; **location de voitures** car hire; **location de vidéos** video rental; **3** reservation, booking (*of theatre seats*).

locomotive *noun Fem.* engine, locomotive.

loge *noun Fem.* **1** lodge (*for the caretaker in a block of flats*); **2** (*in a theatre*) dressing-room (*for an actor*), box (*for a spectator*).

logement *noun Masc.* **1** accommodation; **il a trouvé un logement tout près** he's found somewhere to live just nearby; **2** housing; **la crise du logement** the housing crisis.

loger *verb* [52] **1** to put up; **peux-tu me loger ce soir?** can you put me up tonight?; **2** to stay; **pour l'instant**

a
b
c
d
e
f
g
h
i
j
k
l
m
n
o
p
q
r
s
t
u
v
w
x
y
z

elle loge chez mes parents for the moment she's staying with my parents.

logiciel noun Masc. **1** software; **2** program (for a computer); **un logiciel de jeux** a games program; **un logiciel antivirus** antivirus software.

logique noun Fem. logic.
logique adjective logical.

loi noun Fem. law.

loin adverb **1** (in distance) a long way, far off; **c'est loin** it's a long way; **c'est trop loin** it's too far; **c'est loin d'ici** it's a long way from here; **le cinéma est plus loin** the cinema is further on; **nous ne sommes pas allés plus loin** that's the farthest we went; **2** (in time) far off; **les vacances sont loin** the holidays are a long way off; **il n'est pas loin de midi** it's almost twelve; **3 de loin** from a long way off; **on voit leur maison de loin** you can see their house from a long way off; **4 de loin** by far; **c'est de loin le plus cher** it's by far the most expensive; **5 au loin** in the distance.

lointain adjective distant.

loisirs plural noun Masc. **1** spare time; **je dessine pendant mes loisirs** I draw in my spare time; **2** spare-time activities.

Londonien, Londonienne noun Masc., Fem. Londoner.

Londres noun London; **à Londres** in (or to) London; **les rues de Londres** the streets of London.

long noun Masc. **1 une corde de cinq mètres de long** a rope five metres long; **2 le long de** all along; **le long de la route** all along the road; **3 tout le long du film** all the way through the film.
long (Fem. **longue**) adjective long; **une longue vie** a long life; **un long silence** a long silence; **un long voyage** a long journey; **la rue la plus longue de Paris** the longest street in Paris; **une chemise à manches longues** a long-sleeved shirt; **la pièce est longue de quatre mètres, la pièce fait quatre mètres de long** the room is four metres long; ★ **marcher de long en large** to walk up and down; ★ **à la longue** in the long run.

longtemps adverb (for) a long time; **elle est restée longtemps** she stayed for a long time; **longtemps après** a long time after; **elle est là depuis longtemps** she's been here for a long time; **j'y suis allé, mais il y a longtemps** I've been there, but a long time ago; **ça fait longtemps qu'on ne s'est pas vu!** it's ages since we've seen each other!; **je n'en ai pas pour longtemps** I won't be long.

longuement adverb for a long time.

longueur noun Fem. **1** length; **de quelle longueur est le couloir?** how long is the corridor?; **2 avoir des longueurs** to drag; **le film est intéressant mais il a des longueurs** it's an interesting film but it drags in places.

ngueur d'onde *noun Fem.* wavelength.

rsque, **lorsqu'** (*before a vowel or silent 'h'*) *conjunction* when; **lorsque j'étais petite** when I was a little girl.

t *noun Masc.* **1** batch; **un lot de trois boîtes** a pack of three cans; **2** prize (*in a lottery*); **elle a gagné le gros lot** she won the jackpot.

t *noun Masc.* batch (*in computing*).

terie *noun Fem.* **1** lottery; **2** raffle.

tion *noun Fem.* lotion.

tissement *noun Masc.* housing estate.

to *noun Masc.* lottery.

tte *noun Fem.* monkfish.

uche¹ *noun Fem.* ladle.

uche² *adjective* fishy; **il y a un type louche à la porte** there's a fishy-looking guy at the door.

uer *verb* [1] **1** to let (*a house or flat*); **pendant mon absence j'ai loué mon appartement** while I was away I let my flat; **'à louer'** 'to let'; **2** to rent; **nous avons loué un appartement à Lille** we've rented a flat in Lille; **3** to hire; **nous avons loué une voiture** we hired a car; **4** to praise.

up *noun Masc.* wolf; ★ **j'ai une faim de loup** I'm absolutely starving (*literally: I'm as hungry as a wolf*); ★ **quand on parle du loup (on en voit la queue)** speak of the devil (*literally: when you speak of the wolf (you see its tail)*).

loupe *noun Fem.* magnifying glass.

louper *verb* [1] (*informal*) **1** to miss (*a train*); **on a loupé le train de dix heures** we missed the ten o'clock train; **2** to fail; **elle a loupé son permis** she failed her driving test.

loup-garou *noun Masc.* werewolf.

lourd *adjective* **1** heavy; **ta valise est très lourde** your case is very heavy; **le repas était un peu lourd** the meal was a bit heavy; **2 une lourde erreur** a serious mistake.

loutre *noun Fem.* otter.

loyal (*Masc. plural* **loyaux**) *adjective* faithful.

loyauté *noun Fem.* loyalty.

loyer *noun Masc.* rent; **payer le loyer** to pay the rent.

lu *verb* SEE **lire**.

lucarne *noun Fem.* skylight.

luge *noun Fem.* sledge.

lugubre *adjective* gloomy.

lui *pronoun* **1** him; **c'est lui** it's him; **Hélène travaille avec lui** Hélène works with him; **est-ce qu'il a aimé le bouquin que je lui ai prêté?** did he like the book I lent him?; **2** to him; **Pierre est en colère – qu'est-ce que tu lui as dit?** Pierre's angry – what did you say to him?; **3** to her; **Nadine est en colère – qu'est-ce que tu lui as dit?** Nadine's angry – what did you say to her?; **4** (*for emphasis*) **lui, il n'est jamais content!** he's never pleased!

lui-même *pronoun* **1** himself; **il l'a fait lui-même** he did it himself; **2** (*on telephone*) **'Monsieur**

173

a
b
c
d
e
f
g
h
i
j
k
l
m
n
o
p
q
r
s
t
u
v
w
x
y
z

a b c d e f g h i j k **l** **m** n o p q r s t u v w x y z

Dubois?' – 'lui-même' 'Monsieur Dubois?' – 'speaking'.

lumière *noun Fem.* light.

lumineux (*Fem.* **lumineuse**) *adjective* luminous; **un panneau lumineux** an electronic display board; **une enseigne lumineuse** a neon sign.

lunch *noun Masc.* buffet (*lunch or supper*).

lundi *noun Masc.* **1** Monday; **nous sommes lundi aujourd'hui** it's Monday today; **lundi prochain** next Monday; **lundi dernier** last Monday; **2** on Monday; **je l'ai vu lundi soir** I saw him on Monday evening; **3 le lundi** on Mondays; **fermé le lundi** closed on Mondays; **4 tous les lundis** every Monday.

lune *noun Fem.* moon; ★ **il est dans la lune** he's got his head in the clouds; ★ **il m'a promis la lune** he promised me the earth.

lune de miel *noun Fem.* honeymoon.

lunettes *plural noun Fem.* glasses; **une paire de lunettes** a pair of glasses; **mets tes lunettes!** put on your glasses!; **je porte des lunettes pour lire** I wear glasses for reading.

lunettes de natation *plural noun Fem.* swimming goggles.

lunettes de soleil *plural noun Fem.* sun-glasses.

lutte *noun Fem.* fight, struggle; **la lutte contre la drogue** the fight against drugs.

lutter *verb* [1] to fight, to struggle; **ils luttaient pour la liberté et contre l'oppression** they were fighting for freedom and against oppression.

luxe *noun Masc.* luxury; **une voiture de luxe** a luxury car.

luxueux (*Fem.* **luxueuse**) *adjective* luxurious.

lycée *noun Masc.* secondary school (*for ages 15-18*).

lycéen, **lycéenne** *noun Masc.*, *Fem.* secondary school student.

Mm

M. SHORT FOR **Monsieur**; **M. Dupont** M Dupont.

ma *adjective* my; SEE **mon**.

macaronis *plural noun Masc.* macaroni; **manger des macaroni** to have macaroni.

mâche *noun Fem.* lamb's lettuce.

mâcher *verb* [1] to chew.

machin *noun Masc.* (*informal*) whatsit, thingumajig; **tu n'as pas un machin pour ouvrir les enveloppes?** don't you have a whatsit for opening envelopes with

machine *noun Fem.* **1** machine; **2 taper à la machine** to type.

machine à coudre *noun Fem.* sewing machine.

machine à écrire *noun Fem.* typewriter.

machine à laver *noun Fem.* washing machine.

machine à sous *noun Fem.* fru machine.

âchoire noun Fem. jaw.

âchonner verb [1] to chew.

açon noun Masc. **1** builder; **2** bricklayer.

adame (plural **Mesdames**) noun Fem. **1 Madame Jones** Ms Jones, Mrs Jones; **2 Madame, ...** Dear Madam, ...; **3 bonsoir madame** good evening (when greeting a person you do not know well in French, it is polite to add 'Madame', 'Monsieur', or 'Mademoiselle' to the greeting).

ademoiselle (plural **Mesdemoiselles**) noun Fem. **1** Miss, Ms; **2 bonsoir mademoiselle** good evening. SEE ALSO **Madame**.

agasin noun Masc. shop; **un grand magasin** a department store; **un magasin de vêtements** a clothes shop; **un magasin de sport** a sports shop; **faire les magasins** to go round the shops.

agazine noun Masc. magazine.

aghrébin adjective North African.

aghrébin, Maghrébine noun Masc., Fem. North African.

agicien, magicienne noun Masc., Fem. magician.

agie noun Fem. magic.

agique adjective **1** magic; **2** magical.

agistral (Masc. plural **magistraux**) adjective **un cours magistral** a lecture (at university).

agnétique adjective magnetic.

magnétiser verb [1] **1** to magnetize; **2** to hypnotize.

magnétophone noun Masc. tape recorder.

magnétoscope noun Masc. video recorder.

magnifique adjective splendid.

magouille noun Fem. (informal) fiddling.

magret de canard noun Masc. duck breast.

mai noun Masc. May; **en mai, au mois de mai** in May; **le premier mai** May Day.

maigre adjective thin, skinny; ★ **maigre comme un clou** as thin as a rake (literally: as thin as a nail).

maigrir verb [2] to lose weight; **il a beaucoup maigri** he's lost a lot of weight.

maille noun Fem. stitch (in knitting).

maillot noun Masc. **1** shirt, jersey (in sports such as football); **2 maillot (de corps)** vest.

maillot de bain noun Masc. **1** swimsuit; **2** swimming trunks.

main noun Fem. hand; **avoir quelque chose à la main** to have something in your hand; **serrer la main à quelqu'un** to shake hands with somebody; **se serrer la main** to shake hands; **nous nous sommes serré la main** we shook hands; **se donner la main** to hold hands; **haut les mains!** hands up!; **donner un coup de main à quelqu'un** to give somebody a hand; **tu veux un coup de main?** do you want a hand?; **fait à la main** handmade.

a
b
c
d
e
f
g
h
i
j
k
l
m
n
o
p
q
r
s
t
u
v
w
x
y
z

175

main-d'œuvre *noun Fem.* labour.

maintenant *adverb* **1** now; **il est maintenant trop tard pour sortir** it's too late to go out now; **2** nowadays; **maintenant presque tout le monde a le téléphone** nowadays nearly everybody has a phone.

maintenir *verb* [81] **1** to maintain; **2** to support.

maire *noun Masc.* mayor.

mairesse *noun Fem.* mayoress.

mairie *noun Fem.* **1** town hall; **2** town council.

mais *conjunction* **1** but; **j'ai essayé de t'appeler mais tu n'étais pas là** I tried to phone you but you weren't there; **2 mais oui** yes of course; **mais non** of course not.

maïs *noun Masc.* **1** maize; **2** sweetcorn; **3 des épis de maïs** corn on the cob.

maison *noun Fem.* **1** house; **leur maison est petite mais très confortable** their house is small but very comfortable; **2** home; **rester à la maison** to stay at home; **rentrer à la maison** to go home.

maison de la culture *noun Fem.* cultural centre, arts centre.

maison de retraite *noun Fem.* old people's home.

maître, maîtresse *noun Masc., Fem.* **1** master, mistress; **2** teacher.

maître-nageur *noun Masc.* swimming instructor.

maîtresse *noun Fem.* **1** SEE **maître**; **2** lover.

maîtrise *noun Fem.* **1** mastery; **2** command; **la maîtrise de soi** se control; **3** master's degree.

maîtriser *verb* [1] **1** to control; **2** master.

majestueux (*Fem.* majestueuse *adjective* majestic.

majeur *adjective* **1** major; **2 être majeur** to be over 18.
majeur *noun* middle finger.

majorité *noun Fem.* majority.

majuscule *noun Fem.* capital (letter); **en majuscules** in block capitals; **un R majuscule** a capita R.

mal (*plural* maux) *noun Masc.* **1** pain, ache; **faire mal** to hurt; **se faire mal** to hurt yourself; **avoir m à la gorge** to have a sore throat; **j'** **mal au dos** my back hurts; **ça fai mal** it hurts; **2 faire mal à quelqu'un** to hurt somebody; **aïe!** **me fais mal!** ouch! you're hurting me!; **3 avoir du mal à faire** to hav difficulty in doing; **j'ai du mal à comprendre ce qu'il dit** I have difficulty in understanding what **I** says; **se donner du mal à faire** to a lot of trouble to do; **elle s'est donné beaucoup de mal pour contacter tout le monde** she wer to a lot of trouble to contact everybody; **4** evil.
mal *adjective* **1 pas mal** not bad; **2 être mal** to be uncomfortable.
mal *adverb* **1** badly; **écrire mal t** write badly; **2 je t'entends mal** I can't hear you very well; **3 j'ai ma compris** I misunderstood; **4 être mal à l'aise** to feel uncomfortable

malade *noun Masc. & Fem.* patient.

malade *adjective* ill, sick; **tomber malade** to fall ill.

maladie *noun Fem.* **1** illness; **2** disease.

maladresse *noun Fem.* **1** clumsiness; **2** blunder.

maladroit *adjective* clumsy.

malaise *noun Masc.* **1 avoir un malaise** to feel faint, to pass out; **2 créer un malaise** to make people feel uncomfortable; **ça a créé un malaise** it made everybody feel uncomfortable.

malaxer *verb* [1] **1** to knead; **2** to cream.

malchance *noun Fem.* bad luck.

mal de mer *noun Masc.* **avoir le mal de mer** to be seasick.

mal du pays *noun Masc.* **avoir le mal du pays** to be homesick.

mâle *noun Masc., adjective* male.

malédiction *noun Fem.* curse.

malencontreux (*Fem.* **malencontreuse**) *adjective* unfortunate.

malentendu *noun Masc.* misunderstanding.

malfaiteur *noun Masc.* criminal.

mal famé *adjective* **un quartier mal famé** a rough area.

malgré *preposition* **1** in spite of; **malgré le froid** in spite of the cold; **2 malgré tout** all the same; **mais malgré tout nous avons décidé d'y aller** but we decided to go all the same.

malheur *noun Masc.* misfortune; **porter malheur** to bring bad luck.

malheureusement *adverb* unfortunately; **Vincent était déjà parti, malheureusement** unfortunately, Vincent had already left.

malheureux, malheureuse *noun Masc., Fem.* poor thing; **la malheureuse!** poor woman! **malheureux** (*Fem.* **malheureuse**) *adjective* **1** unhappy; **avoir l'air malheureux** to look unhappy; **rendre quelqu'un malheureux** to make somebody unhappy; **2** unfortunate; **un choix malheureux** an unfortunate choice.

malhonnête *adjective* dishonest.

malice *noun Fem.* mischief.

malicieux (*Fem.* **malicieuse**) *adjective* mischievous.

malin (*Fem.* **maligne**) *adjective* **1** clever; **ce n'était pas très malin** ça that wasn't very clever; **elle se croit maligne** she thinks she's clever; **2** malignant (*tumour*).

malle *noun Fem.* trunk.

malodorant *adjective* smelly.

malpoli *adjective* rude.

malpropre *adjective* dirty.

malsain *adjective* unhealthy.

maltraiter *verb* [1] to ill-treat; **les enfants maltraités** battered children.

malveillance *noun Fem.* malice.

malveillant *adjective* malicious.

maman *noun Fem.* mum, mummy.

mamie *noun Fem.* granny, gran, nan.

mammifère *noun Masc.* mammal.

a
b
c
d
e
f
g
h
i
j
k
l
m
n
o
p
q
r
s
t
u
v
w
x
y
z

177

a **manager** *verb* [52] to manage.

b **manageur** *noun Masc.* manager.

c **manche**[1] *noun Masc.* handle (*of a tool*).

d **manche**[2] *noun Fem.* **1** sleeve; **une chemise à manches courtes** a short-sleeved shirt; **sans manches** sleeveless; **2** leg (*of a match*).

f

g **Manche** *noun Fem.* **la Manche** the Channel; **le tunnel sous la Manche** the Channel Tunnel.

h

i **mandarine** *noun Fem.* mandarin orange.

j **mandat** *noun Masc.* money order.

k **manège** *noun Masc.* **1** merry-go-round; **2** riding school.

l **manette** *noun Fem.* lever.

m **mangeable** *adjective* edible.

n **manger** *noun Masc.* food.
manger *verb* [52] to eat; **qu'est-ce qu'on va manger?** what shall we have to eat?; **manger au restaurant** to go out for a meal; **j'ai déjà mangé** I've already eaten; **j'ai assez mangé** I'm full, I've had enough; **donner à manger à** to feed; **ils mangent trois fois par jour** they have three meals a day; ★ **manger ses mots** to mumble (*literally: to eat your words*).

u **mangue** *noun Fem.* mango.

v **maniaque** *noun Masc. & Fem.* fusspot.
maniaque *adjective* extremely fussy.

w

x **manie** *noun Fem.* **1** odd habit; **2** mania.

y

z **manier** *verb* [1] to handle.

manière *noun Fem.* **1** way; **une manière plus facile** an easier way; **on ne peut pas le faire d'une manière plus facile?** isn't there a easier way of doing it?; **de cette manière** like this, like that; **d'une autre manière** in another way; **d'une manière ou d'une autre** on way or another; **d'une certaine manière** in a way; **2 de toute manière** in any case; **3 de manière à faire** so as to do; **de manière à éviter de dépenser de l'argent** s as to avoid spending money; **4 manières** manners; **ne fais pas de manières!** don't make a fuss!

manifestant, manifestante *noun Masc., Fem.* demonstrator.

manifestation *noun Fem.* demonstration; **une manifestation contre le racisme** a demonstration against racism.

manifester *verb* [1] **1** to demonstrate, to take part in a demonstration; **2 manifester quelque chose** to express something.

manipuler *verb* [1] **1** to handle; **2** to manipulate.

manivelle *noun Fem.* handle.

mannequin *noun Masc.* **1** fashion model; **2** dummy (*either in a shop window or as used by a dressmaker*)

manoir *noun Masc.* manor house.

manque *noun Masc.* **manque de** lack of, shortage of; **leur manque d'imagination** their lack of imagination; **être en manque d'affection** to be in need of affection.

nanqué *adjective* **1** failed; **un acteur manqué** a failed actor; **2** missed; **une occasion manquée** a missed opportunity.

nanquer *verb* [1] **1** manquer **quelque chose** to miss something; **il a manqué son train** he missed his train; **2** manquer un examen to fail an exam; **3** manquer à **quelqu'un** to be missed by somebody; **tu me manques** I miss you; **Londres leur manque** they miss London; **4** il manque **quelque chose** something's missing; **il manque trois fourchettes** there are three forks missing, we're three forks short; **5** manquer de to lack; **nous ne manquons pas de verres** there's no shortage of glasses; **6** manquer de **faire** to fail to do; **il a manqué de fermer la porte à clé** he failed to lock the door.

nansarde *noun Fem.* attic room.

nanteau (*plural* manteaux) *noun Masc.* coat.

nanuel *noun Masc.* **1** manual; **2** textbook; **un manuel scolaire** a school book.
nanuel *adjective* (*Fem.* manuelle) manual.

nanufacture *noun Fem.* **1** factory; **2** manufacture.

nanuscrit *noun Masc.* manuscript.
nanuscrit *adjective* handwritten; **un petit mot manuscrit** a handwritten note.

naquereau (*plural* maquereaux) *noun Masc.* mackerel.

maquette *noun Fem.* scale model.

maquillage *noun Masc.* make-up.

maquiller *verb* [1] **se maquiller** to put on your make-up.

marais *noun Masc.* marsh.

marathon *noun Masc.* marathon.

marbre *noun Masc.* marble; **une cheminée en marbre** a marble fireplace.

marc de café *noun Masc.* coffee grounds.

marchand, marchande *noun Masc., Fem.* **1** shopkeeper; **la marchande de fromage** the woman in the cheese shop; **2** stallholder (*on a market*).

marchand de journaux *noun Masc.* newsagent.

marchander *verb* [1] to haggle (over).

marchandise *noun Fem.* goods.

marche *noun Fem.* **1** walking; **faire de la marche** to go walking; **2** march; **3** step; **les marches d'escalier** the stairs; **attention à la marche** mind the step; **4** mettre en marche to start up (*a machine*); **être en état de marche** to be in working order.

marché *noun Masc.* **1** market; **aller au marché** to go to market; **le marché aux fleurs** the flower market; **un marché aux puces** a flea market; **le marché de l'emploi** the job market; **2** deal.

marche arrière *noun Fem.*
reverse; **faire marche arrière** to
reverse.

marchepied *noun Masc.* step (*on a
train*).

marcher *verb* [1] **1** to walk; **on va
marcher jusqu'à la gare** we'll walk
as far as the station; **2 marcher
dans quelque chose** to tread in
something; **marcher sur quelque
chose** to tread on something; **3** to
march; **4** to work; **ça a marché** it
worked; **la machine à laver ne
marche pas** the washing machine
doesn't work; **les trains ne
marchent pas aujourd'hui** the
trains are not running today; **5 et
ton boulot, ça marche?** (*informal*)
and is your job going all right?;
★ **faire marcher quelqu'un** to pull
somebody's leg.

marcheur, marcheuse *noun
Masc., Fem.* walker.

mardi *noun Masc.* **1** Tuesday; **nous
sommes mardi aujourd'hui** it's
Tuesday today; **mardi prochain**
next Tuesday; **mardi dernier** last
Tuesday; **2** on Tuesday; **je
t'appellerai mardi soir** I'll ring you
on Tuesday evening; **3 le mardi** on
Tuesdays; **c'est fermé le mardi** it's
closed on Tuesdays; **4 tous les
mardis** every Tuesday.

Mardi gras *noun Masc.* Shrove
Tuesday.

mare *noun Fem.* pond.

marécage *noun Masc.* swamp.

marée *noun Fem.* tide; **la marée
monte** the tide's coming in; **la
marée descend** the tide's going out.

marée noire *noun Fem.* oil slick

margarine *noun Fem.* margarine

marge *noun Fem.* **1** margin; **2 en
marge de** on the fringe of.

marguerite *noun Fem.*
1 marguerite; **2** oxeye daisy.

mari *noun Masc.* husband; **le mari d**
Claire Claire's husband.

mariage *noun Masc.* **1** marriage;
2 wedding; **être invité à un
mariage** to be invited to a weddin

Marianne *noun Fem.* Marianne (*
female figure representing the Frenc
Republic in statues and paintings*)

marié, mariée *noun Masc., Fem.*
bridegroom, bride; **les jeunes
mariés** the newlyweds.
marié *adjective* married.

marier *verb* [1] **1 se marier** to ge
married; **ils se sont mariés à
Londres** they got married in
London; **elle s'est mariée avec
Frank** she married Frank; **2 le
prêtre qui les a mariés** the pries
who married them.

marin *noun Masc.* sailor.
marin *adjective* sea.

marine *adjective* **bleu marine** nav
blue.

mariner *verb* [1] to marinate.

marionnette *noun Fem.* puppet.

marjolaine *noun Fem.* marjoram

marketing *noun Masc.* marketing

marmelade *noun Fem.*
marmelade d'oranges amères
orange marmalade.

marmite noun Fem. cooking pot.

marmonner verb [1] to mutter, to mumble.

Maroc noun Masc. Morocco.

marocain adjective Moroccan.

Marocain, **Marocaine** noun Masc., Fem. Moroccan (person).

maroquinerie noun Fem.
1 leather shop; 2 leather goods.

marquant adjective outstanding.

marque noun Fem. 1 brand; **une marque de nourriture pour chats** a brand of cat food; 2 make; **c'est une marque de jean bien connue** it's a well-known make of jeans; 3 mark; 4 point.

marque déposée noun Fem. registered trademark.

marquer verb [1] 1 to mark; 2 to write down; **j'ai marqué ton nom** I've written down your name; 3 **marquer un but** to score a goal.

marqueur noun Masc. marker pen.

marraine noun Fem. godmother.

marrant adjective (informal) funny.

marre adverb (informal) **j'en ai marre** I'm fed up; **j'en ai marre d'écrire** I'm fed up with writing.

marrer verb [1] 1 **se marrer** to have a great time; 2 **se marrer** to have a good laugh.

marron noun Masc. 1 (sweet) chestnut; 2 (horse) chestnut.
marron adjective brown; **des chaussures marron** brown shoes; **marron clair** light brown; **marron foncé** dark brown.

marronnier noun Masc. chestnut tree.

mars noun Masc. March; **en mars, au mois de mars** in March.

Marseillaise noun Fem. **la Marseillaise** the Marseillaise (the French national anthem).

Marseille noun Marseilles.

marteau (plural **marteaux**) noun Masc. 1 hammer; 2 doorknocker.

marteau piqueur noun Masc. pneumatic drill.

marteler verb [45] to hammer.

martinet noun Masc. swift.

martin-pêcheur noun Masc. kingfisher.

martyrisé adjective **un enfant martyrisé** a battered child.

mascotte noun Fem. mascot.

masculin noun Masc. masculine (in French and other grammars); **au masculin** in the masculine.
masculin adjective 1 male; **le sexe masculin** the male sex; 2 men's; **les vêtements masculins** men's clothing; 3 masculine.

masque noun Masc. mask.

masquer verb [1] to hide.

massacre noun Masc. massacre.

massacrer verb [1] to massacre.

massage noun Masc. massage; **faire un massage à quelqu'un** to give somebody a massage.

masse noun Fem. 1 mass; 2 **une masse de** (informal) masses of; **j'ai une masse de boulot à faire avant lundi** I've got masses of work to do for Monday.

a
b
c
d
e
f
g
h
i
j
k
l
m
n
o
p
q
r
s
t
u
v
w
x
y
z

masser *verb* [1] **1** to massage; **2 se masser** to assemble.

massif (Fem. **massive**) *adjective* **1** solid; **une table en pin massif** a solid pine table; **2** massive.

mass media *plural noun* Masc. **les mass media** the mass media.

mastic *noun* Masc. **1** putty; **2** filler.

mastiquer *verb* [1] **1** to chew; **2** to putty (*a window*); **3** to fill (*a crack*).

mat *adjective* matt.

mât *noun* Masc. **1** mast; **2** pole.

match *noun* Masc. match; **un match de foot** a football match; **faire match nul** to draw.

matelas *noun* Masc. mattress.

matelassé *adjective* quilted.

matelot *noun* Masc. sailor.

matériaux *plural noun* Masc. materials; **les matériaux de construction** building materials.

matériel *noun* Masc. equipment; **matériel de sport** sports equipment.

maternel (Fem. **maternelle**) *adjective* **1** motherly; **2** maternal; **ma tante maternelle** my aunt on my mother's side of the family.

maternelle *noun* Fem. (state) nursery school (*for ages 2 - 6*); **aller en maternelle** to go to nursery school.

maternité *noun* Fem. **1** motherhood; **2** pregnancy; **être en congé de maternité** to be on maternity leave; **3** maternity unit.

mathématiques *plural noun* Fem. mathematics.

matheux, matheuse *noun* Masc., Fem. maths genius.

maths *plural noun* Fem. maths.

matière *noun* Fem. subject; **la matière que j'aime le mieux c'es l'histoire** the subject I like best is history; **en matière de: la politiqu du gouvernement en matière de l'éducation** the government's education policy.

matières grasses *plural nou* Fem. fat (*in food*).

matin *noun* Masc. morning; **à quel heure est-ce que tu te lèves le matin?** what time do you get up i the morning?; **à six heures du matin** at six o'clock in the mornin **du matin au soir** from morning t night; **de bon matin** early in the morning.

matinal (Masc. *plural* **matinaux**) **matinal** *adjective* **1** morning; **2 être matinal** to be an early rise

matinée *noun* Fem. **1** morning; **a cours de la matinée** during the morning; **2** matinée.

matou *noun* Masc. tomcat.

matraque *noun* Fem. truncheon, club.

matrimonial (Masc. *plural* **matrimoniaux**) *adjective* **une agence matrimoniale** a marriage bureau.

maturité *noun* Fem. maturity.

maudire *verb* to curse.

maussade *adjective* **1** sullen; **2** dull, dreary (*weather*).

mauvais *adjective* **1** bad; **une mauvaise expérience** a bad experience; **ça sent mauvais ici** there's a nasty smell here; **ça a mauvais goût** it tastes horrible; **c'est du mauvais goût** it's bad taste; **2** wrong; **le mauvais numéro** the wrong number; **la mauvaise adresse** the wrong address; **3 il fait mauvais** the weather's bad; **4 elle a mauvaise mine** she doesn't look well.

mauvaise herbe *noun Fem.* weed.

maux *plural noun Masc.* SEE **mal**.

maximum *noun Masc., adjective* maximum; **au maximum** as much as possible; **au maximum** at the most; **faire le maximum** to do your utmost.

mayonnaise *noun Fem.* mayonnaise.

mazout *noun Masc.* fuel oil.

me, m' *(before a vowel or silent 'h')* *pronoun* me **1** elle me déteste she hates me; **il m'a vu** he saw me; **2** to me; **elle ne me parle jamais** she never speaks to me; **elle m'a donné son adresse** she gave me her address; **il me l'a donné** he gave it to me; **3** myself; **je me fais une salade** I'm making myself a salad; **je me suis blessé** I hurt myself; **je me lève à sept heures** I get up at seven o'clock; **je me brosse les dents** I brush my teeth *(literally: I brush to myself the teeth)*.

mec *noun Masc. (informal)* guy.

mécanicien, mécanicienne *noun Masc., Fem.* **1** mechanic; **2** train driver.

mécanique *noun Fem.* **1** mechanics; **2** mechanism. **mécanique** *adjective* **1** mechanical; **2** clockwork.

mécanisme *noun Masc.* mechanism.

méchamment *adverb* spitefully, nastily.

méchanceté *noun Fem.* **1** nastiness; **2** spite.

méchant *adjective* **1** nasty; **elle a été vraiment méchante avec moi** she was really nasty to me; **2** spiteful; **3** vicious; **'chien méchant'** 'beware of the dog'.

mèche *noun Fem.* **1** lock *(of hair)*; **2** wick.

méconnaissable *adjective* unrecognizable.

mécontent *adjective* dissatisfied.

mécontentement *noun Masc.* **1** annoyance; **2** displeasure.

médaille *noun Fem.* medal.

médecin *noun Masc.* doctor; **aller chez le médecin** to go to the doctor's.

médecine *noun Fem.* medicine; **faire des études de médecine** to go to medical school.

médias *plural noun Masc.* **les médias** the media.

médiathèque *noun Fem.* multimedia library.

médical *(Masc. plural* **médicaux***) adjective* medical.

médicament *noun Masc.* drug.

a
b
c
d
e
f
g
h
i
j
k
l
m
n
o
p
q
r
s
t
u
v
w
x
y
z

a b c d e f g h i j k l m n o p q r s t u v w x y z

médiéval (*Masc. plural* médiévaux) *adjective* medieval.

médiocre *adjective* second-rate, poor; **un travail médiocre** a second-rate piece of work.

méditation *noun Fem.* meditation.

méditer *verb* [1] **1** to meditate; **2 méditer quelque chose** to mull something over.

Méditerranée *noun Fem.* **la Méditerranée** the Mediterranean.

méditerranéen (*Fem.* méditerranéenne) *adjective* Mediterranean; **la cuisine méditerranéenne** Mediterranean cooking.

méduse *noun Fem.* jellyfish.

méfait *noun Masc.* **1** crime; **2 les méfaits de la pollution** the detrimental effects of pollution.

méfiance *noun Fem.* suspicion.

méfiant *adjective* suspicious.

méfier *verb* [1] **se méfier de quelqu'un** not to trust somebody; **méfie-toi!** watch out!

mégère *noun Fem.* shrew.

mégot *noun Masc.* cigarette end.

meilleur *noun Masc.* best; **c'est le meilleur** it's the best one; **le meilleur des deux** the better of the two.
meilleur *adjective* **1** better; **le climat est bien meilleur au sud** the climate's much better in the south; **meilleur que** better than; **ton écriture est meilleure que la mienne** your writing's better than mine; **c'est meilleur que l'autre** it's better than the other one; **2** best; **le**

meilleur the best moment; **c'est m meilleure amie** she's my best friend; **meilleurs voeux** best wishes.

mélange *noun Masc.* mixture.

mélanger *verb* [52] **1** to mix; **2** to mix up; **j'ai mélangé les dates** I g the dates mixed up.

mélasse *noun Fem.* black treacle.

mêlée *noun Fem.* scrum.

mêler *verb* [1] **1 se mêler à** to mingle with; **2 se mêler de** to meddle in; ★ **mêle-toi de ce qui t regarde!** mind your own business

mélodie *noun Fem.* melody, tune.

mélomane *noun Masc. & Fem.* music lover.

melon *noun Masc.* **1** melon; **2 un chapeau melon** a bowler hat.

membre *noun Masc.* **1** member; **2** limb.

même *adjective* **1** same; **j'ai le même anniversaire que toi** I hav the same birthday as you; **ils avaient des chapeaux de la mêm couleur** they had the same colour hats; **2 en même temps** at the sam time; **3 tout de même** all the sam **même** *adverb* even; **il n'a même pas demandé** he didn't even ask.

mémé *noun* (*informal*) *Fem.* **1** granny; **2 une vieille mémé** an old lady.

mémoire *noun Fem.* memory.

mémoriser *verb* [1] to memorize

menace *noun Fem.* threat.

menacer *verb* [61] to threaten.

ménage *noun Masc.* **1** housework; **faire le ménage** to do the cleaning; **une femme de ménage** a cleaning lady; **2** household.

ménager[1] *verb* [52] **ménager quelqu'un** to handle somebody tactfully.

ménager[2] (*Fem.* ménagère) *adjective* household; **les appareils ménagers** household appliances; **les travaux ménagers** housework.

mendiant, mendiante *noun Masc., Fem.* beggar.

mendier *verb* [1] to beg.

mener *verb* [50] **1** to lead; **mener à** to lead to; **le chemin qui mène à la ferme** the track which leads to the farm; **2 mener une société** to run a company; **3 mener une campagne** to conduct a campaign.

méningite *noun Fem.* meningitis.

menottes *plural noun Fem.* handcuffs.

mensonge *noun Masc.* lie; **dire des mensonges** to tell lies.

mensualité *noun Fem.* monthly payment.

mensuel (*Fem.* mensuelle) *adjective* monthly.

mental (*Masc. plural* mentaux) *adjective* mental.

mentalité *noun Fem.* mentality.

menteur, menteuse *noun Masc., Fem.* liar.

menteur (*Fem.* menteuse) *adjective* untruthful.

menthe *noun Fem.* mint; **le sirop de menthe** mint cordial.

mention *noun Fem.* **1** mention; **2** grade (*in an exam or a degree*); **elle a eu son bac avec mention bien** she got a grade B plus pass in her baccalaureate.

mentionner *verb* [1] to mention.

mentir *verb* [53] to lie, to tell lies.

menton *noun Masc.* chin.

menu[1] *noun Masc.* menu; **qu'est-ce qu'il y a au menu?** what's on the menu?; **le menu du jour** today's menu; **est-ce qu'il y un menu à prix fixe?** is there a set menu?

menu[2] *adjective* very small.

menuiserie *noun Fem.* woodwork.

menuisier *noun Masc.* joiner.

mépris *noun Masc.* contempt.

mépriser *verb* [1] to despise.

mer *noun Fem.* sea; **aller à la mer** to go to the seaside; **au bord de la mer** at the seaside; **la mer du Nord** the North Sea; **la mer des Antilles** the Caribbean (Sea).

mercerie *noun Fem.* haberdashery.

merci[1] *exclamation* thank you, thanks; **merci beaucoup, merci bien** thank you very much; **merci de m'avoir rappelé** thank you for calling me back.

merci[2] *noun Fem.* mercy.

mercredi *noun Masc.*
1 Wednesday; **nous sommes mercredi aujourd'hui** it's Wednesday today; **mercredi prochain** next Wednesday; **mercredi dernier** last Wednesday; **2** on Wednesday; **je t'appellerai mercredi soir** I'll ring you on

a
b
c
d
e
f
g
h
i
j
k
l
m
n
o
p
q
r
s
t
u
v
w
x
y
z

Wednesday evening; **3 le mercredi** on Wednesdays; **c'est fermé le mercredi** it's closed on Wednesdays; **tous les mercredis** every Wednesday.

mercure noun Masc. mercury.

mère noun Fem. mother; **la mère de Sophie** Sophie's mother.

merguez noun Fem. spicy lamb sausage.

méridional (Masc. plural méridionaux) adjective southern.

meringue noun Fem. meringue.

mérite noun Fem. merit.

mériter verb [1] to deserve.

merlan noun Masc. whiting.

merle noun Masc. blackbird.

merveille noun Fem. **1** wonder; **ton gâteau est une vraie merveille** your cake's absolutely wonderful; **2 à merveille** wonderfully.

merveilleux (Fem. merveilleuse) adjective marvellous.

mes adjective SEE **mon**.

Mesdames noun SEE **Madame**.

Mesdemoiselles noun SEE **Mademoiselle**.

mesquin adjective petty, mean.

message noun Masc. message.

messager, messagère noun Masc., Fem. messenger.

messe noun Fem. mass; **aller à la messe** to go to mass.

Messieurs noun SEE **Monsieur**.

mesure noun Fem. **1** measurement; **prendre les mesures de la pièce** to take the measurements of the

room; **2 sur mesure** tailor-made; **3** measure; **prendre des mesures pour faire** to take measures to do; **conseil municipal va prendre de mesures pour contrôler la pollution** the town council is goin to take measures to control pollution; **4 être en mesure de faire** to be in a position to do; **nou ne sommes pas en mesure de vous aider** we are not in a positio to help you.

mesurer verb [1] to measure.

met verb SEE **mettre**.

métal (plural métaux) noun Mas metal.

métallique adjective metallic.

métallisé adjective metallic; **ble métallisé** metallic blue.

météo noun Fem. weather forecas

méthode noun Fem. **1** method; **u méthode de faire** a method of doing; **2** manual, tutor.

métier noun Masc. **1** job; **2 un métier à tisser** a weaving loom.

mètre noun Masc. **1** metre; **2 met** rule.

métrique adjective metric.

métro noun Masc. underground; **une station de métro** an underground station.

mets verb SEE **mettre**.

metteur en scène noun Masc **1** director (of a film); **2** producer (a play).

mettre verb [11] **1** to put; **où as-t mis le sel?** where have you put th salt?; **2** to put on; **je vais mettre mon manteau** I'm going to put m

at on; **3** to wear; **mets ta jupe
ose** wear your pink skirt; **4** to turn
n (*radio, television, heating*);
ettre le réveil to set the alarm
ock; **5 mettre quelqu'un en
olère** to make somebody angry;
**j'ai mis trois heures pour le
aire** it took me three hours to do it;
se mettre quelque part to
and (or sit) somewhere; **8 se
ettre debout** to stand up; **9 se
ettre à faire** to start to do; **elle
'est mise à chanter** she started to
ing.

eublé *adjective* furnished.

euble *noun Masc.* **1 des meubles**
rniture; **2 un meuble** a piece of
rniture.

eule *noun Fem.* **1** millstone; **2 une
eule de foin** a haystack.

eurtre *noun Masc.* murder.

eurtrier, meurtrière *noun
asc., Fem.* murderer.
eurtrier (*Fem.* **meurtrière**)
djective **1** deadly; **2** fatal.

exicain *adjective* Mexican.

exicain, Mexicaine *noun
asc. & Fem.* Mexican.

exico *noun* Mexico City.

exique *noun Masc.* Mexico; **aller
u Mexique** to go to Mexico.

i- *prefix* **1** half-; **mi-clos** half-shut;
mid-; **à la mi-février** in mid-
February.

i-bas *noun Masc.* knee sock.

i-chemin *noun* **à mi-chemin**
alfway.

icro *noun Masc.* microphone.

microbe *noun Masc.* germ.

micro-ondes *noun Masc.*
microwave; **faire cuire quelque
chose au micro-ondes** to cook
something in the microwave.

micro-ordinateur *noun Masc.*
microcomputer.

microscope *noun Masc.*
microscope.

midi *noun Masc.* **1** midday, noon; **il
est midi vingt** it's twenty past
twelve; **je viendrai vers midi** I'll
come around twelve; **2** lunchtime; **je
fais mes courses à midi** I do my
shopping in my lunch hour.

Midi *noun Masc.* **le Midi** the South of
France.

miel *noun Masc.* honey.

**mien, mienne, miens,
miennes** *pronoun* **le mien, la
mienne, les miens, les miennes**
mine; **'à qui sont ces
chaussures?' – 'ce sont les
miennes'** 'whose shoes are these?' –
'they're mine'; **puis-je t'emprunter
ton vélo? le mien est chez moi**
can I borrow your bike? mine's at
home.

miette *noun Fem.* crumb.

mieux *adjective, adverb* **1** better; **tu
la connais mieux que moi** you
know her better than I do; **je me
sens mieux** I feel better; **mon
père va mieux maintenant** my
father's better now; **c'est mieux
comme ça** it's better like that; **2 il
vaut mieux que tu restes chez
toi** it would be better if you stayed at
home; **3** best; **c'est le rouge que
j'aime le mieux** I like the red one

a
b
c
d
e
f
g
h
i
j
k
l
m
n
o
p
q
r
s
t
u
v
w
x
y
z

best, I prefer the red one.
mieux noun Masc. **le mieux est de revenir** the best thing is to come back; **au mieux** at best, at least; **pour le mieux** for the best.

mignon (Fem. **mignonne**) adjective sweet.

migraine noun Fem. headache, migraine.

mijoter verb [1] to simmer.

milieu noun Masc. **1** middle; **au milieu de** in the middle of; **2** background; **il vient d'un milieu pauvre** he comes from a poor background; **3** environment.

militaire noun Masc. serviceman.
militaire adjective military; **le service militaire** military service.

mille number a thousand; **mille personnes** a thousand people; **deux mille personnes** two thousand people.

millefeuille noun Masc. vanilla slice.

millénaire noun Masc. millennium.

mille-pattes noun Masc. centipede.

milliard noun Masc. thousand million.

milliardaire noun Masc. & Fem. multimillionaire.

millier noun Masc. thousand; **des milliers de euros** thousands of euros.

milligramme noun Masc. milligramme.

millimètre noun Masc. millimetre.

million noun Masc. million; **deux millions de euros** two million euros.

millionnaire noun Masc. & Fem. millionaire.

mime noun Masc. & Fem. mime arti

mimer verb [1] **1** to mime; **2** to mimic.

minable adjective (informal) **1** pathetic; **ses plaisanteries so minables** her jokes are pathetic; **2** crummy; **un film minable** a crummy film.

mince adjective **1** thin; **une minc tranche de viande** a thin slice of meat; **2** slim; **3 mince alors!** (informal) oh bother!

minceur noun Fem. **1** thinness; **2** slimness.

mine noun Fem. **1 avoir bonne mi** to look well; **tu as mauvaise min** you don't look well; **2** expression; **3** mine; **une mine de charbon** a coalmine; **4** pencil lead.

minéral (plural **minéraux**) nou Masc. mineral.
minéral adjective mineral; **eau minérale** mineral water.

minet, **minette** noun Masc., Fem pussycat.

mineur[1] noun Masc. miner.

mineur[2], **mineure** noun Masc., Fem. minor, person under 18.
mineure adjective **1** minor; **2** under 18.

minijupe noun Fem. mini-skirt.

minimal (Masc. plural **minimaux**) adjective minimal.

inimiser *verb* [1] **1** to minimize; **2** to play down.

inimum *noun Masc.*, *adjective* minimum; **au minimum** at the very least.

inistère *noun Masc.* ministry.

inistre *noun Masc.* minister.

linitel™ *noun Masc.* (*Minitel is France Telecom's online data service; subscribers have a small computer linked to the telephone and can use it to access a large number of services including the telephone directories*).

inorité *noun Fem.* minority.

inou *noun Masc.* pussycat.

inuit *noun Masc.* midnight; **à minuit** at midnight.

inuscule *noun Fem.* small letter (*as opposed to a capital letter*).
minuscule *adjective* tiny.

inute *noun Fem.* minute; **dans dix minutes** in ten minutes; **dix minutes plus tard** ten minutes later; **d'une minute à l'autre** any minute now.

inuterie *noun Fem.* time-switch.

inutieux (*Fem.* **minutieuse**) *adjective* thorough.

irabelle *noun Fem.* small yellow plum.

iracle *noun Masc.* miracle; **par miracle** miraculously.
miracle *adjective* wonder.

iraculeux (*Fem.* **miraculeuse**) *adjective* miraculous.

iroir *noun Masc.* mirror; **au miroir** in the mirror.

inis *verb* SEE **mettre**.

miser *verb* [1] to bet.

misérable *adjective* poor.

misère *noun Fem.* destitution, extreme poverty.

missile *noun Masc.* missile.

missionnaire *noun Masc. & Fem.* missionary.

mistral *noun Masc.* mistral (*a strong cold north wind which blows down the Rhône valley to the Mediterranean*).

mite *noun Fem.* clothes moth.

mi-temps[1] *noun Masc.* part-time job; **travailler à mi-temps** to work part-time.

mi-temps[2] *noun Fem.* half-time (*in a match*).

miteux (*Fem.* **miteuse**) *adjective* seedy, shabby.

mitraillette *noun Fem.* submachine gun.

mixage *noun Masc.* sound mixing.

mixer *verb* [1] to mix.

mixte *adjective* **1** mixed; **2** coeducational.

Mlle SHORT FOR **Mademoiselle**.

Mme SHORT FOR **Madame**.

mobile *noun Masc.* **1** motive; **2** mobile.
mobile *adjective* **1** mobile; **2** **feuilles mobiles** loose sheets (*as opposed to a pad of paper*).

mobilier *noun Masc.* furniture.

mobylette *noun Fem.* moped.

mocassin *noun Masc.* **1** loafer; **2** moccasin.

moche *adjective* (*informal*) **1** awful; **2** ugly.

a
b
c
d
e
f
g
h
i
j
k
l
m
n
o
p
q
r
s
t
u
v
w
x
y
z

a

mode[1] *noun Fem.* fashion; **être à la mode** to be fashionable.

b

mode[2] *noun Masc.* way, mode.

c

mode d'emploi *noun Masc.* instructions for use.

d

mode de vie *noun Masc.* way of life.

e

modèle *noun Masc.* **1** model; **2** style; **ce modèle existe en plusieurs coloris** this style is available in several colours.

f

g

modéré *adjective* moderate.

h

moderne *adjective* modern.

moderniser *verb* [1] to modernize.

i

modernité *noun Fem.* modernity.

j

modeste *adjective* **1** modest; **2** humble.

k

l

modestie *noun Fem.* modesty.

m

modifier *verb* [1] to change.

n

modiste *noun Fem.* milliner.

module *noun Masc.* **1** module; **2** kitchen unit.

o

moelle *noun Fem.* marrow (*of bone*).

p

moelleux (*Fem.* **moelleuse**) *adjective* **1** soft; **2** mellow.

q

mœurs *plural noun Fem.* **1** customs; **2** morals.

r

s

moi *pronoun* **1** me; **c'est pour moi** it's for me; **pas moi** not me; **2 moi, je pense que** ... I think that ...; **3 à moi** mine; **ce n'est pas à moi** it's not mine; **un ami à moi** a friend of mine.

t

u

v

moi-même *pronoun* myself; **je l'ai fait moi-même** I did it myself.

w

x

moindre *adjective* slightest; **le moindre problème** the slightest problem; **je n'ai pas la moindre idée** I haven't the slightest idea.

y

z

moine *noun Masc.* monk.

moineau (*plural* **moineaux**) *noun Masc.* sparrow.

moins *preposition* **1** minus; **sept moins deux égale cinq** seven minus two equals five; **2 il est dix heures moins cinq** it's five to ten. **moins** *adverb* **1** less; **tu en as moins que moi** you've got less than me; **de moins en moins** less and less; **il est moins grand que son frère** he's not as tall as his brother; **c'est moins loin** it's not as far; **j'aime moins le bleu** I don't like the blue one as much; **2 le moins** the least; **le moins difficile** the least difficult; **le moins gros** the smallest; **3 moins de** less, fewer; **moins de beurre** less butter; **moins de voitures** fewer cars; **4 au moins** at least; **5 du moins** at least; **6 à moins que** (+ *subjunctive*) unless; **à moins qu'elle soit malade** unless she's ill.

mois *noun Masc.* month; **au mois de mai** in May; **le mois dernier** last month; **le mois prochain** next month.

moisi *noun Masc.* mould. **moisi** *adjective* mouldy.

moisir *verb* [2] to go mouldy.

moisson *noun Fem.* harvest.

moite *adjective* **1** damp; **2** muggy.

moitié *noun Fem.* **1** half; **la moitié d'une pomme** half an apple; **donne-moi la moitié** give me half; **la moitié du temps** half the time; **2 à moitié** half; **à moitié vide** half empty.

oitié-moitié *adverb* half-and-half; **partager moitié-moitié** to go halves.

olaire *noun Fem.* molar, back tooth.

olle *adjective* SEE **mou**.

ollet *noun Masc.* calf (*of the leg*).
mollet *adjective* **un œuf mollet** a soft-boiled egg.

olleton *noun Masc.* flannel, flannelette.

ôme *noun Masc. & Fem.* (*informal*) kid.

oment *noun Masc.* moment; **un moment, s'il vous plaît** just a moment please; **en ce moment** at the moment; **par moments** at times; **pour le moment** for the moment; **au moment où** just when; **à ce moment-là** just at that moment, just then; **j'ai attendu un bon moment** I waited for a good while.

on, ma, mes *adjective* my; **mon fils** my son; **ma fille** my daughter; **mes enfants** my children.

onarchie *noun Fem.* monarchy.

onastère *noun Masc.* monastery.

onde *noun Masc.* **1** world; **2** people; **il y a beaucoup de monde** there are a lot of people; **peu de monde** not many people; **tout le monde** everybody.

ondial (*Masc. plural* mondiaux) *adjective* **1** world; **la Seconde Guerre mondiale** the Second World War; **2** worldwide.

onétique *noun Fem.* electronic banking.

moniteur[1] *noun Masc.* monitor.

moniteur[2], **monitrice** *noun Masc., Fem.* **1** instructor (*sports or driving*); **un moniteur de ski** a ski instructor; **2** camp leader.

monnaie *noun Fem.* **1** currency; **2 une pièce de monnaie** a coin; **3** change; **je n'ai pas de monnaie** I don't have any change.

monopoliser *verb* [1] to monopolize.

monotone *adjective* monotonous.

Monsieur (*plural* Messieurs) *noun Masc.* **1 Monsieur Lejay** Mr Lejay; **bonsoir monsieur** good evening (*when greeting somebody you do not know well in French it is polite to add 'Monsieur', 'Madame', or 'Mademoiselle' to the greeting*); **2** man; **un grand monsieur** a tall man; **les deux messieurs assis à la table** the two men sitting at the table.

monstre *noun Masc.* monster.
monstre *adjective* huge; **un travail monstre** a huge amount of work.

monstrueux (*Fem.* monstrueuse) *adjective* monstrous.

mont *noun Masc.* mountain; **le mont Blanc** Mont Blanc.

montagne *noun Fem.* **1** mountain; **la montagne** the mountains; **2 une montagne de** a mountain of.

montagneux (*Fem.* montagneuse) *adjective* mountainous.

a
b
c
d
e
f
g
h
i
j
k
l
m
n
o
p
q
r
s
t
u
v
w
x
y
z

montant noun Masc. sum.
montant adjective rising.

montée noun Fem. **1** ascent, way up; **2** rise, increase; **3** slope; **en montée** uphill.

monter verb [1] **1** to go up, to come up; **monter l'escalier** to go (or come) up the stairs; **monter la colline** to go up the hill; **monter se coucher** to go up to bed; **2** **monter dans** to get on (a bus, train, etc); **3** **monter quelque chose** to bring (or take) something up; **je vais monter tes valises** I'll take your cases up; **4** to assemble (a kit); **5** to rise; **les prix ont monté** prices have risen; **6** to increase; **7** **monter à cheval** to ride a horse.

montgolfière noun Fem. hot-air balloon.

montre noun Fem. watch.

montrer verb [1] **1** to show; **montrer quelque chose à quelqu'un** to show somebody something; **montre-moi ton cadeau** show me your present; **2** to point out; **montrer quelque chose du doigt** to point to something.

monture noun Fem. frames (of glasses).

monument noun Masc. **1** monument; **un monument aux morts** a war memorial; **2** historic building.

moquer verb [1] **1** **se moquer de** to make fun of; **tout le monde s'est moqué de moi** everybody made fun of me; **2** **se moquer de** not to care

about; **je m'en moque** I couldn't care less.

moquette noun Fem. fitted carpe

moqueur (Fem. **moqueuse**) adjective mocking.

moral (plural **moraux**) noun Mas morale; **je n'ai pas le moral** I'm feeling really down.
moral (Masc. plural **moraux**) adjective **1** moral; **2** mental.

morale noun Fem. **1** moral; **2** morality.

morceau (plural **morceaux**) nou Masc. piece, bit; **un morceau de pain** a piece of bread; **un morceau de sucre** a sugar lump.

mordre verb [3] to bite.

mordu adjective **être mordu de quelque chose** (informal) to be ma about something.

morne adjective **1** gloomy; **2** dismal, dreary.

morsure noun Fem. bite.

mort[1] noun Fem. death; **trois mois avant sa mort** three months befor he died.

mort[2], **morte** noun Masc., Fem. dead man, dead woman.
mort adjective dead.

mort-aux-rats noun Fem. rat poison.

mortel (Fem. **mortelle**) adjective **1** deadly; **2** fatal.

morue noun Fem. **1** cod; **2** salt cod

mosaïque noun Fem. mosaic.

Moscou noun Moscow.

mosquée noun Fem. mosque.

ot *noun Masc.* **1** word; **mot à mot** word for word; **2 un petit mot** a note.

otard, **motarde** *noun Masc., Fem.* (*informal*) motorcyclist.

ot de passe *noun Masc.* password.

oteur *noun Masc.* engine.

otif *noun Masc.* **1** motive; **2** pattern.

otiver *verb* [1] to motivate.

oto *noun Fem.* motorbike; **je suis venu en moto** I came by motorbike.

otocycliste *noun Masc. & Fem.* motorcyclist.

ots croisés *plural noun Masc.* crossword.

otte *noun Fem.* **1** lump; **2** slab.

ou, **mol** (*before a vowel*) (*Fem.* **molle**) *adjective* **1** soft; **2** flabby.

ouche *noun Fem.* fly.

oucher *verb* [1] **se moucher** to blow your nose.

oucheron *noun Masc.* midge.

ouchoir *noun Masc.* **1** handkerchief; **2** tissue.

oue *noun Fem.* pout; **faire la moue** to pout.

ouette *noun Fem.* seagull.

ouiller *verb* [1] **1** to wet; **2 se mouiller** to get wet.

oulant *adjective* tight-fitting.

oule[1] *noun Masc.* mould.

oule[2] *noun Fem.* mussel.

ouler *verb* [1] to mould.

oulin *noun Masc.* mill.

moulin à vent *noun Masc.* windmill.

moulu *adjective* ground; **le café moulu** ground coffee.

moulure *noun Fem.* moulding.

mourir *verb* [54] to die; **elle est morte en février** she died in February; **je meurs de faim!** I'm starving!; **je meurs d'envie d'y aller** I'm dying to go there.

mousquetaire *noun Masc.* musketeer.

moussant *adjective* foaming.

mousse *noun Fem.* **1** foam; **mousse à raser** shaving foam; **2** lather; **3** froth; **4 mousse au chocolat** chocolate mousse; **5** moss.

mousser *verb* [1] to foam.

mousseux (*Fem.* **mousseuse**) *adjective* **du vin mousseux** sparkling wine.

moustache *noun Fem.* moustache.

moustique *noun Masc.* mosquito.

moutarde *noun Fem.* mustard.

mouton *noun Masc.* **1** sheep; **2** mutton.

mouvement *noun Masc.* **1** movement; **2** activity, bustle.

mouvementé *adjective* hectic, eventful; **j'ai eu une semaine mouvementée** I've had a hectic week.

Moyen-Âge *noun Masc.* Middle Ages.

moyen *noun Masc.* **1** means; **un moyen de transport** a means of transport; **un moyen de faire** a means of doing; **je n'ai aucun moyen de le contacter** I have no

means of contacting him; **2 les moyens** the means, the wherewithal; **je n'ai pas les moyens de m'acheter un ordinateur** I can't afford to buy a computer; **3** way.
moyen (Fem. **moyenne**) adjective **1** medium; **2** medium-sized; **3** average. **un équipe de niveau très moyen** a very average team.

moyenne noun Fem. **1** average; **en moyenne** on average; **2 avoir la moyenne** to pass (an exam).

Moyen-Orient noun Masc. Middle East.

muet (Fem. **muette**) adjective **1** speechless, dumb; **2** silent.

muguet noun Masc. lily of the valley.

mulet noun Masc. mule.

multifonction adjective multipurpose.

multiple adjective **1** multiple; **2** various.

multiplication noun Fem. **1** multiplication; **2 multiplication de** increase in the number of.

multiplier verb [1] **1** to multiply; **2** to increase.

municipal (Masc. plural **municipaux**) adjective **1** local, town; **2** municipal.

municipalité noun Fem. **1** town (or local) council; **2** municipality.

munition noun Fem. ammunition.

mûr adjective **1** ripe; **2** mature.

mur noun Masc. wall.

muraille noun Fem. (defensive) wall; **la Grande Muraille de Chine** the Great Wall of China.

mûre noun Fem. blackberry.

mûrir verb [2] **1** to ripen; **2** to mature; **3** to develop.

murmure noun Masc. murmur.

murmurer verb [1] to murmur.

musc noun Masc. musk.

muscade noun Fem. nutmeg; **une noix de muscade** a nutmeg.

muscle noun Masc. muscle.

musclé adjective muscular.

musculation noun Fem. bodybuilding.

museau (plural **museaux**) noun Masc. muzzle, snout.

musée noun Masc. museum.

musical (Masc. plural **musicaux**) adjective musical.

musicien, **musicienne** noun Masc., Fem. musician.

musique noun Fem. music; **mettre de la musique** to put on some music.

musulman, **musulmane** noun Masc., Fem., adjective Muslim.

mutuel (Fem. **mutuelle**) adjective mutual.

myope adjective short-sighted; ★ **être myope comme une taupe** be as blind as a bat (literally: to be short-sighted as a mole).

myopie noun Fem. short-sightedness.

myosotis noun Masc. forget-me-not.

myrtille noun Fem. bilberry.

mystère *noun Masc.* mystery.

mystérieux *(Fem.* **mystérieuse)** *adjective* mysterious.

mystifier *verb* [1] to fool.

mystique *adjective* mystical.

mythe *noun Masc.* myth.

mythologie *noun Fem.* mythology.

Nn

n' *adverb* SEE **ne.**

nacre *noun Fem.* mother-of-pearl.

nage *noun Fem.* swimming.

nager *verb* [52] to swim.

nageur, nageuse *noun Masc., Fem.* swimmer.

naïf *(Fem.* **naïve)** *adjective* naïve.

nain, naine *noun Masc., Fem., adjective* dwarf.

naissance *noun Fem.* birth; **date de naissance** date of birth.

naître *verb* [55] to be born; **elle est née en 1975** she was born in 1975.

nana *noun Fem.* *(informal)* girl.

naphtaline *noun Fem.* mothballs.

nappe *noun Fem.* tablecloth.

narcisse *noun Masc.* narcissus.

narine *noun Fem.* nostril.

natal *adjective* native; **mon pays natal** my native country.

natalité *noun Fem.* **le taux de natalité** the birthrate.

natation *noun Fem.* swimming; **faire de la natation** to go swimming.

natif *(Fem.* **native)** *adjective* native.

nation *noun Fem.* nation.

national *(Masc. plural* **nationaux)** *adjective* national.

nationaliser *verb* [1] to nationalize.

nationalité *noun Fem.* nationality.

nativité *noun Fem.* Nativity.

natte *noun Fem.* **1** plait; **2** mat.

nature *noun Fem.* nature. **nature** *adjective* **yaourt nature** plain yoghurt; **un thé nature** a cup of tea without milk or sugar.

naturel *noun Masc.* **1** nature; **2 au naturel** plain. **naturel** *(Fem.* **naturelle)** *adjective* natural.

naturellement *adverb* of course.

nausée *noun Fem.* nausea; **avoir la nausée** to feel sick.

nautique *adjective* water; **faire du ski nautique** to go water-skiing.

navet *noun Masc.* turnip.

navette *noun Fem.* shuttle; **j'ai pris la navette de l'aéroport** I took the shuttle from the airport; **faire la navette** to travel back and forth.

naviguer *verb* [1] to sail.

navire *noun Masc.* ship.

navire-citerne *noun Masc.* oil tanker.

navire-école *noun Masc.* training ship.

navré *adjective* sorry; **je suis vraiment navré** I'm terribly sorry.

né, née *verb* SEE **naître.**

ne, n' *(before a vowel or silent 'h') adverb* **1 ne + pas** not; **je n'aime**

a
b
c
d
e
f
g
h
i
j
k
l
m
n
o
p
q
r
s
t
u
v
w
x
y
z

pas le lait I don't like milk; **2 ne + jamais** never; **je ne vais jamais à Londres** I never go to London; **3 ne + que** only; **je n'ai que dix euros** I only have ten euros; **4 ne + plus** no longer; **elle n'habite plus à Londres** she no longer lives in London; **5 ne + rien** nothing; **il ne mange rien** he eats nothing; **rien ne t'empêche d'y aller** there's nothing to stop you going; **6 ne + personne** nobody; **il n'y a personne** there's nobody; **personne n'a compris** nobody understood.

néanmoins *adverb* nevertheless.

nécessaire *noun Masc.* **faire le nécessaire** to do the necessary.
nécessaire *adjective* necessary; **il est nécessaire de faire** it is necessary to do; **est-ce qu'il est nécessaire de réserver?** is it necessary to book?

nécessairement *adverb* necessarily.

nécessité *noun Fem.* necessity.

nécessiter *verb* [1] to require.

nectarine *noun Fem.* nectarine.

néerlandais *noun Masc.* Dutch (*language*).
néerlandais *adjective* Dutch.

nef *noun Fem.* nave (*of a church*).

négatif *noun Masc.* negative.
négatif (*Fem.* **négative**) *adjective* negative.

négligé *adjective* scruffy.

négligent *adjective* careless.

négliger *verb* [52] **1** to neglect; **2 il a négligé de le faire** he didn't bother to do it.

négociant *noun Masc.* merchant.

négocier *verb* [1] to negotiate.

neige *noun Fem.* snow; **un bonhomme de neige** a snowman.

neiger *verb* [52] to snow; **il neige** it snowing.

neigeux (*Fem.* **neigeuse**) *adjective* snowy.

nénuphar *noun Masc.* waterlily.

néon *noun Masc.* neon.

néo-zélandais *adjective* New Zealand.

Néo-Zélandais, Néo-Zélandaise *noun Masc., Fem.* New Zealander.

nerf *noun Masc.* nerve.

nerveux (*Fem.* **nerveuse**) *adjective* nervous.

n'est-ce pas? *adverb* **il fait froi ce soir, n'est-ce pas?** it's cold thi evening, isn't it?; **il habite à Paris n'est ce pas?** he lives in Paris, doesn't he?; **tu as déjà mangé, n'est-ce pas?** you've already eater haven't you?

net (*Fem.* **nette**) *adjective* **1** clear; **c'est très net** it's quite clear; **2** distinct; **une nette différence a** distinct difference; **une nette amélioration** a distinct improvement.
net *adverb* **1 s'arrêter net** to stop dead; **2 refuser net** to refuse flatly

nettement *adverb* far; **nettemen meilleur** much better.

nettoyage *noun Masc.* cleaning; **l nettoyage à sec** dry cleaning.

nettoyer *verb* [39] to clean.

neuf[1] *number* nine; **il est neuf heures du matin** it's nine o'clock in the morning; **Julie a neuf ans** Julie's nine; **le neuf juillet** the ninth of July.

neuf[2] (*Fem.* **neuve**) *adjective* new; **une voiture toute neuve** a brand new car.

neutre *adjective* neutral.

neuvième *noun Masc.* **au neuvième** on the ninth floor.
neuvième *adjective* ninth.

neveu (*plural* **neveux**) *noun Masc.* nephew.

nez *noun Masc.* nose.

ni *conjunction* ni ...ni neither ...nor; **ni lui ni son frère** neither he nor his brother; **il n'y a ni pain ni lait** there's neither bread nor milk; **ni Frank ni Paul ne le sait** neither Frank nor Paul knows; **ni moi non plus** me neither.

niche *noun Fem.* **1** kennel; **2** niche.

nid *noun Masc.* nest.

nièce *noun Fem.* niece.

nier *verb* [1] to deny.

n'importe *adverb* **1** either, it doesn't matter; **'tu veux une aile ou une cuisse?' – 'n'importe'** do you want a wing or a leg?' – 'either, it doesn't matter'; **2 n'importe qui** anybody; **n'importe qui peut le faire** anybody can do it; **3 n'importe quoi** anything; **je ferai n'importe quoi pour t'aider** I'll do absolutely anything to help you; **elle a fait n'importe quoi** she's made a real mess of it; **tu dis n'importe quoi** you're talking complete rubbish; **4 n'importe quand** any time; **tu**

peux m'appeler n'importe quand you can ring me any time; **5 n'importe comment** any old how; **tu peux jeter tous ces papiers dans un tiroir n'importe comment** you can throw all these papers into a drawer any old how; **6 n'importe où** anywhere; **pose tes valises n'importe où** put your cases down anywhere you like; **je ne peux pas habiter n'importe où** I can't live just anywhere.

niveau (*plural* **niveaux**) *noun Masc.* level; **au même niveau** at the same level.

niveau de vie *noun Masc.* standard of living.

noble *adjective* noble.

noces *plural noun Fem.* wedding.

nocif (*Fem.* **nocive**) *adjective* harmful.

nocturne *noun Fem.* late-night opening.
nocturne *adjective* nocturnal.

Noël *noun Masc.* Christmas; **Joyeux Noël** Merry Christmas; **un cadeau de Noël** a Christmas present; **le sapin de Noël** the Christmas tree.

nœud *noun Masc.* knot; **faire un nœud** to tie a knot.

noir *noun Masc.* **1** black; **2 le noir** the dark.
noir *adjective* **1** black; **2** dark; **il fait noir** it's dark.

Noir, Noire *noun Masc., Fem.* black man, black woman; **les Noirs** black people.

noirceur *noun Fem.* blackness.

noircir *verb* [2] to blacken.

197

noisette *noun Fem.* hazelnut.

noix *noun Fem.* **1** walnut; **2 une noix de beurre** a knob of butter.

noix de cajou *noun Fem.* cashew nut.

noix de coco *noun Fem.* coconut.

nom *noun Masc.* **1** name; **nom de famille** surname; **nom de jeune fille** maiden name; **2 au nom de: au nom de la famille Dupont** on behalf of the Dupont family; **3** noun.

nombre *noun Masc.* number; **bon nombre de** a good many; **le nombre de victimes s'élève à 25** the number of dead is 25.

nombreux (*Fem.* **nombreuse**) *adjective* many; **de nombreuses personnes** many people; **ils étaient nombreux** there were a lot of them; **ils étaient peu nombreux** there weren't many of them; **une famille nombreuse** a big family.

nombril *noun Masc.* navel.

nommer *verb* [1] **1** to appoint; **2** to name.

non *adverb* **1** no; **elle a dit non** she said no; **2 non seulement** not only; **non loin de** not far from; **moi non plus** me neither.

non- *combining form* **un non-fumeur** a nonsmoker.

nord *noun Masc.* north; **le nord de l'Espagne** northern Spain; **le vent du nord** the north wind.
nord *adjective* north, northern; **le côté nord** the north side.

nord-américain *adjective* North American.

Nord-Américain, Nord-Américaine *noun Masc., Fem.* North American.

nord-est *noun Masc.* north-east.

nord-ouest *noun Masc.* north-west.

normal (*Masc. plural* **normaux**) *adjective* **1** normal; **2 c'est normal** it's natural; **3 ce n'est pas normal** it's not right.

normalement *adverb* **1** normally; **2** according to plan; **normalement, elle doit être à Rome actuellement** if things have gone according to plan, she should be in Rome at the moment.

normand *adjective* Norman; **la côte normande** the Normandy coast.

Normand, Normande *noun Masc., Fem.* Norman.

Normandie *noun Fem.* Normandy.

norme *noun Fem.* **1** norm; **2** standard; **selon les normes européennes** according to European standards.

Norvège *noun Fem.* Norway.

norvégien (*Fem.* **norvégienne**) *adjective* Norwegian.

nos *adjective* SEE **notre**.

notaire *noun Masc.* notary public.

notamment *adverb* in particular.

note *noun Fem.* **1** bill; **la note, s'il vous plaît** can I have the bill please; **2** mark; **j'ai eu une bonne note en allemand** I got a good mark in German; **3 prendre des notes** to take notes.

noter *verb* [1] **1** to write down; **2** to notice.

notice *noun Fem.* instructions.

notion *noun Fem.* **1** idea; **2 des notions** basic knowledge; **j'ai des notions d'espagnol** I have a basic knowledge of Spanish.

notre (*plural* **nos**) *adjective* our; **notre fille** our daughter; **nos enfants** our children.

nôtre *pronoun* **le nôtre, la nôtre, les nôtres** ours.

nouer *verb* [1] to tie, to knot.

nougat *noun Masc.* nougat.

nouilles *plural noun Fem.* noodles, pasta.

nounours *noun Masc.* (*baby talk*) teddy bear.

nourrice *noun Fem.* childminder.

nourrir *verb* [2] to feed.

nourrissant *adjective* nourishing.

nourrisson *noun Masc.* infant.

nourriture *noun Fem.* food.

nous *pronoun* **1** we; **nous apprenons le français** we are learning French; **2** us; **viens avec nous** come with us; **elle nous aide** she helps us; **elle nous a aidés** she helped us; **3** to us; **elle ne nous a pas parlé** she didn't speak to us; **elle nous a donné son adresse** she gave us her address; **4** ourselves; **nous nous ferons une salade** we'll make ourselves a salad; **5** (*reflexive*) **nous nous levons à sept heures** we get up at seven o'clock.

nous-mêmes *pronoun* ourselves.

nouveau, nouvel (*before a vowel or silent 'h'*) (*Fem.* **nouvelle**) (*Masc.*

plural **nouveaux**) *adjective* **1** new; **viens voir mon nouvel appartement** come and see my new flat; **2 à nouveau, de nouveau** again.

nouveauté *noun Fem.* **1** novelty; **2** new release.

Nouvel An *noun Masc.* New Year.

nouvelle *adjective* SEE **nouveau**

nouvelle *noun Fem.* **1 une nouvelle** news; **j'ai une bonne nouvelle!** I've got good news!; **2** short story; **nous étudions une nouvelle de Camus** we're doing a Camus short story; **3 des nouvelles** news; **nous n'avons pas de nouvelles pour l'instant** we have no news for the moment; **as-tu des nouvelles de lui?** have you heard from him?

Nouvelle-Zélande *noun Fem.* New Zealand.

novembre *noun Masc.* November; **en novembre, au mois de novembre** in November.

noyau (*plural* **noyaux**) *noun Masc.* **1** stone (*in fruit*); **2** nucleus.

noyer[1] *verb* [39] **1** to drown; **2 se noyer** to drown, to drown oneself.

noyer[2] *noun Masc.* **1** walnut tree; **2** walnut; **une table en noyer** a walnut table.

nu *adjective* **1** naked; **2** bare.

nuage *noun Masc.* cloud.

nuageux (*Fem.* **nuageuse**) *adjective* cloudy.

nuance *noun Fem.* **1** shade (*of a colour*); **2** nuance.

a
b
c
d
e
f
g
h
i
j
k
l
m
n
o
p
q
r
s
t
u
v
w
x
y
z

nucléaire *adjective* nuclear; **l'énergie nucléaire** nuclear power.

nœud ferroviaire *noun Masc.* (railway) junction.

nuisible *adjective* harmful.

nuit *noun Fem.* **1** night; **cette nuit** last night, tonight; **dans la nuit** in the night; **toute la nuit** all night; **travailler la nuit** to work at night; **2 il fait nuit** it's dark; **avant la nuit** before dark; **la nuit tombe à sept heures** it gets dark at seven o'clock.

nul (*Fem.* **nulle**) *adjective* **1** (*informal*) hopeless, awful; **le film était nul** the film was awful; **je suis nul en histoire** I'm hopeless at history; **2 un match nul** a draw.

nulle part *adverb* nowhere; **je ne trouve nulle part mon dictionnaire** I can't find my dictionary anywhere.

numéro *noun Masc.* number; **ils habitent au numéro vingt-cinq** they live at number twenty-five.

numéro de téléphone *noun Masc.* telephone number.

nu-pied *noun Masc.* open sandal.

nurse *noun Fem.* nanny.

nutritif (*Fem.* **nutritive**) *adjective* nourishing, nutritious; **valeur nutritive** nutritional value.

nutrition *noun Fem.* nutrition.

nylon *noun Masc.* nylon.

Oo

oasis *noun Fem.* oasis.

obéir *verb* [2] **obéir à** to obey.

obéissance *noun Fem.* obedience.

obéissant *adjective* obedient.

objectif *noun Masc.* objective.
objectif (*Fem.* **objective**) *adjective* objective.

objection *noun Fem.* objection.

objet *noun Masc.* object.

objets trouvés *plural noun Masc.* lost property; **aller aux objets trouvés** to go to the lost property office.

obligatoire *adjective* compulsory.

obligé *adjective* **être obligé de faire** to have to do; **je suis obligé de partir** I have to go.

obliger *verb* [52] **obliger quelqu'un à faire** to force somebody to do.

obscène *adjective* obscene.

obscur *adjective* **1** dark; **2** obscure.

obscurité *noun Fem.* **1** darkness; **dans l'obscurité** in the dark; **2** obscurity.

obséder *verb* [24] to obsess; **être obsédé par quelque chose** to be obsessed by something.

obsèques *plural noun Fem.* funeral.

observateur, observatrice *noun Masc., Fem.* observer.
observateur (*Fem.* **observatrice**) *adjective* observant.

observation *noun Fem.* **1** comment; **2** remark.

office

observatoire *noun Masc.* observatory.

observer *verb* [1] **1** to watch; **elle nous observait de loin** she was watching us from a distance; **2** to observe (*rules*).

obsession *noun Fem.* obsession.

obstacle *noun Masc.* obstacle.

obstination *noun Fem.* obstinacy.

obstiné *adjective* stubborn.

obtenir *verb* [77] to get.

occasion *noun Fem.*
1 opportunity; **avoir l'occasion de faire** to have the opportunity to do; **2 acheter quelque chose d'occasion** to buy something second hand; **une voiture d'occasion** a second-hand car; **3** bargain; **une bonne occasion** a good bargain; **4** occasion; **à l'occasion de** on the occasion of; **5 à l'occasion** some time.

occasionner *verb* [1] to cause.

Occident *noun Masc.* **l'Occident** the West.

occidental (*Masc. plural* **occidentaux**) *adjective* western.

occupation *noun Fem.* occupation; **trouver une occupation** to find something to do.

occupé *adjective* **1** busy; **je suis occupé en ce moment** I'm busy at the moment; **2** engaged (*of a telephone line or toilet*); **3 cette place est occupée** this seat is taken.

occuper *verb* [1] **1** to occupy; **2 s'occuper** to keep yourself busy; **3 s'occuper de** to deal with, to see to; **je vais m'occuper du dîner** I'll go and see to dinner; **je m'en occupe** I'll see to it; **4 s'occuper de quelqu'un** to attend to somebody; **est-ce qu'on s'occupe de vous?** are you being attended to?

occurrence *noun Fem.* **1** case; **plusieurs occurrences de typhoïde** several cases of typhoid; **2** occurrence.

océan *noun Masc.* ocean.

octet *noun Masc.* byte (*in computing*).

octobre *noun Masc.* October; **en octobre, au mois d'octobre** in October.

odeur *noun Fem.* smell; **des odeurs de cuisine** cooking smells.

odorat *noun Masc.* sense of smell.

œil (*plural* **yeux**) *noun Masc.* eye; ★ **cela saute aux yeux** it's obvious (*literally: it jumps into your eyes*).

œillet *noun Masc.* carnation.

œuf *noun Masc.* egg; **un œuf à la coque** a boiled egg; **un œuf dur** a hard-boiled egg; **un œuf mollet** a soft-boiled egg; **un œuf sur le plat** a fried egg; **des œufs brouillés** scrambled eggs.

œuvre *noun Fem.* work (*of art or literature*); **une œuvre d'art** a work of art.

offenser *verb* [1] to offend.

office *noun Masc.* **1** office; **2 office religieux** religious service.

a
b
c
d
e
f
g
h
i
j
k
l
m
n
o
p
q
r
s
t
u
v
w
x
y
z

officiel noun Masc. official.
officiel (Fem. **officielle**) adjective official.

officier noun Masc. officer.

offre noun Fem. 1 offer; 2 'offres d'emploi' 'situations vacant'.

offrir verb [56] 1 **offrir quelque chose à quelqu'un** to give something to somebody; **elle m'a offert une montre pour mon anniversaire** she gave me a watch for my birthday; 2 **s'offrir quelque chose** to treat yourself to something; **je vais m'offrir un nouveau dictionnaire** I'm going to treat myself to a new dictionary; 3 to offer.

oie noun Fem. goose.

oignon noun Masc. onion.

oiseau (plural **oiseaux**) noun Masc. bird.

olive noun Fem. olive; **l'huile d'olive** olive oil.

olivier noun Masc. olive tree.

ombragé adjective shaded (from the sun).

ombre noun Fem. 1 shade; **à l'ombre** in the shade; 2 shadow.

ombre à paupières noun Fem. eyeshadow.

ombrelle noun Fem. sun umbrella.

omelette noun Fem. omelette; **une omelette aux champignons** a mushroom omelette.

omettre verb [11] to omit, to leave out; **omettre de faire quelque chose** to fail to do something.

omoplate noun Fem. shoulder blade.

on pronoun 1 we; **on va au cinéma** we're going to the cinema; **on a oublié de fermer la porte** we forgot to shut the door; 2 you; **de la terrasse on voit la mer** from the terrace you can see the sea; **on ne devrait pas mentir** you shouldn't tell lies; 3 **on leur a dit que ...** they were told that ...; **on a volé leur voiture** their car's been stolen.

oncle noun Masc. uncle.

onde noun Fem. wave (on radio).

ondée noun Fem. shower (of rain).

onéreux (Fem. **onéreuse**) adjective costly.

ongle noun Masc. nail; **se faire les ongles** to do your nails; **je me suis coupé les ongles** I've cut my nails.

ongle de pied noun Masc. toenail.

ONU noun Fem. SHORT FOR **Organisation des Nations unies** UN, United Nations.

onze number eleven; **onze personnes** eleven people; **Marie-Ange a onze ans** Marie-Ange is eleven; **le onze juillet** the eleventh of July.

onzième noun Masc. **au onzième** on the eleventh floor.
onzième adjective eleventh.

opéra noun Masc. 1 opera; 2 opera house.

opérateur, **opératrice** noun Masc., Fem. operator.

opération noun Fem. 1 operation; 2 calculation.

opérer verb [24] to operate; **opérer quelqu'un** to operate on somebody;

202

est-ce qu'il va falloir opérer? will they have to operate; **se faire opérer** to have an operation.

pinion noun Fem. opinion.

pposant, opposante noun Masc., Fem. opponent.

pposé noun **l'opposé** the opposite.

opposé adjective **1** opposite; **2 être opposé à quelque chose** to be opposed to something.

pposer verb [1] **1 le match de samedi prochain oppose les Anglais et les Français** the English are playing the French in next Saturday's match; **2 s'opposer à quelque chose** to oppose something; **ils s'opposent à un changement des règles** they are opposed to a change in the rules.

pposition noun Fem. opposition.

pter verb [1] to opt.

pticien, opticienne noun Masc., Fem. optician.

ptimisme noun Masc. optimism.

ptimiste noun Masc. & Fem. optimist.

optimiste adjective optimistic.

ption noun Fem. option.

ptionnel (Fem. **optionnelle**) adjective optional.

r[1] noun Masc. **1** gold; **une montre en or** a gold watch; **2 une occasion en or** a golden opportunity.

r[2] conjunction now.

rage noun Masc. storm.

rageux (Fem. **orageuse**) adjective **1** stormy; **2** thundery.

oral (plural **oraux**) noun Masc. oral (exam); **l'oral de français** the French oral.
oral (Masc. plural **oraux**) adjective oral; **une épreuve orale** an oral exam.

orange noun Fem., adjective orange.

oranger noun Masc. orange tree.

orbite noun Fem. orbit.

orchestral (Masc. plural **orchestraux**) adjective orchestral.

orchestre noun Masc. **1** orchestra; **2** band.

orchidée noun Fem. orchid.

ordinaire noun Masc. **1** 2-star petrol; **2 sortir de l'ordinaire** to be out of the ordinary; **ça sort un peu de l'ordinaire** it's a bit out of the ordinary; **3 à l'ordinaire, d'ordinaire** usually.
ordinaire adjective ordinary; **une journée ordinaire** an ordinary day.

ordinateur noun Masc. computer; **un ordinateur portable** a portable computer.

ordonnance noun Fem. prescription.

ordonné adjective tidy.

ordonner verb [1] to order.

ordre noun Masc. **1** order; **donner des ordres** to give orders; **2** order; **par ordre alphabétique** in alphabetical order; **mettre de l'ordre** to tidy up; **mettre en ordre** to tidy.

ordures plural noun Fem. rubbish.

a
b
c
d
e
f
g
h
i
j
k
l
m
n
o
p
q
r
s
t
u
v
w
x
y
z

oreille noun Fem. ear.

oreiller noun Masc. pillow.

oreillons plural noun Masc. mumps.

organe noun Masc. organ (of the body).

organique adjective organic.

organisateur, organisatrice noun Masc., Fem. organizer.

organisation noun Fem. organization.

organiser verb [1] **1** to organize; **2** s'organiser to get organized.

organisme noun Masc. **1** organization; **2** body; **3** organism.

organiste noun Masc. & Fem. organist.

orge noun Fem. barley; **le sucre d'orge** barley sugar.

orgeat noun Masc. **le sirop d'orgeat** barley water.

orgue noun Fem. organ; **jouer de l'orgue** to play the organ.

orgueil noun Masc. pride.

orgueilleux (Fem. orgueilleuse) adjective proud.

Orient noun Masc. **l'Orient** the East.

oriental (Masc. plural orientaux) adjective **1** eastern; **2** oriental.

orientation noun Fem. **1** orientation; **2** l'orientation professionnelle careers advice; **3** avoir le sens de l'orientation to have a good sense of direction.

orienter verb [1] **1** to position; **2** to direct; **3** s'orienter to get one's bearings; **4** s'orienter vers to move towards; **Bernard s'oriente vers les langues** Bernard's going in for languages.

originaire adjective **être originaire de** to be a native of; **Giselle est originaire de Dijon** Giselle comes from Dijon.

original (plural originaux) noun Masc. original.

original (Masc. plural originaux) adjective **1** original; **le film est en version originale** the film isn't dubbed; **2** eccentric; **c'est une vieille dame assez originale** she's rather an eccentric old lady.

originalité noun Fem. **1** originality; **2** eccentricity.

origine noun Fem. **1** origin; **2** elle est d'origine écossaise she's Scottish; **3** à l'origine originally; **à l'origine la maison appartenait à mon oncle** the house originally belonged to my uncle.

orme noun Masc. elm tree.

orné adjective **orné de** decorated with.

ornemental (Masc. plural ornementaux) adjective ornamental.

orphelin, orpheline noun Masc. Fem. orphan.

orphelinat noun Masc. orphanag

orteil noun Masc. toe; **gros orteil** b toe.

orthographe noun Fem. spelling

ortie noun Fem. nettle.

os noun Masc. bone.

osé adjective daring; **c'était un pe osé de dire ça** it was a bit daring say that.

seille *noun Fem.* sorrel.

ser *verb* [1] to dare.

sier *noun Masc.* wicker; **un panier en osier** a wicker basket.

sseux (*Fem.* **osseuse**) *adjective* bony (*knees, arms*).

tage *noun Masc.* hostage; **être pris en otage** to be taken hostage.

TAN *noun Fem.* SHORT FOR **Organisation du traité de l'Atlantique Nord** NATO.

ter *verb* [1] **1** to take off; **je vais ôter ma veste** I'll take off my jacket; **2** to take away; **3** to remove.

tite *noun Fem.* earache; **avoir une otite** to have earache.

u *conjunction* **1** or; **est-ce que vous voulez le fromage ou le dessert?** would you like cheese or dessert?; **2 ou ...ou** either ...or; **c'est ou dans ma chambre ou dans le salon** it's either in my bedroom or in the sitting-room; **3 ou bien** or else; **on peut se retrouver au cinéma ou bien chez moi, si tu veux** we can meet at the cinema or else at my place, if you like.

ù *adverb* where; **où es-tu?** where are you?; **ton frère habite où?** where does your brother live?; **tu l'as trouvé où ton sac?** where did you find your bag?; **je sais où elle habite** I know where she lives.

où *pronoun* **1** where; **le village où elle habite** the village where she lives; **la ville d'où il vient** the town he comes from; **2** when, that; **le jour où je suis arrivé** the day I arrived.

uate *noun Fem.* cotton wool.

oubli *noun Masc.* **1** forgetfulness; **2 l'oubli de quelque chose** forgetting something; **3** oversight; **c'était un oubli** I (*or* you, etc.) forgot about it.

oublier *verb* [1] **1** to forget; **j'ai oublié leur adresse** I've forgotten their address; **2** to leave; **j'ai oublié mes clefs chez Jérôme** I've left my keys at Jérôme's.

ouest *noun Masc.* west; **à l'ouest de Paris** west of Paris; **dans l'ouest de la France** in the west of France; **l'Ouest** the West; **l'Europe de l'Ouest** Western Europe.
ouest *adjective* **1** west; **le côté ouest** the west coast; **2** western.

ouf *exclamation* phew!

oui *adverb* yes; **elle a dit oui** she said yes; **dire oui de la tête** to nod.

ouragan *noun Masc.* hurricane.

ourlet *noun Masc.* hem.

ours *noun Masc.* bear.

oursin *noun Masc.* sea urchin.

outil *noun Masc.* tool.

outré *adjective* outraged.

outre *preposition* in addition to.

outremer *noun Masc.*, *adjective* ultramarine.

outre-mer *adverb* overseas.

ouvert *adjective* **1** open; **laisse la porte ouverte** leave the door open; **'ouvert le dimanche'** 'open on Sundays'; **2 laisser le robinet ouvert** to leave the tap on.

ouvertement *adverb* openly.

ouverture *noun Fem.* **1** opening; **les heures d'ouverture** opening

a
b
c
d
e
f
g
h
i
j
k
l
m
n
o
p
q
r
s
t
u
v
w
x
y
z

hours; **2** openness; **ouverture d'esprit** open-mindedness.

ouvre-boîte *noun Masc.* tin-opener.

ouvre-bouteille *noun Masc.* bottle-opener.

ouvrier, ouvrière *noun Masc., Fem.* worker.
ouvrier (*Fem.* **ouvrière**) *adjective* **la classe ouvrière** the working class.

ouvrir *verb* [30] **1** to open; **ouvrir la fenêtre** to open the window;
2 ouvrir le robinet to turn on the tap; **3 elle n'a pas ouvert la bouche** she didn't say a word;
4 s'ouvrir to open; **ça s'ouvre comment?** how do you open it?

ovale *adjective* oval.

overdose *noun Fem.* overdose; **une overdose d'héroïne** an overdose of heroine.

ovni *noun Masc.* SHORT FOR **objet volant non identifié** UFO.

oxygène *noun Masc.* oxygen.

ozone *noun Fem.* ozone.

Pp

Pacifique *noun Masc.* **l'océan Pacifique** the Pacific Ocean.

pagaille *noun Fem.* (*informal*) mess; **quelle pagaille!** what a mess!

page *noun Fem.* page; **à la première/ dernière page** on the first/last page; **les Pages Jaunes** the Yellow Pages.

paie *noun Fem.* pay; **un bulletin de paie, une fiche de paie** a payslip.

paiement *noun Masc.* payment.

paillasson *noun Masc.* doormat.

paille *noun Fem.* straw.

pain *noun Masc.* **1** bread; **une tranche de pain** a slice of bread; **2 un pain** a loaf of bread; **trois pains** three loaves of bread; **un petit pain** a roll; ★ **ils se vendent comme des petits pains** they're selling like hot cakes (*literally: like rolls*).

pain au chocolat *noun Masc.* chocolate pastry.

pain complet *noun Masc.* wholemeal bread.

pain d'épices *noun Masc.* gingerbread.

pain de mie *noun Masc.* sandwich loaf.

pain de seigle *noun Masc.* rye bread.

pain grillé *noun Masc.* toast.

pair *adjective* **1** even (*number*); **2 au pair** au pair; **une jeune fille au pair** an au pair; **travailler au pair** to work as an au pair.

paire *noun Fem.* pair; **une paire de chaussures** a pair of shoes.

paix *noun Fem.* peace.

pakistanais *adjective* Pakistani.

Pakistanais, Pakistanaise *noun Masc., Fem.* Pakistani.

palais *noun Masc.* **1** palace; **2** palate.

palais de justice *noun Masc.* law courts.

âle *adjective* pale; **bleu pâle** pale
blue.

alestine *noun Fem.* Palestine.

alier *noun Masc.* landing (*on a
staircase*).

âlir *verb* [2] **1** to turn pale; **2** to
fade.

alme *noun Fem.* flipper (*for
swimming*).

almier *noun Masc.* palm tree.

alpitant *adjective* thrilling.

amplemousse *noun Masc.*
grapefruit.

anaché *noun Masc.* shandy.

anaché *adjective* **une salade
panachée** a mixed salad.

ancarte *noun Fem.* notice, sign.

ané *adjective* coated in
breadcrumbs.

anier *noun Masc.* basket.

anier à salade *noun Masc.*
salad shaker.

anique *noun Fem.* panic.

aniquer *verb* [1] to panic.

anne *noun Fem.* breakdown (*of a
car or machine*); **la voiture est en
panne** the car's broken down; **la
photocopieuse est en panne** the
photocopier's not working; **tomber
en panne** to break down; **nous
sommes en panne d'essence**
we've run out of petrol; **une panne
de courant** a power cut.

anneau (*plural* **panneaux**) *noun
Masc.* sign, notice board.

anneau indicateur *noun
Masc.* signpost.

panneau publicitaire *noun
Masc.* advertisement hoarding.

panorama *noun Masc.*
1 panorama; **2** viewpoint.

pansement *noun Masc.* **1** sticking
plaster; **2** dressing.

panser *verb* [1] to put a dressing on
(*a wound*).

pantalon *noun Masc.* trousers; **mon
pantalon gris** my grey trousers; **un
pantalon neuf** a new pair of
trousers; **deux pantalons** two pairs
of trousers.

panthère *noun Fem.* panther.

pantoufle *noun Fem.* slipper.

paon *noun Masc.* peacock.

papa *noun Masc.* Dad, Daddy, father.

pape *noun Masc.* pope.

paperasse *noun Fem.* (*informal*)
paperwork, bumph.

papeterie *noun Fem.* **1** stationer's
shop; **2** stationery.

papi *noun Masc.* (*informal*)
granddad.

papier *noun Masc.* paper; **du papier
blanc** white paper; **vos papiers, s'il
vous plaît monsieur** your (identity)
papers please, sir.

papier à lettres *noun Masc.*
writing paper.

papier aluminium *noun Masc.*
kitchen foil.

papier cadeau *noun Masc.* gift
wrap.

papier-calque *noun Masc.*
tracing paper.

papier hygiénique *noun Masc.*
toilet paper.

a
b
c
d
e
f
g
h
i
j
k
l
m
n
o
p
q
r
s
t
u
v
w
x
y
z

papier peint *noun* Masc. wallpaper.

papiers d'identité *plural noun* Masc. identity papers.

papillon *noun* Masc. butterfly.

paquebot *noun* Masc. liner.

pâquerette *noun* Fem. daisy.

Pâques *noun* Masc. Easter; **à Pâques** at Easter; **un œuf de Pâques** an Easter egg; **les vacances de Pâques** the Easter holidays; **le lundi de Pâques** Easter Monday.

paquet *noun* Masc. **1** packet; **un paquet de sucre** a packet of sugar; **2** parcel; **il y a un paquet pour vous** there's a parcel for you; **3** bundle (*of clothes or papers*).

paquet-cadeau *noun* Masc. gift-wrapped parcel; **est-ce que je vous fais un paquet-cadeau?** shall I gift-wrap it for you?

par *preposition* **1** by; **par moi** by me; **par la poste** by post; **payer par chèque** to pay by cheque; **par accident** by accident; **par hasard** by chance; **deux par deux** two by two; **jeter quelque chose par la fenêtre** to throw something out of the window; **aller par Paris** to go via (*or* by) Paris; **par ennui** out of boredom; **2** in; **par endroits** in places; **par cette chaleur** in this heat; **3** per; **50 euros par personne** 50 euros per person; **deux repas par jour** two meals a day; **deux fois par semaine** twice a week.

parachute *noun* Masc. parachute.

parachutiste *noun* Masc. & Fem. parachutist.

paradis *noun* Masc. heaven.

paragraphe *noun* Masc. paragraph.

paraître *verb* [57] **1** to seem; **ça ne paraît étrange** that seems strange to me; **il paraît qu'il est mort** it seems he's dead; **2 paraît-il** apparently; **elle est à Nice, paraît il** she's in Nice, apparently; **3** to appear; **paraître en public** to appear in public; **4** (*of a book*) to come out, to be published; **le roman va paraître en juin** the novel will come out in June.

parallèle *adjective* parallel.

paralysé *adjective* paralysed.

parapente *noun* Masc. **1** paraglider; **2** paragliding.

parapluie *noun* Masc. umbrella.

parasite *noun* Masc. **1** parasite; **2 des parasites** interference (*on TV or radio*).

parasol *noun* Masc. parasol.

parc *noun* Masc. **1** park; **aller au parc** to go to the park; **2** grounds (*a large house*); **3** fleet (*of vehicles*).

parc d'attractions *noun* Masc. amusement park.

parce que *conjunction* because; **parce qu'elle est malade** because she's ill; **c'est parce que je t'aime** it's because I love you.

par-ci *adverb* **par-ci par-là** here and there.

parcmètre *noun* Masc. parking meter.

parc naturel *noun* Masc. natural park.

arcourir verb [29] to go all over, to travel all over; **j'ai parcouru l'Europe** I travelled all over Europe.

arcours noun Masc. **1** route (for a bus or a traveller); **2** course (for a race).

ar-derrière adverb from the back, behind; **elle est passée par-derrière** she went round the back.

ar-dessous adverb underneath.

ar-dessus adverb **1** on top; **2** over it; **il a sauté par-dessus** he jumped over it.

par-dessus preposition over; **elle a sauté par-dessus le ruisseau** she jumped over the stream; **j'aime ça par-dessus tout!** I like that best of all!

ardessus noun Masc. overcoat.

ar-devant adverb by the front.

ardon noun Masc. **1** pardon, forgiveness; **je te demande pardon** I'm sorry; **2** excuse me, sorry.

ardonner verb [1] to forgive; **je ne lui pardonnerai jamais** I'll never forgive him.

are-balles adjective bullet-proof; **un gilet pare-balles** a bullet-proof vest.

are-brise noun Masc. windscreen.

are-chocs noun Masc. bumper (on a car).

areil (Fem. **pareille**) adjective **1** the same; **les deux voitures sont presque pareilles** the two cars are almost the same; **c'est toujours pareil** it's always the same; **mais ce n'est pas du tout pareil!** but it's not the same at all!; **2** such; **je n'ai jamais dit une chose pareille** I never said any such thing; **tu ne**

peux pas sortir par un temps pareil you can't go out in weather like this.

parent noun Masc. **1** parent; **mes parents** my parents; **2** relation; **parents et amis** friends and relations.

parenthèse noun Fem. bracket; **entre parenthèses** in brackets.

paresse noun Fem. laziness.

paresseux (Fem. **paresseuse**) adjective lazy.

parfait adjective perfect.

parfaitement adverb **1** perfectly; **tu le sais parfaitement!** you know perfectly well!; **parfaitement faux** totally wrong; **2 parfaitement!** absolutely!

parfois adverb sometimes.

parfum noun Masc. **1** perfume; **2** flavour; **tu veux quel parfum de yaourt?** what flavour yoghurt would you like?

parfumé adjective **1** perfumed, fragrant; **parfumé à la lavande** lavender-scented; **2** flavoured; **une glace parfumée au chocolat** a chocolate ice cream.

parfumerie noun Fem. perfume shop.

pari noun Masc. bet; **faire un pari** to make a bet.

parier verb [1] to bet.

Paris noun Paris; **à Paris** in (or to) Paris.

parisien (Fem. **parisienne**) adjective **1** Parisian; **2** Paris; **un restaurant parisien** a Paris restaurant.

a
b
c
d
e
f
g
h
i
j
k
l
m
n
o
p
q
r
s
t
u
v
w
x
y
z

Parisien, Parisienne *noun*
Masc., Fem. Parisian.

parking *noun Masc.* car park; **dans
le parking** in the car park.

Parlement *noun Masc.* parliament.

parler *verb* [1] **1** to speak; **parler
(le) français** to speak French;
parler en italien to speak in Italian;
parler fort/doucement to speak
loudly/softly; **parler à quelqu'un** to
speak to someone; **2** to talk; **il parle
très vite** he talks very fast; **parler
cinéma** to talk (about) films;
3 parler de to talk about, to
mention; **tout le monde en parle**
everyone's talking about it; **non, il
n'en a pas parlé** no, he didn't
mention it; **n'en parlons plus!** let's
say no more about it!; **4 se parler** to
talk to each other; ★ **tu parles!**
(*informal*) you must be joking!

parmi *preposition* among; **parmi les
invités** among the guests.

parole *noun Fem.* **1 les paroles** the
lyrics; **les paroles de la chanson**
the lyrics of the song; **2 elle m'a
donné sa parole** she gave me her
word; **3** speech; **perdre la parole** to
lose the power of speech.

parquet *noun Masc.* **1** wooden floor;
2 parquet.

parrain *noun Masc.* godfather.

parrainer *verb* [1] to sponsor.

parsemer *verb* [50] to sprinkle.

part *noun Fem.* **1** portion, helping;
une part de pizza a portion of pizza;
2 share; **il a payé sa part** he paid
his share; **elle a fait sa part du
travail** she did her share of the work;
3 side; **de toutes parts** from all

sides; **4 pour ma part, je pense
que** ... for my part, I think that ...;
5 à part separate, separately; **une
chambre à part** a separate
bedroom; **j'ai mis l'argent à part**
put the money aside; **à part ça,
qu'est-ce qu'il t'a dit?** apart from
that, what did he tell you?; **6 de la
part de quelqu'un** on behalf of
somebody, for somebody; **c'est de
la part de qui?** who's calling?; **dis
lui bonjour de ma part** say hello to
him from me.

partager *verb* [52] **1** to share
(*possessions or food*); **2** to divide; **je
partage mon temps entre mon
travail et les enfants** I divide my
time between my job and the children.

partenaire *noun Masc. & Fem.*
partner.

parterre *noun Masc.* **1** flower bed;
2 stalls (*in a theatre*).

parti *noun Masc.* **1** party, group; **le
parti communiste** the communist
party; **2** side.

participation *noun Fem.*
participation.

participe *noun Masc.* participle;
participe passé past participle.

participer *verb* [1] **participer à
quelque chose** to take part in
something.

particulier *noun Masc.* private
individual.
particulier (*Fem.* **particulière**)
adjective **1** special; **rien de
particulier** nothing special;
2 private; **une voiture particulière**
a private car; **3 en particulier** in
particular; **rien en particulier**

nothing in particular; **4 en particulier** in private.

articulièrement *adverb* particularly.

artie *noun Fem.* **1** part; **une partie de ma vie** part of of my life; **la première partie** the first part; **2 en partie** partly; **3 faire partie de quelque chose** to be part of something; **ce bâtiment fait partie du musée** this building is part of the museum; **elle fait partie de la famille** she's one of the family; **4** game; **faire une partie de tennis** to have a game of tennis; **gagner la partie** to win the game.

artir *verb* [58] **1** to leave, to go; **partir à pied** to go on foot; **tu pars déjà?** are you leaving already?; **elle est partie en Italie** she's gone to Italy; **il est parti à Londres** he's gone to London; **elle est partie au travail** she's left for work; **partir en vacances** to go away on holiday; **elle est partie pour huit jours** she's gone away for a week; **ils sont partis en courant** they ran off; **2 à partir de** from; **à partir de lundi** from Monday (onwards).

artition *noun Fem.* score (*in music*).

artout *adverb* **1** everywhere; **j'ai cherché partout** I've looked everywhere; **2 un peu partout: ça se trouve un peu partout** you can find it/them almost anywhere; **3 trois buts partout** three goals all.

arvenir *verb* [81] **1 parvenir à** to reach; **2 parvenir à faire** to manage to do; **il est parvenu à ouvrir la porte** he managed to open the door.

pas[1] *adverb* **1** (*used with 'ne' to put verbs into the negative*) **je ne suis pas** I am not; **je n'ai pas de stylo** I don't have a pen; **je ne pense pas** I don't think so; **ils n'ont pas le téléphone** they're not on the phone; **2** not; **c'est lui qui paie, pas moi** he's paying, not me; **pas du tout** not at all; **pas vraiment** not really; **une radio pas chère** a cheap radio; **pas de chance!** bad luck!; **pas possible!** I don't believe it!

pas[2] *noun Masc.* **1** step; **faire un grand/petit pas** to take a big/small step; **j'habite à deux pas d'ici** I live very near here; **2** pace; **ralentir le pas** to slow down; **'roulez au pas!'** 'dead slow' (*road sign*).

passage *noun Masc.* **1** traffic; **une rue où il y a beaucoup de passage** a street where there's a lot of traffic; **passage interdit** no through traffic; **2** visit; **je peux te prendre au passage** I can pick you up on my way.

passage à niveau *noun Masc.* level crossing.

passage pour piétons *noun Masc.* pedestrian crossing.

passager, passagère *noun Masc., Fem.* passenger.

passager (*Fem.* **passagère**) *adjective* passing, temporary.

passage souterrain *noun Masc.* subway (*under a road*).

passant, passante *noun Masc., Fem.* passer-by.

passé *noun Masc.* **1** past; **c'est dans le passé** it's in the past now; **2** past tense; **le passé composé** the present perfect.

passé *adjective* **1** l'année passée last year; **2** past; **il est dix heures passées** it's past ten o'clock.

passeport *noun Masc.* passport.

passer *verb* [1] **1** to pass; **le temps passe vite** time passes quickly; **2** to spend (*time*); **j'ai passé deux jours à Paris** I spent two days in Paris; **3 en passant** in passing; **4 passer quelque chose à quelqu'un** to pass somebody something; **passe-moi le sel** pass me the salt; **5** to cross; **passer le pont** to cross the bridge; **6** to drop in; **Pierre est passé ce matin** Pierre dropped in this morning; **est-ce que le facteur est passé?** has the postman been?; **je passerai te prendre à huit heures** I'll pick you up at eight; **7** to get through; **laissez passer l'ambulance!** let the ambulance through!; **8** to be on, to be showing (*films*); **le film est passé à la télé lundi** the film was on telly on Monday; **9** to go; **passer à la caisse** to go to the checkout; **passons au salon** let's go through to the sitting room; **10** to give; **il m'a passé son vélo** he gave me his bike; **11** to put through, to hand over to (*on the telephone*); **je vous passe le responsable** I'll put you through to the manager; **12** to put (on) (*a garment*); **13 passer l'aspirateur** to vacuum; **14** to take, to sit (*a test or an exam*); **15 passer par** to go through; **nous sommes passés par Paris** we went through (or via) Paris; **16 se passer** to happen; **qu'est-ce qui se passe?** what's happening?; **ça s'est passé en Chine** it happened in China; **17 se**

passer de to do without; **se passe d'un manteau** to do without a coa

passerelle *noun Fem.*
1 footbridge; **2** gangway.

passe-temps *noun Masc.* hobby

passif *noun Masc.* passive (*in grammar*).
passif (*Fem.* **passive**) *adjective* passive.

passion *noun Fem.* passion.

passionnant *adjective* exciting.

passionné, passionnée *nou Masc., Fem.* enthusiast; **c'est un passionné de tennis** he's a tenni enthusiast.
passionné *adjective* keen; **c'est une musicienne passionnée** she a keen musician.

passionner *verb* [1] **l'histoire m passionne** history fascinates me.

passoire *noun Fem.* strainer.

patate *noun Fem.* (*informal*) pota

pâte *noun Fem.* **1** pastry; **pâte feuilletée** puff pastry; **2** dough; **3** batter; **pâte à crêpes** pancake batter; **4** paste; **5 les pâtes** pasta; **on va manger des pâtes ce soir** we're having pasta tonight.

pâte à modeler *noun Fem.* Plasticine™.

patience *noun Fem.* patience.

patient, patiente *noun Masc., Fem., adjective* patient.

patienter *verb* [1] to wait; **patientez, s'il vous plaît** please hold the line?

patin *noun Masc.* skate.

patinage *noun Masc.* skating; **patinage artistique** figure skatin

212

atin à glace noun Masc. **1** ice skate; **2** ice skating.

atin à roulettes noun Masc. roller skate.

atiner verb [1] to skate.

atineur, **patineuse** noun Masc., Fem. skater.

atinoire noun Fem. ice rink.

âtisserie noun Fem. **1** cake shop; **2** cake.

atois noun Masc. dialect.

atrie noun Fem. homeland, country.

atron[1] noun Masc. pattern (for dressmaking).

atron[2], **patronne** noun Masc., Fem. boss.

atronner verb [1] to sponsor.

atrouille noun Fem. patrol.

atte noun Fem. **1** paw; **2** leg (of an animal); ★ **à quatre pattes** on all fours.

aume noun Fem. palm (of the hand).

aumer verb [1] (informal) **1** to lose; **2** se paumer to get lost.

aupière noun Fem. eyelid; **le fard à paupières** eyeshadow.

ause noun Fem. **1** break; **faire une pause** to take a break; **la pause café** the coffee break; **2** pause.

auvre noun Masc. & Fem. poor man, poor woman; **les pauvres** the poor; **le pauvre!** poor thing!
pauvre adjective poor.

auvreté noun Fem. poverty.

avé noun Masc. cobblestone.

pavillon noun Masc. **1** detached house; **un pavillon de banlieue** a house in the suburbs; **2** wing (in a hospital).

payant adjective **1** (of a show or event) not free; **c'est payant?** do you have to pay to get in?; **un parking payant** a pay-and-display car park; **2** un hôte payant a paying guest.

paye noun Fem. wages.

payer verb [59] **1** to pay (a bill or a person); **c'est moi qui paie** I'm paying; **être mal payé** to be badly paid; **être payé à l'heure** to be paid by the hour; **2** to pay for; **il a payé le repas** he paid for the meal; **3** (informal) **je te paie à boire** I'll buy you a drink; **4** je me suis payé une semaine à Paris I treated myself to a week in Paris.

pays noun Masc. **1** country; **la France est un beau pays** France is a beautiful country; **2** region; **des fruits du pays** locally grown fruit.

paysage noun Masc. landscape.

paysan, **paysanne** noun Masc., Fem. farmer.

Pays-Bas plural noun Masc. **les Pays-Bas** the Netherlands.

pays de Galles noun Masc. Wales; **au pays de Galles** in (or to) Wales.

PC noun Masc. PC, personal computer.

péage noun Masc. **1** toll; **autoroute à péage** toll motorway (motorists have to pay to travel on motorways in France); **2** tollbooth.

peau (plural **peaux**) noun Fem. **1** skin; **avoir la peau sèche** to have

a
b
c
d
e
f
g
h
i
j
k
l
m
n
o
p
q
r
s
t
u
v
w
x
y
z

a

dry skin; **2** peel (*of fruit*); **peau d'orange** orange peel.

b

pêche *noun Fem.* **1** peach; **2** fishing; **aller à la pêche** to go fishing.

c

péché *noun Masc.* sin.

d

pêcher[1] *verb* [1] **1** to fish for (*trout, salmon, etc*); **2** to catch; **Denise a pêché trois truites** Denise caught three trout.

e

f

pêcher[2] *noun Masc.* peach tree.

g

pêcheur *noun Masc.* fisherman.

h

pédagogique *adjective* educational; **méthode pédagogique** teaching method.

i

j

pédale *noun Fem.* pedal; ★ **perdre les pédales** (*informal*) to lose your grip.

k

l

pédaler *verb* [1] to pedal.

m

pédalo™ *noun Masc.* pedalo, pedal boat.

n

o

pédestre *adjective* **faire une randonnée pédestre** to go walking (*on a long-distance public footpath*).

p

peigne *noun Masc.* comb.

q

peigner *verb* [1] **1** to comb; **2 se peigner** to comb your hair.

r

peindre *verb* [60] to paint.

s

peine *noun Fem.* **1** effort, trouble; **se donner de la peine** to go to a lot of trouble; **il n'a même pas pris la peine d'appeler** he didn't even take the trouble to ring; **2 ce n'est pas la peine** it's not worth it; **3** difficulty; **elle a eu beaucoup de peine à trouver un logement** she had a lot of difficulty finding somewhere to live; **4 faire de la peine à quelqu'un** to upset somebody; **5** penalty (*in law*); **sous peine**

t

u

v

w

x

y

z

d'amende offenders will be fined; **6 à peine** hardly, scarcely; **je le connais à peine** I hardly know him; **il était à peine cinq heures** it wa barely five o'clock.

peine de mort *noun Fem.* death penalty.

peintre *noun Masc.* painter.

peintre-décorateur *noun Mas* decorator.

peinture *noun Fem.* **1** paint; 'peinture fraîche' 'wet paint'; **2** painting; **faire de la peinture** to paint; **3 une peinture** a painting.

pèlerin *noun Masc.* pilgrim.

pèlerinage *noun Masc.* pilgrimage; **faire un pèlerinage** to go on a pilgrimage.

pelle *noun Fem.* **1** spade; **2** shovel.

pelle à poussière *noun Fem.* dustpan.

pelle mécanique *noun Fem.* mechanical digger.

pellicule *noun Fem.* **1** film (*for a camera*); **une pellicule couleur** a colour film; **2 les pellicules** dandruff.

pelouse *noun Fem.* lawn; 'pelous interdite' 'keep off the grass'.

peluche *noun Fem.* soft toy.

pencher *verb* [1] **1** to tilt; **2** to lear **3 se pencher** to bend down; **4 se pencher par la fenêtre** to lean ou of the window.

pendant *preposition* **1** for; **je t'ai attendu pendant deux heures** I waited for you for two hours; **2** during; **pendant l'hiver** during the winter; **3 pendant que** while;

pendant que les enfants sont à l'école while the children are at school; **4 pendant ce temps là** meanwhile; **pendant ce temps là elle attendait à la gare** meanwhile he was waiting at the station.

pendentif noun Masc. pendant.

penderie noun Fem. wardrobe, hanging cupboard.

pendre verb [3] **1** to hang; **2 pendre quelque chose** to hang something up; **3** to hang down.

pendule noun Fem. clock.

pénétrer verb [24] **1 pénétrer dans** to enter; **un voleur a pénétré dans le bureau** a thief got into the office; **2** to penetrate.

pénible adjective **1** difficult, hard; **2 il est pénible** he's a pain.

péniche noun Fem. barge.

pénis noun Masc. penis.

pensée noun Fem. **1** thought; **2** pansy.

penser verb [1] **1** to think; **je pense que tu as raison** I think you're right; **oui, je pense** yes, I think so; **je ne pense pas** I don't think so; **2** to intend; **il pense arriver mardi** he's intending to arrive on Tuesday; **3 penser de** to think of; **qu'est-ce que tu penses de mon idée?** what do you think of my idea?; **4 penser à** to think about; **à quoi penses-tu?** what are you thinking about?; **5 cette chanson me fait penser à ma mère** this song reminds me of your mother; **6** to remember; **pendant que j'y pense** while I remember; **fais-moi penser à**

acheter des citrons remind me to buy lemons.

pension noun Fem. **1** boarding school; **2** boarding house; **3** pension; **4 pension complète** full board; **demi-pension** half board, dinner, bed and breakfast.

pension de famille noun Fem. family hotel.

pensionnaire noun Masc. & Fem. boarder.

pensionnat noun Masc. boarding school.

pente noun Fem. slope; **en pente** sloping.

Pentecôte noun Fem. Whitsun; **à la Pentecôte** at Whitsun.

pépin noun Masc. **1** (grape) pip; **2** (informal) slight problem.

perçant adjective **1** piercing; **2** sharp.

perce-neige noun Masc. OR Fem. snowdrop.

percer verb [61] to pierce; **avoir les oreilles percées** to have pierced ears; **se faire percer les oreilles** to have your ears pierced; **percer un trou** to make a hole.

perceuse noun Fem. drill.

perdant, perdante noun Masc., Fem. loser.

perdre verb [3] **1** to lose; **notre équipe a perdu** our team lost; **2 perdre quelque chose** to lose something; **j'ai perdu mes clefs** I've lost my keys; **j'ai perdu mon chemin** I've lost my way; **3 être perdu** to be lost; **4 se perdre** to get lost; **je me suis perdu dans les**

a
b
c
d
e
f
g
h
i
j
k
l
m
n
o
p
q
r
s
t
u
v
w
x
y
z

215

a   **petites rues** I got lost in the back
streets; **5 perdre du temps** to waste
b   time.

c   **perdrix** noun Fem. (invariable)
partridge.

d

e   **perdu** adjective **1** lost; **un enfant perdu** a lost child; **je suis perdu** I'm
lost; **vous êtes perdu?** are you lost?;
f   **2** stray; **un chien perdu** a stray dog;
3 c'est du temps perdu it's a waste
g   of time.

h   **père** noun Masc. father; **le père Noël**
Father Christmas.

i
perfectionner verb [1] to perfect.

j   **performant** adjective **1** efficient;
2 high-performance.
k

périmé adjective out-of-date.
l
période noun Fem. period.

m   **périphérique** noun Masc. ring
road.
n
perle noun Fem. **1** pearl; **2** bead.
o
permanence noun Fem.
p   **1** service; **'permanence de 8h à
19h'** 'open from 8 a.m. to 7 p.m.';
q   **2 en permanence** permanently, all
the time.
r
permanent adjective
s   **1** permanent; **2** continuous.

t   **permettre** verb [11] **permettre à
quelqu'un de faire** to allow
u   someone to do; **elle leur a permis
de partir** she allowed them to leave;
v   **permettez-moi de vous aider** let
me help you.
w
permis noun Masc. permit, licence.
x
permis de conduire noun
y   Masc. driving licence; **passer son
permis** to sit your driving test.
z

permission noun Fem.
1 permission; **2** leave (from the
army).

perroquet noun Masc. parrot.

perruche noun Fem. budgie.

perruque noun Fem. wig.

persécution noun Fem.
persecution.

persévérer verb [24] to persever

persil noun Masc. parsley.

persister verb [1] to persist.

personnage noun Masc.
1 character (in a book, film, or pla
2 figure, person; **un personnage
célèbre** a famous person.

personnalité noun Fem.
personality.

personne[1] pronoun **1** nobody;
personne ne sait nobody knows;
2 anybody; **je ne vois personne** I
can't see anybody; **je n'ai parlé à
personne** I didn't speak to anybod

personne[2] noun Fem. person; **vin
personnes** twenty people; **les
personnes âgées** the elderly; **en
personne** in person.

personnel noun Masc. **1** staff; **2**
service du personnel the
personnel department.
personnel (Fem. **personnelle**)
adjective personal.

personnellement adverb
personally.

perspective noun Fem.
1 perspective; **2** view; **3** prospect.

persuader verb [1] **1** to persuad
persuader quelqu'un de faire to
persuade somebody to do; **2 être
persuadé** to be sure.

erte *noun Fem.* **1** loss; **2** waste; **une perte de temps** a waste of time.

erturber *verb* [1] to disrupt.

esanteur *noun Fem.* gravity.

èse-personne *noun Masc.* bathroom scales.

eser *verb* [50] **1 peser quelque chose** to weigh something; **2** to weigh; **je pèse 60 kilos** I weigh 60 kilos.

essimiste *noun Masc. & Fem.* pessimist.

essimiste *adjective* pessimistic.

étale *noun Masc.* petal.

étanque *noun Fem.* bowls (*the French version, played outdoors with metal bowls; also called 'boules'*).

étard *noun Masc.* firecracker, banger.

étillant *adjective* sparkling (*wine or mineral water*).

etit[1] *adjective* **1** little, small; **une petite fille** a little girl; **une toute petite maison** a tiny house; **2** short; **une petite distance** a short distance; ★ **petit à petit** little by little.

etit[2] *noun Masc.* little boy; **les petits** the children.

etite *noun Fem.* little girl; **les petites** the little girls.

etit ami *noun Masc.* boyfriend.

etit bassin *noun Masc.* shallow pool (*for non-swimmers*).

etit déjeuner *noun Masc.* breakfast.

etite amie *noun Fem.* girlfriend.

petite annonce *noun Fem.* small ad.

petite-fille *noun Fem.* granddaughter.

petit-fils *noun Masc.* grandson.

petit mot *noun Masc.* note.

petit pois *noun Masc.* garden pea.

petits-enfants *plural noun Masc.* grandchildren.

pétrole *noun Masc.* **1** oil, petroleum; **2** paraffin.

pétrolier *noun Masc.* **1** oil tanker, ship; **2** petroleum engineer.

peu *adverb* **1** not much; **il dort peu** he doesn't sleep much; **elle gagne très peu** she earns very little; **2** not very; **peu intéressant** not very interesting; **peu réaliste** unrealistic; **3 peu de** not much, not many; **il reste peu de temps** there's not much time left; **peu de voitures** not many cars; **4 un peu de** a little, a bit; **il reste un peu de café** there's a bit of coffee left; **un tout petit peu de sel** a tiny amount of salt; **5 parle un peu plus fort** speak a little louder; **juste un petit peu** just a little; **6 à peu près** about; **il y avait à peu près vingt personnes** there were about twenty people.

peuple *noun Masc.* people, nation.

peuplier *noun Masc.* poplar.

peur *noun Fem.* fear; **avoir peur de** to be afraid of; **Nadine a peur des souris** Nadine's afraid of mice; **n'ayez pas peur!** don't be afraid!; **faire peur à quelqu'un** to frighten somebody; **tu m'as fait peur!** you gave me a fright!

peut *verb* SEE **pouvoir**[1].

a
b
c
d
e
f
g
h
i
j
k
l
m
n
o
p
q
r
s
t
u
v
w
x
y
z

peut-être *adverb* perhaps.

peuvent, peux *verb* SEE **pouvoir**[1].

phare *noun Masc.* **1** headlight; **allumer les phares** to turn the headlights on; **2** lighthouse.

pharmacie *noun Fem.* chemist's.

pharmacien, pharmacienne *noun Masc., Fem.* chemist, pharmacist.

phénomène *noun Masc.* phenomenon.

philo *noun Fem.* (*informal*) SHORT FOR **philosophie**.

philosophie *noun Fem.* philosophy.

phoque *noun Masc.* seal.

photo *noun Fem.* **1** photo, photograph; **une photo d'identité** a passport photo; **2** photography.

photocopie *noun Fem.* photocopy.

photocopier *verb* [1] to photocopy.

photocopieuse *noun Fem.* photocopier.

photographe *noun Masc. & Fem.* photographer; **Sean est photographe** Sean's a photographer.

photographie *noun Fem.* **1** photography; **2** photograph.

photographier *verb* [1] to photograph.

photomaton™ *noun Masc.* photo booth.

phrase *noun Fem.* sentence.

physique[1] *noun Fem.* physics.

physique[2] *adjective* physical.

pianiste *noun Masc. & Fem.* pianist.

piano *noun Masc.* piano; **jouer du piano** to play the piano.

piano à queue *noun Masc.* gran piano.

pichet *noun Masc.* jug.

pièce *noun Fem.* **1** room; **notre maison a quatre pièces** our hous has four rooms; **2** coin; **une pièce de deux euros** a two-euro coin; **3** play; **une pièce de Molière** a pla by Molière; **4** bit, piece; **les pièce d'un puzzle** the pieces of a jigsaw **5** item; **dix euros (la) pièce** ten euros each; **6** patch (*for repairs*).

pièce détachée *noun Fem.* spa part.

pièce de théâtre *noun Fem.* play.

pièce d'identité *noun Fem.* identification (*such as a passport* identity card).

pièce jointe *noun Fem.* attachment.

pied *noun Masc.* **1** foot; **être pieds nus** to be barefoot; **aller à pied** to on foot; **un coup de pied** a kick; **donner un coup de pied à quelqu'un** to kick someone; **2** bottom, foot; **au pied du lit** at th foot of the bed; **3 le pied de la tab** the table leg; **4** (*in swimming*) **j'ai pied** I can touch the bottom; **je n'** **plus pied** I'm out of my depth.

piège *noun Masc.* trap.

piéger *verb* [15] to trap; **une voitu piégée** a car bomb.

pierre *noun Fem.* stone.

pierre précieuse *noun Fem.* precious stone.

218

éton, piétonne noun Masc., Fem. pedestrian; **un passage pour piétons** a pedestrian crossing.

étonnier (Fem. **piétonnière**) adjective pedestrian; **une rue piétonnière** a pedestrian street.

euvre noun Fem. octopus.

geon noun Masc. pigeon.

le¹ noun Fem. **1** battery; **2** pile; **une pile de vêtements** a pile of clothes; **3** tails (when tossing a coin); **pile ou face?** heads or tails?

le² adverb (informal) **1** exactly; **à dix heures pile** at ten o'clock on the dot; **2 s'arrêter pile** to stop dead.

ilône noun Masc. pylon.

ilote noun Masc. **1** pilot; **2 un pilote de course** a racing driver.

iloter verb [1] to fly (a plane).

ilule noun Fem. pill.

iment noun Masc. chilli.

in noun Masc. pine tree; **une pomme de pin** a pine cone.

ince noun Fem. **1 une pince** a pair of pliers; **2** dart (in a garment); **3** pincer (of a crab).

ince à épiler noun Fem. tweezers.

ince à linge noun Fem. clothes peg.

inceau (plural **pinceaux**) noun Masc. paintbrush.

incée noun Fem. pinch (of salt, for example).

incer verb [61] to pinch.

ingouin noun Masc. penguin.

ing-pong noun Masc. ping-pong.

intade noun Fem. guinea fowl.

pion¹ noun Masc. **1** counter (in a board game); **2** pawn (in chess); **3** piece (in draughts).

pion² noun Masc. & Fem. student supervisor of school pupils (colloquial) SEE **surveillant**.

pipe noun Fem. pipe; **fumer la pipe** to smoke a pipe.

pipi noun Masc. (informal) wee; **faire pipi** to have a wee.

piquant adjective **1** prickly; **2** spicy.

pique noun Masc. spades (in a pack of cards); **le trois de pique** the three of spades.

pique-nique noun Masc. picnic.

pique-niquer verb [1] to have a picnic.

piquer verb [1] **1** to sting; **j'ai été piqué par une guêpe** I've been stung by a wasp; **2** to bite; **piqué par des moustiques** bitten by mosquitoes; **3 se piquer** to prick yourself; **je me suis piqué le doigt** I've pricked my finger; **4** (informal) to pinch; **quelqu'un a piqué mon stylo** somebody's pinched my pen; ★ **piquer une crise (de nerfs)** (informal) to throw a fit.

piquet noun Masc. **1** post; **2** peg.

piqûre noun Fem. **1** injection; **faire une piqûre à quelqu'un** to give somebody an injection; **2** bite, sting (of an insect).

pirate noun Masc. pirate.

pirate de l'air noun Masc. hijacker (of plane).

pirate de la route noun Masc. hijacker (of lorry).

a
b
c
d
e
f
g
h
i
j
k
l
m
n
o
p
q
r
s
t
u
v
w
x
y
z

pirate informatique *noun*
Masc. computer hacker.

pire *adjective* **1** worse; **pire que**
worse than; **c'est pire que ça!** it's
worse than that!; **c'est encore pire**
it's even worse; **2** worst; **le pire** the
worst; **au pire** if the worst comes to
the worst.

pis *in phrase* **tant pis** too bad; **tant
pis pour lui!** that's his bad luck!

piscine *noun* Fem. swimming-pool;
**est-ce que la piscine est
surveillée?** is there a lifeguard at
the swimming pool?

pissenlit *noun* Masc. dandelion.

pistache *noun* Fem. pistachio.

piste *noun* Fem. **1** trail (*left by an
animal or fugitive*); **la police est
sur sa piste** the police are on his
trail; **2** track (*for racing or sport*);
faire un tour de piste to do a lap;
3 piste, trail (*in skiing*); **4** runway
(*at an airport*).

piste cyclable *noun* Fem. cycle
lane.

pistolet *noun* Masc. pistol.

pitié *noun* Fem. pity; **avoir pitié de
quelqu'un** to feel sorry for someone.

pittoresque *adjective*
picturesque.

pizza *noun* Fem. pizza; **vous voulez
une pizza à quoi?** what kind of
pizza would you like?

placard *noun* Masc. cupboard.

place *noun* Fem. **1** space, room; **il y a
assez de place pour deux** there's
enough room for two; **2** seat (*in a
theatre, cinema, train, or bus*); **trois
places pour ce soir** two seats for

this evening's performance; **3** plac
**remettez tous les livres à leur
place!** put all the books back in
their places!; **si j'étais à ta place**
I were you; **4** place; **en troisième
place** in third place; **5** square; **la
place Rouge** the Red Square; **la
place du village** the village squar
6 à la place de instead of; **il y est
allé à ma place** he went instead c
me; **7 être sur place** to be on the
spot.

placer *verb* [61] **1** to place; **2** to se
(*a person*); **elle m'a placé à côté d
Louis** she put me next to Louis.

plafond *noun* Masc. ceiling.

plage *noun* Fem. beach; **on va à la
plage** we're going to the beach.

plaie *noun* Fem. wound.

plaindre *verb* [31] **1** to feel sorry
for; **je te plains** I feel sorry for yo
2 se plaindre to complain; **je ne m
plains pas** I'm not complaining;
**elle s'est plainte de la qualité d
service auprès du responsable**
she complained to the manager
about the standard of service.

plaine *noun* Fem. plain.

plainte *noun* Fem. complaint;
porter plainte to complain.

plaire *verb* [62] **1 s'il te plaît, s'il
vous plaît** please; **deux billets, s'
vous plaît** two tickets, please; **2 le
tissu me plaît** I like the material; **l
chambre vous plaît?** do you like
your room?; **le film a beaucoup pl
à mon père** my father liked the fil
very much.

plaisanter *verb* [1] to joke.

plaisanterie *noun* Fem. joke.

laisir noun Masc. pleasure; **le plaisir de lire** the pleasure of reading; **'vous venez avec nous?' — 'oui, avec plaisir'** 'will you come too?' — 'yes, with pleasure'; **faire plaisir à quelqu'un** to please someone; **j'y suis allé pour faire plaisir à ma mère** I went to please my mother.

lan noun Masc. **1** map (of a town or underground system); **le plan du métro** the underground map; **2** plan; **le plan du bâtiment** the plan of the building; **3 au premier plan** in the foreground, in the forefront.

lanche noun Fem. plank.

lanche à repasser noun Fem. ironing board.

lanche à roulettes noun Fem. skateboard.

lanche à voile noun Fem. **1** windsurfing board; **2** windsurfing; **faire de la planche à voile** to go windsurfing.

lancher noun Masc. floor.

lan d'eau noun Masc. artificial lake (often for swimming and other water sports).

laner verb [1] **1** to glide; **2** (informal) to have your head in the clouds.

lanète noun Fem. planet.

lante noun Fem. plant; **une plante verte** a house-plant.

lanter verb [1] **1** to plant (a tree, shrub, or plant); **2** to hammer in (a nail); **3 se planter** (informal) to make a blunder.

plaquage noun Masc. **1** tackle; **2** tackling.

plaqué adjective **plaqué or** gold-plated; **plaqué argent** silver-plated.

plaque noun Fem. **1** patch (of damp or ice); **2** plate, sheet (of metal or glass).

plaque d'immatriculation noun Fem. number plate (on a car).

plastique noun Masc. plastic; **un sac en plastique** a plastic bag.

plat noun Masc. **1** dish; **un plat chaud/froid** a hot/cold dish; **le plat du jour** the dish of the day; **2** course (of a meal); **le plat principal** the main course; ★ **faire tout un plat de quelque chose** (informal) to make a big deal of something.
plat adjective **1** flat; **à plat ventre** flat on your stomach; **2 l'eau plate** still water.

platane noun Masc. plane tree.

plateau (plural **plateaux**) noun Masc. **1** tray; **2** plateau.

plate-bande noun Fem. flower bed.

plâtre noun Masc. plaster; **il a une jambe dans le plâtre** he has a leg in plaster.

plein adjective **1** full; **le panier est plein** the basket's full; **elle est pleine d'idées** she's full of ideas; **2 en pleine nuit** in the middle of the night; **en plein été** at the height of summer; **en plein centre-ville** right in the middle of town; **en pleine mer** on the open sea.
plein noun Masc. **faire le plein** to fill up (a car with petrol); **le plein, s'il vous plaît** a full tank, please.
plein adverb **plein de** (informal)

a
b
c
d
e
f
g
h
i
j
k
l
m
n
o
p
q
r
s
t
u
v
w
x
y
z

a b c d e f g h i j k l m n o **p** q r s t u v w x y z

loads of; **elle a plein d'amis** she's got loads of friends.

pleurer verb [1] to cry.

pleut verb SEE **pleuvoir**.

pleuvoir verb [63] to rain; **il pleut** it's raining; **il va pleuvoir** it's going to rain; **il a plu cette nuit** it rained last night.

pli noun Masc. 1 fold; 2 pleat; 3 crease (in trousers).

plier verb [1] 1 to fold; 2 to bend (your arm or leg, or a stem); ★ **être plié en deux/en quatre** (informal) to be doubled up (with laughter or pain).

plomb noun Masc. 1 lead; **de l'essence sans plomb** unleaded petrol; 2 fuse; **faire sauter les plombs** to blow the fuses.

plombage noun Masc. filling (in a tooth).

plombier noun Masc. plumber.

plongée noun Fem. diving; **faire de la plongée** to go diving.

plongeoir noun Masc. diving board.

plonger verb [52] 1 to dive; 2 to plunge.

plongeur, plongeuse noun Masc., Fem. 1 diver; 2 washer-up.

plu verb SEE **plaire**; **pleuvoir**.

pluie noun Fem. rain; **un jour de pluie** a rainy day; **sous la pluie** in the rain.

plume noun Fem. 1 feather; 2 ink pen.

plupart noun Fem. **la plupart de** most; **la plupart des gens** most people; **la plupart du temps** most of the time.

pluriel noun Masc. plural; **au pluriel** in the plural.

plus adverb 1 **plus de** more; **voulez vous un peu plus de fromage?** would you like a little more cheese? 2 **plus de** more than; **il y avait plu de cent personnes** there were more than a hundred people; 3 **plus que** more than; **il mange plus que moi** he eats more than I do; **le film est plus intéressant que le livre** the film's more interesting than the book; **leur maison est plus grand que la nôtre** their house is bigger than ours; 4 **le plus rapide** the fastest; **le plus joli** the prettiest; 5 **plus ...plus** the more ...the more **plus je gagne, plus je dépense** th more I earn the more I spend; 6 **en plus** more; **il nous faut trois côtelettes en plus** we need three more chops; 7 **de plus** more; **trois chaises de plus** three more chair **une fois de plus** one more time; 8 **de plus en plus** more and more **elle fume de plus en plus** she smokes more and more; **je devien de plus en plus fatigué** I'm gettin more and more tired; **il fait de plu en plus chaud** it's getting hotter and hotter; 9 **plus ou moins** more or less; **la cuisine est plus ou moins propre** the kitchen's more c less clean; 10 **le plus** the most; **c'es lui qui gagne le plus** he earns the most; **au plus** at the most; 11 **ne ... plus** no longer; **elle n'habite plus ici** she no longer lives here; 12 **je n veux plus y aller** I don't want to g there any more; 14 **il n'y a plus d lait** there's no milk left; 15 **plus;**

deux plus trois égalent cinq two plus three is five.

plusieurs *adjective* several; **plusieurs personnes** several people; **plusieurs fois** several times.

plutôt *adverb* **1** rather; **prends le jaune plutôt que le vert** take the yellow one rather than the green one; **2** instead; **demande plutôt à Anne** ask Anne instead; **3** pretty; **le repas était plutôt bon** the meal was pretty good; **plutôt bien** pretty good; **4** rather; **elle est plutôt maigre** she's rather thin.

pluvieux (*Fem.* **pluvieuse**) *adjective* rainy.

pneu *noun Masc.* tyre.

pneumopathie atypique *noun Fem.* SARS (*the disease*).

poche *noun Fem.* pocket; **un livre de poche** a paperback; **l'argent de poche** pocket money; ★ **c'est dans la poche** (*informal*) it's in the bag; ★ **je connais Paris comme ma poche** (*informal*) I know Paris like the back of my hand.

poêle[1] *noun Masc.* stove (*for heating*); **un poêle à bois** a wood-burning stove.

poêle[2] *noun Fem.* frying pan.

poème *noun Masc.* poem.

poésie *noun Fem.* poetry.

poète *noun Masc.* poet.

poids *noun Masc.* weight; **prendre du poids** to put on weight; **perdre du poids** to lose weight.

poids lourd *noun Masc.* lorry.

poignée *noun Fem.* **1** handful; **une poignée de cailloux** a handful of pebbles; **2** handle; **3** **une poignée de main** a handshake.

poignet *noun Masc.* wrist.

poil *noun Masc.* hair; **un poil** a hair; **le chat perd ses poils** the cat's moulting; ★ **être de bon/mauvais poil** to be in a good/bad mood.

poilu *adjective* hairy.

poing *noun Masc.* fist; **un coup de poing** a punch.

point *noun Masc.* **1** point; **et mon dernier point** and my last point; **un point de détail** a minor point; **un point faible** a weak point; **2** **un point de rencontre** a meeting-place; **3** **être sur le point de faire** to be just about to do; **j'étais sur le point de t'appeler** I was on the point of phoning you; **4** dot; **un petit point sur la carte** a tiny dot on the map; **5** full stop; **6** point (*when scoring*); **six points contre sept** six points to seven; **marquer/perdre des points** to win/lose points; **7** mark (*in a test*); **8** **à point** just in time; **tu es arrivé à point** you arrived just in time; **un steak cuit à point** a medium-rare steak.

point chaud *noun Masc.* trouble spot.

point de départ *noun Masc.* starting point.

point d'exclamation *noun Masc.* exclamation mark.

point de vue *noun Masc.* point of view; **d'un point de vue politique** from a political point of view.

point d'interrogation *noun Masc.* question mark.

a b c d e f g h i j k l m n o **p** q r s t u v w x y z

pointe noun Fem. **1** point; **la pointe d'un couteau** the point of a knife; **sur la pointe des pieds** on tip-toe; **être en pointe** to be pointed; **2 les heures de pointe** the rush hour, peak time; **3 une pointe de** a touch of; **une pointe d'ail** a touch of garlic; ★ **être à la pointe du progrès** to be in the forefront of progress.

pointillé noun Masc. dotted line.

point mort noun Masc. neutral (gear); **tu es au point mort** you're in neutral.

pointu adjective pointed.

pointure noun Fem. size (of shoes); **quelle est votre pointure?** what size do you take?

point-virgule noun Masc. semi-colon.

poire noun Fem. pear.

poireau (plural **poireaux**) noun Masc. leek.

poirier noun Masc. pear tree; **faire le poirier** to stand on your head.

pois noun Masc. **1** pea; **des petits pois** (garden) peas; **2 à pois** spotted; **un tissu à pois** a spotted fabric.

pois chiche noun Masc. chick pea.

pois de senteur noun Masc. sweet pea.

poison noun Masc. poison.

poisson noun Masc. fish; **j'aime le poisson** I like fish.

poisson d'avril noun Masc. April fool; **il m'a fait un poisson d'avril** he played an April fool trick on me.

poissonnerie noun Fem. fishmonger's.

poissonnier, poissonnière noun Masc., Fem. fishmonger.

poisson rouge noun Masc. goldfish.

Poissons plural noun Masc. Pisces (sign of the Zodiac).

poitrine noun Fem. **1** chest; **2** bust; **quel est votre tour de poitrine?** what is your bust size?

poivre noun Masc. pepper; **poivre noir en grains** whole black peppercorns.

poivrier noun Masc. pepper pot.

poivron noun Masc. pepper (red, green, or yellow).

poker noun Masc. poker.

polar noun Masc. (informal) detective story.

pôle noun Masc. pole; **le pôle Nord/ Sud** the North/South Pole.

poli adjective polite; **être poli avec quelqu'un** to be polite to somebody.

police noun Fem. **1** police; **appeler la police** to call the police; **2** (insurance) policy.

policier noun Masc. police officer; **une femme policier** a woman police officer.
policier adjective **un roman policier** a detective story.

poliment adverb politely.

politesse noun Fem. politeness; **par politesse** out of politeness.

politicien, politicienne noun Masc., Fem. politician.

politique noun Fem. **1** politics; **2** policy; **la politique sociale/ étrangère** social/foreign policy.

politique *adjective* **1** political; **2 un homme politique** a politician.

olluer *verb* [1] to pollute.

ollution *noun Fem.* pollution.

olo *noun Masc.* polo shirt.

ologne *noun Fem.* Poland; **en Pologne** in (*or* to) Poland.

olonais *noun, Masc.* Polish (*language*).

olonais *adjective* Polish.

olonais, Polonaise *noun Masc., Fem.* Pole.

ommade *noun Fem.* ointment.

omme *noun Fem.* **1** apple; **une tarte aux pommes** an apple tart; **2** potato; **pommes frites** chips; ★ **tomber dans les pommes** (*informal*) to faint (*literally: to fall into the apples*).

omme de terre *noun Fem.* potato.

ommier *noun Masc.* apple tree.

ompe *noun Fem.* pump.

ompe à essence *noun Fem.* petrol pump.

ompes funèbres *plural noun Fem.* undertaker's.

ompier *noun Masc.* fire fighter; **appeler les pompiers** to call the fire brigade.

ompiste *noun Masc. & Fem.* petrol pump attendant.

oncer *verb* [61] to sand (*wood*).

onctuation *noun Fem.* punctuation.

oney *noun Masc.* pony.

ont *noun Masc.* **1** bridge; **2** deck (*of a ship*); ★ **faire le pont** to take a long

weekend (*usually when the Thursday before or the Tuesday after is a public holiday*).

populaire *adjective* **1** working-class (*family, housing, or area*); **2** popular (*art or writing*); **3** folk; **la culture populaire** folk culture; **4** popular.

population *noun Fem.* population.

porc *noun Masc.* **1** pig; **un élevage de porcs** a pig farm; **2** pork; **manger un rôti de porc** to have roast pork.

porcelaine *noun Fem.* china, porcelain.

porcherie *noun Fem.* pigsty; **ta chambre est une vraie porcherie** your room is a real pigsty.

port *noun Masc.* **1** port; **2** harbour.

portable *adjective* portable; **un ordinateur portable** a laptop computer.

portail *noun Masc.* gate.

portatif (*Fem.* **portative**) *adjective* portable.

porte *noun Fem.* **1** door; **la porte d'entrée** the front door; **2** gate (*in an airport*); **la porte numéro douze** gate number twelve; **3 l'entreprise a fermé ses portes** the business has closed down; **mettre quelqu'un à la porte** to sack somebody.

porte-bagages *noun Masc.* luggage rack.

porte-clés *noun Masc.* key-ring.

portée *noun Fem.* **à portée de main** within reach.

porte-fenêtre *noun Fem.* French window.

portefeuille noun Masc. wallet; **une jupe en portefeuille** a wrapover skirt.

porte-jarretelles noun Masc. suspender belt.

portemanteau (plural **portemanteaux**) noun Masc. coat rack.

portemine noun Masc. propelling pencil.

porte-monnaie noun Masc. purse.

porte-parole noun Masc. spokesperson.

porter verb [1] **1** to carry; **porter une valise** to carry a suitcase; **2** to take; **porter un paquet à la poste** to take a parcel to the post office; **3** to wear; **elle portait une robe bleue** she was wearing a blue dress; **4 se porter bien** to be well; **se porter mal** to be in a bad way; ★ **porter bonheur/malheur** to bring good/bad luck.

portière noun Fem. door (of a car).

portion noun Fem. portion, helping.

porto noun Masc. port (wine).

portoricain adjective Puerto Rican.

Portoricain, Portoricaine noun Masc., Fem. Puerto Rican (person).

Porto Rico noun Fem. Puerto Rico.

portrait noun Masc. portrait.

portugais noun Masc. Portuguese (language).
portugais adjective Portuguese.

Portugais, Portugaise noun Masc., Fem. Portuguese (person).

Portugal noun Masc. Portugal; **au Portugal** in (or to) Portugal.

poser verb [1] **1** to put down; **il a posé sa tasse sur la table** he pu his cup down on the table; **pose ta valise** put your case down; **2 cela nous pose un problème** that's a problem for us; **3 poser une question** to ask a question.

positif (Fem. **positive**) adjective positive.

position noun Fem. position.

posséder verb [24] to own.

possessif (Fem. **possessive**) adjective possessive.

possibilité noun Fem.
1 possibility; **c'est une possibili** it's a possibility; **2** opportunity; **la possibilité de voyager** the opportunity to travel.

possible adjective possible; **auss grand que possible** as big as possible; **le moins possible** as litt as possible; **dès que possible** as soon as possible; **ce n'est pas possible!** I don't believe it!; ★ **fair tout son possible** to do your best

poste[1] noun Masc. **1** job, post; **un poste de secrétaire** a job as a secretary; **2 un poste de radio/ télévision** a radio/television set; **3** extension (on a telephone system **le poste 578, s'il vous plaît** extension 578, please.

poste[2] noun Fem. post office; **il travaille pour la poste** he works fo the post office; **mettre quelque chose à la poste** to post somethin

poste de police noun Masc. police station.

pot noun Masc. **1** jar; **un pot de confiture** a jar of jam; **2** carton; **u**

pot de crème a carton of cream;
3 un pot de peinture a tin of paint;
★ **prendre un pot** to have a drink.

potable *adjective* **eau (non)
potable** (not) drinking water.

potage *noun Masc.* soup; **potage
aux légumes** vegetable soup.

potager *noun Masc.* vegetable
garden.

pot-au-feu *noun Masc.* boiled beef
with vegetables.

pot d'échappement *noun
Masc.* exhaust, silencer (*for a car*).

poteau (*plural* **poteaux**) *noun
Masc.* post.

poteau télégraphique *noun
Masc.* telegraph pole.

potelé *adjective* chubby.

poterie *noun Fem.* **1** pottery;
2 piece of pottery.

pou (*plural* **poux**) *noun Masc.* louse;
★ **chercher des poux** (*informal*) to
nitpick.

poubelle *noun Fem.* dustbin;
**mettre quelque chose à la
poubelle** to throw something in the
dustbin.

pouce *noun Masc.* **1** thumb; **2** inch;
★ **se tourner les pouces**
(*informal*) to twiddle your thumbs.

poudre *noun Fem.* powder.

pouffer *verb* [1] **pouffer de rire** to
burst out laughing.

poulain *noun Masc.* foal.

poule *noun Fem.* hen; ★ **quand les
poules auront des dents**
(*informal*) when pigs can fly
(*literally: when hens have teeth*).

poulet *noun Masc.* chicken; **une
cuisse de poulet** a chicken leg ; **du
poulet rôti** roast chicken.

poulet fermier *noun Masc.* free-
range chicken.

pouls *noun Masc.* pulse; **le médecin
a pris mon pouls** the doctor took
my pulse.

poumon *noun Masc.* lung; **crier à
pleins poumons** to shout at the top
of your voice.

poupée *noun Fem.* doll.

pour *preposition* **1** for; **un cadeau
pour Marie-Laure** a present for
Marie-Laure; **un billet pour Calais**
a ticket for Calais; **le train pour
Londres** the train for London; **ce
sera prêt pour samedi?** will it be
ready for Saturday?; **être pour** to be
in favour; **je n'y suis pour rien** I had
nothing to do with it; **je n'en ai pas
pour longtemps** it won't take long;
2 pour faire cela in order to do that;
**je suis allé au marché pour
acheter des légumes** I went to the
market to buy some vegetables; **je
suis là pour t'aider** I'm here to help
you; **c'était juste pour rire!** it was
only meant as a joke!; **pour ainsi
dire** so to speak; ★ **le pour et le
contre** the pros and cons;

pourboire *noun Masc.* tip.

pour cent *noun Masc.* per cent; **dix
pour cent** ten per cent.

pourcentage *noun Masc.*
percentage.

pourquoi *adverb* why; **pourquoi
ont-ils refusé?** why did they
refuse?; **je veux savoir pourquoi**

a

b

c

d

e

f

g

h

i

j

k

l

m

n

o

p

q

r

s

t

u

v

w

x

y

z

I want to know why; **pourquoi pas?** why not?

pourri *adjective* rotten.

pourrir *verb* [2] to go bad.

poursuivre *verb* [75] **1** to chase; **2** to continue.

pourtant *adverb* **1** though; **et pourtant c'est vrai** it's true though; **2** yet; **et pourtant ça aurait pu être bien** and yet it could have been good.

pourvu que *conjunction* (*followed by subjunctive*) **1** providing, as long as; **pourvu que tu reviennes samedi** providing you come back on Saturday; **2** let's hope that; **pourvu que ça dure!** let's hope it lasts!

pousser *verb* [1] **1** to push; **elle a poussé la porte** she pushed the door shut (*or* open); **2 pousser un cri** to let out a cry, to cry out; **3** to grow (*of a child, hair, or a plant*); **mes tomates poussent bien** my tomatoes are growing well; **4 se pousser** to move over; **pousse-toi!** move over!

poussette *noun Fem.* pushchair.

poussière *noun Fem.* dust; ★ **dix euros et des poussières** ten euros something, just over 10 euros.

poutre *noun Fem.* beam.

pouvez *verb* SEE **pouvoir**[1].

pouvoir[1] *verb* [12] can; **je peux être là à dix heures** I can be there at ten; **peux-tu m'aider?** can you help me?; **je ne peux pas l'ouvrir** I can't open it; **ils ne pouvaient pas téléphoner avant** they couldn't phone before; **je n'ai pas pu réserver** I wasn't able to book; **elle aurait pu nous le dire** she could have told us; **puis-je**

parler à Cécile, s'il vous plaît ma I speak to Cécile, please; **tu peux toujours essayer** there's no harm in trying.

pouvoir[2] *noun Masc.* power; **après dix ans au pouvoir** after ten years in power.

pouvons *verb* SEE **pouvoir**[1].

prairie *noun Fem.* meadow.

pratique *noun Fem.* practice; **mettre quelque chose en pratiqu** to put something into practice; **il manque de pratique** he lacks practical experience.
pratique *adjective* practical, convenient; **cet ouvre-boîte n'est pas très pratique** this can opener isn't very practical; **le nouvel appartement est très pratique pour les magasins** the new flat's very handy for the shops.

pratiquement *adverb* practically; **c'est pratiquement fin** it's practically finished.

pratiquer *verb* [1] **1** to play, to do (*sport or hobby*); **je pratique le yoga** I do yoga; **2** to practise; **pendant mon séjour à Lille j'aurai la possibilité de pratiquer mon français** during my stay in Lille I'l be able to practise my French.

pré *noun Masc.* meadow.

préalable *adjective* prior; **une condition préalable** a prior condition.

précaution *noun Fem.* precaution **par précaution** as a precaution; **prendre ses précautions** to take precautions.

228

précédent *adjective* previous; **l'année précédente** the previous year, the year before.

précieux (*Fem.* **précieuse**) *adjective* precious, valuable; **une pierre précieuse** a precious stone; **des renseignements précieux** extremely useful information.

précipice *noun Masc.* precipice.

précipitation *noun Fem.* **1** haste; **2 précipitations** rainfall.

précipiter *verb* [1] **se précipiter** to rush; **ils se sont précipités vers la porte** they rushed for the door.

précis *adjective* **1** precise; **2** accurate; **3** specific.

précisément *adverb* precisely.

préciser *verb* [1] **1** to specify (*details or one's intentions*); **2** to explain; **pouvez-vous préciser comment?** could you explain exactly how?

précision *noun Fem.* **1** precision; **2** detail; **voici quelques précisions sur le voyage** here are some details about the journey.

précuit *adjective* precooked.

préfecture *noun Fem.* prefecture (*France is divided into 96 'départements', which are roughly equivalent to British counties. The administration of each of these is done at the local level from the prefecture*).

préfecture de police *noun Fem.* (local) police headquarters.

préférable *adjective* preferable.

préféré *adjective* favourite; **mon plat préféré** my favourite dish.

préférence *noun Fem.* **1** preference; **2 de préférence** preferably; **de préférence avant le dix mai** preferably before the tenth of May.

préférer *verb* [24] to prefer; **elle préfère le poisson à la viande** she prefers fish to meat.

préfet *noun Masc.* prefect (*official with overall responsibility for running a French territorial department*); **le préfet de police** the chief of police; SEE ALSO **préfecture**.

préjugé *noun Masc.* prejudice.

prélavage *noun Masc.* prewash.

prématuré *adjective* premature.

premier (*Fem.* **première**) *adjective* **1** first; **la première fois** the first time; **c'est la première fois que je le fais** it's the first time I've done it; **Michel, tu passes le premier** Michel, you go first; **le premier juin** the first of June; **2** top; **de première qualité** top quality; **3 au premier étage** on the first floor; **4 en premier** first; **arriver en premier** to arrive first.

première *noun Fem.* **1** première (*of a film or play*); **2 une première mondiale** a world first (*an important event or achievement*); **3 voyager en première** to travel first-class; **4** (*in a French school*) the equivalent of Year 12.

premièrement *adverb* firstly.

premier ministre *noun Masc.* prime minister.

prendre *verb* [64] **1** to take; **prends celui-ci!** take this one!; **prendre un taxi** to take a taxi; **2 prendre**

a
b
c
d
e
f
g
h
i
j
k
l
m
n
o
p
q
r
s
t
u
v
w
x
y
z

quelque chose à quelqu'un to take something from somebody; **qui m'a pris mon vélo?** who's taken my bike?; **3** to have (*something to eat or drink*); **je prends une bière** I'll have a beer; **qu'est-ce que tu prends?** what would you like?; **4** to bring; **est-ce que tu as pris ton parapluie?** did you bring your umbrella?; **5 passer prendre quelqu'un** to pick somebody up; **je passerai te prendre à dix heures** I'll pick you up at ten; ★ **c'est à prendre ou à laisser** take it or leave it.

prénom *noun Masc.* first name.

préparatifs *plural noun Masc.* preparations; **les préparatifs du voyage** the preparations for the journey.

préparation *noun Fem.* preparation, training.

préparer *verb* [1] **1** to prepare; **je vais préparer les légumes** I'll go and prepare the vegetables; **Françoise est en train de préparer le dîner** Françoise is busy making dinner; **as-tu préparé tes affaires pour le matin?** have you got your things ready for the morning?; **on a préparé une petite surprise pour elle** we've got a little surprise ready for her; **des plats préparés** ready-to-eat meals; **2 se préparer** to get ready; **je vais me préparer pour partir** I'll go and get ready to leave.

préposition *noun Fem.* preposition.

près *adverb* **1** nearby; **il y a un village tout près** there's a village nearby; **2 près de** near; **près de la gare** near the station; **près de toi** near you; **près de chez nous** near our house, near where we live; **3 près de** nearly, almost; **près de mille euros** nearly a thousand euros; **4 de près** closely; **regarder quelque chose de près** to look closely at something; **5 à peu près** more or less; **à peu près deux heures** two hours, more or less; **j'ai à peu près fini** I've more or less finished.

prescrire *verb* [38] **1** to prescribe; **2** to stipulate.

présence *noun Fem.* presence.

présent *noun Masc.* **1** present (tense; **au présent** in the present; **2 à présent** now; **à présent je n'ai pas le temps** I haven't got time just now; **présent** *adjective* present (*at an event*); **toute la famille était présente** the whole family was ther

présentateur, **présentatrice** *noun Masc., Fem.* **1** presenter (*of a broadcast or programme*); **2** newsreader.

présentation *noun Fem.* **1** presentation; **2** introduction (*to someone you haven't met before*).

présenter *verb* [1] **1** to introduce; **je vous présente mon père** may I introduce my father?; **Alain, je te présente Raphaël** Alain, this is Raphaël; **2** to present (*a ticket, pass or document*); **il faut présenter votre passeport** you must show your passport; **3 présenter ses excuses** to apologize; **4 se présenter** to go, to come; **en arrivant, présentez-vous à la réception** when you get there (*or* here), go (*or* come) to reception; **5 se**

présenter à quelqu'un to introduce yourself to somebody.

réservatif noun Masc. condom.

réservation noun Fem. **1** preservation; **2** conservation.

réserver verb [1] to protect, to preserve.

résident noun Masc. **1** president; **2** chairman.

résidente noun Fem. **1** president; **2** chairwoman.

résidentielles plural noun Fem. **les présidentielles** the presidential elections.

resque adverb **1** nearly; **j'ai presque fini** I've nearly finished; **2 presque rien** hardly anything; **il ne reste presque rien** there's hardly anything left; **3 presque pas de** hardly any; **il ne reste presque pas de lait** there's hardly any milk left.

resqu'île noun Fem. peninsula.

ressant adjective urgent.

resse noun Fem. **la presse** the press, the newspapers; **que dit la presse?** what do the papers say?

ressé adjective **1 être pressé** to be in a hurry; **2** urgent; **ce n'est pas pressé** it's not urgent; **3 un citron pressé** a fresh lemon juice (served with water and sugar).

resser verb [1] **1** to urge (someone to do something); **2** to squeeze; **presser une orange** to squeeze an orange; **3 ça ne presse pas** there's no hurry; **presser le pas** to hurry (on); **4 se presser** to hurry.

ressing noun Masc. dry cleaner's.

pression noun Fem. **1** pressure; **sous pression** pressurized; **2** press stud; **3** (informal) draught beer; **un demi pression** a half of draught beer.

prestidigitateur, **prestidigitatrice** noun Masc., Fem. conjurer.

prestige noun Masc. prestige.

prestigieux (Fem. prestigieuse) adjective prestigious.

présumer verb [1] to assume, to presume.

prêt noun Masc. loan.

prêt adjective ready; **le dîner est prêt!** dinner's ready!; **être prêt à partir** to be ready to leave.

prêt-à-porter noun Masc. ready-to-wear (clothes).

prétendre verb [3] to claim; **elle prétend que ce n'est pas sa faute** she claims it's not her fault.

prêter verb [1] **1** to lend; **prêter quelque chose à quelqu'un** to lend somebody something; **je te prêterai mon vélo** I'll lend you my bike; **2 prêter attention** to pay attention; **3 prêter l'oreille** to listen.

prétexte noun Masc. excuse.

prêtre noun Masc. priest.

preuve noun Fem. **1** proof; **la preuve, c'est que ...** the proof is that ...; **2 faire preuve de** to show; **ils ont fait preuve de beaucoup d'intelligence** they showed considerable intelligence.

prévenir verb [81] **1** to tell (in advance); **préviens-moi de ta visite** tell me when you're coming; **ils arrivent toujours sans nous**

a
b
c
d
e
f
g
h
i
j
k
l
m
n
o
p
q
r
s
t
u
v
w
x
y
z

prévenir they always arrive without letting us know; **2** to call (*the police or a doctor*); **3** to warn; **je te préviens** I warn you.

prévention *noun Fem.* prevention.

prévision *noun Fem.* forecast, forecasting; **les prévisions météorologiques** the weather forecast.

prévoir *verb* [65] **1** to predict (*an event or change*); **2** to plan (*a journey or an arrangement*); **3 tout a été prévu** everything's been taken care of; **4 le départ est prévu pour huit heures** departure is scheduled for eight o'clock; **5** to allow (*time or money*); **prévoyez 10 euros pour le taxi** allow 10 euros for the taxi.

prier *verb* [1] **1 prier quelqu'un de faire** to ask someone to do; **il m'a prié d'excuser son retard** he asked me to forgive him for being late; **les clients sont priés de ne pas fumer** customers are kindly requested not to smoke; **2 je vous en prie** you're welcome, it's nothing; **'merci beaucoup' – 'je vous en prie'** 'thank you very much' – 'you're welcome'; **3** to pray.

prière *noun Fem.* **1** prayer; **2** request; **'prière de fermer la porte'** 'please close the door'.

primaire *adjective* primary; **l'école primaire** primary school.

prime *noun Fem.* **1** bonus; **2** free gift.

primevère *noun Fem.* primrose.

prince *noun Masc.* prince; **le prince Charles** Prince Charles.

princesse *noun Fem.* princess.

principal (*Masc. plural* **principaux**) *adjective* principal, chief.

principe *noun Masc.* **1** principle; **2 en principe** as a rule; **en principe je rentre à six heures** as a rule I get back at six; **3 en principe** in theory; **en principe tout le monde a été informé** in theory, everybody's been informed.

printanier (*Fem.* **printanière**) *adjective* spring-like (*weather*).

printemps *noun Masc.* spring; **au printemps** in (the) spring.

priorité *noun Fem.* **1** priority; **2** right of way; **'vous n'avez pas la priorité'** 'you do not have right of way' (*sign at a roundabout*).

pris *verb* SEE **prendre**
pris *adjective* **1** busy; **je suis très prise ce matin** I'm very busy this morning; **2** taken; **toutes les places sont prises** all the seats are taken; **3** overcome (*with an emotion or a feeling*); **être pris de panique** to be panic-stricken.

prise *noun Fem.* **1** socket, plug (*for an electric appliance*); **2** capture; **la prise de la Bastille** the storming of the Bastille.

prise de courant *noun Fem.* power point.

prise de sang *noun Fem.* blood test.

prise multiple *noun Fem.* adaptor plug.

prison *noun Fem.* prison.

prisonnier, prisonnière *noun Masc., Fem.* prisoner.

232

privé noun Masc. **1** private sector (*of business or the school system*); **2 en privé** in private, off the record.

privé adjective **1** private; **'propriété privée'** 'private property'; **2** without; **nous sommes privés d'électricité** we are without electricity; **privé de sens** senseless.

priver verb [1] **1 priver quelqu'un de quelque chose** to deprive someone of something; **2 se priver de quelque chose** to do without something.

privilège noun Masc. privilege.

privilégié adjective privileged, special, fortunate.

privilégier verb [1] **1** to favour; **2** to give priority to.

prix noun Masc. **1** price; **quel est le prix des places?** what price are the seats?; **le prix a augmenté** the price has gone up; **2 à tout prix** at all costs; **3** prize; **le premier prix** first prize.

probable adjective likely; **c'est peu probable** it's unlikely.

probablement adverb probably.

problème noun Masc. problem; **sans problème!** no problem!

procédé noun Masc. process.

procès noun Masc. **1** trial; **2** lawsuit.

procession noun Fem. procession.

prochain adjective next; **la prochaine fois** the next time; **le mois prochain** next month; **jeudi prochain** next Thursday; **à la prochaine!** see you soon!

prochainement adverb soon.

proche adjective **1** near; **la ville la plus proche est Valence** the nearest town is Valence; **2** close; **c'est une amie très proche de Julie** she' a very close friend of Julie's; **3 proche de** near; **ils ont acheté une maison proche de Nice** they've bought a house near Nice.

Proche-Orient noun Masc. **le Proche-Orient** the Middle East.

proches plural noun Masc. close family and friends.

procurer verb [1] **se procurer quelque chose** to get something.

producteur, productrice noun Masc., Fem. producer.

production noun Fem. production.

produire verb [26] **1** to produce; **2 se produire** to happen; **ça s'est produit au mois de mai** that happened in May.

produit noun Masc. product; **les produits de beauté** beauty products; **les produits d'entretien** household products; **les produits laitiers** dairy produce; **les produits congelés** frozen foods; **les produits d'exportation** export products.

prof noun Masc. (*informal*) SHORT FOR **professeur** teacher; **notre prof de français** our French teacher.

professeur noun Masc. **1** teacher; **ma sœur est professeur de physique** my sister's a physics teacher; **2** university lecturer; **3** university professor.

profession noun Fem. profession, occupation.

a
b
c
d
e
f
g
h
i
j
k
l
m
n
o
p
q
r
s
t
u
v
w
x
y
z

professionnel (*Fem.* **professionnelle**) *adjective* professional.

profil *noun Masc.* profile.

profit *noun Masc.* **1** profit; **les profits de la société** the company's profits; **2 au profit de** in aid of; **au profit des sans-abri** in aid of the homeless.

profiter *verb* [1] **1 profiter de** to take advantage of (*an opportunity*); **j'ai profité des soldes pour m'acheter un manteau** I took advantage of the sales to buy myself a coat; **2** to make the most of; **profite bien de tes vacances!** make the most of your holiday!; **3 profiter à** to benefit.

profond *adjective* deep; **un trou profond de 3 mètres** a hole three metres deep; **la France profonde** provincial France.

profondément *adverb* deeply, profoundly.

profondeur *noun Fem.* depth; **la piscine a une profondeur de 3 mètres** the swimming pool is 3 metres deep; **étudier quelque chose en profondeur** to study something in depth.

programmateur[1] *noun Masc.* **1** timer; **2** programme selector (*on appliance*).

programmateur[2], **programmatrice** *noun Masc., Fem.* programmer (*on radio, tv*).

programme *noun Masc.* **1** programme; **ce n'est pas au programme** it's not on the programme; **2** program (*for a computer*); **3** syllabus; **le programme de maths** the maths syllabus.

programmer *verb* [1] **1** to schedule; **2** to program (*on a computer*).

programmeur, **programmeuse** *noun Masc., Fem.* (computer) programmer.

progrès *noun Masc.* progress; **les progrès de l'informatique** advances in computer science; **faire des progrès** to make progress.

progresser *verb* [1] **1** to progress; **2** to make progress.

projecteur *noun Masc.* **1** floodlight; **2** spotlight; **3** projector.

projet *noun Masc.* **1** plan; **mes projets pour l'été** my plans for the summer; **2** project; **3** rough draft.

projeter *verb* [48] **1** to throw, to hurl; **le choc l'a projeté de sa voiture** the impact hurled him out of his car; **2** to show (*a film*); **3** to cast (*a shadow*); **4 projeter de faire** to plan to do.

prolongation *noun Fem.* **1** continuation; **2** extension; **3** extra time; **jouer les prolongations** to go into extra time.

prolongé *adjective* lengthy; **une discussion prolongée** a lengthy discussion.

prolonger *verb* [52] **1** to extend; **elle a prolongé son congé de maladie** she's extended her sick leave; **2 se prolonger** to go on; **les discussions se sont prolongées**

jusqu'à 23 h discussions went on till 11 p.m.

promenade *noun Fem.* **1** walk; **faire une promenade** to go for a walk; **une promenade en voiture** a drive; **une promenade à vélo** a bike ride; **une promenade en bateau** a boat trip; **2** promenade (*by the sea*).

promener *verb* [50] **1** promener **un enfant** to take a child for a walk; **promener le chien** to walk the dog; **promener quelque chose** to carry something around; **3 se promener** to go for a walk; **se promener en voiture** to go for a drive; **se promener à vélo** to go for a bike ride.

promesse *noun Fem.* promise; **il m'a fait une promesse** he made me a promise; **tenir sa promesse** to keep your promise.

prometteur (*Fem.* prometteuse) *adjective* promising.

promettre *verb* [11] to promise; **promettre de faire** to promise to do; **il a promis de téléphoner ce soir** he promised to ring this evening; **j'ai promis à ma mère de lui écrire une fois par semaine** I promised my mother I would write to her once a week.

promotion *noun Fem.* **1** special offer; **les fraises sont en promotion cette semaine** strawberries are on special offer this week; **2** promotion (*to a higher job*); **avoir une promotion** to be promoted.

pronom *noun Masc.* pronoun.

prononcer *verb* [61] **1** to pronounce (*a word*); **2** to mention (*a name*), to say (*a word or phrase*); **3** to make (*a speech*); **4 se prononcer pour/contre quelque chose** to declare oneself for/against something.

prononciation *noun Fem.* pronunciation.

propagande *noun Fem.* propaganda.

proportion *noun Fem.* proportion; **en proportion de** in proportion to.

propos *noun Masc.* **1 à propos** by the way; **à propos, as-tu appelé maman?** by the way, did you ring Mum?; **2 à propos de** about; **il n'a rien dit à propos de son père** he said nothing about his father; **3 des propos** remarks.

proposer *verb* [1] **1 proposer quelque chose à quelqu'un** to suggest something to somebody; **je leur ai proposé une petite promenade** I suggested we went for a little walk; **2 proposer quelque chose à quelqu'un** to offer somebody something; **on lui a proposé un poste de technicien** she (*or* he) has been offered a job as a technician.

proposition *noun Fem.* offer.

propre *adjective* **1** (*when it comes after the noun*) clean; **une chemise propre** a clean shirt; **2** (*when it comes before the noun*) own; **ma propre voiture** my own car; **leurs propres enfants** their own children.

proprement *adverb* **1** properly; **mange proprement!** eat properly!; **2 à proprement parler** strictly speaking.

propreté *noun Fem.* cleanliness.

propriétaire *noun Masc. & Fem.* **1** owner (*usually of a building or a business*); **2** landlord, landlady.

propriété *noun Fem.* **1** property; **propriété privée** private property; **2** ownership.

prospectus *noun Masc.* leaflet.

prospère *adjective* prosperous.

prostituée *noun Fem.* prostitute.

protecteur, protectrice *noun Masc., Fem.* protector.
protecteur (*Fem.* **protectrice**) *adjective* protective; **une crème protectrice** protective cream.

protection *noun Fem.* protection; **des lunettes de protection** protective goggles.

protéger *verb* [15] to protect; **pour protéger l'environnement** to protect the environment; **se protéger du soleil** to protect yourself from the sun.

protestant, protestante *noun Masc., Fem., adjective* Protestant.

protestation *noun Fem.* protest.

protester *verb* [1] to protest; **protester contre quelque chose** to protest against something.

prouver *verb* [1] to prove.

provenance *noun Fem.* origin; **du fromage en provenance de France** cheese from France; **un passager en provenance de**

Madrid a passenger arriving from Madrid.

provençal (*plural* **provençaux**) *adjective* from Provence, Provença[l]

proverbe *noun Masc.* proverb.

province *noun Fem.* province; **en province** in the provinces; **une vill[e] de province** a provincial town.

provision *noun Fem.* **1** supply; **nous avons fait provision de boi[s]** we've laid in a supply of wood; **2 de[s] provisions** food; **maman est parti[e] prendre des provisions** Mum's gone off shopping for food.

provisoire *adjective* temporary.

provocateur, provocatrice *noun Masc., Fem.* agitator.
provocateur (*Fem.* **provocatrice**) *adjective* provocative.

provoquer *verb* [1] **1** to cause; **provoquer un accident** to cause a[n] accident; **provoquer une discussion** to spark off a discussion; **2 provoquer quelqu'u[n]** to provoke somebody.

proximité *noun Fem.* nearness; **à proximité de** near.

prudemment *adjective* carefully[.]

prudence *noun Fem.* caution; **conduisez avec prudence!** drive carefully!

prudent *adjective* **1** careful; **soye[z] prudents par mauvais temps!** be[ ]careful in bad weather!; **2** wise; **il est plus prudent de réserver** it's [ ] wiser to book.

prune *noun Fem.* plum.

pruneau (*plural* **pruneaux**) *nou[n]* *Masc.* prune.

runier *noun Masc.* plum tree.

sychanalyste *noun Masc. & Fem.* psychoanalyst.

sychiatre *noun Masc. & Fem.* psychiatrist.

sychologie *noun Fem.* psychology.

sychologique *adjective* psychological.

sychologue *noun Masc. & Fem.* psychologist.

u *verb* SEE **pouvoir**[1].

ub *noun Fem.* (*informal*) SHORT FOR **publicité** advert.

ublic *noun Masc.* **1** public; **en public** in public; **ouvert au public** open to the public; **'interdit au public'** 'no admission'; **2** audience, spectators; **pour un public jeune** for a young audience; **3** fans (*of a performer*).

public (*Fem.* **publique**) *adjective* public; **dans un lieu public** in a public place; **une école publique** a state school.

ublicitaire *adjective* **1** advertising; **une campagne publicitaire** an advertising campaign; **2** promotional (*material*).

ublicité *noun Fem.* **1** advertising; **elle travaille dans la publicité** she works in advertising; **faire de la publicité** to advertise; **2** advertisement, ad (*in a magazine, a newspaper, on television, or at the cinema*).

ublier *verb* [1] to publish.

uce *noun Fem.* **1 une puce électronique** a microchip; **une carte à puce** a smart card; **2** flea; **un marché aux puces** a fleamarket.

puer *verb* [1] to stink.

puis *adverb* then; **nous allons à Cannes, puis à Nice** we're going to Cannes, then Nice.

puisque, puisqu' (*before a vowel or silent 'h'*) *conjunction* since; **puisqu'il pleut je prendrai le bus** since it's raining I'll take the bus.

puissance *noun Fem.* power; **un moteur d'une forte puissance** a high-power engine; **une puissance étrangère** a foreign power.

puissant *adjective* powerful, strong.

puits *noun Masc.* well.

pull, pull-over *noun Masc.* jumper.

pulvérisateur *noun Masc.* spray.

punaise *noun Fem.* **1** drawing-pin; **2** bug.

punir *verb* [2] to punish.

punition *noun Fem.* punishment.

pur *adjective* **1** pure; **un shampooing très doux, très pur** an ultra-mild, ultra-pure shampoo; **un croissant pur beurre** an all-butter croissant; **2** sheer, total; **c'est de la folie pure** it's sheer madness.

purée *noun Fem.* mashed potatoes.

puzzle *noun Masc.* jigsaw puzzle.

PV *noun Masc.* SHORT FOR **procès verbal** parking ticket.

pyjama *noun Masc.* (pair of) pyjamas; **où est mon pyjama?** where are my pyjamas?; **un pyjama propre** a clean pair of pyjamas.

pyramide *noun Fem.* pyramid.

Pyrénées *plural noun Fem.* Pyrenees.

a
b
c
d
e
f
g
h
i
j
k
l
m
n
o
p
q
r
s
t
u
v
w
x
y
z

Qq

qu'est-ce que SEE **que**.

qu'est-ce qui SEE **qui**.

quai *noun Masc.* **1** platform; **le train à destination de Paris va arriver au quai numéro trois** the train for Paris is about to arrive at platform number three; **2** quay.

qualifié *adjective* **1** qualified; **2** skilled.

qualifier *verb* [1] to qualify.

qualité *noun Fem.* quality; **des fruits de première qualité** top quality fruit.

quand *conjunction, adverb* when; **quand est-ce que ton frère arrive?** when is your brother arriving?; **quand tu auras dix-sept ans, tu pourras apprendre à conduire** when you're seventeen you'll be able to learn to drive.

quand même *adverb* all the same; **il pleut mais je vais sortir quand même** it's raining but I'm going to go out all the same; **quand même!** honestly!

quant à *preposition* as for; **quant à moi, je reste** as for me, I'm staying here.

quantité *noun Fem.* amount.

quarantaine *noun Fem.* **1** about forty; **une quarantaine de personnes** about forty people; **j'approche la quarantaine** I'll soon be forty; **2** quarantine.

quarante *number* forty.

quart *noun Masc.* **1** (*in time expressions*) quarter; **un quart d'heure** a quarter of an hour; **dix heures et quart** quarter past ten; **2** quarter; **le quart du gâteau** a quarter of the cake; **un quart d'eau minérale** a quarter-litre bottle of mineral water; **trois quarts** three quarters; **les trois quarts du temp** most of the time.

quart de finale *noun Masc.* quarter-final.

quartier *noun Masc.* area (*of a town*); **un quartier résidentiel** a residential area; **les gens du quartier** the local people.

quartier général *Masc.* headquarters.

quartz *noun Masc.* quartz.

quasi *adverb* almost; **quasi parfai** almost perfect.

quasiment *adverb* **1** practically; **c'est quasiment neuf** it's practically new; **2** **quasiment jamais** hardly ever; **il n'est quasiment jamais chez lui** he's hardly ever at home.

quatorze *number* fourteen; **Célin a quatorze ans** Céline's fourteen; **l quatorze juin** the fourteenth of June.

quatre *number* four; **Louis a quatre ans** Louis is four; **le quatr mars** the fourth of March.

quatre-vingt-dix *number* ninety; **quatre-vingt-dix-neuf** ninety-nine.

quatre-vingts *number* eighty; **quatre-vingts personnes** eighty people; **quatre-vingt-trois** eighty-three (*note that the 's' is dropped when another number is added*); **quatre-vingt-seize** ninety-six.

quatrième *noun Fem.* (*in a French school*) the equivalent of Year 9.
quatrième *noun Masc.* **au quatrième** on the fourth floor.
quatrième *adjective* fourth.

que *conjunction, pronoun, adverb*
1 that (*often left out in English*); **elle dit que c'est vrai** she says (that) it's true; **je sais qu'il y habite** I know he lives there; **je veux que tu sois heureux** I want you to be happy; **2** whether; **qu'ils arrivent demain ou mardi, n'importe** whether they come tomorrow or on Tuesday, it doesn't matter; **3 que tout le monde se lève!** everybody stand up!; **4 plus ...que** more ...than; **elle est plus grande que Marie** she's taller than Marie; **5 aussi ...que** as ...as; **elle est aussi grande que moi** she's as tall as me; **6 ne ...que** only; **je n'ai que dix euros** I've only got ten euros; **7** that, which, whom (*often left out in English*); **le livre que je lis** the book (that) I'm reading; **la chemise qu'il a achetée** the shirt (which) he's bought; **8** what; **que veut-il?** what does he want?; **je ne sais pas ce qu'il veut** I don't know what he wants; **9 qu'est-ce que ...?** what ...?; **qu'est-ce que tu as trouvé?** what have you found?; **qu'est-ce que c'est?** what's that?; **qu'est-ce qu'il y a?** what's the matter?; **qu'est-ce qu'elle a?** what's the matter with her?; **10** how (*in an*

exclamation); **que tu as grandi!** how you've grown!

Québec *noun Masc.* **le Québec** Quebec.

québécois *noun Masc.* Canadian French (*language*).
québécois *adjective* from Quebec, Quebecker.

Québécois, Québécoise *noun Masc., Fem.* French Canadian, Quebecker; **les Québécois** the French Canadians, the Quebeckers.

quel, quelle *adjective* **1** (*in a question*) what, which; **quel livre?** which book?; **quelle voiture?** which car?; **quelle heure est-il?** what time is it?; **quel âge as-tu?** how old are you?; **dans quels pays?** in which countries?; **pour quelles raisons?** for what reasons?; **2** (*in an exclamation*) what; **quel beau temps!** what lovely weather!; **quelle coïncidence!** what a coincidence!; **quelle horreur!** how dreadful!

quelconque *adjective* any; **si tu as un problème quelconque** if you have any sort of a problem; **si pour une raison quelconque** if for any reason.

quelle *adjective* SEE **quel**.

quelque chose *pronoun*
1 something; **il faut manger quelque chose, Claire** you must eat something, Claire; **il y a quelque chose de bizarre** there's something strange; **voulez-vous boire quelque chose?** would you like something to drink?; **2** anything; **est-ce que tu as vu quelque chose?** did you see anything?

a
b
c
d
e
f
g
h
i
j
k
l
m
n
o
p
q
r
s
t
u
v
w
x
y
z

quelquefois *adverb* sometimes.

quelque part *adverb*

1 somewhere; **quelque part dans le jardin** somewhere in the garden; 2 anywhere; **est-ce que tu as vu mes lunettes quelque part?** have you seen my glasses anywhere?

quelques *plural adjective* 1 some; **je vais te donner quelques cerises** I'll give you some cherries; 2 a few; **il reste quelques fraises** there are a few strawberries left; **elle est partie pour quelques jours** she's gone away for a few days.

quelqu'un *pronoun* 1 somebody; **quelqu'un a appelé pour toi** somebody rang for you; **quelqu'un d'autre** somebody else; 2 anybody; **il y a quelqu'un?** is there anybody there?

quelques-uns, **quelques-unes** *plural pronoun* some; **quelques-uns des enfants** some of the children.

quels, **quelles** *adjective* SEE **quel**.

querelle *noun Fem.* quarrel.

question *noun Fem.* 1 question; **poser une question à quelqu'un** to ask somebody a question; **elle n'a pas répondu à mes questions** she didn't answer my questions; 2 matter, question; **c'est une question de goût** it's a matter of taste; **c'est hors de question** it's out of the question; **pas question!** no way!

questionnaire *noun Masc.* questionnaire.

questionner *verb* [1] to question.

queue *noun Fem.* 1 tail; **la queue d** **chat** the cat's tail; 2 queue; **faire la queue** to queue; 3 **la queue du train** the rear of the train; 4 stalk (**a** *a flower or a fruit*).

queue de cheval *noun Fem.* ponytail.

qui *pronoun* 1 who; **qui a fermé la porte?** who closed the door?; **qui voulez-vous voir?** who do you war to see?; **la personne qui vous a écrit n'est pas là aujourd'hui** the person who wrote to you is not her today; 2 that; **prends la casserole qui est sur l'évier** take the pan that's on the sink; 3 à qui? whose? **à qui est ce pull?** whose is this jumper?; 4 **à qui parles-tu?** who ar you talking to?; 5 **qu'est-ce qui** ... what ...?; **qu'est-ce qui t'amène?** what brings you here?

quincaillerie *noun Fem.* hardwar shop.

quinzaine *noun Fem.* 1 about fifteen; **une quinzaine d'enfants** about fifteen children; 2 **une quinzaine de jours** a fortnight; **dans une quinzaine** two weeks from now.

quinze *number* 1 fifteen; **Marise a** **quinze ans** Marise is fifteen; **le quinze juillet** the fifteenth of July; 2 **quinze jours** two weeks; **tous le quinze jours** every two weeks.

quitter *verb* [1] 1 to leave; **je quitte** **le bureau à cinq heures** I leave th office at five; **j'ai quitté l'école à seize ans** I left school at sixteen; 2 **se quitter** to part; 3 **ne quittez pas** hold the line please (*on the telephone*).

uoi *pronoun* **1** what; **quoi encore?** what now?; **tu es sourd ou quoi?** are you deaf or what?; **à quoi penses-tu?** what are you thinking about?; **pour quoi faire?** what for?; **à quoi bon continuer?** what's the point in going on?; **il n'y a pas de quoi se fâcher** there's no reason to get angry; **il n'y a pas de quoi** don't mention it; **2** which; **après quoi, il est parti** after which, he left.

uoique *conjunction* although, though; **quoique petit, il est fort** although he's small he's strong.

uotidien (*Fem.* **quotidienne**) *adjective* daily; **la vie quotidienne** daily life; **sa visite quotidienne** her daily visit.

quotidien *noun Masc.* daily newspaper.

uotidiennement *adverb* daily; **les livraisons s'effectuent quotidiennement** deliveries are made daily.

Rr

abais *noun Masc.* discount; **au rabais** at a discount.

accompagner *verb* [1] **raccompagner quelqu'un** to see somebody home.

accourci *noun Masc.* short cut.

accourcir *verb* [2] to shorten.

accrocher *verb* [1] to hang up (*telephone*).

race *noun Fem.* **1** race; **la race humaine** the human race; **2** breed; **un chien de race** a pedigree dog.

racheter *verb* [16] **1** to buy more; **il faut racheter du pain** we'll have to buy more bread; **2 il m'a racheté ma voiture** he bought my car off me.

racine *noun Fem.* root.

raciste *noun Masc. & Fem.*, *adjective* racist; **des propos racistes** racist remarks.

racler *verb* [1] to scrape.

raconter *verb* [1] to tell (*a story*); **raconte-nous ce qui s'est passé** tell us what happened.

radar *noun Masc.* radar.

radeau (*plural* **radeaux**) *noun Masc.* raft.

radiateur *noun Masc.* radiator.

radio *noun Fem.* **1** radio; **je l'ai entendu à la radio** I heard it on the radio; **2** X-ray; **passer une radio** to have an X-ray.

radiocassette *noun Masc. OR Fem.* radio cassette player.

radio-réveil *noun Masc.* clock radio.

radis *noun Masc.* radish.

rafale *noun Fem.* gust (*of wind or rain*), flurry (*of snow*).

raffoler *verb* [1] **raffoler de** to be mad about; **je ne raffole pas des huîtres** I'm not mad about oysters.

rafraîchir *verb* [2] **1 le temps se rafraîchit** the weather's getting cooler; **2** to cool (somebody) down.

rafraîchissement *noun Masc.* **1** refreshment; **2** drop in temperature.

a
b
c
d
e
f
g
h
i
j
k
l
m
n
o
p
q
r
s
t
u
v
w
x
y
z

rage noun Fem. **1** rabies; **2 une rage de dents** raging toothache.

ragoût noun Masc. stew.

raide adjective **1** stiff (body, arm, leg); **2** straight (hair); **3 une pente raide** a steep slope.

raie noun Fem. **1** parting (in your hair); **2** skate (the fish).

rail noun Masc. rail (for trains); ★ **remettre quelque chose sur les rails** to put something back on the right track.

raisin noun Masc. grapes; **j'ai acheté du raisin noir** I bought some black grapes; **une grappe de raisin** a bunch of grapes; **un grain de raisin** a grape; **le jus de raisin** grape juice.

raisin de Corinthe noun Masc. currant.

raisin sec noun Masc. raisin.

raison noun Fem. **1** reason; **pour cette raison** for this reason; **pour raisons de santé** for health reasons; **2 avoir raison** to be right; **oui, tu as raison** yes, you're right.

raisonnable adjective sensible.

raisonnement noun Masc. reasoning.

rajouter verb [1] to add; **on peut rajouter de l'eau si on veut** you can add water if you want.

ralentir verb [2] to slow down.

ralentissement noun Masc. slowing down.

ralentisseur noun Masc. speed bump.

râler verb [1] (informal) to moan; **arrête de râler!** stop moaning!

rallonge noun Fem. **1** extension cord; **2** extra leaf (for a table).

ramasser verb [1] **1** to pick up; **est-ce que tu peux ramasser tou ces papiers, s'il te plaît** can you pick up all these papers please; **2 t** pick (fruit); **ils ont déjà ramassé les framboises** they've already picked the raspberries; **3** to collec **on va ramasser des châtaignes dans les bois** we're going to go ar collect chestnuts in the woods; **4** collect in (books, homework); **Anne, veux-tu ramasser tous les cahiers?** Anne, would you collect all the exercise books?

rame noun Fem. **1** oar; **2 une ram de métro** an underground train.

rameau (plural **rameaux**) noun Masc. branch; **le dimanche des Rameaux** Palm Sunday.

ramener verb [50] **1 ramener quelqu'un (en voiture)** to give somebody a lift home; **tu veux qu je te ramène?** do you want a lift home?; **elle m'a ramené en voitur** she gave me a lift back; **2** to take back; **je dois ramener les livres la bibliothèque** I must take these books back to the library.

ramer verb [1] to row.

rampe noun Fem. **1** banister; **2** ramp.

rançon noun Fem. ransom.

rancune noun Fem. resentment, grudge.

randonnée noun Fem. hike, walk **faire une randonnée pédestre** to go on a hike (on public footpaths); **o a fait une randonnée de vingt**

kilomètres we did a twenty-kilometre walk; **faire une randonnée à cheval** to go pony-trekking; **une randonnée à vélo** a long-distance bike ride.

randonneur, randonneuse *noun Masc., Fem.* **1** hiker, walker, rambler; **2** touring cyclist.

rang *noun Masc.* row; **au cinquième rang** in the fifth row.

rangée *noun Fem.* row; **une rangée de maisons** a row of houses.

ranger *verb* [52] **1** to put away; **ranger la vaisselle** to put away the dishes; **2** to tidy; **je vais ranger ma chambre** I'm going to tidy my room; **3** to arrange; **il range ses livres par ordre alphabétique** he arranges his books alphabetically.

râper *verb* [1] to grate; **le fromage râpé** grated cheese.

rapide *noun Masc.* express train. **rapide** *adjective* quick; **prends le métro, c'est plus rapide** take the underground, it's quicker.

rapidement *adverb* quickly, rapidly.

rappel *noun Masc.* **1** reminder (*for a bill*); **'dernier rappel'** 'final demand'; **2** booster (*vaccination*).

rappeler *verb* [18] **1** to remind; **rappelle-moi de passer par la banque** remind me to go to the bank; **le paysage me rappelle la France** the countryside reminds me of France; **2** to ring back (*on the telephone*); **il va te rappeler dans une heure** he'll ring you back in a hour; **3 se rappeler** to remember; **je ne me rappelle plus** I can't

remember; **je me rappelle qu'elle avait les cheveux longs** I remember she had long hair.

rapport *noun Masc.* **1** report; **un rapport officiel** an official report; **2** connection; **je ne vois pas le rapport** I don't see the connection; **3 être en rapport avec quelqu'un** to be in touch with someone; **4 avoir de bons/mauvais rapports avec quelqu'un** to be on good/bad relations with someone; **5 par rapport à** compared with; **il a fait très beau par rapport à l'année dernière** the weather's been very good compared with last year.

rapporter *verb* [1] **1** to bring back; **est-ce que tu peux le rapporter demain?** can you bring it back tomorrow?; **2** to bring in; **son travail ne rapporte pas beaucoup** her job doesn't bring in much money.

rapprocher *verb* [1] **1** to move (something) closer; **peux-tu rapprocher la lampe de ma chaise?** can you move the lamp closer to my chair?; **2** to bring together (*different people*); **des efforts pour rapprocher les deux pays** efforts to bring the two countries together; **3 se rapprocher** to come (*or* go) closer; **elle s'est rapprochée de la table** she moved closer to the table.

raquette *noun Fem.* **1** racket (*for tennis*); **2** bat (*for ping-pong*).

rare *adjective* rare; **une fleur rare** a rare flower; **il est rare qu'elle arrive à l'heure** she hardly ever arrives on time.

rarement *adverb* rarely.

ras *adjective* **1** short (*hair or fur*); **il a les cheveux coupés ras** his hair is cut short; **2 en rase campagne** in open country; **3 au ras de l'eau/du sol** at water/ground level; ★ **j'en ai ras le bol!** (*informal*) I'm fed up!

raser *verb* [1] **1** to shave, to shave off; **il a rasé sa barbe** he's shaved off his beard; **la mousse à raser** shaving foam; **2 se raser** to shave; **se raser les jambes** to shave your legs.

ras-le-cou *noun Masc.* crew-neck sweater.

rasoir *noun Masc.* razor.

rassemblement *noun Masc.* meeting, rally.

rassembler *verb* [1] to gather (together); **j'ai rassemblé les enfants près de l'entrée** I gathered all the children together by the main entrance; **tout le village s'est rassemblé pour l'écouter** the whole village gathered to listen to him.

rassis *adjective* **du pain rassis** stale bread.

rassurer *verb* [1] **1** to reassure; **ah, cela me rassure!** oh, that sets my mind at rest!; **2 rassure-toi** don't worry.

rat *noun Masc.* rat.

râteau (*plural* **râteaux**) *noun Masc.* rake.

rater *verb* [1] **1** to fail; **Sophie a raté son permis** Sophie failed her driving test; **2** to miss; **j'ai raté mon train** I've missed my train.

rationner *verb* [1] to ration.

RATP *noun Fem.* SHORT FOR **Régie autonome des transports parisiens** (*Paris city-transport system*).

rattacher *verb* [1] **1** to (re)fasten; **rattache ta ceinture** (re)fasten your seat-belt; **2** to attach; **plus rien ne me rattache ici** I no longer have any ties here.

rattraper *verb* [1] **1** to catch up with (*a person*); **ne t'inquiète pas, ils nous rattraperont** don't worry, they'll catch up with us; **2** to make up for (*lost time*); **3 se rattraper** to make up for it; **j'ai très peu joué cet été mais je vais me rattraper** I've played very little this summer but I'll make up for it.

rature *noun Fem.* crossing-out.

ravi *adjective* delighted; **je suis ravi de vous voir** I'm delighted to see you.

ravisseur, ravisseuse *noun Masc., Fem.* kidnapper.

rayé *adjective* striped (*fabric*).

rayer *verb* [59] **1** to cross out (*a mistake*); **j'ai rayé ton nom de la liste** I crossed your name off the list; **2** to scratch (*a surface*).

rayon *noun Masc.* **1** shelf; **un rayon pour mes livres** a shelf for my books; **2** department (*in a department store*); section (*in a supermarket*); **au rayon fraîcheur** in the chilled foods section; **3** ray; **un rayon de soleil** a ray of sunshine; **un rayon laser** a laser beam; **les rayons X** X-rays; **4** radius.

rayure *noun Fem.* **1** stripe; **2** scratch

C noun Masc. SHORT FOR **rez-de-chaussée** ground floor.

réacteur noun Masc. **1** un réacteur nucléaire a nuclear reactor; **2** jet engine.

réaction noun Fem. reaction.

réagir verb [2] to react; **elle n'a pas réagi** she didn't react.

réalisateur, réalisatrice noun Masc., Fem. director (of a film or TV programme).

réalisation noun Fem. **1** carrying out (of a plan or project); **2** production (of a film or a radio/TV programme).

réaliser verb [1] **1** to carry out (a project); **2** to fulfil; **réaliser un rêve** to fulfil a dream; **3** to make (a film); **4** to realize.

réaliste adjective realistic.

réalité noun Fem. reality; **en réalité** in reality.

réanimation noun Fem. resuscitation; **(service de) réanimation** intensive care (unit).

rebelle noun Masc. & Fem. rebel.

rebellion noun Fem. rebellion.

rebondir verb [2] to bounce.

rebord noun Masc. **1** le rebord de la fenêtre the window ledge; **2** edge; **le rebord de la baignoire** the edge of the bath.

récemment adverb recently.

récent adjective recent.

réception noun Fem. **1** reception desk; **demandez la clé à la réception** ask for the key at the reception desk; **2** reception (party).

réceptionniste noun Masc. & Fem. receptionist.

recette noun Fem. recipe; **la recette du gâteau** the recipe for the cake.

recevoir verb [66] **1** to receive, to get; **j'ai reçu ta lettre** I got your letter; **2** to welcome (a visitor or guest); **3** to see (a patient or client); **le dentiste reçoit entre 9h et 17h** the dentist sees patients between 9 a.m. and 5 p.m.; **4** être reçu à un examen to pass an exam; **elle a été reçue première à l'examen** she came top in the exam.

rechange noun Masc. de rechange spare; **une pièce de rechange** a spare part.

recharge noun Fem. refill.

réchaud noun Masc. stove.

réchauffer verb [1] **1** to warm up (food); **peux-tu mettre la soupe à réchauffer?** can you put the soup on to warm?; **2** to warm (hands or feet); **3** se réchauffer to get warm; **va te réchauffer près du feu** go and get warm by the fire.

recherche noun Fem. **1** research; **2** être à la recherche de quelque chose** to be looking for something; **je suis à la recherche d'un logement** I'm looking for somewhere to live.

rechercher verb [1] to look for; **la police le recherche** the police are looking for him; **elle recherche un travail plus flexible** she's looking for a more flexible job.

récipient noun Masc. container.

réciproque adjective mutual.

245

récit *noun Masc.* story; **il nous a fait le récit de son voyage** he told us all about his journey.

réciter *verb* [1] to recite.

réclamation *noun Fem.* claim (*for compensation*).

réclame *noun Fem.*
1 advertisement; **une réclame pour le nouveau modèle** an advertisement for the new model; **2 en réclame** on (special) offer; **le jambon est en réclame cette semaine** the ham is on special offer this week.

réclamer *verb* [1] to demand; **ils réclament trois jours de plus de vacances** they're demanding three more days' holiday.

récolte *noun Fem.* **1** harvest; **2** crop; **faire la récolte** to get the harvest in.

récolter *verb* [1] **1** to harvest; **récolter le blé** to harvest the wheat; **2** to collect (*money*); **3** (*informal*) to get; **récolter une amende** to get a fine.

recommandation *noun Fem.* recommendation.

recommandé *adjective* registered; **une lettre recommandée** a registered letter; **je voudrais l'envoyer en recommandé** I'd like to send it by registered post.

recommander *verb* [1] **1** to advise; **je te recommande de ne rien dire** I advise you to say nothing; **2** to recommend.

recommencer *verb* [61] **1** to start again; **j'ai recommencé ma**

lettre I started my letter again; **il a recommencé à neiger** it's started snowing again; **2** to do it again; **si tu ne fais pas attention, elle va recommencer** if you don't watch out, she'll do it again; **ça recommence!** here we go again!

récompense *noun Fem.* reward.

récompenser *verb* [1] to reward.

réconcilier *verb* [1] **se réconcilier avec quelqu'un** to make it up with somebody.

réconfortant *adjective* comforting.

reconnaissable *adjective* recognizable.

reconnaissance *noun Fem.*
1 gratitude; **en reconnaissance de** in appreciation of; **2** recognition.

reconnaissant *adjective* grateful.

reconnaître *verb* [27] **1** to recognize; **je ne l'ai pas reconnu** I didn't recognize her; **je l'ai reconnu à sa voix** I recognized him by his voice; **2** to admit; **il faut reconnaître que c'est difficile** it must be admitted that it's difficult; **elle reconnaît qu'elle a menti** she admits she lied.

reconstruire *verb* [26] to rebuild.

recopier *verb* [1] to copy out.

record *noun Masc.* record; **un record mondial** a world record; **battre un record** to break a record.

recouvrir *verb* [30] to cover.

récréation *noun Fem.* break; **la cour de récréation** the playground.

rectangle *noun Masc.* rectangle.

ectangulaire *adjective* rectangular.

ectifier *verb* [1] to correct.

eçu *noun Masc.* receipt.

reçu *verb* SEE **recevoir**.

ecueil *noun Masc.* collection (*of poems or essays*).

eculer *verb* [1] **1** to move back; **elle a reculé de quelques pas** she moved back a few steps; **2** to reverse (*in a car*); **3 reculer la date d'une réunion** to postpone a meeting.

eculons *in phrase* **à reculons** backwards.

ecupérer *verb* [24] **1** to get back; **je vais chez Brigitte pour récupérer le bouquin que je lui ai prêté** I'm going round to Brigitte's to get back the book I lent her; **2** to recover (*from an illness*).

ecycler *verb* [1] to recycle.

edaction *noun Fem.* essay.

edemander *verb* [1] **1** to ask again; **tu devrais redemander** you should ask again; **2** to ask for more; **il faut qu'on redemande des cahiers** we'll have to ask for more exercise books.

edescendre *verb* [3] **1** to go (or come) back down; **elle est redescendue à la cave** she went back down to the cellar; **je monte à Glasgow demain et je redescends lundi** I'm going up to Glasgow tomorrow and I'm coming back down on Monday; **2** to bring or take back down; **est-ce que tu peux redescendre ma valise?** can you bring my suitcase back down?

rédiger *verb* [52] to write (*an article*), to write up (*notes*).

redonner *verb* [1] to give again; **je leur ai redonné mon adresse** I gave them my address again; **est-ce que je te redonne un peu de salade?** can I give you a bit more salad?

redoubler *verb* [1] to repeat a year (*at school*).

redresser *verb* [1] **1** to straighten up; **2** to put right; **3 se redresser** to recover.

réduction *noun Fem.* **1** reduction; **une réduction du nombre d'étudiants** a reduction in the number of students; **2** (price) reduction; **une réduction de 20%** a 20% reduction.

réduire *verb* [68] to cut (*prices*); **réduire les impôts** to cut taxes; **des vêtements à prix réduits** cut-price clothing.

rééducation *noun Fem.* physiotherapy.

réel (*Fem.* **réelle**) *adjective* real.

réellement *adverb* really.

refaire *verb* [10] **1** to redo; **je dois refaire mon devoir de maths** I have to redo my maths homework; **c'est tout à refaire** it has to be completely redone; **il ne faut pas refaire la même erreur** we mustn't make the same mistake again; **2** to make more; **elle est en train de refaire du café** she's making some more coffee.

référence *noun Fem.* reference; **faire référence à quelque chose** to refer to something.

a
b
c
d
e
f
g
h
i
j
k
l
m
n
o
p
q
r
s
t
u
v
w
x
y
z

réfléchi *adjective* **1** reflexive
(*verb*); **2** considered (*decision*).

réfléchir *verb* [2] to think; **il faut
bien réfléchir avant d'accepter**
you should think carefully before
accepting; **j'ai réfléchi au
problème** I've thought about the
problem.

reflet *noun Masc.* **1** reflection; **2 des
cheveux aux reflets blonds** hair
with blond highlights.

refléter *verb* [24] to reflect.

réflexe *noun Masc., adjective* reflex.

réflexion *noun Fem.* **1** thought;
2 comment; **il m'a fait des
réflexions désagréables** he made
some nasty comments to me.

refrain *noun Masc.* chorus.

réfrigérateur *noun Masc.*
refrigerator.

refroidir *verb* [2] to cool down.

refroidissement *noun Masc.*
drop in temperature.

refuge *noun Masc.* **1** mountain hut
(*for climbers*); **2** animal sanctuary;
3 traffic island; **4** refuge.

réfugié, réfugiée *noun Masc.,
Fem.* refugee.

réfugier *verb* [1] **se réfugier** to take
shelter, to take refuge.

refus *noun Masc.* refusal; ★ **ce n'est
pas de refus** I wouldn't say no;
'veux-tu boire quelque chose?' –
'ce n'est pas de refus' 'would you
like a drink?' – 'I wouldn't say no'.

refuser *verb* [1] **1** to refuse; **refuser
de faire** to refuse to do; **elle a
refusé de répondre** she refused to
answer; **2** to turn down; **ils ont**

refusé sa candidature they turne
him down for the job.

regagner *verb* [1] **nous avons
regagné nos places** we went bac
to our seats.

régal *noun Masc.* feast; **ça a été u
véritable régal** it was a real feast.

régaler *verb* [1] **on s'est vraimen
régalé!** the food was absolutely
wonderful!

regard *noun Masc.* look.

regarder *verb* [1] **1** to look at; **je
vais regarder la carte** I'll look at
the map; **2** to watch; **regarder la
télé** to watch telly; **veux-tu
regarder le film?** do you want to
watch the film?; **3** to look; **regarde
par la fenêtre** to look out of the
window; **regarde!** look!; **4** to
concern; **cela ne nous regarde pa**
that doesn't concern us; **cela ne le
regarde pas** that's none of his
business.

régate *noun Fem.* regatta.

régime *noun Masc.* **1** diet; **un
régime sans sel** a salt-free diet; **je
fais un régime** I'm on a diet; **2 un
régime de bananes** a bunch of
bananas; **3** régime.

région *noun Fem.* region; **les vins
de la région** the local wines.

régional (*Masc. plural* régionaux)
adjective regional.

registre *noun Masc.* register.

réglable *adjective* adjustable.

règle *noun Fem.* **1** ruler; **2** rule;
selon les règles according to the
rules; **les règles de sécurité** the
safety regulations; **en règle
générale** as a general rule; **3 en**

règle in order (valid); **4 les règles** ...eriod (menstruation); **j'ai mes règles** I've got my period.

règlement noun Masc. regulations.

régler verb [24] **1** to pay (a debt or a bill); **vous réglez comment, monsieur?** how would you like to pay, sir?; **2** to sort out (details or a problem); **3** to adjust; **on peut régler la hauteur** you can adjust the height.

réglisse noun Fem. liquorice.

règne noun Masc. reign.

régner verb [24] to reign.

regret noun Masc. regret; **avec/sans regret** with/without regret; **mille regrets** I'm terribly sorry.

regretter verb [1] **1** to be sorry; **je regrette** I'm sorry; **nous regrettons beaucoup de partir** we're very sorry to be leaving; **2** to regret; **elles regrettent avoir quitté Paris** they regret having left Paris; **je ne regrette rien** I have no regrets; **3** to miss; **je regrette la vie à Paris** I miss the Parisian way of life.

regrouper verb [1] **1** to group together; **les débutants sont regroupés ensemble** beginners are grouped together; **2 se regrouper** to regroup; **les enfants se sont regroupés autour d'elle** the children gathered around her.

régularité noun Fem. regularity.

régulier (Fem. **régulière**) adjective **1** regular; **à intervalles réguliers** at regular intervals; **2 vols réguliers à New York** scheduled flights to New York.

régulièrement adverb regularly.

rein noun Masc. **1** kidney; **2 les reins** the back; **j'ai mal aux reins** I've got back-ache.

reine noun Fem. queen; **la reine Elisabeth** Queen Elizabeth.

reine-claude noun Fem. greengage.

rejeter verb [48] to reject.

rejoindre verb [49] **1** to meet up with; **je vous rejoins au bar** I'll meet you in the bar; **2** to join (other people, a group, or a movement); **3 se rejoindre** to meet up; **alors on se rejoint à onze heures?** so shall we meet up at eleven?; **4 se rejoindre** to merge (motorways, lanes).

rejouer verb [1] to replay.

relâcher verb [1] **1** to loosen (a grip or hold); **2** to set free (a prisoner, hostage, or animal); **3** to relax (your attention or discipline).

relais noun Masc. **1** restaurant, hotel; **2 prendre le relais (de quelqu'un)** to take over (from someone); **il a pris le relais au volant** he took over the driving; **3** relay race.

relatif (Fem. **relative**) adjective relative.

relation noun Fem. **1** connection; **en relation avec** in connection with; **2** acquaintance; **une relation de mon frère** an acquaintance of my brother's; **3** relationship; **il a de bonnes relations avec son patron** he has a good relationship with his boss; **4 les relations publiques** public relations.

a
b
c
d
e
f
g
h
i
j
k
l
m
n
o
p
q
r
s
t
u
v
w
x
y
z

relativement *adverb* relatively; **relativement à** in relation to.

relax *adjective* (*informal*) casual, laid back.

relaxer *verb* [1] to relax.

relent *noun Masc.* lingering smell.

relevé *noun Masc.* **1 faire le relevé de quelque chose** to make a list of something; **2 un relevé de compte** a bank statement.

relever *verb* [50] **1** to raise; **2 relever la tête** to look up; **3** to notice (*details, mistakes, or interesting facts*); **4 relever le compteur** to read the meter; **5 se relever** to pick yourself up (*after a fall*).

relier *verb* [1] **1** to link; **2** to match up.

religieux, religieuse *noun Masc., Fem.* monk, nun.
religieux (*Fem.* religieuse) *adjective* religious.

religion *noun Fem.* religion.

relire *verb* [51] to re-read, to read over.

remarié *adjective* remarried.

remarquable *adjective* remarkable, striking.

remarque *noun Fem.* remark, comment.

remarquer *verb* [1] **1** to notice; **je n'ai rien remarqué** I didn't notice anything; **j'ai remarqué qu'elle est arrivée en retard** I noticed she arrived late; **2 se faire remarquer** to draw attention to yourself; **il n'aime pas se faire remarquer** he doesn't like drawing attention to

himself; **3 faire remarquer quelque chose à quelqu'un** to point something out to somebody; **elle lui a fait remarquer que c'était déjà trop tard** she pointed out to him that it was already too late.

rembobiner *verb* [1] to rewind (*tape or video*).

remboursement *noun Masc.* repayment, refund.

rembourser *verb* [1] **1** to pay back; **je te rembourserai demain** I'll pay you back tomorrow; **2** to refund the price of; **ils m'ont remboursé les billets** they refunded me the price of the tickets; **3** to reimburse; **nous vous rembourserons le voyage** we'll pay your travelling expenses.

remède *noun Masc.* remedy.

remerciement *noun Masc.* thanks; **tous mes remerciements** many thanks; **une lettre de remerciement** a thank-you letter.

remercier *verb* [1] **1** to thank; **je l'ai remerciée pour les fleurs** I thanked her for the flowers; **2 remercier quelqu'un d'avoir fait quelque chose** to thank somebody for doing something; **il nous a remerciés de l'avoir aidé** he thanked us for helping him.

remettre *verb* [11] **1** to put back; **remets la bouteille au frigo** put the bottle back in the fridge; **il a remis la photo sur la table** he put the photo back on the table; **as-tu remis tous les livres à leur place?** have you put all the books back in their place?; **2** to put back on; **je vais**

a
b
c
d
e
f
g
h
i
j
k
l
m
n
o
p
q
r
s
t
u
v
w
x
y
z

remettre ma veste I'm going to put my jacket back on; **3** to hand over; **pouvez-vous me remettre les clés demain?** can you hand over the keys to me tomorrow?; **4** to put off; **ils ont remis la réunion à jeudi** they've put the meeting off until Thursday; **5 se remettre** to start again; **elle s'est remise au piano** she's started playing the piano again; **il s'est remis à pleuvoir** it's started raining again; **6 se remettre de** to recover; **ils ne se sont toujours pas remis du choc** they still haven't recovered from the shock.

emise *noun Fem.* **1** handing out; **la remise des prix** the prizegiving; **2** discount; **nous faisons une remise de 20% sur tous les CD** we're giving a 20% discount on all CDs; **3** garden shed.

emonte-pente *noun Masc.* ski lift.

emonter *verb* [1] **1** to go (*or* come) back up; **Nathalie est remontée dans sa chambre** Nathalie's gone back up to her room; **je descends à Londres ce soir et je remonte lundi** I'm going down to London tonight and coming back up on Monday; **2** to take (*or* bring) back up; **veux-tu remonter les chaises?** would you take the chairs back upstairs?; **3** to put back up; **il m'a remonté ma valise au filet** he put my case up in the luggage rack for me; **4 remonter la pente** to go back up the hill; **5** to get or climb back in; **ils sont remontés dans la car** they got back into the coach; **6 remonter quelqu'un, remonter le moral à quelqu'un** to cheer someone up.

remords *noun Masc.* remorse.

remorque *noun Fem.* **1** trailer (*for a car*); **2** tow-rope.

remplaçant, remplaçante *noun Masc., Fem.* **1** replacement (*for another person*); **2** supply teacher.

remplacer *verb* [61] **1** to stand in for (*a person*); **2** to replace; **il faut remplacer les piles** you need to replace the batteries.

remplir *verb* [2] **1** to fill; **il a rempli son verre de vin** he filled his glass with wine; **la salle était remplie de jeunes** the hall was full of young people; **2 remplir un formulaire** to fill in a form; **3** to carry out (*a duty or a role*).

remue-ménage *noun Masc.* commotion.

remuer *verb* [1] **1** to move (*your head or hand, for example*); **le vent remuait les branches** the wind was shaking the branches; **2** to stir; **peux-tu remuer la sauce, s'il te plaît?** can you stir the sauce, please?

rémunérer *verb* [24] to pay (*a person*), to pay for (*work*).

renard *noun Masc.* fox.

rencontre *noun Fem.* **1** meeting; **elle est venue à ma rencontre** she came to meet me; **2** (*in sport*) match; **la rencontre entre la France et l'Allemagne** the match between France and Germany.

rencontrer *verb* [1] **1** to meet (*a person*); **je l'ai rencontrée en 1993** I met her in 1993; **2** to play (*an opponent or a team*); **3 se rencontrer** to meet; **nous nous**

a
b
c
d
e
f
g
h
i
j
k
l
m
n
o
p
q
r
s
t
u
v
w
x
y
z

a
b
c
d
e
f
g
h
i
j
k
l
m
n
o
p
q
r
s
t
u
v
w
x
y
z

sommes rencontrés à Londres we met in London.

rendez-vous *noun Masc.*
1 appointment; **prendre rendez-vous** to make an appointment; **j'ai rendez-vous chez le dentiste** I've got a dentist's appointment; **le médecin voit les malades sur rendez-vous** the doctor sees patients by appointment; **2** date; **Marc a rendez-vous avec sa copine à trois heures** Marc's got a date with his girlfriend at three; **3 donner rendez-vous à quelqu'un** to arrange to meet somebody; **il m'a donné rendez-vous au café** he arranged to meet me at the cafe.

rendormir *verb* [37] **se rendormir** to go back to sleep; **elle s'est rendormie** she went back to sleep.

rendre *verb* [3] **1** to give back; **je te rendrai les clés demain** I'll give you back the keys tomorrow; **2 rendre quelqu'un heureux** to make somebody happy; **3** to hand in (*homework*); **4 se rendre** to give oneself up, to surrender; **les voleurs se sont rendus à la police** the thieves gave themselves up to the police; **5 se rendre compte de quelque chose** to realize something; **je me suis rendu compte du fait que j'avais oublié mes clés** I realized I had forgotten my keys.

renifler *verb* [1] to sniff.

renne *noun Masc.* reindeer.

renommé *adjective* famous.

renoncer *verb* [61] **1** to give up; **c'est trop difficile, je renonce!** it's too difficult, I give up!; **2 renoncer à**

quelque chose to give something up.

renouveler *verb* [18] to renew (*a passport or a subscription, for example*).

rénover *verb* [1] **1** to renovate (*a house*); **2** to restore (*furniture*).

renseignement *noun Masc.* **1 un renseignement** a piece of information; **un renseignement utile** a useful piece of information; **2 les renseignements** information; **je cherche des renseignements** I'm looking for information; **adressez-vous aux renseignements** ask at the information desk; **3 renseignements** directory enquiries.

renseigner *verb* [1] **1 renseigner quelqu'un** to give someone information; **la brochure vous renseigne sur les horaires** the brochure gives you timetable information; **il était très bien renseigné sur le projet** he was very well-informed about the project; **2 se renseigner** to find out; **je vais me renseigner au bureau de tourisme** I'm going to find out at the tourist office.

rentable *adjective* profitable.

rentrée *noun Fem.* **la rentrée (des classes)** the start of the new school year.

rentrer *verb* [1] **1** to get home; **Maman rentre à dix-huit heures** Mum will be home at six; **je vais rentrer chez moi** I'm going home; **2** to get back; **ils rentrent de Paris jeudi** they'll be back from Paris on

Thursday; **3** to come (or go) in; **rentrez!** do come in!; **elles sont rentrées dans un magasin** they've gone into a shop; **4 rentrer dans quelque chose** to go in something; **tout ça ne rentrera jamais dans ton sac!** all that will never go in your bag!; **5 rentrer dans quelque chose** to crash into something; **la voiture est rentrée dans un mur** the car crashed into a wall; **6 rentrer quelque chose** to bring something in (from outside); **rentre les chaises, il pleut!** bring the chairs in, it's raining!

renverser verb [1] **1** to knock over; **il a renversé sa chaise** he knocked his chair over; **2 être renversé par une voiture** to be knocked down by a car; **3** to spill; **j'ai renversé mon thé** I've spilled my tea.

renvoyer verb [40] **1** to send back; **as-tu renvoyé le formulaire?** have you sent back the form?; **on m'a renvoyé à l'hôpital** they sent me back to hospital; **2** to throw back (a ball); **3** to dismiss; **la secrétaire a été renvoyée** the secretary has been dismissed.

réouverture noun Fem. reopening.

répandu adjective widespread.

réparation noun Fem. repair.

réparer verb [1] to repair.

repartir verb [58] **1** to go off again; **ils ont déposé les enfants et ils sont repartis** they dropped the children and went off again; **2** to go again; **je suis reparti chez moi** I went home again; **3 repartir à zéro** to start from scratch.

repas noun Masc. meal; **le repas de midi** lunch; **le repas du soir** the evening meal.

repassage noun Masc. ironing.

repasser verb [1] **1** to drop in again; **il a dit qu'il repasserait demain** he said he'd drop in again tomorrow; **2** to iron; **Frank est en train de repasser sa chemise** Frank's busy ironing his shirt; **une planche à repasser** an ironing board; **3** to resit (an exam or test); **4** to replay (a video).

repeindre verb [60] to repaint.

repère noun Masc. **un point de repère** a landmark, a reference point.

repérer verb [24] **1** (informal) to spot; **j'ai repéré trois erreurs dans son article** I spotted three mistakes in his article; **2** to locate (a place).

répertoire noun Masc. notebook (with a thumb index); **un répertoire d'adresses** an address book.

répéter verb [24] **1** to repeat; **elle l'a répété trois fois** she repeated it three times; **faire des essais répétés** to make repeated attempts; **2** to rehearse (a play); **3** to practise (a piece of music); **4 se répéter** to repeat oneself; **5 se répéter** to happen again; **espérons que cela ne se répètera pas** let's hope it doesn't happen again.

répétition noun Fem. **1** rehearsal; **la répétition générale** the dress rehearsal; **2** repetition.

replier verb [1] **1** to fold up; **elle a replié la carte** she folded up the map (a sheet); **2 elle a replié ses**

a
b
c
d
e
f
g
h
i
j
k
l
m
n
o
p
q
r
s
t
u
v
w
x
y
z

jambes she tucked her legs up (under her).

répondeur *noun Masc.* answering machine; **j'ai laissé un message sur le répondeur** I left a message on the answering machine.

répondre *verb* [3] **1** to answer; **il n'a pas répondu** he didn't answer; **je ne lui ai pas répondu** I didn't answer him; **2 répondre à une question** to answer a question; **3 répondre à une lettre** to reply to a letter.

réponse *noun Fem.* answer; **donner la bonne/mauvaise réponse** to give the right/wrong answer.

reportage *noun Masc.* **1** report; **un reportage sur la drogue** a report on drugs; **2** (news) story.

reporter[1] *verb* [1] to postpone; **on a reporté le match à jeudi** the match has been postponed until Thursday.

reporter[2] *noun Masc.* reporter.

repos *noun Masc.* rest; **dix jours de repos** ten days' rest.

reposant *adjective* restful.

reposer *verb* [1] **1 reposer quelque chose** to put something back down; **elle a reposé le livre sur la table** she put the book back down on the table; **2 se reposer** to have a rest; **j'ai besoin de me reposer** I need a rest; **repose-toi bien!** have a good rest!

repousser *verb* [1] **1** to grow again; **tes cheveux ont vite repoussé** your hair's grown quickly; **2** to push back; **3** to postpone; **le match a été repoussé** the match has been postponed.

reprendre *verb* [64] **1** to have some more (*food or drink*); **reprends du poulet** have some more chicken; **2** to take back; **est-ce que je peux reprendre les verres que je t'avais prêtés?** can I take back the glasses I lent you?; **3** to start again; **l'école reprend en septembre** school starts again in September; **4 reprendre le travail** to go back to work; **j'ai repris le travail lundi** I went back to work on Monday; **5 reprendre la route** to set off again.

représentant, représentante *noun Masc., Fem.* sales rep.

représentation *noun Fem.* performance (*of a play*); **prochaine représentation à 20h** next performance 8 p.m.

représenter *verb* [1] **1** to depict; **2** to represent.

réprimander *verb* [1] to tell off, to reprimand.

réprimer *verb* [1] to suppress.

reprise *noun Fem.* **1** resumption (*of work or discussions*); **2** rerun (*of a play or film*), repeat (*of a broadcast*); **3 à plusieurs reprises** on several occasions.

reproche *noun Masc.* criticism; **il m'a fait des reproches** he criticized me.

reprocher *verb* [1] **1** to criticize; **il a reproché à son fils de ne pas travailler** he criticized his son for not working; **2 se reprocher** to blame oneself.

reproduction *noun Fem.* reproduction.

reproduire verb [26] **1** to reproduce; **2 se reproduire** to happen again.

républicain adjective republican.

république noun Fem. republic; **la République française** the French Republic.

répugnant adjective revolting.

réputation noun Fem. reputation; **il a la réputation d'être très sévère** he has a reputation for being very strict.

requin noun Masc. shark.

RER noun Masc. SHORT FOR **réseau express régional** (the fast suburban network on the Paris underground).

rescousse noun Fem. **aller à la rescousse de quelqu'un** to go to someone's rescue.

réseau (plural réseaux) noun Masc. network.

réservation noun Fem. reservation.

réservé adjective reserved.

réserve noun Fem. **1** stock; **des réserves de charbon** stocks of coal; **j'ai deux bouteilles en réserve** I have put aside two bottles; **2** reserve (for birds or animals); **une réserve ornithologique** a bird sanctuary.

réserver verb [1] **1** to reserve, to book; **j'ai réservé deux places pour ce soir** I've booked two seats for this evening; **2** to keep; **Philippe t'a réservé du poulet** Philippe's kept some chicken for you.

réservoir noun Masc. **1** tank; **réservoir à essence** petrol tank; **2** reservoir.

résidence noun Fem. **1** home, residence; **une résidence secondaire** a holiday home; **2** block of flats.

résidence universitaire noun Fem. hall of residence.

résident, résidente noun Masc., Fem. resident.

résidentiel (Fem. **résidentielle**) adjective residential.

résistant, résistante noun Masc., Fem. Resistance fighter (in France during World War II). **résistant** adjective tough.

résister verb [1] **résister à** to resist.

résolu adjective **1** determined; **elle est résolue à démissionner** she is determined to resign; **2** resolved; **le problème est résolu** the problem is resolved.

résoudre verb [67] **1** to solve (a problem); **2 se résoudre à faire** to make up one's mind to do; **elle s'est résolue à partir** she made up her mind to leave.

respect noun Masc. respect.

respecter verb [1] to respect.

respectueux (Fem. **respectueuse**) adjective respectful.

respiration noun Fem. breathing.

respirer verb [1] to breathe.

responsabilité noun Fem. **1** responsibility; **2 avoir la responsabilité de quelque chose** to be responsible for something; **il a la responsabilité des livraisons** he's responsible for deliveries.

a
b
c
d
e
f
g
h
i
j
k
l
m
n
o
p
q
r
s
t
u
v
w
x
y
z

255

responsable *noun Masc. & Fem.*
1 person in charge; **le responsable du projet** the person in charge of the project; **2** person responsible; **les responsables de la catastrophe** those responsible for the disaster.
responsable *adjective*
responsible; **il est responsable de l'accident** he's responsible for the accident.

ressemblance *noun Fem.*
similarity.

ressembler *verb* [1]
1 ressembler à to look like; **elle ressemble beaucoup à sa mère** she looks very like her mother; **cela ressemble à du bois mais c'est du plastique** it looks like wood but it's plastic; **2 se ressembler** to be alike; **les deux sœurs ne se ressemblent pas du tout** the two sisters are not at all alike.

ressentiment *noun Masc.*
resentment.

resserrer *verb* [1] **1** to tighten (*a knot or screw, for example*); **2 se resserrer** to move closer together; **resserrez-vous un peu!** squeeze up a bit!

resservir *verb* [58] **1** to give another helping; **je vous ressers un peu?** shall I give you a little more?; **2 se resservir** to help yourself to more; **ressers-toi de la salade** help yourself to some more salad; **je me suis déjà resservi, merci** I've already helped myself to more, thank you.

ressort *noun Masc.* spring (*in a bed or a chair*).

ressortir *verb* [58] to go out agai
**il est revenu pour les clés et il e
ressorti** he came back for the key
and went out again.

ressource *noun Fem.* **1** resourc
des ressources énergétiques
energy resources; **2 il est sans
ressources** he has no means of
support.

restaurant *noun Masc.* restaura
**on mange au restaurant ce soi
we're going out for a meal tonight

restauration *noun Fem.*
1 catering; **la restauration rapid
the fast-food industry; **2** restorati

restaurer *verb* [1] to restore.

reste *noun Masc.* **1 le reste** the re
le reste du temps the rest of the
time; **et tout le reste, tu le sais
déjà** and you know all the rest
already; **2 les restes** the leftover
**j'ai fait un curry avec les restes
du poulet** I made a curry with th
leftover chicken.

rester *verb* [1] **1** to stay; **reste là,
reviens tout de suite!** stay there,
I'll be right back!; **Camille est
restée à la maison** Camille staye
at home; **je ne peux pas rester
longtemps** I can't stay long; **hier
suis resté sans manger** I didn't
have anything to eat yesterday;
2 rester debout to remain
standing; **je préfère rester debo
I prefer to stand; **3 rester assis t
remain seated; **je suis resté assi
toute la journée** I've been sitting
down all day; **4** to be left; **il reste
fromage** there's some cheese left;
nous reste combien d'argent?
how much money have we got left?

ne reste pas beaucoup à faire
there's not much left to do.

estriction *noun Fem.* restriction.

ésultat *noun Masc.* result; **les
résultats des examens** the exam
results.

ésulter *verb* [1] **résulter de** to
result from.

ésumé *noun Masc.* summary,
résumé.

ésumer *verb* [1] to summarize, to
sum up.

établir *verb* [2] **1** to restore; **2 se
rétablir** to recover (*after an illness*).

etaper *verb* [1] to do up (*a house*).

etard *noun Masc.* **1** delay; **ils
annoncent un retard d'une heure
sur notre vol** they say there's an
hour's delay on our flight; **sans
retard** without delay; **2 avoir du
retard** to be late; **excusez mon
retard** I'm sorry I'm late; **ils sont
arrivés avec trois heures de
retard** they arrived three hours late;
3 être en retard to be late; **nous
sommes en retard** we're late.

etarder *verb* [1] **1** to hold up, to
delay; **la grève nous a retardés** the
strike held us up; **l'avion était
retardé** the plane was delayed; **2** to
put off, to postpone; **il a retardé son
départ** he put off his departure.

etenir *verb* [77] **1** to hold up; **j'ai
été retenu au bureau** I was held up
at the office; **je ne vous retiendrai
pas longtemps** I won't keep you
long; **2 retenir son souffle** to hold
your breath; **elle ne pouvait pas
retenir ses larmes** she couldn't
hold back her tears; **3** to book; **j'ai**

retenu des places I've booked
seats; **4** to remember; **je ne retiens
jamais leur adresse** I can never
remember their address.

réticence *noun Fem.* **1** reluctance;
2 reticence.

retirer *verb* [1] **1** to take off; **je vais
d'abord retirer ma veste** I'll take
my jacket off first; **2** to take away; **ils
ont retiré son permis** they took
away his licence; **3 retirer de
l'argent** to take out some money
(*from your bank account*).

retouche *noun Fem.* alteration (*to a
garment*).

retour *noun Masc.* **1** return; **un
billet aller-retour** a return ticket;
dès mon retour as soon as I get
back; **2 être de retour** to be back;
**elle sera de retour vers onze
heures** she'll be back about eleven.

retourner *verb* [1] **1** to go back;
elle est retournée à l'école she
went back to school; **je n'y suis
jamais retourné** I've never been
back there; **2** to turn over; **est-ce
que je retourne les steaks?** shall I
turn the steaks over?; **3** to overturn.

retraite *noun Fem.* retirement;
prendre sa retraite to retire; **une
maison de retraite** an old people's
home.

retraité, **retraitée** *noun Masc.*,
Fem. pensioner.

rétrécir *verb* [2] to shrink.

retrousser *verb* [1] **1** to hitch up;
2 to roll up; **il a retroussé ses
manches** he rolled up his sleeves.

retrouver *verb* [1] **1** to find; **as-tu
retrouvé tes clés?** did you find

a
b
c
d
e
f
g
h
i
j
k
l
m
n
o
p
q
r
s
t
u
v
w
x
y
z

257

your keys?; **2** to meet; **je te retrouve à la sortie** I'll meet you at the exit; **3 se retrouver** to meet; **on se retrouve devant le cinéma?** shall we meet outside the cinema?; **on se retrouvera à Noël** we'll see each other again at Christmas; **4 se retrouver** to end up; **on s'est retrouvé chez Amanda** we ended up at Amanda's place; **5 se retrouver** to find one's way around; **je n'arrive jamais à me retrouver à Londres** I can never find my way around London.

rétroviseur, rétro noun Masc. rearview mirror.

réunion noun Fem. **1** meeting; **2** reunion; **3** gathering; **4** reunification.

réunir verb [2] **se réunir** to meet; **on s'est réuni pour discuter du problème** we met to discuss the problem.

réussi adjective successful.

réussir verb [2] **1** to succeed; **j'espère qu'elle va réussir** I hope she'll succeed; **2 réussir un examen** to pass an exam; **3** to be successful; **ça a très bien réussi** that was very successful; **4 réussir à faire** to manage to do; **je n'ai pas réussi à les persuader** I didn't manage to persuade them.

réussite noun Fem. success.

réutilisable adjective reusable.

revanche noun Fem. **1** return match; **2 prendre sa revanche** to get your own back; **3 en revanche** on the other hand.

rêve noun Masc. dream; **faire un rêve** to have a dream; **votre maiso de rêve** your dream house.

réveil noun Masc. alarm clock.

réveille-matin noun Masc. alar clock.

réveiller verb [1] **1 réveiller quelqu'un** to wake somebody up; **elle m'a réveillé à sept heures** sh woke me at seven; **2 se réveiller** t wake up; **d'habitude je me réveil à sept heures** I usually wake up seven.

réveillon noun Masc. **le réveillon du Nouvel An** the New Year's Eve celebrations.

réveillonner verb [1] **1** to celebrate Christmas Eve; **2** to see the New Year in.

révéler verb [24] to reveal.

revenant, revenante noun Masc., Fem. ghost.

revendre verb [3] to sell, to resel

revenir verb [81] **1** to come back; **elles sont revenues très tard** the came back very late; **tu reviendra nous voir?** will you come back an see us?; **2** to come to; **ça revient quinze euros** that comes to fiftee euros; **ça revient au même** it com to the same thing; **3 je n'en revien pas!** I can't get over it!

revenu noun Masc. income.

rêver verb [1] to dream.

réverbère noun Masc. street lam

revers noun Masc. **1** lapel (on a jacket); turn-up (of trousers,); cuff (on a sleeve); **2** backhand (in tennis

3 setback; **4 le revers de la médaille** the other side of the coin.

éviser *verb* [1] **1** to revise; **2** to service (*a car or machine*).

évision *noun Fem.* **1** revision; **2** service (*for a car*).

evoici *preposition* (*informal*) **me revoici!** here I am again!

evoir[1] *verb* [13] **1** to see again; **et nous ne l'avons jamais revue** and we never saw her again; **2** to revise; **je dois revoir ma chimie** I have to revise my chemistry.

evoir[2] *noun Masc.* **au revoir** goodbye.

évoltant *adjective* appalling.

évolte *noun Fem.* revolt, rebellion.

évolter *verb* [1] to appal.

évolution *noun Fem.* revolution.

évolutionner *verb* [1] to revolutionize.

evolver *noun Masc.* revolver, handgun.

evouloir *verb* [14] to have a second helping of; **est-ce que tu reveux des frites?** would you like a second helping of chips?

evue *noun Fem.* magazine; **une revue d'art** an art magazine; **une revue scientifique** a scientific journal.

ez-de-chaussée *noun Masc.* ground floor (*literally: level with the road*); **la réception est au rez-de-chaussée** reception is on the ground floor.

RF SHORT FOR **République française** French Republic.

Rhin *noun Masc.* **le Rhin** the Rhine.

rhinocéros *noun Masc.* rhinoceros.

rhubarbe *noun Fem.* rhubarb.

rhum *noun Masc.* rum.

rhume *noun Masc.* cold; **attraper un rhume** to catch a cold; **un rhume de cerveau** a head cold.

rhume des foins *noun Masc.* hay fever.

ri *verb* SEE **rire**.

ricaner *verb* [1] to snigger, to giggle.

riche *adjective* **1** well-off; **nous ne sommes pas très riches** we're not terribly well-off; **2** rich; **riche en vitamines** rich in vitamins.

richesse *noun Fem.* **1** wealth; **2 les richesses naturelles** natural resources.

ride *noun Fem.* wrinkle (*on skin*), ripple (*on water*).

rideau (*plural* **rideaux**) *noun Masc.* curtain.

ridicule *adjective* ridiculous; **mais c'est totalement ridicule!** but that's completely ridiculous!

rien[1] *pronoun* **1** nothing; **'qu'est-ce qu'elle a dit?' – 'rien'** 'what did she say?' – 'nothing'; **il n'a rien** he has nothing; **je n'ai rien vu** I didn't see anything; **ce n'est rien** it's nothing; **il ne reste plus rien** there's nothing left; **'merci' – 'de rien'** 'thank you' – 'it's nothing'; **rien d'autre** nothing else; **rien de bon** nothing good; **2 rien que** just; **rien que les livres pèsent 20 kilos** the books by themselves weigh 20 kilos; **'que reste-t-il à faire?' – 'rien que la vaisselle'** 'what's left to do?' – 'just the washing-up'; ★ **rien à faire!** it's no good!

a b c d e f g h i j k l m n o p q r s t u v w x y z

rien[2] *noun* Masc. little thing; **elle se met à hurler pour un rien** the slightest thing starts her shouting.

rigide *adjective* rigid, stiff.

rigoler *verb* [1] (*informal*) **1** to laugh; **elle en a beaucoup rigolé** she had a good laugh about it; **2** to have a good time; **nous avons bien rigolé** we had a great time; **3** to be joking; **je rigolais!** I was only joking!

rigolo (*Fem.* rigolote) *adjective* (*informal*) funny.

rigoureux (*Fem.* rigoureuse) *adjective* **1** rigorous; **2** strict; **3** harsh.

rillettes *plural noun* Fem. **les rillettes de porc** potted pork.

rime *noun* Fem. rhyme.

rimer *verb* [1] to rhyme.

rincer *verb* [61] to rinse; **se rincer les cheveux** to rinse one's hair.

rire *noun* Masc. laughter; **un rire** a laugh.
rire *verb* [68] **1** to laugh; **il nous fait rire** he makes us laugh; **2** to have fun; **on va rire ce soir** we'll have some fun this evening; **c'était pour rire** it was meant as a joke.

ris *noun* Masc. **les ris de veau** calf's sweetbreads.

risque *noun* Masc. risk; **risque d'incendie** fire risk; **c'est sans risque** it's safe.

risqué *adjective* risky.

risquer *verb* [1] **1** to risk; **vas-y, tu ne risques rien** go on, it's quite safe; **2** **il risque de pleuvoir** it might well rain; **tu risques de te brûler** you might burn yourself.

rivage *noun* Masc. shore.

rival, rivale *noun* Masc., Fem. (*Mas plural* rivaux) rival.

rive *noun* Fem. **1** bank (*of a river*); **I Rive gauche** the Left Bank (*when talking about the Seine in Paris an other rivers which flow through cities, the left bank is the left side of the river when you are facing downstream*); **2** shore (*by the sea*).

rivière *noun* Fem. river.

riz *noun* Masc. rice; **riz cantonais** fried rice; **gâteau de riz** rice pudding.

RN *noun* Fem. SHORT FOR **route nationale** A road.

robe *noun* Fem. dress; **une robe d'été** a summer dress; **une robe d mariée** a wedding dress.

robe de chambre *noun* Fem. dressing gown.

robinet *noun* Masc. tap; **l'eau du robinet** tap water.

robot *noun* Masc. robot; **robot ménager** food processor.

robuste *adjective* robust, sturdy.

roche *noun* Fem. rock.

rocher *noun* Masc. rock.

rock *noun* Masc. rock (music).

rôder *verb* [1] to prowl.

rognons *plural noun* Masc. kidney (*for cooking*).

roi *noun* Masc. king; **le roi Charles** King Charles; **les Rois mages** the Three Wise Men; **la fête des Rois** Twelfth Night.

rôle *noun* Masc. role.

roller *noun* Masc. **1** roller-skating; **2** roller-skate.

romain *adjective* Roman.

roman *noun* Masc. novel; **un roman policier** a detective story.

romancier, **romancière** *noun* Masc., Fem. novelist.

romantique *adjective* romantic.

romarin *noun* Masc. rosemary.

rompre *verb* [69] to split up; **Claire et David ont rompu** Claire and David have split up; **Anne a rompu avec son copain** Anne's broken up with her boyfriend; **rompre ses fiançailles** to break off your engagement.

ronce *noun* Fem. bramble.

rond *noun* Masc. circle; **tourner en rond** to go round in circles.
rond *adjective* round.

rondelle *noun* Fem. **1** slice; **une rondelle de tomate** a slice of tomato; **2** washer (*for a tap or screw*).

rond-point *noun* Masc. roundabout.

ronfler *verb* [1] to snore.

ronger *verb* [52] **1** to gnaw; **2 se ronger les ongles** to bite one's nails.

ronronner *verb* [1] to purr.

rosbif *noun* Masc. roast beef.

rose *noun* Fem. rose.
rose *adjective* pink; **rose pâle** pale pink.

rosé *noun* Masc. rosé (wine); **un verre de rosé** a glass of rosé.

rosée *noun* Fem. dew.

rosier *noun* Masc. rosebush.

rossignol *noun* Masc. nightingale.

rôti *noun* Masc. roast; **du rôti de bœuf** roast beef; **un rôti de bœuf** a joint of beef.

rôtir *verb* [2] to roast.

roucouler *verb* [1] to coo.

roue *noun* Fem. wheel; **la roue de secours** the spare wheel; ★ **faire la roue** to turn a cartwheel.

rouge *noun* Masc. **1** (the colour) red; **le rouge ne me va pas** red doesn't suit me; **2** red traffic light; **il est passé au rouge** he jumped the lights; **le feu est passé au rouge** the light changed to red; **3** red wine; **un verre de rouge** a glass of red wine.
rouge *adjective* red; **tes chaussettes rouges** your red socks.

rouge à lèvres *noun* Masc. lipstick.

rouge-gorge *noun* Masc. robin.

rougeur *noun* Fem. redness.

rougir *verb* [2] **1** to blush; **2** to turn red.

rouille *noun* Fem. rust.

rouillé *adjective* rusty.

rouiller, **se rouiller** *verb* [1] to go rusty.

roulade *noun* Fem. **1** stuffed rolled meat; **2** somersault, roll.

roulant *adjective* **un fauteuil roulant** a wheelchair.

a
b
c
d
e
f
g
h
i
j
k
l
m
n
o
p
q
r
s
t
u
v
w
x
y
z

rouleau (*plural* rouleaux) *noun*
Masc. roll; **un rouleau d'essuie-tout**
a roll of kitchen towel.

rouleau à pâtisserie *noun*
Masc. rolling pin.

rouler *verb* [1] **1** to go; **nous
roulons très vite** we're going very
fast; **2** to drive; **il faut rouler à
droite en France** in France you
must drive on the right; **nous avons
roulé toute la nuit** we drove all
night; **3** to roll; **4** to roll up; **il faut
rouler le tapis** we must roll up the
carpet; **5** (*informal*) to cheat; **on m'a
roulé!** I've been done!

Roumanie *noun* Fem. Romania.

rousse *adjective* SEE **roux**.

route *noun* Fem. **1** road; **une grande
route** a main road; **un accident de
la route** a road accident; **Rouen est
à trois heures de route d'ici** Rouen
is three hours' drive from here;
2 route; **il a changé de route à
cause de la neige** he changed his
route because of the snow; **3 en
route** on the way; **être en route** to
be on the way; **nous sommes en
route pour Nice** we're on our way to
Nice; **4 se mettre en route** to set
off; **5 bonne route!** safe journey!

route à quatre voies *noun*
Fem. dual carriageway.

route départementale *noun*
Fem. secondary road, B road.

route nationale *noun* Fem. A
road.

routier, routière *noun* Masc. Fem.
lorry driver.
routier (Fem. **routière**) *adjective*
road; **le transport routier** road

transport; **la gare routière** the bus
station.

routine *noun* Fem. routine.

roux (Fem. **rousse**) *adjective* red-
haired, ginger.

royal (*plural* **royaux**) *adjective*
royal.

royaume *noun* Masc. kingdom.

Royaume-Uni *noun* Masc. United
Kingdom.

ruban *noun* Masc. ribbon.

ruban adhésif *noun* Masc. sticky
tape.

rubéole *noun* Fem. German
measles.

ruche *noun* Fem. beehive.

rudement *adverb* (*informal*)
really; **il est rudement bon ton
gâteau** your cake's really good.

rue *noun* Fem. street; **une rue
piétonne** a pedestrian street;
★ **mettre quelqu'un à la rue** to put
someone out on the street.

rugby *noun* Masc. rugby; **jouer au
rugby** to play rugby.

rugbyman (*plural* **rugbymen**)
noun Masc. rugby player.

ruine *noun* Fem. ruin; **une maison
en ruine(s)** a ruined house.

ruiner *verb* [1] to ruin.

ruisseau (*plural* **ruisseaux**) *noun*
Masc. stream.

rumeur *noun* Fem. **1** rumour;
2 murmur.

rumsteck *noun* Masc. rump steak.

rupture *noun* Fem. break-up.

rural (Masc. *plural* **ruraux**) *adjective*
country; **la vie rurale** country life.

use *noun Fem.* **1** trick; **les ruses du métier** the tricks of the trade; **2** cunning.

usé *adjective* cunning, crafty.

usse *noun Masc.* Russian (*language*).

russe *adjective* Russian.

Russe *noun Masc., Fem.* Russian (*person*).

Russie *noun Fem.* Russia.

ythme *noun Masc.* rhythm; **marquer le rythme** to beat time.

Ss

' *pronoun* SEE **se**.

a *adjective* SEE **son**.

able *noun Masc.* sand.

ablé *noun Masc.* shortbread biscuit.

sablé *adjective* **la pâte sablée** shortcrust pastry.

ac *noun Masc.* **1** bag; **un sac de sucre** a bag of sugar; **un sac de sport** a sports bag; **2** sack; **un sac de charbon** a sack of coal; ★ **vider son sac** (*informal*) to get something off one's chest (*literally: to empty one's bag*).

ac à dos *noun Masc.* rucksack.

ac à main *noun Masc.* handbag.

ac de congélation *noun Masc.* freezer bag.

ac de couchage *noun Masc.* sleeping bag.

achet *noun Masc.* sachet; **un sachet de thé** a teabag.

sacoche *noun Fem.* **1** bag; **la sacoche du facteur** the postman's bag; **2** pannier (*for a bike*).

sacré *adjective* **1** (*informal*) **c'est un sacré problème** it's a hell of a problem; **elle a eu une sacrée chance** she's been damn lucky; **2** sacred.

sacrifice *noun Masc.* sacrifice.

sacrifier *verb* [1] to sacrifice.

sage *adjective* **1** good, well-behaved; **Tom, sois sage** be a good boy, Tom; **2** wise, sensible; **il serait sage de se renseigner sur le prix** it would be wise to enquire about the price.

sage-femme *noun Fem.* midwife.

sagesse *noun Fem.* wisdom; **une dent de sagesse** a wisdom tooth.

Sagittaire *noun Masc.* Sagittarius (*sign of the Zodiac*).

saignant *adjective* rare (*beef*).

saigner *verb* [1] to bleed.

sain *adjective* healthy; ★ **sain et sauf** safe and sound.

saint, sainte *noun Masc., Fem.* saint.
saint *adjective* holy; **le Saint-Esprit** the Holy Spirit; **le vendredi saint** Good Friday; **la Sainte Vierge** the Virgin Mary.

Saint-Jacques *noun* **une coquille Saint-Jacques** a scallop.

Saint-Jean *noun Fem.* Midsummer's Day (*June 24th*).

Saint-Sylvestre *noun Fem.* New Year's Eve.

Saint-Valentin *noun Fem.* St Valentine's Day.

sais *verb* SEE **savoir**[1].

a
b
c
d
e
f
g
h
i
j
k
l
m
n
o
p
q
r
s
t
u
v
w
x
y
z

saisir verb [2] **1** to grab; **il m'a saisi par le bras** he grabbed my arm; **2 saisir l'occasion** to seize the opportunity; **3** to understand; **je n'ai pas tout à fait saisi ...** I didn't entirely understand ...; **4** to catch, (to hear); **je n'ai pas saisi votre nom** I didn't catch your name.

saison noun Fem. season; **il fait froid pour la saison** it's cold for the time of year.

sait verb SEE **savoir**[1].

salade noun Fem. **1** lettuce; **une salade** a lettuce ; **2** salad; **une salade de fruits** a fruit salad.

saladier noun Masc. salad bowl.

salaire noun Masc. salary, wages.

salarié, salariée noun Masc., Fem. salaried employee.

sale adjective **1** (after the noun) dirty; **les mains sales** dirty hands; **2** (before the noun) (informal) horrible; **quel sale temps!** what horrible weather!; **il a une sale tête** he looks awful.

salé adjective **1** salty; **la sauce est un peu trop salée** the sauce is a bit salty; **2** savoury; **des petits gâteaux salés** savoury biscuits; **3 du beurre salé** salt butter.

saler verb [1] to salt.

saleté noun Fem. dirt.

salir verb [2] to dirty, to get (something) dirty; **tu vas salir ta robe** you'll get your dress dirty.

salive noun Fem. saliva.

salle noun Fem. **1** room ('salle' by itself is no longer used to mean a room in a house); **2** dining-room (in a restaurant); **3** hall; **4** auditorium (in a theatre or cinema).

salle à manger noun Fem. **1** dining room; **2** dining-room suite.

salle d'attente noun Fem. waiting room.

salle d'eau noun Fem. shower room.

salle de bains noun Fem. bathroom.

salle de classe noun Fem. classroom.

salle de jeux noun Fem. games room.

salle d'embarquement noun Fem. departure lounge.

salle de séjour noun Fem. living room.

salle des fêtes noun Fem. community centre.

salon noun Masc. **1** sitting room; **2** living-room suite; **3** trade fair; **4** salon; **salon de coiffure** hair salon.

salon de thé noun Masc. tea-room

salopette noun Fem. **1** dungarees; **2** overalls.

saluer verb [1] **1** to say hello to; **je l'ai salué, mais il ne m'a pas entendu** I said hello to him but he didn't hear; **elle l'a salué de la main** she waved at him; **2** to say goodbye to.

salut greeting Masc. Hi!

samedi noun Masc. **1** Saturday; **samedi prochain** next Saturday; **samedi dernier** last Saturday; **2** on Saturday; **samedi soir** on Saturday evening; **3 le samedi** on Saturdays;

fermé le samedi closed on Saturdays; **4 tous les samedis** every Saturday.

AMU noun Masc. SHORT FOR **Service d'assistance médicale d'urgence** ambulance service.

andale noun Fem. sandal.

andwich noun Masc. sandwich; **un sandwich au jambon** a ham sandwich.

andwicherie noun Fem. snack bar.

ang noun Masc. blood; **être en sang** to be covered in blood.

ang-froid noun Masc. calm.

anglier noun Masc. wild boar.

anglot noun Masc. sob; **éclater en sanglots** to burst into tears.

anisette™ noun Fem. automatic public lavatory.

anitaire adjective **les conditions sanitaires** sanitary conditions; **les règlements sanitaires** health regulations.
sanitaire noun Masc. **les sanitaires** the toilet block (in a campsite).

ans preposition without; **une maison sans téléphone** a house without a telephone; **un café sans sucre** a coffee with no sugar; **sans hésiter** without hesitating.

ans-abri noun Masc. & Fem. homeless person; **les sans-abri** the homeless.

ans-emploi noun Masc. & Fem. unemployed person; **les sans-emploi** the unemployed.

santé noun Fem. **1** health; **être en bonne santé** to be in good health; **2 à votre santé!** cheers!

sapeur-pompier noun Masc. fireman; **appeler les sapeurs-pompiers** to call the fire brigade.

sapin noun Masc. fir tree; **un sapin de Noël** a Christmas tree.

sarcasme noun Masc. sarcasm.

sardine noun Fem. sardine.

satellite noun Masc. satellite.

satin noun Masc. satin.

satisfaction noun Fem. satisfaction.

satisfaire verb [10] to satisfy.

satisfaisant adjective satisfactory.

satisfait adjective satisfied; **êtes-vous satisfaits de votre séjour?** are you satisfied with your stay?

sauce noun Fem. **1** sauce; **2** gravy.

saucisse noun Fem. sausage.

saucisson noun Masc. salami.

sauf[1] preposition **1** except; **tous les jours sauf le lundi** every day except Monday; **sauf quand il pleut** except when it rains; **2 sauf si** unless; **c'est tout, sauf s'il y a des questions?** that's all, unless there are any questions?; **3 sauf que** except that; **tout va bien, sauf que ta sur n'est pas encore arrivée** everything's fine, except that your sister hasn't arrived yet.

sauf[2] adjective SEE **sain**.

saule noun Masc. willow; **un saule pleureur** a weeping willow.

saumon noun Masc. salmon.

a
b
c
d
e
f
g
h
i
j
k
l
m
n
o
p
q
r
s
t
u
v
w
x
y
z

a

saupoudrer *verb* [1] to sprinkle.

b

saut *noun Masc.* jump.

c

saut à la perche *noun Masc.* pole vault.

d

saut à l'élastique *noun Masc.* bungee jumping.

e

f

saut en hauteur *noun Masc.* high jump.

g

saut en longueur *noun Masc.* long jump.

h

i

sauter *verb* [1] **1** to jump, to jump over; **elle a sauté la barrière** she jumped over the gate; **elle a sauté dans un taxi** she jumped into a taxi; **2 sauter à la corde** to skip (*with a rope*); **3** to skip; **nous avons sauté trois pages** we've skipped three pages; **4** to blow up; **les terroristes ont fait sauter l'avion** the terrorists blew up the plane; **faire sauter les plombs** to blow the fuses; ★ **ça saute aux yeux!** it's blindingly obvious!

j

k

l

m

n

o

p

sauterelle *noun Fem.* grasshopper.

sauvage *noun Masc., Fem.* savage.
sauvage *adjective* **1** wild;
2 savage.

q

r

s

sauvegarder *verb* [1] **1** to safeguard; **2** to save, to back up (*on a computer*).

t

u

sauver *verb* [1] **1** to save; **vous m'avez sauvé la vie** you saved my life; **2 se sauver** to run away; **ils se sont sauvés** they ran away; **3 je me sauve!** (*informal*) I'm off!

v

w

x

sauvetage *noun Masc.* rescue, life-saving.

y

z

savent, **savez** *verb* SEE **savoir**[1].

savoir[1] *verb* [70] **1** to know; **je sais qu'il habite à Londres** I know he lives in London; **je ne savais pas qu'elle était médecin** I didn't know she was a doctor; **tu sais très bien que** ... you know very well that ...; **je n'en sais rien** I know nothing about it; **comment l'avez-vous su?** how did you find out about it?; **allez savoir!** who knows!; **2 savoir faire** to know how to do; **je ne sais pas le faire** I don't know how to do it; **savoir lire et écrire** to be able to read and write; **tu sais jouer du piano?** can you play the piano?

savoir[2] *noun Masc.* knowledge.

savoir-faire *noun Masc.* know-how.

savon *noun Masc.* soap.

savonnette *noun Fem.* cake of soap.

savons *verb* SEE **savoir**[1].

savoureux (*Fem.* **savoureuse**) *adjective* tasty.

scandale *noun Masc.* scandal; **le discours du ministre a fait scandale** the minister's speech caused a scandal.

scandinave *adjective* Scandinavian.

Scandinavie *noun Fem.* Scandinavia.

scanner *noun Masc.* scanner (*in medicine and for documents*); **passer un scanneur** to have a scan.

scarabée *noun Masc.* beetle.

scénariste *noun Masc. & Fem.* scriptwriter.

cène noun Fem. **1** stage (*in a theatre*); **être sur scène** to be on stage; **mettre en scène** to stage (*a play*), to direct (*a film*); **2** scene; **sur la scène politique** on the political scene; **des scènes de panique** scenes of panic; **faire (toute) une scène** to throw a fit.

ceptique *adjective* sceptical.

chéma noun Masc. diagram.

cie noun Fem. saw.

cience noun Fem. science.

ciences naturelles *plural noun* Fem. biology.

cientifique noun Masc. & Fem. scientist.
scientifique *adjective* scientific.

cier *verb* [1] to saw.

colaire *adjective* school; **les vacances scolaires** the school holidays; **le livret scolaire** the school report.

colarité noun Fem. schooling, education.

corpion noun Masc. Scorpio (*sign of the Zodiac*).

cotch™ noun Masc. Sellotape™.

cout, scoute noun Masc., Fem. boy scout, girl guide.

crutin noun Masc. **1** ballot; **2** polls; **le jour du scrutin** polling day.

culpteur noun Masc. sculptor.

culpteuse noun Fem. sculptress.

culpture noun Fem. sculpture.

DF noun Masc. & Fem. SHORT FOR **sans domicile fixe** of no fixed abode; **les SDF** the homeless.

se, s' (*before a vowel or silent 'h'*) *reflexive pronoun* **1** himself; **il se regarde** he's looking at himself; **2** herself; **elle se regarde** she's looking at herself; **3** itself; **le chien s'est fait mal** the dog has hurt itself; **4** themselves; **ils se sont fait mal** they've hurt themselves; **5** each other; **ils se regardaient** they were looking at each other; **6** yourself, oneself; **se faire mal** to hurt yourself (or oneself); **7** (*sometimes not translated*) **Claudie se lave les cheveux** Claudie's washing her hair; **Jules se brosse les dents** Jules is brushing his teeth.

séance noun Fem. **1** session; **2** showing (*of a film*); **la séance de vingt heures** the eight o'clock showing.

seau (*plural* **seaux**) noun Masc. bucket.

sec (Fem. **sèche**) *adjective* **1** dry; **mes cheveux ne sont pas secs** my hair's not dry; **un vin blanc sec** a dry white wine; **2** dried; **des abricots secs** dried apricots.

sèche-cheveux noun Masc. hair dryer.

sèche-linge noun Masc. tumble dryer.

sèche-mains noun Masc. hand dryer.

sécher *verb* [1] to dry; **des fleurs séchées** dried flowers.

sécheresse noun Fem. drought.

second noun Masc. **au second** on the second floor; **il est arrivé en second** he arrived second.

a
b
c
d
e
f
g
h
i
j
k
l
m
n
o
p
q
r
s
t
u
v
w
x
y
z

second *adjective* second; **la seconde fois** the second time.

secondaire *adjective* secondary; **une école secondaire** a secondary school; **des effets secondaires** side effects.

seconde *noun Fem.* **1** second; **je reviens dans une seconde** I'll be back in a moment; **2** second class; **voyager en seconde** to travel second class; **un billet de seconde** a second class ticket; **3** (*in a French school*) the equivalent of Year 11.

secouer *verb* [1] to shake; **secouer la tête** to shake your head.

secourir *verb* [29] to rescue.

secourisme *noun Masc.* first aid.

secouriste *noun Masc. & Fem.* first aider.

secours *noun Masc.* **1** help; **au secours!** help!; **elle a crié au secours** she shouted for help; **2** ; **les premiers secours** first aid; **3 une sortie de secours** an emergency exit; **4 la roue de secours** the spare wheel.

secret *noun Masc.* secret; **garder un secret** to keep a secret; **en secret** in secret.
secret (Fem. **secrète**) *adjective* secret.

secrétaire[1] *noun Masc., Fem.* secretary.

secrétaire[2] *noun Masc.* writing desk.

secrétariat *noun Masc.* secretary's office.

secteur *noun Masc.* sector; **dans le secteur privé** in the private sector;

dans le secteur public in the public sector.

sécu *noun Fem.* (*informal*) SHORT FOR **Sécurité sociale** Social Security.

sécurité *noun Fem.* **1** safety; **pour votre sécurité** for your own safety; **les règles de sécurité** safety regulations; **la sécurité routière** road safety; **une ceinture de sécurité** a seatbelt; **2 être en sécurité** to be safe; **3** security; **un système de sécurité** a security system; **la sécurité de l'emploi** job security.

Sécurité sociale *noun Fem.* Social Security.

séduisant *adjective* attractive, appealing.

seigle *noun Masc.* rye; **le pain de seigle** rye bread.

seigneur *noun Masc.* lord; **le Seigneur** the Lord.

sein *noun Masc.* **1** breast; **avoir un cancer du sein** to have breast cancer; **2** within; **au sein du gouvernement** within the government.

seize *number* sixteen; **Corinne a seize ans** Corinne's sixteen; **le seize juillet** the sixteenth of July.

seizième *number* sixteenth.

séjour *noun Masc.* **1** stay; **pendant votre séjour en France** during your stay in France; **2 la salle de séjour** the living room.

sel *noun Masc.* salt; **une pincée de sel** a pinch of salt.

sélection *noun Fem.* **1** selection; **2** choice; **3** team; **la sélection française** the French team.

électionner *verb* [1] to select.

elf *noun Masc.* (*informal*) self-service restaurant.

elf-service *noun Masc.* (*informal*) self-service restaurant.

elle *noun Fem.* saddle.

elon *preposition* according to; **selon la météo, il va pleuvoir** according to the forecast, it's going to rain.

emaine *noun Fem.* week; **cette semaine** this week; **la semaine prochaine/dernière** next/last week; **une/deux fois par semaine** once/twice a week; **elle est payée à la semaine** she's paid by the week.

emblable *adjective* similar.

emblant *noun Masc.* **faire semblant de faire** to pretend to do; **elle fait semblant de ne pas entendre** she's pretending not to hear.

embler *verb* [1] to seem; **la maison semble vide** the house seems empty; **il semble bon d'attendre leur retour** it seems a good idea to wait till they get back.

emelle *noun Fem.* sole (*of a shoe*).

emer *verb* [1] **1** to sow (*seeds*); **2** **semer la panique** to spread panic.

emestre *noun Masc.* semester.

emi-remorque *noun Masc.* articulated truck.

emoule *noun Fem.* semolina; **le sucre semoule** caster sugar.

ens *noun Masc.* **1** direction; **dans les deux sens** in both directions; **dans le sens Calais-Paris** in the Calais-Paris direction; **dans tous les sens** in all directions; **sens dessus dessous** upside down; **mets-le dans le bon sens!** put it the right way up!; **2** meaning; **le sens d'un mot** the meaning of a word; **cela n'a pas de sens** it doesn't make sense, it's absurd.

sensation *noun Fem.* **1** feeling; **2** sensation; **le film a fait sensation à Cannes** the film was a sensation at Cannes.

sensationnel (*Fem.* **sensationnelle**) *adjective* sensational, fantastic.

sens commun *noun Masc.* common sense.

sens de l'humour *noun Masc.* sense of humour; **avoir le sens de l'humour** to have a sense of humour.

sensé *adjective* sensible.

sensibiliser *verb* [1] **sensibiliser les gens à un problème** to increase people's awareness of a problem.

sensibilité *noun Fem.* **1** sensitivity; **2** sensibility.

sensible *adjective* **1** sensitive; **c'est une fille très sensible** she's a very sensitive girl; **je suis sensible au froid** I feel the cold; **2** noticeable; **une différence sensible** a noticeable difference.

sensiblement *adverb* noticeably.

sens interdit *noun Masc.* no entry sign, one-way street.

sens unique *noun Masc.* one-way street.

sentier *noun Masc.* path.

a
b
c
d
e
f
g
h
i
j
k
l
m
n
o
p
q
r
s
t
u
v
w
x
y
z

sentier de randonnée noun
Masc. long-distance footpath (a
marked route for ramblers).

sentiment noun Masc. feeling;
sentiments affectueux best
wishes; **veuillez croire à mes
sentiments les meilleurs** yours
sincerely, yours faithfully (one of a
number of fixed formulae for ending
a formal letter).

sentimental (Masc. plural
sentimentaux) adjective
sentimental.

sentir verb [58] **1** to smell; **ça sent
bon!** that smells good!; **2** to smell of;
ça sent les roses it smells of roses;
tu sens la cigarette you smell of
cigarettes; **3** to feel; **je ne sens rien**
I can't feel anything; **on sent que
l'hiver s'approche** you can feel it
will soon be winter; **je sens qu'elle
est sincère** I feel she's sincere; **4 se
sentir** to feel; **je ne me sens pas
bien** I don't feel well; ★ **je ne peux
pas le sentir!** I can't stand him!

séparé adjective **1** separated; **mes
parents sont séparés** my parents
are separated; **2** separate; **dans une
chambre séparée** in a separate
bedroom.

séparément adverb separately.

séparer verb [1] **1** to separate;
séparez les œufs separate the eggs;
séparer les filles des garçons to
separate the girls from the boys;
2 se séparer to separate, to split up;
mes parents se sont séparés my
parents have separated.

sept number seven; **Yasmin a sept
ans** Yasmin's seven; **il est sept**

heures it's seven o'clock; **le sept
mars** the seventh of March.

septante number seventy (used i.
Belgium and Switzerland, instead c
soixante-dix); **septante-sept**
seventy-seven.

septembre noun Masc. September
**en septembre, au mois de
septembre** in September.

septième noun Masc. **au septièm**
on the seventh floor.
septième adjective seventh.

sera, **serai**, **seras**, **serez** ver.
SEE **être**[1].

série noun Fem. series.

sérieusement adverb seriously

sérieux noun **prendre quelque
chose au sérieux** to take
something seriously.
sérieux (Fem. **sérieuse**) adjective
1 serious; **vraiment? tu es
sérieux?** really? are you serious?;
2 responsible; **Camilla est une
jeune fille sérieuse** Camilla is a
responsible young woman;
3 reliable; **il n'est pas sérieux** he'
unreliable; **4 un travail sérieux** a
careful piece of work; ★ **garder so**
sérieux to keep a straight face.

serin noun Masc. canary.

seringue noun Fem. syringe.

séronégatif (Fem. **séronégative**,
adjective HIV-negative.

serons, **seront** verb SEE **être**[1].

séropositif (Fem. **séropositive**)
adjective HIV-positive.

serpent noun Masc. snake.

serpillière noun Fem. floorcloth.

erre *noun Fem.* greenhouse; **l'effet de serre** the greenhouse effect.

erré *adjective* **1** tight; **ma jupe est trop serrée** my skirt's too tight; **un budget serré** a tight budget; **2** close (*match or competition*).

errer *verb* [1] **1** to grip; **elle serrait le volant** she gripped the steering wheel; **il m'a serrée dans ses bras** he hugged me; **2 serrer la main à quelqu'un** to shake somebody's hand; **nous nous sommes serré la main** we shook hands; **3 serrer quelqu'un dans ses bras** to hug somebody; **4 serrer les poings** to clench your fists; **5** to tighten (*a screw or belt*); **6** to be too tight; **mes chaussures me serrent** my shoes are too tight; **7** to push closer together; **serrez les tables** move the tables closer together; **8 se serrer** to squeeze up; **serrez-vous un peu!** squeeze up a bit!

errure *noun Fem.* lock.

erveur, serveuse *noun Masc., Fem.* waiter, waitress.

ervice *noun Masc.* **1** favour; **peux-tu me rendre un petit service?** could you do me a small favour?; **2** service (*bus, train*); **service de dimanche** Sunday service; **3 être en service** to be working; **il n'y a qu'un ascenseur en service** there's only one lift working; **être hors service** to be out of order; **l'ascenseur est hors service** the lift is out of order; **4** duty, service; **la pharmacie de service** the duty chemist; **je suis de service ce soir** I am on duty this evening; **le service militaire** national service;

5 service (*charge*); **le service est compris** service is included; **6** department (*in a town hall or hospital, for example*); **le service des urgences** the casualty department.

service après-vente *noun Masc.* after-sales service.

service clientèle *noun Masc.* customer services.

serviette *noun Fem.* **1** towel; **une serviette de bain** a bath towel; **2** napkin; **3** briefcase.

serviette hygiénique *noun Fem.* sanitary towel.

servir *verb* [71] **1** to serve (*in a shop, for example*); **merci, on me sert** thank you, I'm being served; **2** to serve (*with food or drink*); **est-ce que je peux vous servir du poulet?** can I give you some chicken?; **'servir frais'** 'serve chilled'; **3 se servir** to help yourself; **sers-toi de riz** help yourself to rice; **4 se servir de** to use; **est-ce que tu sais te servir d'une machine à coudre?** do you know how to use a sewing machine?; **5** to serve (*in tennis or in the army*); **à toi de servir!** your service!; **6 servir à** to be used for; **à quoi ça sert?** what's it for?; **ça ne sert à rien!** it's no use!; **ça ne sert à rien de pleurer** there's no point in crying; **7 se servir** to be served (*food or drink*); **ce vin se sert frais** this wine should be served chilled.

ses *adjective* SEE **son**.

set de table *noun Masc.* place mat.

a
b
c
d
e
f
g
h
i
j
k
l
m
n
o
p
q
r
s
t
u
v
w
x
y
z

a
b
c
d
e
f
g
h
i
j
k
l
m
n
o
p
q
r
s
t
u
v
w
x
y
z

seul *adjective* **1** only; **la seule personne** the only person; **c'est le seul Anglais que je connaisse** he's the only English person I know; **j'étais le seul à aimer le film** I was the only one who liked the film; **2** alone; **il ne faut pas y aller seul** you mustn't go there alone; **j'étais tout seul à la maison** I was all alone in the house; **3 se sentir seul** to feel lonely; **4 tout seul** all by yourself; **il l'a fait tout seul** he did it all by himself; **Sophie sait s'habiller toute seule maintenant** Sophie can get dressed all by herself now.

seulement *adverb* **1** only; **trois fois seulement** only three times; **2 non seulement …mais** not only …but; **non seulement elle n'est pas venue, mais elle n'a même pas appelé** not only did she not come, but she didn't even phone; **3 si seulement je l'avais su** if only I'd known.

sévère *adjective* strict.

sexe *noun Masc.* **1** sex; **2** genitals.

sexuel (*Fem.* **sexuelle**) *adjective* **1** sexual; **2 l'éducation sexuelle** sex education.

shampooing *noun Masc.* shampoo.

short *noun Masc.* (pair of) shorts; **où est mon short?** where are my shorts?; **trois shorts** three pairs of shorts.

si, s' (*before 'il' or 'ils'*) *conjunction* if; **si tu veux** if you like; **s'il pleut** if it rains.

si *adverb* **1** so; **je suis si fatigué!** I'm so tired!; **tu chantes si bien!**

you sing so well!; **2** yes (*when you a contradicting somebody*); **'tu ne viens pas avec nous?' –'si!'** 'you' not coming with us?' – 'yes I am!'; **ne reste pas manger' – 'mais si** 'he's not staying for a meal' – 'of course he is!'; **elle ne les aime p du tout, moi si** she doesn't like them at all, but I do.

Sicile *noun Fem.* Sicily.

sida *noun Masc.* SHORT FOR **syndrom immuno-déficitaire acquis** AIDS **avoir le sida** to have AIDS.

siècle *noun Masc.* century; **au vingtième siècle** in the twentieth century.

siège *noun Masc.* **1** seat; **le siège d'avant** the front seat; **2** head offi (*of a company*); **3** siege (*in war*).

sien, sienne, siens, sienne *pronoun* **le sien, la sienne, les siens, les siennes 1** his; **j'ai prê mon vélo à Paul, le sien est che lui** I've lent Paul my bike, his is a home; **'est-ce que ces chaussur sont à Bernard?' – 'oui, ce sont les siennes'** 'are these shoes Bernard's?' – 'yes, they're his'; **2** hers; **j'ai prêté mon vélo à Ann le sien est chez elle** I've lent Anr my bike, hers is at home; **'est-ce que ces chaussures sont à Nathalie?' – 'oui, ce sont les siennes'** 'are these shoes Nathalie's?' – 'yes, they're hers'.

sieste *noun Fem.* nap; **faire la sieste** to have a nap.

siffler *verb* [1] to whistle.

sifflet *noun Masc.* whistle.

ignal (*plural* **signaux**) *noun Masc.* signal.

ignaler *verb* [1] **1** to point out; **je vous signale que je serai absent ce jour-là** I'd like to point out that I shall be away that day; **2** to report; **3** to indicate (*roadworks or danger, for example*).

ignalisation *noun Fem.* signalling, signals.

ignalisation routière *noun Fem.* road signs and markings.

ignature *noun Fem.* signature; **je vous demande une petite signature** just sign here, would you?

igne *noun Masc.* sign; **c'est bon/ mauvais signe** it's a good/bad sign; **faire signe à quelqu'un** to wave to someone; **il m'a fait signe de m'approcher** he beckoned me over to him; **d'un signe de main elle a montré la sortie** she pointed to the exit; **de quel signe êtes-vous?** what star sign are you?

igne astrologique *noun Masc.* star sign.

igner *verb* [1] **1** to sign; **2 se signer** to cross oneself.

ignification *noun Fem.* meaning.

ignifier *verb* [1] to mean.

ilence *noun Masc.* silence; **en silence** in silence.

ilencieux (*Fem.* **silencieuse**) *adjective* silent.

ilhouette *noun Fem.* **1** silhouette, outline; **2** figure.

imilarité *noun Fem.* similarity.

imple *noun Masc.* **le simple messieurs/dames** the men's/ women's singles (*in tennis*).
simple *adjective* simple; **un repas simple** a simple meal; **un simple coup de téléphone** just one telephone call.

simplement *adverb* simply.

simplicité *noun Fem.* simplicity.

simplifier *verb* [1] to simplify.

simuler *verb* [1] to simulate.

simultané *adjective* simultaneous.

sincère *adjective* sincere.

sincérité *noun Fem.* sincerity.

singe *noun Masc.* monkey; **un grand singe** an ape.

singulier *noun Masc.* singular; **au singulier** in the singular.

sinistre *noun Masc.* accident, disaster (*for example, a fire or flood*).
sinistre *adjective* **1** sinister; **2** gloomy.

sinistré, **sinistrée** *noun Masc., Fem.* disaster victim.
sinistrée *adjective* stricken; **de l'aide pour les familles sinistrées** help for the families stricken by the disaster.

sinon *conjunction* otherwise; **il faut partir, sinon on sera en retard** we must leave, otherwise we'll be late.

sirène *noun Fem.* **1** siren; **une sirène d'alarme** a fire alarm; **2** mermaid.

sirop *noun Masc.* **1** syrup; **sirop pectoral** cough mixture; **2 sirop de menthe** mint cordial.

site *noun Masc.* site, area; **site touristique** place of interest (*to visit*); **site classé** conservation area.

a
b
c
d
e
f
g
h
i
j
k
l
m
n
o
p
q
r
s
t
u
v
w
x
y
z

site internet noun Masc. web site.

sitôt adverb as soon as; **sitôt rentrée, elle s'est couchée** as soon as she got home, she went to bed; **sitôt après** immediately afterwards; ★ **sitôt dit, sitôt fait** no sooner said than done.

situation noun Fem. **1** situation; **2** job; **il a perdu sa situation** he's lost his job.

situer verb [1] **1 être situé** to be situated; **l'hôtel est situé au bord de la mer** the hotel is situated by the sea; **bien situé** well situated; **2 se situer** to be situated; **la maison se situe dans un quartier résidentiel** the house is in a residential area; **3 se situer** to be set; **le roman se situe à Moscou** the novel is set in Moscow.

six number six; **Rosie a six ans** Rosie's six; **il est six heures** it's six o'clock; **le six juillet** the sixth of July.

sixième noun Fem. (in a French school) the equivalent of Year 7. **sixième** noun Masc. **au sixième** on the sixth floor. **sixième** adjective sixth.

skate noun Masc. **1** skate-boarding; **2** skate-board.

ski noun Masc. **1** ski; **où sont mes skis?** where are my skis?; **2** skiing; **il adore le ski** he loves skiing; **on va faire du ski ce week-end** we're going skiing this weekend.

ski de fond noun Masc. cross-country skiing.

ski de piste noun Masc. downhill skiing.

skier verb [1] to ski; **il skie plutôt bien** he skis pretty well; **skier hor piste** to ski off-piste.

skieur, skieuse noun Masc., Fer skier.

ski nautique noun Masc. water-skiing.

slip noun Masc. **1** underpants; **2** knickers.

Slovaquie noun Fem. Slovakia.

Slovénie noun Fem. Slovenia.

SMIC noun Masc. SHORT FOR **Salaire minimum interprofessionnel de croissance** guaranteed minimum wage; **elle touche le SMIC** she's o the legal minimum wage.

smoking noun Masc. dinner jacke

snack noun Masc. snack bar.

SNCF noun Fem. SHORT FOR **Société nationale des chemins de fer français** (French national railway.

snob noun Masc. & Fem. snob. **snob** adjective snobbish (of a person), posh (of a restaurant).

sobre adjective sober.

sociable adjective friendly, sociable.

social (Masc. plural **sociaux**) adjective social.

socialiste noun Masc., Fem., adjective socialist.

société noun Fem. **1** society; **dan notre société** in our society; **2** company; **il travaille pour une grande société** he works for a big company.

société anonyme noun Fem. public company.

ociologie *noun Fem.* sociology.

ocquette *noun Fem.* ankle sock.

œur *noun Fem.* sister; **ma grande sœur** my big sister, my older sister.

oi *pronoun* **1** one, oneself; **des amis autour de soi** friends around one; **2 avoir confiance en soi** to have confidence in oneself; **3** itself; **pas très intéressant en soi** not very interesting in itself; **cela va de soi** that goes without saying.

oi-disant *adjective* **1** so-called; **c'est le soi-disant champion** he's the so-called champion; **2** supposedly; **elle est soi-disant malade** she's supposedly ill.

oie *noun Fem.* silk; **un foulard en soie** a silk scarf; **le papier de soie** tissue paper.

oif *noun Masc.* thirst; **avoir soif** to be thirsty.

oigner *verb* [1] to look after.

oigneusement *adverb* carefully.

oi-même *pronoun* yourself, oneself; **il faut le faire soi-même** you have to do it yourself.

oin *noun Masc.* **1** care; **2 prendre soin de quelque chose** to take care of something; **3 les soins** treatment; **4 les premiers soins** first aid.

oir *noun Masc.* evening, night; **ce soir** tonight; **hier soir** last night; **demain soir** tomorrow night; **je sors tous les samedis soirs** I go out every Saturday night; **par un beau soir d'été** one fine summer's evening; **à six heures du soir** at six

in the evening; **à ce soir!** see you tonight!

soirée *noun Fem.* **1** evening; **pendant la soirée** during the evening; **2** party; **elle donne une petite soirée** she's having a little party; **3 en tenue de soirée** in evening dress.

soirée dansante *noun Fem.* dance.

sois *verb* SEE **être**¹; **sois gentil** be good.

soit *conjunction* **soit …soit** either …or; **soit demain, soit jeudi** either tomorrow or Thursday.

soixantaine *noun Fem.* **1** about sixty; **une soixantaine de personnes** about sixty people; **2 avoir la soixantaine** to be in your sixties.

soixante *number* sixty.

soixante-dix *number* seventy; **soixante-dix-huit** seventy-eight.

soja *noun Masc.* soya bean; **la sauce de soja** soy sauce.

sol *noun Masc.* **1** floor; **2** soil.

solaire *adjective* **1** solar; **2 la crème solaire** sun cream.

soldat *noun Masc.* soldier.

solde *noun Masc.* **1 les soldes** the sales; **faire les soldes** to go round the sales; **2 être en solde** to be reduced; **les pulls sont en solde** the jumpers are reduced; **3** balance *(in a bank account)*.

soldé *adjective* reduced.

sole *noun Fem.* sole *(fish)*.

soleil *noun Masc.* sun; **au soleil** in the sun; **il fait soleil** it's sunny; **en**

plein soleil in full sun; **attraper un coup de soleil** to get sunburnt.

solfège *noun Masc.* musical theory.

solide *adjective* **1** strong; **2** solid.

soliste *noun Masc. & Fem.* soloist.

solitaire *adjective* **1** lonely, isolated; **2 un navigateur solitaire** a solo yachtsman.

solitude *noun Fem.* **1** loneliness; **2** solitude.

solution *noun Fem.* solution.

sombre *adjective* dark, gloomy.

somme¹ *noun Fem.* sum; **une somme d'argent** a sum of money.

somme² *noun Masc.* nap; **faire un somme** to have a nap.

sommeil *noun Masc.* sleep; **avoir sommeil** to feel sleepy; **je n'ai plus sommeil** I'm not sleepy any more.

sommes *verb* SEE **être**¹.

sommet *noun Masc.* summit.

somnambule *noun Masc. & Fem.* sleepwalker; **être somnambule** to walk in your sleep.

son¹, **sa**, **ses** *adjective* **1** his; **son fils** his son; **sa fille** his daughter; **ses enfants** his children; **2** her; **son fils** her son; **sa fille** her daughter; **ses enfants** her children; **3** its; **le chat a perdu son collier** the cat's lost its collar.

son² *noun Masc.* **1** sound; **le son d'un piano** the sound of a piano; **2** volume (*on a radio or hi-fi*); **baisser le son** to turn the volume down; **3** bran.

sondage *noun Masc.* survey; **un sondage d'opinion** an opinion poll.

sonner *verb* [1] to ring; **le téléphone sonne** the phone's ringing; **on sonne à la porte** somebody's ringing the doorbell.

sonnerie *noun Fem.* bell; **la sonnerie d'alarme** the alarm bell; **la sonnerie du téléphone** the ring of the telephone.

sonnette *noun Fem.* bell, doorbell.

sono *noun Fem.* (*informal*) sound system.

Sonotone™ *noun Masc.* hearing aid.

sophistiqué *adjective* sophisticated.

sorbet *noun Masc.* sorbet; **un sorbet au cassis** a blackcurrant sorbet.

sorcière *noun Fem.* witch.

sort *noun Masc.* fate; ★ **tirer au sort** to draw lots.

sorte *noun Fem.* sort; **c'est une sorte de poudre** it's a sort of powder; **toutes sortes d'activités** all sorts of activities.

sortie *noun Fem.* **1** exit; **il nous attend à la sortie** he's waiting for us at the exit; **sortie de secours** emergency exit; **2** outing; **3** launch (*of a new product*), release (*of a film*), publication (*of a book*).

sortir *verb* [72] **1** to go out; **tout le monde est sorti dans la rue** everybody went out into the street; **ils sont sortis déjeuner** they've gone out for lunch; **elle est sortie en courant** she ran out; **2** to come out; **c'est l'heure où les gens sortent du cinéma** it's the time when people are coming out of the cinema; **son nouveau film sortira**

en mai her new film is coming out in May; **3** to go out (*for pleasure*); **mes parents sortent peu** my parents don't go out much; **4 sortir avec** to be going out with; **il sort avec ma sœur** he's going out with my sister; **5** to take out; **elle a sorti une bouteille du frigo** she took a bottle out of the fridge; **j'ai oublié de sortir le chien** I forgot to take the dog out; **6 s'en sortir** to manage; **je m'en sortirai d'une manière ou d'une autre** I'll manage one way or another.

sottise *noun Fem.* **1** silliness; **2 dire des sottises** to talk nonsense; **ne fais pas de sottises** don't do anything silly.

sou *noun Masc.* **j'ai dépensé tous mes sous** I've spent all my money; **je n'ai pas un sou** I'm broke; **une machine à sous** a fruit machine; ★ **être près de ses sous** to be tight-fisted.

souci *noun Masc.* **1** worry,; **se faire du souci** to worry; **mon fils me donne bien des soucis** my son's a great worry to me; **j'ai d'autres soucis à présent** I've got other problems just now; **2** marigold.

soucieux (*Fem.* **soucieuse**) *adjective* worried.

soucoupe *noun Fem.* saucer.

soudain *adjective* sudden.
soudain *adverb* suddenly.

souffle *noun Masc.* breath; **être à bout de souffle** to be out of breath; **couper le souffle à quelqu'un** to take someone's breath away.

soufflé *noun Masc.* soufflé; **un soufflé au fromage** a cheese soufflé.

souffler *verb* [1] **1** to blow; **le vent soufflait fort** there was a strong wind; **2** to blow out (*a candle*); **3** to whisper; **elle me soufflait quelque chose à l'oreille** she was whispering something in my ear; ★ **souffler dans le ballon** (*informal*) to be breathalysed.

souffrance *noun Fem.* **1** suffering; **2** misery.

souffrir *verb* [73] **1** to suffer; **a-t-elle beaucoup souffert?** did she suffer much?; **il souffre souvent du dos** he often has back pain; **2 je ne peux pas le souffrir!** (*informal*) I can't stand him!

souhait *noun Masc.* wish; ★ **à tes souhaits!** bless you! (*when somebody sneezes*).

souhaiter *verb* [1] to wish; **je te souhaite bonne chance** I wish you luck; **il nous a souhaité la bienvenue** he welcomed us; **il souhaite se marier** he'd like to get married.

soûl *adjective* drunk.

soulagé *adjective* relieved.

soulagement *noun Masc.* relief.

soulager *verb* [52] to relieve.

soulever *verb* [50] **1** to lift; **je n'arrive pas à soulever ta valise** I can't lift your case; **2** to raise (*problems, objections, or difficulties*); **personne n'a soulevé la question** nobody raised the question.

soulier *noun Masc.* shoe.

a
b
c
d
e
f
g
h
i
j
k
l
m
n
o
p
q
r
s
t
u
v
w
x
y
z

souligner *verb* [1] **1** to underline; **2** to emphasize.

soupçon *noun Masc.* **1** suspicion; **2** spot, drop (*of food or drink*); **juste un soupçon de lait** just a drop of milk.

soupçonner *verb* [1] to suspect.

soupe *noun Fem.* soup; **la soupe aux oignons** onion soup.

souper *verb* [1] to have supper.

soupir *noun Masc.* sigh.

soupirer *verb* [1] to sigh.

souple *adjective* **1** supple (*person*); **2** flexible (*system*); **3** soft (*hair or clean washing*).

source *noun Fem.* spring; **l'eau de source** spring water.

sourcil *noun Masc.* eyebrow.

sourd *adjective* **1** deaf; **2** dull, muffled (*noise*); ★ **faire la sourde oreille** to turn a deaf ear.

souriant *adjective* cheerful.

sourire *noun Masc.* smile; **il faut garder le sourire** you must keep smiling.
sourire *verb* [68] to smile; **sourire à quelqu'un** to smile at somebody.

souris *noun Fem.* mouse (*also for a computer*).

sous *preposition* under, underneath; **sous la chaise** under the chair; **sortir sous la pluie** to go out in the rain; **sous terre** underground; ★ **sous peu** before long.

sous-entendu *noun Masc.* innuendo.
sous-entendu *adjective* implied.

sous-estimer *verb* [1] to underestimate.

sous-marin *noun Masc.* submarine.
sous-marin *adjective* under-water, deep-sea.

sous-sol *noun Masc.* basement; **au sous-sol** in the basement.

sous-tasse *noun Fem.* saucer.

sous-titre *noun Masc.* subtitle.

soustraction *noun Fem.* subtraction.

sous-vêtements *plural noun Masc.* underwear.

soutenir *verb* [77] **1** to support; **elle m'a soutenu à la réunion** she supported me at the meeting; **2 soutenir que** to maintain that; **3 soutenir une conversation** to keep up a conversation; **4** to withstand (*a shock or attack*).

souterrain *adjective* underground.

soutien *noun Masc.* support.

soutien-gorge *noun Masc.* bra.

soutif *noun Masc.* (*informal*) bra.

souvenir *noun Masc.* **1** memory; **mes souvenirs de Londres** my memories of London; **garder un bon souvenir de quelque chose** to have happy memories of something; **je n'ai aucun souvenir de l'avoir rencontrée** I have no memory of meeting her; **2** souvenir.
souvenir *verb* [81] **se souvenir de** to remember; **je me souviens d'elle** I remember her; **je me souviens de l'avoir rencontrée** I remember meeting her; **t'en souviens-tu?** do you remember that?

souvent *adverb* often; **je ne la vois pas très souvent** I don't see her very often; **le plus souvent** more often than not.

spacieux (*Fem.* **spacieuse**) *adjective* spacious.

spaghettis *plural noun Masc.* spaghetti; **manger des spaghettis** to have spaghetti.

sparadrap *noun Masc.* sticking plaster.

speaker, speakerine *noun Masc., Fem.* announcer.

spécial (*Masc. plural* **spéciaux**) *adjective* **1** special; **rien de spécial** nothing special; **les effets spéciaux** special effects; **2** odd; **il est vraiment très spécial** he's really very odd.

spécialement *adverb* specially.

spécialiser *verb* [1] **se spécialiser** to specialize; **elle se spécialise dans la génétique** she's specializing in genetics.

spécialiste *noun Masc. & Fem.* specialist.

spécialité *noun Fem.* speciality.

spécifier *verb* [1] to specify.

spectacle *noun Masc.* show.

spectaculaire *adjective* spectacular.

spectateur, spectatrice *noun Masc., Fem.* **1** member of the audience; **2** spectator.

spéléologie *noun Fem.* potholing.

spirituel, spirituelle *adjective* **1** witty; **2** spiritual.

splendeur *noun Fem.* splendour.

splendide *adjective* magnificent.

sponsoriser *verb* [1] to sponsor.

spontané *adjective* spontaneous.

sport *noun Masc.* sport, sports; **aimez-vous le sport?** do you like sport?; **il fait beaucoup de sport** he does a lot of sport; **mon maillot de sport** my sports shirt; **les sports d'hiver** winter sports; **être bon en sport** to be good at sports.

sportif, sportive *noun Masc., Fem.* sportsman, sportswoman. **sportif** (*Fem.* **sportive**) *adjective* **1** sports; **un club sportif** a sports club; **une rencontre sportive** a sports meeting; **2** sporty, athletic.

spot *noun Masc.* **1** spotlight; **2 un spot publicitaire** a commercial.

square *noun Masc.* public garden.

squelette *noun Masc.* skeleton.

stable *adjective* **1** stable; **2 un emploi stable** a steady job.

stade *noun Masc.* stadium.

stage *noun Masc.* **1** course; **un stage intensif d'anglais** an intensive English course; **faire un stage de formation** to go on a training course; **2 un stage professionnel** work experience; **j'aimerais faire un stage professionnel dans une société française** I'd like to do work experience in a French company.

stagiaire *noun Masc. & Fem.* **1** trainee; **2** person on a work experience placement.

stand *noun Masc.* **1** stand (*in a market or an exhibition*); **2** stall (*in a fairground*).

a
b
c
d
e
f
g
h
i
j
k
l
m
n
o
p
q
r
s
t
u
v
w
x
y
z

a

b

c

d

e

f

g

h

i

j

k

l

m

n

o

p

q

r

s

t

u

v

w

x

y

z

standard noun Masc. switchboard; **il faut passer par le standard** you have to go through the switchboard.

standardiste noun Masc. & Fem. switchboard operator.

standing noun Masc. **un appartement de standing** a luxury flat.

star noun Fem. star (in a film or show).

starter noun Masc. choke (in a car).

station noun Fem. **1 une station de métro** an underground station; **2 une station de taxis** a taxi rank; **3** resort; **une station de ski** a ski resort; **4 une station de radio** a radio station.

station de travail noun Fem. (computer) work station.

stationnaire adjective **1** stationary; **2** stable.

stationnement noun Masc. parking; **'stationnement interdit'** 'no parking'.

stationner verb [1] to park.

station-service noun Fem. service station.

statistique noun Fem. statistic(s).

statue noun Fem. statue.

statut noun Masc. **1** statute; **2** status.

steak noun Masc. steak; **un steak frites** steak and chips; **un steak haché** a burger steak.

sténodactylo noun Masc. & Fem. shorthand typist.

stéréo noun Fem., adjective stereo.

stérile adjective sterile.

stériliser verb [1] to sterilize.

steward noun Masc. flight attendant (male).

stimulant adjective stimulating

stock noun Masc. stock; **en stock** stock.

stop noun Masc. **1** stop sign; **2 fair du stop** to hitch-hike.

stopper verb [1] to stop.

store noun Masc. **1** blind; **2** awnin

strapontin noun Masc. fold-dow seat.

stratégie noun Fem. strategy.

stratégique adjective strategic

stress noun Masc. stress.

stressant adjective stressful.

stressé adjective stressed; **elle avait l'air stressé** she looked stressed; **je suis très stressé en moment** I'm stressed out at the moment.

strict adjective **1** strict; **2** severe.

studieux (Fem. **studieuse**) adjective studious.

studio noun Masc. **1** studio flat; **2** studio.

stupéfait adjective astounded.

stupéfiants plural noun Masc. narcotics.

stupeur noun Fem. astonishment

stupide adjective stupid.

stupidité noun Fem. stupidity.

style noun Masc. style; **c'est bien son style!** that's just like him!

styliste noun Masc. & Fem. design

stylo noun Masc. fountain pen.

ylo-bille noun Masc. ball-point en.

ylo-feutre noun Masc. felt pen.

ylo-plume noun Masc. fountain en.

l verb SEE **savoir**[1].

bir verb [2] **1** to be subjected to *hange, violence, or pressure*); **2** to uffer (*defeat or damage*); **3** subir ne opération to have an operation.

bitement adverb suddenly.

bjonctif noun Masc. subjunctive; u subjonctif in the subjunctive.

bordonné, subordonnée oun Masc., Fem. subordinate.

bstituer verb [1] to substitute.

btil adjective subtle.

bvention noun Fem. subsidy.

ccès noun Masc. success; c'est n grand succès! it's a great uccess!

ccursale noun Fem. branch (*of a* ompany).

cer verb [61] to suck.

cette noun Fem. lollipop.

cre noun Masc. **1** sugar; du jus 'orange sans sucre unsweetened range juice; **2** un sucre a lump of ugar.

cré adjective sweet; c'est trop ucré pour moi it's too sweet for e.

cre cristallisé noun Masc. ranulated sugar.

cre d'orge noun Masc. barley ugar.

cre en morceaux noun Masc. ugar lumps.

sucre en poudre noun Masc. caster sugar.

sucre glace noun Masc. icing sugar.

sucrerie noun Fem. des sucreries sweet things.

sucre roux noun Masc. brown sugar.

sucrier noun Masc. sugar bowl.

sud noun Masc. south; au sud de l'Écosse in the south of Scotland; au sud de Calais south of Calais; un vent du sud a south wind.
sud adjective **1** south; la côte sud the south coast; **2** southern; la partie sud the southern part.

sud-africain adjective South African.

Sud-Africain, Sud-Africaine noun Masc., Fem. South African.

sud-américain adjective South American.

Sud-Américain, Sud-Américaine noun Masc., Fem. South American.

sud-est noun Masc., adjective south-east.

sud-ouest noun Masc., adjective south-west.

Suède noun Fem. Sweden.

suédois noun Masc. Swedish (*language*).
suédois adjective Swedish.

Suédois, Suédoise noun Masc., Fem. Swede.

suer verb [1] to sweat.

sueur noun Fem. sweat; je suis en sueur I'm sweating.

a
b
c
d
e
f
g
h
i
j
k
l
m
n
o
p
q
r
s
t
u
v
w
x
y
z

a

b **suffire** *verb* [74] **1** to be enough; **un kilo suffit** one kilo's enough; **ça**
c **suffit!** that's enough!; **2 il suffit de faire** all you have to do is; **il suffit de**
d **nous téléphoner** all you have to do is give us a call.

e **suffisamment** *adverb* enough; **ce n'est pas suffisamment cuit** it's
f not cooked enough; **il n'y a pas suffisamment de verres** there
g aren't enough glasses.

suffisant *adjective* **1** sufficient;
h **c'est bien suffisant!** that's quite enough!; **2** smug; **je la trouve un**
i **peu suffisante** I find her a bit smug.

j **suffoquer** *verb* [1] to suffocate, to choke.
k
suggérer *verb* [24] to suggest.
l
suggestion *noun Fem.* suggestion.
m
suicider *verb* [1] **se suicider** to
n commit suicide.

o **suis** *verb* SEE **être**[1]; SEE **suivre**.

suisse *adjective* Swiss.
p
Suisse *noun Fem.* Switzerland; **en**
q **Suisse** in (or to) Switzerland; **la Suisse romande** French-speaking
r Switzerland; **la Suisse allemande** German-speaking Switzerland.

s
suite *noun Fem.* **1** rest; **je te**
t **raconterai la suite plus tard** I'll tell you the rest later; **et on connaît**
u **la suite** and we all know what happened next; **2** continuation;
v **'suite page 67'** 'continued on page 67'; **regardez la suite jeudi** watch
w the next instalment on Thursday; **3** suite (*in a hotel*); **4** in succession;
x **trois fois de suite** three times in succession; **5 tout de suite**
y straightaway; **j'arrive tout de suite!**
z

I'll be right there!; **6 par la suite** later; **on s'est rendu compte par suite que c'était une erreur** we realized later that it was a mistak

suivant, suivante *noun Masc., Fem.* next one; **pas ce lundi mais suivant** not this Monday but the next.
suivant *adjective* following; **le jo suivant** the following day.

suivre *verb* [75] **1** to follow; **suive moi** follow me; **2 suivre l'actuali** to keep up with the news; **3 'à suivre'** 'to be continued'; **4 faire suivre son courrier** to have your mail forwarded; **5 suivre un cou** to do a course; **6 suivre un régim** to be on a diet.

sujet *noun Masc.* **1** subject; **au suj de** about; **c'est au sujet de votre fils** it's about your son; **c'est à qu sujet?** what's it about?; **un sujet conversation** a topic of conversation; **2 un sujet d'exame** an exam question.
sujet *adjective* (*Fem.* **sujette**) **êtr sujet à** to suffer from; **elle est sujette à des crises d'asthme** s suffers from asthma attacks.

super *noun Masc.* four-star petrol.
super *adjective* (*informal*) fantastic; **mais c'est super!** but that's fantastic!

superficie *noun Fem.* area.

superficiel (*Fem.* **superficielle**) *adjective* superficial.

supérieur, supérieure *nou Masc., Fem.* superior.
supérieur *adjective* **1** upper; **l'étage supérieur** the upper floor **lèvre supérieure** the upper lip;

greater; **la taille supérieure** the bigger size; **à une vitesse supérieure** at a faster speed; **à une température supérieure** at a higher temperature; **un prix supérieur** a higher price; **3** better, superior (*work, quality*); **c'est de loin supérieur à l'autre!** it's much better than the other one!; **4 supérieur à** greater than; **un nombre supérieur à trois** a number higher than three.

superlatif *noun* Masc. superlative.

supermarché *noun* Masc. supermarket.

superposer *verb* [1] **1** to stack up; **des lits superposés** bunk beds; **2** to superimpose (*an image*).

superstitieux (Fem. **superstitieuse**) *adjective* superstitious.

superstition *noun* Fem. superstition.

supplément *noun* Masc. extra charge; **le vin est en supplément** wine is extra.

supplémentaire *adjective* **1** additional; **2 faire des heures supplémentaires** to do overtime.

supplice *noun* Masc. torture.

supplier *verb* [1] to beg.

support *noun* Masc. **1** support; **2** back-up (material); **un support audiovisuel** audiovisual aids.

supportable *adjective* bearable.

supporter *verb* [1] **1** to stand; **il ne supporte pas qu'on le critique** he can't stand being criticized; **je ne peux plus la supporter!** I can't

stand any more of her!; **2** to support (*a weight*).

supposer *verb* [1] to suppose.

supprimer *verb* [1] **1** to get rid of; **2 supprimer des emplois** to cut jobs; **supprimer un train** to cancel a train.

sur *preposition* **1** on; **c'est sur ton lit** it's on your bed; **un débat sur le racisme** a discussion on racism; **le cinéma est sur la droite** the cinema's on the right; **2** over; **un pont sur la Loire** a bridge over the Loire; **3** by (*in measurements*); **c'est deux mètres sur trois** it's two metres by three; **4** out of; **trois femmes sur cinq** three women out of five; **5** out of; **j'ai eu douze sur vingt en géographie** I got twelve out of twenty in geography.

sûr *adjective* **1** sure; **tu es sûr?** are you sure?; **oui, bien sûr!** yes, of course!; **sûr et certain** certain; **j'en étais sûr!** I knew it!; **2 sûr de soi, de lui, d'elle** (*etc*) self-confident; **elle est très sûre d'elle** she's very self-confident; **3** safe; **en lieu sûr** in a safe place; **le plus sûr est de tout fermer à clé** the safest thing is to lock everything.

surcharger *verb* [52] to overload.

surdité *noun* Fem. deafness.

surdose *noun* Fem. overdose (*of medicine*).

sûrement *adverb* **1** certainly; **sûrement pas!** certainly not!; **2 il doit sûrement arriver à tout instant** he's bound to arrive at any moment; **elle est sûrement partie** she's bound to have left.

sûreté noun Fem. safety, security.

surf noun Masc. surfing; **faire du surf** to go surfing.

surface noun Fem. **1** surface; **2** area; **3 une grande surface** a hypermarket.

surface de réparation noun Fem. penalty area.

surf des neiges noun Masc. snowboarding; **faire du surf des neiges** to go snowboarding.

surfer verb [1] **surfer Internet/le web** to surf the Net/Web.

surfeur, **surfeuse** noun Masc., Fem. surfer (on the sea).

surgelé noun Masc. **les surgelés** frozen food.
surgelé adjective frozen; **les légumes surgelés** frozen vegetables.

sur-le-champ adverb right away.

surlendemain noun Masc. **elle est arrivée le surlendemain** she arrived two days later.

surmonter verb [1] to overcome.

surnaturel (Fem. **surnaturelle**) adjective supernatural.

surnom noun Masc. nickname.

surnommer verb [1] to nickname.

surpeuplé adjective overpopulated.

surprenant adjective surprising.

surprendre verb [64] **1** to surprise; **ça m'a beaucoup surpris** I found that really surprising; **2 surprendre quelqu'un en train de faire quelque chose** to catch somebody doing something; **je l'ai surprise en train de lire mon**

courrier I caught her reading my mail.

surpris adjective surprised; **je su surpris de te voir** I'm surprised t see you.

surprise noun Fem. surprise; **quelle surprise!** what a surprise!; **ma grande surprise elle a accep** to my great surprise she agreed; **faire une surprise à quelqu'un** t give somebody a surprise.

surréaliste noun Masc. & Fem. surrealist.
surréaliste adjective surreal.

surtout adverb **1** especially; **il y beaucoup de touristes, surtout é été** there are lots of tourists, especially in the summer; **2** above all; **il faut surtout rester calme** above all, we must stay calm.

surveillant, **surveillante** noun Masc., Fem. supervisor (in a school, responsible for maintainin, school discipline outside the classroom).

surveiller verb [1] **1** to watch, to keep an eye on; **est-ce que tu peu surveiller mon sac deux secondes?** can you keep an eye o my bag for a couple of minutes?; **2 surveiller une maison** to keep house under surveillance; **3** to supervise; **surveiller le travail de élèves** to supervise the students' work (work or progress); **4 surveiller un examen** to invigilate an exam; **5 je surveille ma ligne** I'm watching my figure.

survêtement noun Masc. tracksuit.

urvie *noun Fem.* survival.

urvivant, **survivante** *noun Masc.*, *Fem.* survivor.

urvivre *verb* [82] to survive; **survivre à un accident** to survive an accident.

urvoler *verb* [1] to fly over.

uspect, **suspecte** *noun Masc.*, *Fem.* suspect.

suspect *adjective* suspicious.

uspense *noun Masc.* suspense (*as in a thriller*).

uture *noun Fem.* **un point de suture** a stitch (*in a wound*).

velte *adjective* slender.

VP SHORT FOR **s'il vous plaît** please.

weat *noun Masc.* SEE **sweatshirt**.

weatshirt *noun Masc.* sweatshirt.

yllabe *noun Fem.* syllable.

ymbole *noun Masc.* symbol.

ymbolique *adjective* symbolic; **un geste symbolique** a token gesture.

ympa *adjective* (*informal*) nice; **je le trouve très sympa, ton copain** he's really nice, your boyfriend.

ympathie *noun Fem.* **j'ai beaucoup de sympathie pour elle** I like her a lot.

ympathique *adjective* nice; **c'est un type sympathique** he's a nice guy.

ympathiser *verb* [1] **sympathiser avec quelqu'un** to get on well with someone.

ymptôme *noun Masc.* symptom.

ynagogue *noun Fem.* synagogue.

yndicat *noun Masc.* trade union.

syndicat d'initiative *noun Masc.* tourist information office.

synthétique *adjective* synthetic.

synthétiseur *noun Masc.* synthesizer.

système *noun Masc.* system; **un système d'éclairage** a lighting system.

Tt

ta *adjective* SEE **ton**[1].

tabac *noun Masc.* **1** tobacco; **2 un bureau de tabac** a tobacconist's.

tabagisme *noun Masc.* addiction to tobacco.

table *noun Fem.* table; **à table!** dinner's ready!; **se mettre à table** to sit down to eat; **mettre la table** to lay the table.

tableau *noun Masc.* **1** painting; **un tableau de Renoir** a painting by Renoir; **2 le tableau noir** the blackboard; **3 le tableau d'affichage** the notice board.

tableau de bord *noun Masc.* dashboard.

table de chevet, **table de nuit** *noun Fem.* bedside table.

table des matières *noun Fem.* (list of) contents (*in a book*).

tablette *noun Fem.* **une tablette de chocolat** a bar of chocolate.

tablier *noun Masc.* apron.

tabouret *noun Masc.* stool.

tache *noun Fem.* **1** stain; **2** spot.

a
b
c
d
e
f
g
h
i
j
k
l
m
n
o
p
q
r
s
t
u
v
w
x
y
z

a **tâche** noun Fem. task.

b **tache de rousseur** noun Fem. freckle.

c **tacher** verb [1] to stain.

d **tacle** noun Masc. tackle (in rugby).

e **tact** noun Masc. tact; **il l'a fait avec beaucoup de tact** he did it very tactfully.

f **tactique** noun Fem. tactics.
tactique adjective tactical.

g **tagueur** noun Masc. graffiti artist.

h **taie** noun Fem. **une taie d'oreiller** a pillowcase.

i **taille** noun Fem. **1** size; **qu'est-ce que vous avez à ma taille?** what have you got in my size?; **quelle taille faites-vous?** what size are you?; **'taille unique'** 'one size'; **la taille au-dessus/au-dessous** the next size up/down; **2** height; **un homme de grande taille** a tall man; **3** waist; **avoir la taille fine** to have a slim waist.

j **taille-crayon** noun Masc. pencil sharpener.

k **tailler** verb [1] **1** to cut; **2** to carve; **3** to prune; **4** to sharpen (a pencil).

l **tailleur** noun Masc. **1** suit (for a woman); **2** tailor; ★ **s'asseoir en tailleur** to sit cross-legged (literally: like a tailor).

m **taire** verb [76] **se taire** to stop talking; **taisez-vous!** be quiet!

n **talent** noun Masc. talent; **c'est un jeune musicien de talent** he's a talented young musician.

o **talon** noun Masc. **1** heel (of your foot or a shoe); **2** stub (of a ticket or cheque book).

talon aiguille noun Masc. stiletto heel.

tambour noun Masc. drum.

tambourin noun Masc. tambourine.

Tamise noun Fem. **la Tamise** the Thames.

tampon noun Masc. **1** pad (for sponging); **un tampon à récurer** a scouring pad; **2** un tampon (hygiénique) a tampon.

tamponneuse adjective **les autos tamponneuses** the dodgems.

tandis que conjunction while.

tant adverb **1** so much; **j'ai tant mangé que ...** I've eaten so much that ...; **ce qu'elle avait tant espéré** what she had so much hoped for; **je ne les aime pas tant que ça** I don't like them as much as that; **2** tant de so much, so many; **tant d'argent** so much money; **tant d'amis** so many friends; **tant de monde** so many people; **3** tant pis never mind; **4** tant mieux so much the better; **5** tant que while; **tant que tu y es passe-moi un stylo** while you're there, pass me a pen; **6** tant que as long as; **tant que Jacques ne sera pas rentré, je ne peux pas sortir** I can't go out until Jacques gets back.

tante noun Fem. aunt.

tantôt adverb sometimes; **tantôt chez elle, tantôt chez moi** sometimes at her place and sometimes at mine.

taper verb [1] **1 taper quelqu'un** to hit somebody; **ça tape aujourd'hui** the sun's really beating down today; **2 taper à la machine** to type; **tape**

une lettre to type a letter; **3 taper des mains** to clap your hands; **taper du pied** to tap your foot; **4 taper à la porte** to knock on the door; **5** (*informal*) **se taper dessus** to knock each other about.

apis *noun Masc.* carpet.

apis de bain *noun Masc.* bathmat.

apis roulant *noun Masc.* **1** walkway; **2** carousel (*for airport luggage*); **3** conveyor belt.

apisser *verb* [1] **1** to wallpaper; **2** to upholster.

apisserie *noun Fem.* **1** tapestry; **2** wallpaper.

aquiner *verb* [1] to tease.

ard *adverb* late; **couche-toi, il est tard** go to bed, it's late; **plus tard** later; **trop tard** too late; **pas plus tard que mardi** no later than Tuesday; **ce sera pour plus tard** there'll be other times.

arder *verb* [1] to be a long time; **ta mère ne va pas tarder** your mother won't be long.

ardif (Fem. **tardive**) *adjective* late.

arif *noun Masc.* **1** rate; **tarif de nuit** night rate (*for the phone*); **2** fare; **plein tarif** full fare; **tarif réduit** reduced fare; **3** price list.

arte *noun Fem.* tart; **une tarte aux abricots** an apricot tart.

artine *noun Fem.* slice of bread and butter (*and/or jam*).

artiner *verb* [1] to spread (*on bread*).

as *noun Masc.* **1** pile; **un tas de bois** a pile of wood; **2** batch; **un tas de lettres** a batch of letters; **3** (*informal*) **un tas de** stacks of; **j'ai un tas de choses à faire ce soir** I've got stacks of things to do tonight.

tasse *noun Fem.* cup; **une tasse de thé** a cup of tea.

tatie *noun Fem.* (*informal*) auntie.

taupe *noun Fem.* mole (*animal*).

taupinière *noun Fem.* mole hill.

taureau (*plural* **taureaux**) *noun Masc.* bull.

Taureau *noun Masc.* Taurus (*sign of the Zodiac*).

taux *noun Masc.* rate; **le taux mensuel** the monthly rate; **le taux de change** the exchange rate.

taxe *noun Fem.* tax; **la boutique hors taxes** the duty-free shop.

taxi *noun Masc.* taxi; **appeler un taxi** to call a taxi.

tchèque *adjective* Czech; **la République tchèque** the Czech Republic.

te, **t'** (*before a vowel or silent 'h'*) *pronoun* you **1** Gaby te cherche Gaby's looking for you; **il t'a vu** he saw you; **il te l'a donné** he gave it to you; **2** to you; **3** yourself; **tu peux te faire une salade** you can make yourself a salad; **tu t'es blessé?** have you hurt yourself?; **tu te lèves quand?** what time do you get up?

technicien, **technicienne** *noun Masc., Fem.* technician.

technique *noun Fem.* technique. **technique** *adjective* technical.

technologie *noun Fem.* technology.

a b c d e f g h i j k l m n o p q r s t u v w x y z

a **teckel** noun Masc. dachshund.

b **tee-shirt** noun Masc. T-shirt.

teint noun Masc. complexion; **avoir
le teint clair** to have a fair
complexion.

c

d **teinturier, teinturière** noun
Masc., Fem. dry-cleaner's.

e **tel, telle** adjective 1 such; **avec un
tel intérêt** with such interest; **une
telle aventure** such an adventure;
de tels mensonges such lies; 2 **tel
que** such as; **les grandes villes
telles que Paris et Lyon** large
towns such as Paris and Lyons;
3 **rien de tel que** nothing like; **il n'y
a rien de tel qu'un bon repas**
there's nothing like a good meal;
4 **servir le saumon tel quel** serve
the salmon just as it is; **je l'ai
acheté tel quel** I bought it just as it
was.

f

g

h

i

j

k

l

m

n **télé** noun Fem. (informal) telly; **je l'ai
vu à la télé** I saw it on telly.

o **télécabine** noun Masc. cable car.

p **télécarte™** noun Fem.
phonecard.

q

r **télécommande** noun Fem.
remote control.

télécopie noun Fem. fax.

s

télécopieur noun Masc. fax
machine, fax.

t

u **téléphérique** noun Masc. cable
car.

v

w **téléphone** noun Masc. telephone;
un numéro de téléphone a phone
number; **Bruno est au téléphone**
Bruno's on the phone.

x

y **téléphone portable** noun Masc.
mobile phone.

z

téléphoner verb [1] to phone; **je
vais téléphoner à Robert** I'll phon▮
Robert.

téléphone sans fil noun Masc.
cordless phone.

téléphonique adjective **une
cabine téléphonique** a phone box▮
un appel téléphonique a phone
call.

télésiège noun Masc. chairlift.

téléski noun Masc. ski-tow.

**téléspectateur,
téléspectatrice** noun Masc.,
Fem. viewer (of TV).

téléviser verb [1] to televize.

téléviseur noun Masc. television
(set); **un téléviseur couleur** a
colour television.

télévision noun Fem. television; **à▮
la télévision** on television.

telle adjective SEE **tel**.

tellement adverb 1 so; **c'est
tellement compliqué!** it's so
complicated!; 2 so much; **c'est
tellement mieux payé** it's so muc▮
better paid; **'tu aimes lire?' – 'pas
tellement'** 'do you like reading?' –
'not much'; 3 **tellement de** so much▮
so many; **j'ai tellement de travail▮**
I've got so much work!; **il y a
tellement de choses à voir!** there▮
are so many things to see!; **il y ava▮
tellement de monde** there were s▮
many people there.

tels, telles adjective SEE **tel**.

témoignage noun Masc. 1 story,
account; **selon les témoignages d▮
l'accident** according to accounts o▮
the accident; 2 evidence (in court);

un témoignage d'amitié a token of friendship.

moigner *verb* [1] to give vidence.

moin *noun Masc.* witness.

mpérature *noun Fem.* emperature.

mpête *noun Fem.* storm.

mple *noun Masc.* **1** temple; (Protestant) church.

mporaire *adjective* temporary.

mps *noun Masc.* **1** weather; **quel emps fait-il?** what's the weather ike?; **par temps de pluie** in rainy veather; **2** time; **je n'ai pas le emps** I haven't got time; **il est emps de partir** it's time to go; **rriver à temps** to arrive in (*or* on) ime; **de temps en temps** from time o time; **en même temps** at the ame time; **ça a pris beaucoup de emps** it took a long time; **il nous este combien de temps?** how nuch time do we have left?; **c'est du emps perdu** it's a waste of time; **il tait temps!** about time too!; **ces erniers temps** recently; **un travail plein temps** a full-time job; **un ravail à temps partiel** a part-time ob; **3** tense (*of a verb*).

ndance *noun Fem.* **1** tendency; voir tendance à faire to tend to do; trend.

ndre[1] *verb* [3] **1** to stretch (*something elastic*); **2** to hold out; elle m'a tendu un crayon** she held ut a pencil to me; **tendre la main à uelqu'un** to hold out one's hand to omeone; **3 tendre le bras** to reach ut.

tendre[2] *adjective* tender.

tendresse *noun Fem.* tenderness.

tendu *adjective* tense.

tenir *verb* [77] **1** to hold; **peux-tu tenir la corde?** can you hold the rope?; **elle tenait l'enfant par la main** she was holding the child by the hand; **2** to run (*a shop, a business*); **le stand est tenu par des bénévoles** the stand is run by volunteers; **3** to keep; **elle tenait les yeux baissés** she kept her eyes down; **'tenir hors de la portée des enfants'** 'keep out of reach of children'; **4** to take up; **cela tient la place de deux personnes** it takes up the space of two people; **5 tenir à** to be attached to; **elle tient beaucoup à ses petits-enfants** she's very attached to her grandchildren; **6 tenir à faire quelque chose** to be determined to do something; **je tiens à le finir aujourd'hui** I'm determined to finish it today; **7 tiens!** oh!; **tiens, il est déjà midi!** oh, it's twelve already!; **tiens! est-ce que je t'ai raconté ...?** listen! have I told you ...?; **tiens, tiens, c'est toi!** well, well, it's you!; **tiens, prends le mien** here, take mine; **8 tenir de quelqu'un** to take after someone; **elle tient de sa mère** she takes after her mother; **9 se tenir** to hold ; **ils se tenaient par la main** they were holding each other by the hand; **10 se tenir** to stand; **elle se tenait devant l'entrée** she was standing by the entrance; **tiens-toi tranquille!** be quiet!; **tiens-toi droit!** stand up straight!; **11 se tenir pour**

a
b
c
d
e
f
g
h
i
j
k
l
m
n
o
p
q
r
s
t
u
v
w
x
y
z

to think yourself; **il se tient pour un génie** he thinks he's a genius.

tennis *noun Masc.* **1** tennis; **jouer au tennis** to play tennis; **un terrain de tennis, un tennis** a tennis court; **tennis de table** table tennis; **2** tennis shoe.

tension *noun Fem.* **1** tension; **2** blood pressure.

tentant *adjective* tempting.

tentation *noun Fem.* temptation.

tentative *noun Fem.* attempt.

tente *noun Fem.* tent.

tenter *verb* [1] **1** to attempt; **il a tenté de s'échapper** he tried to escape; **tenter sa chance, tenter le coup** (*informal*) to give it a try; **2** to tempt.

tenu *adjective* **1** bien/mal tenu well/badly cared for; **2** être tenu de faire** to be required to do.

tenue *noun Fem.* clothes; **être en tenue de sport** to be in sports kit; **en tenue de soirée** in evening dress.

terme *noun Masc.* **1** word, term; **un terme technique** a technical term; **les termes du contrat** the terms of the contract; **2** end; **à court terme** short-term; **à long terme** long-term.

terminaison *noun Fem.* ending.

terminale *noun Fem.* (*in a French school*) the equivalent of Year 13.

terminer *verb* [1] **1** to finish; **2** to end; **la réunion s'est terminée à dix-huit heures** the meeting ended at six p.m.; **ça va mal se terminer!** it'll end in tears!

terminus *noun Masc.* terminus.

terrain *noun Masc.* **1** ground, lan il a acheté du terrain** he's bough some land; **2** pitch, ground (*for sports*); **un terrain de football** a football pitch; **un terrain de golf** golf course; **3** piece of ground; **un terrain à bâtir** a building plot.

terrain de camping *noun Ma* campsite.

terrain de jeu(x) *noun Masc.* playground.

terrain de sport(s) *noun Mas* sports ground.

terrain vague *noun Masc.* wast ground.

terrasse *noun Fem.* terrace.

terre *noun Fem.* **1** ground; **s'assed par terre** to sit on the floor; **tomb par terre** to fall down; **2** la Terre t Earth; **3** soil; **4** land (*not sea*); **aller terre** to go ashore.

terre cuite *noun Fem.* terracott

terrible *adjective* **1** terrible; **des événements terribles** terrible events; **2** (*informal*) terrific; **'c'éta bien, le film?' – 'pas terrible'** 'w the film any good?' – 'not great'.

terrifiant *adjective* terrifying.

terrifier *verb* [1] terrify.

terrine *noun Fem.* pâté.

territoire *noun Masc.* **1** territory **2** country; **il fera beau sur l'ensemble du territoire** the weather will be fine throughout t country.

terrorisme *noun Masc.* terrorisr

terroriste *noun Masc. & Fem.* terrorist.

tes *adjective* your; SEE **ton**[1].

est *noun Masc.* test.

estament *noun Masc.* will.

ester *verb* [1] to test.

étanos *noun Masc.* tetanus.

êtard *noun Masc.* tadpole.

ête *noun Fem.* **1** head; **se laver la tête** to wash your hair; **j'ai la tête qui tourne** my head's spinning; **2** face; **je n'aime pas sa tête** I don't like his face; **3** top; **tu es en tête de la liste** you're first on the list; **4** mind; **j'ai quelque chose en tête** I have something in mind; **où avais-tu la tête?** what were you thinking of?; **5** front (*of a train*); **les deux wagons de tête sont à destination de Bourges** the two front coaches are for Bourges; ★ **faire la tête** to sulk; ★ **un dîner en tête à tête** a private dinner for two; ★ **j'en ai par-dessus la tête!** I'm fed up to the back teeth!

êtu *adjective* stubborn.

exte *noun Masc.* text.

exto™ *noun Masc.* text message; **envoyer un texto à quelqu'un** to text someone.

GV *noun Masc.* SHORT FOR **train à grande vitesse** high-speed train.

halassothérapie *noun Fem.* sea-water treatment (*at a health spa*).

hé *noun Masc.* tea; **un thé au lait** tea with milk.

héâtre *noun Masc.* **1** theatre; **des costumes de théâtre** stage costumes; **un coup de théâtre** a dramatic turn of events; **2** plays; **le théâtre de Molière** Molière's plays;

3 faire du théâtre to belong to a drama group.

théière *noun Fem.* teapot.

thème *noun Masc.* **1** subject; **2** prose (*a text to translate into the foreign language*).

théorie *noun Fem.* theory.

thérapie *noun Fem.* **1** (medical) treatment; **2** therapy.

thermal (*Masc. plural* **thermaux**) *adjective* thermal; **une station thermale** a spa.

thermomètre *noun Masc.* thermometer.

thermos™ *noun Masc.* vacuum flask, thermos™.

thon *noun Masc.* tuna.

thym *noun Masc.* thyme.

tibia *noun Masc.* **1** shin; **2** shinbone.

tic *noun Masc.* nervous twitch.

ticket *noun Masc.* **1** ticket; **un ticket de métro** an underground ticket; **2 un ticket de caisse** a till receipt.

tiède *adjective* **1** warm; **2** lukewarm.

tien, tienne, tiens, tiennes *pronoun* **le tien, la tienne, les tiens, les tiennes** yours; **est-ce que ce stylo est le tien?** is this pen yours?; **ma voiture et la tienne** my car and yours; **mes lettres et les tiennes** my letters and yours.

tiens *verb* SEE **tenir**
tiens *pronoun* SEE **tien**.

tiers *noun Masc.* third; **les deux tiers de la population** two-thirds of the population.
tiers (*Fem.* **tierce**) *adjective* third.

291

a
b
c
d
e
f
g
h
i
j
k
l
m
n
o
p
q
r
s
t
u
v
w
x
y
z

tiers-monde noun Masc. Third World.

tige noun Fem. stem.

tigre noun Masc. tiger.

tilleul noun Masc. 1 lime tree; 2 lime flower tea.

timbre noun Masc. stamp.

timide adjective 1 shy; 2 self-conscious.

timidité noun Fem. shyness.

tiquer verb [1] **sans tiquer** without batting an eyelid.

tir noun Masc. 1 shooting; 2 shot (in football).

tirage noun Masc. **le tirage au sort** the draw (in a lottery, for example); **par tirage au sort** by drawing lots.

tir à l'arc noun Masc. archery.

tire-bouchon noun Masc. corkscrew.

tirelire noun Fem. money box.

tirer verb [1] 1 to pull; **il m'a tiré par le bras** he pulled my arm; **elle m'a tiré les cheveux** she pulled my hair; 2 to draw; **tirer les rideaux** to draw the curtains; **il a tiré la lettre de sa poche** he drew the letter from his pocket; **tirer un trait** to draw a line; **tirer des conclusions** to draw conclusions; **tirer au sort** to draw lots; 3 to fire; **ils ont tiré sur les policiers** they fired on the police; **tirer plusieurs coups de feu** to fire several shots.

tiret noun Masc. dash.

tiroir noun Masc. drawer.

tisane noun Fem. herbal tea.

tisonnier noun Masc. poker (for fire).

tissu noun Masc. material, fabric.

titre noun Masc. 1 title; 2 headline; **les titres de l'actualité** the news headlines; 3 **à juste titre** quite rightly; **à titre d'exemple** as an example.

titre de transport noun Masc. travel ticket.

tituber verb [1] to stagger.

toast noun Masc. 1 piece of toast; **servir avec des toasts** serve with toast; 2 toast (to someone's health).

toboggan noun Masc. slide.

toi pronoun you; **c'est toi!** it's you!; **avec toi** with you; **plus grand que toi** bigger than you; **c'est à toi de jouer** it's your turn; **assieds-toi** sit down; **est-ce que ces chaussettes sont à toi?** are these socks yours?

toile noun Fem. 1 cloth; **toile de lin** linen; **une toile cirée** an oilcloth; 2 painting, canvas; **une toile de Picasso** a painting by Picasso.

Toile noun Fem. **la Toile** the Web.

toile d'araignée noun Fem. spider's web, cobweb.

toilette noun Fem. 1 **faire sa toilette** to have a wash; 2 outfit; **je me suis acheté une toilette pour le mariage de ma sœur** I've bought an outfit for my sister's wedding.

toilettes plural noun Fem. toilet; **aller aux toilettes** to go to the toilet.

toi-même pronoun yourself; **l'as-tu fait toi-même?** did you make it yourself?

toit noun Masc. roof.

tolérant *adjective* tolerant.

tolérer *verb* [24] to tolerate.

tomate *noun Fem.* tomato; **une salade de tomates** a tomato salad.

tombe *noun Fem.* grave.

tombeau *(plural* **tombeaux)** *noun Masc.* tomb.

tomber *verb* [1] **1** to fall; **attention, tu vas tomber!** careful, you'll fall!; **la chaise est tombée** the chair fell over; **Noël tombe un lundi** Christmas falls on a Monday; **2 laisser tomber** to drop; **j'ai laissé tomber mon porte-monnaie** I've dropped my purse; **3 laisser tomber** to give up *(an activity)*; **elle a laissé tomber l'espagnol** she's given up Spanish; **4 tomber malade** to fall ill; **tomber amoureux** to fall in love; **5 tomber sur** to bump into; **je suis tombé sur Georges devant la poste** I bumped into Georges outside the post office; **6 ça tombe bien** that's lucky; ★ **je tombe de sommeil** I can't keep my eyes open *(literally: I'm dropping with sleep)*.

tombola *noun Fem.* tombola, lottery.

ton[1]**, ta, tes** *adjective* your; **ton chat** your cat; **ta sœur** your sister; **tes pieds** your feet.

ton[2] *noun Masc.* **1** tone of voice; **2** colour.

tondeuse *noun Fem.* lawnmower.

tondre *verb* [3] to mow.

tonique *adjective* bracing.

tonne *noun Fem.* tonne, metric ton *(1,000 kg)*; ★ **j'ai des tonnes de choses à faire** *(informal)* I've loads of things to do.

tonneau *(plural* **tonneaux)** *noun Masc.* barrel.

tonnerre *noun Masc.* thunder.

tonton *noun Masc. (informal)* uncle.

tonus *noun Masc.* **1** energy *(for a person)*; **2** tone *(for your muscles)*.

toque *noun Fem.* chef's hat.

torchon *noun Masc.* cloth, tea towel.

tordre *verb* [3] to twist; **se tordre la cheville** to twist your ankle.

tordu *adjective* **1** bent; **2** crooked; **3** weird; **une histoire tordue** a weird story.

tornade *noun Fem.* tornado.

torrent *noun Masc.* waterfall, mountain stream.

torse *noun Masc.* chest, upper body; **il s'est mis torse nu** he stripped to the waist.

tort *noun Masc.* **1 avoir tort** to be wrong; **je crois que tu as tort** I think you're wrong; **il a tort de dire ça** he's wrong to say that; **2 à tort** wrongly; **à tort ou à raison** rightly or wrongly.

torticolis *noun Masc.* stiff neck; **avoir le torticolis** to have a stiff neck.

tortiller *verb* [1] **se tortiller** to wriggle.

tortue *noun Fem.* tortoise, turtle.

torture *noun Fem.* torture.

torturer *verb* [1] to torture.

tôt *adverb* **1** early; **on va partir tôt** we're leaving early; **tôt le matin** early in the morning; **2** soon; **le plus tôt possible** as soon as possible; **tôt ou tard** sooner or later.

a
b
c
d
e
f
g
h
i
j
k
l
m
n
o
p
q
r
s
t
u
v
w
x
y
z

total (*plural* **totaux**) *noun Masc.*
total; **au total** in total.
total (*Masc. plural* **totaux**) *adjective*
total.

totalement *adverb* totally.

totalité *noun Fem.* **la totalité des
élèves** all the pupils; **la totalité du
groupe** the whole group.

touchant *adjective* touching.

touche *noun Fem.* **1** key (*on a piano
or keyboard*); **2** button (*on a
machine*); **la touche
d'enregistrement** the record
button; **appuyez sur la touche**
press the button; **3 (ligne de)
touche** touchline.

toucher *verb* [1] **1** to touch; **ne
touche pas à ma peinture** don't
touch my painting; **2** to touch; **cette
histoire m'a beaucoup touché** that
story really touched me; **3** to affect,
to concern; **ce problème nous
touche tous** this problem affects us
all; **4** to get (*money or wages*); **il
touche 350 euros par semaine**
he's getting 350 euros a week.

touffu *adjective* bushy, thick.

toujours *adverb* **1** always; **il est
toujours en retard** he's always late;
comme toujours as always; **2** still;
**nous habitons toujours au même
endroit** we're still living in the same
place; **ton paquet n'est toujours
pas arrivé** your parcel still hasn't
come; **3 pour toujours** for ever.

tour[1] *noun Masc.* **1 faire le tour de** to
go round; **faire le tour des
magasins** to go round all the shops;
faire le tour du monde to go round
the world; **2 faire un tour** to go for a

walk; **on va faire un petit tour** we'
go for a little walk; **3 faire un tour
vélo** to go for a bike ride; **4 faire u
tour en voiture** to go for a drive;
5 turn; **c'est ton tour de jouer** it'
your turn to play; **à qui le tour?**
whose turn is it?

tour[2] *noun Fem.* **1** tower; **la tour
Eiffel** the Eiffel Tower; **2** tower
block; **3** castle, rook (*in chess*).

tourbillon *noun Masc.* whirlwind
whirlpool.

tourisme *noun Masc.* tourism.

touriste *noun Masc. & Fem.* tourist

touristique *adjective* **un guide
touristique** a tourist guide(book);
une ville touristique a town whic
attracts tourists.

tourmenter *verb* [1] to tease.

tournant *noun Masc.* **1** bend (*in a
road*); **2** turning-point.

tourne-disque *noun Masc.* recor
player.

tournée *noun Fem.* **1** round (*of a
postman or baker, for example*);
2 round (*of drinks*); **c'est ma
tournée** it's my round; **3** tour (*of a
performer*); **être en tournée** to be o
tour.

tourner *verb* [1] **1** to turn; **tourne
à gauche à l'église** turn left at th
church; **2** to toss (*a salad*); **3 mal
tourner** to go wrong; **4 se tourner t
turn; **elle s'est tournée vers moi**
she turned to face me; **5 tourner l
dos à quelqu'un** to have your bac
to somebody.

tournesol *noun Masc.* sunflower.

tournevis *noun Masc.* screwdrive

ournis *noun Masc.* **avoir le tournis** to feel dizzy; **j'ai le tournis** I'm feeling dizzy.

ournoi *noun Masc.* tournament.

ourterelle *noun Fem.* turtle dove.

ous *adjective, pronoun* SEE **tout**.

oussaint *noun Fem.* All Saints' Day (*November 1st*).

ousser *verb* [1] to cough.

out, toute, tous, toutes *adjective* **1** all; **tout le pain** all the bread; **toute la classe** all the class, the whole class; **tous les garçons** all the boys; **toutes les filles** all the girls; **tout le monde** everybody; **toute la journée** all day; **tous les deux** both; **je les achète tous les trois** I'll buy all three of them; **pendant toute une année** for a whole year; **2** any; **à tout âge** at any age; **à tout instant** at any moment; **'service à toute heure'** 'service at any time'; **3** every; **tous les jours** every day; **prenez un comprimé toutes les quatre heures** take one pill every four hours.

tout, toutes, tous, toutes *pronoun* **1** everything; **ils ont tout pris** they took everything; **tout va bien** everything's fine; **2** all; **tous ensemble** all together; **elles étaient toutes là** they were all there; **54 en tout** 54 in all; **et tout ça** and all that; **tout ce que je sais, c'est que ...** all I know is that ...; **3 pas du tout** not at all.

tout *adverb* **c'est tout prêt** it's all ready; **il est tout seul** he's all alone; **tout doucement** very slowly; **tout droit** straight ahead.

out à coup *adverb* suddenly.

tout à fait *adverb* completely, absolutely; **ce n'est pas tout à fait sec** it's not absolutely dry.

tout à l'heure *adverb* **1** just now; **je l'ai vu tout à l'heure** I saw him just now; **2** in a little while; **à tout à l'heure!** see you later!

tout de même *adverb* all the same; **c'est tout de même bizarre** all the same, it is odd.

tout de suite *adverb* at once; **fais-le tout de suite!** do it at once!

tout d'un coup *adverb* suddenly.

toutefois *adverb* however.

toutes *adjective, pronoun* SEE **tout**.

toux *noun Fem.* cough.

toxicomane *noun Masc. & Fem.* drug addict.

toxique *adjective* poisonous, toxic.

trac *noun Masc.* (*informal*) **avoir le trac** to feel nervous.

trace *noun Fem.* **1** tracks; **des traces de skis** ski-tracks; **des traces de pas** footprints; **2** mark; **des traces de doigts** finger marks.

tracer *verb* [61] to draw.

tracteur *noun Masc.* tractor.

tradition *noun Fem.* tradition.

traditionnel (*Fem.* **traditionnelle**) *adjective* traditional.

traducteur, traductrice *noun Masc., Fem.* translator.

traduction *noun Fem.* translation.

traduire *verb* [26] to translate; **traduire en français** to translate into French.

trafic *noun Masc.* **1 le trafic de drogue** drug dealing; **2** traffic.

a
b
c
d
e
f
g
h
i
j
k
l
m
n
o
p
q
r
s
t
u
v
w
x
y
z

trafiquant, **trafiquante** noun Masc., Fem. dealer (in drugs or arms).

tragédie noun Fem. tragedy.

tragique adjective tragic.

trahir verb [2] to betray.

trahison noun Fem. betrayal.

train noun Masc. **1** train; **monter dans le train** to get on the train; **descendre du train** to get off the train; **le train de dix heures** the ten o'clock train; **2 être en train de faire** to be (busy) doing; **Henri est en train de faire la vaisselle** Henri's doing the washing-up.

traîner verb [1] **1** to wander round; **2** to lie around; **il laisse ses affaires traîner partout** he leaves his things lying around everywhere; **3** to dawdle; **ne traînez pas, le train arrive** don't be long, the train's coming; **4** to drag on; **j'ai des projets qui traînent** I've got some projects that are dragging on; **5** to drag; **elle traînait sa valise derrière elle** she was dragging her suitcase behind her; **6 traîner les pieds** to drag your feet.

traire verb [78] to milk.

trait noun Masc. **1** line; **2 les traits** features (of a face); **avoir les traits fins** to have delicate features; **3 d'un seul trait** at one go; **il l'a bu d'un seul trait** he drank it all at one go.

trait d'union noun Masc. hyphen.

traité noun Masc. treaty.

traitement noun Masc. **1** treatment; **2** processing; **le traitement de texte** word processing; **3** salary.

traiter verb [1] **1** to treat; **il la trait très mal** he treats her very badly; **le médecin qui me traite** the doctor who's treating me; **2** to deal with (a question or problem); **3 traiter de** to call; **il m'a traité de menteur** he called me a liar.

traiteur noun Masc. caterer.

trajet noun Masc. **1** journey; **c'est un trajet de deux heures** it's a two hour journey; **2** route.

trampoline noun Masc. trampoline; **faire du trampoline** to trampoline.

tramway noun Masc. tram, tramway.

tranchant adjective sharp.

tranche noun Fem. **1** slice; **deux tranches de jambon** two slices of ham; **2** phase, period (of time).

trancher verb [1] **1** to slice; **2** to decide.

tranquille adjective **1** quiet; **une rue tranquille** a quiet street; **tiens toi tranquille!** be quiet!; **2 laisse-moi tranquille!** leave me alone!; **3 maman n'est pas tranquille si je n'appelle pas** Mum worries if I don't ring.

tranquillité noun Fem. peace.

transat noun Masc. (informal) deck chair.

transférer verb [24] to transfer.

transfert noun Masc. transfer.

transformer verb [1] **1** to change; **ils ont transformé leur jardin** they've completely changed their garden; **nous avons transformé cette chambre en bureau** we've turned this bedroom into a study; **2 se transformer en** to change into; **le têtard se transforme en grenouille** the tadpole changes into a frog.

transfusion *noun Fem.* **une transfusion sanguine** a blood transfusion.

transistor *noun Masc.* transistor.

transmettre *verb* [11] **1 transmettre quelque chose à quelqu'un** to pass something on to somebody; **2** to transmit.

transpiration *noun Fem.* perspiration, sweat.

transpirer *verb* [1] to sweat.

transplantation *noun Fem.* **1** transplant (*medical*); **2** transplantation (*of plants*).

transport *noun Masc.* **1** transport; **les frais de transport** transport costs; **2 les transports en commun** public transport.

transporter *verb* [1] **1** to transport; **2** to carry.

trappe *noun Fem.* trap door.

travail (*plural* travaux) *noun Masc.* **1** work; **j'ai beaucoup de travail à faire** I've got a lot of work to do; **2** job; **je cherche un travail** I'm looking for a job.

travailler *verb* [1] to work; **travailler dans la banque** to work in banking.

travailleur, travailleuse *noun Masc., Fem.* worker. **travailleur** (*Fem.* travailleuse) *adjective* hard-working.

travailliste *adjective* Labour; **le parti travailliste** the Labour party (*in Britain*).

travaux *plural noun Masc.* **1** work; **des travaux de construction** building work; **ils font faire des travaux chez eux** they're having some work done on the house; **2** roadworks; **3 les travaux ménagers** housework; **4 les travaux dirigés** classwork; **les travaux manuels** handicrafts.

travée *noun Fem.* bay (*for coaches*).

travers *noun* **1 à travers** through; **j'ai regardé à travers les rideaux** I looked through the curtains; **voyager à travers le monde** to travel all over the world; **2 de travers** crooked; **le tableau est de travers** the picture's crooked; **3 de travers** wrongly; **c'est boutonné de travers** it's buttoned up wrongly.

traversée *noun Fem.* crossing; **une traversée de l'Atlantique** an Atlantic crossing.

traverser *verb* [1] **1** to cross; **regarde avant de traverser la rue** look before you cross the road; **2** to go through; **traverser la France pour aller en Italie** to go through France on the way to Italy; **la pluie a traversé ma veste** the rain's gone right through my jacket; **ils ont traversé une crise** they went through a crisis.

traversin *noun Masc.* bolster.

trébucher *verb* [1] to stumble.

trèfle *noun Masc.* **1** clover; **2** clubs (*in cards*); **la dame de trèfle** the queen of clubs.

a
b
c
d
e
f
g
h
i
j
k
l
m
n
o
p
q
r
s
t
u
v
w
x
y
z

treize *number* thirteen; **Aurélie a treize ans** Aurélie's thirteen; **à treize heures** at one p.m.; **le treize juillet** the thirteenth of July.

treizième *number* thirteenth.

tremblement de terre *noun Masc.* earthquake.

trembler *verb* [1] to shake, to tremble.

trempé *adjective* soaked.

tremper *verb* [1] to soak.

tremplin *noun Masc.* springboard.

trentaine *noun Fem.* **1** about thirty; **une trentaine de personnes** about thirty people; **2 elle a la trentaine** she's in her thirties.

trente *number* thirty; **elle a trente ans** she's thirty; **le trente juillet** the thirtieth of July.

très *adverb* very; **très heureux** very happy; **j'ai très faim** I'm very hungry; **très bien fait** very well done.

trésor *noun Masc.* treasure.

tresse *noun Fem.* plait.

tréteau (*plural* **tréteaux**) *noun Masc.* trestle.

triangulaire *adjective* triangular.

tribu *noun Fem.* tribe.

tribunal (*plural* **tribunaux**) *noun Masc.* court; **paraître devant le tribunal** to appear in court (*on a charge*).

tricher *verb* [1] to cheat.

tricolore *adjective* three-coloured; **le drapeau tricolore** the French flag (*which is three-coloured, blue, white, and red, in vertical stripes*).

tricoter *verb* [1] to knit.

trier *verb* [1] to sort (out); **hier soir nous avons trié toutes les photos** last night we sorted out all the photographs.

trimestre *noun Masc.* term.

trinidadien (*Fem.* **trinidadienne**) *adjective* Trinidadian.

Trinidadien, **Trinidadienne** *noun Masc., Fem.* Trinidadian.

Trinité *noun Fem.* **(l'île de) la Trinité** Trinidad.

triomphe *noun Masc.* triumph.

triompher *verb* [1] to triumph.

tripes *plural noun Fem.* tripe.

triple *noun Masc.* **le triple** three times as much.

tripler *verb* [1] to treble; **le prix a triplé** the price has tripled.

triplés *plural noun Masc.* triplets.

triste *adjective* sad.

tristesse *noun Fem.* sadness.

trognon *noun Masc.* **un trognon de pomme** an apple core.

trois *number* three; **Tom a trois ans** Tom's three; **à trois heures** at three o'clock; **le trois mars** the third of March; ★ **être haut comme trois pommes** to be knee-high to a grasshopper (*literally: as tall as three apples*).

troisième *noun Fem.* (*in a French school*) the equivalent of Year 10.
troisième *noun Masc.* **au troisième** on the third floor.
troisième *adjective* third.

trombone *noun Masc.* **1** trombone; **2** paperclip (*because of its shape*).

ompe *noun Fem.* trunk *elephant's*).

omper *verb* [1] **1** to deceive; **2 se romper** to make a mistake; **il s'est rompé** he made a mistake; **je me suis trompé de train** I got the wrong train; **vous vous êtes rompé de numéro** you've got the wrong number.

ompette *noun Fem.* trumpet; **ouer de la trompette** to play the rumpet.

onc *noun Masc.* trunk (*of a tree*).

onçonneuse *noun Fem.* chain saw.

op *adverb* **1** too; **c'est trop loin** it's too far; **c'est beaucoup trop cher** t's much too expensive; **2** too much; **'ai trop mangé** I've eaten too much; **u m'en as donné trop** you've given ne too much; **3 trop de** too much, too many; **trop de pain** too much bread; **trop de tomates** too many omatoes; **trop de monde** too many people; **4 de trop** too many, too nuch; **il y a une chaise de trop** here's one chair too many; **il y a dix euros de trop** that's ten euros too much.

opique *noun Masc.* tropic.

ottoir *noun Masc.* pavement.

ou *noun Masc.* hole; **le trou dans la couche d'ozone** the hole in the ozone layer.

oublant *adjective* disturbing.

ou d'incendie *noun Masc.* fire hydrant.

ou de serrure *noun Masc.* keyhole.

trouer *verb* [1] to make a hole in; **des chaussettes trouées** socks with holes in them.

trouille *noun Fem.* **avoir la trouille** (*informal*) to be scared.

troupe *noun Fem.* **1 une troupe de théâtre** a theatre company; **2** flock (*of birds*); **3** troop (*of tourists or children*).

troupeau (*plural* **troupeaux**) *noun Masc.* herd (*of cattle*), flock (*of sheep*).

trousse *noun Fem.* pencil case.

trousseau (*plural* **trousseaux**) *noun Masc.* **un trousseau de clés** a bunch of keys.

trousse de maquillage *noun Fem.* make-up bag.

trousse de secours *noun Fem.* first-aid kit.

trousse de toilette *noun Fem.* toilet bag.

trouver *verb* [1] **1** to find; **as-tu trouvé ton passeport?** did you find your passport?; **2** to think; **j'ai trouvé le film passionnant** I thought the film was wonderful; **3 se trouver** to be (*in a place*); **les gens qui se trouvaient autour de moi** the people who were around me; **savez-vous où se trouve la gare routière?** do you know where the bus station is?

truc *noun Masc.* (*informal*) **1** thing; **un petit truc en bois** a little thing made of wood; **il y a un truc qui ne va pas** something's wrong; **le jazz, ce n'est pas mon truc** jazz just isn't my thing; **2** trick; **il doit y avoir un truc** there must be a trick to it.

a
b
c
d
e
f
g
h
i
j
k
l
m
n
o
p
q
r
s
t
u
v
w
x
y
z

truite noun Fem. trout.

tsigane noun Masc. & Fem. gipsy.

TSVP SHORT FOR **tournez s'il vous plaît** PTO (please turn over).

TTC SHORT FOR **toutes taxes comprises** inclusive of tax.

tu pronoun you ('tu' is used when talking to family members, people you know well, and people of your own age; otherwise 'vous' is used for 'you').

tube noun Masc. **1** tube; **2** (informal) hit (a pop song).

tuer verb [1] **1** to kill; **2 se tuer** to be killed; **elle s'est tuée dans un accident de voiture** she was killed in a car accident; **3 se tuer** to kill yourself.

tue-tête in phrase **crier à tue-tête** to shout at the top of your voice.

tuile noun Fem. **1** tile; **2** thin almond biscuit.

tulipe noun Fem. tulip.

Tunisie noun Fem. Tunisia.

tunisien (Fem. **tunisienne**) adjective Tunisian.

tunnel noun Masc. tunnel; **le tunnel sous la Manche** the Channel Tunnel.

turban noun Masc. turban.

turc noun Masc. Turkish (language). **turc** (Fem. **turque**) adjective Turkish.

Turc, Turque noun Masc., Fem. Turk.

Turquie noun Fem. Turkey.

tuteur, tutrice noun Masc., Fem. **1** guardian; **2** tutor.

tutoyer verb [39] to address somebody as 'tu' (rather than 'vous'); **il ne faut pas tutoyer ton professeur** you mustn't address your teacher as 'tu'; **et si on se tutoyait?** shall we say 'tu' to each other?

tuyau (plural **tuyaux**) noun Masc. **1** pipe; **2** (informal) tip (a helpful hint).

tuyau d'arrosage noun Masc. hosepipe.

TVA noun Fem. SHORT FOR **taxe à la valeur ajoutée** VAT.

type noun Masc. **1** kind; **quel type de papier?** what type of paper?; **2** (informal) guy; **le type qui a ouvert la porte** the guy who opene[s] the door.

typique adjective typical.

tyranniser verb [1] to bully.

tzigane noun Masc. & Fem., adjecti[ve] gypsy.

Uu

ulcère noun Masc. ulcer.

un, une (plural **des**) article, pronoun, number **1** a, an; **un lion** [a] lion; **une fraise** a strawberry; **des cerises** (some) cherries; **2** one; **un pour moi** one for me; **un par un** o[ne] by one; **trente et une personnes** thirty-one people; **les uns pensen[t] que ...** some think that ...; **un jour sur deux** every other day; **3 l'un(e) et l'autre** the one and the other; **l'un est français et l'autre est**

allemand one's French and the other's German; **4 l'un(e) ou l'autre** either of them; **tu peux prendre l'un ou l'autre, ça n'a pas d'importance** you can take either of them, it doesn't matter.

uni *adjective* **1** close-knit (*family or group*); **2** plain (*not patterned*); **un tissu uni** a plain fabric.

uniforme *noun Masc.* uniform.

union *noun Fem.* union; **l'ex-Union soviétique** the former Soviet Union.

Union européenne *noun Fem.* European Union.

unique *adjective* **1** only; **elle est fille unique** she's an only child; **il est fils unique** he's an only child; **l'unique raison** the only reason; **2** single; **'prix unique'** 'all one price'; **3** unique.

uniquement *adverb* only.

unité *noun Fem.* **1** unity; **2** unit (*of currency, measurement, etc*).

unité de disques *noun Fem.* disk drive.

univers *noun Masc.* universe.

universitaire *adjective* university (*degree, town*), academic (*work*).

université *noun Fem.* university.

urbanisme *noun Masc.* town planning.

urgence *noun Fem.* **1** urgency; **il y a urgence!** it's urgent!; **2 d'urgence** immediately, at once; **il faut téléphoner d'urgence** you must phone at once; **3** emergency; **les urgences, le service des**

urgences accident and emergency, the casualty department.

urgent *adjective* urgent.

USA *plural noun Masc.* USA; **aux USA** in (*or* to) the USA.

usage *noun Masc.* **1** use; **à l'usage** with use; **en usage** in use; **à usage externe** for external use only; **2 'hors d'usage'** 'not in service'.

usagé *adjective* **1** worn; **2** used.

usager *noun Masc.* user.

usé *adjective* worn.

user *verb* [1] to wear out (*shoes, clothing*).

usine *noun Fem.* factory.

ustensile *noun Masc.* utensil.

utile *adjective* useful.

utilisable *adjective* usable.

utilisateur, utilisatrice *noun Masc., Fem.* user.

utiliser *verb* [1] to use.

utilité *noun Fem.* usefulness; **un livre d'une grande utilité** a very useful book.

Vv

va *verb* SEE **aller**.

vacances *plural noun Fem.* holidays; **les vacances scolaires** the school holidays; **les grandes vacances** the summer holidays; **être en vacances** to be on holiday; **bonnes vacances!** have a good holiday!

a
b
c
d
e
f
g
h
i
j
k
l
m
n
o
p
q
r
s
t
u
v
w
x
y
z

a **vacancier**, **vacancière** noun Masc., Fem. holiday-maker.

b **vacarme** noun Masc. din; **ils faisaient un vacarme pas possible!** they were making an amazing din!

vaccination noun Fem. vaccination.

vacciner verb [1] to vaccinate; **se faire vacciner** to be vaccinated.

vache noun Fem. cow. **vache** adjective mean.

vachement adverb (informal) really; **c'était vachement bien!** it was really good!

va-et-vient noun Masc. coming and going.

vagabond noun Masc. tramp.

vagin noun Masc. vagina.

vague[1] noun Fem. wave (in the sea).

vague[2] adjective vague.

vaguement adverb vaguely.

vain adjective 1 useless; 2 **en vain** in vain.

vaincre verb [79] 1 to defeat; 2 to overcome.

vainqueur noun Masc. winner.

vais verb SEE **aller**.

vaisseau (plural **vaisseaux**) noun Masc. vessel.

vaisselle noun Fem. dishes; **faire la vaisselle** to do the washing-up.

valable adjective valid.

valet noun Masc. jack; **le valet de pique** the jack of spades.

valeur noun Fem. value; **des objets de valeur** valuables; **c'est sans valeur** it's of no value.

valider verb [1] to stamp (a ticket).

valise noun Fem. suitcase; **faire ses valises** to pack.

vallée noun Fem. valley.

valoir verb [80] 1 to be worth; **ça vaut combien?** how much is it worth?; **ce tableau vaut cher** that painting's worth a lot; 2 **valoir la peine** to be worth it; **ça ne vaut pas la peine d'y aller s'il pleut** it's not worth going if it's raining; **ça vaudrait la peine d'essayer** it would be worth a try; 3 **il vaut mieux faire** it would be better to do **il vaut mieux téléphoner avant** it would be better to phone first.

valse noun Fem. waltz.

vampire noun Masc. vampire.

vandalisme noun Masc. vandalism.

vanille noun Fem. vanilla; **une glace à la vanille** a vanilla ice cream.

vanter verb [1] **se vanter** to boast.

vapeur noun Fem. steam; **faire cuire des légumes à la vapeur** to steam vegetables.

vaporisateur noun Masc. (perfume) spray.

variable adjective variable, changeable.

varicelle noun Fem. chickenpox; **avoir la varicelle** to have chickenpox.

varié adjective varied, various; **'sandwichs variés'** a selection of sandwiches'.

varier verb [1] to vary.

ariété *noun Fem.* **1** variety; **2 un spectacle de variétés** a variety show.

as *verb* SEE **aller**.

ase[1] *noun Masc.* vase.

ase[2] *noun Fem.* mud.

aste *adjective* large, enormous.

a-vite *adverb Fem.* **à la va-vite** in a rush.

eau (*plural* **veaux**) *noun Masc.* **1** calf; **2** veal.

écu *verb* SEE **vivre**.

edette *noun Fem.* star; **une vedette de cinéma** a film star.

égétal *adjective* vegetable; **l'huile végétale** vegetable oil.

égétarien, végétarienne *noun Masc., Fem.* **végétarien** (*Fem.* **végétarienne**) *adjective* vegetarian.

éhicule *noun Masc.* vehicle.

eille *noun Fem.* **la veille** the day before; **je l'avais rencontrée la veille de mon départ** I met her the day before my departure; **la veille de Noël** Christmas Eve; **la veille du jour de l'an** New Year's Eve.

eilleuse *noun Fem.* **1** night-light; **2** pilot light.

einard *noun Masc.* (*informal*) **petit veinard!** you lucky little devil!

eine *noun Fem.* **1 avoir de la veine** (*informal*) to be lucky; **2** vein.

élo *noun Masc.* bike; **je suis venu à vélo** I came by bike; **faire du vélo** to go cycling.

élodrome *noun Masc.* cycle-racing track, velodrome.

vélomoteur *noun Masc.* moped.

vélo tout-terrain *noun Masc.* mountain bike.

velours *noun Masc.* **1** velvet; **2** corduroy.

velouté *noun Masc.* cream soup; **velouté de champignons** cream of mushroom soup.

vendanges *plural noun Fem.* grape harvest.

vendeur, vendeuse *noun Masc., Fem.* **1** shop assistant; **2** salesperson; **3** seller.

vendre *verb* [3] to sell; **vendre quelque chose à quelqu'un** to sell somebody something; **j'ai vendu mon ordinateur à Colette** I've sold my computer to Colette; **'à vendre'** 'for sale'; **'vendu'** 'sold'.

vendredi *noun Masc.* **1** Friday; **nous sommes vendredi aujourd'hui** it's Friday today; **vendredi dernier** last Friday; **vendredi prochain** next Friday; **2** on Friday; **je l'ai vu vendredi soir** I saw him on Friday evening; **3** on Fridays; **fermé le vendredi** closed on Fridays; **4 tous les vendredis** every Friday; **le vendredi saint** Good Friday.

vénéneux (*Fem.* **vénéneuse**) *adjective* poisonous (*plant*).

vengeance *noun Fem.* revenge.

venger *verb* [52] **se venger** to have your revenge.

venimeux (*Fem.* **venimeuse**) *adjective* poisonous (*snake, spider*).

venir *verb* [81] **1** to come; **il vient de Provence** he comes from Provence; **elles sont venues mardi** they came on Tuesday; **viens voir!** come and see!; **2 faire venir** to send for; **il faut faire venir le médecin** we must send for the doctor; **3 venir de faire** to have just done; **ils viennent d'arriver** they have just arrived; **elle venait de partir** she had just left.

vent noun Masc. wind; **un vent du sud** a south wind.

vente noun Fem. sale; **être en vente** to be on sale.

vente aux enchères noun Fem. auction sale.

ventilateur noun Masc. fan.

ventre noun Masc. stomach; **avoir mal au ventre** to have stomachache.

venu verb SEE **venir**.

ver noun Masc. worm.

verbe noun Masc. verb.

verdict noun Masc. verdict.

verger noun Masc. orchard.

verglas noun Masc. black ice.

vérifier verb [1] to check.

véritable adjective real.

vérité noun Fem. truth.

vernir verb [2] to varnish.

vernis à ongles noun Masc. nail varnish.

verre noun Masc. 1 glass; **un verre de vin** a glass of wine; **2** glass; **un vase en verre** a glass vase; **3** lens (of spectacles).

verrou noun Masc. bolt (on a door).

verrouiller verb [1] to bolt (a door).

verrue noun Fem. wart.

vers[1] preposition **1** towards; **il montait vers l'église** he was going up towards the church; **2** about (a time); **vers midi** about twelve; **vers la fin du mois** around the end of the month.

vers[2] noun Masc. line of poetry; **des vers** poetry.

Verseau noun Masc. Aquarius (sign of the Zodiac).

versement noun Masc. payment.

verser verb [1] **1** to pour; **Sylvie m'a versé une tasse de thé** Sylvie poured me a cup of tea; **2** to pay in; **j'ai versé 300 euros sur mon compte** I paid 300 euros into my account.

version noun Fem. **1** version; **2** translation (into your own language).

verso noun Masc. back (of a piece of paper); **voir au verso** see overleaf.

vert adjective green; ★ **avoir la main verte** to have green fingers.

vertical (Masc. plural **verticaux**) adjective vertical, upright.

vertige noun Masc. vertigo.

verveine noun Fem. verbena tea.

veste noun Fem. jacket.

vestiaire noun Masc. **1** cloakroom (in a theatre, restaurant, etc); **2** changing room (in a gym, sports ground).

vêtement noun Masc. garment; **les vêtements** clothes; '**vêtements pour enfants**' 'children's wear'.

vétérinaire noun Masc. & Fem. vet.

veuf, veuve noun Masc., Fem. widower, widow.

vexer verb [1] to annoy, to offend.

viande noun Fem. meat.

ibrer *verb* [1] to vibrate.

ctime *noun Fem.* victim.

ctoire *noun Fem.* victory.

de *adjective* empty.

vide *noun Masc.* **1** space; **dans le vide** in(to) space; **2** vacuum; **emballé sous vide** vacuum-packed.

idéo *noun Fem.* video; **une cassette vidéo** a video cassette; **une caméra vidéo** a video camera; **un jeu vidéo** a video game.

idéoclip *noun Masc.* music video.

idéoclub *noun Masc.* video shop.

idéothèque *noun Fem.* video library.

ider *verb* [1] to empty.

ie *noun Fem.* life; **toute ma vie** all my life; **il est encore en vie** he's still alive; **ton mode de vie** your lifestyle; ★ **c'est la vie** that's life, that's the way it goes.

ieil *adjective* SEE **vieux**.

ieillard, vieillarde *noun Masc., Fem.* old man, old woman.

ieille *adjective* SEE **vieux**.

ieillesse *noun Fem.* old age.

ieillir *verb* [2] to age; **il a beaucoup vieilli récemment** he's aged a lot recently.

ierge *noun Fem.* virgin; **la Sainte Vierge** the Virgin Mary.

vierge *adjective* **1** blank; **une cassette vierge** a blank cassette; **2 laine vierge** pure new wool; **l'huile d'olive vierge** virgin olive oil.

ierge *noun Fem.* Virgo (*sign of the Zodiac*).

vieux, vieil (*before a vowel or silent 'h'*) (*Fem.* **vieille**) (*Masc. plural* **vieux**) *adjective* old; **une vieille ville** an old town; **un vieil arbre** an old tree. **vieux, vieille** *noun Masc., Fem.* **un vieux** an old man; **une vieille** an old woman.

vieux garçon *noun Masc.* bachelor.

vif (*Fem.* **vive**) *adjective* **1** bright; **rose vif** bright pink; **2** lively; **une vive discussion** a lively discussion; **3 avoir l'esprit vif** to be quick-witted.

vigne *noun Fem.* vine, vineyard.

vigneron, vigneronne *noun Masc., Fem.* wine-grower.

vignette *noun Fem.* **1** label; **2** tax disc.

vignoble *noun Masc.* vineyard.

vilain *adjective* **1** ugly; **2** naughty; **c'est vilain, ça!** that's naughty!

villa *noun Fem.* detached house, villa.

village *noun Masc.* village.

ville *noun Fem.* town, city; **une grande ville** a city; **en ville** in (*or* into) town.

vin *noun Masc.* wine.

vinaigre *noun Masc.* vinegar.

vinaigrette *noun Fem.* French dressing.

vingt *number* twenty; **Marion a vingt ans** Marion's twenty; **le vingt juillet** the twentieth of July; **à vingt heures** at 8 p.m.; **vingt et un** twenty-one.

vingtaine *noun Fem.* about twenty; **une vingtaine de personnes** about twenty people.

a
b
c
d
e
f
g
h
i
j
k
l
m
n
o
p
q
r
s
t
u
v
w
x
y
z

vingtième *adjective* twentieth.

viol *noun Masc.* rape.

violemment *adjective* violently.

violence *noun Fem.* violence.

violent *adjective* violent.

violer *verb* [1] to rape.

violet (*Fem.* **violette** [1]) *adjective* purple.

violette [2] *noun Fem.* violet (*the flower*).

violon *noun Masc.* violin; **jouer du violon** to play the violin.

violoncelle *noun Masc.* cello; **jouer du violoncelle** to play the cello.

vipère *noun Fem.* adder, viper.

virage *noun Masc.* bend (*in the road*).

virement *noun Masc.* transfer (*of money*).

virer *verb* [1] **1** to transfer (*money*); **2** to turn; **3** to turn (right) around.

virgule *noun Fem.* **1** comma; **2** decimal point; **sept virgule trois** seven point three.

virus *noun Masc.* virus.

vis [1] *verb* SEE **vivre**.

vis [2] *noun Fem.* screw.

visa *noun Masc.* visa.

visage *noun Masc.* face.

viser *verb* [1] **1** to aim; **2** to aim at (*a target*).

visibilité *noun Fem.* visibility.

visible *adjective* visible, obvious.

visite *noun Fem.* visite; **une visite chez nos cousins** a visit to our cousins; **rendre visite à quelqu'un**

to visit somebody; **elle a de la visi** she's got visitors.

visiter *verb* [1] to visit (*a place*); **o peut visiter l'appartement?** can v see round the flat?

visiteur, visiteuse *noun Masc. Fem.* visitor.

visualisation graphique *noun Fem.* graphics.

vit *verb* SEE **vivre**.

vitamine *noun Fem.* vitamin.

vite *adverb* **1** fast; **tu conduis tro vite** you drive too fast; **parle moir vite** speak more slowly; **2** quick; **vite! le bus arrive!** quick! here's t bus!; **ce sera vite fait** it won't tak long; **3** soon; **on sera vite arrivé** we'll soon be there; **elle a vite compris** she understood immediately.

vitesse *noun Fem.* **1** speed; **elle e partie à toute vitesse** she rushe off; **2** gear; **en deuxième vitesse** second gear.

vitrail (*plural* **vitraux**) *noun Masc* stained glass window.

vitre *noun Fem.* window.

vitrine *noun Fem.* shop window.

vivant *adjective* **1** living; **2** lively.

vive [1] *adjective* SEE **vif**.

vive [2] *exclamation* **Vive le roi!** Lon live the king!

vivement *adverb* **1** **réagir vivement** to react strongly; **2 vivement les vacances!** roll on the holidays!

vivre *verb* [82] to live; **ils vivent ensemble** they live together; **ils o vécu dans plusieurs pays**

différents they've lived in several different countries.

vocabulaire *noun Masc.* vocabulary.

vœu *noun (plural vœux) Masc.*
1 wish; **faire un vœu** to make a wish; **meilleurs vœux!** best wishes! (*especially at the New Year*); **2** vow.

vogue *noun Fem.* fashion; **en vogue** in fashion.

voici *preposition* **1** here is, here are; **voici l'addition** here's the bill; **voici les clés** here are the keys; **me voici!** here I am!; **2** this is; **voici ma sœur** this is my sister.

voie *noun Fem.* **1** way; **être sur la bonne voie** to be on the right track; **2** track (*for trains*); **la voie ferrée** the railway track; **le train de Bourges entre en gare voie dix** the train from Bourges is now arriving at platform ten; **3** lane (*on a main road*); **une route à trois voies** a three-lane road.

voilà *preposition* **1** there is, there are; **voilà tes lunettes, là-bas sur la table** there are your glasses, over there on the table; **la voilà devant la boulangerie** there she is outside the baker's; **2** here is, here are; **voilà Anna qui arrive** here's Anna coming now; **voilà ton café** here's your coffee; **voilà, c'est tout** right, that's all; **3** that is; **voilà ma fille** that's my daughter; **et voilà pourquoi** and that's why.

voile[1] *noun Masc.* veil.

voile[2] *noun Fem.* sail; **des cours de voile** sailing lessons.

voilier *noun Masc.* sailing boat.

voir *verb [13]* **1** to see; **je ne vois rien** I can't see anything; **je viendrai te voir un de ces jours** I'll come and see you one of these days; **oui, je vois, tu veux dire que** … yes, I see, you mean that …; **un film à voir** a film worth seeing; **peut-être, on verra** perhaps, we'll see; **2 se voir** to be noticeable; **ça ne se verra pas** nobody will notice; **3 se voir** to see each other; **ils se voient à Noël** they see each other at Christmas; **4 faire voir quelque chose à quelqu'un** to show somebody something; **je te ferai voir mes photos de vacances** I'll show you my holiday photos; **fais voir!** let's have a look!; **5 ça n'a rien à voir avec mon problème** that's got nothing to do with my problem; ★ **il ne voit pas plus loin que le bout de son nez** he can't see any further than the end of his nose; ★ **elle ne peut pas le voir (en peinture)** she can't stand him (*literally: she can't bear to see him (in a painting)*); ★ **j'en ai vu d'autres** I've seen worse.

voisin, **voisine** *noun Masc., Fem.* neighbour; **Claire est chez les voisins** Claire's round at the neighbours'; **ma voisine de table** the girl sitting next to me at table.

voisinage *noun Masc.* neighbourhood.

voiture *noun Fem.* **1** car; **en voiture** by car; **2** carriage (*on a train*).

voix *noun Fem.* **1** voice; **à haute voix** aloud; **à voix basse** softly; **2** vote; **elle a eu 20 voix** she got 20 votes.

a
b
c
d
e
f
g
h
i
j
k
l
m
n
o
p
q
r
s
t
u
v
w
x
y
z

vol *noun Masc.* **1** flight; **le vol pour Milan** the Milan flight; **2** theft; ★ **à vol d'oiseau** as the crow flies (*literally: by bird flight*).

volaille *noun Fem.* poultry; **les foies de volaille** chicken livers.

volant *noun Masc.* **1** steering wheel; **qui était au volant?** who was driving?; **2** shuttlecock.
volant *adjective* flying.

volcan *noun Masc.* volcano.

volée *noun Fem.* volley.

voler *verb* [1] **1** to fly; **2** to steal; **voler quelque chose à quelqu'un** to steal something from someone; **on leur a volé leur voiture** their car's been stolen; **3 voler quelqu'un** to rob somebody.

volet *noun Masc.* shutter.

voleur, **voleuse** *noun Masc., Fem.* thief.

volley *noun Masc.* volleyball; **jouer au volley** to play volleyball.

volontaire *noun Masc. & Fem.* volunteer.

volonté *noun Fem.* **1** will; **la bonne volonté** goodwill; **2 à volonté** unlimited; **'pizza à volonté'** 'as much pizza as you want'.

volontiers *adverb* gladly; **'tu viens avec nous?' – 'volontiers'** 'will you come too?' – 'I'd love to'; **'tu me le prêtes?' – 'volontiers'** 'will you lend it to me?' – 'of course'.

volume *noun Masc.* volume.

vomir *verb* [2] to be sick, to vomit.

vos *adjective* SEE **votre**.

voter *verb* [1] to vote; **elle vote toujours pour les Verts** she always votes for the Greens.

votre (*plural* **vos**) *adjective* your; **nous connaissons votre fils** we know your son; **vos billets, monsieur** your tickets, sir.

vôtre *pronoun* **le vôtre, la vôtre, les vôtres** yours; **une maison comme la vôtre** a house like yours; **mes parents et les vôtres** my parents and yours; ★ **à la vôtre!** cheers!

vouloir *verb* [14] **1** to want; **elle ne veut rien** she doesn't want anything; **veux-tu venir avec nous?** do you want to come with us?; **je n'ai pas voulu arriver trop tôt** I didn't want to arrive too early; **il veut qu'elle l'appelle** he wants her to phone him; **il m'a vexé sans le vouloir** he annoyed me without meaning to; **2** to like; **si tu veux** if you like; **je voudrais visiter Versailles** I'd like to go to Versailles; **'encore du café?' – 'oui, je veux bien'** 'more coffee?' – 'yes, I'd love some'; **3 voulez-vous m'excuser?** would you excuse me?; **veux-tu fermer la porte?** would you shut the door?; **veux-tu te taire!** will you be quiet!; **4 vouloir dire** to mean; **qu'est-ce que tu veux dire?** what do you mean?; **si tu vois ce que je veux dire** if you see what I mean; **qu'est-ce que ce mot veut dire?** what does this word mean?; **5 en vouloir à quelqu'un** to bear a grudge against someone; **elle leur en veut** she's never forgiven them; ★ **vouloir c'est pouvoir** where there's a will there's a way (*literally: to want is to be able*).

voulu *verb* SEE **vouloir**.

vous *pronoun* **1** you; **avec vous** with you; **est-ce que ce sac est à vous?** is this your bag?; **à vous de jouer!** your turn to play!; **2** to you; **je vous écrirai** I'll write to you; **3** yourself; **ne vous coupez pas!** don't cut yourself!

vous-même(s) *pronoun* yourself, yourselves; **vous me l'avez dit vous-même** you told me yourself; **est-ce que vous l'avez fait vous-mêmes?** did you make it yourselves?

voûte *noun Fem.* vault, arch.

vouvoyer *verb* [39] to use 'vous' to mean 'you' (*rather than 'tu' which you use when talking to friends, family, and people of your own age*); **ils se connaissent depuis des années mais ils continuent à se vouvoyer** they've known each other for years but they still address each other as 'vous'.

voyage *noun Masc.* journey; **bon voyage!** have a good trip!

voyage organisé *noun Masc.* package tour.

voyager *verb* [52] to travel.

voyageur, voyageuse *noun Masc., Fem.* passenger.

voyelle *noun Fem.* vowel.

voyou *noun Masc.* hooligan.

vrac *adverb* **acheter des olives en vrac** to buy olives loose (*as opposed to pre-packaged*).

vrai *adjective* **1** true; **c'est une histoire vraie** it's a true story;

2 real; **c'est un vrai problème** it's a real problem; **c'est vrai?** really?; **pour de vrai** for real; **3 à vrai dire** to tell the truth.

vraiment *adverb* really.

vraisemblable *adjective* likely; **peu vraisemblable** unlikely.

vraisemblablement *adverb* probably.

VTT *noun Masc.* SHORT FOR **vélo tout-terrain** mountain bike.

vu *verb* SEE **voir**

vu *adjective* **1 vu que** seeing that; **vu qu'il pleut, ce n'est pas la peine d'y aller** seeing it's raining, there's no point in going; **2 être mal vu** to be disapproved of; **il est plutôt mal vu** people don't think much of him; **c'est mal vu de faire beaucoup de bruit** they don't like people making a lot of noise; **cette critique a été mal vue** this criticism didn't go down well; **3 être bien vu** to be well thought of; **elle est très bien vue dans la société** people in the company think highly of her.

vue *noun Fem.* **1** eyesight; **perdre la vue** to lose your eyesight; **2** sight; **je le connais de vue** I know him by sight; **nous l'avons perdue de vue** we've lost touch with her; **rien qu'à la vue de la viande** at the very sight of meat; **3** view; **une chambre avec vue sur le lac** a room with a view of the lake.

vulgaire *adjective* **1** vulgar; **2** common.

a
b
c
d
e
f
g
h
i
j
k
l
m
n
o
p
q
r
s
t
u
v
w
x
y
z

Ww

wagon *noun* *Masc.* **1** railway carriage; **2** waggon.

wagon-lit *noun* *Masc.* sleeper (*on a train*).

wagon-restaurant *noun* *Masc.* restaurant car.

wallon *noun* *Masc.* Wallon (*language*).
wallon (*Fem.* **wallonne**) *adjective* Walloon (*of French-speaking Belgium*).

Wallon, Wallone *noun* *Masc.*, *Fem.* Walloon (*French-speaking Belgian*).

WC (*pronounced 'vaysay'*) *plural noun* *Masc.* toilet; **aller aux WC** to go to the toilet; **il est aux WC** he's in the loo.

web *noun* *Masc.* **le web** the Web.

Xx

xylophone *noun* *Masc.* xylophone; **jouer du xylophone** to play the xylophone.

Yy

y *pronoun,*, *adverb* **1** there; **j'y vais demain** I'm going there tomorrow; **2 il y a** there is, there are; **il y a un café à côté** there's a cafe next door; **il y a des tomates dans le frigo** there are some tomatoes in the

fridge; **3 j'y pensais** I was thinking of it; **tu n'y peux rien** you can't do anything about it.

yaourt *noun* *Masc.* yoghurt.

yeux *plural noun* *Masc.* SEE **œil**.

yoga *noun* *Masc.* yoga.

yougoslave *adjective* Yugoslavian.

Yougoslavie *noun* *Fem.* Yugoslavia; **l'ex-Yougoslavie** the former Yugoslavia.

Zz

zapper *verb* [1] to channel hop.

zèbre *noun* *Masc.* zebra.

zéro *noun* *Masc.* zero, nil, love (*in tennis*); **trois à zéro** three-nil; **zéro heure** midnight; **elle a le moral à zéro** she's really depressed; ★ **il faut tout reprendre à zéro** we'll have to start again from scratch.

zézayer *verb* [59] to lisp.

zigzag *noun* *Masc.* zigzag; **une route en zigzag** a winding road; **faire des zigzags** to zigzag.

zodiaque *noun* *Masc.* zodiac.

zone *noun* *Fem.* **1** zone, area; **2 la zone** the slums; **un enfant de la zone** a child who grew up in the slums.

zone euro *noun* *Fem.* eurozone.

zone industrielle *noun* *Fem.* industrial estate.

zoo *noun* *Masc.* zoo.

zoologique *adjective* zoological.

zut *exclamation* (*informal*) damn!

VERB TABLES AND FORMS

aimer
to like *or* to love

Imperative	Past participle
aime	aimé
aimons	
aimez	

Present

j' aime
tu aimes
il aime
nous aimons
vous aimez
ils aiment

Perfect

j' ai aimé
tu as aimé
il a aimé
nous avons aimé
vous avez aimé
ils ont aimé

Future

j' aimerai
tu aimeras
il aimera
nous aimerons
vous aimerez
ils aimeront

Present subjunctive

j' aime
tu aimes
il aime
nous aimions
vous aimiez
ils aiment

Imperfect

j' aimais
tu aimais
il aimait
nous aimions
vous aimiez
ils aimaient

Conditional

j' aimerais
tu aimerais
il aimerait
nous aimerions
vous aimeriez
ils aimeraient

Imperative

finis
finissons
finissez

Past participle

fini

finir
to finish

Present

je finis
tu finis
il finit
nous finissons
vous finissez
ils finissent

Perfect

j' ai fini
tu as fini
il a fini
nous avons fini
vous avez fini
ils ont fini

Future

je finirai
tu finiras
il finira
nous finirons
vous finirez
ils finiront

Present subjunctive

je finisse
tu finisses
il finisse
nous finissions
vous finissiez
ils finissent

Imperfect

je finissais
tu finissais
il finissait
nous finissions
vous finissiez
ils finissaient

Conditional

je finirais
tu finirais
il finirait
nous finirions
vous finiriez
ils finiraient

attendre
to wait

Imperative
attends
attendons
attendez

Past participle
attendu

Present

j'	attends
tu	attends
il	attend
nous	attendons
vous	attendez
ils	attendent

Perfect

j'	ai attendu
tu	as attendu
il	a attendu
nous	avons attendu
vous	avez attendu
ils	ont attendu

Future

j'	attendrai
tu	attendras
il	attendra
nous	attendrons
vous	attendrez
ils	attendront

Present subjunctive

j'	attende
tu	attendes
il	attende
nous	attendions
vous	attendiez
ils	attendent

Imperfect

j'	attendais
tu	attendais
il	attendait
nous	attendions
vous	attendiez
ils	attendaient

Conditional

j'	attendrais
tu	attendrais
il	attendrait
nous	attendrions
vous	attendriez
ils	attendraient

4

Imperative

lave-toi
lavons-nous
lavez-vous

Past participle

lavé

se laver
to wash (oneself)

Present

je me lave
tu te laves
il se lave
nous nous lavons
vous vous lavez
ils se lavent

Perfect

je me suis lavé
tu t'es lavé
il s'est lavé
elles s'est lavée
nous nous sommes lavés
vous vous êtes lavé(s)
ils se sont lavés
elles se sont lavées

Future

je me laverai
tu te laveras
il se lavera
nous nous laverons
vous vous laverez
ils se laveront

Present subjunctive

je me lave
tu te laves
il se lave
nous nous lavions
vous vous laviez
ils se lavent

Imperfect

je me lavais
tu te lavais
il se lavait
nous nous lavions
vous vous laviez
ils se lavaient

Conditional

je me laverais
tu te laverais
il se laverait
nous nous laverions
vous vous laveriez
ils se laveraient

| **avoir** to have | **Imperative** aie ayons ayez | **Past participle** eu |

Present

j' ai
tu as
il a
nous avons
vous avez
ils ont

Perfect

j' ai eu
tu as eu
il a eu
nous avons eu
vous avez eu
ils ont eu

Future

j' aurai
tu auras
il aura
nous aurons
vous aurez
ils auront

Present subjunctive

j' aie
tu aies
il ait
nous ayons
vous ayez
ils aient

Imperfect

j' avais
tu avais
il avait
nous avions
vous aviez
ils avaient

Conditional

j' aurais
tu aurais
il aurait
nous aurions
vous auriez
ils auraient

6

Imperative

sois
soyons
soyez

Past participle

été

être
to be

Present

je **suis**
tu **es**
il **est**
nous **sommes**
vous **êtes**
ils **sont**

Perfect

j' ai **été**
tu as **été**
il a **été**
nous avons **été**
vous avez **été**
ils ont **été**

Future

je **serai**
tu **seras**
il **sera**
nous **serons**
vous **serez**
ils **seront**

Present subjunctive

je **sois**
tu **sois**
il **soit**
nous **soyons**
vous **soyez**
ils **soient**

Imperfect

j' **étais**
tu **étais**
il **était**
nous **étions**
vous **étiez**
ils **étaient**

Conditional

je **serais**
tu **serais**
il **serait**
nous **serions**
vous **seriez**
ils **seraient**

aller
to go

Imperative	Past participle
va	allé
allons	
allez	

Present

je **vais**
tu **vas**
il **va**
nous all**ons**
vous all**ez**
ils **vont**

Perfect

je suis allé
tu es allé
il est allé
nous sommes all**és**
vous êtes allé**(s)**
ils sont all**és**

Future

j' **irai**
tu **iras**
il **ira**
nous **irons**
vous **irez**
ils **iront**

Present subjunctive

j' **aille**
tu **ailles**
il **aille**
nous **allions**
vous **alliez**
ils **aillent**

Imperfect

j' all**ais**
tu all**ais**
il all**ait**
nous all**ions**
vous all**iez**
ils all**aient**

Conditional

j' **irais**
tu **irais**
il **irait**
nous **irions**
vous **iriez**
ils **iraient**

Imperative	Past participle	**devoir**
dois	du	to have to
devons		
devez		

Present

je	**dois**
tu	**dois**
il	**doit**
nous	dev**ons**
vous	dev**ez**
ils	**doivent**

Perfect

j'	ai **dû**
tu	as **dû**
il	a **dû**
nous	avons **dû**
vous	avez **dû**
ils	ont **dû**

Future

je	dev**rai**
tu	dev**ras**
il	dev**ra**
nous	dev**rons**
vous	dev**rez**
ils	dev**ront**

Present subjunctive

je	**doive**
tu	**doives**
il	**doive**
nous	dev**ions**
vous	dev**iez**
ils	**doivent**

Imperfect

je	dev**ais**
tu	dev**ais**
il	dev**ait**
nous	dev**ions**
vous	dev**iez**
ils	dev**aient**

Conditional

je	dev**rais**
tu	dev**rais**
il	dev**rait**
nous	dev**rions**
vous	dev**riez**
ils	dev**raient**

dire
to say

Imperative	Past participle
dis	dit
disons	
dites	

Present

je **dis**
tu **dis**
il **dit**
nous **disons**
vous **dites**
ils **disent**

Perfect

j' ai **dit**
tu as **dit**
il a **dit**
nous avons **dit**
vous avez **dit**
ils ont **dit**

Future

je dir**ai**
tu dir**as**
il dir**a**
nous dir**ons**
vous dir**ez**
ils dir**ont**

Present subjunctive

je **dise**
tu **dises**
il **dise**
nous **disions**
vous **disiez**
ils **disent**

Imperfect

je **disais**
tu **disais**
il **disait**
nous **disions**
vous **disiez**
ils **disaient**

Conditional

je dir**ais**
tu dir**ais**
il dir**ait**
nous dir**ions**
vous dir**iez**
ils dir**aient**

Imperative	Past participle	**faire**
fais	fait	to do *or* to make
faisons		
faites		

Present

je **fais**
tu **fais**
il **fait**
nous **faisons**
vous **faites**
ils **font**

Perfect

j' ai **fait**
tu as **fait**
il a **fait**
nous avons **fait**
vous avez **fait**
ils ont **fait**

Future

je **ferai**
tu **feras**
il **fera**
nous **ferons**
vous **ferez**
ils **feront**

Present subjunctive

je **fasse**
tu **fasses**
il **fasse**
nous **fassions**
vous **fassiez**
ils **fassent**

Imperfect

je **faisais**
tu **faisais**
il **faisait**
nous **faisions**
vous **faisiez**
ils **faisaient**

Conditional

je **ferais**
tu **ferais**
il **ferait**
nous **ferions**
vous **feriez**
ils **feraient**

mettre
to put

Imperative	Past participle
mets	mis
mett**ons**	
mett**ez**	

Present

je	**mets**
tu	**mets**
il	**met**
nous	mett**ons**
vous	mett**ez**
ils	mett**ent**

Perfect

j'	ai **mis**
tu	as **mis**
il	a **mis**
nous	avons **mis**
vous	avez **mis**
ils	ont **mis**

Future

je	mett**rai**
tu	mett**ras**
il	mett**ra**
nous	mett**rons**
vous	mett**rez**
ils	mett**ront**

Present subjunctive

je	mette
tu	mettes
il	mette
nous	mett**ions**
vous	mett**iez**
ils	mett**ent**

Imperfect

je	mett**ais**
tu	mett**ais**
il	mett**ait**
nous	mett**ions**
vous	mett**iez**
ils	mett**aient**

Conditional

je	mett**rais**
tu	mett**rais**
il	mett**rait**
nous	mett**rions**
vous	mett**riez**
ils	mett**raient**

12

Imperative

the imperative of
pouvoir is not used

Past participle

pu

pouvoir
to be able

Present

je **peux**
tu **peux**
il **peut**
nous pouv**ons**
vous pouv**ez**
ils **peuvent**

Perfect

j' ai **pu**
tu as **pu**
il a **pu**
nous avons **pu**
vous avez **pu**
ils ont **pu**

Future

je **pourrai**
tu **pourras**
il **pourra**
nous **pourrons**
vous **pourrez**
ils **pourront**

Present subjunctive

je **puisse**
tu **puisses**
il **puisse**
nous **puissions**
vous **puissiez**
ils **puissent**

Imperfect

je pouv**ais**
tu pouv**ais**
il pouv**ait**
nous pouv**ions**
vous pouv**iez**
ils pouv**aient**

Conditional

je **pourrais**
tu **pourrais**
il **pourrait**
nous **pourrions**
vous **pourriez**
ils **pourraient**

voir
to see

Imperative	**Past participle**
vois	vu
voyons	
voyez	

Present

je vois
tu vois
il voit
nous **voyons**
vous **voyez**
ils voient

Perfect

j' ai **vu**
tu as **vu**
il a **vu**
nous avons **vu**
vous avez **vu**
ils ont **vu**

Future

je verrai
tu verras
il verra
nous verrons
vous verrez
ils verront

Present subjunctive

je voie
tu voies
il voie
nous **voyions**
vous **voyiez**
ils voient

Imperfect

je voyais
tu voyais
il voyait
nous voyions
vous voyiez
ils voyaient

Conditional

je verrais
tu verrais
il verrait
nous verrions
vous verriez
ils verraient

14

Imperative	Past participle	**vouloir**
veuille	voulu	to want
veuillons		
veuillez		

Present

je **veux**
tu **veux**
il **veut**
nous voul**ons**
vous voul**ez**
ils veul**ent**

Perfect

j' ai voul**u**
tu as voul**u**
il a voul**u**
nous avons voul**u**
vous avez voul**u**
ils ont voul**u**

Future

je **voudrai**
tu **voudras**
il **voudra**
nous **voudrons**
vous **voudrez**
ils **voudront**

Present subjunctive

je **veuille**
tu **veuilles**
il **veuille**
nous voul**ions**
vous voul**iez**
ils **veuillent**

Imperfect

je voul**ais**
tu voul**ais**
il voul**ait**
nous voul**ions**
vous voul**iez**
ils voul**aient**

Conditional

je **voudrais**
tu **voudrais**
il **voudrait**
nous **voudrions**
vous **voudriez**
ils **voudraient**

French irregular verb forms

The list shows the main forms of other irregular verbs. The number before the infinitive is the number given after verbs in the dictionary which follow this pattern.

(1) = Present   **(3)** = Imperfect

(2) = Past participle   **(4)** = Future

15 **abréger** (1) j'abrège, nous abrégeons, ils abrègent (2) abrégé (3) j'abrégeais (4) j'abrégerai

16 **acheter** (1) j'achète, nous achetons, ils achètent (2) acheté (3) j'achetais (4) j'achèterai

17 **acquérir** (1) j'acquiers, il acquiert, nous acquérons, vous acquérez ils acquièrent (2) acquis (3) j'acquérais (4) j'acquerrai

18 **appeler** (1) j'appelle, nous appelons (2) appelé (3) j'appelais (4) j'appellerai

19 **apprendre** (1) j'apprends, nous apprenons, vous apprenez, ils apprennent (2) appris (3) j'apprenais (4) j'apprendrai

20 **s'asseoir** (1) je m'assieds, nous nous asseyons, vous vous asseyez, ils s'asseyent (2) assis (3) je m'asseyais (4) je m'assiérai

21 **battre** (1) je bats, il bat, nous battons (2) battu (3) je battais (4) je battrai

22 **boire** (1) je bois, nous buvons, ils boivent (2) bu (3) je buvais (4) je boirai

23 **bouillir** (1) je bous, nous bouillons (2) bouilli (3) je bouillais (4) je bouillirai

24 **céder** (1) je cède, nous cédons, ils cèdent (2) cédé (3) je cédais (4) je céderai

25 **conclure** (1) je conclus, nous concluons (2) conclu (3) je concluais (4) je conclurai

26 **conduire** (1) je conduis, nous conduisons (2) conduit (3) je conduisais (4) je conduirai

27 **connaître** (1) je connais, nous connaissons (2) connu (3) je connaissais (4) je connaîtrai

28 **coudre** (1) je couds, nous cousons, vous cousez, ils cousent (2) cousu (3) je cousais (4) je coudrai

29 **courir** (1) je cours, nous courons (2) couru (3) je courais (4) je courrai

30 **couvrir** (1) je couvre, nous couvrons (2) couvert (3) je couvrais (4) je couvrirai

31 **craindre** (1) je crains, nous craignons (2) craint (3) je craignais (4) je craindrai

32 **créer** (1) je crée, nous créons (2) créé (3) je créais (4) je créerai

33 **croire** (1) je crois, nous croyons, ils croient (2) cru (3) je croyais (4) je croirai

34 **croître** (1) je croîs, nous croissons (2) crû, crue (3) je croissais (4) je croîtrai

35 **cueillir** (1) je cueille, nous cueillons (2) cueilli (3) je cueillais (4) je cueillerai

36 **cuire** (1) je cuis, nous cuisons, ils cuisent (2) cuit (3) je cuisais (4) je cuirai

37 **dormir** (1) je dors, nous dormons (2) dormi (3) je dormais (4) je dormirai

38 **écrire** (1) j'écris, nous écrivons (2) écrit (3) j'écrivais (4) j'écrirai

39 **employer** (1) j'emploie, nous employons, vous employez, ils emploient (2) employé (3) j'employais (4) j'emploierai

40 **envoyer** (1) j'envoie, nous envoyons, vous envoyez, ils envoient (2) envoyé (3) j'envoyais (4) j'enverrai

41 **essuyer** (1) j'essuie, nous essuyons, vous essuyez, ils essuient (2) essuyé (3) j'essuyais (4) j'essuierai

42 **faillir** (1) je faille (2) failli

43 **falloir** (1) je il faut (2) fallu (3) il fallait (4) il faudra

44 **fuir** (1) je fuis, nous fuyons, ils, fuient (2) fui (3) je fuyais (4) je fuirai

45 **geler** (1) je gèle, nous gelons, vous gelez, ils gèlent (2) gelé (3) je gelais (4) je gèlerai

46 **haïr** (1) je hais, nous haïssons, ils haïssent (2) haï (3) je haïssais (4) je haïrai

47 **interdire** (1) j'interdis, nous interdisons, vous interdisez (2) interdît (3) j'interdisais (4) j'interdirai

48 **jeter** (1) je jette, nous jetons, ils jettent (2) jeté (3) je jetais (4) je jetterai

49 **joindre** (1) je joins, nous joignons (2) joint (3) je joignais (4) je joindrai

50 **lever** (1) je lève, nous levons, ils lèvent (2) levé (3) je levais (4) je lèverai

51 **lire** (1) je lis, nous lisons (2) lu (3) je lisais (4) je lirai

52 **manger** (1) je mange, nous mangeons (2) mangé (3) je mangeais (4) je mangerai

53 **mentir** (1) je mens, nous mentons (2) menti (3) je mentais (4) je mentirai

54 **mourir** (1) je meurs, nous mourons, ils meurent (2) mort (3) je mourais (4) je mourrai

55 **naître** (1) je nais, il naît, nous naissons (2) né (3) je naissais (4) je naîtrai

56 **offrir** (1) j'offre, nous offrons (2) offert (3) j'offrais (4) j'offrirai

57 **paraître** (1) je parais, il paraît, nous paraissons (2) paru (3) je paraissais (4) je paraîtrai

58 **partir** (1) je pars, nous partons (2) parti (3) je partais (4) je partirai

59 **payer** (1) je paie/je paye, nous payons, vous payez, ils paient/ils payent (2) payé (3) je payais (4) je paierai/je payerai

60 **peindre** (1) je peins, nous peignons (2) peint (3) je peignais (4) je peindrai

61 **placer** (1) je place, nous plaçons (2) placé (3) je plaçais (4) je placerai

62 **plaire** (1) je plais, il plaît, nous plaisons (2) plu (3) je plaisais (4) je plairai

63 **pleuvoir** (1) je il pleut (2) plu (3) il pleuvait (4) il pleuvra

64 **prendre** (1) je prends, nous prenons, ils prennent (2) pris (3) je prenais (4) je prendrai

65 **prévoir** (1) je prévois, nous prévoyons, vous prévoyez, ils prévoient (2) prévu (3) je prévoyais (4) je prévoirai

66 **recevoir** (1) je reçois, il reçoit, ils reçoivent (2) reçu (3) je recevais (4) je recevrai

67 **résoudre** (1) je résous, nous résolvons, vous résolvez, ils résolvent (2) résolu (3) je résolvais (4) je résoudrai

68 **rire** (1) je ris, nous rions (2) ri (3) je riais (4) je rirai

69 **rompre** (1) je romps, il rompt, nous rompons (2) rompu (3) je rompais (4) je romprai

70 **savoir** (1) je sais, nous savons, ils savent (2) su (3) je savais (4) je saurai (5) pres subj je sache

71 **servir** (1) je sers, nous servons (2) servi (3) je servais (4) je servirai

72 **sortir** (1) je sors, nous sortons (2) sorti (3) je sortais (4) je sortirai

73 **souffrir** (1) je souffre, nous souffrons (2) souffert (3) je souffrais (4) je souffrirai

74 **suffire** (1) je suffis, nous suffisons (2) suffi (3) je suffisais (4) je suffirai

75 **suivre** (1) je suis, nous suivons (2) suivi (3) je suivais (4) je suivrai

76 **taire** (1) je me tais, nous nous taisons (2) tu (3) je me taisais (4) je me tairai

77 **tenir** (1) je tiens, nous tenons, ils tiennent (2) tenu (3) je tenais (4) je tiendrai

78 **traire** (1) je trais, nous trayons, ils traient (2) trait (3) je trayais (4) je trairai

79 **vaincre** (1) je vaincs, il vainc, nous vainquons (2) vaincu (3) je vainquais (4) je vaincrai

80 **valoir** (1) je vaux, il vaut, nous valons (2) valu (3) je valais (4) je vaudrai

81 **venir** (1) je viens, nous venons, ils viennent (2) venu (3) je venais (4) je viendrai

82 **vivre** (1) je vis, nous vivons (2) vécu (3) je vivais (4) je vivrai

Aa

indefinite article **1** (*before a noun which is masculine in French*) un; **a tree** un arbre; **2** (*before a noun which is feminine in French*) une; **a table** une table; **3 five euros a kilo** cinq euros le kilo; **4 fifty kilometres an hour** cinquante kilomètres l'heure; **5 three times a day** trois fois par jour.

abandon *verb* abandonner [1].

abbey *noun* abbaye *Fem.*; **Westminster Abbey** l'Abbaye de Westminster.

abbreviation *noun* abréviation *Fem.*

abide *verb* **I can't abide** ... je ne supporte pas ....

ability *noun* capacité *Fem.*; **the ability to do** la capacité de faire.

able *adjective* **to be able to do** pouvoir [12] faire; **she wasn't able to come** elle n'a pas pu venir.

abnormal *adjective* anormal (*Masc. plural* anormaux).

abolish *verb* abolir [2].

abortion *noun* avortement *Masc.*

about *preposition* **1** (*on the subject of*) sur; **a film about Picasso** un film sur Picasso; **2 what's it about?** de quoi s'agit-il?; **3** (*concerning or in relation to*) au sujet de; **he wants to talk to you about your exam** il veut te parler au sujet de ton examen; **4 to talk about something** parler de quelque chose; **what is she talking about?** de quoi parle-t-elle?; **5 to think about something/**

somebody penser à quelque chose/quelqu'un; **I'm thinking about you** je pense à toi.

about *adverb* **1** (*approximately*) environ, à peu près; **there are about sixty people** il y a environ soixante personnes, il y a à peu près soixante personnes; **2** (*when talking about the time*) vers; **about three o'clock** vers trois heures; ★ **to be about to do** être sur le point de faire; **I'm (just) about to leave** je suis sur le point de partir.

above *preposition* **1** au dessus de; **above the table** au dessus de la table; **2 above all** surtout.

abroad *adverb* à l'étranger; **to go abroad** aller à l'étranger; **to live abroad** vivre à l'étranger.

abscess *noun* abcès *Masc.*

abseiling *noun* descente *Fem.* en rappel.

absent *adjective* absent; **to be absent from** être absent de.

absent-minded *adjective* distrait.

absolute *adjective* complet (*Fem.* complète); **an absolute disaster** un désastre complet.

absolutely *adverb* **1** absolument; **it's absolutely dreadful** c'est absolument affreux; **2** tout à fait; **you're absolutely right** tu as tout à fait raison.

absorb *verb* absorber [1].

abuse *noun* **1 alcohol abuse** abus *Masc.* d'alcool; **drug abuse** usage *Masc.* des stupéfiants; **2** (*violent treatment of a person*) mauvais traitement *Masc.*; **3** (*insulting words*)

a
b
c
d
e
f
g
h
i
j
k
l
m
n
o
p
q
r
s
t
u
v
w
x
y
z

injures *Fem. plural*.

abuse *verb* **to abuse somebody** maltraiter [1] quelqu'un.

academic *adjective* **the academic year** l'année universitaire.

accelerate *verb* accélérer [24].

accelerator *noun* accélérateur *Masc.*

accent *noun* accent *Masc.*; **she has a French accent** elle a l'accent français.

accept *verb* accepter [1].

acceptable *adjective* acceptable.

acceptance *noun* acceptation *Fem.*

access *noun* accès *Masc.*
access *verb* **to access something** accéder [24] à quelque chose.

accessory *noun* accessoire *Masc.*

accident & emergency *noun* les urgences *Fem. plural*.

accident *noun* **1** accident *Masc.*; **to have an accident** avoir un accident; **a road accident** un accident de la route; **a car accident** un accident de voiture; **2** (*chance*) hasard *Masc.*; **by accident** par hasard; **I found it by accident** je l'ai trouvé par hasard.

accidental *adjective* fortuit; **an accidental discovery** une découverte fortuite.

accidentally *adverb* **1** (*without meaning to*) accidentellement; **I accidentally knocked over his glass** j'ai accidentellement renversé son verre; **2** (*by chance*) par hasard;

I accidentally discovered that .. j'ai découvert par hasard que ....

accommodate *verb* recevoir [66]; **the centre can accommodat** **sixty people** le centre peut recevo soixante personnes.

accommodation *noun* logement *Masc.*; **I'm looking for accommodation** je cherche un logement.

accompany *verb* **to accompan somebody** accompagner [1] quelqu'un.

according *in phrase* **according t** selon; **according to Sophie** selon Sophie.

accordion *noun* accordéon *Masc*

account *noun* **1** (*in a bank, shop, or post office*) compte *Masc.*; **a bank account** un compte bancaire; **to open an account** ouvrir un compt **I have fifty pounds in my accoun** j'ai cinquante livres sur mon compte; **2** (*a description of an experience or event*) compte rendu *Masc.*; **3 on account of** à cause de; **the station is closed on accoun of the strike** la gare est fermée à cause de la grève; **4 to take something into account** tenir compte de quelque chose; **we will take his illness into account** nou tiendrons compte de sa maladie.

accountant *noun* comptable *Mas & Fem.*; **she is an accountant** elle e comptable.

accuracy *noun* précision *Fem.*

accurate *adjective* précis.

accurately *adverb* avec précisio

accuse *verb* accuser [1]; **to accuse somebody of something** accuser quelqu'un de quelque chose; **to accuse someone of doing something** accuser quelqu'un d'avoir fait quelque chose; **she accused me of stealing her pen** elle m'a accusé d'avoir volé son stylo.

accustomed to *adjective* ; **to be accustomed to something** être [6] habitué à; **she's accustomed to having lots of homework** elle a l'habitude d'avoir beaucoup de devoirs.

ace *noun* as *Masc.*; **the ace of hearts** l'as de cœur.
ace *adjective* super (*informal*); **he's an ace drummer** c'est un super batteur.

ache *verb* **my arm aches** j'ai mal au bras; **my head aches** j'ai mal à la tête.

achieve *verb* **1** accomplir [2]; **she's achieved a great deal** elle a beaucoup accompli; **2 to achieve an ambition** réaliser [1] une ambition; **3 to achieve an aim** atteindre [60] un objectif; **4 to achieve success** réussir [2].

achievement *noun* **1** réussite *Fem.*; **it's a great achievement** c'est une grande réussite; **2 a sense of achievement** un sentiment de satisfaction.

acid *noun* acide *Masc.*

acid rain *noun* pluies *Fem. plural* acides.

acne *noun* acné *Fem.*

acorn *noun* gland *Masc.*

acrobat *noun* acrobate *Masc. & Fem.*

across *preposition* **1** (*over to the other side of*) **to walk across something** traverser [1] quelque chose; **we walked across the park** nous avons traversé le parc; **to run across the road** traverser la route en courant; **2** (*on the other side of*) de l'autre côté de; **the house across the street** la maison de l'autre côté de la rue; **3 across from** en face de; **she was sitting across from me** elle était assise en face de moi.

acrylic *noun* acrylique *Masc.*

act *noun* acte *Masc.*
act *verb* **1** (*in a play or film*) jouer [1]; **to act the part of** jouer le rôle de; **2** (*to take action*) agir [2].

acting *noun* jeu *Masc.*; **she wants to go into acting** elle veut devenir actrice; **the acting was terrible/sensational** les acteurs jouaient très mal/bien.

action *noun* action *Fem.*

action replay *noun* répétition *Fem.* d'une séquence.

active *adjective* actif (*Fem.* active).

activity *noun* activité *Fem.*

activity holiday *noun* vacances *Fem. plural* sportives.

actor *noun* acteur *Masc.*; **who's your favourite actor?** qui est votre acteur préféré?

actress *noun* actrice *Fem.*; **she's my favourite actress** c'est mon actrice préférée.

actual *adjective* **his actual words** ses paroles précises; ★ **in actual fact** en fait.

actually *adverb* **1** (*in fact, as it happens*)) en fait; **actually, I've changed my mind** en fait, j'ai changé d'avis; **he's not actually here at the moment** en fait il n'est pas là en ce moment; **2** (*really and truly*) vraiment; **did she actually say that?** est-ce qu'elle a vraiment dit ça?

acupuncture *noun* acupuncture *Fem.*

acute *adjective* **1** (*pain*) vif (*Fem.* vive); **2 an acute accent** un accent aigu.

ad *noun* **1** pub *Fem.* (*informal*); **2** (*in a newspaper*) annonce *Fem.*; **to put an ad in the paper** mettre une annonce dans le journal; **the small ads** les petites annonces.

AD *abbreviation* après Jésus-Christ, apr. J-C; **in 400 AD** en quatre cents après Jésus-Christ.

adapt *verb* **1 to adapt something** adapter [1] quelque chose (*a book or film*); **2 to adapt to something** s'adapter [1] à quelque chose; **she's adapted to the new system** elle s'est adaptée au nouveau système.

adaptor *noun* adaptateur *Masc.*

add *verb* ajouter [1]; **add three eggs** ajoutez trois œufs.

● **to add something up** additionner [1] quelque chose.

addict *noun* **1** (*drug addict*) drogué, droguée *Masc.*, *Fem.*; **2** accro *Masc.* & *Fem.* (*informal*); **she's a telly addict** c'est une accro de la télé; **he's a football addict** c'est un accro du foot.

addicted *adjective* **1 to become addicted to heroin** former une dépendance à l'héroïne; **2 I'm addicted to tomatoes** je raffole des tomates.

addition *noun* **1** (*adding up*) addition *Fem.*; **2 in addition** en plus; **3 in addition to** en plus de.

additional *adjective* supplémentaire; **additional costs** les frais supplémentaires.

additive *noun* additif *Masc.*

address *noun* adresse *Fem.*; **what's your address?** quelle est ton adresse?; **to change address** changer d'adresse.

address book *noun* carnet *Masc.* d'adresses.

adequate *adjective* suffisant.

adhesive *noun* colle *Fem.*
adhesive *adjective* collant; **adhesive tape** du papier collant.

adjective *noun* adjectif *Masc.*

adjust *verb* **1 to adjust something** régler [24] quelque chose; **to adjust the height** régler la hauteur; **2 to adjust to something** s'adapter [1] à quelque chose.

adjustable *adjective* réglable.

administration *noun* administration *Fem.*

admiral *noun* amiral *Masc.*

admiration *noun* admiration *Fem.*

admire *verb* admirer [1].

admission *noun* entrée *Fem.*; **'no admission'** 'entrée interdite'; **'admission free'** 'entrée gratuite'.

admit *verb* **1** (*confess*) reconnaître [27]; **she admits she lied** elle

reconnaît qu'elle a menti;
2 (*concede*) admettre [11]; **I must admit that** ... j'admets que ...;
3 (*allow to enter*) laisser [1] entrer; **to admit somebody to a restaurant** laisser entrer quelqu'un dans un restaurant; **4 to be admitted to hospital** être [6] hospitalisé.

dolescence *noun* adolescence *Fem.*

dolescent *noun* adolescent *Masc.*, adolescente *Fem.*

dopt *verb* adopter [1].

dopted *adjective* adoptif (*Fem.* adoptive).

doption *noun* adoption *Fem.*

dore *verb* adorer [1].

driatic Sea *noun* **the Adriatic Sea** la mer Adriatique.

dult *noun* adulte *Masc. & Fem.*
adult *adjective* adulte; **the adult population** la population adulte.

dult Education *noun* enseignement *Masc.* pour adultes.

dvance *noun* progrès *Masc.*; **advances in technology** des progrès dans le domaine de la technologie.
advance *verb* **1** (*make progress*) progresser [1]; **2** (*move forward*) avancer [61].

dvanced *adjective* avancé.

dvantage *noun* **1** avantage *Masc.*; **there are several advantages** il y a plusieurs avantages; **2 to take advantage of something** profiter de quelque chose; **I took advantage of the sales to buy myself some shoes** j'ai profité des soldes pour

m'acheter des chaussures; **3 to take advantage of somebody** (*unfairly*) exploiter quelqu'un.

Advent *noun* Avent *Masc.*

adventure *noun* aventure *Fem.*

adventurous *adjective* aventureux (*Fem.* aventureuse).

adverb *noun* adverbe *Masc.*

advert, advertisement *noun*
1 (*at the cinema or on television*) publicité *Fem.*; **2** (*commercial advertisement in a newspaper*) annonce *Fem.*; **3** (*small ad in a newspaper advertising a job, an article for sale, etc*) petite annonce *Fem.*

advertise *verb* **1 to advertise something in the newspaper** (*in the small ads*) mettre [11] une annonce pour quelque chose dans le journal; **I saw a bike advertised in the paper** j'ai vu une annonce pour un vélo dans le journal; **2 to advertise a product** faire [10] de la publicité pour un produit.

advertising *noun* publicité *Fem.*

advice *noun* conseils *Masc. plural*; **to ask for advice about something** demander des conseils à propos de quelque chose; **a piece of advice** un conseil.

advise *verb* conseiller [1]; **to advise somebody to do** conseiller à quelqu'un de faire; **I advised him to stop** je lui ai conseillé d'arrêter; **I advised her not to wait** je lui ai conseillé de ne pas attendre.

adviser *noun* conseiller *Masc.*, conseillère *Fem.*

aerial *noun* antenne *Fem.*

a
b
c
d
e
f
g
h
i
j
k
l
m
n
o
p
q
r
s
t
u
v
w
x
y
z

333

aerobics *noun* aérobic *Masc.*; **to do aerobics** faire de l'aérobic.

aeroplane *noun* avion *Masc.*

aerosol *noun* **an aerosol can** une bombe.

affair *noun* **1** (*event*) affaire *Fem.*; **international affairs** les affaires internationales; **2 a love affair** une aventure amoureuse.

affect *verb* affecter [1].

affectionate *adjective* affectueux (*Fem.* affectueuse).

afford *verb* **to be able to afford to do** avoir [5] les moyens de faire; **we can't afford to go out much** nous n'avons pas les moyens de sortir beaucoup; **I can't afford a new bike** je n'ai pas les moyens de m'acheter un nouveau vélo.

afraid *adjective* **1 to be afraid of something** avoir peur de quelque chose; **she's afraid of dogs** elle a peur des chiens; **2 I'm afraid there's no milk left** je suis désolé mais il ne reste plus de lait; **I'm afraid so** hélas oui; **I'm afraid not** hélas non.

Africa *noun* Afrique *Fem.*; **in Africa** en Afrique; **to Africa** en Afrique.

African *noun* Africain *Masc.*, Africaine *Fem.*.
African *adjective* africain (*Fem.* africaine).

after *preposition, adverb, conjunction* après; **after 10 o'clock** après dix heures; **after lunch** après le déjeuner; **after school** après l'école; **the day after tomorrow** après-demain; **soon after** peu après; **after I've finished my homework** après que j'aurai fini mes devoirs; **to run after somebody** courir après quelqu'un.

after all *adverb* après tout; **after all, she's only six** elle n'a que six ans après tout.

afternoon *noun* après-midi *Masc. or Fem.*; **this afternoon** cet après-midi; **tomorrow afternoon** demain après-midi; **yesterday afternoon** hier après-midi; **on Saturday afternoon** samedi après-midi; **on Saturday afternoons** le samedi après-midi; **at four o'clock in the afternoon** à quatre heures de l'après-midi; **every afternoon** tou les après-midi.

afters *noun* dessert *Masc.*

after-shave *noun* après-rasage *Masc.*

afterwards *adverb* après; **short afterwards** peu de temps après.

again *adverb* **1** (*one more time*) encore une fois; **try again** essaie encore une fois; **I've forgotten it again** je l'ai oublié encore une fois **2** (*once more*) de nouveau; **she's il again** elle est de nouveau malade; **3 I saw her again yesterday** je l' revue hier; **you should ask again** devrais redemander; **4 I don't war to see her again** je ne veux plus l revoir; **never again!** jamais plus!

against *preposition* contre; **again the wall** contre le mur; **to lean against the wall** s'appuyer contre mur; **I'm against the idea** je suis contre l'idée; **the fight against racism** la lutte contre le racisme.

ge *noun* âge Masc. **1 at the age of fifteen** à l'âge de quinze ans; **she's the same age as me** elle a le même âge que moi; **to be under age** être mineur; **2 I haven't seen Johnny for ages** ça fait une éternité que je n'ai pas vu Johnny; **I haven't been to London for ages** ça fait une éternité que je ne suis pas allé à Londres.

ged *adjective* âgé de; **a woman aged thirty** une femme âgée de trente ans.

genda *noun* ordre Masc. du jour.

gent *noun* agent Masc.; **an estate agent** un agent immobilier; **a travel agent's** une agence de voyage.

ggressive *adjective* agressif (*Fem.* agressive).

go *adverb* **an hour ago** il y a une heure; **three days ago** il y a trois jours; **five years ago** il y a cinq ans; **a long time ago** il y a longtemps; **not long ago** il n'y a pas longtemps; **how long ago was it?** c'était il y a combien de temps?

gree *verb* **1 to agree with somebody** être [6] d'accord avec quelqu'un; **I agree with Laura** je suis d'accord avec Laura; **I don't agree** je ne suis pas d'accord; **2 I agree that** ... je suis d'accord sur le fait que ...; **I agree that it's too late now** je suis d'accord sur le fait qu'il est maintenant trop tard; **3 to agree to do** accepter [1] de faire; **Steve's agreed to help me** Steve a accepté de m'aider; **4 coffee doesn't agree with me** je ne supporte pas le café.

greement *noun* accord Masc.

agricultural *adjective* agricole.

agriculture *noun* agriculture Fem.

ahead *adverb* **1 go ahead!** allez-y!; **2 straight ahead** tout droit; **go straight ahead until you get to the crossroads** allez tout droit jusqu'au carrefour; **3 our team was ten points ahead** notre équipe avait dix points d'avance; **4 to be ahead of time** être en avance.

aid *noun* **1** aide Fem.; **aid to developing countries** l'aide aux pays en voie de développement; **2 in aid of** au profit de; **in aid of the homeless** au profit des sans-abri.

AIDS *noun* sida Masc. (*short for: syndrome immunodéficitaire acquis*); **to have AIDS** avoir le sida.

aim *noun* objectif Masc.; **their aim is to control pollution** leur objectif est de contrôler la pollution. **aim** *verb* **1 to aim to do** avoir [5] l'intention de faire; **we're aiming to finish it today** nous avons l'intention de le finir aujourd'hui; **2 a campaign aimed at young people** une campagne qui vise les jeunes; **3 to aim a gun at somebody** braquer [1] un révolver sur quelqu'un.

air *noun* **1** air Masc.; **in the open air** en plein air; **to go out for a breath of air** sortir prendre l'air; **2 to travel by air** voyager en avion.

airbag *noun* (*in a car*) airbag Masc.

air-conditioned *adjective* climatisé.

air conditioning *noun* climatisation Fem.

a
b
c
d
e
f
g
h
i
j
k
l
m
n
o
p
q
r
s
t
u
v
w
x
y
z

Air Force noun Armée Fem. de l'air.

air hostess noun hôtesse Fem. de l'air; **she's an air hostess** elle est hôtesse de l'air.

airline noun compagnie Fem. aérienne.

airmail noun **by airmail** par avion.

airport noun aéroport Masc.

aisle noun allée Fem. centrale.

alarm noun alarme Fem.; **a fire alarm** une alarme incendie; **a burglar alarm** une alarme contre le vol.

alarm clock noun réveil Masc.

album noun album Masc.

alcohol noun alcool Masc.

alcoholic noun alcoolique Masc. & Fem.

alcoholic adjective alcoolisé; **alcoholic drinks** les boissons alcoolisées.

alert adjective vif (Fem. vive) noun **on the alert: you must be on the alert for pickpockets** faites attention aux pickpockets.

A levels noun plural baccalauréat Masc., bac Masc. (informal) (Students take 'le bac' at the same age as A levels are taken in Britain. You can explain A levels briefly as follows: Les A levels sont répartis en deux niveaux, AS et A2. On passe les examens AS au bout d'une année de préparation, généralement dans quatre ou cinq matières. On passe les examens A2 un an plus tard, dans un plus petit nombre de matières, en choisissant parmi celles qui ont déjà fait l'objet d'un examen AS. La

meilleure note que l'on peut obtenir est A et la note la plus basse est N. Les A levels permettent de s'inscrire à l'université); SEE **baccalauréat**.

Algeria noun Algérie Fem.; **to Algeria** en Algérie; **in Algeria** en Algérie.

alibi noun alibi Masc.

alien noun **1** (foreigner) étranger Masc., étrangère Fem.; **2** (from outer space) extra-terrestre Masc. & Fem.

alike adjective pareil (Fem. pareille) **1** they're all alike ils sont tous pareils; **2 to look alike** se ressembler; **the two brothers look alike** les deux frères se ressemblent.

alive adjective vivant.

all along adverb depuis le début; **knew it all along** je le savais depuis le début.

allergic adjective allergique; **to be allergic to something** être allergique à quelque chose.

allergy noun allergie Fem.; **she has an allergy to cats** elle est allergique aux chats.

alligator noun alligator Masc.

allow verb **1 to allow somebody to do** permettre [11] à quelqu'un de faire; **the teacher allowed them to go out** le prof leur a permis de sortir; **2 to be allowed to do** avoir [5] le droit de faire; **I'm not allowed to go out during the week** je n'ai pas le droit de sortir en semaine.

all right adverb **1** (yes) d'accord; **'come round to my house around six'–'all right'** 'passe chez moi vers six heures'–'d'accord'; **2** (fine) bien; **is everything all right?** est-ce que tout va bien?; **she's all right now** elle va bien maintenant; **it's all right by me** ça ne me dérange pas; **3** (*not bad*) pas mal; **the meal was all right** le repas n'était pas mal; **4 are you all right?** ça va?; **5 is it all right to ...?** est-ce qu'on peut ...?; **is it all right to leave the door open?** est-ce qu'on peut laisser la porte ouverte?

ally *noun* allié *Masc.*, alliée *Fem.*

almond *noun* amande *Fem.*

almost *adverb* presque; **almost every day** presque tous les jours; **almost everybody** presque tout le monde; **she's almost five** elle a presque cinq ans.

alone *adjective* **1** seul; **he lives alone** il habite seul; **2 leave me alone!** laisse-moi tranquille!; **3 leave these papers alone!** ne touche pas à ces papiers!

along *preposition* **1** le long de; **there are trees all along the road** il y a des arbres tout le long de la route; **2** (*there is often no direct translation for 'along' so the sentence has to be expressed differently*) **she lives along the road from me** elle habite dans la même rue que moi; **to go for a walk along the beach** aller se promener sur la plage.

aloud *adverb* à haute voix; **to read something aloud** lire quelque chose à haute voix.

alphabet *noun* alphabet *Masc.*

alphabetical *adjective* alphabétique; **in alphabetical order** par ordre alphabétique.

Alps *plural noun* **the Alps** les Alpes.

already *adverb* déjà; **they've already left** ils sont déjà partis; **it's six o'clock already!** il est déjà six heures!

Alsatian *noun* (*dog*) berger *Masc.* allemand.

also *adverb* aussi; **I've also invited Karen** j'ai aussi invité Karen.

alter *verb* changer [52].

alternate *adjective* **on alternate days** un jour sur deux.

alternative *noun* **1** possibilité *Fem.*; **there are several alternatives** il y a plusieurs possibilités; **2 we have no alternative** nous n'avons pas le choix.
alternative *adjective* autre; **to find an alternative solution** trouver une autre solution.

alternatively *adverb* sinon; **alternatively, we could go together on Saturday** sinon, on pourrait y aller ensemble samedi.

alternative medicine *noun* médecine *Fem.* douce.

although *conjunction* bien que (*followed by subjunctive*); **although she's ill, she's willing to help us** bien qu'elle soit malade, elle est prête à nous aider.

altitude *noun* altitude *Fem.*

altogether *adverb* **1** en tout; **I've spent thirty pounds altogether** j'ai dépensé trente livres en tout; **2** (*completely*) complètement; **I'm not altogether convinced** je ne suis pas complètement convaincu.

aluminium *noun* aluminium *Masc.*

a b c d e f g h i j k l m n o p q r s t u v w x y z

always *adverb* toujours; **I always leave at five** je pars toujours à cinq heures.

am *verb* SEE **be**.

a.m. *abbreviation* du matin; **at 8 a.m.** à huit heures du matin.

amateur *noun* amateur *Masc.*; **amateur dramatics** théâtre *Masc.* amateur.

amaze *verb* surprendre [64]; **what amazes me is** ... ce qui me surprend c'est ....

amazed *adjective* stupéfait; **I was amazed to see her** j'étais stupéfait de la voir.

amazement *noun* stupéfaction *Fem.*; **to my amazement: to my amazement she agreed** à ma grande surprise elle s'est mise d'accord.

amazing *adjective* **1** (*terrific*) fantastique; **your dress is amazing!** ta robe est fantastique!; **they've got an amazing house** ils ont une maison fantastique; **2** (*extraordinary*) extraordinaire; **she has an amazing number of friends** elle a un nombre extraordinaire d'amis; **he told me an amazing story** il m'a raconté une histoire extraordinaire.

ambassador *noun* ambassadeur *Masc.*, ambassadrice *Fem.*.

ambition *noun* ambition *Fem.*

ambitious *adjective* ambitieux (*Fem.* ambitieuse).

ambulance *noun* ambulance *Fem.*

ambulance driver *noun* ambulancier *Masc.*, ambulancière *Fem.*.

amenities *plural noun* équipements *Masc. plural*.

America *noun* Amérique *Fem.*; **in America** en Amérique; **to America** en Amérique.

American *noun* Américain *Masc.*, Américaine *Fem.*.
American *adjective* américain (*Fem.* américaine).

ammunition *noun* munition *Fem.*

among, amongst *preposition* **1** parmi; **I found it amongst my books** je l'ai trouvé parmi mes livres; **2** (*between*) entre; **you can decide amongst yourselves** vous pouvez décider entre vous.

amount *noun* **1** quantité *Fem.*; **an enormous amount of bread** une énorme quantité de pain; **a huge amount of work** un travail énorme; **2** (*of money*) somme *Fem.*; **a large amount of money** une grosse somme d'argent.
amount *verb* **to amount to** s'élever [50] à; **the bill amounts to five hundred euros** la facture s'élève à cinq cents euros.

amp *noun* **1** (*electricity*) ampère *Masc.*; **2** (*amplifier*) ampli *Masc.* (*informal*).

amplifier *noun* amplificateur *Masc.*

amuse *verb* amuser [1].

amusement arcade *noun* salle *Fem.* de jeux électroniques.

amusing *adjective* amusant.

an *article* SEE **a**.

anaesthetic *noun* anesthésie *Fem.*

analyse *verb* analyser [1].

alysis *noun* analyse *Fem.*

cestor *noun* ancêtre *Masc. & Fem.*

chor *noun* ancre *Fem.*

chovy *noun* anchois *Masc.*

cient *adjective* **1** (*historic*) ncien (*Fem.* ancienne); **an ancient bbey** une abbaye ancienne; **2** (*very ld*) très vieux (*Fem.* très vieille); **an ncient pair of jeans** un très vieux ean; **3 ancient Greece** la Grèce ntique.

d *conjunction* **1** et; **Sean and Anna** Sean et Anna; **Rosie and I** Rosie et moi; **your shoes and socks** es chaussures et tes chaussettes; **louder and louder** de plus en plus ort.

gel *noun* ange *Masc.*

ger *noun* colère *Fem.*

gle *noun* angle *Masc.*

grily *adverb* avec colère.

gry *adjective* **to be angry** être en olère; **she was angry with me** elle tait en colère contre moi; **to get ngry** se fâcher [1].

imal *noun* animal *Masc.* (*plural* nimaux).

kle *noun* cheville *Fem.*; **to break our ankle** se casser la cheville.

niversary *noun* anniversaire *Masc.*; **a wedding anniversary** un nniversaire de mariage.

nounce *verb* annoncer [61].

nouncement *noun* annonce em.

nnoy *verb* agacer [61]; **to be nnoyed** être [6] agacé; **to get nnoyed** se fâcher [1]; **she got nnoyed** elle s'est fâchée.

annoying *adjective* agaçant.

annual *adjective* annuel (*Fem.* annuelle).

anorak *noun* anorak *Masc.*

anorexia *noun* anorexie *Fem.*

another *adjective* **1** un autre (*Fem.* une autre); **would you like another cup of tea?** voulez-vous une autre tasse de thé?; **2** encore; **another two years** encore deux ans; **we need another three chairs** il nous faut encore trois chaises.

answer *noun* **1** réponse *Fem.*; **the right answer** la bonne réponse; **the wrong answer** la mauvaise réponse; **2 the answer to a problem** la solution à un problème. **answer** *verb* **1** répondre [3] à; **he hasn't answered our letter** il n'a pas répondu à notre lettre; **2 to answer the door** aller [5] ouvrir la porte.

answering machine *noun* répondeur *Masc.*; **to leave a message on the answering machine** laisser un message au répondeur.

ant *noun* fourmi *Fem.*

Antarctic *noun* Antarctique *Masc.*

anthem *noun* **the national anthem** l'hymne national.

antibiotic *noun* antibiotique *Fem.*

antique *noun* **antiques** les antiquités *Fem.* **antique** *adjective* ancien (*Fem.* ancienne); **an antique table** une table ancienne.

antique shop *noun* magasin *Masc* d'antiquités.

a b c d e f g h i j k l m n o p q r s t u v w x y z

antiseptic *noun* antiseptique *Masc.*

anxious *adjective* inquiet (*Fem.* inquiète).

anxiously *adverb* avec inquiétude.

any *adjective, adverb, pronoun* **1** du, de l', de la, des; **is there any butter?** y a-t-il du beurre?; **is there any oil?** y a-t-il de l'huile?; **is there any flour?** y a-t-il de la farine?; **are there any eggs?** y a-t-il des œufs?; **2** de (*used in negative sentences*); **there isn't any flour** il n'y a pas de farine; **there aren't any eggs** il n'y a pas d'œufs; **3** en (*when 'any' is used on its own without a noun*); **I don't want any** je n'en veux pas; **4** not …any more ne …plus; **there isn't any more butter** il n'y a plus de beurre; **I don't go there any more** je n'y vais plus.

anybody, **anyone** *pronoun* **1** (*in questions and after 'if'*) quelqu'un; **is anybody in?** est-ce qu'il y a quelqu'un?; **if anybody wants some beer, it's in the fridge** si quelqu'un veut de la bière, elle est au frigo; **does anybody want some tea?** qui veut du thé?; **2** not …anybody ne …personne; **there isn't anybody in her office** il n'y a personne dans son bureau; **3** (*absolutely anybody*) n'importe qui; **anybody can go** n'importe qui peut y aller.

anyhow *adverb* SEE **anyway**.

anyone *pronoun* SEE **anybody**.

anything *pronoun* **1** (*in questions*) quelque chose; **is there anything I can do to help?** est-ce que je peux faire quelque chose pour t'aider?;

2 not …anything ne …rien; **there isn't anything on the table** il n'y rien sur la table; **3** (*anything at a* n'importe quoi; **anything could happen** il pourrait arriver n'importe quoi.

anyway, **anyhow** *adverb* de toute façon; **anyway, I'll ring you before I leave** de toute façon, je t'appellerai avant de partir.

anywhere *adverb* **1** (*in question* quelque part; **have you seen my keys anywhere?** est-ce que tu as mes clés quelque part?; **are you going anywhere tomorrow?** est-que tu vas quelque part demain?; **2** not …anywhere ne …nulle part can't find my keys anywhere** je trouve nulle part mes clés; **3** (*absolutely anywhere*) n'importe où; **put your cases down anywhere** pose tes valises n'importe où.

apart *adjective, adverb* **1** (*separat* séparé; **we don't like being apart** nous n'aimons pas être séparés; **2** be two metres apart** être à deux mètres l'un de l'autre; **3 apart fro** à part; **apart from Judy everybod was there** à part Judy tout le mon y était.

apartheid *noun* apartheid *Masc.*

apartment *noun* appartement *Masc.*

ape *noun* (grand) singe *Masc.*

apologize *verb* s'excuser [1]; **he apologizes for his behaviour** il s'excuse de son comportement; **he apologized to Tanya** il s'est excu auprès de Tanya.

340

pology noun excuses Fem. plural.

postrophe noun apostrophe Fem.

pparatus noun 1 (in a gym) agrès Masc. plural; 2 (in a lab) matériel Masc.

pparent adjective apparent.

pparently adverb apparemment.

ppeal noun appel Masc.
appeal verb 1 to appeal for lancer [61] un appel pour; 2 to appeal to somebody tenter [1] quelqu'un; horror films don't appeal to me les films d'épouvante ne me tentent pas.

ppear verb 1 apparaître [57]; Mick appeared at the door Mick est apparu à la porte; 2 to appear on television passer [1] à la télévision; 3 (seem) paraître [57]; it appears that somebody has stolen the key il paraît que quelqu'un a volé la clé.

ppendicitis noun appendicite Fem.

ppendix noun 1 (of book) annexe Fem.; 2 (organ) appendice Masc.

ppetite noun appétit Masc.; it'll spoil your appetite ça te coupera l'appétit.

pplaud verb applaudir [2].

pplause noun applaudissements Masc. plural.

pple noun pomme Fem.

pple core noun trognon Masc. de pomme.

pple tree noun pommier Masc.

pplicant noun candidat Masc., candidate Fem.

pplication noun a job application une candidature.

application form noun (for a job) dossier Masc. de candidature.

apply verb 1 to apply for a job poser [1] sa candidature à un poste; 2 to apply for a course faire [10] une demande d'inscription à un cours; 3 to apply to s'appliquer [1] à; that doesn't apply to students cela ne s'applique pas aux étudiants.

appointment noun rendez-vous Masc.; to make a dental appointment prendre rendez-vous chez le dentiste; I've got a hair appointment at four j'ai rendez-vous chez le coiffeur à seize heures.

appreciate verb I appreciate your advice je vous suis reconnaissant de vos conseils; I'd appreciate it if you could tidy up afterwards je te serais reconnaissant de ranger après.

apprentice noun apprenti Masc., apprentie Fem..

apprenticeship noun apprentissage Masc.

approach verb (come near to) 1 s'approcher de [1]; we were approaching Paris nous nous approchions de Paris; 2 (tackle) aborder [1] (a task or problem).

appropriate adjective approprié.

approval noun approbation Fem.

approve verb to approve of apprécier [1]; they don't approve of her friends ils n'apprécient pas ses amis.

approximate adjective approximatif (Fem. approximative).

a
b
c
d
e
f
g
h
i
j
k
l
m
n
o
p
q
r
s
t
u
v
w
x
y
z

approximately *adverb* environ; **approximately fifty people** environ cinquante personnes.

apricot *noun* abricot *Masc.*

apricot tree *noun* abricotier *Masc.*

April *noun* avril *Masc.*; **in April** en avril.

April Fool *noun* poisson *Masc.* d'avril.

April Fool's Day *noun* le premier avril.

apron *noun* tablier *Masc.*

aquarium *noun* aquarium *Masc.*

Aquarius *noun* Verseau *Masc.*; **Sharon's Aquarius** Sharon est Verseau.

Arab *noun* Arabe *Masc. & Fem.* **Arab** *adjective* arabe; **the Arab countries** les pays arabes.

arch *noun* arche *Fem.*

archaeologist *noun* archéologue *Masc. & Fem.*; **she's an archaeologist** elle est archéologue.

archaeology *noun* archéologie *Fem.*

archbishop *noun* archevêque *Masc.*

architect *noun* architecte *Masc. & Fem.*; **he's an architect** il est architecte.

architecture *noun* architecture *Fem.*

Arctic *noun* Arctique *Masc.*

are *verb* SEE **be**.

area *noun* **1** (*part of a town*) quartier; **a nice area** un quartier bien; **a rough area** un quartier mal

fréquenté; **2** (*region*) région *Fem.*; **in the Leeds area** dans la région de Leeds.

argue *verb* se disputer [1] **1** there's **no point in arguing** ce n'est pas la peine de se disputer; **2 to argue about something** discuter [1] de quelque chose; **they're arguing about the result** ils sont en train de discuter du résultat.

argument *noun* dispute *Fem.*; **to have an argument** se disputer.

Aries *noun* Bélier *Masc.*; **Pauline's Aries** Pauline est Bélier.

arithmetic *noun* arithmétique *Fem.*

arm *noun* bras *Masc.*; **to fold your arms** croiser les bras; **arm in arm** bras dessus bras dessous; **to break your arm** se casser le bras.

armchair *noun* fauteuil *Masc.*

armed *adjective* armé.

armpit *noun* aisselle *Fem.*

army *noun* armée *Fem.*; **to join the army** s'engager dans l'armée.

around *preposition, adverb* **1** (*with time*) vers; **we'll be there around ten** on va arriver vers dix heures; **2** (*with ages or amounts*) environ; **she's around fifteen** elle a environ quinze ans; **we need around six kilos** il nous faut environ six kilos; **3** (*surrounding*) autour de; **the countryside around Edinburgh** le paysage autour d'Édimbourg; **4** (*near*) **is there a post office around here?** est-ce qu'il y a un bureau de poste près d'ici?; **is Phil around?** est-ce que Phil est là?; **5** (*wrapped around*) autour de; **she**

had a scarf around her neck elle avait une écharpe autour du cou.

arrange *verb* **to arrange to do** prévoir [65] de faire; **we've arranged to see a film on Saturday** nous avons prévu de voir un film samedi.

arrangement *noun* **1** (*of things*) disposition *Fem.*; **2** (*agreement*) accord *Masc.*

arrest *noun* **to be under arrest** être en état d'arrestation.
arrest *verb* arrêter [1].

arrival *noun* arrivée *Fem.*

arrive *verb* arriver [1]; **they arrived at 3 p.m.** ils sont arrivés à quinze heures.

arrow *noun* flèche *Fem.*

art *noun* **1** art *Masc.*; **modern art** l'art moderne; **2** (*school subject*) dessin *Masc.*; **the art class** le cours de dessin.

artery *noun* artère *Fem.*

art gallery *noun* (*public*) musée *Masc.* des beaux arts.

artichoke *noun* artichaut *Masc.*

article *noun* article *Masc.*

artificial *adjective* artificiel (*Fem.* artificielle).

artist *noun* artiste *Masc. & Fem.*; **he's an artist** c'est un artiste.

artistic *adjective* artistique.

art school *noun* école *Fem.* de beaux arts.

as *conjunction, adverb, preposition* **1** comme; **as you know** comme vous le savez; **as usual** comme d'habitude; **as I told you** comme je t'avais dit; **2** (*because*) puisque; **as**

there were no trains, we took the bus puisqu'il n'y avait pas de trains, nous avons pris le bus; **3 as ...as** aussi ...que; **he's as tall as his brother** il est aussi grand que son frère; **you must be as tired as I am** tu dois être aussi fatigué que moi; **4 as much ...as** autant de ...que; **you have as much time as I do** tu as autant de temps que moi; **5 as many ...as** autant de ...que; **we have as many problems as he does** nous avons autant de problèmes que lui; **6 as long as** pourvu que (*with subjunctive*); **we'll go tomorrow, as long as it's a nice day** on va y aller demain, pourvu qu'il fasse beau; **7 for as long as** aussi longtemps que; **you can stay for as long as you like** tu peux rester aussi longtemps que tu veux; **8 as soon as possible** dès que possible; **9 to work as** travailler comme; **he works as a taxi driver in the evenings** il travaille comme chauffeur de taxi le soir.

asbestos *noun* amiante *Fem.*

ash *noun* cendre *Fem.*

ashamed *adjective* **to be ashamed** avoir honte; **you should be ashamed of yourself!** tu devrais avoir honte!

ashtray *noun* cendrier *Masc.*

Asia *noun* Asie *Fem.*; **in Asia** en Asie.

Asian *noun* **1** (*from the Far East*) Asiatique *Masc. & Fem.*; **2** (*from India*) Indien *Masc.*, Indienne *Fem.*; **3** (*from Pakstan*) Pakistanais *Masc.*, Pakistanaise *Fem.*
Asian *adjective* **1** asiatique (*from Asia*); **2** (*from India*) indien (*Fem.*

indienne); **3** (*from Pakistan*)
pakistanais (*Fem.* pakistanaise).

ask *verb* **1** demander [1]; **you can
ask at reception** tu peux demander
à l'accueil; **to ask somebody
something** demander quelque
chose à quelqu'un; **I asked him
where he lives** je lui ai demandé où
il habite; **to ask for something**
demander quelque chose; **I asked
for three coffees** j'ai demandé trois
cafés; **to ask somebody for
something** demander quelque
chose à quelqu'un; **to ask
somebody to do** demander à
quelqu'un de faire; **ask Danny to
give you a hand** demande à Danny
de te donner un coup de main; **2 to
ask somebody a question** poser [1]
une question à quelqu'un; **I asked
you a question!** je t'ai posé une
question!; **3** inviter [1]; **they've
asked us to a party at their house**
ils nous ont invité à une soirée chez
eux; **4 Paul's asked Janie out on
Friday** Paul a invité Janie à sortir
avec lui vendredi.

asleep *adjective* **to be asleep**
dormir [37]; **the baby's asleep** le
bébé dort; **to fall asleep** s'endormir
[37].

asparagus *noun* asperges *Fem.*
plural.

aspirin *noun* aspirine *Fem.*

assembly *noun* (*at school*)
rassemblement *Masc.*

assess *verb* évaluer [1].

assignment *noun* (*at school*)
devoir *Masc.*

assist *verb* aider [1].

assistance *noun* aide *Fem.*

assistant *noun* **1** assistant *Masc.*,
assistante *Fem.*; **2 a shop assistan**
un vendeur, une vendeuse.

association *noun* association
Fem.

assorted *adjective* variés (*Fem.*
variées).

assortment *noun* mélange *Masc.*

assume *verb* supposer [1].

assure *verb* assurer [1].

asterisk *noun* astérisque *Masc.*

asthma *noun* asthme *Masc.*; **she
has asthma** elle souffre de l'asthm

astonishing *adjective* étonnant;
her knowledge is astonishing ell
a des connaissances incroyables.

astrologer *noun* astrologue *Masc*
& *Fem.*

astrology *noun* astrologie *Fem.*

astronaut *noun* astronaute *Masc.*
Fem.

astronomer *noun* astronome
Masc. & Fem..

astronomy *noun* astronomie *Fem*

at *preposition* **1** à (*note that 'à + le'
always becomes 'au' and 'à + les'
always becomes 'aux'*); **at home** à l
maison; **at school** à l'école; **at my
office** à mon bureau; **at the marke**
au marché; **at meetings** aux
réunions; **2** (*talking about the time*
à; **at eight o'clock** à huit heures;
3 at night la nuit; **at the weekend**
le weekend; **4 at Emma's house**
chez Emma; **she's at her brother'**
this evening elle est chez son frère
ce soir; **at the hairdresser's** chez l
coiffeur; **5 at last** enfin; **he's foun**

job at last il a enfin trouvé un
mploi; **1** (@ *in email addresses*)
robase *Masc.*; **john-dot-**
mith@easycom-dot-com john-
oint-smith-arobase-easycom-point-
om.

hlete *noun* athlète *Masc. & Fem.*

hletic *adjective* athlétique.

hletics *noun* athlétisme *Masc.*

tlantic *noun* Atlantique *Masc.*

las *noun* atlas *Masc.*

mosphere *noun* atmosphère
em.

om *noun* atome *Masc.*

omic *adjective* atomique.

tach *verb* attacher [1].

tached *adjective* **to be attached**
o être [6] attaché à.

tachment *noun* pièce *Fem.*
ointe.

tack *noun* attaque *Fem.*
attack *verb* attaquer [1].

tacker *noun* agresseur *Masc.*

tempt *noun* tentative *Fem.*; **at the**
irst attempt à la première
entative.

attempt *verb* **to attempt to do**
essayer [59] de faire.

tend *verb* assister [1] à; **to attend**
a class assister à un cours.

tention *noun* attention *Fem.*; **to**
ay attention to faire attention à; **I**
vasn't paying atttention je ne
aisais pas attention.

ttic *noun* grenier *Masc.*; **in the attic**
u grenier.

ttitude *noun* attitude *Fem.*

ttract *verb* attirer [1].

attraction *noun* attraction *Fem.*

attractive *adjective* séduisant.

aubergine *noun* aubergine *Fem.*

auction *noun* vente *Fem.* aux
enchères.

audience *noun* public *Masc.*

August *noun* août *Masc.*; **in August**
en août.

aunt, auntie *noun* tante *Fem.*

au pair *noun* jeune fille *Fem.* au
pair; **I'm looking for a job as an au**
pair je cherche un emploi de jeune
fille au pair.

Australia *noun* Australie *Fem.*; **in**
Australia en Australie; **to Australia**
en Australie.

Australian *noun* Australien *Masc.*,
Australienne *Fem.*
Australian *adjective* australien
(*Fem.* australienne).

Austria *noun* Autriche *Fem.*; **in**
Austria en Autriche; **to Austria** en
Autriche.

Austrian *noun* Autrichien *Masc.*,
Autrichienne *Fem.*
Austrian *adjective* autrichien (*Fem.*
autrichienne).

author *noun* auteur *Masc.*

autobiography *noun*
autobiographie *Fem.*

autograph *noun* autographe *Masc.*

automatic *adjective* automatique.

automatically *adverb*
automatiquement.

autumn *noun* automne *Masc.*; **in**
autumn en automne.

availability *noun* disponibilité
Fem.

a
b
c
d
e
f
g
h
i
j
k
l
m
n
o
p
q
r
s
t
u
v
w
x
y
z

available *adjective* disponible.

avalanche *noun* avalanche *Fem*.

avenue *noun* avenue *Fem*.

average *noun* moyenne *Fem.*; **on average** en moyenne; **above average** au-dessus de la moyenne. **average** *adjective* moyen (*Fem.* moyenne); **the average height** la hauteur moyenne.

avocado *noun* avocat *Masc*.

avoid *verb* éviter [1]; **she avoided me** elle m'a évité; **to avoid doing** éviter de faire; **I avoid speaking to him** j'évite de lui parler.

awake *adjective* **to be awake** être réveillé; **is Lola awake?** est-ce que Lola est réveillée?; **are you still awake?** tu ne dors pas?

award *noun* prix *Masc.*; **to win an award** remporter un prix.

aware *adjective* **to be aware of a noise** être conscient d'un bruit; **to be aware of a problem** être au courant d'un problème; **as far as I'm aware** à ma connaissance.

away *adverb* **1 to be away** être absent; **I'll be away next week** je serai absent la semaine prochaine; **2 to go away** partir; **Laura's gone away for a week** Laura est partie pour une semaine; **go away!** va-t-en!; **3 to run away** partir en courant; **the thieves ran away** les voleurs sont partis en courant; **4 the school is two kilometres away** l'école est à deux kilomètres d'ici; **how far away is it?** c'est à quelle distance d'ici?; **not far away** pas loin d'ici; **5 to put something away** ranger quelque chose; **I'll just**

put my books away je vais juste ranger mes livres; **6 to give something away** donner quelque chose; **she's given away all her tapes** elle a donné toutes ses cassettes.

away match *noun* match *Masc.* l'extérieur.

awful *adjective* **1** affreux (*Fem.* affreuse); **the film was awful!** le film était affreux!; **2 I feel awful** je ne me sens pas bien du tout; **3 I feel awful about it** ça m'ennuie vraiment; **4 an awful lot of** énormément de.

awkward *adjective* **1** difficile; **it an awkward situation** c'est une situation difficile; **it's a bit awkward** c'est un peu difficile; **a awkward child** un enfant difficile; **2 an awkward question** une question gênante.

axe *noun* hache *Fem*.

Bb

baby *noun* bébé *Masc*.

babysit *verb* faire [10] du babysitting.

babysitter *noun* babysitter *Masc. Fem*.

babysitting *noun* babysitting *Masc*.

bachelor *noun* célibataire *Masc*.

back *noun* **1** (*of a person or anime*) dos *Masc.*; **to do something behin someone's back** faire quelque chose dans le dos de quelqu'un; **2**

a piece of paper, your hand, or a garment) dos *Masc.*; **on the back** au dos; **3** (*of a car, a plane, or a building*) arrière *Masc.*; **we have seats at the back** nous avons des places à l'arrière; **a garden at the back of the house** un jardin à l'arrière de la maison; **4 the children at the back of the room** les enfants au fond de la salle; **5** (*of a chair or sofa*) dossier *Masc.*; **6** (*in football or hockey*) arrière *Masc.*; **left back** arrière gauche.

back *adjective* **1** arrière (*a wheel or seat*); **the back seat of the car** le siège arrière de la voiture; **2 the back gate** la porte de derrière; **the back garden** le jardin de derrière.

back *adverb* **1 to go back** rentrer; **to go back to school** rentrer à l'école; **Lisa's gone back to London** Lisa est rentrée à Londres; **2 to come back** rentrer; **they've come back from Italy** ils sont rentrés d'Italie; **she's back at work** elle a repris le travail; **Sue's not back yet** Sue n'est pas encore rentrée; **we went by bus and walked back** nous avons pris le bus pour y aller et nous sommes rentrés à pied; **3 to phone back** rappeler; **I'll ring back later** je rappellerai plus tard; **4 to give something back to somebody** rendre quelque chose à quelqu'un; **I gave him back his cassettes** je lui ai rendu ses cassettes; **give it back!** rends-le-moi!

back *verb* **1** (*to support*) soutenir [81] (*a candidate, for example*); **2** (*to bet on*) parier [1] sur (*a horse*).

● **to back up** (*computing*) **to back up**

a file sauvegarder [1] un fichier sur disquette.

● **to back somebody up** soutenir [77] quelqu'un.

backache *noun* mal *Masc.* de dos.

backbone *noun* colonne *Fem.* vertébrale.

back door *noun* **1** (*of a building*) porte *Fem.* de derrière; **2** (*of a car*) porte *Fem.* arrière.

backfire *verb* (*turn out badly*) échouer [1].

background *noun* **1** (*of a person*) (*social*) milieu *Masc.*; **2** (*of events or a situation*) contexte *Masc.*; **3** (*in a picture or view*) arrière-plan *Masc.*; **the trees in the background** les arbres à l'arrière-plan; **4 background music** la musique d'ambiance; **5 background noise** les bruits *Masc. plural* de fond.

backhand *noun* revers *Masc.*

backing *noun* **1** (*on sticky-back plastic, for example*) revêtement *Masc.* intérieur; **2** (*moral support*) soutien *Masc.*; **3** (*in music*) **a backing group** un groupe d'accompagnement.

backpack *noun* sac *Masc.* à dos. **backpack** *verb* **to go backpacking** partir [58] en voyage avec son sac à dos.

back seat *noun* siège *Masc.* arrière.

backside *noun* derrière *Masc.*

backstage *adverb* **to go backstage** aller dans les coulisses.

backstroke *noun* dos *Masc.* crawlé.

347

back to front *adverb* à l'envers; **your jumper's back to front** ton pull est à l'envers.

backup *noun* **1** (*support*) soutien *Masc.*; **2** (*in computing*) **a backup disk** un disque de sauvegarde.

backwards *adverb* (*to lean or fall*) en arrière.

bacon *noun* **1** (*French streaky bacon*) lard *Masc.*; **2** (*thin-sliced British-type*) bacon *Masc.*; **bacon and eggs** œufs au bacon.

bad *adjective* **1** (*not good*) mauvais (*goes before the noun*) **bad work** du mauvais travail; **a bad meal** un mauvais repas; **his new film's not bad** son nouveau film n'est pas mauvais; **it's bad for your health** c'est mauvais pour la santé; **I'm bad at physics** je suis mauvais en physique; **2** (*serious*) grave; **a bad accident** un accident grave; **a bad cold** un gros rhume; **3** (*rotten*) pourri; **a bad apple** une pomme pourrie; **to go bad** se gâter; **4** (*rude*) **bad language** du langage grossier; **5** (*naughty*) vilain; **bad dog!** vilain!; **bad girl!** vilaine! ★ **too bad!** (*I'm sorry for you*) pas de chance!; (*I don't care*) tant pis!

badge *noun* badge *Masc.*

badly *adverb* **1** mal; **he writes badly** il écrit mal; **I slept badly** j'ai mal dormi; **the exam went badly** l'examen s'est mal passé; **2** (*seriously*) (*to hurt or damage*) gravement; **the car was badly damaged** la voiture a été gravement endommagée; **badly hurt** grièvement blessé.

bad-mannered *adjective* mal élevé.

badminton *noun* badminton *Masc.*; **to play badminton** jouer au badminton.

bad-tempered *adjective* **1** (*for a little while*) irrité; **2** (*always*) **she's very bad-tempered** elle a très mauvais caractère.

bag *noun* sac *Masc.*

baggage *noun* bagages *Masc.* plural

baggage allowance *noun* franchise *Fem.* de bagages.

baggage reclaim *noun* réception *Fem.* des bagages.

bagpipes *plural noun* cornemuse *Fem.*; **to play the bagpipes** jouer de la cornemuse.

bags *plural noun* bagages *Masc.* plural; **to pack your bags** faire ses bagages; ★ **to have bags under your eyes** avoir des valises sous les yeux (*informal*) .

Bahaman *adjective* des Bahamas

Bahamas *noun* (*plural*) **the Bahamas** les Bahamas; **the Bahamas Islands** les îles Bahamas

bake *verb* **to bake a cake** faire [10] un gâteau; **to bake vegetables** faire [10] cuire des légumes au four.

baked *adjective* **1** (*fish or fruit*) au four; **baked apples** les pommes au four; **2 a baked potato** une pomme de terre au four.

baked beans *plural noun* les haricots blancs à la sauce tomate.

baker *noun* boulanger *Masc.*, boulangère *Fem.*; **to go to the baker's** aller à la boulangerie.

akery noun boulangerie Fem.

alance noun **1** équilibre Masc.; **to lose your balance** perdre l'équilibre; **2** (money in your bank account) solde Masc.

alanced adjective équilibré.

alcony noun balcon Masc.

ald adjective chauve.

all noun **1** (for tennis or golf) balle Fem.; **2** (for football or volleyball) ballon Masc.; **3** (of string or wool) pelote Fem.

allet noun ballet Masc.

allet dancer noun danseur Masc. de ballet, danseuse Fem. de ballet.

allet shoe noun chausson Masc. de danse.

alloon noun **1** ballon Masc.; **2** (hot air) montgolfière Fem.

allot noun scrutin Masc.

allpoint (pen) noun stylo Masc. à bille.

an noun interdiction Fem.; **a ban on smoking** une interdiction de fumer.
ban verb interdire [47].

anana noun banane Fem.; **a banana yoghurt** un yaourt à la banane.

and noun **1** (playing music) groupe Masc.; **a rock band** un groupe de rock; **2 a jazz band** un orchestre de jazz; **3 a brass band** une fanfare; **4 a rubber band** un élastique.

andage noun bandage Masc.
bandage verb mettre [11] un bandage à.

ang noun **1** (noise) boum Masc.; **2** (of a door, shutter, or window, etc) claquement Masc.

bang verb **1** (to hit) taper [1] sur (a drum, for example); **he banged his fist on the table** il a tapé du poing sur la table; **2** (to knock) cogner [1]; **to bang on the door** cogner à la porte; **I banged my head on the door** je me suis cogné la tête contre la porte; **I banged into the table** j'ai heurté la table; **3 to bang the door** claquer [1] la porte.

bang exclamation (like a gun) pan!

bangle noun bracelet Masc.

banister(s), **bannister(s)** (plural) noun rampe Fem. (d'escalier).

bank noun **1** (for money) banque Fem.; **I'm going to the bank** je vais à la banque; **2** (of a river or lake) bord Masc.

bank account noun compte Masc. bancaire.

bank balance noun solde Masc. bancaire.

bank card noun carte Fem. bancaire.

bank holiday noun jour Masc. férié.

banking noun banque Fem; milieu Masc. bancaire.

banknote noun billet Masc. de banque.

bank statement noun relevé Masc. de compte.

baptize verb baptiser [1].

bar noun **1** (selling drinks) bar Masc.; **Janet works in a bar** Janet travaille dans un bar; **2** (the counter) comptoir Masc.; **on the bar** sur le bar; **3 a bar of chocolate** une tablette de chocolat; **4 a bar of soap**

a
b
c
d
e
f
g
h
i
j
k
l
m
n
o
p
q
r
s
t
u
v
w
x
y
z

une savonnette; **5** (*made of wood or metal*) barre *Fem.*; **a metal bar** une barre en métal; **6** (*in music*) mesure *Fem.*

bar *verb* **1** (*to block physically*) barrer [1]; **to bar someone's way** barrer le passage à quelqu'un; **2** (*to ban from an activity*) exclure [25].

Barbadian *noun* Barbadien *Masc.*, Barbadienne *Fem.*
Barbadian *adjective* de la Barbade.

Barbados *noun* la Barbade.

barbecue *noun* barbecue *Masc.*; **there's a barbecue tonight** il y a un barbecue ce soir.
barbecue *verb* **to barbecue a chicken** faire [10] griller un poulet au barbecue; **barbecued chicken** du poulet grillé au barbecue.

barbed wire *noun* barbelé *Masc.*

bare *adjective* nu.

barefoot *adjective* **to be barefoot** être nu-pieds; **to walk barefoot** marcher pieds nus.

bargain *noun* (*a good buy*) affaire *Fem.*; **I got a bargain** j'ai fait une affaire; **it's a bargain!** c'est une bonne affaire!

barge *noun* péniche *Fem.*

bark *noun* **1** (*of a tree*) écorce *Fem.*; **2** (*of a dog*) aboiement *Masc.*
bark *verb* aboyer [39].

barley *noun* orge *Masc.*

barmaid *noun* barmaid *Fem.*

barman *noun* barman *Masc.*

barn *noun* grange *Fem.*

barometer *noun* baromètre *Masc.*

barrel *noun* tonneau *Masc.* (*plural* tonneaux).

barrier *noun* barrière *Fem.*

base *noun* base *Fem.*

baseball *noun* base-ball *Masc.*; **a baseball cap** une casquette de base-ball.

based *adjective* **1** **to be based on** être fondé sur; **the film is based on a true story** le film est fondé sur une histoire vraie; **2** **to be based in** être basé à; **he's based in Bristol** il est basé à Bristol.

basement *noun* sous-sol *Masc.*; **in the basement** au sous-sol.

bash *noun* **1** bosse *Fem.*; **it's got a bash on the wing** il y a une bosse à l'aile; **2** **I'll have a bash** je vais essayer un coup.
bash *verb* cogner [1]; **I bashed my head** je me suis cogné la tête.

basic *adjective* **1** de base; **basic knowledge** des connaissances de base; **her basic salary** son salaire de base; **2** **the basic facts** les faits essentiels; **3** (*not luxurious*) rudimentaire; **the flat's a bit basic** l'appartement est un peu rudimentaire.

basically *adverb* **1** au fond; **it's basically all right** au fond ça va; **2** à vrai dire; **basically, I don't want to go** à vrai dire, je ne veux pas y aller.

basics *noun* rudiments *Masc. plural*

basin *noun* (*washbasin*) lavabo *Masc.*

basis *noun* **1** base *Fem.*; **2** **on the basis of** sur la base de; **on a regular basis** régulièrement.

asket noun **1** (*for shopping*) panier *Masc.*; **2** (*other*) corbeille *Fem.*; **a waste-paper basket** une corbeille à papier; **a linen basket** une corbeille à linge.

asketball noun basketball *Masc.*; **to play basketball** jouer au basketball.

ass noun **1** basse *Fem.*; **to play bass** jouer de la basse; **2 a double bass** une contrebasse.

ass drum noun grosse caisse *Fem.*

ass guitar noun guitare *Fem.* basse.

assoon noun basson *Masc.*; **to play the bassoon** jouer du basson.

at noun **1** (*for cricket or baseball*) batte *Fem.*; **2** (*for table tennis*) raquette *Fem.*; **3** (*animal*) chauve-souris *Fem.*

atch noun **1** (*of cakes*) fournée *Fem.*; **2** (*of letters*) tas *Masc.*; **a batch of letters** un tas de lettres; **3** (*in computing*) lot *Masc.*

ath noun **1** bain *Masc.*; **to have a bath** prendre un bain; **I was in the bath** j'étais dans mon bain; **2** (*bathtub*) baignoire *Fem.*; **the bath's pink** la baignoire est rose.

athe verb **1** laver [1] (*a wound*); **2** (*go swimming*) se baigner [1].

athroom noun salle *Fem.* de bains (*plural* salles de bains).

aths plural noun piscine *Fem.*

ath towel noun serviette *Fem.* de bain.

atter noun (*for frying*) pâte *Fem.* à frire; **fish in batter** des beignets de poisson; **pancake batter** la pâte à crêpes.

battery noun **1** (*for a torch or radio, for example*) pile *Fem.*; **2** (*for a car*) batterie *Fem.*

battle noun bataille *Fem.*

bay noun **1** (*on the coast*) baie *Fem.*; **2** (*for coaches*) travée *Fem.*

B.C. (*short for: before Christ*) av. J.-C.

be verb **1** être [6]; **Melanie is in the kitchen** Melanie est dans la cuisine; **where is the butter?** où est le beurre?; **I'm tired** je suis fatigué; **when we were in France** quand nous étions en France; **2** (*with jobs and professions*) être; **she's a teacher** elle est professeur (*note that 'a' is not translated*); **he's a taxi driver** il est chauffeur de taxi; **3** (*in clock times*) être; **it's three o'clock** il est trois heures; **it's half past five** il est cinq heures et demie; **4** (*days of the week and dates*) **what day is it today?** nous sommes quel jour aujourd'hui?; **it's Tuesday today** nous sommes mardi aujourd'hui; **it's the twentieth of May** nous sommes le vingt mai; **5** (*talking about age*) avoir [5]; **how old are you?** quel âge as-tu?; **I'm fifteen** j'ai quinze ans; **Harry's twenty** Harry a vingt ans; **6** (*cold, hot, hungry*) avoir [5]; **I'm hot** j'ai chaud; **I'm cold** j'ai froid; **I'm hungry** j'ai faim; **7** (*weather*) faire [10]; **it's cold today** il fait froid aujourd'hui; **it's a nice day** il fait beau; **8 I've never been to Paris** je ne suis jamais allé à Paris; **have you been to Britain before?** est-ce que tu es déjà venu en Grande Bretagne?; **9 to be loved**

a
b
c
d
e
f
g
h
i
j
k
l
m
n
o
p
q
r
s
t
u
v
w
x
y
z

être aimé; **he has been killed** il a été tué.

beach noun plage Fem.; **to go to the beach** aller à la plage; **on the beach** sur la plage.

bead noun perle Fem.

beak noun bec Masc.

beam noun **1** (of light) rayon Masc.; **2** (for a roof) poutre Fem.

bean noun haricot Masc.; **baked beans** les haricots à la sauce tomate; **green beans** les haricots verts.

bear noun ours Masc.
bear verb **1** supporter [1]; **I can't bear him** je ne peux pas le supporter; **I can't bear the idea** je ne supporte pas l'idée; **2 to bear something in mind** tenir [77] compte de quelque chose; **I'll bear it in mind** je ne l'oublierai pas.
● **to bear up** tenir [77] le coup.

beard noun barbe Fem.

bearded adjective barbu.

bearings plural noun **to get one's bearings** se repérer [24].

beast noun **1** (animal) bête Fem.; **2 you beast!** chameau!

beat noun rythme Masc.
beat verb **1** (defeat) battre [21]; **we beat them!** on les a battus!; **2 to beat the eggs** battre les œufs; **3 you can't beat a good meal** rien ne vaut un bon repas.
● **to beat somebody up** tabasser [1] quelqu'un (informal).

beautician noun esthéticien Masc., esthéticienne Fem.

beautiful adjective beau (Fem. belle) (Masc. plural beaux) (goes before the noun); **a beautiful day** un beau jour; **a beautiful girl** une belle fille; **beautiful pictures** de beaux tableaux; **a beautiful place** un bel endroit ('bel' for masculine nouns beginning with a vowel or silent 'h').

beautifully adverb admirablement.

beauty noun beauté Fem.

beauty spot noun (for tourists) beau site Masc.

because conjunction **1** parce que; **because it's you** parce que c'est toi; **because it's cold** parce qu'il fait froid; **2 because of** à cause de; **because of the accident** à cause de l'accident.

become verb devenir [81].

bed noun **1** lit Masc.; **a double bed** un grand lit; **in bed** au lit; **to go to bed** aller se coucher; **2** (flower bed) parterre Masc.

bedclothes plural noun couvertures Fem. plural.

bedding noun literie Fem.

bedroom noun chambre Fem.; **bedroom furniture** les meubles de chambre; **my bedroom window** la fenêtre de ma chambre.

bedside noun **a bedside table** une table de chevet.

bedsit, bedsitter noun chambre Fem. meublée.

bedspread noun dessus-de-lit Masc.

bedtime noun **it's bedtime** c'est l'heure d'aller se coucher.

ee *noun* abeille *Fem.*

eech *noun* hêtre *Masc.*

eef *noun* bœuf *Masc.*; **we had roast beef** on a mangé du rôti de bœuf.

eefburger *noun* hamburger *Masc.*

eer *noun* bière *Fem.*; **two beers please** deux bières s'il vous plaît; **a beer can** une canette de bière.

eetle *noun* scarabée *Masc.*

eetroot *noun* betterave *Fem.*

efore *preposition, adverb* **1** avant; **before Monday** avant lundi; **he left before me** il est parti avant moi; **2 the day before** la veille; **the day before the wedding** la veille du mariage; **the day before yesterday** avant-hier; **the week before** la semaine d'avant; **3** (*already*) déjà; **I've seen him before somewhere** je l'ai déjà vu quelque part; **I had seen the film before** j'avais déjà vu le film.

efore *conjunction* **1** avant de; **before doing** avant de faire; **I closed the windows before leaving** (or **before I left**) j'ai fermé les fenêtres avant de partir; **2** avant que; **phone me before they leave** appelle-moi avant qu'ils s'en aillent; **oh, before I forget** ... avant que j'oublie ....

eforehand *adverb* (*ahead of time*) à l'avance; **phone beforehand** appelle à l'avance.

eg *verb* **1** (*ask for money*) mendier [1]; **2** (*ask*) supplier [1]; **she begged me not to leave** elle m'a supplié de ne pas partir; **I beg your pardon** je vous demande pardon.

begin *verb* **1** commencer [61]; **the meeting begins at ten** la réunion commence à dix heures; **the words beginning with P** les mots qui commencent par un P; **2 to begin to do** commencer à faire; **I'm beginning to understand** je commence à comprendre.

beginner *noun* débutant *Masc.*, débutante *Fem.*

beginning *noun* début *Masc.*; **at the beginning** au début; **at the beginning of the holidays** au début des vacances.

behalf *noun* **on behalf of** pour.

behave *verb* **1** se comporter [1]; **he behaved badly** il s'est mal comporté; **2 to behave yourself** être sage; **behave yourselves!** soyez sages!

behaviour *noun* comportement *Masc.*

behind *adverb, preposition* **1** derrière; **behind the sofa** derrière le canapé; **behind them** derrière eux; **the car behind** la voiture de derrière; **2** (*not making progress*) **he's behind in class** il a du retard en classe; **3 to leave something behind** oublier quelque chose; **I've left my keys behind** j'ai oublié mes clés.
behind *noun* derrière *Masc.*

beige *adjective* beige.

Belgian *noun* Belge *Masc. & Fem.*
Belgian *adjective* belge.

Belgium *noun* Belgique *Fem.*; **to Belgium** en Belgique; **in Belgium** en Belgique.

a
b
c
d
e
f
g
h
i
j
k
l
m
n
o
p
q
r
s
t
u
v
w
x
y
z

a

b

c

d

e

f

g

h

i

j

k

l

m

n

o

p

q

r

s

t

u

v

w

x

y

z

belief *noun* conviction *Fem.*; **his political beliefs** ses convictions politiques.

believe *verb* **1** croire [33]; **I believe you** je te crois; **they believed what I said** ils ont cru ce que j'ai dit; **I don't believe you!** ce n'est pas vrai!; **2 to believe in** croire à; **to believe in ghosts** croire aux fantômes; **to believe in God** croire en Dieu.

bell *noun* **1** (*in a church*) cloche *Fem.*; **2** (*on a door*) sonnette *Fem.*; **ring the bell!** appuyez sur la sonnette!; **3** (*for a cat or toy*) grelot *Masc*; ★ **that name rings a bell** ce nom me dit quelque chose (*literally: says something to me*).

belong *verb* **1 to belong to** appartenir [81] à; **that belongs to Richard** cela appartient à Richard; **2 to belong to a club** faire [10] partie d'un club; **3** (*go*) aller [5]; **that chair belongs in the study** cette chaise va dans le bureau; **where does this vase belong?** ce vase va où?

belongings *plural noun* affaires *Fem. plural*; **all my belongings are in London** toutes mes affaires sont à Londres.

below *preposition* au-dessous de; **below the window** au-dessous de la fenêtre; **the flat below yours** l'appartement au-dessous du tien. **below** *adverb* **1** (*further down*) en bas; **shouts came from below** des cris venaient d'en bas; **2 the flat below** l'appartement de dessous.

belt *noun* ceinture *Fem.*

bench *noun* banc *Masc.*

bend *noun* **1** (*in a road*) virage *Masc* **2** (*in a river*) courbe *Fem.* **bend** *verb* **1** (*to make a bend in*) plier [1] (*your arm or leg, or a wire*) **2** (*to curve*) (*a road or path*) tourne [1]; **3 to bend down** or **forwards** se pencher [1]; **she bent down to look** elle s'est penchée pour regarder.

beneath *preposition* sous.

benefit *noun* **1** avantage *Masc.*; **2 unemployment benefit** les allocations *Fem. plural* de chômage.

bent *adjective* tordu.

beret *noun* béret *Masc.*

berry *noun* baie *Fem.*

berth *noun* couchette *Fem.*

beside *preposition* (*next to*) à côté de; **she was sitting beside me** elle était assise à côté de moi; ★ **that's beside the point** ça n'a rien à voir.

besides *adverb* **1** (*anyway*) d'ailleurs; **besides, it's too late** d'ailleurs, il est trop tard; **2** (*as well*, en plus; **four dogs, and six cats besides** quatre chiens et six chats en plus.

best *adjective* **1** meilleur; **it's the best** c'est le meilleur; **that's the best car** cette voiture-là est la meilleure; **she's my best friend** c'est ma meilleure amie; **2 she's the best at tennis** c'est elle la meilleure en tennis; **the best thing to do is to phone them** la meilleure chose à faire, c'est de les appeler. **best** *adverb* le mieux; **he plays best** il joue le mieux; **I like Paris best** c'est Paris que j'aime le mieux; **best of all** mieux que tout; ★ **all the best!** (*good luck*) bonne chance!

(*cheers*) à ta santé!; ★ **it's the best I can do** je ne peux pas faire mieux; ★ **to do your best to do** faire de son mieux pour faire;; **I did my best to help her** j'ai fait de mon mieux pour l'aider.

est man *noun* garçon *Masc.* d'honneur.

et *noun* pari *Masc.*
bet *verb* parier [1]; **to bet on a horse** parier sur un cheval; **I bet you he'll forget!** je te parie qu'il va oublier!

etter *adjective, adverb* **1** meilleur; **she's found a better flat** elle a trouvé un meilleur appartement; **this road's better than the other one** cette route est meilleure que l'autre; **2** mieux; **this pen writes better** ce stylo écrit mieux; **it works better than the other one** ça fonctionne mieux que l'autre; **3 even better** encore mieux; **it's even better than before** c'est encore mieux qu'avant; **4** (*less ill*) **to be better** aller mieux; **he's a bit better today** il va un peu mieux aujourd'hui; **to feel better** se sentir mieux; **I feel better** je me sens mieux; **5 to get better** s'améliorer; **my French is getting better** mon français s'améliore; **6 so much the better** tant mieux; **the sooner the better** le plus vite possible.
better *adverb* **you had better phone at once** tu ferais mieux d'appeler de suite; **he'd better not go** il ferait mieux de ne pas y aller; **I'd better go now** je dois partir maintenant.

better off *adjective* **1** (*richer*) plus riche; **they're better off than us** ils sont plus riches que nous; **2** (*more comfortable*) mieux; **you'd be better off in bed** tu serais mieux au lit.

between *preposition* entre; **between London and Dover** entre Londres et Douvres; **between Monday and Friday** entre lundi et vendredi; **between the two** entre les deux.

beware *verb* **beware of the dog!** attention au chien!

beyond *preposition* **1** (*in space and time*) au-delà de; **beyond the border** au-delà de la frontière; **2 it's beyond me!** ça me dépasse!

Bible *noun* **the Bible** la Bible.

bicycle *noun* vélo *Masc.*; **by bicycle** à vélo.

bicycle lane *noun* piste *Fem.* cyclable.

big *adjective* **1** grand (*goes before the noun*); **a big house** une grande maison; **a big city** une grande ville; **my big sister** ma grande sœur; **it's too big for me** c'est trop grand pour moi; **2** gros (*Fem.* grosse) (*before the noun*); **a big dog** un gros chien; **a big car** une grosse voiture; **a big mistake** une grosse erreur.

bigheaded *adjective* **to be bigheaded** avoir la grosse tête.

big screen *noun* grand écran *Masc.*

big toe *noun* gros orteil *Masc.*

bike *noun* **1** (*with pedals*) vélo *Masc.*; **by bike** à vélo; **2** (*with motor*) moto *Fem.*

bikini *noun* bikini *Masc.*

a
b
c
d
e
f
g
h
i
j
k
l
m
n
o
p
q
r
s
t
u
v
w
x
y
z

bilingual *adjective* bilingue.

bill *noun* 1 (*in a restaurant*) addition *Fem.*; **can we have the bill, please** l'addition, s'il vous plaît; 2 (*for gas, electricity, etc.*) facture *Fem.*

billiards *noun* billard *Masc.*; **to play billiards** jouer au billard.

billion *noun* milliard *Masc.*

bin *noun* poubelle *Fem.*

binoculars *noun* jumelles *Fem. plural.*

biochemistry *noun* biochimie *Fem.*

biography *noun* biographie *Fem.*

biologist *noun* biologiste *Masc. & Fem.*

biology *noun* biologie *Fem.*

bird *noun* oiseau *Masc.* (*plural* oiseaux).

bird sanctuary *noun* réserve *Fem.* ornithologique.

birdwatching *noun* **to go birdwatching** observer les oiseaux.

Biro™ *noun* bic™ *Masc.*

birth *noun* naissance *Fem.*

birth certificate *noun* acte *Masc.* de naissance.

birth control *noun* contraception *Fem.*

birthday *noun* 1 anniversaire *Masc.*; **happy birthday!** joyeux anniversaire!; 2 **a birthday present** un cadeau d'anniversaire.

birthday party *noun* 1 (*for a child*) goûter *Masc.* d'anniversaire; 2 (*for an adult*) soirée *Fem.* d'anniversaire.

biscuit *noun* biscuit *Masc.*

bishop *noun* évêque *Masc.*

bit *noun* 1 (*of bread, cheese, wood*) morceau *Masc.*; **a bit of chocolate** un morceau de chocolat; 2 (*of string, paper, garden*) bout *Masc.*; **a bit of string** un bout de ficelle; **with a little bit of garden** avec un petit bout de jardin; 3 (*a small amount*) **a bit of** un peu de; **a bit of sugar** un peu de sucre; **with a bit of luck** avec un peu de chance; **a bit of news** une nouvelle; **to have a bit of trouble with** avoir un petit problème avec; 4 (*in a book or film, for example*) passage *Masc.*; **this bit is brilliant!** ce passage est génial!; 5 **to fall to bits** tomber en morceaux; 6 **a bit** un peu; **a bit hot** un peu chaud; **a bit early** un peu trop tôt; **wait a bit!** attends un peu!; 7 (*for a horse*) mors *Masc.*; ★ **bit by bit** petit à petit.

bite *noun* 1 (*snack*) morceau *Masc.*; **I'll just have a bite before I go** je vais juste manger un morceau avant de partir; 2 (*from an insect*) piqûre *Fem.*; **a mosquito bite** une piqûre de moustique; 3 (*from a dog*) morsure *Fem.*

bite *verb* 1 (*a person or a dog*) mordre [3]; 2 (*an insect*) piquer [1]; ★ **to bite one's nails** se ronger [52] les ongles.

bitter *adjective* (*taste*) amer (*Fem.* amère).

black *adjective* 1 noir; **my black jacket** ma veste noire; **to turn black** noircir [2]; 2 **a Black man** un Noir; **a Black woman** une Noire; 3 **a black coffee** un café noir.

blackberry *noun* mûre *Fem.*

blackbird *noun* merle *Masc.*

blackboard noun tableau Masc. noir.

blackcurrant noun cassis Masc.

black eye noun œil Masc. au beurre noir.

black pudding noun boudin Masc. noir.

blade noun lame Fem.

blame noun responsabilité Fem.; **to take the blame for something** prendre la responsabilité de quelque chose.

blame verb **to blame someone for something** tenir [77] quelqu'un responsable de quelque chose; **they blamed him for the accident** ils l'ont tenu responsable de l'accident; **she is to blame for it** elle en est responsable; **I blame the parents!** à mon avis c'est la faute des parents!; **I don't blame you!** je te comprends!

blank noun blanc Masc.

blank adjective **1** (a page or piece of paper, or a cheque) blanc (Fem. blanche); (a tape or disk) vierge (a screen) vide; **2 my mind went blank** j'ai eu un trou de mémoire.

blanket noun couverture Fem.

blast noun **1** (an explosion) explosion Fem.; **2** (of air) souffle Masc.; **3 to play music at full blast** jouer de la musique à plein volume.

blaze noun incendie Masc.
blaze verb brûler [1].

blazer noun blazer Masc.

bleach noun eau Fem. de javel.

bleed verb saigner [1]; **my nose is bleeding** je saigne du nez.

blend noun mélange Masc.

blender noun mixer Masc.

bless verb bénir [2]; **bless you!** (after a sneeze) à tes souhaits!

blind noun (in a window) store Masc.
blind adjective aveugle; **to go blind** perdre la vue.

blindness noun cécité Fem.

blink verb (your eyes) cligner [1] des yeux.

blister noun ampoule Fem.

blizzard noun tempête Fem. de neige.

blob noun goutte Fem.

block noun **1 a block of flats** un immeuble; **an office block** un immeuble de bureaux; **2** (a square group of buildings) **to run** (or drive) **round the block** faire le tour du pâté de maisons.
block verb **1** bloquer [1] (an exit or a road); **2** boucher [1] (a drain or a hole); **the sink's blocked** l'évier est bouché.

blonde adjective blond.

blood noun sang Masc.

blood test noun prise Fem. de sang.

blossom noun fleurs Fem. plural; **to be in blossom** être en fleurs.

blot noun tache Fem.

blotchy adjective (skin) marbré.

blouse noun chemisier Masc.

blow noun coup Masc.
blow verb **1** (the wind or a person) souffler [1]; **2** (in an explosion) **the bomb blew a hole in the wall** la bombe a fait un trou dans le mur; **3 to blow your nose** se moucher [1].

- **to blow something out** souffler [1] (*a candle*), éteindre [60] (*flames*).
- **to blow up** (*explode*) exploser [1].
- **to blow something up** gonfler [1] (*a balloon or tyre*), faire [10] sauter (*a building*); **they blew up the president's residence** ils ont fait sauter la résidence du président.

blow-dry *noun* brushing *Masc.*; **a cut and blow dry** une coupe brushing.

blue *adjective* bleu; **blue eyes** les yeux bleus.

bluebell *noun* jacinthe *Fem.* des bois.

blues *plural noun* le blues *Masc. singular*.

blunder *noun* gaffe *Fem.*

blunt *adjective* **1** (*a knife or scissors*) émoussé; **2** (*a pencil*) mal taillé; **3** (*person*) brusque.

blurred *adjective* **1** indistinct; **2** (*photo*) flou.

blush *verb* rougir [2].

board *noun* **1** (*plank*) planche *Fem.*; **2** (*blackboard*) tableau *Masc.* noir; **3** (*notice board*) panneau *Masc.* d'affichage; **4** (*for a board game*) jeu *Masc.*; **5 a chess board** un échiquier; **6** (*accommodation in a hotel*) **full board** pension *Fem.* complète; **half board** demi-pension *Fem.*; **7 on board** à bord; **they were on board the ferry** ils étaient à bord du ferry.

boarder *noun* (*in a school*) interne *Masc. & Fem.*

board game *noun* jeu *Masc.* de société (*plural* jeux de société).

boarding *noun* embarquement *Masc.*

boarding card *noun* carte *Fem.* d'embarquement.

boarding school *noun* école *Fem.* privée avec internat.

boast *verb* se vanter [1]; **he was boasting about his new bike** il se vantait de son nouveau vélo.

boat *noun* **1** (*in general*) bateau *Masc.*; **2** (*sailing boat*) voilier *Masc.*; **3** (*rowing boat*) barque *Fem.*

body *noun* **1** corps *Masc.*; **2** (*corpse*) cadavre *Masc.*

bodybuilding *noun* culturisme *Masc.*

bodyguard *noun* garde *Masc.* du corps.

boil *noun* **1 bring the water to the boil** portez l'eau à ébullition; **2** (*swelling*) furoncle *Masc.*
boil *verb* **1** bouillir [23]; **the water's boiling** l'eau bout; **2** faire [10] bouillir; **I'm going to boil some water** je vais faire bouillir de l'eau; **to boil vegetables** faire [10] cuire des légumes à l'eau bouillante **to boil an egg** faire cuire un œuf.
- **to boil over** déborder [1].

boiled egg *noun* œuf *Masc.* à la coque.

boiler *noun* (*for central heating*) chaudière *Fem.*

boiling *adjective* **1** (*water*) bouillant; **2 it's boiling hot today!** il fait une chaleur infernale aujourd'hui!

bolt *noun* (*on a door*) verrou *Masc.*
bolt *verb* (*to lock*) verrouiller [1] (*a door*).

bomb noun bombe Fem.
bomb verb bombarder [1].

bombing noun 1 (in a war)
bombardement Masc.; 2 (a terrorist
attack) attentat Masc. à la bombe.

bone noun 1 os Masc.; 2 (of a fish)
arête Fem.

bonfire noun 1 (for rubbish) feu
Masc. de jardin; 2 (for a celebration)
feu Masc. de joie.

bonnet noun capot Masc. (of a car).

bony adjective 1 (fish) plein d'arêtes;
2 (body) anguleux (Fem. anguleuse);
3 (knee) osseux (Fem. osseuse).

boo verb huer [1]; **the crowd booed
the referee** la foule a hué l'arbitre.

book noun 1 (that you read) livre
Masc.; **a book about dinosaurs** un
livre sur les dinosaures; **a biology
book** un livre de biologie; **2 an
exercise book** un cahier; **3** (of
cheques, stamps, tickets, etc) carnet
Masc.; **a cheque book** un carnet de
chèques.
book verb réserver [1]; **I booked a
table for 8 p.m.** j'ai réservé une
table pour vingt heures.

bookcase noun bibliothèque Fem.

booking noun (for a theatre or a
holiday, for example) réservation
Fem.

booking office noun bureau
Masc. de location.

booklet noun brochure Fem.

bookshelf noun étagère Fem.

bookshop noun librairie Fem.

boom noun 1 (of a sail) bôme Fem.;
2 (time of prosperity) boom Masc.

boot noun 1 (for football, walking,
climbing, or skiing) chaussure Fem.;
walking boots des chaussures de
randonnée; **2** (short fashion boot)
bottine Fem.; **3** (knee-high boots or
wellingtons) botte Fem.; **4** (of a car)
coffre Masc.

border noun (between countries)
frontière Fem.; **we crossed the
border at Basel** nous avons passé la
frontière à Bâle.

bore noun 1 (a boring person)
raseur Masc., raseuse Fem.
(informal); **2** (a nuisance) **what a
bore!** quelle barbe!

bored adjective **to be bored**
s'ennuyer; **je m'ennuie** I'm bored;
to get bored s'ennuyer.

boring adjective ennuyeux (Fem.
ennuyeuse).

born adjective né; **to be born** naître
[55]; **she was born in June** elle est
née en juin.

borrow verb emprunter [1]; **can I
borrow your bike?** puis-je
t'emprunter ton vélo?; **to borrow
something from someone**
emprunter quelque chose à
quelqu'un; **I'll borrow some money
from Dad** je vais emprunter de
l'argent à Papa.

Bosnia noun Bosnie Fem.

boss noun patron Masc., patronne
Fem.

bossy adjective autoritaire.

both pronoun 1 (of people) tous les
deux (Fem. toutes les deux); **they
both came** ils sont venus tous les
deux; **both my sisters were there**
mes sœurs y étaient toutes les deux;

a
b
c
d
e
f
g
h
i
j
k
l
m
n
o
p
q
r
s
t
u
v
w
x
y
z

2 (*of things*) les deux; **they are both sold** les deux sont vendus; **3 both my feet** mes deux pieds; **3 both at home and at school** à la maison comme à l'école; **both in summer and in winter** en été comme en hiver.

bother *noun* ennui *Masc.*; **I've had a lot of bother with the car** j'ai eu beaucoup d'ennuis avec la voiture; **it's too much bother** c'est trop de tracas; **it's no bother** ce n'est pas un problème; **without any bother** sans aucune difficulté.

bother *verb* **1** (*to disturb*) déranger [52]; **I'm sorry to bother you** je suis désolé de vous déranger; **2** (*to worry*) inquiéter [24]; **that doesn't bother me at all** ça ne m'inquiète pas du tout; **don't bother about dinner** ne t'inquiète pas pour le dîner; **3 she didn't even bother to come** elle n'a même pas pris la peine de venir; **don't bother!** ce n'est pas la peine!

bottle *noun* bouteille *Fem.*

bottle bank *noun* conteneur *Masc.* à verre.

bottle opener *noun* ouvre-bouteille *Masc.*

bottom *noun* **1** (*of a hill, a wall, or steps*) pied *Masc.*; **at the bottom of the ladder** au pied de l'échelle; **2** (*of a bag or a bottle, a hole, a stretch of water, or a garden*) fond *Masc.*; **at the bottom of the lake** au fond du lac; **3 at the bottom of the page** en bas de la page; **4** (*buttocks*) derrière *Masc.*

bottom *adjective* **1** inférieur; **the bottom shelf** le rayon inférieur;

2 (*a division, team, or place*) dernier (*Fem.* dernière); **3 the bottom shee**t le drap de dessous; **the bottom fla**t l'appartement du rez-de-chaussée.

bounce *verb* rebondir [2].

bouncer *noun* videur *Masc.*

bound *adjective* (*certain*) **he's bound to be late** il va sûrement êtr**e** en retard; **that was bound to happen** cela devait arriver.

boundary *noun* limite *Fem.* (*for sports*) limites *Fem. plural* du terrain.

bow *noun* **1** (*in a shoelace or ribbon*) nœud *Masc.*; **2** (*for a violin*) archet *Masc.*; **3 a bow and arrow** un arc e**t** une flèche.

bowels *plural noun* intestins *Masc.* plural.

bowl *noun* **1** (*for cereal, for example*) bol *Masc.*; **2** (*larger, for salad or mixing*) saladier *Masc.*; **3** (*for washing up*) cuvette *Fem.*
bowl *verb* lancer [61] (*a ball*).

bowler *noun* (*in cricket*) lanceur *Masc.*

bowling *noun* (*tenpin*) bowling *Masc.*; **to go bowling** jouer au bowling.

bow tie *noun* nœud *Masc.* papillon.

box *noun* **1** boîte *Fem.*; **a box of chocolates** une boîte de chocolats; **2 a cardboard box** un carton; **3** (*on an application form*) case *Fem.*

boxer *noun* **1** (*fighter*) boxeur *Masc.*; **2** (*dog*) boxer *Masc.*

boxer shorts *plural noun* caleçon *Masc. singular.*

boxing *noun* **1** boxe *Fem.*; **2 a boxing match** un match de boxe.

a
b
c
d
e
f
g
h
i
j
k
l
m
n
o
p
q
r
s
t
u
v
w
x
y
z

Boxing Day noun le lendemain de Noël.

box office noun guichet Masc.

boy noun garçon Masc.; **a little boy** un petit garçon.

boyfriend noun copain Masc.

bra noun soutien-gorge Masc.

brace noun (for teeth) appareil Masc.

bracelet noun bracelet Masc.

bracket noun **in brackets** entre parenthèses.

brain noun cerveau Masc. (plural cerveaux).

brainwave noun idée Fem. géniale.

brake noun frein Masc.
brake verb freiner [1].

bramble noun ronce Fem.

branch noun **1** (of a tree) branche Fem.; **2** (of a shop) succursale Fem.; **our Oxford branch** notre succursale à Oxford; **3** (of a bank) agence Fem.

brand noun marque Fem.

brand new adjective tout neuf (Fem. toute neuve).

brandy noun cognac Masc.

brass noun laiton Masc., cuivre Masc. jaune; **a brass candlestick** un chandelier en cuivre jaune.

brass band noun fanfare Fem.

brave adjective courageux (Fem. courageuse).

bravery noun courage Masc.

Brazilian noun Brésilien Masc., Brésilienne Fem.
Brazilian adjective brésilien (Fem. brésilienne).

bread noun pain Masc.; **a slice of bread** une tranche de pain.

break noun **1** (a short rest) pause Fem.; **fifteen minutes' break** une pause de quinze minutes; **to take a break** faire une pause; **2** (in school) récréation Fem.; **3 the Christmas break** les vacances de Noël.
break verb **1** casser [1]; **he broke a glass** il a cassé un verre; **I broke a tooth/my arm** je me suis cassé une dent/le bras; **2** se casser [1]; **the eggs broke** les œufs se sont cassés; **3 to break your arm** se casser le bras; **4 to break your promise** manquer [1] à sa promesse; **he broke the rules** il n'a pas respecté les règlements; **you mustn't break the rules** il faut respecter les règlements; **5 to break a record** battre [21] un record; **6 to break the news** annoncer [61] la nouvelle.
• **to break down** tomber [1] en panne; **the car broke down** la voiture est tombée en panne.
• **to break in** (a thief) entrer [1] par effraction.
• **to break out 1** (a fire) se déclarer [1]; **2** (a fight or a storm) éclater [1]; **3** (a prisoner) s'évader [1].
• **to break up 1** (a family or couple) se séparer [1]; **2** (a crowd or clouds) se disperser [1]; **3** (for the holidays) **we break up on Thursday** les cours finissent jeudi.

breakdown noun **1** (of a vehicle) panne Fem.; **we had a breakdown on the motorway** nous sommes tombés en panne sur l'autoroute; **2** (in talks or negotiations) rupture Fem.; **3** (a nervous collapse) dépression Fem.; **to have a**

a
b
c
d
e
f
g
h
i
j
k
l
m
n
o
p
q
r
s
t
u
v
w
x
y
z

a

b

c

d

e

f

g

h

i

j

k

l

m

n

o

p

q

r

s

t

u

v

w

x

y

z

(nervous) breakdown faire une dépression.

breakdown truck *noun* camion *Masc.* de dépannage.

breakfast *noun* petit déjeuner *Masc.*; **we have breakfast at eight** nous prenons le petit déjeuner à huit heures.

break-in *noun* cambriolage *Masc.*

breast *noun* **1** (*a woman's*) sein *Masc.*; **2** (*of a chicken or other fowl*) blanc *Masc.*

breaststroke *noun* brasse *Fem.*

breath *noun* **1** (*when you breathe in*) souffle *Masc.*; **out of breath** à bout de souffle; **to get one's breath** reprendre son souffle; **to take a deep breath** respirer profondément; **2** (*when you breathe out*) haleine *Fem.*; **to have bad breath** avoir mauvaise haleine.

breathe *verb* respirer [1].

breathing *noun* respiration *Fem.*

breed *noun* (*of dog, for example*) race *Fem.*

breed *verb* **1** élever [50] (*animals*); **2** (*to have babies*) se reproduire [26]; **rabbits breed fast** les lapins se reproduisent vite.

breeze *noun* brise *Fem.*

brew *verb* **1** préparer [1] (*tea*); **2** brasser [1] (*beer*).

brewery *noun* brasserie *Fem.*

brick *noun* brique *Fem.*; **a brick wall** un mur de briques.

bride *noun* mariée *Fem.*; **the bride and groom** les mariés *Masc. plural.*

bridegroom *noun* marié *Masc.*

bridesmaid *noun* demoiselle *Fem.* d'honneur.

bridge *noun* **1** (*over a river*) pont *Masc.*; **a bridge over the Thames** un pont sur la Tamise; **2** (*card game*) bridge *Masc.*; **to play bridge** jouer au bridge.

bridle *noun* bride *Fem.*

brief *adjective* bref (*Fem.* brève).

briefcase *noun* serviette *Fem.*

briefly *adjective* brièvement.

briefs *plural noun* slip *Masc.*

bright *adjective* **1** (*colour, light*) vif (*Fem.* vive); **bright green socks** des chaussettes vert vif; **2 bright sunshine** un soleil éclatant; **3** (*clever*) intelligent; **she's not very bright** elle n'est pas très intelligente; ★ **to look on the bright side** voir le bon côté des choses.

brighten up *verb* **the weather's brightening up** le temps s'éclaircit.

brilliant *adjective* **1** (*very clever*) brillant; **a brilliant surgeon** un chirurgien brillant; **he's brilliant at maths** il est très doué en maths; **2** (*wonderful*) génial (*Masc. plural* géniaux) (*informal*); **the party was brilliant!** la boum était géniale!

bring *verb* **1** apporter [1] (*something you carry*); **they brought a present** ils ont apporté un cadeau; **bring your camera!** apporte ton appareil photo!; **it brings good luck** ça porte bonheur; **2** amener [50] (*a person or an animal*); **she's bringing all the children** elle va amener tous les enfants; **3 to bring something back** rapporter [1] quelque chose;

4 to bring up élever [50] (*children*); **he was brought up by his aunt** il a été élevé par sa tante.

bristle *noun* poil *Masc.*

Britain, Great Britain *noun* Grande-Bretagne *Fem.*; **in Britain** en Grande-Bretagne; **to Britain** en Grande-Bretagne; **Britain is sending aid** la Grande-Bretagne envoie de l'aide.

British *plural noun* **the British** les Britanniques; **the British love animals** les Britanniques adorent les animaux.
British *adjective* britannique; **the British army** l'armée britannique; **the British Isles** les îles Britanniques.

Brittany *noun* Bretagne *Fem.*; **in Brittany** en Bretagne; **to Brittany** en Bretagne.

broad *adjective* (*wide*) large.

broad bean *noun* fève *Fem.*

broadcast *noun* émission *Fem.*
broadcast *verb* diffuser [1] (*a programme*).

broccoli *noun* brocolis *Masc. plural*; **to eat broccoli** manger des brocolis.

brochure *noun* brochure *Fem.*

broke *adjective* **to be broke** (*no money*) être fauché (*informal*).

broken *adjective* cassé; **the window's broken** la vitre est cassée; **to have a broken leg** avoir la jambe cassée.

bronchitis *noun* bronchite *Fem.*; **to have bronchitis** avoir une bronchite.

brooch *noun* broche *Fem.*

broom *noun* **1** (*for sweeping*) balai *Masc.*; **2** (*bush*) genêt *Masc.*

brother *noun* frère *Masc.*; **my little brother** mon petit frère; **my mother's brother** le frère de ma mère.

brother-in-law *noun* beau-frère *Masc.* (*plural* beaux-frères).

brown *adjective* **1** marron (*does not change in the feminine or plural*); **my brown jacket** ma veste marron; **your brown shoes** tes chaussures marron; **light brown** marron clair; **dark brown** marron foncé; **2** châtain (*hair*); **3** (*tanned in the sun*) bronzé; **to go brown** bronzer.

brown bread *noun* pain *Masc.* complet.

brown sugar *noun* sucre *Masc.* brun.

bruise *noun* **1** (*on a person*) bleu *Masc.*; **2** (*on fruit*) tache *Fem.*

brush *noun* **1** (*for your hair, clothes, nails, or shoes*) brosse *Fem.*; **my hair brush** ma brosse à cheveux; **2** (*for sweeping*) balai *Masc.*; **3** (*paintbrush*) pinceau *Masc.*
brush *verb* brosser [1] (*the floor or your clothes*); **to brush your hair** se brosser les cheveux; **she brushed her hair** elle s'est brossé les cheveux; **to brush your teeth** se brosser les dents.

Brussels *noun* Bruxelles.

Brussels sprout *noun* chou *Masc.* de Bruxelles.

bubble *noun* bulle *Fem.*

bubble bath *noun* bain *Masc.* moussant.

a
b
c
d
e
f
g
h
i
j
k
l
m
n
o
p
q
r
s
t
u
v
w
x
y
z

bucket noun seau Masc. (plural seaux).

buckle noun boucle Fem.

Buddhism noun bouddhisme Masc.

Buddhist noun bouddhiste Masc. & Fem.

budget noun budget Masc.

budgie noun perruche Fem.

buffet noun buffet Masc.

buffet car noun voiture Fem. bar.

bug noun 1 (insect) bestiole Fem. (informal,); 2 (germ) microbe Fem.; a stomach bug une gastroentérite; 3 (in a computer) bug Masc.

build verb construire [26]; they are building three houses over there ils construisent trois maisons là-bas.

builder noun maçon Masc.

building noun bâtiment Masc.; (with offices or flats) immeuble Masc.

building site noun chantier Masc.

building society noun société Fem. d'investissement et de crédit immobilier.

built-up adjective urbanisé; a built-up area une agglomération.

bulb noun 1 (for a light) ampoule Fem.; 2 (that you plant) bulbe Masc.

bull noun taureau Masc. (plural taureaux).

bulldozer noun bulldozer Masc.

bullet noun balle Fem.

bulletin noun bulletin Masc.; a news bulletin un bulletin d'informations.

bullfight noun corrida Fem.

bully noun brute Fem.; he's a bully c'est une brute.
bully verb tyranniser [1].

bum noun (bottom) derrière Masc.

bump noun 1 (that sticks up) bosse Fem.; a bump on the head une bosse à la tête; a bump in the road une bosse sur la route; 2 (jolt) secousse Fem.; 3 (noise) bruit Masc. sourd.
bump verb 1 (to bang) cogner [1]; I bumped my head je me suis cogné la tête; 2 to bump into something rentrer [1] dans quelque chose; 3 to bump into somebody (meet by chance) croiser [1] quelqu'un.

bumper noun pare-chocs Masc.

bumpy adjective 1 accidenté (road); 2 agité (plane landing).

bun noun 1 (for a burger) petit pain Masc.; 2 (sugary) petit cake Masc.

bunch noun 1 (of flowers) bouquet Masc.; 2 (of carrots or radishes) botte Fem.; 3 (of keys) trousseau Masc.; 4 a bunch of grapes une grappe de raisin.

bundle noun tas Masc.

bungalow noun pavillon Masc.

bunk noun 1 (on a train or boat) couchette Fem.; 2 bunk beds des lits superposés.

bureau noun agence Fem.

burger noun hamburger Masc.

burglar noun cambrioleur Masc.

burglar alarm noun sonnerie Fem. d'alarme.

burglary noun cambriolage Masc.

burn noun brûlure Fem.
burn verb 1 brûler [1]; I've burned the rubbish j'ai brûlé les ordures;

the fire's burning well le feu brûle bien; **she burnt herself on the grill** elle s'est brûlée au grill; **you'll burn your finger!** tu vas te brûler le doigt!; **2** laisser [1] brûler (*something you're cooking*); **Mum's burnt her cake** maman a laissé brûler son gâteau; **3** (*through sunburn*) **I burn easily** j'attrape facilement des coups de soleil.

burnt *adjective* brûlé.

burst *verb* **1** crever [50] (*a balloon or tyre, for example*); **a burst tyre** un pneu crevé; **2 to burst out laughing** éclater [1] de rire; **3 to burst into tears** fondre [3] en larmes; **4 to burst into flames** prendre [64] feu.

bury *verb* enterrer [1].

bus *noun* **1** (*public transport*) autobus *Masc.*, bus *Masc.*; **we'll take the bus** on va prendre le bus; **on the bus** dans le bus; **a bus ticket** un ticket de bus; **2** (*coach*) car *Masc.*; **to go to London by bus** aller à Londres en car.

bus conductor *noun* receveur *Masc.* d'autobus.

bus driver *noun* conducteur de bus *Masc.*, conductrice de bus *Fem.*

bush *noun* buisson *Masc.*

business *noun* **1** (*commercial dealings*) affaires *Fem. plural*; **to be in business** être dans les affaires; **he's in Leeds on business** il est à Leeds en voyage d'affaires; **he's in the insurance business** il travaille dans l'assurance; **a business letter** une lettre d'affaires; **2** (*firm or company*) entreprise *Fem.*; **small businesses** les petites entreprises;

3 mind your own business! occupe-toi de tes affaires!; **that's my business!** ça me regarde!

business class *noun* classe *Fem.* affaires.

businessman *noun* homme *Masc.* d'affaires.

business trip *noun* voyage *Masc.* d'affaires.

businesswoman *noun* femme *Fem.* d'affaires.

bus lane *noun* couloir *Masc.* d'autobus.

bus pass *noun* carte *Fem.* de bus.

bus route *noun* ligne *Fem.* d'autobus.

bus shelter *noun* abribus™ *Masc.*

bus station *noun* gare *Fem.* routière.

bus stop *noun* arrêt *Masc.* de bus.

bust *noun* **bust size** tour *Masc.* de poitrine.

busy *adjective* **1** occupé (*a person*), chargé (*a day or week*); **2 don't disturb him, he's busy** ne le dérange pas, il est occupé; **a busy day** une journée chargée; **3** (*full of cars or people*) très fréquenté (*a road*); **the shops were busy** il y avait beaucoup de monde dans les magasins; **4** (*phone*) **the line's busy** la ligne est occupée.

but *conjunction* mais; **small but strong** petit mais fort; **not Thursday but Friday** pas jeudi mais vendredi; **I'll try, but it's difficult** j'essaierai, mais c'est difficile. **but** *preposition* sauf; **anything but that** tout, sauf ça; **everyone but**

365

a
b
c
d
e
f
g
h
i
j
k
l
m
n
o
p
q
r
s
t
u
v
w
x
y
z

Roger tout le monde sauf Roger; **the last but one** l'avant-dernier.

butcher noun boucher Masc.; **he's a butcher** il est boucher; **the butcher's** la boucherie.

butter noun beurre Masc.
butter verb beurrer [1].

buttercup noun bouton Masc. d'or.

butterfly noun papillon Masc.

button noun bouton Masc.; **the record button** la touche d'enregistrement.

buttonhole noun boutonnière Fem.

buy noun **a good buy** une bonne affaire; **a bad buy** une mauvaise affaire.
buy verb acheter [16]; **I bought the tickets** j'ai acheté les billets; **to buy something for somebody** acheter quelque chose à quelqu'un; **Sarah bought him a sweater** Sarah lui a acheté un pull; **to buy something from someone** acheter quelque chose à quelqu'un; **I bought my bike from Tim** j'ai acheté mon vélo à Tim.

buyer noun acheteur Masc., acheteuse Fem.

buzz verb (a fly or bee) bourdonner [1].

buzzer noun sonnerie Fem.

by preposition **1** par; **by telephone** par téléphone; **to take somebody by the hand** prendre quelqu'un par la main; **eaten by a dog** mangé par un chien; **by mistake** par erreur; **2** (travel) en; **to come by bus** venir en bus; **to leave by train** partir en train; **by bike** en vélo; **3** (near) à

côté de; **by the fire** à côté du feu; **by the sea** au bord de la mer; **close by** tout près; **4** (before) avant; **ready by Monday** prêt avant lundi; **Kevin was back by four** Kevin est rentré avant quatre heures; **5 by yourself** tout seul; **I was by myself in the house** j'étais tout seul chez moi; **she did it by herself** elle l'a fait toute seule; **6 by the way** au fait; **7 to go by** passer.

bye exclamation au revoir; **bye for now!** à bientôt!

bypass noun rocade Fem.

Cc

cab noun **1** taxi Masc.; **to call a cab** appeler un taxi; **2** (on a lorry) cabine Fem.

cabbage noun chou Masc. (plural choux).

cabin noun cabine Fem.

cable noun câble Masc.

cable car noun téléférique Masc.

cable television noun télévision Fem. par câble.

cactus noun cactus Masc.

cafe noun café Masc.

cage noun cage Fem.

cagoule noun K-way™ Masc.

cake noun gâteau Masc. (plural gâteaux); **would you like a piece of cake?** veux-tu un morceau de gâteau?

calculate verb calculer [1].

calculation noun calcul Masc.

calculator noun calculatrice Fem.

calendar noun calendrier Masc.

calf noun **1** (animal) veau Masc.; **2** (of your leg) mollet.

call noun (telephone) appel Masc.; **I had several calls this morning** j'ai eu plusieurs appels ce matin; **thank you for your call** merci de votre appel; **a phone call** un coup de téléphone.

call verb **1** appeler [18]; **to call a taxi** appeler un taxi; **to call the doctor** appeler le médecin; **they called the police** ils ont appelé la police; **call this number** appelez ce numéro; **thank you for calling** merci de votre appel; **I'll call you back later** je te rappellerai plus tard; **2** appeler [18]; **they've called the baby Julie** ils ont appelé le bébé Julie; **3 to be called** s'appeler [18]; **she has a brother called Dan** elle a un frère qui s'appelle Dan; **what's he called?** il s'appelle comment? **to call in** passer [1]; **I'll call in on the way back from school** je passerai en rentrant de l'école.

call box noun cabine Fem. téléphonique.

calm adjective calme.

calm verb calmer [1].

to calm down se calmer; **he's calmed down a bit** il s'est calmé un peu.

to calm somebody down calmer quelqu'un; **I tried to calm her down** j'ai essayé de la calmer.

calmly adverb calmement.

calorie noun calorie Fem.

camcorder noun caméscope Masc.

camel noun chameau Masc. (plural chameaux).

camera noun **1** appareil Masc. photo (plural appareils photo); **2** (film or TV camera) caméra.

cameraman noun caméraman Masc.

camp noun camp Masc.
camp verb camper [1].

campaign noun campagne Fem.

camper van noun camping-car Masc.

camping noun camping Masc.; **to go camping** faire du camping; **we're going camping in Brittany this summer** nous allons faire du camping en Bretagne cet été.

campsite noun terrain Masc. de camping.

can[1] noun **1** boîte Fem.; **a can of tomatoes** une boîte de tomates; **2** (for petrol or oil) bidon Masc.

can[2] verb **1** pouvoir [12]; **I can't/cannot be there before ten** je ne peux pas y être avant dix heures; **you can leave your bag here** tu peux laisser ton sac ici; **can you open the door, please?** peux-tu ouvrir la porte, s'il te plaît?; **can I help you?** est-ce que je peux vous aider?; **they couldn't come** ils n'ont pas pu venir; **you could ring back tomorrow** tu pourrais rappeler demain; **you could have told me** tu aurais pu me le dire; **2** (not translated) **can you hear me?** est-ce que tu m'entends?; **I can't see him** je ne le vois pas; **I can't remember** je ne me souviens pas; **I can't find my keys** je ne trouve pas mes clés;

a
b
c
d
e
f
g
h
i
j
k
l
m
n
o
p
q
r
s
t
u
v
w
x
y
z

3 (*know how to*) savoir [70]; **she can't drive** elle ne sait pas conduire; **can you play the piano?** est-ce que tu sais jouer du piano?

Canada *noun* Canada *Masc.*; **to Canada** au Canada; **in Canada** au Canada.

Canadian *noun* Canadien *Masc.*, Canadienne *Fem.*.
Canadian *adjective* canadien (*Fem.* canadienne).

canal *noun* canal *Masc.* (*plural* canaux).

canary *noun* canari *Masc.*

cancel *verb* annuler [1]; **the concert's been cancelled** le concert a été annulé.

cancer *noun* cancer *Masc.*; **to have lung cancer** avoir un cancer du poumon.

Cancer *noun* Cancer *Masc.*; **I'm Cancer** je suis Cancer.

candidate *noun* candidat *Masc.*, candidate *Fem.*

candle *noun* bougie *Fem.*

candlestick *noun* bougeoir *Masc.*

candyfloss *noun* barbe *Fem.* à papa.

canned *adjective* en conserve; **canned tomatoes** les tomates en conserve.

cannon *noun* canon *Masc.*

cannot *verb* can².

canoe *noun* canoë *Masc.*

canoeing *noun* **to go canoeing** faire du canoë; **I like canoeing** j'aime faire du canoë.

can-opener *noun* ouvre-boîte *Masc.*

canteen *noun* cantine *Fem.*

canvas *noun* toile *Fem.*

cap *noun* **1** (*hat*) casquette *Fem.*; **a baseball cap** une casquette de baseball; **2** (*on a bottle or tube*) bouchon *Masc.*

capable *adjective* capable.

capacity *noun* capacité *Fem.*

capital *noun* **1** (*city*) capitale *Fem* **Paris is the capital of France** Par est la capitale de la France; **2** (*lette* majuscule *Fem.*; **in capitals** en majuscules.

capitalism *noun* capitalisme *Ma*

Capricorn *noun* Capricorne *Mase* **Linda's Capricorn** Linda est Capricorne.

capsize *verb* chavirer [1].

captain *noun* capitaine *Masc.*

captivity *noun* captivité *Fem.*; **to be kept in captivity** être gardé en captivité.

capture *verb* capturer [1].

car *noun* voiture *Fem.*; **in the car** dans la voiture; **to park the car** garer la voiture; **we're going by ca** nous y allons en voiture; **a car crash** un accident de voiture.

caramel *noun* caramel *Masc.*

caravan *noun* caravane *Fem.*

card *noun* carte *Fem.*; **un jeu de cartes** a card game, a pack of card **faire une partie de cartes** to have game of cards.

cardboard *noun* carton *Masc.*

cardigan *noun* cardigan *Masc.*

ardphone noun téléphone Masc. à
arte.

are noun 1 soin Masc.; **to take care
to do** prendre soin de faire; 2 **to
take care of somebody** s'occuper
de quelqu'un; 3 **take care!** (be
careful) fais attention!, (when saying
goodbye) à bientôt!

care verb 1 **to care about** se
soucier de [1]; **to care about
pollution** se soucier de la pollution;
2 **she doesn't care** ça lui est égal; **I
couldn't care less!** ça m'est
complètement égal!

areer noun carrière Fem.

areful adjective prudent 1 **a
careful driver** un conducteur
prudent; 2 **be careful!** fais
attention!

arefully adverb 1 **read the
instructions carefully** lisez
attentivement les instructions;
listen carefully écoutez bien;
2 (handle) avec précaution; **she put
the vase down carefully** elle a posé
le vase avec précaution; 3 **to copy
something carefully** recopier
soigneusement quelque chose;
4 **drive carefully!** sois prudent!

areless adjective 1 **he's very
careless** il ne fait pas du tout
attention à ce qu'il fait; 2 **this is
careless work** c'est du travail peu
soigné; **a careless mistake** une
faute d'inattention; 3 **careless
driving** la conduite imprudente.

aretaker noun gardien Masc.,
gardienne Fem.

ar ferry noun ferry Masc.

argo noun cargaison Fem.

car hire noun location Fem. de
voitures.

Caribbean noun 1 **the Caribbean
(islands)** les Caraïbes; 2 **the
Caribbean** (sea) la mer des
Caraïbes.

carnation noun œillet Masc.

carnival noun carnaval Masc.

car park noun parking Masc.

carpenter noun menuisier Masc.

carpentry noun menuiserie Fem.

carpet noun 1 (fitted) moquette
Fem.; 2 (loose) tapis Masc.

car phone noun téléphone Masc. de
voiture.

car radio noun autoradio Masc.

carriage noun (of a train) voiture
Fem.

carrier bag noun sac Masc. en
plastique.

carrot noun carotte Fem.

carry verb 1 porter [1]; **she was
carrying a parcel** elle portait un
paquet; 2 (vehicle, plane)
transporter [1]; **the coach was
carrying schoolchildren** le car
transportait des écoliers.

• **to carry on** continuer [1]; **they
carried on talking** ils ont continué
à parler.

carrycot noun porte-bébé Masc.

carsick adjective **to be carsick**
avoir le mal de la route.

cart noun charrette Fem.

carton noun 1 (of cream or yoghurt)
pot Masc.; 2 (of milk or orange)
brique Fem.

a b **c** d e f g h i j k l m n o p q r s t u v w x y z

369

cartoon noun **1** (*a film*) dessin Masc. animé; **2** (*a comic strip*) bande Fem. dessinée; **3** (*an amusing drawing*) dessin Masc. humoristique.

cartridge noun (*for a pen or a video*) cartouche Fem.

carve verb découper [1] (*meat*).

case[1] noun **1** (*suitcase*) valise Fem.; **to pack a case** faire une valise; **2** (*a large wooden box, for wine for example*) caisse Fem.; **3** (*for spectacles or small things*) étui Masc.

case[2] noun **1** cas Masc.; **in that case** en ce cas; **that's not the case** ce n'est pas le cas; **a case of flu** un cas de grippe; **2 in case** au cas où; **in case he's late** au cas où il serait en retard; **check first, just in case** vérifie d'abord, au cas où; **3 in any case** de toute façon; **in any case, it's too late** de toute façon, c'est trop tard.

cash noun **1** (*money in general*) argent Masc.; **I haven't any cash on me** je n'ai pas d'argent; **2** (*money rather than a cheque*) espèces Fem. plural; **to pay in cash** payer en espèces; **£50 in cash** cinquante livres en espèces.

cash card noun carte Fem. de retrait.

cash desk noun caisse Fem.; **pay at the cash desk** payez à la caisse.

cash dispenser noun guichet Masc. automatique.

cashew noun cajou Masc.

cashier noun caissier Masc., caissière Fem.

cash point noun = cash dispenser.

cassette noun cassette Fem.

cassette recorder noun magnétophone Masc. à cassettes.

cast noun les acteurs Masc. plural; **th cast were on stage** les acteurs étaient sur scène.

castle noun **1** château Masc. (*plur* châteaux); **2** (*in chess*) tour Fem.

casual adjective décontracté.

casualty noun **1** (*in an accident*) victime Fem.; **there are 47 casualties** il y a 47 victimes; **2** (*hospital department*) urgences Fem. plural; **he's in casualty** il est au urgences.

cat noun chat Masc.; (*female*) chatte Fem.; **a big black cat** un gros chat noir; ★ **it's raining cats and dogs** pleut des cordes (*literally: it's raining in ropes*).

catalogue noun catalogue Masc.

catastrophe noun catastrophe Fem.

catch noun **1** (*on a door*) fermetur Fem.; **2** (*a drawback*) piège Masc.; **what's the catch?** où est le piège? **catch** verb **1** attraper [1]; **Tom caught the ball** Tom a attrapé le ballon; **you can't catch me!** vous ne m'attraperez pas!; **can you catch hold of the branch?** peux-t attraper la branche?; **2 to catch somebody doing** attraper quelqu'un en train de faire; **he wa caught stealing money** il a été attrapé en train de voler de l'argen **3** prendre [64] (*a bus or plane*); **did Tim catch his plane?** est-ce que Tim a pris son avion?; **4** attraper [1 (*an illness*); **he's caught chickenpox** il a attrapé la varicelle

I've caught a cold j'ai attrapé un rhume; **5** saisir [2] (*what somebody says*); **I didn't catch your name** je n'ai pas saisi votre nom.

to catch up with somebody rattraper [1] quelqu'un.

category *noun* catégorie *Fem.*

catering *noun* restauration *Fem.*

caterpillar *noun* chenille *Fem.*

cathedral *noun* cathédrale *Fem.*; **Winchester cathedral** la cathédrale de Winchester.

Catholic *noun, adjective* catholique *Masc. & Fem.*

cattle *plural noun* bétail *Masc. singular.*

cauliflower *noun* chou-fleur *Masc.* (*plural* choux-fleurs); **cauliflower cheese** un gratin de chou-fleur.

cause *noun* cause *Fem.*; **the cause of the accident** la cause de l'accident; **for a good cause** pour une bonne cause.

cause *verb* **1** causer [1] (*damage or problems*); **to cause problems** causer des problèmes; **2** provoquer [1] (*chaos or disease*); **the strike caused delays** la grève a provoqué des retards.

caution *noun* prudence *Fem.*

cautious *adjective* prudent.

cave *noun* grotte *Fem.*

caving *noun* spéléologie *Fem.*; **to go caving** faire de la spéléologie.

CD *noun* CD *Masc.*

CD player *noun* platine *Fem.* laser.

CD-ROM *noun* CD-ROM *Masc.*

ceiling *noun* plafond *Masc.*; **on the ceiling** au plafond.

celebrate *verb* fêter [1]; **I'm celebrating my birthday** je fête mon anniversaire.

celebrity *noun* célébrité *Fem.*

celery *noun* céleri *Masc.*

cell *noun* cellule *Fem.*

cellar *noun* cave *Fem.*

cello *noun* violoncelle *Masc.*; **to play the cello** jouer du violoncelle.

cement *noun* ciment *Masc.*

cemetery *noun* cimetière *Masc.*

cent *noun* **1** (*in euro system*) centime *Masc.* (d'euro) (*unofficial term*); cent *Masc.* (*official term*); **2** (*in dollar system*) cent *Masc.*

centenary *noun* centenaire *Masc.*

centigrade *adjective* centigrade; **ten degrees centigrade** dix degrés centigrade.

centimetre *noun* centimètre *Masc.*

central *adjective* central (*Masc. plural* centraux); **central London** le centre de Londres; **the office is very central** le bureau est en plein centre-ville.

central heating *noun* chauffage *Masc.* central.

centre *noun* centre *Masc.*; **in the centre of** au centre de; **in the town centre** en centre-ville; **a shopping centre** un centre commercial.

century *noun* siècle *Masc.*; **in the twentieth century** au vingtième siècle; **the twenty-first century** le vingt-et-unième siècle.

cereal *noun* **breakfast cereal** céréales *Fem. plural* pour le petit déjeuner; **to have cereal for**

breakfast prendre des céréales au petit déjeuner.

ceremony noun cérémonie Fem.

certain adjective certain; **a certain number of** un certain nombre de; **are you certain of the address?** es-tu certain de l'adresse?; **I'm certain of it** j'en suis certain; **to be certain that** être sûr que; **Nicola's certain you're wrong** Nicola est sûre que tu as tort; **nobody knows for certain** personne ne sait au juste.

certainly adverb certainement; **certainly not** certainement pas.

certificate noun 1 certificat Masc.; 2 **a birth certificate** un acte de naissance.

chain noun chaîne Fem.

chair noun 1 (upright) chaise Fem.; **a kitchen chair** une chaise de cuisine; 2 (with arms) fauteuil Masc.

chair lift noun télésiège Masc.

chalet noun 1 (in the mountains) chalet Masc.; 2 (in a holiday camp) bungalow Masc.

chalk noun craie Fem.

challenge noun 1 (that excites you) challenge Masc.; **the challenge of new ideas** le challenge des nouvelles idées; 2 (that is difficult) épreuve Fem.; **the exam was a real challenge** l'examen était une vraie épreuve.

champion noun champion Masc., championne Fem.; **world champion** champion du monde.

chance noun 1 (an opportunity) occasion Fem.; **to have the chance to do** avoir l'occasion de faire; **if you have the chance to go to New York** si tu as l'occasion d'aller à New York; **I haven't had the chance to write to him** je n'ai pas eu l'occasion de lui écrire; 2 (likelihood) chance Fem.; **there's little chance of winning** il y a peu de chance de gagner; 3 (luck) **by chance** par hasard; **do you have her address by any chance?** aurais-tu par hasard son adresse?

change noun 1 changement Masc. **a change of plan** un changement de programme; **they've made some changes to the house** ils ont fait des changements dans la maison; **for a change, let's eat out** mangeons au restaurant pour changer; **it makes a change from hamburgers** cela change un peu de hamburgers; 2 **a change of clothes** des vêtements de rechange 3 (cash) monnaie Fem.; **I haven't any change** je n'ai pas de monnaie. **change** verb 1 (transform completely) changer [52]; **it changed my life** cela m'a changé la vie; **Liz never changes** Liz ne change jamais; 2 (to switch from one thing to another) changer [52] de; **we changed trains at Crewe** nous avons changé de train à Crewe; **I must change my shirt** je dois changer de chemise; **they changed places** ils ont changé de place; **to change your mind** changer d'avis; 3 (to exchange in a shop) échanger [52]; **can I change it for the larger size?** puis-je l'échanger contre la taille au-dessus?; 4 (to change your clothes) se changer [52]; **Mike's gone up to change** Mike est monté se changer.

hanging room noun (for sport or swimming) **1** vestiaire Masc.; **2** (in a shop) salon Masc. d'essayage.

hannel noun **1** (on TV) chaîne Fem.; **to change channels** changer de chaîne; **2 the Channel** la Manche.

hannel Islands plural noun les Fem. plural Anglo-Normandes.

hannel Tunnel noun tunnel Masc. sous la Manche.

naos noun pagaille Fem. (informal); **it was chaos!** c'était la pagaille!

hapel noun chapelle Fem.

hapter noun chapitre Masc.; **in chapter two** au chapitre deux.

haracter noun **1** (personality) caractère Masc.; **a house with a lot of character** une maison qui a du caractère; **2** (somebody in a book, play, or film) personnage Masc.; **the main character** le personnage principal.

haracteristic adjective caractéristique.

narcoal noun **1** (for burning) charbon Masc. de bois; **2** (for drawing) fusain Masc.

narge noun **1** (what you pay) frais Masc. plural; **a booking charge** des frais de réservation; **an extra or additional charge** un supplément; **there's no charge** c'est gratuit; **2 to be in charge** être responsable; **who's in charge of these children?** qui est responsable de ces enfants?; **3 to be on a charge of theft** être inculpé de vol.

harge verb **1** (to ask a specific sum) prendre [64]; **they charge fifteen pounds an hour** ils prennent quinze livres de l'heure; **how much do you charge for one day?** combien prenez-vous pour une journée?; **2** (to ask people to pay) faire [10] payer; **we don't charge, it's free** nous ne faisons pas payer les gens, c'est gratuit; **3 to charge somebody with** inculper [1] quelqu'un de (a crime).

charity noun organisation Fem. caritative.

charm noun charme Masc.

charming adjective charmant.

chart noun **1** (table) tableau Masc.; **2 the weather chart** la carte du temps; **3 the charts** le hit-parade; **number one in the charts** numéro un au hit-parade.

charter flight noun vol Masc. charter.

chase noun poursuite Fem.; **a car chase** une poursuite en voiture.
chase verb pourchasser [1] (a person or animal).

chat noun conversation Fem.; **to have a chat with somebody** bavarder avec quelqu'un.

chatroom noun chatroom Masc.

chat show noun talk-show Masc.

chatter verb **1** (gossip) bavarder [1]; **2 my teeth are chattering** je claque des dents.

cheap adjective pas cher (Fem. pas chère); **cheap shoes** des chaussures pas chères; **that's very cheap!** ce n'est vraiment pas cher!

cheaper adjective moins cher (Fem. moins chère).

cheaply *adverb* pas cher; **to eat cheaply** manger pas cher.

cheap rate *adjective* à tarif réduit; **a cheap rate phone call** un appel à tarif réduit.

cheat *noun* tricheur *Masc.*, tricheuse *Fem.*
cheat *verb* tricher [1].

check *noun* **1** (*in a factory or at border controls*) contrôle *Masc.*; **passport check** contrôle des passeports; **2** (*by a doctor*) examen *Masc.*; **3** (*in chess*) **check!** échec au roi!
check *verb* (*to make sure*) vérifier [1]; **he checked the time** il a vérifié l'heure; **check they're all back** vérifiez qu'ils sont tous rentrés; **check with your father** demande à ton père.

● **to check in 1** (*at the airport*) enregistrer [1]; **2** (*at a hotel*) arriver [1] à l'hôtel; **he checked in at five o'clock** il est arrivé à l'hôtel à cinq heures.

● **to check out** quitter [1] l'hôtel; **he checked out at 8.30** il a quitté l'hôtel à 8h30.

check-in *noun* enregistrement *Masc.*

checkout *noun* caisse *Fem.*; **at the checkout** à la caisse.

check-up *noun* examen *Masc.* médical.

cheek *noun* **1** (*part of face*) joue *Fem.*; **2** (*nerve*) **what a cheek!** quel culot! (*informal*).

cheeky *adjective* **1** coquin; **2** (*rude*) impoli.

cheer *noun* **1** **three cheers for Tom!** faisons un ban à Tom!; **2** (*when you have a drink*) **cheers!** la vôtre!
cheer *verb* (*to shout hurray*) applaudir [2].

● **to cheer on** encourager.

● **to cheer up: cheer up!** courage!

● **to cheer somebody up** remonter [1] le moral à quelqu'un; **your visit° cheered me up** ta visite m'a remonté le moral.

cheerful *adjective* gai.

cheese *noun* fromage *Masc.*; **blue cheese** le fromage bleu; **a cheese sandwich** un sandwich au fromag°

cheesecake *noun* cheesecake *Masc.*

chef *noun* chef *Masc.* cuisinier.

chemical *noun* produit *Masc.* chimique.
chemical *adjective* chimique.

chemist *noun* **1** pharmacien *Masc°* pharmacienne *Fem.*; **2 chemist's** pharmacie *Fem.*; **at the chemist's** la pharmacie; **3** (*scientist*) chimist° *Masc. & Fem.*

chemistry *noun* chimie *Fem.*

cheque *noun* chèque *Masc.*; **to pa**° **by cheque** payer par chèque; **to write a cheque** faire un chèque.

chequebook *noun* carnet *Masc. d*° chèques.

cherry *noun* cerise *Fem.*

chess *noun* échecs *Masc. plural*; **to play chess** jouer aux échecs.

chessboard *noun* échiquier *Mas*°

chest *noun* **1** (*part of the body*) poitrine *Fem.*; **2** (*box*) coffre *Masc.*;

374

3 a chest of drawers une commode.

chestnut noun marron Masc.

chestnut tree noun **1** (horse-chestnut) marronnier Masc.; **2** (sweet chestnut) châtaignier Masc.

chew verb mâcher [1] (food).

chewing gum noun chewing-gum Masc.

chick noun (of a hen) poussin Masc.

chicken noun poulet Masc.; **roast chicken** du poulet rôti; **chicken thighs** des cuisses de poulet; **a chicken sandwich** un sandwich au poulet.

chickenpox noun varicelle Fem.

chicory noun endive Fem.

chief noun chef Masc.; **the chief of police** le préfet de police.

child noun enfant Masc. & Fem.; **Jenny's children** les enfants de Jenny.

childish adjective puéril.

child-minder noun nourrice Fem.

chill noun fraîcheur Fem.

chilled adjective (wine) bien frais.

chilli noun piment Masc.

chilly adjective frisquet (Fem. frisquette); **it's chilly today** il fait frisquet aujourd'hui.

chimney noun cheminée Fem.

chimpanzee noun chimpanzé Masc.

chin noun menton Masc.

china noun Chine Fem.; **in China** en Chine.

china noun porcelaine Fem.; **a china plate** une assiette en porcelaine.

Chinese noun **1 the Chinese** (people) les Chinois; **2** (language) chinois Masc.
Chinese adjective chinois; **a Chinese man** un Chinois; **a Chinese woman** une Chinoise; **a Chinese meal** un repas chinois.

chip noun **1** (fried potato) frite Fem.; **I'd like some chips** j'aimerais des frites; **2** (microchip) puce Fem.; **3** (in glass or china) ébréchure Fem.

chipped adjective ébréché.

chives noun ciboulette Fem. singular.

chocolate noun chocolat Masc.; **a chocolate ice cream** une glace au chocolat; **hot chocolate** chocolat Masc. chaud; **a box of chocolates** une boîte de chocolats.

choice noun choix Masc.; **you have a choice of two flights** vous avez le choix entre deux vols.

choir noun **1** (in a school) chorale Fem.; **I sing in the choir** je fais partie de la chorale; **2** (professional) chœur Masc.

choke noun (on a car) starter Masc.
choke verb **1** (by yourself) s'étouffer [1]; **she was choking on a bone** elle s'éttouffait avec une arête; **2** (smoke or fumes) étouffer [1].

choose verb choisir [2]; **you chose well** tu as bien choisi; **Cathy chose the red one** Cathy a choisi le rouge; **it's hard to choose from all these colours** il est difficile de choisir parmi toutes ces couleurs.

chop noun côtelette Fem.; **a lamb chop** une côtelette d'agneau.
chop verb hacher [1].

chopstick noun baguette Fem.

a
b
c
d
e
f
g
h
i
j
k
l
m
n
o
p
q
r
s
t
u
v
w
x
y
z

a

chord noun accord Masc.

b

chorus noun 1 (when you all join in the song) refrain Masc.; 2 (a group of singers) chœur Masc.

c

Christ noun le Christ.

d

christening noun baptême Masc.

e

Christian noun, adjective chrétien Masc., chrétienne Fem.

f

Christian name noun prénom Masc.

g

h

Christmas noun Noël Masc.; **at Christmas** à Noël; **Happy Christmas!** Joyeux Noël!

i

Christmas card noun carte Fem. de Noël.

j

Christmas carol noun chant Masc. de Noël.

k

l

Christmas cracker noun diablotin Masc.

m

Christmas Day noun jour Masc. de Noël.

n

o

Christmas dinner noun repas Masc. de Noël.

p

Christmas Eve noun veille Fem. de Noël; **on Christmas Eve** la veille de Noël.

q

r

Christmas present noun cadeau Masc. de Noël.

s

Christmas tree noun sapin Masc. de Noël.

t

u

chunk noun morceau Masc.

v

church noun église Fem.; **to go to church** aller à l'église.

w

churchyard noun cimetière Masc.

x

chute noun (in a swimming pool or playground) toboggan Masc.

y

cider noun cidre Masc.

z

cigar noun cigare Masc.

cigarette noun cigarette Fem.; **to light a cigarette** allumer une cigarette.

cinema noun cinéma Masc.; **to go to the cinema** aller au cinéma.

circle noun cercle Masc.; **to sit in a circle** s'asseoir en cercle; **to go round in circles** tourner en rond.

circuit noun 1 (for athletes) piste Fem.; 2 (for cars) circuit Masc.

circumference noun circonférence Fem.

circumflex noun accent Masc. circonflexe.

circumstances plural noun **under the circumstances** dans ce circonstances.

circus noun cirque Masc.

citizen noun citoyen Masc., citoyenne Fem.

city noun (grande) ville Fem.; **the city of Paris** la ville de Paris.

city centre noun centre-ville Masc.; **in the city centre** au centre ville.

civilian noun civil Masc., civile Fe

civilization noun civilisation Fe

civil servant noun fonctionnai Masc. & Fem.; **he's a civil servant** il est fonctionnaire.

civil service noun fonction Fem publique.

civil war noun guerre Fem civile.

claim noun 1 (statement) déclaration Fem.; 2 (for compensation) réclamation Fem.; **t make a claim on insurance** faire une demande de remboursement auprès d'une compagnie

claim verb prétendre [3]; **he claimed to know** il prétendait savoir.

lap verb **1** applaudir [2]; **everyone clapped** tout le monde a applaudi; **2 to clap your hands** battre [21] des mains.

lapping noun applaudissements *Masc. plural.*

larinet noun clarinette *Fem.*; **to play the clarinet** jouer de la clarinette.

lash noun (*for example, between police and demonstrators*) affrontement *Masc.*

clash verb **1** (*rival groups*) s'affronter [1]; **2** (*colours*) jurer [1]; **the curtains clash with the wallpaper** les rideaux jurent avec le papier peint.

lasp noun (*of a necklace*) fermoir *Masc.*

lass noun **1** (*a group of students or pupils*) classe *Fem.*; **she's in the same class as me** elle est dans la même classe que moi; **2** (*a lesson*) cours *Masc.*; **an art class** un cours de dessin; **in class** en cours; **3** (*division*) classe *Fem.*; **a social class** une classe sociale.

lassic adjective classique.

lassical adjective classique; **classical music** la musique classique.

lassmate noun camarade *Masc. & Fem.* de classe.

lassroom noun classe *Fem.*

law noun **1** (*of a cat or dog*) griffe *Fem.*; **2** (*of a crab*) pince *Fem.*

clay noun **1** (*for modelling*) argile *Fem.*; **2 a clay court** (*in tennis*) un terrain en terre battue.

clean adjective **1** propre; **a clean shirt** une chemise propre; **my hands are clean** j'ai les mains propres; **2** (*germ-free*) pur (*air or water*).

clean verb nettoyer [39] **1 I cleaned the whole house** j'ai nettoyé toute la maison; **2 to clean your teeth** se laver [1] les dents; **I'm going to clean my teeth** je vais me laver les dents.

cleaner noun **1** (*in a public place*) agent *Masc.* de nettoyage; **2** (*cleaning lady*) femme *Fem.* de ménage; **3 a dry cleaner's** un pressing.

cleaning noun **to do the cleaning** faire le ménage.

cleanser noun **1** (*for the house*) produit *Masc.* d'entretien; **2** (*for your face*) démaquillant *Masc.*

clear adjective **1** (*that you can see through*) transparent; **clear glass** du verre transparent; **2** (*cloudless*) clair; **3** (*easy to understand*) clair; **clear instructions** des instructions claires; **is that clear?** est-ce que c'est clair?; **it's clear that** … il est clair que ….

clear verb **1** enlever [50] (*papers, rubbish, or clothes*); **have you cleared your stuff out of your room?** as-tu enlevé tes affaires de ta chambre?; **2** débarrasser [1] (*a table or a room*); **can I clear the table?** puis-je débarrasser la table?; **3** dégager [52] (*a road or path*); **4** (*fog or snow*) se dissiper [1]; **and then the fog cleared** et puis le

a
b
c
d
e
f
g
h
i
j
k
l
m
n
o
p
q
r
s
t
u
v
w
x
y
z

brouillard s'est dissipé; **5 to clear your throat** se racler [1] la gorge.

● **to clear something up** ranger [52] quelque chose; **I'll just clear up my books** je vais juste ranger mes livres.

clearly *adjective* **1** (*to think, speak, or hear*) clairement; **2** (*obviously*) manifestement; **she was clearly worried** manifestement, elle était inquiète.

clementine *noun* clémentine *Fem.*

clever *adjective* **1** intelligent; **their children are all very clever** leurs enfants sont tous très intelligents; **2** (*ingenious*) astucieux (*Fem.* astucieuse); **a clever idea** une idée astucieuse.

click *noun* **1** (*noise*) petit bruit *Masc.*, déclic *Masc.*; **2** (*with mouse*) clic *Masc.*; **a double-click** un double-clic. **click** *verb* **to click on something**: cliquer [1] sur quelque chose; **click on the icon twice** cliquer deux fois sur l'icône.

client *noun* client *Masc.*, cliente *Fem.*

cliff *noun* falaise *Fem.*

climate *noun* climat *Masc.*

climb *verb* **1** monter [1] (*a hill, stairs*); **2** faire [10] l'escalade de (*a mountain*); **we climbed Mont Blanc** nous avons fait l'escalade du Mont Blanc.

climber *noun* alpiniste *Masc. & Fem.*

climbing *noun* escalade *Fem.*; **they go climbing in Italy** ils font de l'escalade en Italie.

clinic *noun* centre *Masc.* médical (*plural* centres médicaux).

clip *noun* **1** (*from a film*) extrait *Masc.*; **2** (*for your hair*) barrette *Fem.* **clip** *verb* **1** (*to cut*) couper [1]; **2** (*to fasten*) attacher [1].

cloakroom *noun* (*for coats*) vestiaire *Masc.*

clock *noun* (*large*) horloge *Fem.*; (*smaller*) pendule *Fem.*; **an alarm clock** un réveil; **to put the clock forward an hour** avancer les pendules d'une heure; **to put the clocks back** reculer les pendules.

clock radio *noun* radio-réveil *Masc.*

clockwise *adverb* dans le sens des aiguilles d'une montre; **it turns clockwise** ça tourne dans le sens des aiguilles d'une montre.

close¹ *adjective, adverb* **1** (*result*) serré; **2** (*friend or relation*) proche; **3** (*near*) près; **the station's very close** la gare est tout près; **she lives close by** elle habite tout près; **close to the cinema** près du cinéma; **not very close** pas très près.

close² *noun* fin *Fem.*; **at the close** la fin.

close *verb* fermer [1]; **close your eyes!** ferme les yeux!; **she closed the door** elle a fermé la porte; **the post office closes at six** la poste ferme à six heures.

closed *adjective* fermé; **'closed on Mondays'** 'fermé le lundi'.

closely *adverb* de près; **to examine something closely** regarder quelque chose de près.

closing date *noun* date *Fem.* limite; **the closing date for entries** la date limite pour les inscriptions

losing-down sale *noun* liquidation *Fem.*

losing time *noun* heure *Fem.* de fermeture.

loth *noun* **1** (*for the floor*) serpillière *Fem.*; **2** (*for polishing*) chiffon *Masc.*; **3** (*for drying up*) torchon *Masc.*; **4** (*fabric by the metre*) tissu *Masc.*

lothes *plural noun* vêtements *Masc.* plural; **to put your clothes on** s'habiller; **to take your clothes off** se déshabiller; **to change your clothes** se changer.

lothes hanger *noun* cintre *Masc.*

lothes line *noun* corde *Fem.* à linge.

lothes peg *noun* pince *Fem.* à linge.

lothing *noun* vêtements *Masc.* plural.

loud *noun* nuage *Masc.*

to cloud over se couvrir [30]; **it clouded over in the afternoon** ça s'est couvert dans l'après-midi.

loudy *adjective* nuageux (*Fem.* nuageuse).

love *noun* **1** clou *Masc.* de girofle; **2 a clove of garlic** une gousse d'ail.

lown *noun* clown *Masc.*

lub *noun* **1** (*association*) club *Masc.*; **he's in the football club** il fait partie du club de foot; **2** (*in cards*) trèfle *Masc.*; **the four of clubs** le quatre de trèfle; **3** (*golfing iron*) crosse *Fem.*

lue *noun* **1** indice *Masc.*; **they have a few clues** ils ont quelques indices;

2 (*in a crossword*) définition *Fem.*; **★ I haven't a clue** je n'ai aucune idée.

clumsy *adjective* maladroit.

clutch *noun* (*in a car*) embrayage *Masc.*

clutch *verb* **to clutch something** tenir [77] quelque chose fermement.

coach *noun* **1** (*bus*) car *Masc.*; **by coach** en car; **on the coach** dans le car; **to travel by coach** voyager en car; **2** (*sports trainer*) entraîneur *Masc.*, entraîneuse *Fem.*; **3** (*railway carriage*) wagon *Masc.*

coach station *noun* gare *Fem.* routière.

coach trip *noun* excursion *Fem.* en car; **to go on a coach trip** faire une excursion en car.

coal *noun* charbon *Masc.*

coal mine *noun* mine *Fem.* de charbon.

coal miner *noun* mineur *Masc.*

coarse *adjective* grossier (*Fem.* grossière).

coast *noun* côte *Fem.*; **on the east coast** sur la côte est.

coat *noun* **1** manteau *Masc.* (*plural* manteaux); **2 a coat of paint** une couche de peinture.

coat hanger *noun* cintre *Masc.*

cobweb *noun* toile *Fem.* d'araignée.

cockerel *noun* coq *Masc.*

cocoa *noun* (*drink*) chocolat *Masc.* (chaud); (*powder*) cacao *Masc.*

coconut *noun* noix *Fem.* de coco.

cod *noun* cabillaud *Masc.*

code *noun* **1** code *Masc.*; **the highway code** le code de la route;

2 the dialling code for Cambridge l'indicatif pour Cambridge.

coffee noun café Masc.; **a cup of coffee** un café; **a black coffee, please** un café, s'il vous plaît; **a white coffee** un café au lait.

coffee break noun pause-café Fem.

coffee cup noun tasse Fem. à café.

coffee machine noun cafetière Fem.; (electric) cafetière Fem. électrique.

coffee table noun table Fem. basse.

coffin noun cercueil Masc.

coin noun pièce Fem. de monnaie; **a pound coin** une pièce d'une livre.

coincidence noun coïncidence Fem.

Coke™ noun coca Masc.; **two Cokes™ please** deux cocas s'il vous plaît.

colander noun passoire Fem.

cold noun 1 (cold weather) froid Masc.; **to be out in the cold** être dehors dans le froid; 2 (illness) rhume Masc.; **to have a cold** être enrhumé; **Carol's got a cold** Carol est enrhumée; **a bad cold** un gros rhume.

cold adjective 1 froid; **your hands are cold** tu as les mains froides; **cold milk** du lait froid; 2 (weather, temperature) **it's cold today** il fait froid aujourd'hui; **it's cold in the kitchen** il fait froid dans la cuisine; 3 (feeling) **I'm cold** j'ai froid.

cold sore noun bouton Masc. de fièvre.

collapse verb 1 (a roof or a wall) s'écrouler [1]; 2 (a person) **he collapsed in his office** il a eu un malaise dans son bureau.

collar noun 1 (on a garment) col Masc.; 2 (for a dog) collier Masc.

collarbone noun clavicule Fem.

colleague noun collègue Masc. & Fem.

collect verb 1 (as a hobby) collectionner [1]; **I collect stamps** je collectionne les timbres; 2 aller [7] chercher (a person); **she collects the children from school** elle va chercher les enfants à la sortie de l'école; 3 passer [64] prendre (thing) **I have to collect a book at the library** je dois passer prendre un livre à la bibliothèque; 4 encaisser [1] (fares or money); 5 **to collect in the exercise books** ramasser [1] les cahiers.

collection noun 1 (of stamps, CD etc) collection Fem.; 2 (of money) collecte Fem.

collector noun collectionneur Masc., collectionneuse Fem.

college noun 1 (for higher education) établissement Masc. d'études supérieures; **to go to college** faire des études supérieures; 2 (a school) collège Masc.

collie noun colley Masc.

collision noun collision Fem.

colonel noun colonel Masc.

colour noun couleur Fem.; **what colour is your car?** de quelle couleur est ta voiture?; **what colour is it?** c'est de quelle couleur?; **do**

you have it in a different colour?
est-ce que vous l'avez dans une autre
couleur?

colour *verb* (*with paints or crayons*)
colorier [1]; **to colour something
red** colorier quelque chose en rouge.

colour blind *adjective* daltonien
(*Fem.* daltonienne).

colour film *noun* pellicule *Fem.*
couleur (*plural* pellicules couleur).

colourful *adjective* en couleurs
vives.

colouring book *noun* album
Masc. à colorier.

colour scheme *noun* couleurs
Fem. plural.

colour supplement *noun*
supplément *Masc.* illustré.

column *noun* colonne *Fem.*

comb *noun* peigne *Masc.*

comb *verb* **to comb your hair** se
peigner [1]; **I'll just comb my hair** je
vais juste me peigner.

combination *noun* combinaison
Fem.

combine *verb* combiner [1] (*two
separate things*); **they don't
combine well** ils ne se combinent
pas bien.

come *verb* **1** venir [81]; **come
quick!** viens vite!; **come and see!**
venez voir!; **Nick came by bike**
Nick est venu à vélo; **did Jess
come to school yesterday?** est-ce
que Jess est venue à l'école hier?;
Alan comes from Scotland Alan
vient de l'Ecosse; **can you come
over for a coffee?** peux-tu venir
prendre un café?; **2** arriver [1];
coming! j'arrive!; **the bus is**

coming le bus arrive; **3 to come
down** descendre [3] (*the stairs or the
street*); **4 to come up** monter [1];
can you come up a moment?
peux-tu monter un instant?; **5 to
come in** entrer [1]; **come in!**
entrez!; **she came into the kitchen**
elle est entrée dans la cuisine; **6 to
come for** passer [1] prendre (*a
person*); **my father's coming for me**
mon père passe me prendre;
7 come along! dépêche-toi!

● **to come apart** (*to break*) se casser
[1]; **the door handle came apart in
my hands** la poignée m'est restée
dans la main; (*a book*) se déchirer
[1].

● **to come back** revenir [81]; **he's
coming back to collect us** il
revient nous chercher.

● **to come off** (*a button or handle, for
example*) se détacher [1], (*a lid*)
s'enlever [50].

● **to come out 1** sortir [72]; **they
came out when I called** ils sont
sortis quand j'ai appelé; **the CD's
coming out soon** le CD sort bientôt;
2 (*the sun or moon*) se montrer [1].

● **to come up to somebody** aborder
[1] quelqu'un.

comedian *noun* comique *Masc.*

comedy *noun* comédie *Fem.*

comfortable *adjective*
1 confortable; **this chair's really
comfortable** ce fauteuil est très
confortable; **2 to feel comfortable**
(*a person*) se sentir à l'aise; **are you
comfortable there?** êtes-vous bien
là?

comfortably *adverb*
confortablement.

a b c d e f g h i j k l m n o p q r s t u v w x y z

comic noun (magazine) illustré Masc.

comic strip noun bande Fem. dessinée.

comma noun virgule Fem.

command noun ordre Masc.

comment noun (in a conversation) remarque Fem.; **he made some rude comments about my friends** il a fait des remarques impolies sur mes amis.

commentary noun reportage Masc. en direct; **the commentary of the match** le reportage du match.

commentator noun commentateur Masc., commentatrice Fem.; **a sports commentator** un commentateur sportif.

commercial noun spot Masc. publicitaire.
commercial adjective commercial (Masc. plural commerciaux).

commit verb **1** commettre [11] (a crime); **2 to commit yourself** s'engager [52].

committee noun comité Masc.

common adjective **1** courant; **it's a common problem** c'est un problème courant; **2 in common** en commun; **they have nothing in common** ils n'ont rien en commun.

common sense noun bon sens Masc.

communicate verb communiquer [1].

communication noun **1** (message) communication Fem.; **2 communications**

communications Fem. (plural); **the communications are good** les communications sont bonnes.

communion noun communion Fem.

communism noun communism Masc.

communist noun, adjective communiste Masc. & Fem.

community noun communauté Fem.; **the European Community** la Communauté Européenne.

commute verb **to commute between Oxford and London** fair [10] le trajet entre Oxford et Londre tous les jours.

commuter noun navetteur Masc., navetteuse Fem.

compact disc noun disque Masc. compact.

compact disc player noun platine Fem. laser.

company noun **1** (business) société Fem.; **an insurance company** une société d'assurances **she's set up a company** elle a monté une société; **2** compagnie Fem.; **an airline company** une compagnie aérienne; **a theatre company** une compagnie théâtrale **3 to keep somebody company** tenir compagnie à quelqu'un; **the dog keeps me company** le chien me tient compagnie.

comparatively adverb relativement.

compare verb comparer [1]; **if you compare the French with the English** si on compare les Français aux Anglais; **our house is small**

compared with yours notre maison est petite par rapport à la vôtre.

omparison *noun* comparaison *Fem.*; **in comparison with** par rapport à.

ompartment *noun* compartiment *Masc.*

ompass *noun* boussole *Fem.*

ompatible *adjective* (*computing*) compatible.

ompensation *noun* indemnisation *Fem.*

ompete *verb* **1 to compete in something** participer [1] à quelque chose (*race, event*); **2 to compete for something** se disputer [1] quelque chose (*jobs, places*); **thirty people competing for one job** trente personnes qui se disputent un seul emploi.

ompetent *adjective* compétent.

ompetition *noun* concours *Masc.*; **a fishing competition** un concours de pêche.

ompetitor *noun* concurrent *Masc.*, concurrente *Fem.*

omplain *verb* se plaindre [31]; **we complained about the hotel and the meals** nous nous sommes plaints de l'hôtel et des repas.

omplaint *noun* plainte *Fem.*; **to make a complaint** se plaindre [31]; **she made a complaint to the manager about the poor service** elle s'est plainte de la qualité du service auprès du responsable.

omplete *adjective* complet (*Fem.* complète); **the complete collection** la collection complète.

complete *verb* (*to finish*) compléter [24].

completely *adverb* complètement.

complexion *noun* teint *Masc.*

complicated *adjective* compliqué.

compliment *noun* compliment *Masc.*; **to pay somebody a compliment** faire un compliment à quelqu'un.

compose *verb* composer [1]; **composed of** composé de.

composer *noun* compositeur *Masc.*, compositrice *Fem.*

comprehension *noun* compréhension *Fem.*; **a comprehension test** un test de compréhension.

compromise *noun* compromis *Masc.*

compulsory *adjective* obligatoire.

computer *noun* ordinateur *Masc.*; **to work on a computer** travailler sur ordinateur; **to have something on computer** avoir quelque chose sur ordinateur.

computer engineer *noun* technicien *Masc.* en informatique, technicienne *Fem.* en informatique.

computer game *noun* jeu *Masc.* électronique (*plural* jeux électroniques).

computer program *noun* programme *Masc.* informatique, logiciel *Masc.*

computer programmer *noun* programmeur *Masc.*, programmeuse *Fem.*

a
b
c
d
e
f
g
h
i
j
k
l
m
n
o
p
q
r
s
t
u
v
w
x
y
z

computer science *noun* informatique *Fem.*

computing *noun* informatique *Fem.*

conceited *adjective* vaniteux (*Fem.* vaniteuse).

concentrate *verb* se concentrer [1]; **I can't concentrate** je n'arrive pas à me concentrer; **I was concentrating on the film** je me concentrais sur le film.

concentration *noun* concentration *Fem.*

concern *noun* (*worry*) inquiétude *Fem.*; **there is no cause for concern** il n'y a pas lieu de s'inquiéter. **concern** *verb* **1** (*to affect*) concerner [1]; **this doesn't concern you** ceci ne te concerne pas; **2 as far as I'm concerned** en ce qui me concerne.

concert *noun* **1** concert *Masc.*; **to go to a concert** aller à un concert; **2 a concert ticket** un billet de concert.

conclusion *noun* conclusion *Fem.*

concrete *noun* béton *Masc.*; **a concrete floor** un sol en béton.

condemn *verb* condamner [1].

condition *noun* **1** condition *Fem.*; **in good condition** en bonne condition; **weather conditions** les conditions météorologiques; **2** (*something you agree to*) condition *Fem.*; **the conditions of sale** les conditions de vente; **on condition that you let me pay** à condition que tu me laisses payer.

conditional *noun* conditionnel *Masc.*

conditioner *noun* (*for your hair*) après-shampooing *Masc.*

condom *noun* préservatif *Masc.*

conduct *noun* conduite *Fem.*
conduct *verb* diriger [52] (*an orchestra or a piece of music*).

conductor *noun* (*of an orchestra*) chef *Masc.* d'orchestre.

cone *noun* **1** (*for ice cream*) cornet *Masc.*; **2** (*for traffic*) balise *Fem.*

confectionery *noun* confiserie *Fem.*

conference *noun* conférence *Fem.*

confess *verb* avouer [1].

confession *noun* confession *Fem.*

confidence *noun* **1** (*self-confidence*) assurance *Fem.*; **to be lacking in confidence** manquer d'assurance; **2** (*faith in somebody else*) confiance *Fem.*; **to have confidence in somebody** avoir confiance en quelqu'un.

confident *adjective* **1** (*sure of yourself*) assuré; **2** (*sure that something will happen*) sûr.

confirm *verb* confirmer [1]; **we'll confirm the date** nous confirmerons la date.

confuse *verb* **1** troubler [1] (*a person*); **2** confondre [69]; **I confuse him with his brother** je le confonds avec son frère.

confused *adjective* **1** confus; **he gave us a confused story** il nous a raconté une histoire confuse; **2 I'm confused about the holiday dates** je ne comprends pas bien les dates des vacances; **now I'm completely**

confused! là je ne comprends plus rien!

confusing adjective pas clair; **the instructions are confusing** les instructions ne sont pas claires.

confusion noun confusion Fem.

congratulate verb féliciter [1]; **I congratulated Tim on his success** j'ai félicité Tim de son succès; **we congratulate you on winning** nous vous félicitons d'avoir gagné.

congratulations plural noun félicitations Fem. plural; **congratulations on the baby!** félicitations pour le bébé!

conjurer noun prestidigitateur Masc.

connect verb (to plug in to the mains) brancher [1] (a dishwasher or TV, for example).

connection noun 1 (between two ideas or events) rapport Masc.; **there's no connection between his letter and my decision** il n'y a auccun rapport entre sa lettre et ma décision; 2 (between trains or planes) correspondance Fem.; **Sally missed her connection** Sally a raté sa correspondance; 3 (electrical) contact; **a faulty connection** un mauvais contact.

conscience noun conscience Fem.; **to have a guilty conscience** avoir mauvaise conscience.

conscious adjective conscient.

consequence noun conséquence Fem.

consequently adverb par conséquent.

conservation noun (of nature) protection Fem.

conservative noun, adjective conservateur Masc., conservatrice Fem.

conservatory noun jardin Masc. d'hiver.

consider verb 1 (to give thought to) considérer [24] (a suggestion or idea); 2 (to think you might do) envisager [52]; **we are considering buying a flat** nous envisageons d'acheter un appartement; 3 **all things considered** tout compte fait.

considerable adjective considérable; **a considerable number of the students** un pourcentage considérable des étudiants.

considerate adjective attentionné (person).

consideration noun considération Fem.; **no consideration was given to their safety** on ne s'est pas soucié de leur sécurité.

considering preposition étant donné; **considering her age** étant donné son âge; **considering he did it all himself** étant donné qu'il a tout fait lui-même.

consist verb **to consist of** être [6] composé de.

consistent adjective régulier, constant.

consonant noun consonne Fem.

constant adjective permanent.

constipated adjective constipé.

construct verb construire [26].

385

a
b
c
d
e
f
g
h
i
j
k
l
m
n
o
p
q
r
s
t
u
v
w
x
y
z

a

b

c

d

e

f

g

h

i

j

k

l

m

n

o

p

q

r

s

t

u

v

w

x

y

z

construction noun construction Fem.

consul noun consul Masc.

consulate noun consulat Masc.

consult verb consulter [1].

consumer noun consommateur Masc., consommatrice Fem.

consumption noun consommation Fem.

contact noun 1 (touch) contact Masc.; **to be in contact with somebody** être en contact avec quelqu'un; **we've lost contact** nous avons perdu contact; 2 (a person you know) connaissance Fem.; **Rob has contacts in the music business** Rob a des connaissances dans le monde de la musique.

contact verb contacter [1]; **I'll contact you tomorrow** je te contacterai demain.

contact lens noun lentille Fem. de contact (plural lentilles de contact).

contain verb contenir [77].

container noun récipient Masc.

contaminate verb contaminer [1].

contemporary adjective 1 (around today) contemporain; 2 (modern) moderne.

contents plural noun contenu Masc.; **the contents of my suitcase** le contenu de ma valise.

contest noun concours Masc.

contestant noun concurrent Masc., concurrente Fem.

context noun contexte Masc.

continent noun continent Masc.; **on the Continent** en Europe continentale.

continental adjective **a continental holiday** des vacances en Europe continentale.

continue verb continuer [1]; **we continued (with) our journey** nous avons continué notre voyage; **Jill continued chatting** Jill a continué de bavarder; **'to be continued'** 'à suivre'.

continuous adjective continu; **continuous assessment** le contrôle continu.

contraception noun contraception Fem.

contraceptive noun contraceptif Masc.

contract noun contrat Masc.

contradict verb contredire [47].

contradiction noun contradiction Fem.

contrary noun contraire Masc.; **on the contrary** au contraire.

contrast noun contraste Masc.

contribute verb donner [1] (money).

contribution noun (to charity or an appeal) don Masc.

control noun (of a crowd or animals) contrôle Masc.; **the police have lost control** la police a perdu le contrôle; **keep your dogs under control** maîtrisez vos chiens; **everything's under control** tout va bien; **the fire was out of control** on ne maîtrisait plus l'incendie.

control verb 1 maîtriser [1] (a

crowd, animals, or a fire, for example); **2 to control oneself** se contrôler [1].

controversial *adjective* discutable; **a controversial decision** une décision discutable.

convenient *adjective* **1** commode; **frozen vegetables are very convenient** les légumes congelés sont très commodes; **2 to be convenient for somebody** convenir à quelqu'un; **if that's convenient for you** si cela vous convient; **3 the house is convenient for shops and schools** la maison est bien située par rapport aux magasins et aux écoles.

convent *noun* couvent *Masc.*

conventional *adjective* **1** conventionnel (*Fem.* conventionnelle); **2** (*person*) conformiste.

conversation *noun* conversation *Fem.*

convert *verb* transformer [1]; **we're going to convert the garage into a workshop** nous allons transformer le garage en atelier.

convince *verb* convaincre [79]; **I'm convinced you're wrong** je suis convaincu que tu as tort.

convincing *adjective* convaincant.

cook *noun* cuisinier *Masc.*, cuisinière *Fem.*

cook *verb* **1** faire [10] la cuisine; **who's cooking tonight?** qui fait la cuisine ce soir?; **I like cooking** j'aime faire la cuisine; **2** faire [10] cuire (*vegetables, pasta, etc*); **cook the carrots for five minutes** faites cuire les carottes pendant cinq minutes; **3** préparer [1] (*a meal*); **Fran's busy cooking supper** Fran est en train de préparer le dîner; **4** (*food*) cuire [36]; **the sausages are cooking** les saucisses sont en train de cuire; **is the chicken cooked?** est-ce que le poulet est cuit?

cooker *noun* cuisinière *Fem.*; **an electric cooker** une cuisinière électrique; **a gas cooker** une cuisinière à gaz.

cookery *noun* cuisine *Fem.*

cookery book *noun* livre *Masc.* de cuisine.

cooking *noun* cuisine *Fem.*; **to do the cooking** faire la cuisine; **Italian cooking** la cuisine italienne.

cool *noun* **1** (*coldness*) fraîcheur *Fem.*; **stay in the cool** reste à la fraîcheur; **2** (*calm*) **to lose one's cool** perdre son sang-froid; **he kept his cool** il a gardé son sang-froid.
cool *adjective* **1** (*cold*) frais (*Fem.* fraîche); **a cool drink** une boisson fraîche; **it's cool inside** il fait frais dans la maison; **2** (*laid-back*) décontracté; **3** (*sophisticated*) branché (*informal*).
cool *verb* refroidir [2]; **while the engine was cooling (down)** pendant que le moteur refroidissait.

cooperate *verb* coopérer [24].

cop *noun* flic *Masc.* (*informal*).

cope *verb* **1** (*to manage*) se débrouiller [1]; **she copes well** elle se débrouille bien; **2 to cope with** s'occuper [1] de (*children or work*);

a
b
c
d
e
f
g
h
i
j
k
l
m
n
o
p
q
r
s
t
u
v
w
x
y
z

I'll cope with the dishes je m'occuperai de la vaisselle; **3** faire [10] face à (*problems*); **she's had a lot to cope with** elle a été obligée de faire face à beaucoup de choses; **he can't cope any more** il n'arrive plus à faire face.

copper *noun* cuivre *Masc.*

copy *noun* **1** copie *Fem.*; **make ten copies of this letter** faites dix copies de cette lettre; **2** (*of a book*) exemplaire *Masc.*
copy *verb* copier [1]; **I copied (down) the address** j'ai copié l'adresse.

cord *noun* (*for a blind, for example*) cordon *Masc.*

cordless telephone *noun* téléphone *Masc.* sans fil.

core *noun* (*of an apple or a pear*) trognon *Masc.*

cork *noun* **1** (*in a bottle*) bouchon *Masc.*; **2** (*material*) liège *Masc.*

corkscrew *noun* tire-bouchon *Masc.*

corn *noun* **1** (*wheat*) blé *Masc.*; **2** (*sweetcorn*) maïs *Masc.*

corner *noun* coin *Masc.*; **in a corner of the kitchen** dans un coin de la cuisine; **at the corner of the street** au coin de la rue; **out of the corner of your eye** du coin de l'œil; **it's just round the corner** c'est tout près.

cornflakes *noun* corn-flakes *Masc. plural.*

Cornwall *noun* Cornouailles *Fem.*; **in Cornwall** en Cornouailles.

corpse *noun* cadavre *Masc.*

correct *adjective* **1** exact; **yes, that's correct** oui, c'est exact; **2** bon (*Fem.* bonne); **the correct sum** la bonne somme; **the correct answer** la bonne réponse; **the correct choice** le bon choix.
correct *verb* corriger [52].

correction *noun* correction *Fem.*

correctly *adverb* correctement; **have you filled in the form correctly?** est-ce que vous avez rempli le formulaire correctement? **she answered correctly** elle a donné la bonne réponse.

correspond *verb* correspondre [3].

corridor *noun* couloir *Masc.*

Corsica *noun* Corse *Fem.*; **to Corsica** en Corse.

cosmetics *plural noun* produits *Masc. plural* de beauté.

cost *noun* prix *Masc.*; **the cost of a new computer** le prix d'un nouvel ordinateur; **the cost of living** le coût de la vie.
cost *verb* coûter [1]; **how much does it cost?** combien est-ce que ç coûte?; **the tickets cost £10** les billets coûtent dix livres; **it costs too much** cela coûte trop cher.

costume *noun* costume *Masc.*

cosy *adjective* (*a bed or room*) douillet (*Fem.* douillette); **it's cosy by the fire** on est bien à côté du feu

cot *noun* lit *Masc.* d'enfant.

cottage *noun* petite maison *Fem.*

cotton *noun* **1** (*fabric*) coton *Masc.*; **a cotton shirt** une chemise en coton; **2** (*thread*) fil *Masc.* de coton.

otton wool *noun* ouate *Fem.* de coton.

ouch *noun* canapé *Masc.*

ough *noun* toux *Fem.*; **a nasty cough** une mauvaise toux; **to have a cough** tousser.

cough *verb* tousser [1].

ould *verb* **1** **if he could pay** s'il pouvait payer; **I couldn't open it** je ne pouvais pas l'ouvrir; **they couldn't smoke there** ils ne pouvaient pas fumer là; **she did all she could** elle a fait tout ce qu'elle pouvait; **2** (*knew how to*) **he couldn't drive** il ne savait pas conduire; **I couldn't swim** je ne savais pas nager; **3** (*with seeing, hearing, or smelling*) **I could hear the police car** j'entendais la voiture de police; **she couldn't see anything** elle ne voyait rien; **4** (*might*) **could I speak to David?** pourrais-je parler à David?; **you could try telephoning** tu pourrais téléphoner.

ouncil *noun* conseil *Masc.*; **the town council** le conseil municipal.

ouncillor *noun* **1** (*of town council*) membre *Masc.*, du conseil municipal; **2** (*local council*) membre *Masc.*, du conseil régional.

ount *verb* **1** (*reckon up*) compter [1]; **I counted my money** j'ai compté mon argent; **thirty-five not counting the children** trente-cinq sans compter les enfants; **2 to count as** être [6] considéré comme; **children over twelve count as adults** les enfants au-dessus de douze ans sont considérés comme adultes; **3** (*to be allowed*) compter

[1]; **that doesn't count** ça ne compte pas.

counter *noun* **1** (*in a shop or cafe*) comptoir *Masc.*; **2** (*in a post office or bank*) guichet *Masc.*; **3** (*in a big store*) rayon *Masc.*; **on the cheese counter** au rayon fromagerie; **4** (*for board games*) jeton *Masc.*

country *noun* **1** (*France, England, etc*) pays *Masc.*; **a foreign country** un pays étranger; **from another country** d'un autre pays; **2** (*not town*) campagne *Fem.*; **to live in the country** vivre à la campagne; **a country walk** une promenade à la campagne; **a country road** une route de campagne.

country dancing *noun* danse *Fem.* folklorique.

countryside *noun* campagne *Fem.*

county *noun* comté *Masc.*

couple *noun* **1** (*a pair*) couple *Masc.*; **2 a couple of** deux ou trois; **a couple of times** deux ou trois fois; **I've got a couple of things to do** j'ai deux ou trois choses à faire.

courage *noun* courage *Masc.*

courgette *noun* courgette *Fem.*

courier *noun* **1** (*on a package holiday*) accompagnateur *Masc.*, accompagnatrice *Fem.*; **2** (*delivery service*) coursier *Masc.*; **by courier** par coursier.

course *noun* **1** (*lessons*) cours *Masc.*; **a beginners' course** un cours pour débutants; **a computer course** un cours d'informatique; **to go on a course** suivre un cours; **2** (*part of a meal*) plat *Masc.*; **the main course** le plat principal; **a golf course** un golf;

a
b
c
d
e
f
g
h
i
j
k
l
m
n
o
p
q
r
s
t
u
v
w
x
y
z

3 of course bien sûr; **yes, of course!** oui, bien sûr!; **he's forgotten, of course** il a oublié, bien sûr.

court noun **1** (*for tennis or squash*) court *Masc.*; **2** (*for basketball*) terrain *Masc.*

courtyard noun cour *Fem.*

cousin noun cousin *Masc.*, cousine *Fem.*; **my cousin Sonia** ma cousine Sonia.

cover noun **1** (*for a book*) couverture *Fem.*; **2** (*for a duvet or cushion*) housse *Fem.*; **a duvet cover** une housse de couette.
cover verb **1** (*to protect or cover up*) couvrir [30]; **cover the wound** couvrez la blessure; **he was covered in spots** il était couvert de boutons; **2** (*with leaves, snow, or fabric*) recouvrir [30]; **the ground was covered with snow** le sol était recouvert de neige.

cow noun vache *Fem.*; **mad cow disease** maladie *Fem.* de la vache folle.

coward noun lâche *Masc.* & *Fem.*

cowboy noun cowboy *Masc.*

crab noun crabe *Masc.*

crack noun **1** (*in a wall or cup*) fêlure *Fem.*; **2** (*a cracking noise*) craquement *Masc.*
crack verb **1** (*to make a crack in*) fêler [1] (*a cup, a chair, or a bone*); **2** (*to break*) casser [1] (*a nut or an egg*); **3** (*to split by itself: ice, for example*) se fêler [1]; **4** (*to make a noise*) (*a twig*) craquer [1].

cracker noun **1** (*biscuit*) cracker *Masc.*; **2** (*Christmas cracker*) diablotin *Masc.*

crackle verb crépiter [1].

craft noun (*at school*) travaux *Masc. plural* manuels.

crafty adjective ingénieux (*Fem.* ingénieuse); **that was very crafty of her** c'était très ingénieux de sa part.

cramp noun crampe *Fem.*; **to have cramp in your leg** avoir une crampe à la jambe.

crane noun grue *Fem.*

crash noun **1** (*an accident*) accident *Masc.*; **a car crash** un accident de voiture; **2** (*smashing noise*) fracas *Masc.*; **a crash of broken glass** un fracas de verre brisé.
crash verb **1** (*a car or plane*) s'écraser [1]; **the plane crashed** l'avion s'est écrasé; **2 to crash into something** rentrer [1] dans quelque chose; **the car crashed into a tree** la voiture est rentrée dans un arbre.

crash course noun cours *Masc.* intensif.

crash helmet noun casque *Masc.*

crate noun **1** (*for bottles or china*) caisse *Fem.*; **2** (*for fruit*) cageot *Masc.*

crawl noun (*in swimming*) crawl *Masc.*
crawl verb **1** (*a person, a baby*) marcher [1] à quatre pattes; **2** (*cars in a jam*) rouler [1] au pas; **we were crawling along** nous roulions au pas.

crayon noun **1** (*wax*) crayon *Masc.* gras; **2** (*coloured pencil*) crayon *Masc.* de couleur.

craze noun vogue Fem.; **the craze for rollerblades** la vogue des rollers.

crazy adjective fou (Fem. folle).

creak verb (a hinge) grincer [61] (a floorboard) craquer [1].

cream noun crème Fem.; **strawberries and cream** des fraises à la crème.

cream cheese noun fromage Masc. à tartiner.

crease noun pli Masc.

creased adjective froissé.

create verb créer [32].

creative adjective créatif (Fem. créative) (a person).

creature noun créature Fem.

crèche noun crèche Fem.

credit noun crédit Masc.; **to buy something on credit** acheter quelque chose à crédit.

credit card noun carte Fem. de crédit.

cress noun cresson Masc.

crew noun 1 (on a ship or plane) équipage Masc.; 2 (rowing or filming) équipe Fem.

crew cut noun cheveux Masc. plural en brosse.

cricket noun 1 (game) cricket Masc.; **to play cricket** jouer au cricket; 2 (insect) grillon Masc.

cricket bat noun batte Fem. de cricket.

crime noun 1 crime Masc.; **murder is a crime** le meurtre est un crime; 2 (within society) criminalité Fem.;

the fight against crime la lutte contre la criminalité.

criminal noun, adjective criminel Masc., criminelle Fem.

crimson adjective pourpre.

crisis noun crise Fem.

crisp noun chip Fem.; **a packet of (potato) crisps** un sachet de chips. **crisp** adjective 1 (biscuit) croustillant; 2 (apple) croquant.

critical adjective 1 critique (a remark or somebody's condition); 2 décisif (Fem. décisive) (a moment).

criticism noun critique Fem.

criticize verb critiquer [1].

Croatia noun Croatie Fem.

crockery noun vaisselle Fem.

crocodile noun crocodile Masc.

crook noun (criminal) escroc Masc.

crooked adjective de travers; **the picture is crooked** le tableau est de travers; **a crooked line** une ligne pas droite.

crop noun récolte Fem.

cross noun croix Fem.
cross adjective fâché; **she's very cross** elle est très fâchée; **I'm cross with you** je suis fâché contre toi.
cross verb 1 (to cross over) traverser [1]; **to cross the road** traverser la rue; 2 **to cross your legs** croiser [1] les jambes; 3 **to cross into Italy** passer [1] en Italie; 4 (to cross each other) se croiser [1]; **the two roads cross here** les deux routes se croisent ici.
● **to cross out** rayer [59] (a mistake, for example).

a
b
c
d
e
f
g
h
i
j
k
l
m
n
o
p
q
r
s
t
u
v
w
x
y
z

cross-Channel *adjective* trans-Manche; **a cross-Channel ferry** un ferry trans-Manche.

cross-country *noun* **1** cross *Masc.*; **2 cross-country skiing** le ski de fond.

crossing *noun* **1** (*from one place to another*) traversée *Fem.*; **a Channel crossing** une traversée trans-Manche; **2 a pedestrian crossing** un passage piétons; **a level crossing** un passage à niveau.

cross-legged *adjective* **to sit cross-legged** être assis en tailleur.

crossroads *noun* carrefour *Masc.*; **at the crossroads** au carrefour.

crossword *noun* mots *Masc. plural* croisés; **to do the crossword** faire les mots croisés.

crouch *verb* s'accroupir [2].

crow *noun* corbeau *Masc.*; ★ **ten kilometres as the crow flies** dix kilomètres à vol d'oiseau. **crow** *verb* (*a cock*) chanter [1].

crowd *noun* foule *Fem.*; **in the crowd** dans la foule; **a crowd of 5,000** une foule de cinq mille. **crowd** *verb* **to crowd into** or **onto** s'entasser [1] dans (*a room or bus, for example*); **we all crowded into the train** nous nous sommes tous entassés dans le train.

crowded *adjective* bondé.

crown *noun* couronne *Fem.*

crude *adjective* **1** (*rough and ready*) rudimentaire; **2** (*vulgar*) grossier (*Fem.* grossière).

cruel *adjective* cruel (*Fem.* cruelle).

cruelty *noun* cruauté *Fem.*; **they were treated with great cruelty** i[ls] ont été traités avec beaucoup de cruauté.

cruise *noun* croisière *Fem.*; **to go o[n] a cruise** faire une croisière.

crumb *noun* miette *Fem.*

crumple *verb* froisser [1].

crunch *verb* croquer [1] (*an apple*[)]

crunchy *adjective* croquant.

crush *verb* écraser [1].

crust *noun* croûte *Fem.*

crusty *adjective* croustillant (*bread*).

crutch *noun* béquille *Fem.*; **to be o[n] crutches** marcher avec des béquilles.

cry *noun* cri *Masc.* **cry** *verb* **1** (*weep*) pleurer [1]; **2** (*ca[ll] out*) crier [1].

crystal *noun* cristal *Masc.*

cub *noun* **1** (*animal*) petit *Masc.*; **2** (*scout*) louveteau *Masc.*

Cuba *noun* Cuba *Fem.*

Cuban *noun* Cubain *Masc.*, Cubain[e] *Fem.* **Cuban** *adjective* cubain.

cube *noun* cube *Masc.*; **an ice cube** un glaçon.

cubic *adjective* (*for measurements*) cube; **three cubic metres** trois mètres cube.

cubicle *noun* **1** (*in a changing room*) cabine *Fem.*; **2** (*in a public lavatory*) cabinet *Masc.*

cuckoo *noun* coucou *Masc.*

cucumber *noun* concombre *Masc.*

uddle noun **to give somebody a cuddle** faire un câlin à quelqu'un.
cuddle verb câliner [1].

ue noun (billiards, pool, snooker) queue Fem. de billard.

uff noun (on a shirt) manchette Fem.

ul-de-sac noun impasse Fem.

ulture noun culture Fem.

unning adjective rusé.

up noun 1 (for drinking) tasse Fem.; **a cup of tea** une tasse de thé; 2 (a trophy) coupe Fem.

upboard noun placard Masc.; **in the kitchen cupboard** dans le placard de la cuisine.

up tie noun match Masc. de coupe.

ure noun remède Masc.
cure verb guérir [2].

uriosity noun curiosité Fem.

urious adjective curieux (Fem. curieuse).

url noun boucle Fem.
curl verb friser [1] (hair).

urrant noun raisin Masc. de Corinthe.

urrency noun **foreign currency** les devises étrangères.

urrent noun (of electricity or water) courant Masc.
current adjective actuel (Fem. actuelle) (a situation, for example).

urrent affairs noun actualité Fem.

urriculum noun programme Masc.

urry noun curry Masc.; **chicken curry** le curry de poulet.

ursor noun curseur Masc.

curtain noun rideau Masc. (plural rideaux).

cushion noun coussin Masc.

custard noun 1 (runny) crème Fem. anglaise; 2 (baked) flan Masc.

custom noun coutume Fem.

customer noun client Masc., cliente Fem.; **customer services** le service clientèle.

customs plural noun douane Fem. singular; **to go through customs** passer à la douane.

customs hall noun douane Fem.

customs officer noun douanier Masc., douanière Fem.

cut noun 1 (injury) coupure Fem.; 2 (haircut) coupe Fem.
cut verb 1 couper [1]; **I've cut the bread** j'ai coupé le pain; **you'll cut yourself!** tu vas te couper!; **Kevin's cut his finger** Kevin s'est coupé le doigt; 2 **to cut the grass** tondre [3] le gazon; 3 **to get your hair cut** se faire [10] couper les cheveux; **Anne's had her hair cut** Anne s'est fait couper les cheveux; 4 **to cut prices** baisser les prix.

● **to cut down something** abattre [21] (a tree).

● **to cut out something** 1 découper [1] (a shape, a newspaper article); 2 supprimer (sugar, fatty food, etc.).

● **to cut up something** couper [1] (food).

cutlery noun couverts Masc. plural.

CV noun CV Masc.

cycle noun (bike) vélo Masc.
cycle verb faire [10] du vélo; **do you like cycling?** est-ce que tu aimes

a
b
c
d
e
f
g
h
i
j
k
l
m
n
o
p
q
r
s
t
u
v
w
x
y
z

faire du vélo?; **we cycle to school**
nous allons à l'école à vélo.

cycle lane *noun* piste *Fem.*
cyclable.

cycle race *noun* course *Fem.*
cycliste.

cycling *noun* cyclisme *Masc.*

cycling holiday *noun* vacances
Fem. plural à vélo.

cyclist *noun* cycliste *Masc. & Fem.*

cylinder *noun* cylindre *Masc.*

Dd

dad *noun* **1** père *Masc.*; **Anna's dad** le
père d'Anna; **my dad works in a
bank** mon père travaille dans une
banque; **2** (*within the family*) papa
Masc.; **Dad's not home yet** Papa
n'est pas encore rentré.

daffodil *noun* jonquille *Fem.*

daily *adjective* quotidien (*Fem.*
quotidienne); **his daily visit** sa
visite quotidienne.
daily *adverb* quotidiennement; **she
visits him daily** elle lui rend visite
tous les jours.

dairy products *plural noun* les
produits *Masc. plural* laitiers.

daisy *noun* paquerette *Fem.*

dam *noun* barrage *Masc.*

damage *verb* abîmer [1].

damage *noun* dégâts *Masc. plural*;
there's no damage il n'y a pas de
dégâts.
damage *verb* endommager [52].

damn *noun* **he doesn't give a
damn** il s'en fiche complètement
(*informal*).
damn *exclamation* **damn!** zut!
(*informal*).

damp *adjective* humide.
damp *noun* humidité *Fem.*;
because of the damp à cause de
l'humidité.

dance *noun* **1** (*art form*) danse *Fem.*
a folk dance une danse
traditionnelle; **2** (*occasion*) soirée
Fem. dansante.
dance *verb* danser [1].

dancer *noun* danseur *Masc.*,
danseuse *Fem.*

dancing *noun* danse *Fem.*; **I like
dancing** j'aime danser.

dancing class *noun* cours *Masc.*
de danse; **to go to dancing classes**
suivre des cours de danse.

dandruff *noun* pellicules *Fem. plural*

danger *noun* danger *Masc.*; **to be in
danger** être en danger.

dangerous *adjective* dangereux
(*Fem.* dangereuse); **it's dangerous
to drive too fast** il est dangereux de
conduire trop vite.

Danish *noun* danois *Masc.*
Danish *adjective* danois.

dare *verb* **1** oser [1]; **to dare to do**
oser faire; **I didn't dare suggest it**
je n'ai pas osé le suggérer; **2 don't
you dare tell her I'm here!** je
t'interdis de lui dire que je suis là!;
3 I dare you! chiche que tu y vas!
(*informal*); **I dare you to tell him!**
chiche que tu le lui dises! (*informal*)

daring *adjective* osé; **that was a bit
daring!** c'était un peu osé!

dark noun in the dark dans l'obscurité; after dark après la tombée de la nuit; to be afraid of the dark avoir peur du noir.
dark adjective 1 (colour) foncé; a dark blue skirt une jupe bleu foncé; 2 she has dark brown hair elle est brune; 3 it's dark already il fait nuit déjà; it gets dark around five la nuit commence à tomber vers cinq heures; 4 (room) sombre; the kitchen's a bit dark la cuisine est plutôt sombre; it's dark in here il fait sombre ici.

darkness noun obscurité Fem.; in darkness dans l'obscurité.

darling noun chéri Masc., chérie Fem.; see you later, darling! à tout à l'heure, chéri!

dart noun fléchette Fem.; to play darts jouer aux fléchettes.

data plural noun données Fem. plural.

database noun base Fem. de données.

date noun 1 date Fem.; the date of the meeting la date de la réunion; to fix a date for fixer une date pour; 2 what's the date today? nous sommes le combien aujourd'hui?; 3 out of date (passport, driving licence, etc) périmé; (technology, method, information, etc) dépassé; my passport's out of date mon passeport est périmé; 4 (appointment) Laura's got a date with Frank tonight Laura sort avec Frank ce soir; 5 (fruit) datte Fem.

date of birth noun date Fem. de naissance.

daughter noun fille Fem.; Tina's daughter la fille de Tina.

daughter-in-law noun belle-fille Fem. (plural belles-filles).

dawn noun aube Fem.

day noun 1 jour Masc.; three days later trois jours plus tard; the day I went to London le jour où je suis allé à Londres; 2 (just from morning until evening) journée Fem.; we spent the day in London nous avons passé la journée à Londres; it rained all day il a plu pendant toute la journée; 3 it's going to be a nice day tomorrow il va faire beau demain; 4 the day after le lendemain; the day after the wedding le lendemain du mariage; the day after tomorrow après-demain; my sister's arriving the day after tomorrow ma sœur arrive après-demain; 5 the day before la veille; the day before the wedding la veille du mariage; the day before yesterday avant-hier; my sister arrived the day before yesterday ma sœur est arrivée avant-hier.

day off noun jour Masc. de congé; when's your day off? quel est ton jour de congé?

dead adjective mort; her father's dead son père est mort.
dead adverb (really) vachement (informal); he's dead nice il est vachement gentil; it was dead good c'était vachement bien; it's dead easy c'est vachement facile; you're dead right tu as absolument raison; she arrived dead on time elle est arrivée à l'heure pile.

a
b
c
d
e
f
g
h
i
j
k
l
m
n
o
p
q
r
s
t
u
v
w
x
y
z

a
b
c
d
e
f
g
h
i
j
k
l
m
n
o
p
q
r
s
t
u
v
w
x
y
z

dead end *noun* impasse *Fem.*

deadline *noun* date *Fem.* limite.

deaf *adjective* sourd.

deafening *adjective* assourdissant.

deal *noun* **1** (*involving money*) affaire; **it's a good deal** c'est une bonne affaire; **2** marché *Masc.*; **I'll make a deal with you** je ferai un marché avec toi; **it's a deal!** marché conclu!; **3 a great deal of** beaucoup de; **I don't have a great deal of time** je n'ai pas beaucoup de temps. **deal** *verb* (*in cards*) donner [1]; **it's you to deal** c'est à toi de donner.
● **to deal with something** s'occuper [1] de quelque chose; **Linda deals with the accounts** Linda s'occupe de la comptabilité; **I'll deal with it as soon as possible** je m'en occuperai dès que possible.

dear *adjective* **1** cher (*Fem.* chère); **Dear Sylvie** Chère Sylvie; **2** (*expensive*) cher (*Fem.* chère).

death *noun* mort *Fem.*; **after his father's death** après la mort de son père; ★ **you'll frighten him to death** tu lui feras une peur bleue; ★ **I'm bored to death** je m'ennuie à mourir; ★ **I'm sick to death of it** j'en ai marre (*informal*) .

death penalty *noun* peine *Fem.* de mort.

debate *noun* débat *Masc.*
debate *verb* débattre [21].

debt *noun* dette *Fem.*; **to get into debt** s'endetter.

decade *noun* décennie *Fem.*

decaffeinated *adjective* décaféiné.

deceive *verb* tromper [1].

December *noun* décembre *Masc.*; **in December** en décembre.

decent *adjective* **1** convenable; **a decent salary** un salaire convenable; **2 a decent meal** un bon repas; **3 he seems a decent enough guy** il semble être un type plutôt bien (*informal*).

decide *verb* décider [1]; **to decide to do** décider de faire; **she's decided to buy a car** elle a decidé d'acheter une voiture; **she's decided not to buy a car** elle a décidé de ne pas acheter une voiture.

decimal *adjective* décimal (*Masc. plural* décimaux).

decimal point *noun* virgule *Fem.*

decision *noun* décision *Fem.*; **the right decision** la bonne décision; **the wrong decision** la mauvaise décision; **to make a decision** prendre une décision.

deck *noun* (*on a ship*) pont *Masc.*

deckchair *noun* transat *Masc.*

declare *verb* déclarer [1].

decorate *verb* **1** décorer [1]; **to decorate the Christmas tree** décorer le sapin de Noël; **2** peindre; **we're decorating the kitchen this weekend** on va peindre la cuisine ce weekend.

decoration *noun* décoration *Fem.*

decorator *noun* peintre-décorateur *Masc.*

decrease *noun* diminution *Fem.*; **a decrease in the number of** une diminution du nombre de.

decrease *verb* diminuer [1].

deduct *verb* déduire [26].

deep *adjective* profond; **a deep feeling of gratitude** un profond sentiment de reconnaissance; **the river is very deep here** la rivière est très profonde ici; **how deep is the swimming pool?** quelle est la profondeur de la piscine?; **a hole two metres deep** un trou de deux mètres de profondeur.

deep end *noun* **the deep end** (*of a swimming pool*) le grand bassin.

deep freeze *noun* congélateur *Masc.*

deeply *adverb* profondément.

deer *noun* **1** (*red deer*) cerf *Masc.*; **2** (*roe deer*) chevreuil *Masc.*; **3** (*fallow deer*) daim *Masc.*

defeat *noun* défaite *Fem.*
defeat *verb* battre [21].

defect *noun* défaut *Masc.*

defence *noun* défense *Fem.*

defend *verb* défendre [3].

defender *noun* défenseur. *Masc.*

define *verb* définir [2].

definite *adjective* **1** net (*Fem.* nette) (*before the noun*); **a definite change** un net changement; **a definite improvement** une nette amélioration; **2** (*certain*) sûr; **it's not definite yet** ce n'est pas encore sûr; **3** (*exact*) précis; **a definite answer** une réponse précise; **I don't have a definite idea of what I want** je n'ai pas une idée précise de ce que je veux.

definite article *noun* article *Masc.* défini.

definitely *adverb* **1** (*when giving your opinion about something*) sans aucun doute; **the blue one is definitely the biggest** le bleu est sans aucun doute le plus grand; **your French is definitely better than mine** ton français est sans aucun doute meilleur que le mien; '**are you sure you like this one better?' – 'definitely!'** 'tu es sûr que tu préfères celui-ci?' – 'sans aucun doute!'; **2 she's definitely going to be there** elle va y être, c'est sûr; **I'm definitely not going** c'est décidé, je n'y vais pas.

definition *noun* définition *Fem.*

degree *noun* **1** degré *Masc.*; **thirty degrees** trente degrés; **2 a university degree** un diplôme universitaire.

delay *noun* retard *Masc.*; **a two-hour delay** un retard de deux heures.
delay *verb* **1** (*make late*) retarder [1]; **the flight was delayed by bad weather** le vol a été retardé par le mauvais temps; **2** (*postpone*) différer [24]; **the decision has been delayed until Thursday** la décision a été différée juqu'à jeudi.

delete *verb* effacer [61].

deliberate *adjective* délibéré.

deliberately *adverb* exprès; **you did it deliberately** tu l'as fait exprès; **he left it there deliberately** il a fait exprès de le laisser là.

delicate *adjective* délicat.

delicatessen *noun* épicerie *Fem.* fine.

a
b
c
d
e
f
g
h
i
j
k
l
m
n
o
p
q
r
s
t
u
v
w
x
y
z

a
b
c
d
e
f
g
h
i
j
k
l
m
n
o
p
q
r
s
t
u
v
w
x
y
z

delicious *adjective* délicieux (*Fem.* délicieuse).

delighted *adjective* ravi; **they're delighted with their new flat** ils sont ravis de leur nouvel appartement; **I'm delighted to hear you can come** je suis ravi d'apprendre que vous pouvez venir.

deliver *verb* **1** livrer [1]; **they're delivering the washing machine tomorrow** ils vont livrer la machine à laver demain; **2** distribuer [1] (*mail*).

delivery *noun* livraison *Fem.*

demand *noun* demande *Fem.*
demand *verb* exiger [52].

demo *noun* (*protest*) manif *Fem.* (*informal*).

democracy *noun* démocratie *Fem.*

democratic *adjective* démocratique.

demolish *verb* démolir [2].

demonstrate *verb* **1** faire [10] la démonstration de (*a machine, product, or technique*); **2** (*protest*) manifester [1]; **to demonstrate against something** manifester contre quelque chose.

demonstration *noun* **1** (*of machine, product, technique*) démonstration *Fem.*; **2** (*protest*) manifestation.

demonstrator *noun* (*in protest*) manifestant *Masc.*, manifestante *Fem.*

denim *noun* jean *Masc.*; **a denim jacket** un blouson en jean.

Denmark *noun* Danemark *Masc.*; **in Denmark** au Danemark; **to Denmark** au Danemark.

dense *adjective* dense.

dent *noun* bosse *Fem.*
dent *verb* cabosser [1].

dental *adjective* **1** dentaire; **dental floss** du fil dentaire; **dental hygiene** l'hygiène dentaire; **2 a dental appointment** un rendez-vous chez le dentiste.

dental surgeon *noun* chirurgien-dentiste *Masc.*

dentist *noun* dentiste *Masc. & Fem.*; **my mum's a dentist** ma mère est dentiste.

deny *verb* nier [1].

deodorant *noun* déodorant *Masc.*

depart *verb* partir [58].

department *noun* **1** (*in school, university*) département *Masc.*; **the language department** le département de langues; **2** (*in a shop*) rayon *Masc.*; **the men's department** le rayon hommes.

department store *noun* grand magasin *Masc.*

departure *noun* départ *Masc.*

departure lounge *noun* salle *Fem.* d'embarquement.

depend *verb* **to depend on** dépendre [3] de; **it depends on the price** ça dépend du prix; **it depends on what you want** ça dépend de ce que tu veux; **it depends** ça dépend.

deposit *noun* **1** (*when renting or hiring*) caution *Fem.*; **2** (*when booking a holiday or hotel room*) arrhes *Fem. plural*; **to pay a deposit** verser des arrhes; **3** (*on a bottle*) consigne *Fem.*

depressed *adjective* déprimé.

epressing *adjective* déprimant.

epth *noun* profondeur *Fem.*

eputy *noun* adjoint *Masc.*, adjointe *Fem.*.

eputy head *noun* directeur *Masc.* adjoint, directrice *Fem.* adjointe.

escend *verb* descendre [3].

escribe *verb* décrire [38].

escription *noun* description *Fem.*

esert *noun* désert *Masc.*; **in the desert** dans le désert.

esert island *noun* île *Fem.* déserte.

eserve *verb* mériter [1].

esign *noun* **1** conception *Fem.*; **the design of the plane** la conception de l'avion; **2** (*artistic design*) design *Masc.*; **fashion design** le stylisme; **3** (*pattern*) motif *Masc.*; **a floral design** un motif floral.
design *verb* **1** concevoir [66] (*a machine, plane, system*); **2** créer [32] (*costumes, clothes, fabric, scenery*).

esigner *noun* **1** (*fashion designer*) styliste *Masc. & Fem.*; **2** (*graphic designer*) graphiste *Masc. & Fem.*.

esire *noun* désir *Masc.*
desire *verb* désirer [1].

esk *noun* **1** (*in office or at home*) bureau *Masc.*; **2** (*pupil's*) table *Fem.*; **3** **the reception desk** la réception; **the information desk** le bureau des renseignements.

espair *noun* désespoir *Masc.*
despair *verb* **to despair of doing** désespérer [24] de faire.

esperate *adjective* **1** désespéré; **a desperate attempt** une tentative

désespérée; **2** **to be desperate to do** avoir très envie de faire; **I'm desperate to see you** j'ai très envie de te voir.

despise *verb* mépriser [1].

dessert *noun* dessert *Masc.*; **what's for dessert?** qu'est-ce qu'il y a comme dessert?

destination *noun* destination *Fem.*

destroy *verb* détruire [26].

destruction *noun* destruction *Fem.*

detached house *noun* maison *Fem.* individuelle.

detail *noun* détail *Masc.*

detailed *adjective* détaillé.

detective *noun* **1** (*police*) inspecteur *Masc.* de police; **2 a private detective** un détective.

detective story *noun* roman *Masc.* policier.

detention *noun* retenue *Fem.*

detergent *noun* détergent *Masc.*

determined *adjective* résolu; **he's determined to leave** il est résolu de partir.

detour *noun* détour *Masc.*

develop *verb* **1** développer [1]; **to get a film developed** faire développer une pellicule; **2** se développer; **how children develop** comment les enfants se développent.

developing country *noun* pays *Masc.* en voie de développement.

development *noun* développement *Masc.*

devil *noun* diable *Masc.*

a
b
c
d
e
f
g
h
i
j
k
l
m
n
o
p
q
r
s
t
u
v
w
x
y
z

devoted *adjective* dévoué.

dew *noun* rosée *Fem.*

diabetes *noun* diabète *Masc.*

diabetic *noun, adjective* diabète *Masc. & Fem.*; **to be (a) diabetic** être diabète.

diaeresis *noun* tréma *Masc.*

diagnosis *noun* diagnostic *Masc.*

diagonal *adjective* diagonal (*Masc. plural* diagonaux).

diagram *noun* schéma *Masc.*

dial *verb* composer [1] le numéro; **lift the receiver and dial 142** décrochez et composez le 142; **dial 00 33 for France** faites le 00 33 pour la France.

dialling tone *noun* tonalité *Fem.*

dialogue *noun* dialogue *Masc.*

diameter *noun* diamètre *Masc.*

diamond *noun* **1** diamant *Masc.*; **2** (*in cards*) carreau; **the jack of diamonds** le valet de carreau; **3** (*shape*) losange *Masc.*

diarrhoea *noun* diarrhée *Fem.*; **to have diarrhoea** avoir la diarrhoée.

diary *noun* **1** agenda *Masc.*; **j'ai marqué la date de la réunion dans mon agenda** I've noted the date of the meeting in my diary; **2** journal intime; **to keep a diary** tenir un journal (intime).

dice *noun* dé *Masc.*; **to throw the dice** jeter le dé.

dictation *noun* dictée *Fem.*

dictionary *noun* dictionnaire *Masc.*; **to look up a word in the dictionary** chercher un mot dans le dictionnaire.

did *verb* SEE **do**.

die *verb* **1** mourir [54]; **my grannie died in January** ma grand-mère es morte en janvier; **2 to be dying to do** mourir d'envie de faire; **I'm dying to see them!** je meurs d'envie de les voir!

● **to die out** disparaître [27].

diesel *noun* **1** gazole *Masc.*; **2 a diesel engine** un moteur diesel; **a diesel car** une voiture diesel.

diet *noun* **1** alimentation *Fem.*; **to have a healthy diet** avoir une alimentation saine; **2** (*slimming or special*) régime *Masc.*; **to be on a die** être au régime; **a salt-free diet** un régime sans sel.

difference *noun* **1** différence *Fem.* **I can't see any difference between the two** je ne vois pas la différence entre les deux; **what's the difference between ...?** quelle est la différence entre ...?; **2 it makes a difference** ça change quelque chose; **it makes no difference** ça ne change rien; **it makes no difference what I say** je peux dire ce que je veux, ça ne change rien.

different *adjective* différent; **the two sisters are very different** les deux sœurs sont très différentes; **she's very different from her sister** elle est très différente de sa sœur.

difficult *adjective* difficile; **it's really difficult** c'est vraiment difficile; **it's difficult to decide** il est difficile de décider.

difficulty *noun* **1** difficulté *Fem.*; **2 to have difficulty doing** avoir d mal à faire; **I had difficulty finding your house** j'ai eu du mal à trouver ta maison.

dig *verb* **to dig a hole** creuser [1] un trou.

digestion *noun* digestion *Fem.*

digital *adjective* numérique; **a digital recording** un enregistrement numérique; **a digital watch** une montre à affichage numérique.

dim *adjective* **1 a dim light** une lumière faible; **2 she's a bit dim** elle est un peu bouchée (*informal*).

dimension *noun* dimension *Fem.*

din *noun* vacarme *Masc.*; **they were making a dreadful din** ils faisaient un vacarme pas possible; **stop making such a din!** arrêtez de faire ce vacarme!

dinghy *noun* **1 a sailing dinghy** un dériveur; **2 a rubber dinghy** un canot pneumatique.

dining room *noun* salle *Fem.* à manger ; **in the dining room** dans la salle à manger.

dinner *noun* **1** (*evening*) dîner *Masc.*; **to invite somebody to dinner** inviter quelqu'un à dîner; **2** (*midday*) déjeuner *Masc.*; **to have school dinner** manger à la cantine.

dinner party *noun* dîner *Masc.*

dinner time *noun* **1** (*evening*) l'heure du dîner; **2** (*midday*) l'heure du déjeuner.

dinosaur *noun* dinosaure *Masc.*

diploma *noun* diplôme *Masc.*

direct *adjective* direct; **a direct flight** un vol direct.

direct *adverb* directement; **the bus goes direct to the airport** le bus est direct pour l'aéroport.

direct *verb* **1** réaliser [1] (*programme, film*); **2** mettre en scène (*play*); **3** régler (*traffic*).

direction *noun* **1** direction *Fem.*; **in the other direction** dans l'autre direction; **2 to ask somebody for directions** demander son chemin à quelqu'un; **3 directions for use** mode *Masc.* d'emploi.

directly *adverb* **1** directement; **2 directly afterwards** immédiatement après.

director *noun* **1** (*of a company*) directeur *Masc.*, directrice *Fem.*; **2** (*of a programme or film*) réalisateur *Masc.*, réalisatrice *Fem.*; **3** (*of a play*) metteur *Masc.* en scène.

directory *noun* annuaire *Masc.*; **to be ex-directory** être sur la liste rouge.

dirt *noun* saleté *Fem.*

dirty *adjective* sale; **my hands are dirty** j'ai les mains sales; **to get something dirty** salir quelque chose; **you'll get your dress dirty** tu vas salir ta robe; **to get dirty** se salir; **the curtains get dirty quickly** les rideaux se salissent vite.

disability *noun* infirmité *Fem.*, handicap *Masc.*; **does he have a disability?** est-il infirme?

disabled *adjective* handicapé; **disabled people** les handicapés.

disadvantage *noun* **1** désavantage *Masc.*; **2 to be at a disadvantage** être désavantagé.

a
b
c
d
e
f
g
h
i
j
k
l
m
n
o
p
q
r
s
t
u
v
w
x
y
z

disagree *verb* **I disagree** je ne suis pas d'accord; **I disagree with James** je ne suis pas d'accord avec James.

disappear *verb* disparaître [27].

disappearance *noun* disparition *Fem.*

disappointed *adjective* déçu; **I was disappointed with my marks** j'ai été déçu par mes notes.

disappointment *noun* déception *Fem.*

disaster *noun* désastre *Masc.*; **it was a complete disaster** ça a été un désastre complet.

disastrous *adjective* désastreux (*Fem.* désastreuse).

disc *noun* **1 a compact disc** un disque compact; **2 a slipped disc** une hernie discale; **3 a tax disc** (*for a vehicle*) une vignette.

discipline *noun* discipline *Fem.*

disc-jockey *noun* disc-jockey *Masc.*

disco *noun* **1** soirée *Fem.* disco; **they're having a disco** ils font une soirée disco; **2** (*club*) discothèque.

disconnect *verb* **1** (*the telephone, electricity*) couper [1]; **have you disconnected the electricity?** est-ce que vous avez coupé l'électricité?; **2** (*appliance*) débrancher [1].

discount *noun* réduction *Fem.*

discourage *verb* décourager [52].

discover *verb* découvrir [30].

discovery *noun* découverte *Fem.*

discreet *adjective* discret (*Fem.* discrète).

discrimination *noun* discrimination *Fem.*; **racial discrimination** la discrimination raciale.

discuss *verb* **to discuss something** discuter [1] de quelque chose; **we'll discuss the problem tomorrow** nous discuterons du problème demain; **I'm going to discuss it with Phil** je vais en discuter avec Phil.

discussion *noun* discussion *Fem.*

disease *noun* maladie *Fem.*

disgraceful *adjective* scandaleux (*Fem.* scandaleuse).

disguise *noun* déguisement *Masc.*; **to be in disguise** être déguisé. **disguise** *verb* déguiser [1]; **disguised as a woman** déguisé en femme.

disgust *noun* dégoût *Masc.*

disgusted *adjective* dégoûté.

disgusting *adjective* dégoûtant.

dish *noun* **1** plat *Masc.*; **a large white dish** un grand plat blanc; **he cooked my favourite dish** il a préparé mon plat favori; **2 to do the dishes** faire la vaisselle.

dishcloth *noun* (*for drying up*) torchon *Masc.*

dishonest *adjective* malhonnête.

dishonesty *noun* malhonnêteté *Fem.*

dish towel *noun* torchon *Masc.*

dishwasher *noun* lave-vaisselle *Masc.*

disinfect *verb* désinfecter [1].

disinfectant *noun* désinfectant *Masc.*

sk noun disque Masc.; **a floppy disk** une disquette; **the hard disk** le disque dur.

sk drive noun unité Fem. de disque; **the floppy disk drive** le lecteur de disquettes.

skette noun disquette Fem.

slike verb ne pas aimer [1]; **I dislike sport** je n'aime pas le sport.

smay noun consternation Fem.

smiss verb licencier [1] (an employee).

sobedient adjective désobéissant.

sobey verb désobéir à [2] (a person); enfreindre [60] (a rule); **she disobeyed the rules** elle a enfreint les régles.

splay noun 1 exposition Fem.; **a handicrafts display** une exposition d'artisanat; **to be on display** être exposé; 2 **a window display** une vitrine; 3 **a firework display** un feu d'artifice.

display verb exposer [1].

sposable adjective jetable.

spute noun dispute Fem.

squalify verb disqualifier [1].

srupt verb perturber [1].

ssolve verb dissoudre [67].

stance noun distance Fem.; **from a distance** de loin; **in the distance** au loin; **it's within walking distance** on peut y aller à pied.

stant adjective lointain.

stinct adjective net (Fem. nette).

distinctly adverb 1 distinctement; 2 **it's distinctly odd** c'est vraiment bizarre.

distract verb distraire [78].

distribute verb distribuer [1].

district noun 1 (in town) quartier Masc.; **a poor district of Paris** un quartier pauvre de Paris; 2 (in the country) région Fem.

disturb verb déranger [52]; **sorry to disturb you** je suis désolé de vous déranger; **do not disturb** ne pas déranger.

ditch noun fossé Masc.
ditch verb **to ditch somebody** plaquer [1] quelqu'un (informal).

dive noun plongeon Masc.
dive verb plonger [52].

diver noun plongeur Masc., plongeuse Fem..

diversion noun (traffic) déviation Fem.

divide verb diviser [1].

diving noun plongée Fem.

diving board noun plongeoir Masc.

division noun division Fem.

divorce noun divorce Masc.
divorce verb divorcer [61]; **they divorced in Mexico** ils ont divorcé au Mexique.

divorced adjective divorcé; **my parents are divorced** mes parents sont divorcés.

DIY noun bricolage Masc.; **to do DIY** faire du bricolage; **a DIY shop** un magasin de bricolage.

dizzy adjective **I feel dizzy** j'ai la tête qui tourne.

a
b
c
d
e
f
g
h
i
j
k
l
m
n
o
p
q
r
s
t
u
v
w
x
y
z

DJ *noun* disc jockey *Masc.*

do *verb* **1** faire [10]; **what are you doing?** qu'est-ce que tu fais?; **I'm doing my homework** je fais mes devoirs; **what have you done with the hammer?** qu'est-ce que tu as fait du marteau?; **2** (*questions in French are formed either with 'est-ce que' or by putting the pronoun subject after the verb and a hyphen between them*) **do you want some strawberries?** est-ce que tu veux des fraises?, veux-tu des fraises?; **when does it start?** quand est-ce que ça commence?; **how did you open the door?** comment as-tu ouvert la porte?; **3** (*in negative sentences*) **don't, doesn't, didn't** ne ...pas; **I don't like mushrooms** je n'aime pas les champignons; **Rosie doesn't like spinach** Rosie n'aime pas les épinards; **you didn't shut the door** tu n'as pas fermé la porte; **it doesn't matter** ça ne fait rien; **4** (*when it refers back to another verb, 'do' is not translated*) **'do you live here?' – 'yes, I do'** est-ce que tu habites ici?' – 'oui'; **she has more money than I do** elle a plus d'argent que moi; **'I live in Oxford' – 'so do I'** 'j'habite à Oxford' – 'moi aussi'; **'I didn't phone Gemma' – 'neither did I'** 'je n'ai pas appelé Gemma' – 'moi non plus'; **5 don't you?, doesn't he? etc.** n'est-ce pas?; **you know Helen, don't you?** tu connais Helen, n'est-ce pas?; **she left on Thursday, didn't she?** elle est partie jeudi, n'est-ce pas?; **6 that'll do** ça ira; **it'll do like that** ça ira comme ça.

● **to do something up 1** lacer [61]

(*shoes*); **2** boutonner [1] (*cardigan, jacket*); **3** retaper [1] (*house*).

● **to do with 1** regarder [1]; **it has nothing to do with him/you** ça n[e] le/te regarde pas; **2 to do with something: I could do with a re[st]** j'aurai bien besoin de me reposer.

● **to do without** se passer [1] de; **w[e] can do without knives** on peut s[e] passer de couteaux.

doctor *noun* médecin *Masc.*; **her mother's a doctor** sa mère est médecin.

document *noun* document *Masc.*

documentary *noun* documentaire *Masc.*

dodgems *plural noun* **the dodgems** les autos *Fem. plural* tamponneuses.

dog *noun* chien *Masc.*; (*female*) chienne *Fem.*

do-it-yourself *noun* bricolage *Masc.*

dole *noun* allocations *Fem. plural* chômage; **to be on the dole** être a[u] chômage.

doll *noun* poupée *Fem.*

dollar *noun* dollar *Masc.*

dolphin *noun* dauphin *Masc.*

Dominican *noun* Dominicain *Masc.*, Dominicaine *Fem.*
Dominican *adjective* dominicain

Dominican Republic *noun* République *Fem.* dominicaine.

domino *noun* domino *Masc.*; **to pla[y] dominoes** jouer aux dominos.

don't SEE **do**.

donation *noun* don *Masc.*

donkey *noun* âne *Masc.*

door noun **1** porte Fem.; **to open the door** ouvrir la porte; **to shut the door** fermer la porte; **2** (*of a vehicle or train*) portière Fem.

doorbell noun sonnerie Fem.; **to ring the doorbell** sonner à la porte; **there's the doorbell!** on sonne!

doorstep noun pas Masc. de la porte.

dormitory noun dortoir Masc.

dot noun **1** (*written*) point Masc.; **2** (*on fabric*) pois Masc.; **3 at ten on the dot** à dix heures pile.

double adjective, adverb **1** double; **a double helping** une double portion; **a double whisky** un double whisky; **2** le double; **double the time** le double du temps; **double the price** le double du prix; **3 a double room** une chambre pour deux personnes; **4 a double bed** un grand lit.

double bass noun contrebasse Fem.; **to play the double bass** jouer de la contrebasse.

double-breasted adjective **a double-breasted jacket** une veste croisée.

double-decker bus noun autobus Masc. à impériale.

double glazing noun double vitrage Masc.

doubles noun (*in tennis*) double Masc.; **to play a game of doubles** faire un double.

doubt noun doute Masc.; **there's no doubt about it** il n'y a aucun doute là-dessus; **I have my doubts** j'ai des doutes.

doubt verb **to doubt something** douter [1] de quelque chose; **I doubt it** j'en doute; **I doubt that** douter que (+ *subjunctive*); **I doubt they'll do it** je doute qu'ils le fassent.

doubtful adjective **1** pas sûr; **it's doubtful** ce n'est pas sûr; **2 to be doubtful about doing** hésiter à faire; **I'm doubtful about inviting them together** j'hésite à les inviter ensemble.

dough noun pâte Fem.

doughnut noun beignet Masc.

Dover noun Douvres; **to Dover** à Douvres.

down adverb, preposition **1** en bas; **he's down in the cellar** il est en bas dans la cave; **2 down the road** (*nearby*) à côté; **there's a chemist's just down the road** il y a une pharmacie juste à côté; **3 to go down** descendre; **I went down to the kitchen** je suis descendu dans la cuisine; **to walk down the street** descendre la rue; **to run down the stairs** descendre les escaliers en courant; **4 to come down** descendre; **she came down from her bedroom** elle est descendue de sa chambre; **5 to sit down** s'asseoir; **she sat down on the sofa** elle s'est assise sur le canapé.

downstairs adverb **1** en bas; **she's downstairs in the sitting-room** elle est en bas dans le salon; **the dog sleeps downstairs** le chien dort en bas; **2** du dessous; **the flat downstairs** l'appartement du dessous; **the people downstairs** les voisins du dessous.

doze verb sommeiller [1].

a
b
c
d
e
f
g
h
i
j
k
l
m
n
o
p
q
r
s
t
u
v
w
x
y
z

dozen *noun* douzaine *Fem.*; **a dozen eggs** une douzaine d'œufs.

drag *noun* **what a drag!** quelle barbe! (*informal*); **she's a bit of a drag** elle n'est pas marrante (*informal*).
drag *verb* traîner [1].

dragon *noun* dragon *Masc.*

drain *noun* égout *Masc.*
drain *verb* égoutter [1] (*vegetables*).

drama *noun* **1** (*subject*) art *Masc.* dramatique; **2 he made a big drama about it** il en a fait tout un cinéma (*informal*).

dramatic *adjective* spectaculaire.

draught *noun* courant *Masc.* d'air.

draughts *noun* dames *Fem. plural*; **to play draughts** jouer aux dames.

draw *noun* **1** (*in a match*) match nul *Masc.*; **it was a draw** ils ont fait match nul; **2** (*lottery*) tirage *Masc.* au sort.
draw *verb* **1** dessiner [1]; **I can't draw horses** je ne sais pas dessiner les chevaux; **she can draw really well** elle dessine vraiment bien; **2 to draw a picture** faire [10] un dessin; **3 to draw the curtains** tirer [1] les rideaux; **4 to draw a crowd** attirer [1] une foule de spectateurs; **5** (*in a match*) faire [10] match nul; **we drew three all** nous avons fait match nul trois à trois; **6 to draw lots** tirer [1] au sort.

drawback *noun* inconvénient *Masc.*

drawer *noun* tiroir *Masc.*

drawing *noun* dessin *Masc.*

drawing pin *noun* punaise *Fem.*

dreadful *adjective* affreux (*Fem.* affreuse).

dreadfully *adverb* terriblement; **I'm dreadfully late** je suis terriblement en retard; **I'm dreadfully sorry** je suis vraiment navré.

dream *noun* rêve *Masc.*; **to have a dream** faire un rêve; **I had a horrible dream last night** j'ai fait un rêve horrible cette nuit.
dream *verb* rêver [1]; **to dream about something** rêver de quelqu chose.

drenched *adjective* trempé; **to ge drenched** se faire tremper; **we got drenched on the way home** on s'est fait tremper en rentrant.

dress *noun* robe *Fem.*
dress *verb* **to dress a child** habiller [1] un enfant.
● **to dress up** se déguiser [1]; **to dress up as a vampire** se déguise en vampire.

dressed *adjective* **1** habillé; **is Ton dressed yet?** est-ce que Tom est habillé?; **she was dressed in blac trousers and a yellow shirt** elle était habillée d'un pantalon noir et d'une chemise jaune; **2 to get dressed** s'habiller; **I got dressed quickly** je me suis vite habillé.

dresser *noun* (*for dishes*) vaisselie *Masc.*

dressing gown *noun* robe *Fem.* de chambre.

dressing table *noun* coiffeuse *Fem.*

rier *noun* **a hair drier** un sèche-cheveux; **a tumble drier** un sèche-linge.

rift *noun* **a snow drift** une congère.

rill *noun* perceuse *Fem.*

rink *noun* **1** boisson *Fem.*; **a hot drink** une boisson chaude; **a cold drink** une boisson fraîche; **2 would you like a drink?** tu veux boire quelque chose?; **3 to go out for a drink** aller prendre un pot (*informal*).

drink *verb* boire [22]; **he drank a glass of water** il a bu un verre d'eau.

rive *noun* **1 to go for a drive** faire un tour en voiture; **2** (*up to a house*) allée *Fem.*

drive *verb* **1** conduire [26]; **she drives very fast** elle conduit très vite; **to drive a car** conduire une voiture; **I'd like to learn to drive** j'aimerais apprendre à conduire; **can you drive?** tu sais conduire?; **2** aller en voiture; **we drove to Paris** nous somes allés à Paris en voiture; **3 to drive somebody (to a place)** emmener [50] quelqu'un en voiture; **Mum drove me to the station** Maman m'a emmené en voiture à la gare; **to drive somebody home** raccompagner [1] quelqu'un; ★ **she drives me mad!** elle me rend folle!

river *noun* **1** conducteur *Masc.*, conductrice *Fem.*; **2** (*of a taxi or bus*) chauffeur *Masc.*

riving instructor *noun* moniteur *Masc.* d'auto-école.

riving lesson *noun* leçon *Fem.* de conduite.

driving licence *noun* permis *Masc.* de conduire.

driving school *noun* école *Fem.* de conduite.

driving test *noun* permis *Masc.* de conduire; **to take your driving test** passer son permis; **Jenny's passed her driving test** Jenny a eu son permis.

drop *noun* goutte *Fem.*
drop *verb* **1 to drop something** laisser [1] tomber quelque chose; **I dropped my glasses** j'ai laissé tomber mes lunettes; **I'm going to drop history next year** je vais laisser tomber l'histoire l'année prochaine; **drop it!** laisse tomber!; **2** déposer [1] (*a person*); **could you drop me at the station?** est-ce que tu peux me déposer à la gare?

drought *noun* sécheresse *Fem.*

drown *verb* se noyer [39]; **she drowned in the lake** elle s'est noyée dans le lac.

drug *noun* **1** (*medicine*) médicament *Masc.*; **2** (*illegal*) **drugs** la drogue.

drug abuse *noun* usage *Masc.* des stupéfiants.

drug addict *noun* toxicomane *Masc. & Fem.*

drug addiction *noun* toxicomanie *Fem.*

drum *noun* **1** tambour *Masc.*; **2 drums** la batterie; **to play drums** jouer de la batterie.

drum kit *noun* batterie *Fem.*

drummer *noun* batteur *Masc.*, batteuse *Fem.*

drunk noun ivrogne Masc. & Fem.
drunk adjective ivre.

dry adjective sec (Fem. sèche).
dry verb 1 sécher [24]; **to let
something dry** laisser [1] sécher
quelque chose; **2 to dry your hair** se
sécher les cheveux; **3 to dry your
hands** s'essuyer [41] les mains; **to
dry the dishes** s'essuyer [41] la
vaisselle; **4 to dry the washing**
faire [10] sécher le linge.

dry cleaner's noun teinturerie
Fem.

dryer noun SEE **drier**.

dual carriageway noun route
Fem. à quatre voies.

dubbed adjective **a dubbed film** un
film doublé.

duck noun canard Masc.

due adjective, adverb 1 **to be due to
do** devoir faire; **we're due to leave
on Thursday** nous devons partir
jeudi; **Paul's due back soon** Paul
doit bientôt revenir; **2 due to** en
raison de; **the match has been
cancelled due to bad weather** le
match a été annulé en raison du
mauvais temps.

duke noun duc Masc.

dull adjective 1 **dull weather** un
temps maussade; **it's a dull day
today** il fait un temps maussade
aujourd'hui; **2** (boring) ennuyeux
(Fem. ennuyeuse).

dumb adjective 1 muet (Fem.
muette); **to be deaf and dumb** être
sourd-muet; **2** (stupid) bête; **he
asked some dumb questions** il a
posé des questions bêtes.

dummy noun (for a baby) tétine
Fem.

dump verb 1 jeter [48] (rubbish);
2 plaquer [1] (a person) (informal);
she's dumped her boyfriend elle a
plaqué son copain.

dune noun dune Fem.

dungarees plural noun salopett
Fem. singular.

dungeon noun cachot Masc.

Dunkirk noun Dunkerque.

during preposition pendant; **durin
the night** pendant la nuit; **I saw he
during the holidays** je l'ai vue
pendant les vacances.

dusk noun **at dusk** à la nuit
tombante.

dust noun poussière Fem.
dust verb épousseter [48].

dustbin noun poubelle Fem.; **to pu
something in the dustbin** jeter
quelque chose à la poubelle.

dustman noun éboueur Masc.

dusty adjective poussiéreux (Fem.
poussiéreuse).

Dutch noun 1 (language)
hollandais Masc.; **2 the Dutch**
(people) les Hollandais Masc. plural.
Dutch adjective hollandais.

duty noun 1 devoir Masc.; **to have
duty to do** avoir le devoir de faire;
you have a duty to inform us vou
avez le devoir de nous informer; **2 t
be on duty** être de service; **to be o
night duty** être de service de nuit;
I'm off duty tonight je ne suis pas
de service ce soir.

duty-free adjective hors taxes; **th
duty-free shops** les boutiques hor

axes; **duty-free purchases** les achats hors taxes.

uvet noun couette Fem.

uvet cover noun housse Fem. de couette.

VD noun DVD Masc.

warf noun nain Masc., naine Fem.

ye noun teinture Fem.

dye verb teindre [60]; **to dye your hair** se teindre les cheveux; **I'm going to dye my hair pink** je vais me teindre les cheveux en rose.

ynamic adjective dynamique.

yslexia noun dyslexie Fem.

yslexic adjective dyslexique.

Ee

ach adjective chaque; **each time** chaque fois; **curtains for each window** des rideaux pour chaque fenêtre.

each pronoun chacun (Fem. chacune); **my sisters each have a computer** mes sœurs ont chacune un ordinateur; **she gave us an apple each** elle nous a donné une pomme à chacun; **each of you** chacun de vous, chacune de vous; **we each got a present** chacun de nous a reçu un cadeau; **the tickets cost ten pounds each** les billets coûtent dix livres chacun.

ach other pronoun ('each other' is usually translated using a reflexive pronoun) **they love each other** ils s'aiment; **we know each other** nous nous connaissons; **do you** often see each other? est-ce que vous vous voyez souvent?

eagle noun aigle Masc.

ear noun oreille Fem.

earache noun **to have earache** avoir une otite.

earlier adverb **1** (a while ago) tout à l'heure; **your brother phoned earlier** ton frère a appelé tout à l'heure; **2** (not as late) plus tôt; **we should have started earlier** nous aurions dû commencer plus tôt; **earlier in the morning** plus tôt le matin.

early adverb **1** (in the morning) tôt; **to get up early** se lever tôt; **it's too early** il est trop tôt; **2** (for an appointment) en avance; **we're early, the train doesn't leave until ten** nous sommes en avance, le train ne part qu'à dix heures; **Grandma likes to be early** Grand-mère aime être en avance.
early adjective **1** (one of the first) premier (Fem. première); **in the early months** pendant les premiers mois; **I'm getting the early train** je prends le premier train; **2 to have an early lunch** déjeuner tôt; **Jan's having an early night** Jan va se coucher tôt; **we're making an early start** nous partons tôt; **3 in the early afternoon** en début d'après-midi; **in the early hours** au petit matin.

earn verb gagner [1] (money); **Richard earns four pounds an hour** Richard gagne quatre livres de l'heure.

earnings plural noun salaire Masc.

a
b
c
d
e
f
g
h
i
j
k
l
m
n
o
p
q
r
s
t
u
v
w
x
y
z

a

b

c

d

e

f

g

h

i

j

k

l

m

n

o

p

q

r

s

t

u

v

w

x

y

z

earphones noun casque Masc.

earring noun boucle Fem. d'oreille.

earth noun terre Fem.; **life on earth** la vie sur terre; ★ **what on earth are you doing?** mais qu'est-ce que tu fais là?

earthquake noun tremblement Masc. de terre.

easily adverb **1** (without difficulty) facilement; **2** (by far) de loin; **he's easily the best** il est de loin le meilleur.

east noun est Masc.; **in the east** à l'est.

east adjective, adverb est; **the east side** le côté est; **an east wind** un vent d'est; **east of Paris** à l'est de Paris.

Easter noun Pâques Masc.; **they're coming at Easter** ils viennent à Pâques; **Happy Easter** Joyeuses Pâques.

Easter Day noun dimanche Masc. de Pâques.

Easter egg noun œuf Masc. de Pâques.

Eastern Europe noun Europe Fem. de l'Est.

easy adjective facile; **it's easy!** c'est facile!; **it was easy to make** c'était facile à faire.

eat verb **1** manger [52]; **he was eating a banana** il mangeait une banane; **we're going to have something to eat** nous allons manger quelque chose; **2** prendre [64] (a meal); **we were eating breakfast** nous prenions le petit déjeuner; **3 to eat out** manger au restaurant.

EC noun (short for European Community) CE Fem., Communauté Fem. européenne.

echo noun écho Masc.

echo verb retentir [2].

eclipse noun éclipse Fem.

ecological adjective écologique

ecologist noun écologiste Masc. Fem.

ecology noun écologie Fem.

economic adjective **1** (to do with the economy) économique; **2** (profitable) rentable.

economical adjective **1** économe (a person); **2** économique (way of doing something); **it's more economical to buy a big one** c'est plus économique d'acheter un grand.

economics noun économie Fem.

economy noun économie Fem.

eczema noun eczéma Masc.

edge noun **1** bord Masc.; **the edge of the table** le bord de la table; **at the edge of the lake** au bord du lac; **2 to be on edge** être énervé.

edible adjective comestible.

Edinburgh noun Édimbourg.

edit verb éditer [1].

editor noun (of a newspaper) rédacteur Masc. en chef, rédactrice Fem. en chef.

educate verb (a teacher) instruire [26].

education noun éducation Fem.

educational adjective éducatif (Fem. éducative).

effect *noun* effet *Masc.*; **the effect of the accident** l'effet de l'accident; **to have an effect on** avoir un effet sur; **it had a good effect on the whole family** ça a eu un bon effet sur toute la famille; **special effects** les effets spéciaux.

effective *adjective* efficace.

efficient *adjective* efficace.

effort *noun* effort *Masc.*; **to make an effort** faire un effort; **David made an effort to help us** David a fait un effort pour nous aider; **he didn't even make the effort to apologize** il n'a même pas fait l'effort pour s'excuser.

e.g. par ex.

egg *noun* œuf *Masc.*; **a dozen eggs** une douzaine d'œufs; **a fried egg** un œuf au plat; **two boiled eggs** deux œufs à la coque; **a hard-boiled egg** un œuf dur; **scrambled eggs** les œufs brouillés.

egg-cup *noun* coquetier *Masc.*

eggshell *noun* coquille *Fem.* d'œuf.

egg-white *noun* blanc *Masc.* d'œuf.

egg-yolk *noun* jaune *Masc.* d'œuf.

eight *number* huit *Masc.*; **Maya's eight** Maya a huit ans; **at eight o'clock** à huit heures.

eighteen *number* dix-huit *Masc.*; **Jason's eighteen** Jason a dix-huit ans.

eighth *number* **1** huitième; **2 the eighth of July** le huit juillet; **on the eighth floor** au huitième étage.

eighty *number* quatre-vingts; **eighty-five** quatre-vingt-cinq (note

that the 's' disappears when another number follows).

Eire *noun* la République d'Irlande; **in Eire** en République d'Irlande.

either *pronoun* **1** (*one or the other*) l'un ou l'autre; **choose either (of them)** choisis l'un ou l'autre; **I don't like either (of them)** je n'aime ni l'un ni l'autre; **2** (*both*) les deux; **either is possible** tous les deux sont possibles.

either *conjunction* **1 either … or** ou … ou; **either Thursday or Friday** ou jeudi ou vendredi; **either Susie or Judy** ou Susie ou Judy; **he either wrote or phoned** il a ou écrit ou appelé; **2** (*with a negative*) non plus; **he doesn't want to either** il ne veut pas non plus; **I don't know them either** je ne les connais pas non plus.

elastic *noun, adjective* élastique *Masc.*

elastic band *noun* élastique *Masc.*

elbow *noun* coude *Masc.*

elder *adjective* aîné; **her elder brother** son frère aîné.

elderly *adjective* âgé; **the elderly** les personnes *Fem. plural* âgées.

eldest *adjective* aîné; **her eldest brother** son frère aîné.

elect *verb* élire [51]; **she has been elected** elle a été élue.

election *noun* élection *Fem.*; **in the election** aux élections; **to call a general election** fixer les élections législatives.

electric *adjective* électrique.

electrical *adjective* électrique.

electrician noun électricien Masc., électricienne Fem.

electricity noun électricité Fem.; **to turn off the electricity** couper le courant.

electronic adjective électronique.

electronic mail noun courrier Masc. électronique.

electronics noun électronique Fem.

elegant adjective élégant.

element noun élément Masc.

elephant noun éléphant Masc.

eleven number onze Masc.; **Josh is eleven** Josh a onze ans; **at eleven o'clock** à onze heures; **a football eleven** une équipe de football.

eleventh number onzième; **the eleventh of May** le onze mai; **on the eleventh floor** à l'onzième étage.

eliminate verb éliminer [1].

else adverb 1 d'autre; **somebody else** quelqu'un d'autre; **did you see anyone else?** as-tu vu quelqu'un d'autre?; **nothing else** rien d'autre; **I don't want anything else** je ne veux rien d'autre; 2 **something else** autre chose; **would you like something else?** désirez-vous autre chose?; 3 **somewhere else** ailleurs; 4 **or else** sinon; **hurry up, or else we'll be late** dépêche-toi, sinon nous serons en retard.

email noun courrier Masc. électronique.

embankment noun 1 (by a river) quai Masc.; 2 (by a railway) remblai Masc.

embarrassed adjective gêné; **I was terribly embarrassed** j'étais très gêné.

embarrassing adjective gênant

embarrassment noun embarras Masc., gêne Fem.

embassy noun ambassade Fem.; **the French Embassy** l'ambassade de France.

embroider verb broder [1].

embroidery noun broderie Fem.

emergency noun cas Masc. d'urgence; **in an emergency, break the glass** en cas d'urgence, cassez la vitre; **it's an emergency!** c'est urgent!

emergency exit noun sortie Fem. de secours.

emergency landing noun atterrissage Masc. d'urgence.

emotion noun émotion Fem.

emotional adjective 1 ému (a person); **she was quite emotional** elle était tout émue; 2 (a speech or an occasion) chargé d'émotion.

emperor noun empereur Masc.

emphasis noun accent Masc.

emphasize verb **he emphasized that it wasn't compulsory** il a insisté sur le fait que ce n'était pas obligatoire.

empire noun empire Masc.; **the Roman Empire** l'Empire Romain.

employ verb employer [39].

employee noun salarié Masc., salariée Fem.

employer noun employeur Masc., employeuse Fem.

engine

mployment *noun* travail *Masc.*

mpress *noun* impératrice *Fem.*

mpty *adjective* vide; **an empty bottle** une bouteille vide; **the room was empty** la pièce était vide.

empty *verb* vider [1]; **I emptied the teapot into the sink** j'ai vidé la théière dans l'évier.

nchanting *adjective* ravissant.

nclose *verb* (*in a letter*) joindre [49]; **please find enclosed a cheque** veuillez trouver ci-joint un chèque.

ncore *noun* bis *Masc.*; **to give an encore** jouer un bis.

ncourage *verb* encourager [52]; **to encourage somebody to do something** encourager quelqu'un à faire quelque chose; **Mum encouraged me to try again** Maman m'a encouragé à recommencer.

ncouragement *noun* encouragement *Masc.*

ncouraging *adjective* encourageant.

ncyclopedia *noun* encyclopédie *Fem.*

nd *noun* **1** (*last part*) fin *Fem.*; **'The End'** 'Fin'; **at the end of the film** à la fin du film; **by the end of the day** à la fin de la journée; **in the end I went home** finalement je suis rentré chez moi; **Sally's coming at the end of June** Sally viendra fin juin; **2** (*of a table, garden, stick, or road, for example*) bout *Masc.*; **hold the other end** tiens l'autre bout; **at the end of the street** au bout de la rue; **3** (*in tennis or football*) côté

Masc.; **to change ends** changer de côté.

end *verb* **1** (*to put an end to*) mettre [11] fin à (*an arrangement*); **they've ended the strike** ils ont mis fin à la grève; **2** (*to come to an end*) se terminer [1]; **the day ended with a dinner** la journée s'est terminée par un dîner.

• **to end up 1 to end up doing** finir [2] par faire; **we ended up taking a taxi** nous avons fini par prendre un taxi; **2 to end up somewhere** se retrouver [1] quelque part; **Rob ended up in San Francisco** Rob s'est retrouvé à San Francisco.

endangered *adjective* menacé; **an endangered species** une espèce en voie d'extinction.

ending *noun* fin *Fem.*

endless *adjective* interminable (*a day or a journey, for example*).

enemy *noun* ennemi *Masc.*, ennemie *Fem.*; **to make enemies** se faire des ennemis.

energetic *adjective* énergique.

energy *noun* énergie *Fem.*

engaged *adjective* **1** (*to be married*) fiancé; **they're engaged** ils sont fiancés; **to get engaged** se fiancer [61]; **2** (*a phone or toilet*) occupé; **it's engaged, I'll ring later** c'est occupé, j'appellerai plus tard.

engagement *noun* (*to marry*) fiançailles *Fem.* plural.

engagement ring *noun* bague *Fem.* de fiançailles.

engine *noun* **1** (*in a car*) moteur *Masc.*; **2** (*pulling a train*) locomotive *Fem.*

a b c d e f g h i j k l m n o p q r s t u v w x y z

engineer noun 1 (who comes for repairs) technicien Masc.; 2 (who builds roads and bridges) ingénieur Masc.

engineering noun ingénierie Fem.; **to study engineering** faire des études d'ingénieur.

England noun Angleterre Fem.; **in England** en Angleterre; **to England** en Angleterre; **I am from England** je suis anglais.

English noun 1 (the language) anglais Masc.; **do you speak English?** parlez-vous anglais?; **he answered in English** il a répondu en anglais; 2 (English people) **the English** les Anglais Masc. plural. **English** adjective 1 (of or from England) anglais; **the English team** l'équipe anglaise; **2 an English lesson** un cours d'anglais; **our English teacher** notre professeur d'anglais.

English Channel noun **the English Channel** la Manche.

Englishman noun Anglais Masc.

Englishwoman noun Anglaise Fem.

enjoy verb 1 aimer [1]; **did you enjoy the party?** as-tu aimé la soirée?; **we really enjoyed the concert** nous avons beaucoup aimé le concert; **2 to enjoy doing** aimer faire; **I enjoy swimming** j'aime nager; **do you enjoy living in York?** aimez-vous vivre à York?; **3 to enjoy oneself** s'amuser [1]; **we really enjoyed ourselves** nous nous sommes très bien amusés; **enjoy yourselves!** amusez-vous bien!; **did**

you enjoy yourself? tu t'es bien amusé?

enjoyable adjective agréable.

enlarge verb agrandir [2] (a phot for example).

enlargement noun (of a photo) agrandissement Masc.

enormous adjective énorme.

enough adverb, pronoun 1 assez; **there's enough for everyone** il y e a assez pour tout le monde; 2 (followed by a noun) assez de; **is there enough bread?** est-ce qu'il a assez de pain?; 3 (followed by an adjective or adverb) suffisamment; **big enough** suffisamment grand; **slowly enough** suffisamment lentement; **4 that's enough** ça suffit.

enquire verb se renseigner [1]; **I'm going to enquire about the train** je vais me renseigner sur les train

enquiry noun demande Fem. de renseignements; **to make enquirie about something** demander des renseignements sur quelque chose

enrol verb s'inscrire [38]; **I want te enrol on the course** je veux m'inscrire au cours.

enter verb 1 (to go inside) entrer [1 dans (a room or building); **we all entered the church** nous sommes tous entrés dans l'église; **2 to ente for** s'inscrire [38] à (an exam or competition); s'inscrire pour (a race

entertain verb 1 (to keep amused divertir [2]; **something to entertai the children** quelque chose pour divertir les enfants; **2** (to have peop

414

round) recevoir [66]; **they don't entertain much** ils reçoivent peu.

ntertaining *noun* **they do a lot of entertaining** ils reçoivent beaucoup.

entertaining *adjective* amusant.

ntertainment *noun* (*fun*) distractions *Fem. plural*; **there wasn't much entertainment in the evenings** il n'y avait pas beaucoup de distractions le soir.

nthusiasm *noun* enthousiasme *Masc.*

nthusiast *noun* passionné *Masc.*, passionnée *Fem.*; **he's a rugby enthusiast** c'est un passionné de rugby.

nthusiastic *adjective* enthousiaste.

ntire *adjective* entier (*Fem.* entière); **the entire class** la classe entière.

ntirely *adverb* complètement.

ntrance *noun* entrée *Fem.*

ntry *noun* (*the way in*) entrée *Fem.*; **'no entry'** 'défense d'entrer'.

ntry phone *noun* interphone *Masc.*

nvelope *noun* enveloppe *Fem.*

nvious *adjective* envieux (*Fem.* envieuse); **he's envious of my exam results** il est jaloux de mes résultats d'examen.

nvironment *noun* environnement *Masc.*

nvironmental *adjective* écologique.

nvironment-friendly *adjective* écologique.

envy *noun* envie *Fem.*

epidemic *noun* épidémie *Fem.*

epileptic *noun* épileptique *Masc. & Fem.*

episode *noun* épisode *Masc.*

equal *adjective* égal (*Masc. plural* égaux); **in equal quantities** en quantités égales.
equal *verb* égaler [1].

equality *noun* égalité *Fem.*

equalize *verb* égaliser [1]; **they equalized in the last minute** ils ont égalisé dans la dernière minute.

equally *adverb* (*to share*) en parts égales; **we divided it equally** nous l'avons divisé en parts égales.

equator *noun* équateur *Masc.*

equip *verb* équiper [1]; **well equipped for the hike** bien équipé pour la randonnée; **equipped with rucksacks** équipés de sacs à dos.

equipment *noun* **1** (*for sport*) équipement *Masc.*; **2** matériel *Masc.*; **laboratory equipment** le matériel de laboratoire; **3** (*for sports*) équipement *Masc.*

equivalent *adjective* **to be equivalent to** être équivalent à.

error *noun* **1** (*in spelling or typing*) faute *Fem.*; **a spelling error** une faute d'orthographe; **2** (*in maths or on a computer*) erreur *Fem.*

error message *noun* message *Masc.* d'erreur.

escalator *noun* escalier *Masc.* mécanique.

escape *noun* (*from prison*) évasion *Fem.*

a
b
c
d
e
f
g
h
i
j
k
l
m
n
o
p
q
r
s
t
u
v
w
x
y
z

a b c d e f g h i j k l m n o p q r s t u v w x y z

escape *verb* **1** (*a person*) s'évader [1]; **2** (*an animal*) s'échapper [1].

escort *noun* escorte *Fem.*; **a police escort** une escorte de police.

especially *adjective* **1** (*above all*) surtout; **there are lots of tourists, especially in August** il y a beaucoup de touristes, surtout en août; **2** (*unusually*) particulièrement; **'is he rich?' – 'not especially'** 'est-il riche?' – 'pas particulièrement'.

essay *noun* rédaction *Fem.*; **an essay on pollution** une rédaction sur la pollution.

essential *adjective* essentiel (*Fem.* essentielle); **it's essential to reply quickly** il est essentiel de répondre vite.

establishment *noun* (*an organization*) établissement *Masc.*

estate *noun* **1** (*a housing estate*) cité *Fem.*; **2** (*a big house and grounds*) domaine *Masc.*

estate agent's *noun* agence *Fem.* immobilière.

estate car *noun* break *Masc.*

estimate *noun* **1** (*a quote for work*) devis *Masc.*; **2** (*a rough guess*) estimation *Fem.*
estimate *verb* évaluer [1].

etc etc.

ethnic *adjective* ethnique; **an ethnic minority** une minorité ethnique.

EU *noun* (SHORT FOR **European Union**) Union *Fem.* européenne.

euro *noun* euro *Masc.*; **the euro is divided into cents** l'euro est divisé en centimes.

Europe *noun* Europe *Fem.*; **in Europe** en Europe; **to Europe** en Europe.

European *noun* Européen *Masc.*, Européenne *Fem.*
European *adjective* européen (*Fem.* européenne).

European Union *noun* Union *Fem.* européenne.

eurozone *noun* zone *Fem.* euro.

evacuate *verb* faire [10] évacuer; **the police evacuated the building** la police a fait évacuer l'immeuble.

evaporate *verb* s'évaporer [1].

eve *noun* **Christmas Eve** la veille de Noël; **New Year's Eve** la Saint-Sylvestre.

even[1] *adverb* **1** même; **even Lisa didn't like it** même Lisa ne l'a pas aimé; **without even asking** sans même demander; **2 even if** même si; **even if they arrive** même s'ils arrivent; **3 not even** même pas; **I don't like animals, not even dogs** je n'aime pas les animaux, même pas les chiens; **4 even bigger** encore plus grand; **even more embarrassing** encore plus gênant; **even faster** encore plus vite; **5 even more than** encore plus que; **I liked the song even more than their last one** j'ai aimé la chanson encore plus que leur dernière; **6 even so** quand même; **even so, we had a good time** nous nous sommes bien amusés quand même.

even[2] *adjective* **1** (*a surface or layer*) régulier (*Fem.* régulière); **2** (*a number*) pair; **six is an even number** six est un numéro pair; **3** (*with the same score*) à égalité (*competitors*); **Lee and Blair are even** Lee et Blair sont à égalité.

evening *noun* **1** soir *Masc.*; **this evening** ce soir; **at six o'clock in the evening** à six heures du soir; **tomorrow evening** demain soir; **on Thursday evening** jeudi soir; **the evening before** la veille au soir; **every evening** tous les soirs; **I work in the evening(s)** je travaille le soir; **the evening meal** le repas du soir; **2** (*from beginning to end*) soirée *Fem.*; **during the evening** pendant la soirée; **an evening with Pavarotti** une soirée avec Pavarotti.

evening class *noun* cours *Masc.* du soir.

event *noun* **1** (*a happening*) évènement *Masc.*; **2** (*in athletics*) épreuve *Fem.*; **track events** les épreuves de vitesse; **3 in any event, at all events** de toute façon.

eventful *adjective* mouvementé (*a day or an outing*).

eventually *adverb* finalement.

ever *adverb* **1** (*at any time*) jamais; **hardly ever** presque jamais; **have you ever noticed that?** as-tu jamais remarqué ça?; **no-one ever came** personne n'est jamais venu; **hotter than ever** plus chaud que jamais; **more slowly than ever** plus lentement que jamais; **2** (*always*) toujours; **as cheerful as ever** toujours aussi gai; **the same as ever** toujours le même; **3 ever since** depuis; **and it's been raining ever since** et depuis il pleut tout le temps.

every *adjective* **1** tous (*Fem.* toutes); **every house has a garden** toutes les maisons ont un jardin; **every day** tous les jours; **every Monday** tous les lundis; **every ten kilometres** tous les dix kilomètres; **I've seen every one of his films** j'ai vu tous ses films; **2** (*each*) chaque; **every time** chaque fois; **3 every now and then** de temps en temps.

everybody, **everyone** *pronoun* tout le monde; **everybody knows that** ... tout le monde sait que ...; **everyone else** tous les autres.

everything *pronoun* tout; **everything is ready** tout est prêt; **everything's fine** tout va bien; **everything else** tout le reste; **everything you said** tout ce que tu as dit.

everywhere *adverb* partout; **there was mud everywhere** il y avait de la boue partout; **everywhere she went** partout où elle allait; **everywhere else** partout ailleurs.

evidently *adverb* manifestement.

evil *noun* mal *Masc.*
evil *adjective* mauvais.

exact *adjective* exact; **the exact amount** la somme exacte; **it's the exact opposite** c'est exactement le contraire.

exactly *adverb* exactement; **they're exactly the same age** ils ont exactement le même âge; **yes, exactly** oui, exactement.

a
b
c
d
e
f
g
h
i
j
k
l
m
n
o
p
q
r
s
t
u
v
w
x
y
z

a

exaggerate *verb* exagérer [24].

b

exaggeration *noun* exagération *Fem.*

c

exam *noun* examen *Masc.*; **a history exam** un examen d'histoire; **to sit an exam** passer un examen; **to pass an exam** réussir un examen; **to fail an exam** échouer à un examen.

e

f

examination *noun* examen *Masc.*

g

examine *verb* examiner [1].

h

examiner *noun* examinateur *Masc.*, examinatrice *Fem.*

i

example *noun* exemple *Masc.*; **for example** par exemple; **to set a good example** donner l'exemple.

j

k

excellent *adjective* excellent.

l

except *preposition* **1** sauf; **except in March** sauf au mois de mars; **every day except Tuesday** tous les jours sauf le mardi; **except when it rains** sauf quand il pleut; **2 except for** sauf; **except for the children** sauf les enfants.

m

n

o

p

exception *noun* exception *Fem.*; **without exception** sans exception; **with the exception of** à l'exception de.

q

r

s

exchange *noun* échange *Masc.*; **in exchange for his help** en échange de son aide; **an exchange visit** un voyage d'échange.
exchange *verb* échanger [52]; **can I exchange this shirt for a smaller one?** puis-je échanger cette chemise contre une plus petite?

t

u

v

w

exchange rate *noun* taux *Masc.* d'échange.

x

y

z

excite *verb* exciter [1].

excited *adjective* **1** excité (*a person or animal*); **the children are excited** les enfants sont excités; **2 to get excited** s'exciter; **the dogs get excited when they hear the car** les chiens s'excitent quand ils entendent la voiture.

excitement *noun* excitation *Fem.*

exciting *adjective* passionnant; **a really exciting film** un film vraiment passionnant.

exclamation mark *noun* point Masc. d'exclamation.

excursion *noun* excursion *Fem.*

excuse *noun* excuse *Fem.*; **Gary has a good excuse** Gary a une bonne excuse; **that's no excuse** ce n'est pas une excuse.
excuse *verb* (*apologizing*) **excuse me!** excusez-moi!

execute *verb* exécuter [1].

exercise *noun* exercice *Masc.*; **a maths exercise** un exercice de maths; **physical exercise** l'exercice physique.

exercise bicycle *noun* vélo Masc. d'appartement.

exercise book *noun* cahier Masc.; **my French exercise book** mon cahier de français.

exhaust (pipe) *noun* pot *Masc.* d'échappement.

exhausted *adjective* épuisé.

exhaust fumes *noun* gaz Masc. plural d'échappement.

exhibition *noun* exposition *Fem.*; **the Cézanne exhibition** l'exposition Cézanne.

exist *verb* exister [1].

xit noun sortie Fem.

xpand verb s'agrandir [2]; **the town is expanding** la ville se développe.

xpect verb **1** attendre [3] (guests or a baby); **we're expecting thirty people** nous attendons trente personnes; **2** s'attendre [3] à (something to happen); **I didn't expect that** je ne m'attendais pas à ça; **I didn't expect it at all** je ne m'y attendais pas du tout; **3** (as a supposition) imaginer [1]; **I expect you're tired** j'imagine que tu es fatigué; **I expect she'll bring her boyfriend** j'imagine qu'elle amènera son copain; **yes, I expect so** oui, j'imagine.

xpedition noun expédition Fem.

xpel verb **to be expelled** (from school) se faire [10] renvoyer.

xpenses noun frais Masc. plural.

xpensive adjective cher (Fem. chère); **those shoes are too expensive for me** ces chaussures sont trop chères pour moi; **the most expensive CDs** les CDs les plus chers.

xperience noun expérience Fem.

xperienced adjective expérimenté.

xperiment noun expérience Fem.; **to do an experiment** faire une expérience.

xpert noun spécialiste Masc. & Fem.; **he's a computer expert** c'est un spécialiste en informatique.

xpire verb expirer [1].

xpiry date noun date Fem. d'expiration.

explain verb expliquer [1].

explanation noun explication Fem.

explode verb exploser [1].

explore verb explorer [1].

explosion noun explosion Fem.

export noun exportation Fem.; **our chief export is wool** la laine est notre premier produit d'exportation.
export verb exporter [1]; **Russia exports a lot of oil and timber** la Russie exporte beaucoup de pétrole et de bois.

exposure noun (of a film) pose Fem.; **a 24-exposure film** une pellicule de vingt-quatre poses.

express noun (a train) rapide Masc.
express verb **1** exprimer [1]; **2 to express yourself** s'exprimer.

expression noun expression Fem.

extend verb agrandir [2] (a building).

extension noun **1** (to a house) addition Fem.; **2** (telephone) poste Masc.; **can I have extension 2347 please?** est-ce que je peux avoir le poste vingt-trois quarante-sept, s'il vous plaît? (note that in spoken French telephone numbers are usually broken down into groups of two figures; this applies to longer numbers as well); **3** (electrical) rallonge Fem.

extension lead noun rallonge Fem.

extension number noun numéro Masc. de poste.

exterior adjective extérieur.

a
b
c
d
e
f
g
h
i
j
k
l
m
n
o
p
q
r
s
t
u
v
w
x
y
z

extinct *adjective* **1** (*species*) disparu; **2** (*volcano*) éteint.

extinguish *verb* éteindre [60].

extinguisher *noun* (*fire extinguisher*) extincteur *Masc.*

extra *adjective* supplémentaire; **extra homework** des devoirs supplémentaires; **wine is extra** le vin est en supplément; **you have to pay extra** il faut payer un supplément; **at no extra charge** sans supplément.
extra *adverb* **extra hot** extra-chaud; **extra large** extra-grand.

extraordinary *adjective* extraordinaire.

extra-special *adjective* exceptionnel (*Fem.* exceptionnelle).

extra time *noun* (*in football*) prolongation *Fem.*; **to go into extra time** jouer les prolongations.

extravagant *adjective* dépensier (*Fem.* dépensière) (*a person*).

extreme *noun* extrême *Masc.*; **to go to extremes** pousser les choses à l'extrême.
extreme *adjective* extrême.

extremely *adverb* extrêmement; **extremely fast** extrêmement vite.

eye *noun* œil *Masc.* (*plural* yeux); **my left eye** mon œil gauche; **a girl with blue eyes** une fille aux yeux bleus; **shut your eyes!** ferme les yeux!; ★ **to keep an eye on something** surveiller quelque chose; ★ **to make eyes at somebody** faire les yeux doux à quelqu'un.

eyebrow *noun* sourcil *Masc.*

eyelash *noun* cil *Masc.*

eyelid *noun* paupière *Fem.*

eyeliner *noun* eye-liner *Masc.*

eye make-up *noun* maquillage *Masc.* pour les yeux.

eye shadow *noun* fard *Masc.* à paupières.

eyesight *noun* vue *Fem.*

Ff

fabric *noun* (*cloth*) tissu *Masc.*

fabulous *adjective* sensationnel (*Fem.* sensationnelle).

face *noun* **1** (*of a person*) visage *Masc.*; **you've got chocolate on your face** tu as du chocolat sur le visage; **2 to pull a face** faire une grimace; **3** (*of a clock or watch*) cadran *Masc.*
face *verb* **1** (*a person*) faire [10] face à; **she faced her attacker** elle a fait face à son agresseur; **2 the house faces the park** la maison donne sur le jardin public; **3** (*to stand the idea of*) avoir [5] le courage de; **I can't face going back** je n'ai pas le courage de rentrer; **4 to face up to something** faire face à quelque chose.

face cloth *noun* gant *Masc.* de toilette.

facilities *plural noun* **1 the school has good sports facilities** l'école dispose d'un bon ensemble sportif; **2 the flat has cooking facilities** l'appartement a une cuisine équipée.

act noun fait Masc.; **the fact is that ...** le fait est que ...; **in fact** en fait; **is that a fact?** vraiment?

actory noun usine Fem.

ade verb **1** (fabric) se décolorer [1]; **faded jeans** un jean délavé; **2 the colours have faded** les couleurs ont passé.

ail verb **1** rater [1] (a test or exam); **I failed my driving test** j'ai raté mon permis; **2** échouer [1]; **three students failed** trois étudiants ont échoué; **3** (not to do) **to fail to do** manquer [1] de faire; **he failed to contact us** il a manqué de nous contacter; ★ **without fail** sans faute; **ring me without fail** appelle-moi sans faute.

ailure noun **1** échec Masc.; **it was a terrible failure** c'était un échec terrible; **2** (a breakdown in a machine) panne Fem.; **a power failure** une panne de courant.

aint adjective **1 to feel faint** se sentir [58] mal; **2** (slight) léger (Fem. légère); **a faint smell of gas** une légère odeur de gaz; **I haven't the faintest idea** je n'en ai pas la moindre idée; **3** (a voice or sound) faible.

faint verb s'évanouir [2]; **Lisa fainted** Lisa s'est évanouie.

air noun foire Fem.

fair adjective **1** (not unfair) juste; **it's not fair!** ce n'est pas juste!; **2** (hair) blond; **he's fair-haired** il a les cheveux blonds; **3** (skin) clair; **people with fair skin** les gens qui ont la peau claire; **4** (fairly good) assez bon (Fem. assez bonne) (a chance, condition, or performance)

her history is fair son histoire est assez bonne; **5** (weather) **if it's fair tomorrow** s'il ne pleut pas demain.

fairground noun champ Masc. de foire.

fairly adverb (quite) assez; **she's fairly happy** elle est assez contente.

fairy noun fée Fem.

fairy tale noun conte Masc. de fées.

faith noun **1** (trust) confiance Fem.; **to have faith in somebody** avoir confiance en quelqu'un; **2** (religious belief) foi Fem.

faithful adjective fidèle.

faithfully adverb **yours faithfully** veuillez agréer, Monsieur (or Madame) mes salutations distinguées.

fake noun faux Masc.; **the diamonds were fakes** les diamants étaient des faux.

fake adjective faux (Fem. fausse) (goes before the noun); **a fake passport** un faux passeport.

fall noun chute Fem.; **to have a fall** tomber.

fall verb **1** tomber [1]; **mind, you'll fall** attention, tu vas tomber; **Tony fell off his bike** Tony est tombé de son vélo; **she fell downstairs** elle est tombée dans l'escalier; **my jacket fell on the floor** ma veste est tombée par terre; **2** (the temperature) descendre [3]; **it fell to minus eleven last night** il est descendu à moins onze cette nuit; **3** (prices) baisser [1].

false adjective faux (Fem. fausse) (goes before the noun); **a false alarm** une fausse alerte.

421

a b c d e f g h i j k l m n o p q r s t u v w x y z

a
b
c
d
e
f
g
h
i
j
k
l
m
n
o
p
q
r
s
t
u
v
w
x
y
z

false teeth *plural noun* dentier *Masc.*

fame *noun* renommée *Fem.*

familiar *adjective* familier (*Fem.* familière); **your face is familiar** votre visage m'est familier.

family *noun* famille *Fem.*; **a family of six** une famille de six personnes; **Ben's one of the family** Ben fait partie de la famille; **the Barnes family** la famille Barnes.

family name *noun* nom *Masc.* de famille.

famous *adjective* célèbre.

fan *noun* **1** fan *Masc. & Fem.* (*informal;*); **Diana's an Oasis fan** Diana est une fan de Oasis; **2** (*of a team*) supporter *Masc.*; **Brian's a Chelsea fan** Brian est un supporter de Chelsea; **3** (*electric, for cooling*) ventilateur *Masc.*; **4** (*that you hold in your hand*) éventail *Masc.*

fanatic *noun* fanatique *Masc. & Fem.*

fancy *noun* **to take someone's fancy** faire envie à quelqu'un; **the picture took his fancy** le tableau lui a fait envie.
fancy *adjective* (*equipment*) sophistiqué.
fancy *verb* **1** (*to want*) **(do you) fancy a coffee?** tu veux un café?; **do you fancy going to the new film?** ça te dirait d'aller voir le nouveau film?; **2 I really fancy him** il me plaît beaucoup; **3 (just) fancy that!** pas possible!; **fancy you being here!** tiens donc, toi ici!

fancy dress *noun* **in fancy dress** déguisé; **a fancy-dress party** une soirée déguisée.

fantastic *adjective* génial (*Masc. plural* géniaux) (*informal*); **really? that's fantastic!** vraiment? c'est génial!; **a fantastic holiday** des vacances géniales.

far *adverb, adjective* **1** loin; **it's not far** ce n'est pas loin; **is it far to Carlisle?** est-ce que Carlisle est loin d'ici?; **how far is it to Bristol?** Bristol est à quelle distance d'ici?; **he took us as far as Newport** il nous a accompagnés jusqu'à Newport; **2 by far** de loin; **the prettiest by far** de loin le plus joli; **3** (*much*) beaucoup; **far better** beaucoup mieux; **far faster** beaucoup plus vite; **far too many people** beaucoup trop de monde; **4 so far** jusqu'ici; **so far everything's going well** jusqu'ici tout va bien; ★ **as far as I know** pour autant que je sache.

fare *noun* **1** (*on a bus or the underground*) prix *Masc.* du ticket; **2** (*on a train or plane*) prix *Masc.* du billet; **half fare** demi-tarif *Masc.*; **full fare** plein tarif *Masc.*; **the return fare to Cardiff** le prix d'un aller-retour à Cardiff.

Far East *noun* Extrême-Orient *Masc.*

farm *noun* ferme *Fem.*

farmer *noun* agriculteur *Masc.*, agricultrice *Fem.*

farmhouse *noun* ferme *Fem.*

farming *noun* agriculture *Fem.*

farthest *adjective* le plus éloigné; **the farthest hill** la colline la plus éloignée.
farthest *adverb* le plus loin; **that's**

the farthest we went that day
nous ne sommes pas allés plus loin
ce jour-là.

ascinating *adjective* fascinant.

ashion *noun* mode *Fem.*; **in fashion**
à la mode; **out of fashion** démodé.

ashionable *adjective* à la mode.

ashion model *noun* mannequin
Masc.

ashion show *noun* présentation
Fem. de collection.

ast *adjective* **1** rapide; **a fast car**
une voiture rapide; **2 my watch is
fast** ma montre avance; **you're ten
minutes fast** ta montre avance de
dix minutes.

fast *adverb* **1** vite; **he swims fast** il
nage vite; **2 to be fast asleep** être
profondément endormi.

ast food *noun* fast-food *Masc.*

ast forward *noun* avance *Fem.*
rapide.

fat *noun* **1** (*butter, cream, etc*)
matières *Fem. plural* grasses; **2** (*on
meat*) gras *Masc.*; **3** (*on your body*)
graisse *Fem.*

fat *adjective* gros (*Fem.* grosse) (*goes
before the noun*); **a fat man** un gros
monsieur; **to get fat** grossir.

atal *adjective* (*accident*) mortel
(*Fem.* mortelle).

Father's Day *noun* fête *Fem.* des
Pères.

father *noun* père *Masc.*; **my father's
office** le bureau de mon père.

Father Christmas *noun* le père
Noël.

father-in-law *noun* beau-père
Masc.

fault *noun* **1** (*when you are
responsible*) faute *Fem.*; **it's
Stephen's fault** c'est la faute de
Stephen; **it's not my fault** ce n'est
pas ma faute; **2** (*a defect*) défaut
Masc.; **there's a fault in this
sweater** il y a un défaut dans ce pull;
3 (*in tennis*) faute *Fem.*

favour *noun* **1** (*a kindness*) service
Masc.; **to do somebody a favour**
rendre service à quelqu'un; **can you
do me a favour?** peux-tu me rendre
service?; **to ask a favour of
somebody** demander un service à
quelqu'un; **2 to be in favour of
something** être pour quelque chose.

favourite *adjective* préféré; **my
favourite band** mon groupe préféré.

fax *noun* fax *Masc.*

fear *noun* peur *Fem.*
fear *verb* craindre [31]; **to fear the
worst** craindre le pire.

feather *noun* plume *Fem.*

feature *noun* **1** (*of your face*) trait
Masc.; **to have delicate features**
avoir les traits délicats; **2** (*of a car or
a machine*) caractéristique *Fem.*

February *noun* février *Masc.*; **in
February** en février.

fed up *adjective* **I'm fed up** j'en ai
marre (*informal*); **I'm fed up with
working every day** j'en ai marre de
travailler tous les jours.

feed *verb* donner [1] à manger à;
have you fed the dog? est-ce que tu
as donné à manger au chien?

feel *verb* **1** se sentir [58]; **I feel tired**
je me sens fatigué; **I don't feel well**
je ne me sens pas bien; **2** sentir [58];
I didn't feel a thing je n'ai rien

senti; **3 to feel afraid** avoir [5] peur;
to feel cold avoir froid; **to feel
thirsty** avoir soif; **4 to feel like
doing** avoir envie de faire; **I feel like
going to the cinema** j'ai envie
d'aller au cinéma; **5** (*touch*) toucher
[1].

feeling *noun* **1** (*in your mind*)
sentiment *Masc.*; **a feeling of
embarrassment** un sentiment de
gêne; **to show your feelings**
montrer ses sentiments; **to hurt
somebody's feelings** blesser
quelqu'un; **2** (*in your body*)
sensation *Fem.*; **a dizzy feeling** une
sensation de vertige; **3** (*an
impression or intuition*) impression
Fem.; **I have the feeling James
doesn't like me** j'ai l'impression
que James ne m'aime pas.

felt-tip (pen) *noun* feutre *Masc.*

female *noun* (*animal*) femelle *Fem.*
female *adjective* **1** féminin (*person,
population*); **2** femelle (*animal,
insect*).

feminine *adjective* féminin.

feminist *noun, adjective* féministe
Masc. & Fem.

fence *noun* (*round a field*) clôture
Fem.

fern *noun* fougère *Fem.*

ferry *noun* ferry *Masc.*

fertilizer *noun* engrais *Masc.*

festival *noun* (*for films, art, or
music*) festival *Masc.*

fetch *verb* aller [7] chercher; **Tom's
fetching the children** Tom est allé
chercher les enfants; **fetch me the
other knife!** va me chercher l'autre
couteau!

fever *adjective* fièvre *Fem.*

few *adjective, pronoun* **1** peu de; **few
people think that** ... peu de gens
pensent que ...; **very few houses
have a swimming-pool** très peu de
maisons ont une piscine; **2 a few**
(*followed by a noun*) quelques; **a few
weeks earlier** quelques semaines
plus tôt; **in a few minutes** dans
quelques minutes; **3 a few** (*by itself*)
quelques-uns (*Fem.* quelques-unes)
**have you any tomatoes? we want
a few for the salad** avez-vous des
tomates? nous en voulons quelques-
unes pour la salade; **4 quite a few**
pas mal de; **there were quite a few
questions** il y avait pas mal de
questions.

fewer *adjective* moins de; **there are
fewer tourists this year** il y a moins
de touristes cette année.

fiancé *noun* fiancé *Masc.*

fiancée *noun* fiancée *Fem.*

fiction *noun* **I read a lot of fiction**
je lis beacoup de romans.

field *noun* **1** (*with grass or crops*)
champ *Masc.*; **a field of wheat** un
champ de blé; **2** (*for sport*) terrain
Masc.; **3** (*the kind of work you do*)
domaine *Masc.*

fierce *adjective* **1** féroce (*an animal
or person*); **2** violent (*a storm or a
battle*).

fifteen *number* quinze; **Lara's
fifteen** Lara a quinze ans.

fifth *number* cinquième; **the fifth of
January** le cinq janvier; **on the fifth
floor** au cinquième étage.

ifty *number* cinquante Masc.; **my uncle's fifty** mon oncle a cinquante ans.

ig *noun* figue Fem.

ight *noun* **1** (*a scuffle*) bagarre Fem.; **2** (*in boxing*) combat Masc.; **3** (*against illness*) lutte Fem.
fight *verb* **1** (*to have a fight*) se battre [21]; **they were fighting** ils se battaient; **2** (*to quarrel*) se disputer [1]; **they're always fighting** ils sont toujours en train de se disputer; **3** (*struggle against*) lutter [1] contre (*poverty or a disease*).

ighting *noun* **1** (*in the streets or a pub, for example*) bagarre Fem.; **2** (*in war*) combat Masc.

igure *noun* **1** (*number*) chiffre Masc.; **a four-figure number** un nombre de quatre chiffres; **2** (*body shape*) ligne Fem.; **good for your figure** bon pour la ligne; **3** (*a person*) personnage Masc.; **a familiar figure** un personnage familier; **4** (*diagram*) figure Fem.

ile *noun* **1** (*for records of a person or case*) dossier Masc.; **2** (*ring binder*) classeur Masc.; **3** (*cardboard folder*) chemise Fem.; **4** (*on a computer*) fichier Masc.; **5 a nail file** une lime.
file *verb* **1** classer [1] (*documents*); **2 to file your nails** se limer [1] les ongles.

ill *verb* remplir [2] (*a container*); **she filled my glass** elle a rempli mon verre; **a smoke-filled room** une pièce remplie de fumée.

• **to fill in** remplir [2] (*a form*).

• **to fill in for someone** remplacer [61] quelqu'un.

filling *noun* **1** (*for a sandwich*) garniture Fem.; (*of meat, vegetables*) farce Fem.; **with an apricot filling** fourré à l'abricot; **2** (*in tooth*) plombage Masc.

film *noun* **1** (*in a cinema*) film Masc.; **shall we go and see a film?** si on allait voir un film?; **the new film about Picasso** le nouveau film au sujet de Picasso; **2** (*for a camera*) pellicule Fem.; **a 24-exposure colour film** une pellicule couleur de 24 poses.

film star *noun* vedette Fem. de cinéma.

filter *noun* filtre Masc.

filthy *adjective* dégoûtant.

fin *noun* nageoire Fem.

final *noun* (*in sport*) finale Fem.
final *adjective* dernier (Fem. dernière); **the final instalment** le dernier épisode; **the final result** le résultat final.

finally *adverb* finalement.

find *verb* trouver [1]; **did you find your passport?** as-tu trouvé ton passeport?; **I can't find my keys** je ne trouve pas mes clefs.

• **to find out 1** (*to enquire*) se renseigner [1]; **I don't know, I'll find out** je ne sais pas, je me renseignerai; **2 to find something out** découvrir [30] (*the facts or an answer*); **when Lucy found out the truth** quand Lucy a découvert la vérité.

fine *noun* amende Fem. (*for parking or speeding*) contravention Fem.
fine *adjective* **1** (*in good health*) bien; **'how are you?' – 'fine,**

thanks' 'comment ça va?' – 'très bien merci'; **2** (*very good*) excellent; **she's a fine athlete** c'est une excellente athlète; **3** (*convenient*) très bien; **ten o'clock? yes, that's fine** dix heures? oui, très bien; **Friday will be fine** vendredi sera très bien; **4** (*sunny*) beau (*Fem.* belle) (*weather or a day*); **if it's fine** s'il fait beau; **5** (*not coarse or thick*) fin; **in fine wool** en laine fine.

finely *adjective* (*chopped or grated*) finement.

finger *noun* doigt *Masc.*; ★ **I'll keep my fingers crossed for you** je croise les doigts pour toi.

fingernail *noun* ongle *Masc.*

finish *noun* **1** (*end*) fin *Fem.*; **2** (*in a race*) arrivée *Fem.*

finish *verb* **1** finir [2]; **wait, I haven't finished** attends, je n'ai pas fini; **when does school finish?** à quelle heure finit l'école?; **2** (*to finish off*) terminer [1] (*work or a project*); **have you finished the book?** est-ce que tu as terminé le livre?; **3 to finish doing** finir de faire; **have you finished telephoning?** as-tu fini de téléphoner?

● **to finish with** finir avec; **have you finished with the computer?** as-tu fini avec l'ordinateur?

finishing line *noun* ligne *Fem.* d'arrivée.

Finland *noun* Finlande *Fem.*; **in Finland** en Finlande; **to Finland** en Finlande.

Finnish *noun* finnois *Masc.* (*the language*).

Finnish *adjective* finlandais.

fire *noun* **1** (*in a grate*) feu *Masc.*; **to light a fire** allumer un feu; **sitting by the fire** assis près du feu; **2 to catch fire** prendre feu; **3** (*accidental*) incendie *Masc.*; **a fire in a factory** un incendie dans une usine.

fire *verb* **1** (*to shoot*) tirer [1]; **the soldiers were firing** les soldats tiraient; **to fire at somebody** tirer sur quelqu'un; **2** décharger (*a gun*

fire alarm *noun* alarme *Fem.* incendie.

fire brigade *noun* pompiers *Masc. plural*.

fire engine *noun* voiture *Fem.* de pompiers.

fire escape *noun* escalier *Masc.* de secours.

fire extinguisher *noun* extincteur *Masc.*

fire fighter *noun* pompier *Masc.*

fireplace *noun* cheminée *Fem.*

fire station *noun* caserne *Fem.* de pompiers.

firework *noun* feu *Masc.* d'artifice (*plural* feux d'artifice); **there will be a firework display** il y aura un feu d'artifice.

firm *noun* (*business*) entreprise *Fem.*

firm *adjective* ferme.

first *adjective, adverb* **1** premier (*Fem.* première); **Susan's the first** Susan est la première; **the first of May** le premier mai; **for the first time** pour la première fois; **I came first in the 200 metres** je suis arrivé premier aux 200 mètres; **2** (*t begin with*) d'abord; **first, I'm going to make some tea** d'abord je vais faire du thé; **3 at first** au début; **at first he was shy** au début il était timide.

first aid *noun* premiers secours *Masc. plural*.

first-aid kit *noun* trousse *Fem.* de secours.

first class *adjective* **1** de première classe (*a ticket, carriage, or hotel*); **a first-class compartment** un compartiment de première classe; **he always travels first class** il voyage toujours en première; **2** au tarif rapide (*a letter or stamp*); **six first-class stamps** six timbres au tarif rapide.

first floor *noun* premier étage *Masc.*; **on the first floor** au premier étage.

firstly *adverb* premièrement.

first name *noun* prénom *Masc.*

fir tree *noun* sapin *Masc.*

fish *noun* poisson *Masc.*; **do you like fish?** aimez-vous le poisson? **fish** *verb* pêcher [1]; **Dad was fishing for trout** Papa pêchait la truite.

fish and chips *noun* poisson *Masc.* frit avec des frites.

fisherman *noun* pêcheur *Masc.*

fishing *noun* pêche *Fem.*; **I love fishing** j'adore la pêche; **to go fishing** aller à la pêche.

fishing rod *noun* canne *Fem.* à pêche.

fishing tackle *noun* matériel *Masc.* de pêche.

fist *noun* poing *Masc.*

fit *noun* **1** (*of rage*) **to have a fit** piquer une crise; **your dad'll have a fit when he sees your hair!** ton père va piquer une crise quand il va voir tes cheveux!; **2 an epileptic fit** une crise d'épilepsie.
fit *adjective* (*healthy*) en forme; **I feel really fit** je me sens vraiment en forme; **to keep fit** se maintenir en forme.
fit *verb* **1** (*to be the right size for*) (*a garment*) être [6] de la taille de (*a person*); (*shoes*) être à la pointure de; **this skirt doesn't fit me** cette jupe n'est pas à ma taille; **2** (*be able to be put into*) aller [7] dans; **will my cases all fit in the car?** est-ce que mes valises iront dans la voiture?; **the key doesn't fit in the lock** la clé ne va pas dans la serrure; **3** (*install*) installer [1]; **they've fitted an alarm** ils ont installé une alarme.

fitness *noun* forme *Fem.*; **fitness training** exercices *Masc. plural* de mise en forme.

fitted carpet *noun* moquette *Fem.*

fitted kitchen *noun* cuisine *Fem.* intégrée.

fitting room *noun* cabine *Fem.* d'essayage.

five *number* cinq *Masc.*; **Belinda's five** Belinda a cinq ans; **it's five o'clock** il est cinq heures.

fix *verb* **1** (*repair*) réparer [1]; **Mum's fixed the computer** Maman a réparé l'ordinateur; **2** (*to decide on*) fixer [1]; **to fix a date** fixer une date; **at a fixed price** à prix fixe; **3** préparer [1] (*a meal*); **I'll fix supper** c'est moi qui vais préparer le repas du soir.

a
b
c
d
e
f
g
h
i
j
k
l
m
n
o
p
q
r
s
t
u
v
w
x
y
z

fizzy *adjective* gazeux (*Fem.* gazeuse); **fizzy water** eau *Fem.* gazeuse.

flag *noun* drapeau *Masc.* (*plural* drapeaux).

flame *noun* flamme *Fem.*

flamingo *noun* flamant *Masc.* rose.

flan *noun* tarte *Fem.*; **an onion flan** une tarte à l'oignon.

flap *verb* battre [21]; **the bird flapped its wings** l'oiseau battait des ailes.

flash *noun* 1 **a flash of lightning** un éclair; 2 **to do something in a flash** faire quelque chose en un clin d'œil; 3 (*on a camera*) flash *Masc.*
flash *verb* 1 (*a light*) clignoter [1]; 2 **to flash by or past** passer [1] comme un éclair; 3 **to flash your headlights** faire [10] un appel de phares.

flashback *noun* flash-back *Masc.*

flask *noun* 1 (*insulated bottle*) thermos™ *Masc.* or *Fem.*; 2 (*container*) flacon *Masc.*

flat *noun* appartement *Masc.*; **a third-floor flat** un appartement au troisième étage.
flat *adjective* 1 plat; **flat shoes** des chaussures plates; **a flat landscape** un paysage plat; 2 **a flat tyre** un pneu crevé.

flatmate *noun* colocataire *Masc.* & *Fem.*

flatter *verb* flatter [1].

flattering *adjective* flatteur (*Fem.* flatteuse).

flavour *noun* 1 (*taste*) goût *Masc.*; **the sauce had no flavour** la sauce n'avait aucun goût; 2 (*of drink, ice cream, etc.*) parfum *Masc.*; **what flavour of ice cream would you like?** tu veux quel parfum de glace?
flavour *verb* parfumer [1]; **vanilla-flavoured** parfumé à la vanille.

flea *noun* puce *Fem.*

flea market *noun* marché *Masc.* aux puces.

fleet *noun* 1 (*of ships*) flotte *Fem.*; 2 (*of vehicles*) parc *Masc.*

flesh *noun* chair *Fem.*

flex *noun* fil *Masc.*

flexible *adjective* flexible (*an arrangement*).

flight *noun* 1 vol *Masc.*; **a charter flight** un vol charter; **the flight from Moscow is delayed** le vol de Moscou est retardé; 2 **a flight of stairs** un escalier; **four flights of stairs** quatre étages.

flight attendant *noun* 1 (*male*) steward *Masc.*; 2 (*female*) hôtesse *Fem.* de l'air.

fling *verb* lancer [61].

flipper *noun* (*for a swimmer*) palme *Fem.*

flirt *verb* flirter [1].

float *verb* flotter [1].

flood *noun* 1 (*of water*) inondation *Fem.*; **the floods in the south** les inondations au sud; **to be in floods of tears** verser des torrents de larmes; 2 (*of letters or complaints*) déluge *Masc.*
flood *verb* inonder [1].

floodlight *noun* projecteur *Masc.*

floor *noun* 1 (*wooden*) plancher *Masc.* (*concrete*) sol *Masc.*; **to sweep**

the floor balayer; **to sweep the kitchen floor** balayer la cuisine; **your glasses are on the floor** tes lunettes sont par terre; **2** (*a storey*) étage *Masc.*; **on the second floor** au deuxième étage.

floppy disk *noun* disquette *Fem.*

florist *noun* fleuriste *Masc. & Fem.*

flour *noun* farine *Fem.*

flow *verb* couler [1].

flower *noun* fleur *Fem.*; **a bunch of flowers** un bouquet.
flower *verb* fleurir [2].

flu *noun* grippe *Fem.*; **to have flu** avoir la grippe.

fluent *adjective* **she speaks fluent Italian** elle parle couramment l'italien.

fluently *adverb* couramment.

fluid *noun* liquide *Masc.*

flush *verb* **1** (*to go red*) rougir [2]; **2 to flush the lavatory** tirer [1] la chasse.

flute *noun* flûte *Fem.*; **to play the flute** jouer de la flûte.

fly *noun* mouche *Fem.*
fly *verb* **1** (*a bird, a bee, or a plane*) voler [1]; **2** (*in a plane*) prendre [64] l'avion; **we flew to Edinburgh** nous sommes allés à Édimbourg en avion; **we flew from Gatwick** nous sommes partis de Gatwick; **3** faire [10] voler (*a kite*); **4** (*to pass quickly*) (*time*) passer [1] très vite.

fly spray *noun* bombe *Fem.* insecticide.

foam *noun* **1** (*foam rubber*) mousse *Fem.*; **a foam mattress** un matelas mousse; **2** (*on a drink*) mousse *Fem.*

focus *noun* **to be in focus** être au point; **to be out of focus** être flou.
focus *verb* mettre [11] au point (*a camera*).

fog *noun* brouillard *Masc.*

foggy *adjective* brumeux (*Fem.* brumeuse) (*weather*); **it was foggy** il y avait du brouillard.

foil *noun* (*kitchen foil*) papier *Masc.* aluminium.

fold *noun* pli *Masc.*
fold *verb* **1** plier [1]; **to fold something up** plier quelque chose; **2 to fold your arms** croiser [1] les bras.

folder *noun* chemise *Fem.*

folding *adjective* pliant; **a folding table** une table pliante.

follow *verb* suivre [75]; **follow me!** suivez-moi!; **followed by a dinner** suivi d'un dîner; **do you follow me?** vous me suivez?

following *adjective* suivant; **the following year** l'année suivante.

fond *adjective* **to be fond of somebody** aimer beaucoup quelqu'un; **I'm very fond of him** je l'aime beaucoup.

food *noun* **1** nourriture *Fem.*; **to buy food** acheter à manger; **I like French food** j'aime la cuisine française; **2** (*stocks*) provisions *Fem. plural*; **we bought food for the holiday** nous avons acheté des provisions pour les vacances.

food poisoning *noun* intoxication *Fem.* alimentaire.

fool *noun* idiot *Masc.*, idiote *Fem.*

foot noun 1 pied Masc.; **Lucy came on foot** Lucy est venue à pied; 2 (*the bottom*) **at the foot of the stairs** en bas de l'escalier.

football noun 1 (*the game*) football Masc.; **to play football** jouer au football; 2 (*ball*) ballon Masc. de football.

footballer noun joueur Masc. de football, joueuse Fem. de football.

footpath noun sentier Masc.

footprint noun empreinte Fem.

footstep noun pas Masc.

for preposition 1 pour; **a present for my mother** un cadeau pour ma mère; **petrol for the car** de l'essence pour la voiture; **sausages for lunch** des saucisses pour le déjeuner; **it's for cleaning** c'est pour nettoyer; **what's it for?** c'est pour quoi faire?; 2 (*time expressions in the past or future*) pendant; **I studied French for six years** (*but I no longer do*) j'ai étudié le français pendant six ans; **I'll be away for four days** je serai absent pendant quatre jours; 3 (*time expressions in the past but continuing in the present*) depuis; **I've been waiting here for an hour** (*and I'm still waiting*) j'attends ici depuis une heure; **my brother's been living in Paris for three years** (*and he still lives there*) mon frère habite à Paris depuis trois ans; 4 **I sold my bike for fifty pounds** j'ai vendu mon vélo cinquante livres; 5 **what's the French for 'bee'?** comment dit-on 'bee' en français?

forbid verb défendre [3]; **to forbid somebody to do something** défendre à quelqu'un de faire

quelque chose; **I forbid you to go out** je te défends de sortir.

forbidden adjective défendu.

force noun force Fem.
force verb forcer [61]; **to force somebody to do** forcer quelqu'un à faire.

forecast noun (*weather forecast*) météo Fem.

forefinger noun index Masc.

foreground noun premier plan Masc.; **in the foreground** au premier plan.

forehead noun front Masc.

foreign adjective étranger (Fem. étrangère); **in a foreign country** dans un pays étranger.

foreigner noun étranger Masc., étrangère Fem.

foresee verb prévoir [65].

forest noun forêt Fem.

forever adverb 1 pour toujours; **I'd like to stay here forever** j'aimerais rester là pour toujours; 2 (*non-stop*) sans arrêt; **he's forever asking questions** il pose sans arrêt des questions.

forgery noun 1 (*picture*) faux Masc.; 2 (*signature, banknote*) contrefaçon Fem.

forget verb oublier [1]; **I forget his name** j'oublie son nom; **we've forgotten the bread!** nous avons oublié le pain!; **to forget to do** oublier de faire; **I forgot to phone** j'ai oublié d'appeler; **to forget about something** oublier quelque chose.

orgive *verb* pardonner [1] à; **to forgive somebody** pardonner à quelqu'un; **I forgave him** je lui ai pardonné; **to forgive somebody for doing** pardonner à quelqu'un d'avoir fait; **I forgave her for losing my ring** je lui ai pardonné d'avoir perdu ma bague.

ork *noun* fourchette *Fem.*

orm *noun* **1** formulaire *Masc.*; **to fill in a form** remplir un formulaire; **2** (*shape or kind*) forme *Fem.*; **in the form of** sous form de; **3 to be on form** être en forme; **4** (*in school*) classe *Fem.*
form *verb* former [1].

ormal *adjective* officiel (*Fem.* officielle) (*invitation, event, complaint, etc.*).

ormat *noun* format *Masc.*

ormer *adjective* ancien (*Fem.* ancienne) (*goes before the noun*); **a former pupil** un ancien élève.

ormula *noun* formule *Fem.*

ortnight *noun* quinze jours *Masc. plural*; **we're going to Spain for a fortnight** nous allons passer quinze jours en Espagne.

ortress *noun* forteresse *Fem.*

ortunate *adjective* **to be fortunate** avoir [5] de la chance.

ortunately *adverb* heureusement.

ortune *noun* fortune *Fem.*; **to make a fortune** gagner [1] beaucoup d'argent.

orty *number* quarante; **my aunt's forty** ma tante a quarante ans.

forward *noun* (*in sport*) avant *Masc.*
forward *adverb* **to move forward** avancer; **a seat further forward** une place plus en avant.

foster child *noun* enfant *Masc.* adoptif, enfant *Fem.* adoptive.

foul *noun* (*in sport*) faute *Fem.*
foul *adjective* infect; **the weather's foul** il fait un temps infect.

fountain *noun* fontaine *Fem.*

fountain pen *noun* stylo *Masc.* à encre.

four *number* quatre *Masc.*; **Simon's four** Simon a quatre ans; **it's four o'clock** il est quatre heures; ★ **on all fours** à quatre pattes.

fourteen *number* quatorze *Masc.*; **Susie's fourteen** Susie a quatorze ans.

fourth *number* quatrième; **the fourth of July** le quatre juillet; **on the fourth floor** au quatrième étage.

fox *noun* renard *Masc.*

fracture *noun* fracture *Fem.*

fragile *adjective* fragile.

frame *noun* **1** (*of picture*) cadre *Masc.*; **2** (*of door*) encadrement *Masc.*

franc *noun* franc *Masc.*; (*the currency of Switzerland; name of the currencies used in France, Belgium and Luxembourg until replaced by the euro; 100 French francs = 15.24 euros*).

France *noun* France *Fem.*; **in France** en France; **to France** en France; **I like France** j'aime la France; **Nadine's from France** Nadine est française.

a
b
c
d
e
f
g
h
i
j
k
l
m
n
o
p
q
r
s
t
u
v
w
x
y
z

a
b
c
d
e
f
g
h
i
j
k
l
m
n
o
p
q
r
s
t
u
v
w
x
y
z

frantic adjective **1** (very upset) fou (Fem. folle); **Mum was frantic with worry** Maman était folle d'inquiétude; **2** (desperate) désespéré (efforts or a search).

freckle noun tache Fem. de rousseur.

free adjective **1** (when you don't pay) gratuit; **the bus is free** le bus est gratuit; **a free ticket** un billet gratuit; **2** (not occupied) libre; **are you free on Thursday?** es-tu libre jeudi?; **3** sugar-free sans sucre; **lead-free** sans plomb.
free verb libérer [24].

freedom noun liberté Fem.

free gift noun cadeau Masc. (plural cadeaux).

free kick noun coup Masc. franc.

freeze verb **1** (in a freezer) congeler [45]; **frozen peas** des petits pois congelés; **2** (in cold weather) geler [45]; **it's freezing outside** il gèle dehors.

freezer noun congélateur Masc.

freezing noun zéro Masc.; **three degrees below freezing** trois degrés en-dessous de zéro.
freezing adjective **I'm freezing** je suis gelé (informal); **it's freezing outside** il fait très froid dehors.

French noun **1** (the language) français Masc.; **to speak French** parler français; **say it in French** dis-le en français; **to learn French** apprendre le français; **2** (the people) **the French** les Français Masc. plural; **most of the French** la plupart des Français.
French adjective **1** français; Jean-Marc is French Jean-Marc est français; **2** de français (a teacher or a lesson); **the French class** le cours de français.

French bean noun haricot Masc. vert.

French dressing noun vinaigrette Fem.

French fries plural noun frites Fem. plural.

Frenchman noun Français Masc.

French stick noun baguette Fem.

French window noun porte-fenêtre Fem. (plural portes-fenêtres).

Frenchwoman noun Française Fem.

frequent adjective fréquent.

frequently adverb souvent.

fresh adjective frais (Fem. fraîche); **fresh eggs** des œufs frais; **I'm going out for some fresh air** je vais prendre de l'air.

Friday noun vendredi Masc.; **next Friday** vendredi prochain; **last Friday** vendredi dernier; **on Friday** vendredi; **I'll phone you on Friday evening** je t'appellerai vendredi soir; **on Fridays** le vendredi; **closed on Fridays** fermé le vendredi; **every Friday** tous les vendredis; **Good Friday** le Vendredi saint.

fridge noun frigo Masc. (informal); **put it in the fridge** mets-le au frigo.

friend noun ami Masc., amie Fem.; **a friend of mine** un ami (or une amie) à moi; **to make friends** (in a general way) se faire des amis; **he made friends with Danny** il est devenu ami avec Danny.

riendly *adjective* sympathique.

riendship *noun* amitié *Fem.*

ries *plural noun* frites *Fem. plural.*

right *noun* peur *Fem.*; **to have** or **get a fright** avoir peur; **you gave me a fright!** tu m'as fait peur!

righten *verb* effrayer [59].

rightened *adjective* **to be frightened** avoir peur; **Martin's frightened of snakes** Martin a peur des serpents.

rightening *adjective* effrayant.

ringe *noun* frange *Fem.*

rog *noun* grenouille *Fem.*

rom *preposition* de; **a letter from Tom** une lettre de Tom; **100 metres from the cinema** à cent mètres du cinéma; **from Monday to Friday** du lundi jusqu'au vendredi; **he comes from Dublin** il vient de Dublin; **two years from now** d'ici deux ans; **from seven o'clock onwards** à partir de sept heures.

ront *noun* **1** (*of a building, a garment, or a cupboard*) devant *Masc.*; **2** (*of a car*) avant *Masc.*; **sitting in the front** assis à l'avant; **3** (*of a train or a queue*) tête *Fem.*; **there are seats at the front of the train** il y a des places en tête du train; **4** (*of a card or envelope*) recto *Masc.*; **the address is on the front** l'adresse est au recto; **5** (*in a theatre, cinema, or class*) premier rang *Masc.*; **seats at the front** des places au premier rang; **6** in front of devant; **in front of the TV** devant la télé; **in front of me** devant moi.

front *adjective* **1** de devant; **his front paw** sa patte de devant; **in the**

front row au premier rang; **2** avant; **the front seat** (*of a car*) le siège avant; **the front wheel** la roue avant.

front door *noun* porte *Fem.* d'entrée.

frontier *noun* frontière *Fem.*

frost *noun* gel *Masc.*

frosty *adjective* **1** it's frosty this morning il gèle ce matin; **2** couvert de givre (*windscreen, grass, etc.*).

frown *verb* froncer [61] les sourcils; **he frowned at us** il nous a regardés en fronçant les sourcils.

frozen *adjective* (*in a freezer*) surgelé; **a frozen pizza** une pizza surgelée.

fruit *noun* fruits *Masc. plural* (*note that in French 'un fruit' is a piece of fruit, whereas 'fruit' in English meaning several pieces of fruit always has to be 'fruits' in the plural in French*) **we bought cheese and fruit** nous avons acheté du fromage et des fruits; **fruit juice** le jus de fruits.

fruit machine *noun* machine *Fem.* à sous.

fruit salad *noun* salade *Fem.* de fruits.

frustrated *adjective* frustré.

frustrating *adjective* frustrant.

fry *verb* faire [10] frire; **we fried the fish** nous avons fait frire les poissons; **a fried egg** un œuf au plat.

frying pan *noun* poêle *Fem.*

fuel *noun* (*for a vehicle or plane*) carburant *Masc.*

full *adjective* **1** plein; **this glass is full** ce verre est plein; **the train was**

a
b
c
d
e
f
g
h
i
j
k
l
m
n
o
p
q
r
s
t
u
v
w
x
y
z

full of tourists le train était plein de touristes; **2 complet** (*Fem.* complète) (*a hotel or flight*); **3** (*top*) **at full speed** à toute vitesse; **at full volume** à plein volume; **4 I'm full** j'ai assez mangé; **5 to write something out in full** écrire quelque chose en toutes lettres.

full stop *noun* point *Masc.*

full-time *adjective* **a full-time job** un travail à plein temps.

full time *noun* (*in sport*) fin *Fem.* du match.

fully *adjective* entièrement.

fun *noun* plaisir *Masc.*; **to have fun** s'amuser; **have fun!** amusez-vous bien!; **we had fun catching the ponies** nous nous sommes beaucoup amusés en attrapant les poneys; **skiing is fun** c'est amusant de faire du ski; **I do it for fun** je le fais pour m'amuser; ★ **to make fun of somebody** se moquer de quelqu'un.

funds *plural noun* fonds *Masc. plural.*

funeral *noun* enterrement *Masc.*

funfair *noun* fête *Fem.* foraine.

funny *adjective* **1** (*when you laugh*) drôle; **how funny you are!** que tu es drôle!; **a funny story** une histoire drôle; **2** (*strange*) bizarre; **that's funny, I'm sure I paid** c'est bizarre, je suis certain que j'ai payé; **a funny noise** un bruit bizarre.

fur *noun* **1** (*on an animal*) poils *Masc. plural*; **2** (*for a coat*) fourrure *Fem.*; **a fur coat** un manteau de fourrure.

furious *adjective* furieux (*Fem.* furieuse); **she was furious with**

Steve elle était furieuse contre Steve.

furniture *noun* meubles *Masc. plural* **to buy some furniture** acheter des meubles; **a piece of furniture** un meuble.

further *adverb* plus loin; **further than the station** plus loin que la gare; **ten kilometres further on** dix kilomètres plus loin; **further forward** plus en avant; **further back** plus en arrière.

fuse *noun* fusible *Masc.*

fuss *noun* histoires *Fem. plural*; **to make a fuss** faire des histoires; **to make a fuss about the bill** faire toute une histoire à propos de l'addition.

fussy *adjective* **to be fussy about something** être difficile sur quelque chose (*food, for example*).

future *noun* **1** avenir *Masc.*; **in future** à l'avenir; **in the future** dans l'avenir; **2** (*in grammar*) futur *Masc.*; **a verb in the future** un verbe au futur.

Gg

gadget *noun* gadget *Masc.*

gain *verb* **1** gagner [1]; **in order to gain time** pour gagner du temps; **we have nothing to gain** nous n'avons rien à gagner; **2 to gain speed** prendre de la vitesse; **to gain weight** prendre du poids.

galaxy *noun* galaxie *Fem.*

gale *noun* vent *Masc.* violent.

allery noun **an art gallery** (public) un musée; (private) une galerie.

amble verb jouer [1].

ambling noun jeu Masc.

ame noun **1** jeu Masc.; **children's games** les jeux d'enfant; **a game of chance** un jeu de hasard; **a board game** un jeu de société; **2 a game of** une partie de; **to have a game of cards** faire une partie de cartes; **a match** Masc.; **a game of football** un match de foot; **to be good at games: Jack's very good at games** Jack est très bon en sport.

ang noun bande Fem.; **all the gang were there** toute la bande y était.

angster noun gangster Masc.

ap noun **1** (hole) trou Masc.; **2** (in time) intervalle Masc.; **a two-year gap** un intervalle de deux ans; **3 an age gap** une différence d'âge.

ap year noun année Fem. sabbatique avant d'entrer à l'université.

arage noun garage Masc.

arden noun jardin Masc.

ardener noun jardinier Masc.; **he wants to be a gardener** il veut être jardinier.

ardening noun jardinage Masc.

arlic noun ail Masc.

arlic mayonnaise noun aïoli Masc.

arment noun vêtement Masc.

as noun gaz Masc.

as cooker noun cuisinière Fem. à gaz.

gas fire noun radiateur Masc. à gaz.

gas meter noun compteur Masc. à gaz.

gate noun **1** (garden) portail Masc.; **2** (field) barrière Fem.; **3** (at the airport) porte Fem.

gather verb **1** (people) se rassembler [1]; **a crowd gathered** une foule s'est rassemblée; **2** cueillir [35] (fruit, vegetables, flowers); **3 as far as I can gather** autant que je sache.

gay adjective homosexuel (Fem. homosexuelle).

gaze verb **to gaze at something** regarder [1] quelque chose.

GCSEs noun plural You can explain GCSEs briefly as follows: Ce sont des examens que l'on passe à environ 16 ans dans un certain nombre de matières (12 au maximum). La meilleure note que l'on peut obtenir est A-star et la note la plus basse est N. Une fois qu'ils ont obtenu leurs GCSEs, de nombreux étudiants se préparent pour les A levels; SEE **A levels**.

gear noun **1** (in a car) vitesse Fem.; **to change gear** changer de vitesse; **2** (equipment) matériel Masc.; **camping gear** du matériel de camping; **3** (things) affaires; **I've left all my gear at Gary's** j'ai laissé toutes mes affaires chez Gary.

gear lever noun levier Masc. de vitesses.

gel noun **hair gel** le gel pour les cheveux.

Gemini noun Gémeaux Masc. plural; **Steph's Gemini** Steph est Gémeaux.

a
b
c
d
e
f
g
h
i
j
k
l
m
n
o
p
q
r
s
t
u
v
w
x
y
z

gender noun (of a word) genre Masc.; **what is the gender of 'maison'?** quel est le genre de 'maison'?

general noun général Masc. (plural généraux); **General Jackson** le général Jackson.
general adjective général (Masc. plural généraux); **in general** en général.

general election noun élections Fem. plural législatives.

general knowledge noun connaissances Fem. plural générales.

generally adverb généralement.

generation noun génération Fem.

generator noun générateur Masc.

generous adjective généreux (Fem. généreuse).

genetics noun génétique Fem.

Geneva noun Genève; **to Geneva** à Genève; **in Geneva** à Genève; **Lake Geneva** le lac Léman.

genius noun génie Masc.; **Lisa, you're a genius!** Lisa, tu es un génie!

gentle adjective doux (Fem. douce).

gentleman noun monsieur Masc. (plural messieurs); **ladies and gentlemen** mesdames et messieurs.

gently adverb doucement.

gents noun toilettes Fem. plural, (marked on the door) 'Messieurs'; **where's the gents?** où sont les toilettes?

genuine adjective 1 (real) véritable; **a genuine diamond** un véritable diamant; 2 (authentic) authentique; **a genuine signature**

une signature authentique; 3 sincère (person); **she's very genuine** elle est très sincère.

geography noun géographie Fem.

geology noun géologie Fem.

geometry noun géométrie Fem.

germ noun microbe Masc.

German noun 1 Allemand Masc., Allemande Fem.; 2 (language) allemand.
German adjective allemand.

Germany noun Allemagne Fem.; **Germany** en Allemagne; **in Germany** en Allemagne.

get verb 1 (have, receive) avoir [5]; **he's got lots of money** il a beaucoup d'argent; **she's got long hair** elle a les cheveux longs; **I got a bike for my birthday** j'ai eu un vé pour mon anniversaire; **I got your letter yesterday** j'ai eu ta lettre hier; **I got fifteen for my French homework** j'ai eu quinze pour mo devoir français; 2 (fetch) chercher [1]; **I'll go and get some bread** j'irai chercher du pain; **I'll get you bag for you** je te chercherai ton sa 3 (obtain) trouver [1]; **Fred's got a job** Fred a trouvé un emploi; **wher did you get that jacket?** où est-ce que tu as trouvé cette veste?; 4 to **have got to do** devoir [8] faire; **I'v got to phone before midday** je dois appeler avant midi; 5 to get **somewhere** arriver [1] quelque part; **when we got to London** quand nous sommes arrivés à Londres; **to get here (or there)** arriver; **we got here this mornin** nous sommes arrivés ce matin; **what time did they get there?** il

436

sont arrivés à quelle heure?;
6 (*become*) commencer [61] à être;
I'm getting tired je commence à
être fatigué; **it's getting late** il
commence à être tard; **it's getting
dark** il commence à faire nuit; **I'm
getting hungry** je commence à
avoir faim; **7 to get something
done** faire [10] faire quelque chose;
**I'm getting my hair cut this
afternoon** je vais me faire couper
les cheveux cet après-midi.

to get back rentrer [1]; **Mum gets
back at six** Maman rentre à six
heures.

to get something back récupérer
[24] quelque chose; **did you get your
books back?** est-ce que tu as
récupéré tes livres?

to get into something monter [1]
dans quelque chose (*a vehicle*); **he
got into the car** il est monté dans la
voiture.

to get off something descendre [3]
de quelque chose; **I got off the train
at Banbury** je suis descendu du
train à Banbury.

to get on aller [7]; **how's Amanda
getting on?** comment va Amanda?

to get on something monter [1]
dans quelque chose (*vehicle*); **she
got on the train at Reading** elle est
montée dans le train à Reading.

to get on with somebody
s'entendre [3] avec quelqu'un; **she
doesn't get on with her brother**
elle ne s'entend pas avec son frère.

to get out of something descendre
[3] de quelque chose (*vehicle*); **Laura
got out of the car** Laura est
descendue de la voiture.

to get something out sortir [72]

quelque chose; **Robert got his
guitar out** Robert a sorti sa guitare.

● **to get together** se voir; [13]; **we
must get together soon** il faut
qu'on se voie bientôt.

● **to get up** se lever; [50]; **I get up at
seven** je me lève à sept heures.

ghost *noun* fantôme *Masc.*

giant *noun* géant *Masc.*, géante *Fem.*
giant *adjective* énorme; **a giant
lorry** un énorme camion.

giddy *adjective* **to feel giddy** avoir
[5] le tournis; **I'm feeling giddy** j'ai
le tournis.

gift *noun* **1** cadeau *Masc.* (*plural*
cadeaux); **a Christmas gift** un
cadeau de Noël; **2 to have a gift for
something** être doué pour quelque
chose; **Jo has a real gift for
languages** Jo est vraiment douée
pour les langues.

gifted *adjective* doué.

gig *noun* concert *Masc.* de rock.

gigabyte *noun* gigaoctet *Masc.*; **a
twenty gigabyte hard disk** un
disque dur de 20 gigaoctets.

gigantic *adjective* gigantesque.

gin *noun* gin *Masc.*

ginger *noun* gingembre *Masc.*

gipsy *noun* **1** (*in general*) bohémien
Masc., bohémienne *Fem.*; **2** (*from
Spain*) gitan *Masc.*, gitane *Fem.*;
3 (*from Eastern Europe*) tsigane
Masc. & Fem.

giraffe *noun* giraffe *Fem.*

girl *noun* **1** fille *Fem.*; **three boys and
four girls** trois garçons et quatre
filles; **a little girl** une petite fille;
when I was a little girl quand

j'étais petite; **2** (*a teenager or young woman*) jeune fille *Fem.*; **an eighteen-year-old girl** une jeune fille de dix-huit ans.

girlfriend *noun* copine *Fem.*; **Darren's gone out with his girlfriend** Darren est sorti avec sa copine; **Lizzie and her girlfriends have gone to the cinema** Lizzie et ses copines sont allées au cinéma.

give *verb* donner [1]; **to give something to somebody** donner quelque chose à quelqu'un; **I'll give you my address** je te donnerai mon adresse; **give me the key** donne-moi la clé; **Yasmin's dad gave her the money** le père de Yasmin lui a donné l'argent.

● **to give something away** donner quelque chose; **she's given away all her books** elle a donné tous ses livres.

● **to give something back to somebody** rendre [3] quelque chose à quelqu'un; **I gave her back the keys** je lui ai rendu les clés.

● **to give in** céder [24]; **my mum said no but she gave in in the end** maman a dit non, mais elle a fini par céder.

● **to give up** abandonner [1]; **I give up!** j'abandonne!

● **to give up doing** arrêter [1] de faire; **she's given up smoking** elle a arrêté de fumer.

glacier *noun* glacier *Masc.*

glad *adjective* content; **I'm glad to hear he's better** je suis content d'apprendre qu'il va mieux; **I'm glad to be back** je suis content d'être de retour.

glamorous *adjective* **1** (*life*) luxueux (*Fem.* luxueuse); **2** (*job*) prestigieux (*Fem.* prestigieuse); **3** (*woman*) élégant.

glance *noun* coup d'œil *Masc.* **glance** *verb* **to glance at something** jeter [48] un coup d'œil quelque chose; **Sara glanced at th envelope** Sara a jeté un coup d'œil l'enveloppe.

glass *noun* verre *Masc.*; **a glass of water** un verre d'eau; **a glass tabl** une table en verre.

glasses *plural noun* lunettes *Fem. plural*; **to wear glasses** porter des lunettes.

glider *noun* planeur *Masc.*

global *adjective* mondial (*Masc. plural* mondiaux).

global warming *noun* le réchauffement de la planète.

globe *noun* globe *Masc.*

gloomy *adjective* **1** (*expression*) lugubre; **2** (*weather*) déprimant.

glory *noun* gloire *Fem.*

glove *noun* gant *Masc.*; **a pair of gloves** une paire de gants.

glove compartment *noun* boîte *Fem.* à gants.

glue *noun* colle *Fem.*

go *noun* **1** (*in a game*) **whose go is it?** c'est à qui de jouer?; **it's my go** c'est à moi de jouer; **2 to have a go at doing** essayer de faire; **I'll have a go at mending it for you** j'essaiera de le réparer pour toi.

go *verb* **1** aller [7]; **we're going to London tomorrow** nous allons à Londres demain; **Mark's gone to**

he dentist's Mark est allé chez le dentiste; **to go for a walk** aller se **romener**; **2** (*with another verb*) **aller**; **I'm going to make some tea** e vais faire du thé; **he was going to phone me** il allait m'appeler; **3** (*leave*) partir [58]; **Pauline's already gone** Pauline est déjà **partie**; **we're going on holiday tomorrow** nous partons en **vacances demain**; **4** (*an event*) se **passer** [1]; **did the party go well?** est-ce que la soirée s'est bien **passée?**

to go away s'en aller [7]; **go away!** va-t-en!

to go back 1 retourner [1]; **I'm going back to France in March** je retourne en France en mars; **I'm not going back there again!** je n'y retourne plus!; **2** (*to home, school, office*) rentrer [1]; **I went back home** je suis rentré chez moi

to go down 1 descendre [3]; **she's gone down to the kitchen** elle est descendue dans la cuisine; **to go down the stairs** descendre **l'escalier**; **2** (*price, temperature*) **baisser** [1]; **prices have gone down** les prix ont baissé; **3** (*tyre, balloon, airbed*) se dégonfler [1].

to go in entrer [1]; **he went in and shut the door** il est entré et il a **fermé la porte.**

to go into 1 (*person*) entrer dans; **Fran went into the kitchen** Fran **est entrée dans la cuisine; 2** (*object*) entrer [1] dans; **this file won't go into my bag** ce classeur ne rentre **pas dans mon sac**

to go off 1 (*bomb*) exploser [1]; **2** (*alarm clock*) sonner [1]; **my alarm**

clock went off at six mon réveil a sonné à six heures; **3** (*fire or burglar alarm*) se déclencher [1]; **the fire alarm went off** l'alarme d'incendie s'est déclenchée

● **to go on 1** se passer [1]; **what's going on?** qu'est-ce qui se passe?; **2 to go on doing** continuer [1] à faire; **she went on talking** elle a continué à parler; **3 to go on about something** ne pas arrêter [1] de parler de quelque chose; **he's always going on about his dog** il n'arrête pas de parler de son chien

● **to go out 1** sortir [72]; **I'm going out tonight** je sors ce soir; **she went out of the kitchen** elle est sortie de la cuisine; **2 to be going out with somebody** sortir avec quelqu'un; **she's going out with my brother** elle sort avec mon frère; **3** (*light, fire*) s'éteindre [60]; **the light went out** la lumière s'est éteinte

● **to go past something** passer [1] devant quelque chose; **we went past your house** nous sommes passés devant chez toi.

● **to go round: to go round to somebody's house** aller [7] chez quelqu'un; **I went round to Fred's last night** je suis allé chez Fred hier soir.

● **to go round something 1** faire [10] le tour de (*building, park, garden*); **2** visiter [1] (*museum, monument*).

● **to go through** passer [1] par; **the train went through Dijon** le train est passé par Dijon; **you can go through my office** tu peux passer par mon bureau.

● **to go up 1** (*person*) monter [1]; **she's gone up to her room** elle est montée dans sa chambre; **to go up the stairs** monter l'escalier; **2** (*prices*) augmenter [1]; **the price of petrol has gone up** le prix de l'essence a augmenté

goal *noun* but *Masc.*; **to score a goal** marquer un but; **to win by three goals to two** gagner trois buts à deux.

goalkeeper *noun* gardien *Masc.* de but.

goat *noun* chèvre *Fem.*; **goat's cheese** le fromage de chèvre.

God *noun* Dieu *Masc.*; **to believe in God** croire en Dieu.

god *noun* dieu *Masc.* (*plural* dieux).

godchild *noun* filleul *Masc.*, filleule *Fem.*

goddaughter *noun* filleule *Fem.*

goddess *noun* déesse *Fem.*

godfather *noun* parrain *Masc.*

godmother *noun* marraine *Fem.*

godson *noun* filleul *Masc.*

goggles *plural noun* lunettes *Fem. plural*; **swimming goggles** les lunettes de plongée; **skiing goggles** les lunettes de ski.

go-karting *noun* karting *Masc.*; **to go go-karting** faire du karting.

gold *noun* or *Masc.*; **a gold bracelet** un bracelet en or.

goldfish *noun* poisson *Masc.* rouge.

golf *noun* golf *Masc.*; **to play golf** jouer au golf.

golf club *noun* **1** (*place*) club *Masc.* de golf; **2** (*iron*) crosse *Fem.* de golf.

golf course *noun* terrain *Masc.* de golf.

golfer *noun* golfeur *Masc.*, golfeuse *Fem.*

good *adjective* **1** bon (*Fem.* bonne); **she's a good teacher** c'est un bon professeur; **the cherries are very good** les cerises sont très bonnes; **2 to be good for you** être bon pour la santé; **tomatoes are good for you** les tomates sont bonnes pour santé; **3 to be good at** être bon en; **she's good at art** elle est bonne en dessin; **4** (*well-behaved*) sage; **be good!** sois sage!; **5** (*kind*) gentil (*Fem.* gentille); **she's been very good to me** elle a été très gentille avec moi; **6 for good** pour de bon; **I've stopped smoking for good** j'ai arrêté de fumer pour de bon.

good afternoon *exclamation* bonjour.

goodbye *exclamation* au revoir.

good evening *exclamation* bonsoir.

Good Friday *noun* le Vendredi saint.

good-looking *adjective* beau (*Fem.* belle) (*Masc. plural* beaux); **Maya's boyfriend's really good-looking** le copain de Maya est très beau.

good morning *exclamation* bonjour.

goodness *exclamation* mon Dieu; **for goodness sake!** au nom du ci

goodnight *exclamation* bonne nuit.

goods *plural noun* marchandises *Fem. plural*.

goods train *noun* train *Masc.* de marchandises.

oose noun oie Fem.

oose pimples noun chair Fem.
le poule.

orgeous adjective superbe; **a**
gorgeous dress une robe superbe;
t's a gorgeous day il fait un temps
superbe.

orilla noun gorille Masc.

orse noun ajoncs Masc. plural.

osh exclamation ça alors!

ossip noun **1** (person) bavard
Masc., bavarde Fem.; **2** (news)
nouvelles Fem. plural; **what's the**
atest gossip? quoi de neuf?

gossip verb bavarder [1].

overnment noun gouvernement
Masc.

rab verb **1** saisir [2]; **she grabbed**
my arm elle m'a saisi par le bras;
2 to grab something from
somebody arracher [1] quelque
chose à quelqu'un; **he grabbed the**
book from me il m'a arraché le
ivre.

raceful adjective élégant.

rade noun (mark) note Fem.; **to get**
good grades avoir de bonnes notes.

radual adjective progressif (Fem.
progressive).

radually adverb petit à petit; **the**
weather got gradually better le
temps s'est amélioré petit à petit.

raffiti plural noun graffiti Masc.
plural.

rain noun grain Masc.

rammar noun grammaire Fem.

rammar school noun (from
age 11 to 15) collège Masc.; (from age
15 to 18) lycée Masc.

grammatical adjective **a**
grammatical error une faute de
grammaire.

gramme noun gramme Masc.

gran noun mamie Fem. (informal).

grandchildren plural noun
petits-enfants Masc. plural.

granddad noun papy Masc.
(informal).

granddaughter noun petite-fille
Fem.

grandfather noun grand-père
Masc.

grandma noun mamie Fem.
(informal).

grandmother noun grand-mère
Fem.

grandpa noun papi Masc.
(informal).

grandparents plural noun
grandparents Masc. plural.

grandson noun petit-fils Masc.

granny noun mamie Fem.
(informal).

grape noun **a grape** un grain de
raisin; **to buy some grapes** acheter
du raisin; **do you like grapes?** est-
ce que tu aimes le raisin?; **a bunch**
of grapes une grappe de raisin.

grapefruit noun pamplemousse
Masc.

graph noun graphique Masc.

graphic designer noun
graphiste Masc. & Fem.

graphics noun visualisation Fem.
graphique.

grasp verb saisir [2].

grass *noun* **1** herbe *Fem.*; **sitting on the grass** assis sur l'herbe; **2** (*lawn*) pelouse *Fem.*; **to cut the grass** tondre la pelouse.

grasshopper *noun* sauterelle *Fem.*

grate *verb* râper [1]; **grated cheese** du fromage râpé.

grateful *adjective* reconnaissant.

grater *noun* râpe *Fem.*

grave[1] *noun* tombe *Fem.*

grave[2] *noun* accent *Masc.* grave.

gravel *noun* gravillons *Masc. plural.*

graveyard *noun* cimetière *Masc.*

gravity *noun* pesanteur *Fem.*

gravy *noun* sauce *Fem.* au jus de rôti.

grease *noun* graisse *Fem.*

greasy *adjective* gras (*Fem.* grasse); **to have greasy skin** avoir la peau grasse; **I hate greasy food** je déteste la nourriture grasse.

great *adjective* **1** grand; **a great poet** un grand poète; **2** (*terrific*) génial (*Masc. plural* géniaux); **it was a great party!** ça a été une soirée géniale!; **great!** génial!; **3 a great deal of** beaucoup de; **a great many** beaucoup de; **there are a great many things still to be done** il reste beaucoup de choses à faire.

Great Britain *noun* Grande-Bretagne *Fem.*; **in Great Britain** en Grande-Bretagne; **to Great Britain** en Grande-Bretagne; **to be from Great Britain** être britannique.

Greece *noun* Grèce *Fem.*; **to Greece** en Grèce; **in Greece** en Grèce.

greedy *adjective* (*with food*) gourmand.

Greek *noun* **1** (*person*) Grec *Masc.*, Grecque *Fem.*; **2** (*language*) grec *Masc.*
Greek *adjective* grec (*Fem.* grecque).

green *noun* **1** (*colour*) vert *Masc.*; **a pale green** un vert pâle; **2 greens** (*vegetables*) les légumes verts; **3 the Greens** (*ecologists*) les Verts *Masc. plural.*
green *adjective* **1** vert; **a green door** une porte verte; **2** écologiste **the Green Party** le parti écologist

greengrocer *noun* marchand *Masc.* de fruits et légumes.

greenhouse *noun* serre *Fem.*

greenhouse effect *noun* effe *Masc.* de serre.

greetings *plural noun* **Season's Greetings** meilleurs vœux *Masc. plural.*

greetings card *noun* carte *Fem* de vœux.

grey *adjective* gris; **a grey skirt** un jupe grise; **to have grey hair** avoi les cheveux gris.

greyhound *noun* lévrier *Masc.*

grid *noun* **1** (*grating*) grille *Fem.*; **2** (*network*) réseau *Masc.* (*plural* réseaux).

grief *noun* chagrin *Masc.*

grill *noun* (*of a cooker*) gril *Masc.*
grill *verb* **to grill something** fair [10] griller quelque chose; **I grille the sausages** j'ai fait griller les saucisses.

grim *adjective* sinistre.

grin noun sourire Masc.

grin verb sourire [68].

grip noun prise Fem.

grip verb serrer [1].

grit noun (for roads) gravillons Masc. plural.

groan noun 1 (of pain) gémissement Masc.; 2 (of disgust, boredom) grognement Masc.

groan verb 1 (in pain) gémir [2]; 2 (in disgust, boredom) grogner [1].

grocer's noun épicerie Fem.; **I met Jake in the grocer's** j'ai rencontré Jake à l'épicerie.

grocer noun épicier Masc.; **my dad's a grocer** mon père est épicier.

groceries plural noun provisions Fem. plural; **to buy some groceries** acheter des provisions.

groom noun (bridegroom) marié Masc.; **the bride and groom** les jeunes mariés.

gross adjective 1 **a gross injustice** une injustice flagrante; 2 **a gross error** une erreur grossière; 3 (disgusting) dégoûtant; **the food was gross!** la nourriture était dégoûtante!

ground noun 1 terre Fem.; **to sit on the ground** s'asseoir par terre; **to throw something on the ground** jeter quelque chose par terre; 2 (for sport) terrain Masc.; **a football ground** un terrain de foot.

ground adjective moulu; **ground coffee** du café moulu.

ground floor noun rez-de-chaussée Masc.; **they live on the ground floor** ils habitent au rez-de-chaussée.

group noun groupe Masc.

grow verb 1 (plant, hair) pousser [1]; **you hair's grown!** tes cheveux ont poussé!; 2 (person) grandir [2]; **my little sister's grown a lot this year** ma petite sœur a beaucoup grandi cette année; 3 (number) augmenter [1]; **the number of students has grown** le nombre d'étudiants a augmenté; 4 faire [10] pousser (fruit, vegetables); **our neighbours grow strawberries** nos voisins font pousser des fraises; 5 **to grow a beard** se laisser [1] pousser la barbe; 6 **to grow old** vieillir [2].

● **to grow up** grandir [2]; **the children are growing up** les enfants grandissent; **she grew up in Scotland** elle a grandi en Écosse.

growl verb grogner [1].

grown-up noun adulte Masc. & Fem.

growth noun croissance Fem.

grudge noun **to bear a grudge against somebody** en vouloir à quelqu'un; **she bears me a grudge** elle m'en veut.

gruesome adjective horrible.

grumble verb se plaindre [31]; **she's always grumbling** elle est toujours en train de se plaindre; **to grumble about something** se plaindre de quelque chose.

guarantee noun garantie Fem.; **a year's guarantee** une garantie d'un an.

guarantee verb garantir [2].

a
b
c
d
e
f
g
h
i
j
k
l
m
n
o
p
q
r
s
t
u
v
w
x
y
z

guard *noun* **1** a prison guard un gardien de prison; **2** (*on a train*) chef *Masc.* de train; **3** a security guard un vigile.
guard *verb* surveiller [1].

guard dog *noun* chien *Masc.* de garde.

guardian *noun* (*of child*) tuteur *Masc.*, tutrice *Fem.*

guess *noun* have a guess! devine!; it's a good guess tu as deviné.
guess *verb* deviner [1]; guess who I saw last night! devine qui j'ai vu hier soir!; you'll never guess! tu ne devineras jamais!

guest *noun* **1** invité *Masc.*, invitée *Fem.*; we've got guests coming tonight nous avons des invités ce soir; **2** (*in a hotel*) client *Masc.*, cliente *Fem.*; **3** a paying guest un hôte payant.

guesthouse *noun* pension *Fem.* de famille.

guide *noun* **1** (*person or book*) guide *Masc.*; **2** (*girl guide*) guide *Fem.*, (*belonging to a church company of girl guides*) éclaireuse *Fem.*

guidebook *noun* guide *Masc.*

guide dog *noun* chien *Masc.* d'aveugle.

guideline *noun* indication *Fem.*

guilty *adjective* coupable; to feel guilty se sentir coupable.

guinea pig *noun* (*pet*) cochon *Masc.* d'Inde; (*in an experiment*) cobaye *Masc.*; they want me to be a guinea pig ils veulent que je serve de cobaye.

guitar *noun* guitare *Fem.*; to play the guitar jouer de la guitare; on the guitar à la guitare.

guitarist *noun* guitariste *Masc. & Fe*

gum *noun* **1** (*in mouth*) gencive *Fem* **2** (*chewing gum*) chewing-gum *Mas*

gun *noun* **1** revolver *Masc.*; **2** (*rifle*) fusil *Masc.*

gust *noun* a gust of wind une rafal de vent.

gutter *noun* (*in the street*) caniveau (*plural* caniveaux).

guy *noun* type *Masc.* (*informal*); he' a nice guy c'est un type sympa; a guy from Newcastle un type qui vient de Newcastle.

guy rope *noun* corde *Fem.* d'attach

gym *noun* gym *Fem.*; to go to the gym aller à la gym.

gymnasium *noun* gymnase *Masc*

gymnast *noun* gymnaste *Masc. & Fem.*

gymnastics *noun* gymnastique *Fem.*

gym shoe *noun* tennis *Masc.*

Hh

habit *noun* habitude *Fem.*; to be in the habit of doing avoir l'habitud de faire; it's a bad habit c'est une mauvaise habitude.

haddock *noun* églefin *Masc.*; smoked haddock haddock *Masc.*

hail *noun* grêle *Fem.*

hailstone *noun* grêlon *Masc.*

ailstorm *noun* averse *Fem.* de grêle.

air *noun* **1** cheveux *Masc. plural*; **to have short hair** avoir les cheveux courts; **to brush your hair** se brosser les cheveux; **to wash your hair** se laver les cheveux; **to have your hair cut** se faire couper les cheveux; **she's had her hair cut** elle s'est fait couper les cheveux; **2 a hair** (*from the head*) un cheveu; (*from the body*) un poil.

airbrush *noun* brosse *Fem.* à cheveux.

aircut *noun* **1** coupe *Fem.*; **I like your new haircut** j'aime bien ta nouvelle coupe; **2 to have a haircut** se faire couper les cheveux.

airdresser *noun* coiffeur *Masc.*, coiffeuse *Fem.*; **she's a hairdresser** elle est coiffeuse; **at the hairdresser's** chez le coiffeur.

air drier *noun* sèche-cheveux *Masc.*

air gel *noun* gel *Masc.* pour les cheveux.

airgrip *noun* pince *Fem.* à cheveux.

air remover *noun* crème *Fem.* dépilatoire.

airslide *noun* barrette *Fem.*

airspray *noun* laque *Fem.*

airstyle *noun* coiffure *Fem.*

airy *adjective* poilu.

Haiti *noun* Haïti *Masc.*

Haitian *noun* Haïtien *Masc.*, Haïtienne *Fem.*
Haitian *adjective* haïtien (*Fem.* haïtienne).

half *noun* **1** moitié *Fem.*; **half of** la moitié de; **I gave him half of the money** je lui ai donné la moitié de l'argent; **half an apple** la moitié d'une pomme; **you've only eaten half of it** tu n'en as mangé que la moitié; **half the people** la moitié des gens; **2 to cut something in half** couper quelque chose en deux; **3** (*as a fraction*) demi; **three and a half** trois et demi; **she's five and a half** elle a cinq ans et demi; **4** (*in time*) demi, demie; **half an hour** une demi-heure; **an hour and a half** une heure et demie; **it's half past three** il est trois heures et demie; **5** (*in weights and measures*) demi, demie; **half a litre** un demi-litre; **half a cup** une demi-tasse.

half hour *noun* demi-heure *Fem.*; **every half hour** toutes les demi-heures.

half price *adjective, adverb* à moitié prix; **half-price CDs** des CD à moitié prix; **I bought it half price** je l'ai acheté à moitié prix.

half-time *noun* mi-temps *Fem.*; **at half-time** à la mi-temps.

halfway *adverb* **1** à mi-chemin; **halfway between Paris and Dijon** à mi-chemin entre Paris et Dijon; **2 to be halfway through doing** avoir à moitié fini de faire; **I'm halfway through my homework** j'ai à moitié fini mes devoirs.

hall *noun* **1** (*in a house*) entrée *Fem.*; **2** (*public*) salle *Fem.*; **the village hall** la salle des fêtes; **a concert hall** une salle de concert.

a b c d e f g **h** i j k l m n o p q r s t u v w x y z

Hallowe'en *noun* la veille de la Toussaint (*the French do not have any particular customs for this date*).

ham *noun* jambon *Masc.*; **a slice of ham** une tranche de jambon; **a ham sandwich** un sandwich au jambon.

hamburger *noun* hamburger *Masc.*

hammer *noun* marteau *Masc.* (*plural* marteaux).

hammock *noun* hamac *Masc.*

hamster *noun* hamster *Masc.*

hand *noun* **1** main *Fem.*; **to have something in your hand** avoir quelque chose à la main; **to hold somebody's hand** tenir quelqu'un par la main; **2 to give somebody a hand** donner un coup de main à quelqu'un; **can you give me a hand to move the table?** est-ce que tu peux me donner un coup de main pour déplacer la table?; **do you need a hand?** est-ce que tu as besoin d'un coup de main?; **3 on the other hand** ... par contre ...; **4** (*of a watch or clock*) aiguille *Fem.*; **the hour hand** l'aiguille des heures. **hand** *verb* **to hand something to somebody** passer [1] quelque chose à quelqu'un; **I handed him the keys** je lui ai passé les clés.

● **to hand something in** rendre [3] quelque chose; **I've handed in my homework** j'ai rendu mon devoir.

● **to hand something out** distribuer [1] quelque chose; **Claire handed out the exercise books** Claire a distribué les cahiers.

handbag *noun* sac *Masc.* à main (*plural* sacs à main).

handcuffs *plural noun* menottes *Fem. plural.*

handful *noun* **a handful of** une poignée de.

handicapped *adjective* handicapé.

handkerchief *noun* mouchoir *Masc.*

handle *noun* **1** (*of a door or drawer*) poignée *Fem.*; **2** (*on a cup or basket*) anse *Fem.*; **3** (*of a knife, tool, or saucepan*) manche *Masc.*; **4** (*of a frying pan*) queue *Fem.* **handle** *verb* **1** s'occuper [1] de; **Gina handles the accounts** Gina s'occupe de la comptabilité; **2 she's good at handling people** elle a un bon contact avec les gens; **3 I can't handle any more problems!** j'ai assez de problèmes comme ça!

handlebars *plural noun* guidon *Masc.*

hand luggage *noun* bagages *Masc. plural* à main.

handmade *adjective* fait à la main.

handsome *adjective* beau (*Fem.* belle); **he's a handsome guy** c'est un beau type.

handwriting *noun* écriture *Fem.*

handy *adjective* **1** pratique; **this little knife's very handy** ce petit couteau est très pratique; **2** sous la main; **I always keep a notebook handy** je garde toujours un calepin sous la main.

hang *verb* **1** être [6] accroché; **there was a mirror hanging on the wall** il y avait un miroir accroché au mur; **2 to hang something** accrocher [1] quelque chose; **we**

446

hung the mirror on the wall nous avons accroché le miroir au mur.

• to hang around traîner [1]; we were hanging around outside the cinema on traînait devant le cinéma.

• to hang down pendre [3].

• to hang on attendre [3]; hang on a second! attends une seconde!

• to hang up (on the phone) raccrocher [1]; she hung up on me elle m'a raccroché au nez (literally: she hung up on my nose).

• to hang something up accrocher [1] quelque chose; you can hang your coat up in the hall tu peux accrocher ton manteau dans l'entrée.

hang-gliding noun deltaplane Masc.; to go hang-gliding faire du deltaplane.

hangover noun gueule Fem. de bois; to have a hangover avoir la gueule de bois.

happen verb 1 se passer [1]; what's happening? qu'est-ce qui se passe?; it happened in June ça s'est passé en juin; 2 what's happened to the can-opener? où est l'ouvre-boîte?; 3 if you happen to see Jill si par hasard tu vois Jill.

happily adverb 1 joyeusement; she smiled happily elle a souri joyeusement; 2 (willingly) volontiers; I'll happily do it for you je le ferai pour toi volontiers.

happiness noun bonheur Masc.

happy adjective heureux (Fem. heureuse); a happy child un enfant heureux; Happy Birthday! Bon anniversaire!

harbour noun port Masc.

hard adjective 1 dur; to go hard durcir; 2 (difficult) difficile; a hard question une question difficile; it's hard to know ... il est difficile de savoir ....
hard adverb 1 to work hard travailler dur; 2 to try hard faire beaucoup d'efforts.

hard-boiled egg noun œuf Masc. dur.

hard disk noun (in a computer) disque Masc. dur.

hardly adverb 1 à peine; I can hardly hear him je l'entends à peine; 2 hardly any presque pas de; there's hardly any milk il n'y a presque pas de lait; 3 hardly ever presque jamais; I hardly ever see them je ne les vois presque jamais; 4 there was hardly anybody il n'y avait presque personne.

hard up adjective fauché (informal).

hare noun lièvre Masc.

harm noun it won't do you any harm ça ne te fera pas de mal.
harm verb to harm somebody faire [10] du mal à quelqu'un; they did not harm him ils ne lui ont pas fait de mal; a cup of coffee won't harm you une tasse de café ne te fera pas de mal.

harmful adjective nuisible.

harmless adjective inoffensif (Fem. inoffensive).

harvest noun récolte Fem.; to get the harvest in faire [10] la récolte.

hat noun chapeau Masc. (plural chapeaux).

447

a
b
c
d
e
f
g
h
i
j
k
l
m
n
o
p
q
r
s
t
u
v
w
x
y
z

a
b
c
d
e
f
g
h
i
j
k
l
m
n
o
p
q
r
s
t
u
v
w
x
y
z

hate *verb* détester [1]; **I hate geography** je déteste la géographie.

hatred *noun* haine *Fem.*

haunted *adjective* hanté.

have *verb* **1** avoir [5]; **Anna has three brothers** Anna a trois frères; **how many sisters do you have?** tu as combien de sœurs?; **2 to have got** avoir [5]; **we've got a dog** nous avons un chien; **what have you got in your hand?** qu'est-ce que tu as à la main?; **3** (*to form past tenses, some verbs in French take 'avoir' and some 'être'*) **I've finished** j'ai fini; **have you seen the film?** est-ce que tu as vu le film?; **Rosie hasn't arrived yet** Rosie n'est pas encore arrivée; **he had left** il était parti; **4 to have to do** devoir [8] faire; **I have to phone my mum** je dois appeler ma mère; **5** prendre [64] (*food, drink, a shower*); **we had a coffee** nous avons pris un café; **what will you have?** qu'est-ce que tu prends?; **I'll have an omelette** je prends une omelette; **I'm going to have a shower** je vais prendre une douche; **6 to have lunch** déjeuner [1]; **to have dinner** (*in the evening*) dîner [1]; **7 to have something done** faire [10] faire quelque chose; **I'm going to have my hair cut** je vais me faire couper les cheveux.

hawk *noun* faucon *Masc.*

hay *noun* foin *Masc.*

hay fever *noun* rhume *Masc.* des foins.

hazelnut *noun* noisette *Fem.*

he *pronoun* il; **he lives in Manchester** il habite à Manchester; **he's my brother** c'est mon frère.

head *noun* **1** tête *Fem.*; **he had a cap on his head** il avait une casquette sur la tête; **at the head of the queue** à la tête de la queue; **2** (*of school*) directeur *Masc.*, directrice *Fem.*; **3** (*when tossing a coin*) **'heads or tails?' – 'heads'** 'pile ou face?' – 'face' (*note that it is in fact 'tails or heads' in French*).

● **to head for something** se diriger [52] vers quelque chose; **Liz headed for the door** Liz s'est dirigée vers la porte.

headache *noun* **I've got a headache** j'ai mal à la tête.

headlight *noun* phare *Masc.*

headline *noun* gros titre *Masc.*; **to hit the headlines** faire la une.

headmaster *noun* directeur *Masc.*

headmistress *noun* directrice *Fem.*

headphones *plural noun* casque *Masc. singular.*

headquarters *noun* **1** (*of organization*) siège *Masc.* social; **2** (*military*) quartier *Masc.* général.

headteacher *noun* directeur *Masc.*, directrice *Fem.*

health *noun* santé *Fem.*

health centre *noun* centre *Masc.* médico-social.

healthy *adjective* **1** (*person*) **to be healthy** être en bonne santé; **2 a healthy diet** une alimentation saine.

help

heap *noun* tas Masc.; **I've got heaps of things to do** j'ai un tas de choses à faire.

hear *verb* **1** entendre [3]; **I can't hear you** je ne t'entends pas; **I can't hear anything** je n'entends rien; **2** apprendre [64] (*news*); **I hear you've bought a dog** j'apprends que tu as acheté un chien.
 to hear about something entendre [3] parler de quelque chose; **have you heard about the concert?** as-tu entendu parler du concert?
 to hear from somebody avoir [5] des nouvelles de quelqu'un; **have you heard from Amanda?** as-tu des nouvelles d'Amanda?

hearing aid *noun* Sonotone™ Masc.

heart *noun* **1** cœur Masc.; **to learn something by heart** apprendre quelque chose par cœur; **2** (*in cards*) cœur; **the jack of hearts** le valet de cœur.

heart attack *noun* crise Fem. cardiaque.

heat *noun* chaleur Fem.
heat *verb* **1** chauffer [1]; **the soup's heating** la soupe est en train de chauffer; **2 to heat something** faire [10] chauffer quelque chose; **I'll go and heat the soup** je vais faire chauffer la soupe.
 to heat something up faire [10] réchauffer quelque chose; **I'm heating up the sauce** je fais réchauffer la sauce.

heater *noun* radiateur Masc.

heather *noun* bruyère Fem.

heating *noun* chauffage Masc.

heatwave *noun* vague Fem. de chaleur.

heaven *noun* paradis Masc.

heavy *adjective* **1** lourd; **my rucksack's really heavy** mon sac à dos est très lourd; **2** (*busy*) chargé; **I've got a heavy day tomorrow** j'ai une journée chargée demain; **3 heavy rain** des pluies fortes.

heavy metal *noun* (*music*) hard rock Masc.

hectic *adjective* **a hectic day** une journée mouvementée.

hedge *noun* haie Fem.

hedgehog *noun* hérisson Masc.

heel *noun* talon Masc.

height *noun* **1** (*of a person*) taille Fem.; **2** (*of a building*) hauteur Fem.; **3** (*of a mountain*) altitude Fem.

helicopter *noun* hélicoptère Masc.

hell *noun* enfer Masc.; **it's hell here!** c'est infernal ici!

hello *exclamation* **1** (*polite*) bonjour!; **2** (*informal*) salut!; **3** (*on the telephone*) allô!

helmet *noun* casque Masc.

help *noun* aide Fem.; **do you need any help?** est-ce que tu as besoin d'aide?
help *verb* **1** aider [1]; **to help somebody to do** aider quelqu'un à faire; **can you help me move the table?** peux-tu m'aider à déplacer la table?; **2 to help yourself to something** se servir [71] de quelque chose; **help yourselves to vegetables** servez-vous de légumes; **help yourself!** sers-toi!; **3 help!** au secours!

a
b
c
d
e
f
g
h
i
j
k
l
m
n
o
p
q
r
s
t
u
v
w
x
y
z

a
b
c
d
e
f
g
h
i
j
k
l
m
n
o
p
q
r
s
t
u
v
w
x
y
z

helper noun aide Masc. & Fem.; **helpers are needed to run charity stalls** on a besoin de bénévoles pour tenir les stands de la fête de charité.

helpful adjective (person) serviable.

helping noun portion Fem.; **would you like a second helping of chips?** est-ce que tu veux reprendre des frites?

hem noun ourlet Masc.

hen noun poule Fem.

her pronoun 1 la, l' (before a vowel or silent 'h'); **I know her** je la connais; **I can hear her** je l'entends; **listen to her!** écoute-la!; **I saw her last week** je l'ai vue la semaine dernière; 2 (to her) lui; **I gave her my address** je lui ai donné mon adresse; 3 (after a preposition) elle; **with her** avec elle; **without her** sans elle; (in comparisons) **he's older than her** il est plus âgé qu'elle.
her adjective 1 (before a masculine noun) son; **her brother** son frère; **her book** son livre; 2 (before a feminine noun) sa; **her sister** sa sœur; **her house** sa maison (but 'sa' becomes 'son' before a feminine noun beginning with a vowel or silent 'h') **her address** son adresse; 3 (before a plural noun) ses; **her children** ses enfants; 4 (with parts of the body) le, la, les; **she had a glass in her hand** elle avait un verre à la main; **she's washing her hands** elle se lave les mains.

herb noun herbe Fem.

herd noun troupeau Masc (plural troupeaux).

here adverb 1 ici; **not far from here** pas loin d'ici; 2 là; **Tom isn't here at the moment** Tom n'est pas là en ce moment; 3 **here is** voilà; **here's my address** voilà mon adresse; 4 **here are** voilà; **here are the photos** voilà les photos; **and here they are!** et les voilà!

hero noun héros Masc.

heroin noun héroïne Fem.

heroine noun héroïne Fem.

herring noun hareng Masc.

hers pronoun 1 (for a masculine noun) le sien; **I took my hat and she took hers** j'ai pris mon chapeau et elle a pris le sien; 2 (for a feminine noun) la sienne; **I gave her my address and she gave me hers** je lui ai donné mon adresse et elle m'a donné la sienne; 3 (for a masculine plural noun) les siens; **I've invited my parents and Karen's invited hers** j'ai invité mes parents et Karen a invité les siens; 4 (for a feminine plural noun) les siennes; **I showed her my photos and she showed me hers** je lui ai montré mes photos et elle m'a montré les siennes; 5 à elle; **the green one's hers** le vert est à elle; **it's hers** c'est à elle.

herself pronoun 1 **she's hurt herself** elle s'est blessée; 2 **she said it herself** elle l'a dit elle-même; 3 **she did it by herself** elle l'a fait toute seule.

hesitate verb hésiter [1]; **to hesitate to do** hésiter à faire.

heterosexual adjective, noun hétérosexuel Masc., hétérosexuelle Fem.

i *exclamation* salut!

hiccups *plural noun* **to have the hiccups** avoir le hoquet.

hidden *adjective* caché.

hide *verb* **1** (*person*) se cacher [1]; **she hid behind the door** elle s'est cachée derrière la porte; **2 to hide something** cacher [1] quelque chose; **who's hidden the chocolate?** qui a caché le chocolat?

hide-and-seek *noun* **to play hide-and-seek** jouer à cache-cache.

hi-fi *noun* chaîne *Fem.* hi-fi.

high *adjective* **1** haut; **on a high shelf** sur une étagère haute; **the wall is very high** le mur est très haut; **how high is the wall?** quelle est la hauteur du mur?; **the wall is two metres high** le mur fait deux mètres de hauteur; **2** (*number, price, temperature*) élevé; **food prices are very high** les prix de la nourriture sont très élevés; **3 at high speed** à grande vitesse; **4 high winds** des vents violents; **5 a high voice** une voix aiguë.

Highers, Advanced Highers *noun plural* baccalauréat *Masc.*, bac *Masc.* (*informal*) (*Students take 'le bac' at the end of their secondary education. You can explain Highers briefly as follows: Les Highers sont un examen qui sanctionne l'avant-dernière année d'école secondaire en Écosse. On passe les Highers dans cinq matières au maximum. En dernière année, certains lycéens passent également les Advance Highers dans un maximum de trois matières, qui ont déjà fait l'objet de l'un de leurs Highers. Ces deux examens sont notés de A à C et permettent de s'inscrire à l'université*).

high-heeled *adjective* à hauts talons; **high-heeled shoes** des chaussures à hauts talons.

high jump *noun* saut *Masc.* en hauteur.

highly *adverb* extrêmement.

hijack *verb* **to hijack a plane** détourner [1] un avion.

hijacker *noun* pirate *Masc.* de l'air.

hijacking *noun* détournement *Masc.*

hike *noun* randonnée *Fem.*; **to go on a hike** faire une randonnée.

hiker *noun* randonneur *Masc.*, randonneuse *Fem.*

hiking *noun* randonnée *Fem.*

hilarious *adjective* hilarant.

hill *noun* **1** (*in landscape*) colline *Fem.*; **you can see the hills** on voit les collines; **2** (*hillside*) coteau *Masc.* (*plural* coteaux); **the houses on the hill** les maisons sur le coteau; **3** (*sloping street or road*) **to go up the hill** monter; **you go up the hill to the church and then turn right** vous montez jusqu'à l'église et vous tournez à droite.

him *pronoun* **1** le, l' (*before a vowel or silent 'h'*); **I know him** je le connais; **I can hear him** je l'entends; **listen to him!** écoute-le!; **I saw him last week** je l'ai vu la semaine dernière; **2** (*to him*) lui; **I gave him my address** je lui ai donné mon adresse; **3** (*after a preposition*) lui; **with him** avec lui; **without him** sans

a
b
c
d
e
f
g
h
i
j
k
l
m
n
o
p
q
r
s
t
u
v
w
x
y
z

lui; (*in comparisons*) **she's older than him** elle est plus âgée que lui.

himself *pronoun* **1** **he's hurt himself** il s'est blessé; **2** **he said it himself** il l'a dit lui-même; **3** **he did it by himself** il l'a fait tout seul.

Hindu *adjective* hindou.

hip *noun* hanche Fem.

hippie *noun* hippie Masc. & Fem.

hippopotamus *noun* hippopotame Masc.

hire *noun* location Fem.; **car hire** location de voitures; **for hire** à louer. **hire** *verb* louer [1]; **we're going to hire a car** nous allons louer une voiture.

his *adjective* **1** (*before a masculine noun*) son; **his brother** son frère; **his book** son livre; **2** (*before a feminine noun*) sa; **his sister** sa sœur; **his house** sa maison (*but 'sa' becomes 'son' before a feminine noun beginning with a vowel or silent 'h'*) **his address** son adresse; **3** (*before a plural noun*) ses; **his children** ses enfants; **4** (*with parts of the body*) le, la, les; **he had a glass in his hand** il avait un verre à la main; **he's washing his hands** il se lave les mains.

his *pronoun* **1** (*for a masculine noun*) le sien; **I took my hat and he took his** j'ai pris mon chapeau et il a pris le sien; **2** (*for a feminine noun*) la sienne; **I gave him my address and he gave me his** je lui ai donné mon adresse et il m'a donné la sienne; **3** (*for a masculine plural noun*) les siens; **I've invited my parents and Steve's invited his** j'ai invité mes parents et Steve a invité

les siens; **4** (*for a feminine plural noun*) les siennes; **I showed him my photos and he showed me his** je lui ai montré mes photos et il m'a montré les siennes; **5** à lui; **the green car's his** la voiture verte est à lui; **it's his** c'est à lui.

historic *adjective* historique.

history *noun* histoire Fem.

hit *noun* **1** (*song*) tube Masc. (*informal*); **their latest hit** leur dernier tube; **2** (*success*) succès Masc.; **the film is a huge hit** le film a un succès fou.
hit *verb* **1** frapper [1]; **to hit the ball** frapper la balle; **2** **to hit your head on something** se cogner [1] la tête contre quelque chose; **3** heurter [1]; **the car hit a tree** la voiture a heurté un arbre; **4** **to be hit by a car** (*person*) être [6] renversé par une voiture.

hitch *noun* problème Masc.; **there's been a slight hitch** il y a eu un petit problème.
hitch *verb* **to hitch a lift** faire [10] du stop (*informal*).

hitchhike *verb* faire [10] du stop (*informal*); **we hitchhiked to Dijon** nous sommes allés à Dijon en stop.

hitchhiker *noun* autostoppeur Masc., autostoppeuse Fem.

hitchhiking *noun* autostop Masc.

HIV-negative *adjective* séronégatif (Fem. séronégative).

HIV-positive *adjective* séropositif (Fem. séropositive).

hobby *noun* passe-temps Masc.

hockey *noun* hockey Masc.; **to play hockey** jouer au hockey.

ockey stick *noun* crosse *Fem.* de hockey.

old *verb* **1** tenir [77]; **to hold something in your hand** tenir quelque chose à la main; **can you hold the torch?** est-ce que tu peux tenir la lampe?; **2** (*contain*) contenir [77]; **a jug which holds a litre** un pichet qui contient un litre; **3 to hold a meeting** organiser [1] une réunion; **4 can you hold the line, please** ne quittez pas, s'il vous plaît; **5 hold on!** (*wait*) attends!; (*on telephone*) ne quittez pas!

● **to hold somebody up** (*delay*) retenir [77] quelqu'un; **I was held up at the dentist's** j'ai été retenu chez le dentiste.

● **to hold something up** (*raise*) lever [50] quelque chose; **he held up his glass** il a levé son verre.

old-up *noun* **1** retard *Masc.*; **2** (*traffic jam*) bouchon *Masc.*; **3** (*robbery*) hold-up *Masc.*

ole *noun* trou *Masc.*

oliday *noun* **1** vacances *Fem. plural*; **where are you going for your holiday?** où est-ce que vous partez en vacances?; **have a good holiday!** bonnes vacances!; **to be away on holiday** être en vacances; **to go on holiday** partir en vacances; **the school holidays** les vacances scolaires; **2** (*from work*) congé *Masc.*; **I'm taking two days' holiday next week** je prends deux jours de congé la semaine prochaine; **3 a public holiday** un jour férié; **Monday's a holiday** lundi est férié.

oliday home *noun* résidence *Fem.* secondaire.

Holland *noun* Hollande *Fem.*; **to Holland** en Hollande; **in Holland** en Hollande.

hollow *adjective* creux (*Fem.* creuse).

holly *noun* houx *Masc.*

holy *adjective* saint.

home *noun* maison *Fem.*; **I was at home** j'étais à la maison; **to stay at home** rester à la maison; **make yourself at home** fais comme chez toi.

home *adverb* **1** chez soi; **Susie's gone home** Susie est rentrée chez elle; **I'll call in and see you on my way home** je passerai te voir en rentrant chez moi; **2 to get home** rentrer; **we got home at midnight** nous sommes rentrés à minuit.

homeless *adjective* sans abri; **the homeless** les sans-abri *Masc. plural.*

homemade *adjective* fait maison; **homemade cakes** des gâteaux faits maison.

home match *noun* match *Masc.* à domicile.

homeopathic *adjective* homéopathique.

homesick *adjective* **to be homesick** avoir le mal du pays.

homework *noun* devoirs *Masc. plural*; **I did my homework** j'ai fait mes devoirs; **my French homework** mes devoirs de français; (*written*) mon devoir de français.

homosexual *adjective, noun* homosexuel (*Fem.* homosexuelle).

honest *adjective* honnête.

honestly *adverb* franchement.

453

honesty *noun* honnêteté *Fem.*

honey *noun* miel *Masc.*

honeymoon *noun* voyage *Masc.* de noces; **they're going to Paris on their honeymoon** ils partent à Paris en voyage de noces.

honeysuckle *noun* chèvrefeuille *Masc.*

honour *noun* honneur *Masc.*

hood *noun* capuchon *Masc.*

hook *noun* **1** crochet *Masc.*; **2 to take the phone of the hook** décrocher le téléphone.

hooligan *noun* voyou *Masc.*

hooray *exclamation* hourra!

Hoover™ *noun* aspirateur *Masc.*

hoover *verb* passer [1] l'aspirateur; **I hoovered my bedroom** j'ai passé l'aspirateur dans ma chambre.

hope *noun* espoir *Masc.*; **to give up hope** perdre espoir.
hope *verb* espérer [24]; **we hope you'll be able to come** nous espérons que vous allez pouvoir venir; **hoping to see you on Friday** en espérant te voir vendredi; **here's hoping!** espérons que ça marchera!; **I hope so** je l'espère; **I hope not** j'espère que non.

hopefully *adverb* avec un peu de chance; **hopefully, the film won't have started** avec un peu de chance, le film n'aura pas commencé.

hopeless *adjective* nul (*Fem.* nulle) (*informal*); **I'm completely hopeless at geography** je suis complètement nul en géographie.

horizon *noun* horizon *Masc.*

horizontal *adjective* horizontal (*Masc. plural* horizontaux).

horn *noun* **1** (*of an animal*) corne *Fem.*; **2** (*of a car*) klaxon *Masc.*; **to sound your horn** klaxonner; **3** (*musical instrument*) cor; **to play the horn** jouer du cor.

horoscope *noun* horoscope *Masc.*

horrible *adjective* **1** affreux (*Fem.* affreuse); **the weather was horrible** il a fait un temps affreux; **2** (*person*) désagréable; **she's really horrible!** elle est vraiment désagréable; **he was really horrible to me** il a été vraiment désagréable avec moi.

horrific *adjective* terrible; **a horrific accident** un terrible accident.

horror *noun* horreur *Fem.*

horror film *noun* film *Masc.* d'épouvante.

horse *noun* cheval *Masc.* (*plural* chevaux).

horse chestnut *noun* **1** (*tree*) marronnier *Masc.*; **2** (*nut*) marron *Masc.*

horse racing *noun* courses *Fem. plural* hippiques.

horseshoe *noun* fer *Masc.* à cheval.

hose *noun* tuyau *Masc.* (*plural* tuyaux).

hosepipe *noun* tuyau *Masc.* d'arrosage.

hospital *noun* hôpital *Masc.* (*plural* hôpitaux); **to be in hospital** être à l'hôpital; **to be taken into hospital** être hospitalisé.

ospitality *noun* hospitalité *Fem*.

ost *noun* hôte *Masc*., hôtesse *Fem*.; **my host family is very nice** ma famille d'accueil est très sympathique.

ostage *noun* otage *Masc*.

ostel *noun* **youth hostel** auberge *Fem*. de jeunesse.

ostess *noun* hôtesse *Fem*.; **an air hostess** une hôtesse de l'air.

ot *adjective* **1** chaud; **a hot drink** une boisson chaude; **be careful, the plates are hot!** fais attention, les assiettes sont très chaudes!; **2** (*a person*) **to be hot** avoir chaud; **I'm hot** j'ai chaud; **I'm very hot** j'ai très chaud; **I'm too hot** j'ai trop chaud; **3** (*the weather or temperature in a room*) **it's hot today** il fait chaud aujourd'hui; **it's very hot in the kitchen** il fait très chaud dans la cuisine; **4** (*food: spicy*) épicé; **the curry's too hot for me** le curry est trop épicé pour moi.

ot dog *noun* hot-dog *Masc*.

otel *noun* hôtel *Masc*.

our *noun* heure *Fem*.; **two hours later** deux heures plus tard; **we waited for two hours** nous avons attendu pendant deux heures; **two hours ago** il y a deux heures; **to be paid by the hour** être payé à l'heure; **every hour** toutes les heures; **half an hour** une demi-heure; **a quarter of an hour** un quart d'heure; **an hour and a half** une heure et demie.

ourly *adjective* toutes les heures; **there is an hourly bus** il y a un bus

par heure; **the trains leave hourly** il y a des trains toutes les heures.

house *noun* **1** maison *Fem*.; **to buy a house** acheter une maison; **2 at somebody's house** chez quelqu'un; **I'm at Judy's house** je suis chez Judy; **I'm going to Judy's house tonight** je vais chez Judy ce soir; **I phoned from Judy's house** j'ai téléphoné de chez Judy.

housewife *noun* femme *Fem*. au foyer.

housework *noun* ménage *Masc*.; **to do the housework** faire le ménage.

how *adverb* **1** comment; **how did you do it?** comment l'as-tu fait?; **how are you?** comment allez-vous?; **2 how much?** combien?; **how much money do you have?** tu as combien d'argent?; **how much is it?** (*price*) ça coûte combien?; **3 how many?** combien?; **how many brothers do you have?** tu as combien de frères?; **4 how old are you?** quel âge as-tu?; **5 how far is it?** c'est à quelle distance d'ici?; **how far is it to Paris?** Paris est à quelle distance d'ici?; **6 how long will it take?** ça va prendre combien de temps?; **how long have you known her?** tu la connais depuis combien de temps?

however *adverb* cependant.

hug *noun* **to give somebody a hug** serrer quelqu'un dans ses bras; **she gave me a hug** elle m'a serré dans ses bras.

huge *adjective* immense.

hum *verb* fredonner [1].

human *adjective* humain.

human being *noun* être *Masc.* humain.

humour *noun* humour *Masc.*; **to have a sense of humour** avoir le sens de l'humour.

hundred *number* **1** cent; **two hundred** deux cents; **two hundred and ten** deux cent dix (*note that there is no 's' on 'cent' when it is followed by another number*); **a hundred people** cent personnes; **2 about a hundred** une centaine; **about a hundred people** une centaine de personnes; **hundreds of people** des centaines de personnes.

Hungary *noun* Hongrie *Fem.*

hunger *noun* faim *Fem.*

hungry *adjective* **to be hungry** avoir faim; **I'm hungry** j'ai faim.

hunt *verb* **1** chasser [1] (*an animal*); **2** rechercher [1] (*person*).

hunting *noun* chasse *Fem.*; **fox-hunting** la chasse au renard.

hurricane *noun* ouragan *Masc.*

hurry *noun* **to be in a hurry** être pressé; **I'm in a hurry** je suis pressé.

hurry *verb* se dépêcher [50]; **I must hurry** je dois me dépêcher; **he hurried home** il s'est dépêché de rentrer chez lui; **hurry up!** dépêche-toi!

hurt *verb* **1 to hurt somebody** faire [10] mal à quelqu'un; **you're hurting me!** tu me fais mal!; **that hurts!** ça fait mal!; **2 my back hurts** j'ai mal au dos; **3 to hurt yourself** se faire [10] mal; **did you hurt yourself?** est-ce que tu t'es fait mal?
hurt *adjective* **1** (*in an accident*) blessé; **three people were hurt**

trois personnes ont été blessées; **2** (*in feelings*) blessé; **she felt hurt** elle était blessée.

husband *noun* mari *Masc.*

hutch *noun* clapier *Masc.*

hygienic *adjective* hygiénique.

hymn *noun* cantique *Masc.*

hypermarket *noun* hypermarché *Masc.*

hyphen *noun* trait *Masc.* d'union.

hypnotize *verb* hypnotiser [1].

Ii

I *pronoun* **1** je, j' (*before a vowel or a silent 'h'*); **I am Scottish** je suis écossais; **I have two sisters** j'ai deux sœurs; **2** moi; **Robert and I** Robert et moi; **Tony and I left before you** Tony et moi sommes partis avant vous.

ice *noun* **1** glace *Fem.*; **2** (*on the roads*) verglas *Masc.*; **3** (*in a drink*) glaçons *Masc. plural.*

iceberg *noun* iceberg *Masc.*

ice cream *noun* glace *Fem.*; **a chocolate ice cream** une glace au chocolat.

ice-cube *noun* glaçon *Masc.*

ice hockey *noun* hockey *Masc.* sur glace.

ice rink *noun* patinoire *Fem.*

ice-skating *noun* **to go ice-skating** faire [10] du patin à glace.

icing *noun* glaçage *Masc.*

icon *noun* icône *Fem.*

456

cy *adjective* **1** verglacé (*a road*);
2 (*very cold*) glacial; **an icy wind** un
vent glacial.

dea *noun* idée *Fem.*; **what a good
idea!** quelle bonne idée!; **I've no
idea** je n'ai aucune idée.

deal *adjective* idéal (*Masc. plural*
idéaux).

dentical *adjective* identique;
identical twins des vrais jumeaux.

dentification *noun*
identification *Fem.*

dentify *verb* identifier [1].

dentity card *noun* carte *Fem.*
d'identité.

diom *noun* idiome *Masc.*

diot *noun* idiot *Masc.*, idiote *Fem.*

diotic *adjective* bête.

dyllic *adjective* idyllique.

.e. c-à-d (*short for: c'est-à-dire*).

f *conjunction* **1** si, s' (*before 'il' and
'ils'*); **if Sue's there** si Sue est là; **if it
rains** s'il pleut; **if I won the lottery**
si je gagnais la loterie; **if not** sinon;
2 if only ... si seulement ...; **if only
you'd told me** si seulement tu me
l'avais dit; **3 even if** même si; **even
if it snows** même s'il neige; **4 if I
were you** ... à ta place ...; **if I were
you, I'd forget it** à ta place je n'y
penserais plus.

gnore *verb* **1** ignorer [1] (*a person*);
2 ne pas écouter [1] (*what somebody
says*); **3 just ignore it** ne fais pas
attention.

ll *adjective* malade; **to fall ill, to be
taken ill** tomber [1] malade; **I feel ill**
je ne me sens pas bien.

illegal *adjective* illégal (*Masc. plural*
illégaux).

illegible *adjective* illisible.

illness *noun* maladie *Fem.*

illusion *noun* illusion *Fem.*

illustrated *adjective* illustré.

illustration *noun* illustration *Fem.*

image *noun* image *Fem.*; ★ **he's the
spitting image of his father** c'est
son père tout craché.

imagination *noun* imagination
Fem.; **to show imagination** faire
preuve d'imagination.

imaginative *adjective* plein
d'imagination.

imagine *verb* imaginer [1];
imagine that you're very rich
imagine que tu es très riche; **you
can't imagine how hard it was!** tu
ne peux pas t'imaginer combien
c'était difficile!

imitate *verb* imiter [1].

imitation *noun* imitation *Fem.*

immediate *adjective* immédiat.

immediately *adverb*
immédiatement; **I rang them
immediately** je les ai appelés
immédiatement; **immediately
before** juste avant; **immediately
after** juste après.

immigrant *noun* immigré *Masc.*,
immigrée *Fem.*.

immigration *noun* immigration
Fem.

impact *noun* impact *Masc.*

impatience *noun* impatience *Fem.*

a
b
c
d
e
f
g
h
i
j
k
l
m
n
o
p
q
r
s
t
u
v
w
x
y
z

impatient *adjective* **1** impatient; **2 to get impatient with somebody** s'impatienter [1] contre quelqu'un.

impatiently *adverb* avec impatience.

imperfect *noun* (*of a verb*) imparfait *Masc.*; **in the imperfect** à l'imparfait.

import *noun* produit *Masc.* importé.
import *verb* importer [1].

importance *noun* importance *Fem.*

important *adjective* important.

impossible *adjective* impossible; **it's impossible to find a telephone** il est impossible de trouver un téléphone.

impressed *adjective* impressionné.

impression *noun* impression *Fem.*; **to make a good impression on somebody** faire bonne impression sur quelqu'un; **I got the impression he was hiding something** j'avais l'impression qu'il cachait quelque chose.

impressive *adjective* impressionnant.

improve *verb* **1 to improve something** améliorer [1] quelque chose; **2** (*get better*) s'améliorer [1]; **the weather is improving** le temps s'améliore.

improvement *noun* **1** (*a clear change for the better*) amélioration *Fem.*; **2** (*gradual progress*) progrès *Masc.* plural (*in schoolwork, for example*).

in *preposition, adverb* **1** dans; **in my pocket** dans ma poche; **in the newspaper** dans le journal; **in the kitchen** dans la cuisine; **in my class** dans ma classe; **I was in the bath** j'étais dans mon bain; **2** à; **in Oxford** à Oxford; **a house in the country** une maison à la campagne; **in school** à l'école; **in the sun** au soleil; **the girl in the pink shirt** la fille à la chemise rose; **3** en; **in France** en France (*BUT*) **in Portugal** au Portugal (*'en' for feminine countries, 'au' for most masculine countries*); **in town** en ville; **in French** en français; **4** (*time expressions*) **in May** en mai; **in '94** en quatre-vingt-quatorze; **in winter** en hiver; **in summer** en été; (*BUT*) **in spring** au printemps; **in the morning** le matin; **at eight in the morning** à huit heures du matin; **in the night** pendant la nuit; **I'll phone you in ten minutes** je t'appellerai dans dix minutes; **she did it in five minutes** elle l'a fait en cinq minutes; **5** (*talking about a group*) de; **the tallest boy in the class** le garçon le plus grand de la classe; **the biggest city in the world** la ville la plus grande du monde; **6 in time** à temps; **7 in the photo** sur la photo; **8 in the rain** sous la pluie; **9 dressed in white** habillé en blanc; **10 to come in** entrer; **to go in** entrer; **we went into the cinema** nous sommes entrés dans le cinéma; **to run in** entrer en courant; **11 to be in** être là; **Mick's not in at the moment** Mick n'est pas là en ce moment.

incident *noun* incident *Masc.*

include *verb* comprendre [64]; **dinner is included in the price** le dîner est compris dans le prix; **service included** service compris.

including *preposition* (y) compris; **£50 including VAT** cinquante livres TVA comprise; **everyone, including children** tout le monde, y compris les enfants; **including Sundays** y compris les dimanches; **not including Sundays** sans compter les dimanches.

income *noun* revenu *Masc.*

income tax *noun* impôt *Masc.* sur le revenu.

inconvenient *adjective* **1** incommode (*a place or an arrangement*); **2** inopportun (*a time*).

increase *noun* augmentation *Fem.* (*in price, for example*). **increase** *verb* augmenter [1]; **the price has increased by £10** le prix a augmenté de dix livres.

incredible *adjective* incroyable.

incredibly *adverb* (*very*) extrêmement; **the film's incredibly boring** le film est extrêmement ennuyeux.

indeed *adverb* **1** (*to emphasize*) vraiment; **she's very pleased indeed** elle est vraiment très contente; **I'm very hungry indeed** j'ai vraiment très faim; **thank you very much indeed** merci beaucoup; **2** (*certainly*) bien sûr; **'can you hear his radio?' – 'indeed I can!'** 'entends-tu sa radio?' – 'bien sûr que oui!'

indefinite article *noun* (*in grammar*) article *Masc.* indéfini.

independence *noun* indépendance *Fem.*

independent *adjective* indépendant; **an independent school** une école privée.

index *noun* index *Masc.*

index finger *noun* index *Masc.*

India *noun* Inde *Fem.*; **in India** en Inde; **to India** en Inde.

Indian *noun* Indien *Masc.*, Indienne *Fem.* **Indian** *adjective* indien (*Fem.* indienne).

indicate *verb* indiquer [1].

indication *noun* indication *Fem.*

indigestion *noun* indigestion *Fem.*; **to have indigestion** avoir une indigestion.

indirect *adjective* indirect.

individual *noun* individu *Masc.* **individual** *adjective* **1** individuel (*Fem.* individuelle) (*a serving or a contribution, for example*); **2 individual tuition** des cours particuliers.

indoor *adjective* couvert; **an indoor swimming pool** une piscine couverte.

indoors *adverb* à l'intérieur; **it's cooler indoors** il fait plus frais à l'intérieur; **to go indoors** rentrer.

industrial *adjective* industriel (*Fem.* industrielle).

industrial estate *noun* zone *Fem.* industrielle.

industry *noun* industrie *Fem.*; **the advertising industry** l'industrie de la publicité.

inefficient *adjective* inefficace.

a
b
c
d
e
f
g
h
i
j
k
l
m
n
o
p
q
r
s
t
u
v
w
x
y
z

a **inevitable** *adjective* inévitable.

b **inevitably** *adverb* inévitablement.

c **inexperienced** *adjective* inexpérimenté.

d **infant school** *noun* école *Fem.* maternelle.

e **infected** *adjective* qui s'est infecté.

f **infection** *noun* infection *Fem.*; **an eye infection** une infection de l'œil;

g **a throat infection** une angine.

h **infectious** *adjective* contagieux (*Fem.* contagieuse).

infinitive *noun* infinitif *Masc.*; **in the infinitive** à l'infinitif.

j **inflammable** *adjective* inflammable.

k **inflatable** *adjective* pneumatique (*a mattress or a boat*).

l **inflate** *verb* gonfler [1] (*a mattress or boat*).

m **inflation** *noun* inflation *Fem.*

n **influence** *noun* influence *Fem.*; **to be a good influence on somebody** avoir une bonne influence sur quelqu'un.

o **influence** *verb* influencer [61].

p **inform** *verb* informer [1]; **to inform somebody that** informer quelqu'un du fait que; **they informed us that there was a problem** ils nous ont informés du fait qu'il y avait un problème; **to inform somebody of something** informer quelqu'un de quelque chose.

w **informal** *adjective* **1** simple (*a meal or event, for example*); **2** (*language*) familier (*Fem.* familière); **an informal expression** une expression familière.

information *noun* renseignements *Masc. plural*; **I need some information about flights to Paris** j'ai besoin de quelques renseignements sur les vols vers Paris; **a piece of information** un renseignement.

information desk, **information office** *noun* bureau *Masc.* des renseignements.

information technology *noun* informatique *Fem.*

infuriating *adjective* exaspérant.

ingredient *noun* ingrédient *Masc.*

inhabitant *noun* habitant *Masc.*, habitante *Fem.*

initials *plural noun* initiales *Fem. plural*; **put your initials here** marquez vos initiales ici.

initiative *noun* initiative *Fem.*

injection *noun* piqûre *Fem.*; **to give somebody an injection** faire [10] une piqûre à quelqu'un.

injure *verb* blesser [1].

injured *adjective* blessé.

injury *noun* blessure *Fem.*

ink *noun* encre *Fem.*

in-laws *noun* beaux-parents *Masc. plural.*

inner *adjective* intérieur.

innocent *adjective* innocent.

insane *adjective* fou (*Fem.* folle).

inscription *noun* inscription *Fem.*

insect *noun* insecte *Masc.*; **an insect bite** une piqûre d'insecte.

insect repellent *noun* insectifuge *Masc.*

insert *verb* insérer [24].

inside *noun* intérieur *Masc.*; **the inside of the oven** l'intérieur du four.

inside *preposition* à l'intérieur de; **inside the cinema** à l'intérieur du cinéma.

inside *adverb* à l'intérieur; **she's inside, I think** elle est à l'intérieur, je crois; **to go inside** rentrer.

inside out *adjective, adverb* à l'envers.

insincere *adjective* peu sincère.

insist *verb* **1** insister [1]; **if you insist** puisque tu insistes; **to insist on doing** insister pour faire; **he insisted on paying** il a insisté pour payer; **2 to insist that** affirmer [1] que; **Ruth insisted I was wrong** Ruth a affirmé que j'avais tort.

insomnia *noun* insomnie *Fem.*

inspector *noun* inspecteur *Masc.*, inspectrice *Fem.*

install *verb* installer [1].

instalment *noun* (*of a story or serial*) épisode *Masc.*

instance *noun* **for instance** par exemple.

instant *noun* instant *Masc.*; **come here this instant!** viens ici tout de suite!

instant *adjective* **1** instantané (*coffee or soup*); **2** (*immediate*) immédiat (*an effect or a success, for example*).

instantly *adverb* immédiatement.

instead *adverb* **1 Ted couldn't go, so I went instead** Ted ne pouvait pas y aller, donc je suis allé à sa place; **we didn't go to the concert, we went to Lucy's instead** au lieu

d'aller au concert, nous sommes allés chez Lucy; **2 instead of** au lieu de; **instead of pudding I had cheese** j'ai pris le fromage au lieu d'un dessert; **instead of playing tennis we went swimming** au lieu de jouer au tennis nous sommes allés à la piscine.

instinct *noun* instinct *Masc.*

institute *noun* institut *Masc.*

institution *noun* institution *Fem.*

instruct *verb* **to instruct somebody to do** donner [1] l'ordre à quelqu'un de faire; **the teacher instructed us to stay together** le professeur nous a donné l'ordre de rester en groupe.

instructions *plural noun* instructions *Fem. plural*; **follow the instructions on the packet** suivez les instructions sur l'emballage; **'instructions for use'** 'mode d'emploi'.

instructor *noun* moniteur *Masc.*, monitrice *Fem.*; **my skiing instructor** mon moniteur de ski.

instrument *noun* instrument *Masc.*; **to play an instrument** jouer d'un instrument.

insulin *noun* insuline *Fem.*

insult *noun* insulte *Fem.*
insult *verb* insulter [1].

insurance *noun* assurance *Fem.*; **travel insurance** l'assurance voyage; **do you have medical insurance?** est-ce que vous avez une assurance maladie?

intelligence *noun* intelligence *Fem.*

intelligent *adjective* intelligent.

a
b
c
d
e
f
g
h
i
j
k
l
m
n
o
p
q
r
s
t
u
v
w
x
y
z

461

a
b
c
d
e
f
g
h
i
j
k
l
m
n
o
p
q
r
s
t
u
v
w
x
y
z

intend *verb* **1** vouloir [14]; **as I intended** comme je le voulais; **2 to intend to do** avoir [5] l'intention de faire; **we intend to spend the night in Rome** nous avons l'intention de passer la nuit à Rome.

intensive *adjective* intensif (*Fem.* intensive).

intensive care *noun* **in intensive care** en réanimation.

intention *noun* intention *Fem.*; **I have no intention of paying** je n'ai aucune intention de payer.

interest *noun* **1** (*hobby*) centre *Masc.* d'intérêt; **what are your interests?** quels sont vos centres d'intérêt?; **2** (*keenness*) intérêt *Masc.*; **he has an interest in jazz** il a un intérêt pour le jazz.
interest *verb* intéresser [1]; **that doesn't interest me** ça ne m'intéresse pas.

interested *adjective* **to be interested in** s'intéresser à; **Sean's very interested in cooking** Sean s'intéresse beaucoup à la cuisine.

interesting *adjective* intéressant.

interfere *verb* **1 to interfere with something** (*to fiddle with it*) toucher [1] quelque chose; **don't interfere with my computer!** ne touche pas mon ordinateur; **2 to interfere in** se mêler [1] à (*someone else's affairs*).

interior *adjective* intérieur.

interior designer *noun* designer *Masc. & Fem.*

international *adjective* international (*Masc. plural* internationaux).

Internet *noun* Internet *Masc.*; **on the Internet** sur Internet.

Internet cafe *noun* cybercafé *Masc.*; **where is there an Internet cafe?** où est-ce qu'il y a un cybercafé?

interpret *verb* (*act as an interpreter*) faire [10] l'interprète.

interpreter *noun* interprète *Masc. & Fem.*

interrupt *verb* interrompre [69].

interruption *noun* interruption *Fem.*

interval *noun* entracte *Masc.* (*in a play or concert*).

interview *noun* **1** (*for a job*) entretien *Masc.*; **a job interview** un entretien; **2** (*in a newspaper, on TV or radio*) interview *Fem.*
interview *verb* interviewer [1] (*on TV, radio*).

interviewer *noun* interviewer *Masc.*

into *preposition* **1** dans; **he's gone into the bank** il est entré dans la banque; **I put the cat into his basket** j'ai mis le chat dans son panier; **we all got into the car** nous sommes tous montés dans la voiture; **2 to go into town** aller en ville; **Mum's gone into town** Maman est allée en ville; **to get into bed** se mettre au lit; **to translate into French** traduire en français; **to change pounds into euros** changer des livres sterling en euros; **3 to be into jazz** être fana du jazz (*informal*).

introduce *verb* présenter [1]; **she introduced me to her brother** elle m'a présenté à son frère; **can I introduce you to my mother?** je te présente ma mère.

ntroduction *noun* (*in a book*) introduction *Fem.*

ntuition *noun* intuition *Fem.*

nvade *verb* envahir [2].

nvalid *noun* malade *Masc. & Fem.*

nvasion *noun* invasion *Fem.*

nvent *verb* inventer [1].

nvention *noun* invention *Fem.*

nventor *noun* inventeur *Masc.*, inventrice *Fem.*

nverted commas *plural noun* guillemets *Masc. plural*; **in inverted commas** entre guillemets.

nvestigation *noun* (*by police*) enquête *Fem.*; **an investigation into the fire** une enquête sur l'incendie.

nvisible *adjective* invisible.

nvitation *noun* invitation *Fem.*; **an invitation to dinner** une invitation à dîner.

nvite *verb* inviter [1]; **Kirsty invited me to lunch** Kirsty m'a invité à déjeuner; **he's invited me out on Tuesday** il m'a invitée à sortir avec lui mardi.

nviting *adjective* **1** appétissant (*a meal*); **2** accueillant (*a room*).

nvoice *noun* facture *Fem.*

nvolve *verb* **1** nécessiter [1]; **it involves a lot of work** cela nécessite beaucoup de travail; **2** (*to affect*) concerner [1]; **the play will involve everybody** le spectacle va concerner tout le monde; **two cars were involved** deux voitures ont été concernées; **3 to be involved in**

participer [1] à; **I am involved in the new project** je participe au nouveau projet.

Iran *noun* Iran *Masc.*

Iraq *noun* Iraq *Masc.*

Ireland *noun* Irlande *Fem.*; **in Ireland** en Irlande; **to Ireland** en Irlande; **the Republic of Ireland** la République d'Irlande.

Irish *noun* **1** (*the language*) irlandais *Masc.*; **2** (*the people*) **the Irish** les Irlandais *Masc. plural*. **Irish** *adjective* irlandais.

Irishman *noun* Irlandais *Masc.*

Irish Sea *noun* mer *Fem.* d'Irlande.

Irishwoman *noun* Irlandaise *Fem.*

iron *noun* **1** (*for clothes*) fer *Masc.* à repasser; **2** (*the metal*) fer *Masc.* **iron** *verb* repasser [1].

ironing *noun* repassage *Masc.*; **to do the ironing** faire le repassage.

ironing board *noun* planche *Fem.* à repasser.

ironmonger's *noun* quincaillerie *Fem.*

irregular *adjective* irrégulier (*Fem.* irrégulière).

irresponsible *adjective* irresponsable.

irritable *adjective* irritable.

irritate *verb* irriter [1].

irritating *adjective* irritant.

Islam *noun* Islam *Masc.*

Islamic *adjective* islamique.

island *noun* île *Fem.*

isolated *adjective* isolé.

Israel *noun* Israël *Masc.*

a
b
c
d
e
f
g
h
i
j
k
l
m
n
o
p
q
r
s
t
u
v
w
x
y
z

a

b

c

d

e

f

g

h

i

j

k

l

m

n

o

p

q

r

s

t

u

v

w

x

y

z

Israeli *noun* Israélien *Masc.*, Israélienne *Fem.*
Israeli *adjective* israélien (*Fem.* israélienne).

issue *noun* **1** (*something you discuss*) question *Fem.*; **a political issue** une question politique; **2** (*of a magazine*) numéro *Masc.*
issue *verb* (*hand out*) distribuer [1].

IT *noun* (*short for information technology*) informatique *Fem.*

it *pronoun* **1** (*as the subject*) il (*when it stands for a masculine noun*); elle (*when it stands for a feminine noun*); **'where is my bag?' – 'it's in the kitchen'** 'où est mon sac?' – 'il est dans la cuisine'; **'how old is your car?' – 'it's five years old'** 'quel âge a ta voiture?' – 'elle a cinq ans'; **2** (*as the object*) le (*when it stands for a masculine noun*); la (*when it stands for a feminine noun*); l' (*before a vowel or silent 'h'*); **his new book? I know it** son nouveau livre? je le connais; **his address? I know it** son addresse? je la connais; **where's my book? I've lost it** où est mon livre? je l'ai perdu; **3 yes, it's true** oui, c'est vrai; **it doesn't matter** ça ne fait rien; **4 who is it?** qui c'est?; **it's me** c'est moi; **what is it?** qu'est-ce que c'est?; **5 it's raining** il pleut; **it's a nice day** il fait beau; **it's two o'clock** il est deux heures.

Italian *noun* **1** (*the language*) italien *Masc.*; **2** (*person*) Italien *Masc.*, Italienne *Fem.*
Italian *adjective* **1** italien (*Fem.* italienne); **Italian food** la cuisine italienne; **2** d'italien (*a teacher or a*

lesson); **my Italian class** mon cours d'italien.

italics *noun* italique *Masc.*; **in italics** en italique.

Italy *noun* Italie *Fem.*; **in Italy** en Italie; **to Italy** en Italie.

itch *verb* **my back is itching** j'ai le dos qui me démange; **this sweater itches** ce pull me gratte.

item *noun* article *Masc.*

its *determiner* son (*before a masculine noun or a feminine noun beginning with a vowel or silent 'h'*); sa (*before a feminine noun*); ses (*before a plural noun*); **the dog has lost its collar** le chien a perdu son collier; **the dog's in its kennel** le chien est dans sa niche; **its ear** son oreille; **its toys** ses jouets.

itself *pronoun* **1** se, s' (*before a vowel or silent 'h'*); **the cat is washing itself** le chat se lave; **2 he left the dog by itself** il a laissé le chien tout seul.

ivory *noun* ivoire *Masc.*

ivy *noun* lierre *Masc.*

Jj

jack *noun* **1** (*in cards*) valet *Masc.*; **the jack of clubs** le valet de trèfle; **2** (*for a car*) cric *Masc.*

jacket *noun* veste *Fem.*

jacket potato *noun* pomme *Fem.* de terre en robe des champs.

jackpot *noun* gros lot *Masc.*; **to win the jackpot** gagner le gros lot.

agged *adjective* dentelé.

ail *noun* prison *Fem.*

jail *verb* emprisonner [1].

am *noun* **1** (*that you eat*) confiture *Fem.*; **raspberry jam** la confiture de framboises; **2 a traffic jam** un embouteillage.

amaica *noun* Jamaïque *Fem.*

amaican *noun* Jamaïquain *Masc.*, Jamaïquaine *Fem.*
Jamaican *adjective* jamaïquain.

ammed *adjective* coincé.

anuary *noun* janvier *Masc.*; **in January** en janvier.

apan *noun* Japon *Masc.*; **in Japan** au Japon.

apanese *noun* **1** (*the language*) japonais *Masc.*; **2** (*person*) Japonais *Masc.*, Japonaise *Fem.*; **the Japanese** les Japonais *Masc. plural.*
Japanese *adjective* japonais.

ar *noun* (*small*) pot *Masc.*; (*large*) bocal *Masc.* (*plural* bocaux); **a jar of jam** un pot de confiture.

avelin *noun* javelot *Masc.*

aw *noun* mâchoire *Fem.*

azz *noun* jazz *Masc.*

ealous *adjective* jaloux (*Fem.* jalouse).

ealousy *noun* jalousie *Fem.*

eans *noun* jean *Masc.*; **my jeans** mon jean; **a pair of jeans** un jean.

elly *noun* gelée *Fem.*

ellyfish *noun* méduse *Fem.*

ersey *noun* **1** (*a pullover*) pull-over *Masc.*; **2** (*for football*) maillot *Masc.*

Jersey *noun* Jersey *Fem.*

Jesus *noun* Jésus *Masc.*; **Jesus Christ** Jésus-Christ.

jet *noun* jet *Masc.*

jet lag *noun* décalage *Masc.* horaire.

jetty *noun* jetée *Fem.*

Jew *noun* Juif *Masc.*, Juive *Fem.*

jewel *noun* bijou *Masc.* (*plural* bijoux).

jeweller's *noun* bijouterie *Fem.*

jeweller *noun* bijoutier *Masc.*, bijoutière *Fem.*

jewellery *noun* bijoux *Masc. plural.*

Jewish *adjective* juif (*Fem.* juive).

jigsaw *noun* puzzle *Masc.*

job *noun* **1** (*paid work*) emploi *Masc.*; **a job as a secretary** un emploi comme secrétaire; **he's got a job** il a trouvé un emploi; **out of a job** sans emploi; **what's your job?** qu'est-ce que vous faites comme travail?; **a job offer** une offre d'emploi; **2** (*a task*) travail *Masc.*; **it's not an easy job** ce n'est pas un travail facile; **she made a good job of it** elle a fait un bon travail.

jobless *adjective* sans emploi.

jockey *noun* jockey *Masc.*

jog *verb* **to go jogging** faire [10] du jogging.

join *verb* **1** (*become a member of*) s'inscrire [38] à; **I've joined the judo club** je me suis inscrit au club de judo; **2** (*to meet up with*) rejoindre [49]; **I'll join you later** je vous rejoindrai plus tard.
• **to join in 1** participer [1]; **Ruth never joins in** Ruth ne participe jamais; **2 to join in something** participer [1] à quelque chose; **won't**

you join in the game? veux-tu participer au jeu?

joiner *noun* menuisier *Masc.*

joint *noun* **1** (*of meat*) rôti *Masc.*; **a joint of beef** un rôti de bœuf; **2** (*in your body*) articulation *Fem.*
joint *adjective* **1 the joint winners** les lauréats ex aequo.

joke *noun* (*a funny story*) plaisanterie *Fem.*; **to tell a joke** raconter une plaisanterie.
joke *verb* plaisanter [1]; **you must be joking!** tu plaisantes!

joker *noun* (*in cards*) joker *Masc.*

Jordan *noun* Jordanie *Fem.*

journalism *noun* journalisme *Masc.*

journalist *noun* journaliste *Masc. & Fem.*; **Sean's a journalist** Sean est journaliste.

journey *noun* **1** (*a long one*) voyage *Masc.*; **our journey to Turkey** notre voyage en Turquie; **2** (*shorter: to work or school*) trajet *Masc.*; **a bus journey** un trajet en bus.

joy *noun* joie *Fem.*

joy-riding *noun* rodéo *Masc.* à la voiture volée.

joystick *noun* (*for computer games*) manette *Fem.* de jeu.

Judaism *noun* judaïsme *Masc.*

judge *noun* juge *Masc.*
judge *verb* estimer [1] (*a time or distance*).

judgement *noun* jugement *Masc.*

judo *noun* judo *Masc.*; **he does judo** il fait du judo.

jug *noun* pot *Masc.*

juggle *verb* jongler [1].

juice *noun* jus *Masc.*; **two orange juices please** deux jus d'orange s'i vous plaît.

juicy *adjective* juteux (*Fem.* juteuse

jukebox *noun* jukebox *Masc.*

July *noun* juillet *Masc.*; **in July** en juillet.

jumble sale *noun* vente *Fem.* de charité.

jumbo jet *noun* gros-porteur *Masc*

jump *noun* saut *Masc.*; **a parachute jump** un saut en parachute.
jump *verb* sauter [1].

jumper *noun* pull *Masc.*

junction *noun* **1** (*of roads*) carrefour *Masc.*; **2** (*of motorways*) échangeur *Masc.*; **3** (*on railway*) nœud *Masc.* ferroviaire.

June *noun* juin *Masc.*; **in June** en juin.

jungle *noun* jungle *Fem.*

junior *adjective* primaire; **a junior school** une école primaire; **the juniors** les élèves du primaire.

junk *noun* (*real rubbish*) bric-à-brac *Masc.*

junk food *noun* **you shouldn't eat junk food** tu devrais manger correctement (*there is no word for junk food in French, so you will need to express it differently, according to the context*).

junk shop *noun* magasin *Masc.* de brocante.

jury *noun* jury *Masc.*

just *adverb* **1** juste; **just before midday** juste avant midi; **just after**

the church juste après l'église; **just for fun** juste pour rire; **2 to have just done** venir de faire; **Tom has just arrived** Tom vient d'arriver; **Helen had just called** Helen venait d'appeler; **3 to be just doing** être en train de faire; **I'm just finishing the ironing** je suis en train de finir le repassage; **4** (*only*) ne ...que; **he's just a child** il n'est qu'un enfant; **there's just me and Justine** il n'y a que moi et Justine; **5 just coming!** j'arrive!

justice *noun* justice *Fem.*

justify *verb* justifier [1].

Kk

kangaroo *noun* kangourou *Masc.*

karaoke *noun* karaoké *Masc.*

karate *noun* karaté *Masc.*

kebab *noun* brochette *Fem.*

keen *adjective* **1** (*enthusiastic*) enthousiaste; **you don't look too keen** tu n'as pas l'air très enthousiaste; **2** (*committed*) passionné; **he's a keen photographer** c'est un photographe passionné; **3 I'm not keen on fish** je n'aime pas trop le poisson; **4 to be keen on doing** (or **to do**) avoir très envie de faire; **I'm not keen on camping** je n'ai pas très envie de faire du camping.

keep *verb* **1** garder [1]; **I kept the letter** j'ai gardé la lettre; **will you keep my seat?** veux-tu garder ma place?; **they kept her in hospital** ils

l'ont gardée à l'hôpital; **to keep a secret** garder un secret; **2 to keep somebody waiting** faire [10] attendre quelqu'un; **3** (*to store*) ranger [52]; **I keep my bike in the garage** je range mon vélo dans le garage; **where do you keep saucepans?** où rangez-vous les casseroles?; **4 to keep on doing** continuer [1] à faire; **she kept on talking** elle a continué à parler; **keep straight on** continuez tout droit; **5 to keep on doing** (*time after time*) **he keeps on ringing me up** il n'arrête pas de m'appeler; **6** (*stay*) rester [1]; **keep calm!** restez calme!; **keep out of the sun** reste à l'abri du soleil; **7 to keep a promise** tenir [77] sa promesse.

keep fit *noun* gymnastique *Fem.* d'entretien.

kennel *noun* **1** (*for one dog*) niche *Fem.*; **2** (*for boarding*) **kennels** chenil *Masc.*.

kerb *noun* bord *Masc.* du trottoir.

ketchup *noun* ketchup *Masc.*

kettle *noun* bouilloire *Fem.*; **to put the kettle on** mettre l'eau à chauffer.

key *noun* **1** (*for a lock*) clé *Fem.*; **a bunch of keys** un trousseau de clés; **2** (*on a piano or typewriter*) touche *Fem.*

keyboard *noun* (*for a piano or a computer*) clavier *Masc.*

keyhole *noun* trou *Masc.* de serrure.

keyring *noun* porte-clés *Masc.*

kick *noun* **1** (*from a person or a horse*) coup *Masc.* de pied; **to give somebody a kick** donner un coup

a
b
c
d
e
f
g
h
i
j
k
l
m
n
o
p
q
r
s
t
u
v
w
x
y
z

a

de pied à quelqu'un; **2** (*in football*)
tir *Masc.*; ★ **to get a kick out of
doing** prendre plaisir à faire.
kick *verb* **to kick somebody**
donner [1] un coup de pied à
quelqu'un; **to kick the ball** donner
un coup de pied dans le ballon.

• **to kick off** donner [1] le coup
d'envoi.

kick-off *noun* coup *Masc.* d'envoi.

kid *noun* gosse *Masc. & Fem.* (*child*);
Dad's looking after the kids Dad
s'occupe des gosses.

kidnap *verb* enlever [50].

kidnapper *noun* ravisseur *Masc.*,
ravisseuse *Fem.*

kidney *noun* **1** (*part of your body*)
rein *Masc.*; **2** (*for eating*) rognon
Masc.

kill *verb* tuer [1]; **she was killed in
an accident** elle a été tuée dans un
accident.

killer *noun* (*murderer*) meurtrier
Masc., meurtrière *Fem.*

kilo *noun* kilo *Masc.*; **a kilo of sugar**
un kilo de sucre; **five euros a kilo**
cinq euros le kilo.

kilogramme *noun* kilogramme
Masc.

kilometre *noun* kilomètre *Masc.*

kilt *noun* kilt *Masc.*

kind *noun* sorte *Fem.*; **all kinds of
people** toutes sortes de gens.
kind *adjective* gentil (*Fem.* gentille);
Marion was very kind to me
Marion a été très gentille avec moi.

kindness *noun* gentillesse *Fem.*

king *noun* roi *Masc.*; **King George le**
roi Georges; **the king of hearts le**
roi de cœur.

kingdom *noun* royaume *Masc.*; **the
United Kingdom** le Royaume-Uni.

kiosk *noun* **1** (*for newspapers or
snacks*) kiosque *Masc.*; **2** (*for a
phone*) cabine *Fem.*

kipper *noun* hareng *Masc.* fumé.

kiss *noun* baiser *Masc.*; **to give
somebody a kiss** embrasser
quelqu'un.
kiss *verb* embrasser [1]; **kiss me!**
embrasse-moi!; **we kissed each
other** nous nous sommes
embrassés.

kit *noun* **1** (*of tools*) trousse *Fem.*; **a
tool kit** une trousse à outils;
2 (*clothes*) affaires *Fem. plural*;
where's my football kit? où sont
mes affaires de foot?; **3** (*for making
a model, a piece of furniture, etc*) kit
Masc.

kitchen *noun* cuisine *Fem.*; **the
kitchen table** la table de la cuisine

kitchen foil *noun* papier *Masc.*
d'aluminium.

kitchen garden *noun* jardin
Masc. potager.

kitchen roll *noun* essuie-tout
Masc.

kite *noun* (*toy*) cerf-volant *Masc.*; **to
fly a kite** faire voler un cerf-volant

kitten *noun* chaton *Masc.*

kiwi fruit *noun* kiwi *Masc.*

knack *noun* don *Masc.*

knee *noun* genou *Masc.* (*plural
genoux*); **on (your) hands and
knees** à quatre pattes.

neel *verb* se mettre [11] à genoux.

nickers *plural noun* petite culotte *Fem.*

nife *noun* couteau *Masc.* (*plural* couteaux).

night *noun* (*in chess*) cavalier *Masc.*

nit *verb* tricoter [1].

nitting *noun* tricot *Masc.*

nob *noun* bouton *Masc.*

nock *noun* coup *Masc.*; **a knock on the head** un coup à la tête; **a knock at the door** un coup à la porte.

knock *verb* **1** (*to bang*) cogner [1]; **I knocked my arm on the table** je me suis cogné le bras contre la table; **2 to knock on something** (*a person*) frapper [1] à (*the door*).

to knock down 1 (*in a traffic accident*) renverser [1] (*a person*); **2** (*to demolish*) démolir [2] (*an old building*).

to knock out 1 (*to make unconscious*) assommer [1]; **2** (*in sport, to eliminate*) éliminer [1].

nocker *noun* heurtoir *Masc.*

not *noun* nœud *Masc.*; **to tie a knot in something** nouer [1] quelque chose.

now *verb* **1** (*know a fact*) savoir [70]; **do you know where Tim is?** sais-tu où est Tim?; **I know they've moved house** je sais qu'ils ont déménagé; **he knows it by heart** il le sait par cœur; **yes, I know** oui, je sais; **you never know!** on ne sait jamais!; **2** (*be personally acquainted with*) connaître [27] (*a person, place, book, or music, for example*); **do you know the Jacksons?** est-ce que tu connais les Jackson?; **all the people**

I know tous les gens que je connais; **I don't know his mother** je ne connais pas sa mère; **3 to know how to do** savoir [70] faire; **Steve knows how to make couscous** Steve sait faire du couscous; **Liz knows how to mend it** Liz sait le réparer; **4 to know about** être [6] au courant de (*the latest news*); **5 to know about** s'y connaître [27] en (*machines, cooking, etc*); **Lindy knows about computers** Lindy s'y connaît en informatique.

knowledge *noun* connaissance *Fem.*

knuckle *noun* articulation *Fem.* des doigts.

koala *noun* koala *Masc.*

Koran *noun* Coran *Masc.*

kosher *adjective* kascher.

Ll

lab *noun* labo *Masc.*

label *noun* étiquette *Fem.*

laboratory *noun* laboratoire *Masc.*

Labour *noun* les travaillistes *Masc. plural*; **to vote for the Labour party** voter pour les travaillistes; **the Labour Party** le parti travailliste.

lace *noun* **1** (*for a shoe*) lacet *Masc.*; **2** (*for curtains, for example*) dentelle *Fem.*

lad *noun* gars *Masc.*

ladder *noun* (*for climbing, or in your tights*) échelle *Fem.*

ladies noun (lavatory) toilettes Fem. plural; (on a sign) **'Ladies'** 'Dames'.

lady noun dame Fem.; **ladies and gentlemen** mesdames et messieurs.

ladybird noun coccinelle Fem.

lager noun bière Fem. blonde.

laid-back adjective relaxe.

lake noun lac Masc.; **Lake Geneva** le lac Léman.

lamb noun agneau Masc. (plural agneaux); **a leg of lamb** un gigot.

lame adjective boiteux (Fem. boiteuse); **he is lame** il boite.

lamp noun lampe Fem.

lamp-post noun réverbère Masc.

lampshade noun abat-jour Masc. (plural abat-jour).

land noun 1 terre Fem.; **I can see land** je vois la terre; 2 (property) terrain Masc.; **a piece of land** un terrain.
land verb 1 (plane, passenger) atterrir [2]; 2 (leave a ship) débarquer [1].

landing noun 1 (on the stairs) palier Masc.; 2 (of a plane) atterrissage Masc.; 3 (from a boat) débarquement Masc.

landlady noun propriétaire Fem.

landlord noun propriétaire Masc.

landscape noun paysage Masc.

lane noun 1 (a country path) chemin Masc.; 2 (of a motorway) voie Fem.

language noun 1 (French, Italian, etc) langue Fem.; **a foreign language** une langue étrangère; 2 (way of speaking) langage Masc.; **bad language** un langage grossier.

language lab noun laboratoire Masc. de langues.

language school noun école Fem. de langue.

lap noun 1 (your knees) genoux Masc. plural; **on my lap** sur mes genoux; 2 (in races) tour Masc. de piste.

laptop noun portable Masc.

larder noun garde-manger Masc.

large adjective 1 grand (goes before the noun); **a large number** un grand nombre; **a large house** une grande maison; 2 gros (Fem. grosse) (a piece, part, animal) (goes before the noun); **a large piece of cake** un gros morceau de gâteau; 3 nombreux (Fem. nombreuse) (crowd or family); **I come from a large family** je viens d'une famille nombreuse.

laser noun laser Masc.

laser beam noun rayon Masc. laser.

laser printer noun imprimante Fem. laser.

last adjective dernier (Fem. dernière); **the last time** la dernière fois; **last week** la semaine dernière; **last night** (in the evening) hier soir (in the night) cette nuit.
last adverb 1 (in final position) (to arrive or leave) en dernier; **Rob arrived last** Rob est arrivé en dernier; **at last!** enfin!; 2 (most recently) **I last saw him in May** la dernière fois que je l'ai vu était en mai.
last verb durer [1]; **the play lasted two hours** le spectacle a duré deux heures.

ate *adjective, adverb* **1** en retard; **we're late** nous sommes en retard; **they arrived late** ils sont arrivés en retard; **to be late for something** être en retard pour quelque chose; **we were late for the film** nous étions en retard pour le film; **2 to be late** (*a bus or train*) avoir du retard; **the train was an hour late** le train a eu une heure de retard; **3** (*late in the day*) tard; **we got up late** nous nous sommes levés tard; **the chemist is open late** la pharmacie est ouverte tard; **late last night** tard hier soir; **too late!** trop tard!

ately *adverb* ces derniers temps.

ater *adverb* plus tard; **I'll explain later** j'expliquerai plus tard; **see you later!** à tout à l'heure!

atest *adjective* **1** dernier (*Fem.* dernière); **the latest news** les dernières nouvelles; **2 at the latest** au plus tard.

latest *noun* **the latest in audio equipment** le dernier cri en matière d'équipement hifi.

atin *noun* latin *Masc.*

augh *noun* rire *Masc.*; **to do something for a laugh** faire quelque chose pour rigoler (*informal*).

laugh *verb* **1** rire [68]; **everybody laughed** tout le monde a ri; **2 to laugh at** se moquer [1] de; **I tried to explain but they laughed at me** j'ai essayé d'expliquer mais ils se sont moqués de moi.

aughter *noun* rire *Masc.*

aunch *noun* (*of a ship, product, spacecraft*) lancement *Masc.*.

launch *verb* **1** (*product, spacecraft*) lancer [61]; **2** (*ship*) mettre [11] à l'eau.

launderette *noun* laverie *Fem.* automatique.

laundry *noun* **1** (*in hotel etc*) laverie *Fem.*; **2** (*shop*) blanchisserie *Fem.*

lavatory *noun* toilettes *Fem. plural*; **to go to the lavatory** aller aux toilettes.

lavender *noun* lavande *Fem.*

law *noun* **1** loi *Fem.*; **it's against the law** c'est interdit; **2** (*subject of study*) droit *Masc.*

lawn *noun* pelouse *Fem.*

lawnmower *noun* tondeuse *Fem.* à gazon.

lawyer *noun* avocat *Masc.*, avocate *Fem.*

lay *verb* **1** (*put*) poser [1]; **she laid the card on the table** elle a posé la carte sur la table; **2** (*spread out*) étaler [1]; **we laid newspaper on the floor** nous avons étalé du papier journal sur le parquet; **3 to lay the table** mettre [11] la table.

lay-by *noun* aire *Fem.* de stationnement.

layer *noun* couche *Fem.*

laziness *noun* paresse *Fem.*

lazy *adjective* paresseux (*Fem.* paresseuse).

lead[1] *noun* **1** (*when you are ahead*) **to be in the lead** être en tête; **Baxter's in the lead** Baxter est en tête; **we have a lead of three points** nous avons trois points d'avance; **2** (*electric*) fil *Masc.*; **3** (*for a dog*) laisse *Fem.*; **on a lead** en laisse.

a
b
c
d
e
f
g
h
i
j
k
l
m
n
o
p
q
r
s
t
u
v
w
x
y
z

a

b

c

d

e

f

g

h

i

j

k

l

m

n

o

p

q

r

s

t

u

v

w

x

y

z

lead *adjective (a role or a singer)* principal *(Masc. plural* principaux*)*.
lead *verb* **1** mener [50]; **the path leads to the sea** le chemin mène à la mer; **2 to lead the way** montrer [1] le chemin; **3 to lead to something** entraîner [1] quelque chose *(an accident or problems, for example)*.

lead[2] *noun (the metal)* plomb *Masc.*

leader *noun* **1** *(of a gang)* chef *Masc.*; **2** *(of a political party)* dirigeant *Masc.*, dirigeante *Fem.*; **3** *(in a competition)* premier *Masc.*, première *Fem.*.

lead-free petrol *noun* essence *Fem.* sans plomb.

lead singer *noun* chanteur principal *Masc.*, chanteuse principale *Fem.*

leaf *noun* feuille *Fem.*

leaflet *noun* dépliant *Masc.*

league *noun (in sport)* championnat *Masc.*

leak *noun* fuite *Fem.*; **a gas leak** une fuite de gaz.
leak *verb (a bottle or a roof)* fuir [44].

lean *adjective (meat)* maigre.
lean *verb* **1 to lean on something** s'appuyer [41] contre quelque chose; **2** *(prop)* appuyer [41]; **lean the ladder against the tree!** appuie l'échelle contre l'arbre!; **3** *(a person)* se pencher [1]; **to lean out of the window** se pencher par la fenêtre; **lean forward a bit** penche-toi un peu en avant.

leap *verb* sauter [1].
leap year *noun* année *Fem.* bissextile.

learn *verb* apprendre [64]; **to learn Russian** apprendre le russe; **to learn (how) to drive** apprendre à conduire.

learner *noun* apprenant *Masc.*, apprenante *Fem.*; **to be a fast learner** apprendre vite.

learner driver *noun* élève *Masc. Fem.* d'auto-école.

least *adverb, adjective, pronoun* **1** moins; **I like the blue shirt least** c'est la chemise bleue que j'aime le moins; **2** *(followed by a noun)* le moins de; **Tony has the least money** c'est Tony qui a le moins d'argent; **3** *(followed by an adjective)* le moins, la moins, les moins *(according to the gender and number of the noun going with the adjective)*; **the least expensive hotel** l'hôtel le moins cher; **the least expensive car** la voiture la moins chère; **the least expensive shoes** les chaussures les moins chères; **4 the least** *(the slightest)* le moindre, la moindre *(according to the gender of the noun that follows)*; **I haven't the least idea** je n'ai pas la moindre idée; **5 at least** *(at a minimum)* au moins; **at least twenty people** au moins vingt personnes; **6 at least** *(at any rate)* du moins; **at least, I think she's a teacher** du moins, je crois qu'elle est professeur.

leather *noun* cuir *Masc.*; **a leather jacket** un blouson en cuir.

leave *noun* congé *Masc.*; **three days' leave** trois jours de congé.

472

leave *verb* **1** (*go away*) partir [58]; **they're leaving tomorrow** ils vont partir demain; **we left at six** nous sommes partis à six heures; **2** (*go away from*) quitter [1]; **I left the office at five** j'ai quitté le bureau à cinq heures; **Guy left school at sixteen** Guy a quitté l'école à seize ans; **3** (*go out of*) sortir [72] de; **she left the cinema at ten** elle est sortie du cinéma à dix heures; **4** (*deposit*) laisser [1]; **you can leave your coats in the hall** vous pouvez laisser vos manteaux dans l'entrée; **5** (*not do*) laisser [1]; **let's leave the washing up!** laissons la vaisselle!; **6** (*forget*) oublier [1]; **he left his umbrella on the train** il a oublié son parapluie dans le train; **7 be left** rester [1]; **there are two pancakes left** il reste deux crêpes; **we have ten minutes left** il nous reste dix minutes; **I don't have any money left** il ne me reste plus d'argent.

lecture *noun* **1** (*at university*) cours *Masc.* magistral (*plural* cours magistraux); **2** (*public*) conférence *Fem.*

lecturer *noun* professeur *Masc.* à l'université.

ledge *noun* **1** (*of a window*) rebord *Masc.*; **2** (*on a cliff*) corniche *Fem.*

leek *noun* poireau *Masc.* (*plural* poireaux).

left *noun* gauche *Fem.*; **to drive on the left** conduire à gauche; **turn left at the church** tournez à gauche à l'église; **on my left** à ma gauche. **left** *adjective* gauche; **his left foot** son pied gauche.

left-click *noun* clic *Masc.* sur le bouton gauche de la souris. **left-click** *verb* **to left-click the icon** cliquer [1] en appuyant sur le bouton gauche de la souris.

left-hand *adjective* **the left-hand side** la gauche.

left-handed *adjective* gaucher *Masc.*, gauchère *Fem.*

left luggage office *noun* consigne *Fem.*

leftovers *plural noun* restes *Masc. plural.*

leg *noun* **1** (*of a person or a horse*) jambe *Fem.*; **my left leg** ma jambe gauche; **to break your leg** se casser la jambe; **2** (*of other animals*) patte *Fem.*; **3** (*of a table or chair*) pied *Masc.*; **4** (*in cooking*) **a leg of chicken** une cuisse de poulet; **a leg of lamb** un gigot; ★ **to pull somebody's leg** faire [10] marcher quelqu'un.

legal *adjective* légal (*Masc. plural* légaux).

legend *noun* **1** (*story*) légende *Fem.*; **2** (*person*) légende *Fem.*

leggings *plural noun* caleçon *Masc.*

leisure *noun* loisirs *Masc. plural*; **in my leisure time** pendant mes loisirs.

leisure centre *noun* centre *Masc.* de loisirs.

lemon *noun* citron *Masc.*; **a lemon yoghurt** un yaourt au citron.

lemonade *noun* limonade *Fem.*

lemon juice *noun* jus *Masc.* de citron.

lend *verb* prêter [1]; **to lend something to somebody** prêter

a
b
c
d
e
f
g
h
i
j
k
l
m
n
o
p
q
r
s
t
u
v
w
x
y
z

quelque chose à quelqu'un; **I lent Judy my bike** j'ai prêté mon vélo à Judy; **will you lend it to me?** veux-tu me le prêter?

length *noun* longueur *Fem.*

lens *noun* **1** (*in a camera*) objectif *Masc.*; **2** (*in spectacles*) verre *Masc.*; **3 contact lenses** les lentilles *Fem. plural* de contact.

Lent *noun* Carême *Masc.*

lentil *noun* lentille *Fem.*

Leo *noun* Lion *Masc.*; **I'm Leo** je suis Lion.

leotard *noun* justaucorps *Masc.*

lesbian *noun* lesbienne *Fem.*

less *pronoun, adjective, adverb*
1 moins; **Richard eats less** Richard mange moins; **2** (*before a noun*) moins de; **less traffic** moins de circulation; **less time** moins de temps; **3** (*before an adjective or adverb*) moins; **less interesting** moins intéressant; **less quickly than us** moins vite que nous; **4 less than or less than three hours** moins de trois heures; **less than a kilo** moins d'un kilo; **5 less than** (*in comparisons*) moins que; **you spent less than me** tu as dépensé moins que moi.

lesson *noun* **1** (*class*) cours *Masc.*; **the history lesson** le cours d'histoire; **to take tennis lessons** prendre des cours de tennis; **2** (*one in a planned series*) leçon *Fem.*; **a driving lesson** une leçon de conduite.

let[1] *verb* **1** (*allow*) **to let somebody do** laisser [1] quelqu'un faire; **she lets me borrow her bike** elle me

laisse emprunter son vélo; **will you let me go alone?** veux-tu me laisser y aller toute seule?; **the police let us through** la police nous a laissés passer; **let me see** (*show me*) laisse-moi voir; **2** (*as a suggestion or a command*) **let's go!** allons-y!; **let's not talk about it** n'en parlons pas; **let's see, if Tuesday is the third** ... voyons, si mardi est le trois ...; **let's eat out** s on mangeait au restaurant?

• **to let off 1** tirer [1] (*fireworks*); **2** faire [10] exploser (*a bomb*); **3** (*to excuse from*) dispenser [1] de (*homework*).

let[2] *verb* (*to rent out*) louer [1]; **'flat t let'** 'appartement à louer'.

lethal *adjective* mortel (*Fem.* mortelle)

letter *noun* lettre *Fem.*; **a letter for you from Delia** une lettre pour toi de Delia; **G is the letter after F** G es la lettre après F.

letter box *noun* boîte *Fem.* à lettres.

lettuce *noun* salade *Fem.*; **two lettuces** deux salades.

leukaemia *noun* leucémie *Fem.*

level *noun* niveau *Masc.* (*plural* niveaux); **at street level** au niveau de la rue.
level *adjective* **1** droit (*a shelf or floor*); **2** plat (*ground*).

level crossing *noun* passage *Masc.* à niveau.

lever *noun* levier *Masc.*

liar *noun* menteur *Masc.*, menteuse *Fem.*

474

beral *adjective* libéral (*Masc. plural* libéraux); **the Liberal Democrats** le parti libéral-démocrate.

berty *noun* liberté *Fem.*

ibra *noun* Balance *Fem.*; **Sean's Libra** Sean est Balance.

brarian *noun* bibliothécaire *Masc.* & *Fem.*; **Mark's a librarian** Mark est bibliothécaire.

brary *noun* bibliothèque *Fem.*; **the public library** la bibliothèque municipale.

cence *noun* 1 (*for driving or fishing*) permis *Masc.*; **a driving licence** un permis de conduire; 2 (*for a TV*) redevance *Fem.*

ck *verb* lécher [24].

d *noun* couvercle *Masc.*; **she took the lid off** elle a enlevé le couvercle.

e *noun* mensonge *Masc.*; **to tell a lie** (or **lies**) mentir [53].

lie *verb* 1 (*to be stretched out*) être [6] allongé; **Jimmy was lying on the bed** Jimmy était allongé sur le lit; **my coat lay on the bed** mon manteau était sur le lit; **2 to lie down** se coucher [1]; (*for a little while*) s'allonger [52]; **come and lie down in the sun** viens t'allonger au soleil; 3 (*not to tell the truth*) mentir [53].

e-in *noun* **to have a lie-in** faire la grasse matinée.

eutenant *noun* lieutenant *Masc.*

fe *noun* vie *Fem.*; **all her life** toute sa vie; **full of life** plein de vie; **that's life!** c'est la vie!

febelt *noun* bouée *Fem.* de sauvetage.

lifeboat *noun* canot *Masc.* de sauvetage.

lifeguard *noun* maître nageur *Masc.*; **is there a lifeguard at the pool?** est-ce que la piscine est surveillée?

life jacket *noun* gilet *Masc.* de sauvetage.

life-style *noun* style *Masc.* de vie.

lift *noun* 1 ascenseur *Masc.*; **let's take the lift** prenons l'ascenseur; 2 (*a ride*) **to give somebody a lift to the station** déposer quelqu'un à la gare; **Tom gave me a lift home** Tom m'a déposé chez moi; **can I give you a lift?** puis-je vous déposer quelque part?

lift *verb* soulever [50]; **he lifted the box** il a soulevé le carton.

light *noun* 1 (*electric*) lumière *Fem.*; **will you turn the light on?** veux-tu allumer la lumière?; **to turn off the light** éteindre la lumière; 2 (*streetlight*) réverbère *Masc.*; 3 (*a headlight for a car*) phare *Masc.*; **are your lights on?** as-tu allumé tes phares?; 4 (*an indicator on a machine*) voyant *Masc.*; 5 **traffic lights** les feux *Masc. plural*; **the lights were green** le feu était au vert; 6 **have you got a light?** tu as du feu?

light *adjective* 1 (*in colour*) clair; **light blue eyes** des yeux bleu clair; 2 (*not night*) **it gets light at six** il fait jour à six heures; 3 (*not heavy*) léger (*Fem.* légère); **a light sweater** un pull léger; **a light breeze** une brise légère.

light *verb* 1 allumer [1] (*the oven, the fire, or a cigarette*); **we lit a fire**

a
b
c
d
e
f
g
h
i
j
k
l
m
n
o
p
q
r
s
t
u
v
w
x
y
z

nous avons fait un feu; **2** craquer [1] (*a match*).

light bulb *noun* ampoule *Fem.*

lighter *noun* briquet *Masc.*

lighthouse *noun* phare *Masc.*

lightning *noun* éclairs *Masc. plural*; **a flash of lightning** un éclair; **to be struck by lightning** être frappé par la foudre.

light switch *noun* interrupteur *Masc.*

like[1] *preposition, conjunction*
1 comme; **like me** comme moi; **like this** comme ça; **like a duck** comme un canard; **like I said** comme j'ai dit; **what's it like?** c'est comment?; **what was the weather like?** quel temps faisait-il?; **2 to look like** ressembler [1] à; **Cindy looks like her father** Cindy ressemble à son père.

like[2] *verb* **1** aimer [1] (bien); **I like fish** j'aime bien le poisson; **I don't like snakes** je n'aime pas les serpents; **Mum likes travelling** Maman aime bien voyager; **I like Renoir best** je préfère Renoir; **2 I would like** je voudrais; **would you like a coffee?** est-ce que tu voudrais un café?; **what would you like to eat?** qu'est-ce que tu veux manger?; **yes, if you like** oui, si tu veux.

likely *adjective* probable; **it's not very likely** ce n'est pas très probable; **she's likely to phone** elle va probablement appeler.

lilac *noun* lilas *Masc.*

lily *noun* lys *Masc.*

lily of the valley *noun* muguet *Masc.*

lime *noun* citron *Masc.* vert.

limit *noun* limitation *Fem.*; **the speed limit** la limitation de vitess

limp *noun* **to have a limp** boiter [1]

line *noun* **1** ligne *Fem.*; **a straight line** une ligne droite; **six lines of text** six lignes de texte; **to draw a line** tirer un trait; **2 a railway line** (*from one place to another*) une lign de chemin de fer; **on the railway line** (*the track*) sur la voie ferrée; **3** (*a queue of people or cars*) file *Fem* **to stand in line** faire la queue; **4** (*telephone*) ligne *Fem.*; **the line's bad** la ligne est mauvaise; **hold th line, please** ne quittez pas.
line *verb* doubler [1] (*a coat*).

linen *noun* lin *Masc.*; **a linen jacke** une veste en lin.

lining *noun* doublure *Fem.*

link *noun* rapport *Masc.*; **what's th link between the two?** quel est le rapport entre les deux?
link *verb* relier [1] (*two places*); **th terminals are linked by a shuttle service** les terminaux sont reliés par une navette.

lino *noun* linoléum *Masc.*

lion *noun* lion *Masc.*

lip *noun* lèvre *Fem.*

lip-read *verb* lire [51] sur les lèvre

lipstick *noun* rouge *Masc.* à lèvres

liquid *noun, adjective* liquide *Masc*

liquidizer *noun* mixer *Masc.*

list *noun* liste *Fem.*

listen *verb* **1** écouter [1]; **I wasn't listening** je n'écoutais pas; **2 to**

listen to écouter [1]; **listen to the music** écoutez la musique; **you're not listening to me** tu ne m'écoutes pas.

listener *noun* (*to the radio*) auditeur *Masc.*, auditrice *Fem.*

literally *adverb* littéralement.

literature *noun* littérature *Fem.*

litre *noun* litre *Masc.*; **a litre of milk** un litre de lait.

litter *noun* (*rubbbish*) détritus *Masc.* plural.

litter bin *noun* poubelle *Fem.*

little *adjective, pronoun* **1** (*small*) petit (*goes before the noun*); **a little boy** un petit garçon; **a little break** une petite pause; **2** (*not much*) peu (de); **they have little money** ils ont peu d'argent; **we have very little time** nous avons très peu de temps; **3 a little** un peu (de); **4 we have a little money** nous avons un peu d'argent; **just a little, please** juste un peu, s'il vous plaît; **it's a little late** c'est un peu tard; **a little more** un peu plus; **a little less** un peu moins; ★ **little by little** petit à petit.

little finger *noun* petit doigt *Masc.*

live[1] *verb* **1** (*in a house or town*) habiter [1]; **Susan lives in York** Susan habite à York; **we live in a flat** nous habitons dans un appartement; **they live at number 57** ils habitent au numéro cinquante-sept; **we're living in the country now** nous habitons à la campagne maintenant; **2** (*be or stay alive, spend one's life*) vivre [82]; **lions live in Africa** les lions vivent en Afrique; **they live on fruit** ils

vivent de fruits; **they live together** ils vivent ensemble.

live[2] *adjective* **1** en direct (*a broadcast*); **a live concert** un concert en direct; **a broadcast live from Wembley** une émission en direct de Wembley; **2** (*alive*) vivant.

lively *adjective* animé (*a party or restaurant, for example*).

liver *noun* foie *Masc.*

living *noun* vie *Fem.*; **to earn a living** gagner sa vie.

living room *noun* salle *Fem.* de séjour.

lizard *noun* lézard *Masc.*

load *noun* **1** (*on a lorry*) chargement *Masc.*; **a (lorry-)load of bricks** un camion de briques; **2 a bus-load of tourists** un autobus plein de touristes; **3 loads of** des tas de (*informal*); **loads of people** des tas de gens; **they've got loads of money** ils sont bourrés de fric (*informal*).
load *verb* charger [52]; **a lorry loaded with wood** un camion chargé de bois.

loaf *noun* pain *Masc.*; **a loaf of wholemeal bread** un pain complet.

loan *noun* prêt *Masc.*
loan *verb* prêter [1].

loathe *verb* détester [1]; **I loathe getting up early** je déteste me lever tôt.

lobster *noun* homard *Masc.*

local *noun* **1** (*a pub*) pub *Masc.* du coin; **2 the locals** (*people*) les gens du coin.
local *adjective* **the local library** la

a
b
c
d
e
f
g
h
i
j
k
l
m
n
o
p
q
r
s
t
u
v
w
x
y
z

bibliothèque du coin; **the local newspaper** le journal local.

locally *adverb* de façon locale; **they only advertise locally** ils ne font de publicité que dans la région.

lock *noun* **1** (*with a key*) serrure *Fem.*; **2** (*on a canal*) écluse *Fem.*
lock *verb* **to lock the door** fermer [1] la porte à clé; **the door was locked** la porte était fermée à clé.

locker *noun* casier *Masc.*

locker room *noun* vestiaire *Masc.*

lodger *noun* locataire *Masc. & Fem.*

loft *noun* grenier *Masc.*

log *noun* bûche *Fem.*; **a log fire** un feu de bois.

logical *adjective* logique.

lollipop *noun* sucette *Fem.*

London *noun* Londres; **to London** à Londres; **a day in London** une journée à Londres; **the London streets** les rues de Londres.

Londoner *noun* Londonien *Masc.*, Londonienne *Fem.*

loneliness *noun* solitude *Fem.*

lonely *adjective* **1** seul; **to feel lonely** se sentir [53] seul; **2** (*a place*) isolé.

long *adjective, adverb* **1** long (*Fem.* longue); **a long film** un film long; **a long day** une longue journée; **it's an hour long** ça dure une heure; **2 a long time** longtemps; **he stayed for a long time** il est resté longtemps; **I've been here for a long time** je suis là depuis longtemps; **a long time ago** il y a longtemps; **this won't take long** ça ne prendra pas longtemps; **3 how long?** combien de

temps?; **how long have you been here?** tu es là depuis combien de temps?; **long ago** il y a longtemps; **4 a long way** loin; **it's a long way to the cinema** le cinéma est loin d'ici; **5 all night long** toute la nuit long *verb* **to long to do** avoir [5] très envie de faire; **I'm longing to see you** j'ai très envie de te voir.

long-distance call *noun* (*within the country*) appel *Masc.* interurbain.

longer *adverb* **no longer** ne ...plus; **I no longer know** je ne sais plus; **they no longer live here** ils n'habitent plus ici.

long jump *noun* saut *Masc.* en longueur.

longlife milk *noun* lait *Masc.* longue conservation.

loo *noun* toilettes *Fem. plural.*

look *noun* **1** (*a glance*) coup *Masc.* d'œil; **to have a look at something** jeter un coup d'œil à quelque chose; **2** (*a tour*) **to have a look round the town** faire un tour dans la ville; **to have a look round the shops** faire les magasins; **3 to have a look for** chercher (*something you've lost*).
look *verb* **1** regarder [1]; **I wasn't looking** je ne regardais pas; **to look out of the window** regarder par la fenêtre; **2 to look at** regarder [1]; **Andy was looking at the photos** Andy regardait les photos; **3** (*to seem*) avoir [5] l'air; **Melanie looks pleased** Melanie a l'air contente; **the salad looks delicious** la salade a l'air délicieuse; **4 to look like** ressembler [1] à; **Sally looks like her aunt** Sally ressemble à sa tante

they look like each other ils se ressemblent; **what does the house look like?** comment est la maison?; **it looks like rain** on dirait qu'il va pleuvoir

- **to look after 1** s'occuper [1] de; **Dad's looking after the baby** Papa s'occupe du bébé; **2** surveiller [1] (*luggage*)**to look for** chercher [1]; **I'm looking for the keys** je cherche les clés.
- **to look forward to something** attendre [3] quelque chose avec impatience (*a party or a trip, for example*)
- **to look out** (*to be careful*) faire [10] attention; **look out, it's hot!** (fais) attention, c'est chaud!
- **to look something up** chercher [1] quelque chose (*in a dictionary or directory*); **you can look it up in the dictionary** tu peux le chercher dans le dictionnaire.

loose *adjective* **1** (*a screw or knot*) desserré; **2** (*a garment*) ample; **3 loose change** la petite monnaie; ★ **I'm at a loose end** je ne sais pas trop quoi faire.

lorry *noun* camion *Masc.*

lorry driver *noun* routier *Masc.*

lose *verb* **1** perdre [3]; **we lost** nous avons perdu; **we lost the match** nous avons perdu le match; **Sam's lost his watch** Sam a perdu sa montre; **2 to get lost** se perdre [3]; **we got lost in the woods** nous nous sommes perdus dans les bois.

loss *noun* perte *Fem.*

lost *adjective* perdu; **I'm lost** je suis perdu; **are you lost?** vous êtes perdu?

lost property *noun* objets *Masc. plural* trouvés.

lot *noun* **1 a lot** beaucoup; **Jason eats a lot** Jason mange beaucoup; **I spent a lot** j'ai beaucoup dépensé; **he's a lot better** il va beaucoup mieux; **2 a lot of** beaucoup de; **a lot of coffee** beaucoup de café; **lots of people** beaucoup de gens; **'what are you doing tonight?' – 'not a lot'** 'qu'est-ce que tu fais ce soir?' – 'pas grand-chose'.

lottery *noun* loterie *Fem.*; **to win the lottery** gagner à la loterie.

loud *adjective* **1** fort; **in a loud voice** d'une voix forte; **2 to say something out loud** dire quelque chose à haute voix.

loudly *adverb* fort.

loudspeaker *noun* haut-parleur *Masc.* (*plural* haut-parleurs).

lounge *noun* **1** (*in a house or hotel*) salon *Masc.*; **2** (*in an airport*) **the departure lounge** la salle d'embarquement.

love *noun* **1** amour *Masc.*; **to be in love with somebody** être amoureux (*Fem.* amoureuse) de quelqu'un; **she's in love with Jake** elle est amoureuse de Jake; **Gina sends her love** Gina t'embrasse; **with love from Charlie** amitiés, Charlie; **2** (*in tennis*) zéro *Masc.* **love** *verb* **1** aimer [1] (*a person*) **I love you** je t'aime; **2** aimer beaucoup (*place, suggestion*); **she loves London** elle aime beaucoup Londres; **I'd love to come** j'aimerais beaucoup venir; **3** adorer [1] (*activity, thing*); **I love dancing** j'adore danser; **Wayne loves**

a
b
c
d
e
f
g
h
i
j
k
l
m
n
o
p
q
r
s
t
u
v
w
x
y
z

seafood Wayne adore les fruits de mer.

lovely *adjective* **1** (*to look at*) joli; **a lovely dress** une jolie robe; **their garden is lovely** leur jardin est très joli; **a lovely house** une belle maison; **2 it's a lovely day** il fait très beau; **we had lovely weather** il a fait très beau; **3** (*food, meal*) délicieux (*Fem.* délicieuse).

lover *noun* **1** (*general*) partenaire *Masc. & Fem.*; **2** (*of married man*) maîtresse *Fem.*; (*of married woman*) amant *Masc.*

low *adjective* bas (*Fem.* basse); **a low table** une table basse; **at a low price** à prix bas; **in a low voice** à voix basse.

lower *adjective* (*not as high*) inférieur.
lower *verb* baisser [1].

low-fat milk *noun* lait *Masc.* écrémé.

loyalty *noun* loyauté *Fem.*; **loyalty card** carte *Fem.* de fidélité.

luck *noun* chance *Fem.*; **good luck!** bonne chance!; **bad luck!** pas de chance!; **with a bit of luck** avec un peu de chance.

luckily *adverb* heureusement; **luckily for them** heureusement pour eux.

lucky *adjective* **1 to be lucky** (*a person*) avoir de la chance; **we were lucky** nous avons eu de la chance; **2 to be lucky** (*bringing luck*) porter bonheur; **it's supposed to be lucky** c'est censé porter bonheur; **my lucky number** mon numéro porte-bonheur.

luggage *noun* bagages *Masc. plural*; **my luggage is in the boot** mes bagages sont dans le coffre.

lump *noun* **1** (*of earth*) motte *Fem.*; **2** (*piece*) morceau *Masc.* (*plural* morceaux); **3** (*swelling*) grosseur *Fem.*

lunch *noun* déjeuner *Masc.*; **to have lunch** déjeuner [1]; **we had lunch in Oxford** nous avons déjeuné à Oxford.

lunch break *noun* pause-déjeuner *Fem.*

lunch hour, **lunch time** *noun* heure *Fem.* du déjeuner.

lung *noun* poumon *Masc.*

Luxembourg *noun* **1** (*country*) Luxembourg *Masc.*; **to Luxembourg** au Luxembourg; **in Luxembourg** au Luxembourg; **2** (*city*) Luxenbourg; **in Luxembourg** à Luxembourg.

luxurious *adjective* luxueux (*Fem.* luxueuse).

luxury *noun* luxe *Masc.*; **a luxury hotel** un hôtel de luxe.

lyrics *plural noun* paroles *Fem. plural*

Mm

mac *noun* imper *Masc.* (*informal*).

macaroni *noun* macaronis *Masc. plural*; **we had macaroni** nous avons mangé des macaronis.

machine *noun* machine *Fem.*

machinery *noun* machines *Fem. plural*.

mackerel noun maquereau Masc. (plural maquereaux).

mad adjective **1** fou (Fem. folle); **she's completely mad!** elle est complètement folle!; **2** (angry) furieux (Fem. furieuse); **my mum will be mad!** ma mère sera furieuse!; **3 to be mad about something** adorer quelque chose; **she's mad about horses** elle adore les chevaux.

madam noun madame Fem.

madman noun fou Masc.

madness noun folie Fem.

magazine noun magazine Masc.

maggot noun asticot Masc.

magic noun magie Fem.
  magic adjective **1** magique; **a magic wand** une baguette magique; **2** (great) super.

magician noun **1** (wizard) magicien Masc.; **2** (conjurer) prestidigitateur Masc.

magnet noun aimant Masc.

magnificent adjective magnifique.

magnifying glass noun loupe Fem.

magnolia noun magnolia Masc.

mahogany noun acajou Masc.

maiden name noun nom Masc. de jeune fille.

mail noun courrier Masc.; **email** (electronic mail) courrier Masc. électronique.

mail order noun **to buy something by mail order** acheter quelque chose par correspondance; **a mail order catalogue** un catalogue de vente par correspondance.

main adjective principal (Masc. plural principaux); **the main entrance** l'entrée principale.

main course noun plat Masc. principal.

mainly adverb principalement.

main road noun route Fem. principale.

maize noun maïs Masc.

major adjective majeur.
  major noun commandant Masc.

Majorca noun Majorque Fem.

majority noun majorité Fem.

make noun marque Fem.; **what make is your bike?** de quelle marque est ton vélo?
  make verb **1** faire [10]; **I made an omelette** j'ai fait une omelette; **she made her bed** elle a fait son lit; **he made me wait** il m'a fait attendre; **she makes me laugh** elle me fait rire; **two and three make five** deux et trois font cinq; **2** fabriquer [1]; **they make computers** ils fabriquent des ordinateurs; **'made in France'** 'fabriqué en France'; **3** rendre [3]; **to make somebody happy** rendre quelqu'un heureux; **that makes me hungry** ça me donne faim; **4** gagner [1] (money); **he makes forty pounds a day** il gagne quarante livres par jour; **to make a living** gagner sa vie; **5** (force) **to make somebody do something** obliger [52] quelqu'un à faire quelque chose; **she made him give the money back** elle l'a obligé à rendre l'argent; **6 to make a meal**

a b c d e f g h i j k l **m** n o p q r s t u v w x y z

481

préparer [1] un repas; **7 to make a phone call** passer [1] un coup de fil; **I have to make a few phone calls** je dois passer quelques coups de fil; **8 I can't make it tonight** je ne peux pas venir ce soir.

• **to make something up 1** inventer [1] quelque chose; **she made up an excuse** elle a inventé une excuse; **2 to make it up** (*after a quarrel*) se réconcilier [1]; **they've mad it up now** il se sont maintenant réconciliés

make-up *noun* maquillage *Masc.*; **to put on your make-up** se maquiller; **Jo's putting on her make-up** Jo est en train de se maquiller; **I don't wear make-up** je ne me maquille pas.

male *adjective* **1** mâle (*animal*); **a male rat** un rat mâle; **2** (*sex : on a form*) masculin; **3 a male rôle** un rôle pour homme; **a male voice** une voix d'homme; **a male student** un étudiant.

male chauvinist *noun* macho *Masc.*

mall *noun* centre *Masc.* commercial.

Malta *noun* Malte *Fem.*

mammal *noun* mammifère *Masc.*

man *noun* homme *Masc.*; **modern man is taller than his ancestors** l'homme moderne est plus grand que ses ancêtres.

manage *verb* **1** diriger [52] (*business, team*); **she manages a travel agency** elle dirige une agence de voyages; **2** (*cope*) se débrouiller [1]; **I can manage** je me débrouille; **3 to manage to do**

réussir [2] à faire; **he managed to open the door** il a réussi à ouvrir la porte; **I didn't manage to get in touch with her** je n'ai pas réussi à la contacter.

management *noun* **1** gestion *Fem.*; **a management course** un cours de gestion; **2** direction; **a meeting with management** une réunion avec la direction.

manager *noun* **1** (*of a company or a bank*) directeur *Masc.*, directrice *Fem.*; **2** (*of a shop or restaurant*) gérant *Masc.*, gérante *Fem.*; **3** (*in spor and entertainment*) manager *Masc.*

manageress *noun* gérante *Fem.*

managing director *noun* directeur *Masc.* général, directrice *Fem.* générale.

mandarin (orange) *noun* mandarine *Fem.*

mango *noun* mangue *Fem.*

mania *noun* manie *Fem.*

maniac *noun* fou *Masc.*, folle *Fem.*; **she drives like a maniac!** elle conduit comme une folle!

mankind *noun* humanité *Fem.*

man-made *adjective* (*fibre*) synthétique.

manner *noun* **1 in a manner of speaking** pour ainsi dire; **2 to have good manners** être poli; **it's bad manners to talk like that** ce n'est pas poli de parler comme ça.

manpower *noun* main-d'œuvre *Fem.*

mansion *noun* demeure *Fem.*

mantelpiece *noun* cheminée *Fem*

manual *noun* manuel *Masc.*

manufacture *verb* fabriquer [1].

manufacturer *noun* fabricant *Masc.*

manure *noun* fumier *Masc.*

many *adjective, pronoun*
1 beaucoup (de); **does she have many friends?** est-ce qu'elle a beaucoup d'amis?; **we didn't see many people** nous n'avons pas vu beaucoup (de) gens; **not many** pas beaucoup; **there aren't many onions left** il ne reste pas beaucoup d'oignons; **many of them forgot** beaucoup d'entre eux ont oublié; **2 very many** beaucoup (de); **there aren't very many glasses** il n'y a pas beaucoup de verres; **3 so many** tant; **I have so many things to do!** j'ai tant de choses à faire!; **4 so many** autant de; **I've never eaten so many strawberries** je n'ai jamais mangé autant de fraises; **5 as many as** autant que; **you can take as many as you like** tu peux en prendre autant que tu veux; **6 too many** trop (de); **I've got too many things to do** j'ai trop de choses à faire; **there were too many people** il y avait trop de monde; **that's far too many!** c'est beaucoup trop!; **7 how many?** combien?; **how many are there?** il y en a combien?; **how many sisters have you got?** tu as combien de sœurs?; **how many are there left?** il en reste combien?

map *noun* **1** carte *Fem.*; **a road map** une carte routière; **2** (*of a town*) plan *Masc.*

marathon *noun* marathon *Masc.*

marble *noun* **1** marbre *Masc.*; **a marble fireplace** une cheminée en marbre; **2** bille; **to play marbles** jouer aux billes.

march *noun* (*demonstration*) manifestation *Fem.*
march *verb* (*demonstrators*) défiler [1].

March *noun* mars *Masc.*; **in March** en mars.

mare *noun* jument *Fem.*

margarine *noun* margarine *Fem.*

margin *noun* marge *Fem.*

marijuana *noun* marijuana *Fem.*

mark *noun* **1** (*at school*) note *Fem.*; **I got a good mark for my French homework** j'ai eu une bonne note pour mon devoir de français; **what mark did you get for French?** tu as eu combien en français?; **2** (*stain*) tache *Fem.*
mark *verb* corriger [52]; **the teacher marks our homework** le professeur corrige nos devoirs.

market *noun* marché *Masc.*

marketing *noun* marketing *Masc.*

marmalade *noun* confiture *Fem.* d'oranges amères.

maroon *adjective* bordeaux; **a maroon jumper** un pull bordeaux.

marriage *noun* mariage *Masc.*

married *adjective* marié; **a married couple** un couple marié; **they've been married for twenty years** ils sont mariés depuis vingt ans.

marry *verb* **1 to marry somebody** épouser [1] quelqu'un; **she married a Frenchman** elle a épousé un Français; **2 to get married** se marier [1]; **they got married in July** ils se sont mariés en juillet.

a
b
c
d
e
f
g
h
i
j
k
l
m
n
o
p
q
r
s
t
u
v
w
x
y
z

483

a b c d e f g h i j k l m n o p q r s t u v w x y z

marvellous *adjective* merveilleux (*Fem.* merveilleuse); **the weather's marvellous** il fait un temps merveilleux.

marzipan *noun* pâte *Fem.* d'amandes.

mascara *noun* mascara *Masc.*

masculine *noun* (*in French and other grammars*) masculin *Masc.*; **in the masculine** au masculin.

mash *verb* écraser [1] (*vegetables*).

mashed potatoes *noun* purée *Fem.* de pommes de terre.

mask *noun* masque *Masc.*

mass *noun* **1 a mass of** une masse de; **2 masses of** beaucoup de; **they've got masses of money** ils ont beaucoup d'argent; **there's masses left over** il en reste beaucoup; **3** (*religious*) messe *Fem.*; **to go to mass** aller à la messe.

massacre *noun* massacre *Masc.*

massage *noun* massage *Masc.*

massive *adjective* énorme.

master *verb* maîtriser [1].

masterpiece *noun* chef-d'œuvre *Masc.* (*plural* chefs-d'œuvre).

mat *noun* **1** (*doormat*) paillasson *Masc.*; **2** (*to put under a hot dish*) dessous-de-plat *Masc.*; **3 a table mat** un set de table.

match *noun* **1** allumette *Fem.*; **a box of matches** une boîte d'allumettes; **2** (*sports*) match *Masc.* (*plural* matchs); **a football match** un match de foot; **to watch the match** regarder [1] le match; **to win the match** gagner [1] le match; **to lose the match** perdre [3] le match.

match *verb* être [6] assorti à; **the jacket matches the skirt** la veste est assortie à la jupe.

matching *adjective* **matching curtains and cushions** des rideaux et des coussins assortis.

mate *noun* copain *Masc.*, copine *Fem.* (*informal*); **I'm going out with my mates tonight** je sors avec mes copains ce soir.

material *noun* **1** (*fabric*) tissu *Masc.*; **2** (*information*) documentation *Fem.*; **3** (*substance*) matière *Fem.*; **raw materials** les matières *Fem. plural* premières.

mathematics *noun* mathématiques *Fem. plural*.

maths *noun* maths *Fem. plural*; **I like maths** j'aime bien les maths; **Anna's good at maths** Anna est forte en maths.

matter *noun* **what's the matter?** qu'est-ce qu'il y a?
matter *verb* **1 the things that matter** les choses importantes; **it matters a lot to me** c'est très important pour moi; **2 it doesn't matter** ça ne fait rien; **it doesn't matter if it rains** ça ne fait rien s'il pleut; **3 it doesn't matter** (*whether one thing or another*) ça n'a pas d'importance; **you can write it in French or English, it doesn't matter** tu peux l'écrire en français ou en anglais, ça n'a pas d'importance.

mattress *noun* matelas *Masc.*

mature *adjective* mûr.

maximum *noun* maximum *Masc.*; **the maximum possible** le maximum possible.

maximum *adjective* maximum (*does not change in the feminine or plural*); **the maximum temperature** la température maximum; **maximum profits** les bénéfices maximum.

May *noun* mai *Masc.*; **in May** en mai.

may *verb* **1** she may be ill elle est peut-être malade; **we may go to Spain** nous irons peut-être en Espagne; **2** (*asking permission*) **may I close the door?** est-ce que je peux fermer la porte?

maybe *adverb* peut-être; **maybe not** peut-être pas; **maybe he's forgotten** il a peut-être oublié; **maybe they've got lost** ils se sont peut-être perdus.

May Day *noun* le Premier Mai.

mayonnaise *noun* mayonnaise *Fem.*

mayor *noun* maire *Masc.*

mayoress *noun* mairesse *Fem.*

me *pronoun* **1** me, m' (*before a vowel or silent 'h'*); **she knows me** elle me connaît; **can you help me, please?** est-ce que tu peux m'aider, s'il te plaît?; **can you lend me a pen?** peux-tu me prêter un stylo?; **can you give me your address?** peux-tu me donner ton adresse?; **2** (*after a preposition*) moi; **I took her with me** je l'ai emmenée avec moi; **they left without me** ils sont partis sans moi; **3** (*in commands*) moi; **listen to me!** écoute-moi!; **wait for me!** attends-moi!; **excuse me!** excusez-moi!; **4** (*in comparisons*) **than me** que moi; **she's older than me** elle est

plus âgée que moi; **5 me too!** moi aussi!

meadow *noun* pré *Masc.*

meal *noun* repas *Masc.*; **they have three meals a day** ils mangent trois fois par jour.

mean *verb* **1** vouloir [14] dire; **what do you mean?** qu'est-ce que tu veux dire?; **what does that mean?** qu'est-ce que ça veut dire?; **that's not what I meant** ce n'est pas ce que je voulais dire; **2 to mean to do** avoir [5] l'intention de faire; **I meant to phone my mother** j'avais l'intention d'appeler ma mère; **3 to be meant to do** devoir faire; **she was meant to be here at six** elle devait être là à six heures.
mean *adjective* **1** (*with money*) radin (*informal*); **2** (*unkind*) méchant; **she's really mean to her brother** elle est vraiment méchante avec son frère; **what a mean thing to do!** c'est vraiment méchant!

meaning *noun* sens *Masc.*

means *noun* moyen *Masc.*; **a means of transport** un moyen de transport; **a means of doing** un moyen de faire; **we have no means of contacting him** nous n'avons aucun moyen de le contacter; **by means of** au moyen de; **by all means** certainement.

meantime *noun* **for the meantime** pour le moment; **in the meantime** pendant ce temps.

meanwhile *adverb* pendant ce temps; **meanwhile she was waiting at the station** pendant ce temps, elle attendait à la gare.

measles *noun* rougeole *Fem.*

measure *verb* mesurer [1].

measurements *plural noun*
1 (*of a room or an object*) dimensions *Fem. plural*; **the measurements of the room** les dimensions de la pièce; **2** (*of a person*) mensurations *Fem. plural*; **my chest measurement** mon tour de poitrine; **my waist measurement** mon tour de taille.

meat *noun* viande *Fem.*

Mecca *noun* Mecque *Fem.*

mechanic *noun* mécanicien *Masc.*; **he's a mechanic** il est mécanicien.

mechanical *adjective* mécanique.

medal *noun* médaille *Fem.*; **the gold medal** la médaille d'or.

media *noun* **the media** les médias *Masc. plural.*

medical *noun* visite *Fem.* médicale; **to have a medical** passer une visite médicale.
medical *adjective* médical (*Masc. plural* médicaux); **do you have medical insurance?** est-ce que vous avez une assurance-maladie?

medicine *noun* **1** médicament *Masc.*; **I'd like some cough medecine** je voudrais un médicament pour la toux; **2** (*subject of study*) médecine *Fem.*; **she's studying medicine** elle fait des études de médecine; **3 alternative medecine** la médecine douce.

medieval *adjective* médiéval, du moyen-âge.

Mediterranean *noun* **the Mediterranean** la Méditerranée.

medium *adjective* moyen (*Fem.* moyenne).

medium-sized *noun* de taille moyenne.

meet *verb* **1** (*by chance*) rencontrer [1]; **I met Rosie outside the baker's** j'ai rencontré Rosie devant la boulangerie; **2** (*by appointment*) retrouver [1]; **I'll meet you outside the cinema at six** je te retrouverai devant le cinéma à six heures; **3** se retrouver [1]; **we're meeting at six** nous allons nous retrouver à six heures; **4** (*get to know*) faire [10] la connaissance de; **I met a French girl last week** j'ai fait la connaissance d'une Française la semaine dernière; **5 Tom, have you met Oskar?** Tom, est-ce que tu connais Oskar?; **6** (*off a train, bus, etc*) venir [81] chercher; **my dad's meeting me at the station** mon père vient me chercher à la gare.

meeting *noun* réunion *Fem.*; **there's a meeting at ten o'clock** il y a une réunion à dix heures; **she's in a meeting** elle est en réunion.

megabyte *noun* mégaoctet *Masc.*

melody *noun* mélodie *Fem.*

melon *noun* melon *Masc.*

melt *verb* **1** fondre [3]; **it melts in your mouth** ça fond dans la bouche; **2 to melt something** faire [10] fondre quelque chose; **melt the butter in a saucepan** faites fondre le beurre dans une casserole.

member *noun* membre *Masc.*; **she's a member of the Labour Party** elle est membre du parti travailliste.

Member of Parliament *noun* député *Masc.*

membership *noun* adhésion *Fem.*

membership card *noun* carte *Fem.* de membre.

membership fee *noun* cotisation *Fem.*

memorial *noun* **a war memorial** un monument aux morts.

memorial service *noun* messe *Fem.* commémorative.

memorize *verb* **to memorize something** apprendre [64] quelque chose par cœur.

memory *noun* **1** (*of a person or computer*) mémoire *Fem.*; **you have a good memory!** tu as bonne mémoire!; **I have a bad memory** je n'ai pas de mémoire; **2** (*of the past*) souvenir *Masc.*; **I have good memories of my stay in France** j'ai de bons souvenirs de mon séjour en France.

mend *verb* réparer [1].

meningitis *noun* méningite *Fem.*

mental *adjective* mental (*Masc. plural* mentaux); **a mental illness** une maladie mentale; **a mental hospital** un hôpital psychiatrique.

mention *verb* mentionner [1].

menu *noun* menu *Masc.*; **on the menu** au menu; **is there a set menu?** est-ce qu'il y a un menu à prix fixe?

mercy *noun* pitié *Fem.*

merge *verb* **1** (*roads*) se rejoindre [49]; **2** (*documents*) fusionner [1].

meringue *noun* meringue *Fem.*

merit *noun* mérite *Masc.*

mermaid *noun* sirène *Fem.*

merry *adjective* **1** joyeux (*Fem.* joyeuse); **Merry Christmas** Joyeux Noël; **2** (*from drinking*) éméché (*informal*).

merry-go-round *noun* manège *Masc.*

mess *noun* désordre *Masc.*; **my papers are in a mess** mes papiers sont dans le désordre; **to make a mess** mettre du désordre; **to clear up the mess** mettre de l'ordre; **what a mess!** quelle pagaille! (*informal*).

● **to mess about** faire [10] l'imbécile; **stop messing about!** arrête de faire l'imbécile!

● **to mess about with something** jouer [1] avec quelque chose; **it's dangerous to mess about with matches** il est dangereux de jouer avec les allumettes.

● **to mess something up** mettre [11] la pagaille dans quelque chose (*informal*); **you've messed up all my papers** tu as mis la pagaille dans tous mes papiers.

message *noun* message *Masc.*; **a telephone message** un message téléphonique.

messenger *noun* messager *Masc.*

messy *adjective* **1** **it's a messy job** c'est un travail salissant; **2** **he's a messy eater** il mange n'importe comment; **her writing's really messy** elle écrit n'importe comment.

metal *noun* métal *Masc.* (*plural* métaux).

a b c d e f g h i j k l **m** n o p q r s t u v w x y z

487

a
b
c
d
e
f
g
h
i
j
k
l
m
n
o
p
q
r
s
t
u
v
w
x
y
z

meter noun **1** (electricity, gas, taxi) compteur Masc.; **to read the meter** relever le compteur; **2 a parking meter** un parcmètre.

method noun méthode Fem.

Methodist noun méthodiste Masc. & Fem.; **I'm a Methodist** je suis méthodiste.

metre noun mètre Masc.

metric adjective métrique.

Mexican noun Mexicain Masc., Mexicaine Fem.
Mexican adjective mexicain.

Mexico noun Mexique Masc.; **in Mexico** au Mexique; **to Mexico** au Mexique.

microchip noun puce Fem.

microphone noun microphone Masc.

microscope noun microscope Masc.

microwave oven noun four Masc. à micro-ondes.

midday noun midi Masc.; **at midday** à midi.

middle noun **1** milieu Masc.; **in the middle of the room** au milieu de la pièce; **in the middle of the night** au milieu de la nuit; **2 to be in the middle of doing** être en train de faire; **when she phoned I was in the middle of washing my hair** quand elle a appelé j'étais en train de me laver les cheveux.

middle-aged adjective d'un certain âge; **a middle-aged lady** une dame d'un certain âge.

middle-class adjective de la classe moyenne; **a middle-class**

family une famille de la classe moyenne.

Middle-East noun Moyen-Orient Masc.; **in the Middle East** au Moyen Orient.

middle finger noun majeur Masc.

midge noun moucheron Masc.

midnight noun minuit Masc.; **at midnight** à minuit.

Midsummer's Day noun la Saint Jean.

midwife noun sage-femme Fem.

might verb 'are you going to phone him?' – 'I might' 'est-ce que tu vas l'appeler? – 'peut-être'; **I might invite Jo** j'inviterai peut-être Jo; **Amanda might know** Amanda le saurait peut-être; **he might have forgotten** il a peut-être oublié.

migraine noun migraine Fem.

mike noun micro Masc. (informal).

mild adjective doux (Fem. douce); **it's quite mild today** il fait plutôt doux aujourd'hui.

mile noun **1** mille Masc. (the French use kilometres for distances; to convert miles roughly to kilometres, multiply by 8 and divide by 5) **the village is ten miles from Oxford** le village est à seize kilomètres d'Oxford; **2 it's miles better!** c'est dix fois meilleur!

mileage noun kilométrage Masc.; **what's the mileage on your car?** elle a combien de kilomètres, votre voiture?

military adjective militaire.

milk noun lait Masc.; **full-cream milk** le lait entier; **skimmed milk** le lait écrémé; **semi-skimmed milk** le lait demi-écrémé.

milk *verb* traire [78].

milk chocolate *noun* chocolat *Masc.* au lait.

milk jug *noun* pot *Masc.* à lait.

milkman *noun* laitier *Masc.*

milk shake *noun* milk-shake *Masc.*

millennium *noun* millénaire *Masc.*

millimetre *noun* millimètre *Masc.*

million *noun* million *Masc.*; **a million people** un million de personnes; **two million people** deux millions de personnes.

millionaire *noun* millionnaire *Masc.*

mimic *verb* imiter [1].

mince *noun* viande *Fem.* hachée.

mind *noun* **1** esprit *Masc.*; **it crossed my mind that** ... il m'est venu à l'esprit que ...; **2 to change your mind** changer d'avis; **I've changed my mind** j'ai changé d'avis; **3 to make up your mind** se décider; **I can't make up my mind** je n'arrive pas à me décider.

mind *verb* **1** surveiller [1]; **can you mind my bag for me?** est-ce que tu peux surveiller mon sac?; **2** s'occuper [1] de (*baby*); **could you mind the baby for ten minutes?** est-ce que tu peux t'occuper du bébé pendant dix minutes?; **3 do you mind if ...?** est-ce que cela vous dérange si ...?; **do you mind if I close the door?** est-ce que cela vous dérange si je ferme la porte?; **I don't mind** cela ne me dérange pas; **I don't mind the heat** la chaleur ne me dérange pas; **4 mind the step!**

attention à la marche!; **5 never mind!** peu importe!

mine[1] *noun* mine *Fem.*; **a coal mine** une mine de charbon.

mine[2] *pronoun* **1** (*for a masculine noun*) le mien; **she took my hat and I took mine** elle a pris son chapeau et j'ai pris le mien; **2** (*for a feminine noun*) la mienne; **she gave me her address and I gave her mine** elle m'a donné son adresse et je lui ai donné la mienne; **3** (*for a masculine plural noun*) les miens; **Karen's invited her parents and I've invited mine** Karen a invité ses parents et j'ai invité les miens; **4** (*for a feminine plural noun*) les miennes; **she showed me her photos and I showed her mine** elle m'a montré ses photos et je lui ai montré les miennes; **5** à moi; **the green one's mine** le vert est à moi; **it's mine** c'est à moi.

miner *noun* mineur *Masc.*

mineral water *noun* eau *Fem.* minérale.

miniature *noun, adjective* miniature *Fem.*

minibus *noun* minibus *Masc.*

minimum *noun* minimum *Masc.*; **a minimum of** un minimum de.
minimum *adjective* minimum (*does not change in the feminine or plural*); **the minimum age** l'âge minimum; **minimum safety measures** des mesures de sécurité minimum; **the minimum amount** le minimum.

miniskirt *noun* mini-jupe *Fem.*

minister noun **1** (in government)
ministre Masc.; **2** (of a church)
pasteur Masc.

ministry noun ministère Masc.

minor adjective mineur.

minority noun minorité Fem.

mint noun **1** (herb) menthe Fem.;
2 (sweet) bonbon Masc. à la menthe.

minus preposition moins; **seven
minus three is four** sept moins
trois égale quatre; **it was minus ten
this morning** il a fait moins dix ce
matin.

minute¹ noun minute Fem.; **just a
minute!** une minute!; **I'll be ready
in two minutes** je serai prêt dans
deux minutes; **it's five minutes'
walk from here** c'est à cinq minutes
à pied d'ici.

minute² adjective minuscule; **the
bedrooms are minute** les chambres
sont minuscules.

miracle noun miracle Masc.

mirror noun **1** glace Fem.; **I looked
at myself in the mirror** je me suis
regardé dans la glace; **2** (rearview
mirror in a car) rétroviseur Masc.

misbehave verb se conduire [26]
mal.

mischief noun **to get up to
mischief** faire des bêtises.

mischievous adjective coquin.

miser noun avare Masc. & Fem.

miserable adjective
1 malheureux (Fem. malheureuse);
he was miserable without her il
était malheureux sans elle; **I feel
really miserable today** je n'ai
vraiment pas le moral aujourd'hui;

2 it's miserable weather il fait un
sale temps; **3 she gets paid a
miserable wage** elle gagne un
salaire de misère.

misery noun souffrance Fem.; **he
was in misery** il était extrêmement
malheureux.

misfire verb tomber [1] à plat; **our
plans misfired** nos projets sont
tombés à plat.

misfortune noun malheur Masc.

misjudge verb **1** mal évaluer [1];
she misjudged the distance elle a
mal évalué la distance; **2** mal juger
[52] (a person); **everybody had
misjudged her** tout le monde l'avait
mal jugée.

mislay verb égarer [1]; **I've mislaid
my keys** j'ai égaré mes clés.

misleading adjective trompeur
(Fem. trompeuse); **it's a misleading
advertisement** c'est une publicité
trompeuse.

Miss noun Mademoiselle; **Miss
Jones** Mademoiselle Jones; (written
as) Mlle Jones.

miss verb **1** rater [1]; **she missed
her train** elle a raté son train; **I
missed the film** j'ai raté le film; **the
ball missed the goal** le ballon a raté
le but; **missed!** raté!; **2** manquer [1];
he's missed several classes il a
manqué plusieurs cours; **to miss an
opportunity** manquer une occasion;
3 I miss you tu me manques; **she's
missing her sister** sa sœur lui
manque; **I miss France** la France
me manque.

missile noun missile Masc.

missing *adjective* **1** manquant; **she's found the missing pieces** elle a trouvé les pièces manquantes; **the missing link** le chaînon manquant; **2 there's a plate missing** il manque une assiette; **there are three forks missing** il manque trois fourchettes; **3 to go missing** disparaître; **several things have gone missing lately** plusieurs choses ont disparu récemment; **three people are missing** trois personnes ont disparu.

missionary *noun* missionnaire *Masc. & Fem.*

mist *noun* brume *Fem.*

mistake *noun* **1** erreur *Fem.*; **by mistake** par erreur; **it was my mistake** c'était une erreur de ma part; **2** faute *Fem.*; **a spelling mistake** une faute d'orthographe; **you've made lots of mistakes** tu as fait beaucoup de fautes; **3 to make a mistake** (*be mistaken*) se tromper; **sorry, I made a mistake** je suis désolé, je me suis trompé.
mistake *verb* **I mistook you for your brother** je vous ai pris pour votre frère.

mistaken *adjective* **to be mistaken** se tromper; **you're mistaken** tu te trompes.

mistletoe *noun* gui *Masc.*

misty *adjective* brumeux (*Fem.* brumeuse); **a misty morning** un matin brumeux; **it's misty this morning** il y a de la brume ce matin.

misunderstand *verb* mal comprendre [64]; **I misunderstood** j'ai mal compris.

misunderstanding *noun* malentendu *Masc.*; **there's been a misunderstanding** il y a eu un malentendu.

mix *noun* **1** mélange *Masc.*; **a good mix of people** un bon mélange de gens; **2 a cake mix** une préparation pour gâteau.
mix *verb* **1** mélanger [52]; **mix all the ingredients together** mélangez tous les ingrédients; **2 to mix with** fréquenter [1]; **she mixes with lots of interesting people** elle fréquente beaucoup de gens intéressants.
• **1** mélanger [52]; **you've mixed up all my papers** tu as mélangé tous mes papiers; **you've got it all mixed up!** tu mélanges tout! (*story*); **2** (*confuse*) confondre [69]; **I get him mixed up with his brother** je le confonds avec son frère

mixed *adjective* varié; **a mixed programme** un programme varié.

mixed salad *noun* salade *Fem.* composée.

mixed school *noun* école *Fem.* mixte.

mixer *noun* batteur *Masc.* électrique.

mixture *noun* mélange *Masc.*; **it's a mixture of jazz and rock** c'est un mélange de jazz et de rock.

moan *verb* râler [1] (*informal*); **stop moaning!** arrête de râler!

mobile home *noun* mobile home *Masc.*

mobile phone *noun* téléphone *Masc.* portable.

mock *noun* (*mock exam*) examen *Masc.* blanc.

a
b
c
d
e
f
g
h
i
j
k
l
m
n
o
p
q
r
s
t
u
v
w
x
y
z

mock *verb* se moquer [1] de; **stop mocking me!** arrête de te moquer de moi!

model *noun* **1** (*type*) modèle *Masc.*; **the latest model** le dernier modèle; **2** (*fashion model*) mannequin *Masc.*; **she's a model** elle est mannequin de luxe; **3** (*of a plane, car, etc*) modèle *Masc.* réduit; **he makes models** il fait des modèles réduits; **4** (*of a building*) maquette *Fem.*; **a model of Westminster Abbey** une maquette de l'Abbaye de Westminster.

model aeroplane *noun* modèle *Masc.* réduit d'avion.

model railway *noun* chemin *Masc.* de fer miniature.

model village *noun* village *Masc.* miniature.

modem *noun* modem *Masc.*

moderate *adjective* modéré.

modern *adjective* moderne.

modernize *verb* moderniser [1].

modern languages *noun* langues *Fem. plural* vivantes.

modest *adjective* modeste.

modify *verb* modifier [1].

moisture *noun* humidité *Fem.*

moisturizer *noun* **1** (*lotion*) lait hydratant *Masc.*; **2** (*cream*) crème *Fem.* hydratante.

mole *noun* **1** (*animal*) taupe *Fem.*; **2** (*on skin*) graine *Fem.* de beauté.

molecule *noun* molécule *Fem.*

molehill *noun* taupinière *Fem.*

moment *noun* **1** instant *Masc.*; **he'll be here in a moment** il sera là dans un instant; **at any moment** à tout

instant; **2 at the moment** en ce moment; **at the right moment** au bon moment.

Monaco *noun* Monaco.

monarchy *noun* monarchie *Fem.*

monastery *noun* monastère *Masc.*

Monday *noun* lundi *Masc.*; **on Monday** lundi; **I'm going out on Monday** je sors lundi; **see you on Monday!** à lundi!; **on Mondays** le lundi; **the museum is closed on Mondays** le musée est fermé le lundi; **every Monday** tous les lundis; **last Monday** lundi dernier; **next Monday** lundi prochain.

money *noun* argent *Masc.*; **I don't have enough money** je n'ai pas assez d'argent; **to make money** gagner de l'argent; **they gave me my money back** (*in a shop*) ils m'ont remboursé.

money box *noun* tirelire *Fem.*

mongrel *noun* chien *Masc.* bâtard.

monitor *noun* (*on computer*) moniteur *Masc.*

monk *noun* moine *Masc.*

monkey *noun* **1** singe *Masc.*; **2 you little monkey!** petit galopin! (*informal*).

monotonous *adjective* monotone.

monster *noun* monstre *Masc.*

month *noun* mois *Masc.*; **in the month of May** au mois de mai; **this month** ce mois-ci; **next month** le mois prochain; **we're leaving next month** nous allons partir le mois prochain; **last month** le mois dernier; **every month** tous les mois; **in two months' time** dans deux mois; **at the end of the month** à la fin du mois.

monthly *adjective* mensuel (*Fem.* mensuelle); **a monthly payment** une mensualité.

monument *noun* monument *Masc.*

mood *noun* humeur *Fem.*; **to be in a good mood** être de bonne humeur; **to be in a bad mood** être de mauvaise humeur; **I'm not in the mood** ça ne me dit rien.

moody *adjective* lunatique.

moon *noun* lune *Fem.*; **by the light of the moon** au clair de lune; ★ **to be over the moon** être aux anges (*literally: to be at the level of the angels*).

moonlight *noun* clair *Masc.* de lune; **by moonlight** au clair de lune.

moor *noun* lande *Fem.*; **the Yorkshire moors** les landes du Yorkshire.

moor *verb* amarrer [1] (*a boat*).

moped *noun* mobylette™ *Fem.*

moral *noun* morale *Fem.*; **the moral of the story** la morale de l'histoire. **moral** *adjective* moral (*Masc. plural* moraux*).

morale *noun* moral *Masc.*; **to boost somebody's morale** remonter le moral à quelqu'un; **he's been trying to boost morale** il essaie de leur remonter le moral.

morals *noun* moralité *Fem.*

more *adverb* **1** plus; **more interesting** plus intéressant; **more difficult** plus difficile; **more slowly** plus lentement; **more easily** plus facilement; **2 more ...than** plus ...que; **the book's more interesting than the film** le livre est plus intéressant que le film.

more *adjective* **1** plus de; **they have more money than we do** ils ont plus d'argent que nous; **I'll have a little more milk** je prendrai un peu plus de lait; **2** (*of something you have already*) encore de; **would you like some more cake?** voulez-vous encore du gâteau?; **a few more glasses** encore quelques verres.

more *pronoun* **1** plus; **he eats more than me** il mange plus que moi; **2** (*of something you have already*) encore; **we need three more** il nous en faut encore trois; **I'll have a little more** je prendrai un peu plus; **I don't want any more** je n'en veux plus; **3 more and more** de plus en plus; **books are getting more and more expensive** les livres coûtent de plus en plus cher; **it takes more and more time** ça prend de plus en plus de temps; **4 more or less** plus ou moins; **it's more or less finished** c'est plus ou moins fini.

morning *noun* **1** matin *Masc.*; **this morning** ce matin; **tomorrow morning** demain matin; **yesterday morning** hier matin; **in the morning** le matin; **she doesn't work in the morning** elle ne travaille pas le matin; **on Friday mornings** le vendredi matin; **at six o'clock in the morning** à six heures du matin; **2** (*as a period of time spent doing something*) matinée; **I spent the whole morning doing the washing-up** j'ai passé toute la matinée à faire la vaisselle.

a
b
c
d
e
f
g
h
i
j
k
l
m
n
o
p
q
r
s
t
u
v
w
x
y
z

Morocco *noun* Maroc *Masc.*; **to Morocco** au Maroc; **in Morocco** au Maroc.

mortgage *noun* crédit *Masc.* (immobilier).

Moscow *noun* Moscou; **in Moscow** à Moscou.

Moslem *noun* musulman *Masc.*, musulmane *Fem.*

mosque *noun* mosquée *Fem.*

mosquito *noun* moustique *Masc.*; **a mosquito bite** une piqûre de moustique.

most *adjective, adverb, pronoun* **1** (*followed by a plural noun*) la plupart de; **most children like chocolate** la plupart des enfants aiment le chocolat; **most of my friends** la plupart de mes amis; **2** (*followed by a singular noun*) presque tout; **they've eaten most of the chocolate** ils ont mangé presque tout le chocolat; **3** most of the time la plupart du temps; **4** the most (*followed by adjective*) le plus, la plus, les plus; **the most interesting film** le film le plus intéressant; **the most exciting story** l'histoire la plus passionnante; **the most boring books** les livres les plus ennuyeux; **5** the most (*followed by noun*) le plus de; **I've got the most time** c'est moi qui ai le plus de temps; **6** the most (*after verb*) le plus; **what I hate most is the noise** ce que je déteste le plus, c'est le bruit.

moth *noun* **1** (*butterfly*) papillon *Masc.* de nuit; **2** (*clothes moth*) mite *Fem.*

Mother's Day *noun* la fête des Mères (*in France the last Sunday in May*).

mother *noun* mère *Fem.*; **my mother** ma mère; **Kate's mother** la mère de Kate.

mother-in-law *noun* belle-mère *Fem.* (*plural* belles-mères).

motion *noun* mouvement *Masc.*

motivated *adjective* motivé.

motivation *noun* motivation *Fem.*

motor *noun* moteur *Masc.*

motorbike *noun* moto *Fem.*

motorboat *noun* bateau *Masc.* à moteur.

motorcyclist *noun* motocycliste *Masc. & Fem.*

motorist *noun* automobiliste *Masc. & Fem.*

motor racing *noun* course *Fem.* automobile.

motorway *noun* autoroute *Fem.*

mouldy *adjective* moisi.

mountain *noun* montagne *Fem.*; **in the mountains** à la montagne.

mountain bike *noun* VTT *Masc.* (*short for 'vélo tout-terrain'*).

mountaineer *noun* alpiniste *Masc. & Fem.*

mountaineering *noun* alpinisme *Masc.*; **to go mountaineering** faire de l'alpinisme.

mountainous *adjective* montagneux (*Fem.* montagneuse).

mouse *noun* souris *Fem.* (*both the animal and for a computer*).

494

mousse *noun* mousse *Fem.*; **chocolate mousse** la mousse au chocolat.

moustache *noun* moustache *Fem.*; **a man with a moustache** un moustachu.

mouth *noun* bouche *Fem.*

mouthful *noun* bouchée *Fem.*

mouth organ *noun* harmonica *Masc.*; **to play the mouth organ** jouer de l'harmonica.

move *noun* **1** (to a different house) déménagement *Masc.*; **2** (in a game) **your move!** à toi de jouer!
move *verb* **1** bouger [52]; **she didn't move** elle n'a pas bougé; **2 move up a bit** pousse-toi un peu; **3** enlever [50] (an object); **can you move your bag, please?** peux-tu enlever ton sac, s'il te plaît?; **4** (car, traffic) avancer [61]; **the traffic was moving slowly** la circulation avançait lentement; **5 to move forward** avancer [61]; **he moved forward a step** il s'est avancé d'un pas; **6** (move house) déménager [52]; **we're moving on Tuesday** nous déménageons mardi; **they've moved to France** ils se sont installés en France.

● **to move in** emménager [52]; **when are you moving in?** quand est-ce que tu emménages?

● **to move out** déménager [52]; **we're moving out next week** nous déménageons la semaine prochaine.

movement *noun* mouvement *Masc.*

movie *noun* film *Masc.*; **to go to the movies** aller au cinéma.

moving *adjective* **1** en marche; **a moving vehicle** un véhicule en marche; **2** (emotionally) émouvant; **it's a very moving film** c'est un film très émouvant.

mow *verb* tondre [3]; **to mow the grass** tondre la pelouse.

mower *noun* tondeuse *Fem.* à gazon.

MP *noun* député *Masc.*; **she is an MP** elle est député.

Mr *noun* Monsieur (usually abbreviated to 'M.'); **Mr Angus Brown** M. Angus Brown.

Mrs *noun* Madame (usually abbreviated to 'Mme'); **Mrs Mary Hendry** Mme Mary Hendry.

Ms *noun* Madame (usually abbreviated to 'Mme'; note that there is no direct equivalent to 'Ms' in French, but 'Madame' may be used whether the woman is married or not).

much *adjective, adverb, pronoun* **1** beaucoup; **she doesn't eat much** elle ne mange pas beaucoup; **we don't go out much** nous ne sortons pas beaucoup; **much more** beaucoup plus; **much shorter** beaucoup plus court; **2** (followed by a noun) beaucoup de; **we don't have much time** nous n'avons pas beaucoup de temps; **there isn't much butter left** il ne reste pas beaucoup de beurre; **3 very much** beaucoup; **thank you very much** merci beaucoup; **I don't watch television very much** je ne regarde pas beaucoup la télé; **4 very much** (followed by a noun) beaucoup de; **there isn't very much milk** il n'y a pas beaucoup de lait; **5 not much**

a
b
c
d
e
f
g
h
i
j
k
l
m
n
o
p
q
r
s
t
u
v
w
x
y
z

a
b
c
d
e
f
g
h
i
j
k
l

m

n
o
p
q
r
s
t
u
v
w
x
y
z

pas beaucoup; **'do you have a lot of homework?' – 'no, not much'** 'est-ce que tu as beaucoup de devoirs?' – 'non, pas beaucoup'; **6 so much** tellement; **we liked it so much!** nous l'avons tellement aimé!; **I have so much to do!** j'ai tellement de choses à faire!; **7 so much** autant; **you shouldn't have given me so much** tu n'aurais pas dû m'en donner autant; **8 as much as** autant que; **you can take as much as you like** tu peux en prendre autant que tu veux; **9 too much** trop (de); **her parents give her too much money** ses parents lui donnent trop d'argent; **that's far too much!** c'est beaucoup trop!; **10 how much?** combien (de)?; **how much is it?** ça coûte combien?; **how much do you want?** tu en veux combien?; **how much sugar do you want?** tu veux combien de sucre?

mud *noun* boue *Fem.*

muddle *noun* désordre *Masc.*; **to be in a muddle** être en désordre.

muddy *adjective* **1** (*path, road*) boueux (*Fem.* boueuse); **2** (*shoes, clothes*) couverts de boue; **your boots are all muddy** tes bottes sont couvertes de boue.

mug *noun* grande tasse *Fem.*; **a mug of coffee** une grande tasse de café.
mug *verb* **to mug somebody** agresser [1] quelqu'un; **to be mugged** se faire [10] agresser; **my brother was mugged in the park** mon frère s'est fait agresser au parc.

mugging *noun* agression *Fem.*

multiplication *noun* multiplication *Fem.*

multiply *verb* multiplier [1]; **to multiply six by four** multiplier six par quatre.

mum, mummy *noun* **1** mère *Fem.*; **Tom's mum** la mère de Tom; **I'll ask my mum** je vais demander à ma mère; **2** (*within the family or as a name*) maman *Fem.*; **mum's not back yet** maman n'est pas encore rentrée.

mumps *noun* oreillons *Masc. plural.*

murder *noun* meurtre *Masc.*
murder *verb* assassiner [1].

murderer *noun* assassin *Masc.*

muscle *noun* muscle *Masc.*

muscular *adjective* musclé.

museum *noun* musée *Masc.*; **to go to the museum** aller au musée.

mushroom *noun* champignon *Masc.*; **a mushroom salad** une salade aux champignons.

music *noun* musique *Fem.*; **pop music** la musique pop; **classical music** la musique classique.

musical *noun* comédie *Fem.* musicale.
musical *adjective* **1 a musical instrument** un instrument de musique; **2 they're a very musical family** ils sont très musiciens dans la famille.

musician *noun* musicien *Masc.*, musicienne *Fem.*

Muslim *noun* musulman *Masc.*, musulmane *Fem.*

mussel *noun* moule *Fem.*

must *verb* **1** falloir [43] (*to express obligation 'falloir' is used as an impersonal verb*) **we must leave**

Nn

now il faut partir maintenant (*the construction 'il faut que' is followed by a verb in the subjunctive*) **I must tell you something** il faut que je te dise quelque chose; **you must be there at eight** il faut que tu sois là à huit heures; **you must learn the vocabulary** il faut que tu apprennes le vocabulaire; **2** (*expressing probability*) devoir [8]; **you must be tired** tu dois être fatigué; **it must be five o'clock** il doit être cinq heures; **he must have forgotten** il a dû oublier.

nustard *noun* moutarde *Fem.*

nutter *verb* marmonner [1].

ny *adjective* **1** (*before a masculine noun*) mon; **my brother** mon frère; **my book** mon livre; **2** (*before a feminine noun*) ma; **my sister** ma sœur; **my house** ma maison (*but 'ma' becomes 'mon' before a feminine noun beginning with a vowel or silent 'h'*) **my address** mon adresse; **3** (*before a plural noun*) mes; **my children** mes enfants; **4** (*with parts of the body*) le, la, les; **I had a glass in my hand** j'avais un verre à la main; **I'm washing my hands** je me lave les mains.

nyself *pronoun* **1 I've hurt myself** je me suis blessé; **2 I said it myself** je l'ai dit moi-même; **3 by myself** tout seul; **I did it by myself** je l'ai fait tout seul.

nysterious *adjective* mystérieux (*Fem.* mystérieuse).

nystery *noun* **1** mystère *Masc.*; **2** (*book*) roman *Masc.* policier.

nyth *noun* mythe *Masc.*

nythology *noun* mythologie *Fem.*

nail *noun* **1** (*on finger or toe*) ongle *Masc.*; **to bite your nails** se ronger [52] les ongles; **2** (*metal*) clou *Masc.* **nail** *verb* clouer [1].

nailbrush *noun* brosse *Fem.* à ongles.

nailfile *noun* lime *Fem.* à ongles.

nail scissors *noun* ciseaux *Masc. plural* à ongles.

nail varnish *noun* vernis *Masc.* à ongles.

nail varnish remover *noun* dissolvant *Masc.*

naked *adjective* nu.

name *noun* **1** nom *Masc.*; **I've forgotten her name** j'ai oublié son nom; **what's your name?** comment vous appelez-vous?; **my name is Joy** je m'appelle Joy; **2** (*of a book or film*) titre *Masc.*

nanny *noun* nurse *Fem.*

nap *noun* petit somme *Masc.*; **to have a nap** faire un petit somme.

napkin *noun* serviette *Fem.*

nappy *noun* couche *Fem.*

narrow *adjective* étroit; **a narrow street** une rue étroite.

nasty *adjective* **1** (*mean*) méchant; **that was a nasty thing to do** c'était méchant; **2** (*unpleasant*) désagréable; **that's a nasty job** c'est une tâche désagréable; **3** (*bad*) mauvais; **a nasty smell** une mauvaise odeur.

nation *noun* nation *Fem.*

a b c d e f g h i j k l m n o p q r s t u v w x y z

a

b

c

d

e

f

g

h

i

j

k

l

m

n

o

p

q

r

s

t

u

v

w

x

y

z

national *adjective* national (*Masc. plural* nationaux).

national anthem *noun* hymne *Masc.* national.

nationality *noun* nationalité *Fem.*

national park *noun* parc *Masc.* national (*plural* parcs nationaux).

Nativity *noun* nativité *Fem.*

natural *adjective* naturel (*Fem.* naturelle).

naturally *adverb* naturellement.

nature *noun* nature *Fem.*

nature reserve *noun* réserve *Fem.* naturelle.

naughty *adjective* vilain.

nausea *noun* nausée *Fem.*

navel *noun* nombril *Masc.*

navigate *verb* naviguer [1].

navy *noun* marine *Fem.*; **my uncle's in the navy** mon oncle est dans la marine.

navy-blue *adjective* bleu marine; **navy-blue gloves** des gants bleu marine.

near *adjective* proche; **the nearest shop** le magasin le plus proche. **near** *adverb*, *preposition* **1** près; **they live quite near** ils habitent tout près; **to come nearer** s'approcher; **2 near (to)** près de; **near the station** près de la gare.

nearby *adverb* tout près; **there's a park nearby** il y a un parc tout près.

nearly *adverb* presque; **nearly empty** presque vide; **we're nearly there** nous sommes presque arrivés.

neat *adjective* **1** (*well-organized*) bien rangé; **a neat desk** un bureau

bien rangé; **2** soigné (*a garden, you clothes, or the way you look*).

neatly *adverb* avec soin.

necessarily *adverb* not **necessarily** pas forcément.

necessary *adjective* nécessaire; **necessary** si besoin est.

neck *noun* **1** (*of a person*) cou *Masc.* **2** (*of a garment*) encolure *Fem.*

necklace *noun* collier *Masc.*

nectarine *noun* nectarine *Fem.*

need *noun* **there's no need, I've done it already** inutile, c'est fait; **there's no need to wait** inutile d'attendre.

need *verb* **1** avoir [5] besoin de; **we need bread** nous avons besoin de pain; **they need help** ils ont besoin d'aide; **everything you need** tout ce qu'il vous faut; **2** (*to have to*) devoir [8]; **I need to drop in at the bank** je dois passer par la banque; **3 you needn't decide today** tu n'es pas obligé de décider aujourd'hui; **you needn't wait** tu n'es pas obligé d'attendre.

needle *noun* aiguille *Fem.*

negative *noun* (*of a photo*) négatif *Masc.*

neglected *adjective* mal entretenu.

neighbour *noun* voisin *Masc.*, voisine *Fem.*; **we're going round to the neighbours'** on va chez les voisins.

neighbourhood *noun* quartier *Masc.*; **a nice neighbourhood** un quartier agréable.

neither *conjunction* **1 neither ... nor** ni ...ni; **I have neither the time**

nor the money je n'ai ni le temps ni l'argent; **2** neither do I moi non plus; **'I don't like fish'** – **'neither do I'** 'je n'aime pas le poisson' – 'moi non plus' (*translations using 'non plus' can be used for many similar replies*) **'I wasn't invited'** – **'neither was I'** 'je n'ai pas été invité' – 'moi non plus'; **"I didn't like the film'** – **'neither did Kirsty'** 'je n'ai pas aimé le film' – 'Kirsty non plus'; **3 'which do you like?'** – **'neither'** 'lequel aimes-tu?' – 'ni l'un ni l'autre'.

nephew *noun* neveu *Masc.* (*plural* neveux).

nerve *noun* **1** (*in the body*) nerf *Masc.*; **2 to lose one's nerve** perdre son courage; **3 you've got a nerve!** tu as un sacré culot! (*informal*); ★ **he gets on my nerves** il me tape sur les nerfs (*informal*).

nervous *adjective* nerveux (*Fem.* nerveuse); **to feel nervous** (*before a performance or an exam*) avoir le trac (*informal*).

nervous breakdown *noun* dépression *Fem.* nerveuse.

nest *noun* nid *Masc.*

net *noun* **1** (*for fishing or in tennis*) filet *Masc.*; **2** (*in football*) filets *Masc.* *plural*.

Netherlands *noun* Pays-Bas *Masc.* *plural*; **in the Netherlands** aux Pays-Bas.

nettle *noun* ortie *Fem.*

network *noun* réseau *Masc.* (*plural* réseaux).

neutral *noun* (*in a gearbox*) point *Masc.* mort; **to be in neutral** être au point mort.

neutral *adjective* neutre.

never *adjective* **1** ne … jamais; **Ben never smokes** Ben ne fume jamais; **I've never seen the film** je n'ai jamais vu le film; **2** jamais; **'have you ever been to Spain?'** – **'no, never'** 'est-ce que tu es déjà allé en Espagne?' – 'non, jamais'; **3 never again** plus jamais; **4 never mind!** peu importe!

new *adjective* **1** (*different or unknown to you*) nouveau (*Fem.* nouvelle); **have you seen their new house?** as-tu vu leur nouvelle maison?; **Debbie's new boyfriend** le nouveau copain de Debbie; **2** (*brand new*) neuf (*Fem.* neuve); **it's a new car** c'est une voiture neuve.

newcomer *noun* nouveau venu *Masc.* (*plural* nouveaux venus), nouvelle venue *Fem* (*plural* nouvelles venues).

news *plural noun* **1** (*everyday gossip*) nouvelle *Fem.*, nouvelles *Fem.* plural; **a piece of good news** une bonne nouvelle; **I've got good news** j'ai de bonnes nouvelles; **any news?** y a-t-il des nouvelles?; **2** (*on TV*) journal *Masc.*; **the midday news** le journal de midi; **3** (*on the radio*) **the news** les informations.

newsagent *noun* marchand *Masc.* de journaux; **at the newsagent's** chez le marchand de journaux.

newspaper *noun* journal *Masc.* (*plural* journaux).

newsreader *noun* présentateur *Masc.*, présentatrice *Fem.*

New Year *noun* le Nouvel An; **Happy New Year!** Bonne Année!

New Year's Day *noun* le jour de l'An.

a
b
c
d
e
f
g
h
i
j
k
l
m
n
o
p
q
r
s
t
u
v
w
x
y
z

499

a

b

c

d

e

f

g

h

i

j

k

l

m

n

o

p

q

r

s

t

u

v

w

x

y

z

New Year's Eve *noun* la Saint-Sylvestre.

New Zealand *noun* Nouvelle-Zélande *Fem.*

New Zealander *noun* Néo-Zélandais *Masc.*, Néo-Zélandaise *Fem.*

next *adjective* **1** prochain; **the next train is at ten** le prochain train est à dix heures; **next week** la semaine prochaine; **next Thursday** jeudi prochain; **next year** l'année prochaine; **the next time I see you** la prochaine fois que je te verrai; **2** (*following*) suivant; **I saw her the next week** je l'ai vue la semaine suivante; **the next day** le lendemain; **the letter arrived the next day** la lettre est arrivée le lendemain; **3** (*next-door*) voisin; **in the next room** dans la pièce voisine. **next** *adverb* **1** (*afterwards*) ensuite; **what did he say next?** qu'est-ce qu'il a dit ensuite?; **2** (*now*) maintenant; **what shall we do next?** qu'est-ce qu'on fait maintenant?; **3** next to à côté de; **the girl next to Pat** la fille à côté de Pat; **it's next to the baker's** c'est à côté de la boulangerie.

next door *adverb* à côté; **they live next door** ils habitent à côté; **the girl next door** la fille d'à côté.

nice *adjective* **1** (*pleasant*) agréable; **we had a nice evening** nous avons passé une soirée agréable; **Brighton's a nice town** Brighton est une ville agréable; **have a nice time!** amusez-vous bien!; **2** (*attractive to look at*) joli; **that's a nice dress** elle est jolie, cette robe; **3** (*kind, friendly*) sympathique (*a*

person); **she's really nice** elle est vraiment sympathique; **4 to be nice to somebody** être gentil avec quelqu'un; **she's been very nice to me** elle a été très gentille avec moi; **5** (*tasting good*) bon (*Fem.* bonne); **let's have a nice cup of tea** si on prenait une bonne tasse de thé; **6** (*weather*) **it's a nice day** il fait beau; **we had nice weather** il a fait beau.

nick *verb* (*steal*) piquer [1] (*informal*).

nickname *noun* surnom *Masc.*

niece *noun* nièce *Fem.*

night *noun* **1** (*before you go to bed*) soir *Masc.*; **what are you doing tonight?** qu'est-ce que tu fais ce soir?; **see you tonight!** à ce soir!; **I saw Greg last night** j'ai vu Greg hier soir; **2** (*after bedtime*) nuit *Fem.*; **it's cold at night** il fait froid la nuit; **to stay the night with somebody** coucher chez quelqu'un.

night club *noun* boîte *Fem.* de nuit

nightie *noun* chemise *Fem.* de nuit.

nightingale *noun* rossignol *Masc.*

nightmare *noun* cauchemar *Masc.*; **to have a nightmare** faire un cauchemar.

night-time *noun* nuit *Fem.*

nil *noun* zéro *Masc.*; **they won four-nil** ils ont gagné quatre à zéro.

nine *number* neuf *Masc.*; **Jake's nine** Jake a neuf ans.

nineteen *number* dix-neuf *Masc.*; **Kate's nineteen** Kate a dix-neuf ans.

ninety *number* quatre-vingt-dix *Masc.*

ninth *number* neuvième; **on the ninth floor** au neuvième étage; **the ninth of June** le neuf juin.

nitrogen *noun* azote *Masc.*

no *adverb* non; **I said no** j'ai dit non; **no thank you** non merci.
no *adjective* **1** pas de; **we've got no bread** nous n'avons pas de pain; **no problem!** pas de problème!; **2** (*on a notice*) **'no smoking'** 'défense de fumer'; **'no parking'** 'stationnement interdit'.

nobody *pronoun* personne; **'who's there?' – 'nobody'** 'qui est là?' – 'personne'; **there's nobody in the kitchen** il n'y a personne dans la cuisine; **nobody knows me** personne ne me connaît; **nobody answered** personne n'a répondu.

nod *verb* (*to say yes*) faire [10] oui de la tête; **he nodded** il a fait oui de la tête.

noise *noun* bruit *Masc.*; **to make a noise** faire du bruit.

noisy *adjective* bruyant.

none *pronoun* **1** (*not one*) aucun (*Fem.* aucune); **'how many students failed the exam?' – 'none'** 'combien d'étudiants ont raté l'examen?' – 'aucun'; **none of the girls knows him** aucune des filles ne le connaît; **2 there's none left** il n'y en a plus; **there are none left** il n'y en a plus.

nonsense *noun* bêtises *Fem. plural*; **to talk nonsense** dire des bêtises; **nonsense! she's at least thirty!** tu

dis des bêtises! elle a au moins trente ans!

non-smoker *noun* non-fumeur *Masc.*

non-stop *adjective* direct (*a train or flight*).
non-stop *adverb* sans arrêt; **she talks non-stop** elle parle sans arrêt.

noodles *plural noun* nouilles *Fem. plural.*

noon *noun* midi *Masc.*; **at (twelve) noon** à midi.

no-one *pronoun* personne; **'who's there?' – 'no-one'** 'qui est là?' – 'personne'; **there's no-one in the kitchen** il n'y a personne dans la cuisine; **no-one knows me** personne ne me connaît; **no-one answered** personne n'a répondu.

nor *conjunction* **1** neither ...nor ni ...ni; **I have neither the time nor the money** je n'ai ni le temps ni l'argent; **2 nor do I** moi non plus; **'I don't like fish' – 'nor do I'** 'je n'aime pas le poisson' – 'moi non plus'; (*translations using 'non plus' can be used for many similar replies*) **'I wasn't invited' – 'nor was I'** 'je n'ai pas été invité' – 'moi non plus'.

normal *adjective* **1** normal (*Masc. plural* normaux); **2** (*usual*) habituel (*Fem.* habituelle).

normally *adverb* normalement.

Normandy *noun* Normandie *Fem.*; **in Normandy** en Normandie.

north *noun* nord *Masc.*; **in the north** au nord.
north *adjective, adverb* nord (*never agrees*); **the north side** le côté nord;

501

a　**a north wind** un vent du nord; **north of Paris** au nord de Paris.

b

c　**North America** noun Amérique Fem. du Nord.

d　**North American** noun Nord-Américain Masc., Nord-Américaine Fem.

e　**North American** adjective nord-américain.

f

g　**northeast** noun nord-est Masc.
　　northeast adjective **in northeast England** au nord-est de l'Angleterre.

h

i　**Northern Ireland** noun Irlande Fem. du Nord.

j

k　**North Pole** noun pôle Masc. Nord.

l　**North Sea** noun **the North Sea** la mer du Nord.

m　**northwest** noun nord-ouest Masc.
　　northwest adjective **in northwest England** au nord-ouest de l'Angleterre.

n

o　**Norway** noun Norvège Fem.; **in Norway** en Norvège.

p

q　**Norwegian** noun 1 (person) Norvégien Masc., Norvégienne Fem.; 2 (language) norvégien Masc.
　　Norwegian adjective norvégien (Fem. norvégienne).

r

s

t　**nose** noun nez Masc.; **to blow your nose** se moucher [1].

u　**nosebleed** noun **to have a nosebleed** saigner [1] du nez.

v

w　**nostril** noun narine Fem.

x　**not** adverb 1 pas; **not on Saturdays** pas le samedi; **not all alone!** pas tout seul!; **not bad** pas mal; **not at all** pas du tout; **not yet** pas encore; 2 (when used with a verb) ne ...pas;

y

z

it's not my car ce n'est pas ma voiture; **I don't know** je ne sais pas; **Sam didn't phone** Sam n'a pas appelé; **we decided not to wait** nous avons décidé de ne pas attendre; 3 **I hope not** j'espère que non.

note noun 1 (a short letter) mot Masc.; **she left me a note** elle m'a laissé un mot; 2 **to take notes** prendre [64] des notes; 3 (a banknote) billet Masc.; **a ten-pound note** un billet de dix livres; 4 (in music) note Fem.; (on the keyboard) touche Fem.

notebook noun carnet Masc.

notepad noun bloc-notes Masc. (plural blocs-notes).

nothing pronoun 1 rien; **'what did you say?' – 'nothing'** 'qu'est-ce que tu as dit?' – 'rien'; 2 (with an adjective) **nothing new** rien de nouveau; **there's nothing new** il n'y a rien de nouveau; 3 (when used with a verb) ne ...rien; **she knows nothing** elle ne sait rien; **but there was nothing there** mais il n'y avait rien; **I saw nothing** je n'ai rien vu; **nothing's happening** il ne se passe rien; 4 **nothing has changed** rien n'a changé.

notice noun 1 (a sign) panneau Masc. (plural panneaux); 2 (an advertisement) annonce Fem.; 3 **don't take any notice of her!** ne fais pas attention à elle!; 4 **to do something at short notice** faire quelque chose à la dernière minute.
　notice verb remarquer [1]; **I didn't notice anything** je n'ai rien remarqué.

noticeable *adjective* visible.

notice board *noun* panneau *Masc.* d'affichage.

nought *noun* zéro *Masc.*

noun *noun* nom *Masc.*

novel *noun* roman *Masc.*

novelist *noun* romancier *Masc.*, romancière *Fem.*

November *noun* novembre *Masc.*; **in November** en novembre.

now *adverb* **1** maintenant; **where is he now?** où est-il maintenant?; **they've got six children now** ils ont six enfants maintenant; **2 he's busy just now** il est occupé en ce moment; **I saw her just now in the corridor** je viens de la voir dans le couloir; **3 do it right now!** fais-le tout de suite!; **4 now and then** de temps en temps.

nowadays *adverb* de nos jours; **nowadays they are quite common** de nos jours, ils sont assez fréquents.

nowhere *adjective* **1** nulle part; **nowhere in France** nulle part en France; **2 there's nowhere to park** il n'y a pas d'endroit pour se garer.

nuclear *adjective* nucléaire; **a nuclear power station** une centrale nucléaire.

nude *noun* **in the nude** nu. **nude** *adjective* nu.

nuisance *noun* **it's a nuisance** c'est embêtant.

numb *adjective* **1** (*with cold*) engourdi; **my fingers are numb with cold** j'ai les doigts engourdis par le froid; **2** (*with an anaesthetic*) insensible.

number *noun* **1** (*of a house, telephone, or account*) numéro *Masc.*; **I live at number thirty-one** j'habite au numéro trente-et-un; **my new phone number** mon nouveau numéro de téléphone; **2** (*a written figure*) chiffre *Masc.*; **the third number is a 7** le troisième chiffre est un 7; **3** (*an amount*) nombre *Masc.*; **a large number of visitors** un grand nombre de visiteurs.

number plate *noun* plaque *Fem.* d'immatriculation.

nun *noun* religieuse *Fem.*

nurse *noun* infirmier *Masc.*, infirmière *Fem.*; **Janet's a nurse** Janet est infirmière.

nursery *noun* **1** (*for children*) crèche *Fem.*; **2** (*for plants*) pépinière *Fem.*

nursery school *noun* école *Fem.* maternelle.

nursing *noun* profession *Fem.* d'infirmier/d'infirmière; **she went into nursing** elle est devenue infirmière.

nut *noun* **1** (*walnut*) noix *Fem.*; **2** (*almond*) amande *Fem.*; **3** (*peanut*) cacahuète *Fem.*; **4** (*for a bolt*) écrou *Masc.*

nutmeg *noun* noix *Fem.* de muscade.

nylon *noun* nylon *Masc.*

Oo

oak *noun* chêne *Masc.*

a
b
c
d
e
f
g
h
i
j
k
l
m
n
o
p
q
r
s
t
u
v
w
x
y
z

oar *noun* rame *Fem.*

oasis *noun* oasis *Fem.*

oats *noun* avoine *Fem.*; **porridge oats** les flocons d'avoine.

obedient *adjective* obéissant.

obey *verb* obéir [2] à (*a person*); **to obey the rules** respecter [1] les règlements.

object *noun* objet *Masc.*
object *verb* soulever [50] des objections; **if you don't object** si vous n'avez pas d'objection.

objection *noun* objection *Fem.*

oblong *adjective* rectangulaire.

oboe *noun* hautbois *Masc.*; **to play the oboe** jouer du hautbois.

obscene *adjective* obscène.

observe *verb* observer [1].

obsessed *adjective* obsédé; **she's obsessed with her diet** elle est obsédée par son régime.

obsession *noun* obsession *Fem.*; **she has an obsession with cleanliness** elle est obsédée par la propreté.

obstacle *noun* obstacle *Masc.*

obstinate *adjective* têtu.

obstruct *verb* gêner [1] (*people or the traffic*).

obtain *verb* obtenir [77].

obvious *adjective* évident.

obviously *adverb* **1** (*of course*) évidemment; **'do you want to come too?' – 'obviously, but it's a bit difficult'** 'veux-tu nous accompagner?' – 'évidemment, mais c'est un peu difficile'; **2** (*looking at something*) manifestement; **the**

house is obviously empty la maison est manifestement vide.

occasion *noun* occasion *Fem.*; **a special occasion** une grande occasion.

occasional *adjective* **he sends us the occasiona lcard** il nous envoie une carte de temps en temps.

occasionally *adverb* de temps en temps.

occupation *noun* **1** (*job*) profession *Fem.*; **2** (*of territory*) occupation *Fem.*

occupied *adjective* occupé.

occur *verb* **1** **it occurs to me that my cousins live nearby** il me vient à l'esprit que mes cousins habitent tout près; **it never occurred to me** cela ne m'est pas venu à l'idée; **2** (*happen*) avoir [5] lieu; **the accident occurred on Monday** l'accident a eu lieu lundi.

ocean *noun* océan *Masc.*

o'clock *adverb* **at ten o'clock** à dix heures; **it's three o'clock** il est trois heures.

October *noun* octobre *Masc.*; **in October** en octobre.

octopus *noun* pieuvre *Fem.*

odd *adjective* **1** (*strange*) bizarre; **that's odd, I'm sure I heard the phone** c'est bizarre, je suis sûr d'avoir entendu le téléphone; **2** (*number*) impair; **three is an odd number** trois est un chiffre impair; **3 to be the odd one out** être l'exception.

odds and ends *plural noun* bricoles *Fem. plural.*

of *preposition* **1** de; **a kilo of tomatoes** un kilo de tomates; **the end of my work** la fin de mon travail; **2** (*note that 'de le' becomes 'du' and 'de les' becomes 'des'*) **the beginning of the concert** le début du concert; **the name of the flower** le nom de la fleur; **the parents of the children** les parents des enfants; **3 Ray has four horses but he's selling three of them** Ray a trois chevaux mais il en vend trois; **we ate a lot of it** nous en avons mangé beaucoup; **4 two of us** deux d'entre nous; **5 the sixth of June** le six juin; **6 made of** en; **a bracelet made of silver** un bracelet en argent.

off *adverb, adjective, preposition* **1** (*switched off*) éteint; **is the telly off?** est-ce que la télé est éteinte?; **to turn off the lights** éteindre la lumière; **2** (*tap, water, gas*) fermé; **to turn off the tap** fermer le robinet; **3** (*turned off at the meter*) coupé; **the gas and electricity were off** le gaz et l'électricité étaient coupés; **4 to be off** (*to leave*) s'en aller [7]; **I'm off** je m'en vais; **5 a day off** un jour de congé; **Caroline took three days off work** Caroline a pris trois jours de congé; **to be off sick** être malade; **Maya's off school today** Maya n'est pas à l'école aujourd'hui; **6** (*cancelled*) annulé; **the match is off** le match est annulé; **7 '20% off shoes'** '20% de remise sur les chaussures'.

offence *noun* **1** (*crime*) délit *Masc.*; **2 to take offence** s'offenser [1]; **he takes offence easily** il s'offense facilement.

offer *noun* **1** offre *Fem.*; **a job offer** une offre d'emploi; **2 'on (special) offer'** 'en promotion'.
offer *verb* **1** offrir [56] (*a present, a reward, or a job*) **he offered her a chair** il lui a offert une chaise; **2 to offer to do** proposer [1] de faire; **Blake offered to drive me to the station** Blake m'a proposé de me conduire à la gare.

office *noun* bureau *Masc.* (*plural* bureaux); **he's still at the office** il est toujours au bureau; **Sue works in the same office** Sue travaille dans le même bureau.

office block, **office building** *noun* immeuble *Masc.* de bureaux.

officer *noun* officier *Masc.*

official *adjective* officiel (*Fem.* officielle); **the official version** la version officielle.

off-licence *noun* magasin *Masc.* de vins et de spiritueux.

offside *adjective* hors jeu.

often *adverb* souvent; **he's often late** il est souvent en retard; **how often do you see Rosie?** est-ce que tu vois Rosie souvent?; **I'd like to see Eric more often** j'aimerais voir Eric plus souvent.

oil *noun* **1** huile *Fem.*; **olive oil** l'huile d'olive; **suntan oil** l'huile solaire; **2** (*crude oil*) pétrole *Masc.*

oil painting *noun* peinture *Fem.* à l'huile (*both the activity and the object*).

oil rig *noun* plateforme *Fem.* pétrolière.

oil slick *noun* marée *Fem.* noire.

oil tanker *noun* pétrolier *Masc.*

a b c d e f g h i j k l m n o p q r s t u v w x y z

a
b
c
d
e
f
g
h
i
j
k
l
m
n
o
p
q
r
s
t
u
v
w
x
y
z

ointment *noun* pommade *Fem.*

okay *adjective* 1 d'accord; **okay, tomorrow at ten** d'accord, demain à dix heures; **is it okay with you if I don't come till Friday?** ça te va si je ne viens que vendredi?; 2 *(person)* sympa *(informal)*; **Daisy's okay** Daisy est sympa; 3 *(nothing special)* pas mal; **the film was okay** le film n'était pas mal; 4 *(not ill)* **are you okay?** ça va?; **I've been ill but I'm okay now** j'ai été malade, mais ça va mieux maintenant.

old *adjective* 1 *(not young, not new)* vieux, vieil *(before a vowel or silent 'h')* *(Fem.* vieille); **an old man** un vieux monsieur; **an old lady** une vieille dame; **an old tree** un vieil arbre; **old people** les personnes âgées; **bring some old clothes** apporte de vieux vêtements; 2 *(previous)* ancien *(Fem.* ancienne); **our old car was a Rover** notre ancienne voiture était une Rover; **I've only got their old address** je n'ai que leur ancienne adresse; 3 *(talking about age)* **how old are you?** tu as quel âge?; **James is ten years old** James a dix ans; **a two-year-old child** un enfant de deux ans; 4 **my older sister** ma sœur aînée; **she's older than me** elle est plus âgée que moi; **he's a year older than me** il a un an de plus que moi.

old age *noun* vieillesse *Fem.*

old age pensioner *noun* retraité *Masc.*, retraitée *Fem.*

old-fashioned *noun* 1 *(clothes, music, style)* démodé; 2 *(a person)* vieux jeu *(never agrees)*; **my parents**

are so old-fashioned mes parents sont si vieux jeu.

olive *noun* olive *Fem.*

olive oil *noun* huile *Fem.* d'olive.

Olympic Games, Olympics *plural noun* Jeux Olympiques *Masc. plural.*

omelette *noun* omelette *Fem.*; **a cheese omelette** une omelette au fromage.

omit *verb* omettre [11].

on *preposition* 1 sur; **on the desk** sur le bureau; **on the road** sur la route; **on the beach** sur la plage; 2 *(in expressions of time)* **on March 21st** le 21 mars; **he's arriving on Tuesday** il arrive mardi; **it's shut on Saturdays** c'est fermé le samedi; **on rainy days** quand il pleut; 3 *(for buses, trains, etc)* **she arrived on the bus** elle est arrivée en bus; **I met Jackie on the bus** j'ai vu Jackie dans le bus; **I slept on the plane** j'ai dormi dans l'avion; **let's go on our bikes!** allons-y à vélo!; 4 **on TV** à la télé; **on the radio** à la radio; **on video** en vidéo; 5 **on holiday** en vacances; **on strike** en grève.

on *adjective* 1 *(switched on)* **to be on** *(TV, light, oven)* être [6] allumé; *(radio, machine)* être en marche; **all the lights were on** toutes les lumières étaient allumées; **is the radio on?** est-ce que la radio est en marche?; **I've put the oven on** j'ai allumé le four; 2 *(happening)* **what's on on TV?** qu'est-ce qu'il y a à la télé?; **what's on this week at the cinema?** qu'est-ce qui passe cette semaine au cinéma?

once adverb 1 une fois; **I've tried once already** j'ai déjà essayé une fois; **try once more** essaie encore une fois; **once a day** une fois par jour; **more than once** plus d'une fois; **2 at once** (*immediately*) tout de suite; **the doctor came at once** le médecin est venu tout de suite; **3 at once** (*at the same time*) à la fois; **I can't do two things at once** je ne peux pas faire deux choses à la fois.

one's determiner son, sa, ses; **one does one's best** on fait de son mieux; **to pay for one's car** payer sa voiture; **to love one's children** aimer ses enfants; **to wash one's hands** se laver les mains.

one number un (*Fem.* une); **one son** un fils; **one apple** une pomme; **if you want a pen I've got one** si tu veux un stylo j'en ai un; **at one o'clock** à une heure.

one pronoun 1 on; **one never knows** on ne sait jamais; **2 this one** celui-ci (*Fem.* celle-ci); **I like that bike, but this one's cheaper** j'aime bien ce vélo-là, mais celui-ci est moins cher; **do you want the red tie or this one?** veux-tu la cravate rouge ou celle-ci?; **3 that one** celui-là (*Fem.* celle-là); **'which video?'** – **'that one'** 'quelle vidéo?' – 'celle-là'; **4 which one?** lequel? (*Fem.* laquelle?); **'my foot's hurting'** – **'which one?'** 'j'ai mal au pied' – 'auquel?'; **'she borrowed a skirt from me'** – **'which one?'** 'elle m'a emprunté une jupe' – 'laquelle?'

oneself noun 1 **to wash oneself** se laver; **to hurt oneself** se blesser; **2** (*for emphasis*) soi-même; **one has to do everything oneself** il faut

tout faire soi-même; **3 (all) by oneself** tout seul (*Fem.* toute seule).

one-way street noun sens *Masc.* unique.

onion noun oignon *Masc.*; **onion soup** la soupe à l'oignon.

only adjective 1 seul; **the only free seat** la seule place libre; **the only thing to do** la seule chose à faire; **2 an only child** un enfant unique.
only adverb, conjunction 1 (*with a verb*) ne ...que; **they've only got two bedrooms** ils n'ont que deux chambres; **Anne's only free on Fridays** Anne n'est libre que le vendredi; **there are only three left** il n'en reste que trois; **2** seulement; **'how long did they stay?'** – **'only two days'** 'ils sont restés combien de temps?' – 'deux jours seulement'; **3** (*but*) mais; **I'd walk, only it's raining** j'irais à pied, mais il pleut.

onto preposition sur.

open noun **in the open** en plein air.
open adjective 1 (*not shut*) ouvert; **the door's open** la porte est ouverte; **the baker's is not open** la boulangerie n'est pas ouverte; **2 in the open air** en plein air.
open verb 1 ouvrir [30]; **can you open the door for me?** est-ce que tu peux ouvrir la porte?; **Sam opened his eyes** Sam a ouvert les yeux; **the bank opens at nine** la banque ouvre à neuf heures; **2 the door opened slowly** la porte s'est ouverte lentement.

open-air adjective en plein air; **an open-air swimming pool** une piscine en plein air.

a
b
c
d
e
f
g
h
i
j
k
l
m
n
o
p
q
r
s
t
u
v
w
x
y
z

opener noun **1** (*for bottles*) décapsuleur Masc.; **2** (*for cans*) ouvre-boîte Masc.

opening noun **1** (*space*) ouverture Fem.; **2** (*opportunity*) occasion Fem.; **there are few openings for recent graduates** il y a peu de débouchés pour les jeunes diplômés.

opera noun opéra Masc.

operate verb (*medically*) opérer [24]; **will they have to operate?** est-ce qu'il va falloir qu'ils opèrent?

operation noun opération Fem.; **to have an operation** se faire opérer; **she's had an operation** elle s'est fait opérer.

opinion noun avis Masc.; **in my opinion** à mon avis.

opinion poll noun sondage Masc.

opponent noun adversaire Masc. & Fem.

opportunity noun occasion Fem.; **to have the opportunity of doing** avoir l'occasion de faire; **I took the opportunity to visit the museum** j'ai profité de l'occasion pour visiter le musée.

opposed adjective **to be opposed to something** être [6] opposé à quelque chose; **they are opposed to any change of the rules** ils s'opposent à un changement des règles.

opposite noun contraire Masc.; **no, quite the opposite** non, tout le contraire.

opposite adjective **1** opposé (*a direction, side, or view, for example*); **she went off in the opposite direction** elle est partie dans la direction opposée; **2** (*facing*) d'en face; **in the house opposite** dans la maison d'en face.

opposite adverb en face; **they live opposite** ils habitent en face.

opposite preposition en face de; **opposite the station** en face de la gare.

opposition noun opposition Fem.

optician noun opticien Masc., opticienne Fem.

optimistic adjective optimiste.

option noun choix Masc.; **we have no option** nous n'avons pas le choix.

optional adjective facultatif (Fem. facultative).

or conjunction **1** ou; **English or French?** anglais ou français?; **today or Tuesday?** aujourd'hui ou mardi?; **2** (*in negatives*) **I don't have a cat or a dog** je n'ai ni un chat ni un chien; **not in June or July** ni en juin ni en juillet; **3** (*or else*) sinon; **phone Mum, or she'll worry** appelle maman, sinon elle va s'inquiéter.

oral noun (*an exam*) oral Masc. (*plural* oraux); **the French oral** l'oral de français.

orange noun (*the fruit*) orange Fem. **an orange juice** un jus d'orange.

orange adjective orange (*never changes*); **my orange socks** mes chaussettes orange.

orchard noun verger Masc.

orchestra noun orchestre Masc.

order noun **1** (*arrangement*) ordre Masc.; **in the right order** dans le bon ordre; **in the wrong order** dans le mauvais ordre; **in alphabetical**

order dans l'ordre alphabétique;
2 (*in a restaurant or café*) commande
Fem.; **can I take your orders?** puis-
je prendre vos commandes?; **3 'out
of order'** 'en panne'; **4 in order to
do** pour faire; **we hurried in order
to be on time** nous nous sommes
dépêchés pour arriver à l'heure.

order *verb* **1** (*in a restaurant or a
shop*) commander [1]; **we ordered
steaks** nous avons commandé des
steacks; **2** réserver [1] (*a taxi*).

ordinary *adjective* ordinaire.

organ *noun* **1** (*in music*) orgue *Masc.*;
to play the organ jouer de l'orgue;
2 (*of body*) organe *Masc.*

organic *adjective* biologique (*food*).

organization *noun* organisation
Fem.

organize *verb* organiser [1].

orienteering *noun* course *Fem.*
d'orientation.

original *adjective* original (*Masc.
plural* originaux); **the original
version was better** la version
originale était meilleure; **it's a
really original novel** c'est un roman
très original.

originally *adverb* à l'origine;
**originally we wanted to take the
car** à l'origine nous voulions
prendre la voiture.

Orkneys *plural noun* **the Orkneys**
les Orcades *Fem. plural.*

ornament *noun* bibelot *Masc.*

orphan *noun* orphelin *Masc.*,
orpheline *Fem.*

ostrich *noun* autruche *Fem.*

other *adjective* **1** autre; **the other
day** l'autre jour; **we took the other
road** nous avons pris l'autre route;
give me the other one donne-moi
l'autre; **where are the others?** où
sont les autres?; **the other two cars**
les deux autres voitures; **2 every
other week** une semaine sur deux;
3 somebody or other quelqu'un;
something or other quelque chose;
somewhere or other quelque part.

otherwise *adverb* (*in other ways*) à
part ça; **the flat's a bit small but
otherwise it's lovely** l'appartement
n'est pas très grand mais à part ça il
est très bien.
otherwise *conjunction* (*or else*)
sinon; **I'll phone home, otherwise
they'll worry** je vais appeler chez
moi, sinon ils vont s'inquiéter.

ought *verb* (*'ought' is translated by
the conditional tense of 'devoir'* [8]) **I
ought to go now** je devrais partir
maintenant; **they ought to know
the address** ils devraient savoir
l'adresse; **you oughtn't to have any
problems** vous ne devriez pas avoir
des problèmes.

our *adjective* **1** notre; **our house**
notre maison; **2** (*before a plural
noun*) nos; **our parents** nos parents;
3 (*with parts of the body*) le, la, les;
we'll go and wash our hands on va
se laver les mains.

ours *pronoun* **1** (*for a masculine
noun*) le nôtre; **their garden's
bigger than ours** leur jardin est
plus grand que le nôtre; **2** (*for a
feminine noun*) la nôtre; **their house
is smaller than ours** leur maison
est plus petite que la nôtre; **3** (*for a*

a
b
c
d
e
f
g
h
i
j
k
l
m
n
o
p
q
r
s
t
u
v
w
x
y
z

plural noun les nôtres; **they've invited their friends and we've invited ours** ils ont invité leurs amis et nous avons invité les nôtres; **4** à nous; **the green one's ours** le vert est à nous; **it's ours** c'est à nous; **a friend of ours** un ami à nous.

ourselves *pronoun* **1** nous; **we introduced ourselves** nous nous sommes présentés; **2** *(for emphasis)* nous-mêmes; **in the end we did it ourselves** finalement nous l'avons fait nous-mêmes.

out *adverb* **1** *(outside)* dehors; **it's cold out there** il fait froid dehors; **out in the rain** sous la pluie; **they're out in the garden** ils sont dans le jardin; **2 to go out** sortir [72]; **she went out an hour ago** elle est sortie il y a une heure; **Mr. Barnes is out** Monsieur Barnes est sorti; **are you going out this evening?** est-ce que tu sors ce soir?; **Alison's going out with Danny at the moment** Alison sort avec Danny en ce moment; **he's asked me out** il m'a invitée à sortir avec lui; **3 to go out of the room** sortir de la pièce; **he threw it out of the window** il l'a jeté par la fenêtre; **to drink out of a glass** boire dans un verre; **she took the photo out of her bag** elle a pris la photo dans son sac.

out *adjective* *(light, fire)* éteint; **are all the lights out?** est-ce que toutes les lumières sont éteintes?; **the fire was out** le feu était éteint.

outdoor *adjective* *(an activity or sport)* de plein air; **an outdoor restaurant** un restaurant en plein air.

outdoors *adverb* en plein air.

outing *noun* sortie *Fem.*; **to go on an outing** faire une sortie.

outline *noun* *(of an object)* contour *Masc.*

out-of-date *adjective* **1** *(no longer valid)* périmé; **my passport's out of date** mon passeport est périmé; **2** *(old-fashioned)* démodé; **they played out-of-date music** ils ont joué la musique démodée.

outside *noun* extérieur *Masc.*; **it's blue on the outside** c'est bleu à l'extérieur.
outside *adjective* extérieur.
outside *adverb* dehors; **it's cold outside** il fait froid dehors.
outside *preposition* devant *(a building)*; **I'll meet you outside the cinema** on se retrouve devant le cinéma.

outskirts *noun* périphérie *Fem.*; **on the outskirts of York** à la périphérie de York.

outstanding *adjective* exceptionnel *(Fem. exceptionnelle)*.

oval *adjective* ovale.

oven *noun* four *Masc.*; **I've put it in the oven** je l'ai mis au four.

over *preposition* **1** *(above)* au-dessus de; **there's a mirror over the sideboard** il y a un miroir au-dessus du buffet; **2** *(involving movement)* par-dessus; **she jumped over the fence** elle a sauté par-dessus la clôture; **he threw the ball over the wall** il a jeté la balle par-dessus le mur; **3 over here** par ici; **the drinks are over here** les boissons sont par ici; **4 over there** là-bas; **she's over**

there talking to Julian elle est là-bas en train de discuter avec Julian; **5** (*more than*) plus de; **it will cost over a hundred pounds** ça coûtera plus de cent livres; **he's over sixty** il a plus de soixante ans; **6** (*during*) pendant; **over the weekend** pendant le weekend; **over Christmas** à Noël; **7** (*finished*) terminé; **when the meeting's over** quand la réunion sera terminée; **it's all over now** c'est terminé maintenant; **8** on the phone par téléphone; **to ask someone over** inviter quelqu'un; **can you come over on Saturday?** peux-tu venir chez moi samedi?; **9 all over the place** partout; **all over the house** partout dans la maison.

overcast *adjective* couvert.

overcrowded *adjective* bondé.

overdose *noun* **1** (*of drugs*) overdose *Fem.*; **2** (*of medicine*) surdose *Fem.*

overflow *verb* déborder [1].

overseas *adverb* à l'étranger; **Dave works overseas** Dave travaille à l'étranger.

oversleep *verb* se réveiller [1] trop tard.

overtake *verb* doubler [1] (*another car*).

overtime *noun* **to work overtime** faire [10] des heures supplémentaires.

overweight *adjective* (*a person*) trop gros (*Fem.* trop grosse).

owe *verb* devoir [8]; **I owe Rick ten pounds** je dois dix livres à Rick.

owing *adjective* **1** (*to pay*) à payer; **there's five pounds owing** il y a cinq livres à payer; **2 owing to** en raison de; **owing to the snow** en raison de la neige.

owl *noun* hibou *Masc.* (*plural* hiboux).

own *adjective* **1** propre (*goes before the noun*); **my own computer** mon propre ordinateur; **I've got my own room** j'ai une chambre à moi; **2 on your own** tout seul (*Fem.* toute seule); **Annie did it on her own** Annie l'a fait toute seule.
own *verb* posséder [24].

owner *noun* propriétaire *Masc. & Fem.*

oxygen *noun* oxygène *Masc.*

oyster *noun* huître *Fem.*

ozone layer *noun* couche *Fem.* d'ozone.

Pp

pace *noun* **1** (*a step*) pas *Masc.*; **2** (*the speed you walk at*) allure *Fem.*; **at a brisk pace** à vive allure.

Pacific *noun* **the Pacific Ocean** l'océan *Masc.* Pacifique.

pack *noun* **1** paquet *Masc.*; **2 a pack of cards** un jeu de cartes.
pack *verb* **1** faire [10] ses bagages; **I haven't packed yet** je n'ai pas encore fait mes bagages; **2 I'll pack my case tonight** je ferai ma valise ce soir; **have you packed my red shirt?** as-tu mis ma chemise rouge dans la valise?

a b c d e f g h i j k l m n o p q r s t u v w x y z

a

package noun paquet Masc.

b

package holiday, package tour noun voyage Masc. organisé.

c

packed lunch noun panier-repas Masc.

d

packet noun 1 paquet Masc.; **a packet of biscuits** un paquet de biscuits; 2 (bag) sachet Masc.; **a packet of crisps** un sachet de chips.

e

f

g

packing noun **to do your packing** faire ses bagages.

h

pad noun (of paper) bloc-notes Masc.

i

paddle noun (for a canoe) pagaie Fem.
paddle verb (at the seaside) **to go paddling** faire [10] trempette.

j

k

padlock noun cadenas Masc.

l

page noun page Fem.; **on page seven** à la page sept.

m

pain noun douleur Fem.; **I've got a pain in my leg** j'ai mal à la jambe; **to be in pain** souffrir [73]; ★ **Eric's a real pain (in the neck)** Eric est vraiment pénible.

n

o

p

painful adjective douloureux (Fem. douloureuse).

q

r

painkiller noun analgésique Masc.

s

paint noun peinture Fem.; **'wet paint'** 'peinture fraîche'.
paint verb peindre [60]; **to paint something pink** peindre quelque chose en rose.

t

u

v

paintbrush noun pinceau Masc. (plural pinceaux).

w

painter noun peintre Masc.

x

painting noun (picture) tableau Masc. (plural tableaux); **a painting by Monet** un tableau de Monet.

y

z

pair noun 1 paire Fem.; **a pair of socks** une paire de chaussettes; **a pair of scissors** une paire de ciseaux; 2 **a pair of jeans** un jean; **a pair of trousers** un pantalon; **a pair of knickers** un slip; 3 **to work in pairs** travailler en groupes de deux.

Pakistan noun Pakistan Masc.; **in Pakistan** au Pakistan; **to Pakistan** au Pakistan.

Pakistani noun Pakistanais Masc., Pakkistanaise Fem..
Pakistani adjective pakistanais.

palace noun palais Masc.

pale adjective pâle; **pale green** vert pâle (never changes); **pale green curtains** des rideaux vert pâle; **to turn pale** pâlir [2].

palm noun 1 (of your hand) paume Fem.; 2 (a palm tree) palmier Masc.

pan noun (saucepan) casserole Fem. 1 **a pan of water** une casserole d'eau; 2 (frying-pan) poêle Fem.

pancake noun crêpe Fem.

panel noun 1 (on radio or TV) (for a discussion) invités Masc. plural (i.e. guests); (for a quiz show) jury Masc.; 2 (for a wall or a bath, for example) panneau Masc. (plural panneaux).

panel game noun jeu Masc. (plural jeux).

panic noun panique Fem.
panic verb s'affoler [1]; **don't panic!** pas de panique!

pannier noun (on a bike) sacoche Fem.

panther noun panthère Fem.

panties noun petite culotte Fem.

512

pantomime *noun* spectacle *Masc.* pour enfants.

pants *plural noun* slip *Masc.*

paper *noun* 1 papier *Masc.*; **a sheet of paper** une feuille de papier; 2 **a paper cup** un gobelet en carton; **a paper hanky** un mouchoir en papier; 3 (*newspaper*) journal *Masc.* (*plural* journaux); **it was in the paper** c'était dans le journal.

paperback *noun* livre *Masc.* de poche.

paperclip *noun* trombone *Masc.* (*because of its shape*).

paper shop *noun* magasin *Masc.* de journaux.

paper towel *noun* essuie-tout *Masc.*

parachute *noun* parachute *Masc.*

parachuting *noun* parachutisme *Masc.*; **to go parachuting** faire du parachutisme.

parade *noun* défilé *Masc.*

paradise *noun* paradis *Masc.*

paraffin *noun* pétrole *Masc.*

paragraph *noun* paragraphe *Masc.*; **'new paragraph'** 'à la ligne'.

parallel *adjective* parallèle.

paralysed *adjective* paralysé.

parcel *noun* paquet *Masc.*

pardon *noun* **I beg your pardon** pardon; **pardon?** pardon?

parent *noun* parent *Masc.*; **my parents are Scottish** mes parents sont écossais; **a parents' evening** une réunion pour les parents d'élèves.

Paris *noun* Paris; **Marie lives in Paris** Marie habite à Paris.

Parisian *noun* Parisien *Masc.*, Parisienne *Fem.*
Parisian *adjective* parisien (*Fem.* parisienne).

park *noun* 1 parc *Masc.*; **a theme park** un parc à thème; 2 **a car park** un parking.
park *verb* 1 se garer [1]; **you can park outside the house** vous pouvez vous garer devant la maison; 2 **to park a car** garer [1] une voiture; **where did you park the car?** où as-tu garé la voiture?

parking *noun* stationnement *Masc.*; **'no parking'** 'stationnement interdit'.

parking meter *noun* parcmètre *Masc.*

parking space *noun* place *Fem.*

parking ticket *noun* PV *Masc.* (*informal*).

parliament *noun* parlement *Masc.*

parrot *noun* perroquet *Masc.*

parsley *noun* persil *Masc.*

part *noun* 1 partie *Fem.*; **part of the garden** une partie du jardin; **the last part of the concert** la dernière partie du concert; **that's part of your job** ça fait partie de votre travail; 2 **to take part in something** participer à quelque chose; 3 (*a role in a play*) rôle *Masc.*; 4 **spare parts** pièces *Fem. plural* détachées.

particular *adjective* particulier (*Fem.* particulière); **nothing in particular** rien de particulier.

a
b
c
d
e
f
g
h
i
j
k
l
m
n
o
p
q
r
s
t
u
v
w
x
y
z

a
b
c
d
e
f
g
h
i
j
k
l
m
n
o
p
q
r
s
t
u
v
w
x
y
z

particularly *adverb* **1** (*unusually*) spécialement; **not particularly interesting** pas spécialement intéressant; **2** (*in particular*) surtout; **particularly as it's our last day** surtout que c'est notre dernier jour.

parting *noun* (*in your hair*) raie *Fem.*

partly *adverb* en partie.

partner *noun* **1** (*in a game*) partenaire *Masc.*; **2** (*the person you live with*) partenaire *Masc. & Fem.*; **3** (*in business*) associé *Masc.*, associée *Fem.*

partridge *noun* perdrix *Fem.*

part-time *adjective, adverb* à temps partiel; **part-time work** du travail à temps partiel; **to work part-time** travailler à temps partiel.

party *noun* **1** fête *Fem.*; **a Christmas party** une fête de Noël; **to have a birthday party** faire une fête d'anniversaire; **2** (*more formal, in the evening*) soirée *Fem.*; **we've been invited to a party at the Smiths' house** nous sommes invités à une soirée chez les Smith; **3** (*group*) groupe *Masc.*; **a party of schoolchildren** un groupe d'élèves; **a rescue party** une équipe de secouristes; **4** (*in politics*) parti *Masc.*; **the Labour party** le parti travailliste.

party game *noun* jeu *Masc.* de société (*plural* jeux de société).

pass *noun* **1** (*to let you in*) laisser-passer *Masc.* (*plural* laisser-passer); **2 a bus pass** une carte de bus; **3** (*a mountain pass*) col *Masc.*; **4** (*in an exam*) **to get a pass in history** être reçu en histoire.

pass *verb* **1** (*go past*) passer [1] devant (*a place or building*); **we passed your house** nous sommes passés devant chez toi; **2** (*to overtake*) doubler [1] (*a car*); **3** (*give*) passer [1]; **could you pass me the paper please?** peux-tu me passer le journal s'il te plaît?; **4** (*time*) passer [1]; **the time passed slowly** le temps passait lentement; **5** (*in an exam*) être [6] reçu; **did you pass?** as-tu été reçu?; **to pass an exam** être reçu à un examen.

passage *noun* **1** (*a corridor*) couloir *Masc.*; **2** (*a piece of text*) passage *Masc.*

passenger *noun* **1** (*in a car, plane, or ship*) passager *Masc.*, passagère *Fem.*; **2** (*in a train, bus, or underground*) voyageur *Masc.*, voyageuse *Fem.*

passerby *noun* passant *Masc.*, passante *Fem.*

passion *noun* passion *Fem.*

passionate *adjective* passionné.

passive *noun* passif *Masc.*
passive *adjective* passif (*Fem.* passive).

Passover *noun* Pâque *Fem.* juive.

passport *noun* passeport *Masc.*; **an EU passport** un passeport de l'UE.

password *noun* mot *Masc.* de passe.

past *noun* passé *Masc.*; **in the past** au passé.

past *adjective* **1** (*recent*) dernier (*Fem.* dernière) (*goes before the noun*); **in the past few weeks**

pendant les dernières semaines;
2 (*over*) fini; **winter is past** l'hiver
est fini.

past *preposition, adverb* **1 to walk
or drive past something** passer
devant quelque chose; **we went
past the school** nous sommes
passés devant l'école; **Ray went
past in his new car** Ray est passé
dans sa nouvelle voiture; **2** (*the
other side of*) après; **it's just past the
post office** c'est juste après la poste;
3 (*talking about time*) **ten past six**
six heures dix; **half past four** quatre
heures et demie; **a quarter past two**
deux heures et quart.

pasta *noun* pâtes *Fem. plural*; **I don't
like pasta** je n'aime pas les pâtes.

paste *verb* coller [1]; **to cut and
paste the table** copier-coller le
tableau.

pasteurized *adjective* pasteurisé.

pastry *noun* pâte *Fem.*

patch *noun* **1** (*fabric, for mending*)
pièce *Fem.*; **2** (*of snow or ice*) plaque
Fem.; **3** (*of blue sky*) coin *Masc.*

path *noun* chemin *Masc.*; (*very
narrow*) sentier *Masc.*

pathetic *adjective* (*useless,
hopeless*) lamentable.

patience *noun* **1** patience *Fem.*;
2 (*card game*) réussite *Fem.*

patient *noun* patient *Masc.*, patiente
Fem.

patient *adjective* patient.

patiently *adverb* avec patience.

patio *noun* terrasse *Fem.*

patrol *noun* patrouille *Fem.*

patrol car *noun* voiture *Fem.* de
police.

pattern *noun* **1** (*on wallpaper or
fabric*) motif *Masc.*; **2** (*dressmaking*)
patron *Masc.*; **3** (*knitting*) modèle
Masc.

pause *noun* pause *Fem.*

pavement *noun* trottoir *Masc.*; **on
the pavement** sur le trottoir.

paw *noun* patte *Fem.*

pawn *noun* pion *Masc.*

pay *noun* salaire *Masc.*
pay *verb* **1** payer [59]; **I'm paying**
c'est moi qui paie; **to pay cash**
payer comptant; **2 to pay for
something** payer [59] quelque
chose; **Tony paid for the drinks**
Tony a payé les boissons; **it's all
paid for** c'est tout payé; **3 to pay by
credit card** régler [24] par carte de
crédit; **to pay by cheque** régler par
chèque; **4 to pay somebody back**
(*money*) rembourser [1] quelqu'un;
5 to pay attention faire [10]
attention; **6 to pay a visit to
somebody** rendre [3] visite à
quelqu'un.

paydesk *noun* caisse *Fem.*

payment *noun* paiement *Masc.* (*of a
bill*) règlement *Masc.*

pay phone *noun* téléphone *Masc.*
public.

PC *noun* (*computer*) PC *Masc.*

pea *noun* petit pois *Masc.*

peace *noun* paix *Fem.*

peaceful *adjective* paisible (*day,
scene*).

peach *noun* pêche *Fem.*

peacock *noun* paon *Masc.*

peak noun (of a mountain) pic Masc.

peak period (for holidays) période Fem. de pointe.

peak rate noun (for phoning) tarif Masc. rouge.

peak time noun (for traffic) heures Fem. plural de pointe.

peanut noun cacahuète Fem.

peanut butter noun beurre Masc. de cacahuètes.

pear noun poire Fem.

pearl noun perle Fem.

peasant noun paysan Masc., paysanne Fem.

pebble noun 1 (on the road) caillou Masc. (plural cailloux); 2 (on a beach) galet Masc.

peculiar adjective bizarre.

pedal noun pédale Fem.
pedal verb pédaler [1].

pedal boat noun pédalo™ Masc.

pedestrian noun piéton Masc.

pedestrian crossing noun passage Masc. pour piétons.

pedestrian precinct noun zone Fem. piétonne.

pee noun **to have a pee** faire [10] pipi (informal) .

peel noun 1 (of an apple) peau Fem.; 2 (of an orange) écorce Fem.
peel verb éplucher [1] (fruit, vegetables).

peer verb **to peer at something** regarder [1] quelque chose attentivement.

peg noun 1 (hook) patère Fem.; 2 a **clothes peg** une pince à linge; 3 a **tent peg** un piquet.

pen noun stylo Masc.; **a felt pen** un stylo-feutre.

penalty noun 1 (a fine) amende Fem.; 2 (in football) penalty Masc.; 3 (in rugby) pénalité Fem.

penalty area noun surface Fem. de réparation.

pence plural noun pence Masc. plural.

pencil noun crayon Masc.; **to write in pencil** écrire au crayon.

pencil case noun trousse Fem.

pencil sharpener noun taille-crayon Masc.

pendant noun pendentif Masc.

penfriend noun correspondant Masc., correspondante Fem.; **my French pen-friend is called Christelle** ma correspondante française s'appelle Christelle.

penguin noun pingouin Masc.

penis noun pénis Masc.

penknife noun canif Masc.

penny noun penny Masc.

pension noun retraite Fem.

pensioner noun retraité Masc., retraitée Fem.

people plural noun 1 gens Masc. plural; **people round here** les gens d'ici; **nice people** des gens sympathiques; 2 (when you're counting them) personnes Fem. plural; **ten people** dix personnes; **several people** plusieurs personnes; **how many people have you asked?** tu as invité combien de personnes?; 3 **people say he's very rich** on dit qu'il est très riche.

pepper noun **1** (spice) poivre Masc.; **2** (vegetable) poivron; **a green pepper** un poivron vert.

peppermill noun moulin Masc. à poivre.

peppermint noun menthe Fem.; **peppermint tea** le thé à la menthe.

per preposition par; **ten pounds per person** dix livres par personne.

per cent adverb pour cent; **sixty per cent of students** soixante pour cent des étudiants.

percentage noun pourcentage Masc.

percussion noun percussion Fem.; **to play percussion** jouer des percussions.

perfect adjective **1** parfait; **she speaks perfect English** elle parle un anglais parfait; **2** (ideal) idéal (Masc. plural idéaux); **the perfect place for a picnic** l'endroit idéal pour un pique-nique.

perfectly adverb parfaitement.

perform verb **1** jouer [1] (a piece of music or a play); **2** chanter [1] (a song).

performance noun **1** (playing or acting) interprétation Fem.; **a wonderful performance of Macbeth** une superbe interprétation de Macbeth; **2** (show) spectacle Masc.; **the performance starts at eight** le spectacle commence à huit heures; **3** (the results of a team or company) performance Fem.

performer noun artiste Masc. & Fem.

perfume noun parfum Masc.

perhaps adverb peut-être; **perhaps it's in the drawer?** c'est peut-être dans le tiroir?; **perhaps he's missed the train** il a peut-être raté le train.

period noun **1** période Fem.; **a two-year period** une période de deux ans; **2** (in school) cours Masc.; **a forty-five-minute period** un cours de quarante-cinq minutes; **3** (menstruation) règles Fem. plural; **during your period** pendant vos règles.

perm noun permanente Fem.

permanent adjective permanent.

permanently adverb en permanence.

permission noun permission Fem.; **to get permission to do** obtenir la permission de faire.

permit noun permis Masc.
permit verb permettre [11]; **to permit somebody to do** permettre à quelqu'un de faire; **smoking is not permitted** il est interdit de fumer; **weather permitting** si le temps le permet.

person noun personne Fem.; **there's room for one more person** il y a de la place pour une autre personne; **in person** en personne.

personal adjective personnel (Fem. personnelle).

personality noun personnalité Fem.

personally adverb personnellement; **personally, I'm against it** personnellement, je suis contre.

a
b
c
d
e
f
g
h
i
j
k
l
m
n
o
p
q
r
s
t
u
v
w
x
y
z

517

personal stereo *noun* baladeur *Masc.*

perspiration *noun* transpiration *Fem.*

persuade *verb* persuader [1]; **to persuade somebody to do** persuader quelqu'un de faire; **we persuaded Tim to wait a bit** nous avons persuadé Tim d'attendre un peu.

pessimistic *adjective* pessimiste.

pest *noun* **1** (*greenfly for example*) insecte *Masc.* nuisible; **2** (*annoying person*) casse-pieds *Masc. & Fem.*

pester *verb* harceler [45].

pet *noun* **1** animal *Masc.* de compagnie (*plural* animaux de compagnie); **do you have a pet?** avez-vous un animal de compagnie?; **a pet dog** un chien; **2** (*favourite person*) chouchou *Masc.*, chouchoute *Fem.*; **Julie is teacher's pet** Julie est la chouchoute du prof.

petal *noun* pétale *Masc.*

pet name *noun* petit nom *Masc.*

petrol *noun* essence *Fem.*; **to fill up with petrol** faire le plein d'essence; **to run out of petrol** tomber en panne d'essence.

petrol station *noun* station *Fem.* d'essence.

petticoat *noun* jupon *Masc.*

pharmacist *noun* pharmaciste *Masc. & Fem.*

pharmacy *noun* pharmacie *Fem.*

pheasant *noun* faisan *Masc.*

philosophy *noun* philosophie *Fem.*

phone *noun* téléphone *Masc.*; **she's on the phone** elle est au téléphone;

I was on the phone to Sophie j'étais au téléphone avec Sophie; **you can book by phone** on peut réserver par téléphone.

phone *verb* **1** téléphoner [1]; **while I was phoning** pendant que je téléphonais; **2 to phone somebody** appeler [18] quelqu'un; **I'll phone you tonight** je t'appellerai ce soir.

phone book *noun* annuaire *Masc.*

phone box *noun* cabine *Fem.* téléphonique.

phone call *noun* appel *Masc.*; **phone calls are free** les appels sont gratuits; **to make a phone call** téléphoner.

phone card *noun* télécarte *Fem.*

phone number *noun* numéro *Masc.* de téléphone.

photo *noun* photo *Fem.*; **to take a photo** prendre une photo; **to take a photo of somebody** prendre quelqu'un en photo; **I took a photo of their house** j'ai pris leur maison en photo.

photocopier *noun* photocopieuse *Fem.*

photocopy *noun* photocopie *Fem.*
photocopy *verb* photocopier [1].

photograph *noun* photo *Fem.*; **to take a photograph** prendre une photo; **to take a photograph of somebody** prendre quelqu'un en photo.
photograph *verb* photographier [1].

photographer *noun* photographe *Masc. & Fem.*

photography *noun* photographie *Fem.*

a b c d e f g h i j k l m n o **p** q r s t u v w x y z

phrase *noun* expression *Fem.*

phrase-book *noun* manuel *Masc.* de conversation.

physical *adjective* physique.

physicist *noun* physicien *Masc.*, physicienne *Fem.*

physics *noun* physique *Fem.*

physiotherapist *noun* kinésithérapeute *Masc. & Fem.*

physiotherapy *noun* kinésithérapie *Fem.*

pianist *noun* pianiste *Masc. & Fem.*

piano *noun* piano *Masc.*; **to play the piano** jouer du piano; **Steve played it on the piano** Steve l'a joué au piano; **a piano lesson** une leçon de piano.

pick *noun* **take your pick!** choisis!

pick *verb* **1** (*to choose*) choisir [2]; **pick a card** choisis une carte; **2** (*for a team*) sélectionner [1]; **I've been picked for Saturday** j'ai été sélectionné pour samedi; **3** cueillir [35] (*fruit or flowers*).

● **to pick up 1** (*lift*) prendre [64]; **he picked up the papers and went out** il a pris les papiers et il est sorti; **2** (*collect together*) ramasser [1]; **I'll pick up the toys** je ramasserai les jouets; **3** (*to collect*) venir [81] chercher; **I'll pick you up at six** je viendrai te chercher à six heures; **I'll pick up the keys tomorrow** je viendrai chercher les clés demain; **4** (*learn*) apprendre [64]; **you'll soon pick it up** tu vas vite l'apprendre.

pickpocket *noun* pickpocket *Masc.*

picnic *noun* pique-nique *Masc.*; **to have a picnic** pique-niquer.

picture *noun* **1** (*a painting*) tableau *Masc.* (*plural* tableaux); **a picture by Renoir** une tableau de Renoir; **he painted a picture of a horse** il a peint un cheval; **2** (*a drawing*) dessin *Masc.*; **draw me a picture of your little sister** dessine-moi ta petite sœur; **3** (*in a book*) illustration *Fem.*; **a book with lots of pictures** un livre avec beaucoup d'illustrations; **4** (*the cinema*) **the pictures** le cinéma; **to go to the pictures** aller au cinéma.

pie *noun* **1** (*sweet*) tarte *Fem.*; **an apple pie** une tarte aux pommes; **2** (*savoury*) tourte *Fem.*; **a meat pie** une tourte à la viande.

piece *noun* **1** (*a bit*) morceau *Masc.* (*plural* morceaux); **a big piece of cheese** un gros morceau de fromage; **2** (*that you fit together*) pièce *Fem.*; **the pieces of a jigsaw** les pièces d'un puzzle; **to take something to pieces** démonter [1] quelque chose; **3 a piece of furniture** un meuble; **four pieces of luggage** quatre valises; **a piece of information** un renseignement; **that's a piece of luck!** c'est un coup de chance!; **4** (*coin*) pièce *Fem.*; **a two-euro piece** une pièce de deux euros.

pier *noun* jetée *Fem.*

pierced *adjective* percé; **to have pierced ears** avoir les oreilles percées.

pig *noun* cochon *Masc.*

pigeon *noun* pigeon *Masc.*

piggy bank *noun* tirelire *Fem.*

a
b
c
d
e
f
g
h
i
j
k
l
m
n
o
p
q
r
s
t
u
v
w
x
y
z

pigsty noun porcherie Fem.; **your room is a pigsty** ta chambre est une vraie porcherie.

pigtail noun natte Fem.

pile noun 1 (a neat stack) pile Fem.; **a pile of plates** une pile d'assiettes; 2 (a heap) tas Masc.; **a pile of dirty shirts** un tas de chemises sales.
• **to pile something up** (neatly) empiler [1] quelque chose; (in a heap) entasser [1] quelque chose.

pilgrimage noun pèlerinage Masc.; **to go on a pilgrimage** faire [10] un pèlerinage.

pill noun comprimé Masc.; **the pill** (contraceptive) la pilule.

pillar noun pilier Masc.

pillar box noun boîte Fem. aux lettres.

pillow noun oreiller Masc.

pillowcase noun taie Fem. d'oreiller.

pilot noun pilote Masc.

pimple noun bouton Masc.

pin noun 1 (for sewing) épingle Fem.; **2 a three-pin plug** une prise à trois fiches.
• **to pin up 1** épingler [1] (a hem); **2** accrocher [1] (a notice).

PIN noun (personal identification number) code Masc. confidentiel.

pinball noun flipper Masc.; **to play pinball** jouer au flipper; **a pinball machine** un flipper.

pinch noun (of salt, for example) pincée Fem.
pinch verb **1** (steal) piquer [1]; **somebody's pinched my bike** on m'a piqué mon vélo; **2 to pinch somebody** pincer [61] quelqu'un.

pine noun pin Masc.; **a pine table** une table en pin.

pineapple noun ananas Masc.

pine cone noun pomme Fem. de pin.

ping-pong noun ping-pong Masc.; **to play ping-pong** jouer au ping-pong.

pink adjective rose.

pip noun (in a fruit) pépin Masc.

pipe noun **1** (for gas or water) tuyau Masc. (plural tuyaux); **2** (to smoke) pipe Fem.; **he smokes a pipe** il fume la pipe.

pirate noun pirate Masc.

pirated adjective piraté; **a pirated video** une vidéo piratée.

Pisces noun Poissons Masc. plural; **Amanda is Pisces** Amanda est Poissons.

pistachio noun pistache Fem.

pit noun fosse Fem.

pitch noun terrain Masc.; **a football pitch** un terrain de foot.
pitch verb **to pitch a tent** dresser [1] une tente.

pity noun **1 what a pity!** quel dommage!; **it would be a pity to miss the beginning** ce serait dommage de rater le début; **2** (feeling sorry for somebody) pitié Fem.
pity verb **to pity somebody** plaindre [31] quelqu'un.

pizza noun pizza Fem.

place noun **1** endroit Masc.; **in a warm place** dans un endroit chaud;

Rome is a wonderful place Rome est un endroit merveilleux; **all over the place** partout; **2** (*a space*) place *Fem.*; **a place for the car** une place pour la voiture; **is there a place for me?** y a-t-il une place pour moi?; **will you keep my place?** veux-tu me garder ma place?; **to change places** changer de place; **3** (*in a race*) place *Fem.*; **in first place** à la première place; **4 at your place** chez toi; **we'll go round to Zafir's place** on ira chez Zafir; **5 to take place** avoir [5] lieu; **the competition will take place at four** le concours aura lieu à quatre heures.

place *verb* mettre [11]; **he placed his cup on the table** il a mis sa tasse sur la table.

plain *noun* plaine *Fem.*

plain *adjective* **1** simple; **plain cooking** une cuisine simple; **2** (*unflavoured*) nature; **a plain yoghurt** un yaourt nature; **3** (*not patterned*) uni; **plain curtains** des rideaux unis.

plait *noun* natte *Fem.*

plan *noun* **1** projet *Masc.*; **what are your plans for this summer?** quels sont vos projets pour cet été?; **to go according to plan** se passer comme prévu; **everything went according to plan** tout s'est passé comme prévu; **2** (*a map*) plan *Masc.*

plan *verb* **1 to plan to do** avoir [5] l'intention de faire; **we're planning to leave at eight** nous avons l'intention de partir à huit heures; **2** (*make plans for*) préparer [1]; **Ricky's planning a trip to Italy** Ricky prépare un voyage en Italie;

3 (*organize*) organiser [1]; **I'm planning my day** j'organise ma journée; **4** (*to design*) concevoir [66] (*a house or garden*); **a well-planned kitchen** une cuisine bien conçue.

plane *noun* avion *Masc.*; **we went by plane** nous avons pris l'avion.

planet *noun* planète *Fem.*

plank *noun* planche *Fem.*

plant *noun* plante *Fem.*; **a house plant** une plante d'intérieur.
plant *verb* planter [1].

plaster *noun* **1** (*sticking plaster*) pansement *Masc.* adhésif; **2** (*for walls*) plâtre *Masc.*; **3 to have your leg in plaster** avoir la jambe dans le plâtre.

plastic *noun* plastique *Masc.*; **a plastic bag** un sac en plastique.

plate *noun* assiette *Fem.*

platform *noun* **1** (*in a station*) quai *Masc.*; **the train arriving at platform six** le train qui entre en gare quai numéro six; **2** (*for lecturing or performing*) estrade *Fem.*

play *noun* pièce *Fem.*; **a play by Molière** une pièce de Molière; **our school is putting on a play** notre école monte une pièce.

play *verb* **1** jouer [1]; **the children were playing with a ball** les enfants jouaient avec un ballon; **they play all kinds of music** ils jouent toutes sortes de musique; **who's playing Hamlet?** qui est-ce qui joue Hamlet?; **2** jouer [1] à (*a game*); **to play tennis** jouer au tennis; **they were playing cards** ils jouaient aux cartes; **3** jouer [1] de (*a musical instrument*); **Helen plays the violin**

a
b
c
d
e
f
g
h
i
j
k
l
m
n
o
p
q
r
s
t
u
v
w
x
y
z

Helen joue du violon; **4** mettre [11] (*a tape, CD, or record*); **play me your new CD** mets-moi ton nouveau CD.

player *noun* **1** (*in sport*) joueur *Masc.*, joueuse *Fem.*; **a football player** un joueur de foot; **2** (*musician*) musicien *Masc.*, musicienne *Fem.*

playground *noun* cour *Fem.* de récréation.

playgroup *noun* halte-garderie *Fem.*

playing card *noun* carte *Fem.* à jouer.

playing field *noun* terrain *Masc.* de sport.

playroom *noun* salle *Fem.* de jeux.

plaza *noun* **a shopping plaza** un centre commercial.

pleasant *adjective* agréable.

please *adverb* s'il vous plaît; (*less formal*) s'il te plaît; **two coffees, please** deux cafés, s'il vous plaît; **could you turn the TV off, please?** est-ce que tu peux éteindre la télé s'il te plaît?

pleased *adjective* content; **I was really pleased!** j'étais très content!; **she was pleased with her present** elle était contente de son cadeau; **pleased to meet you!** enchanté!

pleasure *noun* plaisir *Masc.*

plenty *pronoun* **1** (*lots*) beaucoup; **there's plenty of bread** il y a beaucoup de pain; **he's got plenty of money** il a beaucoup d'argent; **2** (*quite enough*) **we've got plenty of time for a coffee** nous avons largement le temps de prendre un

café; **thank you, that's plenty!** merci, ça suffit largement!

pliers *noun* pince *Fem.*

plot *noun* (*of a film or novel*) intrigue *Fem.*

plough *verb* labourer [1].

plug *noun* **1** (*electrical*) prise *Fem.*; **2** (*in a bath or sink*) bonde *Fem.*; **to pull out the plug** retirer la bonde.

plum *noun* prune *Fem.*; **a plum tart** une tarte aux prunes.

plumber *noun* plombier *Masc.*; **he's a plumber** il est plombier.

plump *adjective* potelé.

plunge *verb* plonger [52].

plural *noun* pluriel *Masc.*; **in the plural** au pluriel.

plus *preposition* plus; **three children plus the baby** trois enfants plus le bébé.

p.m. *adverb* (*French people usually express times after midday in terms of the 24-hour clock*) **1** **at two p.m.** à quatorze heures; **at nine p.m.** à vingt-et-une heures; **2** (*however, you can also use 'de l'après-midi', for times up to 6 p.m. and 'du soir' for times after that*) **at two p.m.** à deux heures de l'après-midi; **at nine p.m.** à neuf heures du soir.

poached egg *noun* œuf *Masc.* poché.

pocket *noun* poche *Fem.*

pocket money *noun* **1** (*for child*) argent *Masc.* de poche; **2** (*for small purchases*) petites dépenses *Fem. plural.*

poem *noun* poème *Masc.*

poet *noun* poète *Masc.*

poetry noun poésie Fem.

point noun 1 (tip) pointe Fem.; **the point of a nail** la pointe d'un clou; **2** (in time) moment Masc.; **at that point the police arrived** à ce moment-là, la police est arrivée; **3 to get the point** comprendre; **I don't get the point** je ne comprends pas; **what's the point of waiting?** à quoi bon attendre?; **there's no point phoning, he's out** ça ne sert à rien d'appeler, il est sorti; **that's not the point** il ne s'agit pas de ça; **4 that's a good point!** c'est vrai!; **5 from my point of view** de mon point de vue; **6 her strong point** son point fort; **7** (in scoring) point Masc.; **fifteen points to eleven** quinze points à onze; **8** (in decimals) (in French, a comma is used for the decimal point, so 6,75) **6 point 4** 6 virgule 4 (this is how you say it aloud).

point verb 1 indiquer [1]; **a notice pointing to the station** un panneau qui indiquait la gare; **James pointed out the cathedral** James nous a montré la cathédrale; **2** (with finger) montrer [1] du doigt; **he pointed at one of the children** il a montré l'un des enfants du doigt; **3 I'd like to point out that I'm paying** je vous signale que c'est moi qui paie.

pointless adjective inutile; **it's pointless to keep on ringing** c'est inutile de continuer de sonner.

poison noun poison Masc.
poison verb empoisonner [1].

poisonous adjective 1 toxique (chemical or gas); **2** vénéneux (Fem. vénéneuse) (toadstools or berries); **3** venimeux (Fem. venimeuse) (snake or insect).

poker noun 1 (for fire) tisonnier Masc.; **2** (card game) poker Masc.

Poland noun Pologne Fem.; **in Poland** en Pologne.

polar bear noun ours Masc. polaire.

pole noun 1 (for a tent) mât Masc.; **2** (for skiing) bâton Masc.; **3 the North Pole** le pôle Nord.

Pole noun (a Polish person) Polonais Masc., Polonaise Fem.

police noun **the police** la police; **the police are coming** la police arrive (note that a singular verb is used after 'la police').
police verb surveiller [1].

police car noun voiture Fem. de police.

policeman noun agent Masc. de police.

police station noun commissariat Masc. de police.

policewoman noun femme Fem. policier.

policy noun 1 (plan of action) politique Fem.; **2** (document) police Fem.

polish noun 1 (for furniture) cire Fem.; **2** (for shoes) cirage Masc.
polish verb cirer [1] (shoes or furniture).

Polish noun, adjective polonais Masc.

polite adjective poli; **to be polite to somebody** être poli avec quelqu'un.

political adjective politique.

a
b
c
d
e
f
g
h
i
j
k
l
m
n
o
p
q
r
s
t
u
v
w
x
y
z

a

politician noun homme Masc. politique, femme Fem. politique.

b

politics noun politique Fem.

c

polluted adjective pollué.

d

pollution noun pollution Fem.

e

polo-necked adjective à col roulé; **a polo-necked jumper** un pull à col roulé.

f

g

polythene bag noun sac Masc. en plastique.

h

pond noun 1 (large) étang Masc.; 2 (smaller) mare Fem.; 3 (in a garden) bassin Masc.

i

j

pony noun poney Masc.

k

ponytail noun queue Fem. de cheval.

l

poodle noun caniche Masc.

m

pool noun 1 (swimming pool) piscine Fem.; 2 (in the country) étang Masc.; 3 (puddle) flaque Fem.; 4 (game) billard Masc. américain; **to have a game of pool** jouer au billard américain; **5 the football pools** le loto sportif; **to do the pools** jouer au loto sportif.

n

o

p

q

poor adjective 1 pauvre; **a poor area** un quartier pauvre; **a poor family** une famille pauvre; **poor Tanya's failed her exam** la pauvre Tanya a raté son examen; 2 (bad) mauvais; **this is poor work** c'est du mauvais travail; **the weather was pretty poor** le temps était assez mauvais.

r

s

t

u

v

w

pop noun pop Masc.; **a pop concert** un concert de pop; **a pop star** un pop star; **a pop song** une chanson pop.

x

y

z

● **to pop into** faire [10] un saut à; **I'll just pop into the bank** je vais juste faire un saut à la banque.

popcorn noun pop-corn Masc.

pope noun pape Masc.

poppy noun coquelicot Masc.

popular adjective populaire.

population noun population Fem.

porch noun porche Masc.

pork noun porc Masc.; **a pork chop** une côtelette de porc.

porridge noun porridge Masc.

port noun 1 port Masc.; **the ferry was in port** le ferry était au port; 2 (wine) porto Masc.

portable computer noun ordinateur Masc. portable.

porter noun 1 (at a station or airport) porteur Masc.; 2 (in a hotel) portier Masc.

portion noun (of food) portion Fem.

portrait noun portrait Masc.

Portugal noun Portugal Masc.; **to Portugal** au Portugal; **in Portugal** au Portugal.

Portuguese noun 1 (language) portugais Masc.; 2 (a person) Portugais Masc., Portugaise Fem. **Portuguese** adjective portugais.

posh adjective chic (never changes); **a posh house** une maison chic.

position noun position Fem.

positive adjective 1 (sure) sûr; **I'm positive he's left** je suis sûr qu'il est parti; 2 (enthusiastic) positif (Fem. positive); **her reaction was very positive** sa réaction était très

positive; **try to be more positive** essaie d'être plus positif.

possess *verb* posséder [24].

possessions *plural noun* affaires *Fem. plural*; **all my possessions are in the flat** toutes mes affaires sont dans l'appartement.

possibility *noun* possibilité *Fem.*

possible *adjective* possible; **it's possible** c'est possible; **if possible** si possible; **as quickly as possible** le plus vite possible.

possibly *adverb* **1** (*maybe*) peut-être; **'will you be at home at midday?' – 'possibly'** 'est-ce que tu seras chez toi à midi?' – 'peut- être'; **2** (*for emphasis*) **how can you possibly believe that?** mais comment donc peux-tu croire ça?; **I can't possibly arrive before Thursday** je ne peux vraiment pas arriver avant jeudi.

post *noun* **1** poste *Fem.*; **to send something by post** envoyer quelque chose par la poste; **2** (*letters*) courrier *Masc.*; **is there any post for me?** y a-t-il du courrier pour moi?; **3** (*a pole*) poteau *Masc.*; **4** (*a job*) poste *Masc.* **post** *verb* **to post a letter** mettre [11] une lettre à la poste.

postbox *noun* boîte *Fem.* à lettres.

postcard *noun* carte *Fem.* postale.

postcode *noun* code *Masc.* postal.

poster *noun* **1** (*for decoration*) poster *Masc.*; **I've bought an Oasis poster** j'ai acheté un poster d'Oasis; **2** (*advertising*) affiche *Fem.*; **I saw a poster for the concert** j'ai vu une affiche pour le concert.

postman *noun* facteur *Masc.*; **has the postman been?** est-ce que le facteur est passé?

post office *noun* poste *Fem.*; **the post office is on the right** la poste est à droite.

postpone *verb* **to postpone something** remettre [11] quelque chose à plus tard.

postwoman *noun* factrice *Fem.*

pot *noun* **1** (*jar*) pot *Masc.*; **a pot of honey** un pot de miel; **2** (*teapot*) théière *Fem.*; **I'll make a pot of tea** je vais faire du thé; **3 the pots and pans** les casseroles *Fem. plural*; ★ **to take pot luck** manger à la fortune du pot.

potato *noun* pomme *Fem.* de terre; **fried potatoes** des pommes de terre sautées; **mashed potatoes** de la purée.

potato crisps *plural noun* chips *Masc. plural.*

pottery *noun* poterie *Fem.*

pound *noun* **1** (*money*) livre *Fem.*; **fourteen pounds** quatorze livres; **how much is that in pounds?** c'est combien en livres sterling?; **2** (*in weight*) livre *Fem.*; **a pound of apples** une livre de pommes.

pour *verb* **1** verser [1] (*liquid*); **he poured the milk into the pan** il a versé le lait dans la casserole; **2** servir [71] (*a drink*); **to pour the tea** servir le thé; **I poured him a drink** je lui ai servi à boire; **3** (*with rain*) **it's pouring** il pleut à verse.

poverty *noun* pauvreté *Fem.*

powder *noun* poudre *Fem.*

a b c d e f g h i j k l m n o **p** q r s t u v w x y z

power noun **1** (*electricity*) courant Masc.; **2** (*energy*) énergie Fem.; **nuclear power** l'énergie nucléaire; **3** (*over other people*) pouvoir Masc.; **to be in power** être au pouvoir.

power cut noun coupure Fem. de courant.

powerful adjective puissant.

power point noun prise Fem. de courant.

power station noun centrale Fem. électrique.

practical adjective pratique.

practical joke noun farce Fem.

practically adverb pratiquement.

practice noun **1** (*for sport*) entraînement Masc.; **hockey practice** l'entraînement de hockey; **2** (*for an instrument*) **to do your piano practice** travailler [1] son piano; **3 to be out of practice** être rouillé; **4 in practice** en pratique.

practise verb **1** travailler [1] (*music, language, etc*); **a week in Berlin to practise my German** une semaine à Berlin pour travailler mon allemand; **2** (*in a sport*) s'entraîner [1]; **the team practises on Wednesdays** l'équipe s'entraîne le mercredi.

praise verb **to praise somebody for something** féliciter [1] quelqu'un de quelque chose.

pram noun landau Masc.

prawn noun crevette Fem.

pray verb prier [1].

prayer noun prière Fem.

precaution noun précaution Fem.; **to take precautions** prendre ses précautions.

precinct noun **a shopping precinct** un quartier commerçant; **a pedestrian precinct** une zone piétonne.

precious adjective précieux (Fem. précieuse).

precise adjective précis.

precisely adverb précisément; **at eleven o'clock precisely** à onze heures précises.

preface noun préface Fem.

prefer verb préférer [24]; **I prefer coffee to tea** je préfère le café au thé.

pregnancy noun grossesse Fem.

pregnant adjective enceinte.

prejudice noun préjugé Masc.; **a prejudice** un préjugé; **to fight against racial prejudice** lutter contre les préjugés raciaux.

prejudiced adjective **to be prejudiced** avoir des préjugés.

preliminary adjective préliminaire.

première noun première Fem. (*of a play or film*).

prep noun devoirs Masc. plural; **my English prep** mes devoirs d'anglais.

preparation noun **1** préparation Fem.; **2 the preparations** les préparatifs Masc. plural pour; **our preparations for Christmas** nos préparatifs pour Noël.

prepare verb préparer [1]; **to prepare somebody for** préparer quelqu'un à (*a surprise or shock*).

prepared *adjective* prêt; **I'm prepared to pay half** je suis prêt à en payer la moitié; **to be prepared for the worst** s'attendre [3] au pire.

preposition *noun* préposition *Fem.*

prep school *noun* école *Fem.* primaire privée.

prescribe *verb* prescrire [38].

prescription *noun* ordonnance *Fem.*; **on prescription** sur ordonnance.

presence *noun* présence *Fem.*; **in my presence** en ma présence.

presence of mind *noun* présence *Fem.* d'esprit.

present *noun* **1** (*a gift*) cadeau *Masc.* (*plural* cadeaux); **to give somebody a present** offrir un cadeau à quelqu'un; **2** (*the time now*) présent *Masc.*; **in the present (tense)** au présent; **that's all for the present** c'est tout pour le moment. **present** *adjective* **1** (*attending*) présent; **is Tracy present?** est-ce que Tracy est présente?; **to be present at** assister [1] à; **fifty people were present at the funeral** cinquante personnes ont assisté à l'enterrement; **2** (*existing now*) actuel (*Fem.* actuelle); **the present situation** la situation actuelle; **3 at the present time** actuellement. **present** *verb* **1** remettre [11] (*a prize*); **2** (*introduce*) présenter [1].

presenter *noun* (*on TV*) présentateur *Masc.*, présentatrice *Fem.*

presently *adverb* (*soon*) bientôt.

president *noun* président *Masc.*, présidente *Fem.*

press *noun* **the press** la presse. **press** *verb* **1** (*to push*) appuyer [41]; **press here to open** appuyez ici pour ouvrir; **2** appuyer [41] sur (*a button, switch, or pedal*); **he pressed the button** il a appuyé sur le bouton.

press conference *noun* conférence *Fem.* de presse.

pressure *noun* pression *Fem.*

pressure gauge *noun* indicateur *Masc.* de pression.

pressure group *noun* groupe *Masc.* de pression.

pretend *verb* **to pretend to do** faire [10] semblant de faire; **he's pretending not to hear** il fait semblant de ne pas entendre.

pretty *adjective* joli (*goes before the noun*); **a pretty dress** une jolie robe. **pretty** *adverb* plutôt; **it was pretty silly** c'était plutôt bête.

prevent *verb* **to prevent somebody from doing** empêcher [1] quelqu'un de faire; **there's nothing to prevent you from leaving** rien ne vous empêche de partir.

previous *adjective* précédent.

previously *adverb* auparavant.

price *noun* prix *Masc.*; **the price per kilo** le prix du kilo; **CDs have gone up in price** les CD ont augmenté.

price list *noun* liste *Fem.* des prix.

price ticket *noun* étiquette *Fem.*

prick *verb* piquer [1]; **to prick your finger** se piquer le doigt.

pride *noun* fierté *Fem.*

a
b
c
d
e
f
g
h
i
j
k
l
m
n
o
p
q
r
s
t
u
v
w
x
y
z

a **priest** noun prêtre Masc.

b **primary school** noun école Fem.
primaire.

c **primary (school) teacher**
d noun instituteur Masc., institutrice
Fem.

e **prime minister** noun Premier
f ministre Masc.

primrose noun primevère Fem.

g **prince** noun prince Masc.; **Prince**
h **Charles** le prince Charles.

i **princess** noun princesse Fem.;
Princess Anne la princesse Anne.

j **principal** noun (of a college)
k directeur Masc., directrice Fem.
principal adjective (main)
l principal (Masc. plural principaux).

m **principle** noun principe Masc.; **on**
principle par principe; **that's true**
in principle cela est vrai en
n principe.

o **print** noun 1 (letters) caractères
Masc. plural; **in small print** en petits
p caractères; 2 (a photo) tirage Masc.; **a**
colour print un tirage en couleur.
q
printer noun imprimante Fem.

r **print-out** noun copie Fem. papier.

s **prison** noun prison Fem.; **in prison**
t en prison.

prisoner noun prisonnier Masc.,
u prisonnière Fem.

v **private** adjective 1 privé; **a private**
school une école privée; **'private**
w **property'** 'propriété privée';
x 2 particulier (Fem. particulière)
(lesson); **to have private lessons**
y prendre des cours particuliers.

z **privately** adverb en privé.

prize noun prix Masc.; **to win a prize**
gagner un prix.

prize-giving noun distribution
Fem. des prix.

prizewinner noun gagnant Masc.,
gagnante Fem.

probable adjective probable.

probably adverb probablement.

problem noun problème Masc.; **it's**
a serious problem c'est un grave
problème; **no problem!** pas de
problème!

process noun 1 processus Masc.;
2 to be in the process of doing
être en train de faire.

procession noun 1 (in parade)
défilé Masc.; 2 (at religious festival)
procession Fem.

produce noun (food) produits Masc.
plural.
produce verb produire [26]; **I**
produced my passport j'ai produit
mon passeport; **it produces a lot of**
heat ça produit beaucoup de
chaleur.

producer noun (of a film or
programme) metteur Masc. en scène.

product noun produit Masc.

production noun 1 (of a film or
opera) production Fem.; **2** (of a play)
mise Fem. en scène; **a new**
production of Hamlet une nouvelle
mise en scène de Hamlet; **3** (by a
factory) production Fem.

profession noun profession Fem.

professional noun professionnel
Masc., professionnelle Fem.; **he's a**
professional c'est un professionnel.
professional adjective

professionnel (*Fem.* professionnelle); **she's a professional singer** c'est une chanteuse professionnelle.

professor *noun* professeur *Masc.*

profile *noun* profil *Masc.*

profit *noun* bénéfice *Masc.*

profitable *adjective* rentable.

program *noun* **a computer program** un programme informatique.

programme *noun* **1** (*for a play or an event*) programme *Masc.*; **2** (*on TV or radio*) émission *Fem.*

programmer *noun* programmateur *Masc.*, programmatrice *Fem.*

progress *noun* **1** progrès *Masc.*; **to make progress** faire des progrès; **2 to be in progress** être en cours.

project *noun* **1** (*at school*) dossier *Masc.*; **2** (*a plan*) projet *Masc.*; **a project to build a bridge** un projet pour construire un pont.

projector *noun* projecteur *Masc.*

promise *noun* promesse *Fem.*; **to make a promise** faire une promesse; **to break a promise** manquer à sa promesse; **it's a promise!** c'est promis!

promise *verb* **to promise to do** promettre [11] de faire; **I've promised to be home by ten** j'ai promis de rentrer avant dix heures.

promote *verb* **to be promoted** être [6] promu.

promotion *noun* promotion *Fem.*

prompt *adjective* rapide; **a prompt reply** une réponse rapide.

promptly *adjective* **1** (*at once*) immédiatement; **he promptly fell off again** il est retombé immédiatement; **2** (*quickly*) rapidement; **please reply promptly** répondez rapidement s'il vous plaît; **3 promptly at nine o'oclock** à neuf heures précises.

pronoun *noun* pronom *Masc.*

pronounce *verb* prononcer [61]; **it's hard to pronounce** c'est difficile à prononcer.

pronunciation *noun* prononciation *Fem.*

proof *noun* preuve *Fem.*; **there's no proof that ...** rien ne prouve que ....

propaganda *noun* propagande *Fem.*

propeller *noun* hélice *Fem.*

proper *adjective* **1** (*real, genuine*) vrai; **a proper doctor** un vrai médecin; **I need a proper meal** j'ai besoin d'un vrai repas; **2** (*correct*) bon (*Fem.* bonne); **the proper answer** la bonne réponse; **the proper tool** le bon outil; **in its proper place** à sa place.

properly *adverb* comme il faut; **hold it properly** tiens-le comme il faut; **is it properly wrapped?** est-ce que c'est emballé comme il faut?

property *noun* (*your belongings*) affaires *Fem. plural*, propriété *Fem.*; **'private property'** 'propriété privée'.

proposal *noun* proposition *Fem.*

propose *verb* **1** (*suggest*) proposer [1]; **2** (*marriage*) **he proposed to her** il l'a demandée en mariage.

prostitute *noun* prostituée *Fem.*

a
b
c
d
e
f
g
h
i
j
k
l
m
n
o
p
q
r
s
t
u
v
w
x
y
z

a **protect** verb protéger [15].

b **protection** noun protection Fem.

c **protein** noun protéine Fem.

d **protest** noun protestation Fem.; **in spite of their protests** malgré leurs protestations.

e **protest** verb **1** (to grumble) protester [1]; **he protested, but …** il

f a protesté, mais …; **2** (demonstrate) manifester [1].

g **Protestant** noun, adjective

h protestant Masc., protestante Fem.

i **protester** noun manifestant Masc., manifestante Fem.

j **protest march** noun

k manifestation Fem.

l **proud** adjective fier (Fem. fière).

m **prove** verb prouver [1].

proverb noun proverbe Masc.

n **provide** verb fournir [2].

o **provided** conjunction à condition que; **provided you do it now** à

p condition que tu le fasses maintenant (note that a verb in the

q subjunctive is needed).

r **province** noun province Fem.

s **prune** noun pruneau Masc. (plural pruneaux).

t **PS** (at end of letter) P.S.

u **psychiatrist** noun psychiatre Masc. & Fem.; **he's a psychiatrist** il

v est psychiatre.

psychological adjective

w psychologique.

x **psychologist** noun psychologue Masc. & Fem.; **she's a psychologist**

y ele est psychologue.

z

psychology noun psychologie Fem.

PTO TSVP (= tournez s'il vous plaît).

pub noun pub Masc.

public noun **the public** le public; **in public** en public.
public adjective **1** public (Fem. publique); **2 the public library** la bibliothèque municipale.

public address system noun sonorisation Fem.

public holiday noun jour Masc. férié; **January 1 is a public holiday** le premier janvier est férié.

publicity noun publicité Fem.

public school noun école Fem. privée.

public transport noun transports Masc. plural en commun.

publish verb publier [1].

publisher noun éditeur Masc.

pudding noun (dessert) dessert Masc.; **for pudding we've got strawberries** comme dessert nous avons des fraises.

puddle noun flaque Fem.

puff noun (of smoke) bouffée Fem.

puff pastry noun pâte Fem. feuilletée.

pull verb tirer [1]; **pull hard!** tire fort!; **to pull a rope** tirer sur une corde; **he pulled a letter out of his pocket** il a tiré une lettre de sa poche; ★ **you're pulling my leg!** tu me fais marcher!
• **to pull down** baisser [1] (a blind).
• **to pull in** (at the roadside) s'arrêter [1].

pullover noun pull-over Masc.

pulse noun pouls Masc.; **the doctor took my pulse** le médecin a pris mon pouls.

pump noun pompe Fem.; **a bicycle pump** une pompe à vélo.
pump verb pomper [1]; **they were pumping the water out of the cellar** ils pompaient l'eau de la cave.
• **to pump up** gonfler [1] (a tyre).

pumpkin noun citrouille Fem.

punch noun 1 (in boxing) coup Masc. de poing; 2 (drink) punch Masc.
punch verb 1 **to punch somebody** donner [1] un coup de poing à quelqu'un; **he punched me** il m'a donné un coup de poing; 2 composter [1] (a ticket).

punctual adjective ponctuel (Fem. ponctuelle).

punctuation noun ponctuation Fem.

punctuation mark noun signe Masc. de ponctuation.

puncture noun crevaison Fem.; **we had a puncture on the way** nous avons crevé en route.

punish verb punir [2].

punishment noun punition Fem.

pupil noun élève Masc. & Fem.

puppet noun marionnette Fem.

puppy noun chiot Masc.; **a labrador puppy** un chiot labrador.

pure adjective pur.

purple adjective violet (Fem. violette).

purpose noun 1 but Masc.; **what was the purpose of her call?** quel était le but de son appel?; 2 **on purpose** exprès; **she did it on purpose** elle l'a fait exprès; **he closed the door on purpose** il a fait exprès de fermer la porte.

purr verb ronronner [1].

purse noun porte-monnaie Masc. (plural porte-monnaie).

push noun **to give something a push** pousser [1] quelque chose.
push verb 1 pousser [1]; **he pushed me** il m'a poussé; 2 (to press) appuyer [41] sur (a bell or button); 3 **to push somebody to do** pousser [1] quelqu'un à faire; **his teacher is pushing him to sit the exam** son prof le pousse à passer l'examen.
• **to push something away** repousser [1] quelque chose; **she pushed her plate away** elle a repoussé son assiette.

pushchair noun poussette Fem.

put verb 1 mettre [11]; **you can put the cream in the fridge** tu peux mettre la crème au frigo; **where did you put my bag?** où est-ce que tu as mis mon sac?; **put your suitcase here** mets ta valise ici; 2 (write) écrire [38]; **put your address here** écris ton adresse ici.
• **to put away** ranger [52]; **I'll put the shopping away** je vais ranger les courses.
• **to put back 1** remettre [11]; **I put it back in the drawer** je l'ai remis dans le tiroir; 2 (postpone) remettre [11]; **the meeting has been put back until Thursday** la réunion a été remise à jeudi.
• **to put down** poser [1]; **she put the vase down on the table** elle a posé le vase sur la table.
• **to put off 1** (postpone) remettre

[11]; **he's put off my lesson till Thursday** il a remis ma leçon à jeudi; **2** (*turn off*) éteindre [60] (*a light or TV*); **don't forget to put off the lights** n'oublie pas d'éteindre la lumière; **3 to put somebody off something** dégoûter [1] quelqu'un de quelque chose; **it really put me off Chinese food!** ça m'a vraiment dégoûté de la nourriture chinoise!; **4 to be put off** (*doing something*) se décourager [52]; **don't be put off!** ne te décourage pas!

● **to put on 1** mettre [11] (*clothing, make-up, CD*); **I'll just put my shoes on** je vais juste mettre mes chaussures; **il a mis Oasis** he's put on Oasis; **2** (*switch on*) allumer [1] (*a light or heating*); **could you put the lamp on?** est-ce que tu peux allumer la lampe?; **3** monter [1] (*a play*); **we're putting on a French play** nous sommes en train de monter une pièce française.

● **to put out 1** (*put outside*) sortir [72]; **have you put the rubbish out?** as-tu sorti les ordures?; **2** éteindre [60] (*a fire, light, or cigarette*); **I've put the lights out** j'ai éteint la lumière; **3 to put out your hand** tendre [3] la main.

● **to put through** passer [52]; **I'll put you through to the manager** je vous passe le responsable.

● **to put up 1** lever [50] (*your hand*); **I put up my hand** j'ai levé la main; **2** mettre [11] (*picture*); **I've put up some photos in my room** j'ai mis des photos dans ma chambre; **3** afficher [1] (*a notice*); **4** augmenter [1] (*the price*); **they've put up the price of the tickets** ils ont

augmenté le prix des billets; **5** (*for the night*) héberger [52]; **can you put me up on Friday?** est-ce que tu peux m'héberger vendredi?

● **to put up with something** supporter [1]; **I don't know how she puts up with it** je ne sais pas comment elle le supporte.

puzzle *noun* (*jigsaw*) puzzle *Masc.*

puzzled *adjective* perplexe.

pyjamas *plural noun* pyjama *Masc. singular*; **a pair of pyjamas** un pyjama; **where are my pyjamas?** où est mon pyjama?

pylon *noun* pilône *Masc.*

Pyrenees *noun* les Pyrénées *Fem. plural*; **in the Pyrenees** dans les Pyrénées.

Qq

quail *noun* caille *Fem.*

qualification *noun* **1** diplôme *Masc.* (*certificate, exam, degree*); **2 qualifications** qualifications *Fem. plural*; **vocational qualifications** les qualifications professionnelles.

qualified *adjective* **1** qualifié; **she's a qualified ski instructor** c'est une monitrice de ski qualifiée; **2** (*having a degree or a diploma*) diplômé; **a qualified architect** un architecte diplômé.

qualify *verb* **1** (*to be eligible*) avoir [5] droit à; **we don't qualify for a reduction** nous n'avons pas droit à une réduction; **2** (*in sport*) se qualifier [1].

quality *noun* qualité *Fem.*; **good quality vegetables** des légumes de bonne qualité.

quantity *noun* quantité *Fem.*

quarantine *noun* quarantaine *Fem.*

quarrel *noun* dispute *Fem.*; **to have a quarrel** se disputer [1]. **quarrel** *verb* se disputer [1]; **they're always quarrelling** ils sont tout le temps en train de se disputer.

quarry *noun* carrière *Fem.*

quarter *noun* **1** quart *Masc.*; **a quarter of the class** le quart de la classe; **three quarters of the class** les trois quarts de la classe; **2 a quarter past ten** dix heures et quart; **a quarter to ten** dix heures moins le quart; **a quarter of an hour** un quart d'heure; **three quarters of an hour** trois quarts d'heure; **an hour and a quarter** une heure et quart.

quarter-final *noun* quart *Masc.* de finale.

quartet *noun* quatuor *Masc.*; **a jazz quartet** un quatuor de jazz.

quay *noun* quai *Masc.*

queen *noun* reine *Fem.*; **Queen Elizabeth** la reine Elizabeth; **the Queen Mother** la reine mère.

query *noun* question *Fem.*; **are there any queries?** y a-t-il des questions?

question *noun* question *Fem.*; **to ask a question** poser une question; **I asked her a question** je lui ai posé une question; **it's a question of time** c'est une question de temps; **it's out of the question!** c'est hors

de question!
question *verb* interroger [52].

question mark *noun* point *Masc.* d'interrogation.

questionnaire *noun* questionnaire *Masc.*; **to fill in a questionnaire** remplir un questionnaire.

queue *noun* **1** (*of people*) queue *Fem.*; **to stand in a queue** faire la queue; **2** (*of cars*) file *Fem.*. **queue** *verb* faire [10] la queue; **we were queueing for check-in** nous faisions la queue pour l'enregistrement.

quick *adjective* **1** rapide; **a quick lunch** un déjeuner rapide; **it's quicker on the motorway** c'est plus rapide par l'autoroute; **to have a quick look at something** jeter un coup d'il rapide à quelque chose; **2 quick! there's the bus!** vite! voilà le bus!; **be quick!** dépêche-toi!

quickly *adverb* vite; **I'll just quickly phone my mother** je vais vite appeler ma mère.

quiet *adjective* **1** (*silent*) silencieux (*Fem.* silencieuse); **the children are very quiet** les enfants sont très silencieux; **2 to keep quiet** se taire [76]; **please keep quiet** taisez-vous, s'il vous plaît; **3** (*gentle*) doux (*Fem.* douce); **some quiet music** de la musique douce; **in a quiet voice** à voix basse; **4** (*peaceful*) tranquille; **a quiet street** une rue tranquille; **a quiet day at home** une journée tranquille à la maison.

quietly *adverb* **1** (*to move*) sans bruit; **he got up quietly** il s'est levé

sans bruit; **2** (*speak*) doucement;
3 (*read or play*) en silence.

quilt *noun* couette *Fem*.

quite *adverb* **1** assez; **it's quite cold
outside** il fait assez froid dehors;
that's quite a good idea c'est une
assez bonne idée; **he sings quite
well** il chante assez bien; **quite
often** assez souvent; **2** not quite pas
tout à fait; **the meat's not quite
cooked** la viande n'est pas tout à
fait cuite; **3** quite a lot of pas mal
de; **we've got quite a lot of friends
here** nous avons pas mal d'amis ici;
quite a few people pas mal de gens.

quiz *noun* quiz *Masc*.

quotation *noun* (*from a book*)
citation *Fem*.

quotation marks *plural noun*
guillemets *Masc. plural*; **in quotation
marks** entre guillemets.

quote *noun* **1** (*from a book*) citation
Fem.; **2** (*estimate*) devis *Masc*.; **3** in
quotes entre guillemets.
quote *verb* citer [1].

Rr

rabbi *noun* rabbin *Masc*.

rabbit *noun* lapin *Masc*.

rabbit hutch *noun* clapier *Masc*.

rabies *noun* rage *Fem*.

race *noun* **1** (*a sports event*) course
Fem.; **a cycle race** une course
cycliste; **to have a race** faire la
course; **2** (*an ethnic group*) race *Fem*.

racer *noun* (*bike*) vélo *Masc*. de
course.

racetrack *noun* **1** (*for horses*)
champ *Masc*. de course; **2** (*for cars*)
circuit *Masc*.; **3** (*for cycles*) piste *Fem*.

racial *adjective* racial (*Masc. plural*
raciaux); **racial discrimination** la
discrimination raciale.

racing *noun* courses *Fem. plural*.

racing car *noun* voiture *Fem*. de
course.

racing driver *noun* pilote *Masc*. de
course.

racism *noun* racisme *Masc*.

racist *noun, adjective* raciste *Masc. &
Fem*.

rack *noun* (*for luggage*) porte-
bagages *Masc*.

racket *noun* **1** (*for tennis*) raquette
Fem.; **here's your tennis racket**
voici ta raquette de tennis; **2** (*noise*)
vacarme *Masc*.

radar *noun* radar *Masc*.

radiation *noun* radiation *Fem*.

radiator *noun* radiateur *Masc*.

radio *noun* radio *Fem*.; **to listen to
the radio** écouter la radio; **to hear
something on the radio** entendre
quelque chose à la radio.

radioactive *adjective* radioactif
(*Fem*. radioactive).

radio-controlled *adjective*
téléguidé.

radio station *noun* station *Fem*.
de radio.

radish *noun* radis *Masc*.

radius *noun* rayon *Masc*.

raffle *noun* tombola *Fem*.

raft noun radeau Masc.

rag noun chiffon Masc.

rage noun colère Fem.; **she's in a rage** elle est furieuse; ★ **it's all the rage** ça fait fureur.

raid noun **1** hold-up Masc.; **2** (by the police) rafle Fem.

rail noun **1** (the railway) **to go by rail** prendre le train; **2** (on a balcony or bridge) balustrade Fem.; **3** (on stairs) rampe Fem.; **4** (for a train) rail Masc.

railing(s) noun grille Fem.

rail strike noun grève Fem. des cheminots.

railway noun **1** (the system) chemin Masc. de fer; **the railways** les chemins de fer; **2 a railway line** une ligne de chemin de fer (from one place to another); **3 on the railway line** sur la voie ferrée (the rails).

railway carriage noun wagon Masc.

railway station noun gare Fem.; **opposite the railway station** en face de la gare.

rain noun pluie Fem.; **in the rain** sous la pluie.
rain verb pleuvoir [63]; **it's raining** il pleut; **it's going to rain** il va pleuvoir.

rainbow noun arc-en-ciel Masc. (plural arcs-en-ciel).

raincoat noun imperméable Masc.

raindrop noun goutte Fem. de pluie.

rainfall noun niveau Masc. de précipitations.

rainy adjective pluvieux (Fem. pluvieuse).

raise verb **1** (lift up) lever [50]; **she raised her head** elle a levé la tête; **2** (increase) augmenter [1] (a price or a salary); **3 to raise money for something** collecter [1] des fonds pour quelque chose; **4** (to raise the alarm) donner [1] l'alarme; **5** (to raise somebody's spirits) remonter [1] le moral à quelqu'un.

raisin noun raisin Masc. sec.

rake noun rateau Masc. (plural rateaux).

rally noun **1** (a meeting) rassemblement Masc.; **2** (for sport) rallye Masc.; **3** (in tennis) échange Masc.

rambler noun randonneur Masc., randonneuse Fem.

rambling noun randonnée Fem.

ramp noun (for a wheelchair, for example) rampe Fem.

ranch noun ranch Masc.

range noun **1** (a choice) gamme Fem.; **we offer a range of sports** nous vous proposons une gamme de sports; **in a wide range of colours** dans un grand choix de coloris; **a top-of-the-range computer** un ordinateur haut de gamme; **2** (of mountains) chaîne Fem.

rap noun rap Masc. (music).

rape noun viol Masc.
rape verb violer [1].

rare adjective **1** rare; **a rare bird** un oiseau rare; **2** saignant (a steak); **medium-rare** à point.

rarely adverb rarement.

rash noun rougeurs Fem. plural; **I've got a rash on my arms** j'ai des

rougeurs sur les bras.
rash *adjective* irréfléchi; **a rash decision** une décision irréfléchie.

raspberry *noun* framboise *Fem.*; **raspberry jam** la confiture de framboises; **a raspberry tart** une tarte aux framboises.

rat *noun* rat *Masc.*

rate *noun* **1** (*a charge*) tarif *Masc.*; **what are the rates for children?** quels sont les tarifs pour les enfants?; **reduced rates** les tarifs réduits; **2** (*a level*) taux *Masc.*; **a high cancellation rate** un taux élevé d'annulation; **3 at any rate** en tout cas.

rather *adverb* **1** plutôt; **I'm rather busy** je suis plutôt occupé; **2 rather than** plutôt que; **in summer rather than winter** en été plutôt qu'en hiver; **3 I'd rather wait** je préfère attendre; **they'd rather come on Thursday** ils préfèrent venir jeudi; **4 rather a lot of** pas mal de; **I've got rather a lot of shopping to do** j'ai pas mal de courses à faire.

rave *noun* rave *Masc.* (*a party*).

raw *adjective* cru.

ray *noun* rayon *Masc.*

razor *noun* rasoir *Masc.*

razor blade *noun* lame *Fem.* de rasoir.

RE *noun* éducation *Fem.* religieuse.

reach *noun* portée *Fem.*; **out of reach** hors de portée; **within reach** (*of your hand*) à portée de main; **within easy reach of the sea** à proximité de la mer.
reach *verb* **1** arriver [1] à; **when you reach the church** quand vous

arrivez à l'église; **to reach a decision** arriver à une décision; **2 to reach the final** arriver [1] à la finale.

react *verb* réagir [2].

reaction *noun* réaction *Fem.*

read *verb* lire [51]; **what are you reading at the moment?** qu'est-ce que tu lis en ce moment?; **I'm reading a detective novel** je lis un roman policier; **he read out the list** il a lu la liste à haute voix.

reading *noun* lecture *Fem.*; **I don't much like reading** je n'aime pas beaucoup la lecture; **some easy reading for the beach** de la lecture facile pour la plage.

ready *adjective* prêt; **supper's not ready yet** le dîner n'est pas encore prêt; **are you ready to leave?** est-ce que tu es prêt à partir?; **to get ready** se préparer [1]; **I'm getting ready to go out** je me prépare pour sortir; **I was getting ready for bed** je me préparais pour me coucher; **I'll get your room ready** je vais préparer ta chambre.

real *adjective* vrai; **it's a real diamond** c'est un vrai diamant; **he's a real bore** c'est un vrai casse-pieds; **is that his real name?** est-ce que c'est son vrai nom?; **her real father is dead** son vrai père est mort.

realistic *adjective* réaliste.

reality *noun* réalité *Fem.*

realize *verb* se rendre [3] compte; **I hadn't realized** je ne m'en étais pas rendu compte; **I didn't realize he was French** je ne me suis pas rendu compte qu'il était français; **do you**

realize what time it is? tu te rends compte de l'heure qu'il est?

really *adverb* vraiment; **not really** pas vraiment; **is it really midnight?** est-il vraiment minuit?; **the film was really good** le film était vraiment très bon; **really?** c'est vrai?

rear *noun* arrière *Masc.*
rear *adjective* arrière; **the rear door** la porte arrière.

reason *noun* raison *Fem.*; **the reason for the delay** la raison du retard; **the reason why I phoned** la raison pour laquelle j'ai appelé.

reasonable *adjective* raisonnable.

reassure *verb* rassurer [1].

reassuring *adjective* rassurant.

rebel *noun* rebelle *Masc. & Fem.*

rebellion *noun* rébellion *Fem.*, révolte *Fem.*

rebuild *verb* reconstruire [26].

receipt *noun* reçu *Masc.*

receive *verb* recevoir [66].

receiver *noun* combiné *Masc.*; **to pick up the receiver** décrocher [1].

recent *adjective* récent.

recently *adverb* récemment.

reception *noun* **1** réception *Fem.*; **he's waiting at reception** il attend à la réception; **a big wedding reception** une grande réception de mariage; **2 to get a good reception** avoir un bon accueil.

receptionist *noun* réceptionniste *Masc. & Fem.*

recipe *noun* recette *Fem.*; **can I have the recipe for your salad?** est-ce que je peux prendre la recette de ta salade?

reckon *verb* penser [1]; **I reckon it's a good idea** je pense que c'est une bonne idée.

recognize *verb* reconnaître [27].

recommend *verb* conseiller [1]; **can you recommend a dentist?** est-ce que vous pouvez me conseiller un dentiste?; **I recommend the fish soup** je vous conseille la soupe de poisson.

recommendation *noun* recommandation *Fem.*

record *noun* **1** record *Masc.*; **it's a world record** c'est le record mondial; **record sales for the CD** des ventes record pour le CD; **the hottest summer on record** l'été le plus chaud qu'on ait jamais enregistré; **2 to keep a record of something** noter quelque chose; **3** (*music*) disque *Masc.*; **a Miles Davis record** un disque de Miles Davis; **4** (*office files*) dossier *Masc.*; **I'll just check your records** je vais juste vérifier votre dossier.
record *verb* (*on tape or CD*) enregistrer [1]; **they're recording a new album** ils sont en train d'enregistrer un nouvel album.

recorder *noun* **1** flûte *Fem.* à bec; **to play the recorder** jouer de la flûte à bec; **2 a cassette recorder** un magnétophone à cassettes; **a video recorder** un magnétoscope.

recording *noun* enregistrement *Masc.*

537

a b c d e f g h i j k l m n o p q r s t u v w x y z

record player *noun* tourne-disque *Masc.*

recover *verb* se remettre [11]; **she's recovered now** elle s'est maintenant remise.

recovery *noun* (*from an illness*) rétablissement *Masc.*

recovery vehicle *noun* camion *Masc.* de dépannage.

rectangle *noun* rectangle *Masc.*

rectangular *adjective* rectangulaire.

recycle *verb* recycler [1].

red *adjective* **1** rouge; **a red shirt** une chemise rouge; **a bright red car** une voiture rouge vif; **to go red** rougir [2]; **2** roux (*Fem.* rousse) (*hair*); **to have red hair** avoir les cheveux roux.

Red Cross *noun* **the Red Cross** la Croix-Rouge.

redcurrant *noun* groseille *Fem.*; **redcurrant jelly** la gelée de groseilles.

redecorate *verb* refaire [10]; **they've redecorated the kitchen** ils ont refait la cuisine.

redo *verb* refaire [10].

reduce *verb* réduire [68]; **they've reduced the price** ils ont réduit le prix; **to reduce speed** ralentir [2].

reduction *noun* réduction *Fem.*

redundant *adjective* **to be made redundant** être licencié.

reel *noun* (*of cotton*) bobine *Fem.*

refer *verb* **refer to** parler [1] de; **she's referring to you** elle parle de vous.

referee *noun* (*in sport*) arbitre *Masc.*

reference *noun* références *Fem. plural* (*for a job*); **she gave me a good reference** elle m'a fourni de bonnes références.

reference book *noun* ouvrage *Masc.* de référence.

refill *noun* recharge *Fem.*

reflect *verb* refléter [24].

reflection *noun* **1** (*in a mirror*) image *Fem.*; **2** (*thought*) réflexion *Fem.*; **on reflection** à la réflexion.

reflexive *adjective* **a reflexive verb** un verbe réfléchi.

refreshing *adjective* rafraîchissant.

refreshment *noun* rafraîchissement *Masc.*

refrigerator *noun* réfrigérateur *Masc.*

refuge *noun* refuge *Masc.*; **a mountain refuge** un refuge (de montagne); **to take refuge in** se réfugier [1] dans.

refugee *noun* refugié *Masc.*, refugiée *Fem.*

refund *noun* remboursement *Masc.* **refund** *verb* rembourser [1].

refusal *noun* refus *Masc.*

refuse *noun* (*rubbish*) ordures *Fem plural.* **refuse** *verb* refuser [1]; **I refused** j'ai refusé; **he refuses to help** il refuse de nous aider.

regards *plural noun* amitiés *Fem. plural*; **'regards to your parents'** 'mes amitiés à vos parents'; **Nat**

sends his regards tu as le bonjour de Nat.

reggae noun reggae Masc.

region noun région Fem.

regional adjective régional (Masc. plural régionaux).

register noun (in school) cahier Masc. des absences.
register verb s'inscrire [38].

registered letter noun lettre Fem. recommandée.

registration number noun numéro Masc. d'immatriculation (of a vehicle).

regret verb regretter [1].

regular adjective régulier (Fem. régulière); **regular visits** des visites régulières.

regularly adverb régulièrement.

regulation noun règlement Masc.

rehearsal noun répétition Fem.

rehearse verb répéter [24].

reheat verb réchauffer [1].

reign noun règne Masc.

rein noun rêne Fem.

reject verb rejeter [48].

related adjective apparenté; **we're not related** nous ne sommes pas apparentés.

relation noun **my relations** ma famille; **there were just relations and close friends** il n'y avait que la famille et des amis proches; **she's got relations in France** elle a de la famille en France.

relationship noun relations Fem. plural; **we have a good relationship** nous avons de bonnes relations.

relative noun membre Masc. de la famille; **there were a few relatives at the funeral** il y avait quelques membres de la famille à l'enterrement; **all my relatives** toute ma famille.

relatively adverb relativement.

relax verb se détendre [3]; **I'm going to relax and watch telly tonight** je vais me détendre en regardant la télé ce soir.

relaxation noun détente Fem.

relaxed adjective détendu.

relaxing adjective reposant.

relay race noun course Fem. de relais.

release noun **1** nouveauté Fem.; **this week's new releases** les nouveautés de la semaine; **2** (of a prisoner or hostage) libération Fem.
release verb **1** sortir [72] (a record or a video); **2** libérer [24] (a person).

relevant adjective pertinent.

reliable adjective fiable.

relief noun soulagement Masc.; **what a relief!** quel soulagement!

relieve verb soulager [52] (pain).

relieved adjective soulagé; **I was relieved to hear you'd arrived** j'ai été soulagé d'apprendre que tu étais arrivé.

religion noun religion Fem.

religious adjective **1** croyant (a person); **Jane's not religious** Jane n'est pas croyante; **2** religieux (Fem. religieuse) (art or music, for example).

a
b
c
d
e
f
g
h
i
j
k
l
m
n
o
p
q
r
s
t
u
v
w
x
y
z

reluctant *adj* réticent; **he's reluctant to go** il est peu disposé à y aller.

rely *verb* **to rely on somebody** compter [1] sur quelqu'un; **I'm relying on you for Saturday** je compte sur toi pour samedi.

remain *verb* rester [1].

remains *plural noun* restes *Masc. plural*; **the remains of the chicken** les restes du poulet; **the remains of a castle** les restes d'un château.

remark *noun* remarque *Fem.*; **to make remarks about** faire des remarques sur.

remarkable *adjective* remarquable.

remarkably *adverb* remarquablement.

remember *verb* **1** se souvenir [81]; **I don't remember** je ne me souviens plus; **2 to remember something** se souvenir [81] de quelque chose; **I can't remember the number** je ne me souviens pas du numéro; **3 to remember to do** ne pas oublier [1] de faire; **remember to shut the door** n'oublie pas de fermer la porte; **I remembered to bring the CDs** je n'ai pas oublié d'apporter les CD.

remind *verb* rappeler [18] **1 to remind somebody to do** rappeler à quelqu'un de faire; **remind your mother to pick me up** rappelle à ta mère de venir me chercher; **2** faire [10] penser; **it reminds me of Paris** ça me fait penser à Paris; **he reminds me of Frank** il me fait penser à Frank; **oh, that reminds me** ... tiens, j'y pense ....

remote *adjective* isolé.

remote control *noun* télécommande *Fem.*

remove *verb* enlever [50]; **he removed his jacket** il a enlevé sa veste; **the chairs had all been removed** quelqu'un avait enlevé toutes les chaises.

renew *verb* renouveler [18] (*a passport or licence*).

rent *noun* loyer *Masc.*
rent *verb* louer [1]; **Simon's rented a flat** Simon a loué un appartement.

rental *noun* location *Fem.*

reorganize *verb* réorganiser [1].

repair *noun* réparation *Fem.*
repair *verb* réparer [1]; **to get something repaired** faire [10] réparer quelque chose; **we've had the television repaired** nous avons fait réparer la télévision.

repay *verb* rembourser [1]; **he repaid me the money he owed me** il m'a remboursé l'argent qu'il me devait.

repeat *noun* reprise *Fem.* (*of a programme*).
repeat *verb* répéter [24].

repeatedly *adverb* à plusieurs reprises.

repertoire *noun* répertoire *Masc.*

repetitive *adjective* répétitif (*Fem.* répétitive).

replace *verb* remplacer [61].

replacement *noun* **1** (*person*) remplaçant *Masc.*, remplaçante *Fem.*; **2** (*thing*) **can you find me a replacement?** est-ce que vous pouvez le/la remplacer?

540

replay verb **1** (game) rejouer [1]; **2** (video) repasser [1].

reply noun réponse Fem.; **I didn't get a reply to my letter** je n'ai pas reçu de réponse à ma lettre; **there's no reply** ça ne répond pas (on the telephone).
reply verb répondre [3]; **I still haven't replied to the letter** je n'ai toujours pas répondu à la lettre.

report noun **1** (of an event) compte rendu Masc.; **2** (school report) bulletin Masc. scolaire.
report verb **1** signaler [1] (a problem or accident); **we've reported the theft** nous avons signalé le vol; **2** se présenter [1]; **I had to report to reception** je devais me présenter à la réception.

reporter noun journaliste Masc. & Fem.

represent verb représenter [1].

representative noun représentant Masc., représentante Fem..

reproach noun reproche Masc.
reproach verb reprocher [1].

reproduction noun reproduction Fem.

reptile noun reptile Masc.

republic noun république Fem.

reputation noun réputation Fem.; **a good reputation** une bonne réputation; **she has a reputation for honesty** elle a la réputation d'être honnête.

request noun demande Fem.; **on request** sur demande.
request verb demander [1].

rescue noun secours Masc.; **to come to somebody's rescue** venir au secours de quelqu'un.
rescue verb sauver [1]; **they rescued the dog** ils ont sauvé le chien.

rescue party noun équipe Fem. de secours.

rescue worker noun secouriste Masc. & Fem.

research noun recherche Fem.; **for research into Aids** pour la recherche sur le Sida; **to do research** faire des recherches.
research verb **to research into** faire [10] des recherches sur; **a well-researched programme** un programme bien documenté.

resemblance noun ressemblance Fem.

resemble verb ressembler [1] à; **she resembles her aunt** elle ressemble à sa tante.

reservation noun (a booking) réservation Fem.; **to make a reservation** faire une réservation.

reserve noun **1** réserve Fem.; **we have some in reserve** nous en avons en réserve; **2 a nature reserve** une réserve naturelle; **3** (for a match) remplaçant Masc., remplaçante Fem.
reserve verb réserver [1]; **this table is reserved** cette table est réservée.

reservoir noun réservoir Masc.

resident noun résident Masc., résidente Fem.

a
b
c
d
e
f
g
h
i
j
k
l
m
n
o
p
q
r
s
t
u
v
w
x
y
z

residential *adjective* résidentiel (*Fem.* résidentielle); **a residential area** un quartier résidentiel.

resign *verb* démissionner [1].

resignation *noun* (*from a post*) démission *Fem.*

resist *verb* résister [1] à (*an offer or temptation*); **I can't resist!** je ne peux pas résister!

resit *verb* repasser [1] (*an exam*).

resort *noun* **1** (*for holidays*) **a holiday resort** un lieu de villégiature; **a ski resort** une station de ski; **a seaside resort** une station balnéaire; **2 as a last resort** en dernier recours.

respect *noun* respect *Masc.*
respect *verb* respecter [1].

respectable *adjective* respectable.

respectful *adjective* respectueux (*Fem.* respectueuse).

responsibility *noun* responsabilité *Fem.*

responsible *adjective* **1** (*to blame*) responsable; **he's responsible for the delay** il est responsable du retard; **2** (*in charge*) responsable; **I'm responsible for booking the rooms** je suis responsable de la réservation des chambres; **3** (*reliable*) sérieux (*Fem.* sérieuse); **he's not very responsible** il n'est pas très sérieux.

rest *noun* **1 the rest** le reste; **the rest of the day** le reste du jour; **the rest of the bread** le reste du pain; **2** (*the others*) les autres; **the rest have gone home** les autres sont rentrés; **3** repos *Masc.*, ; **ten days'**

complete rest dix jours de repos total; **to have a rest** se reposer [1]; **4** (*a short break*) pause *Fem.*; **to stop for a rest** faire une pause.
rest *verb* (*have a rest*) se reposer [1]

restaurant *noun* restaurant *Masc.*

restful *adjective* reposant.

restless *adjective* nerveux (*Fem.* nerveuse).

restore *verb* restaurer [1]

restrain *verb* retenir [77].

restrict *verb* limiter [1].

restriction *noun* limitation *Fem.*

result *noun* **1** résultat *Masc.*; **the exam results** les résultats des examens; **2 as a result** par conséquent; **as a result we missed the ferry** par conséquent nous avons raté le ferry.

retire *verb* (*from work*) prendre [64] sa retraite; **she retires in June** elle prend sa retraite en juin; **for retired people** pour les retraités.

retirement *noun* retraite *Fem.*

return *noun* **1** retour *Masc.*; **the return journey** le voyage de retour; **by return of post** par retour de courrier; **2 in return** en échange; **in return for his help** en échange de son aide; ★ **many happy returns!** bon anniversaire!
return *verb* **1** (*come back*) revenir [81]; **he returned ten minutes later** il est revenu dix minutes plus tard; **2** (*get home*) rentrer [1]; **to return from holiday** rentrer de vacances; **I'll ask her to phone as soon as she returns** je lui demanderai de vous appeler dès qu'elle rentrera; **3** (*to give back*) rendre [3]; **Gemma's**

never returned the video Gemma n'a jamais rendu la vidéo.

return fare *noun* prix *Masc.* d'un billet aller-retour.

return ticket *noun* billet *Masc.* aller-retour.

reunion *noun* réunion *Fem.*; **a class reunion** une réunion d'anciens élèves.

reveal *verb* révéler [24].

revenge *noun* vengeance *Fem.*; **to get one's revenge on someone** se venger [52] de quelqu'un.

reverse *noun* **1** (*of a coin*) revers *Masc.*; **2** (*of a page*) dos *Masc.*; **3** (*opposite*) **the reverse is true** le contraire est vrai; **4** (*gear*) marche *Fem.* arrière.
reverse *verb* **1** (*in a car*) faire [10] marche arrière; **he reversed the car out of the garage** il a sorti la voiture du garage en marche arrière; **2 to reverse the charges** faire [10] un appel en PCV.

review *noun* (*of a book, play, or film*) critique *Fem.*
review *verb* faire [10] la critique de (*a play or concert*); **the film was well reviewed** le film a eu une bonne critique.

revise *verb* réviser [1]; **Tessa's busy revising for her exams** Tessa est en train de réviser pour ses examens.

revision *noun* révision *Fem.*

revive *verb* ranimer [1].

revolting *adjective* infect; **the sausages are revolting** les saucisses sont infectes.

revolution *noun* révolution *Fem.*; **the Fench Revolution** la Révolution française.

revolving door *noun* porte *Fem.* à tambour.

reward *noun* récompense *Fem.*; **a £100 reward** cent livres de récompense.
reward *verb* récompenser [1].

rewarding *adjective* enrichissant.

rewind *verb* rembobiner [1] (*a cassette or video*).

rhinoceros *noun* rhinocéros *Masc.*

rhubarb *noun* rhubarbe *Fem.*

rhyme *noun* rime *Fem.*

rhythm *noun* rythme *Masc.*

rib *noun* côte *Fem.*

ribbon *noun* ruban *Masc.*

rice *noun* riz *Masc.*; **chicken and rice** du poulet au riz; **rice pudding** le riz au lait.

rich *adjective* riche; **we're not very rich** nous ne sommes pas très riches; **the rich and the poor** les riches et les pauvres.

rid *adjective* **to get rid of something** se débarrasser de quelque chose; **we got rid of the car** nous nous sommes débarrassés de la voiture.

riddle *noun* devinette *Fem.*

ride *noun* tour *Masc.*; **to go for a ride (on a bike)** faire [10] un tour à vélo; **to go for a ride (on a horse)** faire une promenade à cheval.
ride *verb* **1 to learn to ride a bike** apprendre [64] à faire du vélo; **can you ride a bike?** sais-tu faire du vélo?; **2 to learn to ride (a horse)** apprendre [64] à monter à cheval;

a
b
c
d
e
f
g
h
i
j
k
l
m
n
o
p
q
r
s
t
u
v
w
x
y
z

I've never ridden a horse je ne suis jamais monté à cheval.

rider noun **1** (on a horse) cavalier Masc., cavalière Fem.; **2** (on a bike) cycliste Masc. & Fem.; **3** (on a motorbike) motocycliste Masc. & Fem.

ridiculous adjective ridicule.

riding noun équitation Fem.; **to go riding** faire [10] de l'équitation.

riding school noun école Fem. d'équitation.

rifle noun fusil Masc.

right noun **1** (not left) droite Fem.; **on the right** à droite; **on my right** à ma droite; **2** (to do something) droit Masc.; **the right to strike** le droit de grève; **you have no right to say that** tu n'as pas le droit de dire ça. **right** adjective **1** (not left) droit; **my right hand** ma main droite; **2** (correct) bon (Fem. bonne); **the right answer** la bonne réponse; **the right telephone number** le bon numéro de téléphone; **the right amount of** la bonne quantité de; **is this the right address?** est-ce que c'est la bonne adresse?; **3 to be right** (a person) avoir [5] raison; **you see, I was right** tu vois, j'avais raison; **4 you were right to stay at home** tu as bien fait de rester chez toi; **he was right not to say anything** il a bien fait de ne rien dire; **5** (moral) bien; **it's not right to talk like that** ce n'est pas bien de parler comme ça. **right** adverb **1** (direction) à droite; **turn right at the lights** tournez à droite aux feux; **2** (correctly) comme il faut; **you're not doing it right** tu ne le fais pas comme il faut; **3** (completely) tout; **right at the**

bottom tout au fond; **right at the beginning** tout au début; **right now** tout de suite; **right in the middle** en plein milieu; **4** (okay) bon; **right, let's go** bon, allons-y.

right-click noun clic Masc. sur le bouton droit de la souris.

right-hand adjective **on the right-hand side** à droite.

right-handed adjective droitier (Fem. droitière).

rind noun **1** (on fruit) peau Fem.; **2** (on cheese) croûte Fem.

ring noun **1** (on the phone) **to give somebody a ring** appeler [18] quelqu'un; **2** (for your finger) bague Fem.; **3** (circle) cercle Masc.; **4 there was a ring at the door** on a sonné à la porte. **ring** verb **1** (a bell or phone) sonner [1]; **the phone rang** le téléphone a sonné; **2** (phone) appeler [18]; **I'll ring you tomorrow** je t'appellerai demain; **could you ring for a taxi?** est-ce que tu peux appeler un taxi?

● **to ring back** rappeler [18]; **I'll ring you back later** je te rappellerai tout à l'heure.

● **to ring off** raccrocher [1].

ring road noun rocade Fem.

rinse verb rincer [61].

riot noun émeute Fem.

rioting noun émeutes Fem. plural.

rip verb déchirer [1].

ripe adjective mûr; **are the tomatoes ripe?** est-ce que les tomates sont mûres?

rip-off noun **it's a rip-off!** c'est de l'arnaque!

rise noun **1** hausse Fem.; **a rise in price** une hausse de prix; **2 a pay rise** une augmentation.
rise verb **1** (the sun) se lever [50]; **when the sun rose** quand le soleil s'est levé; **2** (prices) augmenter [1].

risk noun risque Masc.; **to take risks** prendre des risques.
risk verb risquer [1]; **he risks losing his job** il risque de perdre son emploi.

rival noun rival Masc. (plural rivaux), rivale Fem.

river noun **1** rivière Fem.; **we picnicked on the edge of a river** nous avons pique-niqué au bord d'une rivière; **2** fleuve Masc.; **the rivers of Europe** les fleuves de l'Europe ('fleuve' is only used for a river which flows directly into the sea like the Thames in Britain or the Seine in France).

Riviera noun **the French Riviera** la Côte d'Azur.

road noun **1** route Fem.; **the road to London** la route de Londres; **2** (in a town) rue Fem.; **the butcher's is on the other side of the road** la boucherie est de l'autre côté de la rue; **3 across the road** en face; **they live across the road from us** ils habitent en face de chez nous.

road accident noun accident Masc. de la route.

road map noun carte Fem. routière.

roadside noun **by the roadside** au bord de la route.

road sign noun panneau Masc. de signalisation (plural panneaux de signalisation).

roadworks plural noun travaux Masc. plural.

roast noun rôti Masc.
roast adjective rôti; **roast potatoes** les pommes de terre rôties; **roast beef** le rôti de bœuf.

rob verb **1** voler [1] (a person); **2** dévaliser [1] (a bank).

robber noun voleur Masc., voleuse Fem.

robbery noun vol Masc.; **a bank robbery** un hold-up.

robot noun robot Masc.

rock noun **1** (a big stone) rocher Masc.; **she was sitting on a rock** elle était assise sur un rocher; **2** (the material) roche Fem.; **3** (music) rock Masc.; **a rock band** un groupe de rock; **to dance rock and roll** danser le rock.

rock climbing noun escalade Fem.; **to go rock climbing** faire de l'escalade.

rocket noun fusée Fem.

rocking horse noun cheval Masc. à bascule.

rock star noun rock-star Fem.

rocky adjective rocailleux (Fem. rocailleuse).

rod noun **a fishing rod** une canne à pêche.

role noun rôle Masc.; **to play the role of** jouer le rôle de.

roll noun **1** rouleau Masc. (plural rouleaux); **a roll of fabric** un rouleau de tissu; **a roll of**

a b c d e f g h i j k l m n o p q r s t u v w x y z

a b c d e f g h i j k l m n o p q **r** s t u v w x y z

sellotape™ un rouleau de scotch™;
a toilet roll un rouleau de papier
hygiénique; **2 a bread roll** un petit
pain.
roll *verb* rouler [1].

• **to roll something up 1** rouler [1]
(*a carpet*); **2** retrousser [1] (*sleeves*);
he rolled up his sleeves il a
retroussé ses manches

roller *noun* rouleau *Masc.* (*plural*
rouleaux).

rollerblades *plural noun* rollers
Masc. plural.

rollercoaster *noun* montagnes
Fem. plural russes (*literally: Russian
mountains*).

roller skates *plural noun* patins
Masc. plural à roulettes.

Roman Catholic *noun, adjective*
catholique *Masc. & Fem.*

romantic *adjective* romantique.

roof *noun* toit *Masc.*

roof rack *noun* galerie *Fem.*

rook *noun* **1** (*in chess*) tour *Fem.*;
2 (*bird*) freux *Masc.*

room *noun* **1** pièce *Fem.*; **she's in the
other room** elle est dans l'autre
pièce; **it's the biggest room in the
house** c'est la pièce la plus grande
de la maison; **a three-room flat** un
appartement à trois pièces; **2** (*a
bedroom*) chambre *Fem.*; **Freda's in
her room** Freda est dans sa
chambre; **I tidied my room last
night** j'ai rangé ma chambre hier
soir; **3** (*space*) place *Fem.*; **enough
room for two** assez de place pour
deux; **very little room** très peu de
place.

roommate *noun* camarade *Masc. &
Fem.* de chambre.

root *noun* racine *Fem.*

rope *noun* corde *Fem.*

rose *noun* rose *Fem.*

rosebush *noun* rosier *Masc.*

rot *verb* pourrir [2].

rota *noun* tableau *Masc.* de service.

rotten *adjective* pourri.

rough *adjective* **1** (*scratchy*)
rugueux (*Fem.* rugueuse); **2** (*vague*)
approximatif (*Fem.* approximative);
a rough idea une idée
approximative; **3** (*stormy*) agité; **a
rough sea** une mer agitée; **in rough
weather** par gros temps; **4** (*difficult*)
to have a rough time passer par
une période dificile; **5 to sleep
rough** dormir à la dure.

roughly *adjective* (*approximately*)
roughly ten per cent à peu près dix
pour cent; **it takes roughly three
hours** ça prend à peu près trois
heures.

round *noun* **1** (*in a tournament*)
manche *Fem.*; **2** (*of cards*) partie *Fem.*;
3 a round of drinks une tournée;
it's my round c'est ma tournée.
round *adjective* rond; **a round table**
une table ronde.
round *preposition* **1** autour de;
round the city autour de la ville;
round my arm autour de mon bras;
they were sitting round the table
ils étaient assis autour de la table;
2 to go round the shops faire les
magasins; **to go round a museum**
visiter un musée; **it's just round the
corner** c'est tout près.
round *adverb* **1 to go round to**

somebody's house aller chez quelqu'un; **we invited Sally round for lunch** nous avons invité Sally à déjeuner; **2 all the year round** toute l'année.

roundabout *noun* **1** (*for traffic*) rond-point *Masc.*; **2** (*in a fairground*) manège *Masc.*

route *noun* **1** (*that you plan*) itinéraire *Masc.*; **the best route is via Calais** le meilleur itinéraire est par Calais; **2 a bus route** un parcours de bus.

routine *noun* routine *Fem.*

row[1] *noun* **1** rang *Masc.*; **in the front row** au premier rang; **in the back row** au dernier rang; **2** rangée *Fem.*; **a row of books** une rangée de livres; **3 four times in a row** quatre fois de suite.

row[2] *verb* (*in a boat*) ramer [1]; **it's your turn to row** c'est à toi de ramer; **we rowed across the lake** nous avons traversé le lac à la rame.

row[3] *noun* **1** (*a quarrel*) dispute *Fem.*; **to have a row** se disputer; **they've had a row** ils se sont disputés; **I had a row with my parents** je me suis disputé avec mes parents; **2** (*noise*) vacarme *Masc.*; **they were making a terrible row!** ils faisaient un vacarme pas possible!

rowing *noun* aviron *Masc.*; **to go rowing** faire [10] de l'aviron.

rowing boat *noun* barque *Fem.*

royal *adjective* royal (*Masc. plural* royaux); **the royal family** la famille royale.

rub *verb* frotter [1]; **to rub your eyes** se frotter les yeux.

● **to rub something out** effacer [61] quelque chose.

rubber *noun* **1** (*an eraser*) gomme *Fem.*; **2** (*material*) caoutchouc *Masc.*; **rubber soles** des semelles en caoutchouc.

rubbish *noun* **1** (*for the bin*) ordures *Fem. plural*; **2** (*nonsense*) bêtises *Fem. plural*; **you're talking rubbish!** tu dis des bêtises!
rubbish *adjective* nul (*Fem.* nulle); **the film was rubbish** le film était nul; **they're a rubbish band** c'est un groupe nul.

rubbish bin *noun* poubelle *Fem.*

rucksack *noun* sac *Masc.* à dos.

rude *adjective* **1** impoli; **that's rude** c'est impoli; **2 a rude joke** une plaisanterie grossière; **a rude word** un gros mot.

rug *noun* **1** tapis *Masc.*; **2** (*a blanket*) couverture *Fem.*

rugby *noun* rugby *Masc.*; **to play rugby** jouer au rugby; **a rugby match** un match de rugby.

ruin *noun* ruine *Fem.*; **in ruins** en ruines.
ruin *verb* **1** abîmer [1]; **you'll ruin your jacket** tu vas abîmer ta veste; **2** gâcher [1] (*day, holiday*); **it ruined my evening** ça m'a gâché la soirée.

rule *noun* **1** règle *Fem.*; **the rules of the game** les règles du jeu; **2 the school rules** le règlement de l'école; **3 as a rule** en général.

ruler *noun* règle *Fem.*; **I've lost my ruler** j'ai perdu ma règle.

rum *noun* rhum *Masc.*

rumour *noun* rumeur *Fem.*

a
b
c
d
e
f
g
h
i
j
k
l
m
n
o
p
q
r
s
t
u
v
w
x
y
z

run *noun* **1 to go for a run** courir [29]; **2** (*in cricket*) point *Masc.*; **to score fifteen runs** marquer quinze points; **3 in the long run** à long terme.

run *verb* **1** courir [29]; **I ran ten kilometres** j'ai couru dix kilomètres; **he ran across the pitch** il a traversé le terrain en courant; **Kitty ran for the bus** Kitty a couru pour attraper le bus; **2** (*organize*) organiser [1]; **who's running this concert?** qui est-ce qui organise ce concert?; **3** diriger [52] (*a business*); **he ran the firm for forty years** il a dirigé l'entreprise pendant quarante ans; **4** (*a train or bus*) circuler [1]; **the buses don't run on Sundays** les bus ne circulent pas le dimanche; **5 to run a bath** faire [10] couler un bain.

● **to run away** s'enfuir [44].

● **to run into** rentrer [1] dans; **the car ran into a lamppost** la voiture est rentrée dans un réverbère.

● **to run out of something: we've run out of bread** il ne reste plus de pain; **I'm running out of money** je n'ai presque plus d'argent.

● **to run somebody over** écraser [1] quelqu'un; **you'll get run over!** tu vas te faire écraser!

runner *noun* coureur *Masc.*, coureuse *Fem.*

runner-up *noun* second *Masc.*, seconde *Fem.*

running *noun* (*for exercise*) course *Fem.*

running *adjective* **1 running water** l'eau courante; **2 three days running** trois jours de suite; **six times running** six fois de suite.

runway *noun* piste *Fem.*

rush *noun* (*a hurry*) **to be in a rush** être pressé; **sorry, I'm in a rush** désolé, je suis pressé.

rush *verb* **1** (*hurry*) se dépêcher [1]; **I must rush!** il faut que je me dépêche!; **2** (*run*) se précipiter [1]; **she rushed into the street** elle s'est précipitée dans la rue; **3 Louise was rushed to hospital** on a emmené Louise d'urgence à l'hôpital.

rush hour *noun* heures *Fem. plural* de pointe; **in the rush hour** aux heures de pointe.

Russia *noun* Russie *Fem.*; **in Russia** en Russie.

Russian *noun* **1** (*a person*) Russe *Masc. & Fem.*; **2** (*the language*) russe *Masc.*

Russian *adjective* russe.

rust *noun* rouille *Fem.*

rusty *adjective* rouillé.

rye *noun* seigle *Masc.*

Ss

Sabbath *noun* **1** (*Jewish*) sabbat *Masc.*; **2** (*Christian*) dimanche *Masc.*

sack *noun* **1** sac *Masc.*; **2 to get the sack** être mis à la porte.

sack *verb* **to sack somebody** mettre [11] quelqu'un à la porte.

sacred *adjective* sacré.

sacrifice *noun* sacrifice *Masc.*

sad *adjective* triste.

saddle *noun* selle *Fem.*

saddlebag noun sacoche Fem.

sadly adverb **1** tristement; **she looked at me sadly** elle m'a regardé tristement; **2** (unfortunately) malheureusement.

safe adjective **1** (out of danger) hors de danger; **to feel safe** se sentir en sécurité; **2** (not dangerous) pas dangereux (Fem. pas dangereuse); **the path is safe** le sentier n'est pas dangereux; **it's not safe** c'est dangereux.

safety noun sécurité Fem.

safety belt noun ceinture Fem. de sécurité.

safety pin noun épingle Fem. de nourrice.

Sagittarius noun Sagittaire Masc.; **Kylie's Sagittarius** Kylie est Sagittaire.

sail noun voile Fem.

sailing noun voile Fem.; **to go sailing** faire [10] de la voile; **she does a lot of sailing** elle fait beaucoup de voile.

sailing boat noun voilier Masc.

sailor noun marin Masc.

saint noun saint Masc., sainte Fem.

sake noun **1 for your mother's sake** par égard pour ta mère; **2 for heaven's sake** nom de Dieu!

salad noun salade Fem.; **a tomato salad** une salade de tomates.

salad dressing noun vinaigrette Fem.

salami noun saucisson Masc.

salary noun salaire Masc.

sale noun **1** (selling) vente Fem.; **the sale of the house** la vente de la maison; **'for sale'** 'à vendre'; **2 the sales** les soldes Fem. plural; **I bought it in the sales** je l'ai acheté en solde.

sales assistant noun vendeur Masc., vendeuse Fem.

salesman noun représentant Masc.; **he's a salesman** il est représentant.

saleswoman noun représentante Fem.

saliva noun salive Fem.

salmon noun saumon Masc.

salt noun sel Masc.

salty adjective salé.

Salvation Army noun armée Fem. du Salut.

same adjective **1** même; **she said the same thing** elle a dit la même chose; **her birthday's the same day as mine** son anniversaire est le même jour que le mien; **at the same time** en même temps; **their car's the same as ours** ils ont la même voiture que nous; **2 the same** (after verb) pareil; **the two bikes are not the same** les deux vélos ne sont pas pareils; **it's not the same** ce n'est pas pareil.

sample noun échantillon Masc.; **a free sample** un échantillon gratuit.

sand noun sable Masc.

sandal noun sandale Fem.; **a pair of sandals** une paire de sandales.

sand castle noun château Masc. de sable (plural châteaux de sable).

sandpaper noun papier Masc. de verre.

a
b
c
d
e
f
g
h
i
j
k
l
m
n
o
p
q
r
s
t
u
v
w
x
y
z

a
b
c
d
e
f
g
h
i
j
k
l
m
n
o
p
q
r
s
t
u
v
w
x
y
z

sandwich *noun* sandwich *Masc.*; **a ham sandwich** un sandwich au jambon.

sanitary towel *noun* serviette *Fem.* hygiénique.

Santa Claus *noun* le père Noël.

sarcasm *noun* sarcasme *Masc.*

sarcastic *adjective* sarcastique.

sardine *noun* sardine *Fem.*

satchel *noun* cartable *Masc.*

SARS *noun* pneumopathie *Fem.* atypique.

satellite *noun* satellite *Masc.*

satellite dish *noun* antenne *Fem.* parabolique.

satellite television *noun* télévision *Fem.* par satellite.

satisfactory *adjective* satisfaisant.

satisfied *adjective* satisfait.

satisfy *verb* satisfaire [10].

satisfying *adjective* 1 (*pleasing*) satisfaisant; 2 **a satisfying meal** un repas consistant.

Saturday *noun* samedi *Masc.*; **on Saturday** samedi; **I'm going out on Saturday** je sors samedi; **see you on Saturday!** à samedi!; **on Saturdays** le samedi; **the museum is closed on Saturdays** le musée est fermé le samedi; **every Saturday** tous les samedis; **last Saturday** samedi dernier; **next Saturday** samedi prochain; **to have a Saturday job** travailler le samedi.

sauce *noun* sauce *Fem.*

saucepan *noun* casserole *Fem.*

saucer *noun* soucoupe *Fem.*

sausage *noun* 1 saucisse *Fem.*; 2 (*salami*) saucisson *Masc.*

savage *noun* sauvage *Masc. & Fem.*

save *verb* 1 (*rescue*) sauver [1]; **to save somebody's life** sauver la vie à quelqu'un; **the doctors saved his life** les médecins lui ont sauvé la vie; 2 mettre [11] de côté (*money, food*); **I've saved £60** j'ai mis soixante livres de côté; 3 (*avoid spending*) économiser [1]; **I walk to school to save money** je vais à l'école à pied pour économiser de l'argent; 4 **to save time** gagner [1] du temps; **we'll take a taxi to save time** on va prendre un taxi pour gagner du temps; 5 (*on a computer*) sauvegarder [1].

● **to save up** mettre [11] de l'argent de côté; **I'm saving up to go to Spain** je mets de l'argent de côté pour aller en Espagne.

savings *plural noun* économies *Fem. plural*; **I've spent all my savings** j'ai dépensé toutes mes économies.

savoury *adjective* salé; **I prefer savoury things to sweet things** j'aime mieux les choses salées que les choses sucrées.

saw *noun* scie *Fem.*

sawdust *noun* sciure *Fem.*

sax *noun* saxo *Masc.* (*informal*); **to play the sax** jouer du saxo.

saxophone *noun* saxophone *Masc.*; **to play the saxophone** jouer du saxophone.

say *verb* 1 dire [9]; **what did you say?** qu'est-ce que tu as dit?; **she says she's tired** elle dit qu'elle est fatiguée; **he said to wait here** il a dit d'attendre ici; **as they say** comme on dit; **that goes without saying** cela va sans dire; **2 to say something again** répéter [24] quelque chose.

saying noun dicton Masc.; **as the saying goes** comme on dit.

scab noun croûte Fem.

scale noun **1** (*of a map or model*) échelle Fem.; **large-scale** à grande échelle; **2** (*extent*) ampleur Fem.; **the scale of the disaster** l'ampleur du désastre; **3** (*in music*) gamme Fem.; **4** (*of a fish*) écaille Fem.

scales noun **1** balance Fem. singular; **kitchen scales** une balance de cuisine; **2 bathroom scales** un pèse-personne Masc. singular.

scallop noun coquille Fem. Saint-Jacques.

scalp noun cuir Masc. chevelu.

scandal noun **1** scandale Masc.; **2** (*gossip*) ragots Masc. plural.

Scandinavia noun Scandinavie Fem.

Scandinavian adjective scandinave.

scanner noun scanner Masc.

scar noun cicatrice Fem.

scarce adjective rare.

scarcely adverb à peine.

scare noun **1** panique Fem.; **it caused a scare** cela a provoqué une panique; **2 a bomb scare** une alerte à la bombe.
scare verb **to scare somebody** faire [10] peur à quelqu'un; **you scared me!** tu m'as fait peur!

scarecrow noun épouvantail Masc.

scared adjective **to be scared** avoir [5] peur; **I'm scared!** j'ai peur; **to be scared of** avoir [5] peur de; **he's scared of dogs** il a peur des chiens; **I'm scared of falling** j'ai peur de tomber.

scarf noun **1** (*silky*) foulard Masc.; **2** (*long, warm*) écharpe Fem.

scary adjective effrayant.

scene noun **1** (*of an incident or a crime*) lieux Masc. plural; **to be on the scene** être sur les lieux; **the scene of the crime** le lieu du crime; **2** (*world*) monde Masc.; **on the music scene** dans le monde de la musique; **3 scenes of violence** des incidents violents; **4 to make a scene** faire une scène.

scenery noun **1** (*landscape*) paysage Masc.; **2** (*theatrical*) décors Masc. plural.

scent noun parfum Masc.

scented adjective parfumé.

schedule noun programme Masc.

scheduled flight noun vol Masc. régulier.

scheme noun projet Masc.

scholarship noun bourse Fem.

school noun école Fem.; **at school** à l'école; **to go to school** aller à l'école.

schoolbook noun livre Masc. scolaire.

schoolboy noun écolier Masc.

schoolchildren plural noun écoliers Masc. plural.

a
b
c
d
e
f
g
h
i
j
k
l
m
n
o
p
q
r
s
t
u
v
w
x
y
z

schoolfriend *noun* camarade *Masc. & Fem.* de classe.

schoolgirl *noun* écolière *Fem.*

science *noun* science *Fem.*; **I like science** j'aime la science; **the science teacher** le prof des sciences.

science fiction *noun* science-fiction *Fem.*

scientific *adjective* scientifique.

scientist *noun* scientifique *Masc. & Fem.*

scissors *plural noun* ciseaux *Masc. plural*; **a pair of scissors** une paire de ciseaux.

scoff *verb* (*eat*) bouffer [1] (*informal*).

scoop *noun* **1** (*utensil*) cuillère *Fem.* à glace; **2** (*content*) boule *Fem.*; **how many scoops would you like?** vous voulez combien de boules?

scooter *noun* **1** (*motor scooter*) scooter *Masc.*; **2** (*for a child*) trottinette *Fem.*

score *noun* score *Masc.*; **the score was three two** le score était trois à deux.
score *verb* **1** marquer [1]; **Lenny scored a goal** Lenny a marqué un but; **I scored three points** j'ai marqué trois points; **2** (*keep score*) compter [1] les points.

Scorpio *noun* Scorpion *Masc.*; **Jess is Scorpio** Jess est Scorpion.

Scot *noun* Écossais *Masc.*, Écossaise *Fem.*; **the Scots** les Écossais *Masc. plural*.

Scotland *noun* Écosse *Fem.*; **in Scotland** en Écosse; **to Scotland** en Écosse; **Pauline's from Scotland** Pauline est écossaise.

Scots *adjective* écossais; **a Scots accent** un accent écossais.

Scotsman *noun* Écossais *Masc.*

Scotswoman *noun* Écossaise *Fem.*

Scottish *adjective* écossais; **a Scottish accent** un accent écossais.

scout *noun* scout *Masc.*

scrambled eggs *noun* œufs *Masc. plural* brouillés.

scrap *noun* **a scrap of paper** un bout de papier.

scrapbook *noun* album *Masc.*

scrape *verb* gratter [1].

scratch *noun* **1** (*on your skin*) égratignure *Fem.*; **2** (*on a surface*) rayure *Fem.*; ★ **to start from scratch** partir de zéro.
scratch *verb* (*scratch yourself*) se gratter [1]; **to scratch your head** se gratter la tête.

scream *noun* cri *Masc.*
scream *verb* crier [1].

screen *noun* écran *Masc.*; **on the screen** à l'écran.

screw *noun* vis *Fem.*
screw *verb* visser [1].

screwdriver *noun* tournevis *Masc.*

scribble *verb* griffonner [1].

scrub *verb* récurer [1] (*a saucepan*); **to scrub your nails** se brosser [1] les ongles.

scuba diving *noun* plongée *Fem.* sous-marine.

sculptor *noun* sculpteur *Masc.*, sculpteuse *Fem*; **Rebecca's a sculptor** Rebecca est sculpteur.

sculpture *noun* sculpture *Fem*.

sea *noun* mer *Fem*.

seafood *noun* fruits *Masc. plural* de mer; **I love seafood** j'adore les fruits de mer.

seagull *noun* mouette *Fem*.

seal *noun* (*animal*) phoque *Masc.* **seal** *verb* coller [1] (*envelope*).

seaman *noun* marin *Masc.*

search *verb* **1** fouiller [1]; **I've searched my desk but I can't find the letter** j'ai fouillé dans mon bureau mais je ne trouve pas la lettre; **the police searched the house/the room** la police a fouillé la maison/la chambre; **2 to search for** chercher [1]; **I've been searching everywhere for the scissors** j'ai cherché les ciseaux partout. **search** *noun* fouille *Fem*.

seashell *noun* coquillage *Masc.*

seasick *adjective* **to be seasick** avoir le mal de mer.

seaside *noun* **at the seaside** au bord de la mer.

season *noun* saison *Fem*; **the rugby season** la saison de rugby; **strawberries are not in season at the moment** ce n'est pas la saison des fraises en ce moment; **off-season prices** des prix hors saison.

season ticket *noun* carte *Fem.* d'abonnement.

seat *noun* **1** siège *Masc.*; (*in a car*) **the front seat** le siège avant; **the back seat** le siège arrière; **take a**

seat assieds-toi; **2** (*in a cinema, theatre, etc*) place *Fem.*; **to book a seat** réserver une place; **can you keep my seat?** est-ce que tu peux garder ma place?

seatbelt *noun* ceinture *Fem.* de sécurité.

seaweed *noun* algues *Fem. plural*.

second *noun* seconde *Fem.*; **can you wait a second?** est-ce que tu peux attendre une seconde? **second** *adjective* **1** deuxième; **for the second time** pour la deuxième fois; **2 the second of July** le deux juillet.

secondary school *noun* **1** collège *Masc.* (*up to the end of the equivalent of Year 10*); **2** lycée *Masc.* (*for the equivalent of Years 11 to 13*).

second class *noun* (*category*) deuxième classe *Fem.*; **a second class team** une équipe de niveau très moyen.

secondhand *adjective, adverb* d'occasion; **a secondhand bike** un vélo d'occasion; **I bought it secondhand** je l'ai acheté d'occasion.

secondly *adverb* deuxièmement.

secret *noun* secret *Masc.*; **to keep a secret** garder un secret; **in secret** en secret. **secret** *adjective* secret (*Fem.* secrète); **a secret plan** un projet secret.

secretarial college *noun* école *Fem.* de secrétariat.

secretary *noun* secrétaire *Masc. & Fem.*; **she's a secretary** elle est

a

secrétaire; **the secretary's office** le secrétariat.

b

secretly adverb secrètement.

c

sect noun secte Fem.

d

section noun section Fem.

e

security noun sécurité Fem.

f

security guard noun vigile Masc.; **he's a security guard** il est vigile.

g

see verb 1 voir [13]; **I saw Lindy yesterday** j'ai vu Lindy hier; **have you seen the film?** est-ce que tu as vu le film?; **I haven't see her for ages** ça fait une éternité que je ne l'ai pas vue; **I'll see what I can do** je vais voir ce que je peux faire; **2 to be able to see** voir [13]; **I can't see anything** je ne vois rien; **3 see you!** salut!; **see you on Saturday!** à samedi!; **see you soon!** à bientôt!

h

i

j

k

l

m

● **to see to something** s'occuper [1] de quelque chose; **Jo's seeing to the drinks** Jo s'occupe des boissons.

n

seed noun graine Fem.; **to plant seeds** semer des graines.

o

p

seem verb 1 paraître [57]; **it seems odd to me** ça me paraît bizarre; **it seems he's left** il paraît qu'il est parti; **2** (look, appear to be) avoir [5] l'air; **he seems a bit shy** il a l'air un peu timide; **the museum seems to be closed** le musée a l'air d'être fermé.

q

r

s

t

u

seesaw noun tapecul Masc.

v

select verb sélectionner [1].

selection noun sélection Fem.

w

self-confidence noun confiance Fem. en soi; **she doesn't have much self-confidence** elle n'a pas beaucoup de confiance en elle.

x

y

z

self-confident adjective plein d'assurance; **he's very self-confident** il est très sûr de lui.

self-conscious adjective timide.

self-contained noun a **self-contained flat** un appartement indépendant.

self-employed noun the self-employed les travailleurs indépendants Masc. plural. **self-employed** adjective **to be self-employed** travailler à son compte; **my parents are self-employed** mes parents travaillent à leur compte.

selfish adjective égoïste.

self-service adjective a **self-service restaurant** un self (informal).

sell verb vendre [3]; **to sell something to somebody** vendre quelque chose à quelqu'un; **I sold him my bike** je lui ai vendu mon vélo; **the house has been sold** la maison a été vendue; **the concert's sold out** il ne reste plus de billets pour le concert.

sell-by date noun date Fem. limite de vente.

seller noun vendeur Masc., vendeuse Fem.

Sellotape™ noun Scotch™ Masc. **Sellotape™** verb **to sellotape something** scotcher [1] quelque chose (informal).

semi noun maison Fem. jumelée (literally: a twinned house); **we live in a semi** nous habitons dans une maison jumelée.

semicircle noun demi-cercle Masc.

semicolon *noun* point-virgule *Masc.*

semi-detached house *noun* maison *Fem.* jumelée (*literally: a twinned house*); **we live in a semi-detached house** nous habitons dans une maison jumelée.

semi-final *noun* demi-finale *Fem.*

semi-skimmed milk *noun* lait *Masc.* demi-écrémé.

send *verb* envoyer [40]; **to send something to somebody** envoyer quelque chose à quelqu'un; **I sent her a present for her birthday** je lui ai envoyé un cadeau pour son anniversaire.

● **to send back: to send somebody back** renvoyer [40] quelqu'un; **to send something back** renvoyer [40] quelque chose.

sender *noun* expéditeur *Masc.*, expéditrice *Fem.*

senior citizen *noun* personne *Fem.* du troisième âge.

sensation *noun* **1** (*feeling*) sensation *Fem.*; **2** (*impact*) sensation *Fem.*; **she caused a sensation** elle a fait sensation.

sensational *adjective* sensationnel (*Fem.* sensationnelle).

sense *noun* **1** sens *Masc.*; **common sense** le bon sens; **it doesn't make sense** ça n'a pas de sens; **it makes sense** ça paraît logique; **to have a sense of humour** avoir le sens de l'humour; **she has no sense of humour** elle n'a aucun sens de l'humour; **2 the sense of smell** l'odorat *Masc.*; **the sense of touch** le toucher.

sensible *adjective* raisonnable; **she's very sensible** elle est très raisonnable; **it's a sensible decision** c'est une décision raisonnable.

sensitive *adjective* sensible; **for sensitive skin** pour peaux sensibles.

sentence *noun* **1** phrase *Fem.*; **écris une phrase en français** write a sentence in French; **2 the death sentence** la peine de mort. **sentence** *verb* condamner [1]; **to be sentenced to death** être condamné à mort.

sentimental *adjective* sentimental (*Masc. plural* sentimentaux).

separate *adjective* **1** à part; **in a separate pile** dans une pile à part; **on a separate sheet of paper** sur une feuille à part; **2** (*different*) autre; **that's a separate problem** c'est un autre problème; **3 they have separate rooms** ils ont chacun leur chambre.
separate *verb* **1** séparer [1]; **2** (*a couple*) se séparer [1].

separately *adverb* séparément.

separation *noun* séparation *Fem.*

September *noun* septembre *Masc.*; **in September** en septembre.

sequel *noun* suite *Fem.*

sequence *noun* **1** série *Fem.*; **a sequence of events** une série d'événements; **2 in sequence** dans l'ordre; **3** (*in a film*) séquence *Fem.*

sergeant *noun* **1** (*in the police*) brigadier *Masc.*; **2** (*in the army*) sergent *Masc.*

a
b
c
d
e
f
g
h
i
j
k
l
m
n
o
p
q
r
s
t
u
v
w
x
y
z

serial *noun* feuilleton *Masc.*

series *noun* série *Fem.*; **a television series** une série télévisée.

serious *adjective* **1** sérieux (*Fem.* sérieuse); **a serious discussion** une discussion sérieuse; **are you serious?** sérieusement?; **2** grave (*illness, injury, mistake, problem*); **we have a serious problem** nous avons un grave problème.

seriously *adverb* **1** sérieusement; **seriously, I have to go now** sérieusement je dois partir maintenant; **seriously?** vraiment?; **2 to take somebody seriously** prendre quelqu'un au sérieux; **3** gravement (*ill, injured*); **she is seriously ill** elle est gravement malade.

servant *noun* domestique *Masc. & Fem.*

serve *noun* (*in tennis*) service *Masc.*; **it's my serve** c'est à moi de servir.
serve *verb* **1** (*in tennis*) servir [71]; **2** servir; **can you serve the vegetables, please?** est-ce que tu peux servir les légumes, s'il te plaît?; **they served the fish with a lemon sauce** ils ont servi le poisson accompagné d'une sauce au citron; ★ **it serves him right** c'est bien fait pour lui.

service *noun* **1** (*in a restaurant, from a company, etc*) service *Masc.*; **the service is very slow** le service est très lent; **service is included** le service est compris; **is there a maid service?** est-ce qu'il y a une femme de ménage?; **2 the emergency services** les services des urgences; **3** (*church service*) office *Masc.*; **4** (*of a car or machine*) révision *Fem.*
service *verb* réviser [1] (*a car or a machine*).

service area *noun* aire *Fem.* de services.

service charge *noun* service *Masc.*; **what is the service charge?** le service est de combien?; **there is no service charge** le service est compris.

service station *noun* station-service *Fem.* (*plural* stations-service).

serviette *noun* serviette *Fem.*

session *noun* séance *Fem.*

set *noun* **1** (*for playing a game*) jeu *Masc.* (*plural* jeux); **a chess set** un jeu d'échecs; **2 a train set** un petit train; **3** (*in tennis*) set *Masc.*
set *adjective* fixe; **at a set time** à une heure fixe; **a set menu** un menu fixe.
set *verb* **1** fixer [1] (*date, time*); **2** établir [2] (*record*); **3 to set the table** mettre [11] la table; **to set an alarm clock** mettre [11] un réveil; **I've set my alarm for seven** j'ai mis mon réveil à sept heures; **4 to set a watch** régler [24] une montre; **5** (*sun*) se coucher [1].

● **to set off** partir [58]; **we're setting off at ten** nous allons partir à dix heures; **they set off for Paris yesterday** ils sont partis pour Paris hier.

● **to set off something 1** faire [10] partir (*firework*); **2** faire [10] exploser (*bomb*); **3** déclencher [1] (*alarm*).

- **to set out** partir [58]; **they set out for Paris yesterday** ils sont partis pour Paris hier.

settee noun canapé Masc.

settle verb régler [24] (a bill or a problem).

seven number sept; **Rosie's seven** Rosie a sept ans.

seventeen number dix-sept; **Jonny's seventeen** Jonny a dix-sept ans.

seventh adjective septième; **on the seventh floor** au septième étage; **the seventh of July** le sept juillet.

seventies plural noun **the seventies** les années soixante-dix; **in the seventies** aux années soixante-dix.

seventieth adjective soixante-dixième; **it's her seventieth birthday** elle fête ses soixante-dix ans.

seventy number soixante-dix; **my grandma's seventy** ma grand-mère a soixante-dix ans.

several adjective, pronoun plusieurs; **I've seen her several times** je l'ai vue plusieurs fois; **I've read several of her novels** j'ai lu plusieurs de ses romans; **he took several** il en a pris plusieurs.

severe adjective **1** (person) sévère; **2** (weather) rigoureux (Fem. rigoureuse); **3** (injuries) grave.

sew verb coudre [28].

sewer noun égout Masc.

sewing noun couture Fem.; **I like sewing** j'aime la couture.

sewing machine noun machine Fem. à coudre.

sex noun **1** (gender) sexe Masc.; **2** (intercourse) rapports Masc. plural sexuels; **to have sex with someone** coucher avec quelqu'un.

sex education noun éducation Fem. sexuelle.

sexism noun sexisme Masc.

sexist adjective sexiste; **sexist remarks** des propos sexistes.

sexual adjective sexuel (Fem. sexuelle).

sexual harassment noun harcèlement Masc. sexuel.

sexuality noun sexualité Fem.

sexy adjective sexy.

shabby adjective miteux (Fem. miteuse).

shade noun **1** (of a colour) ton Masc.; **a pretty shade of green** un joli vert; **2 in the shade** à l'ombre.

shadow noun ombre Fem.

shake verb **1** (tremble) trembler [1]; **my hands are shaking** j'ai les mains qui tremblent; **2 to shake something** secouer [1] quelque chose; **3 to shake hands with somebody** serrer [1] la main à quelqu'un; **she shook hands with me** elle m'a serré la main; **we shook hands** nous nous sommes serré la main; **4 to shake your head** (meaning no) faire [10] non de la tête.

shaken adjective bouleversé; **I was shaken by the news** j'ai été bouleversé par la nouvelle.

shall verb **shall I come with you?** tu veux que je t'accompagne?; **shall**

we stop now? si on s'arrêtait maintenant?

shallow *adjective* peu profond; **the water's very shallow here** l'eau est très peu profonde ici.

shallow end *noun* partie *Fem.* la moins profonde de la piscine.

shambles *noun* pagaille *Fem.* (*informal*); **it was a total shambles!** ça a été la pagaille complète!

shame *noun* **1** honte *Fem.*; **shame on you!** tu devrais avoir honte!; **2 what a shame!** quel dommage!; **it's a shame she can't come** c'est dommage qu'elle ne puisse pas venir (*note that 'c'est dommage que' is followed by a verb in the subjunctive*).

shameful *adjective* honteux (*Fem.* honteuse).

shampoo *noun* shampooing *Masc.*; **I bought some shampoo** j'ai acheté du shampooing.

shamrock *noun* trèfle *Masc.*

shandy *noun* panaché *Masc.*; **a half of shandy** un demi panaché.

shape *noun* forme *Fem.*

share *noun* **1** part *Fem.*; **your share of the money** ta part de l'argent; **he paid his fair share** il a payé sa part; **2** (*in a company*) action *Fem.*
share *verb* partager [52]; **I'm sharing a room with Emma** je partage une chambre avec Emma.
• **to share out** partager [52], répartir [58].

shark *noun* requin *Masc.*

sharp *adjective* **1** (*knife*) bien aiguisé; **this knife isn't very sharp**

ce couteau ne coupe pas très bien; **2 a sharp pencil** un crayon bien taillé; **3 a sharp bend** un virage brusque; **4** (*clever*) intelligent.

sharpen *verb* **1** (*a pencil*) tailler [1]; **2** (*a knife*) aiguiser [1].

sharpener *noun* taille-crayon *Masc.*

shave *verb* **1** (*have a shave*) se raser [1]; **he's just shaving** il est en train de se raser; **2 to shave your legs** se raser [1] les jambes; **to shave off your beard** se raser la barbe.

shaver *noun* **an electric shaver** un rasoir électrique.

shaving cream *noun* crème *Fem.* à raser.

shaving foam *noun* mousse *Fem.* à raser.

she *pronoun* elle; **she's in her room** elle est dans sa chambre; **she's a student** elle est étudiante; **she's a very good teacher** c'est un très bon prof; **here she is!** la voici!; **there she is!** la voilà!

shed *noun* remise *Fem.*

sheep *noun* mouton *Masc.*

sheepdog *noun* chien *Masc.* de berger (*plural* chiens de berger).

sheer *adjective* **1** pur; **it's sheer stupidity!** c'est de la pure bêtise!; **2** (*tights*) extra-fin.

sheet *noun* **1** (*for a bed*) drap *Masc.*; **2 a sheet of paper** une feuille de papier; **a blank sheet** une feuille blanche; **3** (*of glass or metal*) plaque; ★ **to be as white as a sheet** être blanc comme un linge; **she was as white as a sheet** elle était blanche comme un linge.

shelf *noun* **1** (*in the home*) étagère *Fem.*; **a set of shelves** une étagère; **2** (*in a shop, in a fridge*) rayon *Masc.*

shell *noun* **1** (*of an egg or a nut*) coquille *Fem.*; **2** (*seashell*) coquillage *Masc.*; **3** (*explosive*) obus *Masc.*

shellfish *noun* fruits *Masc. plural* de mer.

shelter *noun* **1** abri *Masc.*; **in the shelter of** à l'abri de; **to take shelter from the rain** se mettre à l'abri de la pluie; **2 a bus shelter** un abribus™.

shepherd *noun* berger *Masc.*

sheriff *noun* shérif *Masc.*

sherry *noun* sherry *Masc.*

Shetland Islands *noun* îles *Fem. plural* Shetland.

shield *noun* bouclier *Masc.*

shift *noun* service *Masc.*; **the night shift** le service de nuit; **to be on night shift** être de nuit.
shift *verb* **to shift something** déplacer [61] quelque chose; **can you help me shift this table?** est-ce que tu peux m'aider à déplacer cette table?

shifty *adjective* louche; **he looks a bit shifty** il a l'air un peu louche; **a shifty-looking guy** un type un peu louche.

shin *noun* tibia *Masc.*

shine *verb* briller [1].

shiny *adjective* brillant.

ship *noun* **1** bateau *Masc.*; **2 a passenger ship** un paquebot; **3** (*large naval vessel*) navire *Masc.*

shipbuilding *noun* construction *Fem.* navale.

shipyard *noun* chantier *Masc.* naval.

shirt *noun* **1** (*man's*) chemise *Fem.*; **2** (*woman's*) chemisier *Masc.*

shiver *verb* frissonner [1].

shock *noun* **1** choc *Masc.*; **it was a shock** ça a été un choc; **it gave me a shock** j'ai eu un choc; **2 an electric shock** une décharge; **to get an electric shock** prendre une décharge.
shock *verb* choquer [1].

shocked *adjective* choqué.

shocking *adjective* choquant.

shoe *noun* chaussure *Fem.*; **a pair of shoes** une paire de chaussures.

shoelace *noun* lacet *Masc.*

shoe polish *noun* cirage *Masc.*

shoe shop *noun* magasin *Masc.* de chaussures.

shoot *verb* **1** (*fire*) tirer [1]; **to shoot at somebody** tirer sur quelqu'un; **she shot him in the leg** elle lui a tiré une balle dans la jambe; **he was shot in the arm** il a reçu une balle dans le bras; **2** (*kill*) abattre [21]; **he was shot by terrorists** il a été abattu par des terroristes; **3** (*execute*) fusiller [1]; **4** (*in football, hockey*) shooter [1]; **5 to shoot a film** tourner [1] un film.

shooting *noun* tir *Masc.*

shop *noun* magasin *Masc.*; **a shoe shop** un magasin de chaussures; **to go round the shops** faire les magasins.

shop assistant *noun* vendeur *Masc.*, vendeuse *Fem.*; **Brad's a shop assistant** Brad est vendeur.

a
b
c
d
e
f
g
h
i
j
k
l
m
n
o
p
q
r
s
t
u
v
w
x
y
z

a **shopkeeper** *noun* commerçant
Masc., commerçante Fem.

b **shoplifter** *noun* voleur Masc. à
c l'étalage, voleuse Fem. à l'étalage.

shoplifting *noun* vol Masc. à
d l'étalage.

e **shopping** *noun* courses Fem. plural;
f **can you put the shopping away?**
est-ce que tu peux ranger les
g courses?; **I've got a lot of shopping
to do** j'ai beaucoup de courses à
h faire; **to go shopping** (for food) faire
des courses; (for fun, to buy clothes or
i presents) faire du shopping.

j **shopping bag** *noun* sac Masc. à
provisions.

k **shopping centre** *noun* centre
l Masc. commercial.

shopping trolley *noun* 1 (in a
m supermarket) chariot Masc.;
2 (personal) caddie™ Masc.

n
shop window *noun* vitrine Fem.
o
shore *noun* côte Fem.
p
short *adjective* 1 court; **a short
q dress** une robe courte; **she has
short hair** elle a les cheveux courts;
r 2 **a short break** une petite pause; **to
go for a short walk** faire une petite
s promenade; **it's a short walk from
the station** c'est à quelques minutes
t à pied de la gare; 3 **to be short of
something** ne pas avoir beaucoup
u de quelque chose; **we're a bit short
of money at the moment** nous
v n'avons pas beaucoup d'argent en ce
w moment; **we're getting short of
time** il ne nous reste pas beaucoup
x de temps.

y **shortage** *noun* pénurie Fem.

z **shortbread** *noun* sablé Masc.

shortcrust pastry *noun* pâte
Fem. brisée.

short cut *noun* raccourci Masc.; **we
took a short cut** nous avons pris un
raccourci.

shorten *verb* 1 (clothes) raccourcir
[2]; 2 (a stay, journey) écourter [1].

shortly *adverb* bientôt.

shorts *plural noun* short Masc.
singular; **a pair of shorts** un short;
my red shorts mon short rouge.

short-sighted *adjective* myope;
I'm short-sighted je suis myope.

short story *noun* nouvelle Fem.

shot *noun* 1 (from a gun) coup Masc.
de feu (plural coups de feu); 2 (a
photo) photo Fem.; **I took several
shots of the garden** j'ai pris
plusieurs photos du jardin.

shotgun *noun* fusil Masc. de chasse
(plural fusils de chasse).

should *verb* 1 ('should' meaning
'ought to' is translated by the
conditional tense of 'devoir') devoir
[8]; **you should ask Simon** tu
devrais demander à Simon; **the
potatoes should be cooked now**
les pommes de terre devraient être
cuites maintenant; 2 ('should have'
is translated by the past conditional
tense of 'devoir') **you should have
told me** tu aurais dû me le dire; **I
shouldn't have stayed** je n'aurais
pas dû rester; 3 ('should' meaning
'would' is translated by the
conditional tense of the verb) **I
should forget it if I were you** à ta
place je l'oublierais; 4 **I should
think** à mon avis; **I should think**

he's forgotten à mon avis, il a oublié.

shoulder noun épaule Fem.

shoulder bag noun sac Masc. à bandoulière.

shout noun cri Masc.
shout verb crier [1]; **stop shouting!** arrêtez de crier!; **they shouted at us to come back** ils nous ont crié de revenir.

shovel noun pelle Fem.

show noun **1** (on stage) spectacle Masc.; **we went to see a show** nous sommes allés voir un spectacle; **2** (on TV) émission; **he has a TV show** il a une émission à la télé; **3** (exhibition) salon; **the motor show** le salon des automobiles.
show verb **1** montrer [1]; **to show something to somebody** montrer quelque chose à quelqu'un; **I'll show you my photos** je te montrerai mes photos; **to show somebody how to do** montrer à quelqu'un comment on fait; **he showed me how to make pancakes** il m'a montré comment on fait les crêpes; **2 it shows!** ça se voit!
● **to show off** frimer [1] (informal).

shower noun **1** (in a bathroom) douche Fem.; **to have a shower** prendre une douche; **2** (of rain) averse Fem.

show-jumping noun saut Masc. d'obstacles.

show-off noun frimeur Masc., frimeuse Fem. (informal).

shriek verb hurler [1].

shrimp noun crevette Fem.

shrine noun autel Masc.

shrink verb rétrécir [2].

Shrove Tuesday noun mardi Masc. gras.

shrug verb **to shrug your shoulders** hausser [1] les épaules.

shuffle verb **to shuffle the cards** battre [21] les cartes.

shut adjective fermé; **the shops are shut** les magasins sont fermés.
shut verb fermer [1]; **can you shut the door please?** est-ce que tu peux fermer la porte, s'il te plaît?; **the shops shut at six** les magasins ferment à six heures.
● **to shut up** (be quiet) se taire [76]; **shut up!** tais-toi!

shutter noun volet Masc.

shuttle noun navette Fem.; **there's a shuttle service from the airport** il y a une navette de l'aéroport.

shuttlecock noun volant Masc.

shy adjective timide.

shyness noun timidité Fem.

Sicily noun Sicile Fem.; **to Sicily** en Sicile; **in Sicily** en Sicile.

sick adjective **1** (ill) malade; **2 to be sick** (vomit) vomir [2]; **I was sick several times** j'ai vomi plusieurs fois; **to feel sick** avoir [5] mal au cœur; **3 a sick joke** une plaisanterie malsaine; **4 to be sick of something** en avoir assez de quelque chose; **I'm sick of staying at home every night** j'en ai assez de rester à la maison tous les soirs.

sickness noun maladie Fem.

side noun **1** côté Masc.; **on the other side of the street** de l'autre côté de

561

a b c d e f g h i j k l m n o p q r s t u v w x y z

la rue; **on the wrong side** du mauvais côté; **I'm on your side** (*I agree with you*) je suis de ton côté; **2** (*edge*) bord *Masc.*; **at the side of the road** au bord de la route; **by the side of the pool** au bord de la piscine; **3** (*team*) équipe; **she plays on our side** elle joue dans notre équipe; **4 to take sides** prendre parti; **5 side by side** côte à côte.

sideboard *noun* buffet *Masc.*

sideburns *noun* pattes *Fem. plural.*

side-effect *noun* effet *Masc.* secondaire.

side street *noun* petite rue *Fem.*

siege *noun* siège *Masc.*

sieve *noun* passoire *Fem.*

sigh *noun* soupir *Masc.*
sigh *verb* pousser [1] un soupir.

sight *noun* **1** spectacle *Masc.*; **it was a marvellous sight** c'était un spectacle merveilleux; **2 at the sight of** à la vue de; **3** (*eyesight*) vue *Fem.*; **to have poor sight** avoir une mauvaise vue; **to know somebody by sight** connaître quelqu'un de vue; **out of sight** caché; **4 to see the sights** visiter les attractions touristiques.

sightseeing *noun* tourisme *Masc.*; **to do some sightseeing** faire du tourisme.

sign *noun* **1** (*notice*) panneau *Masc.* (*plural* panneaux); **there's a sign on the door** il y a un panneau sur la porte; **2** (*trace, indication*) signe *Masc.*; **3** (*of the Zodiac*) signe *Masc.*; **what sign are you?** tu es de quel signe?
sign *verb* **1** signer [1]; **to sign a**

cheque signer un chèque; **2** (*using sign language*) communiquer [1] en langage par signes.

● **to sign on** (*as unemployed*) s'inscrire [38] au chômage.

signal *noun* signal *Masc.* (*plural* signaux).

signature *noun* signature *Fem.*

significance *noun* importance *Fem.*

significant *adjective* important.

sign language *noun* langage *Masc.* par signes.

signpost *noun* poteau *Masc.* indicateur (*plural* poteaux indicateurs).

silence *noun* silence *Masc.*

silent *adjective* silencieux (*Fem.* silencieuse).

silicon chip *noun* puce *Fem.* électronique.

silk *noun* soie *Fem.*
silk *adjective* en soie; **a silk shirt** une chemise en soie.

silky *adjective* soyeux (*Fem.* soyeuse).

silly *adjective* idiot; **it was a really silly thing to do** c'était vraiment idiot.

silver *noun* argent *Masc.*
silver *adjective* **a silver spoon** une cuillère en argent; **a silver medal** une médaille d'argent.

SIM card *noun* carte *Fem.* SIM.

similar *adjective* semblable.

similarity *noun* ressemblance *Fem.*

simmer *verb* **to simmer something** faire [10] mijoter quelque chose.

simple *adjective* facile.

simplify *verb* simplifier [1].

simply *adverb* simplement.

sin *noun* péché *Masc.*

since *preposition, adverb, conjunction* **1** depuis (*notice that French uses the present tense where English uses 'have done' or 'have been doing'*) **I have been in Paris since Saturday** je suis à Paris depuis samedi; **I've been learning French since last year** j'apprends le français depuis l'année dernière; **2** depuis que (*the same thing happens with tenses here as above*) **since I have known him** depuis que je le connais; **since I've been learning French** depuis que j'apprends le français; **3 I haven't seen her since** je ne l'ai pas revue depuis; **I haven't seen her since Monday** je ne l'ai pas revue depuis lundi; **since when?** depuis quand?; **4** (*because*) puisque; **since it was raining, the match was cancelled** puisqu'il pleuvait le match a été annulé.

sincere *adjective* sincère.

sincerely *adverb* **Yours sincerely** (*in a business letter*) Veuillez agréer Madame (*or* Monsieur) l'expression de mes sentiments distingués; (*to somebody you know*) Cordialement (*in French there are very formal and rigid formulae for signing letters*).

sing *verb* chanter [1].

singer *noun* chanteur *Masc.*, chanteuse *Fem.*

singing *noun* **1** chant *Masc.*; **a singing lesson** une leçon de chant; **2 I like singing** j'aime chanter.

single *noun* aller *Masc.* simple; **a single to Lyons, please** un aller simple pour Lyon, s'il vous plaît. **single** *adjective* **1** (*not married*) célibataire; **2 a single room** une chambre pour une personne; **a single bed** un lit pour une personne; **3 not a single** pas un seul, pas une seule; **I haven't had a single reply** je n'ai pas reçu une seule réponse.

single parent *noun* **she's a single parent** elle élève ses enfants toute seule; **a single-parent family** une famille monoparentale.

singles *plural noun* (*in tennis*) simple *Masc. singular*; **the women's singles** le simple dames; **the men's singles** le simple messieurs.

singular *noun* singulier *Masc.*; **in the singular** au singulier.

sink *noun* évier *Masc.* **sink** *verb* couler [1].

sir *noun* monsieur *Masc.*; **yes, sir** oui, Monsieur.

siren *noun* sirène *Fem.*

sister *noun* sœur *Fem.*; **my sister's ten** ma sœur a dix ans.

sister-in-law *noun* belle-sœur *Fem.* (*plural* belles-sœurs).

sit *verb* **1** s'asseoir [20]; **you can sit on the sofa** tu peux t'asseoir sur le canapé; **I can sit on the floor** je peux m'asseoir par terre; **2 to be sitting** être [6] assis; **Leila was**

a
b
c
d
e
f
g
h
i
j
k
l
m
n
o
p
q
r
s
t
u
v
w
x
y
z

sitting on the sofa Leila était assise sur le canapé; **3 to sit an exam** passer [1] un examen; **she's sitting her driving test on Thursday** elle passe son permis jeudi.

● **to sit down** s'asseoir [20]; **he sat down on a chair** il s'est assis sur une chaise; **do sit down** asseyez-vous.

sitcom noun comédie Fem. de situation (plural comédies de situation).

site noun **1 a building site** un chantier; **2 a camping site** un camping; **3 an archaeological site** un site archéologique.

sitting room noun salon Masc.

situated adjective **to be situated** être situé; **the house is situated in a small village** la maison est située dans un petit village.

situation noun situation Fem.

six number six; **Harry's six** Harry a six ans.

sixteen number seize; **Alice is sixteen** Alice a seize ans.

sixth adjective sixième; **on the sixth floor** au sixième étage; **the sixth of July** le six juillet.

sixty number soixante; **she's sixty** elle a soixante ans.

size noun **1** grandeur Fem.; **it depends on the size of the house** ça dépend de la grandeur de la maison; **2** (precise measurements) dimensions Fem. plural; **what size is the window?** quelles sont les dimensions de la fenêtre?; **3** (in clothes) taille Fem.; **what size do you**

take? quelle taille faites-vous?; **4** (of shoes) pointure; **I take a size thirty-eight** je fais du trente-huit.

skate noun **1 an ice skate** un patin à glace; **2 a roller skate** un patin à roulettes.
skate verb **1** (ice-skate) faire [10] du patin à glace; **2** (roller-skate) faire [10] du patin à roulettes.

skateboard noun skateboard Masc.

skateboarding noun skateboard Masc.; **to do** (or **go**) **skateboarding** faire du skateboard.

skater noun patineur Masc., patineuse Fem.

skating noun **1** (ice) patin Masc. à glace; **to go skating** faire du patin à glace; **2** roller-skating le patin à roulettes; **to go roller-skating** faire du patin à roulettes.

skating rink noun patinoire Fem.

skeleton noun squelette Masc.

sketch noun **1** (drawing) croquis Masc.; **2** (comedy routine) sketch Masc.

ski noun ski Masc.
ski verb faire [10] du ski; **he can ski** il sait faire du ski.

ski boot noun chaussure Fem. de ski.

skid verb déraper [1]; **the car skidded** la voiture a dérapé.

skier noun skieur Masc., skieuse Fem.

skiing noun ski Masc.; **to go skiing** faire du ski.

ski lift noun remonte-pente Masc.

skill noun compétence Fem.

skimmed milk *noun* lait *Masc.* écrémé.

skin *noun* peau *Fem.* (*plural* peaux).

skinhead *noun* skinhead *Masc. & Fem.*

skinny *adjective* maigre.

skip *noun* (*for rubbish*) benne *Fem.*
skip *verb* **1** sauter [1] (*a meal, part of a book*); **I skipped a few chapters** j'ai sauté quelques chapitres; **2 to skip a lesson** sécher un cours (*informal*).

ski pants *noun* fuseau *Masc. singular;* **I bought some ski pants** j'ai acheté un fuseau.

skipping rope *noun* corde *Fem.* à sauter.

skirt *noun* jupe *Fem.*; **a long skirt** une jupe longue; **a straight skirt** une jupe droite; **a mini-skirt** une mini-jupe.

ski suit *noun* combinaison *Fem.* de ski.

skittles *plural noun* quilles *Fem. plural;* **to play skittles** jouer aux quilles.

skull *noun* crâne *Masc.*

sky *noun* ciel *Masc.*

skyscraper *noun* gratte-ciel *Masc.* (*plural* gratte-ciel).

slam *verb* claquer [1]; **she slammed the door** elle a claqué la porte.

slang *noun* argot *Masc.*

slap *noun* claque *Fem.*
slap *verb* **to slap somebody** donner [1] une claque à quelqu'un.

slate *noun* ardoise *Fem.*

slave *noun* esclave *Masc. & Fem.*

sledge *noun* luge *Fem.*

sledging *noun* **to go sledging** faire [10] de la luge.

sleep *noun* sommeil *Masc.*; **I had a good sleep** j'ai bien dormi; **to go to sleep** s'endormir [37].
sleep *verb* dormir [37]; **she's sleeping** elle dort.

sleeping bag *noun* sac *Masc.* de couchage.

sleeping pill *noun* somnifère *Masc.*

sleepy *adjective* **to be sleepy** avoir [5] sommeil; **I feel sleepy** j'ai sommeil; **he was getting sleepy** il commençait à avoir sommeil.

sleet *noun* neige *Fem.* fondue.

sleeve *noun* manche *Fem.*; **a long-sleeved jumper** un pull à manches longues; **a short-sleeved shirt** une chemise à manches courtes; **to roll up your sleeves** retrousser ses manches.

slice *noun* tranche *Fem.*; **a slice of ham** une tranche de jambon.
slice *verb* **to slice something** couper [1] quelque chose en tranches.

slide *noun* **1** (*photo*) diapositive *Fem.*; **2** (*hairslide*) barrette *Fem.*; **3** (*for sliding down*) toboggan *Masc.*

slight *adjective* léger (*Fem.* légère); **there is a slight problem** il y a un léger problème.

slightly *adverb* légèrement.

slim *adjective* mince.
slim *verb* **I'm slimming** je fais un régime.

sling noun écharpe Fem.; **to have your arm in a sling** avoir le bras en écharpe.

slip noun **1** (mistake) erreur Fem.; **2** (petticoat) (from waist) jupon Masc. (full-length) combinaison Fem.
slip verb **1** (slide) glisser [1]; **2 it had slipped my mind** j'avais oublié.

slipper noun pantoufle Fem.

slippery adjective glissant.

slope noun pente Fem.

slot noun fente Fem.

slot machine noun **1** (games machine) machine Fem. à sous; **2** (vending machine) distributeur Masc. automatique.

slow adjective **1** lent; **the service is a bit slow** le service est une peu lent; **2 my watch is slow** ma montre retarde.

● **to slow down** ralentir [2].

slowly adverb **1** lentement; **he got up slowly** il s'est levé lentement; **2** (speak, drive) doucement; **can you speak more slowly, please?** est-ce que vous pouvez parler plus doucement, s'il vous plaît?

slug noun limace Fem.

slum noun quartier Masc. démuni.

slush noun neige Fem. fondue.

sly adjective (person) rusé; ★ **on the sly** en douce.

smack noun claque Fem.
smack verb **to smack somebody** donner [1] une claque à quelqu'un.

small adjective petit (goes before the noun); **a small dog** un petit chien.

smart adjective **1** (well-dressed, posh) chic; **a smart restaurant** un restaurant chic; **2** (clever) intelligent.

smash noun **a car smash** un accident de voiture.
smash verb casser [1]; **they smashed a window** ils ont cassé une vitre.

smashing adjective formidable.

smell noun odeur Fem.; **a nasty smell** une mauvaise odeur; **there's a smell of burning** ça sent le brûlé.
smell verb **1** sentir [58]; **I can't smell anything** je ne sens rien; **I can smell lavender** ça sent la lavande; **2** (smell bad) sentir [58] mauvais; **the drains smell** les égouts sentent mauvais.

smelly adjective qui sent mauvais; **her smelly dog** son chien qui sent mauvais.

smile noun sourire Masc.
smile verb sourire [68].

smoke noun fumée Fem.
smoke verb fumer [1]; **she doesn't smoke** elle ne fume pas; **he smokes a pipe** il fume la pipe.

smoked adjective fumé; **smoked salmon** du saumon fumé.

smoker noun fumeur Masc., fumeuse Fem.

smoking noun **'no smoking'** 'défense de fumer'; **to give up smoking** arrêter de fumer.

smooth adjective **1** lisse; **a smooth surface** une surface lisse; **2** (person) mielleux (Fem. mielleuse).

smug adjective suffisant.

smuggle verb **to smuggle something** faire [10] passer quelque chose en contrebande.

smuggler *noun* **1** contrebandier *Masc.*, contrebandière *Fem.*; **2 a drugs smuggler** un passeur de drogue.

smuggling *noun* **1** contrebande *Fem.*; **2** (*of drugs or arms*) trafic *Masc.*

snack *noun* casse-croûte *Masc.*

snack bar *noun* sandwicherie *Fem.*, snack-bar *Masc.*

snail *noun* escargot *Masc.*

snake *noun* serpent *Masc.*

snap *noun* (*card game*) bataille *Fem.* **snap** *verb* **1** (*break*) casser [1]; **2 to snap your fingers** faire [10] claquer ses doigts.

snapshot *noun* photo *Fem.*

snarl *verb* gronder [1].

snatch *verb* arracher [1]; **to snatch something from somebody** arracher quelque chose à quelqu'un; **he snatched my book** il m'a arraché mon livre; **she had her bag snatched** on lui a arraché son sac.

sneak *verb* **to sneak in** entrer [1] furtivement; **to sneak out** sortir [72] furtivement; **he sneaked up on me** il s'est approché de moi sans faire de bruit.

sneeze *verb* éternuer [1].

sniff *verb* renifler [1].

snob *noun* snob *Masc. & Fem.*

snobbery *noun* snobisme *Masc.*

snooker *noun* snooker *Masc.*; **to play snooker** jouer au snooker.

snooze *noun* somme *Masc.*; **to have a snooze** faire un petit somme.

snore *verb* ronfler [1].

snow *noun* neige *Fem.*
snow *verb* neiger [52]; **it's snowing** il neige; **it's going to snow** il va neiger.

snowball *noun* boule *Fem.* de neige (*plural* boules de neige).

snowdrift *noun* congère *Fem.*

snowman *noun* bonhomme *Masc.* de neige (*plural* bonshommes de neige).

snowy *adjective* enneigé; **it was very snowy** il y avait beaucoup de neige.

so *conjunction, adverb* **1** tellement; **he's so lazy** il est tellement paresseux; **the coffee's so hot I can't drink it** le café est tellement chaud que je n'arrive pas à le boire; **2 not so** moins; **our house is a bit like yours, but not so big** notre maison est un peu comme la vôtre, mais moins grande; **3 so much** tellement; **I hate it so much!** je le déteste tellement!; **4 so much, so many** tellement de; **I have so much work to do** j'ai tellement de travail à faire; **we've got so many problems** nous avons tellement de problèmes; **5** (*therefore*) donc; **he got up late, so he missed his train** il s'est levé tard, donc il a raté son train; **6** (*starting a sentence*) alors; **so what's your name?** alors, tu t'appelles comment?; **so what shall we do?** alors, qu'est-ce qu'on fait?; **so what?** et alors?; **7 so do I, so am I** moi aussi; **'I live in Leeds' – 'so do I'** 'j'habite à Leeds' – 'moi aussi'; **'I hated the film' – 'so did I'** 'j'ai détesté le film' – 'moi aussi'; **so am I**

567

moi aussi; **so do we** nous aussi; **8 I think so** je crois; **I hope so** j'espère.

soak *verb* tremper [1].

soaked *adjective* trempé; ★ **to be soaked to the skin** être trempé jusqu'aux os (*literally: to be soaked to the bones*).

soaking *adjective* trempé; **soaking wet** trempé.

soap *noun* **1** savon *Masc.*; **a cake of soap** un savon; **2** (*soap opera: on TV*) feuilleton *Masc.*

soap powder *noun* lessive *Fem.*

sober *adjective* **to be sober** ne pas avoir bu; **he's sober** il n'a pas bu; **are you sure she's sober?** tu es sûr qu'elle n'a pas bu?

soccer *noun* football *Masc.*; **to play soccer** jouer au football.

social *adjective* social (*Masc. plural* sociaux).

socialism *noun* socialisme *Masc.*

socialist *noun, adjective* socialiste *Masc. & Fem.*

social security *noun* **1** aide *Fem.* sociale; **to be on social security** recevoir de l'aide sociale; **2 the social security** (*the system*) sécurité sociale *Fem.*

social worker *noun* travailleur *Masc.* social (*plural* travailleurs sociaux), travailleuse *Fem.* sociale; **she's a social worker** elle est travailleuse sociale.

society *noun* société *Fem.*

sociology *noun* sociologie *Fem.*

sock *noun* chaussette *Fem.*; **a pair of socks** une paire de chaussettes.

socket *noun* (*power point*) prise *Fem.* de courant (*plural* prises de courant).

sofa *noun* canapé *Masc.*

sofa bed *noun* canapé-lit *Masc.*

soft *adjective* doux (*Fem.* douce); ★ **to have a soft spot for somebody** avoir un faible pour quelqu'un.

soft drink *noun* boisson *Fem.* non alcoolisée.

soft toy *noun* peluche *Fem.*

software *noun* logiciel *Masc.*

soil *noun* terre *Fem.*

solar energy *noun* énergie *Fem.* solaire.

soldier *noun* soldat *Masc.*

solicitor *noun* **1** (*dealing with property or documents*) notaire *Masc.*; **she's a solicitor** elle est notaire; **2** (*dealing with lawsuits*) avocat *Masc.*, avocate *Fem.*; **she's a solicitor** elle est avocate.

solid *adjective* **1** massif (*Fem.* massive); **a table made of solid pine** une table en pin massif; **a solid gold ring** une bague en or massif; **solid silver** argent massif; **2** (*not flimsy*) solide; **a solid structure** une structure solide.

solo *noun* solo *Masc.*; **a guitar solo** un solo de guitare.
solo *adjective, adverb* en solo; **a solo album** un album en solo; **to play solo** jouer en solo.

soloist *noun* soliste *Masc. & Fem.*

solution *noun* solution *Fem.*

solve *verb* résoudre [67].

some *adjective, adverb* **1** (*followed by a singular noun*), du (*with a masculine noun*), de la (*with a feminine noun*), de l' (*with a noun beginning with a vowel or silent 'h'*); **would you like some butter?** voulez-vous du beurre?; **may I have some salad?** puis-je avoir de la salade?; **can you lend me some money?** est-ce que tu peux me prêter de l'argent?; **2** (*followed by a plural noun*) des; **I've bought some apples** j'ai acheté des pommes; **3** (*referring to something that has been mentioned*) en; **'would you like butter?' – 'thanks, I've got some'** 'veux-tu du beurre?' – 'merci, j'en ai'; **he's eaten some of it** il en a mangé un peu; **4 some people think he's wrong** il y a des gens qui pensent qu'il a tort; **5 some day** un de ces jours.

somebody, **someone** *pronoun* quelqu'un; **there's somebody in the garden** il y a quelqu'un dans le jardin.

somehow *adverb* **1** d'une manière ou d'une autre; **I've got to finish this essay somehow** je dois finir cette rédaction d'une manière ou d'une autre; **2 I somehow think they won't come** quelque chose me dit qu'ils ne viendront pas.

somersault *noun* **1** (*child's*) galipette *Fem.*; **2** (*gymnast's*) roulade *Fem.*; **3** (*diver's*) saut *Masc.* périlleux.

something *pronoun* quelque chose; **I've got something to tell you** j'ai quelque chose à te dire; **something pretty** quelque chose de joli; **something interesting** quelque chose d'intéressant; **there's something wrong** il y a quelque chose qui ne va pas; **their house is really something!** leur maison c'est vraiment quelque chose!; **a guy called Colin something or other** un type qui s'appelle Colin quelque chose.

sometime *adverb* un de ces jours; **give me a ring sometime** appelle-moi un de ces jours; **I'll ring you sometime next week** je t'appellerai dans le courant de la semaine prochaine.

sometimes *adverb* quelquefois; **I sometimes take the train** quelquefois je prends le train.

somewhere *adverb* quelque part; **I've put my bag down somewhere** j'ai posé mon sac quelque part; **I've met you somewhere before** je vous ai déjà vu quelque part.

son *noun* fils *Masc.*

song *noun* chanson *Fem.*

son-in-law *noun* gendre *Masc.*

soon *adverb* **1** bientôt; **it will soon be the holidays** c'est bientôt les vacances; **see you soon!** à bientôt; **2 as soon as** dès que; **as soon as she arrives** dès qu'elle arrivera; **as soon as possible** dès que possible; **3 it's too soon** c'est trop tôt.

sooner *adverb* **1** plus tôt; **we should have started sooner** nous aurions dû commencer plus tôt; **2 I'd sooner wait** je préfère attendre; ★ **sooner or later** tôt ou tard.

soprano *noun* soprano *Masc. & Fem.*

a
b
c
d
e
f
g
h
i
j
k
l
m
n
o
p
q
r
s
t
u
v
w
x
y
z

sore noun plaie Fem.
sore adjective **to have a sore leg** avoir mal à la jambe; **to have a sore throat** avoir mal à la gorge; **my arm's sore** j'ai mal au bras; ★ **it's a sore point** c'est un sujet délicat.

sorry adjective **1** désolé; **I'm really sorry** je suis vraiment désolé; **sorry to disturb you** je suis désolé de vous déranger; **I'm sorry I forgot your birthday** je suis désolé d'avoir oublié ton anniversaire; **2 sorry!** excusez-moi!; **3 sorry?** comment?; **4 to feel sorry for somebody** plaindre [31] quelqu'un.

sort noun sorte Fem.; **what sort of music do you like?** tu aimes quelle sorte de musique?; **all sorts of** toutes sortes de; **for all sorts of reasons** pour toutes sortes de raisons.

● **to sort something out 1** mettre [11] de l'ordre dans (room, desk, papers, possessions); **I must sort out my room tonight** je dois mettre de l'ordre dans ma chambre ce soir; **2** s'occuper [1] de (problem, arrangement); **Liz is sorting it out** Liz s'en occupe.

so-so adjective moyen (Fem. moyenne); **'how was the film?' – 'so-so'** 'c'était comment le film?' – 'moyen'.

soul noun **1** âme Fem.; **2** (music) soul Masc.

sound noun **1** (noise) bruit ; **the sound of voices** le bruit des voix; **2** (volume) volume; **to turn down the sound** baisser le volume.
sound verb **it sounds easy** ça a

l'air facile; **it sounds as if she's happy** elle a l'air d'être heureuse.

sound asleep adjective profondément endormi.

sound effect noun effet Masc. sonore.

soundtrack noun bande Fem. sonore.

soup noun soupe Fem.; **mushroom soup** la soupe aux champignons.

soup plate noun assiette Fem. creuse la soupe.

soup spoon noun cuillère Fem. à soupe.

sour adjective **1** (taste) aigre; **2 the milk has gone sour** le lait a tourné.

south noun sud Masc.; **in the south** au sud.
south adjective, adverb sud (never agrees); **the south side** le côté sud; **a south wind** un vent du sud; **south of Paris** au sud de Paris.

South Africa noun Afrique Fem. du Sud.

South America noun Amérique Fem. du Sud.

South American noun Sud-Américain Masc., Sud-Américaine Fem.
South American adjective sud-américain.

southeast noun sud-est Masc.
southeast adjective **in southeast England** au sud-est de l'Angleterre.

South Pole noun pôle Masc. Sud.

southwest noun sud-ouest Masc.
southwest adjective **in southwest England** au sud-ouest de l'Angleterre.

souvenir *noun* souvenir *Masc.*

soya *noun* soja *Masc.*

soy sauce *noun* sauce *Fem.* de soja.

space *noun* **1** (*room*) place *Fem.*; **is there enough space?** est-ce qu'il y a de la place?; **there's enough space for two** il y a de la place pour deux; **2** (*gap*) espace *Masc.*; **leave a space** laissez un espace; **3** (*outer space*) espace *Masc.*; **in space** dans l'espace.

spacecraft *noun* engin *Masc.* spatial.

spade *noun* **1** pelle *Fem.*; **2** (*in cards*) pique *Masc.*; **the queen of spades** la reine de pique.

spaghetti *noun* spaghetti *Masc. plural.*

Spain *noun* Espagne *Fem.*; **in Spain** en Espagne; **to Spain** en Espagne.

Spaniard *noun* Espagnol *Masc.*, Espagnole *Fem.*

spaniel *noun* épagneul *Masc.*

Spanish *noun* **1** (*language*) espagnol *Masc.*; **I'm learning Spanish** j'apprends l'espagnol; **2 the Spanish** (*people*) les Espagnols *Masc. plural.* **Spanish** *adjective* espagnol; **Pedro is Spanish** Pedro est espagnol.

spank *verb* **to spank somebody** donner [1] une fessée à quelqu'un.

spanner *noun* clé *Fem.* anglaise.

spare *adjective* (*part, battery*) de rechange; **we have a spare ticket** nous avons un billet de trop. **spare** *verb* **I can't spare the time** je n'ai pas le temps; **can you spare a moment?** est-ce que tu as un instant?

spare part *noun* pièce *Fem.* de rechange.

spare room *noun* chambre *Fem.* d'amis.

spare time *noun* temps *Masc.* libre; **in my spare time** dans mon temps libre.

spare wheel *noun* roue *Fem.* de secours.

sparkling *adjective* **sparkling (mineral) water** l'eau (minérale) pétillante; **sparkling wine** le vin mousseux.

sparrow *noun* moineau *Masc.* (*plural* moineaux).

speak *verb* **1** parler [1]; **do you speak French?** est-ce que vous parlez français?; **spoken French** le français parlé; **2 to speak to somebody** parler [1] à quelqu'un; **she's speaking to Mike** elle parle à Mike; **I've never spoken to her** je ne lui ai jamais parlé; **I'll speak to him about it** je vais lui en parler; **3 who's speaking?** (*on the phone*) c'est qui à l'appareil?

speaker *noun* **1** (*on a music system*) enceinte *Fem.*; **2** (*at a public lecture*) conférencier *Masc.*, conférencière *Fem.*; **3** (*of a language*) **a French speaker** un/une francophone; **an English speaker** un/une anglophone.

spear *noun* lance *Fem.*

special *adjective* spécial (*Masc. plural* spéciaux).

specialist *noun* spécialiste *Masc. & Fem.*

a
b
c
d
e
f
g
h
i
j
k
l
m
n
o
p
q
r
s
t
u
v
w
x
y
z

specialize *verb* to specialize in être [6] spécialisé dans; **we specialize in French cars** nous sommes spécialisés dans les voitures françaises.

specially *adverb* **1** spécialement; **not specially** pas spécialement; **the poems have been specially chosen for small children** les poèmes ont été spécialement choisis pour les petits enfants; **2** (*specifically*) exprès; **I came specially in order to see you** je suis venu exprès pour te voir; **I made this cake specially for you** j'ai fait ce gâteau exprès pour toi.

species *noun* espèce *Fem.*

specific *adjective* précis.

spectacles *noun* lunettes *Fem. plural.*

spectacular *adjective* spectaculaire.

spectator *noun* spectateur *Masc.*, spectatrice *Fem.*

speech *noun* discours *Masc.*; **to make a speech** faire un discours.

speechless *adjective* muet (*Fem.* muette); **to be speechless with rage** rester muet de colère; **I was speechless** j'étais stupéfait.

speed *noun* vitesse *Fem.*; **at top speed** à toute vitesse; **what speed was he doing?** il roulait à quelle vitesse?; **a twelve-speed bike** un vélo à douze vitesses.

• **to speed up** accélérer [24].

speeding *noun* excès *Masc.* de vitesse; **he was fined for speeding** il a reçu une contravention pour excès de vitesse.

speed limit *noun* limitation *Fem.* de vitesse.

spell *noun* (*of time*) période *Fem.*; **a cold spell** une période de temps froid; **sunny spells** des éclaircies *Fem. plural.*

spell *verb* **1** (*in writing*) écrire [38]; **how do you spell it?** ça s'écrit comment?; **how do you spell your surname?** ça s'écrit comment, ton nom de famille?; **2** (*out loud*) épeler [18].

spell checker *noun* correcteur *Masc.* orthographique.

spelling *noun* orthographe *Fem.*; **a spelling mistake** une faute d'orthographe.

spend *verb* **1** dépenser [1] (*money*); **I've spent all my money** j'ai dépensé tout mon argent; **2** passer [1] (*time*); **we spent three days in Paris** nous avons passé trois jours à Paris; **she spends her time writing letters** elle passe son temps à écrire des lettres.

spice *noun* épice *Fem.*

spicy *adjective* épicé; **he doesn't like spicy food** il n'aime pas les choses épicées.

spider *noun* araignée *Fem.*

spill *verb* renverser [1]; **I've spilled my wine on the carpet** j'ai renversé mon vin sur la moquette.

spinach *noun* épinards *Masc. plural*; **do you like spinach?** est-ce que tu aimes les épinards?

spine *noun* colonne *Fem.* vertébrale.

spiral *noun* spirale *Fem.*

spiral staircase *noun* escalier *Masc.* en colimaçon.

spire *noun* flèche *Fem.*

spirit *noun* 1 (*energy*) énergie *Fem.*; 2 to get into the spirit of the occasion se mettre dans l'ambiance.

spirits *noun* 1 (*alcohol*) alcools *Masc.* plural forts; 2 to be in good spirits être de bonne humeur.

spit *verb* cracher [1]; to spit something out cracher quelque chose.

spite *noun* 1 in spite of malgré; we decided to go in spite of the rain nous avons décidé d'y aller malgré la pluie; 2 (*nastiness*) méchanceté *Fem.*; to do something out of spite faire quelque chose par méchanceté.

spiteful *adjective* méchant.

splash *noun* 1 (*noise*) plouf *Masc.*; 2 a splash of colour une touche de couleur.
splash *verb* éclabousser [1].

splendid *adjective* splendide.

splinter *noun* écharde *Fem.*

split *verb* 1 (*with an axe or a knife*) fendre [3]; to split a piece of wood fendre un morceau de bois; 2 (*come apart*) se fendre [3]; the lining has split la doublure s'est fendue; 3 (*divide up*) partager [52]; they split the money between them ils ont partagé l'argent entre eux.

• to split up 1 (*a couple or group*) se séparer [1]; 2 she's split up with her boyfriend elle a rompu avec son copain.

spoil *verb* 1 gâcher [1]; it completely spoiled the evening ça a complètement gâché la soirée; to spoil the surprise gâcher la surprise; 2 gâter [1] (*a child*).

spoiled *adjective* gâté; a spoiled child un enfant gâté.

spoilsport *noun* trouble-fête *Masc. & Fem.*

spoke *noun* (*of a wheel*) rayon *Masc.*

spokesman *noun* porte-parole *Masc.* (*plural* porte-parole).

spokeswoman *noun* porte-parole *Masc.* (*plural* porte-parole).

sponge *noun* éponge *Fem.*

sponge bag *noun* trousse *Fem.* de toilette.

sponge cake *noun* génoise *Fem.*

sponsor *noun* sponsor *Masc.*
sponsor *verb* sponsoriser [1].

spontaneous *adjective* spontané.

spooky *adjective* 1 (*atmosphere*) sinistre; 2 a spooky story une histoire qui fait froid dans le dos.

spoon *noun* cuillère *Fem.*; a soup spoon une cuillère à soupe; a teaspoon une petite cuillère.

spoonful *noun* cuillère *Fem.*

sport *noun* sport *Masc.*; to be good at sport être bon en sport; my favourite sport mon sport préféré.

sports bag *noun* sac *Masc.* de sport.

sports car *noun* voiture *Fem.* de sport.

sports centre *noun* centre *Masc.* sportif.

sports club *noun* club *Masc.* sportif.

sportsman *noun* sportif *Masc.*

a
b
c
d
e
f
g
h
i
j
k
l
m
n
o
p
q
r
s
t
u
v
w
x
y
z

sportswear *noun* vêtements *Masc.* plural de sport.

sportswoman *noun* sportive *Fem.*

sporty *adjective* sportif (*Fem.* sportive); **she's very sporty** elle est très sportive.

spot *noun* **1** (*in fabric*) pois *Masc.*; **a red tie with black spots** une cravate rouge aux pois noirs; **2** (*on your skin*) bouton; **I've got spots** j'ai des boutons; **to be covered in spots** être couvert de boutons; **3** (*stain*) tache *Fem.*; **you've got a spot on your tie** tu as une tache sur ta cravate; **4** (*spotlight*) projecteur *Masc.*; (*in the home*) spot *Masc.*; **5 on the spot** (*immediately*) sur-le-champ; **we'll do it for you on the spot** nous le ferons sur-le-champ; **6** (*at hand*) sur place; **they have experts on the spot** ils ont des experts sur place.
spot *verb* repérer [24]; **I spotted her in the crowd** je l'ai repérée dans la foule.

spotless *adjective* impeccable.

spotlight *noun* **1** projecteur *Masc.*; **2** (*in the home*) spot *Masc.*

spotty *adjective* (*pimply*) boutonneux (*Fem.* boutonneuse).

spouse *noun* époux *Masc.*, épouse *Fem.*

sprain *noun* entorse *Fem.*
sprain *verb* **to sprain your ankle** se faire [10] une entorse à la cheville.

spray *noun* (*spray can*) bombe *Fem.*
spray *verb* vaporiser [1] (*liquid*).

spread *noun* pâte *Fem.* à tartiner; **cheese spread** le fromage à tartiner.
spread *verb* **1** (*news or a disease*) se propager [52]; **2** étaler [1] (*butter, jam, cement, glue, etc.*).

spreadsheet *noun* (*on a computer*) tableur *Masc.*

spring *noun* **1** (*the season*) printemps *Masc.*; **in the spring** au printemps; **spring flowers** les fleurs du printemps; **2** (*made of metal*) ressort *Masc.*; **3** (*providing water*) source *Fem.*

spring-cleaning *noun* grand nettoyage *Masc.* de printemps.

springtime *noun* printemps *Masc.*; **in springtime** au printemps.

spring water *noun* eau *Fem.* de source.

sprint *noun* sprint *Masc.*
sprint *verb* courir [2] à toute vitesse.

sprinter *noun* sprinteur *Masc.*, sprinteuse *Fem.*

sprout *noun* (*Brussels sprout*) chou *Masc.* de Bruxelles (*plural* choux de Bruxelles).

spy *noun* espion *Masc.*, espionne *Fem.*
spy *verb* **to spy on somebody** espionner [1] quelqu'un.

spying *noun* espionnage *Masc.*

squabble *verb* se disputer [1].

square *noun* **1** (*shape*) carré; **2** (*in a town or village*) place *Fem.*; **the village square** la place du village; ★ **to go back to square one** retourner à la case départ.
square *adjective* carré; **a square box** une boîte carrée; **three square metres** trois mètres carrés; **the**

room is four metres square la pièce fait quatre mètres carrés.

squash *noun* **1** (*drink*) sirop *Masc.*; **orange squash** le sirop d'orange; **2** (*sport*) squash *Masc.*; **to play squash** jouer au squash.

squeak *verb* **1** (*door, hinge*) grincer [61]; **2** (*person, animal*) pousser [1] un petit cri.

squeeze *verb* **1** serrer [1] (*somebody's arm, hand, etc*); **2** presser [1] (*toothpaste*).

squid *noun* calmar *Masc.*

squirrel *noun* écureuil *Masc.*

stab *verb* poignarder [1].

stable *noun* écurie *Fem.*
stable *adjective* stable.

stack *noun* **1** (*pile*) pile *Fem.*; **2 stacks of** plein de; **she's got stacks of CDs** elle a plein de CD.

stadium *noun* stade *Masc.*

staff *noun* **1** (*of a company*) personnel *Masc.*; **2** (*in a school*) professeurs *Masc. plural.*

stage *noun* **1** (*for a performance*) scène *Fem.*; **on stage** sur scène; **2** (*phase*) stade *Masc.*; **at this stage of the project** à ce stade du projet; **at this stage it's hard to know** pour l'instant il est difficile de savoir.

staggered *adjective* (*amazed*) stupéfié.

stain *noun* tache *Fem.*
stain *verb* tacher [1].

stainless steel *noun* inox *Masc.*; **a stainless steel sink** un évier en inox.

stair *noun* **1** (*step*) marche *Fem.*; **2 stairs** escalier *Masc.*; **I met her on the stairs** je l'ai croisée dans l'escalier.

staircase *noun* escalier *Masc.*

stale *adjective* (*bread*) rassis.

stalemate *noun* (*in chess*) pat *Masc.*

stall *noun* **1** (*at a market or fair*) stand *Masc.*; **2 the stalls** (*in a theatre*) l'orchestre *Masc. singular.*

stammer *noun* **to have a stammer** bégayer [59].
stammer *verb* bégayer [59].

stamp *noun* timbre *Masc.*
stamp *verb* **1** affranchir [2] (*a letter*); **2 to stamp your foot** taper [1] du pied.

stamp album *noun* album *Masc.* de timbres.

stamp collection *noun* collection *Fem.* de timbres.

stand *verb* **1** être [6] debout; **several people were standing** plusieurs personnes étaient debout; **2** (*when you say somebody is standing somewhere 'standing' is not usually translated*) **we were standing outside the cinema** nous étions devant le cinéma; **I'm standing here waiting for you** je suis là en train de t'attendre; **3** (*bear*) supporter [1]; **I can't stand her** je ne la supporte pas; **I can't stand waiting** je ne supporte pas d'attendre.

• **to stand for something** (*be short for*) être [6] l'abréviation de; **'UN' stands for 'United Nations'** 'UN' est l'abréviation de 'United

a

Nations'.

b
- **stand up** se lever [50]; **everybody stood up** tout le monde s'est levé.

c
d
standard noun niveau Masc.; **her work is of a high standard** son travail est d'un bon niveau; **the standard of living** le niveau de vie.

e
standard adjective standard; **the standard price** le prix standard.

f

g
Standard grades noun plural You can explain Standard grades as follows: Ce sont des examens que les lycéens écossais passent à l'âge d'environ 16 ans dans six ou sept matières. La meilleure note que l'on peut obtenir est 1 et la note la plus basse est 7. Une fois qu'ils ont obtenu leurs Standard grades, de nombreux étudiants se préparent pour les Highers; SEE **Highers**.

h
i
j
k
l
m

n
stands noun (in a stadium) tribune Fem. singular.

o
staple noun agrafe Fem.
staple verb agrafer [1]; **to staple the pages together** agrafer les feuilles.

p
q

r
stapler noun agrafeuse Fem.

s
star noun 1 (in the sky) étoile Fem.; 2 (person) vedette; **he's a film star** c'est une vedette de cinéma.
star verb **to star in a film** être [6] la vedette d'un film.

t
u

v
stare verb regarder [1] fixement; **he was staring at me** il me regardait fixement; **what are you staring at?** qu'est-ce que tu regardes?

w
x

y
star sign noun signe Masc. astrologique; **what star sign are you?** de quelle signe êtes-vous?

z

start noun 1 début Masc.; **at the start** au début; **at the start of the book** au début du livre; **from the start** dès le début; **we knew from the start that it was dangerous** nous savions dès le début que c'était dangereux; 2 **to make a start on something** commencer à faire quelque chose; **I've made a start on my homework** j'ai commencé à faire mes devoirs; 3 (of a race) départ Masc.

start verb 1 commencer [61]; **the film starts at eight** le film commence à huit heures; **I've started the book** j'ai commencé le livre; 2 **to start doing** commencer [61] à faire; **I've started learning Spanish** j'ai commencé à apprendre l'espagnol; 3 **to start a business** créer [32] une entreprise; 4 **to start a car** faire [10] démarrer une voiture; **she started the car** elle a fait démarrer la voiture; **the car wouldn't start** la voiture n'a pas voulu démarrer.

starter noun (in a meal) entrée Fem.; **what would you like as a starter?** qu'est-ce que vous voulez comme entrée?

starve verb mourir [54] de faim; **I'm starving!** je meurs de faim!

state noun 1 état Masc.; **the house is in a very bad state** la maison est en très mauvais état; 2 (administrative) état Masc.; **the state** l'État; 3 **the States** les États-Unis Masc. plural; **they live in the States** ils habitent aux États-Unis.
state verb 1 déclarer [1] (intention, opinion); 2 indiquer [1] (address, income, occupation, reason, etc.).

stately home noun château Masc. (plural châteaux).

statement noun déclaration Fem.

station noun gare Fem.; **the railway station** la gare; **the bus station** la gare routière; **the police station** le commissariat; **a radio station** une station de radio.

stationary adjective à l'arrêt.

stationer's noun papeterie Fem.

stationery noun papeterie Fem.

statistics noun 1 (subject) statistique Fem.; 2 **the statistics** (figures) les statistiques.

statue noun statue Fem.

status noun position Fem.

stay noun séjour Masc.; **our stay in Paris** notre séjour à Paris; **enjoy your stay!** bon séjour!
stay verb 1 rester [1]; **I'll stay here** je reste ici; **how long are you staying?** vous restez combien de temps?; 2 (with time) **we're going to stay in Berlin for three days** nous allons passer trois jours à Berlin; 3 (at somebody's house) **to stay with somebody** aller [7] chez quelqu'un; **I'm going to stay with my sister this weekend** je vais chez ma sœur ce weekend; 4 (be temporarily lodged) loger [52]; **where are you staying?** où est-ce que vous logez?

• **to stay in** rester [1] à la maison; **I'm staying in tonight** je reste à la maison ce soir.

steady adjective 1 stable; **a steady job** un emploi stable; 2 régulier (Fem. régulière); **a steady increase** une augmentation régulière;

3 (hand, voice) ferme; 4 **to hold something steady** bien tenir quelque chose.

steak noun steack Masc.; **steak and chips** un steack frites.

steal verb voler [1].

steam noun vapeur Fem.

steam engine noun locomotive Fem. à vapeur.

steam iron noun fer Masc. à vapeur.

steel noun acier Masc.

steep adjective raide; **a steep slope** une pente raide.

steeple noun 1 (spire) flèche Fem.; 2 (bell tower) clocher Masc.

steering wheel noun volant Masc.

step noun 1 pas Masc.; **to take a step forwards** faire un pas en avant; **to take a step backwards** faire un pas en arrière; 2 (stair) marche Fem.; **'mind the step'** 'attention à la marche'.

• **to step back** faire [10] un pas en arrière.

• **to step forward** faire [10] un pas en avant.

• **to step into** entrer [1] dans (a lift).

stepbrother noun demi-frère Masc. (plural demi-frères).

stepdaughter noun belle-fille Fem. (plural belles-filles).

stepfather noun beau-père Masc.

stepladder noun escabeau Masc. (plural escabeaux).

stepmother noun belle-mère Fem.

stepsister noun demi-sœur Fem. (plural demi-sœurs).

a
b
c
d
e
f
g
h
i
j
k
l
m
n
o
p
q
r
s
t
u
v
w
x
y
z

stepson noun beau-fils Masc.
(plural beaux-fils).

stereo noun chaîne Fem. stéréo
(plural chaînes stéréo).

sterling noun sterling Masc.; **in
sterling** en livres sterling.

stew noun ragoût Masc.

steward noun steward Masc.

stewardess noun hôtesse Fem.

stick noun 1 bâton Masc.; **2 a
walking stick** une canne; **3 a
hockey stick** une crosse de hockey.
stick verb 1 (with glue) coller [1];
2 (put) mettre [11]; **stick them on
my desk** mets-les sur mon bureau.

sticker noun autocollant Masc.

sticky adjective 1 poisseux (Fem.
poisseuse); **my hands are sticky**
j'ai les mains poisseuses; **2** adhésif
(Fem. adhésive); **sticky paper** le
papier adhésif.

sticky tape noun Scotch™ Masc.

stiff adjective 1 **to feel stiff** avoir [5]
des courbatures; **to have stiff legs**
avoir des courbatures dans les
jambes; **2 to be bored stiff**
s'ennuyer [41] à mourir; **to be
scared stiff** être [6] mort de peur.

still adjective 1 **sit still!** tiens-toi
tranquille!; **keep still!** ne bouge
pas!; **2 still mineral water** l'eau
minérale non-gazeuse.
still adverb 1 toujours; **do you still
live in London?** est-ce que tu
habites toujours à Londres?; **I've
still not finished** je n'ai toujours
pas fini; **he's still working** il est
toujours en train de travailler;
2 encore; **there's still a lot of beer**

left il reste encore beaucoup de
bière; **3 better still** encore mieux.

sting noun piqûre Fem.; **a wasp
sting** une piqûre de guêpe.
sting verb piquer [1]; **I was stung
by a bee** je me suis fait piquer par
une abeille.

stink noun odeur Fem.; **what a
stink!** ça pue!
stink verb puer [1]; **it stinks of
cigarette smoke in here** ça pue la
cigarette ici.

stir verb remuer [1].

stitch noun 1 (in sewing) point
Masc.; **2** (in knitting) maille Fem.;
3 (surgical) point Masc. de souture
(plural points de souture).

stock noun 1 (in a shop) stock Masc.;
to have something in stock avoir
quelque chose en stock; **2** (supply)
réserve; **I always have a stock of
pencils** j'ai toujours une réserve de
crayons; **3** (for cooking) bouillon;
chicken stock le bouillon de
poulet.
stock verb (in a shop) vendre [3];
they don't stock dictionaries ils
ne vendent pas les dictionnaires.

● **to stock up on something**
s'approvisionner [1] en quelque
chose.

stock cube noun bouillon-cube
Masc.

stock exchange noun Bourse
Fem. (des valeurs).

stocking noun bas Masc.

stomach noun estomac Masc.

stomachache noun **to have
stomachache** avoir mal au ventre.

stone *noun* **1** pierre *Fem.*; **a stone wall** un mur en pierre; **2** (*pebble*) caillou *Masc.*; **3** (*in fruit*) noyau *Masc.* (*plural* noyaux).

stool *noun* tabouret *Masc.*

stop *noun* arrêt *Masc.*; **the bus stop** l'arrêt de bus.
stop *verb* **1** s'arrêter [1]; **he stopped in front of the shop** il s'est arrêté devant le magasin; **the music stopped** la musique s'est arrêtée; **does the train stop in Dijon?** est-ce que le train s'arrête à Dijon?; **2 to stop somebody/something** arrêter [1] quelque chose/quelqu'un; **she stopped me in the street** elle m'a arrêté dans la rue; **3 to stop doing** arrêter [1] de faire; **he's stopped smoking** il a arrêté de fumer; **she never stops asking questions** elle n'arrête pas de poser des questions; **4 to stop somebody doing** empêcher [1] quelqu'un de faire; **there's nothing to stop you going on your own** rien ne t'empêche d'y aller tout seul.

stopwatch *noun* chronomètre *Masc.*

store *noun* (*shop*) magasin *Masc.*
store *verb* **1** garder [1]; **2** (*on a computer*) mémoriser [1].

storey *noun* étage *Masc.*; **a three-storey house** une maison à trois étages.

stork *noun* cigogne *Fem.*

storm *noun* **1** (*wind*) tempête *Fem.*; **a snowstorm** une tempête de neige; **a rainstorm** une tempête de pluie; **2** (*thunderstorm*) orage *Masc.*

stormy *adjective* orageux (*Fem.* orageuse).

story *noun* histoire *Fem.*; **to tell a story** raconter une histoire.

stove *noun* (*cooker*) cuisinière *Fem.*

straight *adjective* **1** droit; **a straight line** une ligne droite; **2 to have straight hair** avoir les cheveux raides.
straight *adverb* **1** (*in direction*) droit; **go straight ahead** continuez tout droit; **2** (*in time*) directement; **he went straight to the doctor's** il est allé directement chez le médecin; **3 straight away** tout de suite.

straightforward *adjective* simple.

strain *noun* stress *Masc.*; **the strain of the last few weeks** le stress de ces dernières semaines; **to be a strain** être stressant.
strain *verb* **1** se faire [10] mal à (*part of the body*); **he's strained his back** il s'est fait mal au dos; **2** (*a muscle*) se froisser [1]; **3** (*vegetables, rice*) égoutter [1].

strange *adjective* bizarre; **a strange situation** une situation bizarre.

stranger *noun* inconnu *Masc.*, inconnue *Fem.*

strangle *verb* étrangler [1].

strap *noun* **1** (*on case, bag, camera*) courroie *Fem.*; **2** (*on a garment*) bretelle *Fem.*; **3** (*of a watch*) bracelet *Masc.*; **a watchstrap** un bracelet de montre; **4** (*on a shoe*) lanière *Fem.*

strapless *adjective* sans bretelles.

a
b
c
d
e
f
g
h
i
j
k
l
m
n
o
p
q
r
s
t
u
v
w
x
y
z

a

b **straw** noun paille Fem. (both the material and for drinking with); **a straw hat** un chapeau de paille.

c **strawberry** noun fraise Fem.; **strawberry jam** la confiture de fraises; **a strawberry yoghurt** un yaourt à la fraise.

d

e **stray** adjective **a stray dog** un chien perdu.

f

g **stream** noun (small river) ruisseau Masc. (plural ruisseaux).

h **street** noun rue Fem.; **I met Simon in the street** j'ai croisé Simon dans la rue.

i

j **streetlamp** noun réverbère Masc.

k **street map** noun plan Masc. de la ville.

l **streetwise** adjective dégourdi.

m **strength** noun force Fem.

n **stress** noun stress Masc. **stress** verb (emphasize) souligner [1]; **to stress the importance of something** souligner l'importance de quelque chose.

o

p

q **stretch** verb 1 (garment) se déformer [1]; **this jumper has stretched** ce pull s'est déformé; 2 (shoes) s'élargir [2].

r **stretcher** noun brancard Masc.

s **stretchy** adjective élastique.

t **strict** adjective strict.

u **strike** noun grève Fem.; **to go on strike** faire grève; **to be on strike** être en grève. **strike** verb 1 (hit) frapper [1]; 2 (clock) sonner [1]; **the clock struck six** l'horloge a sonné six heures; 3 (go on strike) faire [10] grève.

v

w

x

y

z

striker noun 1 (in football) buteur Masc.; 2 (person on strike) gréviste Masc. & Fem.

striking adjective frappant; **a striking resemblance** une ressemblance frappante.

string noun 1 (for tying) ficelle Fem.; 2 (for a musical instrument) corde Fem.

strip noun bande Fem. **strip** verb (undress) se déshabiller [1].

strip cartoon noun bande Fem. dessinée.

stripe noun rayure Fem.

striped adjective rayé.

stroke noun 1 (style of swimming) nage Fem.; 2 (medical) attaque Fem.; **to have a stroke** avoir une attaque; ★ **a stroke of luck** un coup de chance. **stroke** verb caresser [1].

stroll noun **to go for a stroll** faire une petite promenade. **stroll** verb se promener [50].

strong adjective 1 (person, drink) fort; 2 (feeling) puissant; 3 (material) solide.

strongly adverb 1 (believe) fermement; 2 (support) fortement; 3 (advise, oppose) vivement.

struggle noun 1 lutte Fem.; **the struggle for independence** la lutte pour l'indépendance; **a power struggle** une lutte pour le pouvoir; 2 **it's been a struggle** ça a été très dur. **struggle** verb 1 (to obtain something) se battre [21]; **they have struggled to survive** ils se sont battus pour survivre; **2** (*physically, in order to escape or reach something*) se débattre [21]; **3** (*have difficulty in doing*) avoir [5] du mal à faire; **I'm struggling to finish my homework** j'ai du mal à finir mes devoirs.

stub *noun* **a cigarette stub** un mégot.

• **to stub out** écraser [1] (*a cigarette*).

stubborn *adjective* têtu.

stuck *adjective* **1** (*jammed*) coincé; **the drawer's stuck** le tiroir est coincé; **2** (*person*) **to get stuck** rester coincé (*in a lift, traffic jam, or place*).

stud *noun* **1** (*on a belt or jacket*) clou *Masc.*; **2** (*on a boot*) clou *Masc.*; **3** (*earring*) boucle *Fem.* d'oreille.

student *noun* étudiant *Masc.*, étudiante *Fem.*

studio *noun* **1** (*film, TV*) studio *Masc.*; **2** (*artist's*) atelier *Masc.*

studio flat *noun* studio *Masc.*

study *verb* **1** réviser [1]; **he's busy studying for his exams** il est en train de réviser pour ses examens; **2** faire [10] des études de (*a subject*); **she's studying medicine** elle fait des études de médecine.

stuff *noun* **1** (*things*) trucs *Masc. plural* (*informal*); **we can put all that stuff in the attic** on peut mettre tous ces trucs au grenier; **2** (*personal belongings*) affaires *Fem. plural*; **you can leave your stuff at my house** tu peux laisser tes affaires chez moi; **3** (*substance*) truc *Masc.* (*informal*); **some antiseptic stuff** un truc antiseptique.

stuff *verb* **1** (*shove*) fourrer [1] (*informal*); **she stuffed some things into a suitcase** elle a fourré quelques affaires dans une valise; **2** farcir [2] (*chicken, turkey, vegetables*); **stuffed aubergines** des aubergines farcies.

stuffing *noun* (*for cooking*) farce *Fem.*

stuffy *adjective* (*airless*) étouffant.

stumble *verb* (*trip*) trébucher [1].

stunned *adjective* (*amazed*) stupéfait.

stunning *adjective* sensationnel (*Fem.* sensationnelle).

stunt *noun* (*in a film*) cascade *Fem.*

stuntman *noun* cascadeur *Masc.*

stuntwoman *noun* cascadeuse *Fem.*

stupid *adjective* bête; **that was really stupid** c'était vraiment bête; **to do something stupid** faire une bêtise.

stutter *noun* **to have a stutter** bégayer [59].
stutter *verb* bégayer [59].

style *noun* **1** style *Masc.*; **a style of living** un style de vie; **he has his own style** il a son propre style; **2** (*fashion*) mode *Fem.*; **it's the latest style** c'est la dernière mode.

subject *noun* **1** sujet *Masc.*; **the subject of my talk** le sujet de mon exposé; **2** (*at school*) matière *Fem.*; **my favourite subject is biology** ma matière préférée c'est la biologie.

submarine *noun* sous-marin *Masc.* (*plural* sous-marins).

a
b
c
d
e
f
g
h
i
j
k
l
m
n
o
p
q
r
s
t
u
v
w
x
y
z

a
b
c
d
e
f
g
h
i
j
k
l
m
n
o
p
q
r
s
t
u
v
w
x
y
z

subscription noun abonnement Masc.; **to take out a subscription to** s'abonner à.

subsidy noun subvention Fem.

substance noun substance Fem.

substitute noun (person) remplaçant Masc., remplaçante Fem.
substitute verb substituer [1].

subtitled adjective (film) sous-titré.

subtitles plural noun sous-titres Masc. plural.

subtle adjective subtil.

subtract verb soustraire [78].

suburb noun banlieue Fem.; **a suburb of Edinburgh** une banlieue d'Édimbourg; **in the suburbs of London** dans la banlieue de Londres.

suburban adjective de banlieue.

subway noun (underpass) passage Masc. souterrain.

succeed verb réussir [2]; **to succeed in doing** réussir à faire; **we've succeeded in contacting her** nous avons réussi à la contacter.

success noun succès Masc.; **a great success** un grand succès.

successful adjective 1 réussi; **he's a successful writer** c'est un écrivain à succès; **2 to be successful in doing** réussir à faire.

successfully adverb avec succès.

such adverb 1 tellement; **they're such nice people!** ils sont tellement gentils!; **I've had such a busy day!** j'ai eu une journée tellement chargée!; **it's such a long way** c'est tellement loin; **it's such a**

pity c'est tellement dommage; **2 such a lot of** tellement de; **I've got such a lot of things to tell you!** j'ai tellement de choses à te dire!; **3 such as** comme; **in big cities such as Glasgow** dans les grandes villes comme Glasgow; **4 there's no such thing** ça n'existe pas.

suck verb sucer [61].

sudden adjective soudain; ★ **all of a sudden** tout d'un coup.

suddenly adverb 1 tout d'un coup; **he suddenly started to laugh** tout d'un coup il s'est mis à rire; **suddenly the light went out** tout d'un coup la lumière s'est éteinte; **2 to die suddenly** mourir subitement.

suede noun daim Masc.; **a suede jacket** une veste en daim.

suffer verb souffrir [73].

sufficiently adverb suffisamment.

sugar noun sucre Masc.; **would you like sugar?** est-ce que tu veux du sucre?; **brown sugar** le sucre roux.

suggest verb suggérer [24]; **he suggested I should speak to you abou it** il m'a suggéré de vous en parler.

suggestion noun suggestion Fem.; **to make a suggestion** faire une suggestion.

suicide noun suicide Masc.; **to commit suicide** se suicider.

suit noun 1 (man's) costume Masc.; **2** (woman's) tailleur Masc.

suitable adjective 1 (clothing) approprié; **I don't have any suitable shoes** je n'ai pas de

chaussures appropriées;
2 convenable; **a suitable hotel** un hôtel convenable; **3 to be suitable for** convenir à.

suitcase *noun* valise *Fem.*

sulk *verb* bouder [1].

sum *noun* **1** somme *Fem.*; **a sum of money** une somme d'argent; **a large sum** une grosse somme; **2** (*calculation*) calcul *Masc.*

• **to sum up** résumer [1].

summarize *verb* résumer [1].

summary *noun* résumé *Masc.*

summer *noun* été *Masc.*; **in summer** en été; **summer clothes** les vêtements d'été; **the summer holidays** les grandes vacances.

summertime *noun* été *Masc.*; **in summertime** en été.

summit *noun* sommet *Masc.*

sun *noun* soleil *Masc.*; **in the sun** au soleil.

sunbathe *verb* se bronzer [1].

sunblock *noun* crème *Fem.* écran total.

sunburn *noun* coup *Masc.* de soleil.

sunburned *adjective* **1** (*tanned*) bronzé; **2 to get sunburned** (*burned*) attraper un coup de soleil.

Sunday *noun* dimanche *Masc.*; **on Sunday** dimanche; **I'm going out on Sunday** je sors dimanche; **see you on Sunday!** à dimanche!; **on Sundays** le dimanche; **the museum is closed on Sundays** le musée est fermé le dimanche; **every Sunday** tous les dimanches; **last Sunday** dimanche dernier; **next Sunday** dimanche prochain.

sunflower *noun* tournesol *Masc.*; **sunflower oil** l'huile *Fem.* de tournesol.

sunglasses *plural noun* lunettes *Fem. plural* de soleil.

sunlight *noun* soleil *Masc.*

sunny *adjective* **1 it's a sunny day** il fait du soleil; **it's going to be sunny** il va faire du soleil; **2** (*place*) ensoleillé; **in a sunny corner of the garden** dans un coin ensoleillé du jardin.

sunrise *noun* lever *Masc.* du soleil.

sunroof *noun* toit *Masc.* ouvrant.

sunset *noun* coucher *Masc.* du soleil.

sunshine *noun* soleil *Masc.*

sunstroke *noun* insolation *Fem.*; **to get sunstroke** attraper une insolation.

suntan *noun* bronzage *Masc.*; **to get a suntan** bronzer.

suntan lotion *noun* lotion *Fem.* solaire.

suntan oil *noun* huile *Fem.* solaire.

super *adjective* formidable; **we had a super time!** c'était formidable!

supermarket *noun* supermarché *Masc.*

supernatural *adjective* surnaturel (*Fem.* surnaturelle).

superstitious *adjective* superstitieux (*Fem.* superstitieuse).

supervise *verb* surveiller [1].

supervisor *noun* **1** (*in a shop*) responsable *Masc. & Fem.*; **2** (*in a factory*) contremaître *Masc.*

supper *noun* dîner *Masc.*; **I had supper at Sandy's** j'ai dîné chez Sandy.

supplement *noun* supplément *Masc.*

supplies *plural noun* (*of food*) provisions *Fem. plural*.

supply *noun* 1 (*stock*) réserves *Fem. plural*; 2 **to be in short supply** être difficile à trouver.
supply *verb* fournir [2]; **the school supplies the paper** c'est l'école qui fournit le papier; **to supply somebody with something** fournir quelque chose à quelqu'un.

supply teacher *noun* suppléant *Masc.*, suppléante *Fem.*

support *noun* soutien *Masc.*; **he has a lot of support** il a beaucoup de soutien.
support *verb* 1 (*back up*) soutenir [77]; **her teachers have really supported her** ses professeurs l'ont vraiment soutenue; 2 être [6] supporter de (*a team*); **Graeme supports Liverpool** Graeme est supporter de Liverpool; 3 (*financially*) **to support a family** subvenir [81] aux besoins d'une famille.

supporter *noun* supporter *Masc.*; **a Manchester United supporter** un supporter de Manchester United.

suppose *verb* **I suppose she's forgotten** elle a sans doute oublié.

supposed *adjective* **to be supposed to do** être censé faire; **you're supposed to wear a helmet** on est censé porter un casque; **he was supposed to be here at six** il devait être là à six heures.

sure *adjective* sûr; **are you sure?** tu es sûr?; **are you sure you've had enough to eat?** tu es sûr que tu as assez mangé?; **are you sure you saw her?** tu es sûr de l'avoir vue?; **'can you shut the door?' – 'sure!'** 'peux-tu fermer la porte?' – 'bien sûr!'

surely *adverb* quand même; **surely she couldn't have forgotten!** elle ne peut pas avoir oublié quand même!

surf *noun* écume *Fem.*
surf *verb* **to surf the Net/Web** surfer [1] Internet/le web.

surface *noun* surface *Fem.*

surfboard *noun* planche *Fem.* de surf (*plural* planches de surf).

surfer *noun* 1 (*on the sea*) surfeur *Masc.*, surfeuse *Fem.*; 2 (*on the Net*) cybernaute *Masc. & Fem.*, internaute *Masc. & Fem.*

surfing *noun* surf *Masc.*; **to go surfing** faire du surf.

surgeon *noun* chirurgien *Masc.*; **she's a surgeon** elle est chirurgien.

surgery *noun* 1 (*procedure*) chirurgie *Fem.*; **to have surgery** se faire opérer; **laser surgery** la chirurgie au laser; 2 (*doctor's*) cabinet *Masc.* médical; **the dentist's surgery** le cabinet dentaire.

surname *noun* nom *Masc.* de famille (*plural* noms de famille).

surprise *noun* surprise *Fem.*; **what a surprise!** quelle surprise!

surprised *adjective* étonné; **I was surprised to see her** j'ai été étonné de la voir.

surprising *adjective* étonnant.

surrender *verb* **1** (*soldiers*) se rendre [3]; **2** (*country*) capituler [1]; **3** livrer [1] (*a town, castle*).
surrender *noun* (*by sportsman*) abandon *Masc.*; (*by army*) capitulation *Fem.*

surround *verb* **1** encercler [1]; **2 to be surrounded by** être [6] entouré de; **she's surrounded by friends** elle est entourée d'amis.

survey *noun* enquête *Fem.*

survive *verb* survivre [82].

survivor *noun* survivant *Masc.*, survivante *Fem.*

suspect *noun* suspect *Masc.*, suspecte *Fem.*
suspect *adjective* douteux (*Fem.* douteuse).
suspect *verb* soupçonner [1].

suspend *verb* **1** (*hang*) suspendre [3]; **2 to be suspended** (*from school*) être [6] exclu.

suspense *noun* suspense *Masc.*

suspicious *adjective* **1** méfiant; **to be suspicious of** se méfier de; **2 a suspicious parcel** un paquet suspect; **3 a suspicious-looking individual** un individu louche.

swallow *noun* (*bird*) hirondelle *Fem.*
swallow *verb* avaler.

swan *noun* cygne *Masc.*

swap *verb* **1** échanger [52]; **do you want to swap?** tu veux qu'on échange?; **he's swapped his bike** for a computer il a échangé son vélo contre un ordinateur; **2 to swap seats with somebody** changer [52] de place avec quelqu'un.

swear *verb* (*use bad language*) utiliser [1] des gros mots; **he swears a lot** il utilise beaucoup de gros mots.

swearword *noun* gros mot *Masc.*

sweat *noun* transpiration *Fem.*
sweat *verb* transpirer [1].

sweater *noun* pull *Masc.*

sweatshirt *noun* sweatshirt *Masc.*

swede *noun* (*vegetable*) rutabaga *Masc.*

Swede *noun* Suédois *Masc.*, Suédoise *Fem.*

Sweden *noun* Suède *Fem.*; **in Sweden** en Suède; **to Sweden** en Suède.

Swedish *noun* (*language*) suédois *Masc.*
Swedish *adjective* suédois.

sweep *verb* balayer [59].

sweet *noun* **1** bonbon *Masc.*; **I bought her some sweets** je lui ai acheté des bonbons; **2** (*dessert*) dessert *Masc.*
sweet *adjective* **1** (*food*) sucré; **I try not to eat sweet things** j'essaie d'éviter les choses sucrées; **2** (*kind*) gentil (*Fem.* gentille); **she's a really sweet person** elle est vraiment gentille; **it was really sweet of him** c'était vraiment gentil de sa part; **3** (*cute*) mignon (*Fem.* mignonne); **he looks really sweet in that hat!** il est mignon avec ce chapeau!

sweetcorn *noun* maïs *Masc.*

swell *verb* (*part of the body*) enfler [1].

swelling *noun* enflure *Fem.*; **he has a swelling on his knee** il a le genou enflé.

swerve *verb* faire [10] un écart; **the car swerved to avoid the dog** la voiture a fait un écart pour éviter le chien.

swim *noun* **to go for a swim** aller [7] se baigner.

swim *verb* nager [52]; **can he swim?** est-ce qu'il sait nager?; **to swim across a lake** traverser [1] un lac à la nage.

swimmer *noun* nageur *Masc.*, nageuse *Fem.*; **she's a strong swimmer** c'est une bonne nageuse.

swimming *noun* natation *Fem.*; **to go swimming** faire de la natation.

swimming cap *noun* bonnet *Masc.* de bain.

swimming costume *noun* maillot *Masc.* de bain.

swimming pool *noun* piscine *Fem.*

swimming trunks *noun* maillot *Masc.* de bain.

swimsuit *noun* maillot *Masc.* de bain.

swindle *noun* escroquerie *Fem.*; **what a swindle!** quelle escroquerie!

swing *noun* balançoire *Fem.*

Swiss *noun* (*person*) Suisse *Masc.* & *Fem.*; **the Swiss** les Suisses *Masc. plural.*

Swiss *adjective* suisse.

switch *noun* **1** (*button type: electrical*) bouton *Masc.*; **2** (*up-down type*) interrupteur *Masc.*

switch *verb* (*change*) changer [52] de; **to switch places** changer de place.

● **to switch something off** éteindre [60] quelque chose.

● **to switch something on** allumer [1] quelque chose.

Switzerland *noun* Suisse *Fem.*; **in Switzerland** en Suisse; **to Switzerland** en Suisse.

swollen *adjective* enflé.

swop *verb* SEE **swap**.

sword *noun* épée *Fem.*

swordfish *noun* espadon *Masc.*

sycamore *noun* sycomore *Masc.*

syllabus *noun* programme *Masc.*; **to be on the syllabus** être au programme.

symbol *noun* symbole *Masc.*

symbolic *adjective* symbolique.

sympathetic *adjective* compréhensif (*Fem.* compréhensive).

sympathize *verb* **to sympathize with somebody** comprendre [64] quelqu'un; **I sympathize with her** je la comprends.

sympathy *noun* compassion *Fem.*

symphony *noun* symphonie *Fem.*

symphony orchestra *noun* orchestre *Masc.* symphonique.

symptom *noun* symptôme *Masc.*

synagogue *noun* synagogue *Fem.*

synthesizer *noun* synthétiseur *Masc.*

synthetic *adjective* synthétique.

syringe *noun* seringue *Fem.*

system *noun* système *Masc.*

Tt

table *noun* table *Fem.*; **on the table** sur la table; **to lay the table** mettre la table; **to clear the table** débarrasser la table.

tablecloth *noun* nappe *Fem.*

table football *noun* baby-foot *Masc.*

tablemat *noun* **1** (*for individual plates*) set *Masc.* de table; **2** (*for dish*) dessous-de-plat *Masc.*

tablespoon *noun* grande cuillère *Fem.*; (*in recipes*) **a tablespoon of flour** une cuillère à soupe de farine.

tablet *noun* comprimé *Masc.*

table tennis *noun* ping-pong™ *Masc.*; **to play table tennis** jouer au ping-pong.

tabloid *noun* quotidien *Masc.* populaire.

tackle *noun* **1** (*in football*) tacle *Masc.*; **2** (*in rugby*) plaquage *Masc.*
tackle *verb* **1** (*in football or hockey*) tacler [1]; **2** s'attaquer [1] à (*a job or problem*).

tact *noun* tact *Masc.*

tactful *adjective* plein de tact; **that wasn't very tactful** ça a manqué un peu de tact.

tactic *noun* tactique *Fem.*

tadpole *noun* têtard *Masc.*

tail *noun* **1** queue *Fem.*; **2** 'heads or tails?' – 'tails' 'pile ou face?' – 'pile'.

tailor *noun* tailleur *Masc.*

take *verb* **1** prendre [64]; **he took a chocolate** il a pris un chocolat; **take my hand** prends ma main; **I**
took the bus j'ai pris le bus; **to take a holiday** prendre des vacances; **do you take sugar?** est-ce que vous prenez du sucre?; **who's taken my keys?** qui a pris mes clefs?; **it takes two hours** ça prend deux heures; **he took the news badly** il a mal pris la nouvelle; **2** (*to accompany*) emmener [50] (*a person*); **I'm taking Jake to the doctor's** j'emmène Jake chez le médecin; **I must take the car to the garage** je dois emmener la voiture au garage; **3** (*carry away*) emporter [1]; **she's taken some work to do at home** elle a emporté du travail pour faire chez elle; **4 to take something up(stairs)** monter [1] quelque chose; **could you take these towels up?** est-ce que tu peux monter ces serviettes?; **5 to take something down(stairs)** descendre [3] quelque chose; **Cheryl's taken the cups down** Cheryl a descendu les tasses; **6** accepter [1] (*a credit card or a cheque*); **do you take cheques?** est-ce que vous acceptez les chèques?; **7** passer [1] (*an exam*); **she's taking her driving test tomorrow** elle passe son permis demain; **8 it takes a lot of courage** il faut beaucoup de courage; **9 what size do you take?** quelle taille faites-vous?

- **to take something apart** démonter [1] quelque chose.

- **to take something back** rapporter [1] quelque chose.

- **to take off 1** (*a plane*) décoller [1]; **2** enlever [50] (*clothes or shoes*); **he took off his shirt** il a enlevé sa chemise; **3** déduire [26] (*money*); **he**

a
b
c
d
e
f
g
h
i
j
k
l
m
n
o
p
q
r
s
t
u
v
w
x
y
z

a
b
c
d
e
f
g
h
i
j
k
l
m
n
o
p
q
r
s
t
u
v
w
x
y
z

took five pounds off the price il a déduit cinq livres du prix

● **to take out 1** (*from a bag or pocket*) sortir [72]; **Eric took out his wallet** Eric a sorti son porte-feuille; **2 he's taking me out to lunch** il m'emmène déjeuner; **she took me out to the theatre** elle m'a emmenée au théâtre

takeaway *noun* **1** (*a meal*) repas *Masc.* à emporter; **an Indian takeaway** un repas indien à emporter; **2** (*where you buy it*) restaurant *Masc.* qui fait des plats à emporter.

take-off *noun* décollage *Masc.* (*of a plane*).

tale *noun* histoire *Fem.*

talent *noun* talent *Masc.*; **to have a talent for something** être doué pour quelque chose.

talented *adjective* doué; **he's really talented** il est vraiment doué.

talk *noun* **1** (*a chat*) conversation *Fem.*; **I had a talk with Roy about it** j'ai eu une conversation avec Roy à ce sujet; **2** exposé *Masc.*; **she's giving a talk on Hungary** elle fait un exposé sur la Hongrie.
talk *verb* **1** parler [1]; **I was talking to Jeevan about football** je parlais du foot avec Jeevan; **what's he talking about?** de quoi parle-t-il?; **we'll talk about it later** on en parlera plus tard; **2** (*to gossip*) bavarder [1]; **they're always talking** ils n'arrêtent pas de bavarder.

talkative *adjective* bavard; **he's not exactly talkative!** on ne pourrait pas dire qu'il est bavard!

tall *adjective* **1** grand; **she's very tall** elle est très grande; **I'm 1.7 metres tall** je mesure un mètre soixante-dix; **2** haut (*a building or tree*).

tambourine *noun* tambourin *Masc.*

tame *adjective* apprivoisé (*an animal*).

tampon *noun* tampon *Masc.*

tan *noun* bronzage *Masc.*; **to get a tan** bronzer.
tan *verb* bronzer [1]; **I tan easily** je bronze facilement.

tangerine *noun* mandarine *Fem.*

tank *noun* **1** (*for petrol or water*) réservoir *Masc.*; **2 a fish tank** un aquarium; **3** (*military*) char *Masc.*

tanker *noun* **1** (*ship*) navire-citerne *Masc.*; **2** (*on road*) camion-citerne *Masc.*

tanned *adjective* bronzé.

tap *noun* **1** robinet *Masc.*; **to turn on the tap** ouvrir le robinet; **to turn off the tap** fermer le robinet; **the hot tap** le robinet d'eau chaude; **2** (*a pat*) petite tape *Fem.*
tap *verb* taper [1].

tap-dancing *noun* claquettes *Fem. plural*; **to do tap-dancing** faire des claquettes.

tape *noun* **1** cassette *Fem.*; **my tape of the Stones** ma cassette des Stones; **I've got it on tape** je l'ai en cassette; **2 sticky tape** scotch™.
tape *verb* enregistrer [1]; **I want to tape the film** je veux enregistrer le film.

tape measure *noun* mètre *Masc.* à ruban.

tape recorder *noun* magnétophone *Masc.*

tapestry *noun* tapisserie *Fem.*

tar *noun* goudron *Masc.*

target *noun* cible *Fem.*

tart *noun* tarte *Fem.*; **a raspberry tart** une tarte aux framboises.

tartan *adjective* écossais; **a tartan skirt** une jupe écossaise.

task *noun* tâche *Fem.*

taste *noun* goût *Masc.*; **the taste of onions** le goût des oignons; **in bad taste** de mauvais goût.
taste *verb* **1** goûter [1]; **do you want to taste?** tu veux goûter?; **the soup tastes horrible** la soupe a un goût infect; **2 to taste of** avoir [5] un goût de; **it tastes of strawberries** ça a un goût de fraises.

tasty *adjective* savoureux (*Fem.* savoureuse).

tattoo *noun* tatouage *Masc.*; **he's got a tattoo on his arm** il a un tatouage sur le bras.

Taurus *noun* Taureau *Masc.*; **Josephine's Taurus** Josephine est Taureau.

tax *noun* **1** impôts *Masc. plural*; **2** (*on goods*) taxe *Fem.*

taxi *noun* taxi *Masc.*; **by taxi** en taxi; **to take a taxi** prendre un taxi.

taxi driver *noun* chauffeur *Masc.* de taxi.

taxi rank *noun* station *Fem.* de taxis.

TB *noun* tuberculose *Fem.*

tea *noun* **1** thé *Masc.*; **a cup of tea** une tasse de thé; **to have tea** prendre le thé; **2** (*evening meal*) dîner *Masc.*

teabag *noun* sachet *Masc.* de thé.

teach *verb* **1** apprendre [64]; **she's teaching me Italian** elle m'apprend l'italien; **that'll teach you!** ça t'apprendra!; **2** enseigner [1]; **her mum teaches maths** sa mère enseigne les maths; **3 to teach yourself something** apprendre [64] quelque chose tout seul; **Anne taught herself Italian** Anne a appris l'italien toute seule.

teacher *noun* **1** (*in a secondary school*) professeur *Masc.*; **my mother's a teacher** ma mère est professeur; **our biology teacher** notre professeur de biologie; **2** (*in primary school*) instituteur *Masc.*, institutrice *Fem.*; **she's a primary school teacher** elle est institutrice.

teaching *noun* enseignement *Masc.*

team *noun* équipe *Fem.*; **a football team** une équipe de foot; **our team won** notre équipe a gagné.

teapot *noun* théière *Fem.*

tear[1] *noun* (*a rip*) accroc *Masc.*; **I've got a tear in my jeans** j'ai un accroc dans mon jean.
tear *verb* **1** déchirer [1]; **you've torn your shirt** tu as déchiré ta chemise; **she tore up my letter** elle a déchiré ma lettre; **2** se déchirer [1]; **be careful, it tears easily** attention, ça se déchire facilement.

● **to tear off, to tear open 1** (*carefully*) détacher [1]; **2** (*violently*) arracher [1].

tear[2] *noun* (*when you cry*) larme *Fem.*; **to be in tears** être en larmes;

to burst into tears fondre en larmes.

tease *verb* **1** taquiner [1] (*a person*); **2** tourmenter [1] (*an animal*).

teaspoon *noun* petite cuillère *Fem.*; (*in recipes*) **a teaspoonful of ...** une cuillère à café de ....

teatime *noun* l'heure *Fem.* du dîner (*evening meal*).

tea towel *noun* torchon *Masc.*

technical *adjective* technique.

technical college *noun* lycée *Masc.* technique.

technician *noun* technicien *Masc.*, technicienne *Fem.*

technique *noun* technique *Fem.*

techno *noun* techno *Fem.* (*music*).

technological *adjective* technologique.

technology *noun* technologie *Fem.*; **information technology** l'informatique *Fem.*

teddy bear *noun* nounours *Masc.*

teenage *adjective* **1** adolescent (*Fem.* adolescente); **they have a teenage son** ils ont un fils adolescent; **2** (*films, magazines, etc.*) pour les jeunes; **a teenage magazine** un magazine pour les jeunes.

teenager *noun* **1** jeune *Masc. & Fem.*; **a group of teenagers** une bande de jeunes; **2** (*more precisely*) adolescent *Masc.*, adolescente *Fem.*; **when I was a teenager** quand j'étais adolescent.

teens *plural noun* adolescence *Fem.*; **he's in his teens** c'est un adolescent.

tee-shirt *noun* tee-shirt *Masc.*

telegraph pole *noun* poteau *Masc.* télégraphique.

telephone *noun* téléphone *Masc.*; **on the telephone** au téléphone. **telephone** *verb* appeler [18]; **I'll telephone the bank** je vais appeler la banque.

telephone box *noun* cabine *Fem.* téléphonique.

telephone call *noun* coup *Masc.* de téléphone.

telephone card *noun* carte *Fem.* de téléphone.

telephone directory *noun* annuaire *Masc.*

telephone number *noun* numéro *Masc.* de téléphone.

telescope *noun* télescope *Masc.*

televise *verb* téléviser [1]; **they're televising the match** on va téléviser le match.

television *noun* télévision *Fem.*; **she was watching television** elle regardait la télévision; **I saw it on television** je l'ai vu à la télévision.

television programme *noun* émission *Fem.* de télévision.

tell *verb* **1 to tell somebody something** dire [9] quelque chose à quelqu'un; **that's what she told me** c'est ce qu'elle m'a dit; **I told him it was silly** je lui ai dit que c'était idiot; **have you told Sara?** est-ce que tu l'as dit à Sara?; **2 to tell somebody to do** dire [9] à quelqu'un de faire; **he told me to do it myself** il m'a dit de le faire moi-même; **she told me not to wait** elle m'a dit de ne pas attendre;

3 (*explain*) **can you tell me how to do it?** est-ce que vous pouvez m'expliquer comment on le fait?; 4 raconter [1] (*a story*); **tell me about your holiday** raconte-moi tes vacances; 5 (*to see*) voir [13]; **you can tell it's old** on voit bien que c'est ancien; **you can tell she's cross** on voit bien qu'elle est fâchée; **I can't tell them apart** je n'arrive pas à les distinguer.

telly *noun* télé *Fem.*; **to watch telly** regarder la télé; **I saw her on telly** je l'ai vue à la télé.

temp *noun* intérimaire *Masc. & Fem.*

temper *noun* **to be in a temper** être en colère; **to lose your temper** se mettre en colère.

temperature *noun* 1 température *Fem.*; **the oven temperature** la température du four; 2 **to have a temperature** avoir de la fièvre.

temple *noun* temple *Masc.*

temporary *adjective* temporaire.

temptation *noun* tentation *Fem.*

tempted *adjective* tenté; **I'm really tempted to go** je suis vraiment tenté d'y aller.

tempting *adjective* tentant.

ten *number* dix *Masc.*; **Harry's ten** Harry a dix ans.

tend *verb* **to tend to do** avoir [5] tendance à faire; **he tends to talk a lot** il a tendance à beaucoup parler.

tendency *noun* tendance *Fem.*; **to have a tendency to** avoir [5] tendance à.

tender *adjective* tendre.

tennis *noun* tennis *Masc.*; **to play tennis** jouer au tennis.

tennis ball *noun* balle *Fem.* de tennis.

tennis court *noun* tennis *Masc.*

tennis player *noun* joueur de tennis *Masc.*, joueuse de tennis *Fem.*

tennis racket *noun* raquette *Fem.* de tennis.

tenor *noun* ténor *Masc.*

tenpin bowling *noun* bowling *Masc.*; **to go tenpin bowling** jouer au bowling.

tense *noun* **the present tense** le présent; **in the future tense** au futur.
tense *adjective* tendu.

tent *noun* tente *Fem.*

tenth *number* dixième *Masc.*; **on the tenth floor** au dixième étage; **the tenth of April** le dix avril.

term *noun* 1 (*in school*) trimestre *Masc.*; 2 **to be on good terms with somebody** être en bons termes avec quelqu'un.

terminal *noun* 1 (*at an airport*) aérogare *Fem.*; **terminal two** l'aérogare numéro deux; 2 **a ferry terminal** une gare maritime; 3 (*a computer terminal*) terminal *Masc.* (*plural* terminaux).

terrace *noun* 1 (*of a house or hotel*) terrasse *Fem.*; 2 **the terraces** (*at a stadium*) les gradins *Masc. plural*.

terrible *adjective* épouvantable; **the weather was terrible** il a fait un temps épouvantable.

terribly *adverb* 1 (*very*) très; **not terribly clean** pas très propre;

a
b
c
d
e
f
g
h
i
j
k
l
m
n
o
p
q
r
s
t
u
v
w
x
y
z

a **b**

2 (*badly*) affreusement mal; **I played terribly** j'ai joué affreusement mal.

c **d** **e**

terrific *adjective* **1 at a terrific speed** à une vitesse folle; **a terrific amount** une quantité énorme; **2 terrific!** formidable!

f

terrified *adjective* terrifié.

g

terrify *verb* terrifier [1].

h

territory *noun* territoire *Masc.*

terrorism *noun* terrorisme *Masc.*

i

terrorist *noun* terroriste *Masc.* & *Fem.*

j **k** **l** **m** **n** **o** **p** **q** **r**

test *noun* **1** (*in school*) contrôle *Masc.*; **we've got a maths test tomorrow** nous avons un contrôle de maths demain; **2** (*of your skills or patience*) test *Masc.*; **3** (*medical*) analyse *Fem.*; **a blood test** une analyse de sang; **4 a driving test** un examen de permis de conduire; **she's doing her driving test on Friday** elle passe son permis vendredi; **he passed his driving test** il a eu son permis.

test *verb* **1** (*in school*) contrôler [1]; **2 to test something out** essayer [59] quelque chose.

s

test tube *noun* éprouvette *Fem.*

t

text *noun* texte *Masc.*

u **v** **w**

text *verb* **to text someone** envoyer [40] un texto à quelqu'un; **I'll text you tomorrow** je t'enverrai un texto demain.

x

textbook *noun* manuel *Masc.*

y

text message *noun* texto™ *Masc.*

z

Thames *noun* **the Thames** la Tamise.

than *preposition, conjunction* **1** que; **their new album's better than the last one** leur nouveau CD est meilleur que le dernier; **they have more money than we do** ils ont plus d'argent que nous; **2** (*for quantities*) de; **more than forty** plus de quarante; **more than thirty years** plus de trente ans.

thank *verb* remercier [1].

thanks *plural noun* **1** merci; **no thanks** non merci; **thanks a lot** merci beaucoup; **thanks for your letter** merci pour ta lettre; **2 with thanks for** avec mes remerciements pour; **3 thanks to** grâce à; **it was thanks to Micky** c'était grâce à Micky.

thank you *adverb* merci; **thank you very much for the cheque** merci beaucoup pour le chèque; **no thank you** non merci; **a thank-you letter** une lettre de remerciements.

that *adjective* **1** ce (*Fem.* cette) (*but 'ce' becomes 'cet' before a masculine noun beginning with a vowel or a silent 'h'*) **that dog** ce chien; **that man** cet homme; **that blue car** cette voiture bleue; **2 that one** celui-là *Masc.*, celle-là *Fem.*; **'which cake would you like?'** – **'that one, please'** 'tu veux quel gâteau?' – 'celui-là, s'il te plait'; **I like all the dresses but I'm going to buy that one** j'aime toutes les robes mais je vais acheter celle-là.

that *adverb* **1 it's not that silly** ce n'est pas si idiot que ça; **their house isn't that big** leur maison n'est pas si grande que ça; **2 it was that high** c'était haut comme ça.

that *pronoun* **1** (*before verb 'être'*) ce, c' (*before a vowel*); **that's not true** ce n'est pas vrai; **that's not what you told me** ce n'est pas ce que tu m'as dit; **what's that?** qu'est-ce que c'est?; **that smells good** ça sent bon; **who's that?** c'est qui?; **where's that?** c'est où?; **is that Mandy?** c'est Mandy?; **2** ça; **did you see that?** tu as vu ça?; **that's my bedroom** ça c'est ma chambre; **3** qui; **the book that's on the table** le livre qui est sur la table; **4** que, qu' (*before a vowel or a silent 'h'*); **the book that I lent you** le livre que je t'ai prêté.

that *conjunction* que, qu' (*before a vowel or a silent 'h'*); **I knew that he was wrong** je savais qu'il avait tort.

thaw *noun* fonte *Fem.* des neiges.

the *definite article* **1** (*before a noun which is masculine in French*) le, l' (*before a vowel or silent 'h'*) **the cat** le chat; **the tree** l'arbre; **2** (*before a noun which is feminine in French*) la, l' (*before a vowel or silent 'h'*) **the table** la table; **the orange** l'orange; **3** les (*before all plural nouns*); **the windows** les fenêtres.

theatre *noun* théâtre *Masc.*; **to go to the theatre** aller au théâtre.

theft *noun* vol *Masc.*

their *adjective* leur (*plural* leurs); **their flat** leur appartement; **their mother** leur mère; **their presents** leurs cadeaux.

theirs *pronoun* **1** le leur (*when standing for a masculine noun*); **our garden's smaller than theirs** notre jardin est plus petit que le leur; **2** la leur (*when standing for a feminine noun*); **your house is bigger than theirs** votre maison est plus grande que la leur; **3** les leurs (*when standing for a plural noun*); **our children are older than theirs** nos enfants sont plus âgés que les leurs; **4** à eux, à elles; **the yellow car's theirs** la voiture jaune est à eux; **it's theirs** c'est à eux.

them *pronoun* **1** les; **I know them** je les connais; **I don't know them** je ne les connais pas; **listen to them!** écoute-les!; **I saw them last week** je les ai vus la semaine dernière; **2** (*to them*) leur; **I gave them my address** je leur ai donné mon adresse; **3** (*after a preposition*) eux (*Fem.* elles); **I'll go with them** j'irai avec eux; (*if they are all female*) j'irai avec elles; **without them** sans eux, sans elles; (*in comparisons*) **she's older than them** elle est plus âgée qu'eux; (*if all female*) elle est plus âgée qu'elles.

theme *noun* thème *Fem.*

theme park *noun* parc *Masc.* de loisirs.

themselves *pronoun* **1** se; **they've helped themselves** ils se sont servis; **2** (*for emphasis*) eux-mêmes *Masc.*, elles-mêmes *Fem.*; **the boys can do it themselves** les garçons peuvent le faire eux-mêmes; **the girls will tell you themselves** les filles vous le diront elles-mêmes.

then *adverb* **1** (*next*) ensuite; **I wash up and then I make the bed** je fais la vaisselle et ensuite je fais le lit; **I went to the post office and then the bank** je suis allé à la poste et ensuite à la banque; **2** (*at that time*) à l'époque; **we were living in York**

a
b
c
d
e
f
g
h
i
j
k
l
m
n
o
p
q
r
s
t
u
v
w
x
y
z

then nous habitions à York à l'époque; **3** (*in that case*) alors; **then why worry?** alors pourquoi s'inquiéter?; **that's all right then** ça va alors; **4 by then** déjà; **by then it was too late** il était déjà trop tard.

theory *noun* théorie *Fem.*; **in theory** en théorie.

there *adverb* **1** là; **put it there** mets-le là; **stand there** mettez-vous là; **they're in there** ils sont là; **2 over there** là-bas; **she's over there talking to Mark** elle est là-bas en train de discuter avec Mark; **down there** là-bas; **3 up there** là-haut; **look up there!** regarde là-haut!; **4** y (*when the place 'there' stands for has already been mentioned*); **I've seen photos of Oxford but I've never been there** j'ai vu des photos d'Oxford mais je n'y suis jamais allé; **yes, I'm going there on Tuesday** oui, j'y vais mardi; **5 there is** il y a; **there's a cat in the garden** il y a un chat dans le jardin; **there was no bread** il n'y avait pas de pain; **yes, there's enough** oui, il y en a assez; **6 there are** il y a; **there are plenty of seats** il y a beaucoup de places; **7 there they are!** les voilà!; **there she is!** la voilà!; **there's the bus coming!** voilà le bus qui arrive!

therefore *adverb* donc.

thermometer *noun* thermomètre *Masc.*

these *adjective* ces; **these books** ces livres.

they *pronoun* **1** ils (*when standing for a masculine noun*); **'where are the knives?' – 'they're in the drawer'** 'où sont les couteaux?'– 'ils

sont dans le tiroir'; **2** elles (*when standing for a feminine noun*); **I bought some apples but they're not very nice** j'ai acheté des pommes mais elles ne sont pas très bonnes.

thick *adjective* épais (*Fem.* épaisse); **a thick layer of butter** une couche épaisse de beurre.

thickness *noun* épaisseur *Fem.*

thief *noun* voleur *Masc.*, voleuse *Fem.*

thigh *noun* cuisse *Fem.*

thin *adjective* **1** mince (*a slice or a person*); **2** (*too thin, skinny*) maigre; **she's got terribly thin** elle a beaucoup maigri.

thing *noun* **1** (*an object*) chose *Fem.*; **shops full of pretty things** des magasins remplis de jolies choses; **she told me some surprising things** elle m'a raconté des choses étonnantes; **2** (*a whatsit*) truc *Masc.* (*informal*); **tu peux utiliser ce truc-là pour l'ouvrir** you can use that thing to open it; **that thing next to the hammer** ce truc à côté du marteau; **3 things** (*belongings*) affaires *Fem. plural*; **you can put your things in my room** tu peux mettre tes affaires dans ma chambre; **the best thing to do is** ... ce qu'il faut faire, c'est ...; **the thing is, I've lost her address** ce qu'il y a, c'est que j'ai perdu son adresse; **how are things with you?** comment ça va?

think *verb* **1** (*believe*) croire [33]; **do you think they'll come?** tu crois qu'ils vont venir?; **no, I don't think so** non, je ne crois pas; **I think he's already left** je crois qu'il est déjà parti; **2** penser [1]; **I'm thinking**

about you je pense à toi; **Tony thinks it's silly** Tony pense que c'est bête; **what do you think of my new jacket?** qu'est-ce que tu penses de ma nouvelle veste?; **what do you think of that?** qu'en penses-tu?; **3** (*to think carefully*) réfléchir [2]; **he thought for a moment** il a réfléchi un instant; **I've thought it over carefully** j'y ai bien réfléchi; **4** (*imagine*) imaginer [1]; **just think! we'll soon be in Spain!** imagine! on va bientôt être en Espagne!; **I never thought it would be like this!** je n'avais jamais imaginé que ce serait comme ça.

third noun tiers *Masc.*; **a third of the population** un tiers de la population.
third adjective troisième; **on the third floor** au troisième étage; **the third of March** le trois mars.

thirdly adverb troisièmement.

Third World noun tiers-monde *Masc.*

thirst noun soif *Fem.*

thirsty adjective **to be thirsty** avoir [5] soif; **I'm thirsty** j'ai soif; **we were all thirsty** nous avions tous soif.

thirteen number treize *Masc.*; **Ahmed's thirteen** Ahmed a treize ans.

thirty number trente *Masc.*

this adjective **1** ce (*before a masculine noun*), cet (*before a masculine noun beginning with a vowel or a silent 'h'*), cette (*before a feminine noun*); **this paintbrush** ce pinceau; **this tree** cet arbre; **this cup** cette tasse; **this morning** ce

matin; **this evening** ce soir; **this afternoon** cet après-midi; **2 this one** celui-ci *Masc.*, celle-ci *Fem.*; **if you need a pen you can use this one** si tu as besoin d'un stylo tu peux utiliser celui-ci; **if you want a lamp you can borrow this one** si tu veux une lampe tu peux emprunter celle-ci.

this pronoun **1** ça; **can you hold this for a moment?** est-ce que tu peux prendre ça un instant?; **2 what's this?** qu'est-ce que c'est?; **this is Tracy speaking** (*on the phone*) c'est Tracy à l'appareil; **3** (*in introductions*) **this is my sister Carla** je te présente ma sœur Carla.

thistle noun chardon *Masc.*

thorn noun épine *Fem.*

thorough adjective **1** (*search*) minutieux (*Fem.* minutieuse); **2** (*person*) consciencieux (*Fem.* consciencieuse).

those adjective ces; **those books** ces livres.
those pronoun ceux-là *Masc.*, celles-là *Fem.*; **if you want some knives you can take those** si tu veux des couteaux tu peux prendre ceux-là; **if you want some plates you can take those** si tu veux des assiettes tu peux prendre celles-là.

though conjunction, adverb **1** bien que (*followed by a verb in the subjunctive*); **though it's cold** bien qu'il fasse froid; **though he's older than she is** bien qu'il soit plus âgé qu'elle; **2 it was a good idea, though** et pourtant, c'était une bonne idée.

thought noun pensée *Fem.*

a
b
c
d
e
f
g
h
i
j
k
l
m
n
o
p
q
r
s
t
u
v
w
x
y
z

thoughtful *adjective*
1 (*considerate*) gentil (*Fem.* gentille);
it was really thoughtful of you
c'était vraiment gentil de ta part;
2 (*deep in thought*) pensif (*Fem.*
pensive).

thoughtless *adjective* irréfléchi.

thousand *number* **1** mille *Masc.*; **a
thousand** mille; **three thousand**
trois mille; **2 thousands of** des
milliers de; **there were thousands
of tourists in Venice** il y avait des
milliers de touristes à Venise.

thread *noun* fil *Masc.*
thread *verb* enfiler [1] (*a needle*).

threat *noun* menace *Fem.*

threaten *verb* menacer [61]; **to
threaten to do** menacer de faire.

three *number* trois *Masc.*; **Oskar's
three** Oskar a trois ans.

three-quarters *noun* trois-
quarts *Masc. plural*; **three-quarters
full** plein aux trois-quarts.

thrilled *adjective* ravi; **I was
thrilled to hear from you** j'ai été
ravi d'avoir de tes nouvelles.

thriller *noun* thriller *Masc.*

thrilling *adjective* palpitant.

throat *noun* gorge *Fem.*; **to have a
sore throat** avoir mal à la gorge.

through *preposition* **1** (*across*) à
travers; **through the forest** à
travers la forêt; **the water went
right through** l'eau est passée à
travers; **the police let us through**
la police nous a laissés passer;
2 (*via*) par; **the train went through
Leeds** le train est passé par Leeds;
through the window par la fenêtre;
I know them through my cousins
je les connais par mes cousins; **3 to
go through something** traverser
quelque chose; **we went through
the park** nous avons traversé le
parc; **4 right through the day** toute
la journée.
through *adjective* direct (*a train or
flight*).

throughout *preposition*
throughout the match pendant
tout le match; **throughout the
world** partout dans le monde.

throw *verb* **1** jeter [48]; **I threw the
letter into the bin** j'ai jeté la lettre
dans la poubelle; **he threw the
book on the floor** il a jeté le livre
par terre; **2** (*taking aim*) lancer [61];
throw me the ball! lance-moi le
ballon!; **we were throwing
snowballs** on lançait des boules de
neige.
● **to throw something away** jeter
[48] quelque chose; **I've thrown
away the old newspapers** j'ai jeté
les vieux journaux.
● **to throw somebody out** expulser
[1] quelqu'un.
● **to throw something out** jeter [48]
quelque chose (*rubbish*).
● **to throw up** vomir [2].

thumb *noun* pouce *Masc.*

thump *verb* taper [1].

thunder *noun* tonnerre *Masc.*; **a
peal of thunder** un roulement de
tonnerre.

thunderstorm *noun* orage *Masc.*

thundery *adjective* orageux (*Fem.*
orageuse).

Thursday *noun* jeudi *Masc.*; **on
Thursday** jeudi; **I'm going out on
Thursday**

*(left margin alphabet index: a b c d e f g h i j k l m n o p q r s **t** u v w x y z)*

Thursday je sors jeudi; **see you on Thursday!** à jeudi!; **on Thursdays** le jeudi; **the museum is closed on Thursdays** le musée est fermé le jeudi; **every Thursday** tous les jeudis; **last Thursday** jeudi dernier; **next Thursday** jeudi prochain.

thyme *noun* thym *Masc.*

tick *verb* **1** (*tick-tock*) faire [10] tic-tac; **2** (*on paper*) cocher [1]; **tick the box** cochez la case.

ticket *noun* **1** billet *Masc.* (*for a plane, a train, an exhibition, a theatre or cinema*) **two tickets for the concert** deux billets pour le concert; **2** (*for the underground, the bus, or left luggage*) ticket *Masc.*; **a bus ticket** un ticket de bus; **3 a parking ticket** un PV (*informal*).

ticket inspector *noun* contrôleur *Masc.*

ticket office *noun* (*at a station*) guichet *Masc.*

tickle *verb* chatouiller [1].

tide *noun* marée *Fem.*; **at high tide** à marée haute; **the tide is out** c'est la marée basse.

tidy *adjective* **1** bien rangé (*a room*); **2** soigné (*homework*); **3** ordonné (*a person*).
tidy *verb* ranger [52]; **I'll tidy (up) the kitchen** je rangerai la cuisine.

tie *noun* **1** cravate *Fem.*; **a red tie** une cravate rouge; **2** (*in a match*) match *Masc.* nul.
tie *verb* **1** nouer [1]; **to tie your shoelaces** nouer ses lacets; **2 to tie a knot in something** faire [10] un nœud à quelque chose; **3** (*in a*

match) **we tied two all** nous avons fait match nul, deux partout.

tiger *noun* tigre *Masc.*

tight *adjective* **1** juste; **the skirt's a bit tight** la jupe est un peu juste; **these shoes are too tight** ces chaussures me serrent; **2** (*close-fitting*) moulant; **she was wearing a tight dress** elle portait une robe moulante.

tighten *verb* serrer [1].

tightly *adverb* fermement.

tights *plural noun* collant *Masc. singular*; **a pair of purple tights** un collant violet.

tile *noun* **1** (*on a floor or wall*) carreau *Masc.* (*plural* carreaux); **2** (*on a roof*) tuile *Fem.*

till[1] *preposition, conjunction* **1** jusqu'à; **they're here till Sunday** ils sont là jusqu'à dimanche; **till then** jusque là; **till now** jusqu'à présent; **2 not till** pas avant; **she won't be back till ten** elle ne sera pas rentrée avant dix heures; **we won't know till Monday** nous ne le saurons pas avant lundi.

till[2] *noun* caisse *Fem.*; **pay at the till** payez à la caisse.

time *noun* **1** (*on the clock*) heure *Fem.*; **what time is it?** quelle heure est-il?; **it's time for lunch** c'est l'heure du déjeuner; **on time** à l'heure; **ten o'clock French time** dix heures heure française; **2** (*an amount of time*) temps *Masc.*; **we've got lots of time** nous avons beaucoup de temps; **there's not much time left** il ne reste plus beaucoup de temps; **for a long time**

a
b
c
d
e
f
g
h
i
j
k
l
m
n
o
p
q
r
s
t
u
v
w
x
y
z

longtemps; **from time to time** de temps en temps; **3** (*moment*) moment *Masc.*; **is this a good time to phone?** est-ce que c'est le bon moment pour vous appeler?; **at times** par moments; **for the time being** pour le moment; **any time now** d'un moment à l'autre; **4** (*in a series*) fois *Fem.*; **six times** six fois; **the first time** la première fois; **the first time I saw you** la première fois que je t'ai vu; **three times a year** trois fois par an; **three times two is six** trois fois deux égalent six; **5 to have a good time** bien s'amuser [1]; **we had a really good time** nous nous sommes très bien amusés; **have a good time!** amusez-vous bien!

time off *noun* **1** (*free time*) temps *Masc.* libre; **2** (*leave*) congé *Masc.*

timetable *noun* **1** (*in school*) emploi *Masc.* du temps; **2** (*for trains or buses*) horaire *Masc.*; **the bus timetable** l'horaire des bus.

tin *noun* boîte *Fem.*; **a tin of tomatoes** une boîte de tomates.

tin-foil *noun* papier *Masc.* aluminium.

tinned *adjective* en conserve; **tinned peas** des petits pois en conserve.

tin opener *noun* ouvre-boîte *Masc.*

tinted *adjective* teinté.

tiny *adjective* minuscule.

tip *noun* **1** (*the end*) bout *Masc.*; **the tip of my finger** le bout de mon doigt; **2** (*money*) pourboire *Masc.*; **3** (*a useful hint*) tuyau *Masc.* (*plural* tuyaux) (*informal*).

tip *verb* **1** (*to give money to*) donner [1] un pourboire à; **we tipped the waiter** nous avons donné un pourboire au garçon; **2** verser [1] (*liquid*).

tiptoe *noun* **on tiptoe** sur la pointe des pieds.

tired *adjective* **1** fatigué; **I'm tired** je suis fatigué; **you look tired** tu as l'air fatigué; **2 to be tired of** en avoir assez de; **I'm tired of London** j'en ai assez de Londres; **I'm tired of watching TV** j'en ai assez de regarder la télé.

tiring *adjective* fatigant.

tissue *noun* (*a paper hanky*) kleenex™ *Masc.*; **do you have a tissue?** est-ce que tu as un kleenex?

tissue paper *noun* papier *Masc.* de soie.

title *noun* titre *Masc.*

to *preposition* **1** (*to a place or person*) à (*note that 'à + le' becomes 'au' and 'à + les' becomes 'aux'*) **to go to London** aller à Londres; **give the book to Leila** donne le livre à Leila; **I'm going to school** je vais à l'école; **she's gone to the office** elle est partie au bureau; **a letter to parents** une lettre aux parents; **from Monday to Friday** du lundi au vendredi; **2** (*with names of countries*) **they're going to Spain** ils vont en Espagne; (*BUT*) **they're going to Japan** ils vont au Japon (*'en' with feminine countries, 'au' with most masculine countries*); **3** à; **I have nothing to do** je n'ai rien à faire; **I had a lot of homework to do** j'avais beacoup de devoirs à faire; **we're ready to go** nous sommes prêts à partir; **it's easy to do** c'est facile à faire; **4** (*to somebody's house, shop, surgery*) chez; **I went round to Paul's house** je suis allé chez Paul; **we're going to the Browns' for supper** on va dîner chez les Brown; **I'm going to the dentist's tomorrow** je vais chez le dentiste demain; **she's gone to the hairdresser's** elle est allée chez le coiffeur; **5** (*talking about the time*) **it's ten to nine** il est neuf heures moins dix; **it's twenty to** il est moins vingt; **6** (*in order to*) pour; **he gave me some money to buy a sandwich** il m'a donné de l'argent pour acheter un sandwich.

toad *noun* crapaud *Masc.*

toadstool *noun* champignon *Masc.*; **a poisonous toadstool** un champignon vénéneux.

toast *noun* **1** pain *Masc.* grillé; **two slices of toast** deux tranches de pain grillé; **2** (*to your health*) toast *Masc.*; **to drink a toast to the future** lever un verre à l'avenir.

toaster *noun* grille-pain *Masc.*

tobacco *noun* tabac *Masc.*

tobacconist's *noun* bureau *Masc.* de tabac.

today *noun* aujourd'hui *Masc.*; **today's her birthday** c'est son anniversaire aujourd'hui.

toe *noun* doigt *Masc.* de pied; **my big toe** mon gros orteil.

toenail *noun* ongle *Masc.* de pied.

toffee *noun* caramel *Masc.*

together *adverb* **1** ensemble; **Kate and Lenny arrived together** Kate et Lenny sont arrivés ensemble; **2** (*at the same time*) en même temps; **they all left together** ils sont tous partis en même temps.

toilet *noun* toilettes *Fem. plural*; **where's the toilet?** où sont les toilettes?; **she's gone to the toilet** elle est allé aux toilettes.

toilet paper *noun* papier *Masc.* hygiénique.

toilet roll *noun* rouleau *Masc.* de papier hygiénique.

token *noun* **1** (*for a machine or game*) jeton *Masc.*; **2 a record token** un chèque-cadeaux *Masc.* pour disque.

tolerant *adjective* tolérant.

toll *noun* **1** péage *Masc*; **2** (*number of dead*) nombre *Masc.*; **the death toll is now 25** le nombre de victimes s'élève maintenant à 25.

tomato *noun* tomate *Fem.*; **a tomato salad** une salade de tomates; **tomato sauce** la sauce tomate.

tomorrow *adverb* demain; **I'll do it tomorrow** je le ferai demain; **tomorrow afternoon** demain après-midi; **tomorrow morning** demain matin; **tomorrow night** demain soir; **the day after tomorrow** après-demain.

ton *noun* tonne *Fem.*; **she gets tons of letters** elle reçoit des tonnes de lettres.

tone *noun* **1** (*on an answerphone*) tonalité *Fem.*; **speak after the tone** parlez après la tonalité; **2** (*of a voice or a letter*) ton *Masc.*

tongue *noun* langue *Fem.*; **to stick your tongue out** tirer la langue;

a
b
c
d
e
f
g
h
i
j
k
l
m
n
o
p
q
r
s
t
u
v
w
x
y
z

★ **it's on the tip of my tongue** je l'ai sur le bout de la langue.

tonic noun Schweppes™ Masc.; **a gin and tonic** un gin tonic.

tonight adverb 1 (this evening) ce soir; **I'm going out with my mates tonight** je sors avec les copains ce soir; 2 (after bedtime) cette nuit.

tonsillitis noun angine Fem.

too adverb 1 trop; **it's too expensive** c'est trop cher; **too often** trop souvent; 2 **too much, too many** trop; **it takes too much time** ça prend trop de temps; **there are too many accidents** il y a trop d'accidents; **he eats too much** il mange trop; 3 (as well) aussi; **Karen's coming too** Karen vient aussi; **me too!** moi aussi!

tool noun outil Masc.

tool box noun boîte Fem. à outils.

tool kit noun trousse Fem. à outils.

tooth noun dent Fem.; **to brush your teeth** se brosser les dents.

toothache noun mal Masc. de dents; **to have toothache** avoir mal aux dents.

toothbrush noun brosse Fem. à dents.

toothpaste noun dentifrice Masc.

top noun 1 haut Masc. (of a page, a ladder, or stairs); **at the top of the stairs** en haut de l'escalier; 2 (of a container or box) dessus Masc.; **it's on top of the chest-of-drawers** c'est sur la commode; 3 (of a mountain) sommet Masc.; 4 (a lid) (of a pen) capuchon Masc.; (of a bottle) capsule Fem.; 5 (to wear) haut Masc.; 6 **to be at the top of the list** être en

tête de la liste.

top adjective 1 (a step or floor) dernier (Fem. dernière); **it's on the top floor** c'est au dernier étage; 2 de haut (a bunk); 3 du haut (a shelf); 4 **in the top left-hand corner** en haut à gauche; ★ **and on top of all that** et par-dessus le marché; ★ **it was a bit over the top** c'était un peu exagéré.

topic noun sujet Masc.

topping noun garniture Fem.; **which topping would you like on your pizza?** vous voulez une pizza à quoi?

torch noun lampe Fem. de poche.

torn adjective déchiré.

tornado noun tornade Fem.

tortoise noun tortue Fem.

torture noun torture Fem.
torture verb torturer [1].

Tory noun conservateur Masc., conservatrice Fem.

total noun total Masc.
total adjective total (Masc. plural totaux).

totally adverb complètement.

touch noun 1 (contact) **to get in touch with somebody** prendre contact avec quelqu'un; **to stay in touch with somebody** rester en contact avec quelqu'un; 2 **we've lost touch** on s'est perdu de vue; **I've lost touch with her recently** je l'ai perdue de vue récemment; 3 (a little bit) petit peu Masc.; **a touch of vanilla** un petit peu de vanille; **it was a touch embarrassing** c'était un petit peu gênant.

touch verb toucher [1].

touched *adjective* touché.

touching *adjective* touchant.

tough *adjective* **1** dur; **the meat's a bit tough** la viande est un peu dure; **it's a tough area** c'est un quartier dur; **things are a bit tough at the moment** la vie est un peu dure en ce moment; **a tough guy** un dur; **2** robuste; **you need to be tough to survive** il faut être robuste pour survivre!; **a tough fabric** un tissu robuste; **3** (*tough luck*) tant pis; **tough, you're too late** tant pis pour toi, tu arrives trop tard.

tour *noun* **1** visite *Fem.*; **we did the tour of the castle** nous avons fait la visite du château; **a tour of the city** une visite de la ville; **2 a package tour** un voyage organisé; **3** (*by a band or theatre group*) tournée *Fem.*; **to go on tour** partir en tournée. **tour** *verb* (*performer*) être [6] en tournée; **they're touring the States** ils sont en tournée aux États-Unis.

tourism *noun* tourisme *Masc.*

tourist *noun* touriste *Masc. & Fem.*

tourist information office *noun* syndicat *Masc.* d'initiative.

tournament *noun* tournoi *Masc.*; **a tennis tournament** un tournoi de tennis.

tow *verb* **to be towed away** (*by the police*) être [6] emmené à la fourrière; (*by a breakdown truck*) être [6] remorqué.

towards *preposition* en direction de; **she went off towards the lake** elle est partie en direction du lac.

towel *noun* serviette *Fem.*

tower *noun* tour *Fem.*; **the Eiffel Tower** la tour Eiffel.

tower block *noun* tour *Fem.*

town *noun* ville *Fem.*; **to go into town** aller en ville.

town centre *noun* centre-ville *Masc.*

town hall *noun* mairie *Fem.*

toxic *adjective* toxique.

toy *noun* jouet *Masc.*; **a toy car** une petite voiture.

toyshop *noun* magasin *Masc.* de jouets.

trace *noun* trace *Fem.*; **there was no trace of it** il n'en restait aucune trace. **trace** *verb* retrouver [1].

tracing paper *noun* papier *Masc.* calque.

track *noun* **1** (*for sport*) piste *Fem.*; **a track event** une épreuve de vitesse; **a racing track** (*for cars*) un circuit; **2** (*a path*) chemin *Masc.*; **3** (*song*) chanson; **this is my favourite track** c'est ma chanson préférée.

track suit *noun* survêtement *Masc.*

tractor *noun* tracteur *Masc.*

trade *noun* (*a profession*) métier *Masc.*

trademark *noun* marque *Fem.*; **registered trademark** marque déposée.

trade union *noun* syndicat *Masc.*

tradition *noun* tradition *Fem.*

traditional *adjective* traditionnel (*Fem.* traditionnelle).

traffic *noun* circulation *Fem.*

traffic island *noun* refuge *Masc.*

a
b
c
d
e
f
g
h
i
j
k
l
m
n
o
p
q
r
s
t
u
v
w
x
y
z

traffic jam *noun* embouteillage *Masc.*

traffic lights *plural noun* feux *Masc. plural.*

traffic warden *noun* contractuel *Masc.*, contractuelle *Fem.*

tragedy *noun* tragédie *Fem.*

tragic *adjective* tragique.

trail *noun* (*a path*) sentier *Masc.*; **a nature trail** un sentier écologique.

trailer *noun* remorque *Fem.*

train *noun* train *Masc.*; **he's coming by train** il prend le train; **I met her on the train** je l'ai rencontrée dans le train; **the train to York** le train pour York.

train *verb* **1** former [1] (*a student*); **2 to train to be something** suivre [75] une formation de quelque chose; **he's training to be a nurse** il suit une formation d'infirmier; **3** (*in sport*) s'entraîner [1]; **the team trains on Saturdays** l'équipe s'entraîne le samedi.

trainee *noun* stagiaire *Masc. & Fem.*

trainer *noun* **1** (*of an athlete or a horse*) entraîneur *Masc.*, entraîneuse *Fem.*; **2** (*shoe*) basket *Masc.*; **my new trainers** mes nouveaux baskets.

training *noun* **1** (*for a career*) formation *Fem.*; **2** (*for sport*) entraînement *Masc.*

train ticket *noun* billet *Masc.* de train.

train timetable *noun* horaire *Masc.* des trains.

tram *noun* tramway *Masc.*

tramp *noun* clochard *Masc.*, clocharde *Fem.*

trampoline *noun* trampoline *Masc.*

transfer *noun* **1** (*of money*) virement *Masc.*; **2** (*of employee, footballer*) transfert *Masc.*; **3** (*sticker*) décalcomanie *Fem.*

transform *verb* transformer [1].

transistor *noun* transistor *Masc.*

translate *verb* traduire [26]; **to translate something into French** traduire quelque chose en français.

translation *noun* traduction *Fem.*

translator *noun* traducteur *Masc.*, traductrice *Fem.*; **I'd like to be a translator** j'aimerais être traducteur.

transparent *adjective* transparent.

transplant *noun* **1** (*operation*) transplantation *Fem.*; **2** (*organ*) transplant *Masc.*

transport *noun* transport *Masc.*; **air transport** le transport aérien; **public transport** les transports en commun.

trap *noun* piège *Masc.*

travel *noun* voyages *Masc. plural*; **foreign travel** les voyages à l'étranger; **a travel brochure** une brochure de voyages.
travel *verb* voyager [52].

travel agency *noun* agence *Fem.* de voyages.

travel agent *noun* agent *Masc.* de voyages.

traveller's cheque *noun* chèque-voyage *Masc.* (*plural* chèques-voyage).

traveller noun **1** voyageur Masc., voyageuse Fem.; **2** (*gypsy*) nomade Masc. & Fem.

travelling noun voyages Masc. plural; **I like travelling** j'aime partir en voyage.

travel-sick noun **to be** or **get travel-sick** souffrir [73] du mal de voyage.

tray noun plateau Masc. (*plural* plateaux).

tread verb **to tread on something** marcher [1] sur quelque chose.

treasure noun trésor Masc.

treat noun **1 I took them to the circus as a treat** je les ai emmenés au cirque pour leur faire plaisir; **2** (*food*) gâterie Fem.; **it's a little treat** c'est une petite gâterie.
treat verb **1** traiter [1]; **he treats his dog well** il traite bien son chien; **the doctor who treated you** le médecin qui vous a traité; **2 to treat somebody to something** offrir [56] quelque chose à quelqu'un; **I'll treat you to a drink** je vous offre à boire; **I treated myself to a new dress** je me suis offert une nouvelle robe.

treatment noun traitement Masc.

treaty noun traité Masc.

tree noun arbre Masc.

tree trunk noun tronc Masc. d'arbre.

tremble verb trembler [1].

tremendous adjective fantastique; **a tremendous victory/ defeat** une victoire/défaite écrasante.

trend noun **1** (*a fashion*) mode Fem.; **2** (*a tendency*) tendance Fem.

trendy adjective branché.

trial noun (*legal*) procès Masc..

triangle noun triangle Masc.

tribe noun tribu Fem.

tribute noun hommage Masc.; **many tributes were paid to the Pope** de nombreuses personnes ont rendu hommage au Pape.

trick noun **1** (*by a conjuror, or as a joke*) tour Masc.; **to play a trick on somebody** jouer un tour à quelqu'un; **2** (*a knack*) astuce Fem.; **it doesn't work, there must be a trick to it** ça ne marche pas, il doit y avoir une astuce.
trick verb rouler [1]; **he tricked me!** il m'a roulé!

tricky adjective délicat; **it's a tricky situation** c'est une situation délicate.

tricycle noun tricycle Masc.

trim verb couper [1] (*hair or fabric*).

Trinidad noun (île de) la Trinité.

Trinidadian noun Trinidadien Masc., Trinidadienne Fem.
Trinidadian adjective trinidadien (Fem. trinidadienne).

trip noun voyage Masc.; **a trip to Florida** un voyage en Floride; **he's on a business trip** il est en voyage d'affaires; **a day trip to France** une excursion d'une journée en France.
trip verb (*to stumble*) trébucher [1]; **Nicky tripped over a stone** Nicky a trébuché sur un gros caillou.

triple verb tripler [1]; **the price has tripled** le prix a triplé.

a
b
c
d
e
f
g
h
i
j
k
l
m
n
o
p
q
r
s
t
u
v
w
x
y
z

a
b
c
d
e
f
g
h
i
j
k
l
m
n
o
p
q
r
s
t
u
v
w
x
y
z

triumph *noun* triomphe *Masc.*

trolley *noun* chariot *Masc.*

trombone *noun* trombone *Masc.*; **to play the trombone** jouer du trombone.

troops *plural noun* troupes *Fem. plural.*

trophy *noun* trophée *Masc.*

tropical *adjective* tropical (*Masc. plural* tropicaux).

trot *verb* trotter [1].

trouble *noun* **1** problèmes *Masc. plural*; **we've had trouble with the car** nous avons eu des problèmes avec la voiture; **the trouble is, I've forgotten the number** le problème, c'est que j'ai oublié le numéro; **2** (*personal problems*) ennuis *Masc. plural*; **Steph's in trouble** Steph a des ennuis; **what's the trouble?** qu'est-ce qui ne va pas?; **3** (*difficulty*) **to have trouble doing** avoir du mal à faire; **I had trouble finding a seat** j'ai eu du mal à trouver une place; **it's not worth the trouble** cela ne vaut pas la peine; **it's no trouble!** ça ne me dérange pas!

trousers *plural noun* pantalon *Masc. singular*; **my old trousers** mon vieux pantalon; **a new pair of trousers** un pantalon neuf.

trout *noun* truite *Fem.*

truant *noun* **to play truant** faire [10] l'école buissonnière; **she's playing truant** elle fait l'école buissonnière.

truck *noun* camion *Masc.*

true *adjective* vrai; **a true story** une histoire vraie; **is that true?** c'est vrai?; **it's true she's**

absent-minded c'est vrai qu'elle est distraite.

truly *adverb* vraiment.

trump *noun* atout *Masc.*; **spades are trumps** atout pique.

trumpet *noun* trompette *Fem.*; **to play the trumpet** jouer de la trompette.

trunk *noun* **1** (*of a tree*) tronc *Masc.*; **2** (*of an elephant*) trompe *Fem.*; **3** (*a suitcase*) malle *Fem.*

trunks *plural noun* **swimming trunks** maillot *Masc.* de bain.

trust *noun* confiance *Fem.*

trust *verb* **I trust her** je lui fais confiance.

truth *noun* vérité *Fem.*; **to tell the truth, I'd completely forgottten** à vrai dire, j'avais complètement oublié.

try *noun* essai *Masc.*; **it's my first try** c'est mon premier essai; **to have a try** essayer [59]; **you should give it a try** tu devrais l'essayer.

try *verb* essayer [59]; **to try to do** essayer de faire; **I'm trying to open the door** j'essaie d'ouvrir la porte; **to try hard to do** faire [10] de gros efforts pour faire.

● **to try something on** essayer [59] quelque chose (*a garment*).

T-shirt *noun* tee-shirt *Masc.*

tub *noun* **1** (*food container*) pot *Masc.*; **2** (*bath*) baignoire *Fem.*

tube *noun* tube *Masc.*

tuberculosis *noun* tuberculose *Fem.*

Tuesday *noun* mardi *Masc.*; **on Tuesday** mardi; **I'm going out on**

Tuesday je sors mardi; **see you on Tuesday!** à mardi!; **on Tuesdays** le mardi; **the museum is closed on Tuesdays** le musée est fermé le mardi; **every Tuesday** tous les mardis; **last Tuesday** mardi dernier; **next Tuesday** mardi prochain.

tug *verb* tirer [1].

tuition *noun* cours *Masc. plural*; **piano tuition** des cours de piano; **private tuition** des cours particuliers.

tulip *noun* tulipe *Fem*.

tumble-drier *noun* sèche-linge *Masc*.

tumbler *noun* verre *Masc*. droit.

tummy *noun* estomac *Masc*.

tuna *noun* thon *Masc*.

tune *noun* air *Masc*.

Tunisia *noun* Tunisie *Fem*.; **in Tunisia** en Tunisie.

tunnel *noun* tunnel *Masc*.; **the Channel Tunnel** le tunnel sous la Manche.

turban *noun* turban *Masc*.

turf *noun* gazon *Masc*.

turkey *noun* dinde *Fem*.

Turkey *noun* Turquie *Fem*.; **in Turkey** en Turquie; **to Turkey** en Turquie.

Turkish *noun* turc *Masc*. (*language*). **Turkish** *adjective* turc (*Fem*. turque).

turn *noun* **1** (*in a game*) tour *Masc*.; **it's your turn** c'est ton tour; **whose turn is it?** c'est à qui le tour?; **it's Jane's turn to play** c'est à Jane de jouer; **to take turns driving**

conduire à tour de rôle; **2** (*in a road*) virage *Masc*.

turn *verb* **1** tourner [1]; **turn your chair round** tourne ta chaise; **turn left at the next set of lights** tournez à gauche aux prochains feux; **2** (*become*) devenir [81]; **she turned red** elle est devenue rouge.

- **to turn back** faire [10] demi-tour; **we turned back** nous avons fait demi-tour.

- **to turn off 1** (*from a road*) tourner [1]; **2** (*switch off*) éteindre [60] (*a light, an oven, a TV or radio*) fermer [1] (*a tap*) couper [1] (*gas or electricity*).

- **to turn on** allumer [1] (*the oven, TV, radio, or a light*) ouvrir [30] (*a tap*).

- **to turn out 1 to turn out well** bien se terminer [1]; **the holiday turned out badly** les vacances se sont mal terminées; **it all turned out alright in the end** finalement tout s'est arrangé; **2 it turned out that I was wrong** il s'est avéré que j'avais tort

- **to turn over 1** (*roll over*) se retourner [1]; **2** tourner [1] (*a page*).

- **to turn up 1** (*to arrive*) arriver [1]; **they turned up an hour later** ils sont arrivés une heure plus tard; **2** augmenter [1] (*the gas or the heating*); **3** (*make louder*) **can you turn up the volume?** est-ce que tu peux monter le son?

turning *noun* virage *Masc*.; **take the third turning on the right** prenez la troisième rue à gauche.

turnip *noun* navet *Masc*.

turquoise *adjective* turquoise.

turtle *noun* tortue *Fem* marine.

turtle dove *noun* tourterelle *Fem*.

a
b
c
d
e
f
g
h
i
j
k
l
m
n
o
p
q
r
s
t
u
v
w
x
y
z

TV *noun* télé *Fem.*; **I saw her on TV** je l'ai vue à la télé.

tweezers *noun* pince *Fem. singular* à épiler.

twelfth *number* douzième; **on the twelfth floor** au douzième étage; **the twelfth of May** le douze mai.

twelve *number* **1** douze *Masc.*; **Tara's twelve** Tara a douze ans; **2 at twelve o'clock** (*midday*) à midi; (*midnight*) à minuit.

twenty *number* vingt *Masc.*; **Marie's twenty** Marie a vingt ans; **twenty-one** vingt-et-un; **twenty-five** vingt-cinq.

twice *adverb* deux fois; **I've asked him twice** je lui ai demandé deux fois; **twice as much** deux fois plus.

twig *noun* brindille *Fem.*

twilight *noun* crépuscule *Masc.*

twin *noun* jumeau *Masc.* (*plural* jumeaux), jumelle *Fem.*; **Helen and Tim are twins** Helen et Tim sont jumeaux; **her twin sister** sa sœur jumelle.

twin *verb* **Oxford is twinned with Grenoble** Oxford est jumelée avec Grenoble.

twist *verb* tordre [3].

two *number* deux *Masc.*; **Ben's two** Ben a deux ans; **two by two** deux par deux.

type *noun* type *Masc.*; **what type of computer is it?** c'est quel type d'ordinateur?

type *verb* (*on a typewriter*) taper [1]; **I'm learning to type** j'apprends à taper à la machine; **I was busy typing some letters** j'étais en train de taper des lettres.

typewriter *noun* machine *Fem.* à écrire.

typical *adjective* typique.

typing *noun* dactylographie *Fem.*; **her typing is awful** elle tape très , mal.

tyre *noun* pneu *Masc.*

Uu

UFO *noun* ovni *Masc.*

ugly *adjective* laid.

UK *noun* (*short for United Kingdom*) Royaume-Uni *Masc.*

ulcer *noun* ulcère *Masc.*

Ulster *noun* Irlande *Fem.* du Nord.

umbrella *noun* parapluie *Masc.*

umpire *noun* arbitre *Masc.*

UN *noun* O.N.U. *Fem.* (*short for Organisation des Nations Unies*).

unable *adjective* **to be unable to do** ne pas pouvoir faire; **he's unable to come** il ne peut pas venir.

unanimous *adjective* unanime.

unattractive *adjective* peu attrayant (*person, place*).

unavoidable *adjective* inévitable.

unbearable *adjective* insupportable.

unbelievable *adjective* incroyable.

uncertain *adjective* incertain; **I'm uncertain whether they're coming** je ne suis pas sûr qu'ils viennent.

unchanged *adjective* inchangé.

uncivilized *adjective* barbare.

uncle *noun* oncle *Masc.*; **my Uncle Julian** mon oncle Julian.

uncomfortable *adjective* **1** inconfortable (*shoes or a chair*); **2** pénible (*a journey or a situation*).

uncommon *adjective* rare.

unconscious *adjective* (*out cold*) sans connaissance; **Tessa's still unconscious** Tessa est toujours sans connaissance.

under *preposition* **1** (*underneath*) sous; **under the bed** sous le lit; **perhaps it's under there** c'est peut-être là-dessous; **2** (*less than*) moins de; **under £20** moins de vingt livres; **children under five** les enfants de moins de cinq ans.

under-age *noun* **to be under-age** être mineur (*Fem.* mineure).

underclothes *plural noun* sous-vêtements *Masc. plural.*

undercooked *adjective* pas assez cuit.

underestimate *verb* sous-estimer [1].

underground *noun* (*a railway*) métro *Masc.*; **I saw her on the underground** je l'ai vue dans le métro; **shall we go by underground?** on prend le métro? **underground** *adjective* souterrain; **an underground carpark** un parking souterrain.

underline *verb* souligner [1].

underneath *preposition* sous; **it's underneath these papers** c'est sous ces papiers. **underneath** *adverb* dessous; **look underneath** cherche dessous.

underpants *plural noun* slip *Masc. singular*; **my underpants** mon slip.

underpass *noun* **1** (*pedestrian*) passage *Masc.* souterrain; **2** (*for traffic*) passage *Masc.* inférieur.

understand *verb* comprendre [64]; **I don't understand** je ne comprends pas; **I couldn't understand what he was saying** je n'ai pas compris ce qu'il disait.

understandable *adjective* **that's understandable** ça se comprend.

understanding *noun* compréhension *Fem.* **understanding** *adjective* compréhensif (*Fem.* compréhensive); **he was very understanding** il a été très compréhensif.

underwear *noun* sous-vêtements *Masc. plural.*

undo *verb* **1** défaire [10] (*a button or a lock*); **2** ouvrir [30] (*a parcel*).

undone *adjective* **to come undone** se défaire [10].

undress *verb* **to get undressed** se déshabiller [1]; **I got undressed** je me suis déshabillé.

unemployed *noun* **the unemployed** les chômeurs; **work for the unemployed** du travail pour les chômeurs. **unemployed** *adjective* au chômage; **she's unemployed** elle est au chômage.

unemployment *noun* chômage *Masc.*

uneven *adjective* irrégulier (*Fem.* irrégulière).

unexpected *adjective* imprévu.

a **unexpectedly** adverb (to happen, arrive) à l'improviste.

b **unfair** adjective injuste; **it's unfair to young people** c'est injuste pour les jeunes.

c **unfashionable** adjective démodé.

d **unfasten** verb défaire [10].

e **unfit** adjective **I'm terribly unfit** je ne suis pas du tout en forme.

f **unfold** verb déplier [1].

g **unforgettable** adjective inoubliable.

h **unfortunate** adjective regrettable.

i **unfortunately** adverb malheureusement.

j **unfriendly** adjective pas très sympathique.

k **unfurnished** adjective non meublé.

l **ungrateful** adjective ingrat.

m **unhappy** adjective malheureux (Fem. malheureuse).

n **unhealthy** adjective 1 maladif (Fem. maladive) (a person); 2 malsain (food).

o **unhurt** adjective indemne.

uniform noun uniforme Masc.; **in school uniform** en uniforme scolaire.

uninhabited adjective inhabité.

union noun (a trade union) syndicat Masc.

Union Jack noun **the Union Jack** le drapeau du Royaume-Uni.

unique adjective unique.

unit noun 1 (for measuring, for example) unité Fem.; 2 (in a kitchen) élément Masc.; 3 (a hospital department) service Masc.

United Kingdom noun Royaume-Uni Masc.

United Nations noun O.N.U (Organisation des Nations Unies).

United States (of America) plural noun États-Unis Masc. plural; **in the United States** aux États-Unis; **to the United States** aux États-Unis.

universe noun univers Masc.

university noun université Fem.; **to go to university** aller à l'université.

unjust adjective injuste.

unkind adjective pas gentil (Fem. pas gentille).

unknown adjective inconnu.

unleaded petrol noun essence Fem. sans plomb.

unless conjunction **unless he does it** à moins qu'il ne le fasse; **unless you tell her** à moins que tu ne le lui dises (note that 'à moins que' is followed by a subjunctive).

unlike adjective 1 **unlike me, she hates dogs** contrairement à moi, elle déteste les chiens; 2 **it's unlike her to be late** ce n'est pas son genre d'être en retard.

unlikely adjective peu probable; **it's unlikely** c'est peu probable.

unlimited adjective illimité.

unload verb décharger [52].

unlock verb ouvrir [30]; **the car's unlocked** la voiture est ouverte.

unlucky *adjective* **1 to be unlucky** (*a person*) ne pas avoir de chance; **I was unlucky, it was shut** je n'ai pas eu de chance, c'était fermé; **2 thirteen is an unlucky number** le treize porte malheur.

unmarried *adjective* célibataire.

unnatural *adjective* anormal (*Masc. plural* anormaux).

unnecessary *adjective* inutile; **it's unnecessary to book** il est inutile de réserver.

unpack *verb* défaire [10]; **I unpacked my rucksack** j'ai défait mon sac à dos; **I'll just unpack and then come down** je vais juste défaire ma valise et puis je descendrai.

unpaid *adjective* **1** impayé (*a bill*); **2** non rémunéré (*work*).

unpleasant *adjective* désagréable.

unplug *verb* débrancher [1].

unpopular *adjective* impopulaire.

unrealistic *adjective* peu réaliste.

unreasonable *adjective* pas raisonnable; **he's being really unreasonable** il n'est vraiment pas raisonnable.

unrecognizable *adjective* méconnaissable.

unreliable *adjective* peu fiable (*information or equipment*); **he's unreliable** on ne peut pas compter sur lui.

unroll *verb* dérouler [1].

unsafe *adjective* dangereux (*Fem.* dangereuse) (*wiring, for instance*).

unsatisfactory *adjective* insatisfaisant.

unscrew *verb* dévisser [1].

unshaven *adjective* pas rasé.

unsuccessful *adjective* **to be unsuccessful** ne pas réussir; **I tried, but I was unsuccessful** j'ai essayé mais je n'ai pas réussi; **an unsuccessful attempt** un essai vain.

unsuitable *adjective* inapproprié.

untidy *adjective* en désordre; **the house is always untidy** la maison est toujours en désordre.

untie *verb* défaire [10].

until *preposition* **1** jusqu'à; **until Monday** jusqu'à lundi; **until the tenth** jusqu'au dix; **until now** jusqu'à présent; **until then** jusque-là; **2 not until** pas avant; **not until September** pas avant septembre; **it won't be finished until Friday** ce ne sera pas fini avant vendredi.

unusual *adjective* peu commun; **an unusual beetle** un scarabée peu commun; **storms are unusual in June** c'est rare d'avoir des orages au mois de juin.

unwilling *adjective* **to be unwilling to do** ne pas vouloir faire; **he's unwilling to wait** il ne veut pas attendre.

unwrap *verb* déballer [1].

up *preposition, adverb* **1** (*out of bed*) **to be up** être levé; **Liz isn't up yet** Liz n'est pas encore levée; **to get up** se lever [50]; **we got up at six** nous nous sommes levés à six heures; **I was up late last night** je me suis couché tard hier soir; **2** (*higher up*)

a
b
c
d
e
f
g
h
i
j
k
l
m
n
o
p
q
r
s
t
u
v
w
x
y
z

609

en haut; **hands up!** haut les mains!;
up on the roof en haut sur le toit; **up
here** ici; **up there** là-haut; **we went
up the road** nous avons remonté la
rue; **it's just up the road** c'est tout
près; **up in Glasgow** à Glasgow;
3 (*wrong*) **what's up?** qu'est-ce qui
se passe?; **what's up with him?**
qu'est-ce qu'il a?; **4 up to** jusqu'à; **up
to here** jusqu'ici; **up to fifty people**
jusqu'à cinquante personnes; **she
came up to me** elle s'est approchée
de moi; **5 what's she up to?** qu'est-
ce qu'elle fait?; **it's up to you (to
decide)** c'est à toi de décider;
★ **time's up!** c'est l'heure!

update *noun* mise *Fem.* à jour;
here's an update on the delays
voici une mise à jour des retards.
update *verb* **1** (*revise*) mettre [11] à
jour (*timetables or information*);
2 moderniser [1] (*styles or
furnishings*).

upheaval *noun* bouleversement
Masc.

uphill *adverb* en montée.

upright *adjective* droit; **put it
upright** mets-le droit; **to stand
upright** se tenir droit.

upset *noun* **a stomach upset** une
indigestion.
upset *adjective* contrarié; **he's
upset** il est contrarié.
upset *verb* **to upset somebody**
contrarier [1] quelqu'un.

upside down *adjective* à l'envers.

upstairs *adverb* en haut; **Mum's
upstairs** maman est en haut; **to go
upstairs** monter [1].

up-to-date *adjective* **1** (*in fashion*)
moderne; **2** (*information*) à jour.

upwards *adjective* vers le haut.

urgent *adjective* urgent.

urgently *adverb* d'urgence; **she
wants to see you urgently** elle veut
vous voir d'urgence.

US *noun* U.S.A. *Masc. plural.*

us *pronoun* nous; **she knows us** elle
nous connaît; **they saw us** ils nous
ont vus; **he gave us a cheque** il
nous a donné un chèque; **with us**
avec nous.

USA *noun* U.S.A. *Masc. plural.*

use *noun* **1** emploi *Masc.*; **the
instructions for use** le mode
d'emploi; **2 it's no use** ça ne sert à
rien; **it's no use phoning** ça ne sert
à rien de téléphoner.
use *verb* utiliser [1]; **we used the
dictionary** nous avons utilisé le
dictionnaire; **to use something to
do** se servir [71] de quelque chose
pour faire; **I used a knife to open
the parcel** je me suis servi d'un
couteau pour ouvrir le paquet.
● **to use up 1** consommer [1] (*food or
petrol*); **2** dépenser [1] (*money*).

used *adjective* **1 to be used to
something** être [6] habitué à
quelque chose; **I'm not used to cats**
je ne suis pas habitué aux chats; **I'm
not used to it!** je n'ai pas l'habitude;
2 to be used to doing something
avoir [5] l'habitude de faire quelque
chose; **I'm not used to eating in
restaurants** je n'ai pas l'habitude de
manger au restaurant; **3 to get
used to** s'habituer à; **I've got used
to living here** je me suis habitué à

habiter ici; **you'll get used to it!** tu t'y habitueras!

used *verb* **they used to live in the country** ils habitaient à la campagne avant; **she used to smoke** elle fumait avant.

useful *adjective* utile.

useless *adjective* nul (*Fem.* nulle); **this knife's useless** ce couteau est nul; **you're completely useless!** tu es complètement nul!

user *noun* utilisateur *Masc.*, utilisatrice *Fem.*

user-friendly *adjective* convivial (*Masc. plural* conviviaux).

usual *adjective* habituel (*Fem.* habituelle); **it's the usual problem** c'est le problème habituel; **as usual** comme d'habitude; **it's colder than usual** il fait plus froid que d'habitude.

usually *adjective* d'habitude; **I usually leave at eight** d'habitude je pars à huit heures.

utensil *noun* ustensile *Masc.*

Vv

vacancy *noun* **1** (*in a hotel*) 'vacancies' 'chambres libres'; **'no vacancies'** 'complet'; **2 a job vacancy** un poste vacant.

vacant *adjective* libre.

vaccinate *verb* vacciner [1].

vaccination *noun* vaccination *Fem.*

vacuum *noun* vide *Masc.*
vacuum *verb* passer [1] l'aspirateur; **I'm going to vacuum my room** je vais passer l'aspirateur dans ma chambre.

vacuum cleaner *noun* aspirateur *Masc.*

vagina *noun* vagin *Masc.*

vague *adjective* vague.

vaguely *adverb* vaguement.

vain *adjective* vaniteux (*Fem.* vaniteuse); **in vain** en vain.

Valentine's Day *noun* la Saint-Valentin.

valentine card *noun* carte *Fem.* pour la Saint-Valentin.

valid *adjective* valable.

valley *noun* vallée *Fem.*

valuable *adjective* **1** de valeur; **to be valuable** avoir de la valeur; **that watch is very valuable** cette montre a une grande valeur; **2** (*appreciated*) précieux (*Fem.* précieuse); **he gave us some valuable information** il nous a donné des renseignements précieux.

value *noun* valeur *Fem.*
value *verb* apprécier [1] (*somebody's help, opinion, or friendship*).

van *noun* (*small*) fourgon *Masc.*, (*large*) camionnette *Fem.*

vandal *noun* vandale *Masc. & Fem.*

vandalism *noun* vandalisme *Masc.*

vandalize *verb* vandaliser [1].

vanilla *noun* vanille *Fem.*; **a vanilla ice cream** une glace à la vanille.

vanish *verb* disparaître [27].

a
b
c
d
e
f
g
h
i
j
k
l
m
n
o
p
q
r
s
t
u
v
w
x
y
z

a

variety *noun* variété *Fem.*

b

various *adjective* plusieurs; **there are various ways of doing it** il y a plusieurs façons de le faire.

c

vary *verb* varier [1]; **it varies a lot** ça varie beaucoup.

d

vase *noun* vase *Masc.*

e

VAT *noun* TVA *Fem.*

f

VCR *noun* magnétoscope *Masc.*

g

VDU *noun* console *Fem.*

h

veal *noun* veau *Masc.*

i

vegan *noun* végétalien *Masc.*, végétalienne *Fem.*

j

vegetable *noun* légume *Masc.*

k

vegetarian *noun, adjective* végétarien *Masc.*, végétarienne *Fem.*; **he's vegetarian** il est végétarien.

l

vehicle *noun* véhicule *Masc.*

m

vein *noun* veine *Fem.*

n

velvet *noun* velours *Masc.*

o

vending machine *noun* distributeur *Masc.* automatique.

p

ventilation *noun* aération *Fem.*

q

verb *noun* verbe *Masc.*

verdict *noun* verdict *Masc.*

r

verge *noun* 1 (*the roadside*) accotement *Masc.*; 2 **to be on the verge of doing** être [6] sur le point de faire; **I was on the verge of leaving** j'étais sur le point de partir.

s

t

u

version *noun* version *Fem.*

v

versus *preposition* contre; **Bath versus Chelsea** Bath contre Chelsea.

w

vertical *adjective* vertical (*Masc. plural* verticaux).

x

y

vertigo *noun* vertige *Masc.*

z

very *adverb* **it's very difficult** c'est très difficile; **very well** très bien; **very much** beaucoup.
very *adjective* 1 **the very person I need!** exactement la personne qu'il me faut!; **the very thing he was looking for** exactement ce qu'il cherchait; 2 **in the very middle** en plein milieu; **at the very end** tout à la fin; **at the very front** tout devant.

vest *noun* maillot *Masc.* de corps.

vet *noun* vétérinaire *Masc. & Fem.*; **she's a vet** elle est vétérinaire.

via *preposition* **to go via** passer par; **we're going via Dover** nous allons passer par Douvres; **we'll go via the bank** on va passer par la banque.

vicar *noun* pasteur *Masc.*

vicious *adjective* 1 méchant (*a dog*); 2 brutal (*Masc. plural* brutaux) (*an attack*).

victim *noun* victime *Fem.*

victory *noun* victoire *Fem.*

video *noun* 1 (*film*) vidéo *Fem.*; **to watch a video** regarder une vidéo; **I've got it on video** je l'ai en vidéo; 2 (*cassette*) cassette *Fem.* vidéo; **I bought a video** j'ai acheté une cassette vidéo; 3 (*video recorder*) magnétoscope *Masc.*
video *verb* enregistrer [1]; **I'll video it for you** je te l'enregistrerai.

video cassette *noun* cassette *Fem.* vidéo.

video game *noun* jeu *Masc.* vidéo (*plural* jeux vidéo).

video recorder *noun* magnétoscope *Masc.*

video shop *noun* vidéoclub *Masc.*

view *noun* **1** vue *Fem.*; **a room with a view of the lake** une chambre avec vue sur le lac; **2** (*opinion*) avis *Masc.*; **in my view** à mon avis; **a point of view** un point de vue.

viewer *noun* (*on TV*) téléspectateur *Masc.*, téléspectatrice *Fem.*

viewpoint *noun* point *Masc.* de vue.

vigorous *adjective* vigoureux (*Fem.* vigoureuse).

vile *adjective* abominable.

villa *noun* villa *Fem.*

village *noun* village *Masc.*

villager *noun* villageois *Masc.*, villageoise *Fem.*

vine *noun* vigne *Fem.*

vinegar *noun* vinaigre *Masc.*

vineyard *noun* vignoble *Masc.*

violence *noun* violence *Fem.*

violent *adjective* violent.

violin *noun* violon *Masc.*; **to play the violin** jouer du violon.

violinist *noun* violoniste *Masc. & Fem.*

virgin *noun* vierge *Fem.*

Virgo *noun* Vierge *Fem.*; **Robert's Virgo** Robert est Vierge.

virtual reality *noun* réalité *Fem.* virtuelle.

virus *noun* **1** (*in medicine*) virus *Masc.*; **2** (*in computing*) virus *Masc.*; **anti-virus software** un logiciel antivirus.

visa *noun* visa *Masc.*

visible *adjective* visible.

visit *noun* **1** (*stay*) séjour *Masc.*; **my last visit to France** mon dernier séjour en France; **2** visite *Fem.* (*to a house, museum*).

visit *verb* **1** visiter [1] (*museum, castle, town*); **2** aller [7] voir (*a person*); **we visited Auntie Pat at Christmas** nous sommes allés voir tante Pat à Noël.

visitor *noun* **1** invité *Masc.*, invitée *Fem.*; **we've got visitors tonight** on a des invités ce soir; **2** (*a tourist*) visiteur *Masc.*, visiteuse *Fem.*

visual *adjective* visuel (*Fem.* visuelle).

vital *adjective* indispensable; **it's vital to book** il est indispensable de réserver.

vitamin *noun* vitamine *Fem.*

vivid *adjective* **1** (*colour*) vif (*Fem.* vive); **2 to have a vivid imagination** exagérer.

vocabulary *noun* vocabulaire *Masc.*

vocational *adjective* professionnel (*Fem.* professionnelle).

vodka *noun* vodka *Masc.*

voice *noun* voix *Fem.*

volcano *noun* volcan *Masc.*

volleyball *noun* volley-ball *Masc.*; **to play volleyball** jouer au volley-ball.

volume *noun* volume *Masc.*; **could you turn down the volume?** est-ce que tu peux baisser le volume?

voluntary *adjective* **1** (*not compulsory*) volontaire; **2 to do voluntary work** travailler bénévolement.

a
b
c
d
e
f
g
h
i
j
k
l
m
n
o
p
q
r
s
t
u
v
w
x
y
z

a

b

c

d

e

f

g

h

i

j

k

l

m

n

o

p

q

r

s

t

u

v

w

x

y

z

volunteer *noun* **1** (*for a job*) volontaire *Masc. & Fem.*; **2** (*in charity work*) bénévole *Masc. & Fem.*

vomit *verb* vomir [2].

vote *noun* vote *Masc.*; **she got 20 votes** elle a obtenu 20 votes.

vote *verb* voter [1]; **she always votes Green** elle vote toujours pour les Verts.

voucher *noun* bon *Masc.*

vowel *noun* voyelle *Fem.*

voyage *noun* voyage *Masc.*

vulgar *adjective* vulgaire.

Ww

waffle *noun* (*to eat*) gaufre *Fem.*

wage(s) *noun* salaire *Masc.*

wagon *noun* **1** (*for transport*) chariot *Masc.*; **2** (*on railway*) wagon *Masc.* de marchandises.

waist *noun* taille *Fem.*

waistcoat *noun* gilet *Masc.*

waist measurement *noun* tour *Masc.* de taille.

wait *noun* attente *Fem.*; **an hour's wait** une heure d'attente.

wait *verb* **1** attendre [3]; **they're waiting in the car** ils attendent dans la voiture; **she kept me waiting** elle m'a fait attendre; **2 to wait for** attendre [3]; **wait for me!** attends-moi!; **wait for the signal** attendez le signal; **3 I can't wait to open it!** j'ai hâte de l'ouvrir!

waiter *noun* serveur *Masc.*

waiting list *noun* liste *Fem.* d'attente.

waiting room *noun* salle *Fem.* d'attente.

waitress *noun* serveuse *Fem.*

wake *verb* **1** réveiller [1] (*somebody else*); **Jess woke me at six** Jess m'a réveillé à six heures; **2** se réveiller [1]; **I woke (up) at six** je me suis réveillé à six heures; **wake up!** réveille-toi!

Wales *noun* pays *Masc.* de Galles; **in Wales** au pays de Galles; **to Wales** au pays de Galles.

walk *noun* promenade *Fem.* (*a little stroll*) tour *Masc.*; **to go for a walk** faire une promenade; **we went for a walk in the woods** nous avons fait une promenade dans la forêt; **we'll go for a little walk round the village** on va faire un petit tour au village; **to take the dog for a walk** promener [50] le chien; **it's about five minutes' walk from here** c'est à environ cinq minutes à pied d'ici. **walk** *verb* **1** marcher [1]; **I like walking on sand** j'aime marcher sur le sable; **2** (*walk around*) se promener [50]; **we walked around the old town** nous nous sommes promenés dans la vieille ville; **3** (*go*) aller [7]; **I'll walk to the bus stop with you** j'irai avec toi jusqu'à l'arrêt de bus; **4** (*on foot rather than by car or bus*) aller [7] à pied; **it's not far, we can walk** ce n'est pas loin, on peut y aller à pied.

walkie-talkie *noun* talkie-walkie *Masc.* (*plural* talkies-walkies).

walking *noun* (*hiking*) randonnée *Fem.*; **we're going walking in**

Scotland nous allons faire de la randonnée en Écosse.

walking distance *noun* **it's within walking distance of the sea** c'est à quelques minutes à pied de la mer.

walking stick *noun* canne *Fem.*

walkman™ *noun* walkman™ *Masc.*

wall *noun* **1** (*of a house*) mur *Masc.*; **2** (*of a city*) muraille *Fem.*; **the southern wall was destroyed** la muraille sud a été détruite; **the city walls** les fortifications de la ville.

wallet *noun* portefeuille *Masc.*

wallpaper *noun* papier *Masc.* peint.

walnut *noun* noix *Fem.* (*plural* noix).

wander *verb* **to wander around town** se balader [1] en ville; **to wander off** s'éloigner [1].

want *noun* **all our wants** tous nos besoins.

want *verb* vouloir [14]; **do you want some coffee?** tu veux du café?; **what do you want to do?** qu'est-ce que tu veux faire?; **I don't want to bother him** je ne veux pas le déranger.

war *noun* guerre *Fem.*

ward *noun* salle *Fem.* (*in a hospital*).

wardrobe *noun* **1** (*cupboard*) armoire *Fem.*; **2** (*clothes*) garde-robe *Fem.*

warehouse *noun* entrepôt *Masc.*

warm *adjective* **1** chaud; **a warm drink** une boisson chaude; **it's warm today** il fait chaud

aujourd'hui; **I am warm** j'ai chaud; **are you warm enough?** as-tu assez chaud?; **I'll keep your dinner warm** je tiendrai ton dîner au chaud; **2** (*friendly*) chaleureux (*Fem.* chaleureuse); **a warm welcome** un accueil chaleureux.

warm *verb* chauffer [1]; **warm the plates** chauffez les assiettes.

● **to warm up 1** (*the weather*) s'adoucir [2]; **2** (*an athlete*) s'échauffer [1]; **3** (*to heat up*) réchauffer [1] (*food*); **I'll warm up some soup for you** je vous réchaufferai de la soupe

warmth *noun* chaleur *Fem.*

warn *verb* prévenir [81]; **I warn you, it's expensive** je vous préviens que c'est cher; **to warn somebody to do** conseiller [1] à quelqu'un de faire; **he warned me to lock the car** il m'a conseillé de fermer la voiture.

warning *noun* avertissement *Masc.*

wart *noun* verrue *Fem.*

wash *noun* **to give something a wash** laver [1] quelque chose; **to have a wash** se laver.

wash *verb* laver [1]; **I've washed your jeans** j'ai lavé ton jean; **to wash your hands** se laver les mains; **I washed my hands** je me suis lavé les mains; **to wash your hair** se laver les cheveux; **to get washed** se laver; **to wash the dishes** faire [10] la vaisselle.

● **to wash up** faire [10] la vaisselle.

washbasin *noun* lavabo *Masc.*

washing *noun* **1** (*dirty*) linge *Masc.* sale; **2** (*clean*) linge *Masc.*

a b c d e f g h i j k l m n o p q r s t u v **w** x y z

615

washing machine *noun*
machine *Fem.* à laver.

washing powder *noun* lessive
Fem.

washing-up *noun* vaisselle *Fem.*;
to do the washing-up faire la
vaisselle.

washing-up liquid *noun* liquide
Masc. à vaisselle.

wasp *noun* guêpe *Fem.*

waste *noun* **1** (*of food, money,
paper*) gaspillage *Masc.*; **2** (*of time*)
perte *Fem.*; **it's a waste of time** c'est
une perte de temps.

waste *verb* **1** gaspiller [1] (*food,
money, paper*); **2** perdre [3] (*time*);
you're wasting your time tu perds
ton temps.

waste-bin *noun* poubelle *Fem.*

wastepaper-basket *noun*
corbeille *Fem.* à papier.

watch *noun* montre *Fem.*; **my watch
is fast** ma montre avance; **my
watch is slow** ma montre retarde.

watch *verb* **1** (*to look at*) regarder
[1]; **I was watching TV** je regardais
la télé; **2** (*keep a check on*) surveiller
[1]; **watch the time** surveille
l'heure; **3** (*to be careful*) faire [10]
attention; **watch you don't spill it**
fais attention de ne pas le renverser;
watch out for black ice faites
attention au verglas; **watch out!**
attention!

water *noun* eau *Fem.*

water *verb* arroser [1]; **to water
the plants** arroser les plantes.

watercolours *noun* peinture
Fem. pour aquarelle.

waterfall *noun* cascade *Fem.*

watering can *noun* arrosoir
Masc.

water melon *noun* pastèque *Fem.*

waterproof *adjective*
imperméable.

water-skiing *noun* ski *Masc.*
nautique; **to go water-skiing** faire
du ski nautique.

water sports *plural noun* sports
Masc. plural nautiques.

wave *noun* **1** (*in the sea*) vague *Fem.*;
2 (*with your hand*) signe *Masc.*; **she
gave him a wave from the bus** elle
lui a fait signe du bus.

wave *verb* **1** (*with your hand*)
saluer [1] de la main; **2** (*flap*) agiter
[1] (*your ticket or the newspaper, for
example*).

wax *noun* cire *Fem.*

way *noun* **1** (*a route or road*) chemin
Masc.; **the way to town** le chemin
pour aller en ville; **we asked the
way to the station** nous avons
demandé le chemin pour aller à la
gare; **on the way back** sur le
chemin de retour; **on the way** en
route; **'way in'** 'entrée'; **'way out'**
'sortie'; **2** (*direction*) direction *Fem.*;
which way did he go? en quelle
direction est-il parti?; **come this
way** venez par ici; **to be in the way**
gêner le passage; **3** (*side*) sens *Masc.*;
the right way up à l'endroit; **the
wrong way round** à l'envers;
4 (*distance*) **it's a long way** c'est
loin; **Terry went all the way to York**
Terry est allé jusqu'à York;
5 (*manner*) façon *Fem.*; **a way of
talking** une façon de parler; **he does
it his way** il le fait à sa façon; **either
way, she's wrong** de toute façon elle

a tort; **do it this way** fais-le comme ceci; **6 no way!** pas question!; **7 by the way** à propos.

way in *noun* entrée *Fem.*

way out *noun* sortie *Fem.*

we *pronoun* nous; (*informally*) on; **we live in Carlisle** nous habitons Carlisle; **we're going to the cinema tonight** on va au cinéma ce soir.

weak *adjective* **1** (*feeble*) faible; **her voice was weak** sa voix était faible; **2** léger (*Fem.* légère) (*coffee or tea*).

wealth *noun* fortune *Fem.*; **the wealth of the nation** la richesse de la nation.

wealthy *adjective* riche.

weapon *noun* arme *Fem.*

wear *noun* **children's wear** vêtements *Masc. plural* pour enfants; **sports wear** vêtements de sport.
wear *verb* porter [1]; **Tamsin's wearing her trainers** Tamsin porte ses baskets; **she often wears red** elle est souvent en rouge; **to wear make-up** se maquiller [1].

weather *noun* temps *Masc.*; **what's the weather like?** quel temps fait-il?; **in fine weather** quand il fait beau; **the weather was cold** il faisait froid; **the weather here is terrible** il fait un temps affreux ici.

weather forecast *noun* météo *Fem.*; **the weather forecast says it will rain** selon la météo il va pleuvoir.

web *noun* **1** (*spider's*) toile *Fem.*; **2** (*Internet*) **the Web** le web *Masc.*, la Toile *Fem.*

web site *noun* site *Masc.* internet.

wedding *noun* mariage *Masc.*

Wednesday *noun* mercredi *Masc.*; **on Wednesday** mercredi; **I'm going out on Wednesday** je sors mercredi; **see you on Wednesday!** à mercredi!; **on Wednesdays** le mercredi; **the museum is closed on Wednesdays** le musée est fermé le mercredi; **every Wednesday** tous les mercredis; **last Wednesday** mercredi dernier; **next Wednesday** mercredi prochain.

weed *noun* mauvaise herbe *Fem.*

week *noun* semaine *Fem.*; **last week** la semaine dernière; **next week** la semaine prochaine; **this week** cette semaine; **for weeks** pendant des semaines; **a week today** aujourd'hui en huit.

weekday *noun* **on weekdays** en semaine.

weekend *noun* week-end *Masc.*; **last weekend** le weekend dernier; **next weekend** le weekend prochain; **they're coming for the weekend** ils vont passer le weekend chez nous; **I'll do it at the weekend** je le ferai pendant le week-end; **have a nice weekend!** bon weekend!

weekly *adverb* une fois par semaine; **I see her weekly** je la vois toutes les semaines.
weekly *adjective* hebdomadaire; **a weekly magazine** un magazine hebdomadaire.

weigh *verb* peser [50]; **to weigh something** peser quelque chose; **how much do you weigh?** combien pèses-tu?; **I weigh 50 kilos** je pèse cinquante kilos; **to weigh yourself** se peser.

a

b

c

d

e

f

g

h

i

j

k

l

m

n

o

p

q

r

s

t

u

v

w

x

y

z

weight *noun* poids *Masc.*; **to put on weight** prendre du poids; **to lose weight** perdre du poids.

weightlifting *noun* haltérophilie *Fem.*

weird *adjective* bizarre.

welcome *noun* accueil *Masc.*; **they gave us a warm welcome** ils nous ont fait un accueil chaleureux; **welcome to Oxford!** bienvenue à Oxford!

welcome *adjective* bienvenu; **you're welcome any time** vous êtes toujours les bienvenus; **'thank you!'** **– 'you're welcome!'** 'merci!' – 'de rien!'

welcome *verb* accueillir [35].

well ¹ *noun* puits *Masc.*

well ² *adverb* **1 to feel well** se sentir bien; **I'm very well, thank you** ça va très bien, merci; **2** bien; **Terry played well** Terry a bien joué; **the operation went well** l'opération s'est bien passée; **well done!** bravo!; **3 as well** aussi; **Kevin's coming as well** Kevin vient aussi; **4** alors; **well then, what's the problem?** alors, quel est le problème?; **5 very well then, you can go** très bien, tu peux y aller.

well-behaved *adjective* sage.

well-done *adjective* bien cuit (*a steak*).

wellington (boot) *noun* botte *Fem.* en caoutchouc.

well-known *adjective* célèbre.

well-off *adjective* aisé.

Welsh *noun* **1 the Welsh** (*people*) les Gallois *Masc. plural*; **2** (*language*)

gallois *Masc.*

Welsh *adjective* gallois.

Welshman *noun* Gallois *Masc.*

Welshwoman *noun* Galloise *Fem.*

west *noun* ouest *Masc.*; **in the west** à l'ouest.

west *adjective, adverb* ouest (*never agrees*); **the west side** le côté ouest; **a west wind** un vent d'ouest; **west of Paris** à l'ouest de Paris.

western *noun* (*a film*) western *Masc.*

West Indian *noun* Antillais *Masc.*, Antillaise *Fem.*

West Indian *adjective* antillais.

West Indies *plural noun* Antilles *Fem. plural*; **in the West Indies** aux Antilles.

wet *adjective* **1** (*damp*) mouillé; **the grass is wet** l'herbe est mouillée; **we got wet** nous nous sommes fait mouiller; **2 a wet day** un jour de pluie.

whale *noun* baleine *Fem.*

what *pronoun, adjective* **1** qu'est-ce que (*in questions as the object of a verb*); **what did you say?** qu'est-ce que tu as dit?; **what's she doing?** qu'est-ce qu'elle fait?; **what did you buy?** qu'est-ce que tu as acheté?; **what is it?** qu'est-ce que c'est?; **what's the matter?** qu'est-ce qu'il y a?; **2** qu'est-ce qui (*in questions as the subject of the verb*); **what's happening?** qu'est-ce qui se passe?; **3** ce que (*relative pronoun as the object of the verb*); **tell me what you bought** dis-moi ce que tu as acheté; **4** ce qui (*relative pronoun as the* *subject of a verb*); **she told me what had happened** elle m'a dit ce qui s'était passé; **5** quel *Masc.*, quelle *Fem.*; **what's your address?** quelle est ton adresse?; **what country is it in?** c'est dans quel pays?; **what colour is it?** c'est de quelle couleur?; **what make is it?** c'est quelle marque?; **6 what's her name?** elle s'appelle comment?; **what?** comment?

wheat *noun* blé *Masc.*

wheel *noun* roue *Fem.*; **the spare wheel** la roue de rechange; **the steering wheel** le volant.

wheelbarrow *noun* brouette *Fem.*

wheelchair *noun* fauteuil *Masc.* roulant.

when *adverb, conjunction* quand; **when is she arriving?** quand est-ce qu'elle arrive?; **when's your birthday?** c'est quand, ton anniversaire?; **it was raining when I went out** il pleuvait quand je suis sorti.

where *adverb, conjunction* où; **where are the plates?** où sont les assiettes?; **where do you live?** tu habites où?; **where are you going?** où vas-tu?; **I don't know where they live** je ne sais pas où ils habitent.

whether *si*; **I don't know whether he's back or not** je ne sais pas s'il est rentré ou non.

which *adjective* quel (*Fem.* quelle); **which CD did you buy?** quel CD as-tu acheté?

which *pronoun* **1** (*which one*) lequel *Masc.*, laquelle *Fem.*; **'I saw your brother' – 'which one?'** 'j'ai

vu ton frère – lequel?'; **'I saw your sister' – 'which one?'** 'j'ai vu ta sœur' – 'laquelle?'; **which of these jackets is yours?** laquelle de ces vestes est à toi?; **2** (*relative pronoun*) qui (*as the subject of the verb*); **the lamp which is on the table** la lampe qui est sur la table; **3** (*relative pronoun*) que (*as object of the verb*); **the book which you borrowed from me** le livre que tu m'as emprunté.

while *noun* **for a while** pendant quelque temps; **she worked here for a while** elle a travaillé ici pendant quelque temps; **after a while** au bout d'un moment.
while *conjunction* pendant que; **you can make some tea while I'm finishing my homework** tu peux faire du thé pendant que je finirai mes devoirs.

whip *noun* (*for a horse*) cravache *Fem.*
whip *verb* fouetter [1]; **whipped cream** la crème fouettée.

whirlpool *noun* tourbillon *Masc.*

whiskers *plural noun* moustaches *Fem. plural.*

whisky *noun* whisky *Masc.*

whisper *noun* chuchotement *Masc.*; **to speak in a whisper** chuchoter [1].
whisper *verb* chuchoter [1].

whistle *noun* sifflet *Masc.*
whistle *verb* siffler [1].

white *noun* blanc *Masc.*; **an egg white** un blanc d'œuf.
white *adjective* blanc (*Fem.*

a b c d e f g h i j k l m n o p q r s t u v w x y z

blanche); **a white shirt** une chemise blanche.

white coffee *noun* café *Masc.* au lait.

Whitsun *noun* Pentecôte *Fem.*

who *pronoun* 1 (*in questions*) qui; **who wants some chocolate?** qui veut du chocolat?; 2 (*relative pronoun*) qui (*as subject of the verb*); **my friend who lives in Paris** mon ami qui habite à Paris; 3 (*relative pronoun*) que (*as object of the verb*); **the friends who we invited** les amis que nous avons invités.

whole *noun* **the whole of the class** la classe tout entière; **on the whole** dans l'ensemble.
whole *adjective* tout; **the whole family** toute la famille; **the whole morning** toute la matinée; **the whole time** tout le temps; **the whole world** le monde entier.

wholemeal *adjective* complet (*Fem.* complète); **wholemeal bread** le pain complet.

whom *pronoun* 1 que; **the person whom I saw** la personne que j'ai vue; 2 (*after a preposition*) qui; **the person to whom I wrote** la personne à qui j'ai écrit.

whose *pronoun, adjective* 1 à qui; **whose is this jacket?** à qui est cette veste?; **whose shoes are these?** à qui sont ces chaussures?; **whose is it?** à qui c'est?; **I know whose it is** je sais à qui c'est; 2 dont; **the man whose car has been stolen** le monsieur dont la voiture a été volée.

why *adverb* pourquoi; **why did she phone?** pourquoi a-t-elle

appelé?; **nobody knows why he did it** personne ne sait pourquoi il l'a fait.

wicked *adjective* 1 (*bad*) méchant; 2 (*brilliant*) génial (*Masc. plural* géniaux).

wide *adjective* 1 large; **the Thames is very wide here** la Tamise est très large ici; **a piece of paper 20 cm wide** une feuille de papier de vingt centimètres de large; 2 **a wide range** une vaste gamme.
wide *adverb* **the door was wide open** la porte était grande ouverte.

wide awake *adjective* complètement éveillé.

widen *verb* élargir [2].

widow *noun* veuve *Fem.*

widower *noun* veuf *Masc.*

width *noun* largeur *Fem.*

wife *noun* femme *Fem.*

wig *noun* perruque *Fem.*

wild *adjective* 1 sauvage (*an animal or plant*); **wild birds** les oiseaux sauvages; 2 (*crazy*) fou (*Fem.* folle) (*idea, party, person*); 3 **to be wild about something** être un fana de quelque chose.

wild life *noun* **a programme on wild life in Africa** un programme sur la nature en Afrique.

wild life park *noun* réserve *Fem.* naturelle.

will *verb* 1 (*if you are unsure of the future tense of a French verb, you can check in the verb tables in the centre of the dictionary*) **I'll see you soon** te reverrai bientôt; **he'll be pleased**

a b c d e f g h i j k l m n o p q r s t u v **w** x y z

to see you il sera content de te voir; **it won't rain** il ne pleuvra pas; **there won't be a problem** il n'y aura pas de problème; **2** aller [7] (*can be used for the immmediate future*); **I'll phone them at once** je vais les appeler tout de suite; **3** (*in offers and requests*) **will you have a drink?** est-ce que vous prenez quelque chose à boire?; **will you help me?** est-ce que tu peux m'aider?; **'will you write to me?' – 'of course I will!'** 'est-ce que tu m'écriras?' – 'bien sûr que oui!'; **4** he won't open the door il ne veut pas ouvrir la porte; **the car won't start** la voiture ne veut pas démarrer; **the drawer won't open** je n'arrive pas à ouvrir le tiroir.

willing *adjective* **to be willing to do** être prêt à faire; **I'm willing to pay half** je suis prêt à payer la moitié.

willingly *adverb* volontiers.

willow *noun* saule *Masc.*; **a weeping willow** un saule pleureur.

win *noun* victoire *Fem.*; **our win over Everton** notre victoire sur Everton. **win** *verb* gagner [1]; **we won!** nous avons gagné!; **Rovers won by two goals** Rovers ont gagné de deux buts.

wind¹ *noun* vent *Masc.*; **the North wind** le vent du nord.

wind² *verb* **1** enrouler [1] (*a wire or a rope, for example*); **2** remonter [1] (*a clock*).

wind farm *noun* ferme *Fem.* d'éoliennes.

wind instrument *noun* instrument *Masc.* à vent.

window *noun* **1** (*in a building*) fenêtre *Fem.*; **to look out of the window** regarder par la fenêtre; **2** (*in a car, bus, train*) vitre *Fem.*

windscreen *noun* pare-brise *Masc.* (*plural* pare-brise).

windscreen wipers *plural noun* essuie-glace *Masc.*

windsurfing *noun* planche *Fem.* à voile; **to go windsurfing** faire [10] de la planche à voile.

windy *adjective* **1** venteux (*Fem.* venteuse) (*a place*); **2** it's windy today il fait du vent aujourd'hui.

wine *noun* vin *Masc.*; **a glass of white wine** un verre de vin blanc.

wing *noun* **1** aile *Fem.*; **2** (*in sport*) ailier *Masc.*

wink *verb* **to wink at somebody** faire [10] un clin d'œil à quelqu'un.

winner *noun* gagnant *Masc.*, gagnante *Fem.*

winning *adjective* gagnant.

winnings *plural noun* gains *Masc. plural.*

winter *noun* hiver *Masc.*; **in winter** en hiver.

wipe *verb* essuyer [41]; **I'll just wipe the table** je vais juste essuyer la table; **to wipe your nose** se moucher [1].

● **to wipe up** (*dishes*) essuyer [41] la vaisselle.

wire *noun* fil *Masc.*; **an electric wire** un fil électrique.

wire netting *noun* grillage *Masc.*

wise *adjective* sage.

wish *noun* **1** vœu *Masc.* (*plural* vœux); **make a wish!** fais un vœu!;

a
b
c
d
e
f
g
h
i
j
k
l
m
n
o
p
q
r
s
t
u
v
w
x
y
z

2 (*a desire*) désir *Masc.*; **3 best wishes on your birthday** meilleurs vœux pour ton anniversaire.
wish *verb* **1 I wish he were here** si seulement il était ici; **2 I wished him happy birthday** je lui ai souhaité un bon anniversaire.

wit *noun* esprit *Masc.*

witch *noun* sorcière *Fem.*

with *preposition* **1** avec; **with James** avec James; **with me** avec moi; **with pleasure** avec plaisir; **beat the eggs with a fork** battez les œufs avec une fourchette; **he took his umbrella with him** il a pris son parapluie; **2** (*at the house of*) chez; **we're staying the night with Frank** on va passer la nuit chez Frank; **3** (*in descriptions*) **a girl with red hair** une fille aux cheveux roux; **the boy with the broken arm** le garçon au bras cassé; **4** de; **filled with water** rempli d'eau; **covered with mud** couvert de boue; **red with rage** rouge de colère.

without *preposition* sans; **without you** sans toi; **without sugar** sans sucre; **without a sweater** sans pull; **without looking** sans regarder.

witness *noun* témoin *Masc.*

witty *adjective* spirituel (*Fem.* spirituelle).

wizard *noun* magicien *Masc.*

wolf *noun* loup *Masc.*

woman *noun* femme *Fem.*; **a woman friend** une amie; **a woman doctor** une femme médecin.

wonder *noun* **1** merveille *Fem.*; **2 it's no wonder you're tired** ce n'est pas étonnant si tu es fatigué.

wonder *verb* se demander [1]; **I wonder why** je me demande pourquoi; **I wonder where Jake is** je me demande où est Jake.

wonderful *adjective* merveilleux (*Fem.* merveilleuse).

wood *noun* bois *Masc.*; **the lamp is made of wood** la lampe est en bois.

wooden *adjective* en bois.

woodwork *noun* menuiserie *Fem.*

wool *noun* laine *Fem.*

woollen *adjective* en laine.

word *noun* **1** mot *Masc.*; **a long word** un mot long; **what's the French word for 'window'?** comment dit-on 'window' en français?; **in other words** autrement dit; **to have a word with somebody** parler avec quelqu'un; **2** (*promise*) **to give somebody your word** donner sa parole à quelqu'un; **he broke his word** il n'a pas tenu parole; **3 the words of a song** les paroles d'une chanson.

word processing *noun* traitement *Masc.* de texte.

word processor *noun* machine *Fem.* à traitement de texte.

work *noun* travail *Masc.* (*plural* travaux); **Mum's at work** maman est au travail; **I've got some work to do** j'ai du travail à faire; **he's out of work** il est sans emploi; **Ben's off work** (*sick*) Ben est en arrêt de travail; (*on holiday*) Ben est en congé.

work *verb* **1** travailler [1]; **she works in an office** elle travaille dans un bureau; **Dad works at home** papa travaille à domicile;

Ruth works in advertising Ruth travaille dans la publicité; **he works nights** il travaille de nuit; **2** (*to operate*) se servir [71] de; **can you work the video?** sais-tu te servir du magnétoscope?; **3** (*function*) marcher [1]; **the dishwasher's not working** le lave-vaisselle est en panne; **that worked really well!** ça a bien marché!

● **to work out 1** (*understand*) comprendre [64]; **I can't work out why** je ne comprends pas pourquoi; **2** (*exercise*) s'entraîner [1]; **3** (*to go well*) (*a plan*) marcher [1]; **4** (*calculate*) calculer [1]; **I'll work out how much it would cost** je vais calculer combien ç coûterait

worked up *adjective* **to get worked up** s'énerver [1].

worker *noun* (*in a factory*) ouvrier *Masc.*, ouvrière *Fem.*

worker *noun* ouvrier *Masc.*, ouvrière *Fem.*

work experience *noun* stage *Masc.*; **to do work experience** faire un stage; **to be on work experience** être en stage.

working-class *adjective* ouvrier (*Fem.* ouvrière); **a working-class background** un milieu ouvrier.

work of art *noun* œuvre *Fem.* d'art.

workshop *noun* atelier *Masc.*

workstation *noun* (*computer*) poste *Masc.* de travail (*plural* postes de travail).

world *noun* monde *Masc.*; **the best in the world** le meilleur du monde;

the Western world les pays occidentaux.

World Cup *noun* **the World Cup** la Coupe du Monde.

world war *noun* guerre *Fem.* mondiale; **the Second World War** la Seconde Guerre mondiale.

worm *noun* ver *Masc.*

worn out *adjective* **1** (*a person*) épuisé; **2** (*clothes or shoes*) complètement usé.

worried *adjective* inquiet (*Fem.* inquiète); **they're worried** ils s'inquiètent; **to be worried about** s'inquiéter pour; **we're worried about Susan** nous nous inquiétons pour Susan.

worry *noun* soucis *Masc. plural.* **worry** *verb* s'inquiéter [24]; **don't worry!** ne t'inquiète pas!; **there's nothing to worry about** il n'y a pas de quoi s'inquiéter.

worrying *adjective* inquiétant.

worse *adjective* pire; **it was even worse than the last time** c'était encore pire que la dernière fois; **to get worse** empirer [1]; **the weather's getting worse** le temps empire; **things are getting worse and worse** ça va de pire en pire.

worst *adjective* **the worst** le plus mauvais; **it was the worst day of my life** ça a été la journée la plus mauvaise de ma vie; **if the worst comes to the worst** au pire.

worth *adjective* **to be worth** valoir [80]; **how much is it worth?** ça vaut combien?; **to be worth doing** valoir la peine de faire; **it's worth trying** ça vaut la peine d'essayer;

a
b
c
d
e
f
g
h
i
j
k
l
m
n
o
p
q
r
s
t
u
v
w
x
y
z

it's not worth it ça ne vaut pas la peine.

would *verb* **1 would you like something to eat?** voulez-vous quelque chose à manger?; **2 he wouldn't answer** il n'a pas voulu répondre; **the car wouldn't start** la voiture n'a pas voulu démarrer; **3 I would like an omelette** je voudrais une omelette; **I'd like to go to the cinema** j'aimerais aller au cinéma; **that would be a good idea** ce serait une bonne idée; **if we asked her she would help us** elle nous aiderait, si nous le lui demandions.

wound *noun* blessure *Fem*. **wound** *verb* blesser [1].

wrap *verb* emballer [1]; **I'm going to wrap (up) my presents** je vais emballer mes cadeaux; **could you wrap it for me please?** voulez-vous me faire un paquet cadeau, s'il vous plaît?

wrapping paper *noun* papier *Masc*. cadeau.

wreck *noun* **1** (*of a crashed car or plane*) épave *Fem*.; **2 I feel a wreck!** je suis une loque! **wreck** *verb* **1** détruire [26]; **2** gâcher [1] (*plans, occasion*); **it completely wrecked my evening!** ça m'a complètement gâché la soirée!

wrestler *noun* catcheur *Masc*., catcheuse *Fem*.

wrestling *noun* catch *Masc*.

wrinkle *noun* ride *Fem*.

wrinkled *adjective* ridé.

wrist *noun* poignet *Masc*.

write *verb* écrire [38] (*a letter or a story*); **I'll write her a letter** je lui écrirai une lettre; **to write to somebody** écrire à quelqu'un; **I wrote to Jean yesterday** j'ai écrit à Jean hier.

● **to write down** noter [1]; **I wrote down her name** j'ai noté son nom.

writer *noun* écrivain *Masc*.

writing *noun* écriture *Fem*.

wrong *adjective* **1** (*not correct*) mauvais; **the wrong answer** la mauvaise réponse; **it's the wrong address** ce n'est pas la bonne adresse; **I've brought the wrong file** je n'ai pas apporté le bon classeur; **you've got the wrong number** vous vous êtes trompé de numéro; **2 to be wrong** (*mistaken*) se tromper; **I was wrong** je me suis trompé; **I was wrong when I said it was finished** je me suis trompé en disant que c'était fini; **3 what's wrong?** qu'est-ce qu'il y a?; **4** (*false*) faux (*Fem*. fausse); **the information was wrong** les renseignements étaient faux.

Xx

xerox™ *noun* photocopie *Fem*. **xerox**™ *verb* photocopier [1].

Xmas *noun* Christmas.

X-ray *noun* radio *Fem*.; **I saw the X-rays** j'ai vu les radios. **X-ray** *verb* faire [10] une radio de; **they X-rayed her ankle** ils ont fait une radio de sa cheville.

Yy

yacht *noun* **1** (*sailing boat*) voilier *Masc.*; **2** (*large luxury boat*) yacht *Masc.*

yawn *verb* bâiller [1].

year *noun* **1** an *Masc.*; (*the whole period*) année *Fem.*; **six years ago** il y a six ans; **the whole year** toute l'année; **they lived in Moscow for years** ils ont habité Moscou pendant des années; **2** (*for someone's age*) an *Masc.*; **he's seventeen years old** il a dix-sept ans; **a two-year-old child** un enfant de deux ans; **3** (*in secondary schools in France the years go from 'sixième', the equivalent of Year 7, to 'terminale', the equivalent of Year 13*); **I'm in Year 10** je suis en troisième; **I'm in Year 11** je suis en seconde.

yearly *adjective* annuel (*Fem.* annuelle); **a yearly event** un événement annuel.
yearly *adverb* tous les ans; **he goes to Normandy yearly** il va en Normandie tous les ans.

yell *verb* hurler [1].

yellow *adjective* jaune.

yes *adverb* **1** oui; **yes, I know** oui, je sais; **'is Tom in his room?' – 'yes, he is'** 'est-ce que Tom est dans sa chambre?' – 'oui'; **2** (*answering a negative*) si; **'you don't want to go, do you?' – 'yes, I do!'** 'tu ne veux pas y aller, n'est-ce pas?' – 'mais si!'; **'you haven't finished, have you?' – 'yes, I have'** 'tu n'as pas fini?' – 'si si'.

yesterday *adverb* hier; **I saw her yesterday** je l'ai vue hier; **yesterday afternoon** hier après-midi; **yesterday morning** hier matin;
the day before yesterday avant-hier.

yet *adverb* **not yet** pas encore; **it's not ready yet** ce n'est pas encore prêt.

yoga *noun* yoga *Masc.*

yoghurt *noun* yaourt *Masc.*; **a banana yoghurt** un yaourt à la banane.

yolk *noun* jaune *Masc.* d'œuf (*plural* jaunes d'œuf).

you *pronoun* **1** tu (*'tu' is the familiar way of talking to family members, close friends, and people of your own age; 'vous' is more polite*); **do you want to go to the cinema tonight?** tu veux aller au cinéma ce soir?; **2** (*the object form of 'tu'*); **I'll lend you my bike** je te prêterai mon vélo; **I'll invite you** je t'inviterai; **I'll write to you** je t'écrirai; **3** toi (*after prepositions and in comparisons*); **I'll go with you** j'irai avec toi; **he's older than you** il est plus âgé que toi; **4** (*more polite or to several people*) vous; **can you tell me where the station is, please?** est-ce que vous pouvez m'indiquer la gare, s'il vous plaît?; **I'll invite you all!** je vous inviterai tous!

young *adjective* jeune; **he's younger than me** il est plus jeune que moi; **Tessa's two years younger than me** Tessa a deux ans de moins que moi; **young people** les jeunes.

your *adjective* **1** ton *Masc.*, ta *Fem.* (*plural* tes) (*this is the familiar way of talking to family members, close friends, and people of your own age; 'vous' is more polite*) **I met your Dad** j'ai rencontré ton père; **I like your skirt!** j'aime bien ta jupe!; **you've forgotten your CDs!** tu as oublié tes CD; **2** (*more polite or to several people*) votre (*plural* vos); **thank you for your hospitality** merci pour votre hospitalité; **you can all bring your friends** vous pouvez tous amener vos amis.

yours *pronoun* **1** le tien *Masc.*, la tienne *Fem.* (*plural* les tiens *Masc.*, les tiennes *Fem.*) (*this is the familiar way of talking to somebody of your own age or belonging to your family; otherwise you should use 'vôtre'*) **my brother's younger than yours** mon frère est plus jeune que le tien; **2** (*formally or to several people*) le vôtre *Masc.*, la vôtre *Fem.* (*plural* les vôtres); **my children are younger than yours** mes enfants sont plus jeunes que les vôtres; **3** à toi, à vous (*polite form*); **is this pen yours?** est-ce que ce stylo est à toi?

yourself *pronoun* **1** (*informal*) te; (*formal*) vous; **you'll hurt yourself** tu vas te faire mal; **2** (*for emphasis*) toi-même; (*formal*) vous-même; **did you do it yourself?** est-ce que tu l'as fait toi-même?; **3 all by yourself** tout seul (*Fem.* toute seule).

yourselves *pronoun* **1** vous; **help yourselves** servez-vous; **2** (*for emphasis*) vous-mêmes; **did you do it yourselves?** est-ce que vous l'avez fait vous-mêmes?

youth *noun* **1** (*stage in life*) jeunesse *Fem.*; **2** (*young people*) les jeunes *Masc. plural*; **today's youth** les jeunes d'aujourd'hui; **3** (*young male*) jeune *Masc.*

youth hostel *noun* auberge *Fem.* de jeunesse (*plural* auberges de jeunesse).

Yugoslavia *noun* Yougoslavie *Fem.*; **the former Yugoslavia** l'ex-Yougoslavie.

Zz

zany *adjective* loufoque.

zebra *noun* zèbre *Masc.*

zebra crossing *noun* passage *Masc.* pour piétons.

zero *noun* zéro *Masc.*

zigzag *verb* zigzaguer [1].

zip *noun* fermeture *Fem.* éclair™.

zodiac *noun* zodiaque *Masc.*; **the signs of the zodiac** les signes du zodiaque.

zone *noun* zone *Fem.*

zoo *noun* zoo *Masc.*

zoom lens *noun* zoom *Masc.*

FRENCH LIFE AND CULTURE

The year in France

le jour de l'an
New Year's Day. It's a public holiday in France.

Id-al-Fitr
The date of this Muslim festival varies from year to year. It is celebrated mainly by people from North Africa (Algeria, Tunisia, etc), the largest Muslim group in France.

la Fête des Rois
Feast of the Three Kings: 6th January. Cake shops sell a special cake containing a whole bean or almond, or a plastic figure. Whoever gets it in their piece of cake wears the golden cardboard crown that decorates the cake.

la Saint Valentin
St Valentine's Day: 14th February. The custom of people sending a special message to someone they love is growing in France.

le 1er avril
April Fool's Day. People play tricks on each other: the tricks are called *poissons d'avril* (April fish).

Pâques
Easter. Children often look for chocolate eggs or rabbits hidden in the garden. Easter Monday is a public holiday, but Good Friday (le *vendredi saint*) is not.

le 1er mai
1st May: a public holiday.

le huit mai
8th May: a public holiday celebrating the end of World War II.

le quatorze juillet
14th July: the French National Day, and a public holiday. It celebrates the storming of the Bastille prison in 1789, an event which launched the French Revolution. There are street fairs, firework displays, music and dancing in all French towns. Many people set off on holiday at about this time.

le 15 août
15th August: Feast of the Assumption. Many people return home from their summer holidays around the time of this public holiday.

le 1er novembre
1st November: All Saints Day. A public holiday, on which many people put flowers on the graves of relatives and friends who have died.

le 11 novembre
11th November. A public holiday that commemorates the end of World War I, which was largely fought in France.

Noël
Christmas. People often excshange presents on Christmas Eve, before going to Midnight Mass. On Christmas Day they have a big meal, and the traditional cake is a richly decorated Christmas log (*la bûche de Noël*).

le Réveillon
New Year's Eve party. People like to dance and see the New Year in with champagne.

Food and drink

baguette
The name of the most popular French bread.

boucherie
A butcher's shop. A *boucherie chevaline* sells horse meat.

boulangerie
A baker's shop, which sells pain (bread), *croissants, pains au chocolat* (rolls with a chocolate filling), etc

charcuterie
A delicatessen shop that sells ham, sausages, cold meats, salads, etc

café
A French cafe serves coffee, alcoholic drinks, sandwiches and often simple meals. In tourist spots, you often pay more if you sit than if you stand at the counter.

Champagne
The area of Champagne, east of Paris has given its name to the sparkling wine that is produced there. Wines are often called by the areas where they are produced, e.g. Bordeaux, Bourgogne (from Burgundy).

Chantilly
Fresh, sweetened whipped cream.

chips
Crisps. Chips, French fries, are called *frites*.

crêpes
Pancakes. A *crêperie* serves both sweet and savoury pancakes, e.g. pancakes filled with ham or cheese.

fruits de mer
Sea food, such as mussels, shrimps, lobster.

glaces
Ice creams. Flavours include e.g. *cassis* (blackcurrant), *pistache* (pistachio nut), *noisette* (hazelnut), *citron vert* (lime), and many others.

menthe à l'eau
Mint cordial in chilled water: one of the cheapest and most thirst-quenching drinks available in a cafe.

plat du jour
Meal of the day, e.g. in a cafe or restaurant.

pâtisserie
A shop which sells cakes, tarts and biscuits, usually made on the premises.

ratatouille
A spicy vegetable dish made with tomatoes, onions, garlic, courgettes and often aubergine.

salade composée
A mixed salad.

veau
Veal, the meat from a calf, is widely available in France.

Life at School

arts plastiques

The school subject we call 'art'. It is a compulsory subject in French *collèges*.

bac

The end-of-school exam taken by pupils who have stayed at school to the age of 18. *Bac* is short for *baccalauréat*.

brevet

The exam taken at the age of 15 or 16 by pupils leaving school.

Carnet de notes et de correspondance

A book in which pupils write information which the school wants to send home, e.g. information about school trips.

classe de neige

A week which younger pupils (under 12s) spend in the mountains, with skiing lessons as part of their curriculum.

collège

State school for pupils aged 11-15.

éducation civique

A compulsory school subject in which pupils are taught how the country is governed, and what people's rights and duties are.

journée scolaire

The school day. The length of the school day varies, but can be from 8.30 a.m. to 5 p.m.

lycée

State school for 15-18 year olds.

redoubler

Pupils who fail in too many subjects have to repeat the year *(redoubler)* instead of going on to a higher class.

rentrée

The return to school in September. Shops are full of products for pupils going back to school, and the issue of school are widely discussed in the media.

sixième

Pupils begin *collège* when they are about 11 years old. The years are called:

sixième (6th) = Year 7
cinquième (5th) = Year 8
quatrième (4th) = Year 9
troisième (3rd) = Year 10

vacances scolaires

School holidays are usually:

- one week in October / November
- two weeks at Christmas
- two weeks in February
- two weeks at Easter
- about eight weeks in summer, from early July to early September

On holiday in France

aire
Motorway services.

Arc de Triomphe, Paris
A grand arch, built in 1836 at the meeting-point of 13 roads. From the top there is a grand view down the wide avenue called the Champs-Élysées to a similar arch in front of the Louvre palace.

Bretagne
Brittany. A popular tourist area, with a rocky coast and sandy beaches.

Many people speak Breton, a Celtic language, and road signs are often in both French and Breton.

chambre d'hôte
You see this sign outside houses which offer bed-and-breakfast accommodation.

Champs-Élysées
The grandest street in Paris, lined with luxury shops, cafes and hotels. It stretches from the *Arc de Triomphe* to the *Louvre* palace.

Corse
The island of Corsica, in the Mediterranean, has been French since 1768.

Côte d'Azur
The French Riviera, the most fashionable stretch of the French Mediterranean coast, including St Tropez, Cannes, Nice, Monte Carlo, etc

Dordogne
The area along the Dordogne river, famous for its fortified towns and villages.

gîte rural
A self-catering holiday house or flat.

grottes
Underground caves and caverns. Some still have paintings from prehistoric times.

Loire
The longest river in France, famous for its many beautiful castles and palaces (*châteaux*) within a small area near Tours, e.g.

- Chambord, reputed to a have a tower for every day of the year,

- Chenonceaux, built across the river Cher.

Louvre
The Louvre used to be a royal palace. It is now one of the world's largest and richest museums of paintings (e.g. the Mona Lisa), sculptures, and other works of art.

météo
The weather forecast, on the internet, on TV, in newspapers, etc

métro
The Paris underground. The fast trains serving the suburbs are called RER. A carnet of 10 tickets is cheaper than 10 individual tickets.

tour Eiffel
Built by Gustave Eiffel in 1889, 100 years after the French Revolution, the Eiffel Tower was the highest structure in the world. It is 320 metres high. You can climb the stairs to the second storey, or take a lift to the top.

Midi

Midi means 'south', and le Midi refers to the south of France.

Mont Saint-Michel

This tiny island, reached by a causeway from the border between Brittany and Normandy, is one of the most popular tourist attractions in France. It is named after its Benedictine abbey begun in 966 AD.

Monaco

A tiny country on the Mediterranean coast, near Nice, famous for its fashionable luxury marina. The Monaco Grand Prix is raced on the streets of the town.

Monte Carlo

The part of Monaco which houses the famous casino.

Provence

Part of the south of France, near the Rhone delta. Its Roman remains, the associations with the painter Van Gogh, and its hot, sunny climate, make it a popular tourist area.

Routes nationales

The main roads in France. They are numbered in red (N1, N2, etc). Smaller roads, *routes départementales*, are numbered in yellow (D1, D2, etc).

SNCF

The name of French railways. Some main lines operate high-speed trains called *le TGV*.

toutes directions

Follow the *toutes directions* (all directions) signs when you want to leave the town centre.

Versailles

The enormous and magnificent royal palace built in the town of Versailles, outside Paris, as from the 17th century. Louis XIV, sometimes called the Sun King, had his court here.

Life in France

bal public
Many events end with a *bal public:* dancing for all in the town or village square.

boules
A game in which players from two teams throw or roll metal balls on an earth pitch, aiming to get as close as possible to the jack (a small wooden ball). The game, very popular in France, is also called *pétanque.*

carte d'identité
French people have an identity card. It can be used instead of a passport to travel within the EU.

code postal
Postcode. French postcodes have five figures and no letters.

département
France is divided into 95 *départements.* Each has a number, e.g. central Paris is 75. This number is used in postcodes and as the last two numbers on car number plates.

fête
A party. In summer, many towns and villages have *fêtes*, with music, stalls, dancing, etc.

fête nationale
The French national day: 14th July.

Hôtel de Ville
Town hall.

Maghreb
The name given to the North of Africa (Morocco, Algeria, Tunisia). There are many people from these countries living and working in France.

pédalos
Pedal-boats that can be hired on many larger lakes.

République
France is a republic, with a president *(président)* at its head. The president is elected every seven years.

Roland-Garros
A big stadium in Paris. International tennis competitions are held here.

Stade de France
With a capacity of 80 000 for football and rugby matches, 75 000 for athletics or 100 000 for concerts, this stadium in the north of Paris is France's biggest. It was opened in 1998.

Tour de France
The world's most famous cycle race takes place in July.

VTT
Mountain bikes.

Did you know ... ?

★ that most French motorways (autoroutes) charge tolls (péage), but that many are free?

★ that comics (bandes dessinées or BD) are very popular in France?

★ that French letter boxes (boîtes aux lettres) are yellow?

★ that shops are often closed (fermés) at lunchtime, but are open (ouvert) late into the evening?

★ that France is the biggest country in western Europe?

★ that there are about 169 million speakers of French (Francophones) in the world?

★ that the French call the English Channel La Manche (the Sleeve)?

★ that Marseille was founded by the Greeks in about 600BC?

★ that the French national anthem is called the Marseillaise because it was soldiers from Marseille who first sang it in Paris?

★ that Médecins Sans Frontières is an organisation that sends doctors to countries hit by crises such as war or famine?

★ that le Mont Blanc (4807m), on the border between France and Italy, is western Europe's highest mountain?

★ that some museums (musées) are free for young people, and that some are free for all visitors on the first Sunday in the month?

★ that a big piece of meat in a restaurant is called a pavé (paving stone)?

★ that the French national police are organised in two forces (la police, les gendarmes) and that officers in both forces are armed?

★ that the usual place to buy stamps is in a tobacconist's shop (tabac)?

★ that the EU is known as l'UE (Union Européenne) and the UN is known as l'ONU (Organisation des Nations Unies)?